AUSTRALIA
LBC Information Services
Sydney

CANADA and USA
Carswell
Toronto

NEW ZEALAND
Brooker's
Auckland

SINGAPORE and MALAYSIA
Sweet & Maxwell Asia
Singapore and Kuala Lumpur

SCHMITTHOFF'S
EXPORT TRADE

THE LAW AND PRACTICE OF INTERNATIONAL TRADE

TENTH EDITION

By

LEO D'ARCY, M.A. (Dubl.)
Barrister of Gray's Inn,
Senior Lecturer, University of Westminster

CAROLE MURRAY, M.A. (Cantab.)
Barrister of the Middle Temple

BARBARA CLEAVE, LL.B.
Barrister of the Inner Temple

What would this island be without foreign trade, but a place of confinement to the inhabitants, who (without it) could be but a kind of hermites, as being separated from the rest of the world; it is foreign trade that renders us rich, honourable and great, that gives us a name and esteem in the world.

Charles Molloy,
De Jure Maritimo et Navale, 1676

LONDON
SWEET & MAXWELL
2000

First Edition	*1948*
Second Edition	*1950*
Third Edition	*1955 (translated into Russian 1958)*
Fourth Edition	*1962 (translated into Japanese 1968)*
Fifth Edition	*1969 (translated into French 1974)*
Sixth Edition	*1975*
Second Impression	*1977*
Seventh Edition	*1980 (translated into Chinese, Peking, 1985)*
Reprinted	*1982, 1983 and 1985*
Eighth Edition	*1986*
Reprinted	*1988 and 1989*
Ninth Edition	*1990*
Reprinted	*1992, 1993 and 1995 (twice)*
Tenth Edition	*2000 by Leo D'Arcy, Carole Murray and Barbara Cleave*

Published in 2000 by
Sweet & Maxwell Limited
100 Avenue Road
Swiss Cottage
London
NW3 3PF
Typeset by Wyvern 21 Limited, Bristol
Printed in England by Clays Ltd, St Ives plc

No natural forests were destroyed to make this product; only farmed
timber was used and replanted

A CIP catalogue record for this book is available from the British Library.

ISBN Hardback 0 421 61950 3   1002085395
ISBN Paperback 0 421 54680 8

Dedicated to the memory of Leo D'Arcy

[1952–2000]

To

**Geraldine D'Arcy
Robbi
Roger and Olivia and their families**

PREFACE

SADLY this preface must begin by remarking on the death, in 1990, of Professor Clive Schmitthoff. A man of culture, compassion and intellect, Professor Schmitthoff enjoyed a deservedly formidable reputation based on a long career in legal writing, teaching and commitment to various causes. He is greatly missed by those with whom he came into contact either personally or through his work.

Professor Schmitthoff's teaching career disclosed a remarkable dedication to the profession. He taught at a number of institutions both in the United Kingdom and overseas, most notably at the City University, the University of Kent at Canterbury, and the City of London Polytechnic. He also contributed greatly to the work of the Centre for Commercial Studies at Queen Mary and Westfield College.

Professor Schmitthoff's writings are noted for their significant contribution to various aspects of commercial law, conflict of laws and, of course, to the law of international trade. He was involved in *Palmer's Company Law* as editor or co-editor for some 31 years, and was founder of the *Journal of Business Law*, which he edited from 1957 to 1989. His books included *The Sale of Goods, The English Conflict of Laws, Legal Aspects of Export Sales* and, most notably, *Schmitthoff's Export Trade*. The latter made its first appearance in 1948 and continued through nine editions, the last of which was published in 1990.

The aim of this tenth edition of *Export Trade* is to provide a concise account of the law and practice of international trade. It is intended for those engaged in business, their professional advisers and students. The work attempts to reflect the numerous developments which have taken place in international trade law since the ninth edition. Some chapters have changed significantly, whilst others have altered relatively little. Their sequence has been partly reorganised. It has been of paramount importance that the integrity of earlier editions be maintained and as a consequence the original format and, where appropriate, analyses, have been kept much the same.

The recent past has seen some major changes in the law and its context, particularly with the rapidly increasing incorporation of European Community law into many aspects of U.K. domestic law. The full impact of the new Civil Procedure Rules has yet to be observed, nonetheless relevant aspects have been referred to where appropriate, particularly in the area of interim remedies, such as freezing and search orders.

The law relating to sales has been considered in the light of the amendments to the Sale of Goods Act 1979 and the introduction of INCOTERMS 2000, the latter taking effect on the first day of the new century. Trade finance has witnessed the introduction of the 1993 version of the Uniform Customs and Practice for Documentary Credits, the 1995 revised Uniform Rules for Collections and the 1992 Uniform Rules for Demand Guarantees. Carriage of goods by sea has seen the repeal of the Bills of Lading Act 1855 and its replacement by the Carriage of Goods by Sea Act 1992, which dispenses with the requirement that property in goods must have passed to a recipient of a bill of lading in order for them to be able to exercise rights against the carrier under the contract of carriage. The 1992 Act enhances the status of sea waybills and delivery orders and necessitates a more in-depth examination of these documents. The carriage of goods by other means is looked at in the light of recent significant cases and the various amendments to the provisions governing international carriage of goods.

The section on insurance is marked by consideration of the important case of *Pan Atlantic v. Pine Top*, which necessitated a review of the disclosure requirements in contracts of marine insurance. The chapter on export credit guarantees has been recast in the light of the reorganisation of the Export Credits Guarantees Department and the privatisation of its short term facilities.

In the section on International Dispute Resolution, the common law provisions for determining the "proper" law of the contract have been superseded for the most part by the Contracts (Applicable Law) Act 1990 which incorporates the Rome Convention (the Convention on the Law applicable to Contractual Obligations). In order to adequately consider the Convention, the common law rules have been excluded. The Brussels Convention, newly in force when the last edition was published, is extensively considered, together with the Lugano Convention, which came into force in the U.K. in 1992. There is now a considerable body of English law in addition to recent ECJ decisions on aspects of the Brussels Convention. The Arbitration Act 1996 is of great significance. There is a new chapter on Enforcement of Judgments and Arbitral Awards. The creation of the World Trade Organisation has necessitated consideration of that body's dispute resolution mechanism.

In the section on Marketing Organisations Abroad and Competition Law, The Commercial Agents (Council Directive) Regulations 1993, which came into force on January 1, 1994, receive fairly extensive treatment. Further development of European Community law in the areas of company and employment law are included in the chapter on Branch Offices and Subsidiaries Abroad. In addition, the Employment Relations Act 1999 will affect organisations sending employees to work abroad. The U.K.'s Competition Act 1998 is also considered in this section.

The chapters on Construction and Customs law have been extensively revised. For the updating of the Construction chapter we are extremely grateful to Giles Dixon, a partner with Nabarro Nathanson, who specialises in construction. We also extend our grateful thanks to Daren Timson-Hunt, MIEx, for writing the new chapter on Electronic Commerce and EDI, and for revising the chapter on Customs Law and updating the section on SITPRO in Chapter 31. He is currently at the Inns of Court School of Law and was previously an advisor on international trade and customs law at the Simpler Trade Procedures Board.

In addition, the following are thanked for their kind assistance. Clive Williams, Policy Resources and Personnel Directorate, British Trade International for reading and revising the section on government help available to exporters in Chapter 31; Richard Earle, Senior Lecturer at the University of Westminster for his assistance with the chapter on Arbitration; Mark Furse, Senior Lecturer in Law at the University of Westminster for his helpful advice on the Competition Law chapter; Fiona McCallum of ECGD for her assistance in reviewing the section on export credit guarantees; John Price of NCM Ltd for reviewing the passages on short term export credit facilities; David Sandy of Simmons and Simmons for the transcript of an unreported judgment, and finally Evelyn Nwajei is thanked for research assistance.

Thanks are also due to the following organisations for providing access to their publications or for assistance on locating material: ICC, Croners, Tate, UNCITRAL, BIFA and also EUCON for their kind permission to use their transport documentation in the chapter on Containerisation.

Lastly we thank Sweet & Maxwell for their invaluable help. They are to be commended for their patience and tolerance in awaiting this manuscript.

An attempt has been made to present the law as at July 31, 1999 although we have been able to include a few more recent cases and statutory materials.

LDA
CM
BC

December 1999

CONTENTS

Dedications   v–viii
Preface   ix
Table of Cases   xxxv
Table of European Cases   lxxxix
Table of Statutes   xcv
Table of Statutory Instruments   ciii
Table of European Communities Legislation   cvii
  Regulations   cvii
  Directives   cviii
United States Legal Materials   cxi
  Uniform Commercial Code (UCC)   cxi
  Federal Statutes   cxi
  Restatement (Second) of Torts 1965   cxi
International Conventions and other Formulations of
  International Trade Law   cxiii

1. INTRODUCTION   1
  Export transactions based on a contract of sale   1
  Export transactions for the construction of works and
  installations   1
  The export transaction   2
  The parties and the means involved in the export transaction 2

PART ONE

THE INTERNATIONAL SALE OF GOODS

2. SPECIAL TRADE TERMS IN EXPORT SALES   7
  Ex works (named place)   8
  Free carrier (named place)   10
  F.A.S. (named port of shipment)   12
  F.O.B. (named port of shipment)   15
  American practice   17
  Types of f.o.b. contracts   17
  Arrangement of freight and marine insurance   20
  Responsibilities of the parties   21
  Nominating a suitable ship   21
  Suitable ship   22
  Failure to nominate a suitable ship   23
  Nomination of a substitute vessel   24
  The loading operation   24
  Passing of property   25
  Examination of the goods   26

Multi-port f.o.b. terms   27
Duty to procure an export licence   27
F.O.B. airport, free carrier (FCA airport)   28
C.I.F. (named port of destination)   29
Definition   30
The shipping documents   33
The bill of lading   33
The insurance document   34
The invoice   36
Other documents   36
The right to reject the documents and the right to reject the
    goods   36
Responsibilities of the parties   38
Contractual relations of seller and carrier   39
Contractual relations of buyer and carrier   39
Liability of carrier in tort   40
Payment of the price   40
Port of shipment and port of destination   41
Tender of goods afloat   42
Loss of goods   43
Contracts expressed to be c.i.f. but not being true c.i.f.
    contracts   44
Refusal to accept the goods   45
Variants of the c.i.f. contract   45
C. and F. (named port of destination)   47
C.I.F. and c., c.i.f. and e., c.i.f. and c. and i.   48
Carriage and insurance paid to (named place of destination)
    (CIP)   48
Carriage paid to (named place of destination) (CPT)   48
Arrival, ex ship or delivered ex ship (DES) (named port of
    arrival)   49
Ex quay, delivered ex quay (DEQ) (named port of destination)   50
Delivered at frontier (DAF) (named point at frontier)   50
Delivered duty paid (DDP), delivered duty unpaid (DDU)
    (named place of destination in the country of importation)   50
Container trade terms   51

3. FORMATION OF CONTRACT   52
The negotiations   52
Inquiries and invitations to contract   52
The quotation   53
Tenders   53
The offer   53
Firm offers   54
The acceptance   54
The acceptance must be unconditional and unqualified   54

Communication of acceptance	55
Contract by conduct	56
Forms of acceptance	57
The confirmation slip	57
The countersigned acceptance form	57
Comfort letters or letters of intent	57
Acceptance subject to seller's general conditions	58
Incorporation of current edition of general conditions	59
Certainty	59
Parol evidence	61
Special problems relating to general conditions	62
Agreement to standard terms	62
The battle of forms	64
International supply contracts	65

4. PERFORMANCE OF THE CONTRACT
English and foreign sales law	67
	67
Delivery of the goods	68
Passing of the property	69
Unascertained goods	69
Ascertained goods	72
The retention of title clause	74
The simple retention of title clause	74
The extended retention of title clause	74
Passing of the risk	76
Provision of certificates	78
Certificates of quality	78
Certificates of inspection	79
Pre-shipment inspection	80
Liquidated damages and penalties	82

5. ACCEPTANCE AND REJECTION OF GOODS
Conditions, warranties and innominate terms	84
	84
Conditions and warranties	85
The innominate term	87
Examination of goods	89
Acceptance of goods	91
Rejection of goods	93
Right of rejection in c.i.f. contracts	94
Rejection where each delivery to be treated as separate contract	95
Property in rejected goods	96
Rejection and estoppel	96
Relaxation of strict performance of contract	96
The right of the unpaid seller	99

The rights of the unpaid seller 99
The unpaid seller's lien 100
Stoppage in transit 101
The right of resale 103

6. FRUSTRATION OF CONTRACT 104
Legal meaning of frustration 105
Frustration may be a matter of degree 106
Frustration by delay 107
Self-induced frustration 107
Conditions upon which the contract is frustrated 108
Destruction of subject-matter 108
Illegality 109
Outbreak of war 109
Export and import prohibitions 110
Government prohibitions affecting State trading
corporations 111
Fundamental change in circumstances 112
Export and import licences and quotas 114
Partial frustration 117
Apportionment of performance 117
Effect of frustration 118
In general 118
The Law Reform (Frustrated Contracts) Act 1943 119
Different kinds of force majeure clauses 121
The two-stage force majeure clause 122
Force majeure clauses in standard contracts used in the
commodity trade 122
Force majeure clauses which are too vague 123
Force majeure clauses defeated by events 124

7. INVOICES AND PACKING 125
Invoices 125
The invoice must be true and correct 125
The commercial invoice 126
Invoices in letter of credit transactions 127
Official requirements for invoices 127
Packing 128
The obligation to provide suitable packaging 128
Packing in the sale of goods 128
Packing in the law of carriage of goods 129
Packing in containers 130
Packing in insurance law 130
Import regulations relating to packing 130
Dangerous goods 131

8. PRODUCT LIABILITY   132
   The basis of product liability   132
   English law   133
      Liability arising from the contract of sale   133
      The E.C. Directive on Product Liability   134
      The Consumer Protection Act 1987   134
         Liability for defective products   135
         Defences   137
         Examples   138
      Damages   139
   Procedural aspects   139
   Product liability insurance   140
   American law   140
      Restatement (Second) of Torts, s. 402A   141
      The reform of American law   141

PART TWO

FINANCE OF EXPORTS

9. BILLS OF EXCHANGE   145
   Payment on open account   146
   Payment by bills of exchange   146
      Nature of the bill of exchange   147
      Foreign bills   151
      The UN Convention on International Bills of Exchange and
         International Promissory Notes (1988)   152
      The claused bill   152
      The documentary bill   155
      Avalised bills   156
      Bills drawn in a set   157
      Negotiation of bills by exporter   158
      Proceedings on bills of exchange   159

10. COLLECTION ARRANGEMENTS   161
    The Uniform Rules for Collections   161
    Dishonour   164
    Delivery of documents contrary to instructions   164
       Release under a trust receipt   164

11. LETTERS OF CREDIT   166
    Characteristics of the letter of credit   166

Uniform Customs and Practice for Documentary Credits 167
  Application of the UCP 168
The stages of a letter of credit transaction 169
The two fundamental principles 170
The autonomy of the letter of credit 170
  The doctrine of strict compliance 172
The documents tendered to the bank 175
  Time for examination 176
  Discrepancy of the documents 177
  Provisions relating to the documents in the UCP 179
    The transport documents 179
The invoice 182
Insurance documents 182
Several documents to be read together 184
  Linkage of documents 184
Instructions communicated by teletransmission 185
Time of opening of credit 186
The expiry date of the credit 188
  The law applicable to the credit 188
Damages for failure to open or pay a credit 192
Kinds of letters of credit 192
  Payment at sight, deferred payment, acceptance and
    negotiation credits 192
  Revocable and irrevocable credits; confirmed and unconfirmed
    credits 194
  Revocable and unconfirmed credits 195
  Irrevocable and unconfirmed credits 196
  Irrevocable and confirmed credits 196
    Recourse and reimbursement of confirming bank 197
    The confirmation as localisation device 198
    Variants of confirmation 198
  Standby letters of credit 199
  Revolving credits 200
  Packing credits; red clause credits 201
  Back-to-back and overriding credits 202
  Transferable credits 202
    The assignment of the benefit of the credit 203
    The transfer of the credit 204
Anomalous letter of credit situations 206
  Letters of credit and bank indemnities 206
  Payment under reserve 207
  Short-circuiting of letter of credit 208
    The conditional character of the credit 208
    Other instances of short-circuiting 209
  Fraud affecting letters of credit 210
    Evidence of fraud 213

12. BANK GUARANTEES AND OTHER CONTRACT GUARANTEES IN
    GENERAL   214
    Guarantees in the common law and in international trade   214
    Bank guarantees   217
  Bank guarantees procured by the buyer   219
  Bank guarantees procured by the seller   219
    Demand guarantees   219
      Unfair demand or fraud   222

13. FACTORING, FORFAITING, FINANCIAL LEASING AND OTHER FORMS OF
    MERCHANT FINANCE   226
  Factoring   226
    The essence of international factoring   226
    Direct and indirect factoring   227
    Legal forms of factoring   228
    Disclosed factoring   229
    Undisclosed factoring   230
    The Unidroit Convention on International Factoring   231
  Forfaiting   232
    The essence of forfaiting   233
    Avalised bills of exchange and bank guarantees as security for
      the forfaiter   233
    Primary and secondary forfaiting transactions   234
  International financial leasing   235
    The essence of the financial leasing transaction   235
    The Unidroit Convention on International Financial Leasing   235
  Other forms of merchant finance   238
    Non-recourse finance   238

14. COUNTERTRADE   240
    Contracts of sale and of barter   240
    The economic background   241
  Types of countertrade transactions   242
    Reciprocal sales agreements   242
    The definition of the countersale buyer   243
    Barter   244
    The buy-back agreement   245
    Offset arrangements   245
    Disposal and switch transactions   246
    Oil countertrade   246
    The framework agreement   247

PART THREE

TRANSPORTATION OF EXPORTS

15. CARRIAGE OF GOODS BY SEA — 251
    The carriage of goods in export transactions — 251
       Unimodal and multimodal transport — 251
       Traditional methods of transport and container transport — 252
    The course of business in the carriage of goods by sea — 253
    The contract of carriage by sea — 257
       Carriage covered by bill of lading or charterparty — 257
       Conclusion of the contract of carriage by sea — 258
          Shutting out goods — 258
       Freight — 259
          Calculation of freight — 260
          Lump sum freight — 260
          Prepaid freight — 260
          Prepaid freight and freight collect bills of lading — 262
          Pro rata freight — 262
          Back freight — 263
          Dead freight — 263
          Primage — 263
          Freight rates fixed by shipping conferences — 264
          By whom freight is payable — 265
          Shipowner's lien — 266
    Bills of lading and other carriage documents — 267
       Nature of the bill of lading — 267
       The international rules relating to bills of lading — 268
       The territorial and documentary application of the Carriage of
          Goods by Sea Act 1971 — 269
          Territorial application — 269
          Documentary application — 271
       Types of bills of lading — 273
          Charterparty bills of lading — 273
          Negotiable and non-negotiable bills — 275
          "Shipped" and "received" bills — 277
          Clean and "claused" bills — 278
          Through bills of lading — 278
          Container bills of lading — 279
          House bills of lading and groupage bills of lading — 279
          Through bills of lading covering on-carriage by air — 280
          Switch bills — 281
          "Stale" bills of lading — 281
          Sea waybills — 281
          Delivery Orders — 282
       The date of the bill of lading — 283
       The bill of lading as a receipt — 284

The bill of lading as evidence of the contract of carriage 289
The bill of lading as a document of title 289
Indemnities and bills of lading 292
Charterparty indemnity 294
The liability of the carrier 294
Excepted perils 297
The burden of proof 298
Excepted perils and insurance 299
Maximum limits of shipowner's liability 299
The Convention on Limitation of Liability for Maritime
Claims 302
Protection of servants and agents, but not independent
contractors 302
Notice of claim and time limit for claims for loss of or damage
to the goods 304
General average claims and contributions 306
Dangerous goods 307
Proceedings by cargo owner 308
Whom to sue—the legal and actual carrier 308
The right to sue and liability under The Carriage of Goods by
Sea Act 1992 310

16. CONTAINER TRANSPORT 314
The course of business in container transport 314
Container leasing agreements 316
Legal problems of container transport 316
The liability of the container operator 317
The documents used in container transport—the combined
transport document 318
Container bills of lading 319
Deck stowage 321
Definition of "package or unit" in container transport 321

17. CARRIAGE OF GOODS BY AIR 324
History of the statutory scheme 324
Damage during "carriage by air" 325
Basic system of liability—an overview 325
Carrier's defences 326
Those who may claim 327
Carriers who may be sued 327
When do the various regimes apply? 328
1. The original Warsaw Convention 328
2. The amended Convention 329
3. The non-Convention rules 329
Carriage governed by the original Warsaw Convention 330

Document of carriage 330
Basic liability 331
Special rights of consignor and consignee 332
Procedure in the event of a claim 332
Carriage governed by the amended Warsaw Convention 333
Document of carriage 333
Basic liability 333
Special rights of consignor and consignee 334
Procedure in the event of a claim 334
Non-Convention carriage 334
IATA carriage 335

18. CARRIAGE OF GOODS BY LAND 337
Carriage by rail and road 337
Carriage by rail 338
Scope of application 338
Making the contract 338
Liability 339
Carriage by road—CMR 339
Scope of application 339
Successive carriers 341
The consignment note 342
Liability of the carrier 343
Time limits 346
Nullity of stipulations contrary to the Convention 348

PART FOUR

INSURANCE OF GOODS IN TRANSIT

19. MARINE AND AVIATION INSURANCE 351
Marine insurance 351
Stipulations in the contract of sale 351
The assured, the insurer and the broker 352
Kinds of marine insurance 355
Valued and unvalued policies 355
Voyage, time and mixed policies 356
Floating policies 357
Open covers 359
Blanket policies 361
The contract of insurance 361
The slip and the policy 361

Certificates of insurance; brokers' cover notes; letters of
    insurance 362
The duty to disclose 363
The "held covered" clause 366
The insurable interest 367
The premium 370
Assignment 370
Risks covered and risks not covered ("exclusions") 371
The Lloyd's Marine Policy and the Institute Cargo Clauses A,
    B and C 372
Institute Cargo Clauses A 373
Institute Cargo Clauses B 373
Institute Cargo Clauses C 374
The Transit Clause 374
The risks covered 376
Risks not covered (the Exclusion Clauses) 376
General average 380
The general average act 380
The general average loss 381
General average and the contract of carriage by sea 382
General average and the contract of insurance 383
Claims 384
Liability and causation 384
Burden of proof 385
Preparation of claims 386
Total and partial loss 387
Measure of indemnity 388
The insurer's right of subrogation 389
Air cargo insurance 391
Marine clauses 391
Air waybill cover 392

20. EXPORT CREDIT GUARANTEES 394
The Export Credits Guarantee Department 396
Facilities offered by the Export Credits Guarantee Department 396
Supplier's credit finance facility 397
Buyer credits 397
Cover for lines of credit 398
Project financing scheme 399
Export insurance policy 399
Bond risk insurance 399
Insurance for overseas investments 400
One Stop Shopping with the ECGD 401
Comprehensive short term guarantees 401

PART FIVE

INTERNATIONAL COMMERCIAL DISPUTE RESOLUTION

21. ENGLISH LAW AND FOREIGN LAW   407
    Proof of foreign law   408
    Measures of conflict avoidance   409
    The law governing the contract—The Rome Convention   409
      Interpretation   410
      Scope of the Convention   410
      The applicable law   412
        Freedom of choice   412
        Absence of express or implied choice   414
        Limitations on applicable law and mandatory rules   416
        Scope of the applicable law   416
        Burden of proof, formal and material validity   417
        Capacity   419
        Voluntary assignment and subrogation   419
        Specific contracts   419
          Certain consumer contracts   419
          Individual employment contracts   420
      The Foreign Limitation Periods Act 1984   421
    Money of account and of payment—recovery in foreign currency   422
    Foreign state immunity   424
    Extraterritorial effect of foreign state measures   426
      The Protection of Trading Interests Act 1980   427
      Rejection of foreign extraterritorial claims by the courts—
      letters of request   428
    The exclusion of foreign law   430
      Foreign confiscatory or nationalisation laws   431
      Foreign revenue laws, penal laws and other public laws of
        political or administrative character   431
      Other cases of public policy   432
    Foreign illegality   433
      Civil consequences   433
      Criminal consequences   435
    Exchange control   437
      Exchange contracts under the Bretton Woods Agreement   437
        Disguised exchange contracts   438
      Recognition of foreign exchange control regulations   439

22. JURISDICTION   440
    Domicile   441
    Traditional rules   443
      RSC Order 11, rule 1(1)   444
        The application for permission to serve out   444

Stay of English proceedings and restraint of foreign
   proceedings 445
   Stay on the ground of forum non conveniens 445
   Stays and exclusive foreign jurisdiction agreements 447
   Restraint of foreign proceedings 449
   Restraint and exclusive English jurisdiction agreement 450
The Brussels and Lugano Conventions 451
   RSC Order 11, rule 1(2) 451
   Interpretation of the Conventions 452
   Area of application of the Conventions 452
   Jurisdiction provisions 453
     Prorogation of jurisdiction 453
     General jurisdiction 455
     Special jurisdiction 455
       Employment contracts 457
       Tort 458
       Branch, agency or other establishment 459
       Co-defendants, third parties and counterclaims 459
     Insurance contracts 461
     Consumer contracts 461
     Exclusive jurisdiction 462
     Jurisdiction and admissibility 462
     Lis pendens and related actions 463
     The Conventions and *forum non conveniens* 464
Service abroad 464
Interim remedies 465
   The freezing injunction 465
     Its nature 465
     Orders supporting the freezing injunction 467
   The search order 467
In rem jurisdiction 468

23. INTERNATIONAL COMMERCIAL LITIGATION—ARBITRATION 472
   Extrajudicial dispute settlement and court proceedings 472
General aspects of arbitration 473
   Arbitration and litigation compared 473
   Questions of fact and questions of law 474
   The characteristics of an arbitration 475
     The contractual element 475
     The judicial element of arbitration 476
   Ad hoc and institutional arbitration 477
   The law governing the arbitration procedure 477
   Application of the *lex mercatoria* in arbitration proceedings 478
   Arbitration *ex aequo et bono* 479
English arbitration 480
   The arbitration agreement and the arbitrators 480

Examples of arbitration clauses 481
Qualifications 483
Jurisdiction of the tribunal 483
Disputes covered by the arbitration agreement 483
Stays 484
The powers of the tribunal 486
The award 487
The role of the court 488
International arbitration 490
UNCITRAL 490
The UNCITRAL Arbitration Rules 490
The UNCITRAL Conciliation Rules 491
The UNCITRAL model law on international commercial
arbitration 492
The ICC International Court of Arbitration 493
The London Court of International Arbitration 495
The International Centre for Settlement of Investment
Disputes 495

24. ENFORCEMENT OF FOREIGN JUDGMENTS AND ARBITRAL AWARDS
(ENFORCEMENT OF THE WTO AGREEMENT THROUGH THE DISPUTE
SETTLEMENT PROCEDURE) 497
Recognition and enforcement of foreign judgments 497
Brussels Convention 497
Whether the judgment falls within the meaning of "judgment"
under Article 25 498
Whether there is some way in which the jurisdiction of the
adjudicating court can be impeached 498
Grounds for non-recognition 498
Enforcement 500
Enforcement under the common law or statute 500
Enforcement under statute 501
Conditions for enforcement 501
Jurisdiction 502
Fixed sum of money 502
Final and conclusive 502
Penal or revenue sanctions 502
Defences 503
Fraud 503
Recognition contrary to public policy 503
Recognition contrary to natural justice 503
Registration 504
Judgments of the European Court of Justice 504
Enforcement of foreign arbitral awards 504
Grounds for refusal of recognition 505
Other 506

The dispute settlement procedure of WTO 506
  Exporter's standing 506
  The law relating to WTO disputes 507

PART SIX

CONSTRUCTION AND LONG TERM CONTRACTS

25. THE CONSTRUCTION OF WORKS AND INSTALLATIONS ABROAD 511
  The UNCITRAL Legal Guide 512
  Types of procurement 512
    Procurement by inviting tenders and by negotiation 512
    Open and selective tenders 513
    The E.C. Directives on public procurement 514
      Public works 514
      Supplies 514
      Services 515
      Utilities (formerly known as Excluded Sectors) 515
      Compliance 515
  Contract structure 516
  Forms of contract 517
    FIDIC Conditions of Contract 517
    ENAA 518
    UNIDO 518
    The Standard Bidding Documents for the Procurement of
      Works 519
    The Asian Development Bank 519
  The prequalification procedure 519
  The invitation to tender 520
  The tender 521
  The tender guarantee 521
  Opening of tenders 523
  Acceptance of tender 523
  The contract—some key provisions 523
    Pricing 524
    Pricing the risk and changing the contract price 525
    Contract variations 526
    Extensions of time 526
    Standard of design and work 527
  Inspection and acceptance 527
  Assignment and sub-contracting 528
  The engineer or contract administrator 528
  Payment 529
  Performance and repayment guarantees 529
  Liquidated damages and bonus clauses 530

Retention money   530
Currency clauses   531
Insurance and indemnity clauses   531
Other contract clauses   531
Arbitration and the resolution of disputes   531

PART SEVEN

CUSTOMS LAW

26. GOVERNMENT REGULATION OF EXPORTS   537
    Export licensing regulations   537
      The general control of exports   537
      Strategic goods   539
      Antiques   540
    Customs regulations   540
      Introduction   540
      The effect of the Single Market on Customs legislation   541
      Supply of goods to other Member States of the European
        Union   542
        VAT   542
        Statistics   543
        Excise   544
      Supply of goods to countries outside of the European Union   545
        Customs requirements   546
        Normal declaration procedure   547
        Simplified declaration procedures   547
        Information required to be declared to Customs   550
        Postal exports   551
      Customs trader records and accounts   551
      Transit procedures   552
        Common and Community transit   552
        The TIR and ATA Systems   555
      Duty suspense and relief schemes   556
        Outward Processing, Inward Processing Relief and drawback   556
        Return of unused imports   558
        Warehouse goods   559
      E.C. preference arrangements   560
    Customs appeals   562
    Customs offences   563
      The concept of Customs offences   563
      Customs offences and E.C. law   564
      Fines, forfeiture of goods and restoration   565
      Other aspects   568

PART EIGHT

MARKETING ORGANISATIONS ABROAD

27. AGENCY ARRANGEMENTS | 575
Self-employed agents abroad | 575
The contract of agency | 576
  The legal nature of the contract of agency | 576
The agent's authority | 577
  Actual authority | 577
    Disclosure of principal | 577
  Implied, usual and customary authority | 580
  Ostensible (or apparent) authority | 581
  Ratification | 582
  Agency by operation of law | 583
    The agent of necessity | 583
Rights and obligations of agent and principal | 584
  Duties of the agent to his principal | 586
  Duties of the principal | 589
  Exclusive trading rights | 597
Special types of agents | 597
  The Commission agent | 598
  The del credere agent | 599
  The agent carrying stock (the mercantile agent) | 599
  The confirming house | 601
    Nature of the confirming house | 601
    Obligations of the confirming house | 602
    Insolvency of the confirming house | 603
    Illustrations | 604
    Confirmation by confirming house and by bank | 605
  The freight forwarder | 605
    The forwarder acting as principal or as agent | 605
    The forwarder as bailee | 607
    Further duties of the forwarder | 609
Travelling representatives abroad | 610

28. BRANCH OFFICES AND SUBSIDIARIES ABROAD—FOREIGN ACQUISITIONS | 611
Branch offices and subsidiaries abroad | 612
  The choice between branches and subsidiaries | 612
  The legal distinction between branches and subsidiaries | 612
Branch offices abroad | 613
  Jurisdiction over the head office | 613
  The "oversea company" in the United Kingdom | 613
  Dealings between branches | 614
Subsidiary companies abroad | 614

The overseas subsidiary   614
The multinational enterprise   615
The proposed European company   616
Overseas subsidiaries in English and foreign law   616
  Overseas subsidiaries in English law   616
  Overseas subsidiaries in foreign law   618
    Foreign company law   618
    Foreign employment law   619
    Foreign tax law   619
    Foreign investment law   620
    The settlement of international investment disputes   621
Foreign acquisitions   622
  The law relating to take-overs   622
The personnel employed in overseas branches and subsidiaries   623
  English employment law   623
    Restraint of trade clauses   625
  Foreign employment law   625
    Free movement of employees in the E.C.   625
    Legislation pertaining to foreigners in non-E.C. countries   626
    Foreign legislation protecting security of employment   626

29. The Competition Law of the European Community and of the
    United Kingdom   627
The basic provisions of E.C. competition law   627
  Article 81   627
  Article 82   628
  Agreements prohibiting parallel exports or imports   631
  Regulation 17/62   632
  The control of restrictive arrangements in E.C. competition law 633
  Negative clearance and declaration of inapplicability   633
  Measures providing block exemptions and notices   634
  Agreements of minor importance   634
  Exclusive agency contracts   635
  Exclusive distribution agreements   636
  Exclusive purchasing agreements   637
  Joint research and development, joint ventures and
    specialisation agreements   637
  Patent and know-how licensing agreements   638
  Franchising agreements and agreements relating to intellectual
    property rights   638
  Maritime transport and air transport   639
Abuse of dominant position   639
  Powers of Commission to obtain information and to conduct
    investigations   640
The competition law of the United Kingdom   641
  Competition Act 1998   641

Notification 642
Enforcement 642
Appeals 642

30. Sole Distribution Agreements, Licensing and Franchising 644
Nature of sole distribution agreements 645
  Sole and exclusive agreements 645
  Sole distribution agreements distinguished from contracts of
    sale and from agency agreements 645
  Sole distribution agreements and licensing and franchising
    agreements 647
  Export distribution agreements 647
Clauses in sole distribution agreements 649
  Definition of the territory 649
  Definition of the price 650
  Definition of the goods 651
  Sole buying and selling rights 651
  Advertising, market information, protection of patents and
    trade marks 652
  Other clauses 653
Laws relating to restrictive practices 654
Licensing and franchising agreements 654
Franchising 655
  The course of business 655
Franchising agreements and E.C. law 655
Block exemption 656

PART NINE

MARKET INFORMATION

31. Market Information for Exporters—Market Research 659
  Direct market research 659
  Government services for exporters—British Trade
    International 659
    Business links 660
    Export Market Information Centre (EMIC) 660
    The TradeU.K. Export Sales Lead Service 662
    The Export Credits Guarantee Department 663
    Other help available 664
  Export publications 664
    British Trade International publications 664
      Websites for exporters 665
    Croner's Reference Book for Exporters 665
    Tate's Export Guide 665

Export Today 665
Business Matters and International Business Matters 665
Euronews 666
Eurostat 666

PART TEN

STANDARDISATION, UNIFICATION, ELECTRONIC COMMERCE
AND EDI

32. STANDARDISATION OF TERMS AND UNIFICATION OF INTERNATIONAL
    SALES LAW 669
Uniform rules of general character 669
  United Nations Commission on International Trade Law 670
    International conventions 670
    Model Laws 671
    Other instruments 671
    Legal guides 672
  International Chamber of Commerce publications 672
  American Uniform Commercial Code 673
Standard contract forms applying to specified international
  transactions 674
  Standard conditions issued by trade associations 674
  Model contracts sponsored by United Nations Economic
  Commission for Europe 674
  Model contract forms used in construction contracts 676
General terms of business adopted by individual exporters 676
  Some important clauses 676
  Standard terms in domestic transactions 677
Simplifying international trade 678
The Uniform Laws in the United Kingdom 679
  The Uniform Laws on International Sales Act 1967 679
  Application of Uniform Laws only if adopted by parties 679
  Mandatory provisions of applicable law cannot be contracted
    out of 680
General limitations of Uniform Laws 680
  Restriction of contracts between parties in Convention States 681
Contracts of international sale 681
The Uniform Law on International Sales 682
The Uniform Law on Formation 684
UN Convention on Contracts for the International Sale of Goods
  (1980) 685
  The Vienna Convention and the Hague Uniform Laws 685
  Applicability of the Vienna Convention 687
  The Vienna Convention and the national law 687
  The central position of the Vienna Convention 688

Some features of the Vienna Convention 689
    Fundamental and non-fundamental breach 689
Specific performance and repair of non-conforming goods 689
UN Convention on the Limitation Period in the International Sale
    of Goods (1974) 690

33. ELECTRONIC COMMERCE AND ELECTRONIC DATA INTERCHANGE 692
    Standardisation of EDI methods of communication 693
        UN/EDIFACT standard 693
        UNTDED and UNTDID 694
        Interchange agreements 694
    Other legal issues 694
        Electronic commerce and contract law 694
        Selling on the Internet—legal issues 695
        Authentication of messages 696
        Negotiability 696
        Admissibility of electronic data under English law 697
    Electronic Communications Act 698
        UNCITRAL Model Law on Electric Commerce 699

Index 701

TABLE OF CASES

Cases other than those decided by the European Court of Justice and the E.C. Commission; for these see p. lxxxix

A/S D/S Svendborg v. Wansa (t/a Melborne Enterprises), *sub nom.* A/S D/S Svendborg v. Awada (t/a Melborne Enterprises); Estonian Shipping Co Ltd v. Wansa (t/a D&M Impex); A/S D/S Svendborg v. Wansa [1997] 2 Lloyd's Rep. 183, CA; affirming [1996] 2 Lloyd's Rep. 559, QBD (Comm Ct) 22–010
A. Bulloch & Co. v. Distillers Co Ltd [1978] 1 C.M.L.R. 400; [1978] F.S.R. 344, CEC 29–005
Aaronson Bros v. Maderera Del Tropico SA [1967] 2 Lloyd's Rep. 159; 111 S.J. 499, CA 6–012
Adbullah M. Fahem & Co v. Mareb Yemen Insurance and Tomen (U.K.) Ltd [1997] 2 Lloyd's Rep. 738, QBD (Comm Ct) 23–011
Ace Imports Pty v. Companhia de Navegacão Lloyd Brasileiro (The Esmeralda I) [1988] 1 Lloyd's Rep. 206, Sup Ct (NSW) 16–002, 16–009
Acme Transport v. Betts [1981] 1 Lloyd's Rep. 131; [1981] R.T.R. 190, CA 16–006
Actis Co v. Sanko Steamship Co (The Aquacharm) [1982] 1 W.L.R. 119; [1982] 1 All E.R. 390; [1982] 1 Lloyd's Rep. 7; [1981] Com. L.R. 274; 125 S.J. 79, CA; affirming [1980] 2 Lloyd's Rep. 237, QBD (Comm Ct) 15–041
Adamastos Shipping Co Ltd v. Anglo Saxon Petroleum Co [1959] A.C. 133; [1958] 2 W.L.R. 688; [1958] 1 All E.R. 725; 102 S.J. 290; *sub nom.* Anglo Saxon Petroleum Co Ltd v. Adamastos Shipping Co [1958] 1 Lloyd's Rep. 73, HL; reversing *sub nom.* Anglo Saxon Petroleum Co Ltd v. Adamastos Shipping Co [1957] 2 Q.B. 233; [1957] 2 W.L.R. 968; [1957] 2 All E.R. 311; [1957] 1 Lloyd's Rep. 271; 101 S.J. 405, CA; restoring [1957] 2 W.L.R. 509; [1957] 1 All E.R. 673; [1957] 1 Lloyd's Rep. 79; 101 S.J. 267 15–022
Adams v. Cape Industries Plc [1990] Ch. 433; [1990] 2 W.L.R. 657; [1991] 1 All E.R. 929; [1990] B.C.L.C. 479; [1990] B.C.C. 786, CA; affirming *The Times*, June 23, 1988; *The Independent*, June 21, 1988, Ch D 24–005, 24–008, 24–015, 28–008
Adler v. Dickson (The Himalaya) (No.1) [1955] 1 Q.B. 158; [1954] 3 W.L.R. 696; [1954] 3 All E.R. 397; [1954] 2 Lloyd's Rep. 267; 98 S.J. 787, CA; affirming [1954] 3 W.L.R. 450; [1954] 3 All E.R. 21; [1954] 2 Lloyd's Rep. 122; 98 S.J. 592, QBD . 15–047
Advanced Portfolio Technologies Inc v. Ainsworth [1996] C.L.C. 360; [1996] F.S.R. 217; (1996) 19(3) I.P.D. 19021, Ch D 22–009
Aegean Sea Traders Corp v. Repsol Petroleo SA (The Aegean Sea) [1998] 2 Lloyd's Rep. 39; [1998] C.L.C. 1090, QBD (Adm Ct) 15–046
Aga, The. *See* Diestelkamp v. Baynes (Reading) Ltd; Sibaei v. Baynes (Reading) Ltd.
Aggeliki Charis Compania Maritima SA v. Pagnan SpA (The Angelic Grace) [1995] 1 Lloyd's Rep. 87, CA; affirming [1994] 1 Lloyd's Rep. 168, QBD 22–010
Agnew v. Lansforsakringsbolagens AB [1997] 4 All E.R. 937; [1997] L.R.L.R. 671; [1998] C.L.C. 390; [1998] I.L.Pr. 231, CA; affirming [1996] 4 All E.R. 978; [1996] L.R.L.R. 392; [1997] C.L.C. 245; [1997] 6 Re. L.R. 33, QBD (Comm Ct) 22–018
Agricultores Federados Argentinos Sociedad Cooperativa v. Ampro S.A. Commerciale Industrielle et Financiere [1965] 2 Lloyd's Rep. 157 2–012
Agroexport State Enterprise for Foreign Trade v. Compagnic Européene de Céréales [1974] 1 Lloyd's Rep. 449 6–012
Agrosin Pty Ltd v. Highway Shipping Co Ltd (The Mata K) [1998] 2 Lloyd's Rep. 614; [1998] C.L.C. 1300, QBD (Comm Ct) 15–036
Aiglon Ltd v. Gau Shan Co Ltd 1993] 1 Lloyd's Rep. 164; [1993] B.C.L.C. 321, QBD (Comm Ct) 22–022
Airbus Industrie GIE v. Patel [1999] A.C. 119; [1998] 2 W.L.R. 686; [1998] 2 All E.R. 257; [1998] 1 Lloyd's Rep. 631; [1998] C.L.C. 702; [1999] I.L.Pr. 238; (1998) 95(18) L.S.G. 32; (1998) 148 N.L.J. 551; (1998) 142 S.J.L.B. 139, HL; reversing [1997] 2 Lloyd's Rep. 8; [1997] C.L.C. 197; [1997] I.L.Pr. 230; (1996) 93(36)

L.S.G. 35; (1996) 140 S.J.L.B. 214, CA; reversing [1996] I.L.Pr. 465; (1996) 93(24)
L.S.G. 26, QBD 22–009
Akai Pty Ltd v. People's Insurance Co Ltd [1998] 1 Lloyd's Rep. 90; [1997] C.L.C. 1508;
[1999] I.L.Pr. 24, QBD (Comm Ct) 24–008
Aktieselskabet de Danske Sukkerfabrikker v. Bajamar Compania Naviera SA (The Torenia)
[1983] 2 Lloyd's Rep. 210, QBD (Comm Ct) 15–041
Al Adsani v. Government of Kuwait Times, March 29, 1996, CA 21–019
Alan (WJ) & Co Ltd v. El Nasr Export & Import Co [1972] 2 Q.B. 189; [1972] 2 W.L.R.
800; [1972] 2 All E.R. 127; [1972] 1 Lloyd's Rep. 313; 116 S.J. 139, CA; reversing
[1971] 1 Lloyd's Rep. 401 ...... 5–012, 11–024, 11–026, 11–034, 11–036, 11–040, 21–018
Alaska Textile Co. Inc v. Chase Manhattan Bank [1992] 982 Fed. 2d. 813 11–003
Albacora SRL v. Westcott & Laurance Line (The Maltasian) [1966] 2 Lloyd's Rep. 53;
1966 S.C. (HL) 19; 1966 S.L.T. 253; 110 S.J. 525, HL; affirming [1965] 2
Lloyd's Rep. 37; 1965 S.C. 203; 1965 S.L.T. 270, 1 Div; reversing 1965 S.L.T. 3,
OH 15–041, 15–043
Albacruz (Cargo Owners) v. Albazero (Owners) (The Albazero) [1977] A.C. 774; [1976]
3 W.L.R. 419; 120 S.J. 570; *sub nom.* Albazero, The; Owners of the Cargo Lately
Laden on Board the Ship or Vessel Albacruz v. Owners of the Ship or Vessel
Albazero [1976] 3 All E.R. 129; [1976] 2 Lloyd's Law Rep. 467, HL; reversing
sub nom. Albazero, The [1975] 3 W.L.R. 491; 119 S.J. 609; *sub nom.* Albazero,
The; Owners of the Cargo Lately Laden on Board the Ship or Vessel Albacruz v.
Owners of the Ship or Vessel Albazero [1975] 3 All E.R. 21; *sub nom.* Concord
Petroleum Corp v. Gosford Marine Panama SA; Albazero, The [1975] 2 Lloyd's
Rep. 295, CA; affirming *sub nom.* Albazero, The; Owners of Cargo Lately Laden on
Board the Ship or Vessel Albacruz v. Owners of the Ship or Vessel Albazero [1974]
2 All E.R. 906; *sub nom.* Concord Petroleum Corp v. Gosford Marine Panama SA;
Albazero, The [1974] 2 Lloyd's Rep. 38 .... 2–001, 2–027, 4–006, 31–008, 32–008
Albazero, The. *See* Albacruz (Cargo Owners) v. Albazero (Owners).
Albert D Gaon & Co v. Societe Interprofessionelle des Oleagineax Fluides Alimentaires.
See Tsakiroglou & Co Ltd v. Noblee Thorl GmbH.
Alcom v. Republic of Columbia [1984] A.C. 580; [1984] 2 W.L.R. 750; [1984] 2 All E.R.
6; [1984] 2 Lloyd's Rep. 24; (1984) 81 L.S.G. 1837, HL; reversing [1983] 3 W.L.R.
906; [1984] 1 All E.R. 1; [1984] 1 Lloyd's Rep. 368; (1984) 128 S.J. 315, CA 21–019
Aldridge v. Johnson (1875) 7 E. & B. 885 14–007
Alfred (C) Toepfer v. Continental Grain Co [1974] 1 Lloyd's Rep. 11; (1973) 117 S.J.
649, CA; affirming [1973] 1 Lloyd's Rep. 289 .... 4–012, 23–019
Alfred Dunhill of London Inc. v. Republic of Cuba (1976) 96 S.C. 1854 21–019
Alfred Dunhill v. Republic of Cuba 425 U.S. 683 (1976) 21–019
Ali Shipping Corp v. Shipyard Trogir [1999] 1 W.L.R. 314; [1998] 2 All E.R. 136; [1998]
1 Lloyd's Rep. 643; [1998] C.L.C. 566, CA 23–002
Alicia Hosiery v. Brown Shipley & Co [1970] 1 Q.B. 195; [1969] 2 W.L.R. 1268; [1969]
2 All E.R. 504; [1969] 2 Lloyd's Rep. 179; 113 S.J. 466 5–016
Allianz Versicherungs AG v. Fortuna Co Inc [1999] 2 All E.R. 625; [1999] C.L.C. 258,
QBD (Comm Ct)
Almojil (M) Establishment v. Malayan Motor and General Underwriters Pte Ltd (The
Al-Jubail IV) [1982] 2 Lloyd's Rep. 637, CA (Sing) 19–005
Alpha Trading Ltd v. Dunnshaw-Patten Ltd [1981] Q.B. 290; [1981] 2 W.L.R. 169; [1981]
1 All E.R. 482; [1981] 1 Lloyd's Rep. 122; 124 S.J. 827, CA; affirming [1980] 2
Lloyd's Rep. 284, QBD (Comm Ct) 27–012
Alpine Bulk Transport Co Inc v. Saudi Eagle Shipping Co Inc (The Saudi Eagle) [1986]
2 Lloyd's Rep. 221, CA 9–012
Aluminium Industrie Vaassen BV v. Romalpa Aluminium [1976] 1 W.L.R. 676;
[1976] 2 All E.R. 552; [1976] 1 Lloyd's Rep. 443; 120 S.J. 95, CA; affirming
(1975) 119 S.J. 318 .... 4–009, 21–002
Amalgamated Metal Trading Ltd v. Department of Trade and Industry Times, March 21,
1989; Financial Times, February 28, 1989, QBD 21–019
American Airlines Inc v. Hope; Banque Sabbag SAL v. Hope [1974] 2 Lloyd's Rep. 301,
HL; affirming [1973] 1 Lloyd's Rep. 233, CA; affirming *sub nom.* Banque Sabbag
SAL v. Hope; American Airlines Inc v. Hope [1972] 1 Lloyd's Rep. 253   19–010, 19–012
American Express Co v. British Airways Board [1983] 1 W.L.R. 701; [1983] 1 All E.R.
557; (1983) 133 N.L.J. 65; (1983) 127 S.J. 70, QBD 17–003, 17–019
Amin Rasheed Shipping Corp v. Kuwait Insurance Co (The Al Wahab) [1984] A.C. 50;

[1983] 3 W.L.R. 241; [1983] 2 All E.R. 884; [1983] 2 Lloyd's Rep. 365; (1983) 127 S.J. 492, HL; affirming [1983] 1 W.L.R. 228; [1983] 1 All E.R. 873; [1983] 1 Lloyd's Rep. 235; [1983] Com. L.R. 65; (1983) 133 N.L.J. 375, CA; affirming [1982] 1 W.L.R. 961; [1982] 1 Lloyd's Rep. 638; [1982] Com. L.R. 135; 126 S.J. 343, QBD 19–003, 21–007

Amoco Oil Co v. Parpada Shipping Co Ltd (The George S) [1989] 1 Lloyd's Rep. 369, CA; reversing [1987] 2 Lloyd's Rep. 69, QBD (Comm Ct) 15–043

Anders Maersk, The [1986] 1 Lloyd's Rep. 483 15–021

Andrabell, Re [1984] 3 All E.R. 407, Ch.D 4–009

André et Cie SA v. Cook Industries Inc [1987] 2 Lloyd's Rep. 463, CA; reversing [1986] 2 Lloyd's Rep. 200, QBD 6–019

Andre et Cie SA v. JH Vantol Ltd [1952] 2 Lloyd's Rep. 282 .... 2–019, 2–020

Andrew Millar & Co v. Taylor & Co [1916] 1 K.B. 402 6–009

Angelic Grace, The. *See* Aggeliki Charis Compania Maritima SA v. Pagnan SpA.

Angliss (W.) & Co (Australia) Pty v. P&O Steam Navigation Co [1927] 2 K.B. 456 15–041

Anglo African Merchants Ltd v. Bayley [1970] 1 Q.B. 311; [1969] 2 W.L.R. 686; [1969] 2 All E.R. 421; 113 S.J. 281; *sub nom.* Anglo African Merchants and Exmouth Clothing Co Ltd v. Bayley [1969] 1 Lloyd's Rep. 268 .... 19–003, 19–012, 27–011

Anglo African Shipping Co of New York Inc v. J Mortner Ltd [1962] 1 Lloyd's Rep. 610, CA; reversing [1962] 1 Lloyd's Rep. 81 .... 2–004, 27–020

Anglo Iranian Oil Co Ltd v. Jaffrate (The Rose Mary) [1953] 1 W.L.R. 246; 97 S.J. 81 ... 21–025

Anglo Overseas Transport Ltd v. Titan Industrial Corp Ltd [1959] 2 Lloyd's Rep. 152, QBD (Comm Ct) 27–027

Anglo Russian Merchant Traders Ltd v. John Batt & Co (London) Ltd [1917] 2 K.B. 679 .... 6–009, 6–012

Annefield, The. *See* Owners of the Annefield v. Owners of the Carge Lately Laden on Board The Annefield.

Anonima Petroli Italiana SpA and Neste Oy v. Marlucidez Armadora SA (The Filiatra Legacy) [1991] 2 Lloyd's Rep. 337, CA; reversing [1990] 1 Lloyd's Rep. 354 4–006

Antaios Compania Naviera SA v. Salen Rederierna AB (The Antaios) [1985] A.C. 191; [1984] 3 W.L.R. 592; [1984] 3 All E.R. 229; [1984] 2 Lloyd's Rep. 235; (1984) 81 L.S.G. 2776; (1984) 128 S.J. 564, HL; affirming [1983] 1 W.L.R. 1362; [1983] 3 All E.R. 777; [1983] 2 Lloyd's Rep. 473; [1983] Com. L.R. 262; (1983) 127 S.J. 730, CA 3–016, 5–004, 23–019

Antigoni, The [1991] 1 Lloyd's Rep. 209, CA; affirming [1990] 1 Lloyd's Rep. 45, QBD (Adm Ct) 15–043

Anton Piller KG v. Manufacturing Processes Ltd [1976] Ch. 55; [1976] 2 W.L.R. 162; [1976] 1 All E.R. 779; [1976] F.S.R. 129; [1976] R.P.C. 719; (1975) 120 S.J 63, CA 22–032, 26–031

Antonis P Lemos, The. *See* Samick Lines Co v. Owners of the Antonis P Lemos.

Antwerp United Diamond BVBA v. Air Europe [1996] Q.B. 317; [1995] 3 W.L.R. 396; [1995] 3 All E.R. 424; [1995] 2 Lloyd's Rep. 224, CA; affirming [1993] 4 All E.R. 469; [1993] 2 Lloyd's Rep. 413, QBD 17–016

Apioil Ltd v. Kuwait Petroleum Italia SpA; Apioil Ltd v. Sociedade Nacional de Combustiveis de Angola SA [1995] 1 Lloyd's Rep. 124 4–012

Aqualon (UK) Ltd v. Vallana Shipping Corp [1994] 1 Lloyd's Rep. 669, QBD 18–008

Arab African Energy Corp v. Olie Producten Nederland BV [1983] 2 Lloyd's Rep. 419; [1983] Com. L.R. 195, QBD (Comm Ct) 23–011, 23–025

Arab Bank v. Ross [1952] 2 Q.B. 216; [1952] 1 All E.R. 709; [1952] 1 T.L.R. 811; 96 S.J. 229, CA 9–004

Arab Business Consortium International Finance & Investment Co v. Banque Franco-Tunisienne [1997] 1 Lloyd's Rep. 531, CA; Reported [1996] 1 Lloyd's Rep. 485, QBD (Comm Ct) 24–018

Arab Monetary Fund v. Hashim (No.9) [1996] 1 Lloyd's Rep. 589, CA; affirming in part [1993] 1 Lloyd's Rep. 543, QBD 21–017

Aramis, The [1989] 1 Lloyd's Rep. 213, CA; reversing [1987] 2 Lloyd's Rep. 58 .... 4–005, 15–052

Aratra Potato Co Ltd v. Egyptian Navigation Co (The El Amria) [1981] 2 Lloyd's Rep. 119; [1981] Com. L.R. 136, CA; affirming [1980] 1 Lloyd's Rep. 390, QBD (Adm Ct) 22–008, 22–033

Arawa, The. *See* Producers Meats Ltd v. Shaw Savill & Albion Co Ltd.

Arbitration between Moore & Co Ltd and Landauer & Co, Re [1921] 2 K.B. 519; [1921] All E.R. 466; 90 L.J.K.B. 731; 37 T.L.R. 452; 26 Com.Cas 267, CA 7–007

Arbitration between the General Trading Co (Ltd) v. van Stolk's Commissiehandel, Re
 (1911) 16 Com.Cas 95 15–035
Archbolds (Freightage) Ltd v. S Spanglett Ltd [1961] 1 Q.B. 374; [1961] 2 W.L.R. 170;
 [1961] 1 All E.R. 417; 105 S.J. 149, CA 21–027
Arctic Electronics Co (UK) Ltd v. McGregor Sea & Air Services Ltd [1985] 2 Lloyd's
 Rep. 510; [1986] R.T.R. 207, QBD (Comm Ct) 18–007
Argos, The. *See* Gaudet v. Brown; *sub nom.* Cargo ex Argos; Argos, Cargo, ex.
Aries Tanker Corp v. Total Transport Ltd (The Aries) [1977] 1 W.L.R. 185; [1977] 1 All
 E.R. 398; [1977] 1 Lloyd's Rep. 334; 121 S.J. 117, HL; affirming [1976] 2 Lloyd's
 Rep. 256, CA 15–007, 15–048, 18–007
Armagas Ltd v. Mundogas SA (The Ocean Frost) [1986] 2 W.L.R. 1063; [1986] 2 All
 E.R. 385; [1986] 2 Lloyd's Rep. 109; (1986) 83 L.S.G. 2002; (1986) 130 S.J. 430,
 HL; affirming [1986] A.C. 717; [1985] 3 W.L.R. 640; [1985] 3 All E.R. 795; [1985]
 1 Lloyd's Rep. 1; (1984) 81 L.S.G. 2169; (1984) 129 S.J. 362, CA 27–005,
 27–007, 27–011
Arnold Karberg & Co v. Blythe, Green Jourdain & Co [1915] 2 K.B. 379 2–020
Aruna Mills v. Dhanrajmal Gobindram [1968] 1 Q.B. 655; [1968] 2 W.L.R. 101; [1968]
 1 All E.R. 113; [1968] 1 Lloyd's Rep. 304; (1967) 111 S.J. 924 2–032
Asbestos Insurance Coverage Cases, Re [1985] 1 W.L.R. 331; [1985] 1 All E.R. 716;
 [1985] E.C.C. 531; (1985) 82 L.S.G. 1638; (1985) 129 S.J. 189, HL; reversing
 [1985] E.C.C. 355; (1985) 82 L.S.G. 364; (1985) 129 S.J. 131, CA 21–022
Ascot Commodities NV v. Northern Pacific Shipping (The Irini A) (No.2) [1999] 1 Lloyd's
 Rep. 189, QBD (Comm Ct) 24–005
Asfar v. Blundell [1896] 1 Q.B. 127, CA 19–034
Ashmore & Son c. C.S. Cox [1899] 1 Q.B. 436 5–003
Askin v. ABSA Bank Ltd [1999] I.L.Pr. 471; (1999) 96((13)) L.S.G. 32, CA 22–007
Associated Japanese Bank (International) Ltd v. Credit du Nord SA [1989] 1 W.L.R. 255;
 [1988] 3 All E.R. 902; [1989] Fin. L.R. 117; (1989) 86(8) L.S.G. 43; (1988) 138
 N.L.J. 109; (1989) 133 S.J. 81, QBD 6–011, 12–001
Astilleros Canarios SA v. Cape Hatteras Shipping Co Inc (The Cape Hatteras) [1982] 1
 Lloyd's Rep. 518 4–015
Astro Exito Navegacion SA v. Chase Manhattan Bank NA (The Messiniaki Tolmi) [1988]
 2 Lloyd's Rep. 217, CA; affirming [1986] 1 Lloyd's Rep. 455, QBD (Comm Ct) .. 11–008
Astro Exito Navegacion SA v. Southland Enterprise Co (The Messiniaki Tolmi) [1983] 2
 A.C. 787; [1983] 3 W.L.R. 130; [1983] 2 All E.R. 725; [1983] Com. L.R. 217;
 (1983) 80 L.S.G. 3083; (1983) 127 S.J. 461, HL; affirming [1982] Q.B. 1248;
 [1982] 3 W.L.R. 296; [1982] 3 All E.R. 335; [1981] 2 Lloyd's Rep. 595; [1982]
 Com. L.R. 106, CA 11–008
Astro Valiente Compania Naviera SA v. Pakistan Ministry of Food and Agriculture (The
 Emmanuel Colocotronis) (No.2) [1982] 1 W.L.R. 1096; [1982] 1 All E.R. 823;
 [1982] 1 Lloyd's Rep. 286, QBD (Comm Ct) 15–023
Athanasia Comninos and Georges Chr Lemos, The [1990] 1 Lloyd's Rep. 277, QBD
 (Comm Ct) 15–050
Atisa SA v. Aztec AG [1983] 2 Lloyd's Rep. 579, QBD (Comm Ct) 6–012
Atlantic Maritime Co Inc v. Gibbon [1954] 1 Q.B. 105; [1953] 3 W.L.R. 714; [1953] 2
 All E.R. 1086; [1953] 2 Lloyd's Rep. 294; 97 S.J. 760, CA; affirming [1954] 1
 Q.B. 88; [1953] 2 W.L.R. 725; [1953] 1 All E.R. 893; [1953] 1 Lloyd's Rep. 278;
 97 S.J. 248, QBD 6–009
Atlas Express Ltd v. Kafco (Importers and Distributors) Ltd [1989] Q.B. 833; [1989] 3
 W.L.R. 389; [1989] 1 All E.R. 641; (1990) 9 Tr. L.R. 56; (1989) 139 N.L.J. 111;
 (1989) 133 S.J. 977, QBD (Comm Ct) 27–027
Atlas, The. *See* Noble Resources Ltd v. Cavalier Shipping Corp.
Att.-Gen. of Ceylon v. Scindia Steam Navigation Co, India [1962] A.C. 60; [1961]
 3 W.L.R. 936; [1961] 32 All E.R. 684; [1961] 2 Lloyd's Rep. 173; 105 S.J. 865,
 PC 15–036
Att.-Gen. of Hong Kong v. Chan Nai-Keung (Daniel) [1987] 1 W.L.R. 1339; (1987) 3
 B.C.C. 403; (1988) 86 Cr. App. R. 174; [1988] Crim. L.R. 125; (1987) 131 S.J.
 1185, PC 26–028
Att.-Gen. of Hong Kong v. Reid [1994] 1 A.C. 324; [1993] 3 W.L.R. 1143; [1994] 1 All
 E.R. 1; (1993) 143 N.L.J. 1569; (1993) 137 S.J.L.B. 251; [1993] N.P.C. 144, PC . 27–011
Att.-Gen. of Hong Kong v. Tse Hung-lit [1986] A.C. 876; [1986] 3 W.L.R. 320; [1986] 3
 All E.R. 173; (1986) 83 L.S.G. 1995; (1986) 130 S.J. 554, PC 26–030

Att.-Gen. of New Zealand v. Ortiz [1984] A.C. 1; [1983] 2 W.L.R. 809; [1983] 2 All E.R. 93; [1983] 2 Lloyd's Rep. 265; (1983) 133 N.L.J. 537; (1983) 127 S.J. 307, HL; affirming [1982] 3 W.L.R. 570; [1982] 3 All E.R. 432; [1982] 2 Lloyd's Rep. 224; [1982] Com. L.R. 156; (1982) 79 L.S.G. 919; (1982) 126 S.J. 429, CA; reversing [1982] Q.B. 349; [1982] 2 W.L.R. 10; [1982] 1 Lloyd's Rep. 173; 125 S.J. 530, QBD 21–025, 26–030
Att.-Gen. v. Heinemann Publishers Australia [1988] 165 C.L.R. 30 21–025
Att.-Gen. v. Wellington Newspapers Ltd [1988] 1 N.Z.L.R. 129 21–025
Attock Cement Co Ltd v. Romanian Bank for Foreign Trade [1989] 1 W.L.R. 1147; [1989] 1 All E.R. 1189; [1989] 1 Lloyd's Rep. 572; (1989) 86(39) L.S.G. 36; (1989) 133 S.J. 1298, CA 11–020, 12–001
Attorney General of Ghana and Ghana National Petroleum Corp v. Texaco Overseas Tank Ships Ltd (The Texaco Melbourne) [1994] 1 Lloyd's Rep. 473, HL; affirming [1993] 1 Lloyd's Rep. 471, CA; reversing [1992] 1 Lloyd's Rep. 319; [1992] 1 Lloyd's Rep. 303, QBD (Comm Ct) 21–018
Attorney General's Reference (No.1 of 1982), Re [1983] Q.B. 751; [1983] 3 W.L.R. 72; [1983] 2 All E.R. 721; [1983] Crim. L.R. 534; (1984) 148 J.P. 115; (1983) 127 S.J. 377, CA 21–028
Attorney General's Reference (No.1 of 1998), Re (1999) 163 J.P. 390; (1999) 163 J.P.N. 473; (1998) 95(37) L.S.G. 36; (1998) 142 S.J.L.B. 250, CA (Crim Div) 26–031
August 8, The [1983] 2 A.C. 450; [1983] 2 W.L.R. 419; [1983] 1 Lloyd's Rep. 351; (1983) 127 S.J. 450, PC 22–033
Ault & Wiborg Paints v. Sure Service *The Times*, July 2, 1983, CA 30–005, 30–011
Austin Baldwin & Co v. Wilfred Turner & Co (1920) 36 T.L.R. 769 6–009
Australian Coastal Shipping Commission v. Green [1971] 1 Q.B. 456; [1971] 2 W.L.R. 243; [1971] 1 All E.R. 353; [1971] 1 Lloyd's Rep. 16; 115 S.J. 57, CA; affirming [1970] 1 All E.R. 968; [1970] 1 Lloyd's Rep. 209, QBD (Comm Ct) 19–027
Automatic Tube Co Pty Ltd v. Adelaide Steamship (Operations) Ltd (The Beltana) [1967] 1 Lloyd's Rep. 531; 117 N.L.J. 914 15–048
Azov Shipping Co v. Baltic Shipping Co (No.2) [1999] 1 All E.R. (Comm) 716; [1999] 2 Lloyd's Rep. 39; [1999] C.L.C. 624, QBD (Comm Ct) 23–017

B&S Contracts and Design v. Victor Green Publications [1984] I.C.R. 419; (1984) 81 L.S.G. 893; (1984) 128 S.J. 279, CA; affirming [1982] I.C.R. 654 .... 6–003, 6–017
B. & P. Wholesale Distributors v. Marko *The Times*, February 20, 1953 5–005
Bailey (TD) Son & Co v. Ross T. Smyth & Co Ltd (1940) 56 T.L.R. 825 .... 2–019, 2–020, 11–001
Bain Clarkson v. Owners of Sea Friends (The Sea Friends) [1991] 2 Lloyd's Rep. 322, CA 19–003
Baker v. Gibbons [1972] 1 W.L.R. 693; [1972] 2 All E.R. 759; 116 S.J. 313 27–011
Balkanbank v. Taher (No.3) [1995] 1 W.L.R. 1067; (1994) 92(1) L.S.G. 37; (1995) 139 S.J.L.B. 16, CA 22–003
Balli Trading Ltd v. Afalona Shipping Ltd (The Coral) [1993] 1 Lloyd's Rep. 1; (1992) 89(34) L.S.G. 40; (1992) 136 S.J.L.B. 259, CA; reversing [1992] 2 Lloyd's Rep. 158, QBD (Adm Ct) 15–041
Baltimex Baltic Import and Export Co v. Metallo Chemical Refining Co [1956] 1 Lloyd's Rep. 450, CA; affirming [1955] 2 Lloyd's Rep. 438 .... 6–017, 11–018, 11–033
Banco Atlantico SA v. British Bank of the Middle East [1990] 2 Lloyd's Rep. 504, CA .. 22–007
Banco De Vizcaya v. Don Alfonso De Bourbon y Austria [1935] 1 K.B. 140 21–025
Bangladesh Export Import Co Ltd v. Sucden Kerry SA [1995] 2 Lloyd's Rep. 1, CA 6–012
Bank Line Ltd v. Arthur Capel & Co [1919] A.C. 435, HL 6–005
Bank Mellat v. Helleniki Techniki SA [1984] Q.B. 291; [1983] 3 W.L.R. 783; [1983] 3 All E.R. 428; [1983] Com. L.R. 273; (1983) 133 N.L.J. 597; (1983) 127 S.J. 618, CA; affirming [1983] Com. L.R. 174 23–025
Bank Melli Iran v. Barclays Bank (Dominion Colonial & Overseas) [1951] 2 Lloyd's Rep. 367; [1951] 2 T.L.R. 1057 .... 4–012, 11–007, 11–013
Bank Negara Indonesia 1946 v. Lariza (Singapore) Pte Ltd [1988] A.C. 583; [1988] 2 W.L.R. 374; [1988] 1 Lloyd's Rep. 407; [1988] Fin. L.R. 197; (1988) 132 S.J. 125, PC 11–034, 11–036
Bank of America National Trust and Savings Association v. Chrismas (The Kyriaki) [1994] 1 All E.R. 401; [1993] 1 Lloyd's Rep. 137, QBD (Comm Ct) 19–033
Bank of Baroda v. Vysya Bank Ltd [1994] 2 Lloyd's Rep. 87; [1994] 3 Bank. L.R. 216, QBD 11–020, 21–009

Bank of Boston Connecticut (Formerly Colonial Bank) v. European Grain & Shipping Ltd
(The Dominique) [1989] A.C. 1056; [1989] 2 W.L.R. 440; [1989] 1 All E.R. 545;
[1989] 1 Lloyd's Rep. 431; (1989) 86(11) L.S.G. 43; (1989) 133 S.J. 219, HL;
reversing [1988] 3 W.L.R. 60; [1988] 3 All E.R. 233; [1988] 1 Lloyd's Rep. 215;
[1988] 1 F.T.L.R. 327; (1988) 132 S.J. 896, CA; reversing [1987] 1 Lloyd's Rep.
239, QBD (Comm Ct) 6–016, 15–007, 15–010
Bank of Credit & Commerce Hong Kong Ltd v. Sonali Bank [1995] 1 Lloyd's Rep. 227,
QBD (Comm Ct) 11–020
Bank of Cyprus (London) v. Jones (1984) 134 N.L.J. 522 9–004
Bank of Nova Scotia v. Angelic-Whitewear Ltd 36 D.L.R. (4th) 161 11–042
Bank of Nova Scotia v. Hellenic Mutual War Risk Association (Bermuda) (The Good
Luck) [1992] 1 A.C. 233; [1991] 2 W.L.R. 1279; [1991] 3 All E.R. 1; [1991] 2
Lloyd's Rep. 191; (1991) 141 N.L.J. 779, HL; reversing [1990] 1 Q.B. 818; [1990]
2 W.L.R. 547; [1989] 3 All E.R. 628; [1989] 2 Lloyd's Rep. 238; (1990) 87(10)
L.S.G. 34, CA; reversing [1992] 2 Lloyd's Rep. 540 (Note); [1988] 1 Lloyd's Rep.
514, QBD (Comm Ct) 19–012, 19–017
Bank Polski v. KJ Mulder & Co [1942] 1 K.B. 497, CA; affirming [1941] 2 K.B. 266 9–004
Bankers Trust Co v. State Bank of India [1991] 2 Lloyd's Rep. 443, CA; affirming [1991]
1 Lloyd's Rep. 587, QBD (Comm Ct) 11–009, 11–010
Banque de l'Indochine et de Suez SA v. JH Rayner (Mincing Lane) Ltd [1983] Q.B. 711;
[1983] 2 W.L.R. 841; [1983] 1 All E.R. 1137; [1983] 1 Lloyd's Rep. 228; (1983)
127 S.J. 361, CA; affirming [1983] 2 W.L.R. 841; [1983] 1 All E.R. 468; [1982] 2
Lloyd's Rep. 476; [1982] Com. L.R. 205, QBD 2–024, 11–003, 11–008,
11–016, 11–038
Banque des Marchands de Moscou (Koupetschesky) (No.1), Re; Royal Exchange Assurance v. Liquidator; Wilenkin v. Liquidator (No.1) [1952] 1 All E.R. 1269; [1952]
1 T.L.R. 739; [1952] W.N. 151, Ch D 27–009
Banque Financiere de la Cite SA v. Westgate Insurance Co; *sub nom.* Banque Keyser
Ullmann SA v. Skandia (UK) Insurance Co [1991] 2 A.C. 249; [1990] 3 W.L.R.
364; [1990] 2 All E.R. 947; [1990] 2 Lloyd's Rep. 377; (1990) 87(35) L.S.G. 36;
(1990) 140 N.L.J. 1074; (1990) 134 S.J. 1265, HL; affirming [1990] 1 Q.B. 665;
[1989] 3 W.L.R. 25; [1989] 2 All E.R. 952; [1988] 2 Lloyd's Rep. 513; [1989] Fin.
L.R. 1; (1989) 133 S.J. 817, CA; reversing [1987] 2 W.L.R. 1300; [1987] 2 All
E.R. 923; [1987] 1 Lloyd's Rep. 69; [1987] Fin. L.R. 134; (1987) 84 L.S.G. 1965;
(1987) 131 S.J. 775, QBD 19–012
Banque Keyser Ullmann SA v. Skandia (UK) Insurance Co. *See* Banque Financiere de la
Cite SA v. Westgate Insurance Co.
Barber (J) & Sons v. Lloyd's Underwriters [1987] Q.B. 103; [1986] 3 W.L.R. 515; [1986]
2 All E.R. 845; [1987] E.C.C. 154; (1986) 83 L.S.G. 3253; (1986) 136 N.L.J. 658;
(1986) 130 S.J. 730, QBD 21–022
Barclays Bank International Ltd v. Levin Bros (Bradford) Ltd [1977] Q.B. 270; [1976] 3
W.L.R. 852; [1976] 3 All E.R. 900; [1977] 1 Lloyd's Rep. 51; 120 S.J. 801, QBD   9–005,
9–007, 21–018
Barclays Bank Ltd v. Customs and Excise Commissioners [1963] 1 Lloyd's Rep. 81, QBD
(Comm Ct) 15–038
Barclays Bank Plc v. Kapur [1991] 2 A.C. 355; [1991] 2 W.L.R. 401; [1991] 1 All E.R.
646; [1991] I.C.R. 208; [1991] I.R.L.R. 136, HL; affirming [1989] I.C.R. 753;
[1989] I.R.L.R. 387, CA; reversing [1989] I.C.R. 142; [1989] I.R.L.R. 57; (1989)
86(5) L.S.G. 41 28–021
Barclays Bank Plc v. Quincecare Ltd [1988] 1 F.T.L.R. 507; [1988] Fin. L.R. 166, QBD . 11–042
Barlee Marine Corp v. Trevor Rex Mountain (The Leegas) [1987] 1 Lloyd's Rep. 471 3–016
Basma (Abdul Karim) v. Weekes [1950] A.C. 441; [1950] 2 All E.R. 146; 66 T.L.R. (Pt.
1) 1047, PC 27–019
Batchelor (TB & S) & Co Ltd v. Owners of the SS Merak (The Merak) [1965] P. 223;
[1965] 2 W.L.R. 250; [1965] 1 All E.R. 230; [1964] 2 Lloyd's Rep. 527; 108 S.J.
1012, CA; affirming [1964] 3 All E.R. 638; [1964] 2 Lloyd's Rep. 283, PDAD 15–023
Bayer AG v. Winter [1986] 1 W.L.R. 497; [1986] 1 All E.R. 733; [1986] F.S.R. 323;
(1986) 83 L.S.G. 974; (1985) 136 N.L.J. 187; (1985) 130 S.J. 246, CA 22–031
Bayerische Vereinsbank AG v. National Bank of Pakistan [1997] 1 Lloyd's Rep. 59; [1997]
6 Bank. L.R. 319; [1996] C.L.C. 1443, QBD (Comm Ct) 11–007, 11–009,
11–010, 11–019
Baytur SA v. Moona Silk Mills December 20, 1984, unreported, noted in [1985] J.B.L.
324 12–004

Bazias 3, The. *See* Greenmar Navigation v. Owners of Ships Bazias 3 and Bazias 4 and Sally Line.

Beale v. South Devon Rly Co (1864) 3 H. & C. 337 27–011

Beck v. Binks [1949] 1 K.B. 250; [1948] 2 All E.R. 1058; 64 T.L.R. 633; 47 L.G.R. 34; (1950) 113 J.P. 54; [1949] L.J.R. 508, DC 26–031

Belgrano, *The Financial Times*, November 26, 1985, CA 2–010

Beltana, The. *See* Automatic Tube Co Pty Ltd v. Adelaide Steamship (Operations) Ltd.

Bem Dis A Turk Ticaret S/Λ Tr v. International Agri Trade Co Ltd (The Selda) [1999] 1 All E.R. (Comm) 619, CA; affirming [1998] 1 Lloyd's Rep. 416, QBD (Comm Ct) 5–007

Benaim v. Debono [1924] A.C. 514 5–006

Benarty, The. *See* Lister (RA) & Co v. EG Thomson (Shipping) Ltd and PT Djakarta Lloyd.

Bence Graphics International Ltd v. Fasson U.K. Ltd [1998] Q.B. 87; [1997] 3 W.L.R. 205; [1997] 1 All E.R. 979, CA 5–003

Benincasa v. Dentalkit Srl (C269/95) [1998] All E.R. (E.C.) 135; [1997] E.T.M.R. 447; [1997] I.L.Pr. 559, ECJ 22–018

Benmag Ltd v. Barda [1955] 2 Lloyd's Rep. 354, Q.B.D. 27–011

Bergen, The (No.1) [1997] 1 Lloyd's Rep. 380; [1997] C.L.C. 444, QBD (Adm Ct) 22–030

Bergen, The (No.2) [1997] 2 Lloyd's Rep. 710, QBD (Adm Ct) 22–008

Berger & Co v. Gill & Duffus SA. *See* Gill & Duffus SA v. Berger & Co Inc.

Bergerco USA v. Vegoil Ltd [1984] 1 Lloyd's Rep. 440 .... 2–026, 2–032, 5–004, 5–005, 5–006, 5–007

Berk (FW) v. Style [1956] 1 Q.B. 180; [1955] 3 W.L.R. 935; [1955] 3 All E.R. 625; [1955] 2 Lloyd's Rep. 382; 99 S.J. 889 .... 7–010, 19–024

Berndston v. Strang (1868) L.R. 3 Ch.App 588 5–016

Bernstein v. Pamson Motors (Golders Green) Ltd [1987] 2 All E.R. 220; [1987] 6 T.L.R. 33; [1987] R.T.R. 384 5–005

Bessler Waechter Glover & Co v. South Derwent Coal [1938] 1 K.B. 408 5–012

Beverley Acceptances v. Oakley [1982] R.T.R. 417, CA 27–017

Biddell Bros v. E Clemens Horst Co [1912] A.C. 18; [1911] 1 K.B. 214 .... 2–020, 2–027, 2–031, 4–003, 5–005

Bilbee v. Hasse & Co (1889) 5 T.L.R. 677 27–012

Black Clawson International Ltd v. Papierwerke Waldhof-Aschaffenburg AG [1975] A.C. 591; [1975] 2 W.L.R. 513; [1975] 1 All E.R. 810; [1975] 2 Lloyd's Rep. 11; 119 S.J. 221, HL; reversing [1974] Q.B. 660; [1974] 2 W.L.R. 789; [1974] 2 All E.R. 611; [1974] 1 Lloyd's Rep. 573; 118 S.J. 365, CA 24–010

Blackpool and Fylde Aero Club v. Blackpool BC [1990] 1 W.L.R. 1195; [1990] 3 All E.R. 25; 88 L.G.R. 864; (1991) 3 Admin. L.R. 322; (1991) 155 L.G. Rev. 246, CA 3–004

Board of Trade v. Owen [1957] A.C. 602; [1957] 2 W.L.R. 351; [1957] 1 All E.R. 411; (1957) 41 Cr. App. R. 11; 121 J.P. 177; 101 S.J. 186, HL; affirming *sub nom.* R. v. Owen [1957] 1 Q.B. 174; [1956] 3 W.L.R. 739; [1956] 3 All E.R. 432; 120 J.P. 553; 100 S.J. 769, CCA; reversing in part [1956] 3 W.L.R. 252; (1956) 40 Cr. App. R. 103; 100 S.J. 454 21–028

Boardman v. Phipps [1967] 2 A.C. 46; [1966] 3 W.L.R. 1009; [1966] 3 All E.R. 721; 110 S.J. 853, HL; affirming Phipps v. Boardman [1965] Ch. 992; [1965] 2 W.L.R. 839; [1965] 1 All E.R. 849; 109 S.J. 197, CA; affirming [1964] 1 W.L.R. 993; [1964] 2 All E.R. 187; 108 S.J. 619 27–011

Boks & Co Ltd v. JH Rayner & Co Ltd (1921) 37 T.L.R. 800, CA 2–015, 5–005

Bolivinter Oil SA v. Chase Manhattan Bank NA [1984] 1 W.L.R. 392; [1984] 1 Lloyd's Rep. 251; (1984) 128 S.J. 153, CA 11–006, 11–042, 11–043, 12–002, 12–005

Bond Worth Ltd, Re [1980] Ch.D. 228 4–009

Booth Steamship Co Ltd v. Cargo Fleet Iron Co Ltd [1916] 2 K.B. 570 15–013

Boots v. E Christopher & Co [1952] 1 K.B. 89; [1951] 2 All E.R. 1045; [1951] 2 T.L.R. 1169; 95 S.J. 788, CA; reversing [1951] W.N. 269 27–012

Borden (UK) Ltd v. Scottish Timber Products Ltd [1981] Ch. 25; [1979] 3 W.L.R. 672; [1979] 3 All E.R. 961; [1980] 1 Lloyd's Rep. 160; 123 S.J. 688, CA; reversing [1979] 2 Lloyd's Rep. 168; 122 S.J. 825 4–009

Borealis AB v. Stargas Ltd (The Berge Sisar) [1999] Q.B. 863; [1998] 3 W.L.R. 1353; [1998] 4 All E.R. 821; [1998] 2 Lloyd's Rep. 475; [1998] C.L.C. 1589, CA; reversing [1997] 1 Lloyd's Rep. 642 (Note); [1997] 1 Lloyd's Rep. 635, QBD (Comm Ct) 15–052

Borrowman v. Free (1878) 4 Q.B.D. 500 5–007

Boss Group Ltd v. Boss France SA [1997] 1 W.L.R. 351; [1996] 4 All E.R. 970; [1996]
L.R.L.R. 403; [1996] C.L.C. 1419; [1996] I.L.Pr. 544; (1996) 146 N.L.J. 918,
CA 22–018

Boston Deep Sea Fishing & Ice Co v. Ansell (1888) L.R. 39 Ch. D. 339 27–011

Boston Deep Sea Fishing and Ice Co v. Farnham [1957] 1 W.L.R. 1051; [1957] 3 All E.R.
204; [1957] 2 Lloyd's Rep. 238; 50 R. & I.T. 675; 37 T.C. 505; 36 A.T.C. 211;
[1957] T.R. 243; 101 S.J. 834 27–008

Boukadoura Maritime Corp v. Marocaine de l'Industrie et du Raffinage SA (The
Boukadoura) [1989] 1 Lloyd's Rep. 393, QBD 15–036

Bowes Shand (1877) 2 App. Cas 455 5–003

Boyd (David T) & Co Ltd v. Louis Louca [1973] 1 Lloyd's Rep. 209 .... 2–005, 2–016

Boyter v. Thomson [1995] 2 A.C. 628; [1995] 3 W.L.R. 36; [1995] 3 All E.R. 135; 1995
S.C. (HL) 15; (1995) 145 N.L.J. 922; (1995) 139 S.J.L.B. 174; [1995] 2 A.C. 629;
1995 S.L.T. 875; 1995 S.C.L.R. 1009, HL 27–005

BP Exploration Co (Libya) Ltd v. Hunt (No.2) [1983] 2 A.C. 352; [1982] 2 W.L.R. 253;
[1982] 1 All E.R. 925, HL; affirming [1981] 1 W.L.R. 232; 125 S.J. 165, CA;
affirming [1979] 1 W.L.R. 783; 123 S.J. 455, QBD 6–007, 6–015, 21–018

BP Oil International Ltd v. Surena Delmar Navegacion SA (The Irini M) [1988] 1 Lloyd's
Rep. 253, QBD (Comm Ct) 15–043

Bragg v. Villanova (1923) 40 T.L.R. 154 5–005

Brandies, Goldschmidt & Co v. Ecomonic Insurance Co Ltd (1922) 38 T.L.R. 609 19–029

Brandt (HO) & Co v. H. N. Morris & Co Ltd [1917] 2 K.B. 784 .... 2–009, 2–017

Brandt v. Liverpool Brazil and River Plate Steam Navigation Co [1924] 1 K.B. 575 15–052

Brass v. Maitland [1856] 26 L.J.Q.B. 49 15–050

Brauer & Co (Great Britain) Ltd v. James Clark (Brush Materials) Ltd [1952] 2 All E.R.
497; [1952] 2 Lloyd's Rep. 147; [1952] 2 T.L.R. 349; [1952] W.N. 422; 96 S.J.
548, CA; reversing [1952] 1 All E.R. 981; [1952] 1 Lloyd's Rep. 385; [1952] 1
T.L.R. 953; [1952] W.N. 187; 96 S.J. 246, QBD 6–003, 6–012, 6–020

Bremer Handelsgesellschaft GmbH v. Mackprang (C) Jr [1979] 1 Lloyd's Rep. 221, CA;
reversing in part [1977] 2 Lloyd's Rep. 467, QBD (Comm Ct) 6–009

Bremer Handelsgesellschaft GmbH v. Toepfer [1980] 2 Lloyd's Rep. 43, CA; affirming
[1978] 1 Lloyd's Rep. 643, QBD (Comm Ct) 28–007

Bremer Handelsgesellschaft mbH v. Rayner (JH) & Co [1979] 2 Lloyd's Rep. 216, CA;
reversing [1978] 2 Lloyd's Rep. 73 2–009

Bremer Handelsgesellschaft mbH v. Vanden-Avenne Izegem PVBA [1978] 2 Lloyd's Rep.
109, HL; reversing [1977] 2 Lloyd's Rep. 329, CA; reversing [1977] 1 Lloyd's
Rep. 133 .... 2–033, 5–004, 6–018

Bremer Vulkan Schiffbau und Maschinenfabrik v. South India Shipping Corp Ltd; Gregg
v. Raytheon; sub nom. Gregg v. Raytheon; Bremer Vulkan Schiffbau und Maschinenfabrik v. South India Shipping Corp [1981] A.C. 909; [1981] 2 W.L.R. 141;
[1981] 2 All E.R. 289; [1981] 1 Lloyd's Rep. 253; [1981] Com. L.R. 19; [1981]
E.C.C. 151; 125 S.J. 114, HL; affirming [1980] 2 W.L.R. 905; [1980] 1 All E.R.
420; [1980] 1 Lloyd's Rep. 255; 124 S.J. 396, CA; affirming [1979] 3 W.L.R. 905;
[1979] 3 All E.R. 194; (1979) 76 L.S.G. 834; 123 S.J. 504, QBD 6–004, 23–004

Bridges & Salmon Ltd v. Owner of The Swan (The Swan); Marine Diesel Service
(Grimsby) Ltd v. Same [1968] 1 Lloyd's Rep. 5; sub nom. Bridges & Salmon v.
Swan, The (Owner) (1968) 118 N.L.J. 182 27–005

Brimnes, The; Tenax Steamship Co v. Brimnes, The (Owners) [1975] Q.B. 929; [1974] 3
W.L.R. 613; 118 S.J. 808; sub nom. Brimnes, The; Tenax Steamship Co v. Owners
of the Motor Vessel Brimnes [1974] 3 All E.R. 88; sub nom. Tenax Steamship Co
v. Brimnes, The (Owners); Brimnes, The [1974] 2 Lloyd's Rep. 241, CA; affirming
sub nom. Tenax Steamship Co v. Reinante Transoceanica Navegacion SA; Brimnes,
The [1973] 1 W.L.R. 386; 117 S.J. 244; sub nom. Tenax Steamship Co v. Brimnes,
The (Owners) [1972] 2 Lloyd's Rep. 465; [1973] 1 All E.R. 769 3–008

Brinkibon v. Stahag Stahl und Stahlwarenhandels GmbH [1983] 2 A.C. 34; [1982] 2
W.L.R. 264; [1982] 1 All E.R. 293; [1982] 1 Lloyd's Rep. 217; [1982] Com. L.R.
72; [1982] E.C.C. 322; 126 S.J. 116, HL; affirming [1980] 2 Lloyd's Rep. 556,
CA 3–008, 11–018

British Aerospace Plc v. Dee Howard Co [1993] 1 Lloyd's Rep. 368, QBD (Comm Ct) ... 22–008

British Airways Board v. Laker Airways Ltd [1985] A.C. 58; [1984] 3 W.L.R. 413; [1984]
3 All E.R. 39; [1985] E.C.C. 49; (1984) 81 L.S.G. 2849; (1984) 134 N.L.J. 746;

(1984) 128 S.J. 531, HL; reversing [1984] Q.B. 142; [1983] 3 W.L.R. 544; [1983] 3 All E.R. 375; [1983] Com. L.R. 254; [1984] E.C.C. 36; (1983) 80 L.S.G. 2437; (1983) 127 S.J. 646, CA; reversing [1983] Com. L.R. 212; [1983] E.C.C. 503, QBD 21–021, 22–009

British American Tobacco Ltd v. Inland Revenue Commissioners [1943] A.C. 335; [1943] 1 All E.R. 13; 59 T.L.R. 91, HL [1941] 2 K.B. 270, CA 28–008

British Bank for Foreign Trade v. Novinex [1949] 1 K.B. 623; [1949] 1 All E.R. 155; [1949] L.J.R. 658; 93 S.J. 146, CA 27–012

British Electrical and Associated Industries (Cardiff) Ltd v. Patley Pressings Ltd [1953] 1 W.L.R. 280; [1953] 1 All E.R. 94; 97 S.J. 96, QBD 6–020

British Imex Industries v. Midland Bank Ltd [1958] 1 Q.B. 542; [1958] 2 W.L.R. 103; [1958] 1 All E.R. 264; [1957] 2 Lloyd's Rep. 591; 102 S.J. 69 .... 11–008, 11–026, 11–029, 15–036

British Leyland Motor Corp Ltd v. TI Silencers Ltd (1980) [1981] Com. L.R. 3; [1981] 2 C.M.L.R. 75; [1981] F.S.R. 213, CA; reversing [1980] 2 C.M.L.R. 332; [1980] F.S.R. 400, Ch D 29–018

British Movietonews v. London and District Cinemas [1952] A.C. 166; [1951] 2 All E.R. 617; [1951] 2 T.L.R. 571; 95 S.J. 499, HL; reversing [1951] 1 K.B. 190; [1950] 2 All E.R. 390; 66 T.L.R. (Pt. 2) 203; 94 S.J. 504, CA 6–002, 6–003, 6–011

British Nylon Spinners v. Imperial Chemical Industries [1953] Ch. 19; [1952] 2 All E.R. 780; [1952] 2 T.L.R. 669; 69 R.P.C. 288, CA 21–022

British Steel Corp v. Cleveland Bridge & Engineering Co Ltd [1984] 1 All E.R. 504; [1982] Com. L.R. 54; 24 B.L.R. 94 3–015

British Syphon Co v. Homewood (No.2) [1956] 1 W.L.R. 1190; [1956] 2 All E.R. 897; [1956] R.P.C. 225, 330; 100 S.J. 633, Ch D 27–011

Brogden v. Metropolitan Railways [1877] 2 A.C. 666 3–009

Bromarin AB v. IMD Investments Ltd [1999] S.T.C. 301; [1999] B.T.C. 74, CA reversing [1998] S.T.C. 244 6–010

Bronester v. Priddle [1961] 1 W.L.R. 1294; [1961] 3 All E.R. 471; 105 S.J. 683, CA 27–012

Broome v. Pardess Co-operative Society of Orange Growers (Est. 1900) [1939] 3 All E.R. 978 4–010

Brown & Gracie v. Green (FW) & Co Pty [1960] 1 Lloyd's Rep. 289, HL 3–013, 27–019

Brown Jenkinson & Co Ltd v. Percy Dalton (London) Ltd [1957] 2 Q.B. 621; [1957] 3 W.L.R. 403; [1957] 2 All E.R. 844; [1957] 2 Lloyd's Rep. 1; 101 S.J. 610, CA; reversing [1957] 1 Lloyd's Rep. 31, MCLC 15–039

Brown Shipley & Co v. Alicia Hosiery [1966] 1 Lloyd's Rep. 668; 116 N.L.J. 1144, CA 9–012

Browner International Ltd v. Monarch Shipping Co Ltd (The European Enterprise) [1989] 2 Lloyd's Rep. 185, QBD (Comm Ct) 15–022, 15–033

Brrok v. Hook L.R. Exch. 89 27–008

Brushfield Sargent & Co v. Holmwright Engineering Co [1968] 1 Lloyd's Rep. 439; 118 N.L.J. 542, QBD 27–027

Buckley v. Lever Bros Ltd [1953] 4 D.L.R. 16 14–002

Buena Trader, The. *See* Compania de Navegacion Pohing SA v. Sea Tanker Shipping (Pte.).

Bulk Oil (Zug) AG v. Trans Asiatic Oil Ltd SA [1973] 1 Lloyd's Rep. 129, QBD 23–016

Bumper Development Corp v. Commissioner of Police of the Metropolis [1991] 1 W.L.R. 1362; [1991] 4 All E.R. 638; (1991) 135 S.J. 382, CA 21–001, 21–002

Bunge AG v. Sesostrad (The Alkeos C) [1984] 1 Lloyd's Rep. 687; (1984) 134 N.L.J. 705 2–009

Bunge Corp v. Tradax Export SA [1981] 1 W.L.R. 711; [1981] 2 All E.R. 540; [1981] 2 Lloyd's Rep. 1; 125 S.J. 373, HL; affirming [1981] 2 All E.R. 524; [1980] 1 Lloyd's Rep. 294, CA; reversing [1979] 2 Lloyd's Rep. 477 .... 2–010, 5–003, 5–004

Bunge Corp v. Vegetable Vitamin Foods (Pte) Ltd [1985] 1 Lloyd's Rep. 613; (1984) 134 N.L.J. 125, QBD (Comm Ct) 11–018

Bunge GmbH v. Alfred C Toepfer [1978] 1 Lloyd's Rep. 506 2–026

Bunge NV v. Compagnie Noga d'importation et d'Exportation SA (The Bow Cedar) [1980] 2 Lloyd's Rep. 601; [1981] Com. L.R. 92 4–012

Bunge SA v. Deutsche Conti Handelsgesellschaft GmbH [1979] 2 Lloyd's Rep. 435, CA 6–009

Bunge SA v. Kruse [1980] 2 Lloyd's Rep. 142, CA; affirming [1979] 1 Lloyd's Rep. 279 2–033

Bunge SA v. Schleswig-Holsteinische Landwirtschaftliche Hauptgenossenschaft Eingetr
GmbH [1978] 1 Lloyd's Rep. 480 2–026
Bunten & Lancaster (Produce) v. Kiril Mischeff [1964] 1 Lloyd's Rep. 386 2–043
Burke (Raymond) Motors v. Mersey Docks & Harbour Co [1986] 1 Lloyd's Rep. 155 2–007,
15–005, 16–002, 27–025
Butler Machine Tool Co v. Ex-cell-o Corp (England) [1979] 1 W.L.R. 401; [1979] 1 All
E.R. 965; 121 S.J. 406, CA 3–018
Buttes Gas and Oil Co v. Hammer (No.3); Occidental Petroleum Corp v. Buttes Gas and
Oil Co (No.2) [1982] A.C. 888; [1981] 3 W.L.R. 787; [1981] 3 All E.R. 616; [1981]
Com. L.R. 257; 125 S.J. 776, HL; reversing [1981] Q.B. 223; [1980] 3 W.L.R.
668; [1980] 3 All E.R. 475; 124 S.J. 630, CA 21–019, 21–022
Byrne v. Low [1972] 1 W.L.R. 1282; [1972] 3 All E.R. 526; 116 S.J. 762, DC 26–030

Calico Printers Association Ltd v. Barclays Bank (1930) 36 Com.Cas 197, CA 10–004
Camdex International Ltd v. Bank of Zambia (No.3) [1997] 6 Bank. L.R. 44; [1997] C.L.C.
714, CA 21–026
Canada Trust Co v. Stolzenberg (No.2) [1998] 1 W.L.R. 547; [1998] 1 All E.R. 318; [1998]
C.L.C. 23; [1998] I.L.Pr. 290, CA 22–022
Canadian Pacific (Bermuda) Ltd v. Lagon Maritime Overseas (The Fort Kipp) [1985] 2
Lloyd's Rep. 168, QBD (Comm Ct) 15–018
Cape Asbestos Co v. Lloyds Bank [1921] W.N. 274 11–024
Capitan San Luis, The [1994] Q.B. 465; [1994] 2 W.L.R. 299; [1993] 2 Lloyd's Rep. 573,
QBD 15–046
Captain George K. The. *See* Palmco Shipping Inc v. Continental Ore Corp.
Carapanayoti & Co v. ET Green Ltd [1959] 1 Q.B. 131; [1958] 3 W.L.R. 390; [1958] 3
All E.R. 115; [1958] 2 Lloyd's Rep. 169; 102 S.J. 620 6–011
Cargill International SA v. Bangladesh Sugar & Food Industries Corp [1998] 1 W.L.R.
461; [1998] 2 All E.R. 406; [1998] C.L.C. 399; (1998) 95(3) L.S.G. 25; (1998) 142
S.J.L.B. 14, CA; affirming [1996] 4 All E.R. 563; [1996] 2 Lloyd's Rep. 524, QBD
(Comm Ct) 2–020, 12–004
Cargill International SA v. CPN Tankers (Bermuda) Ltd (The Ot Sonja) [1993] 2 Lloyd's
Rep. 435, CA 12–004, 15–048
Cargill UK v. Continental UK [1989] 2 Lloyd's Rep. 290, CA; affirming [1989] 1 Lloyd's
Rep. 193 .... 2–011, 2–012
Carl Zeiss Stiftung v. Rayner & Keeler Rayner & Keeler Ltd v. Courts [1967] 1 A.C. 853,
sub nom. Carl Zeiss Stiftung v. Rayner & Keeler [1966] 3 W.L.R. 125; [1966] 2
All E.R. 536; [1967] R.P.C. 497; 110 S.J. 425, HL; reversing [1965] Ch. 596;
[1965] 2 W.L.R. 277; [1965] 1 All E.R. 300; [1965] R.P.C. 141; 109 S.J. 51, CA;
reversing [1964] R.P.C. 299; [1965] C.L.Y. 557 .... 21–024, 24–005
Carle & Montanari Inc v. American Export Isbrandtsen Lines Inc [1968] 1 Lloyd's Rep.
260 2–007
Carlos Federspiel & Co SA v. Charles Twigg & Co Ltd [1957] 1 Lloyd's Rep. 240 4–005
Carlson v. Rio Tinto Plc [1999] C.L.C. 551, QBD 22–008
Carter v. Boehm (1766) 3 Burr. 1905 19–012
Caspian Basin Caspian Basin Specialised Emergency Salvage Administration v. Bouygues
Offshore SA (No.4); Ultisol Transport Contractors Ltd v. Bouygues Offshore SA
[1997] 2 Lloyd's Rep. 507; [1997] C.L.C. 1463; (1997) 94(35) L.S.G. 35; *The
Times*, July 3, 1997, QBD (Adm Ct) 15–046
Castle Insurance Co v. Hong Kong Islands Shipping Co (The Potoi Chau) [1984] A.C.
226; [1983] 3 W.L.R. 524; [1983] 3 All E.R. 706; [1983] 2 Lloyd's Rep. 376;
(1983) 127 S.J. 616, PC 19–028
Cedar Trading Co Ltd v. Transworld Oil Ltd; (The Gudermes) [1985] 2 Lloyd's Rep.
623 3–003
Cehave NV v. Bremer Handelgesellschaft mbH (The Hansa Nord) [1976] Q.B. 44; [1975]
3 W.L.R. 447; [1975] 3 All E.R. 739; [1975] 2 Lloyd's Rep. 445; 119 S.J. 678,
CA; reversing [1974] 2 Lloyd's Rep. 216 .... 4–010, 5–004, 5–008
Central London Property Trust v. High Trees House [1947] K.B. 130; [1956] 1 All E.R.
256 (Note); 62 T.L.R. 557; 175 L.T. 333; [1947] L.J.R. 77 5–012
Cepheus Shipping Corp v. Guardian Royal Exchange Assurance Plc (The Capricorn)
[1995] 1 Lloyd's Rep. 622, QBD 19–014
Chabbra Corp Pte Ltd v. Owners of the Jag Shakti (The Jag Shakti) [1986] A.C. 337;
[1986] 2 W.L.R. 87; [1986] 1 All E.R. 480; [1986] 1 Lloyd's Rep. 1; (1986) 83
L.S.G. 45; (1986) 130 S.J. 51, PC 15–038, 15–052

Chaigley Farms Ltd v. Crawford Kaye & Grayshire Ltd (t/a Leylands) [1996] B.C.
957 4–009
Channel Island Ferries Ltd v. Cenargo Navigation Ltd (The Rozel) [1994] 2 Lloyd's Rep.
161, QBD 23–018
Channel Tunnel Group and France Manche SA v. Balfour Beatty Construction Ltd [1993]
A.C. 334; [1993] 2 W.L.R. 262; [1993] 1 All E.R. 664; [1993] 1 Lloyd's Rep. 291;
61 B.L.R. 1; 32 Con. L.R. 1; [1993] I.L.Pr. 607; (1993) 137 S.J.L.B. 36; [1993]
N.P.C. 8, HL, affirming [1992] Q.B. 656; [1992] 2 W,L.R. 741; [1992] 2 All E.R.
609; [1992] 2 Lloyd's Rep. 7; 56 B.L.R. 23; (1992) 8 Const. L.J. 150; (1992) 136
S.J.L.B. 54; [1992] N.P.C. 7, CA 23–019
Chaparral, The. *See* Unterweser Reederei GmbH v. Zapata Offshore Co.
Charm Maritime Inc v. Kyriakou [1987] 1 Lloyd's Rep. 433; [1987] 1 F.T.L.R. 265,
CA 24–005
Chas Davis (Metal Brokers) Ltd v. Gilyott & Scott Ltd [1975] 2 Lloyd's Rep. 422, QBD
(Comm Ct) 27–025
Cheetham & Co Ltd v. Thornham Spinning Co Ltd [1964] 2 Lloyd's Rep. 17 .... 2–027, 4–006
Chellew v. Royal Commission on Sugar Supply [1922] 1 K.B. 12 19–028
Chemco Leasing SpA v. Rediffusion [1987] 1 F.T.L.R. 201, CA 3–012
Chevron International Oil Co Ltd v. A/S Sea Team (The TS Havprins) [1983] 2 Lloyd's
Rep. 356; [1983] Com. L.R. 172 3–017
China Ocean Shipping Co (The Xingcheng) v. Andros (The Andros) [1987] 1 W.L.R.
1213; [1987] 2 Lloyd's Rep. 210; (1987) 84 L.S.G. 2364; (1987) 131 S.J. 972,
PC 15–048
China-Pacific SA v. Food Corp of India (The Winson) [1982] A.C. 939; [1981] 3 W.L.R.
860; [1981] 3 All E.R. 688; [1982] 1 Lloyd's Rep. 117; 125 S.J. 808, HL; reversing
[1981] Q.B. 403; [1980] 3 W.L.R. 891; [1980] 3 All E.R. 556; [1980] 2 Lloyd's
Rep. 213; 124 S.J. 614, CA; reversing [1979] 2 All E.R. 35; [1979] 1 Lloyd's Rep.
167, QBD 27–009
Chloride Industrial Batteries Ltd v. F&W Freight Ltd [1989] 1 W.L.R. 823; [1989] 3 All
E.R. 86; [1989] 2 Lloyd's Rep. 274; [1990] R.T.R. 8, CA; affirming [1989] 1
W.L.R. 45; [1989] 1 All E.R. 481; [1989] 1 Lloyd's Rep. 410; [1989] R.T.R. 125;
(1989) 86(1) L.S.G. 40; (1988) 132 S.J. 1697, QBD 18–006
Cho Yang Shipping Co Ltd v. Coral (UK) Ltd [1997] 2 Lloyd's Rep. 641; [1997] C.L.C.
1100, CA 15–037
Chris Foodstuffs (1963) Ltd v. Nigerian National Shipping Line Ltd (The Amadu Bello)
[1967] 1 Lloyd's Rep. 293, CA; affirming [1966] 1 Lloyd's Rep. 677, QBD (Comm
Ct) 15–043
Cia Portorafti Commerciale SA v. Ultramar Panama Inc (The Captain Gregos) (No.1)
[1990] 3 All E.R. 967; [1990] 1 Lloyd's Rep. 310, CA; [1989] 2 All E.R. 54;
[1989] 2 Lloyd's Rep. 63, DC 15–045, 15–048
Cia Portorafti Commerciale SA v. Ultramar Panama Inc (The Captain Gregos) (No.2)
[1990] 2 Lloyd's Rep. 395, CA 15–052
Cicatiello (GL) Srl v. Anglo European Shipping Services Ltd [1994] 1 Lloyd's Rep. 678,
QBD 18–009
Citi-March Ltd v. Neptune Orient Lines Ltd [1996] 1 W.L.R. 1367; [1996] 2 All E.R. 545;
[1997] 1 Lloyd's Rep. 72, QBD 22–008
City of London v. New Hampshire Insurance Co. *See* Wardens and Commonalty of the
Mystery of Mercers of the City of London v. New Hampshire Insurance Co Ltd.
Clarkson Booker v. Andjel [1964] 2 Q.B. 775; [1964] 3 W.L.R. 466; [1964] 3 All E.R.
260; 108 S.J. 580, CA 27–005
Claydon v. Bradley [1987] 1 W.L.R. 521; [1987] 1 All E.R. 522; [1987] F.L.R. 111; (1987)
84 L.S.G. 1571; (1987) 137 N.L.J. 57; (1987) 131 S.J. 593, CA 9–004
Clayton Newbury v. Findlay [1953] 1 W.L.R. 1194 (Note); [1953] 2 All E.R. 826; 97 S.J.
589 27–012
Clough Mill Ltd v. Martin [1985] 1 W.L.R. 111; [1984] 3 All E.R. 982; (1985) 82 L.S.G.
116; (1984) 128 S.J. 850; (1985) L.M.C.L.Q. 15; (1985) 82 L.S.G. 1075, CA;
reversing [1984] 1 W.L.R. 1067; [1984] 1 All E.R. 721; (1984) 81 L.S.G. 2375;
(1984) 128 S.J. 564, Ch D 4–009
Coastal (Bermuda) Petroleum Ltd v. VTT Vulcan Petroleum SA; (The Marine Star) [1993]
1 Lloyd's Rep. 329 .... 2–012, 2–032
Coggins (t/a PC Transport) v. LKW Walter International Transport Organisation AG [1999]
1 Lloyd's Rep. 255, CC (Central London) 18–007

Cohn v. Boulken (1920) 36 T.L.R. 767 9–007
Colin & Shields v. W Weddel & Co Ltd [1952] 2 All E.R. 337; [1952] 2 Lloyd's Rep. 9;
    [1952] 2 T.L.R. 185; [1952] W.N. 420; 96 S.J. 547 .... 2–022, 2–032, 2–035
Colley v. Overseas Exporters [1921] 3 K.B. 302; [1921] All E.R. 596; 90 L.J.K.B. 301;
    126 L.T. 58; 37 T.L.R. 797; 26 Com.Cas 325 .... 2–011, 2–013, 5–011
Colonia Versicherung AG v. Amoco Oil Co (The Wind Star) [1997] 1 Lloyd's Rep. 261;
    [1997] C.L.C. 454; [1997] 6 Re. L.R. 86, CA; affirming [1995] 1 Lloyd's Rep. 570,
    QBD (Comm Ct) 19–017
Colt Industries Inc v. Sarlie (No. 1) [1966] 1 W.L.R. 440; [1966] 1 All E.R. 673; 110 S.J.
    73, CA 22–003
Columbia Pictures Industries v. Robinson [1987] Ch. 38; [1986] 3 W.L.R. 542; [1986] 3
    All E.R. 338; [1986] F.S.R. 367; (1986) 83 L.S.G. 3424; (1986) 130 S.J. 766,
    Ch D 22–032
Comdel Commodities Ltd v. Siporex Trade SA [1997] 1 Lloyd's Rep. 424, CA ... 4–015, 12–004
Commercial Banking Co of Sydney v. Jalsard Pty [1973] A.C. 279; [1972] 3 W.L.R. 566;
    [1972] 2 Lloyd's Rep. 529; 116 S.J. 695, PC 4–013, 11–010
Commercial Fibres (Ireland) Ltd v. Zabaida (t/a Lenmore Trading) [1975] 1 Lloyd's Rep.
    27 .... 2–002, 4–003
Commissioners Customs and Excise v. Dams Inrernational Ltd (1994), (unreported) 26–010
Commissioners of Customs and Excise v. Eastern Pharmaceutics [1995] C3 26–027
Commissioners of Customs and Excise v. Eastwood Care Homes (Ilkeston) Ltd and Others,
    The Times, March 7, 2000 26–027
Commissioners of Customs and Excise v. Invicta Poultry Ltd and Fareway Trading [1996]
    V. & D.R. 291 26–027
Commissioners of Customs and Excise v. Man About Town (Men's Wear) Ltd [1997]
    C65 26–027
Commissioners of Customs and Excise v. Potter & Moore Ltd [1997] C61 26–027
Commissioners of Customs and Excise v. Sidney Barlow Ltd [1997] C64 26–027
Compagnie Algerienne de Meunerie v. Katana Societa di Navigatione Marittima SpA (The
    Nizetti) [1960] 2 Q.B. 115; [1960] 2 W.L.R. 719; [1960] 2 All E.R. 55; [1960] 1
    Lloyd's Rep. 132; 104 S.J. 327, CA; affirming [1959] 1 Q.B. 527; [1959] 2 W.L.R.
    366; [1959] 1 All E.R. 272; [1958] 2 Lloyd's Rep. 502; 103 S.J. 178, QBD 6–009
Compagnie Commerciale Sucres et Denrées v. C. Czarnikow Ltd; (The Naxos) [1990] 1
    W.L.R. 1337; [1990] 3 All E.R. 641; (1990) 134 S.J. 1301; [1991] 1 Lloyd's Rep.
    29, *Financial Times*, October 17, 1990, HL; reversing [1989] 2 Lloyd's Rep. 462;
    Financial Times, July 26, 1989, CA 2–005, 2–010, 2–013, 5–004, 5–005
Compagnie Continentale d'Importation Zurich SA v. Ispahani [1962] 1 Lloyd's Rep. 213,
    CA; affirming [1961] 1 Lloyd's Rep. 293; [1961] C.L.Y. 7992 .... 2–017, 2–027, 11–025
Compagnie de Commerce et Commission, SARL v. Parkinson Stove Co [1953] 2 Lloyd's
    Rep. 487, CA; reversing [1953] 1 Lloyd's Rep. 532 3–010
Compagnie de Renflouement de Récupération et de Travaux Sous-Marins v. S Baroukh et
    Cie v. W Seymour Plant Sales & Hire [1981] 2 Lloyd's Rep. 466 .... 2–005, 2–010
Compagnie Generale Maritime v. Diakan Spirit SA (The Ymnos) (No.2) [1982] 2 Lloyd's
    Rep. 574; [1982] Com. L.R. 228 5–004
Compagnie Tunisienne De Navigation SA v. Compagnie d'Armement Maritime SA [1971]
    A.C. 572; [1970] 3 W.L.R. 389; [1970] 3 All E.R. 71; 114 S.J. 618, HL 15–004
Compania de Navegacion Pohing SA v. Sea Tanker Shipping (Pte.) (The Buena Trader)
    [1978] 2 Lloyd's Rep. 325, CA; reversing [1977] 2 Lloyd's Rep. 27 3–009
Compania Maritima San Basilio SA v. Oceanus Mutual Underwriting Association
    (Bermuda) Ltd [1977] Q.B. 49; [1976] 3 W.L.R. 265; [1976] 3 All E.R. 243; [1976]
    2 Lloyd's Rep. 171; 120 S.J. 486, CA 19–005, 19–024
Compania Naviera General SA v. Kerametal (The Lorna I) [1983] 1 Lloyd's Rep. 373;
    [1982] Com. L.R. 257; (1983) 80 L.S.G. 36, CA; affirming [1981] 2 Lloyd's Rep.
    559, QBD (Comm Ct) 15–007, 15–010
Compania Naviera Vascongada v. Churchill & Sim [1906] 1 K.B. 237 15–036
Compania Portorafti Commerciale SA v. Ultramar Panama Inc (The Captain Gregos). *See*
    Cia Portorafti Commerciale SA v. Ultramar Panama Inc (The Captain Gregos)
    (No.1).
Comptoir d'Achat et de Vente du Boerenbond Belge SA v. Luis de Ridder Limitada
    (The Julia) [1949] A.C. 293; [1949] 1 All E.R. 269; 82 Ll. L. Rep. 270; 65
    T.L.R. 126; [1949] L.J.R. 513; 93 S.J. 101, HL; reversing [1947] 2 All E.R.
    443; 80 Ll. L. Rep. 653; 63 T.L.R. 511; 177 L.T. 648; [1947] W.N. 261;

[1948] L.J.R. 47, CA; affirming [1947] 1 All E.R. 118; (1946) 80 Ll. L. Rep.
140, KBD 2–019, 2–022, 2–035, 4–010, 15–029, 15–034
Concordia Trading BV v. Richco International Ltd [1991] 1 Lloyd's Rep. 475, QBD
(Comm Ct) 2–014
Congimex Companhia Geral de Comercia Importadora e Exportadora Sarl v. Tradax
Export SA [1983] 1 Lloyd's Rep. 250, CA; affirming [1981] 2 Lloyd's Rep.
687 .... 2–020, 6–011, 6–013
Connelly v. RTZ Corp Plc (No.2) [1998] A.C. 854; [1997] 3 W.L.R. 373; [1997] 4
All E.R. 335; [1997] C.L.C. 1357; [1997] I.L.Pr. 805; [1998] Env. L.R. 318;
(1997) 94(32) L.S.G. 28; (1997) 147 N.L.J. 1346; (1997) 141 S.J.L.B. 199, HL;
affirming [1997] I.L.Pr. 643, CA 22–007, 22–008
Container Corporation of America v. Franchise Tax Board 463 U.S. 159 (1983) 28–015
Continental Illinois National Bank & Trust Co of Chicago v. Papanicolaou (The Fedora,
The Tatiana and The Eretrea II) [1986] 2 Lloyd's Rep. 441; [1986] Fin. L.R.
373; (1986) 83 L.S.G. 2569, CA 9–012, 11–006, 11–042, 12–002
Continental Imes Ltd v. HE Dibble [1952] 1 Lloyd's Rep. 220 2–032
Cook Industries Inc v. Tradax Export SA [1985] 2 Lloyd's Rep. 454, CA; affirming
[1983] 1 Lloyd's Rep. 327, QBD (Comm Ct) 6–019
Cook International Inc v. BV Handelmaatschappij Jean Delvaux [1985] 2 Lloyd's Rep.
225, CA; affirming [1985] 1 Lloyd's Rep. 120; (1983) 133 N.L.J. 1042,
DC 23–005
Cooperative Centrale Raiffeisen-Boerenleenbank BA v. Sumitomo Bank (The Royan,
The Abukirk, The Bretagne, The Auvergne) [1988] 2 Lloyd's Rep. 250; [1988]
2 F.T.L.R. 27; [1988] Fin. L.R. 207, CA; affirming in part [1987] 1 Lloyd's
Rep. 345; [1987] 1 F.T.L.R. 233; [1987] Fin. L.R. 275, QBD (Comm Ct) 11–027
Cordova Land Co Ltd v. Victor Bros Inc; Cordova Land Co v. Black Diamond
Steamship Corp [1966] 1 W.L.R. 793; 110 S.J. 290, QBD 15–039
Corocraft Ltd v. Pan American Airways Inc [1969] 1 Q.B. 616; [1968] 3 W.L.R. 1273;
[1969] 1 All E.R. 82; *sub nom.* Corocraft v. Pan American World Airways Inc
(1968) 112 S.J. 903, CA; *sub nom.* Corocraft and Vendome Jewels v. Pan
American Airways Inc [1968] 2 Lloyd's Rep. 459, CA; reversing [1969] 1 Q.B.
622; [1968] 3 W.L.R. 714; 112 S.J. 819; *sub nom.* Corocraft v. Pan American
World Airways Inc [1968] 2 All E.R. 1059; *sub nom.* Corocraft and Vendome
Jewels v. Pan American Airways Inc [1968] 1 Lloyd's Rep. 625 17–011
Cory Brothers Shipping Ltd v. Baldan Ltd [1997] 2 Lloyd's Rep. 58, CC (Central
London) 27–025
Coutlas v. KLM (S.D.N.Y. 1961) Tranport Laws of the World iv/c/1 p. 303 19–024
CPC Consolidated Pool Carriers GmbH v. CTM CIA Transmediterreanea SA (The CPC
Gallia) [1994] 1 Lloyd's Rep. 68 3–015
Credit Suisse Fides Trust SA v. Cuoghi [1998] Q.B. 818; [1997] 3 W.L.R. 871; [1997]
3 All E.R. 724; [1997] C.L.C. 1187; [1998] I.L.Pr. 41, CA 22–030
Crédit Suisse Financial Products v. Societe Generale D'Enterprises [1996] 5 Bank. L.R.
220; [1997] C.L.C. 168; [1997] I.L.Pr. 165, CA 22–016
Crédit Suisse v. Allerdale BC [1997] Q.B. 306; [1996] 3 W.L.R. 894; [1996] 4 All
E.R. 129; [1996] 2 Lloyd's Rep. 241; [1996] 5 Bank. L.R. 249; (1997) 161
J.P. Rep. 88, CA; affirming [1995] 1 Lloyd's Rep. 315; (1995) 159 L.G. Rev.
549, QBD 12–001
Credito Italiano v. M Birnhak & Sons [1967] 1 Lloyd's Rep. 314; 117 N.L.J. 464,
CA 9–003
Cremer v. General Carriers SA [1974] 1 W.L.R. 341; (1973) 117 S.J. 873; [1974] 1
All E.R. 1; *sub nom.* Cremer (Peter), Westfaelische Central Genossenschaft
GmbH and Intergraan NV v. General Carriers SA; Dona Mari, The [1973] 2
Lloyd's Rep. 366 .... 4–012, 15–003, 15–034, 15–036
Crest Homes Plc v. Marks [1987] A.C. 829; [1987] 3 W.L.R. 293; [1987] 2 All E.R.
1074; [1988] R.P.C. 21; (1987) 84 L.S.G. 2362; (1987) 137 N.L.J. 662; (1987)
131 S.J. 1003, HL; affirming [1987] 3 W.L.R. 48; [1987] F.S.R. 305; (1987)
84 L.S.G. 2048; (1987) 137 N.L.J. 318, CA 22–032
Crocker Horlock Ltd v. B Lang & Co Ltd [1949] 1 All E.R. 526; [1949] W.N. 97,
KBD 27–012
Cubazucar v. IANSA. *See* Empresa Exportadora De Azucar (Cubazucar) v. Industria
Azucarera Nacional SA (IANSA) (The Playa Larga and The Marble Islands).

Culford Metal Industries v. Export Credits Guarantee Department, *The Times*, March
25, 1981 20–001
Cummins Engine Co Ltd v. Davis Freight Forwarding (Hull) Ltd [1981] 1 W.L.R.
1363; [1981] 3 All E.R. 567; [1981] 2 Lloyd's Rep. 402; [1981] Com. L.R.
229; [1982] R.T.R. 60; 125 S.J. 775, CA; affirming [1981] 2 Lloyd's Rep. 106,
QBD (Comm Ct) 18–007
Cunningham (J & J) Ltd v. Robert A. Monroe & Co Ltd (1922) 28 Com.Cas. 42,
DC 2–009, 2–010
Customs and Excise Commissioners v. AE Hamlin & Co [1984] 1 W.L.R. 509; [1983] 3
All E.R. 654; [1983] S.T.C. 780; (1983) 80 L.S.G. 2140; (1984) 128 S.J. 246, Ch
D 26–031
Customs and Excise Commissioners v. Air Canada [1991] 2 Q.B. 446; [1991] 2 W.L.R.
344; [1991] 1 All E.R. 570, CA; affirming [1989] Q.B. 234; [1989] 2 W.L.R. 589;
[1989] 2 All E.R. 22; (1989) 86(13) L.S.G. 42; (1989) 133 S.J. 122, QBD 26–030
Customs and Excise Commissioners v. ApS Samex [1983] 1 All E.R. 1042; [1983] Com.
L.R. 72; [1983] 3 C.M.L.R. 194; (1983) 133 N.L.J. 281, QBD (Comm Ct) 26–030
Customs and Excise Commissioners v. Carrier [1995] 4 All E.R. 38; [1995] C.O.D. 323;
(1995) 92(6) L.S.G. 39; (1995) 139 S.J.L.B. 43, QBD 26–031
Customs and Excise Commissioners v. Hare [1996] 2 All E.R. 391; [1996] 2 B.C.L.C.
500; (1996) 93(11) L.S.G. 29, CA 28–007
Customs and Excise Commissioners v. IFS Irish Fully Fashioned Stockings [1957] 1
W.L.R. 397; [1957] 1 All E.R. 108; 101 S.J. 192 26–030
Czarnikow (C) v. Centrala Handlu Zagranicznego Rolimpex (CHZ) [1979] A.C. 351;
[1978] 3 W.L.R. 274; [1978] 2 All E.R. 1043; [1978] 2 Lloyd's Rep. 305; 122 S.J.
506, HL; affirming [1978] Q.B. 176; [1977] 3 W.L.R. 677; [1978] 1 All E.R. 81;
[1977] 2 Lloyd's Rep. 201; (1977) 128 N.L.J. 578; 121 S.J. 527, CA 6–010

Dakin v. Oxley (1864) 15 C.B.N.S. 646 15–007
Dalmia Dairy Industries v. National Bank of Pakistan [1978] 2 Lloyd's Rep. 223; 121 S.J.
442, CA 21–001, 23–007
Daly v. Lime Street Underwriting Agencies [1987] 2 F.T.L.R. 277; [1987] Fin. L.R. 331 . 19–003
Danae Shipping Corp v. TPAO (The Daffodil B) [1983] 1 Lloyd's Rep. 499, QBD (Comm
Ct) 19–027
Danish Mercantile Co v. Beaumont [1951] Ch. 680; [1951] 1 All E.R. 925; 95 S.J. 300,
CA 27–008
Data Card Corp v. Air Express International Corp [1984] 1 W.L.R. 198; [1983] 2 All E.R.
639; [1983] 2 Lloyd's Rep. 81; (1984) 81 L.S.G. 732; (1983) 133 N.L.J. 576;
(1984) 128 S.J. 115, QBD 17–012
Daudruy van Cauwenberghe & Fils SA v. Tropical Product Sales SA; Tropical Product
Sales SA v. Saudi Sabah Palm Oil Corp [1986] 1 Lloyd's Rep. 535 4–012
Daval Aciers D'Usinor et de Sacilor v. Armare Srl (The Nerarno) [1996] 1 Lloyd's Rep.
1, CA 15–023
Davies v. McLean (1873) 28 L.T. 113; 37 J.P. 198; (1873) 21 W.R. 264 2–002
Davis Contractors v. Fareham UDC [1956] A.C. 696; [1956] 3 W.L.R. 37; [1956] 2 All
E.R. 145; 54 L.G.R. 289; 100 S.J. 378, HL; affirming [1955] 1 Q.B. 302; [1955] 2
W.L.R. 388; [1955] 1 All E.R. 275; 99 S.J. 109, CA 6–002, 6–011
Davy International v. Voest Alpine Industrieanlagenblau GmbH [1999] 1 All E.R. 103,
CA 22–027
De Clermont and Donner v. General Steam Navigation (1891) 7 T.L.R. 187 15–003
De Zeven Provincien. *See* South Carolina Insurance Co v. Assurantie Maatshappij "De
Zeven Provincien" NV.
Dearle v. Hall (1828) 3 Russ. 1 13–004
Decro-Wall International SA v. Practitioners in Marketing [1971] 1 W.L.R. 361; [1971] 2
All E.R. 216; (1970) 115 S.J. 171, CA 30–006, 30–013
Deichland, The. *See* Owners of Cargo Lately Laden on Board the Deichland v. Owners
and/or Demise Charterers of the Deichland.
Delfini, The. *See* Enichem Anic SpA v. Ampelos Shipping Co Ltd.
Dempster (R & J) Ltd v. Motherwell Bridge and Engineering Co Ltd 1964 S.C. 308; 1964
S.L.T. 353; 2 B.L.R. 104 .... 14–002, 30–005
Denbigh, Cowan & Co and R. Atcherley & Co, Re (1921) 90 L.J.K.B. 836; 125 L.T. 388;
[1921] All E.R. 245, CA 2–035

Denton v. John Lister Ltd [1971] 1 W.L.R. 1426; [1971] 3 All E.R. 669; 115 S.J. 671,
    DC 26–030
Derby & Co v. Larsson [1976] 1 W.L.R. 202; [1976] 1 All E.R. 401; 120 S.J. 117, HL ... 22–003
Desert Sun Loan Corp v. Hill [1996] 2 All E.R. 847; [1996] 5 Bank. L.R. 98; [1996]
    C.L.C. 1132; [1996] I.L.Pr. 406; (1996) 140 S.J.L.B. 64, CA 24–005
Deutsche Schachtbau und Tiefbohrgesellschaft mbH v. Ras Al-Khaimah National Oil Co
    and Shell International Petroleum Co [1990] 1 A.C. 295; [1988] 3 W.L.R. 230;
    [1988] 2 All E.R. 833; [1988] 2 Lloyd's Rep. 293; (1988) 85(28) L.S.G. 45, HL;
    reversing [1987] 3 W.L.R. 1023; [1987] 2 All E.R. 769; [1987] 2 Lloyd's Rep.
    246; [1987] 1 F.T.L.R. 17; (1987) 131 S.J. 1486, CA 23–008, 24–003
Diamond Alkali Export Corp v. Fl. Bourgeois [1921] 3 K.B. 443; [1921] All E.R. 283; 91
    L.J.K.B. 147; 126 L.T. 379; 15 Asp.M.L.C. 455; 26 Com.Cas 310 2–023,
                                                                                                    19–011, 15–025
Diamond Cutting Works Federation Ltd v. Triefus & Co Ltd [1956] 1 Lloyd's Rep. 216,
    QBD 6–012, 11–018, 11–032
Diamond v. Bank of London and Montreal [1979] Q.B. 333; [1979] 2 W.L.R. 228; [1979]
    1 All E.R. 561; [1979] 1 Lloyd's Rep. 335; 122 S.J. 814, CA 3–008
Dibbins v. Dibbins [1896] 2 Ch. 348 27–008
Didymi Corp v. Atlantic Lines and Navigation Co Inc (The Didymi) [1988] 2 Lloyd's Rep.
    108, CA; affirming [1987] 2 Lloyd's Rep. 166 3–015
Diestelkamp v. Baynes (Reading) Ltd; Sibaei v. Baynes (Reading) Ltd (The Aga) [1968]
    1 Lloyd's Rep. 431; 118 N.L.J. 590, QBD (Comm Ct) 19–028
Discount Records Ltd v. Barclays Bank Ltd [1975] 1 W.L.R. 315; [1975] 1 All E.R. 1071;
    [1975] 1 Lloyd's Rep. 444; (1974) 119 S.J. 133, Ch D 11–025, 11–026, 11–042
Distributori Automatici Italia SpA v. Holford General Trading Co Ltd [1985] 1 W.L.R.
    1066; [1985] 3 All E.R. 750; (1985) 82 L.S.G. 3454; (1985) 129 S.J. 685, QBD ... 22–032
Domicrest Ltd v. Swiss Bank Corp [1999] Q.B. 548; [1999] 1 W.L.R. 364; [1998] 3 All
    E.R. 577; [1999] 1 Lloyd's Rep. 80; [1998] C.L.C. 1451; [1999] I.L.Pr. 146, QBD
    (Comm Ct) 22–020
Dona Mari, The. *See* Cremer v. General Carriers SA.
Donald H Scott & Co v. Barclays Bank [1923] 2 K.B. 1; 92 L.J.K.B. 772; 129 L.T. 108;
    39 T.L.R. 198; 28 Com.Cas. 253, CA 2–023
Donoghue v. Stevenson [1932] A.C. 562; 101 L.J. PC 119; 37 Com.Cas. 350; 1932 S.C.
    (HL) 31; 1932 S.L.T. 317; 48 T.L.R. 494; [1932] W.N. 139; 147 L.T. 281,
    HL 8–009, 21–025
Dowson & Mason v. Potter [1986] 1 W.L.R. 1419; [1986] 2 All E.R. 418; (1986) 83
    L.S.G. 3429; (1986) 130 S.J. 841, CA 27–011
DPP v. Doot [1973] A.C. 807; [1973] 2 W.L.R. 532; [1973] 1 All E.R. 940; (1973) 57 Cr.
    App. R. 600; [1973] Crim. L.R. 292; 117 S.J. 266, HL; reversing *sub nom.* R. v.
    Doot [1973] Q.B. 73; [1972] 3 W.L.R. 33; [1972] 2 All E.R. 1046; [1972] Crim.
    L.R. 500; 116 S.J. 445, CA (Crim Div) 21–028
Dresser UK v. Falcongate Freight Management (The Duke of Yare) [1992] Q.B. 502;
    [1992] 2 W.L.R. 319; [1992] 2 All E.R. 450; [1991] 2 Lloyd's Rep. 557; [1992]
    I.L.Pr. 164; (1991) 135 S.J.L.B. 126, CA 22–027
DSW Silo-und Verwaltungsgesellschaft mbH v. Owners of the Sennar (The Sennar) (No.2)
    [1985] 1 W.L.R. 490; [1985] 2 All E.R. 104; [1985] 1 Lloyd's Rep. 521; (1985)
    82 L.S.G. 1863; (1985) 135 N.L.J. 316; (1985) 129 S.J. 248, HL; affirming [1984]
    2 Lloyd's Rep. 142, CA; reversing [1983] 2 Lloyd's Rep. 399, QBD (Adm
    Ct) 22–008, 24–005
Duffen v. FRA BO SpA [1999] E.C.C 58, CA 27–012
Dufourcet v. Bishop (1886) 18 Q.B.D. 373 .... 15 010
Dunbee Ltd v. Gilman & Co (Australia) Pty Ltd [1968] 2 Lloyd's Rep. 394; 118 N.L.J.
    1126, Sup Ct (NSW) 22 003
Dunlop Pneumatic Tyre Co Ltd v. New Garage & Motor Co Ltd [1915] A.C. 79, HL 4–015
Dunne v. English [1874] L.R. Eq. 524 27–011
Dupont v. British South Africa Co (1901) 18 T.L.R. 24 2–037
Dynamics Corp of America (In Liquidation) (No.2), Re [1976] 1 W.L.R. 757; [1976] 2
    All E.R. 669; 120 S.J. 450, Ch D 21–018

Eagle Star Insurance Co v. Yuval Insurance Co [1978] 1 Lloyd's Rep. 357, CA 23–009
Ebrahim Dawood Ltd v. Heath (Est 1927) Ltd [1961] 2 Lloyd's Rep. 512 5–006

ED & F Man (Sugar) Ltd v. Haryanto Yani (No.2) [1991] 1 Lloyd's Rep. 429; [1991]
I.L.Pr. 393, *Financial Times*, January 23, 1991, CA; affirming [1991] 1 Lloyd's
Rep. 161, QBD (Comm Ct) 24–014
Edward Owen Engineering Ltd v. Barclays Bank International Ltd [1978] Q.B. 159; [1977]
3 W.L.R. 764; [1978] 1 All E.R. 976; [1978] 1 Lloyd's Rep. 166; 6 B.L.R. 1; 121
S.J. 617, CA 12–001, 12–004, 12–005
EE & Smith (Brian) (1928) Ltd v. Wheatsheaf Mills [1939] 2 K.B. 302 5–007
Effort Shipping Co Ltd v. Linden Management SA (The Giannis NK) [1998] A.C. 605;
[1998] 2 W.L.R. 206; [1998] 1 All E.R. 495; [1998] 1 Lloyd's Rep. 337; [1998]
C.L.C. 374; (1998) 95(7) L.S.G. 32; (1998) 148 N.L.J. 121; (1998) 142 S.J.L.B.
54, HL; affirming [1996] 1 Lloyd's Rep. 577; [1996] C.L.C. 943, CA; affirming
[1994] 2 Lloyd's Rep. 171, QBD 15–050
Egmatra AG v. Marco Trading Corp [1999] 1 Lloyd's Rep. 862; [1998] C.L.C. 1552, QBD
(Comm Ct) 24–018
Egon Oldendorff v. Libera Corp (No.1) [1995] 2 Lloyd's Rep. 64; [1996] C.L.C. 482,
QBD (Comm Ct) 21–012, 23–007
Egon Oldendorff v. Libera Corp (No.2) [1996] 1 Lloyd's Rep. 380; [1996] C.L.C. 482,
QBD (Comm Ct) 21–008, 21–009, 23–007, 23–019
Egyptian International Foreign Trade Co v. Soplex Wholesale Supplies and PS Refson &
Co Ltd (The Rafaella). *See* Soplex Wholesale Supplies and PS Refson & Co Ltd
v. Egyptian International Foreign Trading Co.
EI Du Pont de Nemours & Co v. Agnew [1987] 2 Lloyd's Rep. 585; [1987] F.L.R. 376;
[1987] 2 F.T.L.R. 487, CA 21–026, 22–007
Eide UK Ltd v. Lowndes Lambert Group Ltd [1999] Q.B. 199; [1998] 3 W.L.R. 643;
[1998] 1 All E.R. 946; [1998] 1 Lloyd's Rep. 389; [1998] C.L.C. 266; (1998) 95(4)
L.S.G. 34; (1998) 148 N.L.J. 86, CA; affirming (1997) 94(33) L.S.G. 28, QBD 19–003
El Amria, The and El Minia, The (1982) 126 S.J. 411; [1982] 2 Lloyd's Rep. 28; [1982]
Com.L.R. 121, CA 2–007
El Amria, The. *See* Aratra Potato Co Ltd v. Egyptian Navigation Co.
Elder Dempster & Co Ltd v. Paterson Zochonis & Co Ltd; Griffiths Lewis Steam Naviga-
tion Co Ltd v. Paterson, Zochonis & Co Ltd [1924] A.C. 522; (1924) 18 Ll. L.
Rep. 319, HL 15–047
Elder Dempster Lines v. Ionic Shipping Agency, Inc Midland Bank and Marine Midland
Grace Trust Co of New York [1968] 1 Lloyd's Rep. 529, QBD (Comm Ct) 11–023
Electro Motion Ltd v. Maritime Insurance Co Ltd and Bonner [1956] 1 Lloyd's Rep. 420,
QBD 19–031
Eleftheria, The. *See* Owners of Cargo Lately Laden on Board the Eleftheria v. Owners of
the Eleftheria.
Elektronska Industrija Oour TVA v. Transped Oour Kintinentalna Spedicna [1986] 1
Lloyd's Rep. 49, QBD (Comm Ct) 27–025
Ellerman & Bucknall Steamship Co v. Sha Misrimal [1966] All India 1892 15–039
Ellis Shipping Corp v. Voest Alpine Intertrading (The Lefthero) [1992] 2 Lloyd's Rep.
109, CA; affirming [1991] 2 Lloyd's Rep. 599, QBD (Comm Ct) 6–011
Elpis Maritime Co v. Marti Chartering Co (The Maria D) [1992] 1 A.C. 21; [1991] 3
W.L.R. 330; [1991] 3 All E.R. 758; [1991] 2 Lloyd's Rep. 311; (1991) 141 N.L.J.
1109; (1991) 135 S.J.L.B. 100, HL; reversing [1991] 1 Lloyd's Rep. 521, CA 12–001
Emmanuel Colocotronis, The. *See* Astro Valiente Compania Naviera SA v. Pakistan Minis-
try of Food and Agriculture (The Emmanuel Colocotronis) (No.2).
Empresa Cubana Importadora de Alimentos Alimport v. Iasmos Shipping Co SA (The
Good Friend) [1984] 2 Lloyd's Rep. 586, QBD (Comm Ct) 15–041
Empresa Exportadora De Azucar (Cubazucar) v. Industria Azucarera Nacional SA
(IANSA) (The Playa Larga and The Marble Islands) [1983] 2 Lloyd's Rep. 171;
[1983] Com. L.R. 58, CA; affirming [1982] Com. L.R. 171 .... 2–026, 2–042, 6–010,
11–042
Encyclopaedia Britannica, Inc v. Hong Kong Producer, The, and Universal Marine Corp
[1969] 2 Lloyd's Rep. 536, US Ct 16–008
Enichem Anic SpA v. Ampelos Shipping Co Ltd (The Delfini) [1990] 1 Lloyd's Rep. 252,
CA; affirming [1988] 2 Lloyd's Rep. 599, QBD (Comm Ct) 15–039
Enrico Furst & Co v. WE Fischer Ltd [1960] 2 Lloyd's Rep. 340, QBD (Comm Ct) 15–023
Entores Ltd v. Miles Far East Corp [1955] 2 Q.B. 327; [1955] 3 W.L.R. 48; [1955] 2 All
E.R. 493; [1955] 1 Lloyd's Rep. 511; 99 S.J. 384, CA 3–008

Equitable Trust Co of New York v. Dawson Partners (1926) 27 Lloyd's Rep. 49; 25
Lloyd's Rep. 90 .... 4–012, 11–007, 11–010
Ermis Skai Radio and Televison v. Banque Indosuez SA February 26, 1996,
(reported) 12–002
Esso Petroleum Co Ltd v. Milton [1997] 1 W.L.R. 938; [1997] 2 All E.R. 593; [1997]
C.L.C. 634; (1997) 16 Tr. L.R. 250, CA 9–012
Esso Petroleum Co v. Customs and Excise Commissioners [1976] 1 W.L.R. 1; [1976] 1
All E.R. 117; (1975) 120 S.J. 49, HL; affirming [1975] 1 W.L.R. 406; 119 S.J. 205,
CA; reversing [1973] 1 W.L.R. 1240; 117 S.J. 680, DC 14–002
Etablissement Esefka International Anstalt v. Central Bank of Nigeria [1979] 1 Lloyd's
Rep. 445, CA 11–042
Etablissements Chainbaux SARL v. Harbormaster Ltd [1955] 1 Lloyd's Rep. 303   5–012, 11–018
Etablissements Soules et Cie v. International Trade Development Co [1980] 1 Lloyd's Rep.
129, CA; affirming [1979] 2 Lloyd's Rep. 122 4–012
Ethiopian Oilseeds and Pulses Export Corp v. Rio del Mar Foods [1990] 1 Lloyd's Rep.
86, QBD (Comm Ct) 23–015
Eurico SpA v. Philipp Brothers (The Epaphus) [1987] 2 Lloyd's Rep. 215; [1987] 2
F.T.L.R. 213, CA; affirming [1986] 2 Lloyd's Rep. 387 .... 2–033, 6–007
Euro-Diam Ltd v. Bathurst [1990] 1 Q.B. 35; [1988] 2 W.L.R. 517; [1988] 2 All E.R. 23;
[1988] 1 Lloyd's Rep. 228; [1988] F.T.L.R. 242; [1988] Fin. L.R. 27; (1988) 85(9)
L.S.G. 45; (1988) 132 S.J. 372, CA; affirming [1987] 2 W.L.R. 1368; [1987] 2 All
E.R. 113; [1987] 1 Lloyd's Rep. 178; [1987] Fin. L.R. 247; (1987) 84 L.S.G. 1732;
(1987) 131 S.J. 775 .... 7–002, 19–017, 21–027
European Asian Bank AG v. Punjab & Sind Bank (No.2) [1983] 1 W.L.R. 642; [1983] 2
All E.R. 508; [1983] 1 Lloyd's Rep. 611; [1983] Com. L.R. 128; (1983) 127 S.J.
379, CA 9–011, 11–003, 11–022, 11–034
European Enterprise, The. *See* Browner International Ltd v. Monarch Shipping Co
Ltd.
Evans Marshall & Co v. Bertola SA (No.2) [1976] 2 Lloyd's Rep. 17, HL; reversing [1975]
2 Lloyd's Rep. 373, CA 30–006
Evia, The (No. 2). *See* Kodros Shipping Corp of Monrovia v. Empresa Cubana de Fletes
Evpo Agnic, The [1988] 1 W.L.R. 1090; [1988] 3 All E.R. 810; [1988] 2 Lloyd's Rep.
411; (1988) 85(32) L.S.G. 33; (1988) 132 S.J. 1299, CA 22–030
Excomm Ltd v. Guan Guan Shipping Pte Ltd (The Golden Bear) [1987] 1 Lloyd's Rep.
330; [1987] 1 F.T.L.R. 61, QBD (Comm Ct) 6–004
Excomm v. Ahmed Abdul-Qawi Bamaodah (The St Raphael) [1985] 1 Lloyd's Rep. 403;
(1985) 82 L.S.G. 761, CA 23–011
Export Credits Guarantee Department v. Universal Oil Products Co & Procon Inc and
Procon (Great Britain) Ltd [1983] 1 W.L.R. 399; [1983] 2 All E.R. 205; [1983] 2
Lloyd's Rep. 152; 23 B.L.R. 106; (1983) 133 N.L.J. 662; (1983) 127 S.J. 408, HL;
affirming [1983] 1 Lloyd's Rep. 448; [1982] Com. L.R. 232; 126 S.J. 853   4–015, 20–050
Exportelisa SA v. Rocco Giuseppe & Figli Soc Coll [1978] 1 Lloyd's Rep. 433, CA;
affirming [1977] 2 Lloyd's Rep. 494 .... 2–033, 6–003

Faccenda Chicken Ltd v. Fowler; Fowler v. Faccenda Chicken Ltd [1987] Ch. 117; [1986]
3 W.L.R. 288; [1986] 1 All E.R. 617; [1986] I.C.R. 297; [1986] I.R.L.R. 69; [1986]
F.S.R. 291; (1986) 83 L.S.G. 288; (1986) 136 N.L.J. 71; (1986) 130 S.J. 573, CA;
affirming [1985] 1 All E.R. 724; [1984] I.C.R. 589; [1984] I.R.L.R. 61; [1985]
F.S.R. 105; (1984) 134 N.L.J. 255, Ch D 27–011
Fairclough Dodd & Jones v. Vantol (J.H.) [1957] 1 W.L.R. 136; [1956] 3 All E.R. 921;
[1956] 2 Lloyd's Rep. 437; 101 S.J. 86, HL; reversing [1955] 1 W.L.R. 1302;
[1955] 3 All E.R. 750; [1955] 2 Lloyd's Rep. 489; 99 S.J. 888, CA; affirming
[1955] 1 W.L.R. 642; [1955] 2 All E.R. 516; [1955] 1 Lloyd's Rep. 546; 99 S.J.
386 .... 2–033, 6–016, 6–019
Fanti, The. *See* Firma C-Trade SA v. Newcastle Protection and Indemnity Association.
Federal Commerce & Navigation Co Ltd v. Molena Alpha Inc (The Nanfri); Same v.
Molena Beta Inc (The Benfri); Same v. Molena Gamma Inc (The Lorfri) [1979]
A.C. 757; [1978] 3 W.L.R. 991; [1979] 1 All E.R. 307; [1979] 1 Lloyd's Rep. 201;
122 S.J. 843, HL; affirming in part [1978] Q.B. 927; [1978] 3 W.L.R. 309; [1978]
3 All E.R. 1066; [1978] 2 Lloyd's Rep. 132; 122 S.J. 347, CA; reversing [1978] 1
Lloyd's Rep. 581, QBD (Comm Ct) 15–011, 15–023, 15–026

Federal Insurance Co v. Transamerica Occidental Life Insurance Co [1999] 2 All E.R.
(Comm) 138; [1999] 2 Lloyd's Rep. 286; [1999] C.L.C. 1406; (1999) 149 N.L.J.
1037, QBD (Comm Ct) 23–012
Fercometal Sarl v. MSC Mediterranean Shipping Co SA (The Simona) [1989] A.C. 788;
[1988] 3 W.L.R. 200; [1988] 2 All E.R. 742; [1988] 2 Lloyd's Rep. 199; (1988)
138 N.L.J. 178; (1988) 132 S.J. 966; [1987] 2 Lloyd's Rep. 236; [1987] 2 F.T.L.R.
254, CA; affirming [1986] 1 Lloyd's Rep. 171, QBD (Comm Ct) 30–006
Fibrosa Spolka Akcyjna v. Fairbairn Lawson Combe Barbour Ltd [1943] A.C. 32; [1942]
2 All E.R. 122; (1942) 73 Ll. L. Rep. 45, HL; reversing [1942] 1 K.B. 12; (1941)
70 Ll. L. Rep. 30, CA; affirming (1941) 69 Ll. L. Rep. 97, KBD 6–008, 6–016
Fielding & Platt Ltd v. Selim Najjar [1969] 1 W.L.R. 357; [1969] 2 All E.R. 150; 113 S.J.
160 .... 2–016, 7–002, 21–027
Filipinas I, The. *See* Pagnan (R) & Fratelli v. Schouten (NGJ) NV.
Fillite (Runcorn) v. Aqua-Lift 45 B.L.R. 27; 26 Con. L.R. 66; (1989) 5 Const. L.J. 197,
CA 23–015
Finagra (U.K.) Ltd v. O.T. Africa Line Ltd [1998] 2 Lloyd's Rep. 622; [1998] C.L.C.
1419, QBD (Comm Ct) 16–007
Finelvet AG v. Vinava Shipping Co (The Chrysalis) [1983] 1 W.L.R. 1469; [1983] 2 All
E.R. 658; [1983] 1 Lloyd's Rep. 503; [1983] Com. L.R. 126; (1983) 80 L.S.G.
2684; (1983) 127 S.J. 680, QBD 6–008, 6–011
Finnish Government (Ministry of Food) v. H. Ford & Co Ltd (1921) 6 Lloyd's Rep. 188;
(1921) 6 Ll. L. Rep. 188 2–012
Finzel, Berry & Co v. Eastcheap Dried Fruit Co [1962] 2 Lloyd's Rep. 11, CA; affirming
[1962] 1 Lloyd's Rep. 370, QBD 27–005
Firma C-Trade SA v. Newcastle Protection and Indemnity Association (The Fanti); Socony
Mobil Oil Co Inc v. West of England Shipowners Mutual Insurance Association
(London) Ltd (The Padre Island) (No.2) [1991] 2 A.C. 1; [1990] 3 W.L.R. 78;
[1990] 2 All E.R. 705; [1990] 2 Lloyd's Rep. 191; [1990] B.C.L.C. 625; (1990)
134 S.J. 833, HL; reversing [1989] 1 Lloyd's Rep. 239, CA; reversing in part [1987]
2 Lloyd's Rep. 299, QBD (Comm Ct) 19–030
First Energy (UK) v. Hungarian International Bank [1993] 2 Lloyd's Rep. 194; [1993]
B.C.L.C. 1409; [1993] B.C.C. 533; [1993] N.P.C. 34, CA 27–007
Fisher, Reeves & Co v. Armour & Co [1920] 3 K.B. 614; 90 L.J.K.B. 172; 124 L.T. 122;
36 T.L.R. 800; 15 Asp.M.L.C. 91; 26 Com.Cas 46 2–002
Fitzgerald v. Williams; O'Regan v. Williams [1996] Q.B. 657; [1996] 2 W.L.R. 447;
[1996] 2 All E.R. 171; [1996] C.L.C. 646; [1996] I.L.Pr. 275, CA 23–005
Floating Dock Ltd v. Hong Kong and Shanghai Banking Corp [1986] 1 Lloyd's Rep. 65,
QBD (Comm Ct) 11–008
Flowergate, The. *See* Jahn (t/a CF Otto Weber) v. Turnbull Scott Shipping Co Ltd.
Foley v. Classique Coaches [1934] 2 K.B. 1 3–015
Folliott v. Ogden (1789) 1 H.Bl 123 21–025
Food Corp of India v. Antclizo Shipping Corp (The Antclizo) [1988] 1 W.L.R. 603; [1988]
2 All E.R. 513; [1988] 2 Lloyd's Rep. 93; [1988] 2 F.T.L.R. 124; (1988) 138 N.L.J.
135; (1988) 132 S.J. 752, HL; affirming [1987] 2 Lloyd's Rep. 130; [1987] 2
F.T.L.R. 114, CA; affirming [1986] 1 Lloyd's Rep. 181, QBD (Comm Ct) 6–004,
23–004
Ford Motor Co v. Armstrong (1915) 31 T.L.R. 267 4–015
Foreman & Ellams Ltd v. Blackburn [1928] 2 K.B. 60 4–012
Forestal Minosa v. Oriental Credit [1986] 1 W.L.R. 631; [1986] 2 All E.R. 400; [1986] 1
Lloyd's Rep. 329; [1986] Fin. L.R. 171; (1986) 83 L.S.G. 779; (1986) 130 S.J. 202,
CA 11–003, 11–006, 11–022, 11–027
Forsikringsaktieselskapet Vesta v. Butcher [1989] A.C. 852; [1989] 2 W.L.R. 290; [1989]
1 All E.R. 402; [1989] 1 Lloyd's Rep. 331; [1989] Fin. L.R. 223; (1989) 133 S.J.
184, HL; affirming [1988] 3 W.L.R. 565; [1988] 2 All E.R. 43; [1988] 1 Lloyd's
Rep. 19; [1988] 1 F.T.L.R. 78; [1988] Fin. L.R. 67; [1988] 4 Const. L.J. 75; (1988)
85(31) L.S.G. 33; (1988) 132 S.J. 1181, CA; affirming [1986] 2 All E.R. 488;
[1986] 2 Lloyd's Rep. 179, QBD 19–012, 19–017
Fort Sterling Ltd v. South Atlantic Cargo Shipping NV (The Finnrose) [1994] 1 Lloyd's
Rep. 559, QBD 15–048
Forum Craftsman, The [1985] 1 Lloyd's Rep. 291, CA [1984] 2 Lloyd's Rep. 102, QBD
(Adm Ct) 27–025
Foster v. Driscoll [1929] 1 K.B. 470 21–027

Fothergill v. Monarch Airlines Ltd [1981] A.C. 251; [1980] 3 W.L.R. 209; [1980] 2 All
E.R. 696; [1980] 2 Lloyd's Rep. 295; 124 S.J. 512, HL; reversing [1980] Q.B. 23;
[1979] 3 W.L.R. 491; [1979] 3 All E.R. 445; [1980] 1 Lloyd's Rep. 149; [1980]
F.S.R. 145; 123 S.J. 584, CA; affirming [1978] Q.B. 108; [1977] 3 W.L.R. 885;
[1977] 3 All E.R. 616; [1977] 2 Lloyd's Rep. 184; 121 S.J. 774, QBD 17–014
Four Point Garage Ltd v. Carter *The Times*, November 19, 1984; [1985] 3 All E.R. 12 4–009
Francovich v. Italy (C6 and C9/90) [1991] E.C.R. I-5357; [1993] 2 C.M.L.R. 66; [1995]
I.C.R. 722; [1992] I.R.L.R. 84, ECJ 26–029
Frank Pais, The [1986] 1 Lloyd's Rep. 529, QBD (Adm Ct) 15–036
Frankfurther v. WL Exner Ltd [1947] Ch. 629; 177 L.T. 257; [1948] L.J.R. 553; 91 S.J.
532, Ch D 21–024
Frans Maas Logistics (U.K.) Ltd v. CDR Trucking BV [1999] 1 All E.R. (Comm) 737;
[1999] 2 Lloyd's Rep. 179, QBD (Comm Ct) 18–006
Fraser Shipping Ltd v. Colton [1997] 1 Lloyd's Rep. 586, QBD (Comm Ct) 19–033
Fraser v. Thames Television Ltd [1984] Q.B. 44; [1983] 2 W.L.R. 917; [1983] 2 All E.R.
101; (1983) 133 N.L.J. 281; (1983) 127 S.J. 379, QBD 27–011
Fratelli Moretti SpA v. Nidera Handelscompagnie BV [1981] 2 Lloyd's Rep. 47,
CA 3–016, 4–015
Frebold v. Circle Products (1970) 114 S.J. 262; *sub nom.* Frebold and Sturznickel (t/a
Panda OHG) v. Circle Products [1970] 1 Lloyd's Rep. 499, CA 2–005
Freeman & Lockyer v. Buckhurst Park Properties (Mangal) [1964] 2 Q.B. 480; [1964] 2
W.L.R. 618; [1964] 1 All E.R. 630; 108 S.J. 96, CA 27–004, 27–007
Fuerst Day Lawson Ltd v. Orion Insurance Co Ltd [1980] 1 Lloyd's Rep. 656 ..... 4–014, 19–031
Future Express, The [1993] 2 Lloyd's Rep. 542, CA; affirming [1992] 2 Lloyd's Rep. 79,
QBD (Adm Ct) 11–031

G Percy Trentham v. Archital Luxfer [1993] 1 Lloyd's Rep. 25; 63 B.L.R. 44,
CA 3–009, 3–015
G&H Montage GmbH (Formerly Grunzweig und Hartmann Montage GmbH) v. Irvani
[1990] 1 W.L.R. 667; [1990] 2 All E.R. 225; [1990] 1 Lloyd's Rep. 14; [1989] Fin.
L.R. 390; (1990) 87(8) L.S.G. 44; (1990) 134 S.J. 425, CA; affirming [1988] 1
W.L.R. 1285; [1988] 1 Lloyd's Rep. 460; [1989] Fin. L.R. 90, QBD (Comm Ct) .. 9–009
Gabriel & Sons v. Churchill & Sim [1914] 3 K.B. 1272 27–016
Gadd v. Houghton [1876] 1 Ex. D. 357 27–005
Gamerco SA v. ICM/Fair Warning (Agency) Ltd [1995] 1 W.L.R. 1126; [1995] E.M.L.R.
263, QBD 6–003, 6–009, 6–016
Gan Insurance Co Ltd v. Tai Ping Insurance Co Ltd; Royal Reinsurance Co Ltd v. Central
Insurance Co Ltd [1999] 2 All E.R. (Comm) 54, CA; affirming [1999] L.R.L.R.
229; [1998] C.L.C. 1072, QBD (Comm Ct) 21–008
Garcia v. Page & Co (1936) 55 Ll.L.R 391 11–018
Gardano and Giampieri v. Greek Petroleum George Mamidakis & Co [1962] 1 W.L.R. 40;
[1961] 3 All E.R. 919; [1961] 2 Lloyd's Rep. 259; 106 S.J. 76 .... 2–020, 2–035
Garden Cottage Foods Ltd v. Milk Marketing Board [1984] A.C. 130; [1983] 3 W.L.R.
143; [1983] 2 All E.R. 770; [1983] Com. L.R. 198; [1983] 3 C.M.L.R. 43; [1984]
F.S.R. 23; (1983) 127 S.J. 460, HL; reversing [1982] Q.B. 1114; [1982] 3 W.L.R.
514; [1982] 3 All E.R. 292; [1982] 2 C.M.L.R. 542; 126 S.J. 446, CA 29–004, 29–008
Garrett v. Arthur Churchill (Glass) [1970] 1 Q.B. 92; [1969] 3 W.L.R. 6; [1969] 2 All
E.R. 1141; 133 J.P. 509; 113 S.J. 381, DC 26–030
Gatewhite Ltd v. Iberia Lineas Aereas de Espana SA [1990] 1 Q.B. 326; [1989] 3 W.L.R.
1080; [1989] 1 All E.R. 944; [1989] 1 Lloyd's Rep. 160; (1989) 86(39) L.S.G. 35;
(1989) 133 S.J. 1337, QBD 17–005
Gaudet v. Brown; *sub nom.* Cargo ex Argos; Argos, Cargo, ex (1873) L.R. 5 PC
134 .... 15–007, 15–013
Gebruder Metalmann GmbH & Co KG v. NBR (London) [1984] 1 Lloyd's Rep. 614;
(1984) 81 L.S.G. 515, CA; affirming (1983) 133 N.L.J. 642 5–003
Gee & Garnham Ltd v. Whittall [1955] 2 Lloyd's Rep. 562, QBD 19–024
Gefco (UK) Ltd v. Mason [1998] 2 Lloyd's Rep. 585; [1998] C.L.C. 1468; (1998) 95(31)
L.S.G. 35; (1998) 142 S.J.L.B. 206; *The Times*, August 24, 1998, CA 18–006
Geismar v. Sun Alliance and London Insurance Ltd [1978] 1 Q.B. 383; [1978] 2 W.L.R.
38; [1977] 3 All E.R. 570; [1977] 2 Lloyd's Rep. 62; [1977] Crim. L.R. 475; 121
S.J. 201, QBD 21–027

General Accident Fire and Life Assurance Corp Ltd v. Peter William Tanter (The Zephyr)
[1985] 2 Lloyd's Rep. 529, CA; reversing [1984] 1 W.L.R. 100; [1984] 1 All E.R.
35; [1984] 1 Lloyd's Rep. 58; (1984) 134 N.L.J. 35; (1983) 127 S.J. 733, QBD
(Comm Ct) 19–003, 19–010

General Re-Insurance Corp v. Forsakringsaktiebolaget Fennia Patria [1983] Q.B. 856;
[1983] 3 W.L.R. 318; [1983] 2 Lloyd's Rep. 287; (1983) 127 S.J. 389, CA; reversing [1982] Q.B. 1022; [1982] 2 W.L.R. 518; [1982] 1 Lloyd's Rep. 87; [1981]
Com. L.R. 280; 126 S.J. 32, QBD 19–003, 19–010

Geogre Wills & Sons Ltd v. RS Cunningham, Son & Co Ltd [1924] 2 K.B. 220 6–020

Gewa Chartering BV v. Remco Shipping Lines (The Remco) [1984] 2 Lloyd's Rep. 205,
QBD (Comm Ct) 27–005

GH Renton & Co Ltd v. Palmyra Trading Corp of Panama (The Caspiana) [1957] A.C.
149; [1957] 2 W.L.R. 45; [1956] 3 All E.R. 957; [1956] 2 Lloyd's Rep. 379, HL;
affirming [1956] 1 Q.B. 462; [1956] 2 W.L.R. 238; [1956] 1 All E.R. 209; [1955]
2 Lloyd's Rep. 722; 101 S.J. 43, CA; reversing [1955] 3 W.L.R. 535; [1955] 3 All
E.R. 251; [1955] 2 Lloyd's Rep. 301; 99 S.J. 762, QBD 19–022

Gian Singh & Co Ltd v. Banque de L'Indochine [1974] 1 W.L.R. 1234; [1974] 2 All E.R.
754; [1974] 2 Lloyd's Rep. 1; 118 S.J. 644, PC; affirming [1974] 1 Lloyd's Rep.
56 11–007

Gibraltar v. Kenney [1956] 2 Q.B. 410; [1956] 3 W.L.R. 466; [1956] 3 All E.R. 22; 100
S.J. 551, QBD 23–015

Gilchrist Watt & Sanderson Pty v. York Products Pty [1970] 1 W.L.R. 1262; [1970] 3 All
E.R. 825; 114 S.J. 571, PC 15–047

Gill & Duffus Landauer Ltd v. London Export Corp [1982] 2 Lloyd's Rep. 627 2–004

Gill & Duffus SA v. Berger & Co Inc [1984] A.C. 382; [1984] 2 W.L.R. 95; [1984] 1 All
E.R. 438; [1984] 1 Lloyd's Rep. 227; (1984) 81 L.S.G. 429; (1984) 128 S.J. 47,
HL; reversing [1983] 1 Lloyd's Rep. 622; [1983] Com. L.R. 122, CA; reversing
[1981] 2 Lloyd's Rep. 233; [1981] Com. L.R. 253, QBD (Comm Ct) 2–020, 2–025,
2–026, 2–027, 2–037, 4–006, 4–012, 5–008, 11–008

Gill & Duffus SA v. Rionda Futures Ltd [1994] 2 Lloyd's Rep. 67, QBD (Comm Ct) 15–023

Gill & Duffus SA v. Société pour l'Exportation des Sucres SA [1986] 1 Lloyd's Rep. 322,
CA; affirming [1985] 1 Lloyd's Rep. 621 .... 2–005, 2–010

Ginzberg v. Barrow Haematite Steel Co and McKellar [1966] 1 Lloyd's Rep. 343; 116
N.L.J. 752, QBD 2–027, 4–006

Glass's Fruit Markets v. Southwell (A.) & Son (Fruit) [1969] 2 Lloyd's Rep. 398 2–043

Glebe Island Terminals Pty v. Continental Seagram Pty (The Antwerpen) [1994] 1 Lloyd's
Rep. 213, Sup Ct (NSW) 15–038

Glencore Grain Rotterdam BV v. Lebanese Organisation for International Commerce
(LORICO) [1997] 2 Lloyd's Rep. 386; [1997] C.L.C. 1274, CA 2–008, 11–018

Glencore International AG v. Bank of China [1996] 1 Lloyd's Rep. 135; [1996] 5 Bank.
L.R. 1; [1996] C.L.C. 111; [1998] Masons C.L.R. Rep. 78, CA .. 11–007, 11–010, 11–013

Glenroy, The. *See* Procurator General (H. M.) v. MC Spencer (Controller of Mitsui & Co
Ltd).

Glynn (H.) (Covent Garden) Ltd v. Wittleder (t/a W Wittleder, K.G.) [1959] 2 Lloyd's
Rep. 409 2–035

Godley v. Perry, Burton & Sons (Bermondsey) (Third Party), Graham (Fourth Party)
[1960] 1 W.L.R. 9; [1960] 1 All E.R. 36; 104 S.J. 16 8–008

Gold und Silberscheideanstalt v. Customs and Excise Commissioners [1980] Q.B. 390;
[1980] 2 W.L.R. 555; [1980] 2 All E.R. 138; [1980] 1 C.M.L.R. 488; [1980] C.L.Y.
622; 124 S.J. 30, CA; affirming [1978] 2 C.M.L.R. 292 26–030

Goldcorp Exchange Ltd (In Receivership), Re *sub nom.* Kensington v. Unrepresented Non-
Allocated Claimants [1995] 1 A.C. 74; [1994] 3 W.L.R. 199; [1994] 2 All E.R.
806; [1994] 2 B.C.L.C. 578; (1994) 13 Tr. L.R. 434; (1994) 91(24) L.S.G. 46;
(1994) 144 N.L.J. 792; (1994) 138 S.J.L.B. 127, PC 4–004, 4–005

Golden Bay Realty Pte v. Orchard Twelve Investments Pte [1991] 1 W.L.R. 981; (1991)
135 S.J.L.B. 92, PC 4–015

Goldman v. Thai Airways International [1983] 1 W.L.R. 1186; [1983] 3 All E.R. 693;
(1983) 127 S.J. 441, CA; reversing 125 S.J. 413 17–011

Golodetz (M.) & Co Inc v. Czarnikow-Rionda Co Inc (The Galatia) [1980] 1 W.L.R. 495;
[1980] 1 All E.R. 501; [1980] 1 Lloyd's Rep. 453; 124 S.J. 201, CA; affirming
[1979] 2 All E.R. 726; [1979] 2 Lloyd's Rep. 450 ... 2–022, 2–027, 2–034, 2–038, 11–008,
11–010, 11–012, 15–026, 19–031

Gosse Millard Ltd v. Canadian Government Merchant Marine Ltd (The Canadian
    Highlander); American Can Co Ltd v. Same [1929] A.C. 223, HL; [1928] 1 K.B.
    717, CA; [1927] 2 K.B. 432, KBD 15–020, 15–042
Gotha City v. Sotheby's (No.2); Germany v. Same *The Times*, October 8, 1998, QBD 21–017
Goulandris Bros Ltd v. B Goldman & Sons Ltd [1958] 1 Q.B. 74; [1957] 3 W.L.R. 596;
    [1957] 3 All E.R. 100; [1957] 2 Lloyd's Rep. 207; 101 S.J. 762, QBD ... 15–048, 19–028
Government of Sierra Leone v. Marmaro Shipping Co (The Amazona and The Yayamaria)
    [1989] 2 Lloyd's Rep. 130, CA 15–021, 15–048
Grand Metropolitan Plc v. William Hill Group Ltd [1997] 1 B.C.L.C. 390, Ch D 3–016
Grant v. Norway (1851) 10 C.B. 665 .... 15–036, 15–052
Greater Nottingham Co-operative Society v. Cementation Piling and Foundations Ltd
    [1989] Q.B. 71; [1988] 3 W.L.R. 396, CA 8–009
Greenhill v. Federal Insurance Co [1927] 1 K.B. 65 19–012
Greenmar Navigation v. Owners of Ships Bazias 3 and Bazias 4 and Sally Line (The Bazias
    3 and The Bazias 4) [1993] Q.B. 673; [1993] 2 W.L.R. 854; [1993] 2 All E.R. 964;
    [1993] 1 Lloyd's Rep. 101, CA 23–016
Greenock SS Co v. Maritime Insurance Co [1903] 1 K.B. 367 19–013
Greer v. Downs Supply Co [1927] 2 K.B. 28, CA 27–005
Grein v. Imperial Airways [1937] 1 K.B. 50 17–004
Grimaldi Compagnia di Navigazione SpA v. Sekihyo Lines Ltd (The Seki Rolette) [1999]
    1 W.L.R. 708; [1998] 3 All E.R. 943; [1998] 2 Lloyd's Rep. 638; [1998] C.L.C.
    1403; *The Times*, July 20, 1998, QBD (Comm Ct) 15–048, 23–019
Grinsted v. Hadrill [1953] 1 W.L.R. 696; [1953] 1 All E.R. 1188; 97 S.J. 351,
    CA 27–011
Groom Ltd v. Barber [1915] 1 K.B. 316; [1914–15] All E.R. 194; 84 L.J.K.B. 318; 112
    L.T. 301; 31 T.L.R. 66; 12 Asp.M.L.C. 594; 20 Com.Cas. 71 2–034
Group Josi Re Co SA v. Walbrook Insurance Co Ltd; Deutsche Ruckversichering AG v.
    Walbrook Insurance Co Ltd [1996] 1 All E.R. 791; [1996] 1 Lloyd's Rep. 345;
    [1996] 5 Re. L.R. 91, CA; affirming [1995] 1 W.L.R. 1017; [1994] 4 All E.R. 181;
    [1995] 1 Lloyd's Rep. 153; (1994) 91(25) L.S.G. 30; (1994) 138 S.J.L.B. 111,
    QBD 12–005
Groupement National d'Achat Des Tourteaux v. Sociedad Industrial Financiera Argentina
    (The Milton B Medary) [1962] 2 Lloyd's Rep. 192 4–012
Gudermes, The. *See* Cedar Trading Co Ltd v. Transworld Oil Ltd.
Gudermes, The. *See* Mitsui & Co Ltd v. Novorossiysk Shipping Co.
Gulf Bank KSC v. Mitsubishi Heavy Industries Ltd (No.2) [1994] 2 Lloyd's Rep. 145;
    [1994] 3 Bank. L.R. 174, CA 12–001, 12–004
Gur Corp v. Trust Bank of Africa Ltd [1987] Q.B. 599; [1986] 3 W.L.R. 583; [1986] 3
    All E.R. 449; [1986] 2 Lloyd's Rep. 451; (1986) 83 L.S.G. 2659; (1986) 136 N.L.J.
    895; (1986) 130 S.J. 748, CA 21–024
Gurtner v. Beaton [1993] 2 Lloyd's Rep. 369, CA 17–001, 27–007
Gyllenhammar & Partners International Ltd v. Sour Brodogradevna Industrija [1989] 2
    Lloyd's Rep. 403, QBD (Comm Ct) 11–018

H Cousins & Co v. D&C Carriers [1971] 2 Q.B. 230; [1971] 2 W.L.R. 85; [1971] 1 All
    E.R. 55; [1970] 2 Lloyd's Rep. 397; (1970) 114 S.J. 882, CA 19–035
Hackett v. Advanced Medical Computer Systems Ltd [1999] C.L.C. 160, QBD 27–012
Hadley v. Baxendale (1854) 9 Ex. 341 8–009
Hagen, The [1908] P. 189 22–005
Hair and Skin Trading Co v. Norman Airfreight Carriers and World Transport Agencies
    [1974] 1 Lloyd's Rep. 443 27–025
Haiti (Republic of) v. Duvalier (Mareva Injunction) (No.2) [1990] 1 Q.B. 202; [1989] 2
    W.L.R. 261; [1989] 1 All E.R. 456; [1989] 1 Lloyd's Rep. 111; [1989] E.C.C. 449;
    (1988) 138 N.L.J. 234; (1988) 132 S.J. 1495, CA 22–030
Halki Shipping Corp v. Sopex Oils Ltd (The Halki) [1998] 1 W.L.R. 726; [1998] 2 All
    E.R. 23; [1998] 1 Lloyd's Rep. 465; [1998] C.L.C. 583; (1998) 142 S.J.L.B. 44;
    [1998] N.P.C. 4, CA; affirming [1997] 1 W.L.R. 1268; [1997] 3 All E.R. 833;
    [1998] 1 Lloyd's Rep. 49; (1997) 94(28) L.S.G. 26; (1997) 141 S.J.L.B. 172, QBD
    (Adm Ct) 23–016
Hall & Tawse South Ltd v. Ivory Gate Ltd 62 Con. L.R. 117, QBD 3–015
Hallett's Estate, Re (1880) Ch.D. 696 4–009

Hamed el Chiaty & Co (t/a Travco Nile Cruise Lines) v. Thomas Cook Group Ltd (The Nile Rhapsody) [1994] 1 Lloyd's Rep. 382; [1994] I.L.Pr. 367, CA; affirming [1992] 2 Lloyd's Rep. 399 .... 3–016, 22–008, 22–017

Hamilton Finance Co v. Coverley Westray Walbaum & Tosetti and Portland Finance Co [1969] 1 Lloyd's Rep. 53 13–002

Hamzeh Malas & Sons v. British Imex Industries Ltd [1958] 2 Q.B. 127; [1958] 2 W.L.R. 100; [1958] 1 All E.R. 262; [1957] 2 Lloyd's Rep. 549; 102 S.J. 68, CA 11–004, 11–026, 27–020

Hansen-Tangens Rederi III A/S v. Total Transport Corp (The Sagona) [1984] 1 Lloyd's Rep. 194, QBD (Comm Ct) 15–003, 15–038

Hansson v. Hamel & Horley Ltd [1922] 2 A.C. 36, HL 2–032, 11–010

Harbour and General Works Ltd v. Environment Agency [2000] 1 All E.R. 50; [2000] 2 All E.R. 50; [1999] 2 All E.R. (Comm) 686; [2000] 1 Lloyd's Rep. 65, *The Times*, October 22, 1999; affirming [1999] 1 All E.R. (Comm) 953; [1999] C.L.C. 786, QBD (Comm Ct) 23–019

Harbour Assurance Co (UK) Ltd v. Kansa General International Assurance Co Ltd [1993] Q.B. 701; [1993] 3 W.L.R. 42; [1993] 3 All E.R. 897; [1993] 1 Lloyd's Rep. 455, CA; reversing [1992] 1 Lloyd's Rep. 81, QBD (Comm Ct) 23–004, 23–014

Hardwick Game Farm v. Suffolk Agricultural Poultry Producers' Association. *See* Kendall (Henry) & Sons (A Firm) v. Lillico (William) & Sons.

Hardy (MW) & Co v. Pound (AV) & Co. *See* Pound (AV) & Co v. Hardy (MW) & Co

Harlow & Jones Ltd v. Parex (International) Ltd [1967] 2 Lloyd's Rep. 509; (1967) 118 N.L.J. 38 2–012

Harlow & Jones Ltd v. PJ Walker Shipping & Transport Ltd [1986] 2 Lloyd's Rep. 141, QBD (Comm Ct) 27–025

Harper (AC) & Co v. Mackechnie & Co [1925] 2 K.B. 423; 95 L.J.K.B. 162; 134 L.T. 90; 31 Com.Cas 21 2–023

Harris (WM Fergus) & Son v. China Mutual Steam Navigation Co [1959] 2 Lloyd's Rep. 500 .... 15–003, 15–036

Harrods (Buenos Aires) Ltd, Re [1992] Ch. 72; [1991] 3 W.L.R. 397; [1991] 4 All E.R. 334; [1991] B.C.L.C. 666; [1991] B.C.C. 249; [1991] I.L.Pr. 331; (1991) 135 S.J.L.B. 184, CA; reversing [1991] B.C.L.C. 69; [1990] B.C.C. 481, Ch D 22–028

Harvela Investments Ltd v. Royal Trust Co of Canada (CI) Ltd [1986] A.C. 207; [1985] 3 W.L.R. 276; [1985] 2 All E.R. 966; (1985) 82 L.S.G. 3171; (1985) 135 N.L.J. 730; (1985) 128 S.J. 522, HL; reversing [1985] Ch. 103; [1984] 3 W.L.R. 1280; [1985] 1 All E.R. 261; (1984) 81 L.S.G. 2850; (1984) 128 S.J. 701, CA; reversing [1984] 2 W.L.R. 884; [1984] 2 All E.R. 65; (1984) 81 L.S.G. 1837; (1984) 128 S.J. 348 3–004

Harvey v. Johnson [1848] 6 C.B. 295 3–009

Hashwani v. Letherby *sub nom* Hashwani v Customs and Excise Commissioners (1998) 162 J.P. 153; (1998) 162 J.P.N. 266, QBD

Hayler v. Chapman [1989] 1 Lloyd's Rep. 490, CA 19–035

Hecker v. Cunard S.S. July 1898, (unreported) 15–006

Hedley Byrne & Co Ltd v. Heller & Partners Ltd [1964] A.C. 465; [1963] 3 W.L.R. 101; [1963] 2 All E.R. 575; [1963] 1 Lloyd's Rep. 485; 107 S.J. 454; (1963) 107 S.J. 454, HL; affirming [1962] 1 Q.B. 396; [1961] 3 W.L.R. 1225; [1961] 3 All E.R. 891; 105 S.J. 910; (1961) 105 S.J. 910, CA; affirming *The Times*, December 21, 1960 .... 4–013, 8–009, 20–001

Heidberg, The. *See* Partenreederei M/S Heidberg v. Grosvenor Grain & Feed Co Ltd.

Heilbutt v. Hickson (1872) L.R. 7 C.P. 438 5–005

Heisler v. Anglo Dal Ltd [1954] 1 W.L.R. 1273; [1954] 2 All E.R. 770; [1954] 2 Lloyd's Rep. 5; 98 S.J. 698, CA 12–001

Helbert Wagg & Co.'s Claim, Re [1956] Ch. 323; [1956] 2 W.L.R. 183100 S.J. 53 *sub nom*. Helbert Wagg & Co Ltd, Re; Prudential Assurance Co Ltd, Re [1956] 1 All E.R. 129 21–025

Hellenic Steel Co v. Svolamar Shipping Co Ltd (The Komninos S) [1991] 1 Lloyd's Rep. 370, CA; reversing [1990] 1 Lloyd's Rep. 541, QBD (Comm Ct) 15–021, 21–017

Hely-Hutchinson v. Brayhead Ltd [1968] 1 Q.B. 549; [1967] 3 W.L.R. 1408; [1967] 3 All E.R. 98; 111 S.J. 830, CA; affirming [1967] 2 W.L.R. 1312; [1967] 2 All E.R. 14; 111 S.J. 329, QBD 27–006, 27–007

Henderson v. Merrett Syndicates; Hallam-Eames v. Same; Hughes v. Same; Arbuthnott v. Feltrim Underwriting Agencies; Deeny v. Gooda Walker (In Liquidation) [1995] 2

A.C. 145; [1994] 3 W.L.R. 761; [1994] 3 All E.R. 506; [1994] 2 Lloyd's Rep. 468; (1994) 144 N.L.J. 1204, HL; affirming *The Times*, December 30, 1993; *The Independent*, December 14, 1993, CA; affirming [1994] 2 Lloyd's Rep. 193 8–009
Hendy Lennox (Industrial Engines) Ltd v. Grahame Puttick Ltd [1984] 1 W.L.R. 485; [1984] 2 All E.R. 152; [1984] 2 Lloyd's Rep. 422; (1984) 81 L.S.G. 585; (1984) 128 S.J. 220 4–009
Henry (DI) v. Clasen (Wilhelm G.) [1973] 1 Lloyd's Rep. 159, CA; affirming [1972] 1 Lloyd's Rep. 392 .... 2–027, 2–037
Herd (Robert C). & Co Inc v. Krawill Machinery Corp. *See* Krawill Machinery Corporation v. Robert C. Herd & Co Inc.
Heskell v. Continental Express Ltd [1950] 1 All E.R. 1033; 83 Ll. L. Rep. 438; [1950] W.N. 210; 94 S.J. 339, KBD 15–003
Hewitt Brothers v. Wilson [1915] 2 K.B. 739 19–013
Heyman v. Darwins [1942] A.C. 356; [1942] 1 All E.R. 337; (1942) 72 Ll. L. Rep. 65, HL 6–016, 23–015, 27–013
HIB Ltd v. Guardian Insurance Co Inc. *See* Hogg Insurance Brokers Ltd v. Guardian Insurance Co Inc.
Hillas & Co v. Arcos (1932) 147 L.T. 503 3–015
Himalaya, The. *See* Adler v. Dickson.
Hindley & Co Ltd v. General Fibre Co Ltd [1940] 2 K.B. 517; (1940) 67 Ll. L. Rep. 272, KBD 6–013
Hing Yip Hing Fat Co Ltd v. Daiwa Bank [1991] 2 H.K.L.R. 35 .... 11–007, 11–009, 11–010
Hiscox v. Outhwaite [1992] 1 A.C. 562; [1991] 3 W.L.R. 297; [1991] 3 All E.R. 641; [1991] 2 Lloyd's Rep. 435, HL; affirming [1991] 2 W.L.R. 1321; [1991] 3 All E.R. 124; [1991] 2 Lloyd's Rep. 1, CA; affirming [1991] 1 Lloyd's Rep. 99, QBD 23–018
Hispanica de Petroles SA and Compania llberica Refinadera SA v. Vencedora Oceanica Navegacion SA (The Kapetan Markos NL) (No.2) [1987] 2 Lloyd's Rep. 321, CA 2–007, 2–014, 15–052
Hispanica de Petroles SA v. Vencedora Oceanica Navegacion SA (The Kapetan Markos) [1986] 1 Lloyd's Rep. 211, CA; affirming [1986] 1 Lloyd's Rep. 239 .... 2–007, 15–048, 15–052
Hispano Americana Mercantile SA v. Central Bank of Nigeria [1979] 2 Lloyd's Rep. 277; 123 S.J. 336, CA 21–019
Hobbs Padgett & Co (Reinsurance) Ltd v. JC Kirkland Ltd [1969] 2 Lloyd's Rep. 547; (1969) 113 S.J. 832, CA 23–012
Hoecheong Products Co Ltd v. Cargill Hong Kong Ltd [1995] 1 W.L.R. 404; [1995] 1 Lloyd's Rep. 584, PC 6–018
Hogg Insurance Brokers Ltd v. Guardian Insurance Co Inc [1997] 1 Lloyd's Rep. 412, QBD (Comm Ct) 21–009, 22–007
Holding Oil Finance Inc v. Marc Rich & Co AG [1996], CA 22–022
Holland Colombo Trading Society Ltd v. Alawdeen, Segu Mohamed Khaja [1954] 2 Lloyd's Rep. 45, PC 2–032, 2–035
Hollandia, The. *See* Owners of Cargo on Board the Morviken v. Owners of the Hollandia.
Holme v. Brunskill (1877) 3 Q.B. 495 12–001
Holmes (Keiko) v. Bangladesh Biman Corp [1989] A.C. 1112; [1989] 2 W.L.R. 481; [1989] 1 All E.R. 852; [1989] 1 Lloyd's Rep. 444; (1989) 133 S.J. 291, HL; reversing [1988] 2 Lloyd's Rep. 120, CA; affirming [1987] 2 Lloyd's Rep. 192, QBD 17–001, 17–010, 17–030
Home & Overseas Insurance Co v. Mentor Insurance Co (UK) [1990] 1 W.L.R. 153; [1989] 3 All E.R. 74; [1989] 1 Lloyd's Rep. 473; (1989) 86(7) L.S.G. 36; (1989) 133 S.J. 44, CA; affirming *The Times*, August 11, 1988; *The Independent*, August 18, 1988; *Financial Times*, August 10, 1988, QBD 23–009
Home Insurance Co and St Paul Fire and Marine Insurance Co v. Administratia Asigurarilor de Stat [1983] 2 Lloyd's Rep. 674 23–009
Hong Guan & Co v. R Jumabhoy & Sons [1960] A.C. 684; [1960] 2 W.L.R. 754; [1960] 2 All E.R. 100; [1960] 1 Lloyd's Rep. 405; 104 S.J. 367, PC 6–012, 6–017
Hong Kong and Shanghai Banking Corp v. Kloeckner & Co AG [1990] 2 Q.B. 514; [1990] 3 W.L.R. 634; [1989] 3 All E.R. 513; [1989] 2 Lloyd's Rep. 323, QBD 11–001, 11–006, 11–030
Hong Kong and Shanghai Banking Corp Ltd v. GD Trade Co Ltd [1998] C.L.C. 238, CA 9–004

Hong Kong Fir Shipping Co Ltd v. Kawasaki Kisen Kaisha Ltd (The Hong Kong Fir)
[1962] 2 Q.B. 26; [1962] 2 W.L.R. 474; [1962] 1 All E.R. 474; [1961] 2 Lloyd's
Rep. 478; (1961) 106 S.J. 35, CA; affirming [1961] 2 W.L.R. 716; [1961] 2 All
E.R. 257; [1961] 1 Lloyd's Rep. 159; 105 S.J. 347 .... 5–004, 6–003
Hookway (F. E.) & Co Ltd v. Isaacs (Alfred) & Sons; Same v. Graves (Consolidated)
[1954] 1 Lloyd's Rep. 491 4–012
Horabin v. British Overseas Airways Corp [1952] 2 All E.R. 1016; [1952] 2 Lloyd's Rep.
450; [1952] W.N. 519; 96 S.J. 803, QBD 19–024
Hornby v. Lacy (1817) 6 M. & S. 166 27–016
Houda, The. *See* Kuwait Petroleum Corp v. I&D Oil Carriers Ltd.
Hough v. P&O Containers Ltd [1999] Q.B. 834; [1998] 3 W.L.R. 851; [1998] 2 All E.R.
978; [1998] 2 Lloyd's Rep. 318; [1998] C.L.C. 947; [1998] I.L.Pr. 713; (1998)
95(17) L.S.G. 32; (1998) 142 S.J.L.B. 127, QBD (Adm Ct) 22–022
House of Spring Gardens v. Waite [1991] 1 Q.B. 241; [1990] 3 W.L.R. 347; [1990] 2 All
E.R. 990, CA 24–005
Household Fire and Carriage Accident Insurance Ltd v. Grant (1879) 4 Ex.D. 216 3–008
Howe Richardson Scale Co v. Polimex-Cekop [1978] 1 Lloyd's Rep. 161, CA 12–004
Howell Securities Ltd v. Hughes [1974] 1 W.L.R. 155; [1974] 1 All E.R. 161; (1973) 26
P. & C.R. 544; 117 S.J. 912, CA; affirming [1973] 1 W.L.R. 757; [1973] 2 All
E.R. 476; (1973) 26 P. & C.R. 28; 117 S.J. 447 3–008
Hume v. AA Mutual International Insurance Co Ltd [1996] L.R.L.R. 19, QBD 23–016
Huntingdon v. Attrill [1893] A.C. 150, PC 21–025
Hyundai Merchant Marine Co Ltd v. Karander Maritime Inc (The Nizuru) [1996] 2 Lloyd's
Rep. 66; [1996] C.L.C. 749, QBD (Comm Ct) 5–003

I Congreso del Partido. *See* Playa Larga (Cargo Owners) v. I Congreso del Partido
(Owners); Marble Islands (Cargo Owners) v. Same (The I Congreso del Partido,
The Marble Islands and The Playa Larga).
Ian Chisholm Textiles v. Griffiths [1994] 2 B.C.L.C. 291; [1994] B.C.C. 96, Ch D 4–009
Ian Stach v. Baker Bosley [1958] 2 Q.B. 130; [1958] 2 W.L.R. 419; 102 S.J. 177; [1958]
1 All E.R. 542; *sub nom.* Ian Stach v. Baker Bosly [1958] 1 Lloyd's Rep.
127 .... 11–018, 11–026, 11–033, 11–034
ICI Fibres v. Mat Transport [1987] 1 Lloyd's Rep. 354; [1987] 1 F.T.L.R. 145 .... 18–009, 18–010
ICI Ltd v. Berk Pharmaceuticals Ltd. *See* Imperial Chemical Industries Ltd v. Berk Pharma-
ceuticals Ltd.
IE Contractors Ltd v. Lloyds Bank Plc and Rafidain Bank [1990] 2 Lloyd's Rep. 496;
(1990) 51 B.L.R. 5, CA; reversing in part [1989] 2 Lloyd's Rep. 205 12–001,
12–002, 12–004
Ignazio Messina & Co v. Polskie Linie Oceaniczne [1995] 2 Lloyd's Rep. 566 3–015
IMB [1984] 3 C.M.L.R. 147 29–018
Imperial Chemical Industries Ltd v. Berk Pharmaceuticals Ltd [1981] 2 C.M.L.R. 91;
[1981] F.S.R. 1, Ch D 29–018
India (Government of), Ministry of Finance (Revenue Division) v. Taylor [1955] A.C. 491;
[1955] 2 W.L.R. 303; [1955] 1 All E.R. 292; 48 R. & I.T. 98; [1955] T.R. 9; 99
S.J. 94; *sub nom.* Delhi Electric Supply & Traction Co Ltd, Re 34 A.T.C. 10, HL;
affirming [1954] Ch. 131; [1953] 3 W.L.R. 1085; [1953] 2 All E.R. 1452; 46 R. &
I.T. 817; 32 A.T.C. 413; [1953] T.R. 385; 97 S.J. 861, CA; affirming 32 A.T.C.
341; [1953] T.R. 325, Ch D 21–025
India v. India Steamship Co Ltd (The Indian Endurance and The Indian Grace) (No.2)
[1998] A.C. 878; [1997] 3 W.L.R. 818; [1997] 4 All E.R. 380; [1998] 1 Lloyd's
Rep. 1; [1997] C.L.C. 1581; [1998] I.L.Pr. 511; (1997) 94(43) L.S.G. 29; (1997)
147 N.L.J. 1581; (1997) 141 S.J.L.B. 230, HL; affirming [1997] 2 W.L.R. 538;
[1996] 3 All E.R. 641; [1996] 2 Lloyd's Rep. 12; [1996] C.L.C. 1548, CA; reversing
[1994] 2 Lloyd's Rep. 331, QBD 22–033
Indian Oil Corp Ltd v. Greenstone Shipping Co SA (Panama) (The Ypatianna) [1988] Q.B.
345; [1987] 2 W.L.R. 869; [1987] 3 All E.R. 893; [1987] 2 Lloyd's Rep. 286;
[1987] 2 F.T.L.R. 95; (1987) 84 L.S.G. 2768; (1987) 131 S.J. 1121 4–005
Industria Azucarera Nacional SA (IANSA) v. Empresa Exportadora De Azucar
(Cubazucar). *See* Empresa Exportadora De Azucar (Cubazucar) v. Industria Azucarera Nacional SA (IANSA).
Industrial Maritime Carriers (Bahamas) Inc v. Sinoca International Inc (The Eastern Trader)
[1996] 2 Lloyd's Rep. 585, QBD (Comm Ct) 22–010, 24–008

Inglis v. Stock (1885) L.R. 10 App. Cas. 263, HL 19–006, 19–014

Initial Services v. Putterill [1968] 1 Q.B. 396; [1967] 3 W.L.R. 1032; [1967] 3 All E.R. 145; 2 K.I.R. 863; 111 S.J. 541, CA 27–011

Insurance Co of North America v. Japan Line (The Brooklyn Maru) [1975] 2 Lloyd's Rep. 512, US Ct 16–009

Insurance Co v. Lloyd's Syndicate [1995] 1 Lloyd's Rep. 272; [1994] C.L.C. 1303, QBD 23–002

Integrated Container Service v. British Traders Insurance Co [1984] 1 Lloyd's Rep. 154; (1984) 81 L.S.G. 353, CA 19–024

Interdesco SA v. Nullifire Ltd [1992] 1 Lloyd's Rep. 180; [1992] I.L.Pr. 97, QBD 24–003

Interfoto Picture Library Ltd v. Stiletto Visual Programmes Ltd [1989] Q.B. 433; [1988] 2 W.L.R. 615; [1988] 1 All E.R. 348; (1988) 7 Tr. L.R. 187; (1988) 85(9) L.S.G. 45; (1987) 137 N.L.J. 1159; (1988) 132 S.J. 460, CA 3–009, 3–017

International Factors v. Rodriguez [1979] Q.B. 351; [1978] 3 W.L.R. 877; [1979] 1 All E.R. 17; 122 S.J. 680, CA 13–006

International Packers London Ltd v. Ocean Steam Ship Co Ltd [1955] 2 Lloyd's Rep. 218, QBD 15–041

International Petroleum Refining & Supply Sociedad v. Brett (Caleb) & Son, Brett (Caleb) & Son (Continentaal) BV, Brett (Caleb) & Son Italia SpA and Petrinspecteur Srl (The Busiris) [1980] 1 Lloyd's Rep. 569, CA 4–013

International Power Industries Inc, Re [1985] B.C.L.C.; *The Times*, July 25, 1984 21–022

International Sea Tankers Inc of Liberia v. Hemisphere Shipping Co Ltd of Hong Kong (The Wenjiang) (No.2) [1983] 1 Lloyd's Rep. 400; [1983] Com. L.R. 16, QBD (Comm Ct) 6–008, 6–011

International Tank and Pipe SAK v. Kuwait Aviation Fuelling Co KSC [1975] Q.B. 224; [1974] 3 W.L.R. 721; [1975] 1 All E.R. 242; [1975] 1 Lloyd's Rep. 8; 5 B.L.R. 147; 118 S.J. 752, CA 23–007

International Tin Council, Re [1989] Ch. 309; [1988] 3 W.L.R. 1159; [1988] 3 All E.R. 257; (1988) 4 B.C.C. 653; [1989] P.C.C. 90; (1988) 132 S.J. 1494, CA; affirming [1987] Ch. 419; [1987] 2 W.L.R. 1229; [1987] 1 All E.R. 890; [1987] B.C.L.C. 272; [1987] P.C.C. 283; [1987] 1 F.T.L.R. 305; (1987) 84 L.S.G. 1732; (1987) 131 S.J. 690, Ch D 21–019

Intertradex SA v. Lesieur-Tourteaux Sarl [1978] 2 Lloyd's Rep. 509, CA; affirming [1977] 2 Lloyd's Rep. 146 6–014

Intraco Ltd v. Notis Shipping Corp of Liberia (The Bhoja Trader) [1981] 2 Lloyd's Rep. 256; [1981] Com. L.R. 184, CA 11–001, 11–006, 11–020, 12–002

Investors Compensation Scheme Ltd v. West Bromwich Building Society; Investors Compensation Scheme Ltd v. Hopkin & Sons; Alford v. West Bromwich Building Society; Armitage v. West Bromwich Building Society [1998] 1 W.L.R. 896; [1998] 1 All E.R. 98; [1998] 1 B.C.L.C. 531; [1997] C.L.C. 1243; [1997] P.N.L.R. 541; (1997) 147 N.L.J. 989, HL; reversing [1998] 1 B.C.L.C. 521; [1997] C.L.C. 363; [1997] P.N.L.R. 166; [1997] N.PC 104, CA; affirming [1998] 1 B.C.L.C. 493; [1997] C.L.C. 348 3–016

Ireland v. Livingston (1872) L.R. 5 HL 395; 41 L.J.Q.B. 201; 27 L.T. 79; 1 Asp.M.L.C. 389, HL 2–019, 7–003, 27–019

Ishag v. Allied Bank International, Fuhs and Kotalimbora [1981] 1 Lloyd's Rep. 92 15–025

Ismail v. Polish Ocean Lines (The Ciechocinek) [1976] Q.B. 893; [1976] 2 W.L.R. 477; [1976] 1 All E.R. 902; [1976] 1 Lloyd's Rep. 489; 120 S.J. 168, CA; reversing [1975] 2 Lloyd's Rep. 170, QBD (Comm Ct) 15–041

Ispahani v. Bank Melli Iran [1998] Lloyd's Rep. Bank. 133, CA 21–027, 21–029

Italmare Shipping Co v. Tropwood AG (The Tropwind) [1982] 2 Lloyd's Rep. 441 3–015

ITT Schaub Lorenz Vetriebsgesellschaft mbH v. Birkhart Johann Internationale Spedition GmbH [1988] 1 Lloyd's Rep. 487; [1988] F.T.L.R. 463, CA 18–007

J Evans & Son (Portsmouth) Ltd v. Andrea Merzario Ltd [1976] 1 W.L.R. 1078; [1976] 2 All E.R. 930; [1976] 2 Lloyd's Rep. 165; 120 S.J. 734, CA; reversing [1975] 1 Lloyd's Rep. 162 16–008

J. Harris & F. Meisel [1998] L.M.C.L.Q. 568 24–019

J Lauritzen A/S v. Wijsmuller BV (The Super Servant Two) [1990] 1 Lloyd's Rep. 1, CA; affirming [1989] 1 Lloyd's Rep. 148 .... 6–001, 6–005, 6–013

JA Chapman & Co Ltd (In Liquidation) v. Kadirga Denizcilik ve Ticaret AS [1998] C.L.C. 860; [1998] Lloyd's Rep. I.R. 377, CA 19–003

JA Johnston Co Ltd v. Sealion Navigation Co SA (The Tindefjell) [1973] 2 Lloyd's Rep.
253, Fed Ct (Can) 16–009
Jade International Steel Stahl und Eisen GmbH & Co KG v. Robert Nicholas (Steels)
[1978] Q.B. 917; [1978] 3 W.L.R. 39; [1978] 3 All E.R. 104; [1978] 2 Lloyd's
Rep. 13; 122 S.J. 294, CA 9–004
Jaglom v. Excess Insurance Co Ltd [1972] 2 Q.B. 250; [1971] 3 W.L.R. 594; [1972] 1 All
E.R. 267; [1971] 2 Lloyd's Rep. 171; 115 S.J. 639, QBD 19–010
Jahn (t/a CF Otto Weber) v. Turnbull Scott Shipping Co Ltd (The Flowergate) [1967] 1
Lloyd's Rep. 1, QBD (Comm Ct) 15–041, 15–043
Jalamohan, The. *See* Ngo Chew Hong Edible Oil Pte Ltd v. Scindia Steam Navigation Co
Ltd.
James Buchanan & Co Ltd v. Babco Forwarding & Shipping (UK) Ltd [1978] A.C. 141;
[1977] 3 W.L.R. 907; [1977] 3 All E.R. 1048; [1978] 1 Lloyd's Rep. 119; [1978]
R.T.R. 59; [1978] 1 C.M.L.R. 156; 121 S.J. 811, HL; affirming [1977] Q.B. 208;
[1977] 2 W.L.R. 107; [1977] 1 All E.R. 518; [1977] 1 Lloyd's Rep. 234; [1977]
R.T.R. 457; [1977] 2 C.M.L.R. 455; 121 S.J. 10, CA 18–009
James Lamont & Co v. Hyland [1950] 1 K.B. 585; [1950] 1 All E.R. 341; 83 Ll. L. Rep.
477; 66 T.L.R. (Pt. 1) 937; 94 S.J. 179, CA 9–012
James Miller & Partners Ltd v. Whitworth Street Estates (Manchester) Ltd [1970] A.C.
583; [1970] 2 W.L.R. 728; [1970] 1 All E.R. 796; [1970] 1 Lloyd's Rep. 269; 114
S.J. 225, HL; reversing *sub nom.* Whitworth Street Estates (Manchester) Ltd v.
James Miller & Partners Ltd [1969] 1 W.L.R. 377; [1969] 2 All E.R. 210; 113 S.J.
126, CA 23–007
Jayaar Impex Ltd v. Toaken Group Ltd (t/a Hicks Brothers) [1996] 2 Lloyd's Rep. 437,
QBD 3–013
Jet Holdings Inc v. Patel [1990] 1 Q.B. 335; [1988] 3 W.L.R. 295; [1989] 2 All E.R. 648,
CA 24–005
JJ Lloyd Instruments v. Northern Star Insurance Co (The Miss Jay Jay) [1987] 1 Lloyd's
Rep. 32; [1987] F.T.L.R. 14; [1987] Fin. L.R. 120, CA; affirming [1985] 1 Lloyd's
Rep. 264 19–031
John Martin of London Ltd v. A. E. Taylor & Co Ltd [1953] 2 Lloyd's Rep. 589 2–035
Johnson & Bloy (Holdings) Ltd v. Wolstenholme Rink Plc [1987] I.R.L.R. 499; [1987] 2
F.T.L.R. 502; [1989] 1 F.S.R. 135, CA 27–011
Johnson Matthey Bankers Ltd v. State Trading Corp of India Ltd [1984] 1 Lloyd's Rep.
427, QBD (Comm Ct) 6–018
Jones v. European and General Express Co (1920) 90 L.J.K.B. 159 27–025
Jones v. Trollope Colls Cementation Overseas *The Times*, January 26, 1990, CA 21–017
Jordan Grand Prix Ltd v. Baltic Insurance Group [1999] 1 W.L.R. 134; [1999] 1 All E.R.
289; [1999] C.L.C. 527; [1999] 1 Lloyd's Rep. I.R. 93, HL; affirming [1998] 1
W.L.R. 1049; [1998] 3 All E.R. 418; [1998] Lloyd's Rep. I.R. 180; (1997) 94(43)
L.S.G. 30; (1997) 141 S.J.L.B. 230, CA 22–023
Joseph Constantine Steamship Line Ltd v. Imperial Smelting Corp Ltd [1942] A.C. 154;
[1941] 2 All E.R. 165, HL; reversing [1940] 3 All E.R. 211, CA; reversing [1940]
2 All E.R. 46, KBD 6–001, 6–005, 6–007, 6–015
Joseph Pyke & Son (Liverpool) Ltd v. Richard Cornelius & Co [1955] 2 Lloyd's Rep.
747 2–033
Jugoslavenska Oceanska Plovidba v. Castle Investment Co Inc (The Kozara) [1974] Q.B.
292; [1973] 3 W.L.R. 847; [1973] 3 All E.R. 498; [1973] 2 Lloyd's Rep. 1; 117
S.J. 712, CA 21–018

K Lokumal & Sons (London) v. Lotte Shipping Co Pte (The August Leonhardt) [1985] 2
Lloyd's Rep. 28, CA 15–048
K/S A/S Seateam & Co v. Iraq National Oil Co (The Sevonia Team) [1983] 2 Lloyd's
Rep. 640 15–023
Kahler v. Midland Bank Ltd [1950] A.C. 24; [1949] 2 All E.R. 621; 65 T.L.R. 663; [1949]
L.J.R. 1687, HL; affirming [1948] 1 All E.R. 811, CA 21–029
Kapetan Markos NL, The (No.2). *See* Hispanica de Petroles SA and Compania lberica
Refinadera SA v. Vencedora Oceanica Navegacion SA.
Kapetan Markos, The. *See* Hispanica de Petroles SA v. Vencedora Oceanica Navegacion
SA.
Kapur v. Barclays Bank Plc. *See* Barclays Bank Plc v. Kapur.
Karaganda Ltd v. Midland Bank Plc [1999] 1 All E.R. (Comm.) 801, CA; affirming [1998]

Lloyd's Rep. Bank. 173, QBD 11–014
Karlshamns Oljefabriker A/B v. Eastport Navigation Corp (The Elafi) [1982] 1 All E.R.
    208; [1981] 2 Lloyd's Rep. 679; [1981] Com. L.R. 149 .... 4–005, 19–014
Keighley, Maxsted & Co v. Durant [1901] A.C. 240, HL 27–005, 27–008
Kelly v. Cooper [1993] A.C. 205; [1992] 3 W.L.R. 936; [1994] 1 B.C.L.C. 395; [1992]
    E.G.C.S. 119; (1992) 136 S.J.L.B. 303; [1992] N.P.C. 134, PC 27–011
Kendall (Henry) & Sons (A Firm) v. Lillico (William) & Sons; Holland Colombo Trading
    Society v. Grimsdale & Sons; Grimsdale & Sons v. Suffolk Agricultural Poultry
    Producers' Association [1969] 2 A.C. 31; [1968] 3 W.L.R. 110; *sub nom.* Kendall
    (Henry) & Sons (A Firm) v. Lillico (William) and Sons; Holland Colombo Trading
    Society v. Grimsdale and Sons (Consolidated Appeals); Grimsdale and Sons v.
    Suffolk Agricultural and Poultry Producers' Association 112 S.J. 562; Kendall
    (Henry) & Sons (A Firm) v. Lillico (William) & Sons; Holland Colombo Trading
    Society v. Grimsdale & Sons; Grimsdale & Sons v. Suffolk Agricultural Poultry
    and Producers' Association [1968] 2 All E.R. 444; *sub nom.* Hardwick Game Farm
    v. Suffolk Agricultural and Poultry Producers' Association; Lillico (William) (First
    Third Party); Grimsdale & Sons (Second Third Party); Kendall (Henry) & Sons
    (First Fourth Party); Holland-Colombo Trading Society (Second Fourth Party)
    [1968] 1 Lloyd's Rep. 547, HL 2–020, 3–013
Kenya Railways v. Antares Co Pte Ltd (The Antares) (No.1 and 2) [1987] 1 Lloyd's Rep.
    424, CA; [1986] 2 Lloyd's Rep. 633; [1986] 2 Lloyd's Rep. 626, QBD (Comm
    Ct) 15–045, 15–048, 15–051
Kenya Railways v. Antares Co Pte Ltd (The Antares) (Nos. 1 & 2) [1987] 1 Lloyd's Rep.
    424, CA 23–004
Kenya Railways v. Antares Co Pte Ltd (The Antares) [1986] 2 Lloyd's Rep. 633 15–051
KH Enterprise (Cargo Owners) v. Pioneer Container (Owners) (The Pioneer Container)
    [1994] 2 A.C. 324; [1994] 3 W.L.R. 1; [1994] 2 All E.R. 250; [1994] 1 Lloyd's
    Rep. 593; (1994) 91(18) L.S.G. 37; (1994) 138 S.J.L.B. 85, PC 15–047, 15–048,
    22–008, 27–026
Kinnear v. Falconfilms NV [1996] 1 W.L.R. 920; [1994] 3 All E.R. 42; [1994] I.L.Pr. 731,
    QBD 22–022
Kirby v. Cosindit Societa Per Azioni [1969] 1 Lloyd's Rep. 75 19–013
Kirchner v. Venus (1859) 12 Moore PC 361 15–007
Kissavos Shipping Co SA v. Empresa Cubana de Fletes (The Agathon) [1982] 2 Lloyd's
    Rep. 211, CA 6–003
Kite, The [1933] P. 154; [1933] All E.R.Rep. 234; 102 L.J.P. 101; 149 L.T. 498; 49 T.L.R.
    525; (1933) 46 Ll. L. Rep. 83; 18 Asp.M.L.C. 413; 3–013
Kleinwort Benson Ltd v. Glasgow City Council (No.2) [1999] 1 A.C. 153; [1997] 3 W.L.R.
    923; [1997] 4 All E.R. 641; [1998] Lloyd's Rep. Bank. 10; [1997] C.L.C. 1609;
    [1998] I.L.Pr. 350; (1997) 9 Admin. L.R. 721; (1997) 94(44) L.S.G. 36; (1997) 147
    N.L.J. 1617; (1997) 141 S.J.L.B. 237, HL; reversing [1996] Q.B. 678; [1996] 2
    W.L.R. 655; [1996] 2 All E.R. 257; [1996] 5 Bank. L.R. 116; [1996] C.L.C. 759;
    [1996] I.L.Pr. 218, CA 22–018, 22–020
Kleinwort Benson Ltd v. Malaysia Mining Corp Berhad [1989] 1 W.L.R. 379; [1989] 1
    All E.R. 785; [1989] 1 Lloyd's Rep. 556; (1989) 86(16) L.S.G. 35; (1989) 139
    N.L.J. 221; (1989) 133 S.J. 262, CA; reversing [1988] 1 W.L.R. 799; [1988] 1 All
    E.R. 714; [1988] 1 Lloyd's Rep. 556; (1988) 4 B.C.C. 217; [1988] F.T.L.R. 283;
    (1988) 138 N.L.J. 21; (1988) 132 S.J. 497 3–012
Kleinwort Sons & Co v. Ungarische Baumwolle Industrie AG [1939] 2 K.B. 678 21–027
Knotz v. Fairclough Dodd & Jones Ltd [1952] 1 Lloyd's Rep. 226, QBD 11–018
Koch (John) v. C&H Products [1956] 2 Lloyd's Rep. 59, CA; affirming [1956] 1 Lloyd's
    Rep. 302 27–009
Kodros Shipping Corp of Monrovia v. Empresa Cubana de Fletes (The Evia) (No.2) [1983]
    1 A.C. 736; [1982] 3 W.L.R. 637; [1982] 3 All E.R. 350; [1982] 2 Lloyd's Rep.
    307; [1982] Com. L.R. 199; (1982) 126 S.J. 656, HL; affirming [1982] 1 Lloyd's
    Rep. 334; [1982] Com. L.R. 44, CA; reversing [1981] 2 Lloyd's Rep. 613; [1981]
    Com. L.R. 243, QBD (Comm Ct) 6–008, 6–011
Kollerich & Cie SA v. State Trading Corp of India Ltd [1980] 2 Lloyd's Rep. 32, CA;
    affirming [1979] 2 Lloyd's Rep. 442 .... 2–005, 4–013
Komninos S, The. *See* Hellenic Steel Co v. Svolamar Shipping Co Ltd.
Koppel v. Koppel (Wide, Claimant) [1966] 1 W.L.R. 802; [1966] 2 All E.R. 187; 110 S.J.
    229, CA 14–002

Korea Exchange Bank Ltd v. Debenhams (Central Buying) Ltd [1979] 1 Lloyd's Rep. 548;
    123 S.J. 163, CA; reversing [1979] 1 Lloyd's Rep. 100, QBD (Comm Ct) 9–004
Koskas v. Standard Marine Insurance Co Ltd (1927) 32 Com.Cas 160 2–023
Koufos v. Czarnikow (C.) [1969] 1 A.C. 350; [1967] 3 W.L.R. 1491; 111 S.J. 848; *sub
    nom.* Koufos v. Czarnikow (C.) Heron II, The [1967] 3 All E.R. 686; *sub nom.*
    Czarnikow (C.) v. Koufos [1967] 2 Lloyd's Rep. 457, HL; affirming Czarnikow
    (C.) v. Koufos [1966] 2 Q.B. 695; [1966] 2 W.L.R. 1397; [1966] 2 All E.R. 593;
    [1966] 1 Lloyd's Rep. 595, CA; reversing [1966] 1 Lloyd's Rep. 259; 110 S.J.
    287 8–009
Kraut (Jean) AG v. Albany Fabrics Ltd [1977] Q.B. 182; [1976] 3 W.L.R. 872; [1977] 2
    All E.R. 116; [1976] 2 Lloyd's Rep. 350; 120 S.J. 817, QBD 21–018
Krawill Machinery Corporation v. Robert C. Herd & Co Inc (1959) 359 U.S. 297; [1959]
    1 Lloyd's Rep. 305, U.S. Sup.Ct.; affirming [1958] 2 Lloyd's Rep. 159; [1958]
    C.L.Y. 3125, CA (U.S.); affirming [1957] 1 Lloyd's Rep. 40; [1957] C.L.Y.
    3296 2–007
Kredietbank Antwerp v. Midland Bank. *See* Karaganda Ltd v. Midland Bank Plc.
Kronprinsessan Margareta, The [1921] 1 A.C. 486 .... 4–006, 15–038
Kuehne and Nagel Ltd v. W.B. Woolley (Scotland) Ltd Westminster County Court, August
    15, 1973 (unreported) 2–004, 16–003
Kulmerland, The. *See* Royal Typewriter Co v. Owners of the MV Kulmerland.
Kum v. Wah Tat Bank Ltd [1971] 1 Lloyd's Rep. 439, PC 4–003, 15–003, 15–024
Kuo International Oil Ltd v. Daisy Shipping Co Ltd (The Yamatogawa) [1990] 2 Lloyd's
    Rep. 39, QBD (Comm Ct) 15–043
Kurz v. Stella Musical Veranstaltungs GmbH [1992] Ch. 196; [1991] 3 W.L.R. 1046;
    [1992] 1 All E.R. 630; [1992] I.L.Pr. 261, Ch D 22–016
Kuwait Airways Corp v. Iraqi Airways Co (No.1) [1995] 1 W.L.R. 1147; [1995] 3 All
    E.R. 694; [1995] 2 Lloyd's Rep. 317; [1996] I.L.Pr. 339; (1995) 92(28) L.S.G. 28;
    (1995) 139 S.J.L.B. 176, HL; affirming in part [1994] 1 Lloyd's Rep. 276; [1995]
    1 Lloyd's Rep. 25; [1994] I.L.Pr. 427; (1993) 90(45) L.S.G. 39, CA; reversing
    Financial Times, July 17, 1992, QBD 21–019
Kuwait Airways Corp v. Iraqi Airways Co (No.5) *The Times*, May 12, 1998, QBD (Comm
    Ct) 21–026
Kuwait Petroleum Corp v. I. & D. Oil Carriers Ltd (The Houda) [1994] 2 Lloyd's Rep.
    541, CA; reversing [1993] 1 Lloyd's Rep. 333 .... 15–038, 15–039
Kuwait Supply Co v. Oyster Marine Management Inc (The Safeer) [1994] 1 Lloyd's Rep.
    637, QBD 6–011
Kvaerner John Brown Ltd v. Midland Bank Plc [1998] C.L.C. 446, QBD 12–004, 12–005
Kwei Tek Chao (t/a Zung Fu Co) v. British Traders & Shippers, N.V. Handelsmaatschappij
    J. Smith Import-Export, Third Party [1954] 2 Q.B. 459; [1954] 2 W.L.R. 365; 98
    S.J. 163; *sub nom.* Chao v. British Traders & Shippers [1954] 1 All E.R. 779;
    [1954] 1 Lloyd's Rep. 16 .... 2–026, 2–026, 2–027, 4–006, 5–005, 5–006, 5–008, 5–010
Kydon Compania Naviera SA v. National Westminster Bank Ltd (The Lena) [1981] 1
    Lloyd's Rep. 68; [1980] Com. L.R. 12 .... 11–007, 11–008
Kyprianou (Phoebus D) v. Cyprus Textiles [1958] 2 Lloyd's Rep. 60, CA; reversing [1957]
    2 Lloyd's Rep. 353 6–012

Laceys (Wholesale) Footwear Ltd v. Bowler International Freight Ltd [1997] 2 Lloyd's
    Rep. 369, CA 18–009
Lachhani v. Destination Canada (UK) Ltd (1997) 13 Const. L.J. 279 3–015
Laertis Shipping Corp v. Exportadora Espanola de Cementos Portland SA (The Laertis)
    [1982] 1 Lloyd's Rep. 613; [1982] Com. L.R. 39, QBD (Comm Ct) 23–012
Lakeman v. Mountstephen (1874) L.R. 7 HL 17 12–001
Lamb Head Shipping Co Ltd v. Jennings (The Marel) [1994] 1 Lloyd's Rep. 624, CA 19–031
Lamb v. Evans [1893] 1 Ch. 218 27–011
Lambert v. Cooperative Insurance Society Ltd [1975] 2 Lloyd's Rep. 485, CA 19–012
Lamdon Trust v. Hurrell [1955] 1 W.L.R. 391; 99 S.J. 239; *sub nom.* Landom Trust v.
    Hurrell [1955] 1 All E.R. 839 4–015
Landauer v. Asser [1905] 2 K.B. 184 19–016
Landhurst Leasing plc v. Marcq (Leave to Appeal) [1998] I.L.P.R. 822; LTA 97/5577/J,
    CA 24–002
Lark v. Outhwaite [1991] 2 Lloyd's Rep. 132 3–007

Lash Atlantico, The [1987] 2 Lloyd's Rep. 114, CA; reversing [1985] 2 Lloyd's Rep.
464 21–018
Leather's Best Inc v. Moore McCormack Lines Inc (The Mormaclynx) [1971] 2 Lloyd's
Rep. 476; [1970] 1 Lloyd's Rep. 527, US Ct 16–009
Lebeaupin v. Crispin [1920] 2 K.B. 714 6–017
Lecouturier v. Rey [1910] A.C. 262 21–024
Leduc v. Ward [1888] 20 Q.B.D. 457 15–037
Leesh River Tea Co v. British India Steam Navigation Co (The Chyebassa) [1967] 2 Q.B.
250; [1966] 3 W.L.R. 642; [1966] 3 All E.R. 593; [1966] 2 Lloyd's Rep. 193; 110
S.J. 633, CA; reversing [1966] 1 Lloyd's Rep. 450 15–041
Leigh and Sillivan v. Aliakmon Shipping Co (The Aliakmon) [1986] A.C. 785; [1986] 2
W.L.R. 902; [1986] 2 All E.R. 145; [1986] 2 Lloyd's Rep. 1; (1986) 136 N.L.J.
415; (1986) 130 S.J. 357, HL; affirming [1985] Q.B. 350; [1985] 2 All E.R. 44;
[1985] 1 Lloyd's Rep. 199; (1985) 82 L.S.G. 203; (1985) 135 N.L.J. 285; (1985)
129 S.J. 69; [1985] L.M.C.L.Q. 1, CA; reversing [1983] 1 Lloyd's Rep. 203 2–030,
2–035, 4–010, 9–003, 9–008, 15–052, 19–014, 27–025
Lemenda Trading Co Ltd v. African Middle East Petroleum Co Ltd [1988] Q.B. 448;
[1988] 2 W.L.R. 735; [1988] 1 All E.R. 513; [1988] 1 Lloyd's Rep. 361; [1988] 1
F.T.L.R. 123; (1988) 132 S.J. 538, QBD 21–026
Leo Rapp Ltd v. McClure [1955] 1 Lloyd's Rep. 292 .... 2–002, 19–022
Lester v. Balfour Williamson Merchant Shippers [1953] 2 Q.B. 168; [1953] 2 W.L.R.
1068; [1953] 1 All E.R. 1146; [1953] 2 Lloyd's Rep. 13; 51 L.G.R. 357; 117 J.P.
308; 97 S.J. 353, DC 27–005
Lesters Leather & Skin Co Ltd v. Home and Overseas Brokers Ltd (1948–49) 82 Ll. L.
Rep. 202; (1948) 64 T.L.R. 569; [1948] W.N. 437; 92 S.J. 646, CA 5–003
L'Estrange v. Graucob [1934] 2 K.B. 394 3–017
Levy v. Goldhill [1917] 2 Ch. 297 27–012
Lewis Emanuel & Son Ltd v. Sammut [1959] 2 Lloyd's Rep. 629 .... 2–033, 6–002, 6–011
Lexmar Corp and Steamship Mutual Underwriting Association (Bermuda) Ltd v. Nordisk
Skibsrederforening [1997] 1 Lloyd's Rep. 289, QBD (Comm Ct) 22–014
Leyland DAF Ltd v. Automotive Products Plc [1994] 1 B.C.L.C. 245; [1993] B.C.C. 389;
[1994] E.C.C. 289; (1993) 137 S.J.L.B. 133, CA; affirming *The Times*, April 6,
1993, Ch D 29–018
Leyland Shipping Co Ltd v. Norwich Union Fire Insurance Society Ltd [1918] A.C. 350,
HL 19–030
Liberian Insurance Agency Inc v. Mosse [1977] 2 Lloyd's Rep. 560 19–012
Libyan Arab Foreign Bank v. Bankers Trust Co [1989] Q.B. 728; [1989] 3 W.L.R. 314;
[1989] 3 All E.R. 252; [1988] 1 Lloyd's Rep. 259; [1987] 2 F.T.L.R. 509; (1989)
133 S.J. 568, QBD (Comm Ct) 21–027, 28–007
Lickbarrow v. Mason (1794) 5 T.R. 683 .... 5–016, 15–019, 15–038
Lines Bros (In Liquidation), Re [1983] Ch. 1; [1982] 2 W.L.R. 1010; [1982] 2 All E.R.
183; [1982] Com. L.R. 81; 126 S.J. 197, CA; reversing [1981] Com. L.R. 214; 125
S.J. 426 21–018
Lines Bros Ltd (In Liquidation) (No.2), Re [1984] Ch. 438; [1984] 2 W.L.R. 905; (1984)
81 L.S.G. 585; (1984) 128 S.J. 261, Ch D 21–018
Lips Maritime Corp v. President of India (The Lips) [1988] A.C. 395; [1987] 3 W.L.R.
572; [1987] 3 All E.R. 110; [1987] 2 Lloyd's Rep. 311; [1987] 2 F.T.L.R. 477;
[1987] Fin. L.R. 313; (1987) 84 L.S.G. 2765; (1987) 137 N.L.J. 734; (1987) 131
S.J. 1085, HL; reversing [1987] 2 W.L.R. 906; [1987] 1 All E.R. 957; [1987] 1
Lloyd's Rep. 131; [1987] 1 F.T.L.R. 50; [1987] Fin. L.R. 91; (1987) 84 L.S.G.
1333; (1987) 131 S.J. 422, CA; reversing [1985] 2 Lloyd's Rep. 180; (1984) 134
N.L.J. 969, QBD (Comm Ct) 21–018
Lister & Co v. Stubbs (1890) L.R. 45 Ch. D. 1 27–011
Lister (RA) & Co v. EG Thomson (Shipping) Ltd and PT Djakarta Lloyd (The Benarty)
(No.2) [1985] Q.B. 325; [1984] 3 W.L.R. 1082; [1984] 3 All E.R. 961; [1984] 2
Lloyd's Rep. 244; (1984) 81 L.S.G. 2382; (1984) 128 S.J. 684, CA; reversing
[1983] 2 Lloyd's Rep. 50, QBD (Adm Ct) 15–021
Lloyd's Bank v. Bank of America National Trust and Savings Association [1937] 2 K.B.
631; [1938] 2 K.B. 147 .... 10–005, 27–017
Lloyds & Scottish Finance v. Cyril Lord Carpet Sales [1992] B.C.L.C. 609, HL 13–005
Lloyds & Scottish Finance v. Prentice 121 S.J. 847, CA 13–005
Lock International Plc v. Beswick [1989] 1 W.L.R. 1268; [1989] 3 All E.R. 373; [1989]

I.R.L.R. 481; (1989) 86(39) L.S.G. 36; (1989) 139 N.L.J. 644; (1989) S.J. 1297, Ch D 27–011

Logicrose Ltd v. Southend United Football Club Ltd (No.2) [1988] 1 W.L.R. 1256, Ch D 27–011

Lombard Finance Ltd v. Brookplain Trading Ltd [1991] 1 W.L.R. 271; [1991] 2 All E.R. 762, CA 2–026

Lombard Insurance Co Ltd v. Kin Yuen Co Pte Ltd (The Pab) Lloyd's List, July 25, 1995 (I.D.), CA (Sing) 19–005

Lombard North Central Plc v. Butterworth [1987] Q.B. 527; [1987] 2 W.L.R. 7; [1987] 1 All E.R. 267; [1987] 6 T.L.R. 65; (1986) 83 L.S.G. 2750, CA 4–015, 5–002, 5–004

London Drugs Ltd v. Kuehene & Nagel International Ltd [1992] 3 S.C.R. 299 2–007

Lord Advocate v. Crookshanks (1888) 15 R. 995 26–030

Lord Cable (Deceased) Will Trusts, Re (No.1) [1977] 1 W.L.R. 7; [1976] 3 All E.R. 417; 120 S.J. 317, Ch D 21–029

LS Harris (LS) Trustees (t/a Harris & Co) v. Power Packing Services (Hermit Road) [1970] 2 Lloyd's Rep. 65 27–011

Lubbe v. Cape Plc (No.1) [1998] C.L.C. 1559; [1999] I.L.Pr. 113, CA 22–008

Lubbe v. Cape Plc (No. 2) [2000] 1 W.L.R. 1545; *The Times*, July 27, 2000; HL; reversing [2000] 1 Lloyd's Rep 139, [2000] C.L.C. 45, CA 22–008

Lucena v. Craufurd (1806) 2 Bos. & P. (N.S.) 269 19–014

Lusograin Comercio Interacional De Cereas Ltd v. Bunge AG [1986] 2 Lloyd's Rep. 654 .... 2–007, 2–010, 2–016

Luther (AM) Co v. James Sagor & Co [1921] 3 K.B. 532, CA 21–024, 21–025

Lyons (JL) & Co v. May & Baker [1923] 1 K.B. 685 5–010

M. B. Pyramid Sound NV v. Briese Schiffahrts GmbH & Co KG MS "Sina" (The Ines) [1995] 2 Lloyd's Rep. 144, QBD (Comm Ct) 15–038

M/S Aswan Engineering Establishment Co v. Lupdine Ltd [1987] 1 W.L.R. 1; [1987] 1 All E.R. 135; [1986] 2 Lloyd's Rep. 347; [1987] 6 T.L.R. 1; (1986) 83 L.S.G. 2661; (1986) 130 S.J. 712, CA 4–010, 7–007

Mackay v. Dick (1881) 6 App. Cas. 251 5–011

Mackender v. Feldia AG [1967] 2 Q.B. 590; [1967] 2 W.L.R. 119; [1966] 3 All E.R. 847; *sub nom.* Mackenda v. Feldia 110 S.J. 811; *sub nom.* Mackender, Hill and White v. Feldia AG; CH Brachfield and Sons SA and Diamil SRL [1966] 2 Lloyd's Rep. 449; [1966] C.L.Y. 9908, CA 21–027

Mackinnon v. Donaldson Lufkin & Jenrette Securities Corp [1986] Ch. 482; [1986] 2 W.L.R. 453; [1986] 1 All E.R. 653; [1987] E.C.C. 139; [1986] Fin. L.R. 225; (1986) 83 L.S.G. 1226; (1985) 130 S.J. 224, Ch D 21–022

Maclaine Watson & Co Ltd v. International Tin Council (No.1) [1989] Ch. 253; [1988] 3 W.L.R. 1169; [1988] 3 All E.R. 257; (1988) 4 B.C.C. 659; (1988) 132 S.J. 1495, CA; affirming [1988] Ch. 1; [1987] 3 W.L.R. 508; [1987] 3 All E.R. 787; (1987) 3 B.C.C. 346; [1987] P.C.C. 373; [1987] 2 F.T.L.R. 162; (1987) 84 L.S.G. 2764; (1987) 131 S.J. 1062, Ch D 21–019

Maclaine Watson & Co Ltd v. International Tin Council (No.3) *See* Rayner (J.H.) (Mincing Lane) Ltd v. Department of Trade and Industry.

Maclean v. Dunn (1828) 1 Moo. & P. 761 27–009

MacLeod Ross & Co v. Compagnie d'Assurances Generales l'Helvetia of St Gall [1952] 1 All E.R. 331; [1952] 1 Lloyd's Rep. 12; [1952] 1 T.L.R. 314; [1952] W.N. 56; 96 S.J. 90 .... 3–017, 19–007

Macmillan Inc v. Bishopsgate Investment Trust Plc (No.4) [1999] C.L.C. 417, CA 21–002

Macpherson Train & Co v. Howard Ross & Co [1955] 1 W.L.R. 640; [1955] 2 All E.R. 445; [1955] 1 Lloyd's Rep. 518; 99 S.J. 385 2–042

MacShannon v. Rockware Glass Ltd [1978] A.C. 795; [1978] 2 W.L.R. 362; [1978] 1 All E.R. 625; 122 S.J. 81, HL; reversing [1977] 1 W.L.R. 376; [1977] 2 All E.R. 449; 122 S.J. 256, CA 22–007

Maharanee Seethadevi Gaekwar of Baroda v. Wildenstein [1972] 2 Q.B. 283; [1972] 2 W.L.R. 1077; [1972] 2 All E.R. 689; 116 S.J. 221, CA 22–003

Maheno, The [1977] 1 Lloyd's Rep. 81 27–025

Mahesan S/O Thambiah v. Malaysia Government Officers' Cooperative Housing Society [1979] A.C. 374; [1978] 2 W.L.R. 444; [1978] 2 All E.R. 405; 122 S.J. 31, PC 27–011

Mahkutai, The [1996] A.C. 650; [1996] 3 W.L.R. 1; [1996] 3 All E.R. 502; [1996] 2
  Lloyd's Rep. 1; [1996] C.L.C. 799; (1996) 146 N.L.J. 677; (1996) 140 S.J.L.B.
  107, PC 15–047
Makin v. London Rice Mills Co (1869) 20 L.T. 705 7–007
Malca-Amit Ltd and Ors v. British Airways Plc and Ors (1999) Unrep. (LTL 4/5/99) 17–003
Malik Co v. Central European Trading Agency; Central European Trading Agency v. Indu-
  strie Chimiche Italia Centrale SpA [1974] 2 Lloyd's Rep. 279 6–012
Man (ED & F) Ltd v. Nigerian Sweets & Confectionery Co [1977] 2 Lloyd's Rep. 50,
  QBD (Comm Ct) 11–025, 11–040
Manbre Saccharine & Co v. Corn Products Co [1919] 1 K.B. 189 2–034
Manchester Trust v. Furness [1895] 2 Q.B. 539 15–051
Manifest Shipping & Co Ltd v. Uni-Polaris Insurance Co Ltd (The Star Sea) [1997] 1
  Lloyd's Rep. 360; [1997] C.L.C. 481; [1997] 6 Re. L.R. 175, CA; affirming [1995]
  1 Lloyd's Rep. 651, QBD 19–024
Mann v. Nunn [1874] 30 L.T. 526 3–016
Mann, Macneal Boyd v. Dubois (1811) 3 Camp. 133 19–012
Mannai Investment Co Ltd v. Eagle Star Life Assurance Co Ltd [1997] A.C. 749; [1997]
  2 W.L.R. 945; [1997] 3 All E.R. 352; [1997] C.L.C. 1124; [1997] 25 E.G. 138;
  [1997] 24 E.G. 122; [1997] 1 E.G.L.R. 57; (1997) 16 Tr. L.R. 432; [1997] E.G.C.S.
  82; (1997) 94(30) L.S.G. 30; (1997) 147 N.L.J. 846; (1997) 141 S.J.L.B. 130;
  [1997] N.PC 81, HL; reversing [1995] 1 W.L.R. 1508; [1996] 1 All E.R. 55; (1996)
  71 P. & C.R. 129; [1996] 06 E.G. 140; [1996] 1 E.G.L.R. 69; [1995] E.G.C.S. 124;
  (1995) 139 S.J.L.B. 179; [1995] N.PC 117, CA 3–016
Mannesman Handel AG v. Kaunlaran Shipping Corp [1993] 1 Lloyd's Rep. 89 11–035
Mansouri v. Singh [1986] 1 W.L.R. 1393; [1986] 2 All E.R. 619; [1986] F.L.R. 143;
  (1986) 83 L.S.G. 3508; (1986) 136 N.L.J. 260; (1986) 130 S.J. 801, CA; affirming
  in part (1984) 134 N.L.J. 991 21–029
Maran Road Saw Mill v. Austin Taylor & Co. See Ng Chee Chong, Ng Weng Chong, Ng
  Cheng and Ng Yew (A Firm t/a Maran Road Saw Mill) v. Austin Taylor & Co.
Marc Rich & Co AG (Now Glencore International AG) v. Portman; *sub nom.* Glencore
  International AG v. Portman [1997] 1 Lloyd's Rep. 225, CA; affirming [1996] 1
  Lloyd's Rep. 430, QBD 19–012
Marcan Shipping (London) v. Polish Steamship Co (The Manifest Lipkowy) [1989] 2
  Lloyd's Rep. 138, CA; affirming [1988] 2 Lloyd's Rep. 171 27–012
Maredelanto Compania Naviera SA v. Bergbau-Handel GmbH (The Mihalis Angelos)
  [1971] 1 Q.B. 164; [1970] 3 W.L.R. 601; [1970] 3 All E.R. 125; [1970] 2 Lloyd's
  Rep. 43; 114 S.J. 548, CA; reversing [1970] 2 W.L.R. 907; [1970] 1 All E.R. 673;
  [1970] 1 Lloyd's Rep. 118 5–004
Mareva Compania Naviera SA of Panama v. International Bulk Carriers SA (The Mareva)
  [1975] 2 Lloyd's Rep. 509; (1975) 119 S.J. 660, CA 22–030
Margarine Union GmbH v. Cambay Prince Steamship Co (The Wear Breeze) [1969] 1
  Q.B. 219; [1967] 3 W.L.R. 1569; [1967] 3 All E.R. 775; [1967] 2 Lloyd's Rep.
  315; 111 S.J. 943 .... 2–020, 2–021, 2–022
Margaronis Navigation Agency v. Henry W Peabody & Co of London [1965] 2 Q.B. 430;
  [1964] 3 W.L.R. 873; [1964] 3 All E.R. 333; [1964] 2 Lloyd's Rep. 153; 108 S.J.
  562, CA; affirming [1965] 1 Q.B. 300; [1964] 3 W.L.R. 111; [1964] 2 All E.R.
  296; [1964] 1 Lloyd's Rep. 173; 108 S.J. 563, QBD 11–018
Marine Contractors Inc v. Shell Petroleum Development Co of Nigeria Ltd [1984] 2
  Lloyd's Rep. 77; 27 B.L.R. 127; (1984) 81 L.S.G. 1044, CA; affirming [1983]
  Com. L.R. 251 23–025
Maritime National Fish Ltd v. Ocean Trawlers Ltd [1935] A.C. 524, PC 6–005
Marshall v. Harland & Wolff [1972] 1 W.L.R. 899; [1972] 2 All E.R. 715; [1972] 1 R.L.R.
  90; [1972] I.C.R. 101; [1972] I.R.L.R. 90; (1972) 7 I.T.R. 150; 116 S.J. 484,
  NIRC 6–003
Marshall v. NM Financial Management Ltd; *sub nom.* NM Financial Management Ltd v.
  Marshall [1997] 1 W.L.R. 1527; [1997] I.C.R. 1065; [1997] I.R.L.R. 449, CA
  [1995] 1 W.L.R. 1461; [1995] 4 All E.R. 785; [1995] I.C.R. 1042; [1996] I.R.L.R.
  20, Ch D 27–012
Marston Excelsior v. Arbuckle, Smith & Co [1971] 2 Lloyd's Rep. 306; 115 S.J. 654, CA;
  reversing [1971] 1 Lloyd's Rep. 70 27–025

Martin-Baker Aircraft Co v. Canadian Flight Equipment; *sub nom.* Martin-Baker Aircraft
Co v. Murison [1955] 2 Q.B. 556; [1955] 3 W.L.R. 212; [1955] 2 All E.R. 722;
(1955) 72 R.P.C. 236; 99 S.J. 472, QBD 30–013
Mash & Murrell v. Emanuel (Joseph) (I.) [1962] 1 W.L.R. 16; [1962] 1 All E.R. 77n;
[1961] 2 Lloyd's Rep. 326; 105 S.J. 1007, CA; reversing [1961] 1 W.L.R. 862;
[1961] 1 All E.R. 485; [1961] 1 Lloyd's Rep. 46; 105 S.J. 468 .... 2–033, 4–010
Maxine Footwear Co v. Canadian Government Merchant Marine [1959] A.C. 589; [1959]
3 W.L.R. 232; [1959] 2 All E.R. 740; [1959] 2 Lloyd's Rep. 105; 103 S.J. 561,
PC 15–041, 15–043
Mayhew Foods v. Overseas Containers [1984] 1 Lloyd's Rep. 317; (1983) 133 N.L.J.
1103 15–021
McCarren & Co v. Humber International Transport and Truckline Ferries (Poole) (The
Vechstroon) [1982] 1 Lloyd's Rep. 301; [1982] Com. L.R. 11 15–022
McDougall v. Aeromarine of Emsworth [1958] 1 W.L.R. 1126; 102 S.J. 860; [1958] 3 All
E.R. 431; [1958] 2 Lloyd's Rep. 343 .... 2–027, 4–006
McKay Massey Harris Pty Ltd v. Imperial Chemical Industries of Australia & New Zealand
Ltd (The Mahia) (No.2) [1960] 1 Lloyd's Rep. 191 2–008
Mclean v. Dunn [1828] 1 Moo. & P. 761 27–008
McNealy v. Pennine Insurance Co [1978] 2 Lloyd's Rep. 18; [1978] R.T.R. 285; 122 S.J.
229, CA 19–003
McPherson v. Watt [1877] 23 App.Cass 254 27–011
Mecklermedia Corp v. DC Congress GmbH [1998] Ch. 40; [1997] 3 W.L.R. 479; [1998]
1 All E.R. 148; [1997] E.T.M.R. 265; [1997] I.L.Pr. 629; [1997] Info. T.L.R. 132;
[1997] F.S.R. 627; [1998] Masons C.L.R. Rep. 151; (1997) 20(4) I.P.D. 20042, Ch
D 22–020, 22–027
Mediterranean Freight Services Ltd v. BP Oil International Ltd (The Fiona) [1994] 2
Lloyd's Rep. 506, CA; affirming [1993] 1 Lloyd's Rep. 257 .... 15–041, 15–048, 15–050
Medway Packaging Ltd v. Meurer Maschinen GmbH & Co KG [1990] 2 Lloyd's Rep.
112, CA; affirming [1990] 1 Lloyd's Rep. 383; [1990] I.L.Pr. 234, QBD 22–018
Memory Corp Plc v. Sidhu (1999) 96(24) L.S.G. 38, Ch D 22–032
Mendala III Transport v. Total Transport Corp (The Wilomi Tanana) [1993] 2 Lloyd's
Rep. 41 15–035
Merak, The. *See* Batchelor (T. B. & S.) & Co Ltd v. Owners of the SS Merak.
Mercanaut, The. *See* Rederi Kommanditselskaabet Merc-Scandia IV v. Couniniotis SA.
Mercury Communications v. Communications Systems International, LTL, June 1, 1999 . 22–016,
22–029
Meredith (A) Jones & Co Ltd v. Vangemar Shipping Co Ltd (The Apostolis) [1997] 2
Lloyd's Rep. 241, CA; reversing [1996] 1 Lloyd's Rep. 475, QBD 15–041
Metaalhandel JA Magnus BV v. Ardfields Transport [1988] 1 Lloyd's Rep. 197; [1987] 2
F.T.L.R. 319, DC 21–018, 27–025
Metal Scrap Trade Corp Ltd v. Kate Shipping Co Ltd (The Gladys) (No.2) [1994] 2 Lloyd's
Rep. 402 3–015
Metal Scrap Trade Corp Ltd v. Kate Shipping Co Ltd (The Gladys) (No.1) [1990] 1 W.L.R.
115; [1990] 1 All E.R. 397; [1990] 1 Lloyd's Rep. 297; (1990) 87(12) L.S.G. 36;
(1990) 140 N.L.J. 170; (1990) 134 S.J. 261, HL; reversing [1988] 1 W.L.R. 767;
[1988] 3 All E.R. 32; [1988] 2 Lloyd's Rep. 221; (1988) 85(19) L.S.G. 38; (1988)
132 S.J. 993, CA 22–003
Metall und Rohstoff AG v. ACLI Metals (London) Ltd [1984] 1 Lloyd's Rep. 598; [1985]
E.C.C. 502, CA 22–009
Metro Meat Ltd v. Fares Rural Co Pty Ltd [1985] 2 Lloyd's Rep. 13, PC 2–004
Metropolitan Asylums Board Managers v. Kingham & Sons (1890) 6 T.L.R. 217 27–008
Metropolitan Water Board v. Dick, Kerr & Co Ltd [1918] A.C. 119, HL 6–011
MH Smith (Plant Hire) v. DL Mainwaring (t/a Inshore) [1986] 2 Lloyd's Rep. 244, CA .. 19–035
Michael Doyle & Associates Ltd v. Bank of Montreal [1982] 6 W.W.W. 24 .... 11–007, 11–027
Michael Galley Footwear Ltd (In Liquidation) v. Iaboni [1982] 2 All E.R. 200; [1985] 2
Lloyd's Rep. 251, QBD 18–009
Midland Bank Ltd v. Eastcheap Dried Fruit Co [1962] 1 Lloyd's Rep. 359; 106 S.J. 351,
CA; affirming [1961] 2 Lloyd's Rep. 251, QBD 10–005
Midland Bank Ltd v. Seymour [1955] 2 Lloyd's Rep. 147, QBD 11–007, 11–008, 11–015
Midland Bank Plc v. Laker Airways Ltd [1986] Q.B. 689; [1986] 2 W.L.R. 707; [1986] 1
All E.R. 526; [1986] E.C.C. 329; (1985) 129 S.J. 670, CA; reversing [1983] Com.
L.R. 110; (1983) 133 N.L.J. 537, QBD 22–009

Midland Silicones Ltd v. Scruttons Ltd. *See* Scruttons v. Midland Silicones.

Mihalis Angelos, The. *See* Maredelanto Compania Naviera SA v. Bergbau-Handel GmbH.

Milhem (J.) & Sons v. Fuerst Bros & Co Ltd [1954] 2 Lloyd's Rep. 559 3–015

Miliangos v. George Frank (Textiles) Ltd (No.1) [1976] A.C. 443; [1975] 3 W.L.R. 758; [1975] 3 All E.R. 801; [1976] 1 Lloyd's Rep. 201; [1975] 2 C.M.L.R. 585; 119 S.J. 774, HL; affirming [1975] Q.B. 487; [1975] 2 W.L.R. 555; [1975] 1 All E.R. 1076; [1975] 1 Lloyd's Rep. 587; [1975] 1 C.M.L.R. 630; 119 S.J. 322, CA; reversing [1975] 1 Lloyd's Rep. 436; [1975] 1 C.M.L.R. 121; (1974) 119 S.J. 10, QBD 21–018

Miller, Gibb & Co, Re [1957] 1 W.L.R. 703; [1957] 2 All E.R. 266; [1957] 1 Lloyd's Rep. 258; 101 S.J. 392 19–035

Milor Srl v. British Airways Plc [1996] Q.B. 702; [1996] 3 W.L.R. 642; [1996] 3 All E.R. 537; [1996] C.L.C. 816; [1996] I.L.Pr. 426, CA; [1996] C.L.C. 812, QBD (Comm Ct) 17–014, 22–007

Minister of Food v. Reardon Smith Line Ltd [1951] 2 Lloyd's Rep. 265; [1951] 2 T.L.R. 1158, KBD 15–043

Ministry of Food v. Lamport & Holt Line Ltd [1952] 2 Lloyd's Rep. 371, QBD 15–041

Minmetals Germany GmbH v. Ferco Steel Ltd [1999] 1 All E.R. (Comm) 315; [1999] C.L.C. 647; *The Times*, March 1, 1999, QBD (Comm Ct) 23–002

Minnesota v. Philip Morris Inc [1998] I.L.Pr. 170, CA; reversing [1998] I.L.Pr. 158, QBD 21–022

Minories Finance v. Afribank Nigeria Ltd [1995] 1 Lloyd's Rep. 134, QBD 10–002, 22–007

Minster Investments Ltd v. Hyundai Precision & Industry Co Ltd [1988] 2 Lloyd's Rep. 621, QBD 22–020

Minster Trust v. Traps Tractors [1954] 1 W.L.R. 963; [1954] 3 All E.R. 136; 98 S.J. 456 4–012

Miramar Maritime Corp v. Holborn Oil Trading (The Miramar) [1984] A.C. 676; [1984] 3 W.L.R. 1; [1984] 2 All E.R. 326; [1984] 2 Lloyd's Rep. 129; (1984) 81 L.S.G. 2000; (1984) 128 S.J. 414, HL; affirming [1984] 1 Lloyd's Rep. 142, CA; affirming [1983] 2 Lloyd's Rep. 319, QBD (Comm Ct) 15–023

Miserocchi and C. SpA v. Agricultores Federados Argentinos SCL; Same v. Bunge AG (The Sotir and The Angelic Grace) [1982] 1 Lloyd's Rep. 202 .... 2–009, 2–016

Mitchell, Cotts & Co v. Steel Brothers & Co Ltd [1916] 2 K.B. 610 15–050

Mitsubishi Corp v. Alafouzos [1988] 1 Lloyd's Rep. 191; [1988] 1 F.T.L.R. 47 21–026

Mitsui & Co Ltd v. American Lines 1981 A.M.C 331, 2nd Cir. (1981) 16–009

Mitsui & Co Ltd v. Flota Mercante Grancolombiana SA (The Ciudad de Pasto and The Ciudad de Neiva) [1988] 1 W.L.R. 1145; [1989] 1 All E.R. 951; [1988] 2 Lloyd's Rep. 208, CA; reversing [1987] 2 Lloyd's Rep. 392 .... 2–014, 2–028, 4–006, 11–032

Mitsui & Co Ltd v. Novorossiysk Shipping Co (The Gudermes) [1993] 1 Lloyd's Rep. 311, CA; reversing [1991] 1 Lloyd's Rep. 456, QBD (Comm Ct) 15–052

Mizel v. Warren [1973] 1 W.L.R. 899; [1973] 2 All E.R. 1149; 117 S.J. 510, DC 26–031

Modus Vivendi Ltd v. British Products Sanmex Co Ltd [1997] I.L.Pr. 654; [1996] F.S.R. 790; (1996) 19(10) I.P.D. 19089, Ch D 22–020

Mogul Steamship Co Ltd v. McGregor Gow & Co [1892] A.C. 25; [1891–4] All E.R. Rep. 263, HL 15–016

Mohammed v. Bank of Kuwait and the Middle East KSC [1996] 1 W.L.R. 1483; [1996] C.L.C. 1835; [1996] I.L.Pr. 632; (1996) 140 S.J.L.B. 173, CA 22–007

Molling v. Dean (1902) 18 T.L.R. 217 5–005

Montedison SpA v. Icroma SpA (The Caspian Sea) [1980] 1 W.L.R. 48; [1979] 3 All E.R. 378; [1980] 1 Lloyd's Rep. 91; 123 S.J. 551, QBD 15–007

Montes v. HM Advocate (1990) S.C.C.R. 645 26–031

Moore v. Piretta PTA Ltd [1999] 1 All E.R. 174; [1998] C.L.C. 992; [1999] Eu. L.R. 32; (1998) 17 Tr. L.R. 161, QBD 27–012

Moralice (London) Ltd v. E. D. & F. Man [1954] 2 Lloyd's Rep. 526 .... 5–003, 11–037

Morris v. CW Martin & Sons Ltd [1966] 1 Q.B. 716; [1965] 3 W.L.R. 276; [1965] 2 All E.R. 725; [1965] 2 Lloyd's Rep. 63; 109 S.J. 451, CA 27–025

Morris v. Wentworth-Stanley; *sub nom.* Morris v. Molesworth [1999] Q.B. 1004; [1999] 2 W.L.R. 470; [1999] 1 F.L.R. 83, CA 27–005

Morton Norwich Products Inc v. Intercen Ltd [1976] F.S.R. 513; [1978] R.PC 501, Ch D 2–035

Morviken, The. *See* Owners of Cargo on Board the Morviken v. Owners of the Hollandia.

Moschi v. Lep Air Services [1973] A.C. 331; [1972] 2 W.L.R. 1175; 116 S.J. 372; [1972]
  2 All E.R. 393, HL; affirming *sub nom.* Lep Air Services v. Rolloswin Investments
  [1971] 3 All E.R. 45, CA 12–001
Motis Exports Ltd v. Dampskibsselskabet AF 1912, Aktieselkab [1999] 1 Lloyd's Rep.
  837; *The Times*, March 31, 1999, QBD 15–038
Moto Vespa SA v. MAT (Britannia Express) and Mateu & Mateu SA and Vincente Belloch
  Galvez [1979] 1 Lloyd's Rep. 175 27–025
Motor Oil Hellas (Corinth) Refineries SA v. Shipping Corp of India (The Kanchenjunga)
  [1990] 1 Lloyd's Rep. 391, HL; affirming [1989] 1 Lloyd's Rep. 354; (1989) 132
  S.J. 19, CA; affirming [1987] 2 Lloyd's Rep. 509 .... 2–026, 5–011, 5–012
Moukataff v. British Overseas Airways Corp (B.O.A.C.) [1967] 1 Lloyd's Rep. 396,
  QBD 17–019
Mount (DF) v. Jay & Jay (Provisions) Co [1960] 1 Q.B. 159; [1959] 3 W.L.R. 537; [1959]
  3 All E.R. 307; [1959] 2 Lloyd's Rep. 269; 103 S.J. 636 5–016
MSC Mediterranean Shipping Co SA v. BRE-Metro [1985] 2 Lloyd's Rep. 239 30–006
MSC Mediterranean Shipping Co SA v. Polish Ocean Lines (The Tychy) [1999] 1 All
  E.R. (Comm) 819; [1999] 2 Lloyd's Rep. 11; [1999] C.L.C. 1046, CA 22–033
Muduroglu v. TC Ziraat Bankasi [1986] Q.B. 1225; [1986] 3 W.L.R. 606; [1986] 3 All
  E.R. 682; (1986) 83 L.S.G. 2660; (1986) 130 S.J. 749, CA 12–001
Muller Brothers v. GM Power Plant Co *The Guardian*, May 9, 1963; [1963] C.L.Y.
  3114 2–016

N&J Vlassopulos Ltd v. Ney Shipping Ltd (The Santa Carina) [1977] 1 Lloyd's Rep. 478;
  (1976) 121 S.J. 10CA; reversing [1976] 2 Lloyd's Rep. 223, QBD (Comm Ct) 27–005
N. V. Handel My. J. Smits Import-Export v. English Exporters (London) [1957] 1 Lloyd's
  Rep. 517 .... 2–007, 2–008, 11–018
Napier (F. E.) v. Dexters Ltd (1926) 26 Ll.L.R. 184 2–010
National Bank of Sharjah v. Delborg *The Times*, December 24, 1992, CA July 9, 1997
National Bank of South Africa v. Banca Italiana (1922) 10 Ll. L.R. 531 11–026
National Justice Compania Naviera SA v. Prudential Assurance Co Ltd (The Ikarian
  Reefer) [1995] 1 Lloyd's Rep. 455, CA; reversing [1993] 2 Lloyd's Rep. 68; [1993]
  F.S.R. 563; [1993] 37 E.G. 158, QBD (Comm Ct) 19–031
National Petroleum Co, (The Athelviscount), Re (1934) 39 Com.Cas 227 15–036
National Semiconductors (UK) Ltd v. UPS Ltd and Inter City Trucks [1996] 2 Lloyd's
  Rep. 212, QBD 18–009
Naviera Mogor SA v. Societe Metallurgique de Normandie (The Nogar Marin) [1988] 1
  Lloyd's Rep. 412; [1988] 1 F.T.L.R. 349, CA; affirming [1987] 1 Lloyd's Rep.
  456; [1987] 1 F.T.L.R. 243 .... 15–003, 15–036, 15–045
Naxos, The. *See* Compagnie Commerciale Sucres et Denrees v. C. Czarnikow Ltd.
Nea Agrex SA v. Baltic Shipping Co Ltd (The Agios Lazarus) [1976] Q.B. 933; [1976] 2
  W.L.R. 925; [1976] 2 All E.R. 842; [1976] 2 Lloyd's Rep. 47; 120 S.J. 351,
  CA 15–022, 15–048
Nea Tyhi, The [1982] 1 Lloyd's Rep. 606; [1982] Com. L.R. 9 15–036
Nelson Pine Industries Ltd v. Seatrans New Zealand Ltd (The Pembroke) [1995] 2 Lloyd's
  Rep. 290, HC (NZ) 15–045
Neste Chemicals SA v. DK Line SA (The Sargasso) [1994] 3 All E.R. 180; [1994] 2
  Lloyd's Rep. 6; [1995] I.L.Pr. 553, CA; affirming [1993] 1 Lloyd's Rep. 424 22–027
Netherlands Insurance Co Est 1845 Ltd v. Karl Ljungberg & Co AB (The Mammoth Pine)
  [1986] 3 All E.R. 767; [1986] 2 Lloyd's Rep. 19, PC 19–024
New Chinese Antimony Co v. Ocean Steamship Co [1917] 2 K.B. 664 .... 15–036, 16–009
New Zealand Guardian Trust Co Ltd v. Brooks [1995] 1 W.L.R. 96; [1995] 2 B.C.L.C.
  242; [1995] B.C.C. 407; (1995) 92(1) L.S.G. 36; (1994) 138 S.J.L.B. 240, PC 27–005
New Zealand Shipping Co Ltd v. AM Satterthwaite [1975] A.C. 154; [1974] 2 W.L.R.
  865; 118 S.J. 387; [1974] 1 All E.R. 1015; *sub nom.* New Zealand Shipping Co
  Ltd v. AM Satterthwaite & Co (The Eurymedon) [1974] 1 Lloyd's Rep. 534, PC;
  affirming [1972] 2 Lloyd's Rep. 544, CA (NZ); reversing [1971] 2 Lloyd's Rep.
  399; [1972] N.Z.L.R. 385 15–047
New Zealand Shipping Co v. Satterthwaite (A. M.) [1975] A.C. 154; [1974] 2 W.L.R. 865;
  118 S.J. 387; [1974] 1 All E.R. 1015; *sub nom.* New Zealand Shipping Co v.
  Satterthwaite (A. M.) & Co (The Eurymedon) [1974] 1 Lloyd's Rep. 534, PC 2–007
Newman Industries v. Indo-British Industries (Govindram Bros, Third Parties) [1957] 1
  Lloyd's Rep. 211, CA; reversing [1956] 2 Lloyd's Rep. 219 12–001

Ng Chee Chong, Ng Weng Chong, Ng Cheng and Ng Yew (A Firm t/a Maran Road Saw Mill)
v. Austin Taylor & Co [1975] 1 Lloyd's Rep. 156 .... 11–022, 11–025, 11–027, 11–040
Ngo Chew Hong Edible Oil Pte Ltd v. Scindia Steam Navigation Co Ltd (The Jalamohan)
[1988] 1 Lloyd's Rep. 443; [1988] 1 F.T.L.R. 340, QBD (Comm Ct) 15–051
Nichimen Corp v. Gatoil Overseas Inc [1987] 2 Lloyd's Rep. 46, CA 5–012, 11–018
Nicolene Ltd v. Simmonds [1953] 1 Q.B. 543; [1953] 2 W.L.R. 717; [1953] 1 All E.R. 822;
[1953] 1 Lloyd's Rep. 189; (1953) C.L.C. 661; 97 S.J. 247, CA; affirming [1952] 2
Lloyd's Rep. 419 .... 3–015, 6–020, 8–003
Nile Co for the Export of Agricultural Crops v. H&JM Bennett (Commodities) [1986] 1
Lloyd's Rep. 555 6–009
Nile Rhapsody, The. *See* Hamed el Chiaty & Co (t/a Travco Nile Cruise Lines) v. Thomas
Cook Group Ltd.
Nippon Yusen Kaisha v. Ramjiban [1938] A.C. 429 15–003
Noble Resources Ltd v. Cavalier Shipping Corp (The Atlas) [1996] 1 Lloyd's Rep. 642;
[1996] C.L.C. 1148, QBD 15–031, 15–036, 15–045, 16–009
Noirhomme v. Walklate [1992] 1 Lloyd's Rep. 427; [1991] I.L.Pr. 581; *The Times*, August 2,
1991, QBD 24–003
Nordglimt, The [1988] Q.B. 183; [1988] 2 W.L.R. 338; [1988] 2 All E.R. 531; [1987] 2
Lloyd's Rep. 470; [1987] 2 F.T.L.R. 438; (1988) 132 S.J. 262, QBD 15–048
Nordisk Insulinlaboratorium v. Gorgate Products (sued as CL Bencard) [1953] Ch. 430;
[1953] 2 W.L.R. 879; 97 S.J. 298; *sub nom.* Nordisk Insulinlaboratorium v. CL
Bencard (CL) (1934) [1953] 1 All E.R. 986, CA; reversing [1952] 2 All E.R. 1040;
[1952] 2 T.L.R. 964; [1952] W.N. 540; 96 S.J. 850, Ch D 27–011
Nordskog v. National Bank [1922] 10 Ll. L.R. 652 11–031
Norsk Bjergningskompagni A/S v. Owners of the Pantanassa (The Pantanassa) [1970] P. 187;
[1970] 2 W.L.R. 981; *sub nom.* Pantanassa, The 114 S.J. 372; [1970] 1 Lloyd's Rep.
153 *sub nom.* Pantanassa The., Norsk Bjergningskompagni A/S v. Owners of the
Steamship Pantanassa, her Cargo and Freight [1970] 1 All E.R. 848 15–011
North & South Trust Co v. Berkeley; Berkeley v. North & South Trust Co [1971] 1 W.L.R.
470; [1971] 1 All E.R. 980; [1970] 2 Lloyd's Rep. 467; *Sub nom.* North & South Trust
Co v. Berkeley (1970) 115 S.J. 244, QBD 19–032
Northland Airliners v. Dennis Ferranti Meters (1970) 114 S.J. 845, CA; affirming *The Times*,
February 13, 1970 .... 2–006, 3–007
Norway's Application (Nos.1 and 2), Re [1990] 1 A.C. 723; [1989] 2 W.L.R. 458; [1989] 1
All E.R. 745; (1989) 133 S.J. 290, HL; affirming in part [1988] 3 W.L.R. 603; [1989]
1 All E.R. 701; [1989] 1 All E.R. 661; [1988] 1 F.T.L.R. 293, CA 21–021,
21–022, 21–025
Norway's Application, Re [1987] Q.B. 433; [1986] 3 W.L.R. 452; (1986) 83 L.S.G. 3248;
(1986) 130 S.J. 730, CA 21–022, 21–025
Norwich Pharmacal Co v. Customs and Excise Commissioners [1974] A.C. 133; [1973] 3
W.L.R. 164; [1973] 2 All E.R. 943; [1973] F.S.R. 365; [1974] R.P.C. 101; 117 S.J.
567, HL; reversing [1972] 3 W.L.R. 870; [1972] 3 All E.R. 813; [1972] F.S.R. 405;
[1972] R.P.C. 743; 116 S.J. 823, CA; reversing [1972] Ch. 566; [1972] 2 W.L.R. 864;
[1972] 1 All E.R. 972; [1972] F.S.R. 1; (1971) 116 S.J. 315, Ch D 26–031
Nottingham Cooperative Society v. Cementation Piling and Foundations Ltd [1989] Q.B. 71;
[1988] 3 W.L.R. 396; [1988] 2 All E.R. 971; 41 B.L.R. 43; (1988) 4 Const. L.J. 216;
(1988) 138 N.L.J. 112; (1988) 132 S.J. 754 8–009
Nouvion v. Freeman (1889) L.R. 15 App. Cas. 1 24–010
Nova (Jersey) Knit Ltd v. Kammgarn Spinnerei GmbH [1977] 1 W.L.R. 713; [1977] 2 All
E.R. 463; [1977] 1 Lloyd's Rep. 463; 121 S.J. 170, HL; reversing [1976] 2 Lloyd's
Rep., CA 9–012, 11–006
Novaknit Hellas SA v. Kumar Bros International Ltd [1998] Lloyd's Rep. Bank. 287; [1998]
C.L.C. 971, CA 9–004
Nutting v. Baldwin [1995] 1 W.L.R. 201; [1995] 2 All E.R. 321 3–017
Nyholm, Ex p., re Child (1873) 43 L.J.Bk. 21 15–010

Obestain Inc v. National Mineral Development Corp Ltd (The Sanix Ace) [1987] 1 Lloyd's
Rep. 465 .... 2–014, 4–004
Obikoga v. Silvernorth Times, July 6, 1983, CA 22–003
Ocean Tramp Tankers Corp v. V/O Sovfracht (The Eugenia) [1964] 2 Q.B. 226; [1964] 2
W.L.R. 114; [1964] 1 All E.R. 161; [1963] 2 Lloyd's Rep. 381; 107 S.J. 931, CA;
reversing [1963] 2 Lloyd's Rep. 155, QBD (Comm Ct) 6–011

Offshore International SA v. Banco Central SA [1977] 1 W.L.R. 399; [1976] 3 All E.R. 749;
  121 S.J. 252; *sub nom.* Offshore International SA v. Banco Central SA and Hijos de J
  Barreras SA [1976] 2 Lloyd's Rep. 402, QBD 11–019, 11–020,
                                              11–030, 23–025
Oinoussin Pride, The. *See* Pride Shipping Corp v. Chung Hwa Pulp Corp.
OK Petroleum AB v. Vitol Energy SA (The Chemical Venture and The Jade) [1995] 2 Lloyd's
  Rep. 160, QBD 15–024
Olearia Tirrena SpA v. NV Algemeene Oliehandel (The Osterbek) [1973] 2 Lloyd's Rep. 86,
  CA; affirming [1972] 2 Lloyd's Rep. 341 2–011
Oleificio Zucchi SpA v. Northern Sales Ltd [1965] 2 Lloyd's Rep. 496 2–037
Ollett v. Jordan [1918] 2 K.B. 41 4–010
Oppenheimer v. Cattermole (Inspector of Taxes) [1976] A.C. 249; [1975] 2 W.L.R. 347;
  [1975] 1 All E.R. 538; 50 T.C. 159; [1975] S.T.C. 91; [1975] T.R. 13; 119 S.J. 169,
  HL; affirming [1973] Ch. 264; [1972] 3 W.L.R. 815; [1972] 3 All E.R. 1106; 116 S.J.
  802, CA; reversing [1972] Ch. 585; [1972] 2 W.L.R. 1045; [1972] 2 All E.R. 529;
  [1971] T.R. 507; (1971) 116 S.J. 256, Ch D 21–023
Oresundsvarvet Aktiebolag v. Marcos Diamantis Lemos (The Angelic Star) [1988] 1 Lloyd's
  Rep. 122 4–015
Oricon Waren-Handelsgesellschaft MBH v. Intergraan NV [1967] 2 Lloyd's Rep. 82 2–037
Orient Company Ltd v. Brekke & Howlid [1913] 1 K.B. 531; 82 L.J.K.B. 427; 108 L.T. 507;
  18 Com.Cas 101, D.C. 2–023
Oriental Steamship Co Ltd v. Tylor [1893] 2 Q.B. 518 15–010
Osman v. Moss (J Ralph) [1970] 1 Lloyd's Rep. 313, CA 19–003
Osterreichische Landerbank v. S'Elite [1981] Q.B. 565; [1980] 3 W.L.R. 356; [1980] 2 All
  E.R. 651; [1980] 2 Lloyd's Rep. 139; 124 S.J. 326, CA 9–004
OTM v. Hydranautics [1981] 2 Lloyd's Rep. 211 3–018
Overseas Commodities Ltd v. Style [1958] 1 Lloyd's Rep. 546, QBD (Comm Ct) 19–013
Overseas Union Insurance v. AA Mutual International Insurance [1988] 2 Lloyd's Rep. 63;
  [1988] F.T.L.R. 421 .... 21–029, 23–009
Owens Bank Ltd v. Bracco (No.1 and 2) [1992] 2 A.C. 443; [1992] 2 W.L.R. 621; [1992] 2
  All E.R. 193; [1993] I.L.Pr. 24, HL; affirming [1992] 2 A.C. 443; [1992] 2 W.L.R.
  127; [1991] 4 All E.R. 833; [1992] I.L.Pr. 114, CA; affirming *The Times*, August 29,
  1990; *The Independent*, September 3, 1990 (C.S.), QBD 24–013
Owens Bank Ltd v. Etoile Commerciale SA [1995] 1 W.L.R. 44, PC 24–013
Owners of Cargo Lately Laden on Board on the River Gurara v. Nigerian National Shipping
  Line Ltd (The River Gurara) [1998] Q.B. 610; [1997] 3 W.L.R. 1128; [1997] 4 All
  E.R. 498; [1998] 1 Lloyd's Rep. 225; [1997] C.L.C. 1322; (1997) 94(33) L.S.G. 27;
  (1997) 141 S.J.L.B. 175, CA; affirming [1996] 2 Lloyd's Rep. 53; [1996] C.L.C. 927
  .... 7–009, 15–045, 16–009
Owners of Cargo Lately Laden on Board the Deichland v. Owners and/or Demise Charterers
  of the Deichland (The Deichland) [1990] 1 Q.B. 361; [1989] 3 W.L.R. 478; [1989] 2
  All E.R. 1066; [1989] 2 Lloyd's Rep. 113; [1991] I.L.Pr. 135; (1989) 86(24) L.S.G.
  36; (1989) 133 S.J. 596, CA; reversing [1988] 2 Lloyd's Rep. 454, QBD ....
  .... 22–002, 22–033
Owners of Cargo Lately Laden on Board the Eleftheria v. Owners of the Eleftheria (The
  Eleftheria) [1970] P. 94; [1969] 2 W.L.R. 1073; [1969] 2 All E.R. 641; [1969] 1
  Lloyd's Rep. 237; 113 S.J. 407, PDAD 22–009, 23–016
Owners of Cargo Lately Laden on Board The Siskina v. Distos Compania Naviera SA (The
  Siskina); Ibrahim Shanker v. Distos Compania Naviera SA [1979] A.C. 210; [1977]
  3 W.L.R. 818; [1977] 3 All E.R. 803; [1978] 1 Lloyd's Rep. 1; [1978] 1 C.M.L.R.
  190, HL; reversing [1977] 3 W.L.R. 532; [1977] 2 Lloyd's Rep. 230, CA; reversing
  [1977] 1 Lloyd's Rep. 404QBD (Comm Ct) 22–030
Owners of Cargo on Board the Morviken v. Owners of the Hollandia (The Hollandia and The
  Morviken) [1983] 1 A.C. 565; [1982] 3 W.L.R. 1111; [1982] 3 All E.R. 1141; [1983]
  1 Lloyd's Rep. 1; [1983] Com. L.R. 44; 126 S.J. 819, HL 15–021, 15–045,
                                                      22–008
Owners of the Cargo Lately Laden on Board the Rewia v. Caribbean Liners (Caribtainer) Ltd
  (The Rewia) [1991] 2 Lloyds Rep. 325; [1993] I.L.Pr. 507, CA; reversing [1991] 1
  Lloyd's Rep. 69, QBD (Adm Ct) 22–002
Owners of the Annefield v. Owners of the Carge Lately Laden on Board The Annefield (The
  Annefield) [1971] P. 168; [1971] 2 W.L.R. 320; [1971] 1 All E.R. 394; [1971] 1
  Lloyd's Rep. 1, CA 15–023

Owners of the Cargo Lately Laden on Board The Ardennes v. Owners of The Ardennes (The
    Ardennes) [1951] 1 K.B. 55; [1950] 2 All E.R. 517; (1950) 84 Ll. L. Rep. 340; (1950)
    66 T.L.R. (Pt. 2) 312; 94 S.J. 458, KBD 15–037
Owners of the Herceg Novi v. Owners of the Ming Galaxy [1998] 4 All E.R. 238; [1998] 2
    Lloyd's Rep. 454; [1998] C.L.C. 1487, CA; reversing [1998] 1 Lloyd's Rep. 167,
    QBD (Adm Ct) 22–007, 22–008
Ozalid Group (Export) Ltd v. African Continental Bank Ltd [1979] 2 Lloyd's Rep. 231, QBD
    (Comm Ct) 11–021, 21–018

P. H. Grace Pte Ltd v. American Express International Banking Corp [1987] 1 M.L.J.
    437 12–002
Paal Wilson & Co A/S v. Partenreederei Hannah Blumenthal (The Hannah Blumenthal)
    [1983] 1 A.C. 854; [1982] 3 W.L.R. 1149; [1983] 1 All E.R. 34; [1983] 1 Lloyd's Rep.
    103; [1983] Com. L.R. 20; 126 S.J. 835, HL; affirming [1982] 3 W.L.R. 49; [1982] 3
    All E.R. 394; [1982] 1 Lloyd's Rep. 582; [1982] Com. L.R. 117; 126 S.J. 292, CA;
    affirming [1981] 3 W.L.R. 823; [1982] 1 All E.R. 197; [1981] 2 Lloyd's Rep. 438;
    [1981] Com. L.R. 231, QBD 6–004, 6–005
Pacific Molasses Co and United Molasses Trading Co v. Entre Rios Compania Naviera SA
    (The San Nicholas) [1976] 1 Lloyd's Rep. 8, CA 4–006, 15–052
Padre Island, The. (No.2). *See* Firma C-Trade SA v. Newcastle Protection and Indemnity
    Association.
Page v. Combined Shipping & Trading Co Ltd [1997] 3 All E.R. 656; [1996] C.L.C. 1952;
    [1999] Eu. L.R. 1; (1996) 15 Tr. L.R. 357, CA 27–012
Pagnan (R) & Fratelli v. Schouten (NGJ) NV (The Filipinas I) [1973] 1 Lloyd's Rep.
    349 2–005
Pagnan SpA v. Feed Products Ltd [1987] 2 Lloyd's Rep. 601, CA 3–015
Pagnan SpA v. Granaria BV [1986] 2 Lloyd's Rep. 547, CA; affirming [1985] 2 Lloyd's Rep.
    256 .... 3–015, 14–005, 14–010
Pagnan SpA v. Tradax Ocean Transportation SA [1987] 3 All E.R. 565; [1987] 2 Lloyd's
    Rep. 342, CA; affirming [1987] 1 All E.R. 81; [1986] 2 Lloyd's Rep. 646 .... 2–005, 6–012
Paley Olga (Princess) v. Weisz N [1929] 1 K.B. 718 21–024
Palgrave, Brown & Son v. S. S. Turid (Owners) [1922] 1 A.C. 397 3–016
Palmco Shipping Inc v. Continental Ore Corp (The Captain George K) [1970] 2 Lloyd's Rep.
    21, QBD (Comm Ct) 6–011
Pan American World Airways Inc's Application, Re; *sub nom.* Lockerbie Air Disaster, Re
    [1992] Q.B. 854; [1992] 3 W.L.R. 191; [1992] 3 All E.R. 197, CA; reversing 1992
    S.L.T. 268; 1992 S.C.L.R. 257, OH 21–022
Pan Atlantic Insurance Co v. Pine Top Insurance Co [1995] 1 A.C. 501; [1994] 3 W.L.R. 677;
    [1994] 3 All E.R. 581; [1994] 2 Lloyd's Rep. 427; (1994) 91(36) L.S.G. 36; (1994)
    144 N.L.J. 1203; (1994) 138 S.J.L.B. 182, HL; affirming [1993] 1 Lloyd's Rep. 496,
    CA; affirming [1992] 1 Lloyd's Rep. 101, QBD (Comm Ct) 19–012
Panalpina International Transport v. Densil Underwear [1981] 1 Lloyd's Rep. 187,
    QBD 17–014
Panchaud Freres SA v. Etablissements General Grain Co [1970] 1 Lloyd's Rep. 53, CA;
    reversing [1969] 2 Lloyd's Rep. 109 .... 2–026, 4–012, 5–011,
                                                                5–012, 11–007, 11–015
    Pancommerce SA v. Veecheema BV [1983] 2 Lloyd's Rep. 304; [1983] Com. L.R.
    230, CA [1982] 1 Lloyd's Rep. 645 6–014
Pando Compania Naviera SA v. Filmo SAS [1975] Q.B. 742; [1975] 2 W.L.R. 636; [1975] 2
    All E.R. 515; [1975] 1 Lloyd's Rep. 560; 119 S.J. 253 23–013
Panorama Developments (Guildford) Ltd v. Fidelis Furnishing Fabrics Ltd [1971] 2 Q.B. 711;
    [1971] 3 W.L.R. 440; [1971] 3 All E.R. 16; 115 S.J. 483, CA 27–007
Panoutsos v. Raymond Hadley Corp of New York [1917] 2 K.B. 473 11–026
Pantanassa, The. *See*. Norsk Bjergningskompagni A/S v. Owners of the Pantanassa.
Parchim, The [1918] A.C. 157; 87 L.J.P. 18; 117 L.T. 738; 34 T.L.R. 53; 14 Asp.M.L.C. 196,
    PC 2–035
Parkasho v. Singh [1968] P. 233; [1967] 2 W.L.R. 946; [1967] 1 All E.R. 737; (1966) 110 S.J.
    868, DC 21–001
Parker v. South Eastern Railway (1877) L.R. 2 C.P.D. 416 3–017
Paros Shipping Corp v. Nafta (GB) Ltd (The Paros) [1987] 2 Lloyd's Rep. 269, QBD (Comm
    Ct) 15–023

Parsons (Livestock) Ltd v. Uttley Ingham & Co Ltd [1978] Q.B. 791; [1977] 3 W.L.R. 990; [1978] 1 All E.R. 525; [1977] 2 Lloyd's Rep. 522; 121 S.J. 811; (1977) 121 S.J. 811, CA 8–009

Partabmull Rameshar v. Sethia (KC) (1944) [1951] W.N. 389; *sub nom.* Partabmull Rameshar v. Sethia (KC) (1944) [1951] 2 All E.R. 352 (Note); [1951] 2 Lloyd's Rep. 89; *sub nom.* Sethia (1944) v. Partabmull Rameshwar 95 S.J. 528, HL; affirming *sub nom.* Sethia (KC) v. Partabmull Rameshwar [1950] 1 All E.R. 51; [1950] W.N. 5; 94 S.J. 112, CA 6–012, 23–003

Partenreederei M/S Heidberg v. Grosvenor Grain & Feed Co Ltd (The Heidberg) (No.2) [1994] 2 Lloyd's Rep. 287, QBD (Comm Ct) 15–023, 22–014

Partenreederei MS Karen Oltmann v. Scarsdale Shipping Co (The Karen Oltmann) [1976] 2 Lloyd's Rep. 708 3–016

Passmore v. Morland Plc [1999] 1 C.M.L.R. 1129; [1999] 15 E.G. 128; [1999] 1 E.G.L.R. 51; [1999] E.G.C.S. 14; [1999] N.P.C. 14, CA; affirming [1998] 4 All E.R. 468; [1998] E.C.C. 461; [1998] Eu. L.R. 580; [1998] E.G.C.S. 113; [1998] N.P.C. 117, Ch D ......
.... 29–024

Patel (Jitendra) v. Patel & (Dilesh) [1999] 3 W.L.R. 322; [1991] 1 All E.R. (Comm) 923; [1999] B.L.R. 227; 65 Con.L.R. 140, CA 23–016

Pavia & Co SpA v. Thurmann Nielsen [1952] 2 Q.B. 84; [1952] 1 All E.R. 492; [1952] 1 Lloyd's Rep. 153; [1952] 1 T.L.R. 586; 96 S.J. 193, CA; affirming [1951] 2 All E.R. 866; [1951] 2 Lloyd's Rep. 328; [1951] 2 T.L.R. 802; [1951] W.N. 533, KBD 11–018

Payabi v. Armstel Shipping Corp (The Jay Bola); Baker Rasti Lari v. Armstel Shipping Corp (The Jay Bola) [1992] Q.B. 907; [1992] 2 W.L.R. 898; [1992] 3 All E.R. 329; [1992] 2 Lloyd's Rep. 62; (1992) 136 S.J.L.B. 52, QBD 15–048

PCW (Underwriting Agencies) Ltd v. Dixon (PS) [1983] 2 All E.R. 697; [1983] 2 Lloyd's Rep. 197; (1983) 133 N.L.J. 204, CA; affirming [1983] 2 All E.R. 158, QBD 22–030

Peachdart Ltd, Re [1984] Ch. 131; [1983] 3 W.L.R. 878; [1983] 3 All E.R. 204; (1984) 81 L.S.G. 204; 127 S.J. 839, Ch D 4–009

Pearkes, Gunston and Tee Ltd v. Ward [1902] 2 K.B. 1 26–031

Pendle & Rivet v. Ellerman Lines (1927) 33 Com.Cas 70 .... 15–036, 15–045

Perishables Transport Co v. Spyropoulos (N) (London) Ltd [1964] 2 Lloyd's Rep. 379 27–027

Perkins v. Bell [1893] 1 Q.B. 193 5–005

Peter Cassidy Seed Co v. Osuustukkuk-Auppa IL [1957] 1 W.L.R. 273; [1957] 1 All E.R. 484; [1957] 1 Lloyd's Rep. 25; 101 S.J. 149 6–012

Peter der Grosse, The (1875) 1 P.D. 414 15–036

Petraco (Bermuda) v. Petromed International SA [1988] 1 W.L.R. 896; [1988] 3 All E.R. 454; [1988] 2 Lloyd's Rep. 357; (1988) 85(32) L.S.G. 33; 132 S.J. 1091, CA 2–011

Petredec v. Tokumaru Kaiun Co (The Sargasso) [1994] 1 Lloyd's Rep. 162 15–048

Petrograde Inc v. Stinnes Handel GmbH [1995] 1 Lloyd's Rep. 142 5–003

Petrotrade Inc v. Smith [1999] 1 W.L.R. 457; [1998] 2 All E.R. 346; [1998] C.L.C. 298, QBD (Comm Ct) 22–022

Pfeiffer (E.) Weinkellerei-Weineinkauf GmbH & Co v. Arbuthnot Factors Ltd [1988] 1 W.L.R. 150; [1987] B.C.L.C. 522; (1987) 3 B.C.C. 608, QBD 13–004

Pfeiffer (E.) Weinkellerei-Weineinkauf GmbH & Co v. Arbuthnot Factors Ltd [1988] 1 W.L.R. 150; (1988) 132 S.J. 89; [1987] B.C.L.C. 522; (1987) 3 B.C.C. 608 4–009

Phibro Energy AG v. Nissho Iwai Corp. and Bomar Oil Inc (The Honam Jade) [1991] 1 Lloyd's Rep. 38, CA 5–002, 5–003

Philip Alexander Securities & Futures Ltd v. Bamberge; Philip Alexander Securities & Futures Ltd v. Gilhaus [1996] C.L.C. 1757; [1997] Eu. L.R. 63; [1997] I.L.Pr. 73, CA; affirming *The Independent*, July 8, 1996 (C.S.), QBD (Comm Ct) 23–016

Philips Hong Kong Ltd v. Attorney-General of Hong Kong 61 B.L.R. 41; (1993) 9 Const. L.J. 202, PC; affirming 58 B.L.R. 113; (1991) 7 Const. L.J. 340, CA (HK); reversing (1990) 50 B.L.R. 125, HC(HK) 4–015

Philippine Admiral, The; Philippine Admiral (Owners) v. Wallem Shipping (Hong Kong) [1977] A.C. 373; [1976] 2 W.L.R. 214; (1975) 119 S.J. 865 Owners of the Philippine Admiral v. Wallem Shipping (Hong Kong) [1976] 1 All E.R. 78; *sub nom.* Wallem Shipping (Hong Kong) and Telfair Shipping Corp v. Owners of the Ship Philippine Admiral; Philippine Admiral, The [1976] 1 Lloyd's Rep. 234, PC; affirming *sub nom.* Wallem Shipping (Hong Kong) and Telfair Shipping Corp v. Owners of the Ship Philippine Admiral; Philippine Admiral, The [1974] 2 Lloyd's Rep. 568 21–019

Phillips Petroleum Co v. Cabaneli Naviera SA (The Theodegmon) [1990] 1 Lloyd's Rep. 52,
    QBD (Comm Ct) 15–043
Phillipson v. Imperial Airways Ltd [1939] A.C. 332 17–009
Phoenix Distributors v. Clarke (LB) (London) [1967] 1 Lloyd's Rep. 518, CA; affirming
    [1966] 2 Lloyd's Rep. 285; 116 L.J. 1713 4–012
Phoenix General Insurance Co of Greece SA v. Administratia Asiguraliror de Stat; Phoenix
    General Insurance Co of Greece SA v. Halvanon Insurance; Same v. Administration
    Asiguraliror de Stat [1988] Q.B. 216; [1987] 2 W.L.R. 512; [1987] 2 All E.R. 152;
    [1986] 2 Lloyd's Rep. 552; [1987] Fin. L.R. 48; (1987) 84 L.S.G. 1055; (1987) 131
    S.J. 257, CA; reversing [1986] 1 All E.R. 908; [1985] 2 Lloyd's Rep. 599; [1985] Fin.
    L.R. 368; (1985) 135 N.L.J. 1081 .... 5–004, 21–027
Phoenix Insurance Co v. De Monchy (1929) 35 Com. Cas. 67; (1929) 45 T.L.R.
    543 .... 3–017, 19–007, 19–011
Pickstone v. Freemans Plc [1989] A.C. 66; [1988] 3 W.L.R. 265; [1988] 2 All E.R. 803;
    [1988] 3 C.M.L.R. 221; [1988] I.C.R. 697; [1988] I.R.L.R. 357, HL; affirming [1987]
    3 W.L.R. 811; [1987] 3 All E.R. 756; [1987] 2 C.M.L.R. 572; [1987] I.R.L.R. 218;
    [1987] I.C.R. 867, CA; reversing [1986] I.C.R. 886, EAT 28–024
Pierce v. Bemis (The Lusitania) [1986] Q.B. 384; [1986] 2 W.L.R. 501; [1986] 1 All E.R.
    1011; [1986] 1 Lloyd's Rep. 132; (1986) 130 S.J. 202, QBD 19–035
Pioneer Container, The. *See* KH Enterprise (Cargo Owners) v. Pioneer Container (Owners).
Pioneer Shipping Ltd v. BTP Tioxide Ltd (The Nema) (No.2) [1982] A.C. 724; [1981] 3
    W.L.R. 292; [1981] 2 All E.R. 1030; [1981] 2 Lloyd's Rep. 239; [1981] Com. L.R.
    197; 125 S.J. 542, HL; affirming [1980] Q.B. 547; [1980] 3 W.L.R. 326; [1980] 3 All
    E.R. 117; *sub nom.* BTP Tioxide Ltd v. Pioneer Shipping and Armada Marine SA (The
    Nema) [1980] 2 Lloyd's Rep. 339, CA; reversing [1980] 2 Lloyd's Rep. 83 ....
    .... 6–001, 6–003, 23–003, 23–019
Plant Engineers (Sales) v. Davis (1969) 113 S.J. 484 27–005
Plasticmoda Societa Per Azioni v. Davidsons (Manchester) [1952] 1 Lloyd's Rep. 527, CA .
    .... 5–012, 11–018
Playa Larga (Cargo Owners) v. I Congreso del Partido (Owners); Marble Islands (Cargo
    Owners) v. Same (The I Congreso del Partido, The Marble Islands and The Playa
    Larga) [1983] 1 A.C. 244; [1981] 3 W.L.R. 328; [1981] 2 All E.R. 1064; [1981] 2
    Lloyd's Rep. 367; [1981] Com. L.R. 190; 125 S.J. 528, HL; reversing [1981] 1 All
    E.R. 1092; [1980] 1 Lloyd's Rep. 23, CA; affirming [1978] Q.B. 500; [1977] 3 W.L.R.
    778; [1978] 1 All E.R. 1169; [1977] 1 Lloyd's Rep. 536, QBD 6–010, 21–019
Plein & Co Ltd v. Inland Revenue Commissioners [1946] 175 L.T. Rep. 453 .... 9–011, 11–022
Poclain SA v. S.C.A.C. SA [1986] 1 Lloyd's Rep. 404, CA 18–010
Polenghi Bros v. Dried Milk Co (1904) 10 Com.Cas. 42; (1904) 92 L.T. 64 2–037
Port Jackson Stevedoring Pty v. Salmond & Spraggon (Australia) Pty (The New York Star);
    Salmond & Spraggon (Australia) Pty v. Joint Cargo Services Pty [1981] 1 W.L.R.
    138; [1980] 3 All E.R. 257; [1980] 2 Lloyd's Rep. 317; 124 S.J. 756,
    PC 15–047
Poseidon Freight Forwarding Co Ltd v. Davies Turner Southern Ltd [1996] 2 Lloyd's Rep.
    388; [1996] C.L.C. 1264, CA 3–017
Potton Homes Ltd v. Colman Contractors (Overseas) Ltd [1984] Build.L.R. 19 .... 12–002, 12–004
Pound (AV) & Co v. Hardy (MW) & Co Inc [1956] A.C. 588; [1956] 2 W.L.R. 683; 106 S.J.
    208; [1956] 1 All E.R. 639; *sub nom.* Hardy (MW) & Co Inc v. Pound (AV) & Co
    [1956] 1 Lloyd's Rep. 255, HL affirming *sub nom.* Hardy (MW) & Co Inc v. Pound
    (AV) & Co [1955] 1 Q.B. 499; [1955] 2 W.L.R. 589; 99 S.J. 204; [1955] 1 All E.R.
    666; [1955] 1 Lloyd's Rep. 155; [1955] C.L.Y. 2485, CA; reversing [1954] 2 Lloyd's
    Rep. 428 .... 2–004, 2–007, 2–017, 6–012
Power Curber International Ltd v. National Bank of Kuwait SAK [1981] 1 W.L.R. 1233;
    [1981] 3 All E.R. 607; [1981] 2 Lloyd's Rep. 394; [1981] Com. L.R. 224, CA 9–012,
    11–001, 11–006, 11–020
Power v. Butcher (1829) 10 B. 7 Cr. 329 19–003
Practice Direction (Judgment: Foreign currency); *sub nom.* Practice Direction (QBD: For-
    eign currency) [1976] 1 W.L.R. 83; [1976] 1 All E.R. 669; [1976] 1 Lloyd's Rep.
    282, QBD 21–018
Practice Direction (QBD: Admiralty Registry: Retention of Proceeds of Sale in Foreign
    Currency) [1977] 1 W.L.R. 184; [1977] 1 All E.R. 544; [1977] 1 Lloyd's Rep. 455;
    121 S.J. 124, QBD 21–018

Practice Direction (QBD: Comm Ct: Practice Guide) [1994] 1 W.L.R. 1270, QBD (Comm
    Ct) 23–001
Practice Direction (QBD: Practice: Service out of the Jurisdiction) [1989] 3 All E.R. 562,
    QBD 22–028
Practice Note (Comm Ct: Arbitration: New Procedure) [1997] 1 W.L.R. 391; [1997] 1 All
    E.R. 379, QBD (Comm Ct) 23–010
Practice Statement (Alternative Dispute Resolution), *The Times*, June 11, 1996 23–001
Practice Statement (Comm Ct: Alternative Dispute Resolution) [1994] 1 W.L.R. 14 23–001
Prenn v. Simmonds [1971] 1 W.L.R. 1381; [1971] 3 All E.R. 237; 115 S.J. 654, HL 3–016
Presentaciones Musicales SA v. Secunda [1994] Ch. 271; [1994] 2 W.L.R. 660; [1994] 2
    All E.R. 737; (1994) 138 S.J.L.B. 4, CA 27–008
President of India v. Lips Maritime Corp (The Lips). *See* Lips Maritime Corp v. President
    of India (The Lips).
President of India v. Metcalfe Shipping Co (The Dunelmia) [1970] 1 Q.B. 289; [1969] 3
    W.L.R. 1120; [1969] 3 All E.R. 1549; [1969] 2 Lloyd's Rep. 476; 113 S.J. 792,
    CA; affirming [1969] 2 Q.B. 123; [1969] 2 W.L.R. 125; [1969] 1 All E.R. 861;
    [1969] 1 Lloyd's Rep. 32; 113 S.J. 69 .... 2–005, 4–010
President of India v. Taygetos Shipping Co SA (The Agenor) [1985] 1 Lloyd's Rep. 155,
    QBD (Comm Ct) 21–018
Pride Shipping Corp v. Chung Hwa Pulp Corp (The Oinoussin Pride) [1991] 1 Lloyd's
    Rep. 126, QBD (Comm Ct) 15–023
Priestly v. Fernie (1865) 3 H. & C. 977 27–005
Proctor & Gamble Phillipine Manufacturing Corp v. Becher, Kurt A. [1988] 2 Lloyd's
    Rep. 21; [1988] F.T.L.R. 450, CA; affirming [1988] 1 Lloyd's Rep. 88, DC 2–022,
                                                                                 2–026, 5–003, 15–035
Procurator General (H. M.) v. MC Spencer (Controller of Mitsui & Co Ltd) (The Glenroy)
    [1945] A.C. 124, PC 4–006
Produce Brokers New Co (1934) Ltd v. British Italian Trading Co Ltd [1952] 1 Lloyd's
    Rep. 379 .... 2–027, 2–037
Producers Meats Ltd v. Shaw Savill & Albion Co Ltd (The Arawa) [1980] 2 Lloyd's Rep.
    135CA; reversing [1977] 2 Lloyd's Rep. 416, QBD (Adm Ct) 15–005
Promos SA v. European Grain & Shipping [1979] 1 Lloyd's Rep. 375 2–023
PS Chellaram & Co Ltd v. China Ocean Shipping Co (The Zhi Jiang Kou) [1991] 1 Lloyd's
    Rep. 493 3–017
PSA Transport Ltd v. Newton, Landsdowne & Co Ltd [1956] 1 Lloyd's Rep. 121,
    QBD 27–024
Pye Ltd v. BG Transport Service Ltd [1966] 2 Lloyd's Rep. 300; 116 N.L.J. 1713, QBD   21–027
Pyrene Co Ltd v. Scindia Steam Navigation Co Ltd [1954] 2 Q.B. 402; [1954] 2 W.L.R.
    1005; [1954] 2 All E.R. 158; [1954] 1 Lloyd's Rep. 321; 98 S.J. 354 .... 2–007, 2–013,
                                                                                 15–041, 15–045
Pyxis Special Shipping Co Ltd v. Dritsas & Kaglis Bros (The Scaplake) [1978] 2 Lloyd's
    Rep. 380, QBD (Comm Ct) 27–005

Qingdao Ocean Shipping Co v. Grace Shipping Establishment Transatlantic Schiffahrts-
    kontor GmbH (The Xing Su Hai) [1995] 2 Lloyd's Rep. 15, QBD (Comm Ct) 22–003
QRS 1 Aps v. Frandsen; QRS 1A ApS v. Frandsen; QRS 1B ApS v. Frandsen; QRS 2
    ApS v. Frandsen; QRS 2A ApS v. Frandsen [1999] 3 All E.R. 289; [1999] S.T.C.
    616; [1999] B.T.C. 8203; (1999) 96(24) L.S.G. 39, CA; affirming [1999] I.L.Pr.
    432, QBD 21–025, 22–014

R & A Kohnstamm Ltd. *See* Vogel v. R & A Kohnstamm Ltd.
R&J Bow Ltd v. Hill (1930) 37 Ll.L.R. 46 27–019
R. v. Berner (Max Marcus) (1953) 37 Cr. App. R. 113 26–003
R. v. Blackledge (William Stuart); R. v. Grecian (John Paul); R. v. Mason (Bryan Albert);
    R. v. Phillips (Colin William) (1995) 92(23) L.S.G. 32; (1995) 139 S.J.L.B. 139,
    CA 26–003
R. v. Bow Street Magistrates Court, ex p. Noncyp Ltd [1990] 1 Q.B. 123; [1989] 3 W.L.R.
    467; (1989) 89 Cr. App. R. 121; [1989] 1 C.M.L.R. 634; [1989] C.O.D. 357; (1989)
    133 S.J. 1031, CA; affirming [1988] 3 W.L.R. 827; [1988] 3 C.M.L.R. 84; (1988)
    132 S.J. 1063, QBD 26–030
R. v. Carr (Charles Victor) [1957] 1 W.L.R. 165; [1956] 3 All E.R. 979 (Note); (1956) 40
    Cr. App. R. 188; (1957) 121 J.P. 165; 101 S.J. 112, CMAC 27–011

R. v. Chief Metropolitan Stipendiary Magistrate, ex p. Secretary of State for the Home Department [1988] 1 W.L.R. 1204; [1989] 1 All E.R. 151; [1988] Crim. L.R. 835, DC 21–028

R. v. Cohen (Robert Abraham) [1951] 1 K.B. 505; [1951] 1 All E.R. 203; [1951] 1 T.L.R. 251; (1950) 34 Cr. App. R. 239; 49 L.G.R. 216; 115 J.P. 91, CCA 26–031

R. v. Cox (Peter Stanley) [1968] 1 W.L.R. 88; [1968] 1 All E.R. 410; (1968) 52 Cr. App. R. 106; 132 J.P. 162; (1967) 111 S.J. 966, CA (Crim Div) 21–028

R. v. Cross (1987) [1987] Crim. L.R. 43, CA 26–031

R. v. Customs and Excise Commissioners, ex p. Tsahl [1990] C.O.D. 230, QBD 26–030

R. v. Dearlove; R. v. Druker (1989) 88 Cr. App. R. 279; [1988] Crim. L.R. 323, CA 21–028

R. v. Doot. *See* DPP v. Doot.

R. v. Dosanjh (Barjinder) [1998] 3 All E.R. 618; [1999] 1 Cr. App. R. 371; [1999] 1 Cr. App. R. (S.) 107; [1998] Crim. L.R. 593; (1998) 95(22) L.S.G. 28; (1998) 142 S.J.L.B. 163, CA (Crim Div) 26–011

R. v. Dunbar (Ronald Patrick) [1958] 1 Q.B. 1; [1957] 3 W.L.R. 330; [1957] 2 All E.R. 737; (1957) 41 Cr. App. R. 182; 121 J.P. 506; 101 S.J. 594, CCA 26–031

R. v. Governor of Brixton Prison, ex p. Osman [1991] 1 W.L.R. 281; [1992] 1 All E.R. 108; (1991) 93 Cr. App. R. 202; (1991) 3 Admin. L.R. 225; [1991] Crim. L.R. 533 3–008

R. v. Governor of Brixton Prison, ex p. Rush [1969] 1 W.L.R. 165; [1969] 1 All E.R. 316; 133 J.P. 153; 113 S.J. 106, QBD 21–028

R. v. Hayward (1997), (unreported) 26–031

R. v. Hescroff (1990) 154 J.P. 1042; (1990) 154 J.P.N. 562, CA 26–031

R. v. Hurford-Jones (1977) 65 Cr. App. R. 23 26–031

R. v. Latif (Khalid); R. v. Shahzad (Mohammed Khalid) [1996] 1 W.L.R. 104; [1996] 1 All E.R. 353; [1996] 2 Cr. App. R. 92; [1996] Crim. L.R. 414; (1996) 93(5) L.S.G. 30; (1996) 146 N.L.J. 121; (1996) 140 S.J.L.B. 39, HL; affirming [1995] 1 Cr. App. R. 270; (1994) 15 Cr. App. R. (S.) 864; [1994] Crim. L.R. 750; (1994) 91(18) L.S.G. 37; (1994) 138 S.J.L.B. 85, CA (Crim Div) 26–031

R. v. Newland (Alfred Ernest) [1954] 1 Q.B. 158; [1953] 3 W.L.R. 826; [1953] 2 All E.R. 1067; (1953) 37 Cr. App. R. 154; 117 J.P. 573; 97 S.J. 782, CCA 21–028

R. v. Redfern (John Michael) and Dunlop (Aircraft Tyres Division) (1992) 13 Cr. App. R. (S.) 709; [1993] Crim. L.R. 43, CA 26–003, 26–030

R. v. Reiss and John M Potter [1957] Crim. L.R. 404 21–028

R. v. Sang [1980] A.C. 402; [1979] 3 W.L.R. 263; [1979] 2 All E.R. 1222; (1979) 69 Cr. App. R. 282; [1979] Crim. L.R. 655, HL; affirming [1979] 2 W.L.R. 439; [1979] 2 All E.R. 46; (1979) 68 Cr. App. R. 240; [1979] Crim. L.R. 389; 123 S.J. 232, CA 31–028

R. v. Sanusi [1992] Crim. L.R. 43, CA 26–031

R. v. Secretary of State for Transport, ex p. Factortame (Discovery) (1997) 9 Admin. L.R. 591; [1997] C.O.D. 432; (1997) 94(22) L.S.G. 31, QBD 26–029

R. v. Shepherd [1993] A.C. 380, HL 33–011

Radio Corp of America (RCA) v. Rauland Corp (No.2) [1956] 1 Q.B. 618; [1956] 2 W.L.R. 612; [1956] 1 All E.R. 549; 100 S.J. 172, QBD 21–022

Rafsanjan Pistachio Producers Cooperative v. Bank Leumi (UK) Ltd [1992] 1 Lloyd's Rep. 513 .... 11–009, 11–010, 11–042

Raiffeisen Zentralbank Osterreich Aktiengesellschaft v. National Bank of Greece SA [1999] 1 Lloyd's Rep. 408, QBD 22–018

Ralli Bros v. Compania Naviera Sota y Aznar [1920] 2 K.B. 287, CA 21–027

Ralli v. Universal Marine Insurance Co (1862) 31 L.J.Ch. 207 19–016

Rama Corp Ltd v. Proved Tin & General Investments Ltd [1952] 2 Q.B. 147; [1952] 1 All E.R. 554; [1952] 1 T.L.R. 709; 96 S.J. 197, KBD 27–007

Rambler Cycle Co v. Peninsular & Oriental Steam Navigation Co [1968] 1 Lloyd's Rep. 42, Fed Ct (Mal) 15–048

Rank Film Distributors Ltd v. Video Information Centre [1982] A.C. 380; [1981] 2 All E.R. 76; [1981] Com. L.R. 90; [1981] E.C.C. 365; [1981] F.S.R. 363, HL; affirming [1980] 3 W.L.R. 487; [1980] 2 All E.R. 273; [1980] F.S.R. 242, CA 22–032

Rapalli v. Take (KL) [1958] 2 Lloyd's Rep. 469, CA 5–003

Rasnoimport V/O v. Guthrie & Co Ltd [1966] 1 Lloyd's Rep. 1, QBD (Comm Ct) 15–036

Rayner (JH) & Co Ltd v. Hambro's Bank Ltd [1943] 1 K.B. 37 11–007

Rayner (JH) (Mincing Lane) Ltd v. Department of Trade and Industry; Maclaine Watson & Co Ltd v. Department of Trade and Industry; Maclaine Watson & Co Ltd v. Interna-

tional Tin Council; *sub nom.* International Tin Council, Re [1990] 2 A.C. 418;
[1989] 3 W.L.R. 969; [1989] 3 All E.R. 523; [1990] B.C.L.C. 102; (1989) 5 B.C.C.
872; (1990) 87(4) L.S.G. 68; (1989) 139 N.L.J. 1559; (1989) 133 S.J. 1485, HL;
affirming [1989] Ch. 72; [1988] 3 W.L.R. 1033; [1988] 3 All E.R. 257; [1988]
B.C.L.C. 404; (1988) 4 B.C.C. 563; [1989] P.C.C. 68; [1989] P.C.C. 1; (1988) 132
S.J. 1494, CA; affirming [1987] B.C.L.C. 667; (1987) 3 B.C.C. 413; [1988] P.C.C.
150; [1987] 2 F.T.L.R. 328, Ch D 21–019, 21–022
RD Harbottle (Mercantile) Ltd v. National Westminster Bank Ltd [1978] Q.B. 146; [1977]
3 W.L.R. 752; [1977] 2 All E.R. 862; 121 S.J. 745, QBD 11–001, 12–004, 12–005
Reading v. Att.-Gen. [1951] A.C. 507; [1951] 1 All E.R. 617; [1951] 1 T.L.R. 480; 95
S.J.155, HL; affirming *sub nom.* Reading v. R. [1949] 2 K.B. 232; [1949] 2 All
E.R. 68; 65 T.L.R. 405; *sub nom.* Re Reading's Petition of Right, CA; affirming
[1948] 2 K.B. 268; [1948] 2 All E.R. 27; [1949] L.J.R. 280; 92 S.J. 426, KBD 27–011
Reardon Smith Line Ltd v. Ministry of Agriculture, Fisheries and Food; Carlton Steamship
Co Ltd v. Same; Cape of Good Hope Motorship Co Ltd v. Same [1963] A.C. 691;
[1963] 2 W.L.R. 439; [1963] 1 All E.R. 545; [1963] 1 Lloyd's Rep. 12; 107 S.J.
133, HL; reversing in part *sub nom.* Reardon Smith Line Ltd v. Ministry of Agriculture, Fisheries and Food; Garibaldi Societa Cooperativa di Navigazione ARL v.
President of India; Carlton Steamship Co Ltd v. Ministry of Agriculture, Fisheries
and Food; Cape of Good Hope Motorship Co Ltd v. Same; Miramar Compania
Naviera SA v. Government of the Union of South Africa [1962] 1 Q.B. 42; [1961]
3 W.L.R. 110; [1961] 2 All E.R. 577; [1961] 1 Lloyd's Rep. 385; 105 S.J. 567,
CA; affirming [1960] 1 Q.B. 439; [1959] 3 W.L.R. 665; [1959] 3 All E.R. 434;
[1959] 2 Lloyd's Rep. 229; 103 S.J. 920 .... 6–003, 6–013
Reardon Smith Line v. Yngvar Hansen-Tangen; Yngvar Hansen-Tangen v. Sanko Steam-
ship Co [1976] 1 W.L.R. 989; 120 S.J. 719; *sub nom.* Reardon Smith Line v.
Hansen-Tangen; Hansen-Tangen v. Sanko Steamship Co [1976] 3 All E.R. 570;
HL; affirming *sub nom.* Reardon Smith Line v. Yngvar Hansen-Tangen Sanko
Steamship Co (third party) 120 S.J. 329; *sub nom.* Reardon Smith Line v. Yngvar
Hansen-Tangen and Sanko Steamship Co; Diana Prosperity, The [1976] 2 Lloyd's
Rep. 60, CA 3–016, 5–004, 7–007
Reddall v. Union-Castle Mail Steamship Co Ltd (1915) 84 L.J.K.B. 360 5–016
Rederi AB Gustav Erikson v. Dr Fawzi Ahmed Abou Ismail (The Herroe and The Askoe)
[1986] 2 Lloyd's Rep. 281 15–036
Rederi Kommanditselskaabet Merc-Scandia IV v. Couniniotis SA (The Mercanaut) [1980]
2 Lloyd's Rep. 183 30–006
Redler Grain Silos v. BICC [1982] 1 Lloyd's Rep. 435, CA 21–024
Regalian Properties Plc v. London Docklands Development Corp [1995] 1 W.L.R. 212;
[1995] 1 All E.R. 1005; 45 Con. L.R. 37; (1995) 11 Const. L.J. 127; [1994]
E.G.C.S. 176; (1995) 92(4) L.S.G. 34; [1994] N.PC 139 3–015
Regazzoni v. KC Sethia [1958] A.C. 301; [1957] 3 W.L.R. 752; [1957] 3 All E.R. 286;
[1957] 2 Lloyd's Rep. 289; 101 S.J. 848, HL; affirming [1956] 2 Q.B. 490; [1956]
3 W.L.R. 79; [1956] 2 All E.R. 487; [1956] 1 Lloyd's Rep. 435; 100 S.J. 417, CA;
affirming [1956] 2 W.L.R. 204; [1956] 1 All E.R. 229; [1955] 2 Lloyd's Rep. 766;
100 S.J. 55, QBD 21–027
Reinhart Co v. Joshua Hoyle & Sons [1961] 1 Lloyd's Rep. 346, CA; affirming [1960] 1
Lloyd's Rep. 483, QBD 2–023, 2–038, 19–003, 19–022, 19–031
Reinhold & Co and Hansloh, Re (1869) 12 T.L.R. 422 .... 2–025, 4–012
Reischer v. Borwick [1894] 2 Q.B. 548 19–030
Rena K, The [1979] Q.B. 377; [1978] 3 W.L.R. 431; [1979] 1 All E.R. 397; [1978] 1
Lloyd's Rep. 545; 122 S.J. 315, QBD 23–016
Renton (GH) & Co Ltd v. Palmyra Trading Corp of Panama (The Caspiana) [1957] A.C.
149; [1957] 2 W.L.R. 45; [1956] 3 All E.R. 957; [1956] 2 Lloyd's Rep. 379, HL;
affirming [1956] 1 Q.B. 462; [1956] 2 W.L.R. 238; [1956] 1 All E.R. 209; [1955]
2 Lloyd's Rep. 722; 101 S.J. 43, CA; reversing [1955] 3 W.L.R. 535; [1955] 3 All
E.R. 251; [1955] 2 Lloyd's Rep. 301; 99 S.J. 762, QBD 15–013, 15–041
Resolute Maritime Inc v. Nippon Kaiji Kyokai [1983] 1 W.L.R. 857; [1983] 2 All E.R. 1;
[1983] 1 Lloyd's Rep. 431, QBD 27–005
Republic of India v. India Steamship Co Ltd (The Indian Endurance and the The Indian
Grace) (No.1) [1993] A.C. 410; [1993] 2 W.L.R. 461; [1993] 1 All E.R. 998; [1993]
1 Lloyd's Rep. 387, HL; reversing [1992] 1 Lloyd's Rep. 124; [1994] I.L.Pr. 498,
CA 24–005

Rewia, The [1991] 2 Lloyd's Rep. 325; [1993] I.L.Pr. 507, CA; reversing [1991] 1 Lloyd's Rep. 69, QBD (Adm Ct) 22–002

Reynolds (E) & Sons (Chingford) Ltd v. Hendry Bros (London) Ltd [1955] 1 Lloyd's Rep. 258 4–003

RH&D International Ltd v. IAS Animal Air Services Ltd [1984] 1 W.L.R. 573; [1984] 2 All E.R. 203; [1985] R.T.R. 104; (1984) 81 L.S.G. 732; (1984) 128 S.J. 171, QBD 15–007, 18–007

Rhesa Shipping Co SA v. Edmunds (Herbert David); Rhesa Shipping Co SA v. Fenton Insurance Co (The Popi M) [1985] 1 W.L.R. 948; [1985] 2 All E.R. 712; [1985] 2 Lloyd's Rep. 1; (1985) 82 L.S.G. 2995; (1985) 129 S.J. 503, HL; reversing [1984] 2 Lloyd's Rep. 555, CA; reversing in part [1983] 2 Lloyd's Rep. 235 19–031

Rhodian River Shipping Co SA v. Halla Maritime Corp (The Rhodian River and The Rhodian Sailor) [1984] 1 Lloyd's Rep. 373 3–016

Ricardo Biguzzi v. Rank Leisure Plc [1999] 1 W.L.R. 1926 22–030

Richco International Ltd v. Bunge & Co Ltd (The New Prosper); *sub nom.* Bunge & Co v. Tradax Ocean Transportation SA [1991] 2 Lloyd's Rep. 93, QBD (Comm Ct) .. 2–009

Rimeco Riggelsen & Metal Co v. Queenborough Rolling Mill Co Ltd November 9, 1994, CA 3–009

River Gurara, The. *See* Owners of Cargo Lately Laden on Board on the River Gurara v. Nigerian National Shipping Line Ltd.

River Rima, The [1988] 1 W.L.R. 758; [1988] 2 All E.R. 641; [1988] 2 Lloyd's Rep. 193; (1988) 85(28) L.S.G. 46; (1988) 132 S.J. 968, HL; affirming [1987] 3 All E.R. 1; [1987] 2 Lloyd's Rep. 106; [1987] 2 F.T.L.R. 192; (1987) 84 L.S.G. 1967; (1987) 131 S.J. 887, CA; reversing (1987) 84 L.S.G. 1652; (1987) 131 S.J. 657 16–003

Riverstone Meat Co Pty Ltd v. Lancashire Shipping Co Ltd (The Muncaster Castle) [1961] A.C. 807; [1961] 2 W.L.R. 269; [1961] 1 All E.R. 495; [1961] 1 Lloyd's Rep. 57; 105 S.J. 148, HL; reversing [1960] 1 Q.B. 536; [1960] 2 W.L.R. 86; [1960] 1 All E.R. 193; [1959] 2 Lloyd's Rep. 553; 104 S.J. 50, CA; reversing [1959] 1 Q.B. 74; [1958] 3 W.L.R. 482; [1958] 3 All E.R. 261; [1958] 2 Lloyd's Rep. 255; 102 S.J. 656, QBD 15–041

Rivoli Hats v. Gooch [1953] 1 W.L.R. 1190; [1953] 2 All E.R. 823; 97 S.J. 589, QBD 27–012

Roberts v. Elwells Engineers [1972] 2 Q.B. 586; [1972] 3 W.L.R. 1; [1972] 2 All E.R. 890; [1973] 1 Lloyd's Rep. 153; 116 S.J. 431, CA 27–012

Roberts v. Plaisted [1989] 2 Lloyd's Rep. 341, CA 19–012

Robinson Scammell & Co v. Ansell [1985] 2 E.G.L.R. 41; (1985) 135 N.L.J. 752, CA 27–012

Robophone Facilities Ltd v. Blank [1996] 1 W.L.R. 1428; [1996] 3 All E.R. 128; 110 S.J. 544, CA 4–015

Rodacanachi v. Milburn (1886) 18 Q.B.D. 67 15–010

Roger Bullivant Ltd v. Ellis [1987] I.C.R. 464; [1987] I.R.L.R. 491; [1987] F.S.R. 172, CA 27–011

Rogers v. Parish (Scarborough) Ltd [1987] Q.B. 933; [1987] 2 W.L.R. 353; [1987] 2 All E.R. 232; [1987] 6 T.L.R. 55; (1987) 85 Cr. App. R. 312; [1987] R.T.R. 312; (1987) 84 L.S.G. 905; (1987) 131 S.J. 223, CA 4–010

Rolex Watch Co v. Customs and Excise Commissioners [1956] 1 W.L.R. 612; [1956] 2 All E.R. 589; 100 S.J. 419, CA 26–016

Rolfe Lubell & Co v. Keith [1979] 1 All E.R. 860; [1979] 2 Lloyd's Rep. 75; 123 S.J. 32, DC 9–004

Rolls Razor Ltd v. Cox [1967] 1 Q.B. 552; [1967] 2 W.L.R. 241; [1967] 1 All E.R. 397; 110 S.J. 943, CA 27–011

Romalpa. *See* Aluminium Industrie Vaassen BV v. Romalpa Aluminium.

Rome v. Punjab National Bank (No.2) [1989] 1 W.L.R. 1211; [1990] 1 All E.R. 58; [1989] 2 Lloyd's Rep. 354; [1990] B.C.L.C. 20; (1989) 5 B.C.C. 785; (1989) 86(41) L.S.G. 40; (1989) 133 S.J. 1485, CA; affirming [1989] B.C.L.C. 328; (1989) 5 B.C.C. 58, QBD (Comm Ct) 28–005

Rosa S, The [1989] Q.B. 419; [1989] 2 W.L.R. 162; [1989] 1 All E.R. 489; [1988] 2 Lloyd's Rep. 574, QBD (Adm Ct) 15–045

Rose Mary, The. *See* Anglo Iranian Oil Co Ltd v. Jaffrate.

Rosenthal (J.) & Sons v. Esmail (t/a HMH Esmail & Sons) [1965] 1 W.L.R. 1117; [1965] 2 All E.R. 860; [1965] 2 Lloyd's Rep. 171; 109 S.J. 553, HL; affirming [1964] 2 Lloyd's Rep. 447; 108 S.J. 839 5–009

Ross T Smyth & Co (Liverpool) Ltd v. WN Lindsay (Leith) Ltd [1953] 1 W.L.R. 1280; [1953] 2 All E.R. 1064; [1953] 2 Lloyd's Rep. 378; 97 S.J. 744, QBD 6–009, 6–013

Rothmans of Pall Mall (Overseas) v. Saudi Arabian Airlines Corp [1981] Q.B. 368; [1980]
   3 W.L.R. 642; [1980] 3 All E.R. 359; 124 S.J. 542, CA 17–014
Rotterdamsche Bank NV v. British Overseas Airways Corp [1953] 1 W.L.R. 493; [1953]
   1 All E.R. 675; [1953] 1 Lloyd's Rep. 154; 97 S.J. 191, QBD 17–008
Roux v. Salvador [1836] 3 Bing. N.C. 85 19–033
Royal Bank of Scotland Plc v. Cassa di Risparmio delle Provincie Lombarde [1992] 1
   Bank L.R. 251 11–003
Royal Boskalis Westminster NV v. Mountain [1999] Q.B. 674; [1998] 2 W.L.R. 538;
   [1997] 2 All E.R. 929; [1997] L.R.L.R. 523, CA 21–026
Royal Typewriter Co v. Owners of the MV Kulmerland (The Kulmerland); *sub nom.* Divi-
   sion Litton Business Systems Inc v. MV Kulmerland; Hapag-Lloyd AG (Sued as
   Hamburg-America Linie) v. Pioneer Terminal Corp [1973] 2 Lloyd's Rep. 428, US
   Ct; affirming [1973] 1 Lloyd's Rep. 318, US Ct 16–009
Rozel, The. *See* Channel Island Ferries Ltd v. Cenargo Navigation Ltd.
Rudolph A Oetker v. IFA Internationale Frachtagentur AG (The Almak) [1985] 1 Lloyd's
   Rep. 557 .... 15–031, 15–035
Rusholme & Bolton & Roberts Hadfield v. SG Read & Co (London) [1955] 1 W.L.R. 146;
   [1955] 1 All E.R. 180; 99 S.J. 132 .... 1–005, 27–022
Rustenburg Platinum Mines Ltd v. South African Airways and Pan American World Air-
   ways Inc [1979] 1 Lloyd's Rep. 19, CA; reversing [1977] 1 Lloyd's Rep. 564, QBD
   (Comm Ct) 17–011

SA Consortium General Textiles v. Sun & Sand Agencies [1978] Q.B. 279; [1978] 2
   W.L.R. 1; [1978] 2 All E.R. 339; [1978] 1 Lloyd's Rep. 134; 121 S.J. 662, CA;
   affirming *The Times*, February 15, 1977, DC 21–023, 24–011
Saccharine Co v. Corn Products [1919] 1 K.B. 198 7–007
Said v. Butt [1920] 3 K.B. 497, KBD 27–005
Sale Continuation v. Austin Taylor & Co [1968] 2 Q.B. 849; [1967] 3 W.L.R. 1427; [1967]
   2 All E.R. 1092; [1967] 2 Lloyd's Rep. 403; 111 S.J. 472, QBD (Comm Ct) 11–041
Salomon v. Brownfield (1896) 12 T.L.R. 239 27–012
Salsi v. Jetspeed Air Services [1977] 2 Lloyd's Rep. 57 27–025
Samick Lines Co v. Owners of the Antonis P Lemos [1985] A.C. 711; [1985] 2 W.L.R.
   468; [1985] 1 All E.R. 695; [1985] 1 Lloyd's Rep. 283; (1985) 82 L.S.G. 1715,
   HL; affirming [1984] 2 W.L.R. 825; [1984] 2 All E.R. 353; [1984] 1 Lloyd's Rep.
   464; (1984) 81 L.S.G. 740; (1984) 129 S.J. 171, CA; affirming [1983] 2 Lloyd's
   Rep. 310, QBD 23–015
Samuel Montagu & Co Ltd v. Swiss Air Transport Co Ltd [1966] 2 Q.B. 306; [1966] 2
   W.L.R. 854; [1966] 1 All E.R. 814; [1966] 1 Lloyd's Rep. 323; 110 S.J. 347, CA;
   affirming [1965] 2 Lloyd's Rep. 363; 109 S.J. 699, QBD (Comm Ct) 17–011
San Nicholas, The. *See* Pacific Molasses Co and United Molasses Trading Co v. Entre
   Rios Compania Naviera SA.
Santa Clara, The. *See* Vitol SA v. Norelf Ltd.
Sarrio SA v. Kuwait Investment Authority [1999] A.C. 32; [1997] 3 W.L.R. 1143; [1997]
   4 All E.R. 929; [1998] 1 Lloyd's Rep. 129; [1998] Lloyd's Rep. Bank. 57; [1997]
   C.L.C. 1640; [1998] I.L.Pr. 319; (1997) 141 S.J.L.B. 248, HL; reversing [1997] 1
   Lloyd's Rep. 113; [1997] C.L.C. 280; [1997] I.L.Pr. 481, CA; reversing [1996] 1
   Lloyd's Rep. 650; [1996] C.L.C. 211, QBD 22–027
Saudi Crown, The [1986] 1 Lloyd's Rep. 261 .... 15–035, 15–036
Saudi Prince, The (No.2) [1988] 1 Lloyd's Rep. 1, CA; affirming [1986] 1 Lloyd's Rep.
   347, QBD (Adm Ct) 15–021
Saunt v. Belcher and Gibbons (1920) 26 Com.Cas 115 5–005
Sayers v. International Drilling Co NV [1971] 1 W.L.R. 1176; [1971] 3 All E.R. 163;
   [1971] 2 Lloyd's Rep. 105; 11 K.I.R. 65; 115 S.J. 466, CA 28–020
Scammell (G) and Nephew Ltd v. HC & JG Ouston [1941] A.C. 251, HL 3–015
Scancarriers A/S v. Aotearoa International (The Barranduna and The Tarago) [1985] 2
   Lloyd's Rep. 419; (1985) 135 N.L.J. 799, PC 3–003
Scandinavian Trading Co A/B v. Zodiac Petroleum SA and William Hudson (The Al
   Hofuf) [1981] 1 Lloyd's Rep. 81 .... 2–005, 2–007, 2–010
Scarliaris v. Ofverberg Co (1921) 37 T.L.R. 307, CA 5–005
SCCMO (London) Ltd v. Société Générale de Compensation [1956] 1 Lloyd's Rep.
   290 5–012
SCF Finance Co Ltd v. Masri (No.2) [1987] Q.B. 1002; [1987] 2 W.L.R. 58; [1987] 1 All

E.R. 175; [1986] 2 Lloyd's Rep. 366; [1986] Fin. L.R. 309; (1987) 84 L.S.G. 492; (1987) 131 S.J. 74, CA; affirming [1986] 1 All E.R. 40; [1986] 1 Lloyd's Rep. 293; [1986] Fin. L.R. 95; (1985) 135 N.L.J. 914, QBD 21–027

Schiffshypothekenbank Zu Luebeck AG v. Norman Philip Compton (The Alexion Hope) [1988] 1 Lloyd's Rep. 311; [1988] F.T.L.R. 270; [1988] Fin. L.R. 131, CA; affirming [1987] 1 Lloyd's Rep. 60 19–024

Schorsch Meier GmbH v. Hennin [1975] Q.B. 416; [1974] 3 W.L.R. 823; [1975] 1 All E.R. 152; [1975] 1 Lloyd's Rep. 1; [1975] 1 C.M.L.R. 20; 118 S.J. 881, CA 21–018

Schuler (L) AG v. Wickman Machine Tool Sales Ltd; *sub nom.* Wickman Machine Tool Sales Ltd v. L Schuler AG [1974] A.C. 235; [1973] 2 W.L.R. 683; [1973] 2 All E.R. 39; [1973] 2 Lloyd's Rep. 53; 117 S.J. 340; [1973] 2 W.L.R. 6853, HL; affirming [1972] 1 W.L.R. 840; [1972] 2 All E.R. 1173; 116 S.J. 352, CA 30–012

Scott v. Globe Marine Insurance Co Ltd (1896) 1 Com.Cas 370 19–014

Scottish Power Plc v. Britoil (Exploration) Ltd (1997) 94(47) L.S.G. 30; (1997) 141 S.J.L.B. 246; *The Times*, December 2, 1997, CA 3–016

Scruttons Ltd v. Midland Silicones [1962] A.C. 446; [1962] 2 W.L.R. 186; 106 S.J. 34; [1962] 1 All E.R. 1; *sub nom.* Midland Silicones v. Scruttons [1961] 2 Lloyd's Rep. 365, HL; affirming *sub nom.* Midland Silicones v. Scruttons [1961] 1 Q.B. 106; [1960] 3 W.L.R. 372; [1960] 2 All E.R. 737; [1960] 1 Lloyd's Rep. 571; 104 S.J. 603, CA; affirming [1959] 2 Q.B. 171; [1959] 2 W.L.R. 761; [1959] 2 All E.R. 289; [1959] 1 Lloyd's Rep. 289; 103 S.J. 415 . 2–007, 11–047

Sea Calm Shipping Co SA v. Chantiers Navals de l'Esterel SA (The Uhenbels) [1986] 2 Lloyd's Rep. 294 5–012

Seaconsar (Far East) Ltd v. Bank Markazi Jomhouri Islami Iran (Service Outside Jurisdiction) [1994] 1 A.C. 438; [1993] 3 W.L.R. 756; [1993] 4 All E.R. 456; [1994] 1 Lloyd's Rep. 1; [1994] I.L.Pr. 678; (1993) 143 N.L.J. 1479; (1993) 137 S.J.L.B. 239, HL; reversing [1993] 1 Lloyd's Rep. 236, CA 11–007, 11–008, 11–009, 11–010, 22–005

Seaconsar (Far East) Ltd v. Bank Markazi Jomhouri Islami Iran (Documentary Credits) [1999] 1 Lloyd's Rep. 36; [1998] C.L.C. 1543, CA; affirming [1997] 2 Lloyd's Rep. 89; [1997] C.L.C. 611, QBD 11–009, 11–010

Seager v. Copydex Ltd [1967] 1 W.L.R. 923; [1967] 2 All E.R. 415; 2 K.I.R. 828; [1967] F.S.R. 211; [1967] R.P.C. 349; 111 S.J. 335, CA 27–011

Seateam & Co v. Iraq National Oil Co (The Sevonia Team). *See* K/S A/S Seateam & Co v. Iraq National Oil Co.

Seavision Investment SA v. Evennett (Norman Thomas) and Clarkson Puckle (The Tiburon) [1992] 2 Lloyd's Rep. 26, CA; affirming [1990] 2 Lloyd's Rep. 418   19–017

Seaworld Ocean Line Co SA v. Catseye Maritime Co (Kelaniya The) [1989] 1 Lloyd's Rep. 30, CA 23–003

Seely v. Motor Co 63 Cal. 2d. 9 (1965) 8–013

Sellers v. London Counties Newspapers [1951] 1 K.B. 784; [1951] 1 All E.R. 544; 95 S.J. 252, CA 27–012

Sennar, The. *See* DSW Silo-und Verwaltungsgesellschaft mbH v. Owners of the Sennar.

Services Europe Atlantique Sud (SEAS) v. Stockholms Rederiaktiebolag Svea of Stockholm (The Despina R and The Folias) [1979] A.C. 685; [1978] 3 W.L.R. 804; (1978) 122 S.J. 758; [1979] 1 All E.R. 421; [1979] 1 Lloyd's Rep. 1, HL; affirming [1978] 2 W.L.R. 887; [1977] 3 W.L.R. 597; (1978) 122 S.J 366; (1977) 121 S.J. 574; [1978] 2 All E.R. 764; *sub nom.* Owners of the M.V. Eleftherotria v. Owners of the M.V. Despina R [1979] Q.B. 491; [1977] 3 All E.R. 874; [1978] 1 Lloyd's Rep. 535; [1977] 2 Lloyd's Rep. 319, CA; reversing [1978] Q.B. 396; [1977] 3 W.L.R. 176; (1977) 121 S.J. 134, 333; [1977] 3 All E.R. 945; [1977] 1 Lloyd's Rep. 39, QBD (Adm Ct) 21–018

Seth v. British Overseas Airways Corp (BOAC) [1964] 1 Lloyd's Rep. 268, US Ct ... 17–011

Sethia (1944) Ltd v. Partabmull Rameshwar. *See* Partabmull Rameshar v. Sethia (KC) (1944).

Settebello Ltd v. Banco Totta and Acores [1985] 1 W.L.R. 1050; [1985] 2 All E.R. 1025; [1985] 2 Lloyd's Rep. 448; [1986] E.C.C. 15; (1985) 82 L.S.G. 2658; (1985) 135 N.L.J. 658; (1985) 129 S.J. 683, CA; affirming *The Times*, August 4, 1984, QBD 6–010, 21–022

Seven Seas Transportation Ltd v. Pacifico Union Marina Corp (The Satya Kailash and The Oceanic Amity) [1984] 2 All E.R. 140; [1984] 1 Lloyd's Rep. 588, CA; affirming [1983] 1 All E.R. 672; [1982] 2 Lloyd's Rep. 465; [1982] Com. L.R. 236, QBD 15–022

Shaffer (James) v. Findlay Durham & Brodie [1953] 1 W.L.R. 106; 97 S.J. 26, CA .. 30–005
Shamrock S. S. Co v. Storey & Co [1899] 81 L.T. 413 3–015
Shansher Jute Mills v. Sethia London [1987] 1 Lloyd's Rep. 388 .... 11–010, 11–040
Sharif v. Azad [1967] 1 Q.B. 605; [1966] 3 W.L.R. 1285; [1966] 3 All E.R. 785; 110
    S.J. 791, CA 21–029
Shell Chemicals UK Ltd v. P&O Roadtanks Ltd [1995] 1 Lloyd's Rep. 297, CA;
    [1993] 1 Lloyd's Rep. 114 18–010
Shell International Petroleum Co Ltd v. Coral Oil Co Ltd [1999] 1 Lloyd's Rep. 72,
    QBD (Comm Ct) 22–010
Shell International Petroleum Co Ltd v. Seabridge Shipping (The Metula) [1978] 2
    Lloyd's Rep. 5, CA; affirming [1977] 2 Lloyd's Rep. 436, QBD (Comm Ct) .. 15–008
Shell Oil Company v. Iowa Department of Revenue 57 L.W. 4001 (1988) 28–015
Sidney G Jones Ltd v. Martin Bencher Ltd [1986] 1 Lloyd's Rep. 54, QBD   18–010, 27–025
Sidhu v. British Airways Plc [1997] A.C. 430; [1997] 2 W.L.R. 26; [1997] 1 All E.R.
    193, HL affirming [1995] P.I.Q.R. P427, CA 17–003
Silber (JJ) v. Islander Trucking; Patenta GmbH v. Islander Trucking [1985] 2 Lloyd's
    Rep. 243 18–009
Silver v. Ocean Steam Ship Co [1930] 1 K.B. 416, KBD 15–036
Simaan General Contracting Co v. Pilkington Glass Ltd [1988] Q.B. 758; [1988] 2
    W.L.R. 761; [1988] 1 All E.R. 791; 40 B.L.R. 28; [1988] F.T.L.R. 469; (1988)
    138 N.L.J. 53; (1988) 132 S.J. 463, CA 8–009
Simon Engineering Plc v. Butte Mining Plc (No.2) [1996] 1 Lloyd's Rep. 91; [1997]
    I.L.Pr. 599, QBD (Comm Ct) 22–009
Sinason-Teicher Inter-American Grain Corp v. Oilcakes and Oilseeds Trading Co [1954]
    1 W.L.R. 1394; [1954] 3 All E.R. 468; [1954] 2 Lloyd's Rep. 327; 98 S.J.
    804, CA; affirming [1954] 1 W.L.R. 935; [1954] 2 All E.R. 497; [1954] 1
    Lloyd's Rep. 376; 98 S.J. 438 11–018
Singer Co (UK) Ltd v. Tees and Hartlepool Port Authority [1988] 2 Lloyd's Rep. 164;
    [1988] 1 F.T.L.R. 442, QBD (Comm Ct) 27–025
Siporex Trade SA v. Banque Indosuez [1986] 2 Lloyd's Rep. 146, QBD (Comm
    Ct) 11–010, 12–002, 12–003, 12–004
Siskina, The. *See* Owners of Cargo Lately Laden on Board The Siskina v. Distos
    Compania Naviera SA.
Siu Yin Kwan v. Eastern Insurance Co Ltd [1994] 2 A.C. 199; [1994] 2 W.L.R. 370;
    [1994] 1 All E.R. 213; [1994] 1 Lloyd's Rep. 616; (1994) 144 N.L.J. 87; (1994)
    138 S.J.L.B. 26, PC 27–005
Skarp, The [1935] P. 134; [1935] All E.R. Rep. 560; (1935) 52 Ll. L. Rep. 152; 51
    T.L.R. 541; 104 L.J. P. 63, PDAD 15–036
Skips A/S Nordheim v. Syrian Petroleum Co and Petrofina SA (The Varenna) [1984]
    Q.B. 599; [1983] 3 All E.R. 645; [1983] 2 Lloyd's Rep. 592, CA 15–023
SL Sethia Liners Ltd v. State Trading Corp of India Ltd [1985] 1 W.L.R. 1398; [1986] 2
    All E.R. 395; [1986] 1 Lloyd's Rep. 31; (1986) 83 L.S.G. 200; (1985) 129 S.J.
    889, CA 11–006
Slater and Slater and Ors v. Finning Ltd [1997] A.C. 473; [1996] 3 W.L.R. 191; [1996] 3
    All E.R. 398; [1996] 2 Lloyd's Rep. 353, HL 5–003
Smallman v. Smallman [1972] Fam. 25; [1971] 3 W.L.R. 588; [1971] 3 All E.R. 717; 115
    S.J. 527, CA 6–012
Smeaton Hanscomb & Co v. Setty (Sassoon I), Son & Co (No.2) [1953] 1 W.L.R. 1481;
    [1953] 2 All E.R. 1588; 97 S.J. 876, QBD 23–018
Smith Kline & French Laboratories Ltd v. Long [1989] 1 W.L.R. 1; [1988] 3 All E.R.
    887; (1988) 132 S.J. 1553, CA 21–028
Smith v. South Wales Switchgear [1978] 1 W.L.R. 165; [1978] 1 All E.R. 18; 8 B.L.R. 1;
    122 S.J. 61, HL 3–014
Sobell Industries Ltd v. Cory Bros & Co Ltd (Sadikoglu Bros, Third Parties) [1955] 2
    Lloyd's Rep. 82, QBD 1–005, 27–017, 27–022
Société d'Avances Commerciales (London) Ltd v. A Besse & Co (London) Ltd [1952] 1
    Lloyd's Rep. 242; [1952] 1 T.L.R. 644, QBD 6–012
Societe Francaise Bunge SA v. Belcan NV (The Federal Huron) [1985] 3 All E.R. 378;
    [1985] 2 Lloyd's Rep. 189; [1985] Fin. L.R. 282, QBD (Comm Ct) 21–018
Société Italo-Belge Pour le Commerce et L'Industrie SA (Antwerp) v. Palm and Vegetable
    Oils (Malaysia) Sdn Bhd (The Post Chaser) [1982] 1 All E.R. 19; [1981] 2 Lloyd's
    Rep. 695; [1981] Com. L.R. 249 .... 5–004, 5–012

Société Nationale Industrielle Aerospatiale (SNIA) v. Lee Kui Jak [1987] A.C. 871; [1987]
3 W.L.R. 59; [1987] 3 All E.R. 510; (1987) 84 L.S.G. 2048, PC 22–006
Société Nationale Industrielle Aerospatiale (SNIA) v. Lee Kui Jak [1987] A.C. 871; [1987]
3 W.L.R. 59; [1987] 3 All E.R. 510; (1987) 84 L.S.G. 2048, PC 22–009
Society of Lloyd's v. Canadian Imperial Bank of Commerce [1993] 2 Lloyd's Rep. 579,
QBD (Comm Ct) 11–030, 12–005
Sohio Supply Co v. Gatoil (USA) Inc [1989] 1 Lloyd's Rep. 588, CA 22–010
Soleh Boneh International v. Uganda and National Housing Corp [1993] 2 Lloyd's Rep.
208, CA 21–019
Soleimany v. Soleimany [1999] Q.B. 785; [1998] 3 W.L.R. 811; [1998] C.L.C. 779,
CA 21–027, 24–019
Solholt, The. *See* Sotiros Shipping Inc v. Shmeiet Solholt.
Solle v. Butcher [1950] 1 K.B. 671; [1949] 2 All E.R. 1107; 66 T.L.R. (Pt. 1)
448, CA 6–011
Somes v. British Empire Shipping Co (1860) 30 L.J.Q.B. 229 5–015
Sonat Offshore SA v. Amerada Hess Development and Texaco (Britain) [1988] 1 Lloyd's
Rep. 145; 39 B.L.R. 1; [1987] 2 F.T.L.R. 220, CA 6–016, 6–017
Sony Corp v. Time Electronics [1981] 1 W.L.R. 1293; [1981] 3 All E.R. 376; [1981]
F.S.R. 333, Ch D 22–032
Soon Hua Seng Co Ltd v. Glencore Grain Ltd [1996] 1 Lloyd's Rep. 398; [1996] C.L.C.
729, QBD (Comm Ct) 2–032, 2–035, 2–037
Soplex Wholesale Supplies and PS Refson & Co Ltd v. Egyptian International Foreign
Trading Co (The Rafaella) [1985] 2 Lloyd's Rep. 36; [1985] Fin. L.R. 123, CA;
affirming [1984] 1 Lloyd's Rep. 102, DC 27–007
Soproma SpA v. Marine & Animal By-Products Corp [1966] 1 Lloyd's Rep. 367; 116
N.L.J. 867, QBD (Comm Ct) 11–007, 11–039, 11–040, 12–002, 15–024
Sotiros Shipping Inc v. Shmeiet Solholt (The Solholt) [1983] 1 Lloyd's Rep. 605; [1983]
Com. L.R. 114; (1983) 127 S.J. 305 5–003
Source Ltd v. TUV Rheinland Holding AG [1998] Q.B. 54; [1997] 3 W.L.R. 365; [1998]
I.L.Pr. 432; [1997] I.L.Pr. 514, CA 22–018, 22–020
South African Reserve Bank v. Samuel (1931) 40 Ll.L.R 291 4–012
South Carolina Insurance Co v. Assurantie Maatshappij "De Zeven Provincien" NV; Same
v. Al Ahlia Insurance Co [1987] A.C. 24; [1986] 3 W.L.R. 398; [1986] 3 All E.R.
487; [1986] 2 Lloyd's Rep. 317; [1987] E.C.C. 1; (1986) 83 L.S.G. 2659; (1986)
136 N.L.J. 751; (1986) 130 S.J. 634, HL; reversing [1986] Q.B. 348; [1985] 3
W.L.R. 739; [1985] 2 All E.R. 1046; [1985] 2 Lloyd's Rep. 147; [1986] E.C.C.
181; (1985) 82 L.S.G. 3085; (1985) 135 N.L.J. 580; (1985) 129 S.J. 638, CA 21–021,
21–022, 22–009
Soya GmbH Mainz KG v. White [1983] 1 Lloyd's Rep. 122; [1983] Com. L.R. 46; (1983)
133 N.L.J. 64, HL; affirming [1982] 1 Lloyd's Rep. 136; [1982] Com. L.R. 22,
CA; affirming [1980] 1 Lloyd's Rep. 491, QBD (Comm Ct) 19–024
Speed Seal Products Ltd v. Paddington [1986] 1 All E.R. 91; [1986] F.S.R. 309; [1985] 1
W.L.R. 1327; (1985) 82 L.S.G. 3535; (1985) 135 N.L.J. 935, CA 27–011
Speedlink Vanguard, The v. European Gateway [1987] Q.B. 206; [1986] 3 W.L.R. 756;
[1986] 3 All E.R. 554; [1986] 2 Lloyd's Rep. 265; (1986) 83 L.S.G. 3253; (1986)
130 S.J. 748, QBD (Comm Ct) 24–005
Spencer v. Harding [1870] L.R. 5 C.P. 561 3–004
Spiliada Maritime Corp v. Cansulex Ltd (The Spiliada) [1987] A.C. 460; [1986] 3 W.L.R.
972; [1986] 3 All E.R. 843; [1987] 1 Lloyd's Rep. 1; [1987] E.C.C. 168; [1987] 1
F.T.L.R. 103; (1987) 84 L.S.G. 113; (1986) 136 N.L.J. 1137; (1986) 130 S.J. 925,
HL; reversing [1985] 2 Lloyd's Rep. 116; (1985) 82 L.S.G. 1416 22–005,
22–007, 22–008
Sport International Bussum BV v. Hi-Tec Sports [1988] R.P.C. 329, CA 30–012
Spurling (J.) Ltd v. Bradshaw [1956] 1 W.L.R. 461; [1956] 2 All E.R. 121; [1956] 1
Lloyd's Rep. 392; 100 S.J. 317 3–017
St Paul Fire & Marine Insurance Co (UK) Ltd v. McConnell Dowell Constructors Ltd
[1996] 1 All E.R. 96; [1995] 2 Lloyd's Rep. 116; 74 B.L.R. 112; 45 Con. L.R.
89, CA 19–012
St. Enoch Shipping Co Ltd v. Phosphate Mining Co [1916] 2 K.B. 624 15–012
Standard Chartered Bank v. Pakistan National Shipping Corp (No.1) [1998] 1 Lloyd's Rep.
656, CA; [1995] 2 Lloyd's Rep. 365, QBD 15–035

Stapylton Fletcher Ltd (In Administrative Receivership), Re; Ellis Son & Vidler Ltd (In Administrative Receivership), Re [1994] 1 W.L.R. 1181; [1995] 1 All E.R. 192; [1994] 2 B.C.L.C. 681; [1994] B.C.C. 532, Ch D 4–004
State Trading Corp of India Ltd v. M Golodetz Ltd (The Sara D) [1989] 2 Lloyd's Rep. 277, CA; reversing [1988] 2 Lloyd's Rep. 182 .... 2–032, 2–033, 2–034, 2–038, 5–003, 5–004, 11–018, 14–005, 30–006
Steele v. M'Kinlay (1880) L.R. 5 App.Cas. 754, HL 9–009
Stein v. Hambros Bank (1821) 9 Ll. L.R. 507 11–026
Stellar Chartering and Brokerage Inc v. Efibanca-Ente Finanziario Interbancario SpA (The Span Terza) (No.2) [1984] 1 W.L.R. 27; [1984] 1 Lloyd's Rep. 119; [1984] 81 L.S.G. 283, HL; reversing [1983] 1 W.L.R. 632; [1983] 1 Lloyd's Rep. 441, CA; affirming [1982] 2 Lloyd's Rep. 72, QBD (Adm Ct) 22–033
Sterns v. Vickers [1923] 1 K.B. 78 4–010
Stockton v. Mason [1978] 2 Lloyd's Rep. 430; [1979] R.T.R. 130, CA 19–003
Stolt Loyalty, The [1995] 1 Lloyd's Rep. 598, CA; [1993] 2 Lloyd's Rep. 281, QBD (Adm Ct) 15–048, 15–051
Strass v. Spiller and Bakers (1911) 16 Com.Cas 166 19–016
Studebaker Distributors v. Charlton Steam Shipping Co [1938] 1 K.B. 459 15–045
Stumore Weston & Co v. Michael Breen (1886) 12 A.C. 698 15–035
Sucre Export SA v. Northern River Shipping Ltd (The Sormovskiy 3068) [1994] 2 Lloyd's Rep. 266, QBD 15–023, 15–038
Suncorp Insurance and Finance v. Milano Asssicurazioni Spa [1993] 2 Lloyd's Rep. 225 .... 27–007, 27–008
Sunrise Maritime Inc v. Uvisco Ltd (The Hector) [1998] 2 Lloyd's Rep. 287; [1998] C.L.C. 902, QBD (Comm Ct) 15–051
Svenska Traktor AB v. Maritime Agencies (Southampton) [1953] 2 Q.B. 295; [1953] 3 W.L.R. 426; [1953] 2 All E.R. 570; [1953] 2 Lloyd's Rep. 124; 97 S.J. 525 .... 15–022, 15–041
Swiss Bank Corp v. Novorissiysk Shipping Co (The Petr Shmidt) [1995] 1 Lloyd's Rep. 202, QBD (Comm Ct) 15–023
Sykes (F. & G.) (Wessex) v. Fine Fare [1967] 1 Lloyd's Rep. 53, CA; reversing in part [1966] 2 Lloyd's Rep. 205 3–015
Symington & Co v. Union Insurance Society of Canton Ltd (No. 2) (1928) 34 Com.Cas 233 19–010
Sze Hai Tong Bank v. Rambler Cycle Co [1959] A.C. 576; [1959] 3 W.L.R. 214; [1959] 3 All E.R. 182; [1959] 2 Lloyd's Rep. 114; 103 S.J. 561, PC 15–038, 15–039, 15–041
Szeteijn v. J Henry Schroder Banking Corporation (1941) 31 N.Y.S. 2d, 631 11–042

Tai Hing Cotton Mill Ltd v. Liu Chong Hing Bank Ltd [1986] A.C. 80; [1985] 3 W.L.R. 317; [1985] 2 All E.R. 947; [1985] 2 Lloyd's Rep. 313; [1986] F.L.R. 14; (1985) 82 L.S.G. 2995; (1985) 135 N.L.J. 680; (1985) 129 S.J. 503, PC 5–012
Tankreederei Ahrenkeil GmbH v. Frahuil SA (The Multitank Holsatia) [1988] 2 Lloyd's Rep. 486, DC 6–004
Tatem (WJ) Ltd v. Gamboa [1939] 1 K.B. 132; [1938] 3 All E.R. 135; 108 L.J.K.B. 34; 160 L.T. 159; 19 Asp.M.L.C. 216; 43 Com.Cas 343 6–011
Taylor v. Caldwell (1863) 3 B. & S. 826; 2 New Rep. 198; 32 L.J.Q.B. 164; 8 L.T. 356; 27 J.P. 710; 10 W.R. 726; 122 E.R. 309 6–007
Teheran-Europe Co Ltd v. ST Belton (Tractors) Ltd [1968] 2 Q.B. 545; [1968] 3 W.L.R. 205; [1968] 2 All E.R. 886; [1968] 2 Lloyd's Rep. 37; (1968) 112 S.J. 501, CA; affirming in part [1968] 2 Q.B. 53; [1968] 2 W.L.R. 523; [1968] 1 All E.R. 585; [1968] 1 Lloyd's Rep. 211, QBD 27–005, 27–017, 27–020
Tellrite Ltd v. London Confirmers Ltd [1962] 1 Lloyd's Rep. 236, QBD 27–020
Tenax Steamship Co v. Brimnes, The (Owners); Brimnes, The. *See* Brimnes, The; Tenax Steamship Co v. Brimnes, The (Owners).
Terkol Rederierne v. Petroleo Brasileiro SA and Frota Nacional de Petroleiros (The Badagry) [1985] 1 Lloyd's Rep. 395, CA 19–033
Tesam Distribution Ltd v. Schuh Mode Team GmbH [1990] I.L.Pr. 149; (1989) 86(46) L.S.G. 38, CA 22–018
Tetley & Co v. Brisith Trade Corporation (1922) 10 Ll.L.R. 678 27–009
Tetroc Ltd v. Cross-Con (International) Ltd [1981] 1 Lloyd's Rep. 192, QBD 27–025
Texaco Ltd v. The Eurogulf Shipping Co Ltd [1987] 2 Lloyd's Rep. 541 2–011

Thames and Mersey Insurance Co Ltd v. HT Van Laun & Co [1917] 2 K.B. 48   19–006, 19–013
Themehelp Ltd v. West [1996] Q.B. 84; [1995] 3 W.L.R. 751; [1995] 4 All E.R. 215;
    [1995] C.L.C. 703, CA 12–005
Thermo Engineers Ltd and Anhydro A/S v. Ferrymasters Ltd [1981] 1 W.L.R. 1470; [1981]
    1 All E.R. 1142; [1981] 1 Lloyd's Rep. 200; [1981] Com. L.R. 9; 125 S.J. 607 ...   2–007,
                                                                                      18–006
Thomas (T. W.) & Co Ltd v. Portsea Steamship Co Ltd [1912] A.C. 1, HL 15–023
Thomas Borthwick (Glasgow) Ltd v. Bunge & Co Ltd [1969] 1 Lloyd's Rep. 17 ... 2–012, 2–032
Thomas Borthwick (Glasgow) Ltd v. Faure Fairclough Ltd [1968] 1 Lloyd's Rep. 16, QBD
    (Comm Ct) 6–017
Thomas Cook Group Ltd v. Air Malta Co Ltd (t/a Air Malta) [1997] 2 Lloyd's Rep. 399,
    QBD (Comm Ct) 17–016
Thomas Marshall (Exports) Ltd v. Guinle [1979] Ch. 227; [1978] 3 W.L.R. 116; [1978] 3
    All E.R. 193; [1978] I.C.R. 905; [1978] I.R.L.R. 174; [1979] F.S.R. 208; 122 S.J.
    295; [1978] I.R.L.R. 174; [1978] I.C.R. 905; (1978) 122 S.J. 295, Ch D 27–011
Tiburon, The. *See* Seavision Investment SA v. Evennett (Norman Thomas) and Clarkson
    Puckle.
Tilia Gorthon, The [1985] 1 Lloyd's Rep. 552, QBD (Adm Ct) 15–041
Tindefjell, The. *See* JA Johnston Co Ltd v. Sealion Navigation Co SA.
TM Noten BV v. Paul Charles Harding [1990] 2 Lloyd's Rep. 283, CA; reversing [1989]
    2 Lloyd's Rep. 527, QBD (Comm Ct) 19–024
Toepfer (Alfred C) (Hamburg) v. Lenersan-Poortman NV (Rotterdam). *See* Toepfer v.
    Lenersan-Poortman NV; Toepfer v. Verheijdens Veervoeder Commissiehandel.
Toepfer v. Lenersan-Poortman NV; Toepfer v. Verheijdens Veervoeder Commissiehandel
    [1980] 1 Lloyd's Rep. 143, CA; *sub nom.* Toepfer (Alfred C.) (Hamburg) v. Lener-
    san-Poortman NV (Rotterdam); Same v. Verheijdens Veervoeder Commissiehandel
    (1978) 122 S.J. 417; *The Times*, April 26, 1978 .... 2–031, 2–032, 4–002
Toepfer v. Schwarze [1980] 1 Lloyd's Rep. 385, CA; affirming [1977] 2 Lloyd's Rep.
    380 2–033
Tomlinson (A.) (Hauliers) Ltd v. Hepburn [1966] A.C. 451; [1966] 2 W.L.R. 453; [1966]
    1 All E.R. 418; [1966] 1 Lloyd's Rep. 309; 110 S.J. 86, HL; affirming [1966] 1
    Q.B. 21; [1965] 2 W.L.R. 634; [1965] 1 All E.R. 284; [1965] 1 Lloyd's Rep. 1;
    109 S.J. 10, CA; affirming [1964] 1 Lloyd's Rep. 416, QBD (Comm Ct) 19–015
Tool Metal Manufacture Co Ltd v. Tungsten Electric Co Ltd [1955] 1 W.L.R. 761; [1955]
    2 All E.R. 657; 72 R.P.C. 209; 99 S.J. 470, HL; reversing [1954] 1 W.L.R.
    862; [1954] 2 All E.R. 28; 71 R.P.C. 201; 98 S.J. 389, CA; reversing (1953) 71
    R.P.C. 1 5–012
Toprak Mahsulleri Ofisi v. Finagrain Compagnie Commerciale Agricole et Financiere SA
    [1979] 2 Lloyd's Rep. 98, CA 11–006, 11–020, 11–028, 21–027
Torenia, The. *See* Aktieselskabet de Danske Sukkerfabrikker v. Bajamar Compania Naviera
    SA.
Torvald Klaveness A/S v. Arni Maritime Corp (The Gregos) [1994] 1 W.L.R. 1465; [1994]
    4 All E.R. 998; [1995] 1 Lloyd's Rep. 1, HL; reversing [1993] 2 Lloyd's Rep. 335,
    CA; reversing [1992] 2 Lloyd's Rep. 40, QBD 5–003
Total International Ltd v. Addax BV (t/a Addax BV Geneva Branch) [1996] 2 Lloyd's
    Rep. 333, QBD (Comm Ct) 5–003
Total Transport Corp of Panama v. Amoco Transport Co (The Altus) [1985] 1 Lloyd's
    Rep. 423, QBD (Comm Ct) 15–014
Touche Ross & Co v. Baker (Colin) [1992] 2 Lloyd's Rep. 207; (1992) 89 (28) L.S.G. 31;
    [1991] 2 Lloyd's Rep. 230, CA 19–003
Tower Hamlets LBC v. British Gas Corp *The Times*, December 14, 1983, CA; affirming
    (1982) 79 L.S.G. 1025 30–013
Town & City Properties (Development) v. Wiltshier Southern and Gilbert Powell 44 B.L.R.
    109; (1988) B.L.R. 114 23–017
Town & Country Building Society v. Daisystar (1989) 139 N.L.J. 1563, CA
Tracomin SA v. Gibbs Nathaniel (Canada) Ltd and George Jacob Bridge [1985] 1 Lloyd's
    Rep. 586, QBD (Comm Ct) 23–005
Tradax Export SA v. André & Cie SA [1976] 1 Lloyd's Rep. 416, CA; reversing [1975]
    2 Lloyd's Rep. 516 .... 2–033, 6–018
Tradax Export SA v. Italgrani di Francesco Ambrosio; Sosimage SpA v. Italgrani di Fran-
    cesco Ambrosio [1986] 1 Lloyd's Rep. 112, CA; reversing [1983] 2 Lloyd's Rep.
    109; [1983] Com. L.R. 116 2–010

Tradax Export SA v. Volkswagenwerk AG [1970] 1 Q.B. 537; [1970] 2 W.L.R. 339;
    [1970] 1 All E.R. 420; [1970] 1 Lloyd's Rep. 62; 113 S.J. 978, CA; affirming
    [1969] 2 Q.B. 599; [1969] 2 W.L.R. 498; [1969] 2 All E.R. 144; [1969] 1 Lloyd's
    Rep. 494, QBD (Comm Ct) 23–012
Trade Indemnity Plc v. Forsakringsaktiebolaget Njord [1995] 1 All E.R. 796, QBD (Comm
    Ct) 22–018
Trade Star Line Corp v. Mitsui & Co Ltd (The Arctic Trader); Mitsui & Co Ltd v. J
    Lauritzen A/S [1996] 2 Lloyd's Rep. 449; [1997] C.L.C. 174, CA 15–036
Trans Trust SPRL v. Danubian Trading Co Ltd [1952] 2 Q.B. 297; [1952] 1 All E.R. 970;
    [1952] 1 Lloyd's Rep. 348; [1952] 1 T.L.R. 1066; 96 S.J. 312, CA; reversing in
    part [1952] 1 K.B. 285; [1952] 1 All E.R. 89; [1951] 2 Lloyd's Rep. 644; [1952]
    1 T.L.R. 13, KBD 11–018, 11–021, 11–035
Transcontainer Express v. Custodian Security [1988] 1 Lloyd's Rep. 128; [1988] 1 F.T.L.R.
    54, CA 27–025
Transcontinental Underwriting Agency v. Grand Union Insurance Co [1987] 2 Lloyd's
    Rep. 409; [1987] 1 F.T.L.R. 35, QBD (Comm Ct) 19–003
Transworld Oil (USA) Inc v. Minos Compania Naviera SAL (The Leni) [1992] 2 Lloyd's
    Rep. 48, QBD (Comm Ct) 15–048
Trave Shiffahrtsgesellschaft GmbH & Co KG v. Ninemia Maritime Corp (The
    Niedersachsen) (No.2) [1986] Q.B. 802; [1986] 2 W.L.R. 773; [1986] 2 All E.R.
    244; [1986] 1 Lloyd's Rep. 393; (1986) 83 L.S.G. 1474; (1986) 130 S.J. 314, CA   23–018
Travell v. Customs and Excise Commissioners [1998] C.O.D. 92; (1998) 162 J.P. 181,
    QBD 26–030
Trendtex Trading Corp v. Central Bank of Nigeria [1977] Q.B. 529; [1977] 2 W.L.R. 356;
    [1977] 1 All E.R. 881; [1977] 1 Lloyd's Rep. 581; [1977] 2 C.M.L.R. 465; 121
    S.J. 85, CA; reversing [1976] 1 W.L.R. 868; [1976] 3 All E.R. 437; [1976] 2
    C.M.L.R. 668; 120 S.J. 554, QBD 11–025, 21–019
Tropic Plastic and Packaging Industry v. Standard Bank of South Africa Ltd 1969 (4) S.A.
    108 9–007
Tropwind, The. *See* Italmare Shipping Co v. Tropwood AG.
Trucks and Spares v. Maritime Agencies (Southampton) [1951] 2 All E.R. 982; [1951] 2
    Lloyd's Rep. 345; [1951] 2 T.L.R. 1021; [1951] W.N. 597; 95 S.J. 788, CA 15–038
Trygg Hansa Insurance Co Ltd v. Equitas Ltd; *sub nom* Equitas Ltd v. Trygg Hansa Insur-
    ance Co Ltd [1998] 2 Lloyd's Rep. 439; [1998] C.L.C. 979, QBD (Comm Ct) 23–011
Tsakiroglou & Co Ltd v. Noblee Thorl GmbH; Albert D Gaon & Co v. Société Interprofes-
    sionelle des Oleagineax Fluides Alimentaires [1962] A.C. 93; [1961] 2 W.L.R. 633;
    [1961] 2 All E.R. 179; [1961] 1 Lloyd's Rep. 329; 105 S.J. 346, HL; affirming
    [1960] 2 Q.B. 348; [1960] 2 W.L.R. 869; [1960] 2 All E.R. 160; [1960] 1 Lloyd's
    Rep. 349; [1960] C.L.Y. 535, CA; affirming [1960] 2 Q.B. 318; [1959] 2 W.L.R.
    179; [1959] 1 All E.R. 45; [1958] 2 Lloyd's Rep. 515; 103 S.J. 112; [1959] C.L.Y.
    539, QBD 2–022, 6–001
Tsakiroglou & Co Ltd v. Transgrains, SA [1958] 1 Lloyd's Rep. 562, QBD (Comm Ct) .. 11–018
Tukan Timber v. Barclays Bank Plc [1987] 1 Lloyd's Rep. 171; [1987] F.L.R. 208; [1987]
    1 F.T.L.R. 154, QBD 11–006, 11–032, 11–042, 12–004
Turkiye IS Bankasi AS v. Bank of China [1998] 1 Lloyd's Rep. 250; [1998] C.L.C. 182,
    CA; affirming [1996] 2 Lloyd's Rep. 611; [1996] 5 Bank. L.R. 241, QBD
    (Comm Ct) 12–004, 12–005
Turner v. Grovit [1999] 3 W.L.R. 794; [1999] 3 All E.R. 616; [1999] 1 All E.R. (Comm)
    929, CA; reversing [1999] 1 All E.R. (Comm) 445, Ch D 22–027
Tuvyahu v. Yoel Singh, unreported 24–012

U.S. Surgical Corporation v. Hospital Products Ltd [1983] 2 N.S.W.R. 157 30–011
Ulster Swift Ltd v. Taunton Meat Haulage Ltd; Fransen Transport NV (Third Party) [1977]
    1 W.L.R. 625; [1977] 3 All E.R. 641; [1977] 1 Lloyd's Rep. 346; [1977] R.T.R.
    475; [1977] R.T.R. 449; 121 S.J. 169, CA; affirming [1975] 2 Lloyd's Rep. 502,
    QBD (Comm Ct) 18–007, 18–009, 27–025
Ultisol Transport Contractors Ltd v. Bouygues Offshore SA [1996] 2 Lloyd's Rep. 140,
    QBD 22–010
Ultisol Transport Contractors Ltd v. Bouygues Offshore SA. *See* Caspian Basin Specialised
    Emergency Salvage Administration v. Bouygues Offshore SA (No.4).
Union Insurance Society of Canton Ltd v. George Wills & Co [1916] 1 A.C. 281 19–006
Union of India v. Aaby (EB)'s Rederi A/S [1975] A.C. 797; [1974] 3 W.L.R. 269; 118

S.J. 595; [1974] 2 All E.R. 874; *sub nom.* Aaby (EB)'s Rederi A/S v. Union of India (The Evje) [1974] 2 Lloyd's Rep. 57, HL; affirming on other grounds *sub nom.* Aaby (EB)'s Rederi A/S v. Union of India (The Evje) [1973] 1 Lloyd's Rep. 509, CA; affirming [1972] 2 Lloyd's Rep. 129 19–029
Union of India v. NV Reederij Amsterdam (The Amstelslot) [1963] 2 Lloyd's Rep. 223, HL; reversing [1962] 2 Lloyd's Rep. 336, CA; affirming [1962] 1 Lloyd's Rep. 539, QBD (Comm Ct) 15–041
United Bank of Kuwait v. Hammoud [1988] 1 W.L.R. 1051; [1988] 3 All E.R. 418; (1988) 138 N.L.J. 281; (1988) 132 S.J. 1388, CA; reversing (1987) 137 N.L.J. 921 27–007
United Carriers Ltd v. Heritage Food Group (UK) Ltd [1996] 1 W.L.R. 371; [1995] 4 All E.R. 95; [1995] 2 Lloyd's Rep. 269; (1995) 139 S.J.L.B. 83; *The Times*, March 8, 1995, QBD 18–007
United City Merchants (Investments) Ltd v. Royal Bank of Canada (The American Accord) [1983] 1 A.C. 168; [1982] 2 W.L.R. 1039; [1982] 2 All E.R. 720; [1982] 2 Lloyd's Rep. 1; [1982] Com. L.R. 142, HL; reversing [1982] Q.B. 208; [1981] 3 W.L.R. 242; [1981] 3 All E.R. 142; [1981] 1 Lloyd's Rep. 604; [1981] Com. L.R. 98; 125 S.J. 413, CA; affirming [1979] 1 Lloyd's Rep. 267 .... 7–002, 11–042, 12–004, 13–011, 15–035, 21–027
United City Merchants (Investments) Ltd v. Royal Bank of Canada (The American Accord) [1983] 1 A.C. 168; [1982] 2 W.L.R. 1039; [1982] 2 All E.R. 720; [1982] 2 Lloyd's Rep. 1; [1982] Com. L.R. 142, HL; reversing [1982] Q.B. 208; [1981] 3 W.L.R. 242; [1981] 3 All E.R. 142; [1981] 1 Lloyd's Rep. 604; [1981] Com. L.R. 98; 125 S.J. 413, CA; affirming [1979] 1 Lloyd's Rep. 267, QBD (Comm Ct) 11–001, 11–006
United Dominions Trust (Commercial) v. Eagle Aircraft Services; United Dominions Trust (Commercial) v. Eagle Aviation [1968] 1 W.L.R. 74; 111 S.J. 849; [1968] 1 All E.R. 104, CA; reversing *sub nom.* United Dominions Trust (Commercial) v. Eagle Aviation (1967) 117 N.L.J. 324 .... 5–004, 11–018
United States v. Bowe [1990] 1 A.C. 500; [1989] 3 W.L.R. 1256; [1989] 3 All E.R. 315; [1990] Crim. L.R. 196; (1989) 86(39) L.S.G. 35; (1989) 133 S.J. 1298, PC 21–028
United States v. Inkley [1989] Q.B. 255; [1988] 3 W.L.R. 304; [1988] 3 All E.R. 144; [1988] 2 F.T.L.R. 86; (1988) 132 S.J. 995, CA 21–025
United States v. Ivey [1995] 130 D.L.R. (4th) 674 21–025
United Trading Corp SA v. Allied Arab Bank; Murray Clayton v. Rafidair Bank [1985] 2 Lloyd's Rep. 554, CA 11–043, 12–001, 12–002, 12–004, 12–005
Universal Petroleum Co v. Handels und Transport GmbH [1987] 1 W.L.R. 1178; [1987] 2 All E.R. 737; [1987] 1 Lloyd's Rep. 517; [1987] 1 F.T.L.R. 429; (1987) 84 L.S.G. 1238, CA 2–001
Unterweser Reederei GmbH v. Zapata Offshore Co (The Chaparral) [1968] 2 Lloyd's Rep. 158, CA 22–010
Urquhart Lindsay & Co v. Eastern Bank [1922] 1 K.B. 318 .... 11–023, 11–026

Van der Zijden Wildhandel (P. J.) NV v. Tucker & Cross Ltd [1976] 1 Lloyd's Rep. 341; for previous proceedings see [1975] 2 Lloyd's Rep. 240 .... 2–019, 2–033
Vantol (JH) v. Fairclough Dodd and Jones. *See* Fairclough Dodd & Jones v. Vantol (JH).
Vapormatic Co Ltd v. Sparex Ltd [1976] 1 W.L.R. 939; [1976] F.S.R. 451; 120 S.J. 472, Ch D 22–032
Vargas Pena Apezteguia y Cia SAIC v. Peter Cremer GmbH & Co [1987] 1 Lloyd's Rep. 394 2–026
Vaughan Motors and Sheldon Motor Services Ltd v. Scottish General Insurance Co Ltd [1960] 1 Lloyd's Rep. 479, QBD 19–017
Veflings (George) Rederi A/S v. President of India; Monrovia Shipping Co v. Same (The Bellami) [1979] 1 W.L.R. 59; [1979] 1 All E.R. 380; [1979] 1 Lloyd's Rep. 123; 122 S.J. 843, CA; affirming [1978] 1 W.L.R. 982; [1978] 3 All E.R. 838; [1978] 2 Lloyd's Rep. 193; [1978] 1 Lloyd's Rep. 467; 122 S.J. 247, QBD (Comm Ct) 21–018
Velos Group Ltd v. Harbour Insurance Services Ltd [1997] 2 Lloyd's Rep. 461, CC (Central London) 19–003
Ventouris v. Mountain (The Italia Express) (No.2) [1992] 1 W.L.R. 887; [1992] 3 All E.R. 414; [1992] 2 Lloyd's Rep. 216, CA 19–034
Vervaeke v. Smith [1983] 1 A.C. 145; [1982] 2 W.L.R. 855; [1982] 2 All E.R. 144; 126 S.J. 293; (1982) 126 S.J. 293, HL; affirming [1981] Fam. 77; [1981] 2 W.L.R. 901; [1981] 1 All E.R. 55; 125 S.J. 16; [1981] 2 W.L.R. 901; (1980) 125 S.J. 16, CA 21–023

Victoria Laundry (Windsor) v. Newman Industries [1949] 2 K.B. 528; [1949] 1 All E.R. 997; 65 T.L.R. 274; 93 S.J. 371, CA; reversing in part [1948] 2 All E.R. 806; 64 T.L.R. 567; [1948] W.N. 397; 92 S.J. 617 8–009
Virgin Aviation Services Ltd v. CAD Aviation Services [1991] I.L.Pr. 79, QBD 22–027
Viskase Ltd v. Paul Kiefal GmbH [1999] 1 W.L.R. 1305; [1999] 3 All E.R. 362; [1999] 1 All E.R. (Comm.) 641, CA 22–018
Visser, Re [1928] Ch. 877 21–025
Vitol SA v. Esso Australia Ltd (The Wise) [1989] 2 Lloyd's Rep. 451, CA; reversing [1989] 1 Lloyd's Rep. 96 2–014
Vitol SA v. Norelf Ltd (The Santa Clara) [1996] A.C. 800; [1996] 3 W.L.R. 105; [1996] 3 All E.R. 193; [1996] 2 Lloyd's Rep. 225; [1996] C.L.C. 1159; (1996) 15 Tr. L.R. 347; (1996) 93(26) L.S.G. 19; (1996) 146 N.L.J. 957; (1996) 140 S.J.L.B. 147, HL; reversing [1996] Q.B. 108; [1995] 3 W.L.R. 549; [1995] 3 All E.R. 971; [1995] 2 Lloyd's Rep. 128; (1995) 14 Tr. L.R. 451, CA; reversing [1994] 1 W.L.R. 1390; [1994] 4 All E.R. 109; [1993] 2 Lloyd's Rep. 301; (1993) 90(30) L.S.G. 36; 137 S.J.L.B. 146 3–009
Voest Alpine Intertrading GmbH v. Chevron International Oil Co Ltd [1987] 2 Lloyd's Rep. 547, QBD (Comm Ct) 28–006
Vogel v. R & A Kohnstamm Ltd [1973] Q.B. 133; [1971] 3 W.L.R. 537; [1971] 2 All E.R. 1428; 115 S.J. 773, QBD 27–002
Vosnoc Ltd v. Transglobal Projects Ltd [1998] 1 W.L.R. 101; [1998] 2 All E.R. 990; [1998] 1 Lloyd's Rep. 711; [1997] C.L.C. 1345; (1997) 94(34) L.S.G. 28; (1997) 141 S.J.L.B. 215, QBD (Comm Ct) 15–048, 23–019

Wahda Bank v. Arab Bank Plc (1992) [1996] 1 Lloyd's Rep. 470; [1996] 5 Bank. L.R. 128; [1996] C.L.C. 408, CA; affirming [1994] 2 Lloyd's Rep. 411; (1993) 90(4) L.S.G. 38; (1993) 137 S.J.L.B. 24, QBD 12–004
Wait, Re [1927] 1 Ch. 606 4–005
Walek & Co v. Chapman & Ball (International) Ltd [1980] 2 Lloyd's Rep. 279, QBD (Comm Ct) 18–009
Walford v. Miles [1992] 2 A.C. 128; [1992] 2 W.L.R. 174; [1992] 1 All E.R. 453; (1992) 64 P. & C.R. 166; [1992] 11 E.G. 115; [1992] 1 E.G.L.R. 207; [1992] N.PC 4, HL; affirming (1991) 62 P. & C.R. 410; [1991] 28 E.G. 81; [1991] 27 E.G. 114; [1991] 2 E.G.L.R. 185; [1990] E.G.C.S. 158, CA; reversing [1990] 12 E.G. 107; [1990] 1 E.G.L.R. 212 3–015
Walton (Grain and Shipping) Ltd v. British Italian Trading Co Ltd [1959] 1 Lloyd's Rep. 223, QBD (Comm Ct) 6–009
Ward (R. V.) v. Bignall [1967] 1 Q.B. 534; [1967] 2 W.L.R. 1050; [1967] 2 All E.R. 449; 111 S.J. 190, CA 5–017
Wardar's (Import & Export) Co Ltd v. W Norwood & Sons Ltd [1968] 2 Q.B. 663; [1968] 2 W.L.R. 1440; [1968] 2 All E.R. 602; [1968] 2 Lloyd's Rep. 1; *sub nom.* Wardars (Import & Export) v. W Norwood & Sons (1968) 112 S.J. 310 4–010
Wardens and Commonalty of the Mystery of Mercers of the City of London v. New Hampshire Insurance Co Ltd; sub nom, Mercers Co v. New Hampshire Insurance Co Ltd [1992] 1 W.L.R. 792; [1992] 3 All E.R. 57; [1992] 2 Lloyd's Rep. 365; 60 B.L.R. 26; 29 Con. L.R. 30; (1993) 9 Const. L.J. 66, CA; reversing [1991] 1 W.L.R. 1173; [1991] 4 All E.R. 542; [1992] 1 Lloyd's Rep. 431; (1991) 7 Const. L.J. 130; (1991) 135 S.J. 541, QBD 12–001
Waren Import Gesellschaft Krohn & Co v. Internationale Graanhandel Thegra NV [1975] 1 Lloyd's Rep. 146 15–034
Waterford Wedgwood Plc v. David Nagli Ltd (Third Party Notice) [1998] C.L.C. 1011; [1999] I.L.Pr. 9, Ch D 22–022
Waugh v. Morris (1873) L.R. 8 Q.B. 202 6–013
Wayne Tank and Pump Co Ltd v. Employers Liability Assurance Corp Ltd [1974] Q.B. 57; [1973] 3 W.L.R. 483; [1973] 3 All E.R. 825; [1973] 2 Lloyd's Rep. 237; 117 S.J. 564, CA; reversing [1972] 2 Lloyd's Rep. 141, QBD (Comm Ct) 19–031
Weare v. Brimsdown Lead Co (1910) 103 L.T.R. 429 27–012
Weatherby v. Banham [1832] 5 C. & P. 228 3–009
Wessanen's Koninklijke Fabrikien v. Isaac Modiano, Brother & Sons [1960] 1 W.L.R. 1243; [1960] 3 All E.R. 617; [1960] 2 Lloyd's Rep. 257; 104 S.J. 956 23–012
Westacre Investments Inc v. Jugoimport-SPDR Holding Co Ltd [1999] 1 All E.R. (Comm) 865, CA 24–019

Westinghouse Electric Corp Uranium Contract Litigation MDL Docket 235 (No.2) [1978] A.C. 547; [1978] 2 W.L.R. 81; [1978] 1 All E.R. 434; [1978] 1 C.M.L.R. 100; 122 S.J. 32, HL; affirming [1977] 3 W.L.R. 492; [1977] 3 All E.R. 717; [1977] 2 C.M.L.R. 436; 121 S.J. 663, CA 21–022

Westminster Property Group Plc, Re [1985] 1 W.L.R. 676; [1985] 2 All E.R. 426; [1985] P.C.C. 176; (1985) 82 L.S.G. 1085; (1985) 129 S.J. 115, CA; affirming [1984] 1 W.L.R. 1117; (1985) 82 L.S.G. 198; (1984) 128 S.J. 684, Ch D 14–002

Westzucker GmbH v. Bunge GmbH; Bremer Handelsgesellschaft mbH v. Westzucker GmbH [1981] 2 Lloyd's Rep. 130; [1981] Com. L.R. 179, CA 23–018

Whinney v. Moss Steamship Co Ltd (1910) 15 Com.Cas 114 15–018

Whitworth Street Estates (Manchester) Ltd v. James Miller & Partners. *See* Miller (James) & Partners Ltd v. Whitworth Street Estates (Manchester) Ltd.

Wibau Maschinefabrik Hartman SA v. Mackinnon Mackenzie (The Chanda) [1989] 2 Lloyd's Rep. 494, QBD (Comm Ct) 15–045, 15–048

William Tatton & Co Ltd v. Ferrymasters Ltd [1974] 1 Lloyd's Rep. 203, QBD 18–010

William Thomas &Sons v. Harrowing Steamship Co [1915] A.C. 58 15–009

Williams & Glyn's Bank v. Astro Dinamico Comp Nav SA [1984] 1 W.L.R. 438; [1984] 1 All E.R. 760; [1984] 1 Lloyd's Rep. 453; (1984) 128 S.J. 189, HL; affirming [1983] 2 Lloyd's Rep. 485, CA 22–003, 24–008

Williams & Humbert Ltd v. W&H Trade Marks (Jersey) Ltd; Rumasa SA v. Multinvest (UK) [1986] A.C. 368; [1986] 2 W.L.R. 24; [1986] 1 All E.R. 129; (1986) 83 L.S.G. 362; (1986) 136 N.L.J. 15, HL; affirming [1985] 3 W.L.R. 501; [1985] 2 All E.R. 619; (1986) 83 L.S.G. 37, CA; affirming [1985] 2 All E.R. 208; (1985) 129 S.J. 573, Ch D 21–024

Williamson v. Rider [1963] 1 Q.B. 89; [1962] 3 W.L.R. 119; [1962] 2 All E.R. 268; 106 S.J. 263, CA 9–004

Wilson Smithett & Cape (Sugar) v. Bangladesh Sugar and Food Industries Corp [1986] 1 Lloyd's Rep. 378 3–012

Wilson v. Harper, Son & Co [1908] 2 Ch. 370 27–012

Wilson, Holgate & Co v. Belgian Grain and Produce Co [1920] 2 K.B. 1; 89 L.J.K.B. 300; 122 L.T. 524; 35 T.L.R. 530; 14 Asp.M.L.C. 566; 25 Com.Cas 1 .... 2–023, 19–011

Wilson, Smithett & Cope Ltd v. Terruzzi [1976] Q.B. 683; [1976] 2 W.L.R. 418; [1976] 1 All E.R. 817; [1976] 1 Lloyd's Rep. 509; 120 S.J. 116, CA; affirming [1975] 2 W.L.R. 1009; [1975] 2 All E.R. 649; [1975] 1 Lloyd's Rep. 642; 119 S.J. 318 21–029

Wimble, Sons & Co Ltd v. Rosenberg & Sons [1913] 3 K.B. 743; 82 L.J.K.B. 1251; 109 L.T. 294; 29 T.L.R. 752; 12 Asp.M.L.C. 373; 18 Com.Cas 65, 302, CA 2–007, 2–008

Windschuegl (Charles H) v. Alexander Pickering & Co 109583(1950) 84 Lloyd's Rep. 89 6–012

Wingold v. William Looser & Co [1951] 1 D.L.R. 429 30–005

Winkfield, The [1900–03] All E.R. Rep. 346; [1902] P. 42, CA 15–052

Wright v. Commissioners of Customs and Excise [1999] 1 Cr. App. R. 69 26–030

Woodar Investment Development Ltd v. Wimpey Construction UK Ltd [1980] 1 W.L.R. 277; [1980] 1 All E.R. 571; 124 S.J. 184; (1980) 124 S.J. 184, HL 30–006

Woodhouse A.C. Israel Cocoa SA v. Nigerian Produce Marketing Co [1972] A.C. 741; [1972] 2 W.L.R. 1090; [1972] 2 All E.R. 271; [1972] 1 Lloyd's Rep. 439; 116 S.J. 329, HL; affirming [1971] 2 Q.B. 23; [1971] 2 W.L.R. 272; [1971] 1 All E.R. 665; *sub nom.* Woodhouse v. Nigerian Produce Marketing Co (1970) 115 S.J. 56; *sub nom.* Woodhouse A.C. Israel Cocoa S.A. and A.C. Israel Cocoa Inc v. Nigerian Produce Marketing Co [1971] 1 Lloyd's Rep. 25, CA; reversing [1970] 2 All E.R. 124; [1970] 1 Lloyd's Rep. 295 .... 5–012, 21–018

Woolcott v. Sun Alliance and London Insurance Ltd [1978] 1 W.L.R. 493; [1978] 1 All E.R. 1253; [1978] 1 Lloyd's Rep. 629; 121 S.J. 744, QBD 19–012

Woolf v. Collis Removal Service [1948] 1 K.B. 11; [1947] 2 All E.R. 260; 63 T.L.R. 540; 177 L.T. 405; [1947] L.J.R. 1377, CA 23–015

Workers Trust & Merchant Bank v. Dojap Investments [1993] A.C. 573; [1993] 2 W.L.R. 702, PC 4–015

World Transport Agency Ltd v. Royte (England) Ltd [1957] 1 Lloyd's Rep. 381, QBD 27–027

Worldwide Carriers Ltd v. Ardtran International Ltd [1983] 1 All E.R. 692; [1983] 1 Lloyd's Rep. 61; [1982] Com. L.R. 217, QBD 18–010

WT Lamb & Sons v. Goring Brick Co [1932] 1 K.B. 710 27–002

X AG v. Bank, A [1983] 2 All E.R. 464; [1983] 2 Lloyd's Rep. 535; [1983] Com. L.R.
    134; (1983) 133 N.L.J. 400, QBD 21–022
X v. Y and Y Establishment [1990] 1 Q.B. 220; [1989] 3 W.L.R. 910; [1989] 3 All E.R.
    689; [1989] 2 Lloyd's Rep. 561; (1989) 133 S.J. 945, QBD 22–030
Xing Su Hai, The. *See* Qingdao Ocean Shipping Co v. Grace Shipping Establishment
    Transatlantic Schiffahrtskontor GmbH.

Yangtsza Insurance Association v. Lukmanjee [1918] A.C. 585; 87 L.J.PC 111; 118 L.T.
    736; 34 T.L.R. 320; 14 Asp.M.L.C. 296, PC 2–042
Yasuda Fire & Marine Insurance Co of Europe Ltd v. Orion Marine Insurance Underwrit-
    ing Agency [1995] Q.B. 174; [1995] 2 W.L.R. 49; [1995] 3 All E.R. 211; [1995]
    1 Lloyd's Rep. 525, Ch D 27–003
Yasuda Fire & Marine Insurance Co of Europe Ltd v. Orion Marine Insurance Underwrit-
    ing Agency [1995] Q.B. 174; [1995] 2 W.L.R. 49; [1995] 3 All E.R. 211; [1995]
    1 Lloyd's Rep. 525, Ch D 27–011
Yelo v. SM Machado & Co Ltd [1952] 1 Lloyd's Rep. 183 .... 4–012, 15–025
Yeoman Credit v. Latter [1961] 1 W.L.R. 828; [1961] 2 All E.R. 294; 105 S.J. 300,
    CA 12–001
Yukong Line Ltd of Korea v. Rendsburg Investments Corp of Liberia (The Rialto) (No.2)
    [1998] 1 W.L.R. 294; [1998] 4 All E.R. 82; [1998] 1 Lloyd's Rep. 322; [1998] 2
    B.C.L.C. 485; [1998] B.C.C. 870; (1997) 94(39) L.S.G. 39; (1997) 141 S.J.L.B.
    212, QBD (Comm Ct) 27–005

Z Ltd v. A-Z and AA-LL [1982] Q.B. 558; [1982] 2 W.L.R. 288; [1982] 1 All E.R. 556;
    [1982] 1 Lloyd's Rep. 240; [1982] E.C.C. 362; 126 S.J. 100, CA 11–006
Zambia Steel & Building Supplies Ltd v. James Clark & Eaton Ltd [1986] 2 Lloyd's Rep.
    225, CA 23–011
Zimmerman (S) & Son (Merchants) Ltd v. Baxter, Hoare & Co Ltd [1965] 1 Lloyd's Rep.
    88, QBD 27–027
Zuhal K, The and Selin, The [1987] 1 Lloyd's Rep. 151; [1987] 1 F.T.L.R. 76, QBD (Adm
    Ct) 12–001

TABLE OF EUROPEAN CASES

ACEC/Berliet [1968] O.J. L201/7; [1968] C.M.L.R. D35 29–014
Abdoulaye v. Régie Nationale des Usines Renault SA, *The Times*, October 20, 1999 28–024
Agreement of Johs Rieckermann KG and AEG Elotherm GmbH, Re [1968] C.M.L.R.
  D78 29–004
Agreement of the Davidson Rubber Co, Re (No. 72/237/EEC) [1972] C.M.L.R. D52;
  [1972] F.S.R. 451, EC Commission 29–004, 29–014
Ahlstrom Osakeyhtio v. EC Commission (Case C89/85) [1988] E.C.R. 5193; [1988] 4
  C.M.L.R. 901, ECJ 29–004, 29–006
Air Canada v. United Kingdom (Case A/316) (App. No. 18465/91) (1995) 20 E.H.R.R.
  150, ECHR 26–030
AKZO Chemie BV and AKZO Chemie UK v. EC Commission (Case C53/85) [1987] 1
  C.M.L.R. 231; [1987] F.S.R. 203, ECJ 29–019
Arcado Sprl v. Haviland SA (Case 9/87) [1988] E.C.R. 1539; [1989] E.C.C. 1, ECJ 21–006,
                                                                                    22–018
Argyll Group Plc v. Distillers Co 1987 S.L.T. 514; [1986] 1 C.M.L.R. 764 29–018

BASF Lacke Farben / Accinauto SA (Case 95/477) [1995] O.J. L272/16 29–005
Beguelin Import Co v. Import Export SA GL (Case C22/71) [1971] E.C.R. 949; [1972]
  C.M.L.R. 81, ECJ 29–006
Belgische Radio & TV v. SABAM (Case C127/73) [1974] E.C.R. 313; [1974] 2 C.M.L.R.
  238, ECJ 29–002
Benincasa v. Dentalkit Srl (Case C269/95) [1998] All E.R. (E.C.) 135; [1997] E.T.M.R.
  447; [1997] I.L.Pr. 559, ECJ 22–016, 22–023
Bier v. Mines de Potasse D'Alsace. (Case C21/76). *See* Handelswekerij GJ Bier BV and
  Stichtung Reinwater (The Reinwater Foundation) v. Mines de Potasse D'Alsace SA.
Blanckaert and Willems PVBA v. Trost (Case C139/80) [1981] E.C.R. 819; [1982] 2
  C.M.L.R. 1, ECJ 22–021, 27–002
Bosch (Robert) GmbH v. Kleding Verkoopbedrijf de Geus en Uitden bogerd (Case C13/
  61) [1962] C.M.L.R. 1, ECJ 29–004
Brasserie de Haecht v. Wilkin (No.2) (Case C48/72) [1973] E.C.R. 77; [1973] C.M.L.R.
  287, ECJ 29–002
Brenner v. Dean Witter Reynolds Inc (Case C318/93) [1995] All E.R. (E.C.) 278; [1994]
  I.L.Pr. 720; [1994] E.C.R. I–4275, ECJ 22–023
British American Tobacco Co Ltd v. Commission of the European Communities (Case
  C142/84) (No.2) [1988] 4 C.M.L.R. 24 .... 29–004, 29–018
British Leyland Plc v. EC Commission (Case C226/84) [1987] R.T.R. 136; [1987] 1
  C.M.L.R. 185, ECJ 29–018
BRT v. SABAM (Case C127/73). *See* Belgische Radio & TV v. SABAM.
Bulk Oil (Zug) AG v. Sun International Ltd and Sun Oil Trading Co (Case C174/84)
  [1986] 2 All E.R. 744; [1986] E.C.R. 559; [1986] 2 C.M.L.R. 732 29–004
Bulloch (A) & Co v. Distillers Co Ltd [1978] 1 C.M.L.R. 400; [1978] F.S.R. 344 29–005
Bureau National Interprofessionel du Cognac (BNIC) v. Clair (Case C123/83) [1985]
  E.C.R. 391; [1985] 2 C.M.L.R. 430, ECJ 29–004

Centrafarm BV v. Sterling Drug Inc; Same v. Winthrop BV (Case C15 and 16/74) [1974]
  E.C.R. 1183; [1974] E.C.R. 1147; [1974] 2 C.M.L.R. 480; [1975] F.S.R. 161, ECJ ... 29–005
Charles Jourdan [1989] O.J. L35/31; [1989] 4 C.M.L.R. 591 30–017
Christiani and Nielson, Re [1969] O.J. L165/72; [1969] C.M.L.R. D36; [1970] C.M.L.R.
  D19 29–006
COBELPA. *See* Vereeniging Van Nederlandsche Papierfabrikanten (VNP) and the Associ-
  ation des Fabricants de Pates Papiers et Cartons de Belgique (COBELPA), Re
Commercial Solvents Corp v. Commission of the European Communities (Case C6/74 and
  C7/74) [1974] E.C.R. 223; [1974] 1 C.M.L.R. 309, ECJ 28–008, 28–009,
                                                                                    29–006, 29–018
Commission of the European Communities v. United Kingdon (Case C300/95) [1997] All
  E.R. (E.C.) 481, ECJ 8–007

Community, The v. Comptoir Commercial D'Importation (Case C82/53) [1982] 1
  C.M.L.R. 440 29–019
Computerland Europe SA Franchise Agreements, Re (Case IV/32.034) [1987] O.J. L222/
  12; [1989] 4 C.M.L.R. 259; [1989] 1 F.S.R. 397 30–017
Conegate Ltd v. Commissioners of Customs and Excise (Case 121/85) [1986] E.C.R.
  1007 26–030
Consten SA and Grundig Verkaufs GmbH v. Commission of the European Communities
  (Case C56/64) [1966] C.M.L.R. 418, ECJ 29–004, 29–005
Cooperatieve Vereniging Suiker Unie UA v. EC Commission (Case C40/73) [1975] E.C.R.
  1663; [1976] 1 C.M.L.R. 295; [1976] F.S.R. 443, ECJ 29–011
Custom Made Commercial Ltd v. Stawa Metallbau GmbH (Case C288/92) [1994] I.L.Pr.
  516; [1994] E.C.R. I–2913, ECJ 22–018

Daily Mail case. *See* R. v, HM Treasury and Customs and Excise Commissioners, *ex p.*
  Daily Mail and General Trust (C81/87).
Danvaern Production A/S v. Schuhfabriken Otterbeck GmbH & Co (Case C341/93) [1995]
  I.L.Pr. 649; [1995] E.C.R. I–2053, ECJ 22–022
Davidson Rubber Co, Re. *See* Agreement of the Davidson Rubber Co, Re.
De Bloos Sprl v. Etablissements Bouyer SA. *See* Etablissements A De Bloos Sprl v. Etab-
  lissements Bouyer SA.
De Haan Beheer B.V. v. Inspecteor der Invoerrechten en Accijnzen et Rotterdam (Case
  C61/98 [1999] All E.R. (E.C.) 803 26–020
Defrenne v. SABENA (Case C43/75) [1981] 1 All E.R. 122; [1976] E.C.R. 455; [1976] 2
  C.M.L.R. 98; [1976] I.C.R. 547, ECJ 28–024
Denilauler v. SNC Couchet Freres (Case C125/79) [1981] E.C.R. 1553; [1981] 1 C.M.L.R.
  62, ECJ 24–002
Deutsche Grammophon Gesellschaft mbH v. Metro SB Grossmarkte GmbH & Co KG
  (Case C78/70) [1971] C.M.L.R. 631 29–004
Develop DR Eisbein GmbH & Co v. Hauptzollamt Stuttgart-West (Case C35/93) [1994]
  E.C.R. I–2655, ECJ 26–016
Distillers case. *See* A Bulloch & Co v. Distillers Co Ltd.
Distillers Co Ltd v. Commission of the European Communities (Case C30/78) [1980]
  E.C.R. 2229; [1980] 3 C.M.L.R. 121; [1980] F.S.R. 589, ECJ 29–008
Distillers Co Ltd v. EC Commission (Case C30/78) [1980] E.C.R. 2229; [1980] 3 C.M.L.R.
  121; [1980] F.S.R. 589, ECJ 29–004
Drouot Assurances SA v. Consolidated Metallurgical Industries (CMI Industrial Sites)
  (Case C351/96) [1999] Q.B. 497; [1999] 2 W.L.R. 163; [1998] All E.R. (E.C.) 483;
  [1998] C.L.C. 1270; [1998] I.L.Pr. 485, ECJ 22–027
Dumez France SA v. Hessische Landesbank (Case C228/88) [1990] I.L.Pr. 299; [1990]
  E.C.R. 49, ECJ 22–020
Dunlop Slazenger International v. Commission (Case T43/92) [1994] E.C.R. II–441 29–004

Eco Swiss China Time Ltd v. Benetton International NV (Case C126/97) [1999] 2 All E.R.
  (Comm) 44, ECJ 21–027, 24–003, 24–019, 29–002
ECS/AKZO (No. 2) [1985] O.J. L374/1; [1986] 3 C.M.L.R. 273 29–018
Effer SpA v. Hans-Joachim Kantner (Case C38/81) [1982] E.C.R. 825; [1984] 2 C.M.L.R.
  667, ECJ 22–018
Eirpage [1991] O.J. L306/22 29–011
Elefanten Schuh GmbH v. Jacqmain (Case C150/80) [1981] E.C.R. 1671; [1982] 3
  C.M.L.R. 1, ECJ 22–016
Etablissements A De Bloos Sprl v. Etablissements Bouyer SA (Case C14/76) [1976] E.C.R.
  1497; [1977] 1 C.M.L.R. 60, ECJ 22–018, 22–021
Etablissements Somafer SA v. Saar-Ferngas AG (Case C33/78) [1978] E.C.R. 2183; [1979]
  1 C.M.L.R. 490, ECJ 28–003, 22–021
Eurim Pharm GmbH v. Johnson & Johnson Inc [1981] 2 C.M.L.R. 287, EC Commission 29–006
Eurofina, Re [1973] C.M.L.R. (R.P.) 217, EC Commission 29–018
European Music Satellite Venture, Re [1984] 3 C.M.L.R. 162, EC Commission 29–014
Europemballage Corp and Continental Can Co Inc v. EC Commission [1973] E.C.R. 215;
  [1973] C.M.L.R. 199, ECJ 29–018

Fatty Acids, Re [1987] O.J. L3/17; [1989] 4 C.M.L.R. 445 29–004

Ford Werke AG and Ford of Europe Inc v. EC Commission (Bureau Européen des Unions Consommateurs intervening) (Case C25/84) [1985] E.C.R. 2725; [1985] 3 C.M.L.R. 528, ECJ 29–004

Grossfillex-Fillistorf [1964] C.M.L.R. 237 29–008
Gubisch Maschinenfabrik KG v. Palumbo (Case 144/86) [1989] E.C.C. 420; [1987] E.C.R. 4861, ECJ 22–027, 24–003

Handelswekerij GJ Bier BV and Stichting Reinwater (The Reinwater Foundation) v. Mines de Potasse D'Alsace SA (Case C21/76) [1978] Q.B. 708; [1977] 3 W.L.R. 479; [1976] E.C.R. 1735; [1977] 1 C.M.L.R. 284; 121 S.J. 677; (1977) 121 S.J. 677, ECJ 22–020
Hasselblad (GB) Ltd v. EC Commission (Case C86/82 R) [1984] E.C.R. 883; [1984] 1 C.M.L.R. 559; [1984] F.S.R. 321, ECJ 29–004
Hauptzollamt Bielefeld v. Offene Handelsgesellschaft in Firma HC König (Case 185/73) [1974] E.CR. 607, ECJ 26–016
Hendrikman v. Magenta Druck & Verlag GmbH (Case C78/95) [1997] Q.B. 426; [1997] 2 W.L.R. 349; [1996] All E.R. (E.C.) 944; [1996] I.L.Pr. 752; *The Times*, October 17, 1996, ECJ (5th Chamber) 24–003
Henkel/Colgate [1982] O.J. L14/14; [1981] C.M.L.R. D31 29–014
Hoechst AG v. EC Commission (Case 46/87 and 227/88) [1989] E.C.R. 2859; [1991] 4 C.M.L.R. 410, ECJ 29–019
Hoefner v. Macrotron GmbH (Case C41/90) [1991] E.C.R. I–1979; [1993] 4 C.M.L.R. 306; (1991) 135 S.J.L.B. 54; [1991] E.C.R. 1979, ECJ 29–004
Hoffmann La Roche & Co AG v. EC Commission (Case C85/76) [1979] E.C.R. 461; [1979] 3 C.M.L.R. 211; [1980] F.S.R. 13, ECJ 29–018
Hoffman v. Krieg (Case C145/86) [1988] E.C.R. 645; [1990] I.L.Pr. 4, *The Times*, March 26, 1988, ECJ 24–003
Hugin Kassaregister AB and Hugin Cash Registers v. Commission (Case C22/78) [1979] E.C.R. 1869; [1979] 3 C.M.L.R. 345, ECJ 29–018

IAZ International Belgium SA v. Commission of the European Communities (Case C96/82) [1984] 3 C.M.L.R. 276, ECJ 29–006
ICI Plc v. Colmer (Inspector of Taxes) (Case C264/96) [1999] 1 W.L.R. 108; [1998] All E.R. (E.C.) 585; [1998] 3 C.M.L.R. 293; [1998] C.E.C. 861; [1998] B.T.C. 304; [1998] S.T.C. 874, ECJ 28–001, 28–009
ICI v. Commission. *See* Imperial Chemical Industries v. E.C. Commission (Case C48/69).
Imperial Chemical Industries plc v. Colmer (Inspector of Taxes). *See* ICI Plc v. Colmer (Inspector of Taxes) (Case C264/96).
Imperial Chemical Industries v. E.C. Commission (Case C48/69) [1972] C.M.L.R. 557, ECJ 29–004, 29–006
Industrie Tessili Italiana Como v. Dunlop AG (Case C12/76) [1976] E.C.R. 1473; [1977] 1 C.M.L.R. 26, ECJ 22–018
Ioannis Theodorakis Viomikhania Eleou AE v. Greece (Case C109/86) [1989] 2 C.M.L.R. 166, ECJ 6–006
Isabelle Lancray SA v. Peters und Sickert KG (Case C305/88) [1991] I.L.Pr. 99; [1990] E.C.R. I–2725, ECJ 24–003
Iveco Fiat SpA v. Van Hool SA (Case C313/85) [1988] 1 C.M.L.R. 57, ECJ 22–016
Ivenel v. Schwab (Case C133/81) [1982] E.C.R. 1891; [1983] 1 C.M.L.R. 538, ECJ 22–019

Jakob Handte & Co GmbH v. Societe Traitments Mecano-Chimiques des Surfaces (TMCS) (Case C26/91) 10063[1993] I.L.Pr. 5; [1992] E.C.R. I–3967, ECJ 21–006
Jakob Handte & Co GmbH v. Societe Traitments Mecano-Chimiques des Surfaces (TMCS) (Case C26/91) [1993] I.L.Pr. 5, ECJ 22–018

Kalfelis v. Bankhaus Schroder, Munchmeyer, Hengst & Co (Case 189/87) [1988] E.C.R. 5565; [1989] E.C.C. 407, ECJ 22–018, 22–020
Kodak, Re [1970] L147/24; [1970] C.M.L.R. D19 29–005
Kongress Agentur Hagen GmbH v. Zeehaghe BV (Case C365/88) [1990] E.C.R. I–1845; [1991] I.L.Pr. 3, ECJ 22–022
Kraus v. Land Baden-Wurttemberg (Case C19/92) [1993] E.C.R. I–1663; *The Times*, April 6, 1993; *Financial Times*, April 20, 1993, ECJ 28–024

Lancray SA v. Peters und Sickert KG. *See* Isabelle Lancray SA v. Peters und Sickert KG (Case C305/88).
Leathertex Divisione Sintetica SpA v. Bodetex BVBA, *The Times*, October 26, 1999 22–018
Liptons Cash Registers and Business Equipment v. Hugin Kassaregister AB and Hugin Cash Registers (Case 78/68/EEC) [1978] 1 C.M.L.R. D19; [1978] F.S.R. 341 29–018
Lloyd's Register of Shipping v. Societe Campenon Bernard (Case C439/93) [1995] All E.R. (E.C.) 531; [1995] I.L.Pr. 457, ECJ 22–021
LTU v. Eurocontrol (Case C29/76). *See* Lufttransportunternehmen GmbH & Co KG v. Organisation Europeenne pour la Securite de la Navigation Aerienne (Eurocontrol).
Lufttransportunternehmen GmbH & Co KG v. Organisation Europeenne pour la Securite de la Navigation Aerienne (Eurocontrol) (C29/76) [1976] E.C.R. 1541; [1977] 1 C.M.L.R. 88, ECJ 21–005, 22–014

Maciej Rataj, The (Case C406/92). *See* Owners of Cargo Lately Laden on Board the Tatry v. Owners of the Maciej Rataj (The Maciej Rataj); *sub nom.* Owners of Cargo Lately Laden on Board the Tatry v. Owners of the Tatry.
Mainschiffahrts Genossenschaft eG (MSG) v. Les Gravieres Rhenanes Sarl (Case C106/95) [1997] Q.B. 731; [1997] 3 W.L.R. 179; [1997] All E.R. (E.C.) 385; [1997] I.L.Pr. 411, ECJ 22–016
Marc Rich & Co AG v. Societa Italiana Impianti pA (The Atlantic Emperor) (Case C190/89) [1992] 1 Lloyd's Rep. 342; [1991] I.L.Pr. 524; [1991] E.C.R. I–3855, ECJ ....
.... 22–014, 24–018
Marinari v. Lloyds Bank Plc (Case C364/93) [1996] Q.B. 217; [1996] 2 W.L.R. 159; [1996] All E.R. (E.C.) 84; [1996] 5 Bank. L.R. 84; [1996] C.E.C. 14; [1995] I.L.Pr. 737, ECJ 22–020
Meeth v. Glacetal Sarl (Case C23/78) [1978] E.C.R. 2133; [1979] 1 C.M.L.R. 520, ECJ 22–016
Minalmet GmbH v. Brandeis (Case C123/91) [1993] I.L.Pr. 132, ECJ (4th Chamber) 24–003
Ministero delle Finanze v. Esercizio Magazzini Generalli SpA (Case C186 and 187/82) [1984] 3 C.M.L.R. 217, ECJ 26–011
Mulder v. Council of Ministers and Commission of the European Communities (Case C104/89) [1992] E.C.R. I–3061; *Financial Times*, May 27, 1992, ECJ 26–029

Nederlandsche Banden-Industrie Michelin NV v. EC Commission (Case C322/81) [1985] 1 C.M.L.R. 282; [1985] F.S.R. 250, ECJ 29–018
Net Book Agreement [1989] 4 C.M.L.R. 87 29–008
Nugesser KG (LG) and Kurt Eisele v. EC Commision (Case C258/78) [1981] E.C.R. 45; [1983] Com. L.R. 64; [1983] 1 C.M.L.R. 278; [1983] F.S.R. 309 29–004

Omage, Re [1970] O.J. L242/22; [1970] C.M.L.R. D49 29–005
Overseas Union Insurance Ltd v. New Hampshire Insurance Co (Case C351/89) [1992] Q.B. 434; [1992] 2 W.L.R. 586; [1992] 2 All E.R. 138; [1992] 1 Lloyd's Rep. 204; [1991] I.L.Pr. 495, ECJ 22–027
Owens Bank Ltd v. Bracco (No.3) (Case 129/92) [1994] Q.B. 509; [1994] 2 W.L.R. 759, ECJ (6th Chamber) 24–002
Owners of Cargo Lately Laden on Board the Tatry v. Owners of the Maciej Rataj (The Maciej Rataj); *sub nom.* Owners of Cargo Lately Laden on Board the Tatry v. Owners of the Tatry (Case C406/92) [1999] Q.B. 515; [1999] 2 W.L.R. 181; [1995] All E.R. (E.C.) 229; [1995] 1 Lloyd's Rep. 302; [1995] I.L.Pr. 81; [1994] E.C.R. 5439; [1995] All E.R. (EC) 229, ECJ 22–027, 22–033

Partenreederei MS Tilly Russ v. Haven & Vervoerbedrijf Nova NV (The Tilly Russ) (Case 25/76) [1984] E.C.R. 2471, ECJ 22–016
Patrick v. Minister of Cultural Affairs (Case C11/77) [1977] E.C.R. 1199; [1977] 2 C.M.L.R. 523, ECJ 28–024
Pioneer Hi-Fi Equipment, Re [1980] 1 C.M.L.R. 457; [1968] F.S.R. 334 29–004
Pittsburgh Corning Europe, Re [1973] C.M.L.R. D.2 and D7–8, EC Commission 27–016, 9–006, 29–011
Polypropylene, Re [1986] O.J. L230/1; [1988] 4 C.M.L.R. 347
Pronuptia de Paris GmbH v. Prounptia de Paris Irmgard Schillgalis (Case C161/84) [1986] E.C.R. 353; [1986] 1 C.M.L.R. 414, ECJ 29–004, 29–016, 30–017

R. v. HM Treasury and Customs and Excise Commissioners, *ex p.* Daily Mail and General
Trust (Case C81/87) [1989] Q.B. 446; [1989] 2 W.L.R. 908; [1989] 1 All E.R. 328;
[1988] E.C.R. 5483; [1989] B.C.L.C. 206; [1988] 3 C.M.L.R. 713; [1988] S.T.C. 787;
(1989) 133 S.J. 693, ECJ 28–001, 28–024
R. v. Henn (Maurice Donald) (No.2) (Case C34/79) [1981] A.C. 850; [1980] 2 W.L.R.
597; [1980] 2 All E.R. 166; [1979] E.C.R. 3795; (1980) 71 Cr. App. R. 44; [1980] 1
C.M.L.R. 246, ECJ 26–030
R. v. HM Treasury, *ex p.* Centro-Com Srl (Case C124/95) [1997] Q.B. 683; [1997] 3
W.L.R. 239; [1997] All E.R. (E.C.) 193; [1997] 1 C.M.L.R. 555, ECJ 26–029
R. v. Ministry of Agriculture, Fisheries and Food *ex p.* Hedley Lomas (Ireland) Ltd (Case
C5/94) [1996] E.C.R. I-2553 26–030
R. v. Royal Pharmaceutical Society of Great Britain, *ex p.* Association of Pharmaceutical
Importers (Case C266/87) [1990] 1 Q.B. 534; [1990] 2 W.L.R. 445; [1989] 2 All E.R.
758; [1989] E.C.R. 1295; [1989] 2 C.M.L.R. 751; [1990] 2 Med. L.R. 89; (1990)
87(9) L.S.G. 44; (1990) 134 S.J. 933, ECJ 29–005
RPS Prodotti Siderurgici Srl v. Owners of The Sea Maas (The Sea Maas) [1999] 1
All E.R. (Comm) 945; [1999] 2 Lloyd's Rep. 281; [1999] C.L.C. 1336, QBD (Adm
Ct) 22–018
Raimondo v. Italy (Case A/281–A) (1994) 18 E.H.R.R. 237, ECHR 26–030
Reunion Europeeanne SA v. Spliethoffs Bevrachtingskantoor BV (Case C51/97) [1999]
C.L.C. 282; [1999] I.L.Pr. 205, ECJ 22–020, 22–022
Reyners v. Belgium (Case C2/74) [1974] E.C.R. 631; [1974] 2 C.M.L.R. 305, ECJ 28–024
Rieckermann/AEG Elotherm. *See* Agreement of Johs Rieckermann KG and AEG Elotherm
GmbH, Re.
Rockwell International Corp and Iveco Industrial Vehicles Corp BV Agreements, Re (Case
83/390/EEC) [1983] 3 C.M.L.R. 709; [1984] F.S.R. 145 29–004
Rudolf Anterist v. Crédit Lyonnais (Case C22/85) [1986] E.C.R. 1951; [1987] 1 C.M.L.R.
333, ECJ 22–016
Rutili (Roland), Gennevilliers (France) v. Ministry of the Interior of the France (Case C36/
75) [1975] E.C.R. 1219; [1976] 1 C.M.L.R. 140, ECJ 28–024
Rutten v. Cross Medical Ltd (Case C383/95) [1997] All E.R. (E.C.) 121; [1997] I.L.Pr. 199;
[1997] I.C.R. 715; [1997] I.R.L.R. 249, ECJ 22–019, 28–022

Sar Schotte GmbH v. Parfums Rothschild Sarl (Case 218/86) [1989] E.C.C. 431, ECJ 22–021
Segers v. Bestuur van de Bedrijfsvereniging voor Bank-en Verzekeringswezen, Groothan-
del en Vrije Beroepen (Case C79/85) [1987] 2 C.M.L.R. 247, ECJ 28–001
Shenavai v. Kreischer (C266/85) [1987] E.C.R. 239; [1987] 3 C.M.L.R. 782, ECJ 22–018
Shevill v. Presse Alliance SA (Case C68/93) [1995] 2 A.C. 18; [1995] 2 W.L.R. 499;
[1995] All E.R. (E.C.) 289; [1995] I.L.Pr. 267; [1995] E.M.L.R. 543; [1995] E.C.R.
I–415, ECJ 22–019
Sirena Srl v. Eda Srl (Case C40/70) [1971] E.C.R. 69; [1971] C.M.L.R. 260; [1971] F.S.R.
666, ECJ 29–004
Somafer SA v. Saar-Ferngas AG (Case C33/78). *See* Etablissements Somafer SA v. Saar-
Ferngas AG (C33/78).
Spitzley v. Sommer Exploitation SA (Case C48/84) [1985] E.C.R. 787; [1985] 2 C.M.L.R.
507, ECJ 22–016
Stanton v. Institute National d'Assurances Sociales pour Travailleurs Independants
(INASTI) (Case C143/87) [1988] E.C.R. 3877; [1989] 3 C.M.L.R. 761, ECJ 28–024
Suiker Unie. *See* Cooperatieve Vereniging Suiker Unie UA v. EC Commission (Case C40/
73).

Tax Credits, Re; E.C. Commission v. France (Case C270/83) [1986] E.C.R. 273; [1987] 1
C.M.L.R. 401, ECJ 28–001
Tetra Pak Rausing SA v. EC Commission (No.2) [1992] O.J. L72/1; [1992] 4 C.M.L.R.
551 29–004
Theodorakis v. Hellenic Republic (Case C109/86). *See* Ioannis Theodorakis Viomikhania
Eleou AE v. Greece (C109/86).
Thieffry v. Conseil de l'Ordre des Avocats a la Cour de Paris (Case C71/76) [1978] Q.B.
315; [1977] 3 W.L.R. 453; [1977] E.C.R. 765; [1977] 2 C.M.L.R. 373; 121 S.J. 677,
ECJ 28–024
Transocean Marine Paint Association [1989] 4 C.M.L.R. 84 29–014

United Brands Co v. EC Commission (Banana Market) (Case C27/76) [1978] E.C.R. 207;
[1978] 1 C.M.L.R. 429, ECJ 29–018

Van Binsbergen (JHM) v. Bestuur van de Bedrijfsvereniging Voor de Metaalnijverheid
(Case C33/74) [1974] E.C.R. 1299; [1975] 1 C.M.L.R. 298, ECJ 28–024
Van Duyn v. Home Office (Case C41/74) [1975] Ch. 358; [1975] 2 W.L.R. 760; [1975] 3
All E.R. 190; [1974] E.C.R. 1337; [1975] 1 C.M.L.R. 1; (1974) 119 S.J. 302, ECJ ... 28–024
Van Gend en Loos NV v. EC Commission (Case 98/83 and 230/83) [1984] E.C.R.
3763 27–005
Van Uden Maritime BV (t/a Van Uden Africa Line) v. Kommanditgesellschaft in Firma
Deco-Line (Case C391/95) [1999] 2 W.L.R. 1181; [1999] All E.R. (E.C.) 258; [1999]
1 All E.R. (Comm.) 385; [1999] I.L.Pr. 73, ECJ 22–014
Van Zuylen Freres SA v. HAG AG (Case C192/73) [1974] E.C.R. 731; [1974] 2 C.M.L.R.
127; [1974] F.S.R. 511, ECJ 29–004
Verband der Sachversicherer eV v. EC Commission (Case C45/85) [1988] 4 C.M.L.R.
264; [1988] F.S.R. 383; [1987] E.L.R. 265 29–004
Vereeniging van Cement Handelaren v. EC Commission [1973] C.M.L.R. 7, ECJ 29–004
Vereeniging Van Nederlandsche Papierfabrikanten (VNP) and the Association des Fab-
ricants de Pates Papiers et Cartons de Belgique (COBELPA), Re [1977] 2 C.M.L.R.
D28; [1978] F.S.R. 298 29–004
Viho Europe BV v. Commission of the European Communities (Case C73/95 P) [1997]
All E.R. (E.C.) 163; [1997] 4 C.M.L.R. 419; [1997] I.C.R. 130; (1997) 16 Tr. L.R.
59, ECJ 29–006
Völk v. Etablissements Vervaecke SPRL (Case C5/69) [1969] C.M.L.R. 273, ECJ 29–008
Volkswagen AG, Re [1998] O.J. L124/60 29–004

Woodpulp Cartel, Re. *See* Ahlstrom Osakeyhtio v. EC Commission (Case C89/85).

Yves Rocher (Case 87/100) [1987] O.J. L8/49; [1987] 4 C.M.L.R. 592 30–017

Zelger v. Salinitri (Case C56/79) [1980] E.C.R. 89; [1980] 2 C.M.L.R. 635, ECJ 22–016
Zelger v. Salinitri (No. 2) (Case C129/83) [1984] E.C.R. 2397; [1985] 3 C.M.L.R. 366,
ECJ 22–027
Zinc Cartel Producers Group [1984] O.J. L220/27; [1985] 2 C.M.L.R. 108 29–008
Zoja case. *See* Commercial Solvents Corp v. Commission of the European Communities
(Case C6/74 and C7/74).

TABLE OF STATUTES

1677 Statute of Frauds (29 Car. 2, c.
      3) 33–011
      s. 4 28–016
1845 Gaming Act (8 & 9 Vict., c.
      109)
      s. 18 19–014
1855 Bills of Lading Act (18 & 19
      Vict., c. 111) 4–005,
                              5–038, 15–052
      s. 1 15–052
1856 Mercantile Law Amendment
      Act (19 & 20 Vict., c.
      97)
      s. 3 12–001
1870 Extradition Act (33 & 34 Vict.,
      c. 52) 21–028
1873 Extradition Act (36 & 37 Vict.,
      c. 60) 21–028
1875 Explosives Act (38 & 39 Vict.,
      c. 17) 26–015
1876 Customs Consolidation Act
      (39 & 40., c. 36)
      s. 186 26–031
1882 Bills of Exchange Act (45 & 46
      Vict., c. 61) 9–004,
                              9–005, 9–007
      s. 2 9–004
      s. 3 .... 9–004, 9–012
          (4)(b) 9–008
      s. 4 9–005
          (2) 9–005
      s. 5 9–004
      s. 9(1) 9–007
          (a) 9–007
          (d) 9–007
      ss. 10, 11 9–004
      s. 10(1) 9–004
      s. 14(1) 9–004
      s. 17 9–004
      s. 19(2)(c) 9–004
      s. 23 9–004
      s. 26(1), (2) 9–004
      s. 29(1) 9–004
          (3) 9–004
      s. 30(2) 9–004
      s. 31 9–004
      s. 38(2) 9–004
      s. 39(1) 9–004
      s. 44 9–004
      s. 45(3) 9–004
      s. 49 9–009
          (6) 9–004
      s. 51 .... 9–005, 9–009, 10–003
      s. 52(4) 9–004
      s. 55 9–004
          (2) 9–004

1882 Bills of Exchange Act—cont.
      s. 56 .... 9–004, 9–009
      s. 57(1)(b) 9–007
      s. 67 9–004
      s. 71(1) 9–010
      s. 72 .... 9–005, 9–007, 9–009
      s. 74b(1) 9–004
      s. 81a(1) 9–004
      s. 93 10–003
1887 Merchandise Marks Act (50 &
      51 Vic., c. 28)
      s. 11 21–028
1889 Factors Act (53 & 53 Vict., c.
      45) 13–002, 27–017
      s. 1(1) 27–017
      s. 2(1) 15–024
      s. 3 15–024
1893 Sale of Goods Act (56 & 57
      Vict., c. 71) 4–010
1895 Extradition Act (c. 33) 21–028
1906 Prevention of Corruption Act
      (c. 34) 27–011
      Extradition Act (c. 15) 21–028
      Marine Insurance Act (6 Edw.
      7, c. 41) 18–010, 19–001,
                              19–004, 19–012,
                              19–014, 19–018
      s. 2 19–010
      s. 4(2) 19–014
      s. 5(1) 19–014
          (2) 19–014
      s. 6 19–014
      s. 7(1) 19–014
          (2) 19–014
      s. 8 19–014
      s. 9(1), (2) 19–014
      ss. 12, 13 19–014
      s. 14 19–015
      s. 15 19–016
      s. 16 2–023
          (3) 19–004, 19–006
      ss. 17, 18 19–012
      s. 18(1)–(3) 19–012
      s. 19 19–012
          (b) 19–012
      s. 20 19–012
          (1)–(5) 19–012
      s. 23(2)–(5) 19–005
      s. 25 19–004
          (2) 19–005
      s. 26(2) 19–014
      s. 27(2), (3) 19–004
      s. 28 19–004
      s. 29 19–006
      s. 32(2) 19–015

1906 Marine Insurance Act—*cont.*
    s. 33 .... 19–006, 19–017
        (3) 19–017
    s. 39 .... 19–005, 19–024
        (5) 19–024
    s. 41 19–017
    s. 50 19–016
    s. 51 19–016
    s. 52 19–015
    s. 53 19–003
        (2) 19–003
    s. 54 19–003
    s. 55(1) 19–030
        (2)(a) 19–023
        (c) 19–024
    s. 57 .... 19–030, 19–033
    s. 60(2)(iii) 19–030
    s. 61 19–030
    s. 62 19–030
        (7) 19–030
    s. 63 19–035
    s. 66(1), (2) 19–025
        (3) 19–028
        (4), (5) 19–029
    ss. 67, 68 19–034
    ss. 71, 72 19–034
    s. 78 19–024
    s. 79 19–035
    s. 84 19–012
        (2)(e) 19–015
        (3)(f) 19–015
1916 Prevention of Corruption Act
    (c. 64) 27–011
1920 Administration of Justice Act
    (10 & 11 Geo. 5, c.
    81) 24–006, 24–007,
                               24–020
    Pt. II 24–006
    s. 9(2) 24–010
        (a) 24–013
        (c) 24–015
        (f) 24–014
    s. 9(3)(a) 24–020
    s. 9(5) 24–020
1924 Carriage of Goods by Sea Act
    (14 & 15 Geo. 5, c.
    22) 2–007, 15–020,
                               17–001
    s. 4 15–021
    Sched. 1, Art. IV(5) 2–007
1925 Law of Property Act (15 & 16
    Geo. 5, c. 20)
    s. 136 .... 11–035, 13–004
1930 Third Parties (Right against
    Insurers) Act (20 & 21
    Geo. 5, 25) 19–030
1932 Extradition Act (c. 30) 21–028
    Carriage by Air Act (22 & 23
    Geo. 5, c. 36) 17–001,
                               17–004
    s. 2(2) 2–027

1933 Foreign Judgments (Reciprocal
    Enforcement) Act (23 &
    24 Geo. 5, c. 13) 24–006,
                     24–007, 24–020
    s. 4(1)(a)(iii) 24–015
        (iv) 24–013
        (v) 24–014
    s. 5(1) 24–010
    s. 10A 24–020
1936 Air Navigation Act (26 Geo.
    5 & 1 Edw. 8, c. 44)
    s. 29 17–004
1939 Import, Export and Customs
    Powers (Defence) Act (c.
    69) 26–003
1943 Law Reform (Frustrated Con-
    tracts) Act (6 & 7 Geo. 6,
    c. 40) 6–016, 21–001, 23–015
    s. 1(1)–(5) 6–016
    s. 2(3) 6–016
        (5) 6–016
    s. 3(2) 6–016
1945 Bretton Woods Agreements
    Act (9 & 10 Geo. 6,
    c. 19) 7–002, 21–029
    Law Reform (Contributory
    Negligence) Act (8 & 9
    Geo. 6, c. 28) 8–007
1946 United Nations Act (c. 45) 26–003
1947 Exchange Control Act (10 & 11
    Geo. 6, c. 14) 26–002
    Trade Act 26–010
1950 Arbitration Act (14 Geo. 6, c.
    27) 23–010, 23–012
    s. 13A 23–004
    s. 20 23–005
    s. 36(1) 24–018
1952 Customs and Excise Act (15 &
    16 Geo. 6 & 1 Eliz. 2, c.
    44)
    s. 56(2) 26–030
1953 Merchandise Marks Act (1 & 2
    Eliz. 2, c. 48)
    s. 11 21–028
1954 Law Reform (Enforcement of
    Contracts) Act (2 & 3
    Eliz. 2, c. 34) 27–016
1959 Obscene Publications Act (c.
    66) 26–030
    Finance Act (7 & 8 Eliz. 2, c.
    58)
    s. 30(5) 19–005
1962 Carriage by Air (Sup-
    plementary Provisions)
    Act (10 & 11 Eliz. 2, c.
    44) 17–001
    s. 4 17–006
1961 Carriage by Air Act (9 & 10
    Eliz. 2, c. 27) 17–001, 17–004
    s. 1 17–009
    s. 10 17–001
    Sched. 1 17–009

1965 Carriage of Goods by Road Act
(c. 37) 18–001, 18–006, 27–025
s. 2 18–006
s. 6 18–006
s. 7 18–006
s. 9 18–001
s. 13 18–006
Sched. 1, Art. 23(3) 7–008
Sched. 5 18–001
Nuclear Installations Act (c.
57) 8–004
1966 Arbitration (International
Investment Disputes) Act
(c. 41) 23–027, 28–017
1967 Misrepresentation Act (c. 7)
s. 2 3–002
(1) 27–005
s. 3 23–015
s. 4(2) 5–005
Uniform Laws on International
Sales (c. 45) 3–019, 4–002,
5–001, 21–003, 32–018, 32–023,
32–027
s. 1(1) 32–022
(3) 3–007, 32–019, 32–027
(4) 32–020
Sched. 1 ... 32–018, 32–020, 32–024
Sched. 2 ..... 3–007, 32–018, 32–025
Art. 1 32–019
Art. 7(2) 3–007
Fugitive Offenders Act (c. 68) 21–028
1968 Trade Description Act (c. 29) .. 21–028
s. 32 21–028
Theft Act (c. 60)
s. 15 21–028
Civil Evidence Act (c. 64) 33–011
s. 5 33–011
1969 Nuclear Installations Act (c.
18) 8–004
Post Office Act (c. 48)
s. 29(3) 17–019
s. 33 17–019
1970 Tobacco Products Duty Act (c.
7) 26–012
Finance Act (c. 24)
Sched. 7, para. 1(2)(b) 19–010
Agriculture Act (c. 40)
s. 72 2–027
1971 Carriage of Goods by Sea Act
(c. 19) 2–007, 7–008,
15–003, 15–004, 15–010,
15–020, 15–021, 15–022,
15–027, 15–033, 15–036,
17–001, 21–006, 21–010
s. 1A 15–045
(2) 15–045
s. 1(3) 15–021
(4) 15–022, 15–033
(6)(b) 15–022, 15–033
s. 3 15–041

1971 Banking and Financial
Dealings Act (c. 80)
s. 3(2) 9–004
1972 Civil Evidence Act (c. 30)
s. 4(1), (2) 21–002
Carriage by Railway Act
(repealed) (c. 33) 18–001
European Communities Act (c.
68)
s. 3 21–002
1974 Consumer Credit Act (c. 39) 3–019,
13–012
s. 12 13–012
1975 Arbitration Act (c. 3) 23–010
Evidence (Proceedings in Other
Jurisdiction) Act (c. 34) .. 21–021,
21–022
s. 8(2) 28–017
s. 9(4) 21–022
Sched. 2 28–017
Sex Discrimination Act (c.
65) 28–021
1976 Fatal Accidents Act (c. 30) 8–007
Race Relations Act (c. 74) 28–021
1977 Administration of Justice Act
(c. 38) 28–017
s. 4 28–017
Sched. 5
Unfair Contract Terms Act (c.
50) 3–019, 5–003,
8–003, 17–020,
23–015, 32–016
ss. 2–7 32–020
s. 3 32–016
s. 6(2)(a) 8–003
s. 8 23–015
s. 26 .... 8–003, 32–016,
32–020, 32–023
(1) 5–003
(1), (2) 3–019
(3), (4) 5–003
s. 27(2) 32–020
Sched. 4 32–020
1978 Judicature (Northern Ireland)
(c. 23)
Sched. 5 28–017
Civil Liability (Contribution)
Act (c. 47)
s. 3 27–005
Suppression of Terrorism Act
(c. 26) 21–028
Export Guarantees and Over-
seas Investment Act (c.
18) 20–001
State Immunity Act (c. 33) 21–019
ss. 2–17 21–019
s. 3(1)–(3) 21–019
(3)(a)–(c) 21–019
s. 9 21–019
s. 10 21–019
s. 13(4) 21–019
(2)(a) 21–019

1978 State Immunity Act—*cont.*
    s. 14(2) 21–019
       (4) 21–019
    Bills of Sale Act 10–005
    s. 10, 11 26–024
1979 Customs and Excise Manage-
    ment Act (c. 2) 26–012,
       26–015, 26–018, 26–020
    s. 1 26–012
      (1) 26–020, 26–031
    s. 9 26–029
    s. 52(1) 26–015
    s. 53 26–013
    s. 67(9) 26–031
    s. 68 26–030
      (2) 26–031
    s. 75 26–015
    s. 76 26–015
    ss. 92–100 26–011
    s. 92(4) 26–015
    s. 119 26–023
    s. 123 26–024
    s. 133 26–023
    s. 139 .... 26–030, 26–031
    s. 141(1) 26–030
        (a), (b) 26–030
    s. 144–146 26–031
    s. 152–155 26–031
    s. 154 26–031
    s. 167 26–031
      (1) 26–031
      (3) 26–031
    s. 170 26–011
      (2) 26–031
       (b) 26–031
      (3), (4) 26–030
    Sched. 3 .... 26–030, 26–031
    Sched. 3, paras. 1–4 26–030
    Sched 3, para. 16 26–030
    Sched. 3, para. 16(b) 26–030
    Customs and Excise Duties
    (General Reliefs) Act (c. 3) 26–012
    Alcoholic Duties Act (c. 4) 26–012
    Hydrocarbon Oils Duties Act
    (c. 5) 26–012
    Carriage by Air and Road Act
    (c. 28) .. 17–003, 17–012, 18–001
    s. 4 17–001
      (2) 7–008, 18–009
    s. 5 .... 17–003, 18–009
    Sched. 1 .... 17–001, 17–003
    Sched. 1, Art. 22 7–008
    Sched. 2 17–001
    Arbitration Act (c. 42) . 23–010, 23–019
1979 Customs and Excise Manage-
    ment Act (c. 2)................... 26–010
    Sale of Goods Act (c. 54) 3–019,
      4–002, 4–003, 4–004,
      4–010, 5–001, 5–002,
      5–003, 5–006, 5–014,
      5–015, 5–017, 8–003,
      14–002, 15–052, 18–008,
      21–001, 27–019, 32–024

1979 Sale of Goods Act—*cont.*
    ss. 2–5 14–002
    s. 2(1) 14–002
    s. 7 .... 6–007, 6–016
    s. 8(2) 14–002
    s. 11 14–002
      (2) 5–003
      (4) 5–003, 5–006
    ss. 13–15 5–004
    s. 13 .... 2–042, 7–007
      (1) 5–003, 7–007
      A 5–003
      (2) 5–003
    s. 14(2A) 4–010, 8–003
      (2B) 4–010, 4–012
       (a) 5–003
      (2) 4–010, 5–003,
      7–007, 8–003, 27–005
      (3) 5–003, 27–005
      (5) 27–005
      (6) 5–003
    s. 15 5–003
      A 5–004, 8–003
      (1) 5–004
      (2) 5–004
    s. 15(2) 5–003
      (c) 4–010
    s. 16 2–027
    s. 17(1) 4–004
      (2) 4–006
    s. 19 2–014
      (1) 4–006, 4–007,
      4–008, 9–008
      (2) 4–006
      (3) 4–006, 9–008
    s. 20 2–027
      A 2–014, 4–003,
      4–004, 4–005
      B 4–003, 4–005
    s. 20(1) 4–010
    s. 25(1) 4–009, 5–016
    ss. 27–37 4–003
    s. 30 5–006
      (2A) 5–006
    s. 32 .... 5–005, 5–006
      (1) 2–027, 4–003, 5–016
      (3) 2–008, 2–038
    s. 34 5–005
    s. 35 .... 5–003, 5–005, 5–006
      A 5–003, 5–006
      (1)(a) 5–005, 5–006
       (b) 5–006
      (2) 5–005
      (4) 5–006
      (6)(b) 5–006
    s. 36 5–007
    ss. 38–48 5–014
    s. 38 5–015
      (2) 5–015, 19–014,
      27–015, 27–019, 27–020
    s. 39(1) 5–014
    s. 39(2) 5–013
    s. 41(1)(c) 5–015

1979 Sale of Goods Act—*cont.*
    (2) 5–015
    s. 43 5–015
    s. 44 5–016
    s. 45(1) 5–016
    (3) 5–016
    s. 46(1) 5–016
    s. 47(1) 5 016
    (2) 5–016, 15–024
    s. 48(1) 5–017
    (2) 5–017
    s. 50(3) 11–021
    s. 53(1) 5–003
    (3) 5–003
    s. 55 5–003
    (1) 8–003
    s. 59 5–006
    s. 61 .... 4–003, 5–003
    (1) 8–006
    (4) 5–014
    Sched. 2 32–020
1980 Protection of Trading Interests
    Act (c. 11) 15–016, 21–020,
        21–021, 21–021, 28–008
    s. 1 21–021
    (1) 21–021
    (3) 21–021
    s. 2 21–021
    (2) 21–021
    s. 3 21–021
    s. 4 21–021
    Magistrates' Courts Act (c.
    43)
    Sched. 7 21–021
    Sched. 9 21–021
    Limitation Act (c. 58) 5–001,
        8–007, 21–017
    s. 5 .... 8–003, 15–039,
        15–048
    s. 8 15–039
    s. 11A 8–007
    Overseas Development and Co-
    operation Act (c. 63)
    s. 18(1) 6–002
1981 Supreme Court Act (c. 54) 22–033
    s. 20 22–033
    (m) 16–003
    (2)(g) 22–033
    (h) 22–033
    s. 21 22–033
    (4) 22–033
    s. 37 22–030
    s. 49(3) 22–006
    Sched. 2 6–002
    Sched. 5 28–017
1982 Civil Jurisdiction and Judg-
    ments Act (c. 27) .. 3–017, 8–010,
        21–003, 22–001,
        22–002, 22–012
    s. 3(3) 22–013
    B(1), (2) 22–013
    s. 7 24–004
    s. 25 22–030

1982 Civil Jurisdiction and Judge-
    ments Act—*cont.*
    (1), (2) 22–030, 22–031
    (g) 22–031
    (3) 22–030
    s. 26 22–033
    s. 33(1) 22–016
    s. 35(1) 24–006
    s. 34 22–033
    s. 38 21–024
    ss. 41–46 .... 22–001, 22–002
    s. 41(2) 22–002
    (6)(b) 22–002
    (7) 22–002
    s. 42(1) 22–002
    (3) 22–002
    s. 49 22–028
    Sched. 1 22–001
    Art. 16 22–012
    Art. 17 21–012
    Art. 27(1) 21–026
    Sched. 2, Arts. 2, 3 22–013
    Sched 3C 22–001
    Sched. 3C, Art. 27(1) 21–026
    Sched. 4 .... 22–001, 22–002
    Sched. 8 22–002
    Sched. 10 24–006
    Supply of Goods and Services
    Act (c. 29) 3–019, 8–003, 14–002
    Pt. I 14–002
    s. 4(2) 8–003
    (2A) 8–003
    s. 5A 8–003
    s. 11(1) 8–003
    Merchant Shipping (Liner
    Conferences) Act (c. 37) .. 15–016
    Criminal Justice Act (c. 48)
    s. 37 29–030
1983 International Transport Con-
    ventions Act (c. 14) 18–001
1984 Telecommunications Act (c.
    12) 33–012
    s. 12 33–012
    Foreign Judgments (Reciprocal
    Enforcement) Act (c. 13)
    s. 2 21–023
    Foreign Limitation Periods Act
    (c. 16) 21–017
    s. 1(1), (2) 21–017
    (5) 21–017
    s. 2(1)–(3) 21–017
    s. 3 21–017
    s. 5 21–017
    Police and Criminal Evidence
    Act (c. 60) 33–012
    s. 18 33–012
    s. 66 26–030
    s. 67(9) 26–030
    s. 69(1) 33–011
1985 Companies Act (c. 6) 4–009,
        28–011, 28–018, 33–012
    Pt. VII 28–011
    s. 35(3) 27–008

1985 Companies Act—*cont.*
　　　A(1) 27–008
　　　s. 36C(1) 27–008
　　　s. 82(7) 32–025
　　　s. 221–262A 28–011
　　　s. 227(1) 28–008,
　　　　　　　　　　　　　　　　28–011
　　　　　(2) 28–011
　　　s. 228, 229 28–011
　　　s. 395–399 4–008
　　　s. 395 13–004
　　　s. 396 4–009
　　　　　(1)(c) 10–005
　　　　　(e) 13–005
　　　428–430F 28–019
　　　s. 690A 28–003
　　　s. 691 28–003,
　　　　　　　　　　　　　　　　28–005
　　　　　(1)(b)(ii) 28–005
　　　s. 695 28–005
　　　s. 736A 28–011
　　　　　(1) 28–011
　　　Latent Damage Act (c. 37) 8–007
　　　Insolvency Act (c. 65)
　　　s. 251 4–007
　　　Sched. 10 5–014
　　　Interception of Communica-
　　　　tions Act (c. 56) 33–012
1986 Single European Act 30–001
　　　Financial Services Act (c. 60) . 21–010
　　　s. 172 28–019
　　　Sched. 12 28–019
1987 Banking Act (c. 22) 20–005
　　　Consumer Protection Act 1987
　　　　(c. 43) 3–019, 8–002,
　　　　　　　　8–005, 8–006, 8–007,
　　　　　　　　　　　　8–009, 8–011
　　　Pts. I–V 8–005
　　　s. 1(1) 8–005
　　　　　(2), (3) 8–006
　　　s. 2 8–006
　　　　　(1) 8–006
　　　　　(2) 8–007
　　　　　(4)–(6) 8–006
　　　s. 3 8–006
　　　s. 4 8–007
　　　　　(1) 8–007
　　　　　(e) 8–005, 8–007, 8–008
　　　　　(f) 8–006
　　　　　(2) 8–007
　　　　　(2)(a), (b) 8–007
　　　s. 5 8–007
　　　　　(1)–(4) 8–006
　　　s. 6(4) 8–007
　　　　　(7) 8–006
　　　s. 7 8–006
　　　s. 8 8–005
　　　s. 45 8–005
　　　s. 46 8–006
　　　Sched. 1, para. 1 8–007
1988 Criminal Justice Act (c. 33)
　　　Pt. I 21–028
　　　Consumer Arbitration Agree-
　　　　ments Act (c. 21) 23–010

1988 Copyright, Designs and Patents
　　　Act (c. 48)
　　　s. 92(1) 30–002
1989 Extradition Act (c. 33) 21–028
　　　Law of Property Miscellaneous
　　　　Provisions) Act (c. 34) 12–001
　　　Companies Act (c. 40)
　　　s. 108(1) 27–008, 28–019
　　　s. 130(4) 27–008
1990 Contracts (Applicable Law)
　　　Act (c. 36) 3–017, 11–020,
　　　　　　　　　　　21–004, 21–005
　　　s. 2(2) 21–006, 21–010, 21–011
　　　　　(3) 21–006
　　　s. 3(1) 21–004, 21–005
　　　　　(2) 21–004, 21–005
　　　　　(3)(a) 21–005
　　　　　(b) 21–004
　　　Scheds. 1–3 21–004
　　　Sched. 3, Art. 2(a), (b) 21–005
　　　Sched. 3A 21–004
　　　Courts and Legal Services Act
　　　　(c. 41)
　　　s. 102 23–004
1991 Civil Jurisdiction and Judg-
　　　　ments Act (c. 12) 3–017,
　　　　　　　　　　　　　　　22–001
　　　Foreign Corporations Act (c.
　　　　44) 21–024
　　　Exports and Investment Guar-
　　　　antees Act (c. 67) 20–001
　　　Pt. I 20–001
　　　s. 1 20–001
　　　　　(1), (2) 20–001
　　　　　(4) 20–001
　　　s. 2 20–001
　　　　　(1) 20–001
　　　　　(a), (b) 20–001
　　　s. 3 20–001
　　　　　(2)(a), (b) 20–001
　　　s. 4(3) 20–001
　　　s. 6(1)(a) 20–001
　　　　　(3), (4) 20–001
1992 Finance Act (c. 20)
　　　s. 2 26–023
　　　Cheques Act (c. 32) 9–004
　　　Carriage of Goods by Sea Act
　　　　(c. 50) 2–028, 2–029,
　　　　　　　　　2–030, 4–005, 15–025,
　　　　　　　　15–029, 15–033, 15–036,
　　　　　　　　　　　　15–052, 33–010
　　　s. 1(1) 15–052
　　　　　(2)(a), (b) 15–052
　　　　　(3), (4) 15–052
　　　　　(5) 15–052, 33–010
　　　s. 2 2–029
　　　　　(1) 15–034, 15–052
　　　　　(a) 2–028
　　　　　(c) 2–022
　　　　　(2)(a), (b) 15–052
　　　　　(3)–(5) 15–052
　　　s. 3(1) 15–016, 15–052
　　　　　(c) 15–052

1992 Carriage of Goods by Sea Act—*cont.*
   (2) 15–052
   (3) 2–029, 15–052
   s. 4 15–036
   s. 5(2)(c) 15–052
   (3) 15–052
   (4)(a), (b) 15–052
   s. 6(2), (3) 15–052
1993 Criminal Justice Act (c. 56)
   s. 71 26–029
1994 Finance Act 1994 (c. 9) 26–027
   ss. 14–16 26–027
   Sched. 5 26–027
   Sched. 5, para. 2(1)(r) 26–027
   Value Added Tax Act (c. 23) ..
   Sched. 11, para. 2(3) 26–009
   Sale of Goods (Amendment)
     Act (c.32) 8–003
   Sale and Supply of Goods Act
     (c. 35) 4–010, 5–001,
      5–004, 21–001
1995 Proceeds of Crime Act (c. 11) . 21–028
   Merchant Shipping Act (c. 21)
   s. 85 7–012
   s. 87 .... 7–012, 15–050
   s. 185 15–046
   (4) 15–046
   s. 186(1)(a) 15–046
   (2)(a) 15–046
   (5) 15–046
   s. 314 15–045
   Sched. 7, Pt. I 15–046
   Sched. 7, Pt. II 15–046
   Sched. 7, Pt. II, para. 5 15–046
   Sched. 13, para. 45 15–045
   Shipping and Trading Interests
     (Protection) Act (c. 22)
   ss. 1–4 15–016
   Sale of Goods (Amendment)
     Act (c. 28) 4–003, 5–001,
      15–052, 21–001
   Civil Evidence Act (c. 38) 33–011,
     33–012
   s. 1(1) 33–011
   s. 9 33–011
   s. 13 33–011
   Private International Law
     (Miscellaneous
     Provisions) Act (c. 42) 21–018
   ss. 1, 2 21–018
   s. 3 23–005
   s. 4 21–018
1996 Employment Rights Act (c. 18)
   s. 196 28–022
   Arbitration Act (c. 23) 21–018,
     23–002, 23–003,
     23–005, 23–011,
     23–012, 23–016,
     23–017, 23–019
   Pt. 1 .... 23–007, 23–010
   s. 1 .... 22–004, 23–002
   (a) 23–005
   (b) 23–004, 23–016

1996 Arbitration Act—*cont.*
   (c) 23–003, 23–010,
     23–016, 23–019
   s. 2 23–007
   (3)(a)(b) 23–019
   s. 3 23–007
   s. 5 .... 23–011, 24–018
   (2)(a) 23–011
   s. 6 22–004
   (1) 23–011
   (2) 23–011
   s. 7 .... 23–004, 23–014
   s. 9 .... 22–033, 23–016
   (1) 23–016
   (3) 23–016, 23–017
   (4) 23–016
   s. 11 .... 22–033, 23–016
   (1)(a), (b) 23–016
   s. 12 15–048
   s. 15(1) 23–012
   (2) 23–012
   (3) 23–012
   s. 16(5)(b) 23–012
   s. 17 23–012
   s. 18 .... 23–006, 23–012, 23–019
   (3) 23–006
   s. 20 23–006
   s. 21(4) 23–012
   (b) 23–013
   s. 23(4) 23–003
   s. 24 23–019
   (1)(a) 23–005
   s. 30 .... 23–004, 23–014,
     23–017, 23–019
   (1)(a) 23–004
   (b) 23–004
   (c) 23–004
   s. 31 .... 23–004, 23–019
   (1) 23–019
   (4) 23–017
   s. 32 .... 23–004, 23–011, 23–019
   (2) 23–019
   s. 33 23–019
   (1)(a) 23–005
   s. 34 23–017
   (1) 23–017
   (2)(g) 23–017
   s. 37 23–017
   s. 38(3) 23–005, 23–017
   (4), (5) 23–017
   (4)(a) 23–005
   (6) 23–017
   s. 39 23–017
   s. 41 .... 6–004, 23–017
   (3) 23–004, 23–017,
     23–019
   (4), (6) 23–017
   (7) 23–017
   s. 42 23–019
   s. 43 .... 23–017, 23–019
   s. 44 23–019
   (2)(a)–(e) 23–019
   s. 45 23–019

1996 Arbitration Act—*cont.*
 s. 46 .... 23–007, 23–008
  (1)(a) 23–009
  (b) 23–009
 s. 47 23–017
 s. 48 23–018
  (4), (5) 23–005
 s. 49 .... 21–018, 23–005,
  23–018
 s. 52 23–018
  (3), (4) 23–018
 s. 53 23–018
 s. 55(2) 23–018
 s. 56 23–018
 s. 57 23–019
 s. 58 23–002
 s. 58(2) 23–002
 s. 61(1), (2) 23–018
 s. 66 .... 23–002, 23–018
 ss. 67, 68 .... 23–019, 24–018
 s. 68(2) 23–019
 s. 69 23–019
  (3)(a), (b) 23–019
  (c)(i), (ii) 23–019
  (c) 23–019
  (7) 23–018, 23–019
 s. 70 23–019
  (4) 23–018
 s. 81 23–011
 s. 82 .... 23–017, 23–019
 ss. 85–87 .... 23–010, 23–016
 s. 85 23–016
  (2)(a), (b) 23–016
 s. 86(2)(b) 23–016
 s. 93 23–003
  (2) 23–003
 s. 99 24–018
 s. 101 24–018
  (1), (2) 24–018
 s. 103(2) 24–019
  (3), (4) 24–019
 s. 105 23–019
 Sched. 2, para. 7(5) 23–003

1997 Civil Procedure Act (c. 12)
 s. 7 .... 22–032, 26–031
1998 Finance Act (c. 36)
 s. 12 26–011
 Competition Act (c. 41) 29–020,
  29–024
  Chap. I 29–021, 29–024
  Chap. III 29–023
  s. 4 29–021
  s. 45 29–024
  s. 46(3) 29–024
  s. 60(1) 29–020, 29–024
   (2)(b) 29–024
 Human Rights Act (c. 42)
  s. 19 33–012
1999 Finance Act (c.16) 33–012
  Pt VIII 33–012
  ss. 132–133 33–012
 Youth Justice and Criminal
  Evidence Act (c.23) 33–011
 Employee Relations Act (c.
  26) 28–021
  s. 32 28–022
   (3) 28–022
 Contracts (Rights of Third
  Parties) Act (c. 31) 17–006
  s. 6(5)(b) .. 17–006, 18–005, 18–009
  s. 6(8)(a) 18–005
  s. 6(8)(b) 17–006, 18–009
  s. 6(8)(c) 17–006
2000 Electronic Communications
  (EC) Act (c.46) 33–009,
   33–011, 33–012, 33–013
  s. 1 33–012
  s. 1–6 33–012
  s. 2 33–012
  s. 4 33–012
  s. 7(1) 33–012
  s. 8 33–012
   (1) 33–012
   (3) 33–012
   (6)(a) 33–012
   (7) 33–012

TABLE OF STATUTORY INSTRUMENTS

1946 Bretton Woods Agreements
Order in Council (S.R. &
O. 1946, No. 36) 6–002,
21–027, 21–029
1967 Carriage by Air Acts
(Application of Pro-
visions) Order (S.I. 1967,
No. 480) 17–010
Art. 4 17–010
Sched. 1 ... 17–001, 17–010, 17–019
Sched. 2 .... 17–001, 17–008
Pt. B, Art. 25A 17–006
Carriage of Goods by Road Act
1965 (Commencement)
Order (S.I. 1967, No.
819) 18–001
1972 European Communities
(Enforcement of the Com-
munity Judgments) Order
(S.I. 1972, No. 1590) 24–017
1977 Carriage by Air (Parties to
Convention) Order (S.I.
1977, No. 240) 17–009
Carriage by Air (Parties to
Convention) (Supplemen-
tary) Order (S.I. 1977, No.
1631) 17–009
1978 Carriage by Air (Parties to
Convention) (Supplemen-
tary) Order (S.I. 1978, No.
1058) 17–009
1979 Arbitration (Commodity
Contracts) Order (S.I.
1979, No. 754) 31–011
Carriage by Air Acts
(Application of Prov-
isions) (Second Amend-
ment) Order (S.I. 1979,
No. 931) 17–029
1980 Carriage of Goods by Road
(Parties to the Con-
vention) (Amendment)
Order (S.I. 1980, No.
697) 18–006
Carriage by Air and Road Act
1979 (Commencement
No. 1) Order (S.I. 1980,
No. 1966 C.84) 18–009
1985 Police and Criminal Evidence
Act 1984 (Application to
Customs and Excise) (S.I.
1985, No. 1800) 26–031
Value Added Tax (General)
Regulations (S.I. 1985,
No. 886)
Reg. 45, 46 26–024

1985 Merchant Shipping (Liner
Conferences) Act 1982
(Commencement) Order
(S.I. 1985, No. 182) 15–016
Merchant Shipping (Liner
Conferences) (Conditions
for Recognitions) Regula-
tions (S.I. 1985, No.
405) 15–016
Merchant Shipping (Liner
Conferences) (Mandatory
Provisions) Regulations
(S.I. 1985, No. 406) 15–016
International Transport Con-
ventions Act 1983 (Cer-
tification of Commence-
ment of Convention) Order
(S.I. 1985, No. 612) 18–001
1987 Export of Goods (Control)
Order (S.I. 1987, No.
2070) 26–003, 26–031
1988 Excise Warehousing (Etc.)
Regulations (S.I. 1988,
No. 809) 26–011
Consumer Protection Act 1987
(Commencement No. 3)
Order (S.I. 1988, No.
2076) 8–005
1991 Public Supply Contracts Regu-
lations (S.I. 1991, No.
2679) 3–004
Public Works Contracts Regu-
lations (S.I. 1991, No.
2680) 3–004
Excise Duties (Personal
Reliefs) Order (S.I. 1002,
No. 3155) 26–031
1992 Utilities Supply and Works
Contracts Regulations
(S.I. 1992, No. 3279) 3–004
Export of Goods (Control)
Order (S.I. 1992, No.
3092) 26–003, 26–005
s. 4 26–005
Excise Goods (Holding, Move-
ment, Warehouse and
REDS) Regulations (S.I.
1992, No. 3135) 26–011
1992 Revenue Trades (Accounts and
Records) Regulations (S.I.
1992, No. 3150) 26–011
Overseas Companies and
Credit and Financial Institutions (Branch Dis-
closure) Regulations (S.I.
1992, No. 3179) 28–003

1993 Customs and Excise (Transit) Regulations (S.I. 1993, No. 1353) 26–020
Community Customs Code (Consequential Amendment of References) Regulations (S.I. 1993, No. 3014) 26–020
Commercial Agents (Council Directive) Regulations (S.I. 1993, No. 3053) 27–001, 27–010
Pt. III 27–011
IV 27–012
Reg. 1(2) 27–010
Reg. 2(1) 27–010
(i)–(iii) 27–010
(2)(a)–(c) 27–010
(3), (4) 27–020
Reg. 3 27–011
(1) 27–011
(3) 27–011
Reg. 4 27–012
(1) 27–012
(2)(a)–(c) 27–012
Reg. 5 27–012
(1), (2) 27–011
Regs. 6–12 27–012
(1)–(3) 27–012
Reg. 7 27–012
(1)(a), (b) 27–012
(2) 27–013
Reg. 8(a), (b) 27–012
Reg. 9(1) 27–012
Reg. 10(1)–(4) 27–012
Reg. 11(1)–(3) 27–012
Reg. 12(1)–(4) 27–012
Reg. 13(1), (2) 27–012
Regs. 14–20 27–012
Reg. 14 27–012
Reg. 15(1)–(5) 27–012
Reg. 16 27–012
Reg. 17 27–012
(2)–(9) 27–012
Reg. 18 27–012
Reg. 19 27–012
Reg. 20 27–011
(3) 27–011
Reg. 21 27–012
Reg. 23 27–010
Commercial Agents (Council Directive) (Amendment) Regulations (S.I. 1993, No. 3173) 27–001, 27–010
1994 Return of Culture Objects Regulations (S.I. 1994, No. 501) 26–005
Export of Goods (Control) Order (S.I. 1994, No. 1191) 26–003, 26–004
Art. 3 26–003
Art. 6(1) 26–003
Art. 7(1) 26–003
Art. 51 26–004

1994 International Transport Conventions Act 1983 (Amendment Order) (S.I. 1994, No. 1907) 18–001
1995 Excise Drawback Regulations (S.I. 1995, No. 1046) 26–023
Customs Traders (Accounts and Records) Regulations (S.I. 1995, No. 1203) 26–018
reg. 9 26–018
Sched. 1 26–048
2 26–018
Counterfeit and Pirated Goods (Customs) Regulations (S.I. 1995, No. 1403) 26–031
Counterfeit and Pirated Goods (Consequential Provisions) (S.I. 1995, No. 1447) 26–031
Export and Investment Guarantees (Limitation on Foreign Currency Commitments) Order (S.I. 1995, No. 1988) 20–001
1996 Carriage by Air (Sterling Equivalents) Order (S.I. 1996, No. 244) 17–003
Carriage of Dangerous Goods by Road Regulations (S.I. 1996, No. 2095) 33–012
Statistics of Trade (Customs and Excise) (Amendment) Regulations (S.I. 1996, No. 2968) 26–010
Deregulation (Bills of Exchange) Order (S.I. 1996, No. 2993) 9–004
s. 4(1) 9–004
Arbitration Act 1997 (Commencement No. 1 Order) (S.I. 1996, No. 3146) 23–010
Extraterritorial US Legislation (Sanctions against Cuba, Iran and Libya) (Protection of Trading Interests) Order (S.I. 1996, No. 3171) 21–021
Rules of the Supreme Court (Amendment) (S.I. 1996, No. 3215) 23–010
1997 The Civil Jurisdiction and Judgments Act 1982 (Interim Relief) Order (S.I. 1997, No. 302) 22–030
Return of Cultural Objects (Amendment) Regulations (S.I. 1997, No. 1719) 26–005
Merchant Shipping (Dangerous Goods and Marine Pollutants) Regulations (S.I. 1997, No. 2367) .. 7–012, 15–040

1997 Carriage by Air and Road Act
  1979 (Commencement
  No. 2 Order) (S.I. 1997
  No. 2565) 17–001
  State Immunity (Merchant
  Shipping) Order (S.I.
  1997, No. 2591) 21–019
  The Antarctic (Isle of Man)
  Regulations 1997 (S.I.
  1997, No. 2968) 26–010
1998 Carriage by Air (Application
  of Provisions) (Fourth
  Amendment Order) (S.I.
  1998 No. 1058) 17–001
  Working Time Regulations
  (S.I. 1998 No. 1833) 28–021
  Statistics of Trade (Customs
  and Excise) (Amendment)
  Regulations (S.I. 1998 No.
  2973) 26–010
  • Civil Procedure Rules (S.I.
  1998, No. 3132) 26–027,
                                 26–031
  Pt. 1 22–030
  Pts. 1.1, 1.2 .... **22–030**,
                                 22–032
  Pt. 3 9–012
  Pt. 3.7 22–031
  Pt. 6 .... 22–001, 22–005
  Pt. 6.18(g) 22–002, 22–003
  Pt. 6.19 22–011
  Pt. 6.20 .... 22–003, 22–008
  Pt. 6.20(5)(a) 3–008
                    (c) 21–001
  Pt. 6.21(2A) 22–005
  Pt. 6.22 22–012
  Pt. 6.23 22–012
  Pt. 6.24 22–029
  Pt. 6.30 22–029
  Pt. 11 22–003
  Pt. 24 .... 9–012, 22–028,
                             23–016, 24–018
  Pt. 24.1 9–012
  Pt. 24.2 24–005
  Pt. 24.4(1) 9–012
  Pt. 25 .... 22–030, 22–032
  (1)(f) 22–030
  (f)(i), (ii) 22–030
  Pt. 25.1(h) 26–031
  Pt. 25.1(1)(f) 11–006
  Pt. 25.2(1)–(3) 22–030
  Pt. 25.4 22–030
  Pt. 25.10 22–031
  Pt. 25.11 22–031
  Pt. 49 22–033
  Pt. 49(2)(b) 23–010
  Pt. 50.1.3 24–004
  Sched. 1 .... 22–001, 22–003
  Sched. B 22–031
  Practice Direction Pt. 25—
  Interim Injunction 22–030,
                                 22–032

1998 Practice Direction Pt. 49f 22–033
  r.2.2(a) 22–033
  r.2.2(b) 22–033
  r.6 22–033
  r.6.4(1) 22–033
  Pt. 25.7.1 22–032
  Pt. 25.8.1 22–032
  Competition Act (Commence-
  ment No. 1) Order (S.I.
  1998 No. 2750) 29–020
  Competition Act (Commencement No. 2) Order (S.I.
  1998 No. 3166) 29–020
1999 Civil Procedure (Amendment)
  Rules (S.I. 1999, No.
  1008) (L.8) 22–031,
                                 26–031
  Competition Act (Commence-
  ment No. 3) Order (S.I.
  1999 No. 505) 29–020
  High Court and County Courts
  (Allocation of Arbitration
  Proceedings Order) (S.I.
  1999, No. 1010)   23–010, 23–019
  Carriage by Air Acts
  (Implementation of Proto-
  col No. 4) (S.I. 1999 No.
  1312) 17–001
  Carriage by Air (Parties to
  Convention) Order (S.I.
  1999 No. 1313) 17–009
  Carriage by Air Acts
  (Application of Pro-
  visions) (Fifth Amend-
  ment) Order (S.I. 1999
  No. 1737) 17–001
  Unfair Terms in Consumer
  Contracts Regulations
  (S.I. 1999 No. 2083) 3–019,
                                 17–020
  Reg. 3(1) 3–019
  Competition Act (Commence-
  ment No. 4) Order (S.I.
  1999 No. 2859) 29–020
  Carriage by Air (Sterling
  Equivalents) Order (S.I.
  1999 No. 2881) 17–003
  Statistics of Trade (Customs
  and Excise) (Amendment)
  Regulations (S.I. 1999 No.
  3269) 26–010
  Transnational Information and
  Consultation of Employ-
  ees Regulations (S.I. 1999
  No. 3323) 28–010,
                                 28–018
  Working Time Regulations
  (S.I. 1999 No. 3372) 28–021
2000 Export of Goods (Control)
  (Amendment) (No. 3)
  Order (S.I. 2000 No.
  1396) 26–003

RULES OF SUPREME COURT

1965   Rules of Supreme Court (S.I.
          1965, No. 1776)
          Ord. 11 .... 22–003, 22–005,
                                          22–007
             r. 1 22–008
                (A) 22–012
                (B) 22–012
                (1) 22–001, 22–003,
                                          22–004
                   (ii) 21–001
                (2) 22–001, 22–004,

                                          22–011, 22–012, 22–029
                (4) 22–002
             r. 4(2) 22–005
             r. 5 22–029
             r. 6 22–029
          Ord. 14 .... 9–012, 22–027
          Ord. 23 23–005
          Ord. 73 23–010
          Ord. 71 .... 24–004, 24–016
          Ord. 75
             r. 2(1) 22–004
                (2) 22–004
             r. 11 22–033

TABLE OF EUROPEAN COMMUNITIES LEGISLATION

REGULATIONS
1962 Regulation 17/62 O.J. 204/62;
      [1962] O.J. Spec. Ed. 87;
      amended by [1962] O.J.
      Spec. Ed. 1655; [1963]
      O.J. Spec. Ed. 2696,
      and by [1971] O.J.
      L285/49 29–006,
                              29–018, 29–023
      Art. 2 29–008
      Arts. 4, 5 29–006
      Art. 4(2) 29–006
      Art. 11 29–019
      Art. 14 29–019
      Arts. 15, 16 29–004
      Art. 15(1) 29–019, 29–019
         (2) 29–006
      Art. 19 29–018
      Art. 20 29–019
      Regulation 27/62 [1959–1962]
         O.J. 132 29–006
1963 Regulation 99/63 [1963] O.J.
      2268; [1963] O.J. Spec.
      Ed. 47 .... 29–006, 29–018
      Regulation 118/63 29–006
1968 Regulation 1133/68 29–006
1969 Regulation 2603/69 [1969] O.J.
      L324/25
      Art. 1 26–029
1971 Regulation 2822/71 [1971] O.J.
      L285/49 29–006
1975 Regulation 1699/75 29–006
1979 Regulation 954/79 15–016
1981 Regulation 1468/81 26–029
1983 Regulation 1983/83 [1983] O.J.
      L173/1 as amended by
      corrigendum [1983] O.J.
      L281/24 .... 29–012, 29–013
      Arts. 1–3 29–012
1984 Regulation 1984/83 [1983] O.J.
      L173/5, as amended by
      corrigendum [1983] O.J.
      L281/24 29–013
      Recital 12 29–013
      Regulation 2349/84 [1984] O.J.
      L219/15; as amended by
      [1985] O.J. L113/34,
      [1993] O.J. L21/8; Reg.
      70/95 [1995] O.J. L12/12;
      Reg. 2131/95 [1995] O.J.
      L214/6; Reg. 240/96
      [1996] O.J. L31/2 29–015
      Art. 4 29–015
1985 Regulation 418/85 [1985] O.J.
      L53/5; as amended, [1993]
      O.J. L21/10 29–014

1985 Regulation 2137/85 [1985] O.J.
      L199/1 1–005
1986 Regulation 4056/86 [1986] O.J.
      L378/4 .... 15–016, 29–016
1987 Regulation 2658/87 [1987] O.J.
      L256
      Annex I 26–016
      Regulation 3975/87 [1987] O.J.
      L374/1; as amended,
      [1991] O.J. L122/2;
      [1992] O.J. L240/18 29–017
      Regulation 3976/87 [1987] O.J.
      L374/9; as amended by
      [1992] O.J. L240/19 29–017
1988 Regulation 3719/88 26–024
      Regulation 4087/88 [1988] O.J.
      L359/46 29–004,
                        29–016, 30–017, 30–018
      Recitals (4), (5) 30–018
      Art. 1(3) 30–018
      Arts. 3, 4 30–018
      Arts. 6, 7 30–018
1989 Regulation 556/89 (Know-
      How) [1989] O.J. L61/1 ... 29–015
      Regulation 4064/89 [1989] O.J.
      L395/1, as corrected,
      amended and republished
      at [1990] O.J. L257/14.
      Amended by Council
      Regulations 1310/97 of
      June 30, 1997 in [1997]
      O.J. L180/1 28–018
1991 Regulation 3330/91 [1991] O.J.
      L316/1 26–010
1992 Regulation 2913/92 [1992] O.J.
      L302/1 .. 26–012, 26–013, 26–015
      Art. 1 26–012
      Art. 14 26–018
      Art. 16 26–018
      Art. 62(2) 26–014
      Art. 76(1)(a)–(c) 26–015
      Arts. 91–97 26–020
      Art. 99 26–025
      Art. 112(3) 26–025
      Arts. 114–129 26–023
      Art. 114(1)(b) 26–023
      Art. 117(c) 26–023
      Arts. 124–128 26–023
      Arts. 145, 146 26–023
      Art. 118A 26–018
      Art. 161(2) 26–013
         (4) 26–013
      Art. 185(1) 26–014
      Art. 205 26–013
      Art. 243 26–027
      Art. 249 26–027

1992   Regulation—*cont.*
       Annex 37 26–013
       Regulation 3046/92 26–010
       Regulation 3911/92 21–025,
                                                      26–005
1993   Regulation 2454/93 26–012
       Pt. II 26–020
       Art. 199 26–013
       Art. 793 26–014
       Art. 794 26–014
       Arts. 280–287 26–015
       Art. 282 26–015
       Arts 283–287 26–015
       Art. 310 26–020
       Arts. 359–374 26–020
       Art. 454(3) 26–029
       Arts. 549–649 26–023
       Art. 504 26–025
       Art. 551(2) 26–023
       Art. 568(2) 26–023
       Arts. 844–856 26–024
       Annex 70 26–022
       Annex 81 26–022
       Annex 82 26–022
       Annex 98 26–022
       Annex 106 26–022
       Annex 110 26–022
1994   Regulation 40/94 [1994] O.J.
       L011/1 29–016
       Regulation 3295/94 [1994] O.J.
       L341/8 26–031
       Regulation 3381/94 [1994] O.J.
       L367/1 26–003,
                                                      26–004
1995   Regulation 870/95 [1995] O.J.
       L89/7 29–017
       Regulation 1367/95 26–031
1996   Regulation 240/96 [1996] O.J.
       L31/2 29–015,
                                                      30–015
       Regulation 2271/96 [1996] O.J.
       L309/1 21–021
       Art. 2 21–021
       Art. 5 21–021
       Regulation 2469/96 26–005
1997   Regulation 82/97 26–025
       Regulation 515/97 26–029
       Regulation 2236/97 [1997] O.J.
       L306/12 29–014
1999   Regulation 2790/99 [1999] O.J.
       L336/12 29–004

DIRECTIVES
1968   Directive on Co-ordination of
       Safeguards [1968] O.J.
       L065/8 68/151 28–003
1971   Directive on Public Works and
       Construction Contracts 71/
       305 [1971] O.J. L185/1 ... 25–004,
                                                      25–005
1976   Directive 76/308 [1976] L73/
       18 26–029

1977   Directive on Government Pro-
       curement of Supplies of
       Goods Equipment 77/62
       [1977] O.J. L113/1 25–004,
                                                      25–006
       Sixth VAT Directive 77/388
       [1977] O.J. L145/1 26–009
1978   Directive 78/660 [1978] O.J.
       L222/11 .... 28–003, 28–011
1980   Directive 80/767 [1980] O.J.
       L215/1 25–006
1983   Seventh Company Directive
       83/349   [1983]   O.J.
       L193/1 28–011
1984   Eighth Company Directive 84/
       253 [1984] O.J. L126/20 .. 28–011
1985   Council Directive on Product
       Liability 85/374 [1985]
       O.J. L260/29 .... 8–002, 8–003,
                                               8–004, 8–006
       Art. 2 8–006
       Art. 7 8–007
       (e) 8–004, 8–007
       Art. 12 8–004
       Art. 14 8–004
       Art. 15(1)(a) 8–004
       (b) 8–004
       Art. 16 .... 8–004, 8–006
1986   Council   Directive   on   the
       Co-Ordination   of   the
       Laws of the Member
       States Relating to Self-
       Employed   Commercial
       Agents 86/653 [1986] O.J.
       L382/17 .... 27–004, 27–010
       Reg. 13(1) 27–004
       Regs. 14, 15 27–001
1988   Council Directive on Public
       Procurement of Supplies
       and   Equipment   88/295
       [1988] O.J. L217/1 25–006
1989   Directive 89/440 [1989] O.J.
       L210/1 25–005
       Directive 89/665 [1990] O.J.
       L297/1 25–009
       Directive 89/667 [1989] O.J.
       L395/40 28–011
1990   Directive 90/531 [1990] O.J.
       L291/1 25–008
       Directive (Software) 91/250
       [1992] O.J. L122/42 29–016
1992   Directive 92/12 [1992] O.J.
       L76/1 .... 26–011, 26–023
       Directive 92/13 [1992] O.J.
       L76/14 25–009
       Art. 2(b) 3–019
       Art. 3 3–019
       Directive 92/50 [1992] O.J.
       L209/1 25–007
1993   Directive 93/7 [1993] L74/74 . 21–025,
                                                      26–005
       Directive 93/13 [1993] O.J.
       L95/29 .... 3–019, 17–020

1993 Directive 93/36 [1993] O.J.
L199/1 25–006
Directive 93/37 [1994] O.J.
L111/4 25–005
Directive 93/38 [1993] O.J.
L199/84 25–008
1996 Directive 96/100 [1997]
L60/59 26–005
1997 Directive on Distance Selling
97/7 33–008

1997 Directive on Telecommunications Services Licensing
97/13 33–012
Directive 97/52 [1997] O.J.
L328/1 .... 25–005, 25–006,
25–007
1998 Directive 98/4 [1998] O.J.
L101/1 .... 25–008, 25–009

UNITED STATES LEGAL MATERIALS

Uniform Commercial Code (UCC)

Commercial Code (UCC) 2–006, 2–013,
3–006, 3–007,
15–029, 32–009
Art. 2 .... 32–009, 32–028
  A 32–009
Art. 3 32–009
Art. 4 32–009
  A 32–009
Art. 5 32–009
Art. 6 32–009
Art. 7 32–009
  s. 105(4) 4–005
  s. 1–201(6) 15–029
    (17) 4–005
  s. 2–104(1) 3–007
  s. 2–201 32–028
  s. 2–205 .... 3–006, 32–025
  s. 2–207 32–025
  s. 2–207(2) 3–007
  s. 2–304(1) 14–002
  s. 2–305(1) 14–002
  s. 2–318 3–014
  ss. 2–319—2–324 32–028

Commercial Code (UCC)— *cont.*
  s. 2–319 2–004
    (1) 2–006
    (2) 2–004
  s. 2–320(2)(c) 2–023
  s. 2–321(1) 2–037
  s. 2–321(3) 2–037
  s. 2–322 2–043
  ss. 2–401—2–403 32–028
  s. 2–401(1) 4–006
  s. 2–324 2–037
  s. 2–509 4–010
  s. 2–515(b) 4–013
  s. 2–615 6–001
    (b) 6–014

Federal Statutes

1936 Carriage of Goods by Sea
    Act 15–016, 15–047

Restatement (Second) of Torts 1965

s. 402A **8–013**
s   (f) 8–013

INTERNATIONAL CONVENTIONS AND OTHER
FORMULATIONS OF INTERNATIONAL TRADE LAW

1921 Hague Rules relating to Bills of Lading (Hague Rules) 2–007, 15–020,
      15–021, 15–047, 16–007, 32–004
1924 International Convention for the Unification of Certain Rules relating to Bills of
      Lading 16–007
      York-Antwerp Rules 19–028
1927 Geneva Convention on the Execution of Foreign Arbitral Awards 24–018
1929 Warsaw Convention relating to the Unification of certain Rules relating to Interna-
      tional Air Carriage; for Amendment. See Hague Protocol of 1955 15–001,
      16–005, 16–007, 17–001, 17–005,
      17–008, 17–009, 17–010
      Art. 25 17–012
      Art. 28 22–007
      Art. 31 16–005
1930 Geneva Conventions on the Unification of the Law relating to Bills of
      Exchange 9–006
1933 Uniform Customs and Practice for Documentary Credits (UCP 1933) 11–002
1944 Bretton Woods Agreement 21–029
      Art. VIII 21–029
      s. 2(b) 21–029
      Convention on International Civil Aviation 13–013
1947 GATT Agreement 24–021
      Art. XXII 24–022
      Art. XXIII 24–022
1950 British Maritime Law Association Agreement 2–007
      York-Antwerp Rules 19–028
      Rule D 19–028
      European Convention for the Protection of Humans Rights and Fundamental
      Freedoms
      Art. 6 26–027
      Art. 8 33–012
1951 Treaty establishing the European Coal and Steel Community 26–020
      Pt. 3, Arts 23–27 26–007
      Uniform Customs and Practice for Documentary Credits
      (1951 Revision) (UCP 1951) 11–002, 11–007
      Art. 33 11–007
1952 First Protocol to the European Convention of Human Rights—
      Art. 1 26–030
      Art. 6 26–030
      (1) 26–030
      International Convention for Unification of Certain Rules relating to the Arrest
      of Seagoing Ships (Arrest Convention) 22–033
      Art. 7 22–033
1953 Incoterms 2–001
1955 Hague Protocol amending the Warsaw Convention 15–001, 17–003,
      17–009, 17–010
      Arts. 5–9 17–015
      Art. 12 .... 17–005, 17–013
      Art. 13 .... 17–005, 17–013
      (3) 17–005
      Art. 14 .... 17–005, 17–013
      Art. 18 17–016
      (2) 17–004
      Art. 20 17–003
      Art. 21(2) 17–004
      Art. 22 17–016

1955   Hague Protocol amending the Warsaw Convention—*cont.*
        Art. 24(1) 17–003
                (2) 17–003
        Art. 25 .... 17–011, 17–012, 17–016
        Art. 26 .... 17–005, 17–018
                (2) 17–014
        Art. 28 17–014
        Art. 29 .... 17–005, 17–014
        Art. 30(3) 17–005
        Art. 32 17–016
        Art. 34 17–015
1956   Convention on the Contract for the International Carriage of Goods (Convention
        relative au contrat de transport international de merchandise par route—
        CMR) 2–007, 9–002, 15–001, 16–005, 16–007,
                        18–001, 18–006, 18–007, 18–008, 18–009, 18–010, 18–011, 27–025
        Art. 1(1) 18–006
                (2) 18–006
                (3) 18–006
                (4) 18–006
        Art. 2(1) 16–005, 18–006
        Art. 4 18–008
        Art. 5(1), (2) 18–008
        Art. 6 18–008
        Art. 9(1) 18–008
                (2) 18–008
        Art. 11 18–008
        Art. 12(1)–(5) 18–008
        Art. 13 18–008
        Art. 15 18–008
        Art. 17(1)–(4) 18–009
        Art. 18 18–009
                (1) 18–009
                (4) 18–009
        Art. 20 18–009
                (1) 18–010
        Art. 21 18–009
        Art. 22(1) 18–008
        Art. 23(4), (5) 18–009
        Art. 28 18–009
                (2) 18–009
        Art. 30(1) 18–010
                (3) 18–010
        Art. 31 18–006
        Art. 32(1), (2) 18–010
                (1)(a) 18–010
        Art. 32(1)(b) 18–010
        Art. 33 18–006
        Art. 34 .... 18–007, 27–025
        Art. 36 18–007
        Art. 37 .... 18–007, 18–010
        Art. 38 .... 18–007, 18–010
        Art. 39 18–006
        Art. 39(2) 18–007
        Art. 41(1), (2) 18–010
1957   Convention Relating to the Limitation of the Liability of Owners of Seagoing
        Ships 22–007
        EC Treaty (Treaty of Rome) 23–016, 28–024, 30–008
        Pt. I 29–004
        Art. 3(g) 29–004
        Art. 6 23–005
        Art. 8 29–004
        Art. 9 26–008
        Art. 10 26–008

1957   EC Treaty (Treaty of Rome)—*cont.*
Art. 23 .... 26–008, 26–030
Art. 24 26–008
Art. 25 26–030
Art. 28 26–030
Art. 29 26–030
Art. 30 .... 26–007, 26–030
Art. 39 28–024
     (3) 28–024
Art. 39–42 28–024
Art. 43 .... 28–001, 28–024
Art. 43–47 .... 28–001, 28–024
Art. 48 28–001
Art. 81 .... 28–008, 28–009, 29–002, 29–003, 29–004,
                  29–006, 29–010, 29–011, 29–016,
                  29–024, 30–015
     (1) 27–013, 27–016, 29–004, 29–005, 29–006,
                  29–007, 29–008, 29–009, 29–010, 29–012,
                  29–013, 29–014, 29–015, 30–017
     (2) 29–002, 29–004
     (3) 29–002, 29–004, 29–005,
                  29–007, 29–008, 29–009,
                  29–015, 30–015, 30–017
Art. 82 .... 28–008, 28–009, 29–002, 29–004,
                  29–006, 29–016, 29–018, 29–024
Art. 85 15–016
     (1) 26–013
Art. 86 15–016
Art. 90 26–029
Art. 113 26–029
Art. 119 28–024
Art. 133 26–029
Art. 141 28–024
Art. 177 21–005
Arts. 211–219 26–012
Art. 287 29–019
1958   New York Convention on the Recognition of Foreign Arbitral Awards . 24–001, 24–018
1961   Convention supplementary to the Warsaw Convention for the unification of cer-
        tain rules relating to international carriage by air performed by a person other
        than the contracting carrier (Guadalajara Convention) 17–001, 27–025
        International Convention concerning the Carriage of Goods by Rail (Convention
        Internationale concernant le transport de Marchandises par chemin de fer)
        (CIM) 16–005, 16–007,
                  18–001, 18–002
Art. 1 18–003
Art. 2 18–003
Art. 4 18–003
Art. 11 18–004
Art. 12 18–004
Art. 13 18–004
Art. 18 18–004
Art. 19 18–004
Art. 21 18–004
Art. 35(1), (2) 18–005
Art. 36 18–005
Art. 37(1) 18–005
Art. 40 18–005
Art. 44 18–005
Art. 53 18–005
Art. 54 18–005
Art. 55 18–005
     (4) 18–005
Art. 58 18–005

1964   Convention relating to a Uniform Law on the International Sale of Goods
       (Uniform Law on Sales) (The Hague Convention) 4–002, 4–010, 5–001,
                                                        16–005, 32–004, 32–024, 32–026,
                                                                  32–027, 32–028, 32–030
       Art. 1 .... 32–023, 32–025
           (1), (2) 32–022
           (3) 32–023
           (5) 32–023
       Art. 4 .... 32–020, 32–021
       Art. 5(2), (3) 32–025
       Art. 7 .... 32–023, 32–025
       Art. 9 32–024
           (1), (2) 32–025
       Art. 10 .... 32–024, 32–030
       Art. 11 32–024
       Art. 26(1)–(3) 32–024
       Art. 27 32–024
       Art. 33 32–024
       Art. 39(1), (2) 32–024
       Art. 41(1)(a)–(c) 32–024
           (2) 32–024
       Art. 44(1), (2) 32–024
       Art. 49 32–024
       Art. 57 14–002
       Art. 59(1) 22–018
       Art. 78 32–024
       Art. 84 32–024
       Art. 97 4–010
1965   Convention on the Service Abroad of Judicial and Extra-judicial Documents in
       Civil and Commercial Matters (Service Convention) (The Hague) 22–029
       Convention on the Settlement of Investment Disputes between States and Nations
       of other States (Washington Convention) 23–027, 28–017
       Annex II, Art. 4(b) 23–027
1967   Incoterms 2–001
1968   Brussels Protocol revising Hague Rules 1921 relating to Bills of Lading (Hague-Visby
       Rules) 2–007, 7–009, 15–001, 15–004,
                   15–020, 15–022, 15–023, 15–025, 15–027, 15–033, 15–036,
                   15–041, 15–051, 16–005, 16–006, 16–007, 21–004, 21–005,
                                             21–006, 21–010, 32–004, 33–010
       Art. I(b) 15–023, 33–010
           (c) 15–022
       Art. III 15–041
           (a) 15–036
       Art. III, r. 1 .... 15–041, 15–043, 15–050
           (a) 15–041
           2 15–041
           2(a) 15–041
           3 .... 15–003, 15–022, 15–025, 15–036
               (a) 15–036
               (b) 15–036
               (c) 15–036
           4 .... 15–033, 15–036
           5 15–036
           6 .... 15–048, 19–028
               (bis) 15–039, 15–048
           7 15–025
           8 .... 15–021, 15–041, 15–045
       Art. IV 15–041, 15–042
           (bis)(1) 15–045
               (2)–(4) 15–047
               (2) 15–041
           r. 1 .... **15–042**, 15–043
           r. 2 .... **15–042**, 15–043

1968   Brussels Protocol revising Hague Rules 1921 relating to Bills of Lading
         (Hague-Visby Rules)—*cont.*
                   (a) 15–043
                   (b) 15–043
                   (q) 15–043
                   (m) 15–043
               r. 3 15–050
               r. 5 .... 15–022, 15–045, 15–046,
                                                                                       15–050, 16–009
                   (a) 7–008, 7–009, 15–045
                   (c) 16–007, 16–009
                   (d) 15–045
                   (e) 15–045
                   (f) 15–045
                   (g) 15–045
                   (h) 15–045
               r. 6 .... 15–041, 15–050
         Art. X 15–021
         Convention on Jurisdiction and the Enforcement of Judgments in Civil and Com-
               mercial Matters (Lugano Convention) (Lugano, 16 September 1988) 3–017,
                                   8–010, 21–003, 22–001, 22–011, 22–013, 22–014, 22–015,
                                       22–019, 22–028, 22–033, 24–001, 24–002
               Art. 1 .... 22–013, 22–014, 24–003
                   (4) 23–007
               Arts. 2–4 22–013
               Art. 2 .... 22–015, 22–017, 22–018
               Art. 3 .... 22–017, 22–018, 24–002
               Art. 4(1) 22–015
               Art. 5 .... 22–002, 22–015, 22–018
               Art. 5(1) 21–006, 22–016, 22–018, 22–019
                   (3) 22–020
                   (5) 22–021, 27–002, 28–003, 28–004
                   (7) 22–033
               Art. 5(18) 22–017
               Art. 54B 22–013
               Art. 6 22–022
                   A 22–015
               Art. 6(1)–(4) 22–022
               Arts. 7–11 22–023
               Arts. 7–12A 22–015, 22–023
               Art. 12(5) 22–023
               Arts. 13–15 .... 22–015, 22–024
               Art. 13 22–024
               Art. 16 .... 22–015, 22–016, 22–025
               Art. 17 .... 21–006, 22–015, 22–016, 22–017, 22–019, 22–024, 22–033
                   (c) 22–016
                   (1) 3–017
                   (3) 22–016
                   (5) 22–022
               Art. 18 .... 22–015, 22–016
               Art. 19 .... 22–015, 22–025
               Art. 20 .... 22–015, 22–026
               Arts. 21–23 22–015
               Art. 21 .... 22–027, 22–033
               Art. 22 .... 22–018, 22–020, 22–027, 22–033
               Art. 24 22–015
               Art. 25 24–002
               Art. 27 24–003
                   (3), (4), (5) 24–003
               Art. 28(1) 24–002
                   (3), (4), (5) 24–002
               Art. 28 .... 24–002, 24–003
               Art. 29 24–003

1968 Convention on Jurisdiction and the Enforcement of Judgments in Civil and Com-
      mercial Matters (Lugano Convention) (Lugano, 16 September 1988)—*cont.*
      Art. 31 24–004
      Art. 32 24–004
      Art. 33 24–004
      Art. 39 24–004
      Art. 46 24–004
      Art. 47 24–004
      Art. 52 22–002
      Art. 53 22–002
      Art. 54 24–002
      Art. 57 22–033
      Art. 59 24–002
      Art. 68 22–013
1970 Convention on the Taking of Evidence Abroad in Civil or Commercial Matters . 21–022
1974 Convention on a Code of Conduct for Liners Conferences 15–016
      Art. 1 15–016
      UN Convention on the Limitation Period in the International Sale of Goods 4–002,
                                                                                      32–029, 32–032
      Art. 8 32–032
      ICC Uniform Customs and Practice for Documentary Credits (UCP 1974) 11–002,
                                                                                              11–036
      York-Antwerp Rules 15–049
      UNCITRAL Convention on the Limitation Period in International Sale of
      Goods 32–004
1975 Customs Convention on the International Transport of Goods Under the Cover of
      TIR Carnets (TIR Convention) 26–021
      ICC Uniform Rules for a Combined Transport Document 16–006, 32–008
1976 Convention on limitation of Liability for Maritime Claims 15–046
      Art. 4 15–046
      Art. 6 15–046
      Art. 7 15–046
      Art. 8 15–046
      Incoterms 2–001
      UNCITRAL Arbitration Rules 23–022, 32–006
      Art. 6(2) 23–022
      Art. 16(1) 23–022
      Art. 21(1), (2) 23–022
1978 UN Convention on the Carriage of Goods by Sea (Hamburg Rules) (UNCITRAL/
      UNCTAD) 15–016, 16–006,
                                                                                      16–007, 32–004
      Art. 6(2)(a) 16–009, 25–001
      EEC/Switzerland Agreement [1973] O.J. L338/73 26–026
      ICC Uniform Rules for Contract Guarantees (URCG) 12–001, 25–020, 32–008
      Art. 2 12–001
          (a) 25–020
      Art. 4(a) 25–020
      Art. 5(2)(a)–(c) 25–020
      Art. 7(1) 25–020
      Art. 8 25–020
      Art. 9 .... 12–001, 25–020
      Art. 10 25–020
1980 Convention Concerning International Carriage by Rail (COTIF) 15–001, 18–001
      Pt. 3 18–001
      s. 2(1) 18–001
1980 Convention on International Multimodal Transport of Goods 15–001, 16–005
      Art. 14 16–005
      Art. 15 16–005
      Art. 16 .... **16–005**
      Art. 18(1) 16–005
      Art. 19(3) 16–005

1980   Convention on Contracts for the International Sale of Goods (UNCITRAL)
        (Vienna Sales Convention) 2–001, 2–004, 3–006, 3–019, 4–002,
                                        4–010, 5–001, 13–007, 13–013, 21–003,
                                        32–004, 32–026, 32–027, 32–028, 32–029,
                                        32–030, 32–031, 32–032
        Pts. I-IV 32–026
        Pt. III, Chaps. I–V 32–026
        Art. 1(1) 32–027
        Art. 4(a), (b) 32–028
        Art. 5 32–028
        Art. 6 .... 2–001, 32–028
        Art. 7(2) 32–028
        Art. 11 32–028
        Art. 12 2–001
        Art. 16(2) 3–006
        Art. 19(2) 3–007
        Art. 25 32–029
        Art. 30 2–002
        Arts. 30–34 4–003
        Art. 31(a) 2–005
              (c) 2–002
        Art. 32(a) 2–004
        Art. 38 5–005
        Art. 39 .... 5–007, 32–031
        Art. 46 32–031
        Art. 53 2–002
        Art. 55 14–002
        Arts. 64–65 15–013
        Arts. 66–70 4–010
        Art. 67 4–010
        Arts. 71, 72 32–026
        Arts. 74–77 32–026
        Arts 79, 80 32–026
        Arts. 81–84 32–026
        Arts. 85–88 32–026
        Art. 92 32–026
        Convention on the Law Applicable to Contractual Obligations (Private Interna-
        tional Law Convention) (Rome Convention) 3–017, 11–020, 21–002, 21–003,
                                        21–004, 21–007, 21–010, 21–027, 28–021
        Art. 1(1) 11–020, 21–006
              (2) 21–004, 21–006, 23–007
              (h) 21–002, 21–017
        Art. 1(3) 21–004, 21–006
              (4) 21–006
        Art. 2 21–006
        Art. 3 .... 3–017, 11–020, 21–009, 21–010, 21–011, 21–016
              (1) 21–001, 21–004, 21–006, 21–008
              (2) 21–008
              (3) 21–008, 21–010
              (4) 21–008, 21–011
        Art. 4 .... 11–020, 21–015, 21–016
              (1) 11–020, 21–004, 21–006, 21–009
              (2) 11–020, 21–009
              (3) 21–009
              (4) 21–009
              (5) 11–020, 21–009
        Art. 5 .... 21–004, 21–010, 21–011, 21–015
              (2)–(5) 21–015
              (3) 21–010
        Art. 6 .... 21–004, 21–010, 21–011, 21–016
              (1) 21–016
              (2) 21–010, 21–016
        Art. 7 21–008

1980   Convention on the Law Applicable to Contractual Obligations (Private International Law Convention) (Rome Convention)—*cont.*
     (1) 21–006, 21–010, 21–027
     (2) 21–010, 21–027
    Art. 8 21–006
     (1) 21–012
     (2) **21–012**
    Art. 9 .... 21–006, 21–008, 21–012
     (1)–(4) **21–012**, 21–015
     (5) 21–015
     (6) 21–010, **21–012**
    Art. 10 21–011
      (c) 21–011
     (1) 21–011
      (e) 21–006, 21–011
      (d) 21–017
     (2) 21–011
    Art. 11 21–013
    Art. 12 .... 21–011, 21–014
    Art. 13 21–014
    Art. 14 .... 21–006, 21–012
     (2) 21–012
    Art. 15 21–006
    Art. 16 .... 21–010, 21–027
    Art. 18 21–005
    Art. 19(1) 21–006
     (2) 21–006
    Art. 20 21–006
    Art. 21 .... 21–006, 21–029
    Art. 22 21–006
    Sched. 1, Art. 16 21–023
    ICC Incoterms (International Commercial Terms) 2–001, 2–002
    UNCITRAL Conciliation Rules 23–023, 32–006
     Arts. 2, 3 23–023
     Art. 4(2) 23–023
     Art. 7(4) 23–023
     Art. 13 23–023
     Art. 16 23–023
1983   Uniform Customs and Practice for Documentary Credits (UCP 1983) (UCP 400) 11–002, 11–003, 11–004, 11–012, 15–051
    Art. 5 11–003
    Art. 16(c) 11–003, 11–009, 11–012
    Art. 23(a)(i) 11–012
    Art. 26 11–012
    Art. 54(a) 11–036
1985   Convention on the Law Applicable to Contracts for the International Sale of Goods (The Hague) 21–003
    UNCITRAL Model Law on International Commercial Arbitration 23–024, 32–005
    Art. 5 23–010
    Art. 19 23–024
1988   Convention on International Bills of Exchange and International Promissory Notes (Geneva) UNCITRAL 9–006, 32–004
    Convention on International Factoring (Ottawa) 13–001, 13–007, 32–029
    Art. 1 13–007
     (2) 13–007
    Art. 2(c) 13–007
    Art. 3(a), (b) 13–007
    Art. 5(a) 13–007
    Art. 6(1)–(3) 13–007
    Art. 8(1)(b), (c) 13–007
    Art. 10(1), (2) 13–007
    Arts. 11, 12 13–007
    Art. 11(2) 13–007

1988   Convention on International Factoring (Ottawa)—*cont.*
      Art. 14(1) 13–001
      Art. 18 13–007
      Art. 24 22–030
     Convention on International Financial Leasing (Ottawa) 13–001, 13–012,
                                      13–013, 32–029
      Art. 1(1)–(3) 13–013
      Art. 3(1) 13–013
      Art. 5 13–013
      Art. 7 13–013
          (1)–(3) 13–013
          (1)(b) 13–013
      Art. 8(1)(a)–(c) 13–013
      Art. 10 13–013
      Art. 12(1)–(3) 13–013
          (1)(a), (b) 13–013
          (5) 13–013
      Art. 13(1), (2) 13–013
          (2)(b) 13–013
          (3)(b) 13–013
      Art. 16(1) 13–001
1990   CMI Uniform Rules for Sea Waybills 15–033
     CMI Rules on Electronic Bills of Lading 33–010
     IMDG Code (International Maritime Dangerous Goods Code) 7–012
     GAFTA 6–013
     GAFTA Form 100—
     cls. 21, 22 6–019
     GAFTA Form 119 6–012
     Agreement on Preshipment Inspection 4–014
       Art. 1(3) 4–014
          (4) 4–014
       Art. 2(5) 4–014
     Agreement on Rules of Origin 4–014
       Art. 2(a) 4–014
          (e) 4–014
       Art. 9 4–014
     ICC Model International Sale Contract 3–001
     UCPDC 2–023, 2–046
     UCPDC (1993 Revision) UCP 2–032, 2–035
       Art. 11 3–008
       Art. 23 2–032
          (b)–(d) 2–032
       Art. 24 2–032
          (b)–(d) 2–032
       Art. 26 .... 2–032, 2–046
          (b) 2–032
       Art. 37 7–004
       Art. 40(a) 5–009
          (b) 5–006
       Art. 48 7–004
       Art. 48(h) 7–004
     Incoterms 2–001, 2–002
1991   Convention on the Liability of Operators of Transport Terminals in International
     Trade (UN) 32–004
1992   European Economic Agreement—
     Arts. 8–27 26–028
     Rules for Multi modal transport documents (UNCTAD/ICC) 16–006
     UN Model Law on International Credit Transfers 32–005
     Uniform Rules for Demand Guarantees (URDG) (ICC) 11–030, 12–001,
                                        12–004, 12–005
       Art. 1 12–004
       Art. 2(a) 12–004
          (b) 12–004

1992 Uniform Rules for Demand Guarantees (URDG) (ICC)—*cont.*
    (c) 12–001, 12–004
    (d) 12–004
  Art. 19 12–004
  Art. 20 12–004
  Art. 21 12–004
1993 Treaty on Economic Union (Maastricht Treaty)—
  Title II, Art. G(1) 28–001
  Incoterms 2–001, 2–040, 2–043
  Uniform Customs and Practice for Documentary Credits (UCP 1993) (UCP
    500) 11–001, 11–002, 11–003, 11–007, 11–009, 11–010,
          11–011, 11–012, 11–017, 11–019, 11–020, 11–022, 11–023, 11–029,
          11–030, 11–034, 11–035, 11–038, 12–004, 15–002, 15–004, 15–029,
          15–033, 15–051, 16–006, 32–008, 33–010
    Art. 1 11–002
    Art. 2 11–001
    Art. 3 11–006
      (a) 11–006
    Art. 4 .... 11–006, 11–007
    Art. 5(a)(i) 11–010
    Art. 6 11–023
    Art. 7 11–023
    Art. 8 .... 11–023, 11–024
    Art. 9 .... 11–023, 11–025
      (a) 11–022
        (iii) 11–022
      (b) 11–004, 11–010
        (iii) 11–022
    Art. 10(b)(ii) 11–022
    Art. 11 11–017
      (a)(i), (ii) 11–017
      (b) 11–017
    Art. 13(b) 11–009, 11–010
    Art. 14(a) 11–027
      (b) 11–008
      (c) 11–010
      (d)(i), (ii) 11–009, 11–010
      (e) 11–010
      (f) 11–038
    Art. 15 .... 11–042, 10–002
    Art. 17 11–019
    Art. 20, 21 11–014
    Art. 20(b) 11–014
      (c)(i) 11–014
    Arts. 23–30 11–012
    Art. 23(a)(i) 11–012, 15–051
        (ii) 11–012, 15–025
        (iii) 11–012
        (vi) 15–023
      (b) 15–027
      (c) 11–012, 15–027
      (d) 11–012, 15–027
        (i) 11–012
    Art. 24 15–033
    Art. 25 15–023
    Art. 26 .... 15–002, 15–029, 16–006
      (a)(i) 11–012
      (b) 15–027
    Art. 27(a) 11–012
        (i) 11–012
        (ii) 11–012
        (iii) 11–012
      (b) 15–027

1993   Uniform Customs and Practice for Documentary Credits (UCP 1993) (UCP 500)—*cont.*
          Art. 27(c) 15–027
          Art. 28(b) 11–012, 15–027
          Art. 31(i) 11–012
          Art. 32 .... 2–022, 11–012, 15–036
          Arts. 34–36 11–013
          Art. 34(a) 11–014
              (b) 11–014
              (c)–(e) 11–014
              (f)(i) 11–014
              (ii) 2–023, 11–014
          Arts. 35(a), (b) 11–014
          Art. 36 11–014
          Art. 37 11–013
              (a)(i) 11–013
              (ii) 11–013
              (iii) 11–013
              (b) 11–013
              (c) 11–007, 11–013, 11–015, 11–016
          Arts. 43–46 11–019
          Art. 42(a) 11–019
          Art. 43 11–036
              (a) 11–019, 15–032
          Art. 48 .... **11–036**
          Art. 49 11–035
          WTO Agreement 24–021
          Annex 2 24–023
1994   Blue Book (Report of the Standing Advisory Committee on the Carriage of
          Dangerous Goods in Ships) 7–012
          GATT Agreement 24–021
          Art. 2(1) 24–023
          Art. 3 24–023
          Art. 4 24–023
          Art. 5 24–023
          Art. 6 24–023
          Art. 7 24–023
          Art. 8 24–023
          Art. 9 24–023
          Art. 11 24–023
          Art. 14 24–023
          Art. 15 24–023
          Art. 16 24–023
          Art. 17 24–023
          Art. 22 24–023
          Art. 25 24–023
              (4) 24–023
          Intraterms 2–001, 2–013, 2–040, 2–043
          s. 418(2)(c) 2–023
          UNCITRAL Model Law on Procurement of Goods, Construction and
          Services 32–005
          York-Antwerp Rules 19–027, 19–028
          Rule C 19–027
          Rule I 19–027
          Rule XVII 19–028
1995   UN Convention on Independent Guarantees and Standby Letters of Credit 12–001
          Unidroit Convention on Stolen or Illegally Exported Cultural Objects 21–025
          Uniform Rules for Collections (1995 Revision) (ICC) 10–002, 11–001,
                                                                                              32–008
          Pt. A 10–002
          Art. 1(a) 10–002
          Art. 2(a)–(d) 10–002
          Art. 3 10–002
              (a)(i) 10–002

1995   Uniform Rules for Collections (1995 Revision) (ICC)—*cont.*
               (iii) 10–002
               (iv) 10–002
               (b) 10–002
        Art. 4(a)(i)–(iii) 10–002
               (b) 10–002
        Art. 12(a) 10–002
        Arts. 13, 14 10–002
        Arts. 22, 23 10–002
        Art. 24 10–003
        Art. 25 10–002
        Art. 26 10–002
               (a) 10–002
               c(i) 10–002
1996   UN Convention on Independent Guarantees and Stand-by Letters of Credit (New
        York) 11–030, 32–004
        UNCITRAL Model Law on Electronic Commerce 32–005, 33–013
        Arts. 6, 7 33–013
        Arts. 8, 9 33–013
        Art. 11 33–013
        UNCITRAL Notes on Organizing Arbitral Proceedings 32–006
1997   International Carriage of Perishable Foodstuffs (Amendment) Regulations 18–003
        Treaty of Amsterdam 26–009, 26–029, 29–002
        UNCITRAL Model Law on Cross-Border Insolvency 32–005
1998   Code of International Factoring Customs 13–006
        ICC Rules of Conciliation 14–012, 23–025, 32–008
        Art. 4(1), (2) 23–025
        Art. 6(4) 23–025
        Art. 9(3) 23–025
        Rules of Arbitration of the International Chamber of Commerce 23–025
        UNCITRAL Arbitration Rules, the Rules of Arbitration of the ICC 23–006, 23–007,
                                        23–025, 25–020, 25–039
        Art. 8(1), (2) 23–025
        Art. 17(1) 23–008
        Art. 25(3) 23–025
        Art. 28(6) 23–025
1999   International Standby Practices (ISP 98) 11–030
2000   Incoterms 2–001, 2–002, 2–003, 2–005, 32–008
        A2 2–004
        A8 2–004
        B6 2–004
2000   Standard Trading Conditions of the British International Freight Association
        (Standard Trading Conditions) 19–003
        Art. 11(a), (b) 19–003

CHAPTER 1

INTRODUCTION

In this work international trade transactions relate to the exportation of goods **1–001** or services from one country to another. These transactions are referred to as *export transactions* and are divided into two categories: those based on a contract for the international sale of goods and those which involve the supply of services to another country, such as the construction of works and installations.

Export transactions based on a contract of sale

These contracts may be carried out by an exporter selling goods directly to an **1–002** importer abroad or the exporter may choose to create a marketing organisation abroad and conduct business through agents, branch offices, distributors or subsidiary companies.

Selling directly abroad is generally the favoured means of those whose business is usually conducted in the home market or where the volume of exports to any one country does not justify the creation or establishment of a form of representation abroad. The latter is more appropriate where the volume of trade is rather more than occasional. Direct export sales may be transacted regularly or carried out as isolated transactions. Trading through representatives abroad may be carried out under the direct control of the United Kingdom exporter or through looser arrangements such as the use of independent distributors, who may carry the products of other exporters in addition to those of the United Kingdom principal. The exporter may, alternatively, choose the option of establishing a branch office or subsidiary in the country to which the exports are directed. These methods of export trading are examined in Part 8.

Trading by means of sales contracts and through representatives abroad are not exclusive methods of export trading, but are complementary in that the exporter who has appointed permanent representatives abroad normally carries out individual export transactions with them, or through them, by virtue of contracts of sale. This work will examine export trading based on the contract of sale, and also deal with export trading carried out through marketing organisations in other countries.

Export transactions for the construction of works and installations

These transactions generally involve the building of large infrastructure works, **1–003** such as dams or roads or the building of a factory with the attendant transfer of technology, often from an industrialised to a less industrialised nation. The construction contract may proceed by invitation to tender but there also exist other procurement methods. This process is simply stated as the construction phase of the contract and may be accompanied or followed by contracts for the supply of machinery or other equipment to be provided on the basis of an export sale. This type of transaction is examined in Part 6.

THE EXPORT TRANSACTION

1–004   This work is concerned only with the contract of overseas sale, that is a contract under which goods leave the country destined for a buyer abroad, whether by land, sea or air, in containers or as ordinary cargo. All other contracts of sale, though they may be preparatory to the export of goods, are domestic sales and therefore outside the scope of this work. It must be noted that in some sales transactions, for example under an ex works contract, the performance takes place entirely within the country of the seller of the goods and therefore the contract exhibits all the characteristics of a domestic sale. In practice there is no difficulty in determining whether the contract of sale has as its objective the exportation of goods from the country because of the terms of the transaction, such as the arrangements made for the transport of the goods to destination, and the fact that the buyer resides abroad. A great variety of transactions are export transactions and the rights and duties of the parties will vary according to the arrangements they have made regarding the place of delivery, the transportation of the goods and the method of payment of the purchase price. Mercantile custom has developed a number of trade terms and described methods of performance of export transactions. The examination of those terms in the following pages will attempt to indicate the diversity and the practical use of the chosen means of performance.

Contracts for the international sale of goods exhibit a characteristic which is not present in domestic contracts of sale, in that they are entwined with other contracts. These other contracts include the contract for the carriage of goods by whatever means has been agreed, the contract of insurance, and perhaps a contract with a bank or banks under which payment for the goods is to be effected. In many export transactions the delivery of shipping documents to the buyer or the agent of the buyer plays an important, if not pivotal, role in the performance of the transaction. These documents are usually the bill of lading, the commercial invoice and the insurance policy. It is therefore clear that within an export transaction there may be many constituent transactions, each of which will be examined in Parts 1, 2, 3 and 4.

Because of the international character of the transaction and its complexity, regard must be had to the possibility of a dispute arising between the parties. Although this work is based on the presumption that English law will apply to the sale and to all other incidental transactions, it may not do so. Its application or otherwise is determined by examination of an area of law known as the conflict of laws, which will decide where and by what means a dispute may be resolved and in accordance with which law. These matters are set out in Part 5.

The parties and the means involved in the export transaction

1–005   The parties who are involved in an export transaction are numerous and are described variously. The exporter may sell directly to the importer abroad or may sell to an export house or confirming house, which will act either as the agent of the importer or as a principal in its own right. If it acts as agent it will earn commission from the importer; if it acts as principal it will earn the profit on the resale abroad.[1]

The exporter may appoint an agent or set up a branch office, both of which possibilities are examined in Part 8. Alternatively the exporter may conclude a sole distribution agreement, a licensing agreement, franchising agreement or enter a joint venture with a party abroad.

A sole distribution agreement involves the distributor abroad being granted sole or exclusive rights to represent the exporter. Although the distributor is not an agent as such, he does not have to account to the exporter for profits made in selling the goods in question. What this means ought to be specified clearly by the parties, but the agreement will generally involve the granting of sole trading rights, in a specified territory, of specified goods. The exporter will generally agree not to compete with the distributor or allow others to do so. Care must be taken if the distributor is appointed in the territories in which the law of the European Community applies, as there are strict laws safeguarding competition. These interests are set out in Part 8.

A licensing agreement involves the granting by an owner in a particular territory of a form of intellectual property, such as a patent or a trade mark, to a licensee of a right to exploit that property in another territory. The advantage of this type of arrangement is that the licensee provides the capital needed and will carry the commercial risk of the transactions. Two matters are to be noted: the issue of quality control must be dealt with in the licensing agreement and indeed the licensor should protect his reputation by insisting on a right to test samples of the goods produced under licence. Further the issue of compliance with the relevant laws concerning technology transfer when licensing in a less industrialised state must be dealt with, and the relevant European Community law when licensing in a state covered by that legislation.

Where the exporter has a strong and recognisable corporate image, the so-called brand, a particular form of licensing—franchising—may be adopted. Under this arrangement the exporter—franchisor—will rigidly control the way in which the importer—franchisee—conducts the business of selling the goods abroad. The strict control is designed to achieve uniformity between outlets so that customers, wherever they may be, cannot distinguish between outlets owned by the franchisor and those run by the franchisee. Quality control is therefore rigidly maintained. The franchisee will own the outlet and raise his own capital and will source, to the extent of the franchise agreement, goods from the franchisor–exporter.[2]

A joint venture is a common undertaking created by two or more participants for a specific purpose, usually of a commercial nature. The common undertaking may take one of various legal forms and does not necessarily result in the

---

[1] A confirming house may buy goods in this country in its own name or make itself personally responsible to the seller and its profits may be the commission payable by the customer overseas: *Rusholme & Bolton & Roberts Hadfield Ltd v. S.G. Read & Co (London) Ltd* [1955] 1 W.L.R. 146; *Sobell Industries Ltd v. Cory Brothers & Co Ltd* [1955] 2 Lloyd's Rep. 82.

[2] See Chap. 30.

creation of a separate legal entity, as the venture may be purely contractual. Aside from the common project planned, the joint venture partners will pursue their own commercial objects. The joint venture is the preferred vehicle for the conduct of international transactions of certain lesser industrialised nations who have adopted legislation which encourages foreign investment and the protection of their own essential interests. Such a joint enterprise may, in the European context, be in the form of an European Economic Interest Grouping (EEIG),[3] whose purpose is to facilitate and develop the businesses of the participants. The business must be related to the business of the members and its objects must be defined in the contract of formation. In the context of the export trade, the EEIG may be used to create joint buying offices, therefore enabling a more competitive price to be sought from the suppliers, or a joint sales office which could, among other matters, facilitate market studies, thereby ensuring the benefits of an economy of scale. The major forms of overseas organisation, agency, branch offices and subsidiaries are dealt with in Part 8.

The accelerating development of technology has afforded exporters the opportunity of dealing in a paperless environment. The means by which electronic data interchange is conducted and its potential application in export transactions are examined in Part 10.

---

[3] Council Regulation 2137/85 [1985] O.J. L199/1.

CHAPTER 2

SPECIAL TRADE TERMS IN EXPORT SALES

Export sales transactions usually embody trade terms which are not customary **2–001** in the home trade. The most common of these terms are f.a.s., f.o.b. and c.i.f., but there are other less familiar terms which also call for attention. These trade terms have been developed by international mercantile custom and have simplified the sale of goods abroad. They are in universal use in trade transactions but care must be taken as they may be interpreted differently in different countries and their meaning may be modified by agreement of the parties, the custom of a particular trade or the usage prevailing in a particular port.

To avoid any misunderstandings with his buyer abroad, the U.K. exporter should make clear the meaning of any trade term adopted in the transaction. This may be done by, for example, inserting a term into the contract to the effect that the contract will be governed by the law of his own country, the parties may state explicitly what is understood by the use of a particular term or the parties may opt to contract, where appropriate, on standard contract forms issued by trade associations. Alternatively, the exporter may choose to make reference in his own conditions of sale to sets of standard trade terms, for example, *Incoterms*[1] or *Intraterms*[2], the former sponsored by the International Chamber of Commerce under the title of Incoterms 2000, the latter a set of terms developed to eliminate, by the use of plain language, in a "register easily understood by traders", any doubts as to the meaning of terms. An exporter may therefore refer in a contract with a buyer abroad to, as an example, "c.i.f. New York (Incoterms 2000)"[3] or simply provide that "Intraterms 1993 are part of this contract and it should be construed accordingly".[4] Even if the parties agree to trade on the basis of a particular term, the term may nevertheless be adapted by the parties to reflect their particular requirements by the addition of duties on either side. It must be stressed, however, that if a particular sale term is adopted by the parties without reference to any of the published standard sets of terms and if a dispute arises, the English court will apply the traditional meaning of these terms, which

---

[1] Incoterms were first published in 1936. There were revisions and additions in 1953, 1967, 1976, 1980, 1990-ICC No. 460. The new edition, in force on January 1, 2000, is known as ICC No. 560. In some countries Incoterms are given statutory force and in others they are recognised as customs of the trade. In the U.K. neither is the case. Incoterms may be obtained from ICC United Kingdom which is the British National Committee of the International Chamber of Commerce. Their website is *www.iccwbo.org*. Reference should be made to Benjamin, *Sale of Goods* (5th ed.) and to Sassoon, *CIF and FOB Contracts* (4th ed.).

[2] See *International Trade Terms, Standard Terms for Contracts for the International Sale of Goods*, drafted by A.H. Hermann (Graham & Trotman, 1994). They are intended to simplify the language associated with the use of these terms.

[3] In *Universal Petroleum Co Ltd v. Handels und Transport GmbH* [1987] 1 W.L.R. 1178 Incoterms 1980 were incorporated into a contract for the sale of a cargo of oil.

[4] See n. 2 at para. 102 Intraterms.

sometimes differs from the meaning set out in Incoterms and Intraterms or any set of standard terms.[5]

It must also be borne in mind that international conventions, such as the Vienna Convention, sponsored by UNCITRAL, make certain provisions for the sale of goods between parties whose places of business are in two different states. Importantly, the Vienna Convention acknowledges that international trade usages which the parties know about or ought to be aware of, apply to their contracts. It must be emphasised that the Convention, whilst not citing any of the trade terms below, allows parties to exclude its provisions or derogate from certain of them.[6] Whilst setting out the detail of the terms, the appropriate provisions of the Convention will also be cited where relevant.

The special trade terms are designed primarily to define the method of delivery of the goods sold but are also used to indicate the calculation of the purchase price and, in particular, the incidental charges included therein.[7] It is clear that the seller, when quoting f.o.b., will ask for a lower price than when quoting c.i.f. because in the latter insurance and freight charges would be included in the purchase price whereas in an f.o.b. contract they are not. It may be that the seller will quote in his price list or catalogue an ex works price and the buyer abroad may order goods on that basis, but the parties may agree that the goods will be dispatched by mail by the seller who also undertakes to pack, invoice, frank and insure the goods. In this type of situation the term "ex works" refers to the calculation of the purchase price only; the delivery of the goods is governed by other terms.

In the British Customs and Excise practice, the export value is based on the f.o.b. value and the import value on the c.i.f. value, whatever the terms of delivery which have been arranged by the parties. The terms set out below refer to the delivery of the goods and the respective responsibilities of the parties to the contract. The obligations set out are those usually associated with the term but, of course, they may be varied by agreement, by custom or by necessity. The terms, whose duties are summarised below, are derived from Incoterms 2000, Intraterms and the common law.

Ex works (named place)

2–002   In accordance with this term the overseas buyer or his agent must collect the contract goods at the place where the seller's works, factory, warehouse or store are situated. With this in mind, the overseas buyer will have to arrange by himself, or through agents, the collection of the goods by a land carrier to be conveyed to a sea port, airport or railhead so that in pursuance of a further contract for transport of the goods, they may be carried to the country of destination. Insurance will also need to be arranged as the buyer will bear the risks of

---

[5] See Benjamin's *Sale of Goods* (5th ed.), paras 18-002 *et seq.*
[6] See Arts 6 and 12, Vienna Convention on the International Sale of Goods; see Benjamin (*loc. cit.*), para. 1–024.
[7] *Per* Roskill, L.J. in *The Albazero* [1975] 3 W.L.R. 491 at 523, revsd [1977] A.C. 774, HL.

loss or damage to the goods from the time of their delivery to him. The respective obligations of the parties may be summarised as follows:

The seller is required to:

(a) supply conforming goods, which have been weighed, checked, measured and packed for delivery;

(b) supply the invoice and any documents confirming conformity which have been agreed by whatever method has been agreed, or by the agreed means including by electronic communication;

(c) deliver goods to buyer by placing them at the buyer's disposal or otherwise ensuring they may be collected, at the place agreed or at the usual place for such delivery, at the time agreed and give the buyer sufficient notice of the fact without delay[8];

(d) pay any costs incidental to placing the goods at the buyer's disposal;

(e) provide any assistance requested by the buyer in respect of obtaining documents facilitating export or proving information to enable the goods to be insured.

The buyer is required to:

(a) accept delivery of and pay for the goods;

(b) obtain appropriate licences, authorisations for the export of the goods, and comply with customs formalities, whether in the country of delivery or in the exporting country or in a country of transit;

(c) pay any costs incidental to the exportation of the goods including pre-shipment inspection costs, any official charges and the seller's costs in rendering assistance requested by the buyer.

The purchase price becomes due on delivery of the goods unless other arrangements have been made. In an ex works contract the question as to who is to bear the packing costs occasionally arises. The issue will generally be determined by reference to the terms of the contract of sale between the parties. Under Incoterms, the seller is to provide packing at his own expense ". . . which is required for the transport of the goods . . .". It is suggested that this will include export packing, however to avoid any misunderstanding as to whether this obligation extends only to primary packing or is to include export packing, the parties should indicate precisely what is intended.[9]

---

[8] It is generally presumed that in the British practice these obligations arise only if stipulated in the contract. On the duty of the seller under an ex works contract not specifying the locality of the seller's works to notify the buyer of that locality, see n. 10 below. The notes to Incoterms 2000 indicate that should the seller be required to load the goods; this obligation should be specifically agreed.

[9] In *Commercial Fibres (Ireland) Ltd v. Zabaida* [1975] 1 Lloyd's Rep. 27 the sellers undertook to provide export packing at the expense of the buyers.

The ex works clause may either contain the address of the premises from which the goods are to be collected or refer only to the town where the seller's works, factory, store or warehouse is situated. The latter form appears preferable when the seller's business is carried on at various premises in the same locality and it is desired that the sale shall not interfere with the disposition of the goods in the seller's business before they are collected. The seller is then bound to inform the buyer or his agent in time of the local address at which the goods are ready for collection. Failure to do so may ensure that the seller will be unable to maintain an action for non-acceptance and indeed may render himself liable in damages. In one case, Brett J. said[10]: "The words are 'ex quay or warehouse Liverpool.' Liverpool is a large place, and is there not, then, an implied condition for notice to be given?"

The expressions "ex store" and "ex warehouse" are synonymous[11] and denote the place for the storage of goods on land. The terms do not normally include the storage of goods afloat, for example in a lighter, because in this case the goods, when insured, represent a marine risk, whereas goods stored on land are a land risk.[12] The term "ex store" may refer, in certain circumstances, to a particular kind of storage; if, for example, the subject matter of the contract is frozen meat, the term is probably to be construed as meaning "ex refrigerating store."[13] The risk in the goods in an ex works contract passes to the buyer on delivery.

The Vienna Convention requires the seller to "deliver the goods".[14] Under the ex works term this would, by analogy with Article 31(c), be effected by placing the goods at the buyer's disposal at the place where the seller has his business.[15] The buyer is required to "take delivery" and pay for the goods.[16]

Free carrier (named place)

2–003   This term is used frequently when goods are to be transported by container whether by ship, rail, road or a combination of them. It is similar to the f.o.b. term; the seller fulfills his obligations when he delivers the goods into the custody of the carrier at the named point. If no precise point can be stated at the time of the making of the contract, the parties should refer to the place or range of places where the carrier should take the goods into charge; otherwise the place or range is at the seller's choice. The risk of loss or damage is transferred

---

[10] *Davies v. McLean* (1873) 21 W.R. 264 at 265.
[11] *Fisher, Reeves & Co v. Armour & Co* [1920] 3 K.B. 614.
[12] The term "warehouse" has been interpreted in a case concerning burglary insurance as a building and not an enclosed yard (*Leo Rapp Ltd v. McClure* [1955] 1 Lloyd's Rep. 292 at 293). The same interpretation need not necessarily be given to the term in a contract of sale.
[13] The definition "free on rail" and "free on truck", which were contained in the 1980 Incoterms but omitted in the 1990 Revision are not discussed here as they have been made obsolete by the use of the term "free carrier".
[14] Art. 30, Vienna Convention.
[15] Art. 31(c) states "—in placing the goods at the buyer's disposal at the place where the seller had his place of business at the time of the conclusion of the contract".
[16] Art. 53.

at that point. The respective obligations of the parties may be summarised as follows:

The seller is required to:

    (a) supply conforming goods, which have been weighed, checked, measured and packed for delivery;

    (b) supply the invoice and any documents confirming conformity which have been agreed by whatever means have been agreed, including by electronic communication;

    (c) deliver the goods to buyer by placing them in the charge of the carrier named by the buyer at the place agreed for delivery, in the manner agreed or which is customary for the place of delivery, or by loading them onto the carrier's vehicle if that has been agreed;

    (d) if no specific point has been named, and if there are several points available, the seller may select the point at the place of delivery;

    (e) obtain any export licence or other official authorization necessary for the export of the goods if required to do so and pay any taxes, fees and charges associated with exportation;

    (f) bear all costs payable in respect of the goods until delivery;

    (g) provide at his own expense the customary packing of the goods, unless it is the custom of the trade to dispatch the goods unpacked;

    (h) give the buyer without delay appropriate notice of the delivery of the goods;

    (i) assist the buyer in obtaining the contract of carriage and or insurance if agreed.

The buyer is required to:

    (a) accept delivery of and pay for the goods;

    (b) obtain appropriate licences, authorisations for the export of the goods, and comply with customs formalities, whether in the country of delivery, in the exporting country or in a country of transit;

    (c) pay any costs incidental to the exportation of the goods and any costs incurred by the seller in giving any assistance which has been requested by the buyer including costs associated with the provision of documents or electronic messages;

    (d) contract for the carriage of the goods from the agreed point of delivery and give the seller appropriate notice of the name of the carrier and of the time for delivering the goods to him.

Incoterms[17] requires the buyer to bear any additional costs incurred because of his failure to name the carrier, or the carrier named by him fails to take the goods into his charge at the time agreed, and to bear all risks of the goods from the date of expiry of the period stipulated for delivery, so long as the goods have been appropriated to the contract, either by their setting aside or by clear identification as the contract goods.

F.A.S. (named port of shipment)

2–004 This acronym stands for "free alongside ship". This term contains elements not to be found in a sale on the home market. The seller will discharge his responsibility and risk in respect of the goods when they are delivered alongside the ship, which will have been arranged and paid for by the buyer. It may be that the seller has to deliver near the vessel's tying-up berth, so that the goods may be loaded by the ship's own tackle or shore crane or by other means. Delivery alongside carries the implication that the goods are placed in the possession of the carrier. Once delivery has been made, the actual loading of the goods over the ship's rail is the buyer's, and not the seller's, responsibility and the charges for it have to be borne by the buyer. Where the ship is berthed alongside a wharf or quay, the goods have to be placed ashore near her anchorage; where the ship cannot enter the port or is anchored in the stream, the seller has to provide and pay for lighters which will take the consignment alongside the ship, unless the parties agree that delivery should be made "free on lighter", in which case the responsibility of the seller ends when the goods are delivered over the lighter's rail.

The f.a.s. term is frequently used in circumstances where the buyer has a matching contract on c. & f. or c.i.f. terms. An example of such an arrangement is to be found in *Metro Meat Ltd v. Fares Rural Co Pty Ltd*[18] where the seller on f.a.s. terms was the supplier of goods being sold on c. & f. terms.

The respective obligations of the parties may be summarised as follows:

The seller is required to:

    (a) supply conforming goods, packed appropriately or in accordance with the contract, and the commercial invoice or equivalent electronic message which has been agreed;

    (b) deliver the goods to buyer by placing them alongside the vessel or the loading berth which has been notified by the buyer in the manner which is usual or customary at that port for such delivery, at the time agreed and without delay give the buyer sufficient notice of the fact;

    (c) pay any costs incidental to delivery of the goods;

---

[17] See n. 1 above. Incoterms 2000 provides that if delivery is at the seller's place of business, the seller delivers by loading the goods. The carrier is defined as a person who "undertakes to perform or procure performance of transport."

[18] [1985] 2 Lloyd's Rep. 14.

(d) provide proof of delivery[19] in the manner agreed and provide documents confirming conformity if required to do so;

(e) provide any assistance requested by the buyer in respect of obtaining documents facilitating export and providing information to enable the goods to be insured.[20]

The buyer is required to:

(a) give sufficient notice to the seller of the time and location of the delivery having, presumably, contracted for the carriage of the goods from the port of shipment and bear any costs occasioned by his failure to do so;

(b) obtain any appropriate licences, authorisations for the export of the goods, and comply with customs formalities, whether in the country of delivery or in the exporting country or in a country of transit;

(c) pay any costs incidental to the exportation of the goods including pre-shipment inspection costs, any official charges and the seller's costs in rendering assistance requested by the buyer;

(d) pay for the goods.

Strictly speaking, port rates fall due when the goods are "exported", that is when the ship carrying them leaves port. In practice, this obligation is often varied by the rules or custom of the port of shipment. In this respect the obligations under the clause f.a.s. are the same as under that of f.o.b. In order to avoid any dispute as to the responsibility for the payment of port rates, this liability should be covered by express agreement of the parties. Thus, the term "f.a.s. London" (including port rates) would indicate that the export seller wishes to conform with the practice of that port.

Dock dues payable when the goods enter the docks, as well as wharfage, porterage, lighterage and similar charges, have to be borne by the seller,[21] in the absence of a contrary agreement or custom of the port. Where the parties agree that the goods are to be delivered "free to docks" or the phrase "delivery to docks" is used, these charges fall upon the buyer.

As to documentation, the seller is required by Incoterms and Intraterms to provide provide proof of delivery. (The seller need not provide a dock or wharfingers' receipt unless this is stipulated in the contract in terms or necessitated by the custom of the trade.) The seller may be required under the terms of

---

[19] It is thought that in the British practice these obligations arise only if stipulated in the contract. See now Incoterms 2000, A8 where the seller is required to provide proof of delivery—a reversal of the previous position.

[20] Under the agreement of the parties, the duty to obtain an export licence falls normally on the seller. Under Incoterms 2000, the seller is required to clear the goods for export—A2.

[21] The seller has likewise normally to pay or refund to the buyer the "f.o.b. service charge" which freight forwarders often charge. It would appear to make no difference whether the forwarder was chosen by the seller or by the buyer.

the contract of sale to provide additional documentation. The case of *Gill and Duffus Landauer Ltd v. London Export Corporation GmbH*[22] provides an example of this. In that case the seller was obliged by the standard terms of the Dried Fruit Association of California to provide a certificate of quality in respect of the subject matter of the contract, which was shelled almonds.

Under the f.a.s. contract, as under the strict f.o.b.[23] contract, the duty to nominate a suitable ship falls on the buyer unless the parties have made other arrangements.[24] The question whether under an f.a.s. contract an export licence has to be obtained by the seller or the buyer is subject to the same considerations as are explained later with reference to the f.o.b. contract. In the leading case of *M. W. Hardy & Co Inc v. A. V. Pound & Co Ltd* (which dealt with an f.a.s. contract) Lord Goddard C.J., when examining this issue, said: "that in the present case the contract was f.a.s. and not f.o.b. is in my opinion immaterial".[25]

The f.a.s. contract thus creates many, though not all, rights and duties germane to the f.o.b. contract, and it is not surprising that in the American Uniform Commercial Code these two trade terms are treated in the same paragraph.[26]

In container transport the parties sometimes arrange for delivery "free arrival station", meaning that the carrier undertakes to deliver the containers to the arrival station specified in the contract, ready for Customs clearance and emptying by or on behalf of the importers.[27] They may abbreviate this term "f.a.s." but it has, of course, an entirely different meaning from the term here discussed and its meaning should be expressed in unambiguous terms. This type of contract is, in effect, an arrival contract.

In respect of f.c.a. and f.a.s. contracts which involve delivery to a means of carriage, it may be noted that the Vienna Convention provides that the seller's obligation to deliver consists, "if the contract of sale involves carriage of the goods—in handing the goods over to the first carrier for transmission to the buyer".[28] The seller must also give due notice of the consignment, should the goods not already be clearly identified as the contract goods.[29] The buyer's obligation[30] consists of doing all the acts which could reasonably be expected of him to enable the seller to make delivery, including, presumably, entering the appropriate contract of carriage and giving due notices to the seller. He is also obliged to "take over the goods".

---

[22] [1982] 2 Lloyd's Rep. 627.

[23] See *post*, para. 2–007.

[24] *Anglo-African Shipping Co of New York Inc v. J. Mortner* [1962] 1 Lloyd's Rep. 610. In *Gill and Duffus Landauer Ltd v. London Export Corporation GmbH* [1982] 2 Lloyd's Rep. 627 a contract "f.a.s. California" was in issue and Goff J. held, *inter alia*, that the place of performance was in California and the law governing the contract was Californian.

[25] [1955] 1 Q.B. 499 at 512; affd [1956] A.C. 588, HL.

[26] UCC, s.2-319, entitled "F.o.b. and f.a.s. terms". The f.a.s term is defined in s.2-319(2).

[27] *Kuehne and Nagel Ltd v. W. B. Woolley (Scotland) Ltd* (1973, unreported, Westminster county court), see p. 611.

[28] Art. 31(a).

[29] Art. 32(1).

[30] Art. 60 (a) and (b).

F.O.B. (named port of shipment)

The seller when selling f.o.b. ("free on board") assumes still further responsibil- **2–005**
ities than in the preceding instances.[31] He undertakes to place the goods on board
a ship that has been named to him by the buyer and that is berthed at the agreed
port of shipment. All charges incurred up to and including the delivery of the
goods on board ship have to be borne by the seller while the buyer has to pay
all subsequent charges, such as the stowage of the goods in or on board ship,[32]
freight and marine insurance as well as unloading charges, import duties, consular fees and other incidental charges due on arrival of the consignment in the
port of destination.[33] The transaction differs considerably from an ordinary sale
in the home market where no dealings in a port have to be carried out, and yet
it does not exhibit the foreign complexion which is a true characteristic of an
export transaction.

The f.o.b. clause is frequently taken as a basis for the calculation of the goods
sold and not as a term defining the method of delivery. Thus, in the practice of
the U.K. Customs and export licensing authorities, the export value of the goods
is founded on an f.o.b. calculation, whatever the agreed terms of delivery.

The obligations of the seller under the f.o.b. contract may be summarised as
follows:

The seller is required to:

    (a) supply conforming goods, packed appropriately or in accordance with
        the contract, and any documents confirming conformity which have
        been agreed and supply a commercial invoice or its electronic equiva-
        lent;

    (b) deliver the goods to buyer by placing them on board, that is over the
        rail of the vessel which has been notified by the buyer, in the manner
        which is usual or customary at that port for such delivery, at the time
        agreed and without delay give the buyer sufficient notice of the fact;

    (c) place them on the vessel in the position and manner required;

---

[31] On the history of f.o.b. and c.i.f., see D. M. Sassoon, "The Origin of f.o.b. and c.i.f. Terms and
the Factors influencing their Choice" [1967] J.B.L. 32. See also F. Wooldridge, "The Kinds of f.o.b.
Contracts" in *Law and International Trade, Festschrift fur C. M. Schmitthoff* (Frankfurt, 1973),
p. 383.
[32] The parties may, however, agree on "f.o.b. stowed" or "f.o.b. stowed/trimmed" or "f.o.b. in":
President of India v. Metcalfe Shipping Co [1970] 1 Q.B. 289, CA; *David T. Boyd & Co Ltd v.
Louis Louca* [1973] 1 Lloyd's Rep. 209; *The Filipinas I* [1973] 1 Lloyd's Rep. 349; *Kollerich &
Cie SA v. The State Trading Corporation of India* [1980] 2 Lloyd's Rep. 32; *Compagnie de
Rénflouement Baroukh v. W. Seymour Plant Sales & Hire Ltd* [1981] 2 Lloyd's Rep. 466 at 470;
Gill & Duffus SA v. Société pour L'Exportation des Sucres SA [1985] 1 Lloyd's Rep. 621; *Pagnan
SpA v. Tradax Ocean Transportation SA* [1987] 2 Lloyd's Rep. 342 (tapioca pellets, "f.o.b. stowed/
trimmed").
[33] The f.o.b. buyer under an f.o.b. contract has to bear the charges for obtaining the bills of lading.
Unless otherwise agreed, the f.o.b. buyer has also to bear the costs for obtaining documents such as
certificates of origin, consular documents or other documents which he may require for importation
into his country or for transit through other countries. See Incoterms 2000, B6.

(d) pay any costs incidental to delivery of the goods;

(e) obtain an export licence, if so required, or any other document necessary for the exportation of the goods and clear the goods through customs;

(f) provide proof of delivery in the manner agreed—provide any assistance requested by the buyer in respect of obtaining documents facilitating export and providing information to enable the goods to be insured.

The buyer is required to:

(a) give sufficient notice to the seller of the time and location of the delivery having, presumably, contracted for the carriage of the goods from the port of shipment, bear any costs occasioned by his failure to do so and bear the risk of loss or damage to the goods from the time they pass over the ship's rail;

(b) obtain any appropriate licences, authorisations for the import of the goods, and comply with customs formalities for importation whether in the country of destination or in a country of transit;

(c) pay any costs incidental to the importation of the goods, bear the risk in those goods from the time of their delivery and bear the costs of the provision of assistance by the seller at the request of the buyer;

(d) pay for the goods.

In container transport the term f.o.b. is sometimes used as a general delivery term, *e.g.* in such phrases as "f.o.b. container freight station", but this is confusing and should be avoided. It is better in this case to use the term "free carrier".[34]

The liabilities of the parties arising under a contract of sale on f.o.b. terms are sometimes defined by usage prevailing in a particular trade or a particular port. Thus, in the oil trade, for example, a trade usage exists according to which an f.o.b. buyer has to give the seller timely notice of loading.[35] In the port of Stockholm, if wood products are sold "f.o.b. Stockholm", the buyer has to bear the loading costs into the vessel; by this trade usage the f.o.b. delivery is converted into an f.a.s. delivery.

Where a contract is stated to be on f.o.b. terms, the presumption is that the parties intend to give it its established meaning. The seller's instructions to the shipping agents not to hand over the goods until payment has been secured do not nullify the normal consequence that the seller has completed the delivery of the goods when they are placed on board ship or in the hold if so required by

---

[34] See Incoterms, Intraterms and the Vienna Convention, Art. 31(a) which, however, would not equate with a seller's responsibilities under an f.o.b. contract. An f.o.b. seller must deliver goods over a surplus rail.
[35] *Scandinavian Trading Co A/S v. Zodiac Petroleum SA and William Hudson Ltd; The Al Hofuf* [1981] 1 Lloyd's Rep. 81 at 84. See also *The Naxos* [1991] 1 Lloyd's Rep. 29 at *post*, paras 2–010 and 2–013. On notice of readiness to load, see para. 2–010.

agreement or by custom, in the port of despatch.[36] The responsibilities of the parties for the payment of port rates, dock dues, wharfage, porterage and similar charges are the same as were explained in connection with a sale on f.a.s. terms.

American practice

In the United Kingdom and the Commonwealth "f.o.b." is understood as mean- **2–006** ing "f.o.b. vessel." In the American practice "f.o.b." has become a general delivery term which, if used in the form "f.o.b. place of destination", even denotes free delivery at that place.[37] The equivalent to the English meaning of "f.o.b." is the American term "f.o.b. vessel". The American regulation can be gathered from the following provisions of the Uniform Commercial Code[38]:

> "Unless otherwise agreed the term f.o.b. (which means "free on board") at a named place, even though used only in connection with the stated price, is a delivery term under which—
>
> (a) when the term is f.o.b. the place of shipment, the seller must at that place ship the goods . . . and bear the expense and risk of putting them into the possession of the carrier; or
> (b) when the term is f.o.b. the place of destination, the seller must at his own expense and risk transport the goods to that place and there tender delivery of them . . .;
> (c) where under either (a) or (b) the term is also f.o.b. vessel, car or other vehicle, the seller must in addition at his own expense and risk load the goods on board. If the term is f.o.b. vessel the buyer must name the vessel and in the appropriate case the seller must comply with the provisions of this Article on the form of bill of lading . . . ."

Types of f.o.b. contracts

The term f.o.b. is used in transactions of different character and the responsibilit- **2–007** ies which arise under the clause differ according to the nature of the transaction in which the term occurs. The incidental obligations which the term f.o.b. implies have to be ascertained by an analysis of the express or implied intention of the parties.[39]

The term f.o.b. may, for example, be used by an exporter who buys from a manufacturer or merchant in the United Kingdom and who intends to resell the goods abroad; this supply transaction may be concluded f.o.b. U.K. Port. Further, an exporter may sell or resell goods to an overseas buyer f.o.b. U.K. Port; in this case the f.o.b. term is used in the export transaction. The exporter should be aware of the fact that the f.o.b. term when used in the supply transaction may carry different incidental obligations from such a term when used in the export transaction. This point was made clear by Singleton L.J. in *M. W. Hardy & Co Inc v. A. V. Pound & Co Ltd*[40] who explained that this difference might be

---

[36] *Frebold an Sturznickel (Panda OHG) v. Circle Products Ltd* [1970] 1 Lloyd's Rep. 499 at 504.
[37] In this sense the term was used by a Canadian company in *Northland Airliners Ltd v. Dennis Ferranti Meters Ltd* (1970) 114 S.J. 845.
[38] s. 2-319(1).
[39] The different types of f.o.b. clauses and the incidents of the f.o.b. contract in general are analysed in Sassoon, *C.I.F. and F.O.B. Contracts* (British Shipping Laws, 4th ed., 1995).
[40] [1955] 1 Q.B. 499, 508, 510; affd by [1956] A.C. 588, HL.

material for the decision whether an export licence had to be obtained by the seller or the buyer.

A further distinction of considerable practical importance is that between three types of f.o.b. contract, and, here again, it depends on the intention of the parties which of these types is used.

The first type is the "strict" or "classic" f.o.b. contract.[41] Under this arrangement the buyer has to nominate a suitable ship. When it arrives in the port of shipment, the seller places the goods on board under a contract of carriage by sea which he has made with the carrier, but this contract is made for the account of the buyer. The seller receives the bill of lading which normally shows him as consignor and is to his order, and he transfers it to the buyer. Marine insurance is normally arranged by the buyer directly, if he wishes to insure, but he may also ask the seller to arrange marine insurance for his, the buyer's, account.

The second type is the f.o.b. contract "with additional services". Under this arrangement the shipping and insurance arrangements are made by the seller, but this is done for the account of the buyer. In this type of f.o.b. contract the buyer is not under an obligation to nominate a suitable ship but the nomination is done by the seller. Again, as in contracts of the first type, the seller enters into a contract with the carrier by sea, places the goods on board ship and transfers the bill of lading to the buyer.

The third type may be described as the f.o.b. contract (buyer contracting with carrier) or "simple" f.o.b.[42] Here, the buyer himself enters into a contract of carriage by sea directly or through an agent, *e.g.* a forwarder. Naturally, the buyer has nominated the ship, and when it calls at the port of shipment, the seller puts the goods on board. The bill of lading goes directly to the buyer, usually through an agent of the buyer in the port of shipment, such as a freight forwarder, and does not pass through the seller's hands.

Considerable legal differences exist between these three types of f.o.b. contract. They indicate the flexible nature of this arrangement. Indeed, variations and combinations of these types of f.o.b. contract are met in practice. In f.o.b. contracts of the first and third type the duty to nominate the ship falls on the buyer, but in those of the second type it falls on the seller. In contracts of the first and second type the seller is in a contractual relationship with the sea carrier, and for this reason the second type has been described as a variant of the first type.[43] In a contract of the third type, on the other hand, the contract of carriage by sea is made directly with the buyer and the seller is not a party to it.

---

[41] *Per* McNair J. in *NV Handel My. J. Smits Import-Export v. English Exporters (London) Ltd* [1957] 1 Lloyd's Rep. 517 at 519. In *Scandinavian Trading Co A/B v. Zodiac Petroleum SA and William Hudson Ltd; The Al Hofuf* [1981] 1 Lloyd's Rep. 81 an f.o.b. clause used in the oil trade was in issue. Mocatta J. referred to the clause as of the classic type (at 84), but it is more likely that the clause was of a type described here as an f.o.b. (buyer contracting with carrier) clause. See also *Lusograin Comercio Internacional De Cereas Ltd v. Bunge AG* [1986] 2 Lloyd's Rep. 654 as an example of a strict f.o.b. contract.

[42] Although in this type of f.o.b. contract the buyer concludes the contract of carriage with the carrier directly, this type of f.o.b. clause, like any other type of this clause, is, of course, a term of the contract of sale between the seller and buyer and determines the ship's rail as the critical point for the delivery of the goods.

[43] *Per* Donaldson L.J. in *El Amina and El Minia* [1982] 2 Lloyd's Rep. 28 at 32.

The three different types of f.o.b. contract are described by Devlin J. in *Pyrene Co Ltd v. Scindia Navigation Co Ltd* as follows[44]:

"The f.o.b. contract has become a flexible instrument. In . . . the classic type . . . for example, in *Wimble, Sons & Co Ltd v. Rosenberg & Sons*,[45] the buyer's duty is to nominate the ship, and the seller's to put the goods on board for account of the buyer and procure a bill of lading in terms usual in the trade. In such a case the seller is directly a party to the contract of carriage at least until he takes out the bill of lading in the buyer's name. Probably the classic type is based on the assumption that the ship nominated will be willing to load any goods brought down to the berth or at least those of which she is notified. Under present conditions, when space often has to be booked well in advance, the contract of carriage comes into existence at an earlier point of time. Sometimes the seller is asked to make the necessary arrangements; and the contract may then provide for his taking the bill of lading in his own name and obtaining payment against the transfer, as in a c.i.f. contract. Sometimes the buyer engages his own forwarding agent at the port of loading to book space and to procure the bill of lading; if freight has to be paid in advance this method may be most convenient. In such a case the seller discharges his duty by putting the goods on board, getting the mate's receipt and handing it to the forwarding agent to enable him to obtain the bill of lading."

This statement has been referred to with approval by the Court of Appeal in *The El Amria and El Minia*[46]:

"In *Pyrene & Co v. Scindia Steam Navigation Co* Mr. Justice Devlin instanced three types of f.o.b. contract. In the first, or classic type, the buyer nominates the ship and the seller puts the goods on board for account of the buyer, procuring a bill of lading. The seller is then a party to the contract of carriage and if he has taken the bill of lading to his order, the only contract of carriage to which the buyer can become a party is that contained in the bill of lading which is endorsed to him by the seller. The second is a variant of the first, in that the seller arranges for the ship to come on the berth, but the legal incidents are the same. The third is where the seller puts the goods on board, takes a mate's receipt and gives this to the buyer or his agent who then takes a bill of lading. In this latter type the buyer is a party to the contract of carriage *ab initio*."

In the *Pyrene* case an f.o.b. contract of the third type was in issue. The plaintiffs, Pyrene Co Ltd, sold a number of fire tenders to the Government of India for delivery f.o.b. London. The buyers nominated a ship belonging to the defendants and through their forwarding agents made all arrangements for the carriage of the goods to Bombay. While one of the tenders was being lifted into the vessel by the ship's tackle the mast broke and the tender, which had not crossed the ship's rail, was dropped on the quay and damaged; it was repaired at a cost of £966 and later shipped in another vessel. The sellers claimed the cost of the repair from the defendants who admitted negligence but pleaded that, being carriers, their liability was limited under the regulation then in force[47] to £200. Devlin J. held that the sellers, although not parties to the contract of carriage by sea (which was concluded between the buyers and the defendants), participated in the contract so far as it affected them, and took the benefits of the contract which appertained to them subject to the qualifications imposed by the contract,

---

[44] [1954] 2 Q.B. 402 at 424.
[45] [1913] 3 K.B. 743.
[46] [1982] 2 Lloyd's Rep. 28 at 32.
[47] That regulation was Art. IV(5) of the Schedule to the Carriage of Goods by Sea Act 1924, as supplemented by the British Maritime Law Association Agreement of 1950. The 1924 Act is now superseded by the Carriage of Goods by Sea Act 1971; see, para. 15–020 *et seq.*

i.e. subject to the maximum limits of liability. The learned judge held further that as far as the defendants as carriers were concerned the "loading" for which they were responsible was the whole loading operation undertaken by them, and not only that stage of the loading occurring after the goods crossed the ship's rail. Devlin J. gave judgment for the sellers for £200.[48] The position may be different in multimodal transport, where different international conventions apply to different stages of the loading operation. In *Thermo Engineers Ltd v. Ferrymasters Ltd*[49] the issue was whether damage suffered by the cargo during its loading on board ship was governed by the CMR, which applies to the carriage by road,[50] or by the Hague Rules, which then applied to the carriage by sea.[51] The cargo was a huge heat exchanger which had been sold by an English company to buyers in Copenhagen. The exchanger was carried in a trailer and when the trailer drove on the ship, the protruding superstructure of the exchanger struck the bulkhead of the lower deck and was damaged. The trailer had already passed the outward ramp of the vessel and crossed the line of the stern. Neill J. held that the carriage by road had ceased, although the trailer and its load had not been secured in the ship, and that the damage was governed by the Hague Rules. If in this case the damage had occurred before the trailer crossed the ship's rail, the CMR would have applied.

Arrangement of freight and marine insurance

2–008   When goods are sold on f.o.b. terms it is, in principle, the duty of the buyer to arrange the freight and marine insurance cover. The f.o.b. (buyer contracting with carrier) contract is thus the most typical form of f.o.b. contract.[52]

This arrangement is often felt to be inconvenient because the seller who conducts his business in the country where the goods are situated before dispatch has better facilities for arranging these matters than the buyer. This has therefore fostered the development of the classic f.o.b. contract and the f.o.b. contract with additional services. In these two types the parties have agreed that the seller shall enter into a contractual relationship with the carrier and arrange the car-

---

[48] It has been questioned whether *Pyrene Co Ltd v. Scindia Navigation Co Ltd* is good law, in view of the decision of the House of Lords in *Midland Silicones Ltd v. Scruttons Ltd* [1962] A.C. 446. It is thought that this question has to be answered in the affirmative, *per* Viscount Simonds at 471. This view is supported by the fact that in the USA the Supreme Court in *Robert C. Herd & Co Inc v. Krawill Machinery Corpn* (1959) 359 U.S. 297; [1959] 1 Lloyd's Rep. 305 decided similarly to *Midland Silicones*. A New York court gave later a decision similar to *Pyrene* in *Carle & Montanari Inc v. American Export Isbrandtsen Lines Inc* [1968] 1 Lloyd's Rep. 260; see also *New Zealand Shipping Co Inc v. A. M. Satterthwaite & Co Ltd; The Eurymedon* [1975] A.C. 154. On the matter of carrier's limitations and immunities see also para. 15–047, *Burke Motors Ltd v. Mersey Docks & Harbour Co* [1986] 1 Lloyd's Rep. 155, 158–159; *The Kapetan Markos* [1986] 1 Lloyd's Rep. 211; *The Kapetan Markos (No. 2)* [1987] 2 Lloyd's Rep. 321 at 325; *London Drugs Ltd v. Kuehene & Nagel International Ltd* [1992] 3 S.C.R. 299.
[49] [1981] 1 Lloyd's Rep. 200.
[50] See Chap. 18.
[51] When the accident happened the unamended Hague Rules, and not the Hague-Visby Rules, applied; see, para. 15–020.
[52] If the seller under an f.o.b. contract has given the buyer credit, it may be in his interest to take out a contingency insurance relating to the goods because he may have to exercise his right of stoppage in transit. See, para. 5–016.

riage. In both these types of f.o.b. contract the seller will do so normally in his own name. In all types of f.o.b. contract the costs of the freight and insurance ultimately have to be borne by the buyer.[53] In *Glencore Grain Rotterdam BV v. Lebanese Organisation for International Commerce (LORICO)*[54] it was made clear that the seller under an f.o.b. contract is free of any obligation to pay freight and any requirement to do so under the term would, in the absence of special terms otherwise, be contrary to the underlying concept of the f.o.b. contract.

In the f.o.b. contract with additional services the seller may take out the bill of lading in his own name or as an agent of the buyer.[55] In accordance with general principle, the seller is entitled to charge the buyer for the freight and insurance premium, if on the instructions of the buyer he has taken out insurance, and with incidental expenses. He may further charge a commission for having procured the contracts of carriage by sea and marine insurance unless the parties have agreed otherwise or there is a custom of the trade to the contrary. In this case the seller may make out two invoices, one showing the f.o.b. values of the goods including all expenses up to the delivery of the goods over the ship's rail, and another invoice showing the additional services which he performed by request of the buyer, and in particular the costs of prepaid freight and marine insurance and any commission which might be due to him.[56]

Where the seller is to enter the contract of carriage or there are circumstances where the buyer is unaware of the shipping arrangements then, according to English law, the f.o.b. seller has to give the buyer due notice enabling him to insure the goods in sea transit; this duty is provided by the Sale of Goods Act 1979, s.32(3) which states:

> "Unless otherwise agreed, where goods are sent by the seller to the buyer by a route involving sea transit, under circumstances in which it is usual to insure, the seller must give such notice to the buyer as may enable him to insure them during their sea transit, and, if the seller fails to do so, the goods shall be deemed to be at his risk during such sea transit."[57]

The rationale for such a provision is clear; the f.o.b. buyer bears the risk in the goods from the time they cross the rails, and should he not know when the risk passes and the seller does, the seller is obliged to inform him.

RESPONSIBILITIES OF THE PARTIES

Nominating a suitable ship

Sometimes the parties will specify in the contract the ship or the line to which **2–009** the goods are to be delivered, or the parties may agree that the seller will provide the ship. If this is not done, subject to what has been stated, the duty of the

---

[53] *N. V. Handel My. J. Smits Import-Export v. English Exporters Ltd* [1957] 1 Lloyd's Rep. 517, and *per* Herring C.J. in *The Mahia (No. 2)* [1960] 1 Lloyd's Rep. 191 at 198 (Sup. Ct. Victoria).
[54] [1997] 2 Lloyd's Rep. 386, CA.
[55] See para. 2–007.
[56] In the certificate of value required by some Customs authorities the second invoice should be mentioned under "special arrangement".
[57] *Wimble v. Rosenberg & Sons* [1913] 3 K.B. 743.

buyer is to provide the seller with shipping instructions which will enable the
seller to bring the goods alongside and load within the time stipulated by the
contract. The instructions will generally include the name of a suitable ship in
which the goods are to be carried[58] and notice of probable readiness of the ship
to receive the goods. The duty was described by Lord Hewart C.J. in the following words[59]:

> "It was the duty of the purchasers to provide a vessel at the appointed place at such a time
> as would enable the vendors to bring the goods alongside the ship and to put them over the
> ship's rail so as to enable the purchasers to receive them within the appointed time ... the
> usual practice under such a contract is for the buyer to nominate a vessel and to send notice
> of her arrival to the vendor, in order that the vendor may be in a position to fulfil his part of
> the contract."

Suitable ship

2–010   A ship is suitable if it is ready, able and willing to carry the contract goods. It
must be able to load at the specified port; in one instance the contract required
the buyers to provide a ship which complied with size restrictions of a range of
ports, and compliance with this requirement was held to be a condition of the
contract. It is clear that a ship with no refrigeration equipment is not suitable
for a cargo of chilled goods, likewise a general cargo vessel would not be suitable for the carriage of crude oil in bulk. In one case the cargo to be loaded
consisted of large sections of scrap metal. The contract was "fob and stowed
Richards Bay (South Africa)". The buyers nominated The Vicmar Navigator to
carry the goods and the sellers accepted. Mustill J. said[60]:

> "This raises only one issue of principle, which is short but not easy. As I have already stated
> Vicmar was not a suitable ship for her task and the tender of this ship was prima facie a
> breach of contract. Yet [the sellers] expressly accepted her at the time when she was fixed,
> subject to shipper's approval."

The ship to be effective must be able to load the goods within the shipping
period.[61] It may be that the contract will provide that the buyer give notice
within a stated time of the probable readiness of the nominated ship to load. If
there is no such provision the buyer will be required to give such notice as is
reasonable.[62] It has been held that the requirement to give such notice was a

---

[58] A suitable ship is sometimes referred to, as an "effective ship".
[59] In *J. and J. Cunningham Ltd v. Robert A. Monroe & Co Ltd* (1922) 28 Com. Cas. 42 at 45; see
also *per* Scrutton L.J. in *H. O. Brandt & Co v. H. N. Morris & Co Ltd* [1917] 2 K.B. 784 at 798.
For a detailed nomination clause see *Bremer Handelsgesellschaft mbH v. J. H. Rayner & Co Ltd*
[1978] 2 Lloyd's Rep. 73, 85–86. Also *Miserocchi and CSpA v. Agricultores Federados Argentinos
SCL* [1982] 1 Lloyd's Rep. 202 at 207; *Bunge AG v. Sesostrad SA; The Alkeos* [1984] 1 Lloyd's
Rep. 687 at 688. *Richco International v. Bunge and Co (The New Prosper)* [1991] 2 Lloyd's Rep.
93, where the nominated vessel did not comply with the port's load restrictions and was therefore
not contractual.
[60] *Compagnie de Renflouement de Récuperation et de Travaux Sous-Marins VS Baroukh et Cie v.
W. Seymour Plant Sales and Hire Ltd* [1981] 2 Lloyd's Rep. 466, HL at 482.
[61] *J. and J. Cunningham Ltd v. Robert A. Monroe & Co Ltd* (1922) 28 Com. Cas. 42; *Napier (F.E.)
v. Dexters Ltd* (1926) 26 L.l.L.R. 184.
[62] *ibid.*

condition of the contract and not an innominate term.[63] If the f.o.b. is combined with a clause providing a shipment period, for example "shipment in August/September", the buyer must nominate a ship which allows the goods to be shipped within that time. The buyer therefore has the option of determining the time for loading. The goods are in this respect "at the buyer's call".[64]

The seller is obliged to load the goods if the ship nominated is ready to receive them. The seller in this type of contract should insist on a provision whereby he receives sufficient notice of readiness of the ship so that he may bring the goods alongside and commence loading on presentation of the vessel. If the goods are at the buyer's call and sufficient notice of readiness is given the seller will be obliged to comply with that notice and have the contract goods available for loading without delay or interruption.[65]

Failure to nominate a suitable ship

The seller may be entitled therefore to treat the contract as repudiated should the buyer fail to nominate within the stipulated time.[66] Sometimes the buyer may nominate a ship which is unsuitable simply to comply with the requirement of making a timely nomination, with the hope of making a substitution subsequently. Such an artificial and fanciful nomination will entitle the seller to treat the contract as repudiated.[67] **2–011**

The seller is entitled to claim damages for the failure of the buyer to nominate a suitable ship or for his delay in doing so. The purchase price may not be claimed as the seller will still have the goods; the seller must therefore, from any damages, deduct the value of the goods. This is so whether or not the goods have a market value or whether they were uniquely built to the buyer's specification. This rule applies whatever the reason for reason for the buyer's "failure". In view of this position the seller may well insist on a contract clause

---

[63] On this type of loading notice see *Bunge Corporation v. Tradax Export SA* [1980] 1 Lloyd's Rep. 294, CA where it was held that the obligation to give such notice was a condition, and not an innominate term, because in mercantile contracts stipulations as to time are usually of the essence of the contract. Similarly, *Gill & Duffus SA v. Société pour l'Exportation des Sucres SA* [1985] 1 Lloyd's Rep. 621 where in an f.o.b. contract with additional services the duty to nominate the load port within a specified time fell on the seller and his failure to do so was held to be a breach of a condition relieving the buyer from his obligation to perform. Also *Lusograin Comercio Internacional De Cereas Ltda v. Bunge AG* [1986] 2 Lloyd's Rep. 654 (where it was also held that in the case of non-accepted repudiation the seller's damages have to be calculated as on the date of failure to ship, and not as on the date of failure to give notice). See also *Scandinavian Trading Co A/B v. Zodiac Petroleum SA and William Hudson Ltd; The Al Hofuf* [1981] 1 Lloyd's Rep. 81 at 84.
[64] *The Belgrano Financial Times*, November 26, 1985. The term "at buyer's call" means "on demand" of the buyer and a three days' delay of delivery, on the part of the seller, after the ship is ready to load, would entitle the buyer to terminate the contract: *Tradax Export SA v. Italgrani di Francesco Ambrosio Sosimage SpA* [1983] Com. L.R. 116. See also *Cie Commerciale Sucres et Denrées v. C. Czarnikow Ltd; The Naxos* [1991] 1 Lloyd's Rep. 29.
[65] *The Naxos, supra.*
[66] *Olearia Tirrena SpA v. N. V. Algermeene Oliehandel; The Osterbeck* [1972] 2 Lloyd's Rep. 341. On the onus of proving that the buyer would not have been able to provide a suitable ship in time, see *Petraco (Bermuda) Ltd v. Petromed International SA* [1988] 2 Lloyd's Rep. 357.
[67] *Texaco Ltd v. The Eurogulf Shipping Co Ltd* [1987] 2 Lloyd's Rep. 54 at, 545 (such a nomination has been described in previous editions of this work as a "Mickey Mouse" nomination).

to the effect that the purchase price becomes due on a fixed date whether or not a suitable ship has been named.[68]

Nomination of a substitute vessel

2–012 Where the nominated ship is withdrawn or the nomination fails for another reason the buyer is obliged to name a substitute ship as soon as possible and to bear the additional expense caused by the substitution. This rule must be strictly qualified in that substitution may only be allowed if it is made within the contract time, or beyond that time if there is a contractual provision or a trade practice to that effect.[69] In situations where the contractual terms require the buyer to provide notice of a ship which is characterised as "final" or "definite" the buyer may not substitute. The buyer ought to reserve a right to substitute to avoid complications. If a substitute nomination is made the substitution itself must be a valid and effective nomination. Once a suitable ship is nominated the seller is obliged to load.[70]

The loading operation

2–013 If loading on board the vessel is completed uneventfully, it is permissible and indeed convenient to refer to the ship's rail as the legal frontier dividing the responsibilities of the f.o.b. seller and his buyer. If, during the loading operation an accident occurs, for example the ropes break when the cargo is lifted from the shore into the ship, a closer analysis would be required to determine the critical point at which the risk, and possibly the property, passes to the f.o.b. buyer. Such an accident affects two legal relationships, the contract of sale and the contract of carriage by sea. It is, of course, purely fortuitous whether the cargo drops down this side of the ship's rail or that. Devlin J. indicated the fortuitous character of the event in the *Pyrene* case[71]:

> "Only the most enthusiastic lawyer could watch with satisfaction the spectacle of liabilities shifting uneasily as the cargo sways at the end of a derrick across a notional perpendicular projecting from the ship's rail."

---

[68] In *Colley v. Overseas Exporters* [1921] 3 K.B. 302 it was advisable to insert a term in the contract ensuring that the seller receives timely notice of probable readiness of vessel for loading. On the notice of readiness for the substitute vessel see the *Cargill* case n. 69 *infra*.
[69] *Cargill v. Continental* [1989] 1 Lloyd's Rep. 193; *Agricultores Federados Argentinos Sociedad Cooperativa Limitada v. Ampro SA Commerciale Industrielle et Financière* [1965] 2 Lloyd's Rep. 757 at 767. An express contract clause allowing substitution does not, it is thought, normally extend the shipment time: see *Finnish Government (Ministry of Food) v. H. Ford & Co Ltd* (1921) 6 Ll.L.R. 188. Such clauses may in appropriate cases reveal that intention of the parties; see *Thomas Borthwick (Glasgow) Ltd v. Bunge & Co Ltd* [1969] 1 Lloyd's Rep. 17 (however, this was a c.i.f. contract). See also *Coastal (Bermuda) Petroleum Ltd v. VTT Vulcan Petroleum SA; The Marine Star* [1993] 1 Lloyd's Rep. 329, a case involving a c.i.f. contract.
[70] *Harlow & Jones Ltd v. Parex (International) Ltd* [1967] 2 Lloyd's Rep. 509.
[71] [1954] 2 Q.B. 402.

Devlin J. held in this case, as already observed,[72] that in the contract of carriage by sea the loading operation had to be considered as an indivisible whole and the carrier's liability for negligence extended to all stages of that operation irrespective of whether they occured before or after the crossing of the ship's rail. It should be noted, at this point, that stowage is part of the loading operation in circumstances where the goods are taken from their position on the docks directly into the hold of the ship or pumped into the tanks, as would be the case if the cargo was, for example, grain or oil. In the latter example risk passes through the loading flange. If, however, goods are required to be arranged in the cargo holds, stowage is a separate operation and therefore one conducted at the risk of the buyer unless the contract has been concluded on "f.o.b. stowed" or a similar term or if stowage is customarily carried out by the seller in accordance with trade or port usage.[73] If the contract is concluded on , for example, Incoterms, the seller must deliver or load the goods on board the vessel, or if on Intraterms the seller must "load the goods on board". The latter requirement is identical to the requirement expressed in the American Uniform Commercial Code.

As to the contract of sale it is important to discern when the risk, and possibly the property, pass to the f.o.b. buyer if the parties have failed to regulate this point in their contract. Here, two views are possible.[74] It has been suggested that in an f.o.b. contract, the goods are at the buyer's risk when they pass the ship's rail and it is irrelevant whether or not they arrive on the ship safely on completion of the loading operation. According to this view, "loading" has a different meaning in the contract of sale from that attributed to it in the contract of carriage by sea. Alternatively, it can be argued that the seller has fulfilled his obligations under an f.o.b. contract only if the goods are deposited safely on board the vessel and the loading operation is completed. Here, the same meaning is attributed to the concept of loading in both types of contract. It is thought that the second view is correct. The fortuitous element, which Devlin J. rejected as a test for the contract of carriage by sea, should on that basis be rejected for the contract of sale. The manner in which the obligations of the seller are described in Incoterms, Intraterms and the American Commercial Code is relevant as they appear to provide support for the latter view.[75] Under the f.o.b. clause the cost of loading the goods into the ship has to be borne by the seller, but normally this is included in the freight which has to be paid by the buyer.

Passing of property

In an f.o.b. contract, if the goods are unascertained, as is the case when they are **2–014** shipped in bulk but parts of the bulk consignment are sold to several buyers,

---

[72] See *ante*, para. 2–007.
[73] See Sassoon, *CIF and FOB Contracts* (British Shipping Laws, 4th ed., 1995), para. 463.
[74] See Sassoon, *op. cit.*, paras 434, 463, 473 and B. Reynolds [1994] L.M.C.L.Q.R. 119.
[75] Implicit in a reading of UCC 2–319 and 2–504, in Incoterms 2000, A4 and Intraterms §415 delivery "on board" is required: see also J. McCardie in *Colley v. Overseas Exporters* [1921] 3 K.B. at 303. See also *per* Lloyd L.J. in *Cie Sucres et Denrées v. C. Czarnikow Ltd; The Naxos* [1989] 2 Lloyd's Rep. 462 at 474.

the property does not pass, subject to what is set out in Chapter 4 regarding section 20A[76] of the Sale of Goods Act 1979, to these buyers until the various portions are appropriated to them. This is so even if the parties have agreed in their contract that the property shall pass upon the cargo being loaded on board the carrying vessel.[77]

If the goods are ascertained, under an f.o.b. contract property in them passes when they are shipped unless the passing of title is postponed by express or implied stipulation; thus, the seller may have reserved the right of disposal of the goods until the contract terms of payment have been complied with.

Where the seller is in contract with the carrier and obtains the bill of lading, as is the case in the strict f.o.b. contract and in the f.o.b. contract with additional services, the question arises whether title to the goods passes on shipment or on transfer of the bill of lading. The answer depends on the intention of the parties. Normally their intention will be that the passing of title is postponed until the seller makes available the bill of lading to the buyer or his agent,[78] but the facts may disclose a different intention. For example, in *Mitsui & Co Ltd v. Flota Mercante Grancolombiana SA; The Ciudad De Pasto and Ciudad DeNeiva*[79] it was made clear that if the bills of lading were deliverable to the order of the seller, the presumption would be raised that the passing of the property could be postponed until, for example, payment in full of the purchase price.

When the seller has not, by express stipulation or implication of law, retained the property in the goods sold after delivery to the carrier, he may in certain circumstances be entitled to claim the rights of the unpaid seller, and in particular a lien on the goods or the right of stoppage in transit.[80]

Examination of the goods

2–015   The place of examination of the f.o.b. goods depends on the arrangement of the parties and the circumstances of the case. The parties may have agreed on pre-shipment inspection,[81] which plays an increasing role in modern export trade. Where they have not so agreed and the custom of the trade does not provide for it, the buyer is not obliged to inspect the goods when shipped and, if he fails to examine them on that occasion, will not lose his right of rejection if they do not conform to the contract. In this case usually "the only possible place of inspection would be on arrival of the goods at their place of destina-

---

[76] See *post*, para. 4–005.
[77] *Obestain Inc v. National Mineral Development Corporation Ltd; The Sanix Ace* [1987] 1 Lloyd's Rep. 465 at 467. See also *Vitol SA v. Esso Australia Ltd; The Wise* [1989] 2 Lloyd's Rep. 45.
[78] For example, the advising bank under a letter of credit, see Chap. 11.
[79] *Mitsui & Co Ltd v. Flota Mercante Grancolombiana SA* [1988] 2 Lloyd's Rep. 208. The Court of Appeal held that, according to the intention of the parties, the passing of property was postponed until the balance of the purchase price was paid; the bills of lading were deliverable to the order of the sellers and the court considered that the presumption of section 19 of the Sale of Goods Act 1979 was not replaced. See also *The Kapetan Markos (No. 2)* [1987] 2 Lloyd's Rep. 321, and *Concordia Trading BV v. Richco International Ltd* [1991] 1 Lloyd's Rep. 475.
[80] On the rights of the unpaid seller, see, para. 5–014.
[81] See, para. 4–014.

tion".[82] If, however, the goods are bought by the overseas buyers with a view to resale, the court might regard as sufficient an inspection which is carried out at the place where the ultimate buyer resides.

Multi-port f.o.b. terms

The contract provides sometimes for delivery at one of several ports which are **2–016** defined regionally, "f.o.b. United Kingdom port", or "f.o.b. European continental port",[83] The contract terms in *Boyd & Co v. Louca*[84] were "fob stowed good Danish port". Such a term has to be interpreted according to the intention of the parties. Where the contract is a strict f.o.b. contract or an f.o.b. (buyer contracting with carrier) contract it is thought that the buyer's duty to nominate a suitable ship normally includes his duty to elect the port of shipment within the range stipulated in the contract and to inform the seller accordingly in good time.[85] Where the contract is an f.o.b. contract with additional services, it is suggested that the duty to select the appropriate port falls on the seller. In short, the party responsible for the shipment has normally the choice of the port of shipment.

Duty to procure an export licence[86]

Normally, the parties agree expressly or by implication that any export licence **2–017** that may be required shall be procured by the seller. If the contract does not expressly provide for it,[87] such implication is readily prompted when the f.o.b. clause occurs in an export, and not a supply, transaction and, to the knowledge of both parties, regulations requiring an export licence are in existence in the country of shipment at the date of the contract and according to which regulations the seller, or his local supplier, is the only party competent to apply for the licence. In *A. V. Pound & Co Ltd v. M. W. Hardy & Co Inc*[88] an American company agreed to buy from the sellers, an English company, 300 metric tons of Portuguese gum spirits of turpentine "f.a.s. buyers' tank steamer" at Lisbon. The sellers knew at the time they entered into the contract that the buyers contemplated a port in East Germany as the destination of the goods. The sellers

---

[82] *Per* Atkin L.J. in *Boks & Co Ltd v. J. H. Rayner & Co Ltd* (1921) 37 T.L.R. 800 at 801; on examination of the goods, see, para. 5–065.

[83] *Fielding & Platt Ltd v. Najjar* [1969] 1 W.L.R. 357.

[84] [1973] 1 Lloyd's Rep. 209; *Muller Brothers v. GM Power Plant Co* [1963] C.L.Y. 3114.

[85] See n. 84, *supra*. However, in *Miserocchi and CSpA v. Agricultores Federados Argentinos SCL* [1984] 1 Lloyd's Rep. 202 it was held that, although the buyer had to nominate a suitable ship, the choice of the port of shipment under the multi-port f.o.b. clause was intended to be made by the seller. In *Lusograin Comercio Internacional De Cereas Ltda v. Bunge AG* [1986] 2 Lloyd's Rep. 654 the contract gave the sellers an option to choose the port of shipment from the ports specified in the contract.

[86] On export and import licences generally and frustration, see, para. 6–012.

[87] Thus, in *Compagnie Continentale d'Importation Zurich SA v. Ispahani* [1962] 1 Lloyd's Rep. 213, the contract provided that export duties should be based on current rates and that "change of export duties [should be] for buyers' account". Export duties were abolished after part of the shipment was made. The Court of Appeal held that the buyers were entitled to recover from the sellers a sum equivalent to the export duties saved.

[88] [1956] A.C. 588.

then bought the goods from Portuguese suppliers subject to export licence which, however, was refused. The buyers had nominated a tank steamer which arrived in Lisbon in time and was ready to load but as they refused to name another destination and a licence for East Germany was not forthcoming, the goods were not loaded. It was proved that by Portuguese law only the Portuguese suppliers could obtain the export licence and the goods could not be put alongside and cleared through the Customs house before a licence was obtained. The House of Lords, treating the case as being subject to the same rules as apply to an f.o.b. contract, held that, in the circumstances of the case, the parties intended and impliedly agreed that it was the duty of the sellers, and not of the buyers, to obtain the export licence. The court held that the sellers had to do their best to obtain the licence[89] and that as it was not granted, in spite of the efforts to obtain it, the contract was frustrated and they could not recover damages from the buyers.

Where the parties have neither expressly nor impliedly agreed that the f.o.b. seller should obtain the licence and where the transaction is an export transaction, the duty to obtain the export licence is on the seller, and not the buyer. The seller is normally the only person who is sufficiently acquainted with the licensing practices in the country of exportation and is able to obtain the licence. The view expressed here is also adopted by Incoterms. Only if the transaction is a supply transaction, *e.g.* if a U.K. exporter buys goods from a U.K. supplier f.o.b. Liverpool, would the duty to obtain the export licence fall on the buyer, *i.e.* the exporter.

F.O.B. airport, free carrier (FCA airport)[90]

2–018 The most appropriate term for parties contemplating air transport is the free carrier term. The FCA formulation may be completed by the insertion of the name of the airport and the air carrier. If the f.o.b. airport term is used the obligations of the seller and the buyer may be summarised as follows:

The seller is required to:

    (a) supply the goods in conformity with the contract of sale, together with such evidence of conformity as may be required by the contract together with a commercial invoice or equivalent electronic message;

    (b) deliver the goods, on the due date or within the appropriate time period, in the customary manner, into the charge of the air carrier or his agent or any other person named by the buyer;

    (c) obtain, if required, a receipt from the carrier.

---

[89] There is a duty on both parties to co-operate reasonably in obtaining the licence; *A. V. Pound & Co Ltd v. M. W. Hardy & Co Inc* [1956] A.C. 588, 608, 611; see *H.O Brandt & Co v. H. N. Morris & Co* [1917] 3 K.B. 784.

[90] It is suggested that the FCA term is the most appropriate term to be used when carriage by air is contemplated. f.o.b. airport, f.o.b. aircraft, though used, are confusing and should be avoided.

The buyer is required to:

(a) give the seller proper notice and instructions (where required) of the airport of destination for the carriage of the goods by air from the named airport of departure;

(b) bear all costs payable in respect of the goods from the time when they have been delivered in accordance with the provisions of the contract;

(c) pay for the goods.

Two points should be noted. First, in f.o.b. airport the critical point between the responsibilities of the seller and the buyer is the point at which the air carrier takes delivery of the goods at the airport . That will normally be the air carrier's transit shed at the airport. If the goods are lost or damaged between that point and before they are lifted into the aircraft, *e.g.* in the carrier's transit shed or on the tarmac, such loss or damage would fall on the buyer and he should insure against it. Secondly, Incoterms provide that, unlike under f.o.b. vessel, the seller shall be entitled to arrange for air carriage, of course at the buyer's expense, if he or the buyer has not given prompt notice to the contrary. Whether in British practice the seller has that right is doubtful and depends on the intention of the parties. The term f.o.b. aircraft, under which the seller would be responsible until the goods are lifted into the aircraft, is unusual.

C.I.F. (named port of destination)

This is the most recognisable term associated with the export trade which the custom of the merchants has evolved. Lord Wright[91] observed that the term c.i.f. ("cost, insurance, freight"[92]) "is a type of contract which is more widely and more frequently in use than any other contract used for purposes of seaborne commerce. An enormous number of transactions, in value amounting to untold sums, is carried out every year under c.i.f. contracts." Lord Porter[93] indicated the general characteristics of the c.i.f. term in the following passage:

2–019

> "The obligations imposed on a seller under a c.i.f. contract are well known, and in the ordinary case, include the tender of a bill of lading covering the goods contracted to be sold and no others, coupled with an insurance policy in the normal form and accompanied by an invoice which shows the price and, as in this case, usually contains a deduction of the freight which the buyer pays before delivery at the port of discharge. Against tender of these documents the purchaser must pay the price. In such a case the property may pass either on shipment or on tender, the risk generally passes on shipment or as from shipment, but possession does not pass until the documents which represent the goods are handed over in exchange for the price. In the result, the buyer, after receipt of the documents, can claim against the ship for breach of the contract of carriage and against the underwriters for any loss covered by the policy. The strict form of c.i.f. contract may, however, be modified. A provision that a delivery order

---

[91] In *T. D. Bailey Son & Co v. Ross T. Smyth & Co Ltd* (1940) 56 T.L.R. 825 at 828.
[92] T. S. Eliot's explanation (in *Notes on The Waste Land*, 1.210) that c.i.f. denotes "carriage and insurance free", is a use of poetic licence.
[93] In *Comptoir d'Achat v. Luis de Ridder; The Julia* [1949] A.C. 293 at 309; *per* Blackburn J. in *Ireland v. Livingston* (1872) L.R. 5 HL 395 at 406; *per* Sellers J. in *Andre et Cie SA v. Vantol Ltd* [1952] 2 Lloyd's Rep. 282 at 291.

may be substituted for a bill of lading or a certificate of insurance for a policy would not, I think, make the contract be concluded on something other than c.i.f. terms."

Donaldson J. observed in one case[94]:

"The contract called for Chinese rabbits, c.i.f. Their obligation was, therefore, to tender documents, not to ship the rabbits themselves. If there were any Chinese rabbits afloat, they could have bought them."

The nature of the c.i.f. contract is best understood if its economic purpose is kept distinct from the strict legal effect of the transaction.

Definition

2–020   From the business point of view, it has been said that the purpose of the c.i.f. contract is not a sale of the goods themselves but a sale of the documents relating to the goods. "It is not a contract that goods shall arrive, but a contract to ship goods complying with the contract of sale, to obtain, unless the contract otherwise provides, the ordinary contract of carriage to the place of destination, and the ordinary contract of insurance of the goods on that voyage, and to tender these documents against payment of the contract price".[95] McNair J.[96] described the ordinary c.i.f. contract as a contract in which "the seller discharges his obligations as regards delivery by tendering a bill of lading covering the goods". The buyer's aim is to obtain, as early as possible, the right of disposal of the goods in order to resell them or secure a bank advance on them. If the buyer wishes to take physical delivery of the goods he would require, if they are lost, the insurance money. The seller's aim is to accommodate the buyer by providing carriage and insurance cover. The seller would wish to part with the right of disposal of the goods only against payment of the purchase price and not to be answerable for loss of or damage to the goods during the voyage. The aims of both parties are most conveniently achieved when the buyer—or a banker nominated in the contract if the contract so provides—effects payment in the stipulated manner against delivery of the documents relating to the goods. The fact that the delivery of the shipping documents is, "in a business sense, the equivalent of the goods",[97] is of great importance when the goods are lost in transit

---

[94] *P. J. van der Zijden Wildhandel NV v. Tucker & Cross Ltd* [1975] 2 Lloyd's Rep. 240 at 242.
[95] *Per* Scrutton, J. in *Arnold Karberg & Co v. Blythe, Green Jourdain & Co* [1915] 2 K.B. 379 at 388. The phraseology, but not the substance, of Scrutton J.'s observations has been subjected to certain criticism in the Court of Appeal: [1916] 1 K.B. 495. See also *per* Sir John Donaldson M.R. in *Congimex v. Tradax Export SA* [1983] 1 Lloyd's Rep. 250 at 253. *Cargill International SA v. Bangladesh Sugar and Food Industries* [1996] 2 Lloyd's Rep. 524 at 526 *per* Morison J.'s reference to a c. and f. contract as " . . . essentially an agreement for procurement and delivery of documents of title to goods . . ." Vienna Convention A.34.
[96] In *Gardano and Giampieri v. Greek Petroleum George Mamidakis & Co* [1962] 1 W.L.R. 40 at 52. Further, *per* Roskill J. in *Margarine Union GmbH v. Cambay Prince Steamship Co* [1967] 2 Lloyd's Rep. 315 at 332; *per* Lord Morris of Borth-y-Gest in *Kendall & Sons v. William Lillico & Sons Ltd*, appeals from *Hardwick Game Farm v. Suffolk Agricultural Poultry Producers' Association* [1969] 2 A.C. 31 at 101; *per* Lord Diplock in *Berger & Co Inc v. Gill and Duffus SA* [1984] A.C. 382.
[97] *Per* Lord Wright in *T. D. Bailey, Son & Co v. Ross T. Smyth & Co Ltd* (1940) 56 T.L.R. 825 at 829.

but the shipping documents have been delivered to the buyer or can still be delivered to him.

The sale on c.i.f. terms involves the exporter in calculations and operations which, being different from those applied in the home market, require expert knowledge and experience. Export managers and confirming houses possess this expert knowledge and are often in a position to make favourable arrangements as regards freight and insurance. In particular, they will often secure reductions in these charges when engaged in substantial or regular trade with the buyer's country, or they may be able to group several consignments to the same consignee or a number of consignments to different consignees in order to make the best use of the available shipping space[98]; in such circumstances the c.i.f. term offers distinct advantages.

From the legal point of view, the choice of the c.i.f term raises complex issues because the c.i.f. transaction embodies, by necessity, elements of three contracts; the contract of sale, the contract of carriage by sea and the contract of marine insurance. These issues have in the past generated a great deal of litigation, but the implications of dealing under c.i.f. terms have been settled for some time.[99]

The seller's obligations under a c.i.f. contract may be summarised as follows[1]:

(a) to ship goods of the description contained in the contract and clear the goods for export or to buy conforming goods afloat[2];

(b) if the goods are not bought afloat , to procure a contract of carriage by sea under which the goods will be delivered at the destination agreed by the contract and obtain the bill of lading as evidence of having done so;

(c) to arrange, if this has not already been done, insurance on terms current in the trade which will be available for the benefit of the buyer and provide a policy or insurance document which entitles the buyer to make a claim against the insurer;

(d) to make out an invoice which normally will debit the buyer with the agreed price, or the actual cost, commission charges, freight, and insurance premium, and credit him for the amount of the freight which he will have to pay to the shipowner on delivery of the goods at the port of destination.[3]

(e) to tender these documents in the manner agreed whether by presentation directly, transmission by electronic means or otherwise; the bill of

---

[98] On groupage bills of lading and container shipment, see, paras 15–028 and 15–029.

[99] These problems form the subject-matter of Sassoon and Merren, *C.I.F. and F.O.B. Contracts* (British Shipping Laws 4th ed.), Chap. 1 and generally for an analysis of the relationships implicit in a c.i.f. contract.

[1] *Per* Lord Sumner (then Hamilton J.) in *Biddell Brothers v. E. Clemens Horst Co* [1911] 1 K.B. 214 at 220. See, further, *per* Sellers J. in *Andre et Cie SA v. Vantol Ltd* [1952] 2 Lloyd's Rep. 282 at 291.

[2] Or to procure and tender to the buyer goods afloat which have been so shipped.

[3] This definition is founded on the assumption that the parties have arranged "freight collect" and that the freight has not been prepaid by the seller.

lading, insurance policy and invoice to the buyer, together with any other documents which may be agreed between the parties and/or might be required by the customs of the trade so that he may obtain delivery of the goods or recover for their loss, if they are lost on the voyage, and know what freight he has to pay.

The duties of the buyer may be summarised as follows:

(a) to accept the documents when tendered by the seller, if they are in conformity with the contract of sale, and pay the contract price;

(b) to receive the goods at the agreed port of destination and bear, with the exception of the freight and marine insurance, all costs and charges incurred in respect of the goods in the course of their transit by sea until their arrival at the port of destination, as well as unloading costs, including lighterage and wharfage charges, unless such costs and charges have been included in the freight or collected by the carrying company at the time freight was paid;

(c) if war insurance is to be provided, to bear the cost;

(d) to bear all risks of the goods from the time when they shall have effectively passed the ship's rail at the port of shipment;

(e) if the buyer has reserved to himself the right to determine the period within which the goods are to be shipped and/or the right to choose the port of destination, and he fails to give instructions in time, he must bear the additional costs incurred as a result and all risks of the goods from the date of the expiry of the period fixed for shipment, provided always that the goods have been appropriated to the contract, that is to say, clearly set aside or otherwise identified as the contract goods;

(f) to pay the costs and charges incurred in obtaining the certificate of origin and consular documents[4];

(g) to pay all Customs duties as well as any other duties and taxes payable consequent upon the importation;

(h) to obtain and provide at his own risk and expense any import licence or permit or the like which he may require for the importation of the goods at destination.

Note: if the goods are sold "c.i.f. landed", unloading costs, including lighterage and wharfage charges, are borne by the seller.

Traders will adapt these obligations to the particular transaction which they wish to carry out, and will vary and supplement them whenever necessary. They will, in particular, define exactly in their contract the requirements of the ship-

---

[4] It will often be the intention of the parties that these costs and charges have to be borne by the seller, as they are pre-shipment charges (C.M.S.).

ping documents which the seller has to tender to the buyer, and the terms, time, place and currency of payment of the purchase price. They have, however, to take care that these amendments and variations do not destroy the essential characteristics of the c.i.f. term which are that, as the result of the transfer of the shipping documents, a direct relationship is established between the buyer on the one hand and the carrier and insurer on the other, so as to enable the buyer to make direct claims against these persons in case of loss of, or damage to, the goods. If the parties vary this essential character of the shipping documents, for example by providing that the seller shall be at liberty to tender, instead of a bill of lading, a delivery order on his agent in the port of destination or the goods themselves, the contract may cease to be a true c.i.f. contract in the legal sense.[5]

The shipping documents

An examination of the shipping documents is central to any examination of the   **2–021** performance of the c.i.f. transaction. The shipping documents consist, in principle, of a clean bill of lading evidencing a contract of carriage by sea providing continuous cover to the agreed place of destination, a marine insurance policy or certificate covering the usual marine risks and any agreed additional risks and an invoice in the stipulated form.

Two of these shipping documents, the bill of lading and the insurance policy, should provide continuous cover from the port of shipment to the port of discharge, "so that the c.i.f. buyer, whatever happens to the goods, will have either a cause of action on the bill of lading against the ship or a cause of action against the underwriters on the policy".[6] If documents are not to be presented to a bank under an arrangement for payment, it is usual to send the buyer at least two sets of documents by separate secure dispatch.

The bill of lading

The bill of lading, which the seller has to procure, must be a clean bill, that is   **2–022** a bill which must not contain a qualification of, or reservation to, the statement that the goods are shipped in apparent good order and condition.[7] It depends, in the absence of express agreement between the parties, on the custom prevailing in the particular trade whether a "received for shipment" bill or a delivery order on the ship may be substituted for a "shipped" bill.[8] Sometimes the seller will include in his conditions of sale an express clause to the effect that a "received for shipment bill of lading, if tendered, shall be accepted by the buyer." If the

---

[5] See *post*, para. 2–035.
[6] *Per* Roskill J. in *Margarine Union GmbH v. Cambay Prince Steamship Co Ltd* [1969] 1 Q.B. 219 at 245.
[7] On clean bills, see *post*, para. 15–026. See also *Golodetz & Co Inc v. Czarnikow-Rionda Co Inc; The Galatia* [1980] 1 Lloyd's Rep. 453 where a bill "claused" to the effect that cargo had been damaged after loading was nonetheless "clean" but see Article 32 UCPDC (UCP 500) and para. 11–012, *post*.
[8] On "shipped" and "received" bills, see *post*, para. 15–025; on delivery orders, see *post*, para. 5–034.

terms of the contract are silent and no contrary trade custom applies, the buyer is entitled to a "shipped" bill, but in container shipment the intention of the parties is invariably that a "received for shipment" bill of lading may be tendered. The parties may further agree that the seller shall be entitled to substitute a delivery order for a bill of lading. The delivery order should be specified as a ship's delivery order, that is a delivery order addressed to the ship which , if properly acknowledged that is "attorned" by the carrier,[9] would give the buyer a direct right of action against the carrier to receive the goods from the ship.[10] A contract which provides that the seller may substitute a delivery order of a different character, for instance an order addressed to one of his agents or to a warehouseman, would not be a true c.i.f. contract.[11]

The seller under a c.i.f. contract must ship the goods within the agreed shipping period[12] or by the agreed shipping date. They have to be shipped by the customary route, except if a particular route of shipment is stipulated in the contract. If the customary route is unavailable, the seller is not relieved of his contractual obligation but must ship the goods by any reasonable and practicable route.[13]

The insurance document

2–023   The marine insurance policy or certificate, which the seller has to tender to the buyer, should provide cover against the risks which it is customary in the particular trade to cover with respect to the cargo and voyage in question.[14] The parties should not place too much reliance on the custom of the trade, which sometimes varies at the ports of shipment and destination and may be interpreted differently by merchants and courts; they should, in appropriate cases, agree in the contract of sale on the nature of the insurance policy which the seller has to tender, for example, whether the policy should be an all risks policy in the form of Institute Cargo Clauses A to Lloyd's Marine Policy,[15] or should cover war risks. It has been held that a seller, who undertakes to insure "on usual Lloyd's conditions", has not discharged his obligations unless the insurance cover which he obtains is as comprehensive as that provided by the customary transit clause.[16] Another point which should be covered by agreement of the parties to the c.i.f. contract is the value of the insurance cover which the seller has to obtain. The

---

[9] Even before the formal attornment the contract has to be treated as a genuine c.i.f. contract.

[10] *Colin & Shields v. W. Weddel & Co Ltd* [1952] W.N. 420; *Margarine Union GmbH v. Cambay Prince Steamship Co Ltd* [1969] 1 Q.B. 219; see now Carriage of Goods by Sea Act 1992, s. 2(1)(c) and *post*, para. 15–052.

[11] See para. 2–035 and *The Julia, ante.*

[12] On shipment within the shipment period but under a falsely dated bill of lading see *Proctor & Gamble Philippines Manufacturing Corporation v. Kurt A. Becher GmbH & Co KG* [1988] 1 Lloyd's Rep. 88 at 91 and [1988] 2 Lloyd's Rep. 21, CA; see para. 2–026.

[13] *Tsakiroglou & Co Ltd v. Noblee Thorl GmbH* [1962] A.C. 93 at 113, *per* Lord Simonds, 121–122, *per* Lord Radcliffe; see para. 6–011.

[14] *Reinhart Co v. Joshua Hoyle & Sons Ltd* [1961] 1 Lloyd's Rep. 346 at 352. On marine insurance generally, see *post* Chap. 19.

[15] See *post*, Chap. 19.

[16] Which includes the "warehouse to warehouse" clause incorporated as a standard term in the Institute Cargo Clauses A, B and C Policies.

parties often agree on the calculation of that value. Their contract normally provides that the insurable value shall be the invoice value of the goods plus incidental shipping and insurance charges plus a specified percentage of, say, 10 or 15 per cent, representing the buyer's anticipated profits.[17] Indeed, the valuation required by the banks under the UCPDC is, unless the contrary is stipulated, the c.i.f. value plus 10 per cent. It should be noted that the law requires the seller, in the absence of a clear custom of the trade to the contrary, to insure merely the reasonable value of the goods at the place of shipment. Normally this means the cost price of the goods including commission, shipping charges and insurance premium but excluding any rise in the value of the goods, anticipated profits of the buyer and the freight (which, unless it is advance freight, will not be payable if the goods fail to arrive). It is therefore necessary for a buyer who wishes to obtain cover for any of these interests to make express arrangements to that effect with the seller at the time when the contract of sale is concluded.[18]

The seller may have arranged an open cover[19] which covers an unspecified quantity of goods that are to be shipped within a fixed time, and describes the insurance in general terms only, and he will then effect the insurance of the ordered goods by sending the insurers a declaration relating to the details of the consignment in question. In this case he will not receive an insurance policy which he can tender to the buyer, but merely a broker's cover note or certificate or himself issue an insurance certificate.[20] It was held in older English decisions[21] that these documents are not in law equivalent to an insurance policy. The American practice differs from the English practice. In the United States an insurance certificate issued by or on behalf of an insurance company may invariably be tendered in lieu of a policy of insurance[22] but "the term 'certificate of insurance' does not of itself include certificates or 'cover notes' issued by the insurance broker and stating that the goods are covered by a policy".[23] However, it is thought that an insurance certificate or other document entitling the insured (or transferee) to demand the issue of a policy may be acceptable by express or implied agreement of the parties. The decisive criterion is that the document tendered entitles the holder at any time to demand the issue of a formal policy or to be in a position to claim against the insurer. A cover note which does not have this quality need not be accepted by the buyer unless he has so agreed or there is a course of dealing or custom of the trade which provides otherwise. The requirement that an effective insurance policy has to be obtained to cover

---

[17] See Art. 34(f)(ii) UCPDC (UCP500) and Intraterms s. 418(2)(c).
[18] On insurable value, see para. 19–034, and Marine Insurance Act 1906, s. 16.
[19] See *post*, para. 19–007.
[20] See *post*, para. 19–011.
[21] *Wilson, Holgate & Co v. Belgian Grain and Produce Co* [1920] 2 K.B. 1. It was held in *Donald H. Scott & Co v. Barclays Bank* [1923] 2 K.B. 1 that a certificate of insurance is not an "approved insurance policy"; and it was decided in *Harper & Co v. Mackechnie & Co* [1925] 2 K.B. 423 that, even where the buyer accepts a certificate of insurance, the seller impliedly warrants that the assertions in the certificate are correct and that he will produce the insurance policy referred to in the certificate. See also *Promos SA v. European Grain and Shipping Co* [1979] 1 Lloyd's Rep. 375.
[22] Uniform Commercial Code, s.2-320(2)(c).
[23] Official comment to the section quoted in the preceding footnote, para. 9. (7th ed., Gould Publications).

the goods when in transit is an essential condition of the contract, and the buyer under a c.i.f. contract would be entitled to refuse the acceptance of uninsured goods even when they arrived safely at the port of destination.[24]

The invoice

2–024   The invoice must be completed in strict agreement with the terms of the contract. Even the slightest variation may cause difficulties, in particular with the bank which may, in that case, be reluctant to make available finance under the letter of credit.[25] The legal requirements for the trading invoice have been described earlier; they apply unless abrogated by the agreement of the parties or the custom of the trade. On occasion the invoice has to satisfy official requirements of the country of importation of the goods; these requirements are dealt with later. Attention should be paid to the proper linkage of the invoice with the other documents tendered. It must be clear that they all identify the goods sold although some latitude is admitted with respect to their description in the other documents.[26]

Other documents

2–025   The parties may further agree that, in addition to the three principal documents, other documents shall be included in the shipping documents, such as certificates of origin, or quality, or of inspection.[27] Failure to tender these documents in the proper form will normally have the same consequences as a failure to tender the appropriate principal documents.[28]

The right to reject the documents and the right to reject the goods

2–026   In a c.i.f. contract the right to reject the documents is distinct from the right to reject the goods. Devlin J. observed in *Kwei Tek Chao v. British Traders and Shippers Ltd*[29] that:

> "the right to reject the documents arises when the documents are tendered, and the right to reject the goods arises when they are landed and when after examination they are not found to be in conformity with the contract."

The buyer must be aware that the right to reject the documents is lost when he or the bank which advises a letter of credit for the payment of the price takes

---

[24] *Orient Company Ltd v. Brekke & Howlid* [1913] 1 K.B. 531; *Diamond Alkali Export Corp v. Fl. Bourgeois* [1921] 3 K.B. 443; *Koskas v. Standard Marine Insurance Co Ltd* (1927) 32 Com. Cas. 160.
[25] See *post*, para. 11–013.
[26] *Banque de L'Indochine et de Suez SA v. J. H. Rayner (Mincing Lane) Ltd* [1983] Q.B. 711. See also *post*, para. 11–015.
[27] On these certificates see *post*, para. 4–011. A certificate of quality to be obtained on discharge of the goods is not a certificate which can be tendered with the shipping documents: *Gill & Duffus SA v. Berger & Co Inc (No. 2)* [1984] A.C. 382 at 389.
[28] *Re Reinhold & Co and Hansloh* (1869) 12 T.L.R. 422.
[29] [1954] 2 Q.B. 459 at 481; *Proctor & Gamble Philippine Manufacturing Corporation v. Kurt A. Becher GmbH & Co KG* [1988] 2 Lloyd's Rep. 21 at 26.

up the documents, even if inaccurate, and pays against them without objection. The documents are inaccurate if, when taken together[30] they disclose a defect to a person who reads them or could have read them. Thus, in *Panchaud Freres SA v. Establissements General Grain Co*[31] a contract for the sale of a quantity of Brazilian maize, c.i.f. Antwerp, provided for shipment in June/July 1965. The goods were shipped on August 10 to 12 but the bill of lading was backdated to July 31, 1965. The superintendents who supervised the loading of the maize issued a certificate of quantity in which they stated that they had drawn samples on August 10 to 12. That certificate formed part of the shipping documents which were taken up and paid for by the buyers. Later the buyers sought to complain about the false dating of the bill of lading and the delayed shipment. The Court of Appeal rejected this claim. Lord Denning M.R. said[32]:

> "By taking up the documents and paying for them, they are precluded afterwards from complaining of the late shipment or of a defect in the bill of lading."

It must be noted, however, that the loss of the right to reject the documents does not mean that the buyer has lost the right to reject the goods after their arrival on the ground that they do not conform with the specification in the contract. Hobhouse J. observed in one case[33]:

> "The exercise of the right to reject the goods is one which the buyer is entitled to postpone until the goods arrive. He can make up his mind then to exercise the right as it suits him best. He may lose his right meanwhile if he deals with the goods or documents so as to disable himself from restoring title to the sellers or by actual waiver . . . ."

The rejection must be "clear and unequivocal"[34]; it must indicate that the buyer wants to have nothing to do with the documents or goods. If it is couched in ambiguous terms or the buyer engages in contradictory action, such as the resale of the goods, it is ineffective.[35]

Exceptionally, where the buyer or his agent could not have realised that the documents were inaccurate, he does not lose his right to claim damages for a breach of a condition relating to the documents on the ground that he has lost his right to reject the goods. In *Kwei Tek Chao v. British Traders and Shipper Ltd* London exporters sold goods to merchants in Hongkong c.i.f. Hongkong, shipment from continental port not later than October 31, 1951. Unknown to

---

[30] On the rule that all documents forming part of the shipping documents have to be read together, see *post*, para. 11–016.

[31] [1970] 1 Lloyd's Rep. 53, CA.

[32] See para. 5–011. On the question of waiver see also *Bunge GmbH v. Alfred C. Toepfer* [1978] 1 Lloyd's Rep. 506; *Bunge SA v. Schleswig-Holsteinische* [1978] 1 Lloyd's Rep. 480. On cstoppel see *Motor Oil Hellas (Corinth) Refineries SA v. Shipping Corporation of India; The Kanchenjunga* [1990] 1 Lloyd's Rep. 391. On estoppel and waiver see *post*, paras 5–007—5–011.

[33] *Bergerco U.S.A. v. Vegoil Ltd* [1984] 1 Lloyd's Rep. 440 at 446.

[34] *Per* Saville J. in *Vargas Pena Apezteguia y Ciasaic v. Peter Cremer GmbH* [1987] 1 Lloyd's Rep. 394 at 398. Saville J. distinguished this case from *Kwei Tek Chao* (see above) because in the case before him the buyers' loss was not caused by the loss of the right to reject the documents, but it was caused by the fall of the market when the buyers resold the goods. (In *Vargas* the sales contract was on f.o.b. terms, not on c.i.f. terms).

[35] On the right to reject goods, see *post*, paras 5–007 and 5–008.

the sellers, the goods were shipped in Antwerp after that date but the bill of
lading was forged and showed October 31 as the date of shipment. The buyers,
who were unaware of this, accepted the documents and disposed of the goods
after their arrival by placing them into a go-down and by pledging the go-down
warrants with a bank by way of security. Later the buyers discovered the forgery
of the bill of lading and sued the sellers for damages. Devlin J. held that the
two rights to reject the documents and to reject the goods being distinct in a
c.i.f. contract, the disposal of the goods by the buyers did not result in the loss
of their right to reject the documents as not being in accordance with the contract
and that they were entitled to claim damages for being prevented from rejecting
the documents; the amount of damages which they could recover was substantial; it consisted of the difference between the contract price of the goods and
the value of the goods when the buyers discovered the breach of the sellers'
obligation.[36]

Responsibilities of the parties

2–027   Under the c.i.f. term, the seller's responsibility for the goods ends when he
delivers them at the port of shipment on board ship; the goods travel at the
buyer's risk although the seller is responsible for the payment of the freight and
the marine insurance premium. Despite the presumption of section 32(1) of the
Sale of Goods Act 1979, the goods are deemed to be delivered to the buyer
when the bill of lading is delivered to him.[37] The risk passes to the buyer on
shipment, but the property in the goods sold does not normally pass on shipment.
Therefore the two incidents of the passing of the risk and of the property are
separated under the c.i.f. term, in contrast to the provisions of the Sale of Goods
Act, s.20.[38] The property usually passes when the bill of lading is delivered to
the buyer or to the bank, if payment is arranged under a letter of credit and the
buyer thereby acquires the right of disposal of the goods.[39] Normally, however,
he acquires only conditional property, which means property subject to the condition subsequent that the goods shall revert to the seller if, upon examination,

---

[36] [1954] 2 Q.B. 459. The *Kwei Tek Chao* case was referred to in *Empresa Exportadora de Azucar
v. Industria Azucarera Nacional SA; The Playa Larga and Marble Islands* also known as *Cubazucar
v. Iansa* [1983] 2 Lloyd's Rep. 171 at 179; *Gill & Duffus v. Berger & Co Inc* [1984] 2 W.L.R. 95
at 103; *Bergerco U.S.A. v. Vegoil Ltd* [1984] 1 Lloyd's Rep. 440 at 445; *Lombard Finance Ltd v.
Brookplain Trading Ltd* [1991] 1 W.L.R. 271 at 277.
[37] *Biddell Bros v. E. Clemens Horst Co* [1912] A.C. 18 at 22. In exceptional cases, however, the
goods may be released by the seller to the buyer before delivery of the bills of lading. Such procedure
may raise the presumption that property in the goods has been effectively withheld by the seller:
Cheetham & Co Ltd v. Thornham Spinning Co Ltd [1964] 2 Lloyd's Rep. 17; *Ginzberg v. Barrow
Haematite Steel Co Ltd* [1966] 1 Lloyd's Rep. 343. See *post*, para. 4–007 on retention of title.
[38] See *post*, para. 4–004.
[39] Whether property passes in ascertained goods depends on the intention of the parties (Sale of
Goods Act 1979, s. 16). The parties may therefore make other arrangements than the normal arrangements set out in the text. They may arrange that property shall pass on shipment (*per* Roskill L.J.
in *The Albazero* [1975] 3 W.L.R. 491 at 523, revsd [1977] A.C. 774, HL; *per* Donaldson J. in
Golodetz & Co Inc v. Czarnikow-Rionda Co Inc; The Galatia [1980] 1 Lloyd's Rep. 453 at 455).
Or they may arrange for the property to remain in the seller until he receives the purchase price in
cash, see also *post*, para. 4–007 *et seq.*

they are found to be not in accordance with the contract.[40] The buyer's right to inspect the goods is governed by the same rules as apply to these incidents under the f.o.b. term.[41] Import duties and consular fees have to be paid, in the case of the c.i.f. contract, by the buyer, while export licences have to be obtained by the seller, who likewise would be responsible for export duties in the rare cases where they are levied; however these rules of law apply only where the parties have not agreed on another arrangement.[42]

A seller of feeding stuff under a c.i.f. contract who transfers the bills of lading and other shipping documents to his buyer in England, is liable to him under the warranty implied by what was then section 2(2) of the U.K. Fertilisers and Feeding Stuffs Act 1926 which provided that the goods must be suitable for their use as feeding stuff and not contain a prohibited ingredient.[43] The decisive factor is that the transfer of the shipping documents takes place in England; the physical situation of the goods themselves at the date of transfer of the documents is irrelevant.

Contractual relations of seller and carrier

In a c.i.f. contract the seller (consignor) concludes the contract of carriage with   **2–028** the carrier and rights and duties arise from this contract between these parties unless and until they are transferred from the seller to the buyer by virtue of the Carriage of Goods by Sea Act 1992.[44] After such statutory transfer the seller can no longer sue the carrier on the contract of carriage.[45]

Contractual relations of buyer and carrier

Contractual relations between the buyer (consignee)[46] and the carrier are created   **2–029** if the requirements of the Carriage of Goods by Sea Act 1992 are satisfied, that is if the buyer becomes a lawful holder of the bill of lading. Under this section the buyer will acquire a right to sue the carrier and assume the liabilities in respect of the goods.[47] This will be considered later.[48]

---

[40] *Kwei Tek Chao v. British Traders and Shippers Ltd* [1954] 2 Q.B. 459 at 487; *Gill & Duffus SA v. Berger & Co Inc* [1984] 2 W.L.R. 95 at 104. On defeasible property, see also *McDougal v. Aeromarine of Emsworth Ltd* [1958] 1 W.L.R. 1126.

[41] See *ante*, para. 2–015 on examination of the goods, see also *post*, para. 2–036.

[42] *Produce Brokers New Co (1925) Ltd v. British Italian Trading Co* [1952] 1 Lloyd's Rep. 379. *Cf. Compagnie Continentale d'Importation Zurich SA v. Ispahani* [1962] 1 Lloyd's Rep. 213. See also *D. I. Henry Ltd v. Wilhelm G. Clasen* [1973] 1 Lloyd's Rep. 159, CA ("Cape surcharge buyer's account").

[43] Now the Agriculture Act 1970, s. 72(i).

[44] s. 2(1)(a). See *Mitsui & Co Ltd v. Flota Mercante Grancolombiana SA; The Ciudad de Pasto and Ciudad de Neiva* [1988] 2 Lloyd's Rep. 208 at 211 for a discussion on the position of the seller.

[45] See *post*, para. 15–052 on the Carriage of Goods by Sea Act 1992.

[46] See *ante*, n. 44. A pledgee, such as a bank, (who has a special property in the bill of lading) may also acquire rights if the requirements of the Carriage of Goods by Sea Act 1992, s. 2 are satisfied.

[47] In practical terms, these are mainly the obligations to pay the freight and sometimes to pay demurrage. The liability of the consignor as original party to the contract of carriage is preserved by the Carriage of Goods by Sea Act 1992, s. 3(3).

[48] See para. 15–052.

Liability of carrier in tort

2–030   The Law Commission Report, Rights of Suit in Respect of Carriage of Goods by Sea (Law Com. No. 96) which proposed the 1992 Act, deals only with title to sue in contract; the right to sue the carrier in tort has not been excluded under the Act but such an action will indeed be rare and will only be contemplated in residual situations. The right to sue in tort is restricted by *The Aliakmon*[49] to those circumstances where only a person who had legal ownership of or a possessory title to the goods could bring such an action. In *The Aliakmon* English buyers bought a quantity of steel coils from a Japanese company. The contract provided that the goods should be shipped from South Korea c. and f. free out to the English port of Immingham. The sellers arranged for the shipment from South Korea under a clean bill of lading which showed the buyers as consignees and the sellers as notified party. The goods were laden on the eponymous ship. Before the goods arrived, the buyers found it impossible to resell them as they had intended owing to a fall in the market. The parties then agreed that on presentation of the bill of lading to the ship the buyers should take delivery of the goods as agents of the sellers, that they should store them separately from their own goods to the order of the sellers, and that the title in the goods should be reserved to the sellers. The buyers carried out this agreement and paid the purchase price to the sellers. On discharge from the ship it was found that the goods were damaged in transit. Lord Brandon summed up the legal position thus:

> "In the present case . . . what had been originally a usual c. and f. contract had been varied to become a contract of sale ex warehouse . . . Under an ordinary contract of sale ex warehouse, risk and property pass at the same time . . . Under the varied contract, however, the risk had already passed on shipment because of the original c. and f. contract, and there was nothing in the new terms which caused it to revert to the sellers."

The buyers sued the carrier in the tort of negligence but the House of Lords held that this claim could not be sustained because, at the time of the damage, the buyers did not have property of or a possessory title to the goods and the fact that they bore the risk was not sufficient to support their claim.

Payment of the price

2–031   In a c.i.f. contract, unless the parties have agreed otherwise, the payment of the price becomes due when documents conforming to the contract are tendered. Delay in presenting the shipping documents may entitle the buyers to rescind the contract. Thus, in a case[50] concerning the sale of Canadian rapeseed by German sellers to Dutch buyers on a contract form issued by the Oils, Seeds and Fats Association (FOSFA) the contract provided: "Payment: net cash against documents and/or delivery order on arrival of the vessel at port of discharge but not later than 20 days after date of bill of lading". The bills of lading were dated

---

[49] *Leigh and Sillivan Ltd v. Aliakmon Shipping Co Ltd* [1986] A.C. 785.
[50] *Toepfer v. Lenersan-Poortmann NV* [1980] 1 Lloyd's Rep. 143, CA.

December 11, 1974 but the arrival of the ship, which had run aground and had to be repaired, was delayed without fault of the sellers, who received the bills in January 1975 and presented delivery orders on the ship in February 1975. The buyers rejected them on the ground that the presentation was out of time. The Court of Appeal held that in a commodity contract terms as to the time of shipment were prima facie conditions and that the payment clause imposed not only an obligation on the buyers to pay within the stipulated time but also an obligation on the sellers to present the documents within that time; these were correlative obligations and rights. The buyers had therefore rightly rejected the documents. If no time is stipulated for the tender of the documents or the payment of the price, the seller should tender the documents within a reasonable time.[51]

Port of shipment and port of destination

Stipulations in a c.i.f. contract as to the time and place of shipment are, as already observed, ordinarily conditions of the contract, a breach of which entitles the buyer to refuse acceptance of the documents when presented.[52] The contract may provide for shipment in a specified ship "or substitute"[53] or in a "direct ship,", *i.e.* a ship which may not call on an intermediate port.[54] Where a c.i.f. contract provides for shipment from a specified port and prohibits the transhipment of the goods, the buyer is normally[55] entitled to a bill of lading evidencing the continuous carriage from the port of shipment to the port of destination; in this case the bill of lading should not contain a transhipment clause; if the goods are shipped from another port or are transhipped, contrary to the contract of sale, the buyer would be entitled to reject the bill of lading.[56]

2–032

Where the contract of sale does not prohibit transhipment the buyer can claim a bill of lading issued by the ship carrying the goods to the port of destination because it is only on presentation of such bill that he will receive the goods. In such circumstances indirect shipment or transhipment (under an appropriate and usual clause in the bill of lading) is allowed. If the goods are transhipped owing to an emergency, *e.g.* because the first ship cannot continue the voyage in consequence of a mishap, and the oncarrying ship does not issue a bill of lading but its master would deliver the goods on the presentation of a bill issued by the first ship, the tender of such bill is sufficient although it is not issued by the

---

[51] *Biddell Bros. v. E. Clemens Horst Co* [1912] A.C. 18 at 22.
[52] Donaldson J. in *Aruna Mills Ltd v. Dhanrajmal Gobindram* [1968] 1 Lloyd's Rep. 304 at 311; *Thos. Borthwick (Glasgow) v. Bunge & Co* [1969] 1 Lloyd's Rep. 17 at 28; *Alfred C. Toepfer (Hamburg) v. Verheijdens Veervoeder Commissiehandel Rotterdam, The Times,* April 26, 1978.
[53] *Thos. Borthwick (Glasgow) v. Bunge & Co* [1969] 1 Lloyd's Rep. 17. On the substitute clause see also *ante,* para. 2–012 and *Coastal (Bermuda) Petroleum Ltd v. VTT Vulcan Petroleum SA; The Marine Star* [1993] 1 Lloyd's Rep. 329.
[54] *Bergerco USA v. Vegoil Ltd* [1984] 1 Lloyd's Rep. 440 at 443; *State Trading Corporation of India Ltd v. M. Golodetz Ltd* [1988] 2 Lloyd's Rep. 182 at 183–184.
[55] Unless the contract makes special arrangements or a trade custom or practice exists to the contrary. *Hansson v. Hamel and Horley Ltd* [1992] 2 A.C. 36.
[56] *Continental Imes Ltd v. H. E. Dibble* [1952] 1 Lloyd's Rep. 220 at 226.

carrying ship.[57] If transhipment is not prohibited, what is important is to give the buyer rights against the carrier.

Where it is intended that transhipment shall be prohibited and payment is to be made under a letter of credit, the instructions to the bank should state the prohibition in very explicit terms because the UCPDC (1993 Revision),[58] which apply to most bankers' credits, provides[59]:

> "For the purpose of this article transhipment means unloading and reloading from one vessel to another during the course of ocean carriage from the port of loading to the port of discharge stipulated in the Credit."

and

> "Unless transhipment is prohibited by the terms of the Credit, banks will accept a bill of lading which indicates that the goods will be transhipped, provided the entire ocean carriage is covered by one and the same bill of lading."

Where the tendered bill of lading or delivery order does not name as the terminus of the carriage the port stipulated in the contract as the destination, it may be rejected by the buyer. In an import transaction in which hides were bought c. and f. Liverpool but were shipped to Manchester and were from there transhipped to Liverpool in a dumb barge, a delivery order addressed to the master porter of the hide berth in the North Carriers Dock of Liverpool was held to be rightly rejected by the buyers.[60]

Tender of goods afloat

2–033   Normally the seller under a c.i.f. contract has the option either to arrange the actual shipment of the goods in a ship chosen by him or to purchase goods which are already afloat; in either case the seller has to tender to the buyer the appropriate bills of lading.[61] The buyer cannot compel the seller to adopt one or the other of these alternatives; the choice is with the seller. If, however, one alternative becomes impossible, in principle the seller is obliged to use the other to perform; if, for example, the goods cannot be shipped at the contemplated port of shipment because the Government places an embargo on them, the seller is bound to procure the goods afloat and to tender the buyer bills of lading relating to them.[62]

In practice, however, the situation will often be different. The c.i.f. contract

---

[57] *Holland Colombo Trading Society Ltd v. Segu Mohamed Khaja Alawdeen* [1954] 2 Lloyd's Rep. 45. See *Soon Hua Seng Co Ltd v. Glencore Grain Ltd* [1996] 1 Lloyd's Rep. 398 at 401.

[58] On the Uniform Customs and Practice for Documentary Credits see para. 11–002.

[59] In Arts 23(b), (c) and (d), 24(b), (c) and (d) and 26(b). The text quotes from Art. 23 which deals with bills of lading. Arts 24 and 26 deal with Non-Negotiable Sea Waybills and Multimodal Transport Documents respectively, and similar provision is made in those Articles.

[60] *Colin & Shields v. W. Weddell & Co Ltd* [1952] W.N. 420.

[61] *Vantol Ltd v. Fairclough Dodd & Jones Ltd* [1955] 1 W.L.R. 642 at 646; *Pyke (Joseph) & Sons (Liverpool) v. Cornelius (Richard) & Co* [1955] 2 Lloyd's Rep. 747 at 751; *P. J. van der Zijden Wildhandel NV v. Tucker & Cross Ltd* [1975] 2 Lloyd's Rep. 240 at 242.

[62] Per Lord Denning M.R. in *Tradax Export SA v. Andre & Cie SA* [1976] 1 Lloyd's Rep. 416 at 423.

may provide expressly or by necessary implication that the goods shall be "shipped" from a particular port. If shipment from that port becomes impossible owing to a frustrating event, the seller is not obliged to buy goods afloat[63] and the contract is frustrated.[64] Commercial considerations may make this result inevitable as in many circumstances buying afloat would be impracticable and not commercially viable. Lord Denning M.R. observed in one case[65]:

> "Take the usual case of a string of contracts between the shipper and the receiver. If there were an obligation to buy afloat, who is to do the buying? Is each seller to do so in order to fulfil his obligation to the buyer? If that were so there would be 'large numbers of buyers chasing very few goods and the price would reach unheard of levels.' Alternatively, is the first seller in the string to do so? Or the last seller? No one can tell. It seems to me that if there is prohibition of export or force majeure, the sellers are not bound to buy afloat in order to implement their contract."

On the other hand, the c.i.f. contract may expressly provide that the goods should be shipped "afloat", with or without reference to a particular ship.[66]

Loss of goods

It follows from the particular character of the c.i.f. contract that, if the goods are shipped and lost during the ocean transit, the seller is still entitled to tender proper shipping documents to the buyer and to claim the purchase price. Donaldson J. said[67]:

> "the fact that the ship and goods have been lost after shipment or that a liability to contribute in general average or salvage has arisen is no reason for refusing to take up and pay for the documents."

2–034

It has been held[68] that these rules apply even when the seller at the time of tender of the shipping documents knows that the goods are lost. It is immaterial whether before the tender of the documents the property in the goods is vested in the seller or the buyer or a third person or whether the goods are unascertained or have been appropriated. "The seller must be in a position to pass the property in the goods by the bill of lading if the goods are in existence but he need not

---

[63] *Vantol Ltd v. Fairclough Dodd & Jones Ltd* [1955] 1 W.L.R. 642 at 647; *Lewis Emanual & Son Ltd v. Sammut* [1959] 2 Lloyd's Rep. 62; *Tradax Export SA v. Andre & Cie SA* [1976] 1 Lloyd's Rep. 416; *Toepfer v. Schwarze* [1977] 2 Lloyd's Rep. 380 at 390; *Exportelisa SA v. Rocco Giuseppe & Figli Soc Coll* [1978] 1 Lloyd's Rep. 433 at 437; *Bremer Handelsgellschaft mbH v. Vanden Avenne-Izegem PVBA* [1978] 2 Lloyd's Rep. 109; *Bunge SA v. Kruse* [1980] 2 Lloyd's Rep. 142.
[64] See *post*, Chap 6 on frustration of contracts.
[65] *Per* Lord Denning M.R. in *Tradax Export SA v. Andre & Cie SA* [1976] 1 Lloyd's Rep. 416 at 423. See also *Bunge SA v. Kruse* [1980] 2 Lloyd's Rep. 142.
[66] See, for example, *Mash & Murrell Ltd v. Joseph I. Emanuel Ltd* [1961] 1 W.L.R. 862 at 863; [1962] 1 W.L.R. 16. In *Eurico SpA v. Philipp Brothers; The Epaphus* [1987] 2 Lloyd's Rep. 215 at 217 the buyers bought a cargo of rice afloat. See also *State Trading Corporation of India Ltd v. M. Golodetz Ltd* [1988] 2 Lloyd's Rep. 182.
[67] In *Golodetz & Co Inc v. Czarnikow-Rionda Co Inc; The Galatia* [1979] 2 Lloyd's Rep. 452 at 455, affd [1980] 1 Lloyd's Rep. 453, CA. See also *per* MacCardie J. in *Manbre Saccharine Co v. Corn Products Co* [1919] 1 K.B. 198 at 204.
[68] In *Manbre Saccharine Co v. Corn Products Co* [1919] 1 K.B. 198; *State Trading Corporation of India Ltd v. M. Golodetz Ltd* [1988] 2 Lloyd's Rep. 182 at 183.

have appropriated the particular goods in the particular bill of lading to the particular buyer until the moment of the tender, nor need he have obtained any right to deal with the bill of lading until the moment of the tender."[69]

The buyer's remedy, in case of loss of the goods in transit, is normally a claim against the carrier or the insurer. The legal causes of action available for the buyer's claim against the carrier have been considered earlier,[70] but normally the buyer will claim against the insurer, in which case he only has to prove that the loss is caused by a risk covered by the policy. The insurer, when paying, will demand the assignment to himself of the claim against the carrier or to be subrogated to it and, he will, if necessary, pursue this claim, which will only be successful if it is proved that the carrier was at fault.

It may happen that the goods are lost in transit owing to factors which do not entitle the buyer to make a claim against the carrier or insurer. In these circumstances it ought to be remembered that under a c.i.f. contract the buyer, and not the seller, bears the risk from the moment when the goods are delivered to the carrier. Therefore the buyer has to pay the purchase price to the seller upon tender of the appropriate shipping documents or, if he has already paid, cannot recover the price on the ground that there was a total failure of consideration.

Contracts expressed to be c.i.f. but not being true c.i.f. contracts

2–035   These strict rules are peculiar to the c.i.f. contract and do not apply to other contracts, in particular not to arrival contracts and other contracts which are not true c.i.f. contracts though they may be so described by the parties. It should be noted that the terminology employed by the parties is not always a safe guide to their real intentions. In *Comptoir d'Achat v. Luis de Ridder; The Julia*[71] the sellers; who sold on c.i.f. terms; reserved the right to substitute a delivery order on their agents at the port of destination for the bill of lading. The buyers accepted the delivery order and paid the purchase price but the order could not be implemented because the ship carrying the goods had to be diverted because of the Second World War. The House of Lords held that the buyers were entitled to the return of the purchase price because an analysis of the customary course of trading of the parties showed, in the words of Lord Porter,[72] that "payment was not made for the documents but as an advance payment for a contract afterwards to be performed". The contract was, therefore, not a true c.i.f. contract and the sellers' inability to deliver the goods at the port of destination

---

[69] *Per* Atkin J. in *C. Groom Ltd v. Barber* [1915] 1 K.B. 316 at 324.

[70] See *ante*, paras 2–029 and 2–030.

[71] [1949] A.C. 293. See further, *Re Denbigh, Cowan & Co and R. Atcherley & Co* (1921) 90 L.J.K.B. 936; *The Parchim* [1918] A.C. 157 at 163; *Colin & Shields v. W. Weddel & Co Ltd* [1952] W.N. 420; *John Martin of London v. A. E. Taylor* [1953] 2 Lloyd's Rep. 589; *Holland Colombo Trading Society Ltd v. Segu Mohamed Khaja Alawdeen* [1954] 2 Lloyd's Rep. 45; *H. Glynn (Covent Garden) Ltd v. Wittleder* [1959] 2 Lloyd's Rep. 409 at 413; *Gardano and Giampieri v. Greek Petroleum George Mamidakis & Co* [1962] 1 W.L.R. 40 ("Delivery ex Eleussinia Installation"); *Soon Hua Heng Co Ltd v. Glencore Grain Ltd* [1996] 1 Lloyd's Rep. 398 at 401 and 402.

[72] [1949] A.C. 293 at 310.

resulted in a total failure of consideration for the payment of the purchase price by the buyers. The contract was, in law, an "arrival" contract.[73]

Where a contract expressed to be on c.i.f. terms provided that "any tender or delivery of the goods or of the bill of lading" should constitute a valid tender or delivery, the Judicial Committee of the Privy Council, on appeal from Ceylon (now Sri Lanka), advised that the contract was not intended to be a true c.i.f. contract since the tender of the goods was admitted as an alternative to the tender of the documents.[74]

A transport document which on transfer does not give the transferee a direct contractual right against the carrier to claim delivery of the goods does not satisfy the requirements of a genuine c.i.f. contract. Thus, a bill of lading issued by a freight forwarder[75] is not sufficient unless he is himself a carrier by sea. According to the UCP (1993 Revision) certain specified transport documents, which do not qualify as marine bills of lading, will be accepted by a bank unless it is instructed by the credit that the seller shall tender a marine/ocean bill of lading. A contract using the term "c.i.f." in connection with air transport is not a true c.i.f. contract, as Graham J. held in a case[76] which provided for delivery of goods sent from Holland to purchasers in the United Kingdom "c.i.f. Gatwick".

Refusal to accept the goods

The particular qualities of the c.i.f. contract do not prevent the buyer from rejecting the goods[77] when, on delivery and inspection, he finds that they are not in accordance with the terms of the contract; if for example, they are not of the contract description or have been damaged owing to insufficient packing. The payment of the purchase price on delivery of the shipping documents is subject to the condition subsequent that the goods are in accordance with the terms of the contract of sale. If they fall short in that respect, the condition is discharged and the position is the same as in every other contract of sale.[78] If the agreement of the parties as to the quality of the goods was a condition of the contract of sale and not merely a warranty,[79] as is normally the case, the buyer may terminate the contract and recover the purchase price.[80] The buyer's right to inspect and examine the goods is similar to that of a buyer under an f.o.b. contract.[81]

2–036

Variants of the c.i.f. contract

Two variants of the contract, even if described as "c.i.f." by the parties do not, as previously stated,[82] satisfy the essential legal requirements of the c.i.f.

2–037

---

[73] See *post*, para. 2–042. In *The Aliakmon* (*ante*, para. 2–030) an original c. and f. contract was converted by agreement of the parties into an ex warehouse contract.

[74] *Holland Colombo Trading Society Ltd v. Segu Mohamed Khaja Alawdeen, supra*.

[75] See para. 16–010.

[76] *Morton-Norwich Products Inc v. Intercen Ltd* [1976] F.S.R. 513; [1977] J.B.L. 182.

[77] On acceptance see para. 5–006.

[78] See *post*, paras 5–007 and 5–008.

[79] On conditions and warranties in contracts of sale, see *post*, para. 5–002.

[80] See *post*, para. 5–010.

[81] See *ante*, para. 2–026 on examination of goods, see also *post*, para. 5–005.

[82] See *ante*, para. 2–020.

contract. First if it is the intention of the parties that the actual delivery of
the goods is an essential condition of performance, the contract is not a c.i.f.
contract. Secondly, if on transfer of the shipping documents, no direct relationship is created between the transferee on the one hand, and the carrier
and insurer on the other, the contract lacks the essential legal features of a
c.i.f. contract.

If the parties agree that the date of arrival of goods is a determinant for
payment of the price, for example by agreeing c.i.f. terms, adding "payment
on arrival of goods" or "payment x days after arrival of goods", the clause
will be treated as ambiguous and its true meaning will have to be ascertained
from the intention of the parties. It may be that they have intended that the
arrival of the goods shall be a condition for the payment of the price. If so,
the contract is not a c.i.f. contract. English practice has previously been
inclined to interpret the clause in this way,[83] but the better view is that this
interpretation should only be adopted if this intention of the parties can
clearly be gathered from the contract.[84]

Alternatively, it may be that the parties have intended that the clause shall
only refer to the time at which payment has to be made. In short, if the goods
do not arrive, payment shall be made on tender of the documents at the date at
which the goods would normally have arrived. In this case the clause refers only
to the incident of payment but not to that of delivery and the contract is a c.i.f
contract. American practice inclines to this interpretation, as appears from the
Uniform Commercial Code, section 2-321(3):

> "Unless otherwise agreed where the contract provides for payment on or after arrival of the
> goods the seller must before payment allow such preliminary inspection as is feasible; but if
> the goods are lost delivery of the documents and payment are due when the goods should
> have arrived."[85]

If the parties agree on c.i.f. terms and further agree that the price will be calculated on "net landed weights", "delivered weights" "out-turn" quantity or quality, the impression may be created that these are "arrival" contracts, but it has
been held[86] that these or similar clauses are normally intended only to relate to
the determination of the price. They do not affect the character of the contract
as a true c.i.f. contract. These clauses mean that after the goods are landed the
seller must allow a price adjustment.[87] If the goods are lost and the buyer has
already paid an estimated price on tender of the documents, he is not entitled to

[83] *Dupont v. British South Africa Co* (1901) 18 T.L.R. 24; *Polenghi v. Dried Milk Co* (1904) 10
Com. Cas. 42.
[84] Sassoon, *C.I.F. and F.O.B. Contracts* (4th ed.), para. 15.
[85] The term "no arrival, no sale", under which the seller is not obliged to ship, appears to be used
in the American practice (Uniform Commercial Code, s.2-324) but is not customary in the English
practice.
[86] *Soon Hua Heng Co Ltd v. Glencore Grain Ltd* [1996] 1 Lloyd's Rep. 398. Uniform Commercial
Code, s.2-321(1). See *Official Comment* (7th ed., Gould Publications).
[87] See *Oleificio Zucchi SpA v. Northern Sale Ltd* [1965] 2 Lloyd's Rep. 496 at 518, where a contract
c.i.f. Genoa provided for allowances if the goods (Canadian rapeseed screenings in bulk) arrived
damaged. Further: *Oricon Waren & Handels GmbH v. Intergraan NV* [1967] 2 Lloyd's Rep. 83 at
94 ("gross delivered weight"). In *Gill & Duffus SA v. Berger & Co Inc* [1984] 2 W.L.R. 95 the

an adjustment unless he can prove that the shipped goods were less in quantity or quality than he paid for.

If the c.i.f. contract incorporates a provision that a specified element of the charges is to be borne by the buyer, for example a clause such as "increase of export duties for buyer's account"[88] or "Cape surcharge buyer's account"[89], the essential nature of the c.i.f. contract is not destroyed. Such provisions refer only to the ascertainment of the charges and are entirely reconcilable with the character of a c.i.f. contract.

C. and F. (named port of destination)

C. and f. stands for "cost and freight". Under this clause the seller has to arrange **2–038** the carriage of the goods to the named foreign port of destination at his expense (but not at his risk, which ceases when he places the goods on board ship at the place of shipment). However, he is not obliged to arrange marine insurance, which is the concern of the buyer and, if effected, has to be paid by him.[90] In this respect the term differs from the ordinary c.i.f. term, but in all other respects the liabilities and duties of the parties are the same.[91] The c. and f. seller has to bear in mind the provisions of section 32(3) of the Sale of Goods Act 1979[92] because if he fails to give the buyer such notice as may enable him to insure the goods,[93] the goods would, exceptionally, travel at the seller's, and not at the buyer's risk. A c. and f. contract sometimes contains the words "insurance to be effected by buyer" or similar. It has been held[94] that these words are not merely declaratory but constitute a contractual obligation of the buyer to take out the usual insurance policy, *i.e.* a policy which, if the contract had been on c.i.f. terms, would have to be taken out by the seller.

The term "c. and f." is not frequently adopted by exporters, except in the case of some countries which, for political reasons or owing to lack of foreign exchange, require their importers to insure at home rather than to buy on c.i.f. terms. The c. and f. clause leads to an artificial separation of the arrangements for insurance and freight, whereas the c.i.f. stipulation, like the f.o.b. clause, provides a natural division of responsibilities between the exporter and the overseas buyer.

---

parties agreed that "quality final at port of discharge as per certificate of General Superintendance Co Ltd".

[88] *Produce Brokers New Co (1924) Ltd v. British Italian Trading Co* [1952] 1 Lloyd's Rep. 379.

[89] *Henry (D.I.) Ltd v. Wilhelm G. Clasen* [1973] 1 Lloyd's Rep. 159, CA.

[90] Where the c. and f. seller has given the buyer credit, it may be advisable for him to take out a contingency insurance covering the goods in transit, see Chap. 19 on marine insurance.

[91] In particular, the price is payable on tender of the correct shipping documents (exclusive, of course, of an insurance document), even though the parties are aware that the vessel carrying the goods has sunk and the goods are at the bottom of the sea: *State Trading Corporation of India Ltd v. M. Golodetz Ltd* [1988] 2 Lloyd's Rep. 182 at 183.

[92] See *ante*, para. 2–008.

[93] And unless the parties have otherwise agreed.

[94] *Reinhart Co v. Joshua Hoyle & Sons Ltd* [1961] 1 Lloyd's Rep. 346, 354, 357, 359. See also *Golodetz & Co Inc v. Czarnikow-Rionda Co Inc; The Galatia* [1979] 2 Lloyd's Rep. 450, affd [1980] 1 Lloyd's Rep. 453, CA.

C.I.F. and c., c.i.f. and e., c.i.f. and c. and i.

2–039   Other variants of the ordinary c.i.f. stipulation are the terms c.i.f. and c., c.i.f. and e., and c.i.f. and c. and i. The first of these abbreviations stands for "cost, insurance, freight and commission", in the second the letter "e." means "exchange" and in the third the letters "c. and i." denote "commission and interest". These terms should only be used when it is clear that the other party is familiar with their meaning, because they are often misunderstood. The commission referred to in the c.i.f. and c. clause is the exporter's commission which he charges when acting as buying agent for the overseas buyer. Export houses claim this commission as a matter of course and quote their prices "c.i.f. and c." because they wish to inform their customers abroad that the prices include their commission. The expression "exchange" is ambiguous. It is sometimes said to refer to the banker's commission or charge, while others maintain that it refers to exchange rate fluctuations. In the former case it denotes that the banker's charges are included in the price calculation when "c.i.f. and e." prices are quoted. In the latter case it means that the purchase price is not affected by the subsequent rise or fall of the stipulated currency of payment against the pound sterling. It is thought that the former interpretation is more common and that arrangements about currency fluctuations are usually made explicitly. The clause "c.i.f. and c. and i." is used when goods are exported to distant places where some time elapses before the bill drawn on the customer abroad is settled. When the seller negotiates the bill to his bank, the latter charges him commission and interest until payment has been received on the draft in this country, and the seller, by adding, in his contract of export sale, the letter "I." to the clause, indicates to the buyer that the quoted price includes the bank's interest and commission.

Carriage and insurance paid to (named place of destination) (CIP)[95]

2–040   This term is framed on the model of the c.i.f. contract, but whether it is a genuine c.i.f. contract or an arrival contract depends on the documents which the seller is obliged to tender. The seller pays the freight for the carriage of the goods to the named destination. He also has to procure transport insurance against the risk of loss of or damage to the goods during the carriage at his expense. He contracts with both the carrier and the insurer. The risk of loss of or damage to the goods is transferred from the seller to the buyer when the goods have been delivered into the custody of the first carrier. Any increase in the freight and insurance charges between the conclusion of the contract of sale and the delivery of the goods to the first carrier has to be borne by the seller.

Carriage paid to (named place of destination) (CPT)[96]

2–041   Unlike the CIP term above the seller is not obliged to procure insurance cover for the transport. In other respects the observations made on the term "freight/carriage and insurance paid to" apply.

---

[95] Defined in both Incoterms and Intraterms.
[96] *ibid.*

Arrival, ex ship or delivered ex ship (DES) (named port of arrival)

This term[97] has been defined by the Judicial Committee of the Privy Council as   **2–042**
denoting that "the seller has to cause delivery to be made to the buyer from a
ship which has arrived at the port of delivery and has reached a place therein
which is usual for the delivery of goods of the kind in question".[98] The clause is
also defined in Incoterms, Intraterms and in the American Uniform Commercial
Code.[99] Under this clause the seller has to pay the freight or otherwise to release
the carrier's lien, and the buyer is only bound to pay the purchase price if actual
delivery of the goods is made to him at the stipulated port of delivery.

The difference between the arrival (or ex ship) contract and the c.i.f. contract
is that in the former case the documents do not stand in the place of the goods,
but that delivery has to be made *in specie*, *i.e.* the goods sold have to be
delivered to the buyer at the named port of delivery. Consequently, if the goods
are lost in transit, the buyer is not obliged to pay the purchase price upon tender
of the documents, and can, in certain circumstances, claim return of the price
he paid in advance. The delivery of the indorsed bill of lading from the seller
to the buyer is not given with the intention of passing the property in the goods,
but, unless otherwise agreed, the property will pass only when the goods are
handed over to the buyer after arrival of the ship at the agreed port of destination.
As the goods are not at the buyer's risk during the voyage, the seller is not
under an obligation to the buyer to insure the goods. Where the seller actually
insures them and they are lost or damaged in transit, the buyer cannot claim the
insurance money from the insurance company because he has no insurable interest in the goods. He may, however, have an insurable interest in the profits
which he hoped to make on the goods and he may either himself or through the
seller acting as his agent in this behalf insure this interest.[1] The seller must
discharge all liens arising out of the carriage and, if he has not transferred the
bill of lading to the buyer, must give him a delivery order on the ship.

The ex ship clause relates exclusively to the place of delivery of the goods
and does not bring into consideration the special method of payment of the
purchase price against delivery of the shipping documents. In an ex ship contract
the elements of the contract of sale are not combined with those of the contracts
of carriage and insurance in the manner characteristic of the c.i.f. contract.

The reference in a contract of sale to the goods being purchased "ex" or
"afloat per" a particular ship is part of the description of the goods and if the
goods are not shipped in that ship a condition of the contract of sale is breached.[2]
Similarly, the reference to the approximate date of arrival of the named ship is
part of the description of the goods: "there is good commercial sense in that,

---

[97] Contracts containing this term are sometimes referred to as "delivery contracts". This description
is ambiguous and should be avoided.
[98] *Yangtsze Insurance Association v. Lukmanjee* [1918] A.C. 585 at 589; *per* Mustill J. in *Industria
Azucarera Nacional SA (IANSA) v. Expresa Exportadora de Azucar (Cubazucar)* [1982] Com.L.R.
171; affd [1983] 2 Lloyd's Rep. 171, CA (the case is known as *Cubazucar v. IANSA*).
[99] UCC, s.2-322.
[1] *Yangtsze Insurance Association v. Lukmanjee* [1918] A.C. 585 at 589.
[2] Sale of Goods Act 1979, s. 13; see *post*, para. 5–003.

inasmuch as a description of the goods being 'afloat per SS. Morton Bay due approximately 8th June' does give the buyers, not an absolute guarantee of arrival on June 8, but at least some indication of the date on which they may be expected in London."[3]

Ex quay, delivered ex quay (DEQ) (named port of destination)[4]

2–043   Under this term, the seller's duties are the same as under the arrival term but, in addition, the seller accepts responsibility for import duties and unloading charges payable at the port of destination, such as lighterage, dock dues and porterage. "Ex quay" combined with the port of destination, is rarely used in British export practice because the seller will not normally accept responsibilities arising from the landing of the goods unless he has a representative or agent at the port of destination who is acquainted with local practice. The buyer remains, under this clause, liable for the carriage on and from the quay to the ultimate place of destination of the goods, which may be situated inland.[5]

Delivered at frontier (DAF) (named point at frontier)[6]

2–044   This term is used in the Continental export trade where no sea or air carriage is involved. U.K. importers of foodstuffs sometimes buy "delivered at frontier" also described as "franco frontier" of the country where the goods originate. The term, when used in a contract of sale, should specify not only the frontier but also the named place of delivery, for example "Delivered at Franco-Italian frontier (Modane)". The term does not oblige the seller to obtain an insurance policy for the buyer's benefit; the parties should set out in the contract of sale the duties which they should assume with respect to insurance.

Delivered duty paid (DDP), delivered duty unpaid (DDU) (named place of destination in the country of importation)[7]

2–045   These terms, sometimes expressed as "franco domicile" or "free delivery" represent the most favourable terms which the buyer can obtain and the most onerous arrangement for the seller. The term is not often found in the practice of the British export trade, except where the parties have agreed on the delivery of goods of relatively small size by air.

Under these terms the goods are at the seller's risk and expense until placed at the buyer's disposal at the named place of destination. The seller's obligation, under the DDP term, is to pay all charges up to the delivery of the goods at the

---

[3] *Per* McNair J. in *Macpherson Train & Co Ltd v. Howard Ross & Co Ltd* [1955] 1 W.L.R. 640 at 642.

[4] The DEQ terms are defined in both Incoterms and Intraterms.

[5] In *Bunten & Lancaster (Produce) v. Kiril Mischeff* [1964] 1 Lloyd's Rep. 386 an import contract provided for "landed duty paid ex quay Liverpool". See also *Glass's Fruit Markets Ltd v. A. Southwell & Son (Fruit) Ltd* [1969] 2 Lloyd's Rep. 398.

[6] Defined in both Incoterms and Intraterms, para. 410.

[7] *ibid.* at paras 411, 412.

place named by the buyer for delivery, including import duties and inland carriage in the buyer's country. Under the DDU term, the buyer will undertake the costs of importing the goods. An import licence has to be obtained by the seller under the DDP term, but not under the DDU term. In the absence of agreement to the contrary, the buyer is not obliged to pay the purchase price on presentation of the bill of lading or a consignment note, and payment can only be demanded against delivery of the goods themselves.

CONTAINER TRADE TERMS

The terms FCA, CPT and CIP,[8] can be used for all modes of transport, but are **2–046** particularly suitable for container transport and all forms of multimodal traffic, including roll on-roll off operations by trailers and ferries.[9] The main object of these terms is to take account of the increasing consolidation of cargoes. These terms shift the "critical point", when the risk and possibly other legal incidents pass from the seller to the buyer, away from the ship's rail to an earlier point, that is when the first carrier takes charge of the goods. When shipping goods in containers, whether as full container load (FCL) or less than full container load (LCL), the exporter should give preference to one of the container terms rather than use a term appropriate to non-container shipment. The UCPDC provide that transport documents used in container transport are acceptable to banks under letters of credit unless the credit calls for a marine bill of lading, a post receipt or a certificate of posting.[10]

---

[8] See *ante*, para. 2–040.
[9] See *post*, Chap. 16.
[10] UCPDC 1993, Art. 26.

CHAPTER 3

FORMATION OF CONTRACT[1]

3–001   In order to minimise litigation in the event of a dispute, a number of aspects must be borne in mind when drawing up a contract.[2] An international contract should always contain either a jurisdiction and choice of law clause specifying the courts of which country are to have jurisdiction and the law of which country is to govern the contract, or alternatively, the parties may agree that disputes arising should be submitted to arbitration. To do this they would incorporate an arbitration clause specifying where the arbitration is to take place, the number of arbitrators and by whom they are to be appointed, and a choice of law clause.[3]

In English law, to be valid and binding a contract must contain offer, acceptance and consideration, and its terms must be certain. An oral contract is normally equally as binding as a written one, although it is desirable that a commercial contract be in writing and signed.

The Negotiations

Inquiries and invitations to contract

3–002   Negotiations between the parties may or may not lead to the conclusion of a legally binding contract. The first contact between the parties may take the form of an inquiry or an invitation to contract,[4] such as contained in a catalogue, advertisement or invitation to submit tenders for construction or other work. Statements made in the course of negotiation are not contractual statements unless they are subsequently incorporated into the contract.[5] They are not, however, without legal effect, for if a contract results, a pre-contractual false statement may be characterised in law as a misrepresentation.[6] If a contract does not ensue, the information imparted during the negotiations may have been of a confidential nature and its misuse may give rise to a legal remedy.[7] In certain circumstances a pre-contractual statement may be incorporated into the contract.

---

[1] See generally Chitty, *Contracts* (28th ed., 1999); *Halsbury's Laws*, Vol. 9, paras 224–304.
[2] See, *e.g.* the information in ICC Publication No. 556—ICC Model International Sale Contract and diskette.
[3] See Chaps 22 (Jurisdiction), 21 (English Law and Foreign Law) and 23 (Arbitration).
[4] Or an invitation to treat.
[5] In insurance practice the statements on the proposal form are often incorporated into the contract by a "basis of contract" clause.
[6] Misrepresentation Act 1967, s.2.
[7] The cases on confidentiality generally are referred to in Chap. 27.

The quotation

Whether the provision of a quotation is merely an invitation to contract or consti- **3–003**
tutes an offer depends on the intention of the parties, and especially on that of
the person submitting the quotation. Normally, the provision of a quotation is
only an invitation to contract. If the person to whom the quotation is addressed
responds, such response is an offer. It is for the provider of the quotation to
decide whether to accept or reject it. In one case,[8] carriers were invited by
exporters to undertake the shipment of waste paper from New Zealand to India.
The carriers sent the exporters a telex stating the periods of the intended shipments, the freight rate and the manner of stowage, but the telex did not state the
quantity of the cargo, the number of shipments, the dates and the intervals
between them. The exporters presented 919 tonnes of paper for shipment, and
this quantity was shipped in two vessels. The exporters failed to pay the freight
charges for these consignments and the carriers refused all further bookings.
The exporters claimed damages from the carriers for breach of contract. The
Privy Council, on appeal from New Zealand, held that the carriers' telex was
no more than the quotation of a freight rate and that it was not an offer. Consequently, there was no binding contract and the exporters' claim for damages
failed.

On the other hand, a quotation may contain all the elements of an offer and
may qualify in law as such. The decisive test is the intention of the person
providing the quotation.

Tenders

An invitation to submit a tender is generally an invitation to treat[9] but may be **3–004**
an offer where the invitee binds himself to accept the best tender.[10] Where a
local authority invited selected parties to submit tenders, indicating that all tenders would be considered, it was bound to consider each tender.[11]

In the case of tenders for public supply contracts, E.C. Regulations[12] require
that the contracting body inviting tenders accept the lowest tender or that which
is the "most economically advantageous".

THE OFFER

The offer is a statement intended to result in a binding contract if duly accepted **3–005**
by the offeree. The seller should make certain that the essential elements of the
contract are clearly stated in the communications exchanged by the parties. For
example, in a contract for the sale of goods:

---

[8] *Scancarriers A/S v. Aotearoa International Ltd* [1985] 2 Lloyd's Rep. 419. See also *The Gudermes*
[1985] 2 Lloyd's Rep. 623 at 628 where Leggatt L.J. said that there was "no machinery provided
for the ascertainment of a 'market price'", and notice of a price "acceptable to the defendants
represents the very stuff of which agreements to agree are made".
[9] *Spencer v. Harding* [1870] L.R. 5 C.P. 561.
[10] *Harvela Investment Ltd v. Royal Trust of Canada (CI) Ltd* [1986] A.C. 207.
[11] *Blackpool & Fylde Aero Club Ltd v. Blackpool BC* [1990] 1 W.L.R. 1195.
[12] Implemented by S.I. 1991, Nos 2679 and 2680; S.I. 1992, No. 3279.

(a) the goods ordered should be described without ambiguity;

(b) the purchase price and the terms of payment should be stated; and

(c) the terms of delivery should be set out, including instructions for packing and invoicing, transportation and insurance.

Firm offers

3–006 In English law an offer can be revoked until it is accepted. If, however, the offeree has paid "to keep the offer open", it then becomes an option. It can even be revoked if it is given as a "firm offer," that is if it states that the offeror will consider himself bound by it for a specified time.

Other legal systems adopt a different—and less dogmatic—attitude to the firm offer and consider it as binding in certain circumstances. Thus, the UCC, s.2-205, provides that a firm offer for the purchase or sale of goods given by a merchant in a signed writing is not revocable for lack of consideration. The Vienna Convention on Contracts for the International Sale of Goods[13] goes further; it provides in Article 16(2) that a firm offer shall be binding but, unlike the UCC, does not require that it is made by a merchant and in a signed writing.

THE ACCEPTANCE

The acceptance must be unconditional and unqualified

3–007 The acceptance must be unconditional and unqualified. It will fail to take effect if it attempts to vary the terms of the offer or to add new terms.[14] In this instance, it will be a counteroffer and therefore a rejection of the original offer. If the original offeror receives a qualified acceptance and does not express agreement, there is no contract. He is not obliged to reply to the modified acceptance, although complete silence, after its receipt, hardly constitutes good business practice. In *Northland Airliners Ltd v. Dennis Ferranti Meters Ltd*[15] the sellers, a company in North Wales, negotiated with the buyers, a Canadian company, for the sale of an amphibian aircraft. The sellers sent the following telegram: "Confirming sale to you Grummond Mallard aircraft . . . , Please remit £5,000." The buyers replied: "This is to confirm your cable and my purchase Grummond Mallard aircraft terms set out your cable . . . £5,000 sterling forwarded your bank to be held in trust for your account pending delivery . . . Please confirm delivery to be made thirty days within this date". The sellers did not reply but sold the aircraft to a third person at a higher price. The Court of Appeal held that there was no contract. The buyer's reply had introduced two new terms, one as to payment and the other as to delivery, and the sellers were not bound to reply to this counteroffer.

The rule that a modified acceptance always constitutes a counteroffer and can

---

[13] See *post*, paras 32–026 to 32–031.
[14] *Lark v. Outhwaite* [1991] 2 Lloyd's Rep. 132 at 39.
[15] (1970) 114 S.J. 845; *The Times*, October 23, 1970.

be rejected by the original offeror by mere silence may be too rigid in its generality. According to the Uniform Law on the Formation of Contracts[16] which applies to international sales,[17] an acceptance which contains additional or different terms that do not materially alter the offer constitutes a valid acceptance with the proposed modifications, unless promptly objected to by the original offeror.[18] The American Uniform Commercial Code contains a similar—though not identical—regulation. It provides[19]:

> "The additional terms are to be construed as proposals for addition to the contract. Between merchants[20] such terms become part of the contract unless:
>
> (a) the offer expressly limits acceptance to the terms of the offer;
> (b) they materially alter it; or
> (c) notification of objection to them has already been given or is given within a reasonable time after notice of them is received."

Communication of acceptance

The general rule is that a contract is made when the acceptance is communicated to the offeror. Thus, silence cannot amount to acceptance even where the offer so stipulates unless there is a course of dealing between the parties or where circumstances give rise to an estoppel.[21]   **3–008**

If it is necessary to determine where a contract is concluded,[22] it is logical that this is the place at which the acceptance is communicated.[23] "Communication" is a term of art which means that the addressee must have been able to take notice of the statement in question. The statement is duly communicated if it has been received by the addressee, even if for one reason or another he has not read it, for example if, because of his internal office organisation, it has not reached him.[24]

This rule is applied to *instantaneous contracts*. These are contracts made verbally, by telephone or by telex.[25] Contracts made by telex, as already

---

[16] Uniform Laws on International Sales Act 1967, Sched. 2.

[17] But only if it has been chosen by the parties, section 1(3) of the Act.

[18] Sched. 2, Art. 7(2). The UN Convention on Contracts for the International Sale of Goods (Vienna, 1980) contains the same regulation in Art. 19(2). The Vienna Convention is not in force in the U.K.

[19] In s.2–207(2).

[20] A "merchant" is defined in s.2–104(1).

[21] See further Chitty, *Contracts, loc cit.*, Vol. 1, para. 2–066.

[22] *e.g.* for leave to serve a claim form out of the jurisdiction pursuant to CPR, Pt. 6.20(5)(a) (contract made within the jurisdiction).

[23] *Per* Lord Wilberforce in *Brinkibon Ltd v. Stahag Stahl und Stahlwarenhandels GmbH* [1983] 2 A.C. 34 at 41. For a critical review of *Brinkibon* see J. Wightman, "Does Acceptance Matter?" in *Essays for Clive Schmitthoff* (ed. John Adams, 1983), p. 145.

[24] *Cf. The Brimnes* [1975] Q.B. 929.

[25] *Brinkibon Ltd v. Stahag Stahl und Stahlwarenhandels GmbH* [1983] 2 A.C. 34; *Entores Ltd v. Miles Far East Corp.* [1955] 2 Q.B. 327; *The Brimnes* [1975] Q.B. 929. An allegedly false or negligent misrepresentation requires publication and, if made by a person abroad to a person in England by telephone or telex, the place where the tort is committed is the place at which the communication is received, *i.e.* England: *Diamond v. Bank of London and Montreal Ltd* [1979] Q.B. 333. It was held in *R. v. Governor of Pentonville Prison, ex p. Osman* [1991] 1 W.L.R. 281 that the theft of bank funds by telex was committed at the place where the telex was sent (Hong Kong), but the possibility was not ruled out that the appropriation likewise took place at the locality where the telex was received (New York).

observed, are normally regarded as instantaneous contracts. However the rule is not of universal application, as the following observations of Lord Wilberforce in the *Brinkibon* case[26] show:

> "... there are many variants on it. The senders and recipients may not be the principals to the contemplated contract. They may be servants or agents with limited authority. The message may not reach, or be intended to reach, the designated recipient immediately: messages may be sent out of office hours, or at night, with the intention, or upon the assumption, that they will be read at a later time. There may be some error or default at the recipient's end which prevents receipt at the time contemplated and believed in by the sender. The message may have been sent and/or received through machines operated by third persons. And many other variations may occur. No universal rule can cover all such cases: they must be resolved by reference to the intentions of the parties, by sound business practice and in some cases by a judgment where the risk should lie."

In letter of credit transactions, if the issuing bank sends the credit instructions to the advising bank by telex, which is later followed by a mail confirmation, the question arises whether the telex or the mail confirmation is the operative credit document. This situation is regulated by Article 11 of the UCP (1993 Revision)[27] where teletransmission is to constitute the credit unless there is a clear statement of intention to the contrary.

In the case of acceptance by fax, e-mail or electronic data exchange, and where the sender is aware that his communication has not been received, there should be no binding contract. If, however, the sender is unaware that the communication is wholly or partly illegible it may be that the contract is binding.[28]

If the acceptance is by post or telegram, it depends on the intention of the parties whether the general rule for the communication of the statement shall apply or whether the mere posting of such an acceptance, and not its arrival at the address of the offeree, shall be sufficient. Normally, the intention of the parties will be that the general rule shall apply.[29] In exceptional circumstances it may be inferred from the terms of the offer that mere posting of the acceptance shall be sufficient.[30] To exclude ambiguity, the offer should state that the offeror will only be bound if he actually receives the acceptance.

Contract by conduct

3–009   In cases where it cannot be said that the parties were truly in agreement prior to the commencement of performance, a contract may have come into existence as a result of performance.[31] The buyer may accept the goods delivered to him

---

[26] *ibid.* at 42. See also J. Wightman, *op. cit.*, n.23.
[27] See *post*, para. 11–017.
[28] Chitty, *Contracts*, op cit., Vol. 1, para. 2–046. See Chap. 33 for electric commerce and EDI.
[29] *Howell Securities Ltd v. Hughes* [1974] 1 W.L.R. 155.
[30] *Household Fire and Carriage Accident Insurance Ltd v. Grant* (1879) 4 Ex.D. 216 at 223.
[31] *Brogden v. Metropolitan Railways* [1877] 2 A.C. 666; *G. Percy Trentham Ltd v. Archital Luxfor Ltd* [1993] 1 Lloyd's Rep. 25. But see *Rimeco Riggelsen & Metal Co v. Queenborough Rolling Mill Co Ltd* QBCM 1 94/0087/B (arbitration clause was not incorporated by conduct).

by using them,[32] the seller may accept an offer by delivering goods to the buyer,[33] the seller may invite acceptance by conduct[34] or a counteroffer may be accepted by the conduct of the parties.[35] "The fact that the transaction was performed by both sides will often make it unrealistic to argue that there was no intention to enter into legal relations."[36]

Forms of acceptance

The confirmation slip

A contract may be negotiated verbally or by correspondence following which **3–010** one party sends the other an order or acceptance on a printed form with an attached confirmation slip, which has to be returned duly signed by the other party. It is always a matter of construction, in some cases not easy to resolve, whether the parties have agreed to the terms of the contract with sufficient precision.[37] Where an offer stipulates that acceptance must be by return of an attached form "it being expressly understood that no other form of acceptance will be valid or binding", then unless acceptance is by the prescribed form there will be no contract. If, however, the contract is accepted in some other way, the offeror is not entitled to stand by and let the offeree perform and then say there is no contract.[38]

The countersigned acceptance form

Another method of obtaining the offeror's written agreement to the terms of **3–011** acceptance is to send him two forms of acceptance acknowledging his order and to ask him to return one, duly signed by him. This method is frequently used in the export trade, particularly where the goods ordered represent a considerable value or have to be built to the buyer's specification.

In these circumstances, it is essential that the two forms of acceptance should contain identical terms or, at least, that the form retained by the offeror should have a "red hand" clause.[39] This draws attention to the fact that the form which he has signed and returned contains further clauses not included in the form retained by him.

Comfort letters or letters of intent

A typical situation in which a comfort letter is given arises where a company **3–012** wishes to obtain a loan from a bank and the latter asks for some assurance

---

[32] *Weatherby v. Banham* [1832] 5 C. & P. 228.
[33] *Harvey v. Johnson* [1848] 6 C.B. 295; *Cf. Interphoto Picture Library Ltd v. Stilleto Visual Programmes Ltd* [1989] Q.B. 433 at 436.
[34] *The Santa Clara* [1993] 2 Lloyd's Rep. 301 at 304.
[35] *The Bueno Trader* [1977] 2 Lloyd's Rep. 27.
[36] *G. Percy Trentham Ltd v. Archital Luxfor Ltd* [1993] 1 Lloyd's Rep. 25 at 27.
[37] On the parol (extrinsic) evidence rule, see *post*, para. 3–016.
[38] *Compagnie de Commerce et Commission SARL v. Parkinson Stove Co Ltd* [1953] 2 Lloyd's Rep. 487.
[39] On the "red hand" clause, see *post*, para. 3–017, n. 91.

from the company's parent company. The parent company may be unwilling to guarantee the loan because, if it does so, it would have to show the guarantee as a contingent liability in its balance sheet. It may, however, be willing to lend its support to the subsidiary by giving the bank a letter of comfort.

In most cases a comfort letter is intended to create only moral, and not legal, obligations for the parent company. In these cases it is couched in general terms, for example, that the directors of the parent company are aware of the loan facility sought by the subsidiary. In other cases the parent, by the comfort letter, accepts a legal obligation, though not of a financial nature, for example, it undertakes not to sell or otherwise to dispose of the shares in the subsidiary as long as the loan is outstanding.[40]

On occasion, however—and these cases will be rare—the comfort letter is worded in terms which place the parent company under a financial obligation to the bank. In one case[41] the two comfort letters which the parent gave the bank with respect to loans to the subsidiary contained this statement:

> "It is our policy to ensure that the business of [the subsidiary] is at all times in a position to meet its liabilities to you under the above arrangements."

The trial judge (Hirst J.) held that the parent was liable on these undertakings but he was reversed by the Court of Appeal. Ralph Gibson L.J. said[42]:

> ". . . in this case it is clear . . . that the concept of a comfort letter . . . was known to both sides at least to extend to or to include a document under which the defendants would give comfort to the plaintiffs by assuming, not legal liability to ensure repayment of the liabilities of the subsidiary, but a moral responsibility only."

Acceptance subject to seller's general conditions

3–013   The acceptance should invariably incorporate the seller's general conditions of business and here the earlier observations on general terms of business adopted by individual exporters[43] should be kept in mind.[44] When previous export transactions have taken place between the parties and their contracts are governed by the same conditions of sale, the buyer can be presumed to have placed his orders subject to those conditions[45] and the unqualified acceptance by the seller will conclude the contract. In most cases, however, the seller's conditions of

---

[40] In *Chemco Leasing SpA v. Rediffusion plc* [1987] F.T.L.R. 201, the comfort letter written by the defendants, the parent of a subsidiary, stated that the defendants would "take over" the subsidiary's liability to the plaintiffs if they—the defendants—disposed of their interest in the subsidiary and the new shareholders were not acceptable to the plaintiffs; the Court of Appeal held that the defendants' offer of liability was not accepted by the plaintiffs within a reasonable time. See also *Wilson, Smithett & Cape (Sugar) Ltd v. Bangladesh Sugar & Food Industries Corp* [1986] 1 Lloyd's Rep. 378 where a letter of intent amounted to acceptance.

[41] *Kleinwort Benson Ltd v. Malaysia Mining Corporation Berhad* [1989] 1 W.L.R. 379.

[42] At p. 391.

[43] See *post*, para. 32–014.

[44] If the general conditions of the seller conflict with those of the buyer a "battle of forms" may ensue, see *post*, para. 3–018.

[45] See *The Kite* [1933] P. 154 at 164; *Hardwick Game Farm v. Suffolk Agricultural Poultry Producers Association* [1969] 2 A.C. 31.

sale will be unknown to the buyer when making his offer. The acceptance by the seller "subject to our conditions of sale" represents in strict law a rejection of the buyer's offer combined with a counteroffer by the seller. However the courts will be reluctant to reach this conclusion if the transaction and the subsequent conduct of the parties disclose a clear intention to be bound by their agreement. In these situations, the seller who wishes to be on safe ground should obtain the buyer's unqualified confirmation before carrying out the contract, particularly when the negotiations were conducted by correspondence. In practice, the strict requirements of the law are sometimes disregarded which, although understandable, may lead to unfortunate consequences.[46] The reasonable exporter should insist on strict observance of the legal requirements in the case of orders that are not routine transactions.

Incorporation of current edition of general conditions

An exporter's general conditions should be revised from time to time and should   **3–014** provide that the edition current at the date of the conclusion of the contract shall apply. However, even where such a clause is not included, in the absence of indications to the contrary, the same result should be achieved. Where the contract provided that it was subject to general conditions "available on request", it was held[47] that that was a reference to the current edition. "It is common experience that the general conditions of various undertakers are revised from time to time, and anyone requesting a copy of such conditions would reasonably expect to receive the current up-to-date edition."[48]

Certainty

In order for a binding contract to exist its terms must be certain[49] or must be   **3–015** capable of being ascertained. However, the courts will endeavour to give effect to commercial agreements,[50] or where performance has been completed or partially completed.[51] Where its terms are too vague however, the agreement will be unenforceable[52] although in some cases vagueness can be resolved by custom or customary terms in a particular trade,[53] or by applying a standard of reasonableness.[54] The courts will also attempt to interpret a subsidiary term which is

---

[46] *Jayaar Impex Ltd v. Toaken Group Ltd (t/a Hicks Brothers)* [1996] 2 Lloyd's Rep. 437 (oral contract concluded by telephone not modified by written contract when the buyers failed to sign and return it to the sellers). Even where the court decides that there was a valid contract between the parties, as in *Brown & Gracie Ltd v. F. W. Green & Co Pty Ltd* [1960] 1 Lloyd's Rep. 289, costly and protracted litigation might result from the disregard of the simple rules on offer and acceptance or from ambiguity.
[47] *Smith v. South Wales Switchgear Co Ltd* [1978] 1 W.L.R. 165.
[48] *ibid. per* Lord Keith of Kinkel at 177.
[49] *i.e.* not vague or incomplete.
[50] *Hillas & Co Ltd v. Arcos Ltd* [1932] 147 L.T. 503.
[51] *Foley v. Classique Coaches Ltd* [1934] 2 K.B. 1.
[52] *G. Scammell & Nephew Ltd v. Ouston* [1941] A.C. 251.
[53] *Shamrock S.S. Co v. Storey & Co* [1899] 81 L.T. 413.
[54] *Hillas & Co v. Arcos Ltd* [1932] 147 L.T. 503 where the agreement was between parties familiar with the timber trade; *F & G Sykes (Wessex) Ltd v. Fine Fare* [1967] 1 Lloyd's Rep. 53.

meaningless and ought only to reject a provision as meaningless if it is imposs-ible to make sense of it.[55] If no interpretation is possible the court may then ignore it.[56]

Where an agreement is incomplete there is no binding contract. This is so where the agreement is "usual [defendants'] terms to be mutually agreed"[57] or where a standard form has blank spaces[58] or where amendments to a standing form contract remain to be agreed[59] or where a "lock-out" agreement did not contain an expiry date.[60] There are exceptions, however, where the agreement itself provides a means by which an otherwise uncertain term is to be resolved, such as a provision for calculating the price,[61] or where an increased hire rate can be inferred from the contract as a whole.[62] Sometimes lengthy and detailed negotiations take place between the parties, particularly if a major contract is negotiated. In such cases it can be difficult to determine whether the parties have reached agreement or whether the negotiations have failed because they have not been able to overcome the "sticking point".[63] It may be that the parties themselves cannot agree on whether they have a binding contract. It will then be for the tribunal to decide on the exchange of documents between them whether there is in fact a binding contract. Where there is no concluded contract but terms are finalised during performance, the contract is effective retrospect-ively to include pre-contractual part-performance.[64] In *British Steel Corp v. Clev-eland Bridge and Engineering Co Ltd*[65] a letter of intent requested that the other party commence work immediately pending a formal contract. The plaintiffs manufactured and delivered the cast steel nodes to the defendants. No contract was concluded but the plaintiffs' claim for *quantum meruit* succeeded.

If the parties have agreed on all essential points but left details to be settled later, a valid contract may have been concluded. Such an arrangement is some-

---

[55] *The Tropwind* [1982] 1 Lloyd's Rep. 232.
[56] *Nicolene Ltd v. Simmonds* [1953] 1 Q.B. 543.
[57] *CPC Consolidated Pool Carriers GmbH v. CTM Cia Transmediterranea SA; The CPC Gallia* [1994] 1 Lloyd's Rep. 68.
[58] *Metal Scrap Trade Corp v. Kate Shipping Co Ltd; The Gladys (No. 2)* [1994] 2 Lloyd's Rep. 402.
[59] *Ignazio Messina & Co v. Polskie Linie Oceaniczne* [1995] 2 Lloyd's Rep. 566.
[60] *Walford v. Miles* [1992] A.C. 128.
[61] *Hillas & Co Ltd v. Arcos Ltd* [1932] 147 L.T. 503.
[62] *Didymi Crop v. Atlantic Lines & Navigation Co Inc* [1988] 2 Lloyds Rep. 108.
[63] In *J. Milhem & Sons v. Fuerst Brothers & Co Ltd* [1954] 2 Lloyd's Rep. 559, the court held that the parties were never *ad idem*; nor did the negotiations of the parties advance to a binding contract in *Pagnan SpA v. Granaria BV* [1986] 2 Lloyd's Rep. 547 or *The North Sea* [1997] 2 Lloyd's Rep. 324.
[64] *G. Percy Trentham v. Archital Luxfur Ltd* [1993] 1 Lloyd's Rep. 25.
[65] [1984] 1 All E.R. 504, distinguished in *Regalian Properties plc v. London Docklands Development Corporation* [1995] 1 W.L.R. 212, where negotiations were "subject to contract" and in any event the plaintiffs' losses were not incurred at the defendants' request but in putting themselves in a position to obtain and perform the contract which resulted in no benefit to the defendant. See also *Lachhani v. Destination Canada (U.K.) Ltd* [1997] 13 Const.L.J. 279, where, contrary to the belief of both parties, there was no contract and leave was given to include a claim for *quantum meruit*; and *Hall & Tawse South Ltd v. Ivory Gate Ltd* 62 Con L.R. 117 where there was no formal agree-ment following a letter of intent. No contract period or price was agreed; the contractors were allowed a reasonable period to complete the works and were entitled to a reasonable price using JCT valuation machinery.

times referred to as a *heads of agreement*.[66] However, "it is for the parties to decide whether they wish to be bound and, if so, by what terms, whether important or unimportant."[67] Of course, if the agreement of the parties does not extend to all terms which are necessary to make it enforceable there is no "contract" in the legal sense.[68]

Parol evidence

The parol evidence rule states that verbal or other extrinsic evidence is usually   **3–016** not admissible to vary or qualify the written agreement.[69] However, this rule is subject to a number of exceptions, particularly to clarify an ambiguity[70] in the written contract or as an aid to construction. Where the written contract fails to express clearly the contractual terms or where terms are contradictory, it has to be construed in "the commercial, or business, object of the transaction."[71] In *Investors Compensation Scheme Ltd v. West Bromwich Building Society*, Lord Hoffman summarised the principles to be applied to the construction of documents[72]:

> "1. Interpretation is the ascertainment of the meaning which the document would convey to a reasonable person having all the background knowledge which would reasonably have been available to the parties in the situation in which they were at the time of the contract.
> 2. The background . . . includes absolutely anything which would have affected the way in which the language of the document would have been understood by the reasonable man.
> 3. The law excludes from the admissable background the previous negotiations of the parties and their declarations of subjective intent except in an action for rectification . . .
> 4. The meaning which a document (or other utterance) would convey to a reasonable man is not the same thing as the meaning of its words. The meaning of words is a matter of dictionaries and grammars; the meaning of the document is what the parties using those words against the relevant background would reasonably have been understood to mean. The background may not merely enable the reasonable man to choose between the possible meanings of words which are ambiguous but even (as occasionally happens in ordinary life) to conclude that the parties must, for whatever reason, have used the wrong words or syntax (see *Mannai Investment Co Ltd v. Eagle Star Life Assurance Co Ltd* [1997] 3 All E.R. 352.
> 5. The 'rule' that words should be given their 'natural and ordinary meaning' reflects the common sense position that we do not easily accept that people have made linguistic mistakes, particularly in formal documents. On the other hand, if one would nevertheless conclude from the background that something must have gone wrong with the language, the law does not require judges to attribute to the parties an intention which they plainly could not have had. Lord Diplock made this point more vigorously when he said in *Antaios Cia Naviera SA v. Salen Rederii AB; The Antaios* [1985] A.C. 191 at 201:

---

[66] But not all so-called heads of agreement are intended to be binding.

[67] *Per* Lloyd L.J. in *Pagnan SpA v. Feed Products Ltd* [1987] 2 Lloyd's Rep. 601.

[68] *ibid.*

[69] But see Law Commission Report No. 154 on Parol Evidence (January 1986, Cmnd. 9700) that when the question of construction of a contract document is in issue, a so-called parol (extrinsic) evidence rule does not exist, although the Commissioners did not ultimately recommend that the rule be abolished.

[70] *Partenreederei M.S. Karen Oltman v. Scarsdale Shipping Co Ltd; The Karen Oltman* [1976] 2 Lloyd's Rep. 709.

[71] *Per* Lord Wilberforce in *Prenn v. Simmonds* [1971] 1 W.L.R. 1381 at 1385; *Reardon Smith Line Ltd v. Yngvar Hansen-Tangen; The Diana Prosperity* [1976] 1 W.L.R. 989; *Barlee Marine Corporation v. Trevor Rex Mountain; The Leegas* [1987] 1 Lloyd's Rep. 471.

[72] [1998] 1 All E.R. 98, pp.114–115. But see the reservations of Saville and Judge L.JJ in *National Bank of Sharjah v. Delborg*, July 9, 1997 (New Law Publishing) and Staughton L.J. in *Scottish Power plc v. Britoil (Exploration) Ltd. The Times*, December 2, 1997.

'. . . if detailed semantic and syntactical analysis of words in a commercial contract is going to lead to a conclusion that flouts business common sense, it must be made to yield to business common sense.'"

If the parties intend that the document should contain everything, extrinsic evidence is not admissible.

Where the parties have incorporated general terms in a written document, a special agreement in their contract may override these general terms if that is the intention of the parties.[73]

Extrinsic evidence of a custom in the trade is permitted provided it is not contrary to an express provision in the written contract,[74] or to establish that there is a collateral contract.[75] The court may rectify a written agreement which by mistake does not accurately record the agreement of the parties[76] although it may simply consider the amended contract without formally ordering its rectification.[77]

Where one party has given another a verbal promise not to rely on a term in the general conditions and that promise has been accepted by the other party, he cannot rely on that term if it would make the verbal contractual promise wholly illusory. In one case[78] English importers of an Italian injection moulding machine in negotiations with their freight forwarders insisted that, if the machine was to be shipped in a container, it should be carried below deck because they feared that the machine might get rusty. The manager of the forwarders assured the importers orally that "if we use containers, they will not be carried on deck". When the machine was shipped from Rotterdam to Tilbury, the Dutch associated company of the forwarders failed to ensure that the container in which the machine was carried was shipped below deck. The ship met with a slight swell. The container which contained the machine and was shipped on deck fell overboard and became a total loss. In an action for damages by the importers, the forwarders sought to rely on their printed general conditions which gave them complete freedom as to the method of transportation. The Court of Appeal held that the verbal promise of the forwarders not to ship the goods on deck constituted an enforceable contractual promise which overrode the relevant term in the printed general conditions. The court gave judgment for the importers.

SPECIAL PROBLEMS RELATING TO GENERAL CONDITIONS

Agreement to standard terms

3–017   The general terms of business should be printed on price lists, catalogues, estimates, offers, and all contract documents emanating from the seller, such as

---

[73] See *Fratelli Moretti SpA v. Nidera Handelscompagnie BV* [1981] 2 Lloyd's Rep. 47 at 51 where it was held that the parties intended that a general clause adopted by incorporation should prevail over the special clauses in the contract.

[74] *Palgrave, Brown & Son v. S.S. Turid (Owners)* [1922] 1 A.C. 397.

[75] *Mann v. Nunn* [1874] 30 L.T. 526.

[76] See *The Rhodian River* [1984] 1 Lloyd's Rep. 373; *Grand Metropolitan plc v. William Hill Group Ltd* [1997] 1 B.C.L.C. 390.

[77] *The Nile Rhapsody* [1994] 1 Lloyd's Rep. 382.

[78] *J. Evans & Son (Portsmouth) Ltd v. Andrea Merzario Ltd* [1976] 1 W.L.R. 1078. See also *The Ardennes* [1951] 1 K.B. 55 (see *post*, para. 15–005); *Wake v. Renault (U.K.) Ltd, The Times*, August 1, 1996.

acceptances, in a clear, legible and conspicuous manner. They should be incorporated in the context of the seller's offer or acceptance. Where that is not feasible, the text should at least contain a clear and conspicuous reference to the fact that conditions of sale are printed on the reverse or on an attached sheet. Particular care should be taken when negotiating contracts by fax since standard terms are often printed on the back of faxed documents. This situation occurred in a case[79] between two freight forwarding companies. The claimant argued that the defendants' terms were not contained in any of their faxes although some stated that they were. It was held that the claimant had not had reasonable notice of the defendant's standard terms. It is also necessary to obtain the agreement of the buyer to the general terms of business of the seller. It is desirable that the buyer should agree in writing and the question has already been examined as to how to obtain the buyer's written consent.[80]

Particular care should be taken in this connection with the *choice of jurisdiction clause*[81] and *choice of law clause.*[82] The E.C. Convention on Jurisdiction and the Enforcement of Judgments in Civil and Commercial Matters,[83] as amended, to which effect is given in the United Kingdom by the Civil Jurisdiction and Judgments Act 1982[84] as amended, and the Civil Jurisdiction and Judgments Act 1991[85] both set out in Article 17(1) the provisions whereby a jurisdiction clause will be effectively incorporated.[86] The E.C. Convention on the Law Applicable to Contractual Obligations,[87] as enacted in the U.K. by the Contracts (Applicable Law) Act 1990,[88] by Article 3 gives effect to the parties' choice of the law of the country which is to govern their contract.

In certain foreign countries, the courts will not admit general terms of business which are incorporated in the contract only by reference. In English common law, a signed agreement is binding whether or not the party signing it has understood or even read it.[89] Where there is no signed agreement, no terms are incorporated unless reasonable steps have been taken to draw them to the attention of the other party prior to, or at the time of, the agreement.[90] However, "the more unusual a clause is, the greater the notice which must be given of it".[91] Where

---

[79] *Poseidon Freight Forwarding Co Ltd v. Davies Turner Southern Ltd* [1996] 2 Lloyd's Rep. 388.
[80] See *ante*, paras 3–010, 3–011.
[81] See Chap. 22.
[82] See Chap. 21.
[83] The Brussels Convention.
[84] This Act came into force on January 1, 1987.
[85] Enacting the Lugano Convention in respect of EFTA states.
[86] Art. 17(1) is dealt with in detail in para. 22–016, *post.*
[87] The Rome Convention, see *post*, paras 21–004 to 21–016.
[88] Which came into force for contracts made after April 1, 1991.
[89] *L'Estrange v. Graucob Ltd* [1934] 2 K.B. 394; *Chellaram & Co v. China Ocean Shipping Co* [1991] 1 Lloyd's Rep. 493.
[90] *Parker v. South Eastern Ry* [1877] 2 C.P.D. 416.
[91] *J Spurling Ltd v. Bradshaw* [1956] 1 W.L.R. 461. The rule that notice must be given to unusual contract terms is sometimes referred to as the "red hand" rule; the expression has its origin in a dictum of Denning L.J. in this case that "such clauses would need to be printed in red ink with a red hand pointing to it before the notice would be sufficient". See also *Phoenix Insurance Company of Hartford v. De Monchy* (1929) 45 T.L.R. 543. See further *MacLeod Ross & Co Ltd v. Compagnie d'Assurances Generales L'Helvetia of St. Gall* [1952] W.N. 56; *Interfoto Picture Library Ltd v. Stiletto Visual Programmes Ltd* [1988] 2 W.L.R. 615, distinguished in *Nutting v. Baldwin* [1995] 1

there has been a regular and consistent course of dealing between the parties on standard terms they will be incorporated into the contract, particularly standard terms which are customary in the trade.[92] It may happen that the general terms of business of the two parties to the contract conflict. This problem, known as the *battle of forms*, relates to the law of offer and acceptance.

The battle of forms

3–018   It sometimes happens that one party sends the other an offer on his general conditions of business and the other accepts subject to his own general conditions. The two sets of conditions will not normally coincide and the question may arise whether the parties have contracted and, if so, whose general conditions apply. This situation is sometimes referred to as *the battle of forms*.[93]

No battle of forms will arise if one party has taken the precaution of obtaining the other party's consent to his own conditions by a suitably worded confirmation slip or a signed acceptance, as discussed earlier. In one case[94] the sellers quoted for a machine. Their general conditions, which were printed on the reverse of the quotation, contained a price escalation clause. The buyers ordered the machine on their general conditions, which did not contain a price escalation clause. At the bottom of the buyers' order was a detachable slip stating that the order was accepted by the sellers "on the terms and conditions, stated therein". The sellers signed the slip and returned it to the buyers. The Court of Appeal held that the contract was concluded on the buyers' terms and that the sellers were not entitled to increase the price by virtue of the escalation clause. In another case,[95] between Californian sellers and English buyers, Parker J. avoided an apparent conflict of forms by finding that the contract was made by exchange of telex messages prior to the exchange of formal documents. The learned judge came to the conclusion that the "small print clause [in the sellers' formal acknowledgment of the order] is, in the context, meaningless. ... The reference to the original offer was for identification only. ..."

A real difficulty may arise in the battle of forms situation if the operation of the general conditions of one of the parties is not placed beyond doubt by a signed confirmation or acceptance of the other party, or if it cannot be established that the contract was concluded by means other than the exchange of formal documents. In this situation, it may reluctantly be concluded that there is no contract, as the strict application of the offer-acceptance-counteroffer analysis may demand, because that is not what the parties intended. The other terms of the contract and the subsequent conduct of the parties would need to be analysed in order to ascertain whether the conditions

---

W.L.R. 201; E. Macdonald, "The Duty to Give Notice of Unusual Contract Terms" [1988] J.B.L. 375.

[92] *Chevron International Oil Co Ltd v. A/S Sea Team* [1983] 2 Lloyd's Rep. 356.

[93] J. Adams, "The Battle of Forms" [1983] J.B.L. 297.

[94] *Butler Machine Tools Co Ltd v. Ex-Cell-O Corporation (England) Ltd* [1979] 1 W.L.R. 401.

[95] *OTM Ltd v. Hydranautics* [1981] 2 Lloyd's Rep. 211 at 215.

of the man "who fired the last shot" or those of the man "who got in the first blow"[96] were intended to apply.

INTERNATIONAL SUPPLY CONTRACTS

The exporter should be aware that certain enactments under English law protect **3–019** contracting parties of weaker bargaining power, in particular the consumer. These enactments[97] may prohibit or restrict contract terms which purport to exempt or limit a party's liability under the general law. In the normal course of events the exporter will not concern himself with the provisions of the Unfair Contract Terms Act 1977, as the contract concluded will usually be classified as an international supply contract.[98] These contracts are exempted from the provisions of the Unfair Contract Terms Act 1977 by virtue of section 26(1) and (2). An international supply contract is defined[99] as either a contract of sale or one in pursuance of which the possession or ownership of goods passes, and it is made by parties whose places of business, or if none, their habitual residences, are in the territories of different states. The contract must also satisfy the requirements that the goods in issue at the time of the conclusion of the contract are being or will be carried from the territory of one state to another; or the acts of offer and acceptance have been done in the territories of different states; or the contract provides that the goods are to be delivered to the territory of a state other than where the offer or acceptance took place.

In addition, regard must be had to the Unfair Terms in Consumer Contract Regulations 1999[1] which revoke and replace the 1994 Regulations. The modifications in the new Regulations reflect more closely the wording of E.C. Council Directive 93/13.[2] The thrust of the Regulations is to subject all terms of a contract between a seller or supplier of goods or services and a consumer to the requirement that terms which have not been individually negotiated satisfy the requirement of fairness. If the terms are unfair, the consumer is not bound by them. Article 3 of the Directive provides that a term which has not been individually negotiated shall be regarded as unfair if, contrary to the requirement of good faith, it causes a significant imbalance in the parties' rights and obligations arising under the contract to the detriment of the consumer.[3] The definition of

---

[96] *Per* Lord Denning M.R. in the case quoted in n.94.

[97] The Sale of Goods Act 1979, the Supply of Goods and Services Act 1982, the Consumer Credit Act 1974, the Unfair Contract Terms Act 1977 and the Consumer Protection Act 1987 are examples of such enactments.

[98] Exceptionally, an export contract may not satisfy the definition of an international supply contract. The international supply contract is not exempt from the provisions of the Supply of Goods and Services Act 1982, ss. 13–15; the Secretary of State may grant exemption by statutory instrument but has not yet done so.

[99] There are many definitions of an international sales contract: Uniform Law on the International Sale of Goods Act (1964), Art. 1 and the UN Convention on Contracts for the International sale of Goods (Vienna, 1980) among them—for discussion of these see Chap. 32. The above paragraph is concerned only with the definition given in the Unfair Contract Terms Act 1977.

[1] S.I. 1999 No. 2083.

[2] [1993] O.J. L95/29.

[3] The generality of the definition will ensure that much will be left to the discretion of the court.

consumer[4] excludes all other than natural persons. Importantly the definition of consumer applies to those who, in making the contract, are acting for purposes which are outside their trade, business or profession. The exporter, whilst being aware of these Regulations, may rarely in practice encounter situations where they will apply.

---

[4] Reg. 3(1), Art. 2(b).

CHAPTER 4

PERFORMANCE OF THE CONTRACT

In examining the disposal of goods by the seller in performance of the contract **4–001** of sale three issues must be considered; the delivery of the goods, the passing of the property in the goods and the passing of the risk. Normally in overseas sales, in particular on f.o.b. and c.i.f. terms, these three phases do not necessarily coincide and should be clearly distinguished.

English and foreign sales law

The first issue which has to be examined when a dispute arises between the **4–002** parties about the delivery of the goods, the passing of the property or the risk, is whether the dispute is to be considered under English law or the foreign law prevailing in the country of the buyer or some other law chosen by the parties. This question is essentially one relating to the conflict of laws, which will be discussed later.[1] The answer which the rules on the conflict of laws may provide is that the issue is decided by English law, in which case the provisions of the Sale of Goods Act 1979 will apply. If, however, the contract is governed by foreign law, the English courts may still have jurisdiction to hear the case; the substantive question of the law applicable to the contract is distinct from the procedural one of jurisdiction of the court and these two questions should not be confused. The only inference which has to be drawn from the application of foreign law to a particular contract is that the rules of the relevant foreign law displace the provisions of the Sale of Goods Act 1979, and that foreign law can be relied upon in the English courts if its rules can be proved by expert witnesses or in another admissible manner.[2] A third, though from the practical point of view unlikely, possibility is that the parties agree in their contract to apply the Uniform Laws on International Sales; in this case the provisions of the Uniform Laws on International Sales Act 1967 apply. It is, however, intended to replace these laws.[3]

If the contract of sale is governed by a foreign law, it should be borne in mind that the rules of that law may be very different from those of English law. For example, in some continental countries, if the seller delays the delivery of the goods and no time is fixed for the delivery, the buyer must normally demand delivery and allow the seller a reasonable time for performance before he can treat the contract as repudiated; this requirement of *mise en demeure* is unknown

---

[1] See *post*, Chap. 21.
[2] See *post*, Chap. 21, para. 21–002.
[3] See *post*, para. 32–004. It is intended that the Uniform Laws on International Sales will in due course be replaced by the UN Convention on Contracts for the International Sale of Goods (Vienna 1980) but this Convention has not been given effect in the United Kingdom yet (July 2000).

in Anglo-American law which is much stricter in this respect and entitles the innocent party at once to treat the contract as repudiated; when a reasonable time for delivery has expired,[4] if, as is normally the case, time is of the essence of the contract.

In English law, if a buyer wishes to reject goods which are not in accordance with the contract, he has to inform the seller of this intention within "a reasonable time". Under other systems the approach varies; for example, in Swiss and Scandinavian law the defects have to be notified to the seller "at once" (*sofort*); in German law, if the parties are businessmen "without delay" (*unverzueglich*)[5]; in Italian law, in principle, within eight days; in Spanish law, as regards packed goods, within four days and as regards hidden defects (*vicios internos* or *occultos*) within 30 days[6]; and in French law the buyer has to start proceedings "within a short time" (*dans un bref délai*).

According to the Convention on the Limitation Period in the International Sale of Goods sponsored by UNCITRAL and signed in 1974, the limitation period in respect of a claim arising from a defect or lack of conformity of goods in an international sale shall, in principle, be four years.[7]

Further, under the laws of England, the United States of America, and many civil jurisdictions, the property in the goods sold passes when the parties intend it to pass, whether the delivery of the goods did or did not take place. The position is different under the laws of the Netherlands, Spain, Germany, the Argentine, Brazil, Chile and Columbia where the property passes, as a rule, only if the intention of the parties that it should pass is supported by the actual delivery of the goods. It has been suggested by C.M. Schmitthoff[8] that the very considerable differences in the national sales laws are not helpful to international trade and that the general adoption of the UN Convention on Contracts for the International Sale of Goods (Vienna, 1980) which came into operation on January 1, 1988, would be of benefit to the international trading community. The United Kingdom intends to adopt the Convention.

If the U.K. exporter has avoided the application of foreign law by the means of including in his contract an express stipulation that the contract shall be governed, in all respects, by English law, the Sale of Goods Act 1979 would then apply to the sale contract. This Act contains a definition of the term "delivery" and a number of rules on the passing of the property and the risk.

Delivery of the goods

4–003 According to section 61 of the 1979 Act "delivery" means the "voluntary trans-

---

[4] *Toepfer v. Wenersan-Portman NV* [1980] 1 Lloyd's Rep. 143, 147–148, CA. See *post*, para. 4–003.

[5] Para. 377 HGB.

[6] See, generally, *Derecho Civil I and II*, Manuel Albaladejo. Published by Jose Maria Bosch, Editor S.A. Barcelona, 1996.

[7] This Convention and the Protocol amending it (Vienna, 1980) have not been given effect in the U.K. yet.

[8] In previous editions of this work.

fer of possession from one person to another".[9] The goods are normally delivered to the buyer when he, or his agent, acquires custody of them or is enabled to exercise control over them.[10] In cases in which no bill of lading is issued, delivery to the carrier for the purposes of transmission to the buyer is prima facie deemed to be delivery to the buyer.[11] The place and time of delivery are, in export sales, usually defined by the special trade terms which have been considered earlier. These special arrangements displace the provisions of the Sale of Goods Act 1979 on delivery, which are contained mainly in sections 27 to 37, particularly so where the seller has obtained a bill of lading. In c.i.f. or c. and f. contracts, the goods are deemed to be delivered when the bill of lading is delivered to the buyer.[12] If the parties have agreed on one of the container delivery terms, for example, free carrier (FCA), delivery takes place when the carrier takes charge of the goods except in the rare cases in which the seller has undertaken to tender a marine bill of lading; in these cases the same considerations apply as explained above.

Passing of the property

The rules of the Act on the passing of the property in the goods sold are often **4–004** modified by special arrangements made between the parties to an export sale. The Act provides here two fundamental rules, namely that where the contract is for the sale of unascertained goods, the property does not pass to the buyer unless and until the goods are ascertained (s.16). Where the contract is for the sale of specific or ascertained goods, the property passes at such time as the parties intend it to pass (s.17(1)). The effect of this rule has been mitigated by the insertion into the Act of section 20A. The former rule has been discussed in recent cases.[13]

Unascertained goods

The rule that no property can pass in unascertained goods caused difficulty on **4–005** occasions. This was particularly so in two sets of circumstances: first where a

---

[9] The Sale of Goods (Amendment) Act 1995 added to the s.61 definition ". . . except that in relation to sections 20A and 20B above it includes such appropriation of goods to the contract as results in property being transferred to the buyer": see below. The Act inserted into the Sale of Goods Act, sections 20A and 20B. See R. Bradgate & F. White, "Sale of Goods forming part of a bulk: proposals for reform" [1994] L.M.C.L.Q. 315; T. Burns, "Better Late than Never; The Reform of the law on the Sale of Goods Forming Part of a Bulk" (1996) 59 M.L.R. 260 and L. Gullifer, "Constructive possession after the Sale of Goods (Amendment) Act 1995" [1999] L.M.C.L.Q. 93. Vienna Convention, Arts 30–34.

[10] See *E. Reynolds & Sons (Chingford) Ltd v. Hendry Bros. Ltd* [1955] 1 Lloyd's Rep. 258 at 259; *Commercial Fibres (Ireland) Ltd v. Zabaida* [1975] 1 Lloyd's Rep. 27 (delivery ex warehouse or ex dock at place of shipment).

[11] s.32(1). The same applies where the goods are shipped not to the buyer but to a bank to which they are pledged by way of security (*Kum v. Wah Tat Bank Ltd* [1971] 1 Lloyd's Rep. 439).

[12] *Biddell Bros v. E. Clemens Horst Co* [1912] A.C. 18 at 22.

[13] "As a general principle, the passing of full title to the goods depends upon the ability to identify the goods", *per* Hobhouse J. in *Obestain Inc v. National Mineral Development Corporation Ltd; The Sanix Ace* [1987] 1 Lloyd's Rep. 465 at 469. See also *Re Goldcorp Exchange Ltd* [1995] 1 A.C. 74 where it was determined that no property had passed to a purchaser notwithstanding the

buyer buys part of a bulk consignment, *e.g.* 10,000 tonnes of crude oil out of a consignment of 200,000 tonnes carried in a supertanker, or where the buyer has paid the purchase price in advance and the seller becomes insolvent before delivery of the goods. In *Re Wait*,[14] which concerned an import transaction, a British merchant bought 1,000 tonnes of wheat on c.i.f. terms from American suppliers and resold a parcel of 500 tonnes to another British firm which paid the purchase price in spot cash. The wheat was then shipped in bulk to the merchant who became insolvent before the ship arrived. The trustee in bankruptcy successfully resisted the sub-purchaser's claim for delivery of 500 tonnes of the bulk cargo. The court held that his parcel consisted of unascertained goods and the property in them had not passed to the sub-purchaser as there had never been an appropriation or identification of the 500 tonnes of wheat which represented the sub-purchaser's goods.

Unascertained goods may become ascertained by a process of exhaustion and then property may pass in them. In *The Elafi*,[15] the vessel carried 22,000 tonnes of copra in bulk. The claimants, Karlshamns Olje Fabriker, acquired bills of lading relating to 6,000 tonnes and later by a separate contract an additional 500 tonnes of the bulk consignment. The vessel discharged first at Rotterdam and then at Hamburg and the cargo remaining on board consisted only of the copra purchased by the claimants under the two contracts. When the vessel arrived at Karlshamn, water entered one of the holds and the copra therein was damaged. The claimants based their action against the shipowners in the tort of negligence, claiming that they had become owners of the damaged goods.[16] Mustill J. held that the goods which remained in the vessel after discharge in Hamburg had become ascertained goods by exhaustion and the claimants had acquired property in them. It was irrelevant that they were acquired under two separate contracts.

The rule in *Re Wait* was unsatisfactory. Mustill J. qualified it in *The Elafi* by admitting ascertainment by exhaustion but the facts will rarely allow the application of this qualification. A more equitable solution of the problem of undivided shares in bulk would have been for the law to provide that persons interested in the bulk should be regarded as owners in common *pro rata* their interest. The common ownership "rule" was adopted imaginatively by Staughton J. in *The Ypatianna*,[17] a case concerned with a different issue. The defendants, who were the owners of the vessel The Ypatianna, loaded crude oil, the property of the plaintiffs, into their vessel in the port of Novorossisk in what was then the Soviet

---

fact that certificates representing their purchase had been issued. The seller, who became insolvent prior to delivery, had not set aside the gold intended for the purchaser, but see *Re Stapylton Fletcher Ltd* [1994] 1 W.L.R. 1181. See also S. Worthington, "Sorting Out Ownership Interests in a Bulk: Gifts, Sales and Trusts" [1999] J.B.L. 1 (January).
[14] [1927] 1 Ch. 606; *The Aramis* [1989] 1 Lloyd's Rep. 213, CA.
[15] *Karlshamns Olje Fabriker v. Eastport Navigation Corporation; The Elafi* [1981] 2 Lloyd's Rep. 679. See J. Adams (1982) 45 M.L.R. 690.
[16] The claim was also founded on the Bills of Lading Act 1855; The deficiencies of that Act have generally been cured by the Carriage of Goods by Sea Act 1992 as the right to bring an action against a carrier on the bill of lading contract is no longer contingent on the passing of property, to the claimant, in the goods carried under the bill, see para. 15–052.
[17] *Indian Oil Corporation Ltd v. Greenstone Shipping SA* [1988] Q.B. 345.

Union and mixed it in the vessel with their own crude oil. The learned judge found that the mixture could not be separated and that the defendants in mixing the cargo had not done so "for some commercial motive". Reviewing the law, it was noted that it had been held in previous cases[18] that if an owner mixed his goods with those of another in an inextricable manner, the whole of the goods belonged to the other. Relying on those cases, the plaintiffs claimed the value of the whole consignment in The Ypatianna. Staughton J., in an erudite judgment, distinguished the old cases and held that the mixture of crude oil was in the common ownership of the parties. The result was that the plaintiffs were only entitled to the value of their portion in the mixture.

The 1993 Law Commission Report "Sale of Goods Forming Part of Bulk" (Law Com. No. 215) recommended that a new rule be adopted to enable property in an undivided share of a bulk to pass before ascertainment. The enactment, section 20A, provides that a buyer in a contract for a specified quantity of unascertained goods, may, if certain conditions are met, acquire property in an undivided share and become an owner in common of the bulk. The conditions are that the bulk is identified either by the contract or by subsequent agreement between the parties and the seller has paid the price for some or all of the goods. For those interested in sale of goods carried by sea the Law Commission in its Report took the view[19] that reference to goods in bulk on a particular vessel could amount to sufficient identification of the bulk for the purposes of the section.

The common ownership rule is recognised by the American Uniform Commercial Code, which provides that fungible[20] goods which are commingled are owned in common by the persons entitled to them. The person holding them, usually a warehouseman, is seveably liable to each owner for that owner's share.

Section 20A is of undoubted benefit to the merchant who, having purchased part of a bulk from his seller, has resold that part to a sub-buyer. The merchant is given some measure of protection against the insolvency of his seller. Section 20B sets out the consequences of the operation of section 20A, which are that any owner in common falling within the provisions of section 20A shall be deemed to consent to any delivery to any other co-owner or any dealing by that other owner of that co-owner's undivided share. Further, no buyer of a share of the bulk is liable to compensate any other buyer for any shortfall in delivery to them. The purpose of this section was, according to the Law Commission Report,[21] to enable co-owners to deal freely with their undivided share.

A case which is difficult to categorise is *Carlos Federspiel & Co SA v. Charles Twigg & Co Ltd.*[22] It indicates the importance of determining the time at which property passes and the precarious position in which a buyer who has

---

[18] A review referred to in *Re Stapylton, Fletcher Ltd*, and 1198, *ante.*
[19] In para. 4.5. Law Com., no. 215.
[20] s. 7–207(2). "Fungible" is defined in the UCC, s.1-201(17) thus: " 'Fungible' with respect to goods or securities means goods or securities of which any unit is, by nature or usage of trade, the equivalent of any other like unit. Goods which are not fungible shall be deemed to be fungible for the purposes of this Act to the extent that under a particular agreement or document unlike units are treated as equivalents."
[21] Law Com. 215 paras 4.15 and 4.16.
[22] [1957] 1 Lloyd's Rep. 240. See *Re Goldcorp Exchange* [1995] 1 A.C. 74 at 90.

made an advance payment finds himself if the seller becomes insolvent before passing the property in the goods sold. In this case, which concerned an export transaction, a Costa Rican company bought from an English company 85 bicycles f.o.b. British port and paid the price for them in advance. The bicycles were packed into cases, marked with the buyers' name and registered for shipment in a named ship which was to load at Liverpool, but they had not yet been sent to that port and were not yet shipped. A receiver and manager appointed by the debenture holders of the sellers claimed that the bicycles, like the other assets of the sellers, were charged in favour of the debenture holders. Pearson J. held that that contention was correct because the property in the bicycles had not yet passed; in the view of the learned judge the common intention of the parties was that the property should pass on shipment, or possibly later. This finding is also relied upon as authority for the proposition that property in goods will not pass in advance of shipment in an f.o.b. contract. This decision, it is thought, is unsatisfactory in the context of international sales.

Ascertained goods

4–006   In the case of specific or ascertained goods the task is to determine the intention of the parties, who are at liberty to fix the time when the property passes. This is not an easy task, since the clues which the Act furnishes in section 17(2) for ascertaining that intention are couched in vague and general terms, and the five specific presumptions which are laid down in section 18 are not appropriate to the particular circumstances of an export sale. Two possibilities exist here which require separate consideration: the seller may reserve the property in the goods (or, as it is sometimes called, the right of disposal of the goods) until certain conditions have been fulfilled, or he may have made the transfer of the property conditional.

In the first circumstance, property does not pass to the buyer until the conditions imposed by the seller are satisfied, and that will even be the case where the goods have been delivered to the buyer, his agent, or a carrier for transmission to the buyer (s.19(1)). Such a condition may be imposed by the seller inserting into the contract of sale a retention of title[23] clause, *i.e.* a clause making the passing of the property conditional on the receipt of the purchase price in cash— a not unusual condition, particularly in overseas sales unless it is clear that the seller intends to give unsecured credit. The law provides two rebuttable presumptions in favour of a conditional transfer of the property: first, where goods are shipped and by the bill of lading the goods are deliverable to the order of the seller or his agent, it is presumed that the seller reserves the property in the goods until he or his agent delivers the bill to the buyer or his agent (s.19(2))[24] and secondly, where the seller has drawn a bill of exchange on the

---

[23] The terms "title" and "property" are often used interchangeably; see the UCC s.2-401(1).
[24] *Mitsui & Co Ltd v. Flota Mercante Grancolombiana SA; The Ciudad de Pasto and Ciudad de Neiva* [1988] 2 Lloyd's Rep. 208 at 213. The presumption of s.19(2) is rebutted between related companies: *The Albazero* [1975] 3 W.L.R. 491, 512, 513; revsd on other grounds [1977] A.C. 274, HL.

buyer for the purchase price and transmits that bill and the bill of lading together to the buyer to secure acceptance or payment of the bill of exchange, the property does not pass to the buyer if he does not honour the bill of exchange. In this case he would have to return the bill of lading (s.19(3)). These provisions apply to f.o.b. and c.i.f. contracts alike.

The second circumstance arises where the seller has failed to make the passing of the property conditional and where neither of the legal presumptions provided by subsection (2) or (3) of section 19 can be invoked to remedy that failure. Where, for example, the seller has taken out a bill of lading to the order of the buyer or his agent, it depends on whether the seller delivers the bill to the buyer. It has been held[25] that taking out a bill of lading in the name of the buyer does not necessarily reveal the seller's intention of passing the property to him. Where the bill is delivered to the buyer or his agent, the inference is almost[26] conclusive that the seller intended to transfer the property in the goods to the buyer.[27]

These rules apply to all contracts under which it is the seller's duty to deliver a bill of lading. In cases where that duty does not exist, *e.g.* in ex works, f.o.b. (buyer contracting with carrier) or free delivered contracts, the physical delivery of the goods to the buyer or to the carrier is, presumably, the act which passes the property to the buyer.

Where under a c.i.f. or c. and f. contract, or under an f.o.b. contract in which the seller has taken out the bill of lading, the bill is delivered to the buyer or his agent, the inference is that the property which is intended to pass to the buyer is only conditional. This means that the property in the goods shall revert to the seller if upon examination they are found to be not in accordance with the contract.[28]

In exceptional cases the c.i.f. seller may release the goods to the buyer before handing over the bill of lading to him by giving the buyer a delivery order on the ship. It depends here on the intention of the parties whether this procedure is adopted in performance of the c.i.f. contract or merely as "mechanics of delivery".[29] The deliberate retention of the bill of lading by the seller may indicate an intention of the parties that property shall not pass to the buyer on such an anticipated delivery.[30] Further, the fundamental principle should not be overlooked that, from the commercial point of view, the retention of title to the goods is regarded as "security" for the payment of the price. If this "security" is furnished in another way, for example by the provision of a standby letter of

---

[25] *The Kronprinsessan Margareta* [1921] 1 A.C. 486 at 517; *The Glenroy* [1945] A.C. 124.

[26] Exceptionally, the circumstances may support another inference, see the observation of Roskill L.J. in *The Albazero* [1975] 3 W.L.R. 491 at 523, revsd [1977] A.C. 774, HL.

[27] In *The Albazero* [1977] A.C. 774, Brandon J., the Court of Appeal and the House of Lords agreed that by virtue of the transfer of the bill of lading the property and possession had passed to the consignees. See also *The San Nicholas* [1976] 1 Lloyd's Rep. 8, 11, 13.

[28] *Kwei Tek Chao v. British Traders and Shippers Ltd* [1954] 2 Q.B. 459 at 487; *Gill & Duffus SA v. Berger & Co Inc* [1984] 2 W.L.R. 95 at 104, HL. Another case in which the property passed only defeasibly was *McDougall v. Aeromarine of Emsworth Ltd* [1958] 1 W.L.R. 1126.

[29] Per McNair J. in *Ginzberg v. Barrow Haematite Steel Co* [1966] 1 Lloyd's Rep. 343 at 353.

[30] *Cheetham & Co Ltd v. Thornham Spinning Co Ltd* [1964] 2 Lloyd's Rep. 17; *Ginzberg v. Barrow Haematite Steel Co Ltd* [1966] 1 Lloyd's Rep. 343.

credit by a reputable bank, the intention of the parties may well be that property in the goods shall pass when the bank issues the credit.[31]

The retention of title clause

4–007 It has already been stated[32] that English law allows a clause which provides that the seller retains the property in the goods sold until he receives the purchase price in cash. The clause makes the passing of property conditional on a specified event, usually the receipt of the price by the seller. It is clear from section 19(1) of the Sale of Goods Act 1979 that the clause is effective and defeats the general presumption that the property passes when the bill of lading is transferred from the seller (or his agent) to the buyer (or his agent).[33] Retention of title clauses can be divided into two classes, simple and extended clauses.

The simple retention of title clause

4–008 This clause provides that the seller retains the property in the goods sold until a specified condition is satisfied, for example that he receives the purchase price in cash. This type of clause causes little difficulty in law but it is normally considered insufficient by the seller. The validity of the simple retention of title clause cannot be doubted because, as has already been observed,[34] section 19(1) of the Sale of Goods Act 1979 allows it expressly. This clause does not require registration as a charge under sections 395–399 of the Companies Act 1985. There exists a Draft European Convention on the Simple Reservation of Title, sponsored by the Council of Europe in 1982.[35] This Convention has not been finalised yet.[36]

The extended retention of title clause

4–009 Of greater practical importance is the extended retention of title clause but it raises difficult legal problems. Two types of extended clauses are used but other clauses may also be devised. A combination of the features of the two main types is sometimes found in practice. First, the clause may provide that the buyer, if he sells the goods, shall do so as an agent of the seller and shall be a trustee of the proceeds of sale for the benefit of the seller. This clause gives the

---

[31] *Anonima Petroli Italiana SpA v Marlucidez Armadora SA; The Filiatra Legacy* [1991] 2 Lloyd's Rep. 337.

[32] See *ante*, para. 4–006.

[33] A definition of a "retention of title agreement" is provided in section 251 of the Insolvency Act 1986, s.251: "retention of title agreement means an agreement for the sale of goods to a company, being an agreement which does not constitute a charge on the goods, but under which, if the seller is not paid and the company is wound up, the seller will have priority over all other creditors of the company as respects the goods or any property representing the goods."

[34] See *ante*, para. 4–006.

[35] See G. Monti, G. Nejman and W. J. Reuter, "The Future of Reservation of Title Clauses in the European Community" (1997) 46 I.C.L.Q. 866.

[36] July 2000.

buyer a licence to sell and, at the same time, attempts to safeguard the position of the seller. The buyer is made the bailee of the goods supplied by the seller who is in the position of a bailor. This is the most common type of extended retention of title clause. It is recommended that the exporter shall include this clause into his general conditions of business.[37] These extended clauses are frequently used in Germany, the Netherlands and in France.[38] In the United Kingdom such a clause has been upheld in the *Romalpa* case.[39] Aluminium Industrie Vaassen BV (AIV), a Dutch private company, sold a quantity of aluminium foil to Romalpa, an English company. The terms of delivery were ex works AIV in Holland and the price was expressed in Dutch currency. The contract contained an extended title clause which was worded in great detail.[40] A receiver was appointed for Romalpa. Although the contract was closely connected with Dutch law, that law was not pleaded and the case was decided according to English law. The Court of Appeal held that AIV were entitled to the property in the goods supplied by them and which was still in existence. As regards the goods resold by Romalpa, the court held that Romalpa had acted as agents for AIV and were, therefore, in a fiduciary relationship to them; that admitted the application of the equitable doctrine of tracing, as developed in *Re Hallett's Estate*.[41]

It was held by Slade J. in *Re Bond Worth Ltd*[42] that, where the property in the goods was transferred unconditionally to the buyer and the latter was not constituted an agent for the seller the reservation of title clause constituted a floating charge on the goods and on the money obtained on their resale and, as such, was registrable under what is now the Companies Act 1985, s.396. The *Bond Worth* clause was worded differently from the *Romalpa* clause. In *Pfeiffer v. Arbuthnot Factors Ltd*[43] a German retention of title clause was in issue, but the case was decided according to English law; the wording of the clause was similar to, but not identical with, that in *Romalpa*. Phillips J., in his judgment, distinguished *Romalpa* and held that the retention of title clause was invalid because it had not been registered as a charge. Essentially the issue is one of construction of the clause. It is thought that the retention of title clause does not require registration under the Companies Act if it contains two essential provisions.[44] First, the seller should retain the legal property in the goods (possibly with the supporting provisions that the goods shall be kept separate from other goods in the possession of the buyer and its storage be marked with the seller's name), and second that the buyer may resell them only as agent of the seller and receive the repurchase price as agent for and on behalf and on

---

[37] See Croner's *Model Business Contracts* for an example of such a clause.

[38] See [1980] J.B.L. 388.

[39] *Aluminium Industrie Vaassen BV v. Romalpa Aluminium Ltd* [1976] 1 W.L.R. 676. Also *Hendy Lennox (Industrial Engines) Ltd v. Graham Puttick Ltd* [1984] 1 W.L.R. 485; *Clough Mill v. Martin* [1985] 1 W.L.R. 111, CA; *In re Andrabell Ltd* [1984] 2 All E.R. 407; *Chaigley Farms Ltd v. Crawford, Kaye & Grayshire Ltd* [1996] B.C.C. 957.

[40] The clause is reproduced fully in [1976] J.B.L. 209-210.

[41] (1880) Ch. D. 696.

[42] [1980] Ch. 228. See also [1979] J.B.L. 216, where the reservation of property clause in *Bond Worth* is reproduced in full.

[43] The full title of this case is *E. Pfeiffer Weinkellerei & Weineinkauf GmbH & Co v. Arbuthnot Factors Ltd* [1988] 1 W.L.R. 150.

[44] See the discussion in Benjamin (5th ed.), paras 5–139 to 5–150.

account of the seller (possibly with the supporting provision that the buyer shall keep the proceeds of resale in a separate account kept in the seller's name). According to the present state of authorities the requirements of a non-registrable extended retention of title clause cannot be stated with absolute certainty. If only a simple retention of title clause is adopted, an extension to the proceeds of sale is not implied by the law. Such extension must be expressly provided in the clause.[45] Where under a retention of title clause of the type here discussed the buyer obtains possession of the goods and has a licence to resell them, a purchaser in good faith is protected by section 25(1) of the Sale of Goods Act 1979. If the requirements of this provision are satisfied, the title of the original seller is defeated.[46]

Further, the clause sometimes states that if the goods sold are used in the production of other goods, either by admixture or another manufacturing process, the property in the goods so produced shall vest in the seller. This clause is ineffective if the new product has a different commercial identity from the material sold under the reservation of title clause. Thus, if a clause purporting to extend to the new product occurs in a contract of sale of resin it does not extend to chipboard into which the resin is incorporated.[47] If it occurs in a contract for the sale of leather, it does not extend to handbags manufactured from the leather.[48] In any event, even if the clause extended to the finished product, it would be registrable as a charge under section 396 of the Companies Act 1985.

Passing of the risk

4–010   The risk of accidental loss of the goods sold passes prima facie when the property passes (s.20(1)). This is an antiquated rule of the Sale of Goods Act 1979 derived from its predecessor, the Act of 1893. More modern texts, such as the Uniform Commercial Code, the Uniform Laws on International Sales and the Vienna Convention on Contracts for the International Sale of Goods, provide that, as a rule, the risk shall pass on delivery of the goods.[49]

In the law of international trade, contrary to the presumption contained in section 20(1) of the Sale of Goods Act, the two concepts of the passing of the risk and the transfer of property are regularly separated and the statutory presumption may be displaced by agreement of the parties. Special arrangements may be agreed between themselves. In the absence of them[50] the risk will gener-

---

[45] *Hendy Lennox (Industrial Engineers) Ltd v. Graham Puttick Ltd* (1984) 81 L.S. Gaz. 585.
[46] *Cf. Four Point Garage Ltd v. Carter* [1985] 3 All E.R. 12.
[47] *Borden(U.K.) Ltd v. Scottish Timber Products and McNicol Brownlie Ltd* [1981] Ch. 25.
[48] In *Re Peachdart Ltd* [1984] Ch. 131. See also *Ian Chisholm Textiles Ltd v. Griffiths* [1994] B.C.L.C. 291. See T. I. Ogowewo, "When is a Cow Not a Cow? Loss of Title and Retention of Title Clauses" [1996] 12 I.C.C.L.R. 445.
[49] C. M. Schmitthoff, "The Risk of Loss in Transit in International Sales" in *Unification of the Law Governing International Sales of Goods, in The Comparison and possible Harmonisation of National and Regional Unification*, Paris, 1966, pp. 169–199; *Essays*, 277. Arts 97 and 67 respectively and Vienna Convention, Arts 66–70.
[50] In *President of India v. Metcalfe Shipping Co* [1969] 2 Q.B. 123; affd [1970] 1 Q.B. 289, CA passing of the risk (and of the property) under an f.o.b. contract was postponed until delivery of bills of lading.

ally pass in a contract for the sale of goods abroad when the goods leave the custody of the seller. In an ex works contract the risk normally passes when the goods are delivered to the buyer or his agent. In f.a.s. contracts it passes when the goods are placed alongside the ship and in f.o.b. and c.i.f. contracts normally when they are delivered over the ship's rail. If the contract provides for delivery franco domicile or Delivered Duty Paid (DDU) of the buyer, the intention of the parties as regards the passing of the risk can often be gathered from the terms of payment and the insurance arrangement. If the price is prepaid and the buyer is responsible for insurance, there is hardly a doubt that the goods travel at his risk. The result would be reversed if the price were collected on delivery and the seller had to cover the insurance risk. In container delivery terms the risk passes normally when the goods are delivered into the custody of the carrier.

The risk, unlike the property, may pass to the buyer although the goods are unascertained goods which have not been appropriated, but traditionally only if some "special facts" could be established. Such facts included situations where the buyer accepted the delivery order of the seller which instructs a warehouse-man, for example, to deliver a certain quantity from a bulk held at the warehouse, particularly if the buyer by the acceptance of the order undertakes the appropriate charges in respect of the goods comprised in the order.[51] It is suggested by the learned authors of *Benjamin* that buyers who acquire a right of co-ownership in goods forming part of a bulk also acquire the risk in those goods.[52] A buyer to whom the risk, but not property or a possessory title, is transferred by the seller is not entitled to sue the carrier in the tort of negligence.[53]

The risk of accidental loss should not be confused with the risk of deterioration of the goods in transit. In f.o.b. and c.i.f. contracts relating to perishable goods which contain an implied condition that the goods shall be of satisfactory quality (the expression "merchantable quality" was considered of uncertain meaning and obsolete),[54] the seller undertakes, by further implication, that the goods shall be of satisfactory quality not only when they are loaded but also upon arrival at destination and a reasonable time thereafter, allowing for their

---

[51] *Sterns Ltd v. Vickers Ltd* [1923] 1 K.B. 78. Special facts are, *e.g.* the acceptance, by the buyer, of the seller's delivery warrant instructing a storekeeper to deliver to the buyer part of the bulk, particularly if by the terms of the warrant the buyer is liable to pay the charges for his portion of the bulk. See also *per* Croom-Johnson J. in *Comptoir d'Achat v. Luis de Ridder* [1947] 2 All E.R. 443 at 453. Where no special facts could be established, the property and the risk in the sold part of a bulk stored with a third person pass only when the third person has separated that part from the bulk and acknowledges that he holds that part as the buyer's goods; *Wardar's (Import & Export) Co Ltd v. W. Norwood & Sons Ltd* [1968] 2 Q.B. 663. Compare Vienna Convention, Art. 67(2).

[52] *Benjamin's Sale of Goods*, (5th ed., 1997), paras 18-240–245 and generally.

[53] *Leigh and Sillivan v. Aliakmon Shipping Co* [1986] A.C. 785.

[54] See the Sale of Goods Act 1979, ss.14(2) and 15(2)(c), as amended by the Sale and Supply of Goods Act 1994. Section 14(2A) and (2B) contain a definition of satisfactory quality and the matters to be taken into consideration in determining whether goods comply with the implied term or not. For an explanation of the previously used term "merchantable quality", see *Cehave NV v. Bremer Handelsgesellschaft mbh; The Hansa Nord* [1976] 1 Q.B. 44 and *M/S Aswan Engineering Establishment Co v. Lupdine Ltd* [1987] 1 W.L.R. 1 although the latter case would probably not be decided in the same way under the amended provisions , see G. G. Howells, "The Modernization of Sales Law?" [1995] L.M.C.L.Q. 191.

normal disposal,[55] however this implied condition does not apply where the deterioration of the goods is due to an abnormal delay in their transit or disposal.[56] Diplock J. stated this rule thus[57]:

> "It is the extraordinary deterioration of the goods due to abnormal conditions experienced during transit for which the buyer takes the risk. A necessary and inevitable deterioration during transit which will render them unmerchantable on arrival is normally one for which the seller is liable."

Provision of certificates

4–011 An exporter may be required under the contract of sale to provide the buyer with certificates of quality, of pre-shipment inspection, of origin, etc. Such requirements may be in accordance with mandatory provisions of the importer's country or in accordance with agreement of the parties or trade custom.

Certificates of quality

4–012 Certificates of quality, which should not be confused with certificates of origin,[58] are used in the export trade from time to time. The parties may, for example, arrange that the seller should provide a certificate of quality "by experts",[59] a government certificate that certain army surplus goods were "new",[60] that the goods—fruit—should be covered by "phytopathological certificates of freedom from disease"[61] or by a certificate certifying that the goods were of the quality of a trade association's "standard sample",[62] or that "certificates for maize in government elevators"[63] should be produced. The parties may also agree that a certificate as to composition or quality should be given by the seller himself.[64]

Certificates of quality are of two types: certificates of standard quality addressed to all the world (also known as certificates *in rem*) and certificates of contract requirements addressed to the parties to the contract (so-called certificates *in personam*).[65] The type of certificate is required depends on the intention

---

[55] *Mash & Murrell Ltd v. Joseph I. Emanuel Ltd* [1961] 1 W.L.R. 862; revsd on appeal on the facts [1962] 1 W.L.R. 16. See also *Rogers v. Parish (Scarborough) Ltd* [1987] Q.B. 933.

[56] *Broome v. Pardess Co-operative Society* [1939] 3 All E.R. 978 at 985; see also *Ollett v. Jordan* [1918] 2 K.B. 41 at 47. These case dealt with the requirement of "merchantability". It is suggested that, certainly, at least on the basis of business efficacy that goods intended for re-sale should be able to endure the normal incidents of the delivery transit.

[57] *Mash & Murrell Ltd v. Joseph I. Emanuel Ltd, supra*, at 871.

[58] Certificates of origin are generally declarations as to the country of origin of goods and their provision is required under the Customs laws of various countries for import compliance.

[59] *Equitable Trust Company of New York v. Dawson Partners Ltd* (1926) 27 Lloyd's Rep. 49.

[60] *Bank Melli Iran v. Barclays Bank (Dominion, Colonial and Overseas)* [1951] 2 Lloyd's Rep. 367.

[61] *Yelo v. S. M. Machado & Co Ltd* [1952] 1 Lloyd's Rep. 183; *Phoenix Distributors Ltd v. L. B. Clarke (London)* [1966] 2 Lloyd's Rep. 285.

[62] *F. E. Hookway & Co v. Alfred Isaacs & Sons* [1954] 1 Lloyd's Rep. 491.

[63] *South African Reserve Bank v. Samuel* (1931) 40 Ll.L.R. 291. See: *Re Reinhold & Co and Hansloh* (1896) 12 T.L.R. 422; *Foreman & Ellams Ltd v. Blackburn* [1928] 2 K.B. 60; *Panchaud Freres SA v. Etablissements General Grain Co* [1969] 2 Lloyd's Rep. 109.

[64] *Groupement National d'Achat des Tourteaux v. Sociedad Industrial Financiera Argentina* [1962] 2 Lloyd's Rep. 192.

[65] *ibid.*

of the contracting parties. Examples of certificates of standard quality are a certificate of a public analyst or of a recognised engineering, shipbuilding or surveying classification organisation,[66] for example a Lloyd's certificate. Sometimes, a certificate of quality issued by an inspection organisation, such as SGS,[67] a is required.[68]

Certificates of quality *in personam* state sometimes that they shall be "final as to quality". In this case the certificate is binding on the seller and buyer even though the certificate was inaccurate or the certifier acted negligently. It ceases to be binding if it is set aside by a court or arbitration tribunal or revoked by the certifier.[69] Further, the parties to a contract of sale may draw a distinction between the quality of the goods and their condition. In such a case the certificate, though stated to be final, has to be construed restrictively as referring to the quality of the goods only. This does not prevent the buyer from raising a complaint with respect to the condition of the goods.[70] If the parties have omitted to draw that distinction, then "quality of goods" includes their state and condition.[71]

Certificates of inspection

A certificate of inspection is not identical to a certificate of quality although the latter may be issued by an inspection organisation if the contract so provides. The minimum requirements for such a certificate are that the inspector has inspected the goods visually and found them to be in apparent good condition. If a particular method of inspection is adopted or particular information as the result of the inspection is recorded, such as the test results of electrical appliances, the buyer must stipulate this expressly.[72] Of the numerous inspection organisations dealing with general merchandise, one may be mentioned here, as it is represented in many commercial centres of the world: Société Generale de Surveillance SA (SGS) which has its head office in Geneva. It claims to be the

4–013

---

[66] *Minister Trust Ltd v. Traps Tractors Ltd* [1954] 1 W.L.R. 963, 977–979.

[67] Société Générale de Surveillance SA (Geneva).

[68] *Berger & Co Inc v. Gill & Duffus SA* [1984] 2 W.L.R. 95. (The certificate referred to in this case was stated to be issued by "General Superintendence Co Ltd". This company changed its name later to "SGS Inspection Services Ltd". The certificate required in this case was a post-shipment certificate as it had to be issued in the port of discharge. It could, therefore, not be tendered as one of the shipping documents under the contract which was on c.i.f. terms.). On the distinction between an official natural weight certificate of wheat and the certificate of an independent laboratory, see *Ets Soules & Cie v. International Trade Development Co Ltd* [1979] 2 Lloyd's Rep. 122 at 133.

[69] *Alfred C. Toepfer v. Continental Grain Co* [1973] 1 Lloyd's Rep. 289; *Berger & Co. Inc. v. Gill & Duffus SA* [1984] 2 W.L.R. 95. See also *N. V. Bunge v. Compagnie Noga d'Importation et d'Exportation SA; The Bow Cedar* [1980] 2 Lloyd's Rep. 601 at 605 (certificate of chemical analysis did not cover description of the goods): similarly *Ch. Daudruy van Cauwenberghe & Fils SA v. Tropical Products Sales SA* [1986] 1 Lloyd's Rep. 535. As to "finality" see *Apioil Ltd v. Kuwait Petroleum Italia SpA; Apioil Ltd v. Sociedade Nacional de Combustiveis de Angola SA* [1995] 1 Lloyd's Rep.124.

[70] *Cremer v. General Carriers SA* [1974] 1 W.L.R. 341 at 354.

[71] See Sale of Goods Act 1979, s.14(2B).

[72] *Commercial Banking Co of Sydney Ltd v. Jalsard Pty Ltd* [1973] A.C. 279; *International Petroleum Refining and Supply Sociedad Ltd v. Caleb Brett & Son Ltd; The Busiris* [1980] 1 Lloyd's Rep. 569.

world's largest independent inspection organisation and operates in Great Britain through SGS Inspection Services Ltd, London.

The contract between the inspection organisation and the client is known as the contract of goods inspection.[73] The inspector is under a contractual duty to use reasonable care. In one case[74] an inspector was appointed to take tests of oil on its loading at the port of dispatch. The oil was liquid when it was loaded but arrived at its destination in a solidified state. Proceedings were taken against the inspector and the Court of Appeal held that he had failed in his contractual duty because he did not take sufficient samples when the oil was loaded, did not take them at regular intervals and did not check its gravity. He was also liable in tort for negligence on the principle in *Hedley Byrne & Co Ltd v. Heller & Partners Ltd.*[75] In another case[76] the parties agreed on pre-shipment inspection which was to be carried out by one of two nominated inspection organisations referred to in the contract as "firms of international repute". One of them was appointed to carry out the inspection but delegated it to another unspecified company. It then adopted the certificate of the unspecified company as its own certificate without further checking. The court held that the nominated organisation was in breach of the contract of inspection. By the terms of this contract it had to carry out the inspection through its own organisation and was not authorised to delegate this duty.

Pre-shipment inspection

4-014   This type of inspection, briefly referred to as PSI, is of growing importance in modern export trade. It is usually carried out by an independent inspection organisation. If the inspector is properly instructed pre-shipment inspection is very useful. It avoids later disputes between the seller and buyer on whether the goods are in accordance with the contract. It also avoids disputes between the insured and the insurer on whether any loss of or damage to the goods occurred before or after the risk attached.[77] Certain overseas countries insist on pre-shipment inspection. The information on each country in Croner's *Reference Book for Exporters* states whether a pre-shipment certificate is required for imports into the country.

The normal procedure is to have the goods inspected physically when they are delivered to the carrier. The inspection relates normally to the quantity and condition of the goods but the mode of inspection depends on the terms of the contract of goods inspection. Some inspection organisations maintain laborat-

---

[73] See A. Goldstajn, "The Contract of Goods Inspection" (1965) 14 Am.J.Comp.Law 383. For third party inspection of goods in dispute see Uniform Commercial Code, s.2-515(b).
[74] *International Petroleum Refining and Supply Sociedad Ltd v. Caleb Brett & Son Ltd; The Busiris* [1980] 1 Lloyd's Rep. 569.
[75] [1964] A.C. 465.
[76] *Kollerich & Cie SA v. The State Trading Corporation of India* [1980] 2 Lloyd's Rep. 32 (this case arose between the seller and the buyer and it was held that the certificate was false and the seller had failed to tender a correct certificate).
[77] See *Fuerst Day Lawson Ltd v. Orion Insurance Co Ltd* [1980] 1 Lloyd's Rep. 656 at 664 (in this case there was, in fact, a pre-shipment certificate but the court considered it to be insufficient).

ories and other testing facilities and are prepared to carry out more elaborate tests if instructed.

Sometimes, the inspection organisation is instructed, in addition to the quality control, to carry out a price control. In this case they have to advise the buyer whether the price charged is comparable to prices charged by other suppliers for similar goods. Some developing countries will not grant import licences unless an inspection organisation has issued a clean pre-shipment certificate covering price control. In some cases exporters have complained that the inspection organisation insisted on an unjustified reduction of a price firmly agreed with the overseas buyer or that it demanded the disclosure of a price calculation regarded as confidential. Such interference by a third party with the contractual relations of the seller and the buyer may raise legal problems unless it is clearly agreed upon in advance in the contract of sale. The SGS has published a brochure explaining to exporters the procedures and principles employed in the carrying out of pre-shipment inspection.[78]

Such problems were considered by GATT/WTO in the course of negotiations in the so-called Uruguay Round.[79] The result of these negotiations was the Agreement on Preshipment Inspection. The aim of this agreement is to ensure more transparency in the operation of pre-shipment inspection entities and of the laws and regulations relating to such inspections. It also aims to provide for the speedy resolution of disputes between exporters and pre-shipment entities, which are defined [80] as any entity "contracted . . . to carry out pre-shipment inspection activities".

Such activities include the verification of quality, quantity, price, and Customs classification of goods which are the subject matter of an export contract.[81] The Agreement provides for, among other matters, transparency, *i.e.* that entities provide to exporters a list of all the compliance requirements and alert them to any changes.[82] It also provides an appeals procedure under which the entities establish a means by which the grievances of exporters may be considered.[83]

There is also from the same source an Agreement on Rules of Origin, the aim of which is to ensure that the rules of origin as applied in an importing state are such that they do not constitute a restriction on trade. This may be achieved by ensuring that those rules are transparent[84]; and are administered in a consistent, uniform, impartial and reasonable manner[85]; the Agreement looks forward to the harmonisation of such rules.[86]

---

[78] SGS, "Preshipment Inspection: Basic Guide for Exporters" 1997. Obtainable from the local SGS office, SGS House 217–221, London Road, Camberley , Surrey GU15 3EY or from the head office of SGS, at 1 place des Alpes, Caisse postale 898, Ch-1211, Geneva 1, Switzerland. Their website is at *www.sgs.co.uk*. See also Desmond I . Guobadia, "Legal Environment and Procedural Rules for Pre-shipment Inspection" [1997] 7 I.C.C.L.R. 248.
[79] See also EU Council Regulation No. 3287/94.
[80] Agreement on Preshipment Inspection, Art. 1(4).
[81] Art. 1(3).
[82] *ibid.*, Art. 2(5).
[83] *ibid.*, Art. 2(21).
[84] Agreement on Rules of Origin, Art. 2(a).
[85] *ibid.*, Art. 2(e).
[86] *ibid.*, Art. 9.

Liquidated damages and penalties

4–015   The parties may provide in their contract that in the case of non-performance or delayed performance the party in default shall pay a fixed sum, the amount of which may be calculated either as a lump sum or on a scale varying with the length of the default.[87]

In contracts concerning the export of merchandise, clauses fixing the amount recoverable on breach are seldom encountered but they are common in international standard contract forms, such as those used in the commodity trade. In English law,[88] a fixed sum payable on breach of contract may either be liquidated damages or a penalty. It is the former if the contract, upon its proper construction, reveals the intention of the parties genuinely to pre-estimate the damages suffered by the breach of contract. It is the latter if the intention of the parties is to secure the performance of the contract by the imposition of a fine or penalty; such intention is, in particular, evident if the fixed sum is disproportionate to the possible or probable amount of damages, that is, if it is extravagant or unconscionable.[89] The genuine intention of the parties has to be ascertained. The use of the terms "liquidated damages" or "penalties" in the clause, though indicative of the parties' intention, is not conclusive. If the sum fixed in the contract qualifies as liquidated damages, the court will award that sum and it is no obstacle to its recovery that the consequences of the breach are such as to make the pre-estimate of damages almost an impossibility. It is equally irrelevant that the loss actually suffered is lower or higher. A liquidated damages clause, however, cannot be relied upon if the plaintiff himself has contributed to the breach.[90] On the other hand, if the fixed sum qualifies as a penalty, it will be ignored by the court.[91] The differences between these two types of clauses are also important in proving a claim: if the clause stipulates liquidated damages, the party who claims damages need not prove the amount of damages but if it is deemed a penalty clause (which, as has been seen, is ignored) he has to prove the amount of damages which he seeks to recover.

---

[87] See *Dunlop Pneumatic Tyre Co Ltd v. New Garage and Motor Co Ltd* [1915] A.C. 79, *per* Lord Dunedin. See also *Robophone Facilities Ltd v. Blank* [1966] 1 W.L.R. 1428 and *Philips Hong Kong Ltd v. Att.-Gen. of Hong Kong* (1993) 61 B.L.R. 41. See also Chitty, *Contracts* (28th ed., 1999), para. 27–102 *et seq.*

[88] See *Dunlop Pneumatic Tyre Co Ltd v. New Garage and Motor Co Ltd* [1915] A.C. 70 at 87; further, *Ford Motor Co v. Armstrong* (1915) 31 T.L.R. 267; *Lombard North Central plc v. Butterworth* [1987] Q.B. 527 at 540 (*per* Nicolls L.J.), but see *Golden Bay Realty Property Ltd Orchard Twelve Investments Property Ltd* [1991] 1 W.L.R. 981.

[89] An indemnity clause does not operate as a penalty. This was decided in *Export Credit Guarantee Department v. Universal Oil Products Co* [1983] 1 W.L.R. 399 where a clause providing that ECGD should be indemnified by the defendants for payments made to bankers who had financed a construction project of the defendants was upheld by the House of Lords. Carrying charges in the Argentine maize trade are not a penalty: *Fratelli Moretti SpA v. Nidera Handelscompanie BV* [1981] 2 Lloyd's Rep. 47. In a shipbuilding contract a clause providing for immediate payment of all moneys outstanding if the purchasers of the vessel defaulted on a long term loan granted by the shipbuilder was not a penalty clause: *Oresundsvarvet Aktiebolag v. Marcos Diamantis Lemos; The Angelic Star* [1988] 1 Lloyd's Rep. 122.

[90] *Astilleros Canarios SA v. Cape Hatteras Shipping Co Inc; The Cape Hatteras* [1982] 1 Lloyd's Rep. 518 at 526.

[91] *Lamdon Trust Ltd v. Hurrell* [1955] 1 W.L.R. 391.

A liquidated damages clause makes it unnecessary for the parties to have the damages fixed by the court. The clause offers advantages not only to the buyer but also to the supplier because it limits his liability.

It should be noted however that the provision of a performance bond is a "guarantee of due performance and" not a pre-estimate of damages which the beneficiary of the bond may claim in the event of a breach of contract. If the bond exceeds the damages claim the party providing the bond can recover the excess.[92]

---

[92] *Comdel Commodities Ltd v. Siporex Trade SA* [1997] 1 Lloyd's Rep. 424, *per* Potter L.J. at 431. A "deposit" which may be forfeited by a party in the event of his default may be subject to the general law relating to penalties, see *Workers Trust & Merchant Bank Ltd v. Dojap Investments Ltd* [1993] A.C. 573, PC.

CHAPTER 5

ACCEPTANCE AND REJECTION OF GOODS

5–001 In the performance of a contract of international sale the rules relating to the examination, acceptance and rejection of the goods are of great practical importance. If the contract is governed by English law,[1] these rules are founded on the Sale of Goods Act 1979.[2] If the parties to an international sale have adopted the Uniform Laws on International Sales, appended to the Uniform Laws on International Sales Act 1967 or the Vienna Convention on Contracts for the International Sale of Goods (1980), which eventually will take their place,[3] the rules set out therein will govern the examination and acceptance of the goods. These rules will be discussed later.[4]

The general principle on which the regulation of the Sale of Goods Act rests is that if the buyer is deemed to have accepted the goods, he loses his right to reject them. He does not, however, lose all rights with respect to them. Although he is now bound to retain them he can still claim damages if the value of the goods which were actually delivered is less than the value of the goods which the seller promised to supply. This claim for damages is not lost as the result of legal rules peculiar to the sale of goods. It is governed by general legal principles. It is not lost by lapse of time until it becomes barred under the Limitation Act 1980; as most mercantile contracts are in the nature of simple contracts, the seller is normally[5] entitled to plead the defence of limitation after the lapse of six years from the breach of contract. The tendency of English sales law is to discourage the rejection of goods by the buyer but to allow, without serious restriction or qualification, his claim for damages if he has overpaid their value, as expressed in the contract price.

Conditions, warranties and innominate terms

5–002 According to the Sale of Goods Act 1979, the terms of the contract of sale are either conditions or warranties. This simple classification has proved to be insufficient in commercial circumstances and the courts have supplemented it by

---

[1] See *post*, paras 21–002 and 21–004 *et seq.*
[2] As amended by Sale and Supply of Goods Act 1994 and Sale of Goods Amendment Act 1995.
[3] This Convention came into operation on January 1, 1988, but has not been given effect in the U.K. yet.
[4] See *post*, para. 30–026 *et seq.*
[5] The period of limitation may be longer if there is a new accrual of the action as the result of an acknowledgment in writing or part payment, or in case of fraud or of similar circumstances.

recognising a third type of contractual term, the innominate term, also referred to as the intermediate term.[6]

Conditions and warranties

The buyer is entitled to reject the goods if a condition relating to them is broken. **5–003** A condition is a term to which the parties, when making the contract, attribute such importance that it can truly be described as being of the essence of the contract.[7] A condition has to be distinguished from a warranty, which is a contract term of less significance and which relates to matters collateral to the main purpose of the contract.[8] In the case of breach of a warranty the buyer is not entitled to reject the goods. He has to retain them but may claim damages which, if the goods have an available market, are prima facie the difference between the value of the goods as delivered and the value they would have if they had complied with the warranty.[9] As a condition is treated as being of higher legal quality than a warranty, every condition includes a warranty—a statement which cannot be reversed. The buyer is, therefore, at liberty to treat a broken condition as a broken warranty and, instead of rejecting the goods, he may elect to keep them and claim the difference between those two values by way of damages.[10] If the buyer is deemed by law to have accepted the goods[11] and if, consequently, he has lost his right to reject them, he is bound henceforth to treat what, originally, was a condition as a warranty and his only claim is for damages for breach of warranty.[12]

The Sale of Goods Act 1979 implies into a contract of sale certain terms which, in England and Wales, are to be regarded as conditions.[13] If the goods are described then the goods supplied must correspond with their description in the contract.[14] They must be of satisfactory quality.[15] They must be fit for the particular purpose for which, with the knowledge of the seller, they are bought[16] or if the purpose of the goods in question is not made known to the seller they must be fit for all the purposes for which such goods are commonly supplied[17]; they must correspond with the sample, if they have been ordered on the basis

---

[6] *Per* Mustill L.J. in *Lombard North Central plc v. Butterworth* [1987] Q.B. 527 at 537; *Phibro Energy AG v. Nissho Iwai Corp and Bomar Oil Inc (The Honam Jade)* [1991] 1 Lloyd's Rep. 38, CA.

[7] For a discussion whether a term of the contract is a condition, see *State Trading Corporation of India Ltd v. M. Golodetz Ltd; The Sara D* [1989] 2 Lloyd's Rep. 277.

[8] Sale of Goods Act 1979, s.61.

[9] s.53(3). See *Bence Graphics International Ltd v. Fasson U.K. Ltd* [1998] Q.B. 87—appropriate measure is the difference between value of goods on delivery and the value if warranty had been fulfilled. If he has not yet paid the full price, he may set off his claim for damages against the price in diminution or extinction of the latter (s.53(1)).

[10] See s.11(2).

[11] s.35.

[12] s.11(4) now subject to s.35A below.

[13] ss. 13(1)A, 14(6), 15(2).

[14] s.13(1).

[15] s.14(2). As to the difference between words of identity and words of quality see *Total International Ltd v. Addax BV* [1996] 2 Lloyd's Rep. 333 at 341.

[16] s.14(3). *Slater and Slater and Ors v. Finning Ltd* [1996] 2 Lloyd's Rep. 353, Scot. HL.

[17] s.14(2B)(a).

of a sample provided,[18] or with sample and description.[19] These terms are implied by law into contracts of sale but, subject to the Unfair Contract Terms Act 1977 (which does not apply to international supply contracts), may be contracted out of or varied.[20]

In addition to the statutorily implied conditions certain terms in international sales contracts are taken to be conditions. Generally, terms as to time are held to be a condition of the contract.[21] The port of loading in an f.o.b. contract is a condition,[22] as is the name of a vessel and the type of vessel to be used for the carriage of the goods if they have, unusually, been agreed between the parties. In the absence of any such agreement it is a condition of the contract that the goods be carried on a vessel that is usual in the trade for the carriage of such goods.[23]

It may therefore be seen that a breach of a condition operates as a repudiation of the contract by the party in breach.[24] Consequently, a buyer who is entitled to reject the goods is in the same position as a buyer to whom the goods were not tendered[25] at all, unless the breached term has to be treated as an innominate term,[26] or under the *de minimis* rule[27] or special considerations, such as a trade custom or an agreement of the parties to the contrary,[28] apply. In the normal case the buyer is entitled to claim damages from the seller for the non-delivery of the goods.[29] If he has paid the purchase price in advance he can recover it by way of damages, and if he has suffered other reasonably foreseeable loss, he can recover damages as well. The motivation for the buyer's desire to reject the goods is usually that the non-conforming goods which the seller has tendered are useless to him and that the claim for damages is his only remedy. The practical point in the distinction between the buyer's right to reject the goods on the ground that a condition of the contract is broken and his right to claim damages for breach of warranty is that in the former instance the buyer can often claim damages on a considerably higher scale than in the latter. Where a party is entitled to damages, he is bound to take reasonable steps to mitigate his

---

[18] s.15.

[19] s.13(2).

[20] s.55. Sale of Goods Act 1979, see also Unfair Contract Terms Act 1977, s.26(1), (3), (4).

[21] *Bunge Corporation v. Tradax Export SA* [1980] 1 Lloyd's Rep. 294; [1980] CA; [1981] 2 Lloyd's Rep. 1, HL. But see *State Trading Corp of India* (n.7, above); *Phibro Energy AG v. Nissho Iwai Corp (The Honan Jade)* [1991] 1 Lloyd's Rep. 38; *Torvald Klaveness A/S v. Arni Maritime Corp (The Gregos)* [1993] 2 Lloyd's Rep. 335 at 347.

[22] *Petrotrade Inc v. Stinnes Handel GmbH* [1995] 1 Lloyd's Rep. 142.

[23] *Ashmore & Son v. C. S. Cox* [1899] 1 Q.B. 436; *Bowes Shand* (1877) 2 App. Cas. 455.

[24] s.11(2).

[25] The seller may, however, make a second tender of new goods if the time for delivery has not expired. *Hyundai Merchant Marine Co Ltd v. Karander Maritime Inc (The Nizuru)* [1996] 2 Lloyd's Rep. 66. Vienna Convention, Art. 48(1).

[26] See *post*, para. 5–004.

[27] *De minimis non curat lex*; see *Moralice (London) Ltd v. E. D. and F. Man* [1954] 2 Lloyd's Rep. 526; *Rapalli v. K.L. Take Ltd* [1958] 2 Lloyd's Rep. 469.

[28] The conditions of trade associations which, *e.g.* in the commodity trade, are widely adopted, sometimes exclude the rejection of goods.

[29] The measure of damages is the difference between the contract price and the market price, if there is an available market for the goods (s.51(3)). The relevant market price is that ruling at the date of delivery or, failing delivery, that at the date of refusal to deliver. See also *Procter & Gamble Philippine Manufacturing Corp v. Kurt A. Becher GmbH* [1988] 2 Lloyd's Rep. 21.

loss[30] but he is not bound "to go hunting the globe" to find a market in a distant country,[31] nor can it be held against him, if he has acted reasonably, that a method of mitigation more favourable to the defaulting buyer existed.[32]

The innominate term

This is a contractual term which is neither a condition nor a warranty. Its charac-   **5–004**
teristic is that, if the contract is breached, the effect of the breach depends on its nature and gravity.[33] If the breach is grave, the innocent party can treat the contract as repudiated, but if the breach is not serious the contract subsists and the innocent party can only claim damages for any loss which he may have suffered.

The concept of the innominate term was developed in shipping contracts with respect to the stipulation that the ship should be seaworthy.[34] Unseaworthiness could be of serious or unimportant character and its effect on the contract varied according to the facts which made the ship unseaworthy. The concept of the innominate term was extended to other types of contract, notably to the contract of sale.[35] Lord Wilberforce referred to it as "the modern doctrine" when he said[36]:

> "The general law of contract has developed along much more rational lines in attending to the nature and gravity of a breach or departure rather than in accepting rigid categories which do or do not automatically give a right to rescind, and if the choice were between extending cases under the Sale of Goods Act 1893 into other fields, or allowing more modern doctrine to infect those cases, my preference would be clear."

An illustration of the application of the innominate term to the law of international sales is provided by *Cehave NV v. Bremer Handelsgesellschaft mbH; The Hansa Nord*.[37] Bremer Handelsgesellschaft, a German company, sold a quantity of U.S. orange pellets c.i.f. Rotterdam to Cehave, a Dutch company. The pellets were to be used in the manufacture of cattle food. The contract was made on a form of the Cattle Food Trade Association which contained the term "Shipment to be made in good condition". The consignment in issue was about 3,400

---

[30] *The Solholt* [1983] 1 Lloyd's Rep. 605.
[31] *Lesters Leather and Skin Co v. Home and Overseas Brokers Ltd* (1948) 64 T.L.R. 569.
[32] *Gebruder Metelmann GmbH & Co KG v. NBR (London) Ltd* [1984] 1 Lloyd's Rep. 614.
[33] *Hongkong Fir Shipping Co Ltd v. Kawasaki Kisen Kaisha Ltd* [1962] 2 Q.B. 26; *United Dominions Trust (Commercial) Ltd v. Eagle Aircraft Services Ltd* [1968] 1 W.L.R. 74, 80, 82; *The Mihalis Angelos* [1971] 1 Q.B. 164; *Cehave NV v. Bremer Handelsgesellschaft mbH; The Hansa Nord* [1976] 1 Q.B. 44, 60, 70, 82–83; *Reardon Smith Line Ltd v. Yngvar Hansen-Tangen* [1976] 1 W.L.R. 989 at 998; *Compagnie General Maritime v. Diakan Spirit SA; The Ymnos* [1982] 2 Lloyd's Rep. 574 (container guarantee clause guaranteeing the suitability of a chartered ship for container transport); *Phoenix General Insurance Co of Greece SA v. Halvanon Insurance Co Ltd* [1985] 2 Lloyd's Rep. 599 at 614. See also *Bunge v. Tradax supra*, HL.
[34] *Hongkong Fir Shipping Co Ltd v. Kawasaki Kisen Kaisha Ltd* [1962] 2 Q.B. 26.
[35] *Cehave NV v. Bremer Handelsgesellschaft mbH; The Hansa Nord* [1976] 1 Q.B. 44: see below.
[36] In *Reardon Smith Line Ltd v. Yngvar Hansen-Tangen* [1976] 1 W.L.R. 989 at 998; see also *per* Lord Wilberforce in *Bremer Handelsgesellschaft mbH v. Vanden Avenne Izegem PVBA* [1978] 2 Lloyd's Rep. 109, 113, 201, *Krohn & Co v. Mitsui and Co Europe GmbH* [1978] 2 Lloyd's Rep. 419; *Antaios Compañia Naviera SA v. Salen Rederierna AB* [1984] 3 W.L.R. 592 at 597.
[37] [1976] 1 Q.B. 44.

metric tonnes and was carried in The Hansa Nord. The contract price, converted into sterling, was about £100,000 but the market price at the time of arrival of the ship had fallen considerably. On discharge from The Hansa Nord the cargo ex hold no. 1 (1,260 tonnes) was found to be damaged but the cargo ex hold no. 2 (2,053 tonnes) was in good condition. The buyers rejected the whole consignment. The Rotterdam court ordered its sale. It was purchased by a middleman for a sum which, after deduction of the expenses, amounted to an equivalent of £29,903. The middleman sold the pellets the same day for the same price to the original buyers who took them to their factory and used them for the manufacture of cattle food although they received a somewhat smaller quantity of pellets than they would have done if part of the consignment had not been damaged. The total result of the transaction was that the Dutch buyers received goods which they had agreed to buy for £100,000 at the reduced price of about £30,000. The case went to arbitration and then to the courts. The Court of Appeal held that the contractual term "shipment to be made in good condition" was not a condition within the meaning of the Sale of Goods Act but was an innominate term. Lord Denning M.R. said[38]:

> "If a small proportion of the goods sold was a little below that standard, it would be met by commercial men by an allowance off the price. The buyer would have no right to reject the whole lot unless the divergence was serious and substantial."

The court held that the buyers were not entitled to reject the whole consignment but were entitled to damages for the difference in value between the damaged and sound goods on arrival in Rotterdam. The case was remitted to the arbitrators for the determination of these damages.

Section 15A, inserted by the Sale and Supply of Goods Act 1994, provides that where a buyer would have a right to reject goods on the grounds of a breach of sections 13, 14 or 15 and does not deal as a consumer, he may not treat the breach as a breach of condition where it is so slight that it would be unreasonable to do so. The buyer in such a circumstance may only treat the breach as a breach of warranty, although the parties may provide otherwise expressly or implicitly. It is suggested that entry into a contract on f.o.b. and c.i.f. terms implies that the parties do not intend section 15(A) to apply.[39]

However, the concept of the innominate term should not be overused. Many terms are regarded by the parties to the contract as so essential that they qualify as conditions in the legal sense. This applies, in particular, to most time clauses in commercial contracts,[40] *e.g.* in an f.o.b. contract a clause that "buyers shall give at least [15] consecutive days' notice of probable readiness of vessel(s)".[41]

---

[38] *ibid.* at 61.

[39] See ss.15(A)(1), 15(A)(2); Benjamin, *Sale of Goods* (5th ed.), para. 18–224 and Law Com. No. 160, paras 4.23, 4.24.

[40] *Lombard North Central plc v. Butterworth* [1987] Q.B. 527; but not every time clause is a condition, see generally *Bunge v. Tradax, post*, n.41.

[41] *Bunge Corporation v. Tradax Export SA* [1980] 1 Lloyd's Rep. 294, [1980] CA and [1981] 2 Lloyd's Rep. 1, HL; *Société Italo-Belge pour le Commerce et l'Industrie SA v. Palm and Vegetable Oils (Malaysia) Sdn Bhd; The Post Chaser* [1982] 1 All E.R. 19; *State Trading Corporation of India Ltd v. M. Golodetz Ltd* [1988] 2 Lloyd's Rep. 182 at 187; *Compagnie Commerciale Sucres et Denrées v. C. Czarnikow Ltd; The Naxos* [1991] 1 Lloyd's Rep. 29 at 36.

Similarly, in a c. and f. contract a clause that the ship shall sail directly from the port of loading to the port of discharge (direct shipment clause), was held to be a condition and not an innominate term.[42]

Examination of goods

When the seller tenders delivery of the goods, the buyer, unless otherwise agreed, is entitled to request that he be given a reasonable opportunity of examining the goods for the purpose of ascertaining whether they are in conformity with the contract.[43] A buyer who has not previously examined the goods[44] is not deemed to have accepted them and, consequently, has not lost his right to reject them unless and until he has had a reasonable opportunity of examining them.[45]

5–005

There exists a prima facie presumption, where goods are transported, that the place and time of examination are the place and time of delivery of the goods. This presumption is, however, displaced where the arrangements of the parties, the circumstances of the sale or a trade custom point to a different intention of the parties. Bailhache J. observed in one case[46]:

> "In order to postpone the place of inspection it is necessary that there should be two elements: the original vendor must know, either because he is told or by necessary inference, that the goods are going farther on, and the place at which he delivers must either be unsuitable in itself or the nature or packing of the goods must make inspection at that place unreasonable."

An illustration of exceptional circumstances in which the place and time of examination were postponed occurred in *B. & P. Wholesale Distributors v. Marko Ltd*[47] in which the sellers, importers of meat, sold one tonne of fat salted backs with rind to the buyers who were wholesale dealers in meat. The buyers had an opportunity of inspecting the meat cursorily at the docks in London when it arrived, but failed to avail themselves of it and had it taken to their depot in Chester. In the depot the buyers noticed that the meat was not in accordance with the contract. They rejected it and stopped the cheque for the price which they had given the sellers. The latter sued the buyers on the cheque and the buyers counterclaimed for damages for non-delivery of the goods. Pearson J. decided in favour of the buyers. The learned judge held that the place of delivery was the docks in London but that the place of examination was postponed to the buyers' depot in Chester. He observed that the true meaning of section 34 of the Sale of Goods Act (in the form in which it was then in force) was that it must be practicable to make a proper examination of the goods, and until such opportunity was afforded to the buyers they were not deemed to have accepted the goods within the meaning of section 35. In further support of his judgment,

---

[42] *Bergerco USA v. Vegoil Ltd* [1984] 1 Lloyd's Rep. 440 at 444; *State Trading Corporation of India Ltd v. M. Godoletz Ltd* [1988] 2 Lloyd's Rep. 182 at 183–184.
[43] s.34. Vienna Convention, Art. 38.
[44] On preshipment inspection, see para. 4–014.
[45] s.35(2).
[46] *Saunt v. Belcher and Gibbons* (1920) 26 Com.Cas. 115 at 119; see also *Perkins v. Bell* [1893] 1 Q.B. 193 and *Bergerco USA v. Vegoil Ltd* [1984] 1 Lloyd's Rep. 440 at 446; *Cf. Compagnie Commerciale Sucres et Denrées v. C. Czarnikow Ltd; The Naxos* [1991] 1 Lloyd's Rep. 29.
[47] *The Times*, February 20, 1953.

the learned judge could now refer to the additional words contained in section 35 of the Sale of Goods Act 1979.[48] These words make it clear that the buyer's right to reject exists until he is given a genuine opportunity of examining the goods.

In export sales the place and time of examination are frequently not those of delivery but are postponed. In a contract of export sale the place and time of delivery is usually defined by the special trade clause which the parties have adopted.[49] Where the seller is not obliged to tender a bill of lading to the buyer, as in sales ex works, f.a.s., f.o.b. (buyer contracting with carrier), or in container delivery contracts, physical delivery of the goods takes place in his—the seller's—country.[50] Where bills of lading have to be tendered, as in f.o.b. contracts of the classic type or providing additional services, c.i.f. contracts, and c. and f. contracts, the delivery of the goods is constructive and completely divorced from the actual situation of the goods. Whether in an export sale the delivery is physical or constructive, the two conditions postulated by Bailhache J. in the case referred to[51] for the postponement of the place of examination are normally satisfied. The goods are usually ordered and packed for export, and these facts alone indicate to the seller that they are going farther on. The locality at which the delivery takes place is usually unsuitable for the examination of the goods, so that it is unreasonable to expect the buyer to carry out the examination there. Consequently, in an export sale, unless the parties have otherwise agreed, for example by arranging pre-shipment inspection,[52] or a trade custom provides a different practice, it has to be assumed that the parties intend that the examination of the goods shall be postponed until the goods have arrived at the place of their destination and that that place is the agreed place of examination.[53] Thus, in a case concerning a c. and f. contract Hobhouse J. said[54] that "the exercise of the right to reject goods is one which the seller is entitled to postpone until the goods arrive." Further, in *Molling & Co v. Dean & Son Ltd*[55] the sellers, colour printers in Germany, sold the buyers 40,000 toy books which, as they knew, the buyer had resold to sub-purchasers in the United States of America. The books were packed specially for carriage to America and the buyers, without opening the cases, sent them on to their sub-purchasers who rejected them rightly as not being in conformity with their contract and re-shipped them to the original buyers (their sellers). It was held that the place of examination was postponed to America and that the buyers were entitled to reject the books and

---

[48] In s.35 the reference to s.34 was already added by the Misrepresentation Act 1967, s.4(2).
[49] See *ante*, para. 4–003.
[50] Normally, when the goods are delivered to the carrier for transmission to the buyer (s.32).
[51] *Saunt v. Belcher and Gibbons, supra*, n.46.
[52] See para. 4–014.
[53] *Molling v. Dean* (1902) 18 T.L.R. 217; *Boks v. Rayner* (1921) 37 T.L.R. 800; *Bragg v. Villanova* (1923) 40 T.L.R. 154; *Scarliaris v. Ofverberg & Co* (1921) 37 T.L.R. 307, CA; *Biddell Bros v. E. Clemens Horst Co* [1911] 1 K.B. 934 at 960; *Kwei Tek Chao v. British Traders and Shippers Ltd* [1954] 2 Q.B. 459; *Bergerco USA v. Vegoil Ltd* [1984] 1 Lloyd's Rep. 440.
[54] *Bergerco USA v. Vegoil Ltd* [1984] 1 Lloyd's Rep. 440 at 446. For a fuller quotation from this judgment see para. 2–026.
[55] (1902) 18 T.L.R. 217.

to claim as damages the cost of sending them to America and from there back
to England, as well as the duty paid on them in New York.

In international sales, where the wharf at which the goods are landed or the
Customs house into which they are taken after landing is unsuitable for examination, the place of examination is the business premises of the buyer[56] (or that of
his agent in performance of the contract[57]). Where the place of destination is
situated inland and the goods, after having been landed, have to be taken to that
locality, the intended place of examination will normally be the place of ultimate
destination.

It should be noted that the Act does not make the examination of the goods
a condition precedent of their acceptance. It merely requires that the buyer be
given a "reasonable opportunity" of examining the goods and provides that he
is not deemed to have accepted the goods until he is given that opportunity.[58]
Whether the buyer avails himself of that opportunity or waives his right of
examination is for him to decide. He waives this right, if for example, he refrains
from inspecting the goods when given that opportunity. In such a case the buyer
loses his right to reject the goods. Thus, a buyer who after arrival of the goods
orders them to be taken to his warehouse without inspecting them cannot reject
them when many months later he discovers that they are faulty, because the
retention of goods after a reasonable amount of time has elapsed[59] without
intimation that the goods are rejected is deemed to be an acceptance of the
goods.[60] It is always prudent to examine the goods as early as practicable after
their arrival at the place of examination, whether that is the place of delivery,
the place of final destination or another place.

Where the goods have hidden defects, "not discoverable by any reasonable
exercise of care or skill on an inspection",[61] the time of examination with respect
to that defect is postponed to the time at which such examination could have
been carried out effectively. If the defect can only be discovered when the goods
are used, but not on prior examination, the buyer would still be entitled to reject
them on discovery of the defect, provided that he has not kept them for longer
than a reasonable time.[62]

Acceptance of goods

The test adopted by section 35 is whether the buyer is "deemed to have   **5–006**
accepted" the goods.[63] The receipt of the goods is not acceptance and the section

---

[56] This follows from *B & P Wholesale Distributors v. Marko Ltd The Times*, February 20, 1953.
[57] As contrasted with an agent for the purposes of transmission (whose authority is limited to that
purpose), such as a carrier, forwarder or warehouseman (unless, exceptionally, a buyer has a reasonable opportunity of inspecting the goods in the possession of any of those persons).
[58] s.35(2).
[59] Assuming that he kept the goods in his warehouse unexamined for an unreasonably long time.
[60] s.35(1)(a).
[61] *Per* Brett J. in *Heilbutt v. Hickson* (1872) L.R. 7 C.P. 438 at 456.
[62] In *Bernstein v. Pamson Motors (Golders Green) Ltd* [1987] 2 All E.R. 220 Rougier J. held, *obiter*,
that a buyer could be deemed to have accepted the goods by retention although he had no knowledge
of the defect; this statement might be too general; in the case before him the judge found, as a fact,
that the buyer retained the goods although he had an opportunity of discovering the defect.
[63] See I. Brown, "Acceptance in the Sale of Goods" [1988] J.B.L. 56.

does not provide that the mere receipt of the goods shall be deemed to be acceptance. On the other hand, approval is not always required by the section: in two of the three circumstances set out by section 35 a buyer is deemed to have accepted the goods though he may not have approved them.

The buyer is deemed to have accepted the goods:

(a) when he intimates to the seller that he has accepted them (s.35(1)(a));

(b) when the goods have been delivered to him, and he does any act in relation to them which is inconsistent with the ownership of the seller (s.35(1)(b)); or

(c) when, after the lapse of a reasonable time, he retains the goods without intimating to the seller that he has rejected them (s.35(4)).

The first of these three cases is obvious and does not need clarification. As regards the third, it should be noted that indecision on the part of the buyer may lead to the loss of his right to reject the goods, that is, if he retains them for an unreasonably long time without intimating that he has rejected them. The Act refrains from requiring a fixed period of time within which the buyer has to intimate his rejection. "Reasonable time" is a flexible requirement which varies according to the circumstances of the case; the question of what is a reasonable time is always a question of fact.[64] The prudent buyer will, as observed earlier,[65] examine the goods as soon as they arrive at the place of examination and will then decide whether to reject them or to keep them.

Of particular importance is the second case. First, this circumstance arises only after the buyer has been afforded a reasonable opportunity of examining the goods. Secondly, "an act inconsistent with the ownership of the seller" is deemed to be an acceptance of the goods only after the goods have been delivered to the buyer, but the delivery need not be physical. A delivery to a carrier for transmission to the buyer, *e.g.* under an f.o.b. or c.i.f. contract, would be sufficient.[66] An act inconsistent with the ownership of the seller is any act by which the buyer behaves as if he were the owner of the goods. Whereas any disposal of the goods, *e.g.* a resale and dispatch or delivery of the goods to a sub-purchaser, or the pledging of them as a security, was deemed an act inconsistent with the ownership of the seller, because thereby the buyer accepts the title to the goods although he might not have accepted their quality,[67] this no longer reflects the law. The Sale of Goods Act now provides that[68] the buyer is not deemed to have accepted the goods merely because the goods have been delivered to another under a sub-sale or other disposition. The thrust of the

---

[64] s.59.

[65] See para. 2–026.

[66] See s.32; *Kwei Tek Chao v. British Traders and Shippers* [1954] 2 Q.B. 459; *Bergerco USA v. Vegoil Ltd* [1984] 1 Lloyd's Rep. 440 at 445; see also *Benaim v. Debono* [1924] A.C. 514.

[67] A mere resale of the goods (unaccompanied by a disposal or an attempted disposal of them, such as a dispatch to the sub-purchaser), or an inquiry whether the goods are saleable, is not an act inconsistent with the ownership of the seller.

[68] s.35(6)(b).

subsection ensures that where a buyer passes on the contract goods without examination to a sub-buyer, he is not necessarily deemed to have accepted the goods although there has been a delivery from the prima facie place of inspection. This amendment is rather easier to understand in the context of international sales where often the buyer is merely the supplier of goods under a subsale and in situations where the delivery is effected by the presentation of documents. In the latter example it is clear that the acceptance of the documents amounts to only conditional acceptance of the goods themselves. The right to reject is not lost simply because the documents are "sold" on to a subpurchaser.[69]

If the contract is not severable, that is where goods are to be delivered in instalments which are to be completed before payment is to be made, and the buyer has accepted part of the goods, he can no longer reject the other part of the goods.[70] This, however, is subject to section 35A which provides that if a buyer has a right to reject goods by reason of a breach that affects some or all of the goods he does not lose his right to reject the remainder of the goods by accepting some of them.

The position is different, however, if the seller tenders the wrong quantity of goods. The buyer is entitled to reject the whole consignment or to accept the contract quantity and to reject the others, but if he accepts a smaller or larger quantity than he bought he has to pay for what he accepted.[71] The above is again subject to the proposition that the section will not apply generally in overseas sales,[72] that a buyer, other than a consumer, may not reject an excess or shortfall in quantity of goods if that excess or shortfall is so slight that it would be unreasonable to do so. Where the buyer has bought "assorted" goods but is tendered only one type of goods he is entitled to accept a reasonable percentage of the tendered goods and to reject the remainder.[73]

Rejection of goods

A buyer who wishes to reject the goods has to intimate within a reasonable time[74] to the seller that he refuses to accept them. This notice should be clear and definite and should not be contradicted by an act relating to the goods by which the buyer denies the title of the seller to them. No form is prescribed for the notice of rejection, which may be given verbally, by telex, fax or in writing, but the buyer should make certain that it reaches the seller, otherwise it is ineffective.   **5–007**

The buyer who rejects the goods is not bound to return them to the seller unless this is agreed[75] but, being a bailee, he has to exercise reasonable care

---

[69] Or pledged to a bank by way of security, see *Kwei Tek Chao, supra* and para. 5–008, below.
[70] s.11(4). This, however, is subject to s.35A.
[71] s.30.
[72] s.30(2A). See n.39, above.
[73] *Ebrahim Dawood v. Heath (est. 1927)* [1961] 2 Lloyd's Rep. 512.
[74] s.36. See Vienna Convention, Art. 39 on buyer's loss of right to reject.
[75] *ibid.* But the buyer who wrongly rejects or otherwise refuses to accept conforming goods is liable in damages for non-acceptance, s.50. The measure is set out in s.50(2)(3), see *Bem Dis A Turk Ticaret S/A Tr v. International Agri Trade Co Ltd (The Selda)* [1999] 1 Lloyd's Rep. 729.

with respect to them. Subject to this obligation, if the goods are rejected for good reason and in good time, the risk of loss of, or damage to, the goods is with the seller.

Unless a different intention of the parties is expressed in the contract or can be gathered from its terms by necessary implication, the buyer's right to reject the goods is postponed until the goods arrive and he has a reasonable opportunity of examining them.[76] In appropriate cases the buyer may reject the goods even before having received them, that is, if he notices from a provisional invoice or advice note that the seller has dispatched goods which are not in accordance with the contract.[77] A seller, except in c.i.f. sales,[78] who has tendered goods not in accordance with the contract may cancel the original tender and make another tender, but only if he can make the other tender within the time stipulated in the contract.[79] Branson J. said in one case[80]:

> "It does not prevent the seller, if he has time within which to do so, from tendering another parcel of goods, which may be goods which accord with the contract, and which the buyer must, therefore, accept and pay for. It cannot be predicated in any particular case that, if the first tender is not a proper tender, there may not yet be another tender which is a proper tender."

Right of rejection in c.i.f. contracts

5–008   Some observations have to be added on c.i.f. contracts. As has been explained earlier,[81] the characteristic feature of these contracts is the importance attributed to the shipping documents. It has been held, *obiter*, in *Kwei Tek Chao v. British Traders and Shippers Ltd*,[82] that a disposal of the bill of lading (which is part of the shipping documents) is not necessarily an act inconsistent with the seller's ownership of the goods and that, in principle, a c.i.f. buyer does not lose his right to reject the goods by dealings with forged documents, *e.g.* by pledging the bill of lading to a bank. In that case, the question whether by dealing with the documents the buyers had done an act inconsistent with the sellers' ownership in the goods did not arise, but in the interest of "those who may be concerned" Devlin J. observed that so long as a buyer was merely dealing with the documents, he did not commit an act inconsistent with the seller's ownership in the goods and retained the right of rejecting the goods if upon examination after their arrival they were found not to be in conformity with the contract. The argument that the buyer, when reselling the bill of lading or pledging it to a bank, intended to give the sub-purchaser or pledgee a proprietary interest in the goods and passed title to him, was rejected by Devlin J. on the grounds that the buyer himself had only conditional property, *viz.* property conditional on the

---

[76] *Bergerco USA v. Vegoil Ltd* [1984] 1 Lloyd's Rep. 440 at 446.

[77] *E. E. & Brian Smith (1928) Ltd v. Wheatsheaf Mills Ltd* [1939] 2 K.B. 302.

[78] Where it is important that the tendered documents are in order.

[79] *Borrowman v. Free* (1878) 4 Q.B.D. 500; Lord Devlin, "The Treatment of Breach of Contract" [1966] Cam. L.J. 192.

[80] *E. E. & Brian Smith (1928) Ltd v. Wheatsheaf Mills Ltd* [1939] 2 K.B. 302 at 314.

[81] See *ante*, para. 2–019.

[82] [1954] 2 Q.B. 459; see also *ante*, para. 2–026.

goods being in accordance with the contract and that therefore he could not deal with more than conditional property. Devlin J. said[83]:

> "I think that the true view is that what the buyer obtains when the title under the documents is given to him, is the property in the goods, subject to the condition that they revest if upon examination he finds them to be not in accordance with the contract. That means that he gets only conditional property in the goods, the condition being a condition subsequent. All his dealings with the documents are dealings only with that conditional property in the goods. It follows, therefore, that there can be no dealing which is inconsistent with the seller's ownership unless he deals with something more than the conditional property."

Rejection where each delivery to be treated as separate contract

The contract may provide that "each delivery is to be treated as a separate contract".[84] Unless delivery by instalments is arranged, this term gives the seller an option; he may deliver in one consignment, in which case there is one indivisible contract, or he may make several deliveries, in which case there are several separate contracts. The seller exercises this option by the mode of performance.[85] Where the contract is on c.i.f. terms, the fact that the seller has shipped under separate bills of lading in different vessels indicates clearly that he has exercised the option in favour of several contracts. The position is difficult if he ships under separate bills of lading in the same vessel; here it is a question of intention of the parties, *i.e.* whether they intend that there should be one transaction or several contracts. In one case[86] a seller in Hong Kong sold 140 bales of grey cotton poplin to cotton converters in Manchester. The contract was c.i.f. Liverpool and provided that each delivery was to be treated as a separate contract. The seller shipped the whole consignment in the same ship but for reasons connected with the quota regulation in Hong Kong the goods were shipped under two bills of lading, each relating to half the consignment. The buyers accepted one bill of lading and rejected the other. The House of Lords held that in the special circumstances of this case—the buyers requiring the goods for their own use and not for resale—the parties, in spite of the shipment under two separate bills of lading, treated the transaction as one, and the buyers, having accepted part of the goods, could no longer reject the other part.[87] This case, however, was founded on special facts. Normally, when the contract contains a separation clause and the goods are shipped under separate bills of lading, it has to be inferred that the parties intend that there should be several contracts.[88]

5–009

---

[83] [1954] 2 Q.B. 459 at 487. See *Gill & Duffus SA v. Berger & Co Inc* [1984] A.C. 382 where it is provided that conforming documents must be accepted even if the buyer is aware that he will have a right to reject the goods on arrival.

[84] In *Cehave NV v. Bremer Handelsgesellschaft mbH; The Hansa Nord* [1976] 1 Q.B. 44 the contract provided: "each shipment shall be considered a separate contract".

[85] *J. Rosenthal & Sons Ltd v. Esmail* [1965] 1 W.L.R. 1117.

[86] *ibid.*

[87] See para. 5–007.

[88] A different question is whether shipments under several bills of lading constitute "partial shipments" for the purposes of letters of credit, entitling the bank to reject such bills of lading. Here the UCP (1993 Revision) provide in Art. 40(a) that partial shipments are allowed unless the credit stipulates otherwise. Further, it is provided in Art. 44(b) that "Transport documents which appear on their face to indicate that shipment has been made on the same means of conveyance and for the same journey provided they indicate the same destination, will not be regarded as covering partial

Property in rejected goods

5–010 The property in the rejected goods revests in the seller when he accepts the rejection.[89] When he does not accept the rejection it is believed that if it is later decided by the court or arbitration tribunal that the rejection was justified, the property likewise revests in the seller because, as Devlin J. observed in the *Kwei Tek Chao* case,[90] the property passes to the buyer subject to a condition subsequent that on examination the goods are found to be in accordance with the contract. A buyer who has paid the price in advance and then rejects the goods is not entitled to retain them by virtue of an "unpaid buyer's lien"[91] until the price is refunded. In the case of c.i.f. contracts dealings with the documents do not affect the right of the buyer to reject the goods. This right normally arises only after the arrival of the goods when they can be examined.[92]

Rejection and estoppel

5–011 If the buyer has a valid ground for rejection of the goods but so conducts himself as to lead the seller to believe that he is not relying on that ground, he is estopped—precluded—from setting up that ground of rejection when it would be unfair or unjust to allow him so to do.[93] On the other hand, if a buyer has rejected the goods on a ground which he has notified to the seller, he is not confined to that ground and can later rely on other grounds for the rejection.[94] If owing to a frustrating event the rejection of the goods becomes impossible, it would appear that the buyer has lost the right to reject the goods.[95]

Relaxation of strict performance of contract[96]

5–012 It sometimes happens that a party to a contract of international sale does not insist on strict performance of the contract when the other party asks for indulgence. The buyer may ask the seller to defer the date of delivery of the goods or the date of payment of the price, or the seller may ask for extension of the shipping time. The party to whom such request is addressed may fully realise that, according to the terms of the contract, he is entitled to refuse it and, if the other party does not perform, he may treat the contract as repudiated and claim

---

shipments, even if the transport documents indicate different dates of shipment and/or different ports of loading, places of taking in charge, or despatch."

[89] *J. L. Lyons & Co v. May & Baker* [1923] 1 K.B. 685 at 688.

[90] [1954] 2 Q.B. 459; see *ante*, para. 2–026.

[91] An analogy to the unpaid seller's lien (see *post*, para. 5–015) is not allowed: *J. L. Lyons & Co v. May & Baker* [1923] 1 K.B. 685.

[92] See *ante*, para. 5–008.

[93] *Panchaud Freres SA v. Etablissements General Grain Co* [1970] 1 Lloyd's Rep. 53 at 57; *Motor Oil Hellas (Corinth) Refineries SA v. Shipping Corporation of India; The Kanchenjunga* [1990] 1 Lloyd's Rep. 391.

[94] *Panchaud Freres SA v. Etablissements General Grain Co* [1970] 1 Lloyd's Rep. 53 at 56.

[95] *Mackay v. Dick* (1881) 6 App.Cas. 251; *Colley v. Overseas Importers* [1921] 3 K.B. 302.

[96] This paragraph is based on C. M. Schmitthoff, *Legal Aspects of Export Sales* (3rd ed., Institute of Export, 1978), pp. 14–16.

damages. He may not wish to insist on his rights for reasons of business policy. From the legal point of view this reasonable attitude might cause considerable difficulty. If the party who has been asked to relax the terms of the contract asks for a consideration in return for the favour, there is a true contract to vary the terms of the original contract and the new agreement is binding on both parties. If the favour is merely a voluntary forbearance to insist on strict performance, the position is different. In that case, if "one party has by its conduct led the other to alter his position"[97] it is probable that the former party cannot change his mind at once and insist again on his strict rights. For instance, an overseas buyer of computers asks the export seller to defer shipment for one month, and the seller agrees. It is probable that the seller cannot arbitrarily set aside this arrangement. This view is founded either on what has become known as the doctrine of waiver or on that of equitable estoppel.[98] The latter was formulated by Denning L.J.[99] as follows:

"If one party, by his conduct, leads another to believe that the strict rights arising under the contract will not be insisted upon, intending that the other should act on that belief, and he does act on it, then the first party will not afterwards be allowed to insist on the strict rights when it would be inequitable for him to do so."

But this does not mean that the terms of the original contract are varied, and can no longer be relied upon. Goddard J. said in this connection[1]:

"If what happens is a mere voluntary forbearance to insist on delivery or acceptance according to the strict terms of the written contract, the original contract remains unaffected and the obligation to deliver and to accept the full contract quantity still continues."

And Lord Simonds observed[2]:

"I would not have it supposed, particularly in commercial transactions, that mere acts of indulgence are apt to create rights."

---

[97] *Per* Lord Simonds in *Tool Manufacturing Co Ltd v. Tungsten Electric Co Ltd* [1955] W.L.R. 761 at 764.
[98] These two doctrines are frequently equated and usually overlap but strictly speaking they are distinct and separate doctrines, see *per* Denning L.J. in *Panchaud Freres SA v. Etablissements General Grain Co* [1970] 1 Lloyd's Rep. 53 at 57, and J. Adams, "Waiver Redistributed" (1973) 36 Conveyancer 245. Different from equitable estoppel is estoppel by previous conduct, technically known as "estoppel by convention". This arises where the parties have acted on an agreed assumption that a state of facts is true (see Chitty, *Contracts* (28th ed., 1999), paras 25–005—25–009). A party who has acted in such a manner would not act in good faith if he suddenly decided to act differently (*venire contra factum proprium*). See also *The Kanchenjunga, supra,* n.93.
[99] *Plasticmoda SpA v. Davidsons (Manchester) Ltd* [1952] 1 Lloyd's Rep. 527. There are numerous older cases on this subject; the most famous of them is *Central London Property Trust Ltd v. High Trees House Ltd* [1947] K.B. 130. The following, *inter alia,* are also of interest *Panchaud Freres SA v. Etablissements General Grain Co* [1970] 1 Lloyd's Rep. 53; *Woodhouse A.C. Israel Cocoa Ltd SA v. Nigerian Produce Marketing Co Ltd* [1972] A.C. 741; *W. J. Alan & Co Ltd v. El Nasr Export & Import Co* [1972] 2 W.L.R. 800 at 814; *Société Italo-Belge pour le Commerce et l'Industrie SA v. Palm and Vegetable Oils (Malaysia) Sdn Bhd; The Post Chaser* [1982] 1 All E.R. 19; *Hing Cotton Mill Ltd v. Liu Chong Hing Bank Ltd* [1985] 3 W.L.R. 317 at 333; *Sea Calm Shipping Co SA v. Chantiers Navals de L'Esterel SA; The Uhenbels* [1986] 2 Lloyd's Rep. 294 at 298.
[1] *Bessler Waechter Glover & Co v. South Derwent Coal Co* [1938] 1 K.B. 408 at 416.
[2] In *Tool Manufacturing Co Ltd v. Tungsten Electric Co Ltd* [1955] 1 W.L.R. 761 at 764.

If, therefore, in the above example, the buyer, after expiry of one month, is still unwilling to accept delivery of the goods, the seller would be entitled to revert to the original terms of the contract. Goulding J. said in one case[3]:

> "Indeed, the mere extension of the period to a new fixed period would on the authorities have preserved the position that time was of the essence without fresh stipulation to that effect."

Moreover, if no time limit is provided for the indulgence, the party who has agreed to relax the strict terms can likewise unilaterally notify the other party that the indulgence is over and that the strict terms of the contract shall again apply. Normally, the party who has shown indulgence has to give the other party notice of reasonable length "for readjustment before he is allowed to enforce his strict rights".[4] Such notice is not always essential: it is not required if it is clear from the circumstances that the period of suspension is over or that, even if notice had been given, the other party could not have complied with it. In one case,[5] a French company bought goods from an English company under an f.o.b. contract which provided that the price should be paid in sterling under a banker's letter of credit to be opened in London "within a few weeks". The time for the opening of the credit expired, as the court found, on August 19. There were extensions, and on October 22 the sellers informed the buyers peremptorily that, having regard to the delay in the establishment of the credit, they considered the contract cancelled. Devlin J. held that the peremptory notice of October 22 was sufficient and that the sellers were not obliged to give the buyers further time because even if they had given them, say, a fortnight's notice, the buyers could not have complied with it as they could not obtain transferable sterling from their bank; the legal principle was expressed by the learned judge[6] as follows:

> "The position of a party who has started out with a contract where time is of the essence and has allowed the time to go by is, I think, quite clearly laid down in the authorities. He has got to make time of the essence of the contract again in the normal case, and that means that he has to give notice giving the other side what is a reasonable time in all the circumstances to comply with their obligations. But in my judgment, although that is the ordinary doctrine, the giving of a notice is not always essential."

---

[3] (1973) 26 P.C.R. 89; quoted with approval by Kerr L.J. in *Nichimen Corporation v. Gatoil Overseas Inc* [1987] 2 Lloyd's Rep. 46 at 53.
[4] Per Lord Tucker in *Tool Manufacturing Co Ltd v. Tungsten Electric Co Ltd* [1955] 1 W.L.R. 761 at 785; *SCCMO (London) Ltd v. Société Générale de Compensation* [1956] 1 Lloyd's Rep. 290 at 300.
[5] *Etablissements Chainbaux SARL v. Harbormaster Ltd* [1955] 1 Lloyd's Rep. 303; See also *Nichimen Corporation v. Gatoil Overseas Inc* [1987] 2 Lloyd's Rep. 46 (failure to open letter of credit was breach of a condition of the contract of sale and this position was not changed by the sellers granting the buyers indulgence for the opening of the credit).
[6] In the *Chainbaux* case at 312.

These equitable principles are of great importance in international sales. They enable a seller who has voluntarily forborne to insist on the strict performance of the contract to reintroduce those strict terms again if the necessity arises.

The right of the unpaid seller

In international sales transactions the seller normally parts with the possession **5–013** of the goods before receiving the purchase price because he wants to dispatch the goods with due expedition. Even where the sale is on a cash basis, some time will elapse before the buyer's remittance reaches the seller. Where the sale is a credit transaction more time will pass before the bill of exchange drawn by the seller on the buyer is settled. Much may happen during that time. The buyer may become insolvent, he may issue debentures taking priority over ordinary trading debts, he may amalgamate with a firm that is heavily indebted, or the buyer's country may prohibit payment in the stipulated currency. It is imperative that the seller should be properly protected here.

The law would fail in its task if it omitted to devise special rules for the protection of the seller during the vulnerable period which commences when he gives up possession of the goods and continues until he has received the price. However, here again, the best protection is the seller's foresight. The seller who parts with his goods before obtaining the price should insert into the contract of sale a clause reserving the title in the goods until he receives the purchase price. Section 39(2) entitles the unpaid seller, who has reserved the property in the goods,[7] to withhold their delivery until the price is paid, and provides that[8] his rights against the goods shall be similar to and coextensive with the rights of lien and stoppage in transit which can be claimed by an unpaid seller who has not retained title in the goods.

The rights of the unpaid seller

Where the seller has failed to reserve the property in the goods, the rights of the **5–014** unpaid seller are defined in sections 38–48 of the Sale of Goods Act 1979. These rights, which can be claimed by implication of the law, are[9] (section 39(1)):

(a) a lien on the goods for the price while he is in possession of them;

(b) in case of the insolvency of the buyer,[10] a right of stopping the goods in transit after he has parted with the possession of them;

(c) a right of resale, as limited by the Act.

---

[7] Sale of Goods Act 1979, s.34(2). The retention of title clause is discussed at *ante*, para. 4–007 *et seq.*

[8] In addition to his other remedies. As to the sellers' remedies under the Vienna Convention see Arts 64–65.

[9] Sale of Goods Act 1979, ss.38–48.

[10] The Sale of Goods Act 1979, s.61(4), as amended by the Insolvency Act 1985, Sched. 10, defines insolvency thus: "A person is deemed to be insolvent within the meaning of this Act if he has either ceased to pay his debts in the ordinary course of business or he cannot pay his debts as they become due". Insolvency of companies and individuals is regulated by the Insolvency Act 1986.

The Act also provides[11] a definition of the unpaid seller, who becomes such:

(a) when the whole of the price has not been paid or tendered; or

(b) when a bill of exchange or other negotiable instrument has been received as conditional payment and the condition on which it was received has not been fulfilled by reason of the dishonour of the instrument or otherwise.

The rights of the unpaid seller may likewise be claimed by an agent of the seller to whom the bill of lading has been indorsed or by a consignor or confirming agent who has himself paid or is directly responsible for the price or who, for other reasons, is in the position of a seller.[12]

The unpaid seller's lien

5–015 The unpaid seller can exercise his lien on the sold goods only if he still has actual possession of them. Where he has delivered them to a carrier for the purpose of transmission to the buyer, or to the buyer or his agent, the lien on the goods is lost.[13] If the goods are still in transit and have not yet been delivered into the possession of the buyer or his agent authorised to accept them on his behalf, the question arises whether the unpaid seller can exercise his right of stoppage in transit. This question will be examined in the next section. It will be seen that the conditions on which the Act allows stoppage in transit are very strict. In international sales transactions the unpaid seller's lien on the goods plays a relatively minor role.

The seller's right of lien is merely a right to retain the goods until the purchase price is paid and is not a right to resell them. He has, however, in certain circumstances such a right under the Act[14]; sometimes such right is given by mercantile custom, *e.g.* in the tea trade. The lien cannot be claimed for storage charges incurred when the goods are stored during the buyer's default.[15] In the case of a credit sale, the unpaid seller has no right of lien during the credit period unless, during that period, the buyer becomes insolvent.[16] After the expiration of the credit period he can exercise the lien in any event. The seller is entitled to the lien even if he is in possession of the goods as an agent for the buyer.[17] A confirming house, which acts as agent for a principal abroad, may exercise the lien on goods bought on behalf of the principal if he fails to pay the commission or incidental charges.

---

[11] s.38.
[12] s.38(2).
[13] s.43.
[14] See para. 5–017.
[15] *Somes v. British Empire Shipping Co* (1860) 30 L.J.Q.B. 229.
[16] s.41(1)(c).
[17] s.41(2).

Stoppage in transit

This right is of much greater practical value for the exporter than the right of **5–016**
lien, particularly as it has always been interpreted favourably for the seller by
the courts, but it should be noted that it can only be claimed if the buyer is
insolvent.[18] Stoppage in transit operates, as it were, as the seller's outstretched
arm, which snatches back goods from the route leading to the insolvent buyer.

This right can only be exercised during the transit of the goods. This
period begins when the goods have left the possession of the seller or his
agent, and ends when the goods have reached the possession of the buyer
or his agent who is authorised to accept the goods on his behalf. The Act
defines the duration of transit as the time when the goods "are delivered to
a carrier by land or water, or other bailee for the purpose of transmission
to the buyer, until the buyer or his agent in that behalf takes delivery of
them from such carrier or other bailee."[19] It follows that the term "transit"
has in law a technical meaning which is entirely different from its natural
meaning. Goods may be "in transit" although not in motion, and goods
which are in motion may never have been "in transit" in the eyes of the
law. If, *e.g.* the seller under an ex works contract delivers the goods to the
buyer's purchasing agent in this country, the goods pass from the possession
of the seller directly to that of the buyer, and the seller cannot claim a right
of stoppage while the goods are being shipped to the place of destination.
Only where the goods, having left the seller's possession, and are in neutral
hands, *e.g.* in the custody of a carrier, shipping agent or other independent
intermediary, and only so long as they are in those hands for the purposes
of transmission, can the right of stoppage be claimed. The right operates
against the goods themselves. Its aim is to revest possession of the goods in
the seller as long as they are in the course of transit and to enable him to
retain them and claim a lien on them until the purchase price is paid.[20] If
the goods are damaged, the seller who exercises his right of stoppage has
no claim for the insurance money, as was decided in a case concerning the
importation of timber from Sweden.[21] The plaintiff, a timber merchant in
Sweden, sold timber to a firm in London; the timber was duly shipped but
damaged during the voyage. The buyers, who had the timber insured, stopped
payment before it arrived in England. The seller gave notice of stoppage to
the captain of the ship, and the question was whether he was entitled to the
insurance money which had been paid for the damage to the timber. It was
held that the claim was untenable; in the words of Lord Cairns L.C.:

> "The right to stop in transitu is a right to stop the goods in whatever state they arrive. If they
> arrive injured or damaged in bulk or quality the right to stop in transitu is so far impaired;
> there is no contract or agreement which entitles the vendor to go beyond those goods in the
> state in which they arrive."

---

[18] See n.10, *supra.*
[19] s.45(1).
[20] s.44.
[21] *Berndtson v. Strang* (1868) L.R. 3 Ch.App. 588.

The right of stoppage in transit is exercised by the seller giving notice of his claim to the carrier or the carrier's principal, or by the seller taking actual possession of the goods if he can do so without breach of the peace. The notice to the carrier's principal, that is the line in whose ships the goods are carried, is only effective if given in such time and under such circumstances that the principal, by the exercise of reasonable diligence, can communicate it to his servant or agent in time to prevent a delivery to the buyer.[22]

The right of stoppage in transit, which originally arose by mercantile custom, gave rise to much litigation before it was cast in its present form. It is outside the scope of this work to examine the matter exhaustively. Three points however, may be mentioned briefly.

First, delivery of the goods to a carrier or agent, who takes his instructions from the buyer, does not necessarily lead to a loss of the right of stoppage. In connection with that right, section 32(1) of the Act, which has been discussed earlier,[23] does not apply. If the carrier or agent is merely the buyer's agent for the purposes of transmitting the goods, the right of stoppage in transit can still be claimed, provided that the goods are still in the agent's possession. If, on the other hand, the agent is authorised to accept delivery of the goods in accordance with the terms of the contract of sale and has to dispose of them in compliance with the instructions of the buyer, the right is lost. The courts will generally incline to the view that the master of the ship obtains possession of the goods in his capacity as carrier and not as agent of the buyer to take delivery under the contract of sale, and this applies even where the goods are delivered on a vessel chartered by him. Thus, where the seller, under an ordinary f.o.b. contract, delivers the goods to the master of the ship, who makes out the bill of lading in the buyer's name, the goods are still "in transit", and the right of stoppage can be exercised by the seller. Where, however, in the course of the shipment,[24] or after arrival of the goods at the place of destination, the carrier acknowledges—"attorns"—to the buyer or his agent that he holds the goods on his behalf, the transit has come to an end even if the buyer orders the transshipment of the goods to another place.[25]

Secondly, the right of stoppage is not lost when the bill of lading is made out in the name of the buyer (or his agent), or, if originally made out in the seller's name, is delivered to the buyer. The latter act is, as has been seen,[26] decisive for the passing of the property unless the seller has reserved the right of disposal; but these acts are irrelevant for the exercise of the right of stoppage. In fact, that right acquires particular practical importance after the bill of lading has reached the buyer and he has thus obtained the right of disposal of the goods.

Thirdly, while normally the unpaid seller's lien or right of stoppage in transit is not affected by a sale or other disposition which the buyer has made with

---

[22] s.46(1).
[23] See *ante*, para. 4–003.
[24] *Reddall v. Union-Castle Mail Steamship Co Ltd* (1915) 84 L.J.K.B. 360.
[25] s.45(3).
[26] See *ante*, para. 4–006.

respect to the goods without the seller's assent,[27] the position is different in one case: if the bill of lading was delivered to the buyer and he has indorsed it for valuable consideration to a third person who is acting in good faith, the unpaid seller's rights are defeated and the third party acquires a valid title to the goods.[28] This rule is now laid down in the 1979 Act in section 47(2) but was first established in 1794 in the celebrated case of *Lickbarrow v. Mason*[29] after six years of litigation.

The right of resale

The Sale of Goods Act gives the unpaid seller the right to resell the goods[30]:   **5–017**

   (a) where they are of a perishable nature, without further notice to the buyer; or

   (b) where they are not perishable, after he—the unpaid seller—has given notice to the buyer of his intention to resell, and the buyer has not within a reasonable time paid or tendered the price.

By the exercise of the right of resale the unpaid seller has placed it beyond his power to perform the original contract which is rescinded.[31] The property in the goods has reverted to the seller who transfers it to the second buyer. The seller is entitled to retain the proceeds of the resale, whether they be greater or less than the original contract price.[32] If the seller makes a loss on the resale, he can recover damages from the defaulting buyer for breach of contract.[33] A third person who buys the goods on resale acquires a good title to them as against the original buyer.[34]

---

[27] s. 47(1). A case in which the seller assented to the sale by the buyer and thereby lost his rights against the goods was *D. F. Mount v. Jay & Jay (Provisions) Co Ltd* [1960] 1 Q.B. 159.

[28] The same rule applies to other documents of title, *e.g.* a delivery order addressed to a wharfinger; but the third person who acquires the goods from the buyer is only protected if the buyer indorses to him the same delivery order which he himself received from the seller; the third person is not protected by s.47(2) if the buyer delivers to him a "back-to-back" delivery order, *i.e.* a new delivery order corresponding to that received by the buyer from the seller; in that case the third person may, however, claim the protection of what under the 1979 Act is s.25(1) if the requirements of that section are satisfied: *D. F. Mount v. Jay & Jay (Provisions) Co Ltd* [1960] 1 Q.B. 159.

[29] (1794) 5 T.R. 683. A delivery order addressed to a warehouseman is either a promise by the seller that the goods be delivered to the buyer or a mere authority to the buyer entitling him to receive the goods; whether it is one or the other, depends on the intention of the parties: *Alicia Hosiery Ltd v. Brown Shipley & Co Ltd* [1970] 1 Q.B. 195.

[30] An unpaid seller who has not exercised the right of lien or stoppage in transit but is still in possession of the goods has likewise a right of resale: *per* Diplock L.J. in *R. v. Ward Ltd v. Bignall* [1967] 1 Q.B. 534 at 545.

[31] *R. v. Ward Ltd v. Bignall* [1967] 1 Q.B. 534. The exercise of the right of lien or retention or stoppage in transit—as contrasted with the exercise of the right of resale—does not rescind the contract (s.48(1)).

[32] *ibid.*

[33] s.48(1).

[34] s.48(2).

CHAPTER 6

FRUSTRATION OF CONTRACT

6–001   Sometimes the commercial aims of the parties to a contract are defeated, through no fault of their own, by the impact of supervening circumstances. Where such a situation occurs, English law provides that the contract will be considered frustrated if certain requirements are met. The principles on which the doctrine of frustration is based are well settled. However the application of the doctrine is not without difficulty, for whether the circumstances in a particular situation amount to frustration is often difficult to decide. The words of Lord Diplock[1] highlight this difficulty. Frustration is:

> "... never a pure question of fact but does in the ultimate analysis involve a conclusion of law as to whether the frustrating event or series of events has made the performance of the contract a thing radically different from that which was undertaken by the contract."

Frustration must therefore be established by the court. The court needs to be satisfied that there was an outside event which occurred through no fault or blame on the party which seeks to rely on the event in order to claim the contract as frustrated. If frustration is established, the consequences are that the contract is effectively "killed" or brought to an end forthwith and the parties are free from further liability under it.[2]

The doctrine of frustration is of great importance in international trade transactions because there is a greater element of uncertainty than in purely domestic transactions, as such transactions are subject to diverse political and economic influences. It is noteworthy that litigation which was primarily concerned with international trade[3] has contributed greatly to the shaping of the doctrine in its present form.

Other legal systems make provision for the occurrence of frustrating events. The American Uniform Commercial Code, for example, provides for commercial "impracticability" where such impracticability affects the basic assumption on which the contract was made.[4] The French system admits *force majeure* whereas the German system advances the notion of *Wegfall der Geschäftsgrundslage*—collapse of the basis of the transaction. It is intended to deal first

---

[1] In *Pioneer Shipping Ltd v. BTP Tioxide Ltd; The Nema* [1982] A.C. 724; see also *Tsakiroglou & Co Ltd v. Noblee Thorl GmbH* [1962] A.C. 93. See Chitty, *Contracts* (28th ed.), paras 24–001–24–068; Treitel, *Frustration and Force Majeure* (1994) and *Force Majeure and Frustration of Contract* (McKendrick ed., 2nd ed., 1994).
[2] *Per* Bingham L.J. in *J. Lauritzen AS v. Wijsmuller BV; The Super Servant Two* [1990] 1 Lloyd's Rep. 1.
[3] See for example, *Joseph Constantine Steamship Line Ltd v. Imperial Smelting Corporation Ltd* [1942] A.C. 154 and *Tsakiroglou & Co Ltd v. Noblee Thorl GmbH, supra.*
[4] UCC s.2-615.

with the conditions under which the doctrine may be invoked and then with the effect of its application.

LEGAL MEANING OF FRUSTRATION

Frustration occurs only where, subsequent to the conclusion of the contract, a **6–002** fundamentally different situation has unexpectedly emerged. Not every turn of events satisfies the test imposed by the doctrine. The emergence of some new set of circumstances might make the performance of the contract more difficult, onerous or costly than was envisaged by the parties when entering the contract. Examples of such circumstances may include a sudden, even abnormal, rise or fall in prices or the failure of a particular source of supply requiring the seller to obtain supplies from another more expensive source.[5] These events will not normally operate to frustrate a contract. They will do so only when they create such a fundamental change in circumstances that the parties cannot perform the contract they have made. Lord Radcliffe in *Davis Contractors Ltd v. Fareham UDC* put it thus:

> ". . . frustration occurs whenever the law recognises that without default of either party a contractual obligation has become incapable of being performed because the circumstances in which performance is called for would render it a thing radically different from that which was undertaken by the contract. *Non haec in foedera veni*. It was not this that I promised to do."

Lord Simon stated[6]:

> "The parties to an executory contract are often faced, in the course of carrying it out, with a turn of events which they did not at all anticipate—a wholly abnormal rise or fall in prices, a sudden depreciation of currency, an unexpected obstacle to execution, or the like. Yet this does not in itself affect the bargain they have made. If, on the other hand, a consideration of the terms of the contract, in the light of the circumstances, existing when it was made, shows that they never agreed to be bound in a fundamentally different situation which has now unexpectedly emerged, the contract ceases to bind at that point—not because the court in its discretion thinks it just and reasonable to qualify the terms of the contract, but because on its true construction it does not apply in that situation."

In the words of Bingham L.J. in *The Super Servant Two*[7]:

> "The object of the doctrine was to . . . achieve a just and reasonable result . . . as an expedient to escape from injustice where such would result from enforcement of a contract in its literal terms after a significant change of circumstances."

---

[5] The doctrine of frustration can be applied to a c.i.f. contract relating to unascertained goods but, in view of the nature of such contract and the possibility of buying goods afloat, it is more difficult to find a frustrating event in this case than in others: *Lewis Emanuel & Son Ltd v. Sammut* [1959] 2 Lloyd's Rep. 629. See also *Davis Contractors Ltd v. Fareham UDC* [1956] A.C. 696 at 729 and case note at [1996] LMCLQ 170.

[6] *British Movietonews Ltd v. London and District Cinemas Ltd* [1952] A.C. 166 at 185.

[7] See *ante*, n. 2. See also *Gamerco SA v. ICM/Fair Warning (Agency) Ltd* [1995] 1 W.L.R. 1226.

It is evident from these observations that the international merchant is expected to have a considerable degree of foresight. He should therefore protect himself against an unexpected, but in the view of the law, foreseeable, turn of events by ordinary commercial safeguards, such as an appropriate *force majeure* clause,[8] insurance or a hedging transaction.

Frustration may be a matter of degree

6–003　　Frustration in the legal sense may occur in some cases at a stage—often not easily predictable—in a sequence of events which are in gradual transition, and it then becomes a matter of degree whether an uncontemplated event does, or does not, amount in law to frustration. Lord Roskill stated this rule as follows[9]:

> "... in some cases where it is claimed that frustration has occurred by reason of the happening of a particular event, it is possible to determine at once whether or not the doctrine can be legitimately invoked. But in others, where the effect of that event is to cause delay in the performance of contractual obligations, it is often necessary to wait upon events in order to see whether the delay already suffered and the prospects of further delay from that cause, will make any ultimate performance of the relevant contractual obligations 'radically different' ... from that undertaken by the contract."

Denning L.J. recognised this in one case[10] in which the Court of Appeal held that the sellers of Brazilian piassava, a woody fibre used in the making of brushes and the like, under a c.i.f. contract containing the clause "subject to any Brazilian export licence" were not relieved of their obligation to obtain the licence by a rise in prices by 20 to 30 per cent in excess of the prices agreed upon with their buyers. Denning L.J. said: "Was that [payment of the higher price] a step which they could reasonably be expected to take? This depends on how much was the price they had to pay to get the licence. If it was ... 100 times as much as the contract price, that would be a "fundamentally different situation" which had unexpectedly emerged, and they would not be bound to pay it."[11]

A similar question of degree arises where it is alleged that a contract is frustrated as the result of a government prohibition of exportation or importation, or as the result of a strike[12] or other industrial action.[13] In those cases the contract might, at the beginning of the event in question, merely be suspended and might become frustrated only after the lapse of a reasonable time when it becomes clear that the delay caused by the intervening event affects the foundation of the

---

[8] See *post*, paras 6–017–6–021.

[9] *Pioneer Shipping Ltd v. BTP Tioxide Ltd; The Nema* [1982] A.C. 724 at 752; *Kissavos Shipping Co SA v. Empresa Cubana de Fletes; The Agathon* [1982] 2 Lloyd's Rep. 211 at 213.

[10] *Brauer & Co (Great Britain) Ltd v. James Clark (Brush Materials) Ltd* [1952] 2 All E.R. 497 at 501. See also *Hong Kong Fir Shipping Co Ltd v. Kawasaki Kisen Kaisha Ltd; The Antrim* [1962] 2 Q.B. 26, CA; *Exportelisa SA v. Rocco Guiseppe & Figli Soc Coll* [1978] 1 Lloyd's Rep. 433.

[11] Denning L.J. supported this statement by a reference to *British Movietonews Ltd v. London and District Cinemas Ltd* [1952] A.C. 166.

[12] *Per* Lord Roskill in *The Nema*, at 752. If a party fails to take reasonable steps to avoid a strike, he may not be able to rely on a *force majeure* clause: *B & S Contracts and Design v. Victor Green Publications* [1982] I.C.R. 654.

[13] On the effect of war as a frustrating event, see *post*, para. 6–008.

contract.[14] What is a reasonable time is again a question of degree.[15] In these cases it is not necessary to ascertain the exact date on which the contract was frustrated but it is sufficient to state that the contract was frustrated by not later than a certain date.[16]

Frustration by delay

Whether delay for which neither party is responsible operates as a frustrating **6–004** event is a matter of degree and has been considered in the preceding paragraph.

However, the following must be added. Arbitration was sometimes promoted with such inordinate delay that a party contends later in court proceedings that the arbitration agreement is "frustrated" because a fair trial before the arbitrator is no longer possible.[17] Lord Diplock observed[18] that the virtual impossibility of having a fair trial in consequence of inordinate dilatoriness on the part of the parties is "incapable of qualifying as a frustrating event, even if it has come about without default by either party." Inordinate delay in arbitration proceedings may have allowed the inference that the parties have abandoned the arbitration by mutual agreement or that one party has repudiated it and the other has accepted the repudiation.[19] In both cases the arbitration has come to an end but neither case constitutes "frustration" in the legal sense.[20]

Self-induced frustration

An act or omission of one of the parties rendering the performance of the con- **6–005** tract impossible or otherwise creating a fundamentally different situation does not qualify as a frustrating event. The first requirement of the doctrine of frustration is that the frustrating event must be an event beyond the control of the parties, *i.e.* an event for which neither of them is responsible.[21] The event must,

---

[14] *Reardon Smith Line Ltd v. Ministry of Agriculture, Fisheries and Food* [1962] 1 Q.B. 42; revsd in part on different grounds [1963] A.C. 691.
[15] Andrew J. Bateson, "Time as an Element of Frustration" [1954] Business Law Review, 173; see also the same, "Time in the Law of Contract" [1957] J.B.L. 357.
[16] *Marshall v. Harland & Wolff Ltd* [1972] 1 W.L.R. 899 at 904.
[17] *Bremer Vulkan Schiffbau und Maschinenfabrik v. South India Shipping Corporation Ltd* [1981] A.C. 909; *Paal Wilson & Co. A/S v. Partenreederei Hannah Blumenthal* [1983] 1 A.C. 854. In *Food Corporation of India v. Antclizo Shipping Corporation; The Antclizo* [1988] 2 Lloyd's Rep. 93, 95, 101, the House of Lords expressed concern about so-called "sleeping arbitrations" and suggested that, by a legislative measure, the court should be empowered to dismiss arbitrations for want of prosecution, which was done by s.41 of the Arbitration Act 1996.
[18] In the *Paal Wilson & Co A/S v. Partenreederei Hannah Blumenthal* [1983] 1 A.C. 854.
[19] Silence and inactivity may, in a particular case, constitute an offer and acceptance to discontinue the arbitration but the clearest possible evidence is required that this was the intention of the parties: *Excomm Ltd. Guan Guan Shipping (Pte) Ltd; The Golden Bear* [1987] 1 Lloyd's Rep. 330 at 341. See also *Tankrederei Ahrenkeil GmbH v. Frahuil SA; The Multitank Holsatia* [1988] 2 Lloyd's Rep. 486 at 493, where that intention of the parties was not proved.
[20] See Chap. 23 for the effect of delay on arbitration.
[21] *Bank Line Ltd v. A. Capel & Co* [1919] A.C. 435 at 452: "Reliance cannot be placed on self-induced frustration" (*per* Lord Sumner); *Maritime National Fish Ltd v. Ocean Trawlers Ltd* [1953] A.C. 524. See also *The Super Servant Two, supra.*

in the words of Lord Brandon of Oakbrook in the *Hannah Blumenthal* case,[22] be "some outside event or extraneous change of situation." The expression "self-induced frustration" is thus a contradiction in terms—but it is widely used and has the advantage of being shorter than the correct phrase "self-induced inability to perform."

The onus of proving that the "frustrating" event was self-induced rests on the party raising this point.[23]

CONDITIONS UPON WHICH THE CONTRACT IS FRUSTRATED

6–006   It is impossible to give a complete catalogue of frustrating events. The following are typical sets of circumstances in which it has been contended—often success-fully—that the contract was frustrated.[24]

Destruction of subject-matter

6–007   The simplest case of frustration occurs where the performance depends on the continued existence of a given person or thing and, after the conclusion of the contract, that person or thing has been physically destroyed. In these cases, "a condition is implied that the impossibility of performance arising from the per-ishing of the person or thing shall excuse the performance."[25]

Where a ship was chartered but failed to load because it had been disabled by an explosion which was not due to the negligence of the shipowners or their servants, the commercial object of the contract of carriage by sea was held to be frustrated.[26] When the subject-matter of the contract is the sale of specific goods, as, for instance, is the case in the sale of secondhand machinery or antiques, this effect is expressly provided for by section 7 of the Sale of Goods Act 1979 which lays down:

> "Where there is an agreement to sell specific goods, and subsequently the goods, without any fault on the part of the seller or buyer, perish before the risk passes to the buyer, the agreement is thereby avoided."

However, frustration cannot be pleaded if the event which made performance impossible existed *before* the conclusion of the contract and could have been covered by an appropriate clause in the contract. A c. and f. contract for the sale of rice provided for delivery per vessel *Epaphus* "at one main Italian port." The buyers, who under the contract were entitled to nominate the port of delivery, nominated Ravenna, but the draught of the vessel was too deep for this port and

[22] See [1983] 1 A.C. 854 at 909.

[23] *Joseph Constantine Steamship Line Ltd v. Imperial Smelting Corporation* [1942] A.C. 154 at 179.

[24] On the view of the European Court of Justice on frustration see Case 109/86 *Joannis Theodorakis Viomikhania Eleou AE v. The State (Greece)* [1989] 2 C.M.L.R. 166.

[25] *Per* Blackburn J. in *Taylor v. Caldwell* (1863) 3 B. & S. 826 at 839. See L. E. Trakman, "Frus-trated Contracts and Legal Fictions" (1983) 46 M.L.R. 39.

[26] *Joseph Constantine Steamship Line Ltd v. Imperial Smelting Corporation Ltd* [1942] A.C. 154. Frustration also takes place where parties enter into a joint venture agreement for the development of an oilfield in a foreign country and subsequently the foreign government expropriates the interests of the parties in the oilfield: *B.P. Exploration Co (Libya) Ltd v. Hunt (No. 2)* [1979] 1 W.L.R. 783.

the port authorities refused permission for the *Epaphus* to discharge. The vessel went to Ancona, where it was lightened by partial discharge of the cargo. The court refused to imply a term prohibiting the buyers from nominating an Italian port where discharge was impossible.[27]

Illegality

Outbreak of war

When, after the parties have entered into the contract, war breaks out, the question arises whether the performance of the contract is rendered illegal by that event or is only indirectly affected by the outbreak of war. **6–008**

If, say, a United Kingdom exporter has sold goods to an importer in another country and war breaks out between the United Kingdom and that country, the performance of the contract by the United Kingdom exporter would become illegal because it would constitute an act of trading with the enemy, and the contract is frustrated. The same is true if in the course of the war the importer's country has fallen under the control of the enemy. Thus, in the *Fibrosa* case,[28] a Polish company had ordered certain flax-hackling machines from manufacturers in Leeds shortly before the outbreak of the Second World War. The machines had to be delivered c.i.f. Gdynia within a certain time and the contract provided that in case of war or other events beyond the control of the parties, a reasonable extension of the time of delivery should be granted. After the outbreak of the war, Gdynia was occupied by the Germans. It was held by the House of Lords that the contract was frustrated owing to war and the British manufacturers were discharged from delivering the machines. The clause allowing for extension of the time of delivery did not save the contract because it was intended to cover merely minor delay as distinguished from a prolonged and indefinite interruption of contractual performance.

If, on the other hand, the contract is for the exportation of goods from the United Kingdom to country X and war breaks out between country X and country Y, the outbreak of war affects the contract only indirectly. In this case the legality of performance is not affected by the war and the contract does not automatically become frustrated by that event. It is, of course, an entirely different question whether in those circumstances the contract might be frustrated for other reasons, in particular on the ground that its performance is prohibited by the government of the United Kingdom or of country X, or that in consequence of the effect of war[29] there has been a vital change in circumstances. These questions will be examined later.[30]

---

[27] In *Eurico SpA v. Philipp Brothers; The Epaphus* [1987] 2 Lloyd's Rep. 215.
[28] *Fibrosa Spolka Akcyjna v. Fairbairn Lawson Combe Barbour Ltd* [1943] A.C. 32. The effect of frustration on the *Fibrosa* case is discussed at *post*, para. 6–015.
[29] The effect of war is here contrasted with the outbreak of war, see *Kodros Shipping Corporation v. Empresa Cubana de Fletes; The Evia (No. 2)* [1983] 1 A.C. 736; *International Sea Tankers Inc v. Hemisphere Shipping Co; The Wenjiang (No. 2)* [1983] 1 Lloyd's Rep. 400; *Finelvet AG v. Vinava Shipping Co Ltd; The Chrysalis* [1983] 1 W.L.R. 1469.
[30] See *post*, para. 6–011.

Export and import prohibitions

6–009   A contract may be frustrated because subsequent to its conclusion the government has prohibited its performance, for instance by placing an embargo on the
exportation or importation of the goods sold in situations other than wartime.[31]
       Here, however, great care should be taken. Not every governmental prohibi-
tion has the effect of rendering the contract illegal. Sometimes the effect is
merely to suspend and postpone the performance of the contract. It is always
necessary to relate the prohibition to the terms of the contract, especially those
governing the time of performance. The prohibition operates as a frustrating
event only if it is final and extends to the whole time still available for the
performance of the contract. If these conditions are not satisfied a party would
be well advised to wait until the time of performance has expired before treating
the contract as frustrated because the prohibition may be removed in time to
allow performance.[32] If the government prohibition extends beyond the stipulated time for performance, it is normally safe to assume that the contract is
frustrated because there is an implied condition in every contract that its performance shall be legal at the date when the contract is to be performed.[33]
       The rule that a subsequent government prohibition operates as a frustrating
event only if it covers the whole of the contract period applies also if the prohibition does not come into operation at once and exporters are allowed a time of grace
during which they may perform existing contracts. In one case[34] the contract provided for the shipment of horse beans from a Sicilian port c.i.f. Glasgow during
October and November 1951. By an Italian regulation dated October 20, 1951, the
exportation was prohibited as and from November 1, 1951, except under special
licence. The sellers failed to ship and the buyers claimed damages. Devlin J. held
that they were entitled to succeed. The prohibition did not operate as a frustrating
event. It merely reduced the time of shipment from two months to one month and
after the issue of the Italian regulation the sellers still had 10 days' grace within
which they could have effected shipment. If the prohibition of export had been
instantaneous it would have operated as a frustrating event, and the same would
have been the case if the sellers could have proved that they had no shipping facilities during the remaining 10 days.
       Sometimes the government prohibition may allow exporters to perform at
least some of the contracts into which they have entered. It may thus leave
"loopholes". It may, for instance, allow exporters who have goods already on
lighters or have begun to load them on vessels to fulfil their contracts. In such

---

[31] On the requirement of export and import licences and quotas, see *post*, para. 6–012.
[32] *Andrew Millar & Co Ltd v. Taylor & Co Ltd* [1916] 1 K.B. 402; *Austin, Baldwin & Co v. Wilfred Turner & Co* (1920) 36 T.L.R. 769; *Atlantic Maritime Co Inc v. Gibbon* [1954] 1 Q.B. 105, 114, 132; *Compagnie Algerienne de Meunerie v. Katana Societa di Navigatione Marittima SpA; The Nizetti* [1960] 2 Q.B. 115, 125–126.
[33] *Walton (Grain & Shipping Ltd) v. British Italian Trading Co Ltd* [1959] 1 Lloyd's Rep. 223. *Cf. Nile Company for the Export of Agricultural Crops v. H. & J. M. Bennett, Commodities Ltd* [1986] 1 Lloyd's Rep. 555 at 582.
[34] *Ross T. Smyth & Co Ltd (Liverpool) v. W. N. Lindsay Ltd (Leith)* [1953] 1 W.L.R. 1280; explaining *Re Anglo-Russian Merchant Traders Ltd, and John Batt & Co (London)* [1917] 2 K.B. 679. See also *Gamerco SA v. I.C.M./Fair Warning (Agency) Ltd* [1995] 1 W.L.R. 1226, *ante*.

circumstances an exporter who wishes to plead frustration has the heavy burden of proving that he could not avail himself of one of these "loopholes".[35]

Government prohibitions affecting State trading corporations

The question has arisen whether a State trading corporation can plead a government prohibition of exports as a frustrating event. Normally the State trading corporation which has separate legal personality will not be so closely connected with its own government as to be precluded from relying on the prohibition. There might, however, be exceptional cases in which it can be proved that the foreign government had taken action in order to extricate the State enterprise from its contractual obligations and in these cases the courts might arrive at a different conclusion. This proposition can be inferred from a case[36] in which a Polish State trading corporation sold a quantity of sugar to English sugar merchants. The contracts, which were subject to the standard rules of the Refined Sugar Association (RSA), were made in May and July 1974 and provided for delivery in November/December of that year. The Polish State corporation had been authorised to enter into these contracts and the sugar which formed the subject matter of the contracts was intended to be Polish beet sugar. The force majeure clause of the RSA provided, *inter alia*, that if "government intervention" occurred, there should be an extension and ultimately a cancellation of the contracts. Owing to heavy rains in August, the sugar crop failed in Poland and on November 5 the Polish Minister of Foreign Trade signed a decree making the export of sugar illegal by Polish law. This export ban remained in force until July 1975. The State corporation failed to deliver the sugar and pleaded force majeure. The House of Lords held that the claim was justified. The State trading corporation was independent of the government and the evidence showed that the export ban was imposed in order to avoid serious domestic, social and political unrest. That was " government intervention" within the meaning of the force majeure clause in the rules of the RSA. It would thus appear that the courts are entitled to inquire into the motives of the government prohibition preventing the State trading organisation from performing its contract,[37] but they will be reluctant to exercise this jurisdiction if they think that it may constitute an unwarranted interference with a foreign State's sovereignty. In *Settebello Ltd v. Banco Totta and Acores*[38] the Court of Appeal refrained from expressing a view on the question whether the English courts should analyse the motivation of foreign legislation which was allegedly designed to interfere with contracts concluded by a State trading corporation and its guarantors. The court decided

6–010

---

[35] *Per* Lord Denning M.R. in *Bunge SA v. Deutsche Conti Handelsgesellschaft mbH* [1979] 2 Lloyd's Rep. 435 at 437; *Bremer Handelsgesellschaft mbH v. C. Mackprang Jr.* [1979] 1 Lloyd's Rep. 221 at 223. (These are two of the *Soya Bean Meal* cases considered at *post*, para. 6–019.

[36] *C. Czarnikow Ltd v. Rolimpex* [1979] A.C. 351. See also the cases referred to in the next footnote.

[37] In addition to *C. Czarnikow Ltd v. Rolimpex, ante*, see *I Congreso del Partido* [1983] 1 A.C. 244; *Empresa Exportadora de Azucar v. Industria Azucarera Nacional SA (Iansa); The Playa Larga and the Marble Islands* [1983] 2 Lloyd's Rep. 171 at 189. But see *Bromarin AB v. IMD Investments Ltd* [1999] S.T.C. 301, a change in legislation did not frustrate a share scheme—the parties had accepted the risk of change.

[38] [1985] 1 W.L.R. 1050.

that letters of request relating to these issues should not be addressed to the courts of a friendly foreign State if the request would be "deeply embarrassing and indeed offensive" to those courts.

Fundamental change in circumstances

6–011   A contract is further frustrated if, after it was made,[39] such a radical change of circumstances has occurred that the foundation of the contract has gone and the contract, if kept alive, would amount to a new and different contract from that originally concluded by the parties. To hold the parties to their original bargain after the original common design is gone would mean that a different contract was substituted for their original contract.

While it is usually relatively easy to ascertain whether a contract is frustrated by impossibility be it physical (destruction of the subject-matter) or legal (illegality), it is often extremely difficult to decide whether in cases in which performance would still be possible, a fundamentally different situation has unexpectedly arisen in which the contract ceases to bind.[40] The English decisions show that the courts consider the principle of sanctity of contract as of infinitely higher importance than the requirements of commercial convenience and that they will not lightly assume that a contract which is still capable of performance is frustrated. Only if the change in circumstances is so profound that the parties would have replied to another person—"the officious bystander"—when the contract was made: "of course, if that event happens, the contract is off", is the contract regarded as frustrated.[41]

If, for instance, the performance of a contract for the supply of goods is delayed inordinately for reasons beyond the control of the parties and consequently the prices which were fixed in relation to the then existing conditions of labour and costs of raw material are entirely outdated, it may well be argued that the foundation of the contract has gone.[42] Into this category fall further cases in which the contract aimed at the execution of a particular object which has been defeated by supervening events. Normally an event which was within the contemplation of the parties when they entered into the contract does not operate as a frustrating event even though they did not expect or consider it probable that it would happen.[43] In exceptional cases the doctrine has been

---

[39] That circumstances existing *before* the conclusion of the contract cannot constitute frustration, was discussed at *ante*, para. 6–002. They may, of course, constitute a common mistake (*Solle v. Butcher* [1950] 1 K.B. 671); *Associated Japanese Bank International Ltd v. Credit du Nord SA* [1988] 3 All E.R. 902.

[40] See the statements by Lord Radcliffe in *Davis Contractors Ltd v. Fareham UDC* [1956] A.C. 696 at 729, and *per* Lord Simon in *British Movietonews Ltd v. London and District Cinemas Ltd* [1952] A.C. 166.

[41] *Per* McNair J. in *Carapanayoti & Co Ltd v. E.T. Green Ltd* [1959] 1 Q.B. 131 at 148; *Per* Pearson J. in *Lewis Emanuel & Son Ltd v. Sammut* [1959] 2 Lloyd's Rep. 629.

[42] *Metropolitan Water Board v. Dick, Kerr & Co* [1918] A.C. 119 at 139.

[43] *Davis Contractors Ltd v. Fareham UDC* [1956] A.C. 696. See also *The Lefthero* [1992] 2 Lloyd's Rep. 109 and *Kuwait Supply Co v. Oyster Marine Management Inc (The Safeer)* [1994] 1 Lloyd's Rep. 637—a Kuwait case.

applied where the parties were aware of the possibility that the frustrating event might occur but omitted to provide for that eventuality.[44]

The difficulty of successfully contending that a change in circumstances is so fundamental that it results in frustration may be seen from the so-called *Suez Canal* cases.[45] These resulted from the closure of the Suez Canal on November 2, 1956, as a result of military operations between Egypt and Israel. In these cases exporters in East Africa had sold certain goods for shipment c.i.f. specified European destinations; the contracts were made before the date of the closure of the Canal but had to be performed after that date. On the date of performance the Canal was no longer open for shipment but it was still possible to ship the goods to their destination via the Cape of Good Hope. That route was very much longer than the voyage via the Canal and caused considerable additional expense. It was clear that the additional expense was not of such magnitude as to support the view that the contracts were frustrated on that account. More difficult was the question whether the necessity to ship by the alternative route round the Cape constituted a radical difference in the character of the seller's obligation. The House of Lords[46] answered that question in the negative; the court held that the sellers were under a duty when the usual route—via the Canal—was no longer available to send the goods by a reasonable and practicable route; such a route was in the present case still available in the route around the Cape. In the Court of Appeal Harman L.J. stated the general attitude of the English courts to issues of frustration in the following terms[47]:

> "Frustration is a doctrine only too often invoked by a party to a contract who finds performance difficult or unprofitable, but it is very rarely relied upon with success. It is, in fact, a kind of last ditch, and, as Lord Radcliffe says in his speech in the most recent case,[48] it is a conclusion which should be reached rarely and with reluctance."

Another line of cases, the so-called *Shatt-al-Arab* cases,[49] indicates that frustration is a legal conclusion which should not be reached lightly or prematurely. When war broke out between Iran and Iraq in September 1980, a large number of vessels were trapped in the Shatt-al-Arab, a waterway separating the two hostile countries. Legal disputes concerning some of these vessels arose, mainly on

---

[44] *W. J. Tatem Ltd v. Gamboa* [1939] 1 K.B. 132.

[45] *Tsakiroglou & Co Ltd v. Noblee Thorl GmbH* [1962] A.C. 93, HL; *Gaon (Albert D.) & Co v. Société Interprofessionelle des Oléagineux Fluides Aliméntaires; Carapanayoti & Co Ltd v. E. T. Green Ltd* [1959] 1 Q.B. 131, *per* McNair J.; *The Eugenia* [1964] 2 Q.B. 226, CA and *The Captain George K.* [1970] 2 Lloyd's Rep. 21 (where contracts of affreightment were in issue).

[46] In the *Tsakiroglou* case, *ante*, n. 45. In the court of first instance there was a considerable difference of opinion. McNair J. in *Carapanayoti*'s case decided in favour, and Diplock J. in *Tsakiroglou*'s and Ashworth J. in *Gaon*'s case against frustration; see [1959] J.B.L. 366.

[47] [1960] 2 Q.B. 318 at 370. An event affecting only a minor aspect of performance does not necessarily frustrate the contract: *Congimex Compania Geral de Commercio Importadora e Exportadora Sarl v. Tradax Export SA* [1956] 1 Lloyd's Rep. 250.

[48] In *Davis Contractors v. Fareham UDC* [1956] A.C. 696 at 727.

[49] *Kodros Shipping Corporation of Monrovia v. Empresa Cubana de Fletes; The Evia (No. 2)* [1983] 1 A.C. 736; *International Sea Tankers Inc v. Hemisphere Shipping Co; The Wenjiang (No. 2)* [1983] 1 Lloyd's Rep. 400; *Finelvet AG v. Vinava Shipping Co Ltd; The Chrysalis* [1983] 1 W.L.R. 1469. Reference has already been made to a Gulf War case at n. 43, *"The Safeer."*

the issue when the charterparties relating to these vessels were frustrated.[50] The opinions of the maritime arbitrators who dealt with these cases varied between October 4, 1980 and December 9, 1980,[51] but many considered November 24, 1980 as the date of frustration. The House of Lords in *The Evia (No. 2)*[52] declined to lay down one date for all these cases because their factual matrix might be different, the charterparties may be of different length, the discharge of the cargo may have been completed on different dates, or the masters and crews of the various vessels may have left their vessels on different dates. The only principle which emerges from the *Shatt-al-Arab* cases is that already noted,[53] namely, that *outbreak* of war between two foreign countries does not normally act as a frustrating event, but that the *effect* of such war may lead to frustration. Mustill J. summed up the position in the *Chrysalis*[54] thus:

> "Except in the case of supervening illegality, arising from the fact that the contract involves a party in trading with someone who has become an enemy, a declaration of war does not prevent the performance of a contract; it is the acts done in furtherance of the war which may or may not prevent performance, depending on the individual circumstances of the case."

Export and import licences and quotas

6–012   Considerable difficulty is often caused by the imposition or strengthening of restrictive government regulations affecting the exportation and importation of goods, such as licences and quotas. Where a contract cannot be performed because the licence is not granted or revoked or the quota is too small, it is often contended that the contract is frustrated.[55] Here the following propositions should be borne in mind:

(1) *Where the contract of sale does not contain the terms "subject to licence", "subject to quota" or a similar term making it conditional*, the question arises whether the parties intended that the party on whom the duty falls to obtain the licence or quota[56] shall be bound absolutely by his undertaking or whether he merely shall use due diligence and take all reasonable steps to obtain the licence or quota.[57] The legal position is different in each case. Where a party has undertaken to perform, he has warranted to obtain the licence or quota and if he fails to do so he is in breach, but where he has merely undertaken to take all reasonable steps the contract is frustrated if he can prove that he has discharged that

---

[50] But other issues, such as whether the ship was directed to a "safe port", also arose; see *The Evia (No. 2), ante.*
[51] See *The Wenjiang* [1982] 1 Lloyd's Rep. 128 at 130.
[52] See *ante*, n. 29.
[53] See *ante*, para. 6–008.
[54] [1983] 1 W.L.R. 1469 at 1481.
[55] On government prohibitions rendering performance illegal, see *ante*, para. 6–010. See also *Bangladesh Export Import Co Ltd v. Sucden Kerry SA* [1995] 2 Lloyd's Rep. 1.
[56] On the duty to procure an export licence under an f.o.b. contract, see *ante*, para. 2–017 (where *A. V. Pound & Co Ltd v. M. W. Hardy & Co Inc* [1956] A.C. 588, is discussed). On the question of whether in a c.i.f. contract the seller is bound to procure goods afloat if he cannot ship from the port of shipment, see *ante*, para. 2–033.
[57] *Re Anglo-Russian Merchant Traders Ltd, and John Batt & Co (London) Ltd* [1917] 2 K.B. 679, 685, 689; *Diamond Cutting Works Federation Ltd v. Triefus & Co Ltd* [1956] 1 Lloyd's Rep. 216 at 224; *Pagnan Spa v. Tradax Ocean Transportation SA* [1986] 2 Lloyd's Rep. 646 at 650.

duty but failed. The question is one of construction of his contractual undertakings.

If a party has failed to make the nature of his obligation explicit in the contract by using such a phrase as "subject to"—"a piece of phraseology", as Devlin J. observed,[58] "with which all commercial men must be very familiar"—it is very doubtful and depends entirely on the circumstances of the case what interpretation the courts will place on this undertaking. Devlin J. once said[59] that "when nothing is said in the contract it is usually, indeed I think it is probably fair to say almost invariably, the latter class of warranty that is implied", *i.e.* the warranty to use all due diligence, and Steyn J. said[60]:

> "In accordance with the principles governing the implication of terms, the court will usually incline towards implying the minimal provision necessary to give business efficacy to the contract, *viz.* that the duty is one of reasonable diligence only."

There are however also dicta[61] to the contrary, and, in view of the widespread use of the phrase "subject to" by exporters there is always considerable risk that, in the absence of such a phrase, the court may hold the undertaking to be absolute.

In one case[62] Indian sellers of jute who had sold the goods under c.i.f. contracts not containing the clause "subject to quota" found themselves unable to supply the whole quantity of goods because the quota allotted to them was too small. At the time the contracts were concluded the exportation of jute from India was prohibited except under licence and a quota system was already in force. The sellers contended that a term should be implied into the contracts to the effect that they were subject to the necessary licences and quotas being obtainable. The House of Lords rejected this view and held that the obligation of the sellers to deliver the goods was absolute. In another instance[63] sellers in Finland sold to an English company a quantity of ant eggs f.o.b. Helsinki, "delivery: prompt, as soon as export licence granted". The sellers were unable to obtain the export licence and to ship, although they used all due diligence, because they were not members of the Finnish Ant Egg Exporters' Association. Devlin J. held that "as soon as" was not the same as "subject to" and that the sellers had undertaken absolutely to obtain the licence sooner or later; the learned judge upheld an award holding the sellers liable to pay damages to the buyers. Another example[64] concerned the exportation of Thailand tapioca pellets

---

[58] In *Peter Cassidy Seed Co Ltd v. Osuustukkukauppa IL* [1957] 1 W.L.R. 273 at 279. It should not be thought that the phrase "subject to" is a general escape clause enabling the party in whose favour it is directed to withdraw from the contract in any circumstances; see *Hong Guan & Co Ltd v. R. Jumabhoy & Sons Ltd* [1960] A.C. 684.

[59] [1957] 1 W.L.R. 273 at 277; see also the cases quoted in *ante*, n. 56.

[60] *Pagnan SpA v. Tradax Transportation SA* [1986] 2 Lloyd's Rep. 646 at 650.

[61] *Per* Jenkins L.J. (approved by the House of Lords) in *Partabmull Rameshwar v. K. C. Sethia (1944) Ltd* [1951] 2 Lloyd's Rep. 89, 97–98; Denning L.J. in *Brauer & Co (Great Britain) Ltd v. James Clark (Brush Materials) Ltd* [1952] 2 All E.R. 497 at 501.

[62] *Partabmull Rameshwar v. K. C. Sethia (1944) Ltd* [1951] 2 Lloyd's Rep. 89, 97–98.

[63] *Peter Cassidy Seed Co Ltd v. Osuustukkukauppa IL* [1957] 1 W.L.R. 273. In *Atisa SA v. Aztec AG* [1983] 2 Lloyd's Rep. 579 the sellers specifically undertook to obtain the export licence; consequently the contract was not frustrated when the licence was refused.

[64] *Pagnan SpA v. Tradax Ocean Transportation SA* [1986] 2 Lloyd's Rep. 646.

to the E.C., which operated a quota system restricting the importation of these goods into the E.C. The contract of sale, which was on GAFTA Form 119, contained a special condition according to which the sellers had to provide a Thai export certificate enabling the buyers to import the goods into the E.C. at a reduced Customs rate. The sellers failed to obtain the certificate and the buyers claimed damages. Steyn J. held that the special condition constituted an absolute undertaking on the part of the sellers to obtain the export certificate.[65]

(2) *Where the contract of sale contains the term "subject to licence", "subject to quota" or a similar term making it conditional*, this clause gives the seller some, but not complete, protection: the seller is free from his obligation to deliver the goods but only if he can show that although he used *due diligence and took all reasonable steps* he was unable to obtain the licence or to comply with the government regulation, or that he could do so only on prohibitive terms which he could not reasonably be expected to accept. If he remains inactive and makes no attempt to obtain the licence because, as he alleges, such an attempt would have been useless, the burden that the attempt would have failed rests on him and, in the words of Devlin J., it "is always a difficult burden for a party to assume".[66] If the seller is ignorant of a local requirement of an export licence and therefore has failed to obtain such licence when, in all probability, he might have been granted it, he has not used his best endeavours to obtain the licence.[67]

The duty to co-operate in order to comply with government requirements regulating the exportation or importation of goods arises from a general condition implied into every contract that the parties shall reasonably co-operate to ensure the performance of their bargain.[68] This duty rests on the seller and buyer alike. In *Kyprianov v. Cyprus Textiles Ltd*[69] buyers of cotton seed which was to be shipped from Syria failed to send the seller a certificate stating that they did not intend to re-export the goods to Israel (against which Syria maintained an embargo) and consequently the seller was unable to obtain a Syrian export licence and to ship the goods. The court dismissed the action by the buyers against the seller for damages for non-performance because the buyers themselves had failed to co-operate by sending the seller the necessary information to obtain the export licence which, as both parties knew, was required.

While, as has already been observed,[70] it is always wise to stipulate expressly

---

[65] But the claim of the buyers for damages failed; Steyn J. held that the special condition did not override the clause in GAFTA 119 providing for cancellation of the contract in case of restriction of exports by governmental action of the country of origin, and the sellers, though in breach of their absolute obligation, were excused of performance by virtue of that clause.

[66] *Per* Devlin J. in *Charles H. Windschuegl Ltd v. Pickering & Co Ltd* (1950) 84 Lloyd's Rep. 89 at 93; Sellers J. in *Société D'Avances Commerciales (London) Ltd v. A. Besse & Co (London) Ltd* [1952] 1 T.L.R. 644 at 646; Denning L.J. in *Brauer & Co (Great Britain) Ltd v. James Clark (Brush Materials) Ltd* [1952] 2 All E.R. 497 at 501; *Joseph Pike & Sons (Liverpool) Ltd v. Richard Cornelius & Co* [1955] 2 Lloyd's Rep. 747 at 750; *Aaronson Bros Ltd v. Maderera del Tropico SA* [1967] 2 Lloyd's Rep. 159 at 160; *Smallman v. Smallman* [1972] Fam. 25 at 32.

[67] *Malik Co v. Central European Trading Agency Ltd* [1974] 2 Lloyd's Rep. 279 at 283.

[68] Andrew J. Bateson, "The Duty to Co-operate" in [1960] J.B.L. 187. Whether best endeavours have been used as a question of fact see *Agroexport State Enterprise for Foreign Trade v. Compagnie Européene de Céréales* [1974] 1 Lloyd's Rep. 499.

[69] [1958] 2 Lloyd's Rep. 60.

[70] See *ante*, para. 6–012.

"subject to licence or quota", it is possible in appropriate cases to imply such term into the contract by way of necessary implication in order to give it business efficacy.[71] In this case the obligations of the parties are the same as if the term had been expressly adopted.

Partial frustration

Where a contract gives a party the right of electing one of several modes of performance and one mode has become frustrated, the contract is not completely destroyed but has to be performed in one of the remaining modes.[72] Thus, under a contract concluded shortly before the Second World War goods were to be shipped from Calcutta to Hamburg, Antwerp, Rotterdam or Bremen and the buyers had to declare the port of destination; the outbreak of war did not frustrate the contract as delivery in Antwerp and Rotterdam (which at that time were not occupied by Germany) was still legal.[73] Further, where United States/Brazilian soya bean meal—a commodity having a world market—was sold c.i.f. Lisbon under a GAFTA contract but the Portuguese authorities refused an import licence, the contract was held not to be frustrated because it was not proved that the prohibition would have prevented the reshipment or transhipment to a non-Portuguese destination. A similar conclusion was reached where a contract for carriage of a rig by one particular vessel was not frustrated by its sinking. The contract could have been performed by using another vessel which had been specifically named in the contract.[74]

6–013

Apportionment of performance

It has been seen that self-induced frustration does not qualify as frustration in the legal sense, *i.e.* it is not allowed as an excuse for non-performance.[75]

6–014

This rule creates a difficulty if a person has entered into several contracts but, owing to a supervening event which qualifies in law as frustration, is unable to perform them all. For example, if an exporter sells 1,000 tonnes of sugar to A and another 1,000 tonnes to B and if subsequent to the sale but before delivery a quota scheme is introduced which allocates only 1,000 tonnes to the exporter, what can be done? The traditional view is that whatever he elects to do, whether to supply each with 500 tonnes or deliver the lot to A, he could not escape liability to both in the former case or to B in the latter. Any

---

[71] *Re Anglo-Russian Merchant Traders Ltd, and John Batt & Co (London) Ltd* [1917] 2 K.B. 679, 685, 689; *Diamond Cutting Works Federation Ltd v. Triefus & Co Ltd* [1956] 1 Lloyd's Rep. 216 at 225; *Peter Cassidy Seed Co Ltd v. Osuustukkukauppa IL* [1957] 1 W.L.R. 273; *Pagnan SpA v. Tradax Ocean Transportation SA* [1986] 2 Lloyd's Rep. 646 at 650 (see the quotations at para. 6–012).

[72] *Waugh v. Morris* (1873) L.R. 8 Q.B. 202; *Reardon Smith Line Ltd v. Ministry of Agriculture, Fisheries and Food* [1963] A.C. 691; see the notes by R. P. Colinvaux on this case in [1960] J.B.L. 236 and [1961] J.B.L. 407. See Treitel chapters.

[73] *Hindley & Co Ltd v. General Fibre Co Ltd* [1940] 2 K.B. 517; see also *Ross T. Smyth & Co Ltd (Liverpool) v. W.N. Lindsay Ltd (Leith)* [1953] 1 W.L.R. 1280 and *J. Lauritzen AS v. Wijsmuller BV (The Super Servant Two)* [1990] 1 Lloyd's Rep. 1 respectively.

[74] *Congimex v. Tradax Export SA* [1983] 1 Lloyd's Rep. 250 at 253.

[75] See *ante*, para. 6–005.

action undertaken would be of his own volition and any "frustration" would therefore be self-induced. In *Intertradax SA v. Lesieur-Tourteaux Sarl*[76] it was however suggested that the party who cannot perform all contracts into which he has entered because a frustrating event prevents him from doing so should act in a fair and reasonable manner. If he does so, he may plead frustration in so far as he cannot perform all contracts. In this case Lord Denning M.R. quoted with approval the following observations of the judge of first instance, Donaldson J.[77]:

> ". . . if the seller appropriates the goods in a way which the trade would consider to be proper and reasonable—whether the basis of appropriation is pro rata, chronological order of contracts or some other basis—the effective cause is not the seller's appropriation, but whatever caused the shortage."

When apportioning, the seller should only take into account his legal commitments. He must disregard any moral commitments, even to regular customers with whom, at the relevant time, he is not in contract.[78]

It is appropriate here to refer to American law. The Uniform Code provides[79]:

> "Where the causes mentioned in paragraph (a) affect only a part of the seller's capacity to perform, he must allocate production and deliveries among his customers but may at his option include regular customers not then under contract as well as his own requirements for further manufacture. He may so allocate in any manner which is fair and reasonable."

English law thus now adopts the same principle of apportionment as American law, namely that it has to be done in a fair and reasonable manner and, if so done, does not disentitle the seller from raising the plea of frustration in respect of the part which he has not performed. There is, however, an important difference between English and American law. English law does not allow the seller to take into account moral commitments to his regular customers but American law does.[80] Further, the English courts have not yet been called upon to decide whether a seller in this situation may include his own requirements in the apportionment. It is very doubtful that they will allow him to do so when he is under contractual obligations to others. Here again, there may be a significant difference between English and American law.

EFFECT OF FRUSTRATION

In general

6–015   The consequences of frustration have been stated by Lord Simon L.C.[81] with admirable brevity: "When frustration in the legal sense occurs, it does not merely provide one party with a defence in an action brought by the other. It

---

[76] [1978] 2 Lloyd's Rep. 509. (See Treitel, paras 5–020–5–027).
[77] *ibid.* at 513.
[78] *Pancommerce SA v. Veecheema BV* [1983] 2 Lloyd's Rep. 304 at 307.
[79] UCC, s.2-615(b).
[80] Sir John Donaldson M.R. emphasised this point in *Pancommerce SA v. Veecheema BV*. In referring to what he termed the "pro rata" defence, *ante* at n. 78.
[81] *Joseph Constantine Steamship Line Ltd v. Imperial Smelting Corporation Ltd* [1942] A.C. 154 at 163.

kills the contract itself and discharges both parties automatically". The contract is consequently avoided as from the date when the frustrating event occurs: the liability of the parties in respect of the future performance of the contract is discharged, and all that remains to be done is to provide for an adjustment of the mutual rights and liabilities which arose under the contract prior to the time of discharge. This adjustment may involve difficult problems. Thus, in the *Fibrosa* case[82] the Polish buyers had paid £1,000 on account of the purchase price of £4,800 when the frustrating event took place, and the British manufacturers had incurred considerable expense in building the machines, which were of an unusual type, to the specification of the buyers. In such a case, can the buyer recover the advance paid on the purchase price? Is the seller entitled to retain his expenses, and, if so, how are they to be calculated? These and similar problems arise when the adjustment is made between the parties.

The Law Reform (Frustrated Contracts) Act 1943

When the contract is discharged by frustration, the adjustment of the contractual **6–016** rights of the parties has to be carried out in most cases[83] in compliance with the provisions of the Law Reform (Frustrated Contracts) Act 1943. This Act was passed following the *Fibrosa* litigation with the aim of enabling the courts to adjust these differences on the basis of equity and justice.[84] Under section 1(2) of the Act, all advances paid before the time of discharge can be recovered by the party who paid them, but the recipient of the money is entitled to retain such expenses incurred before that time in or for the purpose of the performance of the contract as the court may consider just. Where no advance was paid and consequently expenses cannot be retained, the court may allow a claim for payment of just expenses against the party who, at the time of the discharge of the contract, had obtained a valuable benefit at the cost of the claimant (s.1(3)). The Act provides expressly that overhead expenses and personal labour may be included in the claim for retention or recovery of expenses (s.1(4)) and that, when the adjustment is made, the court shall not take into account the fact that a party may have insured voluntarily against the frustrating event and obtained the insurance money. However if the insurance was effected in consequence of an express term of the frustrated contract (or under an enactment), for example if it was a c.i.f. contract, the insurance money has to be taken into account when the adjustment is made (s.1(5)). The Act aims at the prevention of unjust enrichment of either party at the expense of the other.[85]

---

[82] See *ante*, para. 6–008.

[83] For exceptions, see *infra*.

[84] In the *Fibrosa* case it was held that the Polish buyers could recover the deposit of £1,000 on the ground that there was total failure of consideration. This rigid rule was abrogated by the Act of 1943.

[85] *BP Exploration Co (Libya) Ltd v. Hunt (No. 2)* [1979] 1 W.L.R. 783 at 799; [1983] 2 A.C. 352, HL. See also *Bank of Boston Connecticut v. European Grain and Shipping Ltd; The Dominique* [1989] 2 W.L.R. 440 at 454, HL. See further A. M. Haycroft and D. M. Waksman, "Frustration and Restitution" [1984] J.B.L. 207. See also *Gamerco*, n. 34, *supra*.

The Act does not apply in the following exceptional cases:

"(1) Where the contract is not governed by English law (s.1(1)). This provision lacks precision because it does not state what is to happen when different aspects of the contract are governed by different laws.[86] Where, *e.g.*, a contract is concluded in England but is to be performed in Brazil, the essential validity of the contract is likely to be governed by English law, but the incidents of performance by the law of Brazil. It is believed that such a contract, if frustrated, cannot be adjusted under the provisions of the Act, but that those provisions apply only where English law governs the performance of the contract.

(2) Where section 7 of the Sale of Goods Act 1979 applies (s.2(5) of the Law Reform (Frustrated Contracts) Act 1943). Section 7 provides for the avoidance of a contract for the sale of specific goods which have perished before the risk passed to the buyer.[87] In this case, advances paid on the purchase price can be recovered by the buyer, but the seller is not entitled to retain or recover just expenses.

(3) Certain contracts of insurance; certain charterparties and other contracts of carriage by sea (s.2(5)). The contracts dealing with these topics normally contain special provisions for the adjustment of the rights of the parties when frustration occurs.

(4) When the contract contains provisions which are intended to have effect in the event of commercial frustration; in this case the court has to give effect to the contractual provisions and to apply the provisions of the Act only to such extent as appears to be consistent with the contractual provisions (s.2(3))."

The Act specifically provides (s.3(2)) that it shall also apply when the dispute is to be determined by an arbitrator. An arbitration clause is normally not invalidated when a party maintains that the contract is frustrated, and the arbitrator has to determine whether the contract has been frustrated or not.[88]

An exporter will reflect that it may be wiser to introduce a clause in agreements defining in advance mutual rights and duties if certain events beyond control occur, whether or not such events result, in the eyes of the law, in the frustration of the contract.[89] Such clauses are, in fact, frequently employed in practice. They are known as *force majeure clauses* and vary considerably in ambit and effect.[90] That an event falls within the ambit of a force majeure clause must be proved by the party pleading it—a difficult burden as such clauses are very narrowly construed.[91]

---

[86] See *post*, Chap. 22.
[87] As to risk see *ante*, para. 4–010.
[88] *Heyman v. Darwins Ltd* [1942] A.C. 356; see para. 23–015.
[89] *Per* Lord Tucker in *Fairclough Dodd & Jones Ltd v. J. H. Vantol Ltd* [1957] 1 W.L.R. 136 at 143. See also B. J. Cartoon, "Drafting an Acceptable Force Majeure Clause" [1978] J.B.L. 230.
[90] A force majeure clause differs from an exception clause in that the latter is intended to protect a party who is in breach, whereas the former applies when a certain event happens, whether or not, in consequence of that event, the party would be in breach; *per* Lord Tucker, *ibid.*
[91] *Sonat Offshore SA v. Amerada Hess Development Ltd and Texaco (Britain) Ltd* [1988] 1 Lloyd's Rep. 145.

Different kinds of force majeure clauses

As regards the ambit of the clause, *i.e.* the events covered by the clause, it is **6–017** sufficient to state simply that it shall apply in case of force majeure. This term has a clear meaning in law[92]; it includes every event beyond the control of the parties. Sometimes, however, the parties modify the normal meaning of the clause and it is therefore necessary to construe the clause in each case "with a close attention to the words which precede or follow it, and with a due regard to the nature and general terms of the contract. The effect of the clause may vary with each instrument."[93] Sometimes the parties define the ambit of the clause in considerable detail, as may be illustrated by the following clause[94]:

> "Strikes, lockouts, labour disturbances, anomalous working conditions, accidents to machinery, delays en route, policies or restrictions of governments, including restrictions on export or import or other licences, war (whether declared or not), riot, civil disturbances, fire, act of god, or any other contingency whatsoever beyond the control of either party, to be sufficient excuse for any delay or non-performance traceable to any of these causes."

This force majeure clause, like most clauses of this type, consists of two parts, *viz.* a catalogue of "the various catastrophes there listed"[95] and at the end a general clause operating as a safety net to include any event not listed in the catalogue; in the preceding illustration the general clause is worded "any other contingency whatsoever beyond the control of either party".[96]

As regards the effect of the force majeure clause, sometimes these clauses provide for the extension of the time of performance, or the automatic suspension or cancellation of the contract in case of the occurrence of the interrupting event. Sometimes they give each party or one party only an option of suspending or cancelling the contract in that event. Expressions such as "force majeure excepted" or "subject to force majeure" mean that in the event of force majeure the parties shall be excused from further performing the contract, subject to their obligation to co-operate reasonably to ensure the performance of their bargain.[97]

---

[92] Although Donaldson J. said in *Thomas Borthwick (Glasgow) Ltd v. Faure Fairclough Ltd* [1968] 1 Lloyd's Rep. 16 at 28 that "the precise meaning of this term, if it has one, has eluded the lawyers for years". For the interpretation of the *force majeure* clause by the E.C.J. see *Theodorakis v. Hellenic Republic* (Case 109/86 [1989] 2 C.M.L.R. 166).

[93] *Per* McCardie J. in *Lebeaupin v. Crispin* [1920] 2 K.B. 714 at 720. The protection of the clause "subject to force majeure and shipment" is not available to a seller who has, in fact, received a shipment of the goods sold from his supplier but uses it for the performance of other commitments: *Hong Guan & Co Ltd v. R. Jumabhoy & Sons Ltd* [1960] A.C. 684. A party who has not taken reasonable steps to avoid a strike may not be able to rely on a force majeure clause: *B & S Contracts and Design v. Victor Green Publications* [1984] I.C.R. 419.

[94] This clause is founded on the model of force majeure clauses in *Baltimex Ltd v. Metallo Chemical Refining Ltd* [1955] 2 Lloyd's Rep. 438 at 446, and *Sonat Offshore SA v. Amerada Hess Development Ltd and Texaco (Britain) Ltd* [1988] 1 Lloyd's Rep. 145 at 148.

Another (more complicated) form of a force majeure clause is suggested in ICC Brochure No. 421 on *Force majeure and Hardship*.

[95] *Per* Purchas L.J. in the *Sonat* case (n. 94, *ante*), at 158.

[96] In the *Sonat* case the general clause was worded "or other cause beyond the reasonable control of such party"; the Court of Appeal held that these words had to be construed *ejusdem generis*, and not disjunctively, with the words in the catalogue, and did not extend to breakage or failure of drilling equipment of an oil rig caused by alleged negligence or wilful default of a party.

[97] See *ante*, n. 68.

The two-stage force majeure clause

6–018 The form of force majeure clause which is increasingly used provides for two stages with respect to the effect of force majeure. In the first stage the time for the performance of the contract is extended for a specified period, *e.g.* 28 days. If the event which constitutes force majeure continues after the expiration of that period, each party is entitled to cancel the contract.

Sometimes it is provided that the party claiming extension of the time for performance shall give the other party notice or even several notices, such as a warning notice and a final notice. These provisions, as with those relating to the exercise of the option to cancel the contract, must be carefully adhered to.[98]

Force majeure clauses in standard contracts used in the commodity trade

6–019 Sometimes contracts, particularly standard contracts in the commodity trade, contain a more elaborate provision. A contract[99] on a form of the London Oil and Tallow Trades Association provided for the shipment of Egyptian cottonseed oil from Alexandria to Rotterdam during December and January. The contract contained two force majeure clauses, one to the effect that in case of war or other specified events *preventing* shipment the contract should be cancelled, and the other providing that if another event *delayed* shipment, the period of shipment should be extended by two months. The Egyptian Government prohibited the exportation of the goods from December 12 to January 3 (during which period the sellers, in fact, intended to ship) but shipment was possible on January 31 when the shipment period expired. The sellers did not ship within the original shipment period, and the buyers claimed damages. The defence of the sellers was that, by virtue of the second clause, the performance of the contract was extended by two months. The House of Lords held, on the construction of the force majeure clause, that that contention was correct and that the clause became operative through the intermittent delay although the delay was no longer in existence at the end of the shipment period.

Elaborate force majeure and cancellation clauses were in issue in the so-called *Soya Bean Meal* cases, which concerned the interpretation of standard contract forms of the Grain and Feed Trade Association (GAFTA).[1] In the *Vanden Avenne* case Bremer Handelsgesellschaft, of Hamburg, sold a quantity of soya bean meal of American origin to Vanden Avenne, of Antwerp. The contracts,

---

[98] *Bremer Handelsgesellschaft mbH v. Vanden Avenne Izegem PVBA* [1978] 2 Lloyd's Rep. 109. See also *Hoecheong Products Co v. Cargill HK* [1995] 1 W.L.R. 404. In *Tradax Export SA v. Andre & Cie SA* [1976] 1 Lloyd's Rep. 416 the Court of Appeal held that a "rolled up" notice, *i.e.* a notice combining several required notices, was sufficient, as long as it contained all the required information. In *Johnson Matthey Bankers Ltd v. State Trading Corporation of India Ltd* [1984] 1 Lloyd's Rep. 427 a provision in a force majeure clause that the seller, an Indian State trading company, if unable to deliver the goods—silver bullion—should pay damages to the buyers was held not to be against Indian public policy when the contract was frustrated by an export prohibition of the Indian government.

[99] In *Fairclough Dodd & Jones Ltd v. J. H. Vantol Ltd* [1957] 1 W.L.R. 136.

[1] *Bremer, etc. v. C. Mackprang Jr* [1979] 2 Lloyd's Rep. 221; [1981] 1 Lloyd's Rep. 292; *Cook Industries Inc v. Tradax Export SA* [1985] 2 Lloyd's Rep. 454; *André et Cie v. Cook Industries Inc* [1987] 2 Lloyd's Rep. 463 and many others.

which were dated April 5, 1973 and provided for monthly instalment deliveries c.i.f. Rotterdam, were made on GAFTA form no. 100 which in clauses 21 and 22 contained detailed prohibition of exports and force majeure clauses. Owing to the flooding of the Mississippi in the spring of 1973, the export of soya bean meal by American shippers was greatly impeded and the shortage caused the market price to rise sharply. On June 27, 1973 the United States Government imposed an embargo on the export of soya bean meal but after a few days, on July 2, it allowed exporters a quota by which they could export 40 per cent of their contracted obligations. The sellers claimed that by virtue of the prohibition and force majeure clauses in GAFTA form no. 100 they were relieved of their obligation to ship the prohibited portion of the June 1973 instalment and the House of Lords, interpreting clauses 21 and 22, upheld that contention. One of the arguments of the buyers was that clause 21 (which provided for notices) was a condition precedent, that the onus of satisfying it was on the sellers and, since the findings of fact by the arbitrators did not deal with that point, the case had to be remitted to them. The House of Lords rejected this argument. Lord Wilberforce said that clause 21 was an innominate term[2] and not a condition precedent and that no such finding was necessary. The House of Lords further held that there was no obligation on the sellers to purchase the goods afloat,[3] and decided in favour of the sellers.[4]

Force majeure clauses which are too vague

While, as has been seen, the meaning of the phrase "force majeure" is clear in law, although perhaps not in all its implications, and its use does not render the agreement of the parties invalid on the ground of uncertainty, the position is different where the contract contains an unspecified reference to the "usual" force majeure clause and it is impossible to state with certainty which of the numerous force majeure clauses used in practice the parties had in mind. In these cases the courts have held that the clause is too vague; if it is of the essence, it makes the whole contract in which it occurs invalid,[5] but if the meaningless clause is severable from the other terms of the contract it is ignored and leaves the other obligations unaffected and enforceable.[6] The position is different if the phrase "usual force majeure clause", by necessary implication, has a definite meaning, for instance if it clearly refers to a clause usual in a particular trade. In that case it has full legal effect.

6–020

Further, it would be unwise for the parties to adopt words which have no clear legal connotation. Thus, in one case[7] a judge had to decide whether a contract embodying the clause "u.c.e." (unforeseen circumstances excepted)

---

[2] See *ante*, para. 5–002.
[3] See *ante*, para. 2–033.
[4] In some of the cases listed in n. 1 *ante*, the facts were found to be different from those in *Vanden Avenne*, and the decision was for the buyers.
[5] *British Electrical and Associated Industries (Cardiff) Ltd v. Patley Pressings Ltd* [1953] 1 W.L.R. 280 at 285.
[6] *Nicolene Ltd v. Simmonds* [1953] 1 Q.B. 543.
[7] *Per* Greer J. in *George Wills & Sons Ltd v. R.S. Cunningham, Son & Co Ltd* [1924] 2 K.B. 220 at 221.

was discharged when unforeseen circumstances prevented the seller from obtaining the goods, which he had sold to the buyer, from the source of supply contemplated by him; the judge observed:

> "It is a pity that merchants will continue to use shorthand expressions of this kind, if I may so term them, without a definition of them in the contract, and thus leave them to be interpreted by the court,"

and held that the clause did not mean that the seller should be free if the goods could not be obtained from that particular source of supply but were still obtainable elsewhere.

Force majeure clauses defeated by events

6–021　Exceptionally a force majeure clause may be defeated by events. The courts have disregarded such clauses where the supervening event rendered the performance of the contract illegal or was of such an unforeseeable magnitude that the contract, if upheld, would have constituted a new and different contract from the original one.

A force majeure clause does not protect a seller who claims that he is not bound to deliver the goods for the reason that he cannot obtain an export licence unless he pays a price 20 to 30 per cent higher than the contract price. This is not a case of force majeure; there is no physical or legal prevention of the exportation, such as a prohibition or an embargo.[8]

---

[8] *Brauer & Co (Great Britain) Ltd v. James Clark (Brush Materials) Ltd* [1952] 2 All E.R. 497 at 499; see *ante*, para. 6–009.

CHAPTER 7

INVOICES AND PACKING

INVOICES

Correct invoicing is a matter of great importance in the export trade. The smooth **7–001**
performance of the contract of sale will often depend on it. The seller may
sometimes regard the buyer's instructions on this point as too exacting, but it
should be borne in mind that the buyer may require certain details in order to
comply with regulations in force in his own country with respect to such matters
as import licences, Customs duties and exchange restrictions. In certain circumstances the buyer may request a *pro forma* invoice in advance, or for the invoice
to be dated a month, or some other fixed time, later than the date of the last
invoice.

The invoice must be true and correct

The exporter should make it a firm principle of business policy in international **7–002**
sales and other international supply contracts only to issue invoices which are
correct in all respects.

He is sometimes requested by the buyer abroad to insert inaccurate particulars
into the invoice. The buyer may ask that the price for the goods be understated
in the invoice because he wants to reduce or evade taxes or import duties in his
country.[1] Or, alternatively, he may ask that the invoice price be inflated and the
excess be transferred to an account outside his country because he wishes to
evade local exchange control on the transfer of funds abroad.[2]

False invoicing almost invariably has an improper motive. A contract in which
the parties agree that a false invoice be issued is often unenforceable in law.
The exporter should, in his own interest, decline to accommodate the buyer if
he requests that the invoice contain false statements. If the seller agrees to the
request, knowing that the contract stipulating for a false invoice is illegal under
the buyer's law, the English courts will refuse to enforce the contract because
they give no legal assistance to a party who intends to break the laws of a
friendly foreign country.[3] If in such circumstances the buyer fails to perform his
obligations, the seller may be without a contractual remedy in the English or

---

[1] *Euro-Diam Ltd v. Bathurst* [1990] 1 Q.B. 35 (where a U.K. exporter, complying with the request
of a German importer, underpriced in the invoice goods (diamonds) delivered to the importer on
sale or return terms and thereby committed an offence under the German tax code. Nevertheless,
when the unsold goods were stolen in Germany, he could recover from the U.K. insurer because
the insurance contract was not tainted by the illegality of the sale or return contract).
[2] *United City Merchants (Investments) Ltd v. Royal Bank of Scotland (The American Accord)* [1983]
1 A.C. 168; see *post*, para. 21–030.
[3] See *post*, para. 21–027.

foreign courts, unless in English proceedings the court holds that the remainder of the contract can be severed from the illegal part.[4] Moreover, false invoicing may infringe English law directly. Overpricing in the invoice in order to evade foreign exchange control may contravene the Bretton Woods Agreements,[5] which form part of English law. If this is the case, the contract is unenforceable in the English courts as far as the excess price is concerned.[6]

The refusal of the exporter to be a party to the issue of a false invoice will thus avoid a potential source of subsequent legal embarrassment to himself. Normally the seller's statement that the issue of a false invoice is contrary to his business practice will be accepted by the buyer.

The commercial invoice

7–003   The trading invoice should state the names and addresses of the seller and buyer, the date and reference number of the buyer's order, a description of the goods sold, details of package (including the weight of every bale or case), exact marks and numbers appearing on the package, and the price. If possible, the shipping details (including the name of the vessel and the route) should be added. It is not unusual for the invoice to contain the note *"e. and o.e."* (errors and omissions excepted). A typical reference to the shipping details would be:

> "INVOICE of 4 Cases Worsted Tweeds supplied by Messrs. Bubble and Squeak, of Liverpool, to Messrs. Bow and Line, of Sydney, Australia, to be shipped in SS. Aurora from Liverpool. Order Number XYZ/1345."

The invoice price has to be stated in accordance with the agreed terms of the contract, as explained earlier; it may be the ex works price, or the f.o.b. price, or the c.i.f price and so on. In the case of a c.i.f. contract, the price calculation in the invoice has to comply, in the absence of an agreement of the parties to the contrary, with the principles explained earlier.[7] The buyer will often ask that a detailed breakdown of the price be shown on the invoice, setting out separately the actual net price ex factory and the further charges, because these details are required for submission to his own authorities. In an f.o.b. contract with additional services[8] the seller is requested by the buyer to arrange freight and insurance for the consignment. As this goes beyond the normal duty of the f.o.b. seller and represents a separate arrangement, the buyer should be debited for these items not on the goods invoice, but on a separate invoice which would

---

[4] *Fielding & Platt Ltd v. Najjar* [1969] 1 W.L.R. 357 at 362 (where the court found that the British manufacturer had no knowledge of the illegality under the buyer's law); see also *The American Accord*, ante, n. 2.

[5] The U.K. is a member of the Bretton Woods Agreements. The Bretton Woods Agreements Act 1945 was repealed by the Overseas Development and Co-operation Act 1980, s.18(1) and Sched. 2, but the Bretton Woods Agreements Order in Council 1946 (S.R. & O. 1946 No. 36) is still in operation. See further para. 21–029 *et seq.*

[6] *United City Merchants (Investments) Ltd v. Royal Bank of Canada (The American Accord)* [1983] 1 A.C. 168; see *post*, para. 21–030.

[7] At *ante*, para. 2–020. *Per* Blackburn J. in *Ireland v. Livingston* (1872) L.R. 5, HL.

[8] See *ante*, para. 2–007.

cover the prepaid freight, the insurance premium and the incidental commissions and charges.[9]

Invoices in letter of credit transactions

Where payment under a letter of credit is agreed, it is normal that the commer- **7–004**
cial invoice is one of the documents which have to be tendered to the advising
bank. Here the invoice is an important—if not the most important—document.
Great care should be taken that it contains the correct description of the goods
and any other particulars relating to them, as specified in the contract of sale.
These details are likely to be transmitted by the buyer (the applicant for the
credit) to the issuing bank when instructed to open the credit; they are passed
on to the advising bank and the documents may be rejected by either bank if
the required details are not stated, or are stated incorrectly, in the invoice. Article
37 of the UCP (1993 Revision) provides:

"a. Unless otherwise stipulated in the Credit, commercial invoices:

    i. must appear on their face to be issued by the Beneficiary named in the Credit

    (except as provided in Article 48)[10] and

    ii. must be made out in the name of the Applicant (except as provided in sub-Article
    48(h)).[11]

    and

    iii. need not be signed:

b. Unless otherwise stipulated in the Credit, banks may refuse commercial invoices issued
for amounts in excess of the amount permitted by the Credit. Nevertheless, if a bank
authorised to pay, incur a deferred payment undertaking, accept Draft(s), or negotiate under
a Credit accepts such invoices, its decision will be binding upon all parties, provided that
such bank has not paid, incurred a deferred payment undertaking, accepted Draft(s) or
negotiated for an amount in excess of that permitted by the Credit.

c. The description of the goods in the commercial invoice must correspond with the description in the Credit. In all other documents, the goods may be described in general terms not
inconsistent with the description of the goods in the Credit."

The details in the invoice must also correspond with the general description of
the goods in the other documents tendered to the bank.[12]

Official requirements for invoices

Although consular invoices, which had to be completed on an official form and **7–005**
certified by the local consul, are now abolished, some countries prescribe that

---

[9] See *ante*, para. 2–008.
[10] Which regulates transferable credits.
[11] Which allows the name of the first beneficiary to be substituted for that of the applicant, though
if required by the original credit the applicant's name must appear on any document other than the
invoice.
[12] On the linkage of documents tendered to the bank see *post*, para. 11–016.

the commercial invoice should be in a particular form or should satisfy certain requirements, for example, that it should be combined with a certificate of value and/or origin. The requirements of foreign laws in respect of invoices vary greatly and are altered from time to time. The exporter who does not employ the services of a freight forwarder should keep himself informed of these changes and make certain that he dispatches the goods in accordance with the latest invoice requirements in force in the country of destination. They are recorded in Croner's *Reference Book for Exporters* and the other trade publications mentioned earlier. In case of doubt the exporter can obtain the desired information from the consulate of the country of destination, his chamber of commerce or British Trade International.[13]

PACKING

The obligation to provide suitable packaging

7–006   The exporter has to give careful consideration to the packing of the goods to be shipped abroad. Unless otherwise agreed in the contract of sale, it is his duty to pack the goods in a manner which assures their safe arrival and facilitates their handling in transit and at the place of destination. Neglect in this respect will invariably result in delay in the delivery of the goods and might entitle the overseas customer to reject the goods or to claim damages.

Packing in the sale of goods

7–007   The buyer is, in certain circumstances, entitled to refuse the acceptance of the goods if they are not packed in accordance with his instructions or with the custom of the trade. Where a particular package is stipulated, the packing of the goods often forms part of the description of the goods within the meaning of section 13 of the Sale of Goods Act 1979. It may be essential for the overseas buyer that the goods should be supplied in the stipulated packings.[14] If he has ordered jam in one and two pound jars, the contract is breached if the jam is supplied in 10 pound tins. According to section 13(1) of the 1979 Act it is an implied condition, where goods are sold by description, that the goods shall correspond with the description. This, however, has to be read in the light of the doctrine of the innominate term,[15] according to which it depends on the nature and gravity of the breach whether it entitles the buyer to rescind the contract or whether the contract still subsists and he is only entitled to dam-

---

[13] See generally Chap. 31.
[14] Although in *M/S Aswan Engineering Establishment Co v. Lupdine Ltd* [1987] 1 W.L.R. 1 the failure to perform the contract for the sale of a liquid waterproofing compound by a U.K. seller to a buyer in Kuwait was due to the quality of the packing (heavy duty pails purchased for export collapsed in intensive heat in Kuwait), the issues in this case did not concern the point here treated; they were whether the pails were of merchantable quality within the Sale of Goods Act 1979, s.14(2) (which the court held they were) and whether the buyer had a claim in the tort of negligence against the manufacturer of the pails (which the court rejected).
[15] See *ante*, para. 5–004.

ages.[16] If the deficiency in the packing affects the "substantial identity" of the goods, it will be treated as a breach of the condition implied by section 13(1).

In one case, where the description qualified as a condition, the buyer of Australian canned fruit was held to be entitled to reject the whole consignment because the cases did not all contain 30 tins each, as agreed upon, but there were included in the consignment smaller cases containing 24 tins each, and this, although an umpire had declared that there was no difference in the market value of the goods whether packed 24 or 30 tins in a case.[17] This case, if decided correctly, would indicate a remarkable extension of the rule. In an earlier case, where Siam rice was rejected because it was supplied in single bags instead of double bags, (*i.e.* gunny bags) as stipulated, the buyer was required to prove that the rice was more easily saleable in double bags,[18] and today this kind of evidence or other evidence as to the gravity of the breach is necessary to establish breach of a condition. When goods are sold on f.o.b. or c.i.f. terms, the price quotation includes export packing charges, unless it is stated expressly that an extra charge will be made for package. The exporter who wishes to make an extra charge for package should state this clearly when sending out the quotation or confirmation.

Packing in the law of carriage of goods

In the law of carriage of goods by sea, freight is paid on the weight or measurement or value of the cargo and the carrier is entitled to demand the calculation of the freight at the highest rate.[19] The seller should consult his freight forwarder in order to ascertain the mode of packing which is required to secure a favourable rate of freight, but he should not place this consideration higher than the safety of the consignment and the convenience of the customer, whose agents have to handle the packages on arrival. Where stowage on deck is agreed upon, presumably stronger package will have to be provided than where the goods are stowed in the holds, unless the goods are stowed in containers. The master of the ship will refuse to sign a clean bill of lading if the package is defective, and the seller, who under his contract with the buyer may be obliged to tender him a clean bill, will be unable to do so. The individual packages should be marked and branded in strict compliance with the directions of the buyer, who is entitled to refuse the acceptance of a bill of lading which refers to goods that are marked and branded differently. The description of the goods in the bill of lading or other transport document should, at least in general terms, correspond to that in the invoice and other documents, so that an identification of the goods throughout the whole set of documents is possible.

7–008

---

[16] *Per* Lord Wilberforce in *Reardon Smith Line Ltd v. Yngvar Hansen-Tangen* [1976] 1 W.L.R. 989 at 998.
[17] *Re an Arbitration between Moore & Co Ltd and Landauer & Co* [1921] 2 K.B. 519. It is doubtful if this case would be decided in the same manner today; it is possible that the term in question may be classified as an innominate term. See also *Manbre Saccharine Co v. Corn Products Co* [1919] 1 K.B. 198 at 207.
[18] *Makin v. London Rice Mills Co* (1869) 20 L.T. 705.
[19] See *post*, para. 15–008.

Under Article IV, Rule 5(a) of the Hague-Visby Rules, to which effect was given in the United Kingdom by the Carriage of Goods by Sea Act 1971, the liability of the carrier for loss of or damage to the goods in transit is limited in amount. Unless the nature and value of the goods have been declared before shipment and inserted in the bill of lading, the liability does not exceed 666.67 units of account per package or unit, or two units of account per kilo of gross weight of the goods lost or damaged, whichever is higher.[20] In the case of transportation by air, the statutory maximum limitation of liability of the carrier is calculated by weight and not by the number of packages.[21] In international transport by road, it is likewise expressed by reference to weight, and not to package or unit.[22]

Packing in containers

7–009 In container transport by sea a difficult legal problem arises: is the container itself a "package" within the meaning of Article IV, Rule 5(a) of the Hague-Visby Rules, or is each of the pieces of cargo carried in the container a separate "package" within the meaning of that provision?[23] The practical importance of this problem is obvious. If the container is the "package", the liability of the carrier is limited as indicated earlier. But if each part of its contents is a "package", and the container carries *e.g.* 100 pieces of cargo, the maximum liability of the carrier under the Hague-Visby Rules would be 100 times higher than in the former case. This and other important legal aspects of container transport are discussed in Chapter 16.[24]

Packing in insurance law

7–010 Insufficient packing may, in certain circumstances, be regarded as inherent vice of the goods and deprive the assured of the protection of an all risks cover under Cargo Clauses A attached to Lloyd's Marine Policy.[25]

Import regulations relating to packing

7–011 The package should conform with the legislation in force in the country of destination. In some countries, certain types of packing are prohibited or restricted and import duties may be levied on particular types of packing material, *e.g.* glass containers or metal sheeting. Many countries have strict regulations about the marking and branding of packages. The seller, if in doubt, should

---

[20] The units of account are the SDRs of the World Bank. For the conversion of the SDRs into pounds sterling see *post*, para. 15–045.
[21] Carriage by Air and Road Act 1979, Sched. 1, Art. 22, see *post*, paras 17–003 and 17–012.
[22] Carriage of Goods by Road Act 1965, Sched. 1, Art. 23(3), as amended by section 4(2) of the Carriage by Air and Road Act 1979; see *post*, para. 18–009.
[23] See, *e.g. The River Gurara* [1998] 1 Lloyd's Rep. 225.
[24] See *post*, para. 16–009.
[25] *F. W. Berk & Co Ltd v. Style* [1956] 1 Q.B. 180; see *post*, para. 19–023.

obtain full instructions from his buyer or, if it is more convenient, consult the trade publications or inquire of the institutions referred to subsequently.[26]

Dangerous goods

There exist stringent legal requirements for the packing and labelling of danger- **7–012** ous goods in transit.[27] These regulations are different for transportation by sea, air, road and rail.[28] Information about these requirements can be obtained from firms specialising in export packing, freight forwarders and in the *Hints to Exporters* booklets mentioned earlier.[29]

As far as sea transport is concerned, detailed information, including classifications of dangerous goods, is contained in the IMDG Code (International Maritime Dangerous Goods Code).[30]

---

[26] See Chap. 31.
[27] Merchant Shipping (Dangerous Goods and Marine Pollutants) Regulations 1997, S.I. 1997 No. 2367; see also Merchant Shipping Act 1995, ss. 85 and 87.
[28] See Croner's *Reference Book for Exporters*.
[29] See *post*, para. 31–009. Guides to Packaging Dangerous Goods for Transport can also be obtained from Aurigny Ltd, Menzies, Manor House, 1 The Crescent, Leatherhead, Surrey KT22 8DY, England.
[30] Obtainable from International Maritime Organisation, Imco Building, 4 Albert Embankment, London SE17 and see *http://www.imo.org/imo/pubs* and *post*, para. 15–050.

CHAPTER 8

PRODUCT LIABILITY[1]

8–001   Product liability is the liability of the producer of a product which, owing to a defect, causes injury, damage or loss to the ultimate user. The defect may consist in the quality—or rather lack of it—of the product itself, but may also be due to insufficiency in the instructions for use or in the failure to give adequate warning of a dangerous propensity of the product.

Clearly the issue of product liability is of great concern to the manufacturer who sells part of his produce abroad. It may also concern other suppliers. Of importance too is the question of whether they can cover the risk of claims in respect of defective products by insurance and, if so, on what terms.

A claim for damages caused by a defective product may be based on contract, tort, a statutory right, or a combination of these.

The Basis of Product Liability

8–002   Liability for defective products is based on one of the following:

(a) strict liability;

(b) qualified liability; or

(c) fault liability.

In all three types of product liability, the claimant has to prove that the product was defective and that he has suffered damage. If a legal system adopts the principle of *strict liability*, all the claimant has to prove—in addition to the facts mentioned above—is causation, *i.e.* that the damage was caused by the defect of the product. If he succeeds in discharging that burden of proof, the producer has no defence and, in principle, is liable.

If the principle of *qualified liability* is applied, the claimant has similarly to prove causation, but the producer has the defence available that in view of the state of scientific or technical knowledge existing at the time the product was put into circulation, he could not have been expected to have discovered the defect. This defence is known as the development risk, or state of the art defence.

If a claim is founded on *fault liability*, the claimant, in addition to causation,

---

[1] See generally *Encyclopaedia of Consumer Law* (Sweet & Maxwell); Miller, *Butterworths Trading and Consumer Law* (both looseleafs); B. W. Harvey and D. L. Parry, *The Law of Consumer Protection and Fair Trading* (5th ed., 1996); for country by country Product Liability in Europe: *Product Liability: European Laws and Practice* (1993) ed. C. Hodges; P. Kelly and R. Attree, *European Product Liabilities* (2nd ed., 1997).

has to prove that the producer was at fault, for instance that he was negligent in the manufacture of his product.

In English law all three principles are applied. The strict principle applies if the action can be founded in contract. The qualified principle applies if it is based on the Consumer Protection Act 1987, which implements the E.C. Directive on Product Liability. The fault principle is applied if the action is brought in the tort of negligence.

ENGLISH LAW

Liability arising from the contract of sale

In English law, liability for defective goods of the seller arises under the Sale   **8–003** of Goods Act 1979 and in the transfer of property in the goods under the Supply of Goods and Services Act 1982, both as amended by the Sale of Goods (Amendment) Act 1994. Liability under these two Acts is not limited to the producer of the goods, nor is it relevant that the supplier is a manufacturer selling his own goods or a merchant selling goods produced by others.

These Acts provide for an implied condition as to satisfactory quality if the seller sells,[2] or the transferor supplies,[3] goods in the course of a business. The goods sold or supplied are of satisfactory quality if a reasonable person would regard them as satisfactory, taking all relevant circumstances into account.[4]

If the goods are defective and the defect amounts to a lack of satisfactory quality, the buyer or transferee, if a consumer, is entitled to reject them and/or claim damages for breach of an implied condition of the contract, but a non-consumer may not reject them if the breach is so slight that rejection would be unreasonable.[5] The seller's, or supplier's, liability is in the nature of strict liability, in the sense in which this term was used earlier.[6] The provisions of the Acts are considered in detail in Chapters 4 and 5.

As against a consumer, the implied condition of satisfactory quality cannot be excluded or restricted by a contract term[7] and any terms which are not individually negotiated must satisfy the requirement of fairness. If they are unfair they are not binding on the consumer.[8] In other sales or supply contracts and in particular in international supply contracts,[9] contractual exemption and restriction clauses are admissible.

The limitation period for a claim founded on simple contract is six years from the date on which the cause of action accrued.[10]

---

[2] Sale of Goods Act 1979, s.14(2).
[3] Supply of Goods and Services Act 1982, s.4(2).
[4] Sale of Goods Act 1979, s.14(2A); Supply of Goods and Services Act 1982, s.4(2A).
[5] Sale of Goods Act 1979, s.15A; Supply of Goods and Services Act 1982, s.5A.
[6] *Cf.* the observations of Sellers J. in *Nicolene Ltd v. Simmonds* [1958] 2 Lloyd's Rep. 419 at 425.
[7] 1979 Act, s.55(1); 1982 Act, s.11(1), and Unfair Contract Terms Act 1977, s.6(2)(a).
[8] EEC Council Directive: Unfair Terms in Consumer Contract Regulations, Art. 3; for Unfair Contract Terms Act and the E.C. Directive see para. 3–019.
[9] Unfair Contract Terms Act 1977, s.26.
[10] Limitation Act 1980, s.5.

The E.C. Directive on Product Liability

8–004 This Directive was approved by the Council of Ministers on July 25, 1985.[11] The harmonisation of the national laws of the Member States was no easy task.[12] The principal difficulties were agreement on the basis of product liability by resolving the conflict between strict and fault liability, and determination as to whether the liability of the producer should be capped, *i.e.* whether a maximum limit of liability should be imposed.[13] The first of these difficulties raised a particularly delicate issue of policy in the countries of Western Europe. Traditionally, tort liability was founded on fault, but modern technological progress made this attitude unrealistic and favoured the introduction of strict liability in one form or another. This demand became even more acute as the United States had already accepted the principle of strict liability.[14] The problem for the E.C. was to adopt a system which, though admitting strict liability, did not discourage progress in scientific and technological development.

The Directive solved these difficulties by giving Member States the option of derogating from specified Regulations. As regards the basis of liability, it adopts the principle of qualified liability[15] as a compromise between strict and fault liability, with a strong leaning towards strict liability. However, it allows Member States to opt out of this regulation by adopting the principle of unqualified strict liability.[16] There is no option for fault liability.

As regards the limits of liability, the Directive provides that the producer's liability shall not be limited or excluded by a provision limiting his liability or exempting him from liability,[17] but a Member State may admit a limitation to an amount of not less than 70 million ECUs in case of damage resulting from death or personal injury.[18]

A third option is provided by the Directive with respect to primary agricultural products and game. The definition of "product" in the Directive excludes these items[19] but a Member State may opt to include them.[20]

The Consumer Protection Act 1987

8–005 This Act, which became fully operative on March 1, 1989,[21] aims in Part I,

---

[11] 85/374 [1985] O.J. L260/29.

[12] The preparation of the Directive took nine years.

[13] As is provided, *e.g.* by international conventions relating to nuclear damage, see Nuclear Installations Acts 1965 and 1969. The E.C. Directive does not apply to injury or damage arising from nuclear accidents and covered by international conventions ratified by the Member States (Art. 14).

[14] See *post*, paras 8–012 to 8–014.

[15] Art. 7(e).

[16] Art. 15(1)(b).

[17] Art. 12.

[18] Art. 16.

[19] See *ante*, para. 8–006.

[20] Art. 15(1)(a).

[21] Consumer Protection Act 1987 (Commencement No. 3) Order 1988 (S.I. 1988 No. 2076).

entitled "Product Liability",[22] to give effect to the E.C. Directive on this subject[23] and provides[24]:

> "This Part shall have effect for the purpose of making such provision as is necessary in order to comply with the Product Liability Directive and shall be construed accordingly."

The Act follows closely the provisions of the Directive. The liability of the producer is founded on the principle of qualified liability.[25] The United Kingdom has not availed itself of any of the options permitted by the Directive, but has reserved the right to do so at any time by Order in Council.[26]

Liability for defective products

The Act gives a statutory right of action to a user who suffers damage caused **8–006** wholly or partly by a defect in a product.[27] Product is defined in the Act thus[28]:

> "'product' means any goods[29] or electricity and (subject to subsection (3) below[30]) includes a product which is comprised in another product, whether by virtue of being a component part or raw material or otherwise."

A product is defective if its safety is not such as persons are generally entitled to expect (including its component parts), taking into account how it is marketed, its get-up, instructions for its use including any warnings, what might reasonably be expected to be done with it and the time when it was supplied; but a defect in a subsequent product does not alone establish that the defect existed in the product complained of.[31]

Damage means "death or personal injury or any loss of or damage to any property (including land)"[32] but there is no liability for loss or damage to property which is not intended for private use, occupation or consumption or so

---

[22] Part II deals with Consumer Safety, Part III with Misleading Price Indications and Parts IV and V with enforcement and miscellaneous matters.

[23] See *ante*, para. 8–004.

[24] s.1(1).

[25] s.4(1)(e).

[26] s.8.

[27] s.2(1).

[28] This definition should be compared with that in Article 2 of the Directive. For the purposes of this Directive, "product" means all movables with the exception of primary agricultural products and game, even though incorporated into another movable or into an immovable. "Primary agricultural products" means the products of the soil, of stock-farming and of fisheries, excluding products which have undergone initial processing. "Product" includes electricity.

[29] As regards "goods", s.45 states that "'goods' includes substances, growing crops and things comprised in land by virtue of being attached to it and any ship, aircraft or vehicle". This definition of "goods" differs from that in s.61(1) of the Sale of Goods Act 1979. The liability for defective products does not extend to any game or agricultural produce, except if it has undergone an industrial process (s.2(4)).

[30] s.3(3) reads: "For the purposes of this Part a person who supplies any product in which products are comprised, whether by virtue of being component parts or raw materials or otherwise, shall not be treated by reason only of his supply of that product as supplying any of the products so comprised."

[31] s.3.

[32] s.5(1).

mainly intended by the person suffering loss or damage,[33] nor is there liability for the defective product itself or any component part.[34] Any claim must be for more than £275 excluding interest[35] but there is no maximum limit in the case of death or personal injury in the Act, although the Directive provides for an optional limit.[36]

The following are liable[37]:

1. the producer of the product;
2. the person who, by putting his brand name on the product, has held himself out to be the producer;
3. the importer into a Member State of the E.C.; or
4. a supplier, who when asked by the claimant within a reasonable period to identify any of those in 1–3 above, fails to give this information within a reasonable time.

Producer (No. 1 above) is defined thus[38]:

"producer", in relation to a product, means

(a) the person who has manufactured it;
(b) in the case of a substance which has not been manufactured but has been won or abstracted, the person who won or abstracted it;
(c) in the case of a product which has not been manufactured, won or abstracted but essential characteristics of which are attributable to an industrial or other process having been carried out (for example in relation to agricultural produce), the person who carried out that process.

The supplier (No. 4 above) may be a wholesaler, distributor, retailer, principal or agent. Supplying the goods includes[39]:

(a) selling, hiring out or lending the goods;
(b) entering into a hire-purchase agreement to furnish the goods;
(c) providing the goods in exchange for any consideration (including trading stamps) other than money;
(e) providing the goods in or in connection with the performance of any statutory function; or
(f) giving the goods as a prize or otherwise making a gift of the goods.

---

[33] s.5(3).
[34] s.5(2).
[35] s.5(4). It is pointed out by Hodges, *ante* n.1 that this provision has been incorrectly implemented since the Directive states that this is the sum to be deducted from an award of damages "whereas the Act makes it a jurisdictional threshold" (at p. 671).
[36] Art. 16.
[37] s.2.
[38] s.1(2).
[39] s.46.

As can be seen from the foregoing, it would appear that any person who had any connection with the defective product prior to its reaching the claimant is potentially liable. However, there are saving provisions for the supplier where the product contains defective component parts or raw materials[40] and for the producer of a defective component if the defect was wholly attributable to the design or instructions of the producer of the final product.[41]

Liability under this Part of the Act cannot be limited or excluded by any contract term, by any notice or by any other provision[42] and liability is joint and several where two or more persons are liable for the same damage.[43]

The right of action for damages caused by a defective product provided by the Act is without prejudice to any other cause of action which the claimant may have,[44] *i.e.* in contract or tort. The statutory cause of action provided by the Act is treated as an action founded in tort for jurisdictional purposes.[45]

Defences

The defences to the statutory action for damages for a defective product, apart **8–007** from those denying the pre-conditions of the action, are listed in section 4(1) of the 1987 Act. They are so important that this provision has to be quoted in full:

"In any civil proceedings by virtue of this Part against any person ('the person proceeded against') in respect of a defect in a product it shall be a defence for him to show—

(a) that the defect is attributable to compliance with any requirement imposed by or under any enactment or with any Community obligation; or

(b) that the person proceeded against did not at any time supply the product to another; or

(c) that the following conditions are satisfied, that is to say—

(i) that the only supply of the product to another by the person proceeded against was otherwise than in the course of a business of that person's; and

(ii) that section 2(2) above does not apply to that person or applies to him by virtue only of things done otherwise than with a view to profit; or

(d) that the defect did not exist in the product at the relevant time; or

(e) that the state of scientific and technical knowledge at the relevant time was not such that a producer of products of the same description as the product in question might be expected to have discovered the defect if had existed in his products while they were under his control; or

(f) [dealt with above]."

The wording of the "state of the art" defence in the Act is different from that in the Directive.[46] However, the E.C.J. has held that section 4(1)(e) does not clearly conflict with Article 7 and the Commission's argument that the section 4(1)(e) wording considerably broadened the defence was not made out.[47]

---

[40] s.1(3).
[41] s.4(1)(f).
[42] s.7.
[43] s.2(5).
[44] s.2(6).
[45] s.6(7).
[46] Art. 7(e).
[47] Case C-300/95 *Commission of the European Communities v. United Kingdom* [1997] All E.R. (E.C.) 481.

Three factors of importance to the producer or supplier are causation, limitation periods and contributory negligence.

As mentioned earlier[48] it is for the claimant to establish that the damage was caused by the defective product and the Act has not changed this requirement.

In relation to limitation periods, where the action is founded on the statutory right of the Consumer Protection Act 1987, the action must be brought within three years from the date when the cause of action occurred or from knowledge of the cause of action.[49] But there is an overriding time bar of 10 years from the relevant time within the meaning of section 4[50] or, in relation to electricity, when it is generated.[51] The relevant time in relation to any other product is, in general, when the product was supplied.[52]

Where an action for damages caused by a defective product is founded on the tort of negligence, it is subject to the ordinary time limits set out in the Limitation Act 1980, amended, with respect to negligence actions, by the Latent Damage Act 1986.[53]

The Law Reform (Contributory Negligence) Act 1945 and the Fatal Accidents Act 1976[54] apply to a claim for damages caused by a defective product where any damage is caused partly by a defect in a product and partly by the person suffering the damage.[55]

Examples

8–008 Three hypothetical examples may illustrate the position. First, a boy of six years of age bought a catapult from a stationer.[56] When he used it in the ordinary way, it broke in his hands as it had been made in an indifferent manner and part of it ruptured the boy's eyes. The stationer had bought a quantity of these catapults from a wholesaler who had bought them from an importer; the catapults had been manufactured abroad. Under the 1987 Act the boy can sue the importer directly, basing his claim on the statutory right of action.[57]

Secondly, a manufacturer of commercial storage freezers markets them in the United Kingdom and in his export markets under his own brand name, but indicating that they are made for him abroad by another manufacturer. One of these freezers is wrongly wired and malfunctions; the food stored therein per-

---

[48] See *ante*, para. 8–002.
[49] Sched. 1, para. 1 of the Consumer Protection Act 1987, which has inserted a new s.11A into the Limitation Act 1980. The Schedule has also made consequential amendments of the 1980 Act.
[50] *ibid.*
[51] s.4(2).
[52] s.4(2)(a)(b).
[53] Negligence actions involving damage to property must be brought within six years from the accrual of the cause of action or three years from knowledge, but there is an overriding bar of 15 years from the damage-causing event. Claims for personal injury must be brought within three years from accrual or knowledge, and for death within three years from accrual or knowledge of the personal representative.
[54] s.5.
[55] s.6(4).
[56] This example is modelled on the facts of *Godley v. Perry* [1960] 1 W.L.R. 9.
[57] In 1959, when *Godley v. Perry* was decided, the liability was founded on the chain of contracts, *i.e.* the boy had to sue the stationer, the latter the wholesaler and he in turn the importer who may have had a contractual claim against the supplier abroad.

ishes and its loss causes the shopowner considerable damage. The manufacturer is liable because the defective product was marketed under his brand name.

Thirdly, a pharmaceutical manufacturer produces a drug which has an excellent therapeutic effect after long and careful tests, and being satisfied that it is harmless, he puts it on the market. After some time it is unexpectedly discovered that the drug has a harmful side-effect on a small number of users allergic to one of its components. Under section 4(1)(e) of the Act the manufacturer may be able to avail himself of the development risk defence.

Damages[58]

Where the action can be founded on breach of contract, damages for physical **8–009** loss, *i.e.* for death, personal injury or damage to property, as well as for economic loss, *i.e.* loss of profit or other financial loss, can be recovered to the extent that the loss is not too remote.[59]

Where the action is founded on the Consumer Protection Act 1987, physical damage is recoverable but pure economic loss is not provided for.

If the action for damages for a defective product is founded on the tort of negligence, it has been clear since *Donoghue v. Stevenson*[60] that damages for physical loss, both with respect to the person and to property, are recoverable. As regards the recovery of pure economic loss, the courts have recently tended to be more restrictive. The present law is, it is thought, stated correctly by Purchas L.J. in *Greater Nottingham Co-operative Society Ltd*,[61] when observing[62] that an action in negligence for the recovery of economic loss is only admissible if is "possible to cull from the close relationship of the parties the assumption by the tortfeasor of a duty not to cause pecuniary loss to the victim". Where the action is founded on a defect of a product, this will be possible only in rare circumstances.[63] Such a circumstance might be if the plaintiff were able to establish a relationship of proximity between himself and the supplier akin to reliance, which might result in the supplier owing him a duty of care regarding financial loss[64] but this is unlikely.

PROCEDURAL ASPECTS

Disputes concerning product liability, or insurance or re-insurance covering the **8–010** risk, often raise procedural issues.

If the defective product is produced in the United Kingdom and exported to

---

[58] H. McGregor, *McGregor on Damages* (16th ed., 1997).
[59] *Hadley v. Baxendale* [1854] 9 Exch. 341; *Victoria Laundry v. Newman Industries* [1949] 2 K.B. 528; *Czarnikow Ltd v. Koufos* [1969] 1 A.C. 350; *H. Parsons (Livestock) Ltd v. Uttley Ingham & Co Ltd* [1978] Q.B. 791.
[60] [1932] A.C. 562.
[61] [1988] 3 W.L.R. 396.
[62] At 413. Purchas L.J. called this type of proximity the *Hedley-Byrne* type of relationship, after *Hedley Byrne & Co Ltd v. Heller & Partners Ltd* [1964] A.C. 465.
[63] *Per* Bingham L.J. in *Simaan Contracting Co v. Pilkington Glass Ltd (No. 2)* [1988] 2 W.L.R. 761 at 777.
[64] *Henderson v. Merritt Syndicates Ltd* [1995] 2 A.C. 145.

another country, where it is ultimately acquired by a user who suffers damage, the question arises whether the user may sue in this country or in his own country.[65]

Further, in cases to which the Brussels or Lugano Conventions on Jurisdiction and Enforcement of Judgments in Civil and Commercial Matters of 1968 apply the victim has a choice: he may either sue in the courts of the producer's country or in his own courts.[66]

PRODUCT LIABILITY INSURANCE

8–011 A manufacturing exporter will have to give serious consideration to the question of whether he should cover by insurance the risk caused by a defective product bearing in mind that even the best run and most carefully supervised production line on occasion turns out a "rogue elephant". The same considerations apply to other persons who may be sued under the Consumer Protection Act 1987 or may otherwise become liable for the supply of a defective product. Product liability insurance is available, but depending on the product, may be costly.

Product liability cover is often part of a public liability policy, either incorporated within it or as a separate schedule, the cover varying from insurer to insurer and possibly subject to negotiation.[67]

Cover would include damage for financial loss caused as a direct result of the defective product, although not the loss suffered where the product did not work. However, the policy is certain to contain an upper limit for which the insurer is liable. This is particularly likely in the case of U.S. claims where the policy may contain other specific exclusions. Legal costs are included but, in the case of U.S. claims, may be subject to a limit or included in the upper limit of the insurer's liability.

An insurance policy is a policy of indemnity and therefore extends only to the amount for which the insured is legally liable so the insured may not admit liability or negotiate a settlement.

The general principles of insurance law similarly apply to product liability insurance, foremost of them the duty to disclose, the requirement of an insurable interest on the part of the insured and the object of insurance as indemnity for the loss sustained by the insured. These principles are discussed later in the chapter on Marine and Aviation Insurance.[68]

AMERICAN LAW

8–012 A brief survey of the legal position in the United States has to be added for two reasons. The United States is an important export market and the British exporter and his legal adviser should be aware of the problems which arise in that market. Further, the United States has led the world in imposing liability on suppliers

---

[65] See Chap. 22.
[66] The Convention is given effect in the U.K. by the Civil Jurisdiction and Judgments Act, 1982, see *post*, Chap. 22.
[67] For a specimen policy see *European Product Liability*, Appendix 1.
[68] See Chap. 19.

for defective goods and has influenced the acceptance of the qualified principle by the E.C.

Restatement (Second) of Torts, s. 402A

The law on product liability of all the American States is founded on section **8–013** 402A of the Restatement (Second) of Torts. This provision adopts the principle of strict liability by expressly providing (in sub-section 2(a)) that the rule applies although "the seller[69] has exercised all possible care in the preparation and sale of his product".[70]

Section 402A states[71]:

> "**402A**. Special Liability of Seller of Product for Physical Harm to User or Consumer
>
> (1) One who sells any product in a defective condition unreasonably dangerous to the user or consumer or to his property is subject to liability for physical harm thereby caused to the ultimate user or consumer, or to his property, if
>
> (a) the seller is engaged in the business of selling such a product, and
> (b) is expected to and does reach the user or consumer withoutut substantial change in the condition in which it is sold.
>
> (2) The rule stated in Subsection (1) applies although
>
> (a) the seller has exercised all possible care in the preparation and sale of his product, and
> (b) the user or consumer has not bought the product from or entered into any contractual relation with the seller."

The section provides only for liability for physical damage to a person or his property. As regards purely economic damage, the preponderance of judicial opinion seems to favour the view that purely economic loss is not recoverable without privity of contract.[72] It is important to note that the Restatement quoted above, although persuasive, is not of binding authority and has not uniformly been adopted by all the States.[73]

The reform of American law

In the United States the reform of the law relating to product liability is widely **8–014** discussed and the conflicting lobbies of producers and consumers are strong.

---

[69] Unlike the position in English law, the term "seller" in the American Restatement applies to any person engaged in the business of selling, including a manufacturer, wholesaler or retail dealer or distributor, even the operator of a restaurant (Comment to s.402A(f)).

[70] But American law admits the defence of "unavoidably unsafe products". This defence applies, in particular, to experimental drugs. If such a product, properly prepared and accompanied by proper directions and warning, is used by a knowing user, it is not considered as defective or unreasonably dangerous and the "seller" (see note *ibid.*) would escape strict liability (comment (k)).

[71] This rule is, as is usual in the Restatement, followed by an extensive Comment which is not reproduced here.

[72] See S. J. Leacock, "A General Conspectus of American Law on Product Liability" [1989] J.B.L. 273, the author refers, in particular, to the judgment of Chief Justice Trayner in *Seely v. White Motor Co* 63 Cal. 2d. 9 (1965).

[73] J. H. Tipler and M. J. Christensen, "The Possibility of Bringing a United States Lawsuit for Product Liability Damages arising in the United Kingdom" [1995] J.P.I.L. 185.

UCC section 2-318 extends a warranty to anyone in the buyer's household who suffers personal injury. This may be varied by individual States to include any natural person or omit the personal injury requirement. Many States have introduced "caps", *i.e.* maximum limits of liability for specified cases of non-economic damages, *e.g.* for damages for pain and suffering, while others have capped all derivative non-economic damages[74] but the situation varies from State to State.

---

[74] N. L. Manzer, "1986 Tort Reform Legislation: A Systematic Evaluation of Caps on Damages and Limitations on Joint and Several Liability" (1988) 73 Cornell Law Review 628n at 637–648.

PART TWO

FINANCE OF EXPORTS

CHAPTER 9

BILLS OF EXCHANGE

In every contract for the sale of goods abroad, the clause dealing with the pay- **9–001**
ment of the purchase price embodies four elements: time, mode, place and currency of payment. The various methods of paying for exports represent, in law,
variations and permutations of these four elements.

Mercantile custom has developed methods of payment which attempt to
reconcile the conflicting economic interests involved in export transactions. The
exporter's interest is to obtain the purchase price as soon as possible, however,
if the transport documents are documents of title to the goods, the exporter will
not wish to part with these before having received payment, or at least confirmation that his draft has been accepted. The buyer, on the other hand, will wish to
postpone payment of the price until the documents—and notably the bills of
lading—are no longer in the disposition of the seller. To achieve a reconciliation
of these conflicting interests, the interposition of a bank, or of banks, is necessary.

The most frequent payment methods in which banks are involved are a *collection arrangement* or payment under a *letter of credit*. In a collection arrangement
the bank receives its instructions from the seller. The exchange of the documents
of title representing the goods and the payment of the price is normally effected
at the place at which the buyer carries on business. Conversely, in the case of a
letter of credit the instructions to the bank usually emanate from the buyer. The
exchange of the documents and the price is normally effected at the seller's
place of business. A considerable amount of business is transacted under letters
of credit under which the banker, on the instructions of the buyer, promises to
accept, honour or negotiate bills of exchange drawn by the seller. Both these
methods, the collection arrangement and the letter of credit, enable the interposed bank or banks to use the documents of title as a collateral security.

Occasionally, payment arrangements are made which do not require the interposition of banks. The buyer may transfer the price to the seller on open account
or the seller may send the buyer a documentary bill of exchange, *i.e.* a bill of
exchange to which the bill of lading is attached.[1]

This chapter considers methods of payment which do not necessarily involve
the interposition of a bank and deals, in particular, with bills of exchange. These
instruments are not only used where the buyer makes direct payment to the seller
but are also very frequently used in collection and letter of credit arrangements.

The following chapters will consider collection arrangements,[2] letters of

---

[1] See *post*, para. 9–008.
[2] See *post*, para. 10–001.

credit,[3] bank guarantees,[4] and factoring, forfaiting, financial leasing and other forms of merchant finance for exports.[5]

PAYMENT ON OPEN ACCOUNT

9–002   In the simplest case, the parties agree on "cash with order" terms. An exporter who is able to sell on these terms reduces the financial risk of the export transaction to a minimum.

Sometimes the parties agree on "sight payment", either in sterling or in a foreign currency. Here, the buyer has to remit the purchase price when presented with the documents of title to the goods sold.

Sight payment is arranged when the exporter is acquainted with the financial status of the buyer and has no doubt about his solvency. The exporter sends the documents to the buyer who remits the agreed price by telegraphic transfer (T/T), mail (M/T) or by a SWIFT[6] transfer. These remittances are usually carried out through the buyer's bank. Sight payment is sometimes arranged when the exporter sells goods to his own overseas branch or subsidiary. Here, "the seller ships to his branch and settlement is usually a matter of periodical remittance. There may even be a two-way trading, as where raw materials are drawn from the territory where the products are finally marketed, in which case settlement between parent and offspring is a matter of running accounts and periodical remittances of balances due."[7]

If the exporter is not familiar with the financial status of the buyer or other circumstances demand it, he can arrange that the purchase price shall be paid "cash against documents" or "cash on delivery". These clauses are particularly suitable when delivery of the goods sold is to take place ex works. "Cash on delivery" can also be arranged for transportation of goods by land under the CMR.[8] In f.o.b. or c.i.f. contracts direct payment by the buyer is not the normal method of payment; usually payment is effected through a bank, either under a collection arrangement[9] or under a letter of credit.[10]

PAYMENT BY BILLS OF EXCHANGE[11]

9–003   Normally, the buyer does not remit the purchase price on open account, but

---

[3] See *post*, para. 11–001.
[4] See *post*, para. 12–001.
[5] See *post*, para. 13–001.
[6] An independent network operated by the Society for World Wide International Financial Communications. See Geva, *The Law of Electronic Funds Transfers* (1992); Brindle and Cox, *Law of Bank Payments* (1996).
[7] W. W. Syrett, "Finance of Exports", in *Talks about Exports*, published by the Institute of Export, Pitman, p. 441; on countertrade see *post*, para. 14–001.
[8] See *post*, para. 18–001.
[9] See *post*, para. 10–001.
[10] See *post*, para. 11–001.
[11] On Bills of Exchange generally see Chalmers and Guest, *Bills of Exchange, Cheques and Promissory Notes* (15th ed., 1998); Chitty, *Contracts* (28th ed., 1999), Chap. 34; Hedley, *Bills of Exchange and Bankers' Documentary Credits*, (3rd. ed., 1997).

allows the exporter to draw a bill of exchange[12] on him.[13] This arrangement offers advantages to both parties. The exporter obtains a negotiable instrument which he can turn into cash by negotiation at once, and the buyer is allowed a definite period of credit for settlement unless the bill is payable at sight.[14] If the parties fail to make express arrangements, the custom prevailing in the particular trade determines whether the price is to be paid on open account or by bill, and on which terms the latter has to be drawn.

Nature of the bill of exchange

The law governing bills of exchange is codified in the Bills of Exchange Act 1882. This Act, which has been described[15] as "the best drafted Act of Parliament ever passed", should be studied carefully by everyone who has to deal with bills of exchange. The Act defines in section 3 a bill of exchange as:

9–004

> "... an unconditional order in writing, addressed by one person to another, signed by the person giving it, requiring the person to whom it is addressed to pay on demand or at a fixed or determinable future time a sum certain in money to or to the order of a specified person, or to bearer."

This definition can be expressed in graphic form as follows:

	London, January 10, 20 . . . .
£10,000	*On demand** pay *Britannia Bank Limited or Order*** the sum of ten thousand pounds for value received. Exports Limited
To Imports Inc, Boston, U.S.A.	

*or—On March 10, 19 . . . **or—Bearer
*or—Ninety days after sight.

There are three original parties to a bill of exchange: the drawer, the drawee and the payee. They are, in the preceding example: Exports Ltd (the drawer),

---

[12] The expression "bill of exchange" and "draft" have the same meaning.
[13] For an example of such a transaction, see *Credito Italiano v. M. Birnhak & Sons Ltd* [1967] 1 Lloyd's Rep. 314 at 320. A similar arrangement was agreed upon by the parties to a c. and f. contract in *Leigh and Sillivan Ltd v. Aliakmon Shipping Co Ltd* [1985] Q.B. 350, CA, affd [1986] A.C. 785, HL, but in this case the bill of exchange was to be endorsed by the buyer's bank (in the circumstances the bank declined to back the bill).
[14] On negotiation, see *post*, para. 9–011; on sight bills and time bills, see *post*, para. 9–004.
[15] *Per* MacKinnon L.J. in *Bank Polski v. K.J. Mulder & Co* [1942] 1 K.B. 497 at 500.

Imports Inc (the drawee), and Britannia Bank Ltd (the payee). The drawer and the payee, or the drawee and the payee may be the same person, but where the drawer and the drawee are the same person the bill may be treated, at the option of the holder of the bill, as a promissory note or a bill of exchange (s.5).[16]

The characteristics of a bill of exchange are:

(a) Every obligation arising under the bill must be expressed in writing on the bill and signed by the party liable (s.23).

(b) The obligations stipulated in the bill can be transferred easily by "negotiation" of the bill, often in performance of the sale of the bill at a discount if the bill is a time bill, *i.e.* contains a credit element. The negotiation is done, in the case of a bill to bearer, by mere delivery of the bill, and, in the case of a bill to order, both by delivery of the bill and indorsement (s.31).[17]

(c) Performance of the obligations stipulated in the bill can only be claimed by a person holding the document. This person is called the holder of the bill and is defined, in section 2, as the payee or indorsee or bearer of the bill, who is in possession of the bill.

(d) The person to whom a bill is negotiated may acquire a better right under it than his predecessors possess. This is a remarkable exception to the common law principle that no transferee can acquire a better title than his transferor. The object of this rule is to facilitate the negotiation of bills.

Section 38(2) expresses the rule as follows:

> "where he [*i.e.* the holder of a bill] is 'holder in due course', he holds the bill free from any defect of title of prior parties, as well as from mere personal defences available to prior parties amongst themselves, and may enforce payment against all parties liable on the bill."

A *holder in due course* is a holder who took a bill, which is complete and regular on the face of it, in good faith and for value and without notice of any defect in the title of the person negotiating it to him, and before it was overdue and without notice that it was dishonoured (s.29(1)). A holder who derives his title through a holder in due course and who is not himself a party to any fraud or illegality affecting the bill, has all the rights of that holder in due course as regards the acceptor and all parties to the bill prior to that holder (s.29(3)). Consequently, where a bill is negotiated to a holder in due course but later on dishonour is returned into the possession of the drawer, the latter, by virtue of

---

[16] References here and on the following pages are to the Bills of Exchange Act 1882.
[17] Since the passing of the Cheques Act 1992, cheques bearing the words "account payee" or "a/c payee" are not transferable and thus are now no longer negotiable instruments; s. 81A(1) as inserted by Cheques Act 1992, s.1.

section 29(3), has all the rights of that holder in due course.[18] A holder of a bill is prima facie presumed to be a holder in due course, but if it is admitted or proved that the acceptance, issue or subsequent negotiation of the bill is affected by fraud,[19] duress or force and fear, or illegality, the burden of proof is shifted. In these circumstances the holder has to prove, first, that value was given at the relevant time and, secondly, that he acted in good faith (s.30(2)).[20]

It should be noted that a bill of exchange does not represent an individual obligation but contains a number of obligations which, while being independent in certain respects, are in others closely interconnected since they are embodied in the same document. Generally, all three original parties are liable to honour the bill: the drawer by drawing it (s.55); the drawee by writing his acceptance on, or usually across, the bill, whereby he becomes the acceptor (s.17); and the payee by indorsing the bill when negotiating it, whereby he becomes the indorser (s.55(2)(a)).

Sometimes, a bill may be considered to be irregular if, for instance, it bears an irregular indorsement. "When is an indorsement irregular? Lord Denning held that it is irregular whenever it is such as to give rise to doubt whether it is the indorsement of the named payee. A bill of exchange is like currency. It should be above suspicion."[21]

In principle, every person signing a bill of exchange, even the mere "backer" of the bill (s.56), incurs liability,[22] but the drawer or an indorser can negative his liability by adding the words "without recourse" (*sans recours*) to his signature.

Further, a person signing a bill as drawer, indorser or acceptor can negative his liability by adding words to his signature indicating that he signs for or on behalf of a principal or in a representative capacity[23]; but the addition of descriptive words, such as "commission agent" or "company director", may not be sufficient to exempt him from personal liability (s.26(1)).

The primary liability to pay the bill rests upon the drawee. The drawer and indorsers are only liable on recourse, *i.e.* if the drawee dishonours the bill and they have received notice of dishonour by the holder or a subsequent indorser. Return of the dishonoured bill is a sufficient notice of dishonour (s.49(6)).

A bill payable on demand (*sight bill*) is dishonoured if it is not paid on presentation. A *time bill* is dishonoured if it is not accepted by the drawee when presented to him for acceptance (unless presentment is excused) or if not paid

---

[18] *Jade International Steel Stahl und Eisen GmbH & Co KG v. Robert Nicholas (Steels) Ltd* [1978] Q.B. 917.
[19] "Fraud" means here a common law fraud, *i.e.* dishonesty: *Osterreichische Landerbank v. S'Elite Ltd* [1981] Q.B. 565.
[20] *Bank of Cyprus (London) Ltd v. Jones* (1984) 134 N.L.J. 522.
[21] *Per* Denning L.J. in *Arab Bank Ltd v. Ross* [1952] 2 Q.B. 216 at 227. "Face" was held to mean both the front and back of the bill.
[22] See *post*, para. 9–009.
[23] But where the bill was accepted by a company and later indorsed by a director "for and on behalf of the company" the director was held to be personally liable because the company was already liable on the acceptance and his intention must have been to bind himself (s.26(2)): *Rolfe Lubbell & Co v. Keith and Greenwood* [1979] 2 Lloyd's Rep. 75; this decision rests on its facts and does not reveal a general principle; see also *Novaknit Hellas SA v. Kumas Bros International Ltd* [1998] C.L.C. 971, CA.

by him. Presentment for acceptance is required where the bill is payable a certain time after sight in order to fix the maturity of the bill (s.39(1)). There is, of course, no presentment for acceptance in the case of a sight bill. In the case of a time bill, the bill is due and payable on the last day of the time of payment as fixed by the bill. If that is a non-business day, the bill is due on the succeeding business day.[24]

Bills of exchange must be presented for payment "by the holder or by some person authorised to receive payment on his behalf at a reasonable hour on a business day, at the proper place as hereinafter defined, either to the person designated by the bill as payer, or to some person authorised to pay or refuse payment on his behalf if with the exercise of reasonable diligence such person can be found" (s.45(3)). Further, the holder must exhibit the bill to the person from whom he demands payment and deliver it to him when it is honoured. (s. 52(4)).

The Deregulation (Bills of Exchange) Order 1996[25] now allows collecting banks to present cheques for payment by notification of the "essential features by electronic means or otherwise" of the cheque, instead of presenting the cheque itself.[26]

The drawer or any indorser may insert in the bill the name of a person to whom the holder may resort if the bill is dishonoured by non-acceptance or non-payment (s.15). Such person is called "the referee in case of need". The bill must be protested or noted[27] before it can be presented to the referee (s.67). In the United Kingdom presentment in case of need is optional, but in many overseas countries such presentment is obligatory.

The time of payment is normally inserted in the bill when it is drawn. The bill is either a sight bill or a time bill, in banking language also called a term bill or usance bill. The latter expression originally referred to a time bill drawn for a period customary in a particular trade. A sight bill is defined in section 10(1) of the Act, as a bill:

> "(a) which is expressed to be payable on demand, or at sight, or on presentation, or
>
> (b) in which no time for payment is expressed."

A time bill is payable at a fixed future time or a determinable future time (ss.10, 11). In the latter case it is usually payable a fixed period after date or sight, *e.g.* "ninety days after sight". A bill payable at an uncertain date or on a contingency is not a bill of exchange in the meaning of the law; consequently, a bill would be bad if payable "on or before" a certain date[28]; "by" a certain date,[29] "after sight", or "on arrival of steamer".[30]

---

[24] s.14(1) as substituted by the Banking and Financial Dealing Act 1971, s.3(2).
[25] S.I. 1996 No. 2993.
[26] See s.74B(1) as amended by s.4(1) of the Deregulation (Bills of Exchange) Order 1996.
[27] See *post*, paras 9–005 and 10–003.
[28] *Williamson v. Rider* [1963] 1 Q.B. 89.
[29] *Claydon v. Bradley* [1987] 1 W.L.R. 521.
[30] It was held in *Korea Exchange Bank v. Debenhams (Central Buying) Ltd* [1979] 1 Lloyd's Rep. 548 at 551, CA that the words "At 90 days documents against acceptance . . . pay" were "gibberish" and the instrument was not payable at a fixed or determinable future time and thus was not a bill

The place of payment is specified in the bill by the drawer or, if the drawer fails to do so, by the acceptor when accepting the bill. Usually, a bill is made payable at a banker's office, but this is not a requirement of the law. Where a particular place is specified as the place of payment, that place is not regarded as the exclusive place of payment (s.19(2)(c)), and the acceptor can be sued for payment at another place. But where it is expressly stated that the bill shall be paid at the particular place only and not elsewhere, the acceptor can only be sued at that place. Where the acceptor adds an exclusive place of payment to his acceptance, the holder of the bill is entitled to treat the acceptance as qualified and the bill as dishonoured (s.44), but he cannot claim this right if the place of payment is not made exclusive. In one case[31] a Polish firm drew a bill on "X Y, Plantation House, Mincing Lane, London, payable in Amsterdam at the A B Bank". The bill was drawn on May 1, 1939, and payable in Dutch florins on November 1, 1939. It was duly accepted by X Y, but could not be presented in Amsterdam owing to the outbreak of the Second World War. Although the place of payment was in Holland and the stipulated currency Dutch florins, the court held that the plaintiff was entitled to recovery from X Y in London because Amsterdam was not stipulated as the only place of payment.

Foreign bills

The Bills of Exchange Act 1882 contains important provisions dealing with foreign bills.[32] A foreign bill is a bill which: **9–005**

(a) either is drawn by a person who is not resident in the British Islands[33];

(b) or is drawn by a person resident in the British Islands on a person resident abroad *and* is payable abroad.

All other bills are inland bills (s.4). It should be noted that a bill is not necessarily a foreign bill if it is payable abroad or if the drawee resides abroad; only if these two elements are combined is the bill a foreign bill, while it is always a foreign bill if the drawer resides abroad. If it is uncertain whether a bill is an inland bill or a foreign bill, it is treated as an inland bill (s.4(2)). The main difference between inland bills and foreign bills is that the latter, as a rule, must be formally protested upon dishonour by non-acceptance or by non-payment (s.51), while no protest is required for inland bills. In this respect English law differs from many foreign laws which likewise prescribe a protest for inland bills. In view of these and other differences between English and foreign law,

---

of exchange. See also *Novaknit Hellas SA v. Kumar Bros International Ltd* [1998] C.L.C. 971, CA; *Hong Kong and Shanghai Banking Corp Ltd v. GD Trade Co Ltd* [1998] C.L.C. 238, CA.
[31] *Bank Polski v. K.J. Mulder & Co* [1942] 1 K.B. 497.
[32] Dicey and Morris, *The Conflict of Laws* (13th ed., 2000), Vol. 2, p. 1435 *et seq.*
[33] The term "British Islands" includes any part of the United Kingdom of Great Britain and Ireland, the Islands of Man, Guernsey, Jersey, Alderney and Sark, and the islands adjacent to any of them being part of the dominions of the Crown.

it is often important to know whether the obligation of a person who signed a bill is to be judged by English law or a particular system of foreign law. The Act contains, in section 72, detailed rules on the conflict of laws relating to bills of exchange.[34]

Where the bill is expressed in foreign currency, but is payable in England, judgment can be obtained in the English courts in foreign currency.[35]

The UN Convention on International Bills of Exchange and International Promissory Notes (1988)

9–006   Globally, the law of bills of exchange is divided into two legal families. They are the Geneva system, founded on the Geneva Conventions,[36] which has been adopted in civil law jurisdictions, and the Anglo-American system, which applies in the United Kingdom, most countries of the Commonwealth, the United States and other common law jurisdictions.

In order to reconcile these two systems, UNCITRAL prepared a Convention on International Bills of Exchange and Promissory Notes[37] which was approved by the General Assembly of the United Nations on December 9, 1988. The Convention's aim is to create special instruments which persons engaged in international trade might use in place of the existing instruments to make payment or to give credit. Its provisions will apply only if the instrument in question is designated "International Bill of Exchange (UNCITRAL Convention)" or "International Promissory Note (UNCITRAL Convention)" and this designation must appear in the heading and the text of the instrument.

At the time of writing, the Convention has not been adopted in the United Kingdom. It will come into operation 12 months after the date of deposit of the instrument of ratification or accession by 10 States.

The claused bill

9–007   The draft customary in the export trade is not normally in the simple form set out at *ante*, para. 9–003, but contains a number of additional clauses. The following is an example of a draft as used in export transactions:

---

[34] This section is reproduced in Dicey and Morris, *op. cit.* as Rule 195, on p. 1453 *et seq.* where it is commented upon.
[35] Administration of Justice Act 1977, s.4 (repealing BOE ss. 57(2) and 72(4) and see *Barclays Bank International Ltd v. Levin Brothers (Bradford) Ltd* [1977] Q.B. 270; Chalmers and Guest (15th ed.), paras. 1824–28.
[36] There are three Geneva Conventions on the Unification of the Law relating to Bills of Exchange of June 7, 1930, and three further Conventions signed at Geneva on the Unification of the Law relating to Cheques of March 19, 1931.
[37] The text of the Convention may be found in Chalmers and Guest (15th ed.) and at *http://www.uncitral/.org*; see also Ademuni-Odeke, *The United Nations Convention on International Bills of Exchange and Promissory Notes* [1992] J.B.L. 281.

No. 1285

Liverpool, February 15,
20 . . . .

Ninety days after sight of this our First of Exchange (Second and Third of the same date and tenor unpaid) pay Britannia Bank Limited or Order the sum of ten thousand Pounds Sterling, payable at the collecting Bank's selling rate for sight drafts on $10,000 London, with interest at 12 per cent per annum added thereto from date hereof to due date of payment, value received.

$10,000

Exports Limited.

To:
Imports Inc,
Boston,
U.S.A.

Particular regard should be had to the clauses providing for payment at a specific rate of exchange or adding, to the sum payable, interest or specified charges. Thus, payment is stipulated "at the collecting bank's selling rate for sight drafts on London" and it is provided that "interest at 12 per cent per annum . . . from date hereof to due date of payment" shall be added to the stipulated sum. Such clauses are very common, particularly when the bill is made payable in foreign currency because various rates of exchange normally exist for the currencies in force at the buyer's and seller's residence, and it is unavoidable, when the bill is negotiated, that incidental expenses, such as bankers' charges or foreign stamp duties, are incurred. Even where payment has to be made by sterling draft it is advisable to insert exchange and charges clauses in the bill in order to define with certainty the financial obligations of the parties in the case of any unforeseen fluctuations in the rate of exchange.

The following "floating" exchange clauses are found in drafts used in export transactions:

(a) payable at the bank's drawing rate for demand drafts on London;

(b) payable at collecting bank's selling rate for Telegraphic Transfer;

(c) payable at collecting bank's selling rate for sight drafts on London;

(d) payable at collecting bank's selling rate for 90 days after sight drafts on London;

(e) payable by approved bank's draft on London, exchange per indorsement.

Some of these clauses are customary in the trade with particular overseas countries and others are used where the buyer intends to obtain finance in a particular manner. Thus, "exchange as per indorsement" clauses are mainly used where the seller wishes to discount the bill to bank; the bank then includes its discount in the sum payable when converting the stipulated currency into the local currency of the drawee.[38]

As alternatives to the clause stated in the example, *supra*, the following clauses relating to charges and interest are found, sometimes combined with one another and added to an exchange clause:

(a) payable with interest at ... per cent per annum from date hereof to due date of arrival of remittance in London;

(b) payable with exchange;

(c) payable without loss in exchange;

(d) payable with stamps;

(e) payable with bankers' charges;

(f) payable with collecting bank's charges;

(g) payable with negotiating bank's charges.

If the bill does not provide for payment of interest from the date of the bill, interest can only be demanded from the time of maturity of the bill (s.57(1)(b)). If the bill does not provide that the incidental charges should be borne by the drawee, they fall upon the drawer.

From the legal point of view, no objection exists to inserting in the bill clauses regulating the rate of exchange or the payment of interest or charges. The Bills of Exchange Act 1882 provides that the sum payable by the bill has to be "a sum certain in money",[39] but adds in section 9(1) that:

> "the sum payable by a bill is a sum certain within the meaning of this Act, although it is required to be paid—
>
> (a) With interest
>
> ...
>
> (d) According to an indicated rate of exchange or according to a rate of exchange to be ascertained as directed by the bill."

The clause "payable with interest at ... per cent per annum from date hereof to due date of arrival of remittance in London" is of doubtful legal validity. It was held by a court in Australia[40] that the clause was invalid on the ground of uncertainty, mainly because the terminal date of interest could not be ascertained from anything appearing on the face of the bill. It is submitted, with great

---

[38] In view of the possibility of currency devaluations, it is advisable to specify the exchange calculation expressly in the indorsement and not to rely on the details on the front of the bill: *Tropic Plastic and Packaging Industry v. Standard Bank of South Africa Ltd* 1969 (4) S.A.L.R. 108; see the note in [1970] J.B.L. 121–122.

[39] See *ante*, para. 9–004.

[40] *Commonwealth Bank of Australia v. Rosenhain & Co* [1922] Vic.L.R. 155 (High Court of Australia).

respect, that this view is incorrect. That the requirement of payment of interest does not invalidate the bill is expressly provided by section 9(1)(a) of the Act of 1882. The payment of interest is merely ancillary to the payment of the main sum, and it is thought that the requirement of certainty does not extend to ancillary sums, such as interest and exchange, with the same rigour as to the main sum. But the rate of interest must be specified in the bill. Banks in the City of London sometimes consider the clause under examination as unacceptable on the ground of uncertainty. However, the English courts have not yet been called upon to give their ruling on the clause.

The clause "payable without loss in exchange" is designed to protect the drawer against loss caused by an adverse alteration of the rate of exchange, particularly during the time which might elapse between the deposit of the price by the buyer in local currency with his bank and the release of the currency of exchange by the latter—or the foreign central bank—to the seller after compliance with the foreign exchange control regulations.

A draft expressed in foreign currency need not contain an exchange clause; the provisions of section 9(1)(d) of the Act are purely permissive.[41] If no exchange clause is inserted and the rate of exchange cannot be ascertained by reference to the custom of the trade, it is calculated according to the rate of sight drafts at the place of payment on the day the bill is payable (s.72), but instead of claiming that rate of exchange, judgment may be obtained in the foreign currency in which the draft is expressed and the date of conversion into sterling is then the date on which enforcement of the judgment is sought.[42]

The documentary bill

The seller often attaches to a bill of exchange which he has drawn on the buyer   **9–008**
the bill of lading to the goods sold. Such a bill of exchange is known as a *documentary bill*. The purpose of issuing a documentary bill is mainly to ensure that the buyer shall not receive the bill of lading and with it, the right of disposal of the goods, unless he has first accepted or paid the attached bill of exchange according to the arrangement between the parties. If the buyer fails to honour the bill of exchange, he has to return the bill of lading, and, if he wrongfully retains the latter, the law presumes that the property in the goods sold has not passed to him.[43]

Occasionally, the tenor of the documentary bill contains a clear reference to the export transaction to which the bill relates. Such statements do not render the bill of exchange void though they are, of course, superfluous (s.3(4)(b)). The practice of inserting them is convenient, and facilitates the careful checking of bills and documents which is a paramount responsibility of those dealing with the financial aspects of the export trade.

---

[41] *Cohn v. Boulken* (1920) 36 T.L.R. 767.
[42] *Barclays Bank International Ltd v. Levin Brothers (Bradford) Ltd* [1977] Q.B. 270.
[43] Sale of Goods Act 1979, s.19(3) *ante*, para. 4–006. *Cf. Leigh and Sillivan Ltd v. Aliakmon Shipping Co Ltd* [1985] Q.B. 350, CA, affd [1986] A.C. 785, HL (This case concerned, however, subs. (1), and not (3), of s.19.). On the *Aliakmon* case see *ante*, para. 2–030.

Avalised bills

9–009   An aval is the signature on a bill of exchange by a person who wants to "back" it and to guarantee its payment to the holder in due course.[44] Lord Blackburn[45] described the term "aval" as an antiquated term signifying "underwriting". But, influenced by the continental practice, it has come again into use in the United Kingdom, particularly in connection with forfaiting.[46]

Section 56 provides:

> "Where a person signs a bill otherwise than as drawer or acceptor, he thereby incurs the liabilities of an indorser to a holder in due course."

Although the avaliser incurs the liabilities of an indorser to a holder in due course, he is not in the position of an indorser.[47] He is, as observed, a guarantor of the liabilities of an immediate party to the bill. It depends on the wording of the aval on the instrument whose liabilities the avaliser guarantees. He may guarantee payment by the acceptor, or by one of the indorsers, or payment by all immediate parties, the acceptor and those liable on recourse.

In *G. & H. Montage GmbH v. Irvani*[48] the plaintiffs, a German company, sold in 1976 three cold stores to an Iranian company of which the defendant Irvani was chairman and managing director. The balance of the purchase price was payable in 30 semi-annual bills of exchange; these bills were in DM payable in London. It was further agreed that the defendant should guarantee the bills. The plaintiffs posted the 30 drafts to the Iranian buyers who duly accepted them and the defendant Irvani signed them on the back. When the plaintiffs sent the drafts to their bank in Germany—apparently for collection—the bank advised that the defendant should be asked to add the words "*bon pour aval pour les tirés*" (good as a guarantee for the drawees) above his signature. On the authority of the defendants, the plaintiffs added these words. After the Iranian revolution in February 1979 some of the outstanding bills were dishonoured. No notice of dishonour was given with respect to these bills, and in the case of some of them the protest was not carried out in the time required by section 51 of the Bills of Exchange Act.

The plaintiffs sued the defendant Irvani, who had fled from Iran, in the English courts on the aval. Saville J. and the Court of Appeal decided in favour of the plaintiffs, though on different grounds,[49] but both courts agreed that section 56 did not apply. It is thought that in a case to which section 56 applies,

---

[44] See *ante*, para. 9–004.
[45] In *Steele v. M'Kinlay* (1880) 5 App.Cas. 754 at 772.
[46] See *post*, para. 13–008.
[47] He is sometimes described, not very happily, as a quasi-indorser.
[48] For the decision of Saville J. see [1988] 1 W.L.R. 1285. The case is reported in [1988] 1 Lloyd's Rep. 460 *sub nom. Grunzweig und Hartmann GmbH v. Irvani*. For the CA decision see [1990] 1 W.L.R. 667.
[49] Saville J. held that section 56 was not applicable because the plaintiffs were not holders in due course and the defendant was liable, by virtue of German law as a guarantor and not as an indorser. The Court of Appeal held that German law was the law governing the aval (although the bills were dishonoured in London) and under German law no notice of dishonour to the avaliser was required.

notice of dishonour[50] to the avaliser is required because this is a condition precedent of his liability.

Only a time bill, and not a sight bill, can be avalised. An original party to the bill of exchange, *e.g.* the drawer or the acceptor, cannot avalise a bill himself as he is liable on the bill in any event and the aval, by its nature, is the added liability of another person though he becomes "a party" to the bill.[51] But their own liability of an original party may be avalised by a third party.

As a rule, a bill is avalised only after it has been accepted by the drawee. Usually, bills are avalised by banks[52] but there is no rule of law to that effect and anybody whose signature carries weight may avalise a bill. Banks usually carry out the aval by stamping across the bill "per aval" or similar words; this notation must, of course, be signed by an authorised person.

Commercially, the aval of a bank of good standing is of great value. It is one of the forms of security which a finance house requires when providing non-recourse finance to an exporter by way of a forfaiting arrangement or a similar transaction.[53] The charges of the avaliser for adding his liability to the bill are likely to be high.

Avals can also be used in connection with the transport documents. Thus, if under a collection arrangement the documents are to be presented to the acceptor of the bill (who in the sales transaction will be the buyer) it may be a condition precedent of the release of the documents to him that he obtains a good aval. Or, conversely, the acceptor can make the procurement of the aval by him conditional on the documents being released to him first. This combination of the financial and the documentary aspects bears some similarity to a letter of credit transaction but it cannot replace the latter and does not give the export seller the same financial assurance as an irrevocable and confirmed letter of credit.

Bills drawn in a set

It has been seen earlier[54] that the seller usually presents the buyer with several sets of transport documents. In this case, the seller does not draw the bill of exchange as a "sola" but as "parts of a set" and attaches a part of the bill to every set of transport documents which he despatches. The tenor of every part indicates that the bill represents a part in a set, and states the number of parts existing in all. In the example at *ante*, para. 9–007, the words "First of Exchange (Second and Third of the same date and tenor unpaid)" indicate that the bill is drawn in triplicate. The Bills of Exchange Act 1882 regulates this practice by providing, in section 71(1), that:

9–010

---

[50] And compliance with other provisions of the Act for recourse to the indorser, such as timely protest.

[51] As the avaliser is a "party" to the bill, section 72 is applicable, *per* Saville J. in *G. & H. Montage GmbH v. Irvani* [1988] 1 W.L.R. 1285 at 1295.

[52] The difference between a bank signing as avaliser and an acceptance credit by the bank is that in the former case the bank, as a stranger, adds its signature to that of the acceptor, but in the latter case the bill is drawn on the bank and the bank signs as one of the original parties to the bill.

[53] See *post*, para. 13–001.

[54] See *ante*, para. 2–021.

"where a bill is drawn in a set, each part of the set being numbered, and containing a reference to the other parts, the whole of the parts constitute one bill."

The parts of the set may be indorsed to different persons, but only one part is accepted by the drawee. If he is so foolish as to write his acceptance on more than one part and the accepted parts reach different holders in due course, he is liable on each part as if it were a separate bill. In the normal case, payment of the accepted part discharges the whole bill and the acceptor is entitled to claim delivery of the accepted part.

Negotiation of bills by exporter

9–011   It is vital for the exporter as for every other businessman to turn over his capital as quickly as possible. The exporter, therefore, frequently asks his bank to make an advance on the security of a documentary bill handed to the bank for collection[55] or to discount or purchase bills which he is entitled to draw on the issuing or advising bank under an accepted letter of credit[56] opened by the buyer. A bill which bears a bank's acceptance is known in banking circles as a "fine trade bill".

In the case of advances, specific advances against individual bills are distinguished from general overdrafts allowed on security of a steady flow of bills for collection held by the bank. These advances are in law in the nature of bankers' loans to customers[57]; in case of the exporter's failure, the bank would be in the position of a secured creditor in respect of the documentary bills held by it and the proceeds thereof.

Where the buyer has agreed to pay the purchase price under a letter of credit, the exporter who wishes to obtain finance before delivery of the transport documents to the advising bank might negotiate the draft drawn on the buyer or the bank to another bank[58] for cash. Here, bankers distinguish two transactions: bills are said to be discounted where the exporter (drawer) pays the bank's interest; and they are said to be purchased where the drawee pays the bank's interest and the exporter receives the nominal value of the bill. Whether a bill is purchasable or discountable depends on the clauses in a bill.[59] The rates of discount are here of great practical importance. In law, no difference is drawn between purchased and discounted bills. They are both negotiated to the bank by indorsement and delivery of the bill, and in both cases the bank which has become the indorsee is entitled to have recourse to the drawer.

The negotiation of a bill of exchange under a letter of credit differs from the discount of the letter of credit itself, which may occur where the credit provides for deferred payment.[60] This subject is discussed in Chapter 11.[61]

---

[55] On collection arrangements, see *post*, para. 10–001.
[56] On letters of credit, see *post*, para. 11–001.
[57] *Plein & Co Ltd v. Inland Revenue Commissioners* (1946) 175 L.T.Rep. 453.
[58] On negotiation credits where the advising bank is authorised to negotiate the bill drawn by the seller, see *post*, para. 11–022.
[59] See *ante*, para. 9–007.
[60] See *European Asian Bank AG v. Punjab & Sind Bank (No 2)* [1983] 1 W.L.R. 642.
[61] See *post*, para. 11–022.

Proceedings on bills of exchange

It is well established in English law that the courts are unwilling to allow **9–012**
defences to actions on bills of exchange. The holder of a bill is entitled to bring
an action for summary judgment[62] and, save in exceptional circumstances, a
defendant may not establish a counterclaim or set off for unliquidated damages
for breach of the underlying contract.

Lord Wilberforce referred in one case[63] to time bills, *i.e.* bills payable at
future dates, as "deferred instalments in cash" and said that since a bill is an
"unconditional order in writing", as stated in section 3, "English law ... does
not allow cross-claims, or defences, except such limited defences as those based
on fraud, invalidity or failure of consideration, to be made."[64]

Where one of the parties to a bill of exchange defaults, *e.g.* the acceptor
dishonours the bill by non-payment, an application for summary judgment[65]
against him may now be made under Part 24 of the new Civil Procedure Rules
1998.[66] Summary judgment is defined as "a procedure by which the court may
decide a claim or a particular issue without a trial"[67] and covers matters previously dealt with under RSC Order 14. It is submitted that previous practice with
regard to bills of exchange is unlikely to be departed from under the new rules.

Summary judgment may now be given if:

    (a) the court considers that—

        (i) the claimant has no real prospect of succeeding on the claim or
        issue; or
        (ii) the defendant has no real prospect of successfully defending the
        claim or issue; and

    (b) there is no other reason why the case or issue should be disposed of at
    a trial.

The former "no triable issue" test has now been replaced by the *Saudi Eagle*[68]
test that "the defendant has no real prospect of success".

---

[62] Most other countries provide also for summary proceedings in case of default under a bill of
exchange.

[63] *Nova (Jersey) Knit Ltd v. Kammgarn Spinnerei GmbH* [1977] 2 All E.R. 593, CA.

[64] This rule has now been extended to include direct debit instructions, which are regarded as
equivalent to cheques: *Esso Petroleum Co Ltd v. Milto*n [1997] 1 W.L.R. 938, [1997] 2 All E.R.
593, CA.

[65] Dealt with under RSC Ord. 14 of the previous High Court Rules, see Supreme Court Practice
1999, Note 14/4/20. The statement in the text is supported by reference to the following cases:
James Lamont & Co Ltd v. Hyland Ltd [1950] 1 K.B. 585; *Brown Shipley & Co Ltd v. Alicia
Hosiery Ltd* [1966] 1 Lloyd's Rep. 668 and *Nova (Jersey) Knit Ltd v. Kammgarn Spinnerei GmbH*
[1977] 1 W.L.R. 713; [1977] 2 All E.R. 463, HL. See also Lord Denning M.R. in *Power Curber
International Ltd v. National Bank of Kuwait SAK* [1981] 2 Lloyd's Rep. 394 at 398; *Continental
Illinois National Bank & Trust Co of Chicago v. John Paul Papanicolaou; The Fedora, Tatiana
and Eretrea II* [1986] 2 Lloyd's Rep. 441 at 445; see further Chitty, *Contracts* (29th ed., 1999),
para. 34–097.

[66] Supplemented by 1/PD/24—*Practice Direction—The Summary Disposal of Claims.*

[67] CPR Part 24.1.

[68] *Alpine Bulk Transport Co Inc v. Saudi Eagle Shipping Company Ltd; The Saudi Eagle* [1986] 2
Lloyd's Rep., CA.

A respondent must be given at least 14 days' notice of the hearing and the application must be supported by evidence. Any evidence from the respondent should be filed and served at least seven days before the date of the hearing and evidence in reply must be served three clear days before the summary judgment hearing. Under the new rules, this evidence will usually be in the form of witness statements (rather than by affidavit as previously) and/or by a verified statement of case.

Under the court's new case management powers[69] the issue of summary judgment can also be raised by the court itself. The claimant may not apply for summary judgment until the defendant has responded to the claim by filing either an acknowledgment of service or a defence[70] unless the court gives permission or a practice direction provides otherwise.

---

[69] CPR Part 3.
[70] CPR Part 24.4(1).

CHAPTER 10

COLLECTION ARRANGEMENTS[1]

Where the parties have not arranged for payment of the purchase price to take **10–001** place in the seller's country the problem arises as to who is to present the bill of exchange drawn by the seller on the buyer at his residence and, if it is a documentary bill,[2] who is to deliver the transport documents to him when he accepts or pays the draft? Normally the exporter asks his bank to arrange for the collection of the price, *i.e.* the acceptance or payment of the bill, and the bank will carry out this task through its own branch office abroad or a correspondent bank in the buyer's country. Sometimes the seller entrusts these duties to his representative or subsidiary company, if he is represented at the buyer's place of business, or to his forwarders.

The seller's instructions to present for acceptance or for payment the bill drawn for the price will pass through many hands and will have to be carried out abroad. They must be precise and complete and deal with the various contingencies which may arise in the course of their execution. The banks ask their customers to issue instructions on a *documentary bill lodgment form* which is designed to obtain instructions for all eventualities.

In modern practice the documentary bill lodgment form is arranged in a tabular manner. The table contains all contingencies which occur in the ordinary course of business, and the customer is requested to complete the form and to tick off the instructions which he wants to give the bank. This layout is followed by a space in which further instructions may be given if desired.[3]

The Uniform Rules for Collections

Banking practice relating to collection arrangements is standardised by the *Uni-* **10–002** *form Rules for Collections* (1995 Revision), sponsored by the International Chamber of Commerce.[4] The Uniform Rules apply only if incorporated by the parties into their contract.[5] This is widely done, particularly in the interaction between the remitting bank, instructed by the seller, and the collecting bank,

---

[1] See generally Benjamin (5th ed., 1997), Chap. 22, para. 22-067.
[2] On documentary bills of exchange, see *ante*, para. 9–008.
[3] See, *e.g.* SITPRO standard form collection request, widely used.
[4] ICC Brochure No. 522. These took effect as from January 1, 1996. See also the *ICC Uniform Rules for Collections: A Commentary (Brochure No. 550)* and the *ICC Guide to Collection Operations for URC 522 (Brochure No. 561)*. The Uniform Rules for Collections should not be confused with the Uniform Customs and Practice for Documentary Credits; on the latter, see para. 11–002. Details of countries and territories in which banks have indicated adherence to the Uniform Rules for Collection are available from the ICC and at *http://www.iccwbo*.
[5] URC, Art. 1(a). Note that the Uniform Rules for Collection do not apply when documents are negotiated under a documentary credit.

which presents the bill to the buyer at his place on the instructions of the remitting bank. Specific provisions may be excluded expressly by the parties if so required.

The current revision of the Uniform Rules,[6] considerably more detailed than its predecessors, is divided into seven Parts. Part A contains "General Provisions and Definitions", of which the following are of interest.

Under Article 2(a) "Collection" means the handling by banks, in accordance with instructions received, of documents in order to:

"(i) obtain payment and/or acceptance, or

(ii) deliver documents against payment and/or against acceptance, or

(iii) deliver documents on other terms and conditions."

Under Article 2(b), "Documents" means financial documents and/or commercial documents:

"(i) 'Financial documents' means bills of exchange, promissory notes, cheques, or other similar instruments used for obtaining the payment of money;

(ii) 'Commercial documents' means invoices, transport documents, documents of title or other similar documents, or any other documents whatsoever, not being financial documents."

A "clean collection", defined at Article 2(c), means "collection of financial documents not accompanied by commercial documents". A "documentary collection", defined in Article 2(d), means the collection of:

"(i) Financial documents accompanied by commercial documents;

(ii) Commercial documents not accompanied by financial documents."

In the latter type of documentary collections the commercial documents are presented by the collecting bank to the buyer, together with the financial documents. It is this type of collection arrangement which is of interest to the exporter.

Parties to the transaction are defined in Article 3 as follows:

(a) The "principal" (Art. 3(a)(i)), is the party (usually the seller) "entrusting the handling of a collection to a bank".

(b) The "drawee" (Art. 3b) is the party "to whom presentation is to be made in accordance with the collection instruction."

(c) The "collecting bank" (Art. 3(a)(iii)), is stated to be "any bank, other than the remitting bank, involved in processing the collection".

---

[6] *i.e.* URC 522. The Uniform Rules were first published in 1956, with revisions appearing in 1967 and 1978.

(d) The "presenting bank" (Art. 3(a)(iv)) is "the collecting bank making presentation [of the documents] to the drawee".

The Uniform Rules provide[7] that all documents sent for collection must be accompanied by a "collection instruction" incorporating the Rules and giving complete and precise instructions. The collecting bank may only act upon instructions contained in this collection instruction.[8] Article 4(b) sets out the details which must be included in each instruction and states that it must identify the principal, the drawee, the remitting bank and the presenting bank. It should state clearly the amount and currency to be collected, list the accompanying documents, the terms of the delivery of the documents, together with any other matters relating to interest and charges, and state how payment is to be made and what steps are to be taken in the event of dishonour.

In the case of a documentary collection, the exporter must instruct the remitting bank and the latter must instruct the collecting bank as to whether the documents shall be delivered to the buyer on acceptance of the bill (D/A terms), on actual payment (D/P terms), or in accordance with special instructions (which have to be stated on the form). Instructions must also be given as to whether the documents shall be handed to a *representative in case of need*[9] in the event of non-payment and/or non-acceptance, and what the powers of that representative are, whether the buyer shall be allowed a rebate for payment before maturity, and, if the documents are not taken up, whether the goods are to be warehoused and what insurance is to be effected.

By Article 12(a), a bank must establish that the documents they have received appear to be as listed in the collection instruction. If such is not the case they must notify "by telecommunication or if that is not possible, by other expeditious means, without delay", the party from whom the collection instruction was received, identifying any documents missing or which are found to be other than listed. The collecting bank must advise the remitting bank of the fate of the collection immediately[10]; and this advice must[11] include appropriate details. The remitting bank must specify the method by which such advice is to be given, failing which the collecting bank may choose which method to employ. Clause 26(c) contemplates three types of advice, namely advice of payment, advice of acceptance[12] and advice of non-payment and/or acceptance (*i.e.* dishonour). The advice of payment must show (a) the sum collected; (b) charges and/or disbursements and/or expenses and, (c) if appropriate, the methods of disposal of the funds.[13]

---

[7] At Art. 4(a)(i).

[8] Under Art. 4(a)(ii) banks will not examine documents in order to obtain instructions and under Art. 4(a)(iii) banks are to disregard any instructions given by any party other than the one from whom they receive the collection.

[9] Art. 25.

[10] URC, Art. 26.

[11] URC, Art. 26(a).

[12] *Cf.* the position under URC 322, as expressed by Longmore J. in *Minories Finance Ltd v. Afribank Nigeria Ltd* [1995] 1 Lloyd's Rep. 134.

[13] URC, Art. 26(c)(i).

Article 13[14] exempts banks from liability for the form, sufficiency and genuineness of the documents. By Article 14 they are exempt from responsibility for the consequences of various events such as delay, loss in transit of messages and the like, and also from responsibility for delays caused by the need to obtain clarification of instructions received. In addition, banks do not accept responsibility for the authenticity of signatures on bills of exchange, promissory notes, or similar documents.[15]

Dishonour

10–003 Specific directions should be included in the collection instruction as to the steps to be taken by the collecting banker in the event of dishonour of the bill of exchange. These should provide precise instructions relating to the noting or protest (or other legal process in lieu) where the bill of exchange is dishonoured by non-acceptance or non-payment.[16] In the absence of such instructions, banks are not obliged to have the documents protested. Noting means obtaining a minute on the bill by a notary public at the time of refusal of acceptance or payment. The minute, which is dated and initialled by the notary is, in practice, a sufficient assurance for all parties concerned that the bill has been dishonoured, and only in particular cases, for instance when the matter leads to litigation, is the notary public required to procure a formal protest. Acccording to English law, where a bill has been noted[17] on the day of dishonour or the next succeeding business day, the protest may be drawn up subsequently and dated back to the date of noting (Bills of Exchange Act 1882, ss. 51 and 93).

The instructions for collection may contain additional requests. The exporter may, for instance, require the collecting bank to "cable advice if not paid".

Delivery of documents contrary to instructions

10–004 If the collecting bank releases the documents to the buyer contrary to instructions, for example, by not insisting on payment or the acceptance of a time bill, the bank is liable in damages to the seller for breach of contract[18] and for conversion of the documents.

Release under a trust receipt

10–005 Sometimes the collecting bank finds itself in a predicament. It realises that it takes a considerable risk if it releases the documents, and particularly the bill of lading, without insisting on the performance of the conditions set out in the collection instruction but, on the other hand, the buyer may be one of its

---

[14] Reflecting Art. 15 of UCP 500.
[15] Arts 22 and 23.
[16] Art. 24.
[17] See para. 9–004.
[18] Privity of contract exists between the seller and the collecting bank because, when, in the collection order, the remitting bank passes on the seller's instructions, it acts as authorised agent of the seller, see *Calico Printers Association Ltd v. Barclays Bank* (1930) 36 Com. Cas. 197, CA.

customers. In these cases an indemnity by the buyer would not protect the bank if the buyer becomes insolvent. The bank may therefore be tempted to release the documents prematurely under a *trust receipt*. Under such a document a genuine trust is constituted, the buyer being the trustee, the bank the beneficiary, and the trust property being the bill of lading, the goods obtained by the buyer from the vessel and, if the buyer is authorised to sell them, the proceeds of sale.[19] Under this form of trust receipt the buyer undertakes to pay the bank— he may be able to do so out of the proceeds of sale of goods—and thus to discharge the condition imposed on the bank in the collection instruction. Under another form of trust receipt the buyer is not entitled to sell the goods obtained from the vessel but is obliged to warehouse them in the bank's name and to deliver the warehouse receipt to the bank. As observed, however, if the release under a trust receipt does not go according to plan, the collecting bank is liable to the seller unless it has first obtained his authority. Moreover, if a buyer who qualifies as a mercantile agent sells the bill of lading to a bona fide purchaser in breach of the trust constituted by the trust receipt, the title of the bona fide purchaser prevails over that of the bank.[20]

In *Midland Bank Ltd v. Eastcheap Dried Fruit Co*[21] the bank was instructed to release the documents, including the bill of lading, to the buyers against payment in cash.[22] The bank, which was in the position of the collecting bank, released the documents without insisting on cash payment, but did so under a "collection note", which stated that the documents were released only for inspection and were left with the buyers in trust and had to be returned to the bank if no immediate payment was made. The buyers sold the documents to a bona fide purchaser. The bank paid the seller and the sued the buyers. The Court of Appeal held that the buyers were liable to the bank for breach of contract and for conversion of the bill of lading.

---

[19] A trust receipt is not a bill of sale within the meaning of the Bills of Sale Act 1978 and consequently need not be registered as a charge under the Companies Act 1985, s.396(1)(c).
[20] *Lloyd's Bank v. Bank of America National Trust and Savings Association* [1937] 2 K.B. 631; [1938] 2 K.B. 147; see *post*, para. 27–017.
[21] [1962] 1 Lloyd's Rep. 359.
[22] This case did not involve a documentary bill of exchange, but the collecting bank was instructed to deliver the documents against cash payment.

CHAPTER 11

LETTERS OF CREDIT

CHARACTERISTICS OF THE LETTER OF CREDIT

11–001 Letters of credit,[1] also called documentary credits or bankers commercial credits, are the most common method of payment for goods in the export trade and have been described by English judges as "the life blood of international commerce".[2] Donaldson L.J., with the concurrence of Ackner L.J., said[3]:

> "Irrevocable letters of credit and bank guarantees given in circumstances such that they are equivalent to an irrevocable letter of credit have been said to be the life blood of commerce. Thrombosis will occur if, unless fraud is involved, the courts intervene and thereby disturb the mercantile practice of treating rights thereunder as being equivalent to cash in hand."

There are various types of letter of credit. The most important distinctions are made between revocable and irrevocable credits and between confirmed and unconfirmed credits.[4] The feature common to all is that in accordance with the agreement between the seller and the buyer in the contract of sale ("the underlying contract"[5]), the buyer arranges for payment of the price to be made by a bank, normally at the seller's place, on presentation of specified documents (usually including the transport documents) and on the performance of other conditions stated in the credit and advised by the bank to the seller. On presentation of the documents the bank pays the purchase price, according to the terms of the credit, by sight payment, deferred payment, or by acceptance or negotiation of a bill of exchange drawn by the seller.[6]

The essence of the letter of credit transaction lies in its documentary character, *i.e.* where the goods are represented by a bill of lading, this document of title is

---

[1] For further reading: H.C. Gutteridge and Maurice Megrah, *The Law of Bankers' Commercial Credits* (7th ed., 1983); R. Jack, *Documentary Credits* (2nd ed., 1993); L. Sarna, *Letters of Credit: The Law and Current Practice* (3rd ed., 1997, Canada); *Benjamin's Sale of Goods* (5th ed., 1997); W. Hedley, *Bills of Exchange and Bankers' Documentary Credits* (3rd ed., 1997); P. Todd, *Bills of Lading and Banker's Documentary Credits*, (3rd ed., 1998).

[2] *Per* Kerr L.J. in *R.D. Harbottle (Mercantile) Ltd v. National Westminster Bank Ltd* [1978] Q.B. 146 at 155; *per* Griffiths L.J. in *Power Curber International Ltd v. National Bank of Kuwait SAK* [1981] 2 Lloyd's Rep. 394 at 400; *per* Donaldson L.J. in *Intraco Ltd v. Notis Shipping Corporation of Liberia; The Bhoja Trader* [1981] 2 Lloyd's Rep. 256 at 257; *per* Ackner L.J., *ibid.*; and *per* Stephenson L.J. in *United City Merchants (Investments) Ltd v. Royal Bank of Canada* [1982] Q.B. 208 at 222; *per* Hirst J. in *Hong Kong and Shanghai Banking Corporation v. Kloeckner & Co AG* [1989] 2 Lloyd's Rep. 323 at 330.

[3] In *Intraco Ltd v. Notis Shipping Corporation of Liberia; The Bhoja Trader, supra.*

[4] As to which see *post*, para 11–023.

[5] The underlying contract may be another type of contract, *e.g.* a construction contract or a contract for services.

[6] See *post*, para. 11–022.

used as a means of financing the transaction. Lord Wright[7] describes the function of the letter of credit as follows:

> "The general course of international commerce involves the practice of raising money on the documents so as to bridge the period between the shipment and the time of obtaining payment against documents."

The documentary character of this type of bankers' credit, as used in international trade, cannot be over-emphasised. The paying bank is prepared to pay the exporter because it holds the documents as collateral security and, if necessary, can have recourse to the issuing bank, which in turn can have recourse to the buyer as instructing customer. Where the transport documents consist of bills of lading, the bank invariably asks for the delivery of a full set of original bills; otherwise a fraudulent shipper would be able to obtain payment under the letter of credit on one of them and advances from other bankers on the security of the other originals constituting the set.[8]

A comprehensive definition of the letter of credit is to be found in the *Uniform Customs and Practice for Documentary Credits (1993 Revision)*[9] where it is provided[10]:

> "For the purposes of these Articles, the expressions 'Documentary Credit(s)' and 'Standby Letter(s) of Credit'[11] (hereinafter referred to as 'Credit(s)'), mean any arrangement, however named or described, whereby a bank (the 'Issuing Bank') acting at the request and on the instructions of a customer (the 'Applicant')[12] or on its own behalf."
>
> (i) is to make a payment to or to the order of a third party (the 'Beneficiary')[13] or is to accept and pay bills of exchange (Draft(s)) drawn by the Beneficiary,
>
> or
>
> (ii) authorises another bank[14] to effect such payment, or to accept and pay such bills of exchange (Draft(s)),
>
> or
>
> (iii) authorises another bank to negotiate,
>
> against stipulated document(s), provided that the terms and conditions of the Credit are complied with."

Uniform Customs and Practice for Documentary Credits

Banking practice relating to letters of credit is standardised by the *Uniform* **11–002** *Customs and Practice for Documentary Credits (1993 Revision)*, which are a set

---

[7] In *T.D. Bailey, Son & Co v. Ross T. Smyth & Co Ltd* (1940) 56 T.L.R. 825 at 828.

[8] This passage was quoted with approval by Ackner L.J. in *United City Merchants (Investments) Ltd v. Royal Bank of Canada* [1982] Q.B. 208 at 247.

[9] ICC Brochure 500. The *Uniform Customs and Practice for Documentary Credits 1993* (Brochure 500) must not be confused with the *Uniform Rules for Collection 1995* (Brochure 522), discussed at *ante*, Chap. 10. A list of countries and territories in which banks have notified their adherence to the UCP is available from the ICC and at *http://www.iccwbo.org*.

[10] In Art. 2.

[11] On standby letters of credit, see *post*, para. 11–030.

[12] This is usually the buyer.

[13] This is usually the seller (exporter), but as the underlying contract may be of a type other than a contract of sale, the neutral expression "beneficiary" is used.

[14] This is normally the advising bank at the seller's place.

of rules issued by the International Chamber of Commerce. These are commonly referred to as the UCP. In this area of law attempts at unification have been highly successful and after more than 60 years of effort and periodic revision,[15] the UCP now have almost universal effect.

Application of the UCP

11–003 In principle, the UCP apply only if the parties have incorporated them into their contract. Article 1 of the UCP makes this clear:

> "The Uniform Customs and Practice for Documentary Credits, 1993 Revision, ICC Publication No. 500, shall apply to all Documentary Credits (including to the extent to which they may be applicable, Standby Letter(s) of Credit) where they are incorporated into the text of the Credit. They are binding on all parties thereto, unless otherwise expressly stipulated in the Credit."

In English law the UCP do not have the force of law[16] or the status of a trade custom and in accordance with Article 1, apply only if the parties have incorporated them into their contract. This is normally done by British banks, when contracting with a United Kingdom party, an overseas merchant or other banks, and consequently English courts are familiar with the provisions of the UCP and have frequently interpreted them.[17] In certain states of the United States, the provisions of the Uniform Commercial Code on letters of credit[18] are replaced by the UCP where the parties have agreed to apply them or where they are customarily applicable. In countries which have national banking associations, the general standard conditions applied by the members of these associations often incorporate the UCP. If the automated international transfer system SWIFT[19] is used by banks in letter of credit transactions, the UCP apply to the contractual relations between the banks and between them and SWIFT.

Even where the UCP are adopted specifically or generally , the parties are at liberty to contract out of them, as is clearly expressed in Article 1, quoted earlier.

The ICC has attempted to standardise documentation relating to letters of credit, and has published the *ICC Standard Documentary Credit Forms (UCP 500)*,[20] as well as a useful guide to the 1993 Revision.[21] On occasion, the ICC Banking Commission is asked to express its view on the interpretation and

---

[15] The first issue of the UCP was published in 1933, the second in 1951, the third in 1962, the fourth in 1974 and the fifth in 1983. The present—sixth—revision, *viz.* the 1993 revision, came into operation on January 1, 1994.

[16] See, *e.g. Royal Bank of Scotland v. Cassa di Risparmio delle Province Lombard* [1992] 1 Bank L.R. 251.

[17] *e.g.* in *Banque de l'Indoschine et de Suez v. J.H. Rayner (Mincing Lane) Ltd* [1983] Q.B. 711; *European Asian Bank AG v. Punjab & Sind Bank (No. 2)* [1983] 1 W.L.R. 642; *Forestal Mimosa v. Oriental Credit Ltd* [1986] 1 W.L.R. 631.

[18] UCC, Art. 5; for a discussion of the interaction between the UCP and the Uniform Commercial Code see *Alaska Textile Co Inc v. Chase Manhattan Bank* [1992] 982 Fed. 2d. 813.

[19] SWIFT stands for Society for Worldwide Interbank Financial Telecommunications.

[20] ICC Brochure No. 516, which contains a standard application form for a documentary credit.

[21] "ICC Guide to Documentary Credit Operations for UCP 500" (ICC Brochure 515).

application of the UCP by the banks and its published collections of opinions[22] provide valuable source material.

The stages of a letter of credit transaction

Where payment under a letter of credit is arranged, four stages can normally be **11–004** distinguished:

(a) The exporter and the overseas buyer agree in the contract of sale that payment shall be made under a letter of credit.

(b) The overseas buyer (acting as "applicant for the credit") instructs a bank at his place of business (known as the "issuing bank") to open a letter of credit for the United Kingdom exporter (known as "the beneficiary") on the terms specified by the buyer in his instructions to the issuing bank.

(c) The issuing bank arranges with a bank at the locality of the exporter (known as the "advising bank") to negotiate, accept, or pay the exporter's draft upon delivery of the transport documents by the seller.

(d) The advising bank informs the exporter that it will negotiate, accept or pay his draft upon delivery of the transport documents. The advising bank may do so either *without its own engagement* or it may *confirm* the credit opened by the issuing bank.[23]

Sometimes, when the bank is represented at the overseas buyer's and the exporter's place, stages (c) and (d) are combined and the issuing bank advises the exporter of the credit opened in his favour, either directly or through a branch at the exporter's place.

Two points emerge from this structure. First, stages (a) and (d) are of great importance to the exporter, *viz.* the arrangement, in his contract of sale of the most appropriate type of credit; and the corresponding notification from the advising bank.

Second, provided the correct documents are tendered and this is done before the expiry of the credit, there is a binding undertaking of the issuing bank, if

---

[22] Decisions (1975–1979) of the ICC Banking Commission (ICC Doc. No. 371); Opinions (1980–1981) of the ICC Banking Opinion (ICC Doc. No. 399) and Opinions of the ICC Banking Commission on Queries relating to Uniform Customs and Practice for Documentary Credits (1984–1986) (ICC Doc. No. 434); Opinions of the ICC Banking Commission (1989–1991) (ICC Doc. No 494); Opinions of the ICC Banking Commission (1995–1996) (ICC Doc. No. 565). Opinions covering the period between 1981 and 1984 have not been published. Further useful ICC publications include "ICC Case Studies on Documentary Credits under UCP 500" (ICC Brochure 535) and Documentary Credits: UCP 500 and 400 Compared—1993 Revision (ICC Doc. 511); "More Queries and Responses on UCP 500" (ICC Brochure 596).

[23] Sometimes the situation is more complicated. The issuing bank may authorise another bank, (*e.g.* at a major trading centre in the seller's country) to confirm, and this bank may instruct a third bank, (*e.g.* in a small place at which the seller carries on business) to advise the irrevocable and confirmed credit. However, no bank would confirm a credit if the issuing bank has not made it irrevocable, see UCP, Art. 9(b). On confirmed and unconfirmed credits, see *post*, para. 11–023.

the credit is irrevocable, and also of the confirming bank, if it is confirmed, to the beneficiary to pay the purchase price. These undertakings are contractual in nature. A bank which has given such an undertaking will refuse to accept instructions from the buyer not to pay a seller who has performed the conditions of the credit,[24] and will not accept a revocation of the credit.

The two fundamental principles

11–005 The law relating to letters of credit is founded on two principles:

(a) the autonomy of the credit; and

(b) the doctrine of strict compliance.

The autonomy of the letter of credit

11–006 According to this principle, the credit is separate from and independent of the underlying contract of sale or other transaction. A bank which operates a credit is concerned only with whether the documents tendered by the seller correspond to those specified in the instructions. The letter of credit transaction is thus a paper transaction. It is irrelevant to the bank whether the underlying contract concerns the purchase of timber, oil, machinery or whether it concerns another transaction. The only case in which—exceptionally—the bank should refuse to pay under the credit occurs if it is proved to its satisfaction that the documents, though apparently in order on their face, are fraudulent and that the beneficiary (the seller) was involved in the fraud.[25] This is usually referred to as the "fraud exception".

The principle of autonomy of the credit is stated in Articles 3(a) and 4 of the UCP in these terms:

> *Article 3*
>
> (a) Credits, by their nature, are separate transactions from the sales or other contract(s) on which they may be based and banks are in no way concerned with or bound by such contract(s), even if any reference whatsoever to such contract(s) is included in the Credit. Consequently, the undertaking of a bank to pay, accept and pay Draft(s) or negotiate and/or to fulfil any other obligation under the Credit, is not subject to claims or defences by the Applicant resulting from his relationships with the Issuing Bank or the Beneficiary.
>
> *Article 4*
>
> In Credit operations all parties concerned deal with documents, and not with goods, services and/or other performances to which the documents may relate.

By virtue of its autonomous character, the letter of credit is approximated, to

---

[24] *Hamzeh Malas & Sons v. British Imex Industries Ltd* [1958] 2 Q.B. 127, see *post*, para. 11–026.
[25] *United City Merchants (Investments) Ltd v. Royal Bank of Canada* [1983] 1 A.C. 168; *Tukan Timber Ltd v. Barclays Bank plc* [1987] 1 Lloyd's Rep. 171 at 174. On fraud affecting letters of credit, see *post*, para. 11–042.

some extent, to the bill of exchange.[26] This development was noted by Lord Denning M.R. in *Power Curber International Ltd v. National Bank of Kuwait*,[27] when he said[28]:

> "It is vital that every bank which issues a letter of credit should honour its obligations. The bank is in no way concerned with any dispute that the buyer may have with the seller. The buyer may say that the goods are not up to contract. Nevertheless the bank must honour its obligations. The buyer may say that he has a cross-claim in a large amount. Still the bank must honour its obligations. A letter of credit is like a bill of exchange given for the price of the goods. It ranks as cash and must be honoured. No set off or counterclaim is allowed to detract from it: see *Nova Jersey (Knit) Ltd. v. Kammgarn Spinnerei GmbH*.[29] All the more so with a letter of credit. Whereas a bill of exchange is given by buyer to seller, a letter of credit is given by a bank to the seller with the very intention of avoiding anything in the nature of a set off or counterclaim."

In this case distributors in Kuwait bought machinery from Power Curber, an American company carrying on business in North Carolina. The National Bank of Kuwait issued an irrevocable letter of credit, instructing the Bank of America in Miami to advise the credit to the sellers through a bank in Charlotte, North Carolina. The machinery was duly delivered but the Kuwaiti buyers raised a large counterclaim against the sellers in the courts of Kuwait and obtained from them a provisional attachment order which prevented the bank, which was willing to honour the irrevocable credit, from paying under it. The sellers sued the bank, which had a registered address in London, in the English courts and Parker J. gave summary judgment against the bank. The Court of Appeal upheld this decision. It was held that the order of the court in Kuwait did not affect the obligation of the bank to honour the credit and, moreover, it could not have extraterritorial effect.[30] As can be seen from this case, a summary judgment[31] can in many instances be obtained against a bank which tries to negate its obligations under an irrevocable or irrevocable and confirmed credit. Moreover, the courts will normally refuse to issue a freezing injunction[32] preventing a bank from paying under the credit.[33] However the courts are prepared in appropriate cases to issue such an order against the beneficiary (the seller), attaching the

---

[26] This statement should not be misunderstood. The concept of a holder in due course (see *ante*, para. 9–004) does not apply to letters of credit. Further, a letter of credit is not negotiable; if it is made transferable, it can be transferred only once (see *post*, para. 11–036).

[27] [1981] 2 W.L.R. 1233. See also *Toprak Mahsulleri Ofisi v. Finagrain Compagnie Commerciale Agricole et Financiere SA* [1979] 2 Lloyd's Rep. 98; *Intraco Ltd v. Notis Shipping Corporation; The Bhoja Trader* [1981] 2 Lloyd's Rep. 256.

[28] [1981] 1 W.L.R. at 1241.

[29] [1977] 1 W.L.R. 713 (this case concerned bills of exchange, and not letters of credit).

[30] See Jack (1993), paras 13.8–13.11.

[31] See *ante*, para. 9–012. See also *S.L. Sethia Liners Ltd v. State Trading Corporation of India Ltd* [1985] 1 W.L.R. 1398 at 1401; *Forestal Mimosa Ltd v. Oriental Credit Ltd* [1986] 1 W.L.R. 631; *Continental Illinois National Bank & Trust Company of Chicago v. John Paul Papanicolaou; The Fedora, Tatiana and Eritrea II* [1986] 2 Lloyd's Rep. 441, CA (this case concerned a guarantee).

[32] Under CPR r.25.1(1)(f), formerly known as a "Mareva" injunction.

[33] *Intraco Ltd v. Notis Shipping Corporation; The Bhoja Trader* [1981] 2 Lloyd's Rep. 256; *Bolivinter Oil SA v. Chase Manhattan Bank NA* [1984] 1 W.L.R. 392; [1984] 1 Lloyd's Rep. 251; see *post*, paras 22–027 and 22–028. If the fraud exception is established, a court may be persuaded to grant a freezing injunction.

proceeds which he has received from the bank under the credit. Lord Denning said in one case[34]:

> "The injunction does not prevent payment under a letter of credit or under a bank guarantee, but it may apply to the proceeds as and when received by the defendant."

On the other hand, it has been held[35] that a bank may set off a claim for liquidated damages which has accrued to it against its own letter of credit liability to the beneficiary in a case in which the claim for liquidated damages arose directly out of the same banking transaction to which the letter of credit related.

The doctrine of strict compliance

11–007 The legal principle that the bank is entitled to reject documents which do not strictly conform with the terms of the credit is conveniently referred to as the doctrine of strict compliance. The reason underlying this rule—which is not always appreciated by exporters—is that the advising bank is a special agent of the issuing bank[36] and the latter is the special agent of the buyer. If an agent with limited authority acts outside that authority (in banking terminology: his mandate) the principal is entitled to disown the act of the agent, who cannot recover from him and has to bear the commercial risk of the transaction. In a falling market a buyer is easily tempted to reject documents which the bank accepted, on the ground that they do not strictly conform with the terms of the credit. Moreover, the bank deals in finance, not in goods[37]; it normally has no expert knowledge of the usages and practices of a particular trade. If the documents tendered are not strictly in conformity with the terms of the credit and the bank refuses to accept them, the exporter should at once contact his overseas buyer and request him to instruct the bank to accept the documents as tendered. The refusal of the bank to depart in even a small and apparently insignificant matter not sanctioned by the instructions or the UCP, where applicable, from its instructions will, in the overwhelming majority of cases, be upheld by the courts if litigation ensues. Lord Sumner expressed the doctrine of strict compliance in the following classic passage: "There is no room for documents which are almost the same, or which will do just as well."[38]

The doctrine of strict compliance may be illustrated by the following examples:

---

[34] *Z. Ltd v. A-Z and AA-LL* [1982] Q.B. 558 at 574.

[35] *Hong Kong and Shanghai Banking Corporation v. Kloeckner & Co AG* [1989] 2 Lloyd's Rep. 342 (the decision is founded on exceptional facts).

[36] See Jack (1993), para. 6.4.

[37] See UCP, Art. 4, quoted at para. 11–006.

[38] In *Equitable Trust Co of New York v. Dawson Partners Ltd* [1927] 27 L.I.R. 49 at 52; *per* Devlin J. in *Midland Bank v. Seymour* [1955] 2 Lloyd's Rep. 147; *per* Parker J. in *Kydon Compañía Naviera SA v. National Westminster Bank Ltd; The Lena* [1981] 1 Lloyd's Rep. 68 at 75. See also *Hing Yip Hing Fat Co Ltd* [1991] 2 H.K.L.R. 35, discussed in Murphy "Documentary Credits and Rejected Documents" (1992) L.M.C.L.Q. 26; *Seaconsar Far East Ltd v. Bank Markazi Iran* [1993] 1 Lloyd's Rep. 236 at 239; *Glencore International AG v. Bank of China* [1996] 1 Lloyd's Rep. 135; *Bayerische Vereinsbank Aktiengesellschaft v. National Bank of Pakistan* [1997] 1 Lloyd's Rep. 59.

In *Equitable Trust Company of New York v. Dawson Partners Ltd*[39] the defendants bought vanilla beans from a seller in Batavia (now Jakarta). They instructed the plaintiff bank to open a confirmed letter of credit in favour of the seller and to make finance available thereunder on delivery of certain documents including a certificate of quality to be issued "*by experts*". Owing to an ambiguity in the cabled codeword, the advising bank in Batavia informed the seller that the credit was available on the tender of a certificate "*by expert*". The seller, who was fraudulent, shipped mainly rubbish and the expert failed to discover the fraud. The House of Lords held that the plaintiff bank was not entitled to be reimbursed by the buyers because, contrary to their instructions, it made available finance on the certificate of one expert only instead of at least two experts.

In *Soproma SpA v. Marine & Animal By-Products Corporation*[40] the buyers, an Italian company, bought a quantity of Chilean fish full meal from a New York company. The contract, which was on a London Cattle Food Trade Association form, was c. and f. Savona and provided that the buyers should open a letter of credit with a New York bank. The documents to be presented by the sellers to that bank had to include bills of lading issued to order and marked "freight prepaid" and further an analysis certificate stating that the goods had a content of minimum 70 per cent protein. The credit was subject to the UCP (1951 Revision). The sellers tendered to the advising bank in New York bills of lading which were not to order and consequently were not negotiable.[41] They did not bear the remark "freight prepaid" but, on the contrary, bore the remark "collect freight"; the analysis certificate showed only a protein content of 67 per cent minimum; and the goods, although described in the invoice as "Fish Full Meal," were described in the bills of lading only as "Fishmeal". The buyers rejected the documents. Thereupon (the time of validity of the credit having expired) the sellers made a second tender of documents to the buyers directly,[42] adding a freight receipt showing that they had paid the freight and an analysis certificate of minimum 70 per cent protein. The buyers likewise rejected the second tender and, after arbitration in London, the dispute came before the English court. McNair J. decided that the buyers had rightly rejected the documents, for the following reasons:

(1) the second—direct—tender of documents was irrelevant[43] and had to be disregarded completely;

(2) the first tender, *i.e.* the tender to the correspondent bank in New York, was defective because—

   (a) the bills of lading did not bear the remark "freight prepaid"[44] but were in fact marked "freight collect". Further, they were not nego-

---

[39] (1927) 27 L.I.L.R. 49. See also *Gian Singh & Co Ltd v. Banque de l'Indochine* [1974] 1 W.L.R. 1234.
[40] [1966] 1 Lloyd's Rep. 367.
[41] See *post*, para. 15–024.
[42] Not to the advising bank in New York.
[43] For reasons discussed at *post*, para. 11–039.
[44] Nor was the freight deducted from the price or a freight receipt tendered with the bills.

tiable as they were not to order and consequently were not proper
bills which could be tendered under a c.i.f. or c. and f. contract;

(b) the analysis certificate showed too low a minimum protein content;
(c) but the description of the goods in the bill of lading in general
terms (as "Fishmeal") was sufficient, since the goods were correctly described in the commercial invoice; the learned judge
referred here to the UCP (1951 Revision), Art. 33[45] where it is
provided that a general description in the bills of lading is sufficient if the goods are correctly described in the commercial
invoice.

In *J.H. Rayner & Co Ltd v. Hambro's Bank Ltd*[46] the correspondent bank
advised the sellers that a letter of credit in their favour was available upon
delivery of certain documents evidencing the shipment of "Coromandel
groundnuts". The sellers tendered a bill of lading describing the goods as
"machine shelled groundnut kernels" and having in its margin the letters
"C.R.S." which were an abbreviation of "Coromandels", but in the invoice the
goods were described correctly as "Coromandel groundnuts". The Court of
Appeal held that the bank had rightly refused payment under the credit, in view
of the doctrine of strict compliance. McNair J. rightly distinguished the *Soproma*
case from the *Rayner* case because the UCP applied to the former but not to the
latter.

Where a bank pays under a confirmed letter of credit although the documents
tendered are defective, the principal—the issuing bank or the buyer, as the case
may be—forfeits his right to refuse reimbursement if he ratifies the unauthorised
payment.[47] The intention to ratify may, in appropriate circumstances, even be
inferred from prolonged inaction or silence.[48] In a c.i.f. contract the documents
should be rejected by the principal on their face value; if, *e.g.* the buyer who is
aware of their irregularity remains inactive and attempts to reject them after the
arrival and inspection of the goods at the port of destination, he is likely to be
deemed to have ratified the payment by the bank. In *Bank Melli Iran v. Barclays
Bank DCO*[49] an Iranian buyer purchased American trucks from English sellers.
On the instructions of the buyer Bank Melli Iran opened a credit for the sellers,
Barclays acting as the advising bank. The instructions of the issuing bank to the
advising bank stated that the credit was for the price of "100 new Chevrolet
trucks" and required the presentation of a certificate of the United States Government to that effect. The documents tendered to Barclays were ambiguous and
contradictory. The invoice stated that the trucks were "in a new condition," the
Government certificate referred to them as "new, good," and the delivery order

---

[45] This provision of the 1951 edition is substantially the same as Art. 37(c) of the 1993 Revision.
[46] [1943] 1 K.B. 37.
[47] *Bank Melli Iran v. Barclays Bank (Dominion, Colonial and Overseas)* [1951] 23 Lloyd's Rep.
376. *Cf.* also *Panchaud Freres SA v. Etablissements General Grain Company* [1970] 1 Lloyd's Rep.
53 at 57 (in this case payment was not to be made under a documentary credit).
[48] *Bank Melli Iran v. Barclays DCO, ibid.* and the Canadian case *Michael Doyle & Associates Ltd
v. Bank of Montreal* [1982] 6 W.W.R. 24 (bank unconditionally accepted draft drawn on it although
the documents were defective; bank could not recover from beneficiary).
[49] [1951] 2 Lloyd's Rep. 367.

described them as "new-good" [*sic*]. Barclays paid against these documents and passed them on to Bank Melli Iran. The latter informed Barclays that they considered the documents faulty but did not reject them. Indeed, they later authorised Barclays to increase the credit and the buyer surveyed the first consignment of the goods on arrival in Iran.

After approximately six weeks Bank Melli rejected the documents. McNair J. held (1) that the documents were faulty and should have been rejected by Barclays, (2) but in the circumstances Bank Melli had ratified the transaction and lost its right of rejection.

The documents tendered to the bank

The bank must determine on the basis of the documents alone whether or not **11–008** they comply with the mandate.[50] According to the doctrine of strict compliance the bank is within its rights when refusing documents tendered by the seller which do not contain all the particulars specified in the credit.[51] Beyond this the bank is not obliged to go and should not go. In particular, it need not concern itself with the legal significance and value of the documents which it is instructed to demand. Even if their legal value appears questionable, documents in the required form may have commercial value for the buyer and, as Devlin J. said,[52] "it is not for the bank to reason why". An illustration is the requirement of a credit that the bill of lading shall contain a specific description of the goods; the value of such description is nugatory in view of the—usual—clause in the bill that "weight, measure, marks, numbers, quality, contents and value if mentioned in the bill of lading are to be considered unknown"; nevertheless, the bank must insist that the bill contains the specified description but, unless instructed otherwise, need not reject such bill on the ground that the "weight, etc., unknown" clause is not deleted.[53] In the absence of instructions to the contrary, banks are not under a duty to concern themselves with the clauses— the "small print"—on a bill of lading. All they have to do, in the words of Salmon J.,[54] is "to satisfy themselves that the correct documents are presented to them, and that the bills of lading bear no indorsement or clausing by the shipowners or shippers which could reasonably mean that there was, or might be, some defect in the goods or their packing."[55]

---

[50] UCP Art.14(b).

[51] The bank is entitled to demand documentary evidence that the conditions in the instructions are complied with: *Floating Dock Ltd v. Hongkong and Shanghai Banking Corporation* [1986] 1 Lloyd's Rep. 65 at 80. See also *Banque de l'Indochine et de Suez SA v. J. H. Rayner (Mincing Lane) Ltd* [1983] Q.B. 711, CA; *Astro Exito Navegacion SA v. Chase Manhattan Bank NA; The Messiniaki Tolmi* [1988] 2 Lloyd's Rep. 217, CA (gas free certificate not endorsed by Taiwan authorities); *Seaconsar Far East Ltd v. Bank Markazi Jomhouri Islami Iran* [1993] 1 Lloyd's Rep. 236.

[52] In *Midland Bank Ltd v. Seymour* [1955] 2 Lloyd's Rep. 147 at 151. Also *per* Donaldson J. in *Golodetz & Co Inc v. Czarnikow-Rionda Co Inc; The Galatia* [1979] 2 Lloyd's Rep. 450 at 457; and *per* Parker J. in *Kydon Compañía Naviera SA v. National Westminster Bank Ltd; The Lena* [1981] 1 Lloyd's Rep. 68 at 75.

[53] See *ibid.*

[54] In *British Imex Industries Ltd v. Midland Bank Ltd* [1958] 1 Q.B. 542 at 552.

[55] Sometimes the credit instructions incorporate unusual requirements. Thus, in *Astro Exito Navegacion SA v. Southland Enterprise Co Ltd (No. 2)* [1982] 2 Q.B. 1248, which concerned the sale of a vessel intended to be broken up, the instructions required a certificate signed on behalf of the buyers

Time for examination

11–009 UCP 400 did not provide[56] clear guidance as to what was a reasonable time for the examination of documents. UCP 500, Article 13(b) differs significantly from its predecessor in this regard and states as follows:

> "The Issuing Bank, the Confirming Bank, if any, or a Nominated Bank acting on their behalf, shall each have a reasonable time, not to exceed seven banking days[57] following the day of receipt of the documents, to examine the documents and determine whether to take up or to refuse the documents and to inform the party from which it received the documents accordingly."

This Article, which applies not only to the issuing bank, but also to a confirming or nominated bank, thus places a maximum limit on "reasonable time" of seven banking days following the day of receipt of the documents.

The question of what amounts to a reasonable time was addressed by the Court of Appeal in *Banker's Trust Co v. State Bank of India*[58] a case in which the plaintiff had issued an irrevocable letter of credit which was confirmed by the defendant. The credit was subject to the UCP (1983 revision). The plaintiff examined some 967 pages of documentation within three days and upon discovering discrepancies, notified its customer, the applicant for the credit. A further 72 hours elapsed during which time the applicant was allowed to check the documents again. The notice of rejection was given by the plaintiff to the defendant some eight working days after the documents were received. The plaintiff contended that a reasonable time included the time necessary to consult the applicant for the credit. Hirst J., at first instance,[59.] held that a period of eight working days exceeded a reasonable time for the plaintiff to examine the documents. Affirming this decision, the Court of Appeal held that a reasonable time for the bank to examine the documents was not to be extended by a further period of time in which the customer was allowed to conduct its own examination and concluded that the issuing bank had exceeded a reasonable time between presentation and rejection.[60] The length of the reasonable time depends in each case on the circumstances. Relevant factors are the number and complexity of the tendered documents, their language, the need for urgency in view of the early arrival of the vessel carrying the goods, and possible objections to payment by the buyer on the ground of a suspected or actual fraud by the seller.[61] In *Banker's Trust*, expert evidence was adduced by the defendant to the effect

---

that the vessel had arrived safely at its destination. See also *Gill & Duffus SA v. Berger & Co Inc (No. 2)* [1984] A.C. 382, where the shipping documents to be tendered under a c.i.f. contract were to include a certificate of quality of the goods on discharge; these instructions were obviously nonsense.

[56] In Art. 16(c): "The issuing bank shall have a reasonable time in which to examine the documents and to determine . . . whether to take up or to refuse the documents."

[57] Though banking day is not defined.

[58] [1991] 2 Lloyd's Rep. 443, CA.

[59] [1991] 1 Lloyd's Rep. 587.

[60] [1991] 2 Lloyd's Rep. 443 at 449.

[61] See also Jack (1993), para. 5.41.

that the major U.K. clearing banks generally aim at accepting or rejecting the documents within three working days of their receipt.[62]

In the light of the *Bankers Trust* case, amendments were made to UCP 500 resulting in the seven day time limit set out in Article 13 (b).[63]

Should the bank decide that the documents do not comply with the terms of the credit, notice to that effect must be given without delay, and in any event no later than the close of the seventh banking day following receipt.[64]

Discrepancy of the documents

The law on this subject is summed up by Sir John Donaldson M.R. in the **11–010** following passage,[65] where he observed that the basis was:

> ". . . that the banker is not concerned with why the buyer has called for particular documents,[66] that there is no room for documents which are almost the same, or which will do just as well, as those specified,[67] that whilst the bank is entitled to put a reasonable construction upon any ambiguity in its mandate, if the mandate is clear there must be strict compliance with that mandate,[68] that documents have to be taken up or rejected promptly and without opportunity for prolonged inquiry,[69] and that a tender of documents which properly read and understood calls for further inquiry or is such as to invite litigation is a bad tender."[70]

Two situations have thus to be distinguished. There may be an ambiguity in the credit instructions (mandate), or there may be an ambiguity with respect to the tendered documents.

If the credit instructions are ambiguous,[71] the best course for the bank is to ask for clarification. If this is not possible the bank is protected if it has acted reasonably. Lord Diplock said[72]:

---

[62] *Banker's Trust Co v. State Bank of India* [1991] 1 Lloyd's Rep. 587 at 594; see also *Hing Yip Hing Fat Co Ltd v. Daiwa Bank* [1991] 2 H.K.L.R. 35; *Seaconsar Far East Ltd v. Bank Markazi* [1993] 1 Lloyd's Rep. 236. See also E.P. Ellinger [1985] J.B.L. 406; H. Bennett, "Documentary Credits: A Reasonable Time for What?" [1992] L.C.M.L.Q. 169. On the liability of the bank for delaying payment of the credit beyond a reasonable time without excuse, see *post*, para. 11–021.

[63] And see Jack, (1993), para. 5.41: "It must be emphasised that article 13(b) does not allow seven banking days; it allows a reasonable time up to seven banking days. A reasonable time will in many circumstances be less."

[64] UCP, Art.14(d)(i) and (ii); and see *Rafsanjan Pistachio Producers v. Bank Leumi Cooperative (U.K.) plc* [1992] 1 Lloyd's Rep 513 at 531 where "without delay" was held to mean "without unreasonable delay"; also *Bayerische Vereinsbank v. Bank of Pakistan* [1997] 1 Lloyd's Rep. 59; *Seaconsar (Far East) Ltd v. Bank Markazi Jomhouri Islami Iran* [1997] 2 Lloyd's Rep. 89; affd. [1999] 1 Lloyd's Rep. 36. See further para. 11–010 below.

[65] *Banque de l'Indochine et de Suez SA v. J.H. Rayner (Mincing Lane) Ltd* [1983] Q.B. 711, 729–730. See also *Shamsher Jute Mills Ltd v. Sethia (London) Ltd* [1987] 1 Lloyd's Rep. 388. Further, C.M. Schmitthoff, "Discrepancy of Documents in Letter of Credit Transactions" [1987] J.B.L. 93, *Essays*, 431.

[66] *Commercial Banking Co of Sydney Ltd v. Jalsard Pty Ltd* [1973] A.C. 279.

[67] *Equitable Trust of New York v. Dawson Partners Ltd* (1926) 27 Ll. L. Rep. 49.

[68] *Jalsard's* case, *supra*.

[69] *Hansson v. Hamel and Horley Ltd* [1922] 2 A.C. 36.

[70] *M. Golodetz & Co Inc v. Czarnikow-Rionda Co Inc; The Galatia* [1980] 1 W.L.R. 495.

[71] Which would contravene Article 5(a)(i) the UCP. It is thought that any discrepancy between the underlying contract and the tendered documents should be disregarded by banks because, in principle (and subject to the fraud exception) banks are not concerned with the underlying contract; see *Siporex Trade SA v. Banque Indosuez* [1988] 2 Lloyd's Rep. 147, 161 (a performance bond case).

[72] In *Jalsard's* case, *ante*.

"... where the banker's instructions from his customer are ambiguous or unclear he commits no breach of his contract with the buyer if he has construed them in a reasonable sense, even though upon the closer consideration which can be given to questions of construction in an action in a court of law, it is possible to say that some other meaning is to be preferred."

If the tendered documents are ambiguous, the tender is, in principle, a bad tender. However the bank, when examining the tendered documents, should not insist on the rigid and meticulous fulfilment of the precise wording in all cases.[73] If, "properly read and understood", the words in the instructions and in the tendered documents have the same meaning, if they correspond though not being identical, the bank should not reject the documents. It has been said in an Opinion of the Banking Commission of the ICC that "banks could not act like robots, but had to check each case individually and use their judgment".[74]

However, the margin allowed to the bank in interpreting the documents is very narrow and the bank will be at risk if it does not insist on strict compliance. In *Seaconsar Far East Ltd v. Bank Markazi Jomhouri Islami Iran*[75] the credit stipulated that each tendered document should state the name of the buyer and give the letter of credit number. These did not appear on one of the documents and the bank then rejected the tender. The seller contended that the omissions were trivial in nature, however the court held that since the credit number and buyer's name were specifically required by the credit the bank was in fact entitled to reject the documents.

In practice, the bank may in exceptional cases be prepared to accept an ambiguous document at its risk under reserve[76] or against an indemnity.[77]

Articles 14(d)(i) and (ii) set out the prescribed procedure for refusal of documents. If the bank decides to reject the documents, it must specify *all* of the discrepancies in the notice of rejection and must also state whether it is holding the documents at the disposal of, or returning them to, the presenter.[78] The notice must be given by telecommunication or, if this is not possible, by other expeditious means, without delay[79] and no later than the seven day period prescribed by Article 13(b), and should be given to the party who has remitted the documents to the bank, *i.e.* the bank from which the documents were received, or the beneficiary if the documents were received directly from him.[80] If an issuing bank determines that the documents are discrepant it may, however, exercise a discretion to approach the applicant for a waiver of the discrepancies. This is usually done before a notice of

---

[73] See, *e.g. Hing Yip Hing Fat Co Ltd v. Daiwa Bank Ltd* [1991] 2 H.K.L.R. 35.

[74] Opinions (1980–1981) of the ICC Banking Commission (ICC Publications No. 399), 35.

[75] [1993] 1 Lloyd's Rep. 236; reversed on other grounds [1994] 1 A.C. 438.

[76] See *post*, para. 11–038.

[77] See *post*, para. 11–037.

[78] Both are required under UCP, Art. 14(d) (ii); in *Glencore International AG v. Bank of China* [1996] 1 Lloyd's Rep. 135, it was common ground that the bank could not later rely on any discrepancies other than those contained in the notice; see also *Hing Yip Hing Fat Co Ltd v. Daiwa Bank Ltd* [1991] 2 H.K.L.R. 35.

[79] UCP, Art. 14(d)(i); and see *Rafsanjan Pistachio Producers Co-operative v. Bank Leumi (U.K.) plc* [1992] 1 Lloyd's Rep. 513; *Bayerische Vereinsbank v. Bank of Pakistan* [1997] 1 Lloyd's Rep. 59 at 70, *Seaconsar (Far East) Ltd v. Bank Markazi Jomhouri Islami Iran* [1997] 2 Lloyd's Rep. 89; affd. [1999] 1 Lloyd's Rep. 36.

[80] UCP, Art. 14(d)(i).

rejection is sent. If the applicant for the credit agrees to waive the discrepancy then the documents will usually be taken up.[81]

Failure to comply with the rejection procedure outlined by the UCP precludes the bank from claiming that the documents are discrepant.[82] In *Bayerische Vereinsbank Aktiengesellschaft v. National Bank of Pakistan*[83] the issuing bank forwarded the documents to the applicant in order that the latter might examine them for discrepancies. In the judgment of Mance J., the issuing bank acted as "no more than a postbox"[84] in passing documents to the applicant and then conveying the latter's response to the confirming bank. If the applicant had been referred to only for a waiver of discrepancies identified by the issuing bank, the procedure would have been quicker and thus the issuing bank did not act "within a reasonable time" nor "without delay" and was subject to the provisions of Article 14(e) in that it was precluded from claiming that the documents were not in compliance with the terms and conditions of the credit.

Rejection of non-conforming documents does not preclude the beneficiary from remedying the defects and representing conforming documents provided that this is done within the period of validity of the credit.

Provisions relating to the documents in the UCP

When a question of sufficiency of documents under a letter of credit issued **11–011** under the UCP arises and this question cannot be resolved by reference to the instructions to the bank, it is necessary to turn to the UCP, which set out in considerable detail the documents normally acceptable to the bank. The UCP 500 expands and amends the provisions relating to documents and in particular those which concern transport documentation.

The transport documents

It is common for buyers to require presentation of an invoice, an insurance **11–012** document and a bill of lading or other transport document under the credit. The most commonly required transport document is a bill of lading or a combined transport document. Whereas the UCP 400 referred to three categories of transport documents (marine bills of lading, post receipts and other transport documents) under a credit, the UCP 500, taking account of the increased use of other types of transport documentation, introduces individual Articles which distinguish between various types of transport document and which set out the circumstances under which banks may accept them. These individual Articles refer to:

---

[81] UCP, Art. 14(c) though as stated therein, 14(c) does not extend the period of seven banking days as mentioned in Art. 13(b); and see the expert evidence in *Banker's Trust Co v. State Bank of India* [1991] 2 Lloyd's Rep. 443 at 449, that discrepancies are found in nearly half of all credits and that, in the vast majority of cases, the buyers are prepared to waive the discrepancy.

[82] UCP, Art. 14(e).

[83] [1997] 1 Lloyd's Rep. 59.

[84] At 69.

(a) marine/ocean bills of lading (Art. 23);

(b) non-negotiable sea waybills (Art. 24);

(c) charterparty bills of lading (Art. 25);

(d) multimodal transport documents (Art. 26);

(e) air transport documents (Art. 27);

(f) road, rail and inland waterway transport documents (Art. 28);

(g) courier and post receipts (Art. 29);

(h) transport documents issued by freight forwarders (Art. 30).

(a) **Marine ocean bills of lading (Art. 23)** In English law a marine bill of lading is recognised as a negotiable document of title.[85] Article 23 generally reflects the provisions concerning marine bills of lading found in Article 26 of the 1983 revision. Where a credit calls for a bill of lading covering a port-to-port shipment, it specifies that the following requirements shall apply. The bill of lading must appear on its face to indicate the name of the carrier and be signed or authenticated by the carrier, master or a named agent of either (who must indicate on whose behalf he is acting).[86] It must also indicate that the goods have been loaded on board or shipped on a named vessel. Loading on board may be evidenced by a notation or by a pre-printed clause to this effect on the bill of lading.[87] Further, the bill of lading must indicate the port of loading and the port of discharge stipulated in the credit.[88] Even though transhipment may be prohibited under the credit, Article 23(c)–(d) permits the tender of a bill which includes a clause authorising transhipment.[89]

For other types of transport documentation, the UCP 500 revisions generally apply the principles which govern marine bills of lading but with appropriate modifications.

(b) **Non-negotiable sea waybills (Art. 24)** Unlike bills of lading, sea waybills are not negotiable documents of title. They provide evidence of the shippers' receipt of the goods and of the contract of carriage to a nominated consignee. The provisions for non-negotiable sea waybills are new, but are substantially similar to those for marine ocean bills of lading and permit a bank to accept such documents if the stipulated conditions are met.

(c) **Charter Party bills of lading (Art. 25)** The requirements for charter party bills of lading also reflect those for marine bills of lading. Under this Article, a bank may accept a charter party bill of lading, but it is not obliged to examine the charter party contract. Should a charter party contract be presented,

---

[85] As to marine bills of lading generally, see Chap. 15.

[86] UCP, Art. 23 (a)(i). *Cf.* UCP 400, Art. 23(a)(i): where the bill of lading only had to appear to have been issued by a named carrier.

[87] UCP, Art. 23(a)(ii).

[88] UCP, Art. 23(a)(iii).

[89] As long as the relevant cargo is shipped in container(s), trailer(s) and/or "LASH" barge(s), evidenced by the bill of lading, provided that the entire ocean carriage is covered by one and the same bill of lading (UCP, Art. 23(d)(i)).

the bank will not examine it, and will pass it on without incurring responsibility on its part.

(d) Multimodal transport documents (combined transport documents) (Art. 26) This provision again corresponds with the requirements for a marine bill of lading. The Article applies where the credit calls for "a transport document covering at least two different modes of transport (multimodal transport)". Banks must accept a document which covers carriage of the goods from one mode of transport to another. Even though the credit may prohibit transhipment, the bank will accept a multimodal transport document indicating that transhipment will or may take place, provided the entire carriage is covered by one and the same multimodal transport document.[90] The document must indicate on its face the name of the carrier or multimodal transport operator and must be signed or authenticated by the carrier, the operator or his agent, or by a master or an agent acting on his behalf.[91] Combined transport documents may also be issued by a freight forwarder acting as principal.[92]

(e) Air Transport Documents (Art. 27) This new provision governing air transport requires that the carrier or his named agent acting on his behalf sign the document.[93] The document must show that the goods have been accepted for carriage[94] and also should show the airport of departure and destination stipulated in the credit. If the credit calls for an actual date of despatch, that date must be indicated by a specific notation on the air transport document, otherwise the date of issuance of the air transport document is deemed to be the date of shipment.[95]

Article 28, also a new provision, governs carriage by road, rail or inland waterways and applies similar principles to those cited above. In the absence of any indication on the rail, road or inland waterway transport documents as to the numbers issued, banks will accept the transport document(s) presented as constituting a full set. Banks will also accept such transport documents as originals, whether or not they are marked as originals.[96]

Documentation concerning transport by post or courier is regulated by Article 29.

(f) Transport documents issued by Freight Forwarders (Art. 30) Under UCP 400 only two types of documents issued by freight forwarders were considered acceptable, the "FIATA Combined Transport Bill of Lading" approved by the ICC, and any transport document issued by a freight forwarder who was acting as a carrier or agent of a named carrier. Under this new provision, unless otherwise stipulated in the credit, transport documents issued by a freight forwarder are acceptable if the freight forwarder executes them as a carrier or as a multimodal transport operator or as agent acting on their behalf. The references to FIATA documents have been removed.

---

[90] UCP, Art. 26(b).
[91] UCP, Art. 26(a)(i).
[92] UCP, Art. 30.
[93] UCP, Art. 27(a)(i).
[94] UCP, Art. 27(a)(ii).
[95] UCP, Art. 27(a)(iii).
[96] UCP, Art. 28(b).

In the case of carriage by sea, or by more than one means of conveyance including carriage by sea, unless specifically authorised by the credit banks will not accept a transport document which states that the goods are or will be loaded on deck. A transport document which states that the goods may be carried on deck, or which does not indicate where the goods will be carried, is acceptable.[97] Article 32 provides that, unless the credit expressly stipulates clauses or notations which may be accepted, transport documents presented to the bank must be "clean", *i.e.* they must not bear any clause or notation which "expressly declares a defective condition of the goods and/or the packaging".[98]

The invoice

11–013 Article 37 deals with commercial invoices and sets out the requirements to be met in the absence of any stipulation to the contrary. The commercial invoice for the goods must appear on its face to be issued by the beneficiary named in the credit though it need not be signed.[99] It should be made out in the name of the buyer/applicant for the credit.[1] and the description of the goods must correspond exactly with that found in the credit, though other documents may contain a description in general terms not inconsistent with the terms of the credit.[2] A bank has a discretion to reject a set of documents containing an invoice issued for an amount in excess of the credit.[3]

Insurance documents

11–014 These are governed by Articles 34 to 36. Such documents are to be stipulated in the credit and issued and signed by the insurance company, or underwriters or their agents. If the insurance document indicates that it has been issued in more than one original, all the originals must be presented.[4] Unless specifically authorised by the credit, broker's cover notes are not acceptable,[5] though (unless otherwise stipulated) banks will accept an insurance certificate or a declaration under an open cover, presigned by insurance companies or underwriters or their agents.[6] Cover must be effective at the latest from the date of loading on board or dispatch or taking in charge[7] and the insurance documents must be expressed in the same currency as the credit.[8]

---

[97] UCP, Art. 31(i).
[98] See *M. Golodetz & Co Inc v. Czarnikow-Rionda Co Inc; The Galatia* [1979] 2 Lloyd's Rep. 450 [1980], also C.M. Schmitthoff, "Discrepancy of Documents in Letter of Credit Transactions" [1987] J.B.L. 94.
[99] UCP, Art. 37(a)(i) and (iii).
[1] UCP, Art. 37(a)(ii).
[2] UCP, Art. 37(c); and see, *e.g. Bank Melli Iran v. Barclays Bank Dominion, Colonial & Overseas* [1951] 2 Lloyd's List Rep. 367; *Glencore International AG v. Bank of China* [1996] 1 Lloyd's Rep. 135 at 153.
[3] UCP, Art. 37(b).
[4] UCP, Art. 34(a) and (b).
[5] UCP, Art. 34(c).
[6] UCP, Art. 34(d).
[7] UCP, Art. 34(e).
[8] UCP, Art. 34(f)(i).

The goods are to be insured for at least their c.i.f. value plus 10 per cent. Should the bank be unable to determine the c.i.f. value from the face of the documents, it will accept an insurance document stating that the minimum amount of cover is 110 per cent of the amount for which payment, acceptance or negotiation is requested under the credit, or 110 per cent of the gross amount of the invoice, whichever is greater.[9]

The credit should stipulate the type of insurance required and any additional risks covered. In the absence of such stipulation, the bank will accept the insurance documents as presented by the seller and bears no responsibility for any risks not covered therein.[10]

If the credit stipulates "all risks" terms, the insurance document need not bear such a heading provided it contains a clear "all risks" clause or notation.[11]

The seller may, of course, require the tender of documents other than the commercial invoice, transport and insurance documents. Where other documents are called for under the credit, it should stipulate by whom such documents are to be issued and their wording or data content. In accordance with Article 21, if a bank has no precise instructions as to the required content of such documents, then it will accept documents as presented, providing their content is not inconsistent with any other stipulated documents tendered. The bank is under an obligation to check for inconsistencies in such additional documentation and must ensure that there is a consistency between the documents and that there is unequivocal reference to the same goods in all the documents.

The general rule is that the buyer is entitled to receive original documents.[12] Article 20 attempts to clarify the circumstances in which documents presented for payment can be said to be original. Article 20(b) makes it clear that unless otherwise stipulated in the credit, a document produced by reprographic, automated or computerised systems or a carbon copy may be treated as an original if it is marked as original[13] and where necessary appears to be signed. The signature may be by handwriting, facsimile signature, or perforated signature and signatures executed by "stamp, by symbol or by any other mechanical or electronic method of authentication".[14]

The effect of Article 20(b) was considered in *Glencore International AG v. Bank of China*[15] where the issuing bank rejected documents, *inter alia*, on grounds that a certificate issued by the beneficiary was not marked "original". The document had originally been generated on a word-processing system and printer and then photocopied. One of the photocopies was signed by the beneficiary with an original signature in blue ink. The Court of Appeal determined that the original signature was not enough to render the document an original for the purposes of Article 20(b) if the document itself was not otherwise original.

---

[9] UCP, Art. 34(f)(ii).

[10] UCP, Art. 35(a) and (b).

[11] UCP, Art. 36.

[12] See Jack (1993), para. 8.40.

[13] And see Bennett, "Strict Compliance Under the UCP 500" [1997] L.C.M.L.Q. 7.

[14] UCP, Art. 20(b). The ICC Commission on Banking Technique and Practice has issued a Policy Statement dated July 12, 1999 concerning the correct intepretation of Article 20(b). See *http://www.iccwbo.org*.

[15] [1996] 1 Lloyd's Rep. 135.

Article 20(c)(i) further states that a copy is a document so labelled or a document not marked as an original.[16]

Several documents to be read together

11–015 The bank is usually instructed to make finance available on tender of several documents in a set, and as stated, these would normally be the transport document, *e.g.* a bill of lading, the invoice and the insurance policy or certificate. In that case, in the absence of instructions to the contrary, it is sufficient if all the documents in the set, taken together, contain the particulars required by the bank's mandate and it is not necessary that every document in the set should contain them. The goods must be fully described in the invoice in accordance with the credit instructions, but in the other documents they may be described in general terms. This rule is now contained in Article 37(c) of the UCP which mitigates, to some extent, the effect of the doctrine of strict compliance.

The rule in Article 37(c) is founded on the English case of *Midland Bank Ltd v. Seymour*.[17] In this case a merchant in England bought a quantity of ducks' feathers from sellers in Hong Kong c. and f. Hamburg. The instructions to the bank were that the documents had to evidence "shipment from Hong Kong to Hamburg of the undermentioned goods", and then, under "Description, Quantity and Price" it was stated "Hong Kong duck feathers—85 per cent clean; 12 bales each weighing about 190 lb.; 5s per lb". The bill of lading described the goods merely as "12 bales; Hong Kong duck feathers" but all the documents, namely the bills of lading, invoices, weight account and certificate of origin, when read together, contained a complete description of the goods. The seller shipped worthless goods and the buyer claimed that the bank was not entitled to debit him with the credit since the bill of lading did not contain a full description of the goods. Devlin J. rejected this contention and held that the bank had complied with its mandate.

Linkage of documents

11–016 Whilst some latitude is allowed in the description of the goods in the documents other than the invoice, all documents tendered to the bank must clearly and unequivocally relate to the same goods. This question of *identification* of the goods is different from that of their *description* in the documents. If the documents are not linked by an unambiguous reference to the same goods, the tender is bad. But it is not necessary that the *documents themselves* be linked by mutual references. In one case[18] concerning the sale of sugar, the credit instructions

---

[16] Although this does not apply to originally handwritten or typed documents, which do not need to be marked as original; see *Glencore International AG v. Bank of China* [1996] 1 Lloyd's Rep. 135; see further *Kredietbank Antwerp v. Midland Bank plc*, *The Times*, October 31, 1997; *The Times*, May 1, 1999, CA.

[17] [1955] 2 Lloyd's Rep. 147; see also *Panchaud Freres SA v. Etablissements General Grain Co* [1970] 1 Lloyd's Rep. 53, CA, *ante*, para. 2–026.

[18] *Banque de l'Indochine et de Suez SA v. J.H. Rayner (Mincing Lane) Ltd* [1983] Q.B. 711; another issue which arose in this case is located at *post*, para. 11–038.

required certificates of origin, EUR 1 certificates, and a full set of clean on board bills of lading evidencing shipment from an E.C. port to Djibouti in transit to Yemen. The bills of lading showed that shipment was made in the vessel *Markhor*. One of the certificates of origin referred to the goods as shipped in "m.v. Markhor or substitute" and the other to "transport mixed à destination Djibouti Port in Transit Yemen". The Court of Appeal held that, although the requirements relating to description provided in what is now Article 37(c) of the 1993 UCP were satisfied, the linkage between the bills of lading and the certificate of origin was missing. "Clearly this [m.v. Markhor or substitute] *could* be a different vessel and accordingly refer to a different parcel of sugar".[19] Although the decision of the Court of Appeal was unanimous, it is respectfully submitted that on this issue[20] the requirement of linkage was applied by the court too strictly.

Instructions communicated by teletransmission

The provisions of the UCP which deal with credit instructions communicated **11–017** by teletransmission[21] are contained in Article 11. The essence of these provisions is that unless there is a clear statement of intention to the contrary, the teletransmission is to constitute the operative credit instrument or the operative amendment, and a bank is not obliged to check a mail confirmation even if one is sent.

Article 11 is worded as follows:

"(a) (i) When an Issuing Bank instructs an Advising Bank by an authenticated teletransmission to advise a Credit or an amendment to a Credit, the teletransmission will be deemed to be the operative Credit instrument or the operative amendment, and no mail confirmation should be sent. Should a mail confirmation nevertheless be sent, it will have no effect and the Advising Bank will have no obligation to check such mail confirmation against the operative Credit instrument or the operative amendment received by teletransmission.

(ii) If the teletransmission states "full details to follow" (or words of similar effect) or states that the mail confirmation is to be the operative Credit instrument or the operative amendment, then the teletransmission will not be deemed to be the operative Credit instrument or the operative amendment. The Issuing Bank must forward the operative Credit instrument or the operative amendment to such advising Bank without delay.

(b) If a bank uses the services of an Advising Bank to have the Credit advised to the Beneficiary, it must also use the services of the same bank for advising an amendment(s).

(c) [omitted]."

---

[19] *Per* Sir John Donaldson M.R., *ibid.* at 732.
[20] There were other discrepancies on the documents and, having regard to them, the decision of the Court was clearly correct.
[21] Which appears to include telegrams, telexes and telefaxes, though not telephone conversations; Opinions of the ICC Banking Commission (1984–1986) ICC Publication No. 434, p.19, cited in *Todd* (1998), p. 153.

Time of opening of credit

11–018 Often the contract of sale will make express provision as regards the date at
which the credit has to be opened. Sometimes it is stated that the credit shall
be opened by a certain date, sometimes it is provided that it shall be opened
"immediately", which means that the credit has to be opened at once within
such time as is required for a person of reasonable diligence to establish the
credit,[22] or sometimes the opening of the credit is made dependent on an act by
the seller relating to the delivery of the goods, *e.g.* the sending of a provisional
invoice[23] or of an advice that the goods are, or will soon be, ready for shipment.[24]
The opening of the credit may also be made dependent on the seller providing
a performance guarantee.[25] The credit is regarded as "opened" when the advice
of the confirmation, as the case may be, is communicated to the beneficiary (the
seller).[26]

Where the contact does not provide when the credit shall be opened, the
parties are not normally entitled to assume that the existence of the contract of
sale depends on the opening of the credit by the buyer. Although the parties are
at liberty to agree that the contract shall be "subject to the opening of a credit"
in which case the opening of the credit is a condition precedent to the *formation*
of the contract and in the words of Denning L.J., "if no credit is provided, there
is no contract between the parties",[27] such interpretation of the buyer's promise
is only possible where the parties have expressly or impliedly agreed that this
promise shall be subject to that condition. In the normal cases in which the
contract is unqualified, the stipulation to open a letter of credit is only a condition precedent to the *performance* of the contract; it is the mechanism agreed
upon for the payment of the price, the failure of the buyer to open the credit
within the stipulated time may be treated by the seller as a breach of a condition
of the contract and as repudiation of it.[28]

---

[22] *Garcia v. Page & Co* [1936] 55 Ll. L.R. 391. The seller may waive the rights arising from the
delay in the opening of the credit expressly or impliedly: *Baltimex v. Metallo Chemical Refinery Co
Ltd* [1956] 1 Lloyd's Rep. 450.

[23] *Knotz v. Fairclough, Dodd & Jones Ltd* [1952] 1 Lloyd's Rep. 226.

[24] *Plasticmoda SpA v. Davidsons (Manchester)* [1952] 1 Lloyd's Rep. 527. See also *Etablissements
Chainbaux SARL v. Harbormaster Ltd* [1955] 1 Lloyd's Rep. 303.

[25] *Cf. State Trading Corporation of India Ltd v. M. Golodetz Ltd; The Sara D* [1989] 2 Lloyd's
Rep. 277; see *ante*, para. 14–005 and *post*, n. 26.

[26] *Bunge Corporation v. Vegetable Vitamin Foods (Pte) Ltd* [1985] 1 Lloyd's Rep. 613 with reference to *Brinkibon Ltd v. Stahag Stahl und Stahlwarenhandels GmbH* [1983] 2 A.C. 34; *State Trading
Corporation of India v. M. Golodetz Ltd; The Sara D* [1988] 2 Lloyd's Rep. 182 (where Evans J.
held that the "opening" of a bank guarantee required the person obliged to procure it to take "the
appropriate steps" with the bank rests on the facts of this case). Evans J. was overruled by the CA
on other grounds [1989] 2 Lloyd's Rep. 277, see *ante*, para. 14–005. On the moment when an
irrevocable or a confirmed credit becomes binding on the bank, see *post*, para. 11–023.

[27] *Trans Trust SPRL v. Danubian Trading Co Ltd* [1952] 2 Q.B. 297 at 304; see also *United Dominions Trust (Commercial) Ltd v. Eagle Aircraft Services Ltd* [1968] 1 W.L.R. 74, 80, 82; *Gyllenhammar & Partners International Ltd v. Sour Brodogradevna Industria* [1989] 2 Lloyd's Rep. 403
("subject to" obtaining a bank guarantee).

[28] *Nichimen Corporation v. Gatoil Overseas Inc* [1987] 2 Lloyd's Rep. 46 (this repudiation, like
every repudiation (see *ante*, para. 12–005, n. 12) has, of course, to be accepted by the innocent
party).

Where the contract of sale is unconditional but does not provide a date on which the credit shall be opened, the credit has to be opened within "a reasonable time".[29] This means a reasonable time calculated back from the first date of the shipment, not calculated forward from the date of the conclusion of the contract.[30] Taking the first date of shipment as the starting point, the buyer has, it is thought, to open the credit a sufficient time in advance of that event to enable the seller to know before he sends the goods to the docks that his payment will be secured by the credit for which it is stipulated. Where a certain period for shipment is stipulated in the contract, *e.g.* shipment in February, March or April, in the absence of a stipulation to the contrary, the buyer has to open the credit not when the seller is ready to ship, but he has to give the seller the benefit of the whole shipment period; as Somerwell L.J. observed in one case[31]:

> "When a seller is given a right to ship over a period and there is machinery for payment, that machinery must be available over the whole of that period. If the buyer is anxious, as he might be if the period of shipment is a long one, not to have to put the credit machinery in motion until shortly before the seller is likely to want to ship, then he must insert some provision in the contract by which the credit shall be provided, *e.g.* fourteen days after a cable received from the seller."

These rules apply equally to c.i.f. contracts[32] and f.o.b. contracts in which the seller has to make arrangements for freight and marine insurance for the account of the buyer[33] and there is at least a prima facie rule that they likewise apply to f.o.b. contracts of the strict type[34] although in that case the shipping period is arranged for the benefit of the buyer and not the seller, because only in that way, in the words of Diplock J.,[35] can one get "certainty into what is a very common commercial contract".

In *Glencore Grain Rotterdam BV v. Lebanese Organisation for International Commerce*[36] it was held by the Court of Appeal that in the absence of any special agreement, the sellers under an f.o.b. contract were entitled to see a conforming letter of credit in place before commencing shipment of the goods. Then, their obligation was to ship the contract goods on board the vessel provided by the buyers for carriage on whatever terms as to freight or otherwise the buyers had agreed with the shipowners.

---

[29] This is an implied term of the contract: *Diamond Cutting Works Federation v. Triefus & Co Ltd* [1956] 1 Lloyd's Rep. 216 at 225.
[30] *Sinaison-Teicher Inter-American Grain Corporation v. Oilcakes and Oilseeds Trading Co Ltd* [1954] 1 W.L.R. 935.
[31] *Pavia & Co SpA v. Thurmann-Nielsen* [1952] 2 Q.B. 84 at 88; see also *Tsakiroglou & Co Ltd v. Trangrains SA* [1958] 1 Lloyd's Rep. 562 (shipping period and nomination of port of destination by buyers); *Margaronis Navigation Agency Ltd v. H.W. Peabody & Co of London Ltd* [1964] 1 Lloyd's Rep. 173 (laydays under charterparty).
[32] *Pavia & Co SpA v. Thurmann-Nielsen* [1952] 2 Q.B. 84; *Sinaison-Teicher Inter-American Grain Corporation v. Oilcakes and Oilseeds Trading Co Ltd* [1954] 1 W.L.R. 935.
[33] See para. 2–007; *NV Handel My. J. Smits Import-Export v. English Exporters (London) Ltd* [1957] 1 Lloyd's Rep. 517 at 519.
[34] See *ante*, para. 2–007; particularly when they are string contracts in which the credit of the ultimate buyer is of overriding character: *Ian Stach Ltd v. Baker Bosley Ltd* [1958].
[35] *ibid.* at 144.
[36] [1997] 2 Lloyd's Rep. 386.

The expiry date of the credit

11–019 The letter of credit must stipulate an expiry date on or before which documents must be presented by the seller (at the stipulated place of presentation). Article 42(a) of the UCP provides:

> "All Credits must stipulate an expiry date and a place for presentation of documents for payment, acceptance, or with the exception of freely negotiable Credits, a place for presentation of documents for negotiation. An expiry date stipulated for payment, acceptance or negotiation will be construed to express an expiry date for presentation of documents."

The UCP further contains detailed provisions for the ascertainment of the expiry date and its extension should it fall on a day when the bank is closed[37] or in case of interruption of the bank's business owing to events beyond its control.[38]

The expiry date of the credit should not be confused with the shipment date. The shipment date is the—earlier—date shown in the bill of lading as the date when the goods were loaded. The credit sometimes stipulates, in addition to its expiry date, that the bills presented to the bank shall indicate a certain shipment date.[39] If the bills of lading presented by the seller to the bank show a later date or if the bills are stale,[40] the bank will refuse to accept the documents even if presented before the expiry date. Article 43(a) provides that in addition to stipulating an expiry date for presentation of documents, where the credit calls for the tender of transport documents, the period of time after the date of shipment during which presentation must be made should also be specified. If no such time period is specified, then the banks will not accept documents presented to them later than 21 days after the date of the shipment.

Exceptionally, in long-term transactions, the credit may have to be kept open for a considerable time. In one case[41] the parties agreed that upon expiration of the period of three years the credit was considered automatically invalidated but in the event of the matter being submitted to arbitration it should be deemed extended automatically without amendment for one year from any expiry date. A letter of credit may also contain a provision under which it is extended automatically for another fixed period from the expiry date unless the bank notifies the beneficiary, for instance 30 days prior to the expiry date by registered mail, that it has elected not to renew the credit. Such a provision, known as an *evergreen clause*, should not be confused with a revolving credit.[42]

The law applicable to the credit

11–020 It will rarely be necessary to ascertain the law governing a letter of credit because, as has been seen,[43] banks in most countries operate credits under the

---

[37] UCP, Art. 44 and see further *Bayerische Vereinsbank AG v. National Bank of Pakistan* [1997] 1 Lloyd's Rep. 59.
[38] UCP, Art.17.
[39] The UCP contains detailed provisions on the ascertainment of the loading date in Articles 43–46.
[40] See *post*, para. 15–032.
[41] *Offshore International SA v. Banco Central SA* [1976] 2 Lloyd's Rep. 402.
[42] See *post*, para. 11–031.
[43] See *ante*, para. 11–002.

UCP and that uniformity excludes the possibility of a conflict of laws with respect to most legal problems. The question of the law governing the credit is, of course, entirely separate from the ascertainment of the law governing the relationship between the seller and the buyer, *i.e.* the underlying contract of sale.

The UCP itself does not contain any provisions concerning the conflict of laws. If it is necessary to determine the law governing a letter of credit and the credit itself does not contain a choice of law clause[44] then this has traditionally been determined in accordance with general principles governing choice of law.[45] At common law the law applicable was the law of the country with which the credit had its closest and most real connection,[46] generally the place of presentment and examination of documents stipulated under the credit and where payment was to be made by or on behalf of the issuing bank.

In relation to letter of credit contracts entered into since April 1, 1991, the ascertainment of the applicable law is to be determined by reference to the Articles of the Rome Convention.[47] Under Article 3 of the Convention a contract is to be governed by the law chosen by the parties. The choice must be expressed or demonstrated with reasonable certainty by the terms of the contract or the circumstances of the case. Where the parties have not chosen a law to govern the contract, Article 4(1) preserves the general position at common law that the applicable law is to be that of the country with which it is most closely connected. By Article 4(2) (and subject to the presumption contained in Article 4(5)) it shall be presumed that the contract is most closely connected with the country where the party who is to effect the performance which is characteristic of the contract has, at the time of conclusion of the contract, its principal place of business or, where the performance is to be effected through another place of business, the country in which that other place is business is situated. Article 4(5) states that Article 4(2) shall not apply if the characteristic performance cannot be determined and "the presumption in paragraph 2 . . . shall be disregarded if it appears from the circumstances as a whole that the contract is more closely connected with another country".

When attempting to ascertain the law governing the credit, it should be borne in mind that the credit involves several contractual relationships and that these relationships are not all governed by the same applicable law:

1. As between the buyer and the issuing bank, the characteristic performance is likely to be that of the bank and the governing law of the country in which the bank carries on business and has issued the credit. In practice, inasmuch as this contract will often be made between two parties in the same country it is less likely that a "situation involving a choice between the laws of different

---

[44] Standard form letters of credit do not ordinarily specify a choice of law.
[45] See Chap. 21.
[46] *Offshore International SA v. Banco Central SA* [1976] 2 Lloyd's Rep. 402 at 403.
[47] Incorporated in the U.K. by the Contracts (Applicable Law) Act 1990 and see Chap. 21; see also C.J.G. Morse, "Letters of Credit And the Rome Convention" [1994] L.C.M.L.Q. 560.

countries"[48] will arise and that the Rome Convention will be brought into operation.

2.   As between the issuing bank and the beneficiary (*i.e.* the seller), this contract will generally be governed by the law of the place in which the beneficiary is to present documents in order to obtain payment. When the letter of credit is also confirmed, this creates an independent contract between the beneficiary and the bank which confirms the credit.

In a leading common law case[49] an irrevocable credit was opened by a Spanish bank in favor of an oil rig company incorporated in Panama but operating from Houston, Texas. The credit was advised by a New York bank but was not confirmed by it. The beneficiary sued the issuing bank in the English courts and the preliminary question arose whether the contract between the beneficiary and the issuing bank was governed by Spanish law (the law of the issuing bank) or by New York law (the law of the advising bank). Applying the common law test, Ackner J. decided in favor of New York law on the ground that this was the law with which the transaction had its closest and most real connection. He observed[50]:

> "... I am satisfied that .... very great inconvenience would arise, if the law of the issuing bank were to be considered as the proper law. The advising bank would have constantly to be seeking to apply a whole variety of foreign laws [if a different view were adopted]."

Under the Rome Convention, the characteristic performance would appear to be that of the issuing bank. By virtue of Article 4(2), the governing law would, accordingly, be that of the country in which the principal place of business or the place of business of the bank is situated.[51]

3.   The relationship between the issuing bank and the advising bank causes the greatest difficulty. In these inter-bank transactions general conditions of business or a course of dealing may allow some conclusions as to a choice of law by the parties, but in the absence of such indication, the common law position was that the contract was considered as having the closest and most real connection with the country where the branch of the bank at which payment was to be made was situated.

In *Bank of Credit & Commerce Hong Kong Ltd (in liquidation) v. Sonali Bank*[52] it was the defendant's contention that the law of Bangladesh was the proper law governing seven claims for reimbursement under five letters of credit.

---

[48] Art. 1(1) of the Convention and see *Jack* (1993), para. 13.16; Morse [1994] L.M.C.L.Q. 560 at 570.
[49] *Offshore Internationa SA v. Banco Central SA* [1977] 1 W.L.R. 399.
[50] The observations of Ackner J. were approved by the Court of Appeal in *Power Curber International Ltd v. National Bank of Kuwait SK* [1981] 2 Lloyd's Rep. 394, 399 and 400. See also *Toprak Mahsulleri Ofisi v. Finagrain Compagnie Commercial Agricole et Financiere SA* [1979] 2 Lloyd's Rep. 98 at 114; *Intraco Ltd v. Notis Shipping Corporation; The Bhoja Trader* [1981] 2 Lloyd's Rep. 256 at 258; *Attock Cement Company Ltd v. Romanian Bank for Foreign Trade* [1989] 1 Lloyd's Rep. 572.
[51] Though see *Bank of Baroda, post.*
[52] [1995] 1 Lloyd's Rep. 227.

The plaintiffs were the confirming bank in all but one case and in all cases the beneficiary presented documents to and was paid by the plaintiffs in Hong Kong. Applying the common law test, Cresswell J. held[53] that the law governing the contracts between BCCHK and Sonali was in each case the law of Hong Kong because: (a) it was common ground that in each case BCCHK (in Hong Kong) would add its confirmation to the credit; (b) when it confirmed the credit, BCCHK was incurring an obligation in addition to that of Sonali; (c) in requesting BCCHK to add its confirmation, Sonali authorised BCCHK to negotiate against documents which appeared on their face to be in accordance with the terms and conditions of the credit, and undertook to reimburse BCCHK; (d) having confirmed the credit, BCCHK was *obliged*[54] to negotiate the documents and; (e) the credits contemplated that negotiation of documents presented by or on behalf of the Hong Kong beneficiary would take place in Hong Kong (which is what happened, with payment made by BCCHK to the beneficiary).

In *Bank of Baroda v. Vysya Bank*,[55] one of the first English cases to be decided under the Rome Convention, the plaintiff had confirmed letters of credit through its City of London office. The law applicable to the contract between Vysya, the issuing bank and Bank of Baroda as confirming bank fell to be determined by reference to Article 4 of the Rome Convention,[56] requiring the identification of the performance which characterised the contract between the parties. The applicable law would then be that of the country of the principal place of business or place of business, of the party who was to effect the characteristic performance. Mance J. observed[57] that "under a contract between an issuing bank and a confirming bank the performance which is characteristic of the contract is the adding of its confirmation by the latter and its honouring of the obligations accepted thereby in relation to the beneficiary. The liability on the part of the issuing bank to reimburse or indemnify the confirming bank is consequential on the character of the contract; it does not itself characterise the contract". Thus, the characteristic performance was that of the Bank of Baroda, through a "place of business other than [its] principal place of business". As confirmation took place in London, the contract between the two parties was, accordingly, governed by English law.

Mance J. also considered the law governing certain of the other contracts associated with the letter of credit, and determined that as between Bank of Baroda as confirming bank and the beneficiary, English law was the governing law whether one considered Article 4(2) or Article 4(5) of the Rome Convention. He held that the relationship between Vysya as issuing bank and the beneficiary was also subject to English law. Whilst the application of Article 4(2) raised the presumption that this relationship would be governed by Indian law, Mance J. determined that this presumption was to be rebutted by Article 4(5) in favour of the law of the country where payment was to be made against presentation

---

[53] At 237; the letters of credit in this case predated April 1, 1991 and thus the Rome Convention did not apply.
[54] See Jack (1993), para 6.17.
[55] [1994] 2 Lloyd's Rep. 87.
[56] See para. 11–020.
[57] At 90.

of documents. The application of Article 4(2) would lead to a confusion and a lack of clarity and simplicity in the issue and in the operation of international letters of credit and great inconvenience would be caused by having different legal systems governing the relationship of each of the two banks (issuing and confirming) with the beneficiary.[58]

Damages for failure to open or pay a credit

11–021 Where the buyer fails to open a credit as stipulated, the seller is entitled to claim damages for breach of that stipulation, which qualifies as a condition.[59] The amount of damages recoverable under this heading is sometimes higher than the amount which the seller can recover for breach of the buyer's obligation to accept delivery of the goods. In the latter case, if the goods have an available market, the presumption of section 50(3) of the Sale of Goods Act 1979 applies. This provides that the measure of damages is prima facie the difference between the contract price and the market price at the date when the goods ought to have been accepted. In a rising market damages for non-acceptance of goods are nominal but damages for failure to open a commercial credit are not subject to the restriction of section 50(3) and may, in appropriate cases, include the loss of profit which the seller would have made had the transaction been carried out.[60] Where the advising bank delays the payment of the credit without excuse beyond a reasonable time, although the documents were presented on time, it may be liable to the seller in damages.[61]

KINDS OF LETTERS OF CREDIT

Payment at sight, deferred payment, acceptance and negotiation credits

11–022 It is of importance to the seller to know in what manner he will obtain the moneys due to him under the credit. Four possibilities exist[62]: the credit may be available by sight payment, by deferred payment, by acceptance or by negotiation. The credit itself should state which of these four methods has been chosen by the parties and this issue should be settled beforehand in the contract under which the credit is opened.

1.   If the parties have arranged a *payment at sight credit*, the advising bank is instructed to pay, or arrange for payment, to the seller the moneys due on presentation of the documents. This is a case of payment against documents.

---

[58] At 93, citing Ackner J. in *Offshore International SA v. Banco Central SA* [1977] 2 W.L.R. 399 at 401.
[59] See *ante*, para. 5–003.
[60] *Trans Trust SPRL v. Danubian Trading Co Ltd* [1952] 2 Q.B. 297 at 305.
[61] *Ozalid Group (Export) Ltd v. African Continental Bank Ltd* [1979] 2 Lloyd's Rep. 231. On the length of a "reasonable time" for the examination of documents, see *ante*, para. 11–009.
[62] UCP, Art. 9(a).

2.   If the parties have arranged a *deferred payment credit*, the advising bank is authorised to pay, or make arrangements for payment, at some future date determinable in accordance with the terms of the credit.

The deferred payment credit may, for example, provide for payment 180 days from the date of the bill of lading. In this case an acceptance credit[63] providing for a time bill would be inappropriate because a bill of exchange cannot be made payable at a time which can only be determined by reference to the uncertain date of the issue of the bill of lading.[64]

If the seller requires cash before the deferred payment credit matures, he can only provide it by negotiating the letter of credit.[65] The issuing bank sometimes provides in the credit that such negotiation shall be restricted to a specified bank, "perhaps because this [is] a bank with which [it has] a commercial relationship".[66] The negotiation of the deferred payment credit is normally done at a discount, which reduces the amount of the credit due to the seller.

3.   If the credit is an *acceptance credit*, the seller draws the bill of exchange on the advising bank in the specified manner. The bill will normally be a time draft. By accepting the bill, the bank signifies its commitment to pay the face value on maturity to the party presenting it. The bill accepted by the advising bank provides the seller with a considerable degree of security. If he does not want to hold the bill until it matures, he may turn it into money by negotiating, *e.g.* by discounting it or selling it to his own bank.[67] On negotiation, he is unlikely to receive the full amount of money stated in the tenor of the bill because the negotiating bank will deduct a discount or interest and commission.

Another form of acceptance credit is a credit which, according to the arrangement of the parties to the contract of sale, shall be accepted by the issuing bank or by the buyer (the applicant for the credit). Where the issuing bank issues the credit as irrevocable, it holds itself under the UCP, Art. 9(a)(iii), responsible that the bill will be accepted and paid by the buyer. Where the advising bank confirms the credit, a similar obligation is placed on it by the UCP, Art. 9(b)(iii). It follows that, even if the arrangement of the parties is that only the buyer has to accept, if the credit is made irrevocable or irrevocable and confirmed and is made subject to the UCP, the seller has a considerable degree of security.[68]

There is no recourse by a bank which has accepted a bill against the seller. If that bank dishonours the bill by non-payment, *e.g.* because it becomes insolvent, the seller has still his claim for the purchase price against the buyer because the acceptance credit is only a conditional performance of the buyer's obligation to pay.[69]

---

[63] For acceptance credit see "3", below.
[64] See *ante*, para. 9–004.
[65] *European Asian Bank AG v. Punjab & Sind Bank (No. 2)* [1983] 1 W.L.R. 642. See E.P. Ellinger, "Discount of Letter of Credit," [1984] J.B.L. 379.
[66] *Per* Robert Goff L.J. (handing down the judgment of the CA), in the *European Asian Bank AG* case, *supra*, n. 65 at 655.
[67] See *ante*, para. 9–011.
[68] See *Forestal Mimosa Ltd v. Oriental Credit Bank Ltd* [1986] 1 W.L.R. 631, CA.
[69] See *post*, para. 11–040.

4.   Under the *negotiation credit* the advising bank is only authorised to negoti-ate[70] a bill of exchange drawn by the seller on the buyer or the issuing bank. The advising bank will indorse the bill and negotiate it, subject to deduction of discount or interest and commission. The bill may be a sight draft or a time draft, according to the terms of the credit.

The negotiation credit is subject to recourse against the seller as drawer of the bill because the bank has become an indorser of the bill of exchange, but if the negotiating bank is the confirming bank (and the tender of the documents is in order), it cannot avail itself of this facility since it is liable to the seller on the confirmation.[71]

Sometimes, the bank is only authorised to make an advance on the security of the documentary bill.[72]

Revocable and irrevocable credits; confirmed and unconfirmed credits

11–023   It is essential to distinguish between these types of credit. The quality of the credit as "revocable" or "irrevocable" refers to the obligation of the issuing bank to the beneficiary (the seller). The quality of the credit as "confirmed" or "unconfirmed"[73] refers to the obligation of the advising bank to the beneficiary.

Article 6 of the UCP states that a credit may either be revocable or irrevoc-able. Reversing the previous position, the 1993 revision now provides that a credit is deemed to be irrevocable unless there is a clear indication that it is revocable. This principle is stated as follows.

"(b) The Credit . . . should clearly indicate whether it is revocable or irrevocable.

(c) In the absence of such indication the Credit shall be deemed to be irrevocable."

Of course, no advising or nominated bank would ever confirm a credit unless the issuing bank has made it irrevocable. The UCP contains detailed provisions entitling the advising bank, which has taken up the documents in accordance with the instructions, to reimbursement from the issuing bank[74]; these provisions apply to revocable as well as irrevocable credits.[75]

It is controversial at which moment the irrevocable credit becomes binding on the issuing bank and the confirmed credit on the advising bank.[76] It is thought

---

[70] See *ante*, para. 9–004; UCP, Art. 10(b)(ii) defines negotiation as the giving of value for draft(s) and or document(s) by the bank authorised to negotiate.

[71] The treatment of a time draft as a sight draft does not operate automatically as confirmation and does not prevent recourse: *Maran Road v. Austin Taylors Co Ltd* [1975] 1 Lloyd's Rep. 156 at 161.

[72] *Plein & Co Ltd v. Inland Revenue Commissioners* [1946] 175 L.T. 453.

[73] The UCP use the term "without engagement" for "unconfirmed" credits: Art. 7.

[74] Provided the documents have been taken up before the credit was revoked.

[75] UCP, Arts 8 and 9.

[76] The difficulty is due to the fact that the bank makes the beneficiary a unilateral offer of a contract and the question arises when this offer is accepted. Some authors, like Treitel, *The Law of Contract*, (9th ed., 1995), p. 140, suggest that the acceptance takes place when the beneficiary has "taken steps in the performance," *i.e.* the performance of the contract of sale. This view can refer to the statement of Rowlatt J. in *Urquhart Lindsay & Co Ltd v. Eastern Bank Ltd* [1922] 1 K.B. 318, that the beneficiary must have "acted upon" the bank's undertaking. Other authors, like Gutteridge and Megrah, *The Law of Bankers' Commercial Credits* (7th ed.), p. 34 take the view that the question is academic; they state that the bank becomes bound to the seller the moment the credit is communic-

that these obligations become binding on the banks before the tender of the documents, namely when the beneficiary receives the communication of the bank and accepts it.[77] The relationships between the banks which undertake these obligations and the beneficiary are, as already observed, contractual.

From the exporter's perspective, a particularly important feature of the credit is whether it is irrevocable or irrevocable and confirmed. He has to arrange in the contract of sale (or other underlying contract) the most appropriate of these two types of credit and all the other details of it, including the mode of payment.[78] He must later check the notification sent to him by the bank; this notification should contain the terms of the credit, as arranged in the underlying contract.

Revocable and unconfirmed credits

In practice, revocable credits are not widely used. Irrevocable credits, which **11–024** may be confirmed or unconfirmed, are the norm.

The UCP provides at Article 8(a) that a revocable credit may be amended or cancelled by the issuing bank at any moment and without prior notice to the beneficiary. The Article further provides that the issuing bank has to reimburse another bank which has already paid the credit.

If the credit is revocable its nature is reflected in the advice sent by the advising bank to the beneficiary (the seller) which also states expressly that the credit is not confirmed. The following clause in the advice note is typical:

> "We have no authority from our clients to confirm this credit. The credit is therefore subject to cancellation or modification at any time without notice."

From the exporter's point of view, an unconfirmed credit is a very unsatisfactory method of finance, but unconfirmed credits are sometimes preferred to confirmed credits because they are cheaper in respect of bank charges than the latter. The precarious nature of an unconfirmed credit is well illustrated by the facts in *Cape Asbestos v. Lloyd's Bank.*[79] Importers in Warsaw bought a consignment of asbestos sheets from the plaintiffs and opened an unconfirmed credit in favour of the latter with the defendants. The defendants duly advised the plaintiffs of the credit, adding the clause "this is merely an advice of opening of the above-mentioned credit and is not a confirmation of the same". The plaintiffs shipped part of the consignment and their draft on the bank was duly accepted. The plaintiffs then shipped the remainder, but, on presenting their draft to the bank, acceptance of the draft was refused. In the meantime, the importers in

---

ated to him but its liability is unenforceable until the seller complies with the conditions of the credit. See also Todd, *Bills of Lading and Bankers Documentary Credits*, (3rd ed., 1998), p. 278.

[77] This is the view which practice takes. It is founded on the ruling that the credit is regarded as "opened" when the advice is communicated to the beneficiary; see *ante*, para. 11–018. See also *per* Donaldson J. in *Elder Dempster Lines Ltd v. Ionic Shipping Agency Inc* [1968] 1 Lloyd's Rep. 529 at 535.

[78] Whether by sight payment, deferred payment, acceptance or negotiation; see *ante*, para. 11–022.

[79] [1921] W.N. 274; see also *per* Lord Denning M.R. in *W.J. Alan & Co Ltd v. El Nasr Export and Import Co* [1972] 2 Q.B. 189 at 207.

Warsaw had cancelled the credit, but the defendant bank had failed to notify the plaintiffs of the cancellation. It was held that the bank was entitled to refuse the acceptance of the draft for the remainder and Bailhache J. said in the course of that judgment that "an unconfirmed credit is practically worthless".

The case was based on unusual facts because normally the bank will notify the creditor of the revocation of an unconfirmed credit. The exporter who sells under such a credit should at least ask the bank to insert a *notice clause* in the advice. Under this clause the bank is obliged to inform the exporter forthwith of the cancellation of the credit.

Irrevocable and unconfirmed credits

11–025 The obligations of the issuing bank in terms of an irrevocable credit are set out in Article 9. Where this type of credit[80] is used, the issuing bank cannot revoke its undertaking to the beneficiary, but the advising bank does not enter into its own obligation to make payment under the credit. The advice of an irrevocable and unconfirmed credit would state:

> "This credit is irrevocable on the part of the above-mentioned issuing bank but we are not instructed to confirm it and therefore it does not involve any undertaking on our part."

These credits are sometimes issued by leading banks, particularly American and British banks, which consider a local confirmation as unnecessary.

While unconfirmed credits are somewhat cheaper than confirmed credits, they have the disadvantage that they do not localise the performance of the contract of sale in the seller's country. If the advising bank refused to pay on tender of the documents, the beneficiary might be compelled to institute proceedings overseas—a situation which largely defeats the main purpose of the commercial credit.[81]

Irrevocable and confirmed credits

11–026 This is the type of letter of credit most favourable to the exporter because the advising bank stipulates in terms that it will honour the exporter's drafts provided they are drawn and presented in conformity with the terms of credit.

In the case of a confirmed credit, the engagement of the advising bank to the beneficiary is expressly stated in the letter of advice which that bank sends him. The following clause in the advice note is typical:

> "We undertake to honour such drafts on presentation provided that they are drawn and presented in conformity with the terms of this credit."

---

[80] For examples, see *Cie Continentale d'Importation v. Ispahani Ltd* [1960] 1 Lloyd's Rep. 293 at 301; *Maran Road v. Austin Taylor & Co Ltd* [1975] 1 Lloyd's Rep. 156; *Discount Records Ltd v. Barclays Bank Ltd* [1975] 1 W.L.R. 315; *Trendtex Trading Corporation v. Central Bank of Nigeria* [1977] 2 W.L.R. 356; *E.D. & F. Man Ltd v. Nigerian Sweets & Confectionery Co Ltd* [1977] 1 Lloyd's Rep. 50.
[81] C.M. Schmitthoff, "Confirmation in Export Transactions" [1957] J.B.L. 17.

The effect of a confirmed credit has been described by Diplock J.[82] as constituting "a direct undertaking by the banker that the seller, if he presents the documents as required in the required time, will receive payment." The bank cannot withdraw from its liability to the exporter even if instructed by the buyer to cancel the credit. This is illustrated by *Hamzeh Malas & Sons v. British Imex Industries Ltd*[83] where the plaintiffs, a Jordanian firm, contracted to buy from the defendants, a British firm, a quantity of reinforced steel rods, to be delivered in two instalments. Payment was to be made under two confirmed credits, one for each instalment, to be opened with the Midland Bank, London. Both credits were duly opened and confirmed by the bank to the sellers. The first was realised on shipment of the first instalment, but a dispute arose with respect to the second credit. The buyers complained that the first instalment was not of contract quality and applied to the court for an injunction restraining the sellers from drawing on the second credit or recovering any money under it. Donovan J. and the Court of Appeal refused to grant the injunction, on the grounds stated by Jenkins L.J. in a lucid judgment:

> "It seems to be plain enough that the opening of a confirmed letter of credit constitutes a bargain between the banker and the vendor of the goods, which imposes upon the banker an absolute obligation to pay, irrespective of any dispute there may be between the parties as to whether the goods are up to the contract or not. An elaborate commercial system has been built up on the footing that bankers' commercial credits are of that character, and, in my judgment, it would be wrong for this court in the present case to interfere with that established practice.
>
> There is this to be remembered, too. A vendor of goods selling against a confirmed letter of credit is selling under the assurance that nothing will prevent him from receiving the price. That is no mean advantage when goods manufactured in one country are being sold in another."

Where the credit does not conform to the terms of the contract of sale, two courses are open to the seller. He may reject the non-conforming credit; thus, where under the terms of the contract of sale he is entitled to a confirmed credit but is only advised of the opening of an unconfirmed credit, he need not ship the goods.[84] Alternatively, he may accept the non-conforming credit. If he does so without objection, he is treated as having waived irrevocably his right to a conforming credit.[85]

Recourse and reimbursement of confirming bank

Under a confirmed credit the paying bank does not have a right of recourse **11–027** against the seller, even if the credit is only a negotiation credit,[86] except if the

---

[82] In *Ian Stach Ltd v. Baker Bosley Ltd* [1958] 2 Q.B. 130.
[83] [1958] 2 Q.B. 127; a sequel of this litigation was the case of *British Imex Industries Ltd v. Midland Bank Ltd* [1958] 1 Q.B. 542, mentioned at *ante*, para. 11–008. See also *Urquhart Lindsay v. Eastern Bank* [1922] 1 K.B. 318; further, see *Stein v. Hambros Bank* (1821) 9 Ll. L.R. 507; *National Bank of South Africa v. Banca Italiana* (1922) 10 Ll. L.R. 531; *Discount Records v. Barclays Bank Ltd* [1975] 1 W.L.R. 315.
[84] *Panoutsos v. Raymond Hadley Corp* [1917] 2 K.B. 473.
[85] *W.J. Alan & Co Ltd v. El Nasr Export & Import Co* [1972] 2 Q.B. 189 at 212, *per* Lord Denning, CA.
[86] See para. 11–022, and *Maran Road v. Austin Taylor & Co* [1975] 1 Lloyd's Rep. 156 at 161. On the liability of the confirming bank under an acceptance credit, see *Forestal Mimosa Ltd v. Oriental Credit Ltd* [1986] 2 All E.R. 400, CA.

bank has paid "under reserve",[87] or has obtained an indemnity from the seller,[88] or the seller has acted fraudulently.[89]

The confirming bank, which has paid the seller in accordance with the terms of the credit, is entitled to reimbursement from the issuing bank and/or the applicant for the credit (the buyer).[90]

Where the confirming bank pays the beneficiary under reserve but the issuing bank retains the documents beyond a reasonable time without electing whether to accept or reject them and in the end accepts them, the issuing bank is regarded as having waived the right to rely on discrepancies and has to reimburse the confirming bank for the financing charges (including interest) which arise from the late acceptance.[91]

The confirmation as localisation device

11–028 Confirmed credits are very popular in export trade because they act as a means of localising the all-important payment obligation of an export transaction in the seller's country. If he has obtained the confirmation of a bank of good standing in his own country, he can be sure of obtaining payment, acceptance of his draft or its negotiation, as arranged in the contract with his buyer, if he tenders the correct documents in good time. The export transaction is thus assimilated to a home transaction as far as the payment obligation is concerned and the credit risk of the export transaction is practically eliminated. Confirmed letters of credit are in many trades the normal terms of settlement. The banks have made an invaluable contribution to the smooth discharge of export transactions by making available this type of commercial credit.[92]

Variants of confirmation

11–029 The practice has developed two variants of the advising bank's confirmation: the "seller's confirmation" and the "soft confirmation".

The *seller's confirmation* is an arrangement under which the bank charges for the confirmation have to be borne by the beneficiary (the seller), and not by the

---

[87] See *post*, para. 11–038.

[88] See *post*, para. 11–037.

[89] See *post*, para. 11–042. It is thought that, apart from the case of fraud or dishonesty on the part of the seller, a claim for restitution by the confirming bank against the seller is admissible if such claim is admitted under the general principles of law; *e.g.* in the case of payment by the confirming bank under a common mistake; but the view is controversial, see Gutteridge-Megrah (7th ed.), pp. 86–87.

[90] See UCP, Art. 14(a).

[91] *Co-operative Centrale Raiffeisen-Boereleenbank BA (Rabobank Nederland) v. Sumitomo Bank Ltd; The Royan* [1987] 1 Lloyd's Rep. 345; in the Canadian case of *Michael Doyle & Associates Ltd v. Bank of Montreal* [1982] 6 W.W.R. 24 (which concerned an irrevocable but unconfirmed credit) the advising bank accepted a draft drawn on it by the sellers although the documents showed a discrepancy. The issuing bank rejected the documents. The Court of Appeal of British Columbia held that the advising bank could not take recourse on the sellers.

[92] Where the credit had to be confirmed by a first-class West European or U.S. bank, the fact that the opening of the credit was illegal under Turkish law (the law of the buyers) was immaterial because the sellers were not concerned with the machinery of providing the credit; *Toprak Mahsulleri Ofisi v. Finagrain Cie Commerciale* [1979] 2 Lloyd's Rep. 98 at 114.

applicant for the credit (the buyer), as is normally the case.[93] This arrangement is made where the seller is anxious to minimise the risk of the sales transaction by obtaining an absolute undertaking of a reputable bank at his place of business, but the buyer is unwilling to bear the cost of providing the seller with this additional security.

The *soft confirmation* is a conditional—and not a definite and absolute—undertaking of the advising bank. This practice has arisen where imports into a lesser industrialised country are financed by loans granted by international institutions, such as the International Bank or Reconstruction and Development (the World Bank) or by a regional or national foreign aid institution. The advising bank in the exporter's country may find it difficult to obtain reimbursement form the issuing bank, if, *e.g.* the government of the importing country prohibits the reimbursement or exchange control regulations delay it. The advising bank, if apprehending that such a complication may arise, may make its confirmation conditional on being reimbursed by the financing institution. The advising bank would then qualify its confirmation, *e.g.* by stating:

> "We clause our confirmation to the extent that we shall only be able to honour it after we have obtained reimbursement from. . . ."

The ICC Banking Commission has ruled[94] that such qualified undertaking by the advising bank is permissible, provided that the conditions under which payment will be made are indicated clearly to the beneficiary. However, as far as the UCP are concerned, such credit does not rank as an "irrevocable credit" nor does the advising bank's undertaking constitute a "confirmation" within the meaning of the UCP.

Standby letters of credit

A standby letter of credit[95] is an undertaking by a bank to make payment to a **11–030** third party (the beneficiary) or to accept bills of exchange drawn on him, provided that he complies with the stipulations of the credit which, in international trade transactions, invariably include the tender of one or several documents. The bank may also be instructed to authorise another bank to pay, accept or negotiate bills of exchange against the stipulated comments.

In international trade transactions the standby letter of credit, like the ordinary letter of credit, is activated by the tender of documents in accordance with the requirements of the credit. The two types of credit differ significantly however. The ordinary letter of credit is a payment instrument which normally[96] obliges the beneficiary to tender, together with other specified documents, the transport documents. The standby credit is intended to protect the beneficiary in case of default of the other party to the (underlying) contract. In a standby credit the

---

[93] *British Imex Industries Ltd v. Midland Bank Ltd* [1958] 1 Q.B. 542 at 544, concerned a seller's confirmation. In this case the seller agreed to pay the bank a confirming commission.
[94] Opinions (1980–1981) of the ICC Banking Commission, pp. 10–13 (Ref. 68).
[95] See further Benjamin (1997) paras 23–217 *et seq.*
[96] But there may be other documents, see on packing credits, see *post*, para. 11–032.

required documents need not include the transport documents; this type of credit may be activated by a document of any description, *e.g.* a demand by the beneficiary or a statement from him that the other party is in default. The standby letter of credit is thus often functionally similar in effect to a bank guarantee or performance bond.[97]

The standby letter of credit originated in the United States, where, according to federal law and the laws of some States, national banking associations traditionally were prohibited from issuing guarantees. These American banks therefore extended the letter of credit concept to domestic banking but varied it with respect to the documents to be tendered. As observed earlier,[98] standby letters of credit are covered by the UCP,[99] if the parties subject them to this regulation. Recently, the ICC, in collaboration with the Institute of International Banking Law and Practice, has also promulgated a separate code for standby credits, known as International Standby Practices (ISP 98),[1] which took effect on January 1, 1999. This new set of rules has been designed to be compatible with the United Nations Convention on Independent Guarantees and Standby Letters of Credit. Parties are still at liberty to issue standby credits subject to the UCP[2] if they so wish, and it remains to be seen whether the new standby credit provisions will gain popularity.

The principles relating to ordinary letters of credit likewise apply to standby credits, *mutatis mutandis*.[3] In particular, the principles of the autonomy of the credit and the requirement of strict compliance also apply to this type of credit.

Revolving credits

11–031 Where the export sale is not an isolated transaction but the overseas buyer is a regular customer of the exporter, the buyer will arrange a revolving credit in favour of the latter.[4] The buyer gives the bank standing instructions to arrange for a credit in favour of the exporter which at no time shall exceed a fixed maximum. The advantage of this arrangement is than no renewal is required and clerical labour is saved; a revolving credit is, for instance, a corollary to a sole distribution agreement.[5] The joint general manager of Lloyds Bank, when called in one case[6] as an expert witness to explain the meaning of this term, gave the following definition:

---

[97] See *post*, Chap. 12.
[98] See *ante*, para. 11–003.
[99] UCP, Art.1.
[1] ICC Brochure No. 590.
[2] They may also be issued subject to the ICC Uniform Rules for Demand Guarantees (ICC Brochure No. 458) and see para. 12–004.
[3] See, *e.g. Offshore International SA v. Banco Central SA* [1977] 1 W.L.R. 239; *Hong Kong and Shanghai Banking Corporation v. Kloeckner & Co AG* [1989] 2 Lloyd's Rep. 323; *Society of Lloyd's v. Canadian Imperial Bank of Commerce* [1993] 2 Lloyd's Rep. 579.
[4] See, *e.g. The Future Express* [1993] 2 Lloyd's Rep. 542, CA, affirming [1992] 2 Lloyd's Rep. 79.
[5] See Chap. 3.
[6] *Nordskog v. National Bank* [1922] 10 Ll. L.R. 652.

"A revolving credit is one for a certain sum which is automatically renewed by putting on at the bottom that which is taken off at the top. If you have a revolving credit for £50,000 open for three months to be operated on by drafts at 30 days' sight, as drafts are drawn they temporarily reduce the amount of the credit below the £50,000. As these drafts run off and are presented and paid they are added again to the top of the credit and restore it again to the £50,000. That is what is known technically as a revolving credit, and it is automatic in its operation and does not need renewal."

Several varieties of revolving credit are in use. The revolving credit should not be confused with the evergreen credit,[7] although both have in common that they are not limited to a single period of currency.

Packing credits; red clause credits

The packing credit, sometimes called anticipatory credit, is intended to assist **11–032** the exporter in the production or procurement of the goods sold. The credit is payable at a time prior to the shipment of the goods, and against a document other than a transport document. The bank is instructed to pay the purchase price, or part of it, on production of, *e.g.* a warehouse receipt (evidencing that the goods are in existence) or a forwarder's certificate (FCR)[8] (affirming that the goods have been received for shipment or have been shipped), or an air dispatch registered post receipt.[9]

The packing credit is a convenient method of finance for the small exporter who is not familiar with shipping practice; if, for example, he sells cloth ex London store and arranges that the purchase price shall be paid under a letter of credit against delivery of a forwarder's receipt, he is not concerned with the actual shipping arrangements which will be made by the forwarder on instructions of the buyer. The buyer, on the other hand, is certain that the goods sold are no longer in the possession of the seller when receiving the purchase price. In more complicated transactions, which are nearer in nature to letters of credit proper, the bank, when advising the exporter of the credit, inserts the so-called *red clause*[10] into the letter of advice and is prepared to honour the exporter's sight drafts to a certain amount against production of the stipulated documents, *e.g.* the warehouse receipts[11]; when the exporter ships the goods and delivers the transport documents to the bank, he presents a draft for the purchase price less the amount received by way of advance.

In the case of a packing credit, the arrangement can be construed as an agreement that the buyer, through the bank, is to make an advance on the purchase price, the advance being payable on production of the stipulated documents, and

---

[7] See *ante*, para. 11–019.
[8] See para. 15–029.
[9] *Diamond Cutting Works Federation v. Triefus & Co Ltd* [1956] 1 Lloyd's Rep. 216.
[10] Gutteridge and Megrah, *loc cit*. p. 12. This clause is called the red clause because it was originally written in red ink.
[11] In *Tukan Timber Ltd v. Barclays Bank plc* [1987] 1 Lloyd's Rep. 171 the red clause provided that no advance could be made on the credit without the countersignature of one of the directors of the buyers. In *Mitsui & Co Ltd v. Flota Mercante Granco Iombiana SA* [1988] 1 W.L.R. 1145 the red clause provided that 80 per cent of the price was payable "when the goods were available for consignment but before shipment".

the balance of the price being payable on delivery of the proper transport documents (and/or other specified documents).

Back-to-back and overriding credits

11–033 Back-to-back credits, also called countervailing credits, are mainly used in the *external trade* where a U.K. merchant buys goods in one overseas country and sells them in another, and in *string contracts*[12] where the same goods are sold or resold by several middlemen before being bought by the ultimate purchaser.

The characteristic feature of the back-to-back credit is that the confirmed credit opened by the ultimate purchaser in favour of his immediate seller is used by the latter as security for the credit which he has to open for his own supplier. If there are several middlemen, each will use the credit in his favour as security for the credit which he has to open for his predecessor in the chain of contracts until the first buyer in the chain opens a credit in favour of the original supplier. The terms of these credits are literally identical, except as far as relating to prices and invoices.

The easiest method of operating back-to-back credits is to have the various credits controlled by the same bank but they can also be operated when several banks are concerned. Back-to-back arrangements can also be operated by means of a transferable credit[13] or by combining a documentary credit with a collection arrangement.[14]

Of particular importance in these arrangements is the credit to be opened by the ultimate purchaser. That credit, known as the *overriding credit*, is, as the middlemen are usually aware, the foundation on which the whole financial structure of the arrangement rests. For this reason, the courts pay special attention to the terms of that credit if issues involving the whole chain of contracts arise.[15]

Transferable credits

11–034 A more popular method of financing the supply transaction than the back-to-back credit is the practice of making a credit transferable.[16] The UCP provide, in Article 48, that a transferable credit is automatically divisible, provided that partial shipments are not prohibited. Credits are transferable only if so designated by the issuing bank.

As has been observed earlier,[17] the letter of credit is not negotiable in the sense

---

[12] This type of trading is used particularly often in the commodity trades but is also found in other trades.

[13] See *post*, para. 11–034.

[14] See *post*, para. 11–041.

[15] *Ian Stach Ltd v. Baker Bosley Ltd* [1958] 2 Q.B. 130 at 138; *Baltimex v. Metallo Chemical Refinery Co Ltd* [1956] 1 Lloyd's Rep. 450 at 455.

[16] See, *e.g. Ian Stach v. Baker Bosley Ltd* [1958] 2 Q.B. 130; *W.J. Alan & Co Ltd v. El Nasr Export and Import Co* [1972] 2 Q.B. 189; *European Asia Bank AG v. Punjab and Sind Bank (No. 2)* [1981] 2 Lloyd's Rep. 651 at 129; [1983] 1 W.L.R. 642 at 649, CA; *Bank Negara Indonesia 1946 v. Lariza (Singapore) Pte Ltd* [1988] A.C. 583. See also R.M. Goode [1981] J.B.L. 150; C.M. Schmitthoff, "The Transferable Credit" [1988] J.B.L. 49.

[17] See para. 11–006, n. 26.

in which a bill of exchange or other negotiable instrument can be transferred to another person.[18] The advising bank is not authorised, unless receiving instructions to the contrary, to pay the credit to *any* person satisfying the conditions of the credit; indeed, if it paid on tender of the stipulated documents by a person other than the named beneficiary (or his agent) it would contravene its mandate.

If it is intended to make the benefit of the credit available to a person other than the named beneficiary, two possibilities exist: the assignment of the benefit of the credit and the transfer of the credit as such with its attendant rights and duties, but it should again be emphasised that the latter possibility only exists if the parties have made the credit transferable. These two possibilities require separate consideration.

The assignment of the benefit of the credit

A letter of credit is a *chose* in action.[19] Where it is an irrevocable credit or a **11–035** confirmed credit, it is a conditional debt of the bank, which has undertaken an obligation to the seller, *i.e.* an obligation subject to the condition precedent that the seller tenders the stipulated documents timely. The seller can assign this conditional debt, *viz.* the benefit accruing to him under the credit, without authority of the buyer or the paying bank, even though the credit is not advised to be transferable or assignable, provided that he complies with the requirements laid down for the assignment of *choses* in action in section 136 of the Law of Property Act 1925, which are that the assignment has to be absolute and not in part, that it has to be in writing under the hand of the assignor, and that notice in writing of the assignment must be given to the debtor, *viz.* the bank. The assigned debt continues to be conditional and the condition can only be discharged by the seller (or his agent) but not by the assignee. This condition constitutes a liability which, according to general principles of law, cannot be assigned without the consent of the other party, *viz.* the paying bank which, in that respect, has to act on the instructions of its principal, the issuing bank or the buyer. The UCP expressly allow the assignability of the benefit of a letter of credit even if the credit is not stated to be transferable,[20] but the assignability of such benefit may be excluded by a term to that effect in the credit. The usefulness of an assignment of the benefit of a credit is limited to the cases in which the seller himself intends to ship and to present the documents to the bank. Any assignment is, of course, subject to prior equities.

Assignment may be used where a buyer intends to utilise a credit in his favour opened by one bank as security for the issue of a letter of credit with a different bank.[21]

---

[18] On the distinction between the negotiability of a transferable credit, *e.g.* to the supplier, and the negotiability of a deferred payment credit by the beneficiary (in order to obtain ready cash), see *European Asian Bank AG v. Punjab and Sind Bank (No. 2)* [1981] 1 W.L.R. 642 at 654–655.
[19] *Per* Denning L.J. in *Trans Trust SPRL v. Danubian Trading Co Ltd* [1952] 2 Q.B. 297 at 305.
[20] UCP, Art. 49, which also clearly states that it refers only to the assignment of the proceeds of the credit and not to the assignment of the right to perform under it. The assignability of the latter is a matter of debate. See Jack (1993), para. 10.41, Gutteridge & Megrah (7th ed.), p. 105.
[21] See, *e.g. Mannesman Handel AG v. Kaunlaren Shipping Corp* [1993] 1 Lloyd's Rep. 89.

Other, less formal, methods of making the benefit of the credit available to the supplier are also in use. In *Trans Trust SPRL v. Danubian Trading Co Ltd*,[22] A gave B an option to buy; B sold to C; C sold to D. In the contract of sale between B and C, the latter undertook to procure a credit to be opened by D in favour of A, and B undertook to refund to C the difference between C's buying price and selling price which was thus disclosed to B. When D failed to open the credit, C was held to be liable to B for loss of profit.

A mere undertaking by the seller that he will pay the supplier out of the proceeds of the credit to be opened by the buyer affords little security to the supplier. This may operate as an equitable assignment but even if the seller notifies the bank of it, his interest in the credit may be defeated by a subsequent fraudulent transfer of the credit (if it is transferable) or a legal assignment of the benefit under it. Mere instructions by the seller to the bank to pay over the credit (or part of it) to the supplier on presentation of the proper documents by the seller also do not protect the supplier because they can be countermanded by the seller. The supplier's position would be strengthened by a requirement that any instructions or mandate given by the seller to his bank be irrevocable in nature.

The transfer of the credit

11–036 The transfer of the credit is very different from the assignment of the benefit under it. It means that the seller transfers the rights and at least certain of the duties arising under the credit to another person, usually his supplier, in such a manner that that person steps into the credit and in advance is assured payment out of funds made available by the ultimate buyer, provided that the conditions of the original credit are complied with. Such an arrangement requires the consent of the buyer (who is not obliged to provide a transferable credit unless he has agreed to do so), and of the issuing bank; the credit should be stated in terms to be transferable. Where a credit is made transferable, it can, unless otherwise stated in the credit, be transferred once only.

A transferable credit made subject to the UCP is, as already observed[23] divisible automatically and can be transferred in fractions, provided that partial shipments are not excluded. A transferable credit governed by English law, which is not subject to this provision of the UCP, would not appear to be divisible automatically. If this effect is desired, the credit should, it is thought, be made expressly subject to the UCP and be designated as transferable.

The UCP provide in Article 48:

"(a) A transferable Credit is a Credit under which the Beneficiary (First Beneficiary) may request the bank authorised to pay, incur a deferred payment undertaking, accept or negotiate (the 'Transferring Bank'), or in the case of a freely negotiable Credit, the bank specifically authorised in the Credit as a Transferring Bank, to make the Credit available in whole or in part to one or more other Beneficiary(ies) (Second Beneficiary(ies)).

(b) A Credit can be transferred only if it is expressly designated as 'transferable' by the

---

[22] [1952] 2 Q.B. 297.
[23] At *ante*, para. 11–034.

Issuing Bank. Terms such as 'divisible', 'fractionable', 'assignable', and 'transmissible' do not render the Credit transferable. If such terms are used they shall be disregarded.

(c) The Transferring Bank shall be under no obligation to effect such transfer except to the extent and in the manner expressly consented to by such bank.

(d) At the time of making a request for transfer and prior to transfer of the Credit, the First Beneficiary must irrevocably instruct the Transferring Bank to advise amendments to the Second Beneficiary(ies). If the Transferring Bank consents to the transfer under these conditions, it must, at the time of transfer, advise the Second Beneficiary(ies) of the First Beneficiary's instructions regarding amendments.

(e) If a Credit is transferred to more than one Second Beneficiary(ies), refusal of an amendment by one or more Second Beneficiary(ies) does not invalidate the acceptance(s) by the other Second Beneficiary(ies) with respect to whom the Credit will be amended accordingly. With respect to the Second Beneficiary(ies) who rejected the amendment, the Credit will remain unamended.

(f) Transferring Bank charges in respect of transfers including commissions, fees, costs or expenses are payable by the First Beneficiary, unless otherwise agreed. If the Transferring Bank agrees to transfer the Credit it shall be under no obligation to effect the transfer until such charges are paid.

(g) Unless otherwise stated in the Credit, a transferable Credit can be transferred once only. Consequently, the Credit cannot be transferred at the request of the Second Beneficiary to any subsequent Third Beneficiary. For the purpose of this Article, a retransfer to the First Beneficiary does not constitute a prohibited transfer.

Fractions of a transferable Credit (not exceeding in the aggregate the amount of the Credit) can be transferred separately, provided partial shipments/drawings are not prohibited, and the aggregate of such transfers will be considered as constituting only one transfer of the Credit.

(h) The Credit can be transferred only on the terms and conditions specified in the original Credit, with the exception of:

— the amount of the Credit,
— any unit price stated therein,
— the expiry date,
— the last date for presentation of documents in accordance with Article 43,
— the period for shipment,

any or all of which may be reduced or curtailed.

The percentage for which insurance cover must be effected may be increased in such a way as to provide the amount of cover stipulated in the original Credit, or these Articles.

In addition, the name of the First Beneficiary can be substituted for that of the Applicant, but if the name of the Applicant is specifically required by the original Credit to appear in any document(s) other than the invoice, such requirement must be fulfilled.

(i) The First Beneficiary has the right to substitute his own invoice(s) (and Draft(s) for those of the Second Beneficiary(ies), for amounts not in excess of the original amount stipulated in the Credit and for the original unit prices if stipulated in the Credit, and upon such substitution of invoice(s) (and Draft(s)) the First Beneficiary can draw under the Credit for the difference, if any, between his invoice(s) and the Second Beneficiary's(ies') invoice(s).

When a Credit has been transferred and the First Beneficiary is to supply his own invoice(s) and Draft(s)) in exchange for the Second Beneficiary's(ies') invoice(s) (and Draft(s) but fails to do so on first demand, the Transferring Bank has the right to deliver to the Issuing Bank the documents received under the transferred Credit, including the Second Beneficiary's(ies) invoice(s) (and Draft(s)) without further responsibility to the First Beneficiary.

(j) The First Beneficiary may request that payment or negotiation be effected to the Second beneficiary(ies) at the place to which the Credit has been transferred up to and including the expiry date of the Credit, unless the original Credit expressly states that it may not be made available for payment or negotiation at a place other than that stipulated in the Credit. This is without prejudice to the First Beneficiary's right to substitute subsequently his own invoice(s) (andDraft(s)) for those of the Second Beneficiary(ies) and to claim any difference due to him."

A transferable credit can be used in a back-to-back arrangement in the following manner. Company A in country (A) sells goods to company B in country (B) and B undertakes to pay by an irrevocable and confirmed credit. Company B then resells the goods to company C in country (C), and C undertakes to pay B by (another) irrevocable and confirmed credit, which is made transferable. B then transfers to A the part of the credit opened by C which corresponds to the purchase price due to A. In such a case it is of the utmost importance that the credit of C is expressed in the same currency as that opened by B because otherwise currency fluctuations may affect the arrangement. In one case[24] the credit opened by B was expressed in Kenyan shillings and that opened by C in United Kingdom shillings. At the time of the transfer the two currencies were equivalent and company A did not object when the credit in United Kingdom currency was transferred to it. Later, the United Kingdom currency was devalued but the Kenyan currency remained at its original value. The Court of Appeal held that by accepting the credit in the United Kingdom currency, company A had lost its right to claim payment in the undervalued Kenyan currency although the latter was the currency of account of the transaction.

It would appear that a bank which has issued or advised a transferable credit may still refuse to effect the transfer although all the conditions of the credit are fulfilled.[25] The UCP state in Article 48(a) that, if the credit is made transferable, "the Beneficiary (First Beneficiary) may *request* the bank" to make it available to a second beneficiary (the transferee of the credit).[26] Thus, though the bank may accept the transfer of the credit, it does not mean that it is *obliged* to do so. This interpretation is supported by paragraph (c) of Article 48, according to which the bank is "under no obligation to effect such transfer "except to the extent and in the manner expressly consented to" by it. It was held by the Privy Council in an appeal from Singapore[27] that the bank's consent "has to be an express consent made after the request (for transfer) and it has to cover both the extent and the manner of the transfer requested." This means that the designation of the credit as "transferable", when issued, is not a sufficient consent of the bank within Article 48(b) of the UCP (1993 Revision). The decision has been criticised as reducing the usefulness of the transferable credit for financing supply transactions.[28] Fortunately, major international banks do not in practice refuse to accept a request for transfer of a credit which they have issued as "transferable", unless they think that there is good reason for doing so (but they are not bound in law to disclose this reason).

ANOMALOUS LETTER OF CREDIT SITUATIONS

Letters of credit and bank indemnities

11–037 Where the seller tenders non-conforming documents, the advising bank, instead of refusing to accept them, as it is entitled to do, may ask the seller to supply an

---

[24] *W.J. Alan & Co Ltd v. El Nasr Export and Import Co* [1972] 2 Q.B. 189.
[25] Though see Benjamin (5th ed., 1997), para. 23–059, which suggests that banks ought only to be able to refuse such transfer on reasonable grounds, and draws an analogy with a landlord's limited right of refusal to grant consent to the transfer of a lease.
[26] The corresponding Article 54(a) of the 1983 Revision of the UPC stated that "the beneficiary has the right to request the bank" to effect the transfer.
[27] *Bank Negara Indonesia 1946 v. Lariza (Singapore) Pte Ltd* [1988] A.C. 583 (this case arose under the 1974 Revision of the UCP).
[28] See C.M. Schmitthoff, in the article quoted at para. 11–034, n. 16.

indemnity and, on the strength of such indemnity, may make the credit available. Sometimes, where the advising bank is not identical with the exporter's bank, it will ask for an indemnity from the exporter's bank. This procedure is adopted where there are discrepancies between the documents presented by the exporter and the instructions received by the advising bank, or when documents are presented after the expiry date of the credit and no arrangements have been made for its extension. An indemnity which the seller gives to the advising bank cannot be transferred or extended by that bank to the issuing bank without the seller's consent.

The exporter, when giving an indemnity in order to avail himself of the credit, should be aware that the bank may have recourse against him and may hold him liable on the indemnity[29]; he should, therefore, endeavour to settle the point which has given rise to the discrepancy forthwith by agreement with the overseas buyer.

An alternative to giving the bank an indemnity is for the seller to ask the advising bank to forward the documents as *collection under protection of the credit*.[30] In this case the advising bank will pay the seller when the buyer has taken up the documents. This substitute arrangement, while avoiding the hazards of an indemnity by the seller, defeats the purpose of the letter of credit which the buyer was obliged to open by virtue of the underlying contract of sale.

If the buyer's refusal to amend the instructions to the bank is so serious as to amount to a repudiation of the buyer's undertaking to open the credit in accordance with the terms of the contract of sale, the seller has the further alternative of claiming damages from the buyer for breach of that contract.

Payment under reserve

Another possibility for a bank which has doubts whether the tendered documents **11–038** conform to the instructions received by it but wishes to accommodate the beneficiary (the seller) is to make payment[31] "under reserve". The bank will do so when it considers the beneficiary to be of good standing and able to make repayment if a difficulty arises or when it thinks that the alleged discrepancy is unimportant and the issuing bank and the buyer are likely to take up the documents in spite of it. In particular, the bank will be prepared to make payment under reserve if the beneficiary is a valued customer and a genuine dispute has arisen with him whether the documents are in order.

The expression "payment under reserve" occurs in the UCP[32] but is not defined therein.[33] Its meaning was considered by the Court of Appeal in *Banque de*

---

[29] *Moralice (London) Ltd v. E.D. & F. Man* [1954] 2 Lloyd's Rep. 526.

[30] On collection arrangements see Chap. 10.

[31] Or to accept or negotiate.

[32] See UCP, Art. 14(f) which states that where a remitting bank has accepted documents under reserve or against an indemnity, such terms concern only the parties to that arrangement and do not affect the obligations of the issuing or confirming bank.

[33] *Per* Sir John Donaldson M.R. in *Banque de l'Indochine et de Suez SA v. J.H. Rayner (Mincing Lane) Ltd* [1983] Q.B. 711 at 727 suggested that a future revision of the UCP should define this term.

l'Indochine et Suez SA v. J.H. Rayner (Mincing) Lane Ltd.[34] In this case the bank advised the beneficiaries of an irrevocable credit opened by a bank in Djibouti and added its own confirmation. The bank considered the tendered documents to be defective on various specified grounds but, by arrangement with the beneficiaries, made payment under reserve. The question arose whether the reservation entitled the bank to recover the money if the issuing bank refused to take up the documents or whether it could reclaim the money only if it was established that the tendered documents were genuinely defective. The court decided that, according to the intention of the parties, the expression "under reserve" had the former meaning. "What the parties meant," said Kerr L.J.[35] "was that the payment was to be made under reserve in the sense that the beneficiary would be bound to repay the money on demand if the issuing bank should reject the documents, whether on its own initiative or on the buyer's instructions." The court did not have to decide[36] whether the advising bank could recover its money only if the issuing bank rejected the documents on the same grounds—or at least some of them—as those originally notified by the advising bank to the beneficiaries, but it inclined to this view. It is thought that this is doubtful; the advising bank should be entitled to recover the money paid under reserve whenever the documents are rejected by the issuing bank or the buyer.

Short-circuiting of letter of credit

11–039 In principle, where the parties to the contract of international sale have arranged for the payment mechanism of a letter of credit, they must abide by their agreement and cannot short-circuit the credit by making direct claims connected with the payment of the price against each other. The letter of credit arrangement, said McNair J. in the *Soproma* case[37]:

> "is of mutual advantage to both parties—of advantage to the seller in that by the terms of the contract he is given what has been called in the authorities a 'reliable paymaster' generally in his own country whom he can sue, and of advantage to the buyer in that he can make arrangements with his bankers for the provision of the necessary funds. . . ."

For this reason, McNair J. in the *Soproma* case regarded the second—direct—tender of documents by the sellers as ineffective.

The conditional character of the credit

11–040 Exceptionally, however, the short-circuiting of the letter of credit arrangement is permissible. In the ordinary way, the credit operates as conditional payment of the price; it does not operate as absolute payment.[38]

---

[34] [1983] Q.B. 711.

[35] *ibid.* at 734.

[36] Because the documents were in fact defective, in particular because there was no linkage between them; see *ante*, para. 11–016.

[37] *Soproma SpA v. Marine & Animal By-Products Corporation* [1966] 1 Lloyd's Rep. 367 at 385, see *ante*, para. 11–007.

[38] *W.J. Alan & Co Ltd v. El Nasr Export and Import Co* [1972] 2 Q.B. 189, CA. See also *Maran Road v. Austin Taylor & Co Ltd* [1977] 1 Lloyd's Rep. 50; *E.D. & F. Man Ltd v. Nigerian Sweets & Confectionery Co Ltd* [1977] 2 Lloyd's Rep. 50.

If, for example the bank whom the parties have interposed as intermediary becomes insolvent, the seller normally can claim the price from the buyer directly, making a direct tender of documents to the latter.[39] The implied condition is discharged by the insolvency of the intermediary.

Thus, in one case[40] Nigerian buyers bought a quantity of sugar from London sugar merchants. Payment was to be made under an irrevocable letter of credit to be opened with Merchant's Swiss Ltd, a merchant bank most shares in which were owned by the Nigerian buyers. The credit was an acceptance credit providing for 90 days' drafts on the bank. The sugar was supplied and the buyers transferred the purchase price to Merchants' Swiss Ltd. Before the bank paid over the price to the London sellers, it went into a creditors' voluntary winding up. The sellers claimed the price from the buyers in arbitration in London which eventually resulted in court proceedings. Ackner J. held that the sellers could claim the price from the buyers although they had already transferred the money to the bank. He said[41]:

> "It follows from the finding that the letters of credit were given only as a conditional payment, that if they were not honoured the respondents' debt has not been discharged. This is because the buyers promised *to pay* by letter of credit not to provide by letter of credit the source of payment which did not pay . . . The respondents' liability to the sellers was a primary liability. This liability was suspended during the period available to the issuing bank to honour the drafts and was activated when the issuing bank failed."[42]

However if payment under the credit is not made because the seller is at fault, *e.g.* he tenders non-conforming documents, he cannot rely on the conditional character of the credit and the buyer is discharged.[43]

Other instances of short-circuiting

Similar considerations were applied in *Sale Continuation Ltd v. Austin Taylor &* **11–041** *Co Ltd*.[44] In this case N, a timber exporter in Malaysia, used the services of A, the defendant, as selling agent for the sale of timber. A sold N's timber to G, a Belgian timber importer. Payment was arranged by a back-to-back arrangement[45] which consisted of a combination of an irrevocable credit and a collection arrangement. A Belgian bank was instructed to collect the price from G against the documents, and A, through the plaintiffs, an English merchant bank which acted as issuing bank in this transaction, opened a credit in favour of N, the seller, who drew a bill of exchange on the plaintiffs; that bill was accepted by the latter. The plaintiffs then passed the documents to A under a trust receipt,

---

[39] *Soproma SpA* [1966] 1 Lloyd's Rep. 367 at 386.
[40] *E.D. & F. Man Ltd v. Nigerian Sweets & Confectionery Co Ltd* [1977] 2 Lloyd's Rep. 50; *Shamsher Jute Mills Ltd v. Sethia (London) Ltd* [1987] 1 Lloyd's Rep. 388. The credit constitutes absolute payment only if the seller stipulates, expressly or impliedly, that it should be so.
[41] [1977] 2 Lloyd's Rep. at 56.
[42] The fact that the parties had agreed on a particular bank as issuing and correspondent bank did not convert the conditional obligation into an absolute one.
[43] *Shamsher Jute Mills Ltd v. Sethia (London) Ltd* [1987] 1 Lloyd's Rep. 388.
[44] [1967] 2 Lloyd's Rep. 403.
[45] See para. 11–033.

and A handed them to G who paid the purchase price to A under a trust receipt, and A handed them to G who paid the purchase price to A and received the timber. The plaintiffs sued A, claiming that they were entitled to the price and that N had merely a claim in their insolvency. Paull J. rejected the plaintiff's argument and held that the defendant A had rightly transferred the purchase price directly to N. Since the plaintiffs had evinced the intention not to honour the bill drawn by N on them, A was free from his obligation to put the plaintiffs in funds to enable them to meet N's bill. As to the effect of the trust receipt, N was entitled to cancel the contract of pledge of the documents with the plaintiffs when the latter intimated that they would not honour his bill. No doubt, this decision of Paull J. is clear common sense.

Fraud affecting letters of credit

11–042 It has been seen earlier[46] that one of the maxims on which the letter of credit system is founded is the autonomy of the institution. This means that the banks engaged in a letter of credit transaction are, in principle, not involved in any dispute arising between the parties to the underlying contract of sale or other contract. Only one exception is admitted to this rule; the fraud exception, which permits a court to consider evidence other than the actual terms and conditions of the credit and is founded on the maxim *ex turpi causa non oritur actio*. Where it can be pleaded successfully, the bank—the issuing bank under an irrevocable credit and the advising bank if it has added its confirmation—should refuse to honour the undertaking which it has given the beneficiary, *viz.* to pay, accept or negotiate according to the terms of the credit, if the correct documents are tendered before the expiry of the credit.

In circumstances where the documents are discrepant, the defects are apparent on their face.[47] Here, we are dealing with circumstances in which the documents appear to be in order on their face, but they or their tender are tainted by fraud. This fraud will usually relate to the documents themselves. They may be forged or untrue in relation to the goods to which they refer, however on their face they appear to be correct and good tender under the documentary credit.

The allegation of fraud is normally raised by the buyer, who will attempt to prevent the bank from honouring the credit or the seller from drawing on it. The buyer may allege that the seller shipped rubbish instead of conforming goods or that he shipped no goods at all, or that the bills of lading were forged or fraudulently false,[48] in that they were antedated to show shipment within the stipulated shipping time whereas the goods were actually shipped out of time.

The bank is not obliged actively to ascertain whether the alleged fraud can

---

[46] See para. 11–006.
[47] See para. 11–010.
[48] The courts appear to draw no distinction between forged and fraudulently false bills of lading in this respect but there may be a difference; in the case of the forged bill of lading it can be argued that it is a non-document but a false bill (even if fraudulent) is a genuine bill of lading having an untrue content; in the *United City Merchants* case (see next page) the House of Lords dealt with a false bill of lading but did not deal with a forged bill.

be proved.[49] It may adopt a passive attitude and evaluate the evidence placed before it by the buyer. If court proceedings ensue, the issue of whether a relevant fraud has occurred has to be decided according to the facts then known to the court and it is irrelevant that an earlier stage the fraud was unknown to the bank.[50]

In ascertaining whether the fraud exception applies, three sets of circumstances have to be distinguished.

First, where there is only an allegation, communicated by the buyer to the bank, that fraud has occurred. This allegation may be founded on a suspicion, even a grave one. Or the bank itself, without instigation by the buyer, may entertain such suspicion. If no more can be established, the bank should pay. Megarry J. said[51]: "I would be slow to interfere with bankers' irrevocable credits, and not least in the sphere of international banking, unless a sufficiently grave cause is shown", and the Court of Appeal stated in a case in which it refused an application for an injunction restraining the bank to pay[52]:

> "The wholly exceptional case where an injunction may be granted is where it is proved that the bank knows that any demand for payment already made or which may thereafter be made will be clearly fraudulent. But the evidence must be clear, both as to the fact of fraud and as to the bank's knowledge. It would certainly not normally be sufficient that this rests upon the uncorroborated statement of the customer, for irreparable damage can be done to a bank's credit in the relatively brief time which must elapse between the granting of such an injunction and an application by the bank to have it discharged."

Secondly, where it is clearly established to the satisfaction of the bank that a fraud has occurred. There is unambiguous evidence before it, for instance that the documents, or some of them, are fraudulent or forged. But there is no evidence before the bank which shows *that the beneficiary (the seller) knew of the fraud*. There is the possibility that the fraud was committed by a third party, *e.g.* a forwarder or loading broker, who intended to cover up the fact that the goods were shipped out of time, and that the beneficiary himself was unaware of this fraud. One should have thought that even in this case the rule applies that "fraud unravels all".[53] But not so. The House of Lords decided in *United City Merchants (Investments) Ltd v. Royal Bank of Canada*[54] that in this case

---

[49] *Barclays Bank plc v. Quincecare Ltd, Financial Times*, March 1, 1989 (relating to the general duty of the bank to exercise care).

[50] *Bolivinter Oil SA v. Chase Manhattan Bank NA* [1984] 1 Lloyd's Rep. 251 at 256.

[51] In *Discount Records Ltd v. Barclays Bank Ltd* [1975] 1 W.L.R. 315 at 320. See also *Etablissements Esefka International Anstalt v. Central Bank of Nigeria* [1979] 1 Lloyd's Rep. 455 and *Tukan Timber Ltd v. Barclays Bank plc* [1987] 1 Lloyd's Rep. 171 (the fact that two forgery attempts were made before did not support the assumption that on a future third occasion again forged documents would be tendered).

[52] *Bolivinter Oil SA v. Chase Manhattan Bank NA* [1984] 1 W.L.R. 392 at 393. See also *Continental Illinois National Bank and Trust Company of Chicago v. John Paul Papanicolau; The Fedora, Tatiana and Eretrea II* [1986] 2 Lloyd's Rep. 441. The English courts have not adopted the practice of the American courts to grant temporary restraining orders on the basis of strong suspicion or/of fraud.

[53] *Szteijn v. J. Henry Schroder Banking Corporation* (1941) 31 N.Y.S. 2d, 631 at 634.

[54] [1983] 1 A.C. 168. See, further, *Tukan Timber Ltd v. Barclays Bank plc* [1987] 1 Lloyd's Rep. 171. See also the important decision of the Supreme Court of Canada in *Bank of Nova Scotia v. Angelica-Whitewear Ltd* [1987] 36 D.L.R. (4th) 161.

the bank must pay. The case concerned the purchase of a glass fibre manufacturing plant by Peruvian buyers from English sellers and at the request of the buyers the purchase price was doubled in the invoice in order to evade Peruvian exchange control regulations. The case raised two issues: the "Bretton Woods Agreement point", which was considered earlier,[55] and the letter of credit point, which arose in the following manner. The bills of lading were antedated. They showed a the date of shipment December 15, 1976, which was the latest date for shipment required by the credit, but the goods were, in fact, loaded a day later, which was out of time. The bank (the Royal Bank of Canada) which had confirmed the credit, knew of this fraud because in the first tender of the bills of lading the date was blanked out and the date of December 15, 1976 was superimposed, but later, before the expiry of the credit, a second tender of unamended bills of lading was made which showed the date of December 15, 1976. The documents were thus correct on their face. The false date was inserted by an employee of the loading brokers and the sellers knew nothing about it. The House of Lords held, as observed that the bank was obliged to pay, in spite of its knowledge of the fraud, because not only the bank and the buyers, but also the sellers, were deceived by the fraud of the third party. Lord Diplock observed[56]:

> ". . . what rational ground can there be for drawing any distinction between apparently conforming documents that, unknown to the seller, in fact contain a statement of fact that is inaccurate where the inaccuracy was due to inadvertence by the maker of the document, and the like document where the same inaccuracy had been inserted by the maker of the document with intent to deceive, among others, the seller/beneficiary himself?"

The *United City Merchants* decision caused unease in banking circles. It is contrary to the common sense of the ordinary banker to pay under a credit if he knows that the tendered documents,[57] though apparently correct on their face, are in fact fraudulent or forged. Moreover, he fears that, by doing so, he may incur legal liability. The beneficiary (seller) may raise a contractual claim on the ground that the bank has paid against a document which, as it knew, was a nullity, owing to its forgery or the fraud. It is thought that in some of these cases, if the credit is operated under the UCP, the bank is protected by Article 15, which provides:

> "Banks assume no liability or responsibility for the form, sufficiency, accuracy, genuineness, falsification or legal effect of any documents . . ."

But these questions were not decided in *United City Merchants* and the legal position remains doubtful.

Thirdly, where the bank has positive proof that a fraud has been committed *and that the beneficiary knew of this fraud.* If both these facts are clearly established to the satisfaction of the bank, it must not honour its obligation under the credit. Such a case may arise, *e.g.* if the beneficiary (seller) himself tenders

---

[55] See para. 21–030.
[56] [1983] 1 A.C. 168 at 167.
[57] On the possible differentiation in the treatment of forged and false bills of lading, see *ante*, n. 48.

documents which, to his knowledge, are false or if somebody else does so with his knowledge or connivance.[58] Another illustration would be if the seller tenders documents evidencing the transportation of the goods to the buyer but the seller has recalled the goods from the person carrying out the transport and knows that the goods will not reach the buyer. The legal position here is clear from *United City Merchants* and other cases.[59]

Evidence of fraud

The courts require, in principle, that the facts on which the fraud exception is **11–043** pleaded are established clearly and unambiguously. But, as Ackner L.J. pointed out in one case,[60] a requirement of excessive strictness with respect to the proof of fraud would make it impossible for the courts to apply this exception to the principle of autonomy of the credit at all. The learned Judge gave the following guidance for the degree of proof required for establishing fraud[61]:

> "We would expect the court to require strong corroborative evidence of the allegation, usually in the form of contemporary documents, particularly emanating from the buyer . . . If the court considers that on the material before it the only realistic inference to draw is that of fraud, then the seller would have made out a sufficient case for fraud."

---

[58] See, *e.g. Rafsanjan Pistachio Producers Co-operative v. Bank Leumi (U.K.) plc* [1992] 1 Lloyd's Rep. 513.

[59] *Empresa Exportadora de Azucar v. Industria Azucarera Nacional SA (IANSA); The Playa Larga and the Marble Islands* [1983] 2 Lloyd's Rep. 171 (this case did not involve the bank but arose between the buyer and the seller, however, the facts are relevant to the discussion in the text); *Tukan Timber Ltd v. Barclays Bank plc* [1987] 1 Lloyd's Rep. 171 at 176.

[60] *United Trading Corporation SA v. Allied Arab Bank Ltd* [1985] 2 Lloyd's Rep. 554 at 561 (this case concerned a performance guaranteee given by the seller, and not a letter of credit, but where fraud is alleged, the legal issues are the same), see E.P. Ellinger [1985] J.B.L. 232; *Bolivinter Oil SA v. Chase Manhattan Bank NA* [1984] 1 W.L.R. 392 at 393; [1984] 1 Lloyd's Rep. 251 at 255–257.

[61] [1985] 2 Lloyd's Rep. 554 at 561.

CHAPTER 12

BANK GUARANTEES AND OTHER CONTRACT GUARANTEES IN GENERAL

Guarantees in the common law and in international trade

12–001 In the common law the guarantee,[1] or suretyship, is an arrangement involving three parties: the *creditor*, who has a claim against the *principal debtor*, and a third party, the *guarantor* (the surety), who undertakes to be liable to the creditor if the principal debtor fails to discharge his obligation to him.[2] The arrangement between the creditor and the guarantor is the *contract of guarantee*. It is a secondary obligation, subsidiary to the contract between the creditor and the principal debtor.

As with any contract, in a contract of guarantee there must be an intention to create legal relations between parties who have the capacity to contract and the agreement itself must be supported by valid consideration.[3] To be enforceable, the material terms of a contract of guarantee[4] must either be in writing or must be evidenced by a note or memorandum in writing signed by the guarantor or his agent.[5] The absence of any such written agreement or memorandum affects the enforceability rather than the underlying validity of the contract.[6]

Since the contract of guarantee is accessory in nature, it follows that an agreement may only be a guarantee if there is another, principal, obligation to which it is subsidiary. In the words of Lord Selborne[7]:

> "There can be no suretyship unless there be a principal debtor, who of course may be constituted in the course of the transaction by matters *ex post facto* and need not be so at the time, but until there is a principal debtor there can be no suretyship. Nor can a man guarantee anybody else's debt unless there is a debt or some other person to be guaranteed."

---

[1] On contracts of guarantee generally see *Halsbury's Laws* (4th ed., 1994 reissue), Vol. 20, para. 101.

[2] The creditor can claim against the guarantor if the principal debtor is in default. It is not necessary for the creditor first to make a claim aginst the principal debtor or first to sue him, but the parties may so provide in the contract of guarantee.When the guarantor has paid the creditor, he has normally a claim for reimbursement against the principal debtor: *The Zuhal K and Selin* [1987] 1 Lloyd's Rep. 151.

[3] Unless the guarantee is made by deed, in which case it must comply with the requirements of the Law of Property (Miscellaneous Provisions) Act 1989 concerning deeds.

[4] As well as any subsequent variation of such terms.

[5] Statute of Frauds (1677), s. 4 (as amended). But the consideration for the guarantor's undertaking need not be specified: Mercantile Law Amendment Act 1856, s.3.

[6] Where the contract of guarantee is evidenced by a note or memorandum, the agreement itself may be oral; see *Elpis Maritime Co Ltd v. Marti Chartering Co Inc* [1992] 1 A.C. 21.

[7] *Lakeman v. Mountstephen* (1874) L.R. 7 HL 17 at 24.

The liability guaranteed may consist of something other than the payment of a debt, such as the performance of some other type of obligation. The extent of the guarantor's liability depends upon the terms of the contract of guarantee.[8] In general, under what is known as the principle of co-extensiveness, a guarantor is only liable to the same extent that the principal debtor is liable.[9]

A guarantor may be released from his obligation by a variety of means. If the obligation of the principal debtor is discharged, either by performance or otherwise, or if the liability to pay is extinguished by operation of law, the guarantor may be correspondingly discharged from his obligations. Conduct of the creditor which results in either a variation or extinction of any of the rights which the guarantor may have against the debtor will also operate to release the guarantor from liability. Thus, if the principal contract is varied without the guarantor's consent,[10] *e.g.* if the creditor grants the principal debtor an extension of time or releases a co-surety,[11] liability under the guarantee may be discharged. If the principal contract is invalid the guarantor will also be exempt from liability to the creditor.[12]

A distinction must be made between between demand guarantees[13] and conditional guarantees. Demand guarantees are widely used in contracts for the international sale of goods and in construction contracts. They are payable upon first demand by the beneficiary against presentation of specified documents to the bank and are unconditional.[14] Banks will not normally enquire as to the circumstances giving rise to the demand.[15] In the case of a *conditional guarantee*, the obligation of the guarantor is normally activated by the non-performance of an underlying obligation. Banks are sometimes reluctant to issue conditional guarantees because they wish to avoid being involved in disputes arising from the underlying contract. However other financial institutions, such as insurance or surety companies, are prepared to issue conditional guarantees.

Contracts of guarantee should be distinguished from contracts of indemnity. These often have similar characteristics and perform similar functions to contracts of guarantee, in that they also act to secure the performance of an obligation by a third party. However, in contrast to the contract of guarantee, the contract of indemnity is a two-party arrangement under which the indemnor undertakes to hold the other harmless if the latter suffers loss in his dealings with another.[16] It is a primary obligation to the creditor, a separate and autonomous

---

[8] *Moschi v. Lep Air Services Ltd* [1973] A.C. 331 at 345.

[9] See Steyn J., "Guarantees: The Co-extensiveness Principle" (1974) 90 L.Q.R. 246.

[10] *Holme v. Brunskill* (1877) 3 Q.B. 495 and see *City of London v. New Hampshire Insurance Co* [1992] 2 Lloyd's Rep. 365; *Crédit Suisse v. London Borough of Allerdale* [1995] 1 Lloyd's Rep. 315.

[11] Unless the contract of guarantee provides that the creditor may allow the principal debtor such indulgence.

[12] *Associated Japanese Bank (International) v. Crédit du Nord* [1989] 1 W.L.R. 255.

[13] See *post*, para. 12–004.

[14] *IE Contractors v. Lloyds Bank plc* [1989] 2 Lloyd's Rep. 205 at 207 ("under what are sometimes called first demands bonds the obligation to pay arises without any evidence of the validity of the claim on a simple demand, or on a demand either in a specified form or accompanied by a specified document.")

[15] See *post*, para. 12–004.

[16] *Yeoman Credit v. Latter* [1961] 1 W.L.R. 828.

undertaking which does not depend for its validity on the existence of a contract between the other parties. Moreover, whereas the liability of a guarantor is generally co-extensive with that of the principal debtor, this principle does not apply to indemnities. In *Gulf Bank KSC v. Mitsubishi Heavy Industries (No. 2)*[17] the customer agreed to indemnify the bank for claims made "under or in connection with the issue of the guarantee". The obligations under the counter indemnity were expressed not to be "in any way discharged or diminished" by the guarantee's total or partial invalidity and the bank was held entitled to claim on the indemnity even if the guarantee was at no time legally valid.

In international trade, a bank guarantee or other contract guarantee often—though not always—describes a primary and independent undertaking by the guarantor to pay if the conditions of the guarantee are satisfied.[18] Rarely will the bank guarantee be a guarantee in the strict common law sense. *i.e.* an undertaking to pay only if the bank's customer is in default. In the words of Somervell L.J.[19] "the word 'guarantee' is often used in other than its legal sense." It simply means 'undertaking'.[20]

This is the meaning attributed to the term "guarantee" in this chapter. And this is the meaning in which the term "guarantee" is used in the brochure *Uniform Rules for Contract Guarantees, (URCG)* published by the ICC in 1978.[21]

The Uniform Rules for Contract Guarantees deal only with guarantees, bonds, indemnities, sureties or similar undertakings ("guarantees") given on behalf of the seller or supplier but do not deal with those given on behalf of the buyer. They deal with three types of guarantee: the tender guarantee, which in this work is discussed in Chapter 25 on the construction of works and installations abroad[22]; the performance guarantee; and the repayment guarantee. The URCG are intended to regulate guarantees given by banks, insurance companies or other third parties, and apply only if the guarantee states that "it is subject to the Uniform Rules for Tender, Performance and Repayment Guarantees ('Contract Guarantees') of the International Chamber of Commerce (Publication No. 325)".

---

[17] [1994] 2 Lloyd's Rep. 145.

[18] In some civil law jurisdictions, this is called an "abstract guarantee".

[19] In *Heisler v. Anglo-Dal Ltd* [1954] 1 W.L.R. 1273 at 1276.

[20] In *Heisler v. Anglo-Dal Ltd* [1954] 1 W.L.R. 1273 the seller gave the buyers a personal "guarantee" to pay them 10 per cent of the value of the goods should he fail to deliver them. The buyers insisted on a bank or third-party guarantee. The Court of Appeal, affirming Devlin J., held that on the true construction of the contract the buyer was not entitled to a third-party guarantee and the seller's personal guarantee was sufficient. The Court of Appeal approved the statement of Devlin J. that, although to a lawyer a "guarantee" by a person to perform what he had undertaken quite worthless, to a commercial man it had some value as underlining the promise which had been given. Moreover, it might be construed as a promise to pay the fixed amount by way of liquidated damages if the contract was not performed. See also *Newman Industries v. Indo-British Industries* [1957] 1 Lloyd's Rep. 211 and *Attock Cement Ltd v. Romanian Bank for Foreign Trade* [1989] 1 W.L.R. 1147 (autonomous character of performance bond).

[21] ICC Brochure No. 325 (1978).

[22] See *post*, Chap. 25.

In practice, however, the URCG have not achieved widespread acceptance, due mainly to the requirement[23] that a judgment or arbitral award be produced as a condition of obtaining payment. Attempts to revise them foundered and instead, in April 1992, the ICC promulgated the Uniform Rules for Demand Guarantees[24] (URDG), which were drafted to take account of international banking practice and to produce a more even balance between the paying party and the beneficiary. Though rarely used, the Uniform Rules for Contract Guarantees have not been withdrawn, however, and may still be incorporated into performance guarantees.

The United Nations Conference on International Trade Law (UNCITRAL) has also published its UN Convention on Independent Guarantees and Standby Letters of Credit[25] which has yet to obtain the required number of ratifications before it can enter into force.

In addition to the tender, performance and repayment guarantee,[26] defined in and regulated by the ICC Uniform Rules for Contract Guarantees[27], a great variety of guarantees are issued by banks, insurance companies and other third parties.

Counter-guarantees[28] arise where a buyer (or employer in a construction contract) asks the seller (or contractor) to provide a performance guarantee. The seller obtains such a guarantee from a bank in his own country but the bank gives the guarantee to a local bank in the buyer's country, and not to the buyer directly. The local bank then gives the buyer a counter-guarantee.[29] It is of great importance that the terms of the counter-guarantee are identical with those of the primary guarantee.[30]

Bank guarantees

Bank guarantees may be procured by the buyer or by the seller. If they are **12–002** procured by the buyer, their aim is to secure the payment of the price to the seller by substituting a "reliable paymaster"[31] for the buyer. If they are procured

---

[23] At Art. 9.

[24] ICC Brochure No. 458 (1992), See further Goode, "Guide to the ICC Uniform Rules for Demand Guarantees", ICC Brochure No. 510 and Goode, "The new I.C.C. Uniform Rules for Demand Guarantees" [1992] L.M.C.L.Q. 190. See para. 12–004, *post*.

[25] On January 26, 1996, adopted by the General Assembly on December 11, 1995. See further Gorton, *The Draft UNCITRAL Convention on Independent Guarantees* [1997] J.B.L. 240.

[26] A repayment guarantee for an advance payment made by the employer in a construction contract was in issue in *Muduroglu Ltd v. T.C. Ziraat Bankasi* [1986] Q.B. 1225.

[27] Art. 2.

[28] Defined in Art. 2(c) of the URDG.

[29] Sometimes, the terminology is reversed and the guarantee given by the local bank is called "the guarantee" and that by the seller's bank the "counterguarantee", see *I.E. Contractors Ltd v. Lloyd's Bank plc and Rafidain Bank* [1989] 2 Lloyd's Rep. 205. This is a purely terminological difference and does not affect the observations in the text.

[30] Counterguarantees were issued in *Edward Owen Engineering Ltd v. Barclays Bank International Ltd* [1978] Q.B. 159, and *United Trading Corporation SA v. Allied Arab Bank Ltd* [1985] 2 Lloyd's Rep. 554; *Muduroglu Ltd v. T.C. Ziraat Bankasi* [1986] Q.B. 1225. Some countries, particularly in the Middle East, require performance guarantees to be operated by way of counter-guarantees.

[31] *Per* McNair J. in *Soproma SpA v. Marine & Animal By-Products Corporation* [1966] 1 Lloyd's Rep. 367 at 385.

by the seller, their purpose is to secure the buyer if he has a claim for damages against the seller for non-delivery of the goods, for defective delivery or other cases of non-performance. Such guarantees are known as *performance guarantees*. But, as has been observed earlier, bank guarantees are also given to secure a great variety of other contingencies.

A bank guarantee is normally an absolute undertaking[32] by the bank to pay if the conditions for payment are satisfied. A confusing terminology has arisen to describe these undertakings. In practice, demand guarantees, performance bonds, performance guarantees and standby letters of credit have a similar legal character and resemble documentary credits in that they are primary in form, and generally conditional only upon presentation of a written demand for payment together with any other stipulated documents. The issuing bank is not concerned as to whether there has been any actual default by the principal.

Many considerations which apply to documentary credits likewise apply to the bank guarantee. In particular, the principles of the autonomy of the bank's undertaking[33] and of strict compliance with the conditions stated in the bank's instructions (mandate)[34] apply, *mutatis mutandis*, to bank guarantees as well.[35] The application of the doctrine of strict compliance to demand notices was considered in *IE Contractors Ltd v. Lloyds Bank plc*[36] where Leggatt J. stated that the "demand must conform strictly to the terms of the bond in the same way that documents tendered under a letter of credit must conform strictly to the terms of the credit". On appeal[37] Staughton L.J. held that the application of the principle of strict compliance depends in each case upon the construction of the guarantee or bond and that the conditions specified in each case must be adhered to.

The obligation of the bank to honour its undertaking is subject to the fraud exception in the same circumstances[38] as have been explained when letters of credit were discussed.[39] Indeed, some of those rules were developed in cases in which bank guarantees were involved.[40]

---

[32] A bank guarantee often contains a clause obliging the guarantor to pay "free of set-off or counterclaim" (see *The Fedora* [1986] 2 Lloyd's Rep. 441); sometimes this clause may be implied into a bank guarantee as a matter of construction, see the Singapore case *P.H. Grace Pte Ltd v. American Express International Banking Corp* [1987] 1 M.L.J. 437.

[33] See *ante*, para. 11–006. See in particular *Siporex Trade SA v. Banque Indosuez* [1986] 2 Lloyd's Rep. 146; also *Ermis Skai Radio and Television v. Banque Indosuez SA*, February 26, 1997, unreported.

[34] See *ante*, para. 11–007.

[35] Hirst J. in *Siporex*, see n. 33, *ante*. See also *Potton Homes Ltd v. Colman Contractors (Overseas) Ltd* [1984] 28 Build. L.R. 19.

[36] [1989] 2 Lloyd's Rep. 205 at 207.

[37] [1990] 2 Lloyd's Rep. 496.

[38] See *ante*, para. 11–042. But if the guarantee is a demand performance guarantee given by the seller, the question is whether the buyer (and not the seller, as under a letter of credit) has acted fraudulently, when making a demand under the guarantee, see *post*, para. 12–005.

[39] *Siporex Trade SA v. Banque Indosuez* [1986] 2 Lloyd's Rep. 146.

[40] *United Trading Corporation SA v. Allied Arab Bank Ltd* [1985] 2 Lloyd's Rep. 554; *Bolivinter Oil SA v. Chase Manhattan Bank NA* [1984] 1 W.L.R. 392; *Intraco Ltd v. Notis Shipping Corporation; The Bhoja Trader* [1981] 2 Lloyd's Rep. 256; *Potton Homes Ltd v. Coleman Contractors (Overseas) Ltd* [1984] 28 Build. L.R. 19.

Bank Guarantees Procured by the Buyer

The bank guarantee procured by the buyer for the benefit of the seller[41] may **12–003** provide that the bank is liable to the seller for the guaranteed amount if no letter of credit is issued in his favour or no payment of the price is made in the manner and at the time stipulated in the underlying contract. In a case[42] in which the defendant bank provided a so-called performance guarantee obliging it to pay in the event that no letter of credit was issued in favour of the plaintiff sellers by a certain date, and no credit was in fact issued, Hirst J. held that the bank was liable on the guarantee because its obligation was an absolute undertaking. The learned judge said,[43] in words reminiscent of the famous "life blood" passage relating to letters of credit[44]:

> "The whole commercial purpose of a performance bond is to provide a security which is to be readily, promptly and assuredly available when the prescribed event occurs."

Devlin J. observed[45] that "the bank guarantee is not a general performance guarantee but only a a guarantee of a limited performance," *i.e.* of the payment of the price.

Where the buyer is obliged to obtain a confirmed letter of credit and the advising bank, instead of confirming the credit, absolutely guarantees payment of the price on the same conditions as were stipulated for the confirmed credit, it is thought that the bank guarantee is an adequate substitute for the confirmed credit.

Bank Guarantees Procured by the Seller

Demand guarantees[46]

These are guarantees procured by the seller in order to protect the buyer against **12–004** non performance.[47] Performance bonds are simply a form of demand guarantee.

---

[41] Or the beneficiary under another type of underlying contract.
[42] *Siporex Trade SA v. Banque Indosuez* [1986] 2 Lloyd's Rep. 146.
[43] *ibid.*, at 158.
[44] See para. 11–001.
[45] In *Sinaison-Teicher Inter-American Grain Corporation v. Oilcakes and Oilseeds Trading Co Ltd* [1954] 1 W.L.R. 935 at 941; affd [1954] 1 W.L.R. 1394, CA.
[46] See generally Pierce, *Demand Guarantees in International Trade* (Sweet & Maxwell, 1993).
[47] See, *e.g. R.D. Harbottle (Mercantile) Ltd v. National Westminster Bank Ltd* [1978] Q.B. 146; *Edward Owen Engineering Ltd v. Barclays Bank International Ltd* [1978] Q.B. 150; *Potton Homes Ltd v. Coleman Contractors (Overseas) Ltd* [1984] 28 B.L.R. 19; *United Trading Corporation SA v. Allied Arab Bank Ltd* [1985] 2 Lloyd's Rep. 554; *Siporex Trade SA v. Banque Indosuez* [1986] 2 Lloyd's Rep.146; *Tukan Timber Ltd v. Barclays Bank plc* [1987] 1 Lloyd's Rep. 171, *Wadha Bank Ltd v. Arab Bank plc* [1996] 1 Lloyd's Rep. 470, *Turkiye Is Bankasi AS v. Bank of China* [1998] 1 Lloyd's Rep. 250, *Cargill International SA v. Bangladesh Sugar Food Industries Corp* [1998] 2 All E.R. 406, CA, *Kvaerner John Brown Ltd v. Midland Bank plc* [1998] C.L.C. 446.

Similar in nature are *advance (or repayment)* guarantees which have to be pro-cured by the seller in order to secure a refund to the buyer in cases in which part or all of the purchase price has been paid in advance.[48]

The condition on which the bank is obliged to pay is usually a first demand[49] by the buyer. It must pay on a demand presented in accordance with the terms of the guarantee and is not concerned with the underlying contract. Here again, the bank enters into an absolute and autonomous undertaking, similar to the confirmation of a letter of credit, and must meet its obligations even if the seller objects and there are circumstances strongly supporting his contention that the buyer's demand is unjustified. However, if it is clearly established to the satis-faction of the bank that the demand is fraudulent and that the buyer knew of the fraud, the bank should not pay, or at least it should interplead, *i.e.* apply to pay the money into court and leave it to the parties to litigate about who is entitled to it. In *Edward Owen Engineering Ltd v. Barclays Bank International Ltd*[50] the sellers in the United Kingdom agreed to supply greenhouses to a State enterprise in Libya. The buyers undertook to open an irrevocable confirmed credit in favour of the sellers through Barclays International. The sellers had to provide a demand performance guarantee of 10 per cent of the purchase price. They instructed Barclays International to issue such guarantee to the Umma Bank in Libya, which gave its own counter-guarantee to the buyers. Barclays Interna-tional's guarantee was payable "on demand without proof or conditions". The buyers failed to open a satisfactory credit, as stipulated in the contract, and the sellers refused to supply the greenhouses. The buyers claimed under the demand guarantee from the Umma Bank and the latter claimed from Barclays Interna-tional under their guarantee. The Court of Appeal refused an injunction by the sellers enjoining Barclays International to pay. The court treated payment under a demand guarantee as analogous to payment under a confirmed letter of credit. Lord Denning M.R. observed:

> "All this leads to the conclusion that the performance guarantee stands on a similar footing to a letter of credit. A bank which gives a performance guarantee must honour that guarantee according to its terms. It is not concerned in the least with the relations between the supplier and the customer: nor with the question whether the supplier has performed his contracted obligation or not; nor with the question whether the supplier is in default or not. The bank must pay according to its guarantee, on demand, if so stipulated, without proof or conditions. The only exception is when there is a clear fraud of which the bank has notice."

The bank will issue a demand performance guarantee normally only on the counter-indemnity of the seller.[51] The guarantee will usually state the maximum liability of the bank and has an expiry date.

---

[48] *Howe Richardson Scale Co Ltd v. Polimex Cekop and National Westminster Bank* [1978] 1 Lloyd's Rep. 161, CA.

[49] The demand must be made strictly in the manner prescribed by the guarantee (or counter-guarantee) otherwise it is invalid; *IE Contractors Ltd v. Lloyd's Bank plc and Rafidain Bank* [1989] 2 Lloyd's Rep. 205. See *ante*, para. 12–002.

[50] [1978] Q.B. 159.

[51] Indeed, the counter-indemnity may be operative even where the underlying performance bond may never have had legal effect, *Gulf Bank KSC v. Mitsubishi Heavy Industries Ltd (No. 2)* [1994] 2 Lloyd's Rep. 145. See para. 12–001.

 If the seller (or contractor under a construction contract) fails to perform the contract, the buyer (or employer) is entitled to recover full damages but, if he has called in the performance guarantee, he has to give credit for the amount of the guarantee in the computation of the damages.[52] In *Cargill International SA v. Bangladesh Sugar & Food Industries Corporation*,[53] the Court of Appeal affirmed the decision of Morison J.[54] that it was implicit in the nature of a performance bond that in the absence of clear words to a different effect, there would at some stage in the future be an "accounting" between the parties. Thus, although the buyer could demand the full amount of the bond, if that amount exceeded the true loss which had been sustained, the provider of the bond was entitled to recover the overpayment.

The Uniform Rules for Demand Guarantees[55] have attempted to codify international market practice and to establish a balance between the beneficiary and the party for whose account a peformance bond is opened. The Rules, which reflect many of the provisions of the UCPDC, apply to any demand guarantee or counter-guarantee[56] provided they are expressly incorporated.[57]

Demand Guarantees are defined by Article 2(a) of the URDG as:

> "any guarantee, bond or other payment undertaking, however named or described, by a bank, insurance company or other body or person (hereinafter called the 'Guarantor') given in writing for the payment of money on presentation in conformity with the terms of the undertaking of a written demand for payment and such other document(s) (for example, a certificate by an architect or engineer, a judgment or an arbitral award) as may be specified in the Guarantee, such undertaking being given
>
> (i) at the request or on the instructions and under the liability of a party (hereinafter called 'the Principal'); or
> (ii) at the request or on the instructions and under the liability of a bank, insurance company or any other body or person (hereinafter 'the Instructing Party') acting on the instructions of a Principal to another party (hereinafter the 'Beneficiary')."

The autonomy of demand guarantees is described in Article 2(b):

> "Guarantees by their nature are separate transactions from the contract(s) or tender conditions on which they may be based, and the Guarantors are in no way concerned with or bound by such contract(s), or tender conditions, despite the inclusion of a reference to them in the Guarantee. The duty of the Guarantor under a Guarantee is to pay the sum or sums therein stated on the presentation of a written demand for payment and other documents specified in the Guarantee which appear on their face to be in accordance with the terms of the Guarantee."

---

[52] *Baytur SA v. Moona Silk Mills* December 20, 1984, unreported, noted in [1985] J.B.L. 324. This case concerned the interpretation of a clause in GAFTA Form No. 62. The buyers claimed damages *in addition* to the performance guarantee but Mustill J. held, on the construction of the clause, that they had to give credit for the guarantee.

[53] [1998] 2 All E.R. 406, CA.

[54] [1996] 2 Lloyd's Rep. 524; see also *Comdel Commodities Ltd v. Siporex Trade SA* [1997] 1 Lloyd's Rep. 424.

[55] See *ante*, para. 12–001. See also Goode, *Guide to the Uniform Rules for Demand Guarantees*, ICC Publication No. 510. The text of these Rules is available in Jack, *Documentary Credits* (1993), Appendix 4.

[56] As defined in Art. 2(c).

[57] URDG, Art. 1—the Rules will apply to any demand guarantee or amendment which states that it is subject to the Uniform Rules for Demand Guarantees of the International Chamber of Commerce (Publication No. 458).

These Rules contain certain requirements with regard to the making of a demand by the beneficiary, which attempt to afford some protection against unfair calling whilst maintaining the essential character of the demand guarantee. They state that the demand must be in writing,[58] must be transmitted to the principal without delay[59] and must be presented at the place at which the guarantee is issued and before its expiry.[60] Article 20 sets out the formal requirements of the demand as follows:

> "(a) Any demand for payment under the Guarantee shall be in writing and shall (in addition to such other documents as may be specified in the Guarantee) be supported by a written statement (whether in the demand itself or in a separate document or documents accompanying the demand and referred to in it) stating:
>
>> (i) that the Principal is in breach of his obligation(s) under the underlying contract(s) or, in the case of a tender guarantee, the tender conditions; and
>> (ii) the respect in which the Principal is in breach.
>
> (b) Any demand under the Counter-Guarantee shall be supported by a written statement that the Guarantor has received a demand for payment under the Guarantee in accordance with its terms and with this Article."

Therefore, although the guarantee may require only presentation of a written demand, it must still be accompanied by a statement that the principal is in breach of his obligations and must also identify the nature of the breach. It is thought that such a provision may have the effect of discouraging fraudulent calls under guarantees which incorporate these Rules.[61]

Unfair demand or fraud

12–005 The unconditional demand guarantee or performance bond involves the exporter in a heavy risk. The beneficiary may make an unfair demand under the guarantee, *i.e.* a demand which is wholly unjustified in the circumstances, having regard to the mutual undertakings of the parties in the underlying contract. Kerr J. observed correctly[62] that "performance guarantees in such unqualified terms seem astonishing, but I am told that they are by no means unusual, particularly in transactions with customers in the Middle East." Competitive conditions of business may make it necessary for the exporter to accept this risk.

The Export Credit Guarantees Department is prepared, subject to certain conditions, to cover the risk of unfair demand.[63] In addition, policies against the unjustified calling of demand guarantees are also available in the private insurance market.[64] It is submitted that parties will improve their position if they

---

[58] "Writing" includes EDI messages and other tested and authenticated teletransmissions, URDG, Art. 2(d).
[59] URDG, Art. 21.
[60] URDG, Art. 19.
[61] See, *e.g.* Jack (1993) para. 12.71; Goode, "The New I.C.C. Uniform Rules for Demand Guarantees" [1992] L.C.M.L.Q., 203.
[62] In *R.D. Harbottle (Mercantile) Ltd v. National Westminster Bank Ltd* [1978] Q.B. 146 at 150.
[63] "Bond Risk" cover under a Bond Insurance Policy, where ECGD facilities are being provided for the related export contract.
[64] From, *e.g* Lloyd's of London, NCM Credit Insurance Ltd.

provide for guarantees to be made subject to the ICC Uniform Rules for Demand Guarantees.

As stated previously, the fraud exception, recognised in relation to documentary credits, is also applicable to demand guarantees or bonds[65] and in principle, application may be made for an order restraining a bank from making payment on the ground that a demand is fraudulently made. In practice, however, the courts' reluctance to interfere with the autonomous nature of guarantees means that such orders are granted only in exceptional circumstances. Banks assume irrevocable obligations in relation to these facilities and only when fraud is clearly established is a bank justified in refusing to pay.

In *Bolivinter Oil SA v. Chase Manhattan Bank NA*[66] the Court of Appeal considered the grant of *ex parte* injunctions restraining payment under letters of credit, performance bonds and guarantees and made the following observations:

> "The unique value of such a letter, bond or guarantee is that the beneficiary can be completely satisfied that whatever disputes may thereafter arise between him and the bank's customer in relation to the performance or indeed existence of the underlying contract, the bank is personally undertaking to pay him provided that the specified conditions are met. In requesting a bank to issue such a letter, bond or guarantee, the customer is seeking to take advantage of this unique characteristic. If, save in the most exceptional cases, he is to be allowed to derogate from the bank's personal and irrevocable undertaking, given be it again noted at his request, by obtaining an injunction restraining the bank from honouring that undertaking, he will undermine what is the bank's greatest asset, however large and rich it may be, namely its reputation for financial and contractual probity. Furthermore, if this happens at all frequently, the value of all irrevocable letters of credit and performance bonds and guarantees will be undermined.
>
> Judges who are asked, often at short notice and *ex parte*, to issue an injunction restraining payment by a bank under an irrevocable letter of credit or performance bond or guarantee should ask whether there is any challenge to the validity of the letter, bond or guarantee itself. If there is not or if the challenge is not substantial, prima facie no injunction should be granted and the bank should be left free to honour its contractual obligation, although restrictions may well be imposed upon the freedom of the beneficiary to deal with the money after he has received it. The wholly exceptional case where an injunction may be granted is where it is proved that the bank knows that any demand for payment already made or which may thereafter be made will clearly be fraudulent. But the evidence must be clear, both as to the fact of fraud and as to the bank's knowledge. It would certainly not normally be sufficient that this rests upon the uncorroborated statement of the customer, for irreparable damage can be done to a bank's credit in the relatively brief time which must elapse between the granting of such an injunction and an application by the bank to have it discharged."

Emphasis is thus placed on the autonomy of the contract between the beneficiary and the bank which has issued the bond or guarantee. If the stipulated conditions are met, in principle an injunction enjoining payment under the facility will not be granted.

In *United Trading v. Allied Arab Bank*[67] the Court of Appeal considered the evidential burden on the applicant for an injunction, and concluded that if it could be established as seriously arguable that on the evidence available the only

---

[65] *Edward Owen Engineering Ltd v. Barclays Bank International Ltd* [1978] Q.B. 159; [1978] 1 All E.R. 976; *United City Merchants (Investments) Ltd v. Royal Bank of Canada* [1983] 1 A.C. 168; [1982] 2 All E.R. 720.
[66] [1984] 1 Lloyd's Rep. 251, DC.
[67] [1985] 2 Lloyd's Rep. 554 at 561.

realistic inference was fraud by the beneficiary, then this would be sufficient to warrant the grant of an injunction.[68] Ackner L.J. observed:

> "The evidence of fraud must be clear, both as to the fact of fraud and as to the Bank's knowledge. The mere assertion or allegation of fraud would not be sufficient. We would expect the Court to require strong corroborative evidence of the allegation, usually in the form of contemporary documents, particularly those emanating from the buyer. In general, for the evidence of fraud to be clear, we would also expect the buyer to have been given an opportunity to answer the allegation and to have failed to provide any, or any adequate answer, in circumstances where one could properly be expected. If the Court considers that on the material before it the only realistic inference to draw is that of fraud, then the seller would have made out a sufficient case of fraud."

In practice, the stringent onus of proof borne by the applicant is difficult to discharge. Rarely is it possible to establish a clear and obvious case of fraud to the degree required in order to successfully invoke the fraud exception. The mere suspicion of fraud is inadequate. In *Society of Lloyd's v. Canadian Imperial Bank of Commerce*,[69] which concerned a standby credit, the Court held that it was insufficient for a bank to plead that it had been provided with information which its customer alleged amounted to a sufficient case of fraud such as to justify rejection of a tender.

The case of *Turkiye I S Bankasi AS v. Bank of China*[70] concerned a counter-guarantee provided by the BOC in favour of TIB to cover a performance bond issued by TIB. A demand was made under the bond. The issue was whether or not TIB, on the material before it, should have refused payment on the basis of the fraud exception. It was BOC's contention that the Turkish bank would have been aware that its customer's demand under the bond in relation to which the counter-guarantee had been issued was fraudulent. Waller J. held that TIB was entitled to enforce its counter-guarantee against BOC and observed[71]:

> "It is simply not for a bank to make enquiries about the allegations that are being made one side against the other. If one side wishes to establish that a demand is fraudulent it must put the irrefutable evidence before the bank. It must not simply make allegations and expect the bank to check whether those allegations are [well-) founded or not . . . it is not the role of a bank to examine the merits of allegations and counter-allegations of breach of contract. To hold otherwise would be to place banks in a position where they would in effect have to act as courts in deciding whether to make payment or not . . ."

The problem of enjoining banks from paying out against unfair calls has led, in recent years, to applications for injunctions restraining the beneficiary from making a call on the guarantee. In *Themehelp Ltd v. West*[72] the purchaser of a business provided a third party first demand guarantee to the seller in order to secure the price payable under a share sale agreement. The purchase price was

---

[68] Though in this instance it was held that the plaintiff did not satisfy this test.
[69] [1993] 2 Lloyd's Rep. 579; and see *Kvaerner John Brown v. Midland Bank plc* [1998] C.L.C. 446 where the court granted an application to maintain an injunction on the grounds that the demand had been fraudulently made.
[70] [1996] 2 Lloyd's Rep. 611; [1998] 1 Lloyd's Rep. 250, CA.
[71] At 617.
[72] [1995] C.L.C. 703; [1995] 4 All E.R. 215, CAS, considered in *Group Josi Re v. Walbrook Insurance Co Ltd* [1996] 1 W.L.R. 1152; [1996] 1 All E.R. 791, CA.

payable in instalments. Upon subsequently learning of misrepresentations concerning the state of the business, the buyer successfully applied for an injunction restraining the seller from calling on the guarantee. In upholding the trial judge's grant of the injunction, Waite L.J. held[73] that the grant of an injunction restraining the beneficiary's rights of enforcement did not amount to a threat to the autonomy of the performance guarantee. He said that if a demand had not yet been made there was no risk to the integrity of the performance guarantee and consequently no occasion to involve the guarantor in the question of whether or not the fraud was established. In this way the buyer succeeded in preventing payment in a manner which did not involve the bank.

In a strong dissenting judgement, Evans L.J. concluded, *inter alia*, that the grant of the injunction was contrary to legal principle and harmful to the integrity of the banking system, and that the solution was for the plaintiff to apply for a Mareva injunction (now known as a "freezing injunction") restraining the beneficiary from using funds received from the performance bond. This would thereby not derogate from the principle of the autonomy of the bond.

---

[73] *ibid.* at 98–99.

CHAPTER 13

FACTORING, FORFAITING, FINANCIAL LEASING AND OTHER FORMS OF MERCHANT FINANCE

13–001 In addition to the financing methods described in the preceding chapters, a variety of other financing procedures, where finance is made available by banks or finance houses, are used in modern export trade. Four of these additional financing methods call for treatment here, namely factoring, forfaiting, financial licensing and non-recourse finance.

Two of these methods, international factoring and international financial leasing, form the subject matter of international Conventions, each dealing with the respective topic. The Conventions were prepared by Unidroit[1] and adopted by a Diplomatic Conference at Ottawa on May 28, 1988. The Conventions are not yet in force since they require ratification by at least three States.[2] They are examples of sound draftsmanship and contribute to the understanding of the legal principles on which these financial transactions are founded. The main features of the Conventions will be reviewed later on.[3]

FACTORING

The essence of international factoring

13–002 The essence of export factoring[4] is that a finance house, called the factor, agrees to relieve the exporter of the financial burden of the export transaction, in particular the collection of the price due from overseas buyers, so that the exporter can concentrate on his real business, the selling and marketing of his products. There is thus a division of labour, in that the exportation, including the despatch of the goods, the documentation and the transfer of the transport documents, is carried out by the exporter (the seller), but the credit management, to the extent agreed upon, is the responsibility of the factor.

International factoring is of considerable importance in modern export trade. It helps to ease the cash flow of the exporter's business, an important considera-

---

[1] Unidroit stands for the International Institute for the Unification of Private Law in Rome.

[2] Leasing Convention, Art. 16(1); Factoring Convention, Art. 14(1).

[3] Factoring Convention, see *post*, para. 13–007; Leasing Convention, see *post*, para. 13–012.

[4] See generally F. R. Salinger, *Factoring: The Law and Practice of Invoice Finance* (3rd ed., 1999); R.M. Goode, "Some Aspects of Factoring Law" [1982] J.B.L. 240, 338, 410, and 427; R.M. Goode, "Conclusion of the Leasing and Factoring Conventions" [1988] J.B.L. 347 at 510. The trading association of finance houses engaged in factoring is the Factors & Discounters Association, Boston House, the Little Green, Richmond, Surrey, TW9 1QE, tel: 020 8332 9955; fax: 020 8332 2585; Website: *www.factors.org.uk*

tion, as most export transactions contain a credit element. If the factoring is on a non-recourse basis,[5] it affords protection against bad debts.

When entering into a factoring agreement, two points, both of legal nature, are of particular importance to the exporter: what is the legal form of the factoring arrangement, *i.e.* is it disclosed or undisclosed; and does the factor have a claim of recourse against the exporter if the overseas buyer fails to pay, or is the factoring arrangement on a non-recourse basis?

As regards the legal form, in *disclosed factoring* the overseas buyer is notified—or at least can be notified—of the financing arrangement, but the *undisclosed factoring* arrangement is confidential between the export seller and the finance house and no notification is given to the overseas buyer. In both cases the international factor is not a factor in the legal sense.[6]

Where the factoring agreement is on a non-recourse basis, the factor, to whom the exporter's claim for the price is assigned, bears the credit risk and is not entitled to reimbursement if the buyer defaults. However if the factoring agreement admits recourse, *e.g.* for unapproved receivables assigned to the factor,[7] the factor has a claim for indemnification.

Direct and indirect factoring

Factoring may be either direct or indirect.[8] In direct factoring there is only one **13–003** factor, namely the export factor in the exporter's (seller's) country, with whom the exporter has concluded the factoring agreement. In indirect factoring, there are two factors, the export factor and the import factor in the importer's (buyer's) country. Under a direct factoring arrangement, upon assignment of the claim for the price, the export factor enters into direct contractual relations with the overseas buyer. In the case of indirect factoring, the overseas buyer, to whom this arrangement is disclosed, makes payment to an import factor in his country. The import factor will pay the export factor in the seller's country and the latter provides the arranged finance to the export seller. There is no contractual relationship between the exporter and the import factor. Indirect factoring has the advantage that each of the finance houses—the export factor and the import factor—deals with a local customer whose creditworthiness it can best appraise. The relationship between the export factor and import factor, who may be associated companies, is sometimes one of mutuality.

The factoring contract is, of course, separate from the export sales contract. The law governing the factoring contract is normally that of the place at which the factor carries on business.

Whether the factoring arrangement is with or without recourse to the export seller is a matter of arrangement between the two parties to the agreement. If, to the knowledge of the seller, non-conforming goods are supplied or another

---

[5] See *post*, para. 13–003.
[6] On factors within the meaning of the Factors Act 1889 see *post*, para. 27–017, Mocatta J. in *Hamilton Finance Co v. Coverley Westray* [1969] 1 Lloyd's Rep. 53 at 58, described the expression "factoring" as somewhat confusing.
[7] See *post*, para. 13–005.
[8] This distinction should not be confused with that between disclosed and undisclosed factoring.

condition of the sales contract is breached by the seller and the buyer rightly refuses to pay under the contract of export sale, the factor is normally entitled to recourse, even if the contract with him provides for non-recourse finance.

Legal forms of factoring

13–004 The legal structure of disclosed and undisclosed factoring is different. Disclosed factoring is, in essence, founded on a legal assignment of the exporter's claim for payment of the purchase price to the factor as assignee. The assignment has to comply with the requirements of section 136 of the Law of Property Act 1925 which regulates the assignment of debts. According to this provision, the assignment must be in writing, signed by the assignee (the export seller), it must be absolute[9] and express notice in writing must be given to the debtor (the overseas buyer). In practice, the notice is often given simply on the invoice. On receipt of notice by the debtor, the assignee then obtains a legal right to the debt. Assignments which do not comply with one or more of the requirements of section 136 take effect as equitable assignments.

The most common forms of undisclosed factoring constitute merely an equitable assignment of the seller's claim to the finance house. They do not satisfy the requirements of a legal assignment, as no notice is given to the overseas buyer. Some foreign legal systems do not recognise an equitable assignment and for this reason finance houses are in some cases reluctant to agree to this form of factoring. Other forms of undisclosed factoring are likewise in use.[10]

The overseas buyer (the debtor for the price) should be notified of the assignment to the factor as early as possible. Such notification may secure the factor priority over other secured creditors of the debtor. If several equitable interests compete, the order of notification to the debtor determines the priority.[11] In one case[12] a German wine producer sold a quantity of wine to an English wine merchant. The contract contained a reservation of title clause which was void against the creditors of the buyer because it was not registered as a charge under section 395 of the Companies Act 1985[13]; the unregistered charge was merely an equitable charge. Later, the buyer resold the wine to a sub-purchaser and entered into a factoring agreement with the defendant factors,[14] to whom he assigned the claim for the sub-purchase price by way of a legal assignment. The sub-purchaser was notified of the assignment and made payments to the factors. When the original buyer ceased paying the German wine seller, the latter sued the factors for the moneys received from the sub-purchasers. Phillips J. felt compelled—rather surprisingly—to treat the legal assignment to the factors as

---

[9] This means that the whole claim, and not only part of it, must be assigned, so that the debtor is not inconvenienced by having to deal with several creditors.
[10] See *post*, para. 13–006.
[11] Under the rule in *Dearle v. Hall* (1828) 3 Russ, 1.
[12] *E. Pfeiffer Weinkellerei-Weineinkauf GmbH v. Arbuthnot Factors Ltd* [1988] 1 W.L.R. 150.
[13] On reservation of title clauses, see *ante*, paras 4–007—4–009.
[14] This was a domestic factoring arrangement, and not an international factoring contract.

an equitable assignment.[15] The learned judge held that the (later) equitable assignment to the factors took priority over the (earlier) equitable charge in favour of the German seller because *notification to the debtor* of the assignment to the factors was earlier in time.

Disclosed factoring

The *price collection service* in disclosed factoring transactions is carried out in **13–005** the following way. The factor enters into the factoring contract with the exporter whereby he agrees to purchase from him certain specifically approved short-term debts ("approved receivables") owed by the overseas buyers. When the exporter sells goods abroad, the claim for the price is assigned to the factor and the overseas buyer is asked to pay to him. The buyer is thus notified of the fact that the price shall not be paid to the exporter. Assignments of approved receivables may—and often do—form the subject-matter of non-recourse finance. Receivables which are not approved by the factor ("unapproved receivables") are purchased by him on a recourse basis. Factoring arrangements are usually made on a "whole turnover" basis and the factor's commission is calculated accordingly. Under such an arrangement the export seller is obliged to offer all his receivables to the finance house for factoring.

In addition to the price collection service, the factor may carry out some functions of the exporter's *credit management*. These functions will be set out in the factoring agreement, and several options are available. They may include the handling, by the factor, of the internal credit control and sales accounting ("ledgering") of the exporter, an arrangement whereby the exporter passes duplicate invoices to the factor to enable him to carry out these activities.

The factor may make payment to the exporter on a calculated average settlement date which is called "average maturity factoring". Under this arrangement, the exporter receives an assured payment regularly on a specified date, instead of a number of small payments which fall due on the varying maturity dates of the purchase price from the overseas buyers. However, if the exporter prefers, he may also arrange that the finance house pays him on those maturity dates, which is called *"pay as paid factoring"*.

If the exporter wants the factor to finance the transaction, in addition to providing price collection and/or credit management services, the factor will make an immediate payment to the exporter, usually up to 80 per cent of the book value of approved invoices, while extending credit to the overseas buyer. Here again, the factor may assume the credit risk and make payment to the exporter for approved receivables on a non-recourse basis. Where an export factor finances the transaction, he will often use the services of an import factor in the overseas buyer's country. This enables the latter to pay the price in his own currency. If the factor provides immediate finance in

---

[15] If Phillips J. had treated the assignment as a legal assignment, he could have founded his decision in favour of the factors on this ground because a legal assignment normally takes priority over equitable interests.

addition to the debt collecting services, a charge will be made which varies with the money rates and is usually 3 to 4 per cent per annum above the appropriate bank's base rate. The factor selects the exporters whom he accepts as clients with great care.

If the provision of finance by the factor is combined with the assignment of receivables under a price collection arrangement—a combination which is often met in practice—and the supplier is a company, the question arises whether the assignment of present and future receivables has to be registered as a book debt by virtue of section 396(1)(e) of the Companies Act 1985. It is thought that no registration under this section is required because the object of the assignment is debt collection and not the provision of security for a loan, and the assignment of the receivables is absolute, and not by way of a charge.[16]

Undisclosed factoring

13–006 The most common type of undisclosed factoring is known as *invoice discounting*. It is carried out in the form of an equitable assignment of the purchase price by the export seller to the factor. In this arrangement the factoring arrangement is not disclosed to the overseas buyer. He pays the purchase price to the export seller. The factoring contract will provide that the export seller receives the price as a trustee of the factor and has to place it into a separate account nominated by the latter. Where the contract so provides, the director of the exporting company would commit the tort of conversion and have to refund such payment to the factor if, on receipt of the payment, he put it into the company's account.[17] Invoice discounting is usually on a recourse basis.

Some finance houses use other legal forms which do not involve the disclosure of the financing arrangement to the overseas buyer. They require the exporter to sell the goods to them outright for cash and then authorise the exporter to resell them to the overseas buyer as their undisclosed agent.[18] The resale to the overseas buyer is often on credit terms. In this arrangement the exporter receives the price from the overseas buyer as agent of the finance house and has to account for it to the latter.

Worldwide chains of correspondent factors have been established which have produced common rules for the regulation of factoring transactions. One example of this is the Code of International Factoring Customs[19] promulgated by Factors Chain International, which includes a provision[20] that disputes between member export and import factors are to be settled by an arbitration procedure.

---

[16] See *Lloyd's and Scottish Finance Ltd v. Prentice* (1977) S.J. 147; see also *Lloyd's and Scottish Finance Ltd v. Cyril Lord Carpets Sales Ltd* [1992] B.C.L.C. 609, HL.
[17] *International Factors Ltd v. Rodriguez* [1979] Q.B. 351.
[18] See *ante*, para. 27–005.
[19] The latest revision of this appeared in June 1998. Full text available in Salinger, 3rd ed.
[20] At Art. 2.

The Unidroit Convention on International Factoring

The Convention, when in force,[21] applies[22] whenever the receivables assigned **13–007** pursuant to a factoring contract arise from a contract of sale of goods between a supplier (the seller) and a debtor (the buyer) whose places of business are in different States and:

(a) these States and the State in which the factor has its place of business are Contracting States; or

(b) both the contract of sale of goods and the factoring contract are governed by the law of a Contracting State.

The purpose of this provision is to align the International Factoring Convention with the Vienna Convention on Contracts for the International Sale of Goods.[23]

The application of the Convention may be excluded by the parties to the factoring contract or by the parties to the sale contract in respect of receivables arising at or after notification of this exclusion to the factor (Art. 3(a) and (b)).

The Unidroit Convention governs factoring contracts, and for its purposes a factoring contract must satisfy the following requirements[24]:

(a) The supplier may or will assign to the factor receivables arising from contracts of sale of goods made between the supplier and its customers (debtors) other than those for the sale of goods bought primarily for their personal, family or household use.

(b) The factor is to perform at least two of the following functions:
   (i) finance for the supplier, including loans and advance payments;
   (ii) maintenance of accounts (ledgering) relating to the receivables;
   (iii) collection of receivables;
   (iv) protection against default in payment by debtors.

The Convention applies to undisclosed and disclosed factoring.

A difficult issue is whether a prohibition of the assignment of the claim for the price in the supply contract prevents the supplier from assigning the claim to the factor. As already observed, the supply contract and the factoring contract are two different contractual relationships. The solution which the Convention adopts is to provide[25] that the assignment of a receivable by the supplier to the factor shall be effective, notwithstanding any agreement between the supplier and the debtor prohibiting such assignment. But a Contracting State may contract out of this provision by declaring that it shall not apply when, at the time of conclusion of the contract of sale of goods, the debtor has his place of business in the Contracting State.[26] Further, the assignment to a factor in spite of a prohibition in the supply contract does not affect any obligation of good faith

---

[21] See *ante*, para. 13–001.
[22] Art. 2(c).
[23] See para. 32–026.
[24] Art. 1(2).
[25] Art. 6(1).
[26] Arts 6(2) and 18.

owed by the supplier to the debtor or any liability for breach of a term in the supply contract.[27]

As regards the notice of assignment to the debtor, it is provided[28] that it shall be in writing and reasonably identify the factor to whom payment has to be made and the receivables to which the assignment relates. A notice relating to the assignment of receivables which form the subject-matter of a future supply contract is invalid,[29] and so is a general notice of assignment with respect to all future supply contracts.

Where the debtor has made payment to the factor and never receives the goods or receives non-conforming goods, he has, in principle, no right to recover payment from him but has only a claim against the supplier.[30] In two exceptional cases, however, the debtor may claim recovery against the factor[31]: if the debtor has paid the factor but the factor has not paid the supplier in respect of the receivable in question, and if the factor paid the supplier with knowledge that the supplier had defaulted on his obligations to the debtor.

The Convention also regulates indirect factoring.[32] Where the supplier assigns to the export factor and he makes a second assignment to the import factor, it often happens that the debtor is only notified of the second assignment, but not of the first. The Convention provides[33] that notification of the second assignment shall also operate as notice of the first assignment. While, in principle, the Convention applies to subsequent assignments, this is not the case if the (first) factoring agreement prohibits subsequent assignments.[34]

FORFAITING

13–008 Forfaiting,[35] or to use the French expression,[36] an *à forfait* transaction, is the purchase of a debt expressed in a negotiable instrument, such as a bill of exchange or a promissory note, from the creditor on a non-recourse basis. The purchaser, known as the forfaiter, undertakes to waive—to forfeit—his right of recourse against the creditor if he cannot obtain satisfaction from the debtor. However, the forfaiter will purchase the negotiable instrument only if he is given security by a bank of good standing. This security is given either in the form of an aval on the negotiable instrument itself,[37] or in the form of a separate bank

---

[27] Art. 6(3).

[28] Art. 8(1) (b) and (c).

[29] This statement applies only to the notice to be given to the debtor. The factoring contract (between the supplier and the factors) may provide for the supplier's obligation to assign future receivables (Art. 5(a)) and even for their assignment without a new act of transfer (Art. 1).

[30] Art. 10(1).

[31] Art. 10(2).

[32] Art. 11.

[33] Art. 11(2).

[34] Art. 12.

[35] See Ripley, *Forfaiting for Exporters—Practical Solutions for Global Trade Finance* (International Thomson Business Press, 1996).

[36] Forfaiting has its origin on the European Continent and is said to have been first developed in Switzerland. London has become an important forfaiting market and forfaiting transactions are undertaken by most London banks engaged in international finance.

[37] See *ante*, para. 9–009.

guarantee,[38] guaranteeing due and punctual observance of all obligations under the negotiable instrument. The purchase of the negotiable instrument by the forfaiter is, of course, at a discount. The forfaiter will be a bank, finance house or discount company.

Forfaiting agreements have traditionally been based on a single underlying transaction and often for high value transactions, though they are now increasingly available for less substantial values and shorter credit periods.

The essence of forfaiting

The essence of the transaction is that the debtor's obligation, which matures at **13–009** some future date, can be turned by the creditor at once into ready cash, by selling that obligation to the forfaiter who, however, agrees to the purchase of the obligation on a non-recourse basis only if it is secured by a third party. The forfaiting technique is used in two types of transactions: in a financial transaction, to make a long-term financial facility liquid; and in an export transaction, to help the cash flow of the exporter who has allowed the overseas buyer credit. This chapter is concerned only with the second type of forfaiting.

Avalised bills of exchange and bank guarantees as security for the forfaiter

In international trade, the export seller will obtain from the overseas buyer **13–010** time bills of exchange or promissory notes maturing at specified future dates. These negotiable instruments will be avalised by a bank in the importer's country or that bank will guarantee their performance. The negotiable instruments so secured will then be negotiated by the export seller to his own bank, without recourse by that bank to him. The exporter's bank thus acts as the forfaiter. The forfaiting arrangement has to be agreed between the seller and the buyer in the contract of export sale and normally this is only done after agreement is first obtained from the banks, *i.e.* agreement between the seller and his bank that it will forfait the negotiable instruments, and agreement between the buyer and the bank in his country that it will avalise or guarantee them. Forfaiting is particularly appropriate to the export of capital goods where the contract of sale may provide for payment by instalments extending over two to five years. A typical transaction would be the sale of machinery to be paid by 10 promissory notes from the buyer maturing at six-monthly intervals over five years. Banks prefer promissory notes from the buyer but bills of exchange are also acceptable.

The forfaiter is naturally particularly interested in the effectiveness of the security supporting the negotiable instrument which he purchases. If it is an aval, it has already been observed[39] that such a commitment is valid in English law and the avaliser as a backer is under the same liability as an indorser of the document. If the security takes the form of a bank guarantee, it will state that it

---

[38] See *ante*, para. 12–002, or a standby credit, at para. 11–030 *ante*.
[39] See *ante*, para. 9–009.

is a primary guarantee and the guarantor is in the position of a principal debtor, that it is irrevocable and unconditional, that it is divisible and assignable, and it will contain a statement such as:

> Notice in writing of any default on the part of the said [acceptor/promissor] is to be given to us [the guaranteeing bank] and forthwith upon receipt of such notice payment shall be made by us of all sums then due from us under this guarantee.

The security for the negotiable instrument is abstract and does not depend on incidents concerning the underlying sale or other export transaction for which the overseas importer has given the negotiable instruments. In this respect the security is autonomous. The contract between the forfaiter and the export seller usually so states in express terms, but nevertheless the forfaiter normally asks to be advised of the underlying transaction.

The contract between the export seller and the forfaiter usually contains a choice of law clause and a jurisdiction clause and, if the security is a guarantee, similar clauses will be inserted into the guarantee which the bank in the importer's country gives the forfaiter. If the forfaiter is located in England and Wales, these contracts are normally governed by English law and there is a non-exclusive jurisdiction clause in favour of the English courts.

Primary and secondary forfaiting transactions

13–011 The forfaiter will often renegotiate the negotiable instruments which he has purchased by way of a forfaiting transaction, in order to place himself in funds or to spread the risk. Financial circles refer to a primary and a secondary forfait market and refer to the original forfaiter as the introducing bank. Secondary market operations may raise complicated legal problems. Normally the exporter is not concerned with these, but on occasion they may have repercussions which concern him. For this reason a bank which has a forfaiting unit might word the non-recourse clause in its forfait contract with the seller in cautious terms such as the following:

> We confirm that we waive our right of recourse against you as drawer of these bills and will endeavour to obtain a similar undertaking from any subsequent purchaser from us.

Further, it has been argued that the non-recourse clause does not protect the seller if he fails to deliver the goods to the buyer without legal excuse. It is doubtful whether the courts will accept this argument in view of the autonomous character of the security (aval or bank guarantee), but it will certainly be successful if it can be proved that the seller was involved in a fraud.[40]

If the forfaiter is a bank operating export finance transactions, it will normally obtain the forfaitable paper through its documentary credit collection system.[41] Documents of title to the goods are transmitted to the importer's bank with

---

[40] On the principle accepted by the House of Lords in *United City Merchants Investments Ltd v. Royal Bank of Canada* [1983] 1 A.C. 168; see para. 11–042, *ante.*
[41] See *ante*, para. 10–001.

instructions that they must only be released against acceptance of the bills of exchange or signature of the promissory notes, plus the per aval indorsement or the issue of the letter of guarantee by the importer's bank, according to the previous arrangement with the forfaiter.

INTERNATIONAL FINANCIAL LEASING

The essence of the financial leasing transaction

Banks and finance houses are sometimes asked to provide financial assistance **13–012** to international leasing transactions. These transactions normally concern capital goods, such as the leasing of ships or aircraft, containers, or heavy equipment for the exploration of oil or mineral resources. The lessee who wishes to use the equipment pays the lessor a rental. As the period of the lease may be lengthy, the lessor incurs a considerable financial risk.

If the owner of the equipment is prepared to accept this risk, he will himself act as the lessor. The ordinary lease is thus a two-party agreement between the lessor and the lessee. If the owner does not want to accept the financial risk, a financial leasing transaction is entered into. Under such a transaction a bank or finance house is interposed between the owner and the user. The owner (known as the supplier) sells the goods outright to the finance house (known as the creditor), possibly on a cash basis, and the finance house acts as lessor *vis à vis* the user (the lessee, known as the debtor). This is a three-party transaction. It is an application, in the international sphere, of the principle on which, in the domestic sphere, the concept of the hire-purchase contract and the debtor-creditor-supplier agreement under the Consumer Credit Act 1974[42] is founded.

Financial leasing agreements are of two types. In the pure leasing transaction, possession reverts to the lessor when the lease is terminated. Under other leasing agreements the lessee has the option of acquiring the property in the leased goods; in this instance a deferred price component is included in the rental. In both types of financial leasing agreements the rental payable by the lessee sometimes includes an amortisation element for the wear and tear of the equipment.

The Unidroit Convention on International Financial Leasing

The Convention,[43] when in force, applies[44] if the lessor and the lessee have their **13–013** places of business in different States and:

(a) these States and the State in which the supplier has its place of business are Contracting States; or

(b) both the supply agreement and the leasing agreement are governed by the law of a Contracting State.

---

[42] Consumer Credit Act 1974, s.12.
[43] See *ante*, para. 13–001.
[44] Convention, Art. 3(1).

The application of the Convention may be excluded only if each of the parties to the supply agreement and each of the parties to the leasing agreement agree to do so (Art. 5).

The Convention governs a transaction which includes the following characteristics[45]:

    (a) The lessee specifies the equipment and selects the supplier without relying primarily on the skill and judgment of the lessor.

    (b) The equipment is acquired by the lessor in connection with a leasing agreement which, to the knowledge of the supplier, either has been made or is to be made between the lessor and the lessee; and

    (c) The rentals payable under the leasing agreement are calculated so as to take into account, in particular, the amortisation of the whole or a substantial part of the cost of the equipment.

The Convention applies whether or not the lessee has the option to buy the equipment or to hold it on lease for a further period, and whether or not for a nominal price or rental.[46]

The Convention distinguishes between two agreements:

    (a) *the supply agreement* concluded between the lessor and the supplier; and

    (b) *the leasing agreement* between the lessor and the lessee.[47]

The main objective of the Convention is to remove, with respect to the equipment, liability from the lessor to the supplier, as the lessor has only a financial interest in the transaction.[48] Except as otherwise agreed, the lessor does not incur liability to the lessee in respect of the equipment, except if the loss is caused by the reliance of the lessee on the skill and judgment of the lessor or the lessor has intervened in the selection of the supplier or the equipment.[49] Further, the lessor, in his capacity as such, is not liable to third parties for death, personal injury or damage to property caused by the equipment[50] though he may be liable in another capacity, for example as owner.[51]

Where the equipment is not delivered or is delivered late or does not conform to the terms of the supply contract, the rights of the parties to the leasing agreement are as follows:

    (a) The lessee has the right as against the lessor to reject the equipment or to terminate the leasing agreement[52];

---

[45] Art. 1(2).
[46] Art. 1(3).
[47] Art. 1(1).
[48] R.M. Goode, "Conclusion of the Leasing and Factoring Conventions—1" [1988] J.B.L. 347.
[49] Art. 8(1)(a).
[50] Art. 8(1)(b).
[51] Art. 8(1)(c).
[52] Art. 12(1)(a).

(b) The lessor is entitled to remedy the failure by tendering equipment in conformity with the supply contract[53]; and

(c) The lessee may withhold payment of the rental until the lessor has made a remedial tender of the equipment.[54]

These rights are aligned with those of the seller and buyer under the Vienna Convention on Contracts for the International Sale of Goods.[55] The rights conferred on the lessor and lessee under the Convention are exercisable as if the lessee had agreed to buy the equipment from the lessor under the terms of the supply agreement.[56]

The Convention contains further safeguards for the protection of the lessor. It provides[57] that the lessor shall not be responsible for a default by virtue of non-delivery or misdelivery of the equipment to the lessee, except if it is due to an act or omission of the lessor. In addition, it provides that the duties of the supplier under the supply contract shall also be owed to the lessee as if he were a party to the supply agreement.[58]

Two further provisions of the Convention may be mentioned here. First, in the case of default by the lessee the lessor may recover the accrued unpaid rentals, together with interest and damages.[59] Where the default is substantial, the lessor may claim acceleration of future rentals or termination of the leasing agreement, and after termination he may recover possession of the equipment and damages.[60] If he terminates the leasing agreement however, he cannot claim accelerated rentals, though their value may be taken into account in computing the damages.[61] In any event, the damages which the lessor may claim are only compensatory. A contract clause providing for the payment of excessive liquidated damages is not enforceable against the lessee.[62]

Secondly, the lessor's real rights in the equipment are protected in the event of the insolvency of the lessee. They are valid against the trustee in bankruptcy[63] and the creditors, including creditors who have obtained an attachment or execution.[64] Where a legal system recognises as valid in the lessee's insolvency real rights in the equipment only if a prescribed form of public notice has been given, for instance by registration of those rights, this requirement of the applicable law[65] has to be complied with.

---

[53] Art. 12(1)(b).
[54] Art. 12(3), or he—the lessee—has lost the right to reject the equipment.
[55] See *post*, para. 32–026.
[56] Art. 12(2) and 12(1), end. This provision, and that of Art. 10, modifies, to some extent, the English doctrine of privity of contract.
[57] Art. 12(5).
[58] Art. 10. But the supplier is not liable to both the lessor and lessee for the same damage.
[59] Art. 13(1)
[60] Art. 13(2).
[61] Art. 13(2).
[62] Art. 13(2)(b) and 3(b).
[63] Art. 7(1)(b) gives a wide definition of this term; it includes a liquidator and an administrator.
[64] Art. 7(1).
[65] Art. 7(2). For the purposes of this provision, the applicable law is defined in Art. 7(3) as the law of the State which, at the time when the lessor becomes entitled to invoke the rules of Art. 7 is:
  (a) in the case of a registered ship, the State in which it is registered in the name of the owner (for the purposes of this sub-paragraph a bare boat charterer is deemed not to be the owner);
  (b) in the case of an aircraft which is registered pursuant to the Convention on International Civil

OTHER FORMS OF MERCHANT FINANCE

Non-recourse finance

13–014 This type of finance occupies a half-way position between the facilities offered by the confirming house[66] and by the confirming bank under a letter of credit.[67] The typical transaction of this kind differs from the activities of a confirming house in so far as the finance house does not undertake to export the goods and does not concern itself with making arrangements for transport, insurance or export documentation. It differs from the position of the confirming bank in so far as the exporter is not required to undertake personal liability as the drawer of a bill of exchange.[68] Consequently, in this type of transaction the finance house accepts the financial risk of the transaction.

The terms on which finance houses make non-recourse finance available differ considerably and the rights and obligations of the exporter depend largely on his arrangement with the finance house. In a typical non-recourse transaction—always bearing in mind that other arrangements are possible—the finance house enters into two contracts, one with the exporter and the other with the overseas buyer.

In the contract with the exporter the finance house undertakes to pay him at once the purchase price in full, less a deposit paid by the overseas buyer to the exporter,[69] such payment to be made on delivery of specified transport documents to the finance house. Some finance houses undertake this liability only after the name of the buyer is disclosed to them and they are satisfied as to his financial standing. Normally the finance house itself is covered by an ECGD policy and further agrees in its contract with the exporter to relieve him of the credit and political risk attending the transaction, as far as it is itself covered by that policy.[70] The contract will then contain a clause making it clear that the finance house is not involved in the goods aspects of the transaction, for example:

> We shall not be responsible for any claim arising out of or in connection with your transactions with the buyer, on whatever legal ground such claim may be founded or whether it is for loss, damage or otherwise or made by you against the buyer or by the buyer against you.

The contract also provides for a particular and a general lien in favour of the finance house, for the application of English law and for London arbitration.

Aviation done at Chicago on December 7, 1944, the State in which it is so registered..
   (c) in the case of other equipment of a kind normally moved from one State to another, including an aircraft engine, the State in which the lessee has its principal place of business;
   (d) in the case of all other equipment, the State in which the equipment is situated.

[66] See *ante*, para. 27–018.
[67] See *ante*, para. 11–026.
[68] Under the terms of his contract with the finance house, the exporter will, however, be liable to the finance house if the buyer refuses to pay for reasons for which the exporter is responsible, *e.g.* if he has supplied goods not conforming to the contract.
[69] The payment of such a deposit is normal in this type of transaction.
[70] The policy must not be disclosed to the buyer.

The second contract relating to the same transaction is concluded between the finance house and the overseas buyer. This contract contains an obligation on the part of the buyer to pay to the finance house the purchase price and the charges of the finance house, less the deposit paid directly to the exporter. Usually the buyer, on presentation of the transport documents to him, has to accept drafts drawn on him by the finance house. This procedure enables the finance house to grant the buyer credit or to accept instalment payments from him. The contract does not, of course, refer to the ECGD policy of the finance house. Some finance houses request an indemnity from the buyer and ask for confirmation that he has any necessary import licences and exchange control permissions for the transfer of funds to the finance house. In other respects, the contract with the buyer contains clauses similar to those with the exporter.

CHAPTER 14

COUNTERTRADE

14–001 Countertrade is a collective term which denotes various methods of linking two export transactions, one emanating from the exporter's country and the other from that of the importer. The simplest forms of countertrade are reciprocal sales and barters but, as will be seen later, other types of countertrade are also in use, some of great complexity.[1]

Contracts of sale and of barter

14–002 Normal dealings in international trade are founded on the concept of the sale of goods. The sale of goods means an exchange of goods for money. The money consideration is called the price.[2] It is irrelevant whether the price is payable on delivery of the goods,[3] or in advance, or whether credit is allowed. In English law, unlike some other legal systems,[4] it is equally irrelevant that the price is not fixed in the contract of sale or that the contract does not contain machinery for the determination of the price. The Sale of Goods Act 1979 admits "open price" contracts and states[5] that in these cases the buyer must pay "a reasonable price". However, if the contract provides for an exchange of goods for goods or services, it is not a contract of sale in the legal sense, but a barter.[6]

The rules governing a contract of barter are not well defined in English law.[7] It is obvious that the Sale of Goods Act 1979 does not apply directly. However,

---

[1] See generally *Countertrade and Offset—a Guide for Exporters* (1998 ed.) published by the Department of Trade and Industry, see DTI website: see also *Countertrade*, ICC Publications No. 944; UNCITRAL Legal Guide on International Countertrade Transactions, 1992 (http://www.uncitral.org).

[2] The Sale of Goods Act 1979, s.2(1) provides: "A contract of sale of goods is a contract by which the seller transfers the property in goods to the buyer for a money consideration, called the price".

[3] Unless otherwise agreed, the price is so payable. In the terminology of the Sale of Goods Act 1979, unless otherwise agreed, the delivery of the goods and payment of the price are "concurrent conditions" (s.28).

[4] French law (Civil Code, Art. 1583) requires the fixing of the price, or a method of ascertaining it, in the contract of sale. U.S. law, like English law, admits "open price" contracts (Uniform Commercial Code, s.2-305(1)), in which case a "reasonable price" is payable. The Uniform Law on the International Sale of Goods (Hague Convention, 1964), Art. 57, and the UN Convention on Contracts for the International Sale of Goods (Vienna, 1980), Art. 55, follow, in principle, the U.K. and U.S. regulation. On "open price" contracts generally see *R. & J. Dempster Ltd v. Motherwell Bridge and Engineering Co Ltd* 1964 S.C. 308.

[5] In s.8(2).

[6] See *Re Westminster Property Group plc* [1985] 1 W.L.R. 676. The American concept of the contract of sale is wider than the English concept. The UCC, s.2-304(1) provides that "the price can be made payable in money or otherwise". A contract of barter is thus a contract of sale in American law.

[7] See *Benjamin's Sale of Goods* (5th ed., 1997), paras 1–034—1–037. See also *Esso Petroleum Co Ltd v. Customs and Excise Commissioners* [1976] 1 W.L.R. 1 at 11.

the provisions of the Supply of Goods and Services Act 1982, Part I[8] apply to a contract of barter. By virtue of this Act the contract of barter is assimilated to the contract of sale, as far as the terms implied by law into contract are concerned.[9] The property in the goods supplied in a barter by each party to the other passes when the parties intend it to pass.[10] In this respect, as in others not covered by the 1982 Act, many provisions of the Sale of Goods Act 1979 apply to barter by way of analogy.[11]

The economic background

The reasons for countertrade arrangements are not difficult to find. Some countries, particularly those which lack hard currency and credit facilities to pay for their imports, may wish to expand their export markets by demanding these facilities. The oil exporting countries want to establish stability of market conditions and use the oil which they produce as consideration in kind for industrial and other products which they require. In some countries administrative rules having a similar effect are applied. **14–003**

Countertrade may not be the most desirable form of international trade. It is not in harmony with the concept of an open, cash-based, multilateral trading system, which the WTO/GATT and the Organisation for Economic Co-operation and Development (OECD) aim to maintain and promote.

In practice, however, importers in many overseas markets may insist on countertrade measures. The large or medium-sized exporter cannot ignore this possibility. He should realise that countertrade arrangements often involve considerable additional risks. The disposal of the countertraded goods received may cause difficulty, in particular if they cannot be sold in a readily available commodity market. The exporter may require for their disposal the services of a third party, such as a trading house, and he may be charged more for the countertraded goods than the goods will fetch when sold. This price difference, plus the trading house's commission, is known as the *disagio*. It may be considerable and has to be calculated into the price for which the exporter is prepared to sell his goods. Sometimes the exporter may find it difficult to turn the countertraded goods into money in consequence of exchange control restrictions or other trade barriers which exist between various countries, and it may be necessary for him to engage in a complicated swap transaction involving a third country in order to obtain the consideration due to him for the export sale. Finally, ECGD cover is not available for a countertrade transaction, except in the case of a reciprocal sales agreement under which the ordinary export sale is unconnected with the countersale.[12] Private insurance may offer more favourable terms. Some of these additional risks can be reduced or avoided if the exporter enters into a factoring

---

[8] Which came into operation on January 1, 1983; see [1982] J.B.L. 357–358.
[9] These terms relate to title, etc. (s.2), description (s.3), quality of fitness (s.4), sample (s.5), and the exclusion of implied terms by express agreement, course of dealing or usage binding both parties (s.11).
[10] *Cf. Koppel v. Koppel* [1966] 1 W.L.R. 802 at 811.
[11] *Buckley v. Lever Bros Ltd* [1953] 4 D.L.R. 16.
[12] See *post*, para. 14–005.

agreement with a confirming house, broker, bank or other finance institution.[13] The exporter then assigns his obligations to the factor and is no longer involved in the countertrade transaction. The factor provides him at once with cash, charging, of course, a fee for his services and sometimes demanding a bank guarantee from him.

An exporter who has to agree to the demand for countertrade is well advised to make use of the specialist services available to assist him. Reference has been made to the brochure *Countertrade and Offset—A Guide for Exporters*, published by the Department of Trade and Industry (1998 edition). Appended to this brochure is a list of some British companies experienced in countertrading with addresses and information about their activities.

TYPES OF COUNTERTRADE TRANSACTIONS

14–004 The forms which countertrade transactions assume are infinite and vary from country to country and case to case. However some types of countertrade transaction can be discerned. Normally it is advisable to conclude a *framework agreement* (also known as a memorandum of understanding), within which the individual transactions shall operate. The essential features of the framework agreement will be considered later.[14] Exceptionally, no separate framework agreement is necessary. Thus in a long-term or major construction contract[15] it is usual to build the countertrade provisions into the main contract. To give a hypothetical example, if a company in country A undertakes to build a mine for a public undertaking in country B and it further contracts to buy back the output of the mine, the buy-back clauses are likely to be included in the mining contract. Strictly speaking, these clauses, although appearing as terms of the main contract, constitute a framework agreement for the individual contracts, whereby the company in country A will purchase the minerals from the public undertaking in country B.

Reciprocal sales agreements

14–005 Under this arrangement the export seller enters into a separate contract with the overseas buyer, whereby he (the export seller) or another person undertakes to purchase certain specific goods produced in the buyer's country. There are thus two parallel contracts of sale, the export contract and the countersale. It is left to the agreement of the parties whether the countersale shall cover the total value of the export sale or only part of it.[16] In the latter case the balance has to be paid by the overseas buyer in cash or additional goods have to be supplied in order to achieve equivalence. The reciprocal sales agreement is the most frequently used form of countertrade.

Two variants of reciprocal sales agreements exist. In the first, the obligation

---

[13] On factoring, see *post*, para. 13–001.
[14] See *post*, para. 14–012.
[15] See *post*, para. 25–001.
[16] In *State Trading Corporation of India Ltd v. M. Golodetz Ltd; The Sara D* [1989] 2 Lloyd's Rep. 277 the countersale covered only 60 per cent of the principal sale.

of the export seller to enter into the countersale is linked with the countersale only in the framework agreement but, apart from this linkage, the two contracts of sale are entirely independent of each other. In the second variant, the export sale is conditional on the export seller entering into, or possibly performing, the countersale. The first variant is preferable for two reasons. First, the exporter can obtain cover for the export sale under a comprehensive short-term guarantee (CST guarantee).[17] Secondly, the usual bank guarantees, letters of credit and/or performance bonds are more easily arranged for the export sale if it is entirely independent of the countersale.[18] Even if the first variant is chosen, the linkage between the export sale and the countersale is so close that, if one of these contracts cannot be performed, for instance, because it is frustrated, there is merit in the argument that the parties intended the other contract likewise to be invalidated.

The remedies of the parties to the export sale and the countersale for non-performance or breach of contract are exactly the same as in a single sales transaction.

A reciprocal sales agreement was contemplated in *Pagnan SpAro v. Granaria BV*[19] where one contract was for the sale of Thai tapioca and the countersale for Chinese manioc.[20] The parties negotiated but, according to the finding of the court, never entered into binding contracts. In the course of his judgment, Sir John Donaldson M.R. said[21]:

> "The idea was that each would buy from the other and that there would therefore be a 'swap' transaction. I think it is inherent in that concept that if either of these contracts were still under negotiation at the crucial moment, they both were."

The definition of the countersale buyer

In reciprocal sales agreements a difficulty arises. Only in rare cases will the **14–006** export seller wish to acquire the countersold goods for his own use. Normally he wants to dispose of them and to realise their value, which means that he has to find a trader who is willing to buy them. This difficulty is particularly great if the goods do not have a readily accessible commodity market. Usually the exporter, before agreeing to a countertrade transaction in goods not traded at a commodity market, will approach a trading house specialising in these transac-

---

[17] See *post*, para. 20–012.
[18] In *State Trading Corporation of India Ltd v. M. Golodetz Ltd; The Sara D* [1989] 2 Lloyd's Rep. 277 a reciprocal sales agreement, in which the sale and the countersale were independent, was in issue. Unfortunately, there was a linkage of the financial arrangements. The buyers were obliged to open a letter of credit and the sellers were to give a so-called countertrade guarantee with respect to their obligations under the countersale. To make things worse, both the obligations of the buyer and those of the seller had to be performed simultaneously. The buyers failed to open the letter of credit and the sellers failed to give the countertrade guarantee. The Court of Appeal held that the seller's obligation to procure the countertrade guarantee was not a condition precedent to the buyer's obligation to open the letter of credit and that the buyers were in breach of contract, owing to their failure to open the credit.
[19] [1986] 2 Lloyd's Rep. 547.
[20] Which is another name for tapioca although there is a difference in quality between the Chinese and the Thai product.
[21] *ibid.*, at 549.

tions in order to ascertain whether it is willing to purchase the countertraded goods.

From the legal point of view, the important question is: who is the buyer in the countersale? Often exporter A will conclude the contract of export sale with overseas importer B and importer B will sell by way of countersale to trading house C in the exporter's country, with C acting as a principal in the countersale transaction. However it is also possible that importer B will insist that C should act as agent of A, in which case the countersale contract is concluded between B and A.

Sometimes, even though the reciprocal sales agreements are independent of each other, the exporter will insist that the countersold goods are shipped before he is willing to ship his goods. The foreign importer will, however, be unwilling to ship unless he is sure of his money. The foreign counterseller may have to provide a performance guarantee,[22] but it is more usual to resolve this difficulty by constituting an *escrow account* with a bank. Under such an arrangement the bank undertakes to pay out the money only if certain specified conditions are satisfied, for instance the counterpurchaser would pay the price for the counterbought goods into the escrow account, and the bank would release it to the counterseller or his bank when notified that the countersold goods are shipped.

Barter

14–007 This term is employed loosely in commercial circles. It is sometimes used—incorrectly—for all types of countertrade, irrespective of the legal nature of the arrangements made by the parties.

In law a barter, as already observed,[23] is an exchange of goods for goods or services, *e.g.* sugar from Cuba is exchanged for screws produced in Britain.

A barter arrangement is sometimes described as a *compensation contract* because the delivery of the goods by one of the parties is "the compensation"—in legal terms "the consideration"—for the delivery of the goods by the other. If one of them fails to make delivery in accordance with the contract, this may provide a ground for non-performance by the other.

Here again, two types can be distinguished. In the true barter, there is a simple exchange and no value is placed on the goods exchanged. For example, the owner of a motor cycle arranges with his friend to exchange it for the friend's minicar. In the second type of barter, some value is placed on the exchanged goods. It is obvious that in commercial transactions only the valued barter is used.

A valued barter is not the same as a reciprocal sales contract, although in some cases the courts have been inclined to treat it as such.[24] The essential difference is that a valued barter, like an unvalued one, is a one-contract transaction in which the obligations of the parties are made dependent on each other,

---

[22] See *post*, para. 12–004.
[23] See *ante*, para. 14–002.
[24] *Aldridge v. Johnson* (1857) 7 E. & B. 885; see *Benjamin's Sale of Goods* (5th ed., 1997), para. 1–037.

whereas the reciprocal sales agreement is always a two-contract arrangement, even if the contracts are linked together in the manner indicated earlier.[25]

In the valued barter two problems arise. The first is the disposal of the goods received by the exporter from the overseas customer. The position here is the same as has been discussed for the reciprocal sale.[26] In other words, the exporter will normally deal with these goods by way of a disposal or swap transaction, requiring the services of a third party who will charge a fee, commission or *disagio*. Secondly, arrangements have to be made for the payment of the settlement balance, which at the end will arise in favour of one of the parties to the barter. A *settlement account* or *evidence account* will have to be constituted, preferably in a hard currency country which does not operate an exchange control system. The value of the bartered goods is set off in the settlement account and on termination of the transaction the credit balance is paid in cash or kind to the party entitled thereto.

The buy-back agreement

This kind of arrangement is made in mining, oil exploration or other major **14–008** export transactions. The contractor who carries out the work agrees that the purchase price be paid in full or partly by his purchase of the produce of the installation. The buy-back clauses, which may be lengthy, are normally incorporated into the main contract.[27]

The buy-back terms will often contain a most favoured customer (m.f.c.) clause, according to which the employer (the seller of the produce) will grant the contractor (the buyer) the most favourable price which he charges another customer purchasing goods on comparable conditions.[28] The m.f.c. price will be reduced by a discount which includes the amortisation element for the installation price. In view of the need to include the amortisation factor, the duration of the buy-back agreement may be lengthy.

Offset arrangements

An offset transaction is an arrangement by which the exporter of goods **14–009** is obliged to incorporate in the goods specified materials, components or sub-assemblies produced in the importing country or otherwise to perform specified services in that country. Offset arrangements are an established feature in the sale of advanced technology products, such as defence systems and aircraft. Sometimes the exporter is required to open or equip a factory producing components or to maintain an assembly plant in the importing country.

---

[25] See *ante*, para. 14–005.
[26] As footnote 25.
[27] See *ante*, para. 14–004.
[28] For an example of a m.f.c. clause see *post*, para. 30–009.

Disposal and switch transactions

14–010 In reciprocal sales and barter agreements the disposal of the countertraded goods causes, as already discussed,[29] a problem. Here, two situations have to be distinguished. The goods may have an easily accessible commodity market at which they are regularly traded,[30] or they may not be so easily marketable.

If the goods have a commodity market, like oil or other commodities, the exporter will ask a dealer at the market to sell the goods. If, for instance an aircraft manufacturer sells aircraft to an oil producing country, which pays in oil, it is relatively easy for the manufacturer to sell the oil through a dealer at the oil market in Rotterdam. Even such a simple disposal may involve a string of dealers. In these string contracts the property in the countertraded goods (the oil), which may still be afloat, is passed by transfer of negotiable bills of lading or similar document of title.

The position is more complicated if no commodity market exists for the goods. The U.K. exporter may be unable to obtain payment from the overseas importer because the importer's country may not permit the transfer of the price to the U.K., owing to lack of hard currency or for other reasons. On the other hand, the importer's country may have a bilateral clearing arrangement with a third country, which has a credit surplus with the importer's country. Here this credit surplus can be utilised by way of a triangular swap transaction for the payment of the price due to the U.K. exporter. The U.K. exporter arranges the countersale in the following manner. He sells his goods to the overseas buyer in country A. The overseas buyer sells produce of his own country to country B which has the clearing arrangement with A. The buyer in country B (which has no currency restrictions *vis-a-vis* the U.K.) then pays the U.K. seller. In this manner the U.K. exporter is paid out of the credit surplus accumulated by country B in its trade with country A. Other forms of swap transactions are also in use. They need not always be triangular and some of them are simply currency swaps. It is obvious that swap deals in any form require the assistance of an experienced countertrade expert.

Oil countertrade

14–011 In the oil business, countertrade transactions are frequently used. For this reason, the illustrations given in the preceding sections often refer to oil transactions. Countertrade in oil usually takes the form of reciprocal sales contracts or barter transactions. The disposal of the countertraded goods is relatively easy as oil has a commodity market, but sometimes the services of an oil distributing company are required to carry out the disposal of the oil.

---

[29] See *ante*, para. 14–006. There may be other problems. Some of them came to light in *Pagnan SpA v. Granaria BV* [1986] 2 Lloyd's Rep. 547 at 549, *viz.* the price differential between the sold and the countersold goods, the differential in the dates of payment, and the different requirements of an export certificate. There may be also problems relating to the exchange rate.

[30] In commercial terminology, these markets are referred to as "terminal commodity markets".

The framework agreement

In countertrade transactions great care should be given to the proper drafting of **14–012** the initial framework agreement, sometimes also referred to as the *countertrade agreement*. Sometimes this agreement takes the form of a letter of intent. This is unsatisfactory because a letter of intent is not enforceable in law.

The framework agreement should be an enforceable contract. It should contain a clear definition of the mutual obligations of the parties. The countertraded goods must be specified and it should be stated whether their value will be ascertained on an f.o.b. or c.i.f. basis. Arrangements should be made for a settlement account or evidence account and for the payment or other settlement of the credit balance at regular intervals and on termination of the agreement. The agreement should provide that the exporter's obligations under the countertrade contract may be performed by an affiliated company or another company nominated by him, and should also allow for the transferability of the obligation to counterpurchase. This will enable the exporter to transfer these obligations to a third party, such as a trading house, which will then become the buyer of the countersold goods in the capacity of principal. Moreover, there should be no restrictions relating to the markets in which the countersold goods can be traded. Sometimes countries which insist on countertrade offer a variety of their produce for countertrade and in this case the U.K. exporter should attempt to secure for himself the widest possible choice of countertraded goods.

The framework agreement should also contain a link between the reciprocal sales agreements if this form is chosen. It should be provided that the exporter's countersale obligations shall only become effective when the main export contract is concluded or the counterseller has provided a performance guarantee.

If the exporter intends to realise the countertrade proceeds at once by a disclosed factoring arrangement,[31] the factor should be a party to the framework agreement. The framework agreement often contains penalty provisions for non-performance of the countertrade obligations by the exporter. The conditions on which these penalties become payable should be kept separate from, and independent of, the exporter's obligations under the contract of export sale. In other words, if the countertrade transaction is in the form of a reciprocal sales arrangement, the penalty provisions should only relate to the countersale but should not relate to the export sale.

In addition, the framework agreement should contain the terms normally inserted into an international trade contract.[32] In particular, a choice of law clause must be included. It simplifies matters if all contracts, namely the framework agreement, the export sale and the countersale, are subject to the same legal system. There should also be an arbitration clause wide enough to cover any dispute arising out of, or in connection with, the framework agreement itself and all connected contracts. The parties may provide for *ad hoc* arbitration,

---

[31] See *post*, para. 13–005.
[32] See *post*, para. 32–014.

e.g. so-called "neutral arbitration",[33] but generally their best course would be to agree to arbitration under institutional rules, such as those of the ICC Court of Arbitration. In any event, the arbitration clause should lay down the venue and the language of the arbitration.

---

[33] As to institutional arbitration and arbitration under ICC Rules, see *post*, Chap. 23.

PART THREE

TRANSPORTATION OF EXPORTS

CHAPTER 15

CARRIAGE OF GOODS BY SEA[1]

THE CARRIAGE OF GOODS IN EXPORT TRANSACTIONS

Unimodal and multimodal transport

Goods which are the subject matter of an export transaction, whether a contract **15–001** of sale or of construction, have to be moved from the place of dispatch to that of destination. This carriage invariably has an international character. It may be executed by sea, air or land or by a combination of these modes of transportation. If it is done by only one of them, the international transport is *unimodal* and if it is carried out by a combination of them, it is *multimodal* or combined transport. To give examples: a Swiss manufacturer sells watches to a store in London; the consignment is flown by air from Zurich to Heathrow. This is unimodal international transport. A merchant in Bradford, England, sells knitwear to an importer in Canberra, Australia; the goods are loaded into a door-to-door container in Bradford, taken by lorry or trailer to Liverpool; there the container is loaded on a vessel which proceeds to Sydney where it is unloaded and taken by land to Canberra. Here the international transport is multimodal as it consists of three stages, land, sea, and again land.

Unimodal international transport is governed by international Conventions. They have been adopted by many countries and are of great practical effect. The most important of them are:

  (a) *Sea transport*: the Hague-Visby Rules relating to Bills of Lading.

  (b) *Air transport*: the Warsaw Convention; or the Warsaw Convention as amended.[2]

  (c) *Land transport by road*: the CMR.[3]

These Conventions will be considered later.[4]

The UN Convention on International Multimodal Transport of Goods was

---

[1] See generally Scrutton, *Charterparties and Bills of Lading* (20th ed., 1996); *Halsbury's Laws of England*, Vol. 43(2) (Reissue), Part 14.

[2] In air transport, there exists, however, also non-Convention carriage, see Chap. 17.

[3] The acronym CMR stands for *Convention relative au contrat de transport international des marchandises par route*. There exists also an international convention relating to transport of goods by rail; it is known as CIM, which stands for *Convention international concernant le transport des marchandises par chemin de fer*. The CIM is embodied in the Convention concerning International Carriage by Rail, known as COTIF, which stands for *Convention relative aux transports internationaux ferroviaires*. On international rail transportation, see Chap. 18.

[4] On the Hague-Visby Rules, see *post*, paras 15–021, 15–022, 15–041 to 15–045, 15–047, 15–048, 15–050; on the Warsaw Convention, see Chap. 17; on the CMR see Chap. 18.

adopted at Geneva on May 24, 1980[5] but is not yet operative. However, a model form for the Convention has been produced by UNCTAD and ICC.[6]

Traditional methods of transport and container transport

15–002 Traditionally, the carriage of goods by sea is effected by two methods determined by the nature of the goods. If they are to be carried in bulk, *e.g.* grain, coal or oil, the shipper[7] may hire a whole vessel by means of a *charterparty*.[8] If individual packages of goods have to be carried, they are normally loaded in a ship's hold or on deck and are carried under *bills of lading*.[9] The traditional method of carriage of goods by air is done under *air consignment notes*[10] or *air waybills*.[11] In the case of international carriage by road, *consignment notes*[12] are used.

In modern international transport goods other than bulk cargoes are often carried in containers.[13] Here, traditional transport documents may be used, or more frequently, variants of these. The most important of these are *combined transport documents*[14] and *FIATA combined transport bills of lading*.[15] A high percentage of international cargoes is nowadays carried in containers under documents which are not traditional transport documents. For this reason UCP (1993 Revision)[16] provides for the acceptance by banks of a multimodal transport document as long as the same transport document covers the entire carriage.

To a large extent the international carriage of goods has, historically, been conducted on the basis of paper work, namely by using transport documents, although the nature and form of these documents has changed greatly. It is anticipated that in the not too distant future, traditional written transport documentation may be superseded by the paperless electronic communication of trade data.[17]

Modern developments in transport technology can only be understood when the exporter has a knowledge of the traditional methods of international transport. For this reason the law relating to the traditional carriage of goods by sea will be considered in this chapter. The following chapter deals with the special legal aspects of container transport. The law of carriage of goods by air and by land will be treated in separate chapters.

---

[5] See J. Ramberg in *International Carriage of Goods: Some Legal Problems and Possible Solutions* (C.M. Schmitthoff and R.M. Goode ed., London, 1988).

[6] UNCTAD/ICC Rules for Multimodal Transport Documents; ICC Publication No. 481 which includes explanatory notes.

[7] This is the designation applied to the person who contracts with the carrier by sea. He will usually be the exporter, *i.e.* the seller, but he may also be the buyer or the buyer's agent.

[8] See *post*, para. 15–003. But bills of lading may be issued with respect to goods carried in chartered vessels: see *post*, para. 15–023.

[9] See *post*, para. 15–019.

[10] See Chap. 17.

[11] *ibid.*

[12] See Chap. 18.

[13] See Chap. 16.

[14] *ibid.*

[15] See *post*, para. 15–029.

[16] Art. 26. See Chap. 11.

[17] On electronic commerce and electronic data interchange, see Chap. 33.

THE COURSE OF BUSINESS IN THE CARRIAGE OF GOODS BY SEA

The general course of business in traditional sea transport may be illustrated by **15–003** the following example. A United Kingdom exporter is obliged, by his contract of sale with the overseas buyer, to arrange for the carriage of goods by sea to the place of destination and wishes to carry out this arrangement himself. Evidently he has to conclude a contract of carriage with a shipowner,[18] whereby the latter undertakes to carry the goods in his ship from the United Kingdom port of dispatch to the overseas port of destination. This contract is known as the contract of carriage by sea.[19] The remuneration to be paid to the shipowner is the freight, the shipowner is the carrier, and the exporter, as a party to the contract of carriage by sea, is referred to as the shipper. The exporter first has to decide whether the quantity of goods to be exported warrants the charter of a complete ship, in which case the terms of the contract of carriage are embodied in a document called the charterparty. In most cases, however, the goods form only part of the intended cargo of the ship and are carried in the ship together with goods belonging to other shippers. Here the terms of the contract of carriage are evidenced by a document called a bill of lading which, in effect, is a receipt by the shipowner acknowledging that goods have been delivered to him for the purpose of carriage[20] and reiterating the terms of the contract. However, this document is generally issued only after the contract of carriage is well on its way to performance.[21]

Usually, the shipper instructs a forwarder to procure freight space for the cargo. The shipowner likewise employs an agent, the loading broker, to obtain cargoes for his ships. Devlin J. described the duties of these agents as follows[22]:

"The forwarding agent's normal duties are to ascertain the date and place of sailing, obtain a space allocation if that is required, and prepare the bill of lading. The different shipping lines have their own forms of bill of lading which can be obtained from stationers in the City, and it is the duty of the forwarding agent to put in the necessary particulars and to send the draft . . . to the loading broker. His duties include also arranging for the goods to be brought alongside, making the customs entry and paying any dues on the cargo. After shipment he collects the completed bill of lading and sends it to the shipper. All the regular shipping lines operating from the United Kingdom appear to entrust the business of arranging for cargo to a loading broker. He advertises the date of sailings in shipping papers or elsewhere, and generally prepares and circulates to his customers a sailing card. It is his business to supervise the arrangements for loading, though the actual stowage is decided on by the cargo superintendent who is in the direct service of the shipowner. It is the broker's business also to sign the bill of lading, and issue it to the shipper or his agent in exchange for the freight. His remuneration is by way of commission on freight[23]; and that is doubtless an inducement to him to carry out his primary function, at any rate when shipping is plentiful, of securing enough cargo to fill the ship . . .

The loading broker and the forwarding agent thus appear to discharge well-defined and

---

[18] Or with a person who, for the time being, as against the shipowner has the right to enter into a contract of carriage of goods in his ship, *e.g.* a charterer. On the question of whether the exporter as shipper contracts with the shipowner or charterer, see *post*, para. 15–051.

[19] Or "contract of affreightment".

[20] Scrutton, *Charterparties and Bills of Lading* (20th ed., 1996), pp. 2, 3.

[21] See *post*.

[22] *Heskell v. Continental Express Ltd* [1950] 1 All E.R. 1033 at 1037.

[23] The commission of the loading broker is paid by the shipowner, while the commission of the forwarder is paid by the shipper.

separate functions, but in practice the same firm is often both the loading broker and the forwarding agent, though the two sets of dealings may be kept in two separate compartments of the business. The firm generally acts as loading broker only for one line and does all the line's business, so that it is free in respect of other business to act as it will."

In due course, the shipowner, through his loading broker, advises the shipper or his agent of the name of the ship that is to carry the consignment, the locality where the goods should be sent for loading and the time when the ship is ready to receive the goods. This is often done by a printed notice, called the sailing card, which contains a reference to the closing date, *i.e.* the last date when goods will be received by the ship for loading. The closing date is usually a few days in advance of the actual sailing date in order to give the ship an opportunity to get ready for the voyage. If the goods are not sent to the appointed locality in good time, *i.e.* if they arrive after the closing date, the shipowner is entitled to shut them out even if the ship has not sailed.

When the goods are sent to the docks, the shipper sends shipping instructions to the shipowner which briefly state the particulars of the intended shipment, and a shipping note to the superintendent of the docks which advises him of the arrival of the goods and states their particulars and the name of the ship for which they are intended.

The place and mode of delivery of the goods to the shipowner are subject to agreement of the parties or fixed by the custom of the port. At common law, in the absence of special agreement or custom, the shipper has to deliver the goods alongside the ship or within reach of her tackle at his own expense. When the goods are delivered to the shipowner, the shipper receives a document known as the mate's receipt, unless there are special customs of the port to the contrary. In the Port of London, for instance, the shipper receives a mate's receipt only if waterborne goods are delivered alongside the ship. Where goods are sent to the docks by land, they are stored in a shed of the Port of London Authority which issues a wharfinger's note or dock receipt. The mate's receipt is issued later when the goods are placed on board ship. In some foreign ports, mate's receipts are issued for all cargo, whether received by water or land.

The *mate's receipt* is a document of some importance. When the goods are at the docks for loading on board ship, they are inspected by tally clerks who take down a "record or tally of their date of loading, identification marks, individual package, numbers, their weight and/or measurement, and any defect or comment about the condition in which the goods are received."[24] In particular, the tally clerks note any damage to packages, lack of protection, old cases, ambiguous markings, etc. When the loading is completed, the ship's officer in charge of loading operations signs the mate's receipt, which is based on the notes of the tally clerks and embodies any comments and qualifications in respect of the condition of the goods received. If the mate's receipt is qualified, it is said to be claused[25]; if it does not contain adverse observations, it is a clean

---

[24] *Harris & Son Ltd v. China Mutual Steam Navigation Co Ltd* [1959] 2 Lloyd's Rep. 500 at 501. See also *Naviera Mogor SA v. Societe Metallurgique de Normandie; The Nogar Marin* [1988] 1 Lloyd's Rep. 412 at 420, CA.

[25] See *Cremer v. General Carriers SA* [1973] 2 Lloyd's Rep 366 (the qualifications on the mate's receipt were not transferred to the bill of lading which was issued clean).

receipt. The qualifications on the mate's receipt are later incorporated in the bill of lading and make that document a claused or clean bill respectively. The issue of the mate's receipt has two consequences:

(a) The mate's receipt is an acknowledgement by the shipowner that he has received the goods in the condition stated therein, and that the goods are in his possession and at his risk. It sometimes contains a statement to the effect that:

> "these goods are received subject to the conditions contained in the bill of lading to be issued for the same"[26]

but it has been held[27] that, even where no such clause is expressly inserted, the goods are held by the shipowner subject to the conditions and exemptions of his usual bill of lading.

(b) The mate's receipt is prima facie evidence of ownership of the goods. The shipowner may safely assume, unless he has knowledge to the contrary, that the holder of the receipt or the person named therein[28] is the owner of the goods and the person entitled to receive the bill of lading in exchange for the mate's receipt. However the mate's receipt is not a document of title; its transfer does not pass possession of the goods and therefore it is of less significance than the bill of lading.[29] Consequently, the shipowner is within his rights if he issues a bill of lading without insisting on the return of the mate's receipt.[30]

The records of loading which the tally clerks take during the loading operation are handed to the shipowner's clerks, who compare them with the draft bills of lading sent by the shipper to the shipowner's office. Shipping companies which run regular shipping services publish their printed forms of bills of lading, which are revised from time to time and are obtainable from stationers. The shipper or his agent usually completes a set of two or three original bills of lading in respect of the consignment, and when the particulars on the bills agree with the tally notes taken during the loading, the bills are signed by the loading broker or another agent on behalf of the shipowner and the completed and signed bills are handed over to the shipper.[31] However a bill is not always clean; if it is

---

[26] *De Clermont and Donner v. General Steam Navigation Co* (1891) 7 T.L.R. 187.
[27] *ibid.*
[28] If a person is named; the majority of receipts do not name a person.
[29] Exceptionally, however, by local custom the mate's receipt may be a document of title but the addition of the words "not negotiable" would destroy its character as a document of title: *Kum v. Wah Tat Bank Ltd* [1971] 1 Lloyd's Rep. 439 at 443 (such local custom was found to exist in the trade. between Singapore and Sarawak).
[30] *Nippon Yusen Kaisha v. Ramjiban Serowgee* [1938] A.C. 429.
[31] In practice, the bill of lading is sometimes handed over to the shipper only when the ship leaves port. Where the bill is issued under the Carriage of Goods by Sea Act 1971, as is the case for consignments loaded in British ports (see *post*, para. 15–021), the Hague-Visby Rules appended to the Act provide in Art. III, r.3 that the shipper can demand the issue of the bill after the carrier has received the goods into his charge. See *post*, para. 15–025.

disputed complications might arise because, where payment is arranged under a letter of credit, the advising bank is likely to refuse the shipper finance when he presents a claused, instead of a clean, bill of lading. These complications, and the proper and improper means of resolving them, will be considered later.[32]

The particulars of all bills of lading are entered on the ship's manifest. The manifest must contain full particulars of marks, numbers, quantity, contents, shipper, and consignee, with the particulars required by the consular authorities of the country to which the goods are being forwarded. The ship's manifest is produced to naval, port, customs or consular authorities; it contains details of the complete cargo of the ship.

Bills of lading are usually issued in a set of two or more original parts, all of the same tenor and date. If one of them is "accomplished", *i.e.* the goods are delivered against it, the others stand void. Unless payment is arranged under a letter of credit, the various parts of the set are forwarded to the consignee by subsequent air mails, preferably registered, to secure their speedy and safe arrival. It is of great importance that at least one part of the set should be in the consignee's hands before or at the time of the arrival of the goods, because the shipowner is not bound to hand over the goods unless a bill of lading is delivered to him. Sometimes one part of the bill, together with the other papers forming the shipping documents,[33] is dispatched by letter in the ship's bag of the ship carrying the goods. Control of the contents of ship's bags is exercised in the United Kingdom by the Senior Naval Officer at the port of departure. The exporter sends the documents in the ship's bag in an unsealed envelope addressed to the overseas buyer or to his own representative or a referee in case of need.[34] Correspondence not relating to the cargo and remittances must not be included, and the dispatch is covered by a cover letter addressed to the master and asking him to deliver the dispatch to the addressee. On arrival, the master delivers the letter to the addressee who, if he has not received a part of the bill of lading before, delivers the bill of lading to the shipowner's representative or agent—known as the ship's agent[35]—at the port of destination. The ship's agent will then issue a *delivery order* which the holder presents to the ship's officer in charge of unloading.

If the exporter sells under a letter of credit, he normally hands all parts of the bill, together with the other required documents, to the advising or nominated bank, and that bank then forwards the documents by air mail to the issuing bank. Where various parts of a bill of lading are in the hands of different persons, the shipowner or the master (acting as the shipowner's agent) may hand over the cargo to the first person presenting a bill, "provided that he has no notice of any other claims to the goods, or knowledge of any other circumstances which

---

[32] See *post*, para. 15–039.
[33] See *ante*, paras 2–021 to 2–025.
[34] See *ante*, para. 10–002.
[35] The function of the ship's agent is described by Staughton J. in *A/S Hansen-Tangens Rederi III v. Total Transport Corporation; The Sagona* [1984] 1 Lloyd's Rep 194, 198–199. On arrival of the ship, he deals with the port, immigration and customs formalities and arranges its proper discharge. In law he is normally the agent of the shipowner but, if the ship is on a time charter, he is generally the agent of the charterer.

raise a reasonable suspicion that the claimant is not entitled to the goods. If he has any such notice or knowledge, he must deliver at his peril to the rightful owner or must interplead. He is not entitled to deliver to the consignee named in the bill of lading without the production of the bill of lading, and does so at his risk if the consignee is not in fact entitled to the goods."[36]

On presentation of the delivery order, the goods are delivered from the ship to the person authorised by the order to take delivery. In the absence of agreement of the parties or a custom of the port of discharge to the contrary, the shipowner or master is not bound to notify the consignee of the arrival of the ship or his readiness to unload. It is the duty of the consignee to ascertain these facts. Where nothing else is arranged or customary, delivery has to take place over the ship's rail, and the consignee has to pay for lighters and stevedores to take delivery. The shipowner's responsibility for the goods does not cease when the ship arrives at the port of destination but only after he has duly delivered the goods to the consignee in accordance with the provisions of the contract of carriage, as evidenced by the bill of lading or as stipulated by law. However, delivery does not necessarily mean transfer of the goods into the physical custody of the consignee. Often delivery to a dock company or appropriate warehousing of the goods is sufficient. Normally, the bill of lading contains detailed provisions about the methods of delivery and the cessation of the shipowner's liability.

THE CONTRACT OF CARRIAGE BY SEA

Carriage covered by bill of lading or charterparty

The two types of contract of carriage by sea, namely contracts evidenced by bills **15–004** of lading and contracts contained in charterparties, have few points in common.

Charterparties are mainly governed by the rules of common law. The principle of liberty of contracting applies to them[37]; and the shipowner may, by agreement with the charterer, modify his normal liability as a carrier without any limitations, apart from those postulated by the general principles of common law. Contracts of carriage evidenced by bills of lading, on the other hand, are to a large measure regulated by statute law, in particular by the Carriage of Goods by Sea Act 1971.[38] This Act qualifies the contractual liberty of the parties and especially restrains the shipowner from introducing exemptions from his liability beyond those admitted by the Rules relating to Bills of Lading, the Hague-Visby Rules, appended to the Act.

Charterparties are of little interest to the average exporter, because only in exceptional cases is the quantity or bulk of his shipments such that the hire of

---

[36] Scrutton, *loc. cit.*, p. 292.
[37] By virtue of their liberty of contracting, the parties to a charterparty often adopt a standard form, such as, *inter alia*, the Gencon Charter, the Baltimore 1939 Charter or the New York Product Exchange form, but sometimes they vary the clauses in the standard form to suit their own requirements; see *Compagnie Tunisienne de Navigation SA v. Compagnie d'Armement Maritime SA* [1971] A.C. 572.
[38] See *post*, paras 15–021, 22; 15–041 to 15–045; 15–047, 48; 15–050.

a whole ship would be profitable for him. The exporter who has chartered a whole ship may issue bills of lading under the charterparty and terms from the charterparty may be incorporated in the bill of lading.[39] If payment is to be made under a banker's letter of credit, bills which contain a clause incorporating the terms of the charterparty will be accepted by the bank unless it is otherwise stipulated in the credit.[40]

Conclusion of the contract of carriage by sea

15–005 It has been seen earlier that the contract of carriage by sea is concluded prior to the issue of the bill of lading, and that the latter merely evidences the terms of a contract which has already been partly performed.[41] Consequently, a special term of the contract of carriage, even if agreed upon only orally, may override the general clauses printed in the bill of lading. This proposition is best illustrated by reference to *The Ardennes*.[42] In this case a shipper of mandarin oranges in Spain agreed orally with a carrier that the goods should be shipped directly to England so that they would reach this country before December 1, 1947, when the import duty on these goods was to be raised. The bill of lading covering the consignment contained the usual clause providing that the carrier was at liberty to proceed by any route and to carry the goods directly or indirectly to the port of destination. The ship proceeded first to Antwerp and then to London, which it did not reach until December 4. Lord Goddard C.J. held that the contract of carriage was concluded before the issue of the bill of lading, that it was an express warranty in the contract of carriage that the carrier would not rely on a liberty which otherwise would have been open to him, and that that oral warranty overrode the terms set out in the bill of lading. Accordingly, he awarded the consignor damages.

If the vessel carrying the goods is let by the owner to a charterer who makes it available as a general ship, the question arises whether the party with whom the shipper enters into the contract of carriage is the shipowner or the charterer. This question is considered later.[43]

Shutting out goods

15–006 When the goods of a shipper are shut out by the shipowner for want of room, even though the goods were sent to the appointed place of loading before the closing date, two cases have to be distinguished. If, in reliance on the statement in the sailing card, the shipper sends the goods to the docks without previous agreement with the shipowner, he cannot claim damages because no contract

---

[39] See *post*, para. 15–023.
[40] UCP (1993 Revision), Art. 25.
[41] See *ante*, para. 15–003 and see *post*, para. 15–019. A *draft* bill of lading sent by the shipper to the carrier is often an offer but the contract of carriage is only concluded when the carrier accepts this offer by receiving the shipper's goods for carriage: *Burke Motors Ltd v. Mersey Docks and Harbour Co* [1986] 1 Lloyd's Rep. 155.
[42] [1951] 1 K.B. 55. But bill of lading clauses which have not been varied by an overriding special agreement remain effective: *The Arawa* [1980] 2 Lloyd's Rep. 135 at 138.
[43] See *post*, para. 15–051.

has been concluded. The notification on the sailing card is in the nature of an invitation to make an offer, the dispatch of the goods to the docks is the offer, and the shipowner is free to accept or refuse this offer. However, the position is different if, as is the modern practice, the shipper has booked freight space in advance. Here, "the contract of affreightment is prima facie breached and an action will lie against the shipowner."[44] Even in this case, actions are rarely brought for damage caused by "shutting out". There are several reasons for this. First, shipowners' notifications of closing dates usually contain the reservation that:

> "last day for goods is . . . unless the ship is previously full."

Secondly, in such a case the shipowner normally refunds freight, if already paid, without dispute and loss of profits on goods shut out may or may not be recoverable, depending on whether such loss is foreseeable.[45]

Freight

"Freight is the reward payable to the carrier for the safe carriage and delivery **15–007** of the goods; it is payable only on safe carriage and delivery; if the goods are lost on the voyage, nothing is payable."[46] This definition requires explanation, since the carrier's obligation is readiness to deliver the goods rather than their actual delivery[47] and "safe" does not refer to the condition of the goods. Thus ". . . freight is earned by the carriage and arrival of the goods ready to be delivered to the merchant . . ."[48] The shipowner is not entitled to claim freight unless he is ready to deliver the cargo to the consignee at the port of destination, except if he is prevented by some default of the cargo owner.[49] If the cargo arrives, though damaged, the shipowner is entitled to freight, unless the damage is so serious that the goods have completely lost their merchantable character.[50] Freight is not payable before the goods have arrived at the port of destination and the shipowner is ready to deliver them. In practice, the contract of carriage as evidenced in the bill of lading usually contains a clause stipulating that freight is payable/non-refundable "vessel and/or cargo lost or not lost".

Since the carrier is entitled to the full freight if he delivers the goods at their destination, even though they are damaged, it follows that the cargo owner is not entitled to make a deduction from the freight for the damage to the goods

---

[44] Scrutton, *loc. cit.*, p. 123.

[45] *Per* Bigham J. in the unreported case of *Hecker v. Cunard S.S.*, July 1898 (referred to by Scrutton, *loc. cit.*, p. 123 n.(2)).

[46] *Kirchner v. Venus* (1859) 12 Moore PC 361 at 390; *Compañía Naviera General SA v. Kerametal Ltd; The Lorna I* [1983] 1 Lloyd's Rep. 373 at 374. On prepaid freight and "freight collect" see *post*, paras 15–010, 11.

[47] *The Argos (Cargo ex), Gaudet v. Brown* (1873) L.R. 5 PC 134.

[48] *Dakin v. Oxley* (1864) 15 C.B.N.S. 646.

[49] *The Argos (Cargo ex), Gaudet v. Brown* (1873) L.R. 5 PC 134.

[50] *Asfar v. Blundell* [1896] 1 Q.B. 123; on the meaning of "merchantable character" in this connection, see *per* Donaldson J. in *Montedison SpA v. Icroma SpA* [1980] 1 Lloyd's Rep. 91 at 95.

or delay in the delivery, or to set off his claim for damages against the carrier's claim for freight.[51] However, the cargo owner is entitled to pursue such a claim for damages by way of action or counterclaim.[52]

Calculation of freight

15–008 Freight payable under bills of lading is normally calculated by weight or measurement, in accordance with the carrier's tariff. Some goods decrease in weight or bulk during shipment and others increase, *e.g.* due to loss or increase in moisture. In the absence of express agreement, or custom of the port or trade, where the weight or measurement has decreased, freight is calculated on the delivered weight or measurement. Where it has increased, it is calculated on shipment.[53]

There are several different types of freight: lump sum, prepaid, pro rata, back, dead and primage.

Lump sum freight

15–009 While freight is normally arranged according to weight, measurement or value, the shipper may agree to pay a lump sum as freight for the use of the entire ship or a portion thereof.[54] In this case, the amount of freight payable by the shipper is fixed and invariable and, if the shipowner is ready to perform his contract, is payable whether the shipper uses the hired space to full capacity, or loads below capacity or does not load at all. Moreover, in the absence of agreement to the contrary, the whole lump sum freight is payable if only part of the loaded cargo is delivered by the shipowner at the port of destination and the remainder is lost.[55] However, the shipowner cannot claim lump sum freight if he is unable to deliver at least part of the cargo.

Lump sum freight is not customary in a contract of carriage evidenced by bills of lading, but is sometimes arranged under charterparties when the shipper is uncertain of the quantity or species of the goods which he has to ship.

Prepaid freight

15–010 It has been seen that, in law, the shipowner is not entitled to claim freight before the cargo has arrived and he is ready to deliver it. The parties are at liberty to modify these rules by agreement, and their discretion is not qualified by the Carriage of Goods by Sea Act 1971.

In respect of freight payable under a bill of lading, the rules of law are, in

---

[51] *Aries Tanker Corporation v. Total Transport Ltd* [1977] 1 W.L.R. 185; *Bank of Boston Connecticut v. European Grain and Shipping Ltd; The Dominique* [1989] A.C. 1056; See also *R H & D International Ltd v. I A S Animal Air Services Ltd* [1984] 1 W.L.R. 573 (application to CMR freight).
[52] Scrutton, *loc. cit.*, p. 331.
[53] See *The Metula* [1978] 2 Lloyd's Rep. 5.
[54] Scrutton, *loc. cit.*, p. 329.
[55] *William Thomas & Sons v. Harrowing Steamship Co* [1915] A.C. 58.

practice, invariably abrogated by express agreement of the parties. Clauses in bills of lading stipulating prepayment of freight vary considerably. The following is fairly typical:

> "Freight for the said goods . . . shall be due and payable by the shipper on shipment at port of loading in cash, without deduction, and shall not be repayable, vessel or goods lost or not lost."

Most freight clauses in bills of lading contain the words "ship lost or not lost", often supplemented by the words "freight deemed to have been earned on shipment". Where words to this effect are inserted in the bill of lading, the nature of prepaid freight is beyond dispute: it is, in legal terminology, *advance freight*. Such freight is due and earned when the stipulated event happens, *e.g.* on the signing of the bill of lading. It is due if, under the terms of the contract, it is payable at a later date. Even if before it is payable, the contract is terminated by acceptance of a repudiatory breach, the claim for advance freight, when it becomes due, survives such termination.[56] Apart from exceptional cases, the right of the shipowner to claim freight is not affected by the subsequent loss of the goods, and the shipowner is not only entitled to retain the full amount of prepaid freight but may even sue the shipper for it, if, for one reason or another, due prepaid freight has not been paid.[57] These rules are subject to three exceptions. The shipowner has to return advance freight if:

(a) "the ship never earned freight and never began to earn freight",[58] *e.g.* because she did not sail; or

(b) the goods are lost before advance freight becomes due[59]; or

(c) the goods are lost by an event other than an excepted peril.[60]

If the bill of lading omits to state when advance freight shall become payable, it appears to be payable on the final sailing of the ship. As the shipper bears the risk in respect of prepaid freight, he has an insurable interest therein which he may cover by marine insurance.[61]

In modern practice the wording of freight clauses in the bill of lading or charterparty normally puts it beyond doubt that prepaid freight is intended by the parties to be advance freight. In the past it was sometimes doubtful whether prepaid freight was in the nature of advance freight or merely a loan by the shipper on account of freight payable in accordance with the general rules of

---

[56] *Bank of Boston Connecticut v. European Grain and Shipping Ltd; The Dominique* [1989] A.C. 1056.

[57] *Oriental Steamship Co Ltd v. Tylor* [1893] 2 Q.B. 518.

[58] *Per* James L.J. in *Ex p. Nyholm, re Child* (1873) 43 L.J.Bk. 21 at 24.

[59] If, *e.g.* the advance freight is payable, say, five days after the master signed the bill, and the cargo is lost by a frustrating event within the five days and the bill does not contain an "earned upon shipment" or similar clause, the carrier cannot demand payment of the (unpaid) advance freight: *Compañía Naviera General SA v. Kerametal Ltd; The Lorna I* [1983] 1 Lloyd's Rep. 373. But see *The Dominique* [1989] A.C. 1056.

[60] *Dufourcet v. Bishop* (1886) 18 Q.B.D. 373; *Rodocanachi v. Milburn* (1886) 18 Q.B.D. 67.

[61] See Chap. 19.

the common law, namely, on safe arrival of the cargo. The difference in the
interpretation of the prepayment clause is considerable when the goods are lost
in transit. The prepaid sum, if advance freight, cannot normally be recovered,
but, if paid as a loan, can be recovered by the shipper. The interpretation of the
clause depends entirely on the intention of the parties, which is not always easy
to ascertain. The courts have evolved the rule that, when freight has to be insured
by the shipowner, the prepayment is likely to be a loan, but, if it has to be
insured by the shipper, it is likely to be advance freight.

Prepaid freight and freight collect bills of lading

15–011 We have so far considered the obligations arising from the contract of carriage
by sea, as far as they concern the questions of who has to pay the freight and
when freight is payable. Another problem arises between the seller and the buyer
under a c.i.f. contract. It is obvious that the c.i.f. price includes a freight element,
but the question is whether that freight element has to be paid by the seller by
way of prepaid freight or by the buyer on arrival of the goods, in which case
the seller has to give the buyer credit for the freight, by deducting the freight
element from the invoice price. Whether one or other method is used, depends
on the agreement of the parties. "When the first method is used the seller provides freight prepaid bills of lading. When the second method is used, he provides what have been conveniently called freight collect bills of lading, that is
to say, bills of lading under which freight is payable by the receiver (who may
be the buyer himself or a sub-buyer from the buyer) to the ship at the port of
discharge."[62]

The distinction is of considerable commercial importance. If freight collect
bills are used, the buyer's obligation to pay freight to the shipowner is conditional on the arrival of the goods. Notwithstanding this condition, the contract
is a true c.i.f. contract.[63]

Pro rata freight

15–012 *Pro rata* freight is payable in exceptional circumstances only, namely, where
the parties to the contract of carriage conclude a new contract[64] to the effect that
the goods shall be delivered at an intermediate port, and not the port of destination named in the bill of lading. Such agreement, unless concluded expressly, is
only inferred from the circumstances where the shipper has a genuine choice of
having his goods carried to the destination originally agreed upon. The shipper
is, therefore, not obliged to pay *pro rata* freight where the shipowner leaves the
goods at an intermediate port and is unable or unwilling to carry them to the
port of destination. The shipowner is entitled to *pro rata* freight where he
loads only part of the agreed cargo or delivers only part of the total loaded

---

[62] Brandon J. in *The Pantanassa* [1970] 1 Lloyd's Rep. 153 at 163. See also *Federal Commerce
and Navigation Ltd v. Molena Alpha Inc; The Nanfri* [1979] A.C. 757.
[63] *ibid.*
[64] *St. Enoch Shipping Co Ltd v. Phosphate Mining Co* [1916] 2 K.B. 624.

cargo, the delivery of the remainder having become impossible through excepted perils.[65]

Back freight

The shipper is liable to pay back freight where the goods shipped are carried, **15–013** on his instructions or in his interest, to a place other than the port of destination.[66] Where the shipper, in his capacity of unpaid seller, exercises his right of stoppage in transit[67] and instructs the shipowner to deliver the goods at a port other than the port of destination named in the bill of lading, the shipper is liable for any additional freight and, if he instructs the shipowner to deliver the goods short of the original port of destination, he has to pay the total original freight as damages because, by giving notice of stoppage, he was in breach of the contract of carriage concluded with the shipowner and prevented the latter from earning the freight.[68] Where the master, in the interest of the shipper, considers it advisable to carry the goods to a place other than the bill of lading destination, because, for example, that port is strikebound,[69] the shipper is liable to pay the additional freight as back freight.

Dead freight

Where the shipper fails to load the cargo or the full cargo after arranging with **15–014** the shipowner for its carriage, he is in breach of the contract of carriage and is liable to pay the agreed freight as damages (dead freight). But the shipowner who uses the freight space which would have been taken up by the goods of the defaulting shipper, and carries therein goods of other shippers, has to deduct the earned freight when claiming damages. He may claim from the defaulting shipper the difference between the agreed and actually earned freight, *e.g.* if he had to accept cargo which earned a lower rate of freight.[70]

Primage

Some bills of lading refer to the remuneration payable to the shipowner as **15–015** "freight and primage (if any)". Primage was originally a small payment made by the shipper to the master in consideration of the care and attention which he was to give during the voyage to the shipper's cargo. However, such payment is no longer customary.

In modern practice, primage is not normally charged. Where it is claimed, it

---

[65] Scrutton, *loc. cit.*, p. 333; on excepted perils, see *post*, para. 15–042.
[66] *The Argos (Cargo ex)* (1873) L.R. PC 134.
[67] See *ante*, para. 5–016.
[68] *Booth Steamship Co Ltd v. Cargo Fleet Iron Co Ltd* [1916] 2 K.B. 570.
[69] *G. H. Renton & Co Ltd v. Palmyra Trading Corporation of Panama; The Caspiana* [1957] A.C. 149.
[70] *Cf. Total Transport Corporation of Panama v. Amoco Transport Co; The Altus* [1985] 1 Lloyd's Rep. 423.

means hardly more than a percentage added to the freight which is payable to the shipowner.

Freight rates fixed by shipping conferences

15–016 The standard freight rates for shipments in liner vessels are often fixed by so-called *shipping conferences*. These are combinations or pools of shipowners maintaining regular liner services to particular parts of the world. The rates which they offer are frequently lower than those which non-conference ship-owners are able to quote, but regular services can only be profitably maintained if supported by regular freight bookings.

The validity, in common law, of a conference arrangement was upheld in the famous *Mogul* case,[71] where a non-conference shipowner sued members of the conference formed for the shipment of tea from China to Europe. It was held that the conference arrangement was not illegal as being a conspiracy because its members pursued the lawful object of protecting and extending their own trade and had not employed unlawful means to achieve this object.

The liner conference system was also criticised by some developing countries which claimed that in some instances it operated in a discriminatory fashion against their shipowners, shippers and foreign trade. On the suggestion of UNCTAD, a *Convention on a Code of Conduct for Liner Conferences* was signed at Geneva on April 6, 1974 and became effective on October 6, 1983.[72] An E.C. Regulation[73] provides for ratification of the Convention by E.C. States but subject to reservations. The aims of the Convention have been described thus[74]:

> "The Code aims at striking a just and fair balance between many interests. Discrimination between the members of a liner conference and non-members which are recognised national shipping lines shall be avoided; this provision,[75] it is thought, modifies the ruling of the House of Lords in the *Mogul* case.[76] The relations between the members of a liner conference, who often have disputes among themselves, are regulated. Transactions between conference members and shippers, including the grant of loyalty rebates, are covered. Important rules for freight determination, including promotional freight rates for non-traditional exports, are laid down. Altogether, this is a very comprehensive code."

The Code also provides a mandatory conciliation procedure for certain specified disputes. Prior to the Convention coming into effect, the United Kingdom passed enabling legislation, *viz.* the Merchant Shipping (Liner Conferences) Act 1982, to which the Code was appended in the Schedule. The Act came into force on March 14, 1985.[77]

---

[71] *Mogul Steamship Co v. McGregor, Gow & Co* [1892] A.C. 25.
[72] See L. Juda, "The UNCTAD Liner Code: A Preliminary Examination of the Implications of the Code of Conduct for Liner Conferences", (1985) 16 Journal of Maritime Law and Commerce, 181.
[73] Council Regulation 954/79 (O.J. L121, May 17, 1979).
[74] In an Editorial in [1982] J.B.L. 441.
[75] Art. 1 of the Code.
[76] *Mogul Steamship Co v. McGregor, Gow & Co* [1892] A.C. 25.
[77] Merchant Shipping (Liner Conferences) Act 1982 (Commencement) Order 1985 (S.I. 1985 No. 182). The following S.I.s have also been issued: Merchant Shipping (Liner Conferences) (Conditions for Recognitions) Regulations 1985 (S.I. 1985 No. 405); and Merchant Shipping (Liner Conferences) (Mandatory Provisions) Regulations 1985 (S.I. 1985 No. 406).

The arrangements which the owners combined in a shipping conference make between themselves and with their customers have undoubtedly a restrictive element which can, however, be justified in view of the benefit which the international trading community derives from the maintenance of scheduled liner services to distant places. This restrictive element came under review in the E.C. In the E.C. a Council Regulation of 1986[78] exempts, subject to certain conditions, shipping conference arrangements, including agreement of rates, from the prohibitions of Articles 81 and 82 of the E.C. Treaty. A further Council Regulation[79] provides for a block exemption in relation to the joint operation of liner services.

The Protection of Trading Interests Act 1980[80] and Shipping and Trading Interests (Protection) Act 1995[81] provide extensive protection for British shippers and shipping conferences. The original legislation which these Acts replaced was enacted largely in response to U.S. anti-trust legislation.

By whom freight is payable

From the point of view of the exporter, the question of to whom freight is **15–017** payable normally causes little difficulty, except if the vessel is under charter and the question arises as to whether the shipper is in contract with the shipowner or the charterer.[82] On the other hand, the question of from whom the shipowner may demand payment of the freight is of great practical significance. This question cannot be answered by reference to the contract of sale under which the exporter sold and shipped the goods. That contract regulates the ultimate responsibility for freight between the two parties to the sale but is irrelevant as far as the liability for freight to the shipowner is concerned.

Where the bill of lading does not contain express provisions, the following rules apply:

(a) The shipper is primarily liable for payment of the freight, because he is the person with whom the shipowner concludes the contract of carriage. This liability is purely contractual. It is irrelevant, in this respect, whether the shipper was at the time of the shipment the owner of the goods or not, or whether under the bill of lading the goods were made deliverable to the shipper or his order, or to a third person.

(b) The consignee is in an entirely different position. He is not liable for freight under the contract of carriage because he is not a party thereto unless, of course, he is himself the shipper, as would be the case under an f.o.b. contract, or the shipper concluded the contract as his agent. Notwithstanding this fact, the shipowner may demand freight from him

---

[78] Council Regulation 4056/86, in force July 1, 1987, known as the Maritime Transport (Antitrust) Regulation 1986, see [1986] O.J. L378/4.
[79] 870/95.
[80] See *post*, para. 21–021.
[81] ss. 1–4, in force January 1, 1996.
[82] See *post*, para. 15–051.

in any of the circumstances set out in section 3(1) of the Carriage of Goods by Sea Act 1992.[83]

(c) The seller who exercises his right of stoppage in transit[84] is liable to pay the freight to the shipowner.

Shipowner's lien

15–018 The shipowner has a lien on the goods of the shipper which are in his possession. The shipowner's lien is based on the common law or by express agreement.

At common law the shipowner has a lien:

(a) for freight which is payable on delivery of the goods, but not for advance freight, dead freight, or freight payable after delivery of the goods[85];

(b) for general average contributions[86];

(c) for "expenses incurred by the shipowner or master in protecting and preserving the goods".[87]

The common law lien of the shipowner is a possessory lien. It can be exercised only as long as the goods are in the shipowner's possession on board ship or, subject to the notice of lien discussed below, in a warehouse ashore. This shipowner's lien is lost when the goods are duly delivered or the shipowner agrees to accept freight subsequent to delivery.

At common law the shipowner's lien attaches to all goods carried to the same consignee on the same voyage under the same contract. It is immaterial that several bills of lading have been issued in respect of them. If part of the goods is delivered without payment of freight the shipowner may still claim his lien on the remainder of the goods for the whole freight due to him. But the position is different where goods are shipped under different contracts of carriage. Where, for example, the shipowner carries goods under one contract of carriage and delivers them without insisting on payment of freight, and then later ships goods of the same shipper to the same consignee under another contract of carriage, he cannot in common law claim a lien on these goods for the unpaid freight due under the previous contract.

The lien of the shipowner is usually extended beyond the limits of the common law lien by agreement of the parties. Bills of lading normally contain special clauses dealing with the shipowner's lien. The following clause is typical:

---

[83] See *post*, para. 15–052.
[84] See *ante*, para. 5–016.
[85] *Canadian Pacific (Bermuda) Ltd v. Lagon Maritime Overseas; The Fort Kipp* [1985] 2 Lloyd's Rep. 168.
[86] See *post*, para. 19–028.
[87] Scrutton, *loc. cit.*, p. 378.

"The carrier, his servants or agents shall have a lien on the goods and a right to sell the goods whether privately or by public auction for all freight (including additional freight payable as above stipulated), primage, dead freight, demurrage, detention charges, salvage, average of any kind whatsoever, and for all other charges and expenses whatsoever, which are for account of the goods or of the shipper, consignee or owner of the goods under this bill of lading, and for the costs and expenses of exercising such lien and of such sale and also for all previously unsatisfied debts whatsoever due to him by the shipper, consignee or owner of the goods. Nothing in this clause shall prevent the carrier from recovering from the shipper, consignee or owner of the goods the difference between the amount due from them or any of them to him and the amount realised by the exercise of the rights given to the carrier under this clause."

The shipowner's lien is often extended by these special clauses to cover dead freight, advance freight, freight payable after delivery of the goods, unsatisfied previous freight, inland or forwarding charges, porterage, fines, costs and other charges or amounts due from the shippers or consignees, to the shipowners or their agents.[88] The clauses dealing with the shipowner's lien usually authorise the shipowner to realise the lien by sale of the goods by public auction or otherwise.

BILLS OF LADING AND OTHER CARRIAGE DOCUMENTS

Nature of the bill of lading

One of the principal purposes of the bill of lading is to enable the owner of the **15–019** goods, to which it relates, to dispose of them rapidly, although the goods are not in his hands but are in the custody of a carrier. When goods are on the high seas in transit from London to Singapore and the bill of lading has been air-mailed to the buyer in Singapore and the buyer has thus become the owner of the goods, the bill of lading representing the goods enables the buyer to pledge the goods with his bank in Singapore or to resell them to a repurchaser in New York. The bill of lading is a creation of mercantile custom, a typical institution of international trade. It came into use in the sixteenth century. A book on mercantile law, published in 1686, stated that "bills of lading are commonly to be had in print in all places and several languages".[89] The character of the bill of lading as a document of title was first recognised by the courts in 1794 in *Lickbarrow v. Mason.*[90]

From the legal point of view, a bill of lading is:

(a) a formal receipt by the shipowner acknowledging that goods alleged to be of the stated species, quantity and condition are shipped to a stated destination in a certain ship, or at least are received in the custody of the shipowner for the purpose of shipment;

---

[88] *Whinney v. Moss Steamship Co Ltd* (1910) 15 Com.Cas. 114.
[89] Malynes, *Lex Mercatoria* (3rd ed., 1686), p. 97.
[90] (1794) 5 T.R. 683.

(b) evidence of the contract of carriage, repeating in detail the terms of the contract which was in fact concluded prior to the signing of the bill; and

(c) a document of title to the goods enabling the consignee to dispose of the goods by indorsement and delivery of the bill of lading.

Before considering in more detail the above three properties of the bill of lading, it is necessary to summarise the international rules which govern them and differentiate between the various types of bills of lading and other transport documents.

The international rules relating to bills of lading

15–020 Although the clauses contained in a duly tendered and signed bill of lading represent in law the terms of agreement between the shipper and the carrier, the shipper has little discretion in the negotiation of these terms. The terms of the contract which he concludes are fixed in advance, and his position is not unlike that of a railway passenger who, when buying a ticket, concludes an elaborate standard contract with the railway authority for the carriage of his person from one locality to another. The shipper, like the railway passenger, is protected by Act of Parliament against abuse of the greater bargaining power of the other party. As far as the shipper is concerned, this protection is contained in the Carriage of Goods by Sea Act 1971 which implements the Hague-Visby Rules. The legislative intention is, in the words of Lord Sumner,[91] to "replace a conventional contract, in which it was constantly attempted, often with much success, to relieve the carrier from every kind of liability, by a legislative bargain, under which . . . his position was to be one of restricted exemption."

The Act of 1971 was preceded by the Carriage of Goods by Sea Act 1924, implementing the Hague Rules, which has an interesting history.[92] The clauses in bills of lading exempting the carrier from liability had become so complex and diffuse that the usefulness of bills of lading as "currency of trade"[93] was seriously threatened. This was particularly unsatisfactory to holders of bills of lading who were not the original parties to the contract of carriage and consequently had no influence on its formation, such as further purchasers of goods, bankers who accepted the bills as security for advances, or insurers who were subrogated to the rights of the shipper.

The Hague Rules were revised by the Brussels Protocol of 1968. The revised Rules, known as the Hague-Visby Rules, are appended to the Carriage of Goods by Sea Act 1971 and form part of it. That Act came into operation on June 23, 1977.

The Hague-Visby Rules were fundamentally revised by the United Nations Convention on the Carriage of Goods by Sea 1978, which accepted the so-called

---

[91] In *Gosse Millard Ltd v. Canadian Government Merchant Marine* [1929] A.C. 223 at 236 (in respect of the Carriage of Goods by Sea Act 1924, which preceded the 1971 Act).
[92] A. Diamond Q.C., "The Hague-Visby Rules" [1978] L.M.C.L.Q., 225.
[93] Scrutton, *loc. cit.*, p. 404.

Hamburg Rules. They were prepared by UNCITRAL and adopted by a United Nations conference at Hamburg on March 30, 1978. The Hamburg Rules came into force on November 1, 1992 having been ratified in 20 States. The main alterations incorporated in the Hamburg Rules are: they apply to all contracts for the carriage of goods by sea between two different States, except charterparties, even if the carriage is not carried out under a bill of lading; the period of responsibility of the carrier is extended so as to cover the whole period during which the goods are in his charge; the exclusion of the carrier's liability in case of error in navigation is abolished; a distinction is drawn between the contractual carrier and actual carrier, the contractual carrier being liable for the actual carrier and, in principle, both being liable to the shipper jointly and severally; the maximum limits of the carrier's liability are greatly increased and fixed by reference to the Special Drawing Rights of the International Monetary Fund (SDRs); and the Hamburg Rules may apply to transport documents other than bills of lading.

The present position is that the Hamburg Rules have not been ratified by the United Kingdom. The Hague-Visby Rules are law in the United Kingdom but a number of States have not adopted them and still adhere to the original Hague Rules, amongst them, in particular, the United States of America.[94] It should thus be noted that the original Hague Rules may still be relevant in proceedings before arbitrators or in the courts in the United Kingdom, *e.g.* if a dispute concerns a bill of lading relating to a shipment from a State which is not a Contracting State under the Hague-Visby Rules but still adheres to the original Hague Rules. The original unity of international regulation in the law relating to bills of lading is thus lost, at least temporarily, until all sea-going States have again adopted uniform Rules.

The following treatment is founded on the United Kingdom Carriage of Goods by Sea Act 1971 (the Act) and the Hague-Visby Rules (the Rules) in the Schedule to that Act.

In brief, the Act and the Rules provide for the carrier's duty and liability in respect of goods shipped from a port in a contracting state, or where the bill is issued in a contracting state, but only to goods in respect of which a bill of lading or similar document of title has been issued. However, the Rules may be expressly incorporated in other shipping documents to which they would not otherwise apply. They do not apply to charterparties. Exceptions and limits to the carrier's liability are provided for, as well as a time limit within which the cargo-owner must make a claim for loss or damage to the goods.

The territorial and documentary application of the Carriage of Goods by Sea Act 1971

Territorial application

The Act provides[95] that it applies to every bill of lading relating to the carriage **15–021** of goods by sea, where the port of shipment is a port in the United Kingdom. Article X of the Rules provides:

---

[94] See U.S. Carriage of Goods by Sea Act 1936.
[95] s.1(3).

"The provisions of these Rules shall apply to every bill of lading relating to the carriage of goods between ports in two different States if:

    (a) the bill of lading is issued in a Contracting State; or
    (b) the carriage is from a port in a Contracting State; or
    (c) the contract contained in or evidenced by the bill of lading provides that these Rules or legislation of any State giving effect to them are to govern the contract, whatever may be the nationality of the ship, the carrier, the consignee, or any other interested person whatever may be the nationality of the ship, the carrier, the shipper, the consignee, or any other interested person."

The Rules thus apply by statute to outward bills of lading relating to all goods exported from ports in Great Britain and Northern Ireland or from any other Contracting State and also to bills issued in these countries.

The Rules apply to bills of lading relating to coastal as well as to international voyages.[96] They apply by force of law only "in relation to and in connection with the carriage of goods by sea"[97]; they do not apply to the preceding and subsequent land transport. Thus, in one case[98] the carrier contracted to take frozen chicken in a refrigerated container from Uckfield in Sussex to Jeddah in Saudi Arabia. A bill of lading evidencing shipment from an English port to Jeddah was issued. However, without the knowledge of the shipper, the carrier, after having taken the container by land from Uckfield to Shoreham, shipped it from there to Le Havre, stored it for five or six days, and then shipped it from Le Havre in another vessel to Jeddah. When the goods arrived, they were found to be contaminated, owing to heating in the container. It was clear that they could not have thawed on the short land journey from Uckfield to Shoreham, but they could have deteriorated on the voyage from there to Le Havre. Bingham J. held (1) that the Hague-Visby Rules did not apply to the land journey from Uckfield to Shoreham, (2) but that the sea voyage, according to the contract of carriage, began in Shoreham, and not in Le Havre, and (3) that the short storage on land in Le Havre was "in connection with" the sea voyage. The learned judge held that the Rules applied when the goods were loaded in Shoreham and that the shipper could recover damages under the Rules.

Carriers cannot contract out of their liability for loss of or damage to, or in connection with, goods arising from their negligence, fault or failure in their duties imposed by the Rules. A clause in the contract of carriage purporting to relieve them of these obligations would be null and void and without effect.[99] In *The Hollandia*, also known as *The Morviken*,[1] the House of Lords had to consider the ambit of this provision in the following circumstances. A road-finishing machine was shipped from the Scottish port of Leith on board a Dutch vessel, The Haico Holwerda, to Bonaire, in the Dutch West Indies. The bill of lading contained a clause providing that the contract of carriage by sea should

---

[96] The original Hague Rules did not apply to coastal transport (Carriage of Goods by Sea Act 1924, s.4; see 1971 Act, s.1(3)).
[97] s.1(3).
[98] *Mayhew Foods Ltd v. Overseas Containers Ltd* [1984] 1 Lloyd's Rep. 317; see also *The Anders Maersk* [1986] 1 Lloyd's Rep. 483.
[99] Art. III, r.8.
[1] [1983] A.C. 565. See also *The Saudi Prince (No. 2)* [1988] 1 Lloyd's Rep. 1 (Art. III, r. 8 applied under Italian Law); *Sierra Leone Government v. Margaritis Marine Co Ltd; The Amazona, The Yayamaria* [1989] 2 Lloyd's Rep. 130. (Construction of Art. III, r.8 in the light of *The Hollandia*.)

be governed by the law of the Netherlands and that all actions should be brought in the court of Amsterdam. The machine was transshipped in Amsterdam into a Norwegian vessel, The Morviken. When the machine was unloaded in Bonaire, it was damaged, as the owners alleged, by the negligence of the carrier's employees. In the United Kingdom, under the Hague-Visby Rules the cargo owners could recover about £11,000 if they could prove their case, but in the Netherlands, where at that time the unamended Hague Rules applied, the maximum liability of the carrier was limited to about £250. In proceedings in the English courts on the preliminary point of whether they had jurisdiction[2] the House of Lords held that the choice of law in favour of Netherlands law was ineffective, under Article III, Rule 8, as far as it would lead to the lessening of the carrier's liability under the Hague-Visby Rules, because otherwise a carrier could avoid this liability by the simple device of opting in the bill of lading for a law which did not apply these Rules.[3] The court also held that the choice of jurisdiction clause in favour of the court of Amsterdam was likewise ineffective, but only in so far as it would lead to the reduction of the carrier's liability; it would remain valid if the dispute did not concern his liability, *e.g.* if it concerned a claim for unpaid freight.[4] It should be noted that the decision in *The Hollandia* concerned a situation in which a clause in the bill of lading adopted a legal system which had not given effect to the enlarged liability of the carrier under the Hague-Visby Rules. However, an implied choice of English law does not imply an intention to incorporate the Rules where the territorial requirements for their application are not fulfilled.[5]

Documentary application

The Act, including the Rules, applies to all shipments where "the contract **15–022** expressly or by implication provides for the issue of a bill of lading or any similar document of title".[6]

   The carrier can thus escape the application of the Act and the Rules if his contract with the shipper does not provide for the issue of a bill of lading and shipment is carried out under a sea waybill, data freight receipt or a similar transport document acknowledging only the receipt of the goods[7]; such non-negotiable receipts are invariably issued instead of bills of lading by English cross-channel operators.[8] These non-negotiable receipts can, however, be sub-

---

[2] The case arose in the English jurisdiction because a sister ship of The Haico Holwerda, The Hollandia, was arrested in the English jurisdiction.
[3] But it was held in *The Benarty* [1985] Q.B. 325 that a foreign jurisdiction clause in favour of the court of Jarkarta was valid although that court would apply the Indonesian Commercial Code which provided for a *tonnage* limitation of the charterer that was lower than the *package* limitation of the Hague-Visby Rules. For the U.K. provision on tonnage limitation see *post*, para. 15–046.
[4] It was further decided in *The Hollandia* that the time at which to ascertain whether a choice of jurisdiction clause had the effect of reducing the liability of the carrier, contrary to the Rules, was the time when the carrier sought to rely on the relieving clause.
[5] *Hellenic Steel Co v. Sudamar Shipping Co; The Kominos S* [1991] 1 Lloyd's Rep 371.
[6] s.1(4).
[7] See *post*, para. 15–033.
[8] *Browner International Transport Ltd v. Monarch S.S. Company Ltd; The European Enterprise* [1989] 2 Lloyd's Rep. 185.

jected to the application Rules by marking the receipt that the Rules shall apply "as if the receipt were a bill of lading".[9]

In addition, in many instances, what is known as a "clause paramount" is inserted into bills of lading in order to incorporate the Rules in a contract of carriage to which they would otherwise not apply.

Lord Denning M.R. described the effect of the clause paramount as follows[10]:

> "When a paramount clause is incorporated into a contract, the purpose is to give the Hague Rules contractual force; so that, although the bill of lading may contain very wide exceptions, the Rules are paramount and make the shipowners liable for want of due diligence to make the ship seaworthy and so forth."

Whether the Rules are incorporated as a matter of law or contract depends on the wording of the clause. They apply as a matter of law if the clause is intended to subject such bills or receipts to the Rules, and as a matter of contract if the clause is only intended to restate the position existing under the Act but varies certain provisions, such as limitation.

The difference between the statutory and contractual application of the rules is illustrated in *The European Enterprise*.[11] Here the contract of carriage was evidenced by a sea waybill which expressly incorporated the Rules but did not contain the words "as if the receipt were a bill of lading".[12] The sea waybill also contained a limit of liability provision which was in excess of the limit in the Rules.[13] Steyn J. held that since the words were not included, the Rules had contractual and not statutory force and therefore the limitation provision could be varied. He disagreed with the ruling in an earlier case.[14]

The Rules are adopted by non-negotiable transport documents[15] and charterparties[16] as far as applicable.

In cases where the contract of carriage is not governed by the Rules, or in the absence of their contractual incorporation, the common law rules apply. According to common law, the carrier impliedly undertakes the same liability as a common carrier, namely to carry the goods at his own absolute risk, except if the goods are lost or damaged by act of God, the Queen's enemies, inherent defect of the goods themselves or the shipper's default.[17]

"Goods" includes "articles of every kind whatsoever, except live animals and cargo which by the contract of carriage is stated as being carried on deck and

---

[9] Carriage of Goods by Sea Act 1971, s.1(6)(b).

[10] *Adamastos Shipping Co Ltd v. Anglo-Saxon Petroleum Co Ltd* [1957] 2 Q.B. 233 at 266; *Nea Agrex SA v. Baltic Shipping Co Ltd* [1976] Q.B. 933 at 943.

[11] *Browner International Transport Ltd v. Monarch S.S. Co Ltd; The European Enterprise* [1989] 2 Lloyd's Rep. 185.

[12] As required by s.1(6)(b).

[13] Art. IV, r.5.

[14] *McCarren v. Humber International Transport Ltd; The Vechscroon* [1982] 1 Lloyd's Rep. 301.

[15] Such as, *e.g.* a commercial vehicle movement order, see *McCarren v. Humber International Transport Ltd; The Vechscroon* [1982] 1 Lloyd's Rep. 301.

[16] *Adamastos Shipping Co Ltd v. Anglo-Saxon Petroleum Co Ltd* [1959] A.C. 133; *The Merak* [1964] 2 Lloyd's Rep. 527 at 536; *Seven Seas Transportation Ltd v. Pacifico Union Marina Corporation; The Stya Kailash and Oceanic Amity* [1984] 1 Lloyd's Rep. 588.

[17] *Halsbury's Laws of England* (4th ed., Reissue), Vol. 43(2), "Shipping and Navigation", para. 1483.

is so carried".[18] Where cargo is carried on deck without specific agreement between the parties as to the carriage on deck, and there is no statement in compliance with Article 1(c), the carriage is subject to the Rules.[19] Where the bill of lading contains the usual clause that the shipowner shall be at liberty to carry on deck, he is free to do so but is not relieved, by that clause, of his obligations under Article III, Rule 2, *e.g.* to stow properly and carefully.[20]

The extent of the carrier's liability and excepted perils, and other provisions of the Rules are dealt with later in this chapter.

Types of bills of lading

Charterparty bills of lading

Where a charterer ships goods himself, the terms of the contract of carriage are **15–023** contained in the charterparty and not the bill of lading. However, in the hands of a consignee or indorsee the bill of lading constitutes the contract of carriage, since they cannot be expected to have knowledge of the terms of the charterparty. The Hague-Visby Rules do not apply to charterparty bills[21] although most charterparties expressly incorporate them.

A charterparty bill of lading is a bill which incorporates, by reference, some of the terms of the charterparty, so that they might have effect against the consignee or the indorsee of the bill. But a bill, though issued under a charterparty, which does not incorporate the terms of the charterparty into the contract with the consignee or indorsee, is not a charterparty bill of lading in the technical sense.[22] Unless instructed to the contrary, banks will refuse to accept a charterparty bill of lading as good tender under a letter of credit. The UCP (1993 Revision) state in Article 23(a)(vi) that banks will reject a document which contains any indication that it is subject to a charterparty unless otherwise stipulated in the credit.[23]

Sometimes, the charterparty provides that bills of lading issued under it shall be charterparty bills, incorporating all or any of the clauses of the charterparty. Such a provision is inserted in the interest of the shipowner who wants to preserve the protection of the charterparty against the shipper (cargo owner).[24] A charterparty bill of lading may be issued in the negotiable or non-negotiable form.

Charterparty bills give rise to two potential problems for the cargo-owner.

---

[18] Art. 1(c).
[19] *Svenska Traktor Akt v. Maritime Agencies (Southampton) Ltd* [1953] 2 Q.B. 295.
[20] *ibid.*
[21] Art. 1(b) which provides that the *bill of lading* must regulate relations between the carrier and the holder of the bill.
[22] *Enrico Furst & Co v. W. E. Fischer Ltd* [1960] 2 Lloyd's Rep. 340.
[23] Art. 25 further provides that banks are not required to examine the charterparty, even if tendered, and are relieved of any responsibility for failing to do so.
[24] *Federal Commerce and Navigation Ltd v. Molena Alpha Inc; The Nanfri, The Benfri, the Lorfri* [1979] A.C. 757; *Paros Shipping Corporation v. Nafta (G.B.) Ltd; The Paros* [1987] 2 Lloyd's Rep. 269 (in this case the bills of lading, in breach of the charterparty, were not issued in the form prescribed by the charterparty).

The first relates to which, if any, of the charterparty terms are incorporated in the bill of lading and whether the incorporation clause is effective.[25] In the event that he has to sue the carrier for loss or damage to the goods, his second problem is to identify whom to sue, the shipowner or the charterer.[26]

Where the bill is a charterparty bill of lading in the technical sense, *i.e.* a bill issued under a charterparty, a problem for the cargo-owner is which terms of the charterparty are incorporated into the bill by reference. Here, the observations of Sir John Donaldson M.R.[27] should be borne in mind that:

> "the starting point . . . must be the contract contained in or evidenced by the bill of lading, for this is the only contract to which the shipowners and consignees are both parties. What the shipowners agreed with the charterers, whether in the charterparty or otherwise, is wholly irrelevant, save in so far as the whole or part of any such agreement has become part of the bill of lading contract. Such an incorporation cannot be achieved by agreement between the owners and the charterers. It can only be achieved by the agreement of the parties to the bill of lading contract and thus the operative words of incorporation must be found in the bill of lading itself."

Two possibilities exist: the incorporation clause may expressly refer to one or several specific terms in the charterparty, or the reference may be in a general manner, for example by stating that "all the terms, provisions and exceptions of the aforesaid charterparty are deemed to be incorporated into this bill of lading."[28]

The main problem for the cargo-owner is the extent to which a general incorporation clause can successfully incorporate the charterparty terms. Provided the "operative words of incorporation" are in the bill of lading, ascertaining whether some or all of the charterparty terms have been effectively incorporated in the bill appears to be a two-stage process. The first is whether the specific words of incorporation describe clearly the term or terms to be incorporated and secondly, the term or terms to be incorporated must be consistent with the bill of lading (the description and consistency issues).[29]

Where there is more than one charterparty, it will be necessary to ascertain which is the relevant one. The date of the charterparty may identify it, but in the absence of a date the head charter is taken to be the one referred to in the incorporation clause in the bill,[30] unless the facts point to a sub-charter. A charterparty that has not yet been reduced to writing is incapable of being incorported into a bill of lading[31] and an oral agreement will not qualify.[32]

A general incorporation clause will, it seems, suffice to incorporate terms which are germane to the shipment, carriage and discharge of the cargo and

---

[25] See *post.*
[26] See *post*, para. 15–051.
[27] *Skips A/S Nordheim v. Syrian Petroleum Co Ltd; The Varenna* [1984] Q.B. 599 at 615.
[28] The wording of incorporation clauses varies greatly; see Scrutton, *op. cit.*, Art. 37.
[29] *The Emmanuel Coloctronis (No. 2)* [1982] 1 Lloyd's Rep. 286.
[30] *Seateam & Co v. Iraq National Oil Co; The Sevonia Team* [1983] 2 Lloyd's Rep. 640 at 644.
[31] *The Heidberg* [1994] 2 Lloyd's Rep. 287; *cf. Gill & Duffus SA v. Rionda Futures* [1994] 2 Lloyd's Rep. 67; *Swiss Bank Corp v. Novorissiysk Shipping Co; The Petr Schmidt* [1995] 1 Lloyd's Rep. 509 where no charterparty was drawn up.
[32] *The Heidberg, ante.*

freight payment[33] but the words in the charterparty will not be manipulated such that they conflict with the words in the bill of lading.[34]

The courts are slower to accept that an arbitration clause is incorporated here, the parties' intention must be demonstrated by specific words in the bill of lading[35] and in this case the words may be manipulated to give effect to the intention of the parties.[36]

Negotiable and non-negotiable bills

Bills of lading can perform their principal function of enabling a person to **15–024** dispose of goods which are not in his possession only if they are, at least to some extent, negotiable. But a bill of lading is not a negotiable instrument as is a bill of exchange[37]; the term negotiable when used in relation to a bill of lading merely means transferable.[38] However, recent cases still refer to a bill of lading as being negotiable, or "a negotiable instrument".[39]

Bills of lading, like bills of exchange, may be made out to bearer, or to a particular person or his order. If made out to bearer, they are transferred by delivery while, if made out to order, they are transferred by indorsement and delivery of the bill. In practice, bills of lading made out to bearer are rarely used, as the bill of lading is a document of title which is a symbol of the goods represented by the bill.[40] A transfer of the bill of lading passes such rights in the goods as the parties wish to pass, *e.g.* the property if the goods are sold and the parties intend to pass the property on delivery of the bill, or a charge if the goods are pledged. It is the quality of the bill of lading as a document of title which, though logically distinct from its mode of transfer, confers great practical significance on the latter: by making the bill of lading "negotiable" the cargo is, in fact, made negotiable. It follows that a buyer, who in the contract of sale has stipulated for negotiable bills of lading, is entitled to reject non-negotiable bills.[41]

The negotiability of bills of lading is less developed than that of bills of exchange in two respects. First, while a bill of exchange is negotiable *unless* its negotiability is expressly *excluded*, a bill of lading is only negotiable if *made* negotiable. The shipper, when making out the draft bill, has the choice of creating a transport document that can generally be used by the consignee as a

---

[33] *Thomas & Co Ltd v. Portsea S.S. Co Ltd* [1912] A.C. 1; *The Merak* [1964] 2 Lloyd's Rep. 527; *The Annefield* [1971] 1 Lloyd's Rep. 1.
[34] *Miramar Maritime Corp v. Holborn Trading Ltd; The Miramar* [1984] A.C. 676 where the word "charterer" in the charterparty would not be substitued for "consignee" in the bill of lading; *SA Sucre Export v. Northern River Shipping Ltd; The Sormovskiy 3068* [1994] 2 Lloyd's Rep. 266.
[35] *Thomas & Co Ltd v. Portsea S.S. Co Ltd* and *The Annefield, supra*; *Daval Aciers D'Usinor et de Sacilor v. Armare Srl; The Nerano* [1996] 1 Lloyd's Rep. 1.
[36] *The Nerano, ante*; *The Ouinoussin Pride* [1991] 1 Lloyd's Rep. 126.
[37] See *ante*, para. 9–004.
[38] *Kum v. Wah Tat Bank Ltd* [1971] 1 Lloyd's Rep. 439 at 446.
[39] *e.g. OK Petroleum AB v. Vitol Energy SA* [1995] 2 Lloyd's Rep. 160 at 163.
[40] See *post*, para. 15–038.
[41] *Soproma SpA v. Marine & Animal By-Products Corporation* [1966] 1 Lloyd's Rep. 367. As to pledges, see Factors Act 1889, s.3.

medium of transfer of the goods represented by the bill, or of merely obtaining from the shipowner a formal receipt stipulating delivery to a named person.

In the modern bill of lading a box on the left-hand corner of the bill usually provides:

"Consignee (if 'Order' state Notify Party)."

If the shipper intends to obtain a negotiable bill he completes this box by inserting "order" and adding as "notify party" the name of the consignee.[42]

A shipper who wishes to obtain a bill of lading which is not negotiable does not insert the word "order" in the appropriate box of the bill but inserts the name of the consignee in the following box. The effect of this procedure is that, although the shipper can transfer title in the goods to the consignee by delivering the bill of lading to him, the consignee cannot further pass on title in them to a third party by transfer of the bill of lading.

The second respect in which the negotiability of bills of lading differs from that of bills of exchange is that a holder of a bill of lading, unlike the holder in due course of a bill of exchange, cannot acquire a better title than that of his predecessor.[43] He does not take "free of equities". This is a significant difference; it means that, where a negotiable bill of lading is obtained by fraud and indorsed to a bona fide indorsee for value, the latter does not acquire a title to the goods represented by the bill. If the same happens in case of a bill of exchange which is regular on its face, and not overdue or dishonoured, the indorsee is entitled to all rights arising under the bill of exchange.

In two exceptional cases, however, statutory provisions enable the bona fide indorsee of a bill of lading to acquire, upon certain carefully defined conditions, a better title than his predecessor possessed. The Factors Act 1889, s.2(1), protects an indorsee who takes a bill from a factor acting in excess of his authority[44]; and the Sale of Goods Act 1979, s.47(2) provides that the unpaid seller's rights of lien and of stoppage in transit are defeated by a previous transfer of a bill from the buyer to an indorsee who takes the bill in good faith and for valuable consideration.[45]

The traditional form of negotiable bills of lading is preferred in some kinds of international business but in others the non-negotiable form is favoured. Negotiable bills are normally used in the commodity trade, such as trade in grain or oil, where bills of lading relating to goods in transit are purchased and sold in string contracts[46]; under which the intermediaries do not intend to take delivery and only the last purchaser in the string will take physical delivery of the goods from the ship on its arrival. Negotiable bills of lading are also used if the buyer intends, or at least contemplates, pledging the bills as a collateral security to a bank before the goods arrive. There are other cases in which a

---

[42] The shipper may name himself as consignee.
[43] See *ante*, para. 9–004.
[44] See *post*, para. 27–017.
[45] See *ante*, para. 5–016.
[46] A string contract is a series of contracts of sale under which the same goods or bills of lading relating to them are sold by A to B, by B to C, and so forth, possibly through the whole alphabet.

negotiable bill of lading is stipulated in the contract between the exporter and the overseas importer. On the other hand, where it is anticipated that the consignee himself will take delivery of the goods on arrival of the ship and will not deal in the bills of lading, a non-negotiable bill is perfectly sufficient. Non-negotiable transport documents will be considered later.[47]

"Shipped" and "received" bills

Unless the goods are shipped in containers, bills of lading are usually "shipped" **15–025** bills but sometimes "received for shipment" bills (also called "alongside" bills) are used. The difference between these types of bills may be seen from the following examples:

> "*Shipped* in apparent good order and condition by . . . on board the steam or motor vessel . . ."

and

> "*Received* in apparent good order and condition from . . . for shipment on board the ship . . ."

A "shipped" bill is also called an "on board" bill, particularly in the United States. United Kingdom businessmen buying in the United States of America usually call for an "on board ocean" bill of lading if they wish to get a "shipped bill of lading", as understood in this country. The practical difference between a shipped and received bill is considerable.

Where the shipowner issues a "shipped" bill, he acknowledges that the goods are loaded on board ship. Where he issues a "received for shipment" bill, he confirms only that the goods are delivered into his custody; in this case the goods might be stored in a ship or warehouse under his control. The "received" bill is, thus, less valuable than the "shipped" bill because it does not confirm that the shipment has already begun. The buyer under a c.i.f. contract need not accept a "received for shipment" bill as part of the shipping documents but may insist on a "shipped" bill, unless the contrary is expressly agreed upon by the parties to the contract of sale or is customary in a particular trade.[48] In *Yelo v. S. M. Machado & Co Ltd*,[49] the terms of the credit provided for "shipped" bills; Sellers J. held that the tender of "received" bills (which were not indorsed with the date of shipment) was insufficient.

In all cases to which the Hague-Visby Rules apply,[50] the shipper is entitled to demand from the shipowner a bill of lading after he has received the goods,[51] and a "shipped" bill after the goods are loaded[52] but the shipowner may notate

---

[47] See *post*, paras 15–033, 34.
[48] See *post*, para. 22–022, and *Diamond Alkali Export Corporation v. Fl. Bourgeois* [1921] 3 K.B. 443. On the wording of a "received for shipment" bill of lading see *per* Lloyd J. in *Ishag v. Allied Bank International, Fuhs and Kotalimbora* [1981] 1 Lloyd's Rep. 92 at 97.
[49] [1952] 1 Lloyd's Rep. 183.
[50] See *ante*, paras 15–021, 22.
[51] Art. III, r.3.
[52] Art. III, r.7.

a "received" bill with the name of the ship and the date of shipment[53] which then equates to a "shipped" bill. Where payment is arranged under a letter of credit, UCP (1993 Revision)[54] similarly provides for a notation of the bill, giving the date on which the goods have been loaded. The Carriage of Goods by Sea Act 1992 applies equally to shipped and received for shipment bills.

A container bill of lading issued at an inland loading depot of the container shipping line is invariably a "received" bill of lading.[55]

Clean and "claused" bills

15–026 The difference between these types of bills and the consequences attending the issue of a qualified or "claused" bill of lading are dealt with elsewhere.[56]

It may be added that a clause which does not refer to the *state of the goods when loaded* but refers to the subsequent fate of the goods and their state when discharged does not make a bill a claused bill. It was held in one case[57] that the clause on the bill "Cargo covered by this bill of lading has been discharged . . . damaged by fire and/or water used to extinguish fire for which general average declared" did not deprive the bill of its character of a clean bill.[58]

Through bills of lading

15–027 Where the ocean shipment forms only part of the complete journey and subsequently[59] the goods have to be carried by other land or sea carriers, it is more convenient for the shipper to take out a through bill of lading than to contract with the various carriers who have to carry the goods at the consecutive stages of the journey. Through bills of lading are also used where "the sea transit may itself be divided into separate stages to be performed by different shipowners by a process of transhipment"[60] but whether the contract of carriage, as evidenced by the bill of lading, allows transhipment is a different question.[61] Through bills of lading are increasingly used in modern transport.

The shipper, who takes out a through bill, has only to deal with the carrier who signs the through bill. This carrier undertakes to arrange the transhipment with the on-carriers. The carrier charges an inclusive freight, which, if prepayable, is due on the stipulated event[62] and governed by the rules explained earlier

---

[53] Art. III, r.7.

[54] Art. 23(a)(ii).

[55] See *post*, para. 16–007.

[56] See *ante*, para. 15–003, and *post*, para. 15–036.

[57] *Golodetz & Co Inc v. Czarnikow-Rionda Co Inc; The Galatia* [1980] 1 W.L.R. 495, CA.

[58] Sometimes a charterparty bill of lading (which refers to the terms of the charterparty) is described as a "claused" bill, but this terminology is confusing and should be avoided, see *Federal Commerce and Navigation Ltd v. Molena Alpha Inc; The Nanfri, The Benfri, The Lorfri* [1979] A.C. 757.

[59] Through bills are also used where the on-carriage occurs prior to shipment. The observations in the text apply to such bills *mutatis mutandis*.

[60] Scrutton, *op. cit.*, Art. 180, p. 369.

[61] See *ante*, paras 2–032 and 11–012, where the rules of the UCP relating to the acceptability by banks of bills of lading prohibiting transshipment (Arts 23(b)-(d), 26(b), 27(b)-(c), 28(b)) are also discussed.

[62] See *ante*, para. 15–010.

in respect of prepaid freight.[63] The goods are only delivered by the last on-carrier upon delivery of one original part of the through bill which has to be dispatched to the consignee. The principal contract of sea carriage is superimposed upon the contracts with the on-carriers.

Through bills frequently contain a clause exempting the carrier arranging on-carriage from all liability or stating that transhipment is at owner's risk, or that the responsibility of the shipowner shall cease on delivery of the goods to the on-carrier.

Where legal difficulties arise between the shipper and an on-carrier, it may become relevant to ascertain whether the on-carrier is a party to a contract with the shipper or not. The answer depends, in the first instance, on the construction of the terms of the through bill. If the shipper contracted exclusively with the carrier, and the on-carrier is merely the carrier's servant or a sub-contractor, the carrier alone can claim against the on-carrier in contract. He alone is responsible to the shipper and the direction of the on-carriage rests solely with him. If, on the other hand, the carrier, when contracting with the shipper, acts as agent of the on-carrier, a direct contract of carriage has come into existence between the shipper and the on-carrier. Both alternatives are used in practice.

The Carriage of Goods by Sea Act 1971 and the Rules adopted by the Act apply to through bills issued in respect of goods dispatched from a port in the United Kingdom and Northern Ireland, or of any other Contracting State or issued in those countries, even after the goods have been transshipped at a foreign port. If and when the Hamburg Rules become law, the relationship between the shipper and the contractual and actual carrier will be fundamentally altered.[64]

Container bills of lading

These bills are issued by container shipping lines to cover the multimodal trans- **15–028** port of goods in a container from an inland place of dispatch to the final place of arrival. Container bills have features not present in other bills and are considered later in this work.[65]

House bills of lading and groupage bills of lading

House bills of lading are issued by freight forwarders, who consolidate several **15–029** cargoes belonging to different owners or forming the subject-matter of different export transactions, in one consignment shipped under a groupage bill of lading issued by the carrier to the forwarder. Such a consolidation of cargoes is particularly frequent in the case of groupage containers.[66] An example of such a document is the *FIATA Combined Transport Bill of Lading (FBL)*[67]. This document

---

[63] *ibid.*
[64] See *ante*, para. 15–020.
[65] See Chap. 16.
[66] *ibid.*
[67] FIATA stands for *Federation Internationale des Associations de Transitaires et Assimiles*; its headquarters are at 24, Baumackerstrasse, P.O. Box 8493, Zurich, Switzerland, CH-8050. Three FIATA documents are in use: the FIATA FCR (Forwarder's Certificate of Receipt), the FIATA

states in its title that it is "negotiable"[68] and, in its amended version of 1992, incorporates the UNCTAD/ICC rules for Multimodal Transport Documents and satisfies the requirements of an ICC Combined Transport Document.[69] According to UCP 500 (1993 edition),[70] such combined transport documents are acceptable by banks in letter of credit transactions unless the credit states to the contrary.

A house bill of lading is a misnomer because such a document is not a bill of lading in the technical legal sense.[71] It is not a document of title giving the consignee or assignee a right to claim the goods from the carrier. The provisions of the Carriage of Goods by Sea Act 1992[72] do not apply to it. It follows that a house bill of lading is not good tender under a c.i.f. contract as a proper bill of lading and, if the contract allows such a tender, the contract cannot be regarded as a proper c.i.f. contract.[73]

A transport document issued by a freight forwarder will be rejected by banks unless the document indicates that the forwarder is acting as a carrier or as an agent of a carrier, or, of course, the credit instructions provide otherwise.

Shipping certificates are of two kinds. They are issued either by a carrier, especially on short sea routes, or by a forwarder (who is not the carrier). In both cases they are merely receipts confirming that the person who has issued them has taken the goods in his charge.

Through bills of lading covering on-carriage by air

15–030   This type of through bill is used where the goods, after having been unloaded at the port of discharge, are carried to their ultimate inland destination by air.

There is no reason why a through bill should not cover on-carriage by air. The legal difficulty is that the bill of lading is a document of title[74] but the air consignment note is not.[75] It is thought that a combination of these two documents does not give the combined through bill the character of a document of title. While, in practice, the goods might sometimes not be delivered to the consignee at the final place of destination without surrender of the through bill of lading by him, no commercial custom exists to that effect. The exporter cannot rely on this practice and has no legal remedy if it is not observed.

FCT (Forwarder's Certificate of Transport) and the FBL (Negotiable FIATA Combined Transport Bill of Lading).
[68] The "negotiability" of the FIATA documents means merely assignability of the rights under the contract of carriage but not transfer of obligations. The FIATA Combined Transport Bill of Lading is further not a document of title, but contractually the surrender of the duly indorsed document is a condition precedent for the delivery of the goods.
[69] See Chap. 16.
[70] Art. 26.
[71] The definition of "bill of lading" in the UCC, s.1-201(6), is wider than the English definition; the definition of the UCC includes receipts of goods for shipment issued by persons engaged in the business of transporting and forwarding goods including airbills.
[72] See *ante*, para. 15–052.
[73] *Comptoir d'Achat v. Luis de Ridder; The Julia* [1949] A.C. 293.
[74] See *post*, para. 15–038.
[75] See Chap. 17.

Switch bills

Switch bills may be issued by the carrier in exchange for the original set, the **15–031**
the new bills containing some altered details. There may be a number of reasons
for altering such details, such as to conceal the origin of the goods or the identity
of the original supplier,[76] or to fraudulently evade customs duty. In *The Almak*,[77]
switch bills were issued to alter the date of shipment which governed the price
of the goods. Even where switch bills are issued for a legitimate reasons "it is
a practice fraught with danger . . ."[78]

"Stale" bills of lading

The expression "stale bill of lading" is used in banking practice. A bank which **15–032**
is instructed by or on behalf of a buyer to make finance available under a letter
of credit upon presentation by the seller of a bill of lading (and of other
documents) might feel obliged, in order to safeguard the interest of its principal,
to reject the bill as being "stale". This means that the bill, though conforming
in all respects with the requirements of the credit, is presented so late that, as
the result of the delay in its presentation, the consignee might become involved
in legal or practical complications or might have to pay additional costs, *e.g.* for
the warehousing of goods.

The UCP (1993 Revision) provide in Article 43(a), that transport documents
must be presented within a specified time after issuance and that, if no time is
specified, banks may refuse documents if presented to them later than 21 days
after issuance of the bill of lading or other transport document. In many
instances, the introduction of a definite time limit has reduced the uncertainty
inherent in the concept of the stale bill.

The bank will often accept a bill of lading or other transport document which
it might regard as stale on an indemnity given by the seller.

Sea waybills

A sea waybill is a non-negotiable transport document and its great advantage is **15–033**
that its presentation by the consignee is not required in order for him, on production of satisfactory identification, to take delivery of the goods, thus avoiding
delay both for him and the carrier where the goods arrive before the waybill. It
is not a document of title but contains, or is evidence of, the contract of carriage
as between the shipper and carrier[79] in that it incorporates the standard terms of
the carrier on its face. However, unlike a bill of lading, these terms are not
detailed on the reverse of the waybill which is blank. A waybill is usually issued
in the "received for shipment" form but may, like a bill of lading, be notated
once the goods have been loaded.

---

[76] *Noble Resources Ltd v. Cavalier Shipping Corp; The Atlas* [1996] 1 Lloyd's Rep. 642.
[77] *Rudolf Oetker v. IFA Internationale Frachtagentur AG; The Almak* [1985] 1 Lloyd's Rep. 557.
[78] *The Atlas, ante* at 645.
[79] As to the position between consignee and carrier see *post*, para. 15–052.

It has already been observed[80] that a non-negotiable document is sufficient where the intention is that the consignee shall take delivery of the goods on arrival of the ship but that in some kinds of business, particularly commodities, in which bills of lading are traded, a negotiable bill of lading is required. Further, where payment is to be by documentary credit, a sea waybill is not as acceptable to banks as a bill of lading, since it is not a document of title and so does not provide them with the security of a bill of lading. Nevertheless, UCP 500[81] provide for acceptance of sea waybills.[82]

In modern times the use of a non-negotiable sea waybill issued by the carrier has greatly increased, especially as the result of the growth of ocean container transport. Provision for the consignee to sue the carrier under the contract of carriage contained in the Carriage of Goods by Sea Act 1992[83] may well result in their even wider use,[84] as may the introduction of the CMI Uniform Rules for Sea Waybills, which may be voluntarily incorporated in the contract of carriage. In addition, due to its non-negotiability, the sea waybill "could easily be replaced by messages sent between the interested parties by Electronic Data Interchange".[85]

A non-negotiable transport document may be a non-negotiable bill of lading or it may simply be a receipt by the carrier, acknowledging that he has received the goods in his charge or that he has shipped them.[86] If the document is a non-negotiable bill of lading, the Hague-Visby Rules apply to the contract of carriage, provided that the conditions for the application of the Carriage of Goods by Sea Act 1971 are satisfied.[87] If the transport document is a sea waybill, the Rules do not apply[88] but may be expressly incorporated.[89]

Delivery orders

15–034 The splitting up of a bulk cargo, or a consignment shipped under one bill of lading into smaller parcels sold to different buyers, can be achieved by the use of delivery orders relating to specified portions of the whole consignment. Such a delivery order may be a *ship's delivery order* or a *merchant's delivery order*[90] and, although neither is a document of title, from the legal point of view the

---

[80] See *ante*, para. 15–024.
[81] Art. 24.
[82] See para. 11–012.
[83] See *post*, para. 15–052.
[84] See the *Law Commission Report*, para. 5.9 in relation to the provisions of the 1992 Act.
[85] CMI Rules for Electronic Bills of Lading, Introduction, p. 22. On EDI see Chap. 33.
[86] To give examples: in an f.o.b. (buyer contracting with carrier) contract (see Chap. 2) the non-negotiable document, even if described as a bill of lading, is merely a receipt of the carrier, but in a strict f.o.b. contract, an f.o.b. contract, with additional services, or a c.i.f. contract, the non-negotiable bill of lading may well be a true bill of lading.
[87] See *ante*, para. 15–022.
[88] s.1(4) of the 1971 Act and Art. III, r.4 which applies only to bills of lading.
[89] See 1971 Act, s.1(6)(b); see *The European Enterprise* [1989] 2 Lloyd's Rep. 185; and *ante*, para. 15–022.
[90] Also called a "mere" delivery order.

distinction is important.[91] A ship's delivery order is either issued by or on behalf of the carrier or by the shipper directing the carrier to deliver the goods to the holder.[92] A merchant's delivery order may be issued by a seller undertaking delivery to the buyer or directed to his agent[93] or a freight forwarder at the port of destination, and the order directs the agent to deliver the portion or quantity of the goods stated in it to the holder of the order. In this case the consignment is consigned to the agent or freight forwarder.

The importance of the distinction between the two types of delivery orders is that a ship's delivery order gives the person to whom delivery relates rights of suit against the carrier,[94] whereas the person named in a merchant's shipping order has no such rights.

The date of the bill of lading

The correct dating of the bill of lading is a matter of great importance. The **15–035** correct date of a "shipped" bill is the date when all the goods are loaded and it must not be dated earlier[95]; and that of a "received for shipment" bill is the date when they are taken into the charge of the carrier. If a "received for shipment" bill is notated "shipped", the date of shipment of the goods is that of the notation, and not that of the receipt of the goods by the carrier. Where the loading extends over several days, the bill should be dated when the loading is completed[96] but there may be a trade custom admitting the insertion of the date when the loading commences.

The date of the bill of lading is material in three legal relationships: in the contract of carriage, in the contract of sale, and in relation to the banks if payment is arranged under a letter of credit.

As to the contract of carriage, it has already been observed that the shipper is entitled to demand that the bill of lading should be dated correctly. If the master (or another agent of the carrier) negligently misdates the bill, the carrier as principal is liable in damages, provided that the shipper can prove that he has suffered a loss as the result of the misdating, because there is an implied obligation that due care should be exercised in the dating of the bill.[97] However, the

---

[91] See *Rights of Suit in Respect of Carriage of Goods by Sea* (Law Com. No. 196), paras 5.23–5.31.
[92] An excellent explanation of the various types of delivery orders is contained in the judgment of Kerr J. in *Cremer v. General Carriers SA; The Dona Mari* [1974] 1 W.L.R. 341 at 349; *Waren Import Gesellschaft Krohn & Co v. Internationale Graanhandel Thegra NV* [1975] 1 Lloyd's Rep. 146. *ibid.*
[93] *Comptoir d'Achat v. Luis de Ridder; The Julia* [1949] A.C. 293.
[94] Carriage of Goods by Sea Act 1992, s.2(1); see *post*, para. 15–052.
[95] *Mendala III Transport v. Todd Transport Corp; The Wiloma Tanana* [1993] 2 Lloyd's Rep. 41. In the case of a "shipped" bill it is not the earlier date when the goods are placed into a "full load" container at an inland container collection depot: *per* Mocatta J. in *United City Merchants (Investments) Ltd v. Royal Bank of Canada; The American Accord* [1979] 1 Lloyd's Rep. 267 at 271–273.
[96] *Rudolf A. Oetker v. IFA International Frachtagentur AG; The Almak* [1985] 1 Lloyd's Rep. 557 at 558.
[97] *Stumore Weston & Co v. Michael Breen* (1886) 12 A.C. 698 (and the carrier may have a claim against the master to be indemnified). See also *The Saudi Crown* [1986] 1 Lloyd's Rep. 261.

position may be different if the misdating is due to want of care on the part of the shipper.[98]

The date of the bill of lading may also be relevant in the contract of sale. The tender of a wrongly dated bill of lading qualifies, at least in a c.i.f. contract, as a breach of condition and entitles the buyer to reject the bill and to treat the contract as repudiated,[99] even if the goods are in fact shipped within the contract time.[1] In *The Almak*[2] it was agreed that the purchase price of the goods—gas oil—should be the price ruling at the date of the bill of lading. The goods were loaded on June 27 but the bill bore the date of June 22, and the master signed it without noticing that it was incorrectly dated. The price was calculated by reference to June 22, instead of June 27. The market fell by £7 between these two dates, with the result that the buyer paid the seller more than he would have done if the bill had been correctly dated. The action of the buyer (who had chartered the ship to carry the goods which he had purchased) against the disponent owner of the ship failed, because the inclusion of the wrong date in the bill of lading was due to want of care on his part, as he—the buyer—had tendered the (inadvertently) incorrectly dated bill to the master for signature.

Where payment is arranged under a letter of credit, the credit often states a date for shipment of the goods, in addition to the expiry date which every credit contains.[3] Here the date of the bill of lading is likewise relevant. An issuer of a bill of lading, who deliberately backdates it in order to bring it within the shipment time in the credit, acts fraudulently, and, as far as the *issue* of the bill is concerned, there is no difference between the case where he has forged the bill and where he has deliberately backdated it. However, in the hands of an innocent person, the fraudulently backdated bill is far from being a nullity; in fact, it is perfectly valid. In *United City Merchants (Investments) Ltd v. Royal Bank of Canada*[4] the bill was backdated by an employee of the forwarder but the shipper had no knowledge of the fraud. It was held that the bank, which had confirmed the credit, was bound to pay on tender of the backdated bill.

In certain circumstances, where the shipment date is incorrect because of a genuine mistake, it may be amended by the carrier.[5]

The bill of lading as a receipt

15–036 The bill of lading, being a receipt of the shipowner for the goods, contains in its free space, known as the margin, a description of the goods. This description is perhaps the most vital part of the whole bill, because the consignee or indorsee

[98] *The Almak, ante* at 560.
[99] Unless the breach can be regarded as a breach of an innominate term; see para. 5–004.
[1] *Re an Arbitration between the General Trading Co (Ltd) v. van Stolk's Commissiehandel* (1911) 16 Com.Cas. 95; *Procter & Gamble Philippine Manufacturing Corporation v. Kurt A. Becher GmbH & Co KG* [1988] 2 Lloyd's Rep. 21, CA.
[2] [1985] Lloyd's Rep. 557.
[3] See para. 11–019.
[4] [1983] A.C. 168; *cf. Standard Chartered Bank v. Pakistan National Shipping Corp* [1995] 2 Lloyd's Rep. 365 (shipowner and agent liable to the bank which paid out under a letter of credit against a falsely dated bill); see para. 11–042.
[5] *Mendala III Transport v. Total Transport Corp; The Wiloma Tanana* [1993] 2 Lloyd's Rep. 41.

of the bill, who wishes to buy the goods by having the bill indorsed to him, normally has no opportunity of verifying the representations of the buyer as to their quantity and quality by examining them. The consignee or indorsee therefore parts with the purchase price in reliance upon the shipowner's description of the goods in the bill of lading. In numerous cases disappointed buyers have tried, often successfully, to hold the shipowner responsible for an inaccurate description of the goods in the bill and ingenious clauses have been devised by shipowners to restrict that liability.

By the provisions of the Hague-Visby Rules,[6] the shipper is entitled to demand that the bill of lading which the owner is obliged to issue to him should contain the following:

"(a) The leading marks necessary for identification of the goods are the same as furnished in writing by the shipper before the loading of such goods starts, provided such marks are stamped or otherwise shown clearly upon the goods if uncovered, or on the cases or coverings in which such goods are contained, in such a manner as should ordinarily remain legible until the end of the voyage;

(b) Either the number of packages or pieces, or the quantity, or weight, as the case may be, as furnished in writing by the shipper;

(c) The apparent order and condition of the goods:

Provided that no carrier, master or agent of the carrier, shall be bound to state or show in the bill of lading any marks, number, quantity, or weight which he has reasonable ground for suspecting not accurately to represent the goods actually received, or which he has had no reasonable means of checking."

An accurate statement as to the apparent order and condition of the goods is required and reasonable care on the part of the carrier or master is not sufficient.[7]

When the shipowner affirms that the goods received are in "apparent good order and condition", he issues a "clean" bill. When this statement is qualified, the bill is "claused".[8] The following definition of a clean transport document of lading is provided by the UCP (1993 Revision), Art. 32:

"A clean transport document is one which bears no superimposed clause or notation which expressly declares a defective condition of the goods and/or the packaging."

The words "in apparent good order and condition" denote that "apparently, and so far as met the eye, and externally [the goods] were placed in good order on board this ship",[9] but the statement does not extend to qualities of the goods "which were not apparent to reasonable inspection having regard to the circumstances of loading".[10] The statement does not constitute a promise or undertaking by the shipowner, but is merely a statement of fact, an affirmation that

---

[6] Art. III, r.3.
[7] *Trade Star Line Corp v. Mitsui & Co Ltd; The Arctic Trader* [1996] 2 Lloyd's Rep. 449 at 458.
[8] *Per* Salmon J. in *British Imex Industries Ltd v. Midland Bank Ltd* [1958] 2 Q.B. 542 at 551.
[9] *Per* Sir R. Phillimore in *The Peter der Grosse* (1875) 1 P.D. 414 at 420.
[10] *Per* Branson J. in *Re National Petroleum Co; The Athelviscount* (1934) 39 Com.Cas. 227 at 236; *Harris & Son Ltd v. China Mutual Steam Navigation Co Ltd* [1959] 2 Lloyd's Rep. 500 at 501 (inherent defect); see also Art. IV, r. 2, of the Rules.

certain facts are correct.[11] The shipowner who gives a clean bill does not promise to deliver goods "in apparent good order and condition" to the consignee, and may prove that the goods were damaged subsequent to the issue of the bill by an excepted peril, but he is prevented ("estopped") from denying that he received the goods in apparent good order and condition and cannot escape liability by alleging that an excepted peril *e.g.* insufficient packing existed prior to the issue of the clean bill.[12] This estoppel operates only in favour of a consignee who *relies* on the statement in the bill that goods were in apparent good order and condition,[13] but, as was said by Scrutton L.J.[14]:

> "the mercantile importance of clean bills is so obvious and important that I think the fact that he (*i.e.* the consignee) took the bill of lading which in fact is clean, without objection, is quite sufficient evidence that he relied on it."

In one case[15] the master, who was instructed to sign bills of lading "as presented", refused to sign a bill which showed a larger quantity of goods—fuel oil shipped in Saudi Arabia—than actually loaded.[16] This necessitated a further survey[17] and caused delay in the departure of the vessel. Evans J. held that the "as presented" clause did not mean that the master was obliged to sign irregular bills. "There is a basic and implied requirement that the bills as presented should relate to goods actually shipped, and that they should not contain a misdescription of the goods which was known to be incorrect".[18]

The carrier, when asked to issue a clean bill contrary to the facts, is in an evident predicament. If he obliges, he may be liable to the consignee; if he refuses, he inconveniences his client, the shipper, who might have difficulties in negotiating the bill. This explains why sometimes a dangerous attempt is made to induce the carrier, upon receipt of an indemnity from the shipper or his bank, to issue a clean bill contrary to facts.[19] It further explains the tendency of clausing the bill in an apparently innocent form which, while protecting the carrier, does not frighten off the unwary consignee. This accounts for vague qualifying remarks such as "weight unknown", "quality unknown", or "condition unknown" which are occasionally found in the margin of the bill. Some forms of bills of lading have the following or similar words imprinted in their context:

> "Measurement, weight, quantity, brand, contents, condition, quality and value as declared by shipper but unknown to the carrier."

The protective value, from the point of view of the carrier, of qualifying clauses

---

[11] *Per* Channel J. in *Compañía Naviera Vascongada v. Churchill & Sim* [1906] 1 K.B. 237 at 247.
[12] *Silver v. Ocean Steamship Co* [1930] 1 K.B. 416; *Cremer v. General Carriers SA* [1974] 1 W.L.R. 341 at 500; *Naviera Mogor SA v. Société Metallurgique de Normandie; The Nogar Marin* [1988] 1 Lloyd's Rep. 412 (clean bill issued although wire coils, which were to be shipped, were obviously rusty; shipowner held to be liable).
[13] Hague-Visby Rules, Art. III, r. 4.
[14] In *Silver v. Ocean Steamship Co* [1930] 1 K.B. 416.
[15] *Boukadoura Maritime Corporation v. SA Marocaine de' Industrie et du Raffinage Boukadoura; The Boukadoura* [1989] 1 Lloyd's Rep. 393.
[16] The reason may have been that the shore measurements differed from the loading measurements.
[17] The measurements of the master proved to be approximately correct.
[18] *Per* Evans J., in *The Boukadoura, ante,* at 399.
[19] See *post,* para. 15–039.

is greatly diminished in the cases to which the Carriage of Goods by Sea Act 1971 applies, because under this Act the shipper is entitled to demand a clear statement in the bill of lading as to some of the particulars in question.[20] Where the required particulars are stated they cannot be negatived or contradicted by a clause that they are "unknown" to the shipowner; such a qualifying clause is ineffective in law.

It should, however, be noted that the carrier is only obliged, by Article III, Rule 3b of the Rules, to state in the bill *either* the number of packages or pieces, *or* the quantity *or* the weight, but not *all* these particulars. Where he states the number of packages, and adds a qualifying clause in respect of other particulars, *e.g.* "weight and quality unknown", the qualifying clause affords him protection in respect of the latter particulars.[21] Where the quantity is expressed to be "unknown", the bill of lading is not prima facie evidence of the quantity shipped.[22] However, the "unknown" clause does not provide absolute protection. A shipowner who acknowledges having received the goods in apparent good order and condition cannot nullify this admission by adding "condition unknown", as was held in one case[23] where the cargo consisted of timber which was loaded in a deteriorated condition. The master recorded in his log that the timber was "very black, wet and partly musty" but issued a clean bill qualified only by the words "condition unknown". Langton J. held that the clause was insufficient to convey to the consignee that the timber was damaged. The learned judge said[24]:

> "The straightforward thing to do was surely to put upon the bill of lading, in the ample margin which is apparently provided for that purpose, a clause which would clearly advertise to any buyer of a particular bill of lading that the goods he was going to receive were not in good order and condition. It would not have been beyond the master's power to take the entry from his own log and to put upon the bill of lading 'very black, wet and partly musty'. If he could see it for the purposes of his log, he could with the same eyes have seen it for the purposes of the bill of lading."

Another question is whether the shipowner can escape the effect of the estoppel created by a clean bill of lading by pleading that under the terms of the contract of sale the consignee was bound to accept the defective goods in any event.[25] Kerr J.[26] rejected this contention because the consequences of the issue of a

---

[20] See *ante*.

[21] *New Chinese Antimony Co v. Ocean Steam Ship Co* [1917] 2 K.B. 664; *Pendle & Rivet v. Ellerman Lines* (1927) 33 Com.Cas. 70 at 77; *Re National Petroleum Co; The Athelviscount* (1934) 39 Com.Cas. 227; *Rederiaktiebolaget Gustav W. Erikson v. Dr. Fawzi Ahmed Abou Ismail; The Herroe and The Askoe* [1986] 2 Lloyd's Rep. 281 at 283; *The Boukadoura* [1989] 1 Lloyd's Rep. 393 at 399.

[22] *Noble Resources v. Cavalier Shipping Corp; The Atlas* [1996] 1 Lloyd's Rep. 642, the tally documents prepared on behalf of the port authority were extrinsic evidence of the quantity shipped. *Agrosin Pty Ltd v. Highway Shipping Co Ltd; The Mata K* [1998] 2 Lloyd's Rep. 614.

[23] *The Skarp* [1935] P. 134; in *The Herroe and The Askoe, ante*, the effect of the "unknown" clause was superseded by the master expressly attaching his signature and stamp against the number of potato bags stated to be loaded in the bill of lading.

[24] *The Skarp, ante*, at 142.

[25] Essentially, this is a question of reliance on the estoppel. In *The Skarp* [1935] P. 134 Langton J. held, on the facts of the case before him, that the consignee would have accepted the goods even in their defective condition.

[26] In *Cremer v. General Carriers SA* [1974] 1 W.L.R. 341 at 353.

clean bill of lading arise from the contract of carriage, and a party thereto cannot avail himself of a defence which originates in quite a different contract, namely the contract of sale.[27]

The shipper is deemed to have guaranteed to the carrier the accuracy of the marks, number, quantity and weight as furnished by him, and the shipper has to indemnify the carrier against loss or damage arising from inaccuracies in such particulars. The right of the carrier to be indemnified by the shipper in these circumstances cannot be pleaded by the carrier in defence against a consignee who tries to hold him responsible.[28] Where the shipowner is hesitant to issue a clean bill, the shipper sometimes gives him an express indemnity in order to induce him to issue a clean bill, but such indemnity might be illegal and in that case does not protect the carrier.[29] Bills of lading sometimes contain clauses providing that in case of incorrect or insufficient declaration of the cargo the shipper shall be obliged to pay double freight by way of liquidated damages.[30]

A bill of lading issued under the Carriage of Goods by Sea Act 1971 is prima facie evidence of the receipt of the goods by the carrier as described in accordance with Article III, Rule (3)(a)–(c) but so far as leading marks are concerned the estoppel only operates against the carrier where the marks are "necessary for the identification of the goods".[31] This provision[32] applies to "shipped" and "received" bills[33] alike. The Hague-Visby Rules further provide[34] that the bill shall be *conclusive evidence* regarding those particulars in the hands of a third party acting in good faith; such a third party would be the consignee, to whom the bill is transferred, or an indorsee.[35] It is obvious that the bill is conclusive evidence of shipment against the person who actually signed it, *e.g.* the master of the ship. However, the question is whether the carrier as principal is also liable if the master (or another agent) signs an inaccurate bill and its holder suffers a loss in consequence of the misrepresentation in the bill. Prior to the coming into force of the Carriage of Goods by Sea Act 1992 it had been held in *Grant* v. *Norway*[36] that the master had no ostensible authority to knowingly sign a bill containing a misstatement. In order to dispose of this rule section 4 was included in the 1992 Act.[37] Where the bill containing a misstatement is signed by someone other than the master, the liability of the principal will depend on the normal principles of agency.[38] In one case,[39] where plywood was

---

[27] This would be *res inter alios acta* (a transaction between other parties).

[28] Hague-Visby Rules, Art. III, r. 5.

[29] See *post*, para. 15–039.

[30] See *ante*, para. 4–015.

[31] Art. III, r.3(a).

[32] Rules, Art. III, r.4; *Att-Gen of Ceylon* v. *Scindia Steam Navigation Co India* [1962] A.C. 60 (but the bill is not even prima facie evidence as to the weight or contents of the packages; see also *The Frank Pais* [1986] 1 Lloyd's Rep. 529 at 533.

[33] See *ante*, para. 15–025.

[34] Rules, Art. III, r.4, second sentence.

[35] As is a bill signed by the Master under The Carriage of Goods by Sea Act 1992, s. 4, see *post*, para. 15–052.

[36] *Grant* v. *Norway* (1851) 10 C.B. 665.

[37] See *post*, para. 15–052.

[38] See Chap. 27.

[39] *The Nea Tyhi* [1982] 1 Lloyd's Rep. 606.

shipped from Port Kelang in Malaysia to Newport in the United Kingdom, the bill of lading, signed by charterer's agents, stated that the goods were shipped below deck whereas they were actually shipped on deck. The plywood was damaged by rain-water. The buyers contended that they would never have accepted bills claused "shipped on deck" because it was essential that the goods be kept dry during the voyage. The buyers' claim for damages against the carrier was successful. Sheen J. said[40]:

> "... the charterers' agents had ostensible authority to sign bills of lading on behalf of the master. Accordingly that signature binds the shipowners as principals to the contract contained in or evidenced by the bills of lading."

The—unauthorised—agent himself may be liable for breach of an implied warranty of authority.[41]

The bill of lading as evidence of the contract of carriage

It has long been accepted that the terms set out on the reverse of the bill of lading are only evidence of the contract of carriage as between shipper and carrier, since the contract is agreed before the bill is issued.[42] It is equally accepted that as between the carrier and a bona fide transferee, the bill of lading terms of the contract of carriage are conclusive and the carrier is estopped from adducing external evidence to the contrary.[43] **15–037**

The bill of lading as a document of title

It has been seen[44] that a principal purpose of the bill of lading is to enable the person entitled to the goods represented by the bill to dispose of the goods while they are in transit. By mercantile custom, possession of the bill is in many respects equivalent to possession of the goods[45] and the transfer of the bill of lading has normally the same effect as the delivery of the goods themselves. The bill of lading is thus a symbol of, or a key to, the goods themselves. This is why it is referred to as a document of title. **15–038**

Two points should be noted in this connection: first, the transfer of the bill of lading is merely deemed to operate as a symbolic transfer of possession of the goods, but not necessarily as a transfer of the property in them. The transfer of the bill passes such rights in the goods as the parties intend to pass. Where the consignee or indorsee of the bill is the agent of the shipper at the port of destination, it is evident that the parties, by transferring the bill of lading, intend only to pass the right to claim delivery of the goods from the carrier upon arrival of

---

[40] *ibid.* at 611. See also *The Saudi Crown* [1986] 1 Lloyd's Rep. 261.
[41] *V/O Rasnoimport v. Guthrie & Co Ltd* [1966] 1 Lloyd's Rep. 1.
[42] See *The Ardennes* [1951] 1 K.B. 55; *Choyang Shipping Co Ltd v. Coral (U.K.) Ltd* [1997] 2 Lloyd's Rep. 641.
[43] *Leduc v. Ward* [1888] 20 Q.B.D. 457.
[44] See *ante*, para. 15–019.
[45] The holder of the bill of lading has constructive possession of the goods; the actual possession is with the carrier as long as the goods are in his charge.

the goods, but not the property in them. Where the consignee or indorsee is a banker who advances money on the security of the goods represented by the bill, the parties are likely to intend, by the transfer of the bill, the creation of a charge or pledge on the goods in favour of the banker, but not the transfer of the property in them to him, although the pledgee can demand delivery of the goods and then sell them. In the seller and buyer relationship, the rules relating to the passing of property apply.[46] Whether the property in the goods shall pass on the transfer of the bill of lading depends on the intention of the parties. Often this will be the case as the seller in a c.i.f. contract (and other types of international sales) will have this intention, but it may be recalled that taking out a bill of lading in the name of the buyer does not necessarily reveal the seller's intention of passing the property to him.[47]

Secondly, only a person holding a bill of lading is entitled to claim delivery of the goods from the carrier. The carrier is protected if he delivers the goods to the holder of the first original bill presented to him—even if it is only one in a set[48]—and need not inquire into the title of the holder of the bill or the whereabouts of the other parts of the bill. The bill of lading retains its character of document of title until the contract of carriage by sea is discharged by delivery of the goods against the bill,[49] and the carrier is not responsible for wrongful delivery of the goods against the bill unless he knows of the defect in the title of the holder. If the carrier (or his agent) delivers the goods to a person who is not the holder of the bill of lading, he does so at his peril. If that person is not the true owner, the carrier is liable to the latter for conversion of the goods. In practice, carriers normally rigorously insist on the production of a bill of lading, but, where the bill is produced and the identity of the consignee is in doubt or in other exceptional cases,[50] they sometimes deliver the goods against letters of indemnity which, in some instances, have to be provided by a bank.

The difficulties which can arise when the carrier releases the goods without insisting on the production of the bill of lading, are demonstrated by *Sze Hai Tong Bank v. Rambler Cycle Co Ltd*[51] In that case an English company had sold

---

[46] See *ante*, paras 4–004 to 4–006.

[47] *The Kronprinsessan Margareta* [1921] 1 A.C. 486 at 517. For the right of the consignor to sue when the bill of lading has been transferred to the consignee or an indorsee, see *post*, para. 15–052.

[48] See *ante*, para. 15–003. In *Motis Exports Ltd v. Dampskibsselskabet AF1912, Aktieselskab* [1999] 1 Lloyd's Rep. 837 it was held that a shipowner who delivered goods on presentation of a forged bill of lading was liable to the holder of the genuine bill. It was no defence to be deceived into delivering the goods since he could not be held liable for refusing to deliver them against a forged bill.

[49] *Barclays Bank Ltd v. Commissioners of Customs and Excise* [1963] 1 Lloyd's Rep. 81 (the bill does not lose its character of document of title by "exhaustion", *i.e.* by non-presentation immediately on arrival of the ship).

[50] In the oil trade the goods sometimes arrive before the bills of lading are in the hands of the last indorsee. The reason is that the bills are traded in string contracts. In these cases the carrier may release the goods against a bank indemnity but he does so at his risk.

[51] [1959] A.C. 576. See also *Chabbra Corporation Pte Ltd v. Jag Shakti (Owners); The Jag Shakti* [1986] A.C. 337; *Glebe Island Terminals Pty Ltd v. Continental Seagram Pty Ltd; The Antwerpen* [1994] 1 Lloyd's Rep. 213; *SA Sucre Export v. Northern River Shipping Ltd; The Somovskiy 3068* [1994] 2 Lloyd's Rep. 266; *Kuwait Petroleum Corp v. I & D Oil Carriers Ltd; The Houda* [1994] 2 Lloyd's Rep. 541; *MB Pyramid Sound NV v. Briese Shiffahrts GmbH; The Ines* [1995] 2 Lloyd's Rep. 144.

bicycle parts to importers in Singapore; the goods were shipped in the S.S. Glengarry, which belonged to the Glen Line Ltd. The sellers instructed the Bank of China to collect the proceeds and release the bills of lading to the buyers on payment. The buyers, however, induced the carriers to deliver the goods to them without bills of lading on an indemnity given by the buyers and their bank, the Sze Hai Tong Bank. When the sellers discovered what had happened, they brought proceedings in the courts of Singapore against the carriers for damages for breach of contract and conversion, and the carriers brought in as third parties the Sze Hai Tong Bank, against which the carriers claimed a declaration of indemnity. The High Court of Singapore held the carriers to be liable and held further that the bank was obliged to indemnify them. The bank appealed without success to the Court of Appeal in Singapore and eventually to the Judicial Committee of the Privy Council. Lord Denning, who gave the judgment of the court, said[52]:

> "It is perfectly clear that a shipowner who delivers without production of the bill of lading does so at his peril. The contract is to deliver, on production of the bill of lading, to the person entitled under the bill of lading. ... The shipping company did not deliver the goods to any such person. They are therefore liable for breach of contract unless there is some term in the bill of lading protecting them. And they delivered the goods, without production of the bill of lading, to a person who was not entitled to receive them. They are, therefore, liable in conversion unless likewise protected."

The Judicial Committee rejected the argument that the carriers, and consequently the bank, were relieved from liability by a clause in the bill of lading that the responsibility of the carriers should cease absolutely after the goods were discharged from the ship, because that exemption clause was not intended to protect a carrier who deliberately disregarded his obligation and committed a fundamental breach of contract by releasing the goods without production of a bill of lading.

On the other hand, even the true owner of the goods cannot claim the goods if unable to produce a bill of lading. In one case[53] a Canadian company bought six trucks and certain spare parts from a seller in England. The seller shipped the goods from Southampton to Montreal and paid the freight but the carriers refused to deliver the bills of lading (which were duly drawn up and signed) to the seller until he paid them certain shipping charges incurred in respect of previous shipments. The carriers, who alleged to have a general lien on the bills of lading, forwarded them to their agents at Montreal with instructions to hold them until they sanctioned their release. The Canadian company claimed to be the owners of the goods and applied to the English court for an interim injunction ordering the carriers to deliver the goods to them without production of a bill of lading. The Court of Appeal refused to make such an order. Denning L.J. said[54]: "Whether the property has passed or not, in my opinion, they [the buyers] ought to produce the bills of lading duly endorsed in order to make a good title

---

[52] [1959] A.C. 576 at 586.
[53] *Trucks & Spares Ltd v. Maritime Agencies (Southampton) Ltd* [1951] 2 All E.R. 982.
[54] *ibid.*, at 983.

at this stage", and Lloyd-Jacob J. observed[55]: "A decision affirming title at this stage may create grave injustice to some person or persons acquiring a title through the bills of lading in ignorance of the circumstances with which this action is concerned."

However, subject to the terms of the contract, the master may deliver the goods without presentation of a bill of lading, provided that he is reasonably satisfied that the person requesting the goods is entitled to them and there is a reasonable explanation for the absence of the bill.[56]

In the oil cargo trade the strict requirement that an original bill of lading must be produced on arrival of the goods sometimes appears to be treated with laxity. If the tanker is on a time charter and the charterer instructs the master to deliver the cargo to a party who cannot produce a bill of lading, the master is entitled to refuse compliance with the instructions. However, if, without reason to suspect that anything is wrong, he complies with them and the owner of the cargo suffers a loss, the shipowner, who normally would have to bear responsibility as principal of the master, can claim indemnity from the charterer who has given the unlawful order.[57]

Logically, the function of the bill of lading as a document of title is distinct from its negotiable quality.[58] Even a bill of lading which is not made negotiable operates as a document of title, because the consignee named therein can only claim delivery of the goods from the shipowner if able to produce the bill of lading. However, the great practical value of the bill of lading as a means of making goods in transit rapidly transferable is due to the customary combination of the two features of the bill, namely its quasi-negotiability and its function as a document of title.

Indemnities and bills of lading

15–039 It has already been observed[59] that a difficult situation develops if the carrier feels compelled to refuse the issue of a clean bill of lading. Where payment is arranged under a letter of credit, the exporter will be unable to obtain finance from the bank if he presents a claused, instead of a clean, bill. On the other hand, the carrier who issues a clean bill although he knows that the goods are not in apparent good order and condition when shipped or received for shipment, is estopped from denying as against the bona fide consignee or assignee that he received the goods in such condition and might be liable to him.[60]

The obvious way out of this difficulty is for the exporter to offer the carrier an indemnity, under which the exporter will recompense him for any loss sus-

---

[55] *ibid.*, at 984.
[56] *SA Sucre Export v. Northern River Shipping; The Sormovskiy 3068* [1994] 2 Lloyd's Rep. 266.
[57] *A/S Hansen-Tangens Rederi III v. Total Transport Corporation; The Sagona* [1984] 1 Lloyd's Rep. 194.
[58] See *ante*, para. 15–024. The quality of the bill of lading as a document of title originates in the custom of the merchants and was first recognised by the courts in *Lickbarrow v. Mason* (1794) 5 T.R. 683; the character of the bill of lading as a quasi-negotiable instrument is derived from the Bills of Lading Act 1855.
[59] See *ante*, para. 15–036.
[60] *ibid.*

tained as the result of the issue of a clean bill of lading. Such indemnity, however, does not provide a solution in all circumstances. If both parties, the exporter and the carrier, know that the clean bill for which the indemnity is given should never have been issued in view of the condition of the cargo, they have conspired to defraud the bona fide consignee or indorsee, who will take up the bill and part with his money, thinking that the goods did not show any defect when shipped or received for shipment. Such fraud vitiates the indemnity and renders it illegal; the carrier cannot claim under it against the exporter and, from the carrier's point of view, such indemnity is completely worthless. Not all indemnities given for clean bills of lading are illegal. Two cases have to be distinguished: the clausing of the bill may concern a technicality which, as the exporter well knows, does not entitle the buyer to reject the goods; in this case the tender of an indemnity is legitimate and convenient. Only if the clausing of the bill concerns a serious matter which would entitle the buyer to reject the goods, is the indemnity tainted by fraud[61] and invalid. The proper course for the exporter here is to inform the buyer at once of the true facts and to ask him to amend the credit and to authorise the bank to pay against the bills of lading as issued. These principles were stated in *Brown, Jenkinson & Co Ltd v. Percy Dalton (London) Ltd*[62] where the majority of the Court of Appeal held that an indemnity was invalid which was given by the exporters (the defendants) to the plaintiffs, who were loading brokers for the shipowners. The cargo consisted of 100 barrels of orange juice and the tally clerk had described the casks on his tally card as "old and frail" and recorded some leaking, but the plaintiffs, on the request of the defendants, had issued clean bills of lading against the defendant's indemnity. Pearce L.J. said[63]:

> "Trust is the foundation of trade; and bills of lading are important documents . . . In trivial matters and in cases of bona fide dispute where the difficulty of ascertaining the correct state of affairs is out of proportion to its importance, no doubt the practice [of accepting indemnities] is useful. But here the plaintiffs went outside those reasonable limits . . . Recklessness is sufficient to make a man liable in damages for fraud. Here the plaintiffs intended their misrepresentation to deceive, although they did not intend that the party deceived should ultimately go without just compensation."

For some time London banks have by mutual consent refused to issue and countersign indemnities required to obtain clean bills of lading.[64]

An indemnity given to the carrier in order to induce him to deliver the goods to the consignee without production of the bill of lading, although in some instances equally reprehensible, is valid and enforceable by the carrier, as has been seen from the discussion of *Sze Hai Tong Bank v. Rambler Cycle Co Ltd.*[65]

---

[61] A consignee or indorsee of a fraudulently issued clean bill of lading can sue for fraudulent misrepresentation: *Cordova Land Co Ltd v. Victor Brothers Inc* [1966] 1 W.L.R. 793 at 800.
[62] [1957] 2 Q.B. 621. Referred to with approval in the Indian case of *Ellerman & Bucknall Steamship Co v. Sha Misrimal* [1966] All India Rep. 1892.
[63] [1957] 2 Q.B. 621 at 639.
[64] [1957] J.B.L. 173.
[65] [1959] A.C. 576, see *ante*, para. 15–038 for discussion of this case; see also *The Delfini* [1990] 1 Lloyd's Rep. 252 and *The Houda* [1994] 2 Lloyd's Rep. 541.

The carrier is not obliged to deliver the goods against an indemnity in the absence of the bill of lading[66] unless the contract so provides.[67]

The limitation period for an action for an indemnity can be brought within the time allowed by the law of the court seized of the case.[68] In English law the limitation period for a claim founded on a simple contract is six years after the cause of action accrued.[69]

Charterparty indemnity

15–040 The charterparty usually provides that the charterer shall indemnify the shipowner against all liabilities that may arise from the signing of the bills of lading in accordance with the directions of the charterer. Consequently, even if the shipowner is liable to the holder of the bill of lading, he can pass on this liability under the indemnity clause in the charterparty to the charterer.[70]

THE LIABILITY OF THE CARRIER

15–041 The responsibilities of the carrier in respect of the safety of the goods entrusted to his care are described in detail in the Hague–Visby Rules,[71] Article III:

> "1.   The carrier shall be bound, before and at the beginning of the voyage, to exercise due diligence to—
>
> (a) Make the ship seaworthy.
> (b) Properly man, equip and supply the ship.
> (c) Make the holds, refrigerating and cool chambers, and all other parts of the ship in which goods are carried, fit and safe for their reception, carriage and preservation.
>
> 2.   Subject to the provisions of Article IV, the carrier shall properly and carefully load, handle, stow, carry, keep, care for and discharge the goods carried."

The principle underlying these provisions is that the shipowner is only liable if he is negligent. This is clearly expressed by the words, in rule 1, enjoining the shipowner "to exercise due diligence", and, in rule 2, postulating that he should act "properly and carefully". The responsibilities of the shipowner under the Act are thus lighter than they are at common law, though this is compensated for by the provision that he cannot contract out of the Rules.[72] In particular, at common law the shipowner is under an absolute obligation to provide a seaworthy ship, *i.e.* a ship that in all respects is fit to load, carry and discharge the cargo safely, having regard to the ordinary perils encountered on the voyage.

---

[66] *The Houda* [1994] 2 Lloyd's Rep. 541.

[67] *The Delfni* [1990] 1 Lloyd's Rep. 252.

[68] Hague-Visby Rules Art. III, r. 6 *bis*, *post*, para. 15–048.

[69] Limitation Act 1980, s.5. If the indemnity is given by deed, it would be 12 years (Limitation Act 1980, s.8).

[70] The shipowner's claim for indemnity against the charterer frequently gives rise to disputes; a consideration of these cases is outside the ambit of this work.

[71] The Rules are commented upon in detail in Scrutton, *op. cit.*, section XX.

[72] Art. III, r.8.

Under the Carriage of Goods by Sea Act 1971, he is only responsible if he fails, upon reasonable inspection, to discover the lack of seaworthiness of his ship.[73] "Under the old rule, the only relevant question was whether the ship was seaworthy or unseaworthy. That rule was no doubt well adapted to more simple days when ships were not very complicated wooden structures . . . but in modern times, when ships are complicated steel structures full of complex machinery, the old unqualified rule imposed too serious an obligation on carriers by sea . . . he is to be liable for all such duties as appertain to a prudent and careful carrier acting as such by the servants and agents in his employment."[74]

Seaworthiness, within the meaning of Article III, Rule 1(a) (and in common law) includes cargoworthiness. Consequently the vessel is unseaworthy if its condition before loading the cargo constitutes a major and permanent obstacle to the completion of the contract voyage. A vessel is unseaworthy if before loading it is infested with insects and for this reason the discharge of the cargo is prohibited by the authorities at the port of destination.[75] However, the concept of unseaworthiness cannot be extended to cover *activities* which might damage the cargo, rather than the *intrinsic attributes* of the ship which threaten the cargo.[76]

The provisions of Article III, Rule 1 are overriding; thus where the shipper, contrary to Article IV, Rule 6,[77] does not warn the shipowner of the dangerous nature of the goods shipped, the shipowner cannot claim indemnity from the shipper.[78]

The obligation of the carrier to use due diligence in the cases stated in Article III, Rules 1 and 2 is not limited to his personal diligence. He is liable if servants and agents[79] in his employment fail to act with due diligence[80] and he has been even held liable for a reputable independent contractor whom he instructed to repair his ship and whose workman acted negligently, although neither the shipowner himself, nor his servants and agents, were guilty of any negligence.[81] Under Article III, Rules 1 and 2 the carrier is liable for the negligence of his

---

[73] s.3. On the duty of the carrier to use due dililgence to make the ship seaworthy see *per* Sheen J. in *The Tilia Gorthon* [1985] 1 Lloyd's Rep. 552.

[74] *Per* Wright J. in *W. Angliss & Co (Australia) Proprietary v. Peninsular and Oriental Steam Navigation Co* [1927] 2 K.B. 456 at 461; *Ministry of Food v. Lamport and Holt Line Ltd* [1952] 2 Lloyd's Rep. 371; *International Packers London Ltd v. Ocean S.S. Co Ltd* [1955] 2 Lloyd's Rep. 218 at 236; *Riverstone Meat Co Pty Ltd v. Lancashire Shipping Co Ltd; The Muncaster Castle* [1961] A.C. 807; *Union of India v. NV Reederij Amsterdam, The Amstelslot* [1963] 2 Lloyd's Rep. 223; *Albacora SRL v. Westcott & Laurance Line Ltd; The Maltasian* [1966] 2 Lloyd's Rep. 53; *The Flowergate* [1967] 1 Lloyd's Rep. 1 at 7; *The Torenia* [1983] 2 Lloyd's Rep. 210.

[75] *Empresa Cubana Importadora de Alimentos "Alimport" v. Iasmos Shipping Co SA; The Good Friend* [1984] 2 Lloyd's Rep. 586. But there is no unseaworthiness within the Rules where the vessel, as such, is seaworthy and had only to be lightened to get through the Panama Canal: *Actis Co Ltd v. The Sanko Steamship Co Ltd; The Aquacharm* [1982] 1 Lloyd's Rep. 7.

[76] *A. Meredith Jones & Co Ltd v. Vangemar Shipping Co Ltd; The Apostolis* [1997] 2 Lloyd's Rep. 241.

[77] See *post*, para. 15–050.

[78] *Mediterranean Freight Services Ltd v. BP Oil International Ltd; The Fiona* [1994] 2 Lloyd's Rep. 506.

[79] On the protection of servants and agents by the Rules, see *post*, para. 15–047.

[80] See the cases referred to in n.74, *ante*.

[81] *Riverstone Meat Co Pty Ltd v. Lancashire Shipping Co Ltd; The Muncaster Castle* [1961] A.C. 807.

servants and agents. This is an important extension of his liability and should be contrasted with Article IV, Rule 2(a) which provides that the carrier is not liable for the neglect or the fault of his servants in the navigation or management of the ship. On the other hand, a servant or agent of the carrier—but not an independent contractor[82]—if sued, is entitled to the same defences and limits of liability which the carrier may invoke under the Rules.[83]

The liability of the carrier for the negligent acts or omissions of his servants exists not only in the cases listed in Article III, Rule 1 but also in those mentioned in Article III, Rule 2. Thus, carriers were held liable to owners of a cargo of maize for damage caused by bad stowage. Above the maize, which was carried mostly in bulk in a lower hold, a cargo of tallow in casks was carried. During the voyage some of the casks were broken and the tallow, which became heated, began to leak and penetrate to the hold in which the maize was stowed, causing it damage.[84] Carriers were likewise held liable for damage caused during the loading operation by the negligence of their servants[85]; for the destruction, of the goods by negligently caused fire, after they were loaded but before the ship sailed[86]; and for the loss of a tractor carried on deck without specific agreement with the shipper that it should be deck cargo, which was washed overboard because it was not properly secured.[87] In contrast, carriers did not act negligently and were not held to be responsible when in an intermediate port, in spite of a careful watch, the cover plate of a storm valve in a hold was stolen by stevedores during unloading and loading and sea water damaged the cargo in the hold on the continued voyage.[88] But if the master, when stowing the goods, follows strictly the instructions of the shipper's agent (who acts within his authority), the shipper may be estopped by conduct from asserting that the stowage was defective.[89]

The carrier is practically bound to play some part in the loading operation but the scope and area of the part which he has to play is determined by the contract of the parties, and may further depend upon the custom and practice of the port and the nature of the cargo. The phrase "shall properly and carefully load" in Article III, Rule 2 is not designed to define the scope and area of the carrier's part in the loading operation but defines the terms on which that service is to be performed.[90] Thus, where goods sold under an f.o.b. contract and loaded from the quay in the ship's tackle were damaged by the negligence of the carrier's servants before they crossed the ship's rail (they were dropped on the quay), the carriers were liable because *under the contract of carriage* in question they were

---

[82] Art. IV *bis*, r.2. See *post*, para. 15–047.
[83] *ibid.*
[84] *Ministry of Food v. Lamport and Holt Line Ltd.* [1952] 2 Lloyd's Rep. 371.
[85] *Pyrene Co Ltd v. Scindia Navigation Co Ltd* [1954] 2 Q.B. 402; see *ante*, para. 2–007.
[86] *Maxine Footwear Co Ltd v. Canadian Government Merchant Marine Ltd* [1959] A.C. 589.
[87] *Svenska Traktor Akt v. Maritime Agencies (Southampton) Ltd* [1953] 2 Q.B. 295.
[88] *Leesh River Tea Co Ltd v. British India Steam Navigation Co Ltd; The Chyebassa* [1966] 1 Lloyd's Rep. 450.
[89] *Ismael v. Polish Ocean Lines* [1976] Q.B. 893.
[90] *G. H. Renton & Co Ltd v. Palmyra Trading Corporation of Panama; The Caspiana* [1957] A.C. 149; *Balli Trading Ltd v. Afalona Shipping Co Ltd; The Coral* [1993] 1 Lloyd's Rep. 1.

responsible for the *whole* of the loading, and not only for the part following the crossing of the rail.[91]

The duty of the carrier properly and carefully to discharge the goods carried, which is stipulated in Article III, Rule 2, is normally ended when the goods are delivered from the ship to a person entitled to receive them[92] in the same apparent order and condition as on shipment.[93] However, where they are discharged into a lighter, the shipowner continues to be liable if the goods loaded into the lighter are damaged by other cargoes stowed negligently on top of them.[94] Since the words of Article III, Rule 2 likewise define the terms on which the contract of carriage is to be performed and have no geographical connotation, they do not invalidate a clause according to which the carrier is entitled, if the port of discharge is strikebound, to discharge the goods at any other safe and convenient port[95]; the costs of on-carriage to the agreed port of discharge have to be borne by the shipper.

Any term in a contract of carriage which seeks to relieve or lessen the carrier's liability in respect of the goods is null and void by virtue of Article III, Rule 8.[96]

EXCEPTED PERILS

The Rules contain, in Article IV,[97] a "long list of matters in respect of loss or damage arising or resulting from which the carrier is not liable".[98] This Article provides in Rules 1 and 2: **15–042**

> "1.   Neither the carrier nor the ship shall be liable for loss or damage arising or resulting from unseaworthiness unless caused by want of due diligence on the part of the carrier to make the ship seaworthy, and to secure that the ship is properly manned, equipped and supplied, and to make the holds, refrigerating and cool chambers and all other parts of the ship in which goods are carried fit and safe for their reception, carriage and preservation in accordance with the provisions of paragraph 1 of Article III. Whenever loss or damage has resulted from unseaworthiness the burden of proving the exercise of due diligence shall be on the carrier or other person claiming exemption under this article.
>
> 2.   Neither the carrier nor the ship shall be responsible for loss or damage arising or resulting from—

---

[91] *Pyrene Co Ltd v. Scindia Navigation Co Ltd* [1954] 2 Q.B. 402; see para. 2–007.

[92] *Sze Hai Tong Bank Ltd v. Rambler Cycle Co Ltd* [1959] 2 Lloyd's Rep. 114 at 120.

[93] *Per* Wright J. in *Gosse Millard v. Canadian Government Merchant Marine; American Can Co v. Same* [1927] 2 K.B. 432 at 434.

[94] *Per* Roche J. in *Goodwin, Ferreira & Co Ltd v. Lamport and Holt Ltd* (1920) 34 Ll.L.R. 192 at 194; see also *East & West Steamship Co v. Hossain Brothers* [1968] 2 Lloyd's Rep. 145 at 149 (Pakistan Sup.Ct.).

[95] *G. H. Renton & Co Ltd v. Palmyra Trading Corporation of Panama; The Caspiana* [1957] A.C. 149.

[96] *The Saudi Prince (No. 2)* [1988] 1 Lloyd's Rep. 1. But in the case of a freight receipt, which is not governed by the Hague-Visby Rules, such exclusion might be possible if the general law so allows; see *Browner International Transport Ltd v. Monarch S.S. Company Ltd; The European Enterprise* [1989] 2 Lloyd's Rep. 185.

[97] Article IV (which comprises six Rules and is followed by Article IV *bis* is too long to be produced here in full; the solution of a practical problem requires the examination of the whole Article.

[98] *Per* Wright J. in *Gosse Millard v. Canadian Government Merchant Marine* [1927] 2 K.B. 432 at 434.

(a) Act, neglect, or default of the master, mariner, pilot, or the servants of the carrier in the navigation or in the management of the ship.

(b) Fire, unless caused by the actual fault or privity of the carrier.

(c) Perils, dangers and accidents of the sea or other navigable waters.

(d) Act of God.

(e) Act of war.

(f) Act of public enemies.

(g) Arrest or restraint of princes, rulers or people, or seizure under legal process.

(h) Quarantine restrictions.

(i) Act or omission of the shipper or owner of the goods, his agent or representative.

(j) Strikes or lockouts or stoppage or restraint of labour from whatever cause, whether partial or general.

(k) Riots and civil commotions.

(l) Saving or attempting to save life or property at sea.

(m) Wastage in bulk or weight or any other loss or damage arising from inherent defect, quality or vice of the goods.

(n) Insufficiency of packing.

(o) Insufficiency or inadequacy of marks.

(p) Latent defects not discoverable by due diligence.

(q) Any other cause arising without the actual fault or privity of the carrier, or without the fault or neglect of the agents or servants of the carrier, but the burden of proof shall be on the person claiming the benefit of this exception to show that neither the actual fault or privity of the carrier nor the fault or neglect of the agents or servants of the carrier contributed to the loss or damage.

The burden of proof

15–043   Under Article IV, Rule 1 the burden is on the cargo-owner to establish that the ship was unseaworthy *and* that the unseaworthiness caused loss or damage to the cargo.[99] The burden then shifts to the carrier to prove due diligence in respect of the ship's seaworthiness.[1] However, if the ship is unseaworthy resulting in loss or damage to the goods, the effect of Article III, Rule 1 is that the shipowner is deprived of reliance on the Article IV, Rule 2 exceptions[2] but may still limit his liability.[3]

It is for the shipowner to establish that the loss or damage comes within an Article IV, Rule 2 exception and then for the cargo-owner to prove negligence[4], except in cases within (a) or (b) which provide for negligence or fault and (q) where the burden is on the shipowner to disprove negligence.[5] Among the grounds on which the shipowner will frequently try to rely, is inherent defect of the cargo (Art. IV, Rule 2(m)).[6]

The burden of proof causes problems in cases of short delivery, *i.e.* if a smaller quantity of a cargo is unloaded than was loaded according to a (clean) bill of lading. This is a not uncommon event in the transportation of oil in bulk.

---

[99] *Minister of Food v. Reardon Smith Line Ltd* [1951] 2 Lloyd's Rep. 265; *Kuo International Oil v. Daisy Shipping Co; The Yamatogawa* [1990] 2 Lloyd's Rep. 39.

[1] *Phillips Petroleum Co v. Cabanali Naviera SA; The Theodegmon* [1990] 1 Lloyd's Rep. 52; *The Antigoni* [1991] 1 Lloyd's Rep. 9.

[2] *Maxine Footwear v. Canadian Government Merchant Marine* [1959] A.C. 589.

[3] Art. IV, r.5 see *post*, para. 15–045.

[4] *The Theodegmon, supra.*

[5] Scrutton *op. cit.*, p. 446.

[6] *Albacora SRL v. Westcott & Laurance Line Ltd; The Maltasian* [1966] 2 Lloyd's Rep. 53; *The Flowergate* [1967] 1 Lloyd's Rep. 1 at 7; *Chris Foodstuffs (1963) Ltd v. Nigerian National Shipping Line; The Amadu Bello* [1967] 1 Lloyd's Rep. 293 (concealed pre-shipment damage).

In such a case the onus of proving the shortage falls on the cargo owner who will normally be the plaintiff,[7] but he need not prove the cause of the shortage, which, in any event, may be speculative.[8]

Excepted perils and insurance

From the point of view of the shipper, the catalogue of exceptions is not so **15–044** disconcerting as would appear at first glance. A comparison of the catalogue with Lloyd's Marine Policy and the Institute Cargo Clauses A, B and C supplementing it[9] shows that some exceptions, which are not based on the carrier's neglect (such as fire damage to the cargo aboard), are covered by these standard clauses. If they are not covered by them, additional insurance, at the cost of a further premium, can always be obtained. It is of great practical importance for the shipper to make certain that the clauses of his contract of carriage and contract of marine insurance are duly co-ordinated. Risks which the shipper has to bear under the contract of carriage should be covered by his marine insurance policy. Bills of lading sometimes contain a clause drawing the attention of the shipper to the necessity of obtaining adequate insurance cover.

Maximum limits of shipowner's liability

The Hague-Visby Rules provide in Article IV, Rule 5 the following maximum **15–045** limits for the carrier's liability for damage to or loss of the goods shipped:

"(a) Unless the nature and value of such goods have been declared by the shipper before shipment and inserted in the bill of lading, neither the carrier nor the ship shall in any event be or become liable for any loss or damage to or in connection with the goods in an amount exceeding 666.67 units of account[10] per package or unit or 2 units of account per kilogramme of gross weight of the goods lost or damaged, whichever is the higher.

(b) The total amount recoverable shall be calculated by reference to the value of such goods at the place and time at which the goods are discharged from the ship in accordance with the contract or should have been so discharged.

The value of the goods shall be fixed according to the commodity exchange price, or, if there be no such price, according to the current market price, or, if there be no commodity exchange price or current market price, by reference to the normal value of goods of the same kind and quality.

(c) Where a container, pallet or similar article of transport is used to consolidate goods, the number of packages or units enumerated in the bill of lading as packed in such article of transport shall be deemed the number of packages or units for the purpose of this paragraph as far as these packages or units are concerned. Except as aforesaid such article of transport shall be considered the package or unit.

(d) The unit of account mentioned in this Article is the special drawing right as defined by the International Monetary Fund. The amounts mentioned in sub-paragraph (a) of this paragraph shall be converted into the national currency on the basis of the value of that currency on a date to be determined by the law of the court seized of the case.[11]

---

[7] *Amoco Oil Co v. Parpada Shipping Co Ltd; The George S.* [1987] 2 Lloyd's Rep. 69.
[8] *BP International Ltd v. Surena Delmar Navegacion SA; The Irini M* [1988] 1 Lloyd's Rep. 253.
[9] See *post*, para. 19–018.
[10] The units of account are the SDRs of the International Monetary Fund, as is stated in Art. IV, r.5(d); see below in the text.
[11] These references to units of account were substituted for provisions relating to the "Poincare gold franc" by (now) section 314 of the Merchant Shipping Act 1995, Schedule 13 para 45, inserting section 1A in the Carriage of Goods by Sea Act 1971 which gave effect to the 1979 Protocol. It

(e) Neither the carrier nor the ship shall be entitled to the benefit of the limitation of liability provided for in this paragraph if it is proved that the damage resulted from an act or omission of the carrier done with intent to cause damage, or recklessly and with knowledge that damage would probably result.

(f) The declaration mentioned in sub-paragraph (a) of this paragraph, if embodied in the bill of lading, shall be prima facie evidence, but shall not be binding or conclusive on the carrier."

In the United Kingdom the value of the SDRs mentioned in sub-paragraph (a) of Article IV, Rule 5 is ascertained by conversion into pounds sterling on a daily basis.[12]

The maximum limits provided by the Rules for the carrier's liability are not of an absolute character. They may be *increased* by agreement of the parties or by declaration of the nature and value of the shipped goods by the shipper before shipment, *and* insertion of the declaration in the bill of lading.[13] However, the maximum limits for the liability of the carrier cannot, by agreement, be *reduced* below the limits provided in Rule 5(a) of Article IV.[14]

Where the declared value of the goods is embodied in the bill, the shipper may, in case of damage or loss due to other than excepted perils, claim damages in excess of the maximum limits. The measure of damages is the loss actually suffered by the shipper, and it is open to the carrier to prove that that loss is smaller than the value of the goods stated in the bill.

The shipper who wishes to hold the carrier liable in excess of the statutory maximum limit should note that two conditions have to be satisfied, namely the declaration of the nature and value of the goods, and the insertion of these particulars in the bill. In one case,[15] the shipper had satisfied the first condition, but the value of the goods was not embodied in the bill. MacKinnon J. said: "Though the plaintiffs did declare the value of the goods before shipment, that was not inserted in the bill of lading; and in those circumstances only one of the conditions on which the defendants could be liable for more than £100 was fulfilled", and ruled that the maximum limits applied.[16] Where the parties arrange for the carrier's liability in excess of the maximum limits, the freight rate is higher than in the case where the limits apply.

The carrier can plead the maximum limits of liability not only against the party to the contract of carriage by sea and his assignee but, in the case of an f.o.b. (buyer contracting with carrier) contract,[17] also against the seller who loads the goods on board a ship contracted for and nominated by the buyer, if the

---

was held in *The Rosa S* [1989] 2 W.L.R. 162, that the original reference to gold franc in the Rules was to the gold value converted into sterling.

[12] The conversion value of an SDR on a particular day can be ascertained from a bank or by reference to the financial press. If necessary, a certificate by or on behalf of the Treasury can be obtained which shall be conclusive evidence of the equivalent sterling value on a particular day, section 1A(2) of the Act.

[13] Art. IV, r.5(a) and (f).

[14] Art. IV, r.5(g). See also Art. III, r.8 and *The Hollandia* (also called *The Morviken*) [1983] A.C. 565; see *ante*, para. 15–021.

[15] *Pendle & Rivet Ltd v. Ellerman Lines Ltd* [1927] 29 Ll. L. Rep. 133.

[16] On the date when this case was decided £100 was the maximum limit of the carrier's liability under the Hague Rules.

[17] See *ante*, para. 2–007.

goods are damaged by the negligence of the shipowner's servants before they cross the ship's rail.[18]

The package limitation of Article IV, Rule 5(a) cannot be relied upon by the shipowner if, without agreement of the cargo owner, he carries delicate equipment of the latter on deck (and not below it) and as the result of this breach of his obligations the cargo is damaged.[19]

Where the maximum limits apply, the liability of the carrier may be calculated per package or unit or per gross weight, whichever is higher. "Package", in the words of a former Lord Chief Justice,[20] "must indicate something packed". Therefore, a car put on a ship without a box, crate or any form of covering is not a package.[21] The reference to "unit" is to freight units in use in various trades, for instance in the case of bulk shipment of grain. If the measure of damages is calculated on the number of packages or units, their weight is irrelevant.

Where the bill of lading lists containers "said to contain" a specified number of separately packed items, the parcels and not the containers constituted the relevant unit, but the bill of lading was not conclusive and it was for the cargo-owner to establish by extrinsic evidence the number of parcels loaded.[22]

In two cases the protective provisions of the Rules do not operate. First, *as against the carrier*, he (and the ship) cannot rely on the maximum limits of liability if it is proved that the damage resulted from an act or omission of the carrier done with intent to cause damage, or recklessly and with knowledge that damage would probably result.[23] Secondly, as *against the shipper* where he has knowingly misstated in the bill of lading the nature or value of the goods, he cannot hold the carrier or the ship responsible for loss or damage to the goods[24] unless the master, on inspection, could have noticed the misstatement and failed to clause the bill of lading.[25]

However, against a claim of deliberate misappropriation of the cargo, the carrier may rely on the one-year time bar for commencing action in Article III, r.6.[26]

Article IV *bis*(1) provides that the defences and limits of liability apply to actions both in contract and tort.

---

[18] *Pyrene Co Ltd v. Scindia Navigation Co Ltd* [1954] 2 Q.B. 402; see para. 2–007.

[19] But this is a matter of construction of the terms in the bill of lading, see *Kenya Railways v. Antares Co Pte Ltd: The Antares (Nos. 1 and 2)* [1987] 1 Lloyd's Rep. 424; *Wibau Machinenfabric Hartman SA v. Mackinnon Mackenzie & Co; The Chanda* [1989] 2 Lloyd's Rep. 494 the learned judge, Hirst J., distinguishing *The Antares; Nelson Pine Industries Ltd v. Seatrans New Zealand Ltd; The Pembroke* [1995] 2 Lloyd's Rep. 290.

[20] Per Goddard J. in *Studebaker Distributors Ltd v. Charlton Steam Shipping Co Ltd* [1938] 1 K.B. 459 at 467.

[21] *ibid.*

[22] *The River Gurara* [1998] 1 Lloyd's Rep. 225; see also *The Atlas* [1996] 1 Lloyd's Rep. 642.

[23] Art. IV, r.5(e).

[24] Art. IV, r.5(h). *Compañía Portorafti Commerciale SA v. Ultramar Panama Inc; The Captain Gregos.*

[25] See *Naviera Mogor SA v. Société Metallurgique de Normandie; The Nogar Marin* [1988] 1 Lloyd's Rep. 412; in this case the negligence of the master (who was the servant of the shipowner) broke the chain of causation and the shipowner was estopped from raising this defence.

[26] *Compañía Portorafti Commerciale SA v. Ultramar Panama Inc; The Captain Gregos* [1990] 1 Lloyd's Rep. 310. On Art. III, r.6, see *post*, para. 15–048.

The Convention on Limitation of Liability for Maritime Claims

15–046 In addition to limiting his liability under Article 4, Rule 5 of the Rules, the shipowner may rely on the limitation provisions of the Convention on Limitation of Liability for Maritime Claims 1976 which is given the force of law by section 185 of the Merchant Shipping Act 1995. The Convention is appended to the Act as Part I of Schedule 7; Part II contains modifications for the Convention to operate in the United Kingdom.

The general limits of liability are set out in Article 6 and are expressed in Units of Account[27] in relation to the tonnage of the ship, with a higher limit for death and personal injury[28] than other loss or damage. There is a lower limit for small ships of less than 300 tons.[29]

Further, in accordance with section 186 the owner[30] of a British ship is not liable for any loss or damage caused by fire or loss by theft of gold, silver, watches or precious stones[31] unless their value was declared in the bill of lading or in writing at the time of shipment.

There is no limit or exclusion of liability "if it is proved[32] that the loss resulted from his personal act or omission, committed with the intent to cause such loss, or recklessly and with knowledge that such loss would probably result".[33]

A limitation action under the Act may be comenced and a declaration made before liability is·established or admitted.[34]

Protection of servants and agents, but not independent contractors

15–047 The question arises whether persons whom the carrier employs in the performance of his duties can, when sued by the cargo owner (*e.g.* for negligent damage to the cargo), plead the protection of the maximum limits of liability and other defences which the carrier could have pleaded under the Rules if he had been sued. The Rules admit the extension of these protective provisions to servants and agents of the carrier but not to independent contractors.[35] The Rules provide in Article IV, *bis* Rules 2–4:

> "2. If such an action is brought against a servant or agent of the carrier (such servant or agent not being an independent contractor), such servant or agent shall be entitled to avail himself of the defences and limits of liability which the carrier is entitled to invoke under these Rules.

---

[27] This is the special drawing right as defined by the International Monetary Fund: Art. 8.

[28] Except for passengers where the limit is in accordance with Art. 7. The limits of liability do not apply to crew members whose contracts of employment are governed by U.K. law: s. 185(4).

[29] Part II, para. 5.

[30] By s.186(5) "owner" includes part-owner, charterer, manager or operator of the ship and by s.186(2)(a) the liability of the master, crew member or servant is also excluded. However, a charterer is not entitled to limit claims as against a shipowner: *Aegean Sea Traders Corp v. Repsol Petroleo SA; The Aegean Sea* [1998] 2 Lloyd's Rep. 39.

[31] s.186(1)(a) and (b).

[32] The burden of proof is on the claimant: *The Captain San Luis* [1993] 2 Lloyd's Rep. 573.

[33] Art. 4.

[34] *Ultisol Transport Contractors Ltd v. Bouygues Offshore SA, The Times*, July 3, 1997.

[35] The original Hague Rules did not even admit the extension to servants and agents and the only way to protect these auxiliary persons was to insert into the bill of lading the *Himalaya* clause described *infra* in the text.

3. The aggregate of the amounts recoverable from the carrier, and such servants and agents, shall in no case exceed the limit provided for in these Rules.

4. Nevertheless, a servant or agent of the carrier shall not be entitled to avail himself of the provisions of this article, if it is proved that the damage resulted from an act or omission of the servant or agent done with intent to cause damage or recklessly and with knowledge that damage would probably result."

That independent contractors employed by the carrier are not protected by the Rules was decided in *Midland Silicones Ltd v. Scruttons Ltd.*[36] In that case the House of Lords held that stevedores (employed by the carrier) who negligently damaged cargo when unloading it, in an action for negligence brought against them by the cargo owners, could not claim the maximum limitation of liability under the contract of carriage which embodied the Hague Rules[37] because there was no privity of contract between the stevedores and the cargo owners.

If it is intended, in addition to the carrier's servants and agents, to protect independent contractors employed by the carrier or, in the case of a bill of lading governed by the original Hague Rules, to provide protection to all three categories of auxiliary persons, it is necessary to insert into the bill of lading the so-called *Himalaya* clause[38] which provides that the *carrier*, as agent of his own servants and agents (including independent contractors from time to time employed by the carrier), contracts with the cargo owner that these servants, agents and independent contractors shall be protected by the limits of liability and other defences arising from the contract of carriage. A majority of the Privy Council in *New Zealand Shipping Co Ltd v. A. M. Satterthwaite & Co Ltd; The Eurymedon*[39] held that such a clause achieved the desired effect.

However, a *Himalaya* clause in a bill of lading which provides that a third party shall have the benefit of exceptions and limitations does not extend to the benefit of an exclusive jurisdiction clause since, as a matter of construction, that provision is not an exception or limitation but creates mutual rights and obligations between the contracting parties.[40]

The law of bailment[41] has been invoked to bypass the doctrine of privity of contract.[42] In *The Pioneer Container*,[43] where the contract of carriage provided for the sub-contracting of carriage "on any terms", the Privy Council held that a

---

[36] *Scruttons Ltd v. Midland Silicones Ltd sub nom. Scruttons v. Midland Silicones Ltd* [1962] A.C. 446. Stevedores and ship's agents may be liable to the owner for loss of goods on mere acceptance of the goods for bailment; no contract or attornment is necessary: *Gilchrist Watt and Sanderson Pty Ltd v. York Products Pty Ltd* [1970] 1 W.L.R. 1262.

[37] By virtue of the U.S. Carriage of Goods by Sea Act 1936.

[38] So-called after *Adler v. Dickson; The Himalaya* [1955] 1 Q.B. 158 where in a case concerning personal injury to a passenger (she travelled in The Himalaya) it was held that an exclusion clause in favour of the carrier did not bar an action in negligence against the master of the ship. According to Pearce L.J. in the *Midland Silicones* case [1961] 1 Q.B. 106 at 128 the principles governing the liability of carriers under contracts of passage and of carriage of goods by sea are, in that respect, the same. The object of the *Himalaya* clause is to remedy the difficulties resulting from *Adler v. Dickson* for the carrier's servants, agents and independent contractors.

[39] [1975] A.C. 154; *Port Jackson Stevedoring Pty Ltd v. Salmond and Spraggon (Australia) Pty Ltd; The New York Star* [1981] 1 W.L.R. 138.

[40] *The Mahkutai* [1996] A.C. 650.

[41] See *ante*, para. 27–026.

[42] *Elder, Dempster & Co Ltd v. Paterson, Zochonis & Co Ltd* [1924] A.C. 522; *The Pioneer Container* [1994] 2 A.C. 324.

[43] [1994] 2 A.C. 324.

sub-contractor, as sub-bailee, could rely on the terms of the contract of carriage, including the exclusive jurisdiction clause.

In *The Mahkutai*,[44] Lord Goff sets out the development of the acceptance by the courts of *Himalaya* clauses and the application of the principles of agency and bailment in order to accommodate commercial need. He felt that although effective, these were technical solutions and the time could come when the courts would take the final step and recognise "a fully-fledged exception to the doctrine of privity of contract, thus escaping from all the technicalities with which courts are now faced in English law."[45]

The Law Commission has addressed the privity of contract issue in a recent Report[46] and recommended that in certain circumstances a third party should be entitled to enforce a contractual provision. Their recommendation is reflected in the Contracts (Rights of Third Parties) Bill. However, by clause 6(5), no rights are conferred on a third party in the case of a contract for the carriage of goods by sea, except that he may avail himself of an exclusion of limitation of liability in such a contract.

Notice of claim and time limit for claims for loss of or damage to the goods

15–048 The Rules provide in Article III, Rule 6 strict requirements for a claim against the carrier for loss of or damage to the goods. However, Article III, Rule 6 *bis* provides for a time limit in accordance with the law of the forum, with a three month extension if necessary in respect of a claim for indemnity, since this cannot be instituted until the main action is decided or settled, which would almost inevitably be after the expiry of the one year time bar:

> "6. Unless notice of loss or damage and the general nature of such loss or damage be given in writing to the carrier or his agent at the port of discharge before or at the time of removal of the goods into the custody of the person entitled to delivery thereof under the contract of carriage, or, if the loss or damage be not apparent, within three days, such removal shall be prima facie evidence of the delivery by the carrier of the goods as described in the bill of lading.
>
> The notice in writing need not be given if the state of the goods has at the time of their receipt been the subject of joint survey or inspection. Subject to paragraph 6 *bis* the carrier and the ship shall in any event be discharged from all liability whatsoever in respect of the goods, unless suit is brought within one year of their delivery or of the date when they should have been delivered.[47] This period may, however, be extended if the parties so agree after the cause of action has arisen.
>
> In the case of any actual or apprehended loss or damage the carrier and receiver shall give all reasonable facilities to each other for inspecting and tallying the goods.
>
> (6)*bis*. An action for indemnity against a third person may be brought even after the expiration of the year provided for in the preceding paragraph if brought within the time allowed

---

[44] *ante.*
[45] At 665.
[46] No. 242, 1996.
[47] For cases in which the period of limitation does not operate against the cargo owners, see *Goulandris Brothers v. B. Goldman & Sons Ltd* [1958] 1 Q.B. 74; *Rambler Cycle Co v. P & O Steam Navigation Co* [1968] 1 Lloyd's Rep. 42 (Malaysia Fed.C. (Appellate)). "Delivery" within Art. III, r.6 occurs when the goods are landed on the quay or at the latest when placed at the consignee's disposal: *The Beltana* [1967] 1 Lloyd's Rep. 531 (Aust.).

by the law of the court seized of the case.[48] However, the time allowed shall be not less than three months, commencing from the day when the person bringing such action for indemnity has settled the claim or has been served with process in the action against himself."

The time bar in Article III, Rule 6 is absolute, *i.e.* the claim ceases to exist.[49]

These provisions are sometimes modified in slight but significant detail by clauses in the bill of lading. Thus, the bill of lading might provide:

"The ship's protest[50] relating to facts and circumstances exempting carriers from liability duly sworn by the captain and/or one or more members of the crew will be deemed sufficient proof by parties to this bill of lading of such facts and circumstances."

In considering Article III, Rule 6 the courts have referred to the purpose behind the Rules: speedy commencement of litigation[51]; to allow fresh proceedings to be instituted after initial proceedings have been dismissed for want of prosecution would be counter to the purpose of the Rule[52]; and thus the Rule is to be interpreted purposively.[53]

The limitation period of one year is only interrupted if "suit" is brought by a competent claimant, that is, one having title to sue[54] in a competent court (which may be a foreign court).[55] Accidental misdescription of a party will not cause the suit to be invalidated,[56] nor will amendment of detail in the pleadings,[57] but an amendment to incorporate a cause of action not previously pleaded will invalidate the suit.[58]

The time limit of Article III, Rule 6 applies to claims for loss of or damage to the goods but is not restricted to physical loss or damage. It also includes loss or damage related to the goods,[59] and financial loss where the goods were

---

[48] In English law this is six years, Limitation Act 1980, s. 5. Art. III, r.6 *bis* is independent of r.6; r.6 *bis* applies if shipowner A, being under actual or potential liability to cargo-owner B, claims an indemnity by way of damages against ship or shipowner C: *China Ocean Shipping Co (Owners of Xingcheng) v. Andros (Owners of The Andros)* [1987] 1 W.L.R. 1213.

[49] *Mediterranean Freight Services Ltd v. BP Oil International Ltd; The Fiona* [1994] 2 Lloyd's Rep. 506; *Aries Tanker Corp v. Total Transport; The Aries* [1977] 1 Lloyd's Rep. 334; *Compañía Portorafti Commerciale SA v. Ultramar Panama Inc; The Captain Gregos* [1990] 1 Lloyd's Rep. 310 (an action for conversion was time-barred).

[50] Also called the master's protest, see *post*, para. 19–032.

[51] *Kenya Railways v. Antares Co Pte Ltd; The Antares (Nos. 1 and 2)* [1987] 1 Lloyd's Rep. 424 (the carrier was not deprived of his right to rely on the time limit by his unauthorised act of stowing the goods on deck); but see *Wibau Maschinenfabric Hartman SA v. Mackinnon Mackenzie & Co; The Chanda* [1989] 2 Lloyd's Rep. 494.

[52] *Fort Sterling Ltd v. South Atlantic Cargo Shipping NV; The Finnrose* [1994] 1 Lloyd's Rep. 559.

[53] *Government of Sierra Leone v. Marmaro Shipping Co. Ltd; The Amazona and Yayamaria* [1989] 2 Lloyd's Rep. 130 (defendant could not rely on the time bar where the proceedings instituted by the plaintiff were as agreed by the parties).

[54] *Transworld Oil (U.S.A.) Inc v. Minos Compañia Naviera SA; The Leni* [1992] 2 Lloyd's Rep. 48.

[55] *The Nordglimt* [1988] Q.B. 183. "Suit" includes arbitration proceedings: *The Merak* [1965] P. 223; *Nea Agrex SA v. Baltic Shipping Co Ltd* [1976] Q.B. 933 (letter to carrier requesting that an arbitrator be named fulfilled the "suit is brought" requirement); *Petredec v. Tokumaru Kaiun Co; The Sargasso* [1994] 1 Lloyd's Rep. 162. *Allianz Versicherungs Aktiengessellschaft v. Fortuna Co Inc* [1999] C.L.C. 258 (faxed notice of appointment of arbitrator sufficient).

[56] *The Leni, ante.*

[57] *The Kapetan Markos* [1986] 1 Lloyd's Rep. 211; *Continental Fertiliser Co Ltd v. Pionier Shipping CV; The Pioneer* [1995] 1 Lloyd's Rep. 223.

[58] *The Leni, supra; Payabi v. Armstel Shipping Corp Ltd; The Jay Bola* [1992] 2 Lloyd's Rep. 62.

[59] *Goulandris Bros v. B. Goldman & Sons* [1957] 2 Lloyd's Rep. 207; *Cargill International SA v. CPN Tankers (Bermuda); The OT Sonja* [1993] 2 Lloyd's Rep. 435.

never loaded.[60] It does not apply to other claims against the carrier, such as pleading unseaworthiness as a defence to a claim by the carrier for loss resulting from the shipment of dangerous goods.[61]

If it is intended to extend the limitation period provided in the Rules or in the bill of lading by agreement, great care has to be taken to establish that a clear agreement on the extension has been reached. Mere inactivity or silence by one of two parties may lead to an ambiguous situation and may raise difficult questions of estoppel.[62]

If a bill of lading issued under the Rules contains an arbitration clause, an apparent conflict occurs between the Rules and arbitration law. The Rules provide the one year time limit but the Arbitration Act 1996 provides in section 12 that the High Court shall have power to extend a time limit agreed upon in the arbitration agreement "only if satisfied" of circumstances outside the reasonable contemplation of the parties whereby an extension would be just,[63] or that one party's conduct makes it unjust to hold the other party to the strict terms of the agreed time limit. The conflict is apparent because the power of the court to extend the time limit applies only to *contractual* time limits, but the time limit in Article III, Rule 6 is a *statutory* time limit which is imposed by force of law; consequently the discretionary power under section 12 of the Arbitration Act 1966 does not enable the court to extend the one-year time limit of Article III, Rule 6.[64]

Article III, Rule 6 *bis* applies to an action for indemnity against a third party and is independent of Article III, Rule 6.[65]

GENERAL AVERAGE CLAIMS AND CONTRIBUTIONS

15–049 The law of general average, so far as it affects the rights and duties of the shipper under the contract of carriage by sea, has been discussed in the chapter on insurance[66] as a necessary preliminary to an explanation of the rules of insurance law, protecting the shipper in case of general average loss or expenditure.

Bills of lading regularly contain a clause providing that general average shall be adjusted in acccordance with the York-Antwerp Rules 1974. Sometimes, it

---

[60] *The OT Sonja, ante.*

[61] *Mediterranean Freight Services v. BP Oil International; The Fiona* [1994] 2 Lloyd's Rep. 506.

[62] *K. Lokumal & Sons (London) Ltd v. Lotte Shipping Co Pte Ltd; The August Leonhardt* [1985] 2 Lloyd's Rep. 28; see also *The Stolt Loyalty* [1993] 2 Lloyd's Rep. 281 affd [1995] 1 Lloyd's Rep. 598.

[63] *Vosnoc Ltd v. Trans Global Ltd* [1998] 1 Lloyd's Rep. 711; *cf. Grimaldi ETAL v. Sekihyo Lines Ltd, The Times,* July 20, 1998.

[64] *Kenya Railways v. Antares Co Pte Ltd; The Antares (Nos. 1 and 2)* [1987] 1 Lloyd's Rep. 424, CA. It was also held in this case that the carrier was not deprived of his right to rely on the time limit by his unauthorised act of stowing the goods on deck; but see *Wibau Maschinenfabric Hartman SA v. Mackinnon Mackenzie & Co; The Chanda.* See also *Government of Sierra Leone v. Marmaro Shipping Co Ltd; The Amazona and Yayamaria* [1989] 2 Lloyd's Rep. 130.

[65] Art. III, r.6 *bis* would apply in a situation where shipowner A, being under actual or potential liability to cargo-owner B, claims an indemnity by way of damages against ship or shipowner C: *China Ocean Shipping Co (Owners of Xingcheng) v. Andros (Owners of The Andros)* [1987] 1 W.L.R. 1213.

[66] See *post,* para. 19–028.

is added that the practice of English Average Adjusters shall apply to all points on which the Rules do not contain provisions.

DANGEROUS GOODS

Bills of lading sometimes contain a clause cautioning shippers against shipping **15–050** dangerous or damaging goods; *e.g.*:

> "Shippers are cautioned against shipping goods of a dangerous or damaging nature as by so doing they may become responsible for all consequential damage and also render themselves liable to penalties imposed by statute."

Article IV, Rule 6 of the Rules provides:

> "Goods of an inflammable, explosive or dangerous nature to the shipment whereof the carrier, master or agent of the carrier, has not consented, with knowledge of their nature and character may at any time before discharge be landed at any place or destroyed or rendered innocuous by the carrier without compensation, and the shipper of such goods shall be liable for all damages and expenses directly or indirectly arising out of or resulting from such shipment.
>
> If any such goods shipped with such knowledge and consent shall become a danger to the ship or cargo, they may in like manner be landed at any place or destroyed or rendered innocuous by the carrier without liability on the part of the carrier except to general average, if any."

The leading authority on dangerous goods is now *The Giannis NK*.[67] In this case a cargo of ground-nut extraction meal pellets was shipped, which, unknown to both the shipper and the carrier, was infested with Khapra beetle. The vessel was also carrying a cargo of wheat pellets. The beetle infestation was discovered at the port of discharge and the vessel was ordered to leave port. At a further port the vessel was ordered to return the cargo to its port of shipment or dump it at sea. Both the ground-nut and wheat cargos (although the wheat cargo was not infested) were dumped at sea and the vessel fumigated. The carriers claimed damages against the shippers for, *inter alia*, the loss caused by delay and fumigation expenses. The decision for the House of Lords was whether the infested cargo was dangerous within the meaning of Article IV, Rule 6, and if so, whether the shippers' liability was qualified by Article IV, Rule 3.[68] The bill of lading under which the goods were carried incorporated the Hague Rules but the two Rules under consideration are identical to the corresponding Hague-Visby Rules.

The House of Lords decided that the words "goods of . . . [a] dangerous nature" were to be given a broad interpretation and were not restricted to goods which were liable to cause direct physical damage, but included goods which were indirectly dangerous in that they were liable to give rise to the loss of other cargo. The ground-nut cargo was dangerous and consented to its shipment with knowledge of its dangerous character. Article IV, r.6 was not subject to Article IV, r.3 and the shippers were liable.

---

[67] *Effort Shipping Co Ltd v. Linden Management SA* [1998] 2 W.L.R. 206.
[68] "The shipper shall not be responsible for loss or damage sustained by the carrier or the ship arising or resulting from any cause without the act, fault or neglect of the shipper, his agents or his servants".

As to the relationship between Articles IV, Rule 6 and IV, Rule 3, the House of Lords decided that Article IV, Rule 6 created free-standing rights and obligations which were neither expressly nor impliedly qualified by Article IV, Rule 3. Accordingly, although the shippers acted without fault or neglect, Article IV, Rule 3 did not exempt them from the strict liability imposed by Article IV, Rule 6. They went on to decide that the shipper's liability under common law was the same as that under Article IV, Rule 6, that is, his liability did not depend on his knowledge, or means of knowledge, that the goods were dangerous.

In an earlier case it was held that the shipper was liable for delay in discharging the goods due to import restrictions or prohibitions, where the goods themselves were not physically dangerous.[69] The carrier's knowledge in Article IV, Rule 6 includes those matters of which he ought to be aware.[70]

In *The Fiona*,[71] the relationship between Articles IV, Rule 6 and III, Rule 1[72] was considered. A cargo of fuel oil damaged the carrier's vessel during discharge. The carrier was not warned that it could produce an explosive mixture. The explosion was caused by contamination of the cargo by a previous cargo carried by the vessel. The Court of Appeal held that the carrier could not claim an indemnity under Article IV, Rule 6 where he was in breach of his Article III, Rule 1[73] obligation, since this was an overriding obligation.

Under the Merchant Shipping Acts 1995[74] a shipper is liable to fines for shipping in any vessel, British or foreign, goods designated as "dangerous" without giving the shipowner notice and distinctly marking the nature of the goods on the outside of the packages, or for knowingly sending dangerous goods under false description of the goods or the sender. In addition, the carriage of dangerous goods is covered by extensive Regulations.[75] Failure to comply with these regulations will result in the cargo being refused for shipment and renders the sender liable to heavy penalties.

PROCEEDINGS BY CARGO OWNER

Whom to Sue—The Legal and Actual Carrier

15–051 In the event that the cargo-owner needs to sue the carrier, it is essential for him to know whether the contract of carriage is made with the shipowner or the charterer. The identity of the carrier is sometimes difficult to determine.[76] In other words, the actual carrier may not be the legal carrier. It is the legal carrier

---

[69] *Mitchell, Cotts & Co v. Steel Brothers & Co Ltd* [1916] 2 K.B. 610.
[70] *Brass v. Maitland* [1856] 26 L.J.Q.B. 49; *The Athanasia Cominos* [1990] 1 Lloyd's Rep. 277.
[71] *Mediterranean Freight Services v. BP Oil International; The Fiona* [1994] 2 Lloyd's Rep. 506.
[72] See *ante*, para. 15–041.
[73] *ibid.*
[74] s. 87.
[75] Merchant Shipping (Dangerous Goods and Marine Pollutants) Regulations 1997 (S.I. 1997/2367). Dangerous goods are those classified as such by the IMDG (International Maritime Dangerous Goods) Code, consolidated edition, 1994 as amended, published by the International Maritime Organisation. The IMDG Code is currently updated every two years. The most recent amendment (Amendment 29) became effective on January 1, 1999. It includes changes to harmonise the Code with the 10th edition of the UN Recommendations on the Transport of Dangerous Goods.
[76] See Scrutton, *loc. cit*, p. 80.

with whom the contract of carriage is concluded. The word "shipowner" may be confusing in that it may be used to denote a registered shipowner, a demise charterer, a disponent owner (sub-charterer), or a contracting carrier.[77]

In general, if the charter is a demise[78] charter, under which the charterer employs his own master and crew, it is probable that the master has signed the bills of lading as agent of the charterer and the latter would be the carrier. If, however, the charter is not a demise charter (*i.e.* is a time or voyage charter), the master and crew are the employees of the shipowner and the contract of carriage is usually made with the shipowner. This will even be the case if the charter provides that the master shall sign the bills of lading as agent of the charterer and the shipper does not know that the charterparty contains such a clause.[79]

The bill of lading may contain a clause stating that the party contracting with the shipper shall be the shipowner (or demise charterer), and not the (ordinary) charterer[80] but such clauses may themselves be confusing. The signature on the bill and the capacity of the signer might be of assistance. In cases where it is simply not possible to determine the correct party to sue, it may be necessary to incur the expense of suing both the charterer and the shipowner. This is because if the cargo-owner erroneously makes a claim for loss of, or damage to, the cargo against the charterer, thinking that he is the shipowner, the charterer cannot be regarded as agent of the owner, except if he has authority from the latter,[81] and a later claim against the owner would fail if the action against him is brought outside the time limit of the Hague-Visby Rules.[82] Circumstances vary and in each case the issue as to whether a bill is a charterers' or owners' bill is a matter of construction, depending on all the surrounding circumstances.[83]

If payment is to be made under a banker's letter of credit, UCP (1993 Revision) provides that a bill will be accepted which[84]:

> "appears on its face to indicate the name of the carrier and to have been signed or otherwise authenticated by:
>
> — the carrier or a named agent for or on behalf of the carrier, or
> — the master or a named agent for or on behalf of the master.
>
> Any signature or authentication of the carrier or master must be identified as carrier or master, as the case may be. An agent signing or authenticating for the carrier or master must also indicate the name and capacity of the party, *i.e.* carrier or master, on whose behalf that agent is acting."

---

[77] *The Stolt Loyalty* [1995] 1 Lloyd's Rep. 598.
[78] Also called a bareboat charter.
[79] *Manchester Trust v. Furness, Withy & Co* [1895] 2 Q.B. 539.
[80] This clause is usually referred to as the "demise clause", *Kenya Railways v. Antares Co Pte Ltd*; *The Antares (No. 2)* [1986] 2 Lloyd's Rep. 633; *Ngo Chew Hong Edible Oil Pte Ltd v. Scindia Steam Navigation Co Ltd; The Jalamohan* [1988] 1 Lloyd's Rep. 443. But these clauses may themselves be confusing. Also potentially confusing are the "identity of carrier" clauses in bills of lading, as these are notoriously difficult to interpret.
[81] In *The Antares (No. 2)* he had no authority but in *The Jalamohan* he had such authority.
[82] *The Antares (Nos 1 and 2)* [1987] 1 Lloyd's Rep. 424, CA; on the time limits under the Hague-Visby Rules, see *ante*, para. 15–048.
[83] *Sunrise Maritime Inc v. Uvisco Ltd; The Hector* [1998] 2 Lloyd's Rep. 287.
[84] Art. 23(a)(i).

This improvement on the provisions in the earlier UCP,[85] which omitted requirements as to signature, may well assist cargo-owners in identifying the correct
party to sue if payment is made under a letter of credit.

The right to sue and liability under The Carriage of Goods by Sea Act 1992

15–052 The contract of carriage by sea is often concluded by the consignor, particularly
where he has sold the goods on delivery terms such as strict f.o.b., f.o.b. with
additional services, or c.i.f. terms. If it is necessary to bring an action against the
carrier, the question arises who is entitled to sue, the consignor or the consignee.

Prior to the coming into force of the Carriage of Goods by Sea Act 1992,[86]
where the bill of lading was transferred to the consignee or indorsee and the
property had passed by reason of such consignment or indorsement, the consignee or indorsee had title to sue on the contract of carriage by virtue of section
1 of the Bills of Lading Act 1855. In other words, this provision operated as a
statutory transfer of the right to sue and the consignee or indorsee was entitled
to bring an action against the carrier for damages for any loss of or damage to
the cargo, since he had suffered these damages himself as the owner of the
goods.[87] The right of suit did not pass to the consignee under the Bills of Lading
Act 1855 if the property in the goods passed to him otherwise than "upon or by
reason of" indorsement of the bill of lading, for example, if it passed to him
before shipment.[88]

The Carriage of Goods by Sea Act 1992 ("the 1992 Act")[89] repeals the Bills
of Lading Act 1855.[90] In summary, the 1992 Act provides for rights of suit in
respect of bills of lading, sea waybills and delivery orders; dispenses with the
requirement for property to have passed[91]; separates the transfer of rights and
liabilities of the transferee; provides that a holder may sue on behalf of another
who has suffered loss even though he has himself suffered no loss; and makes
provision for rights of suit in respect of bulk cargo prior to ascertainment.

The 1992 Act applies to[92]:

(a) any bill of lading;

(b) any sea waybill; and

(c) any ship's delivery order.

---

[85] (1983 Revision).

[86] September 16, 1992.

[87] See *The San Nicholas* [1976] 1 Lloyd's Rep. 8.

[88] *Hispanica de Petroleos SA (Hispanoil) v. Vencedora Oceanica Navegacion SA; The Kapetan Markos* [1986] 1 Lloyd's Rep. 211 at 213 and *The Kapetan Markos (No. 2)* [1987] 2 Lloyd's Rep. 321 at 329.

[89] For a full explanation of the 1992 Act see The Law Commission's *Rights of Suit in Respect of Carriage of Goods by Sea* (Law Com. No. 96). The Draft Bill appended to the Report was enacted without amendment. The Draft Bill itself contains explanatory notes.

[90] s. 6(2), but the 1992 Act is not retrospective so does not apply to any document issued before it came into force, s. 6(3).

[91] See *post*, paras 4–004 to 4–006.

[92] s. 1(1).

Under the 1992 Act a bill of lading which is incapable of transfer by indorsement is excluded,[93] but the Law Commissioners felt such a bill would come within the definition of sea waybill.[94] A received for shipment bill is included.[95] A sea waybill is any document which is not a bill of lading but is a receipt for goods containing or evidencing the contract of carriage and identifies the person to whom, under the contract, delivery is to be made.[96] A ship's delivery order is any document, not being a bill of lading or a sea waybill, which contains an undertaking relating to the contract of carriage and an undertaking by the carrier to deliver the goods to an identified person.[97]

A person who is the lawful holder[98] of a bill of lading, the identified consignee in a sea waybill, or the person entitled to delivery of goods to which a delivery order relates, has title to sue the carrier under the contract of carriage "as if he had been a party to that contract"[99] but this provision is subject to exceptions. These occur where the bill of lading no longer gives the holder a right to possession of the goods, unless he becomes the holder by contract or arrangement before the bill ceased to be a transferable document of title,[1] or "as a result of the rejection to that person by another person of goods or documents delivered to the other person in pursuance of such arrangements."[2] The latter provision is clarified in the explanatory notes to the Draft Act by this example[3]:

> "... S [seller] and B [buyer] make a contract of sale in March for delivery in June. After delivery of the goods, the bill ceases to be a transferable document of title. The goods are rejected upon arrival, and the documents make their way back up the chain until they reach S in October. Although by October the bill of lading has ceased to grant constructive possession of the goods, S is able to sue the carrier because he became the holder of the bill as a result of the rejection of goods delivered under an arrangement (the March sale) made before the bill ceased to be a transferable document of title."

Under a ship's delivery order the rights of suit relate to the terms of the order and are confined to the goods in the order.[4] Section 5(4)(b) provides that rights of suit can exist under a delivery order where goods cannot be identified, whether because they are mixed with other goods or for any other reason.[5]

Provision is made for a person who has not suffered any loss to sue on behalf

---

[93] s. 1(2)(a).
[94] para. 2.50 of the Report.
[95] s. 1(2)(b).
[96] s. 1(3). Although sea waybills are non-negotiable, since the person is "identified by description", this allows for the person to be varied after the issue of the sea waybill, s. 5(3).
[97] s. 1(4).
[98] Including one who has become the holder in good faith, s. 5(2)(c).
[99] s. 2(1). Section 5 defines that contract as either the contract contained in the bill of lading or evidenced by it, *cf.* Bills of Lading Act 1855, s.1.
[1] s. 2(2)(a). The notes to the Draft Act, p. 49, make it clear that included are cases where delivery has been made and where the goods are destroyed.
[2] s. 2(2)(b).
[3] p. 49.
[4] s. 2(3).
[5] In relation to unascertained goods see also the Sale of Goods Act 1979 as amended by the Sale of Goods (Amendment) Act 1995.

of a person who has suffered loss[6]; and the extinguishing of rights of suit of the holder where the bill of lading has been indorsed to another or the right to delivery of the goods has passed to another.[7]

A person in section 2(1) only assumes liability[8] under the contract of carriage when he[9]:

(a) takes or demands delivery from the carrier of any of the goods to which the document relates;

(b) makes a claim under the contract of carriage against the carrier in respect of any of those goods; or

(c) is a person who, at a time before those rights were vested in him, took or demanded delivery from the carrier of any of those goods.

It has recently been held that the holder of a bill of lading, who had become liable by taking one of the steps contained in section 3(1), would be discharged by the subsequent endorsement of the bill of lading and transfer of the goods to a third party.[10] In this case the holder of the bill of lading demanded samples of the cargo,[11] rejected it after testing the samples and sold it on. He was liable only until he indorsed the bill to the buyer.

In the case of a bulk shipment under a ship's delivery order liability is restricted to the goods to which the delivery order relates.[12] All the foregoing are without prejudice to the liabilities of the shipper or carrier as original parties to the contract of carriage.[13]

Prior to the coming into force of the 1992 Act, where the shipowner delivered the goods on presentation of the bill of lading and the holder did not have property in the goods,[14] the court could imply a *Brandt v. Liverpool*[15] contract between the carrier and the bill of lading holder. A *Brandt v. Liverpool* contract was implied where the shipowner delivered goods to a person without presentation of the bill of lading.[16]

The provisions relating to representations in bills of lading implements

---

[6] s. 2(4), although there is no obligation on him to do so. If he does, the Commissioners feel that he would hold any damages on account for the person who suffered the loss, paras 2.24–2.29 of the Report.

[7] s. 2(5).

[8] Including liability for freight, see *ante*, para. 15–017.

[9] s. 3(1). The separation of rights and liabilities means that a pledgee (such as a bank holding the bill as security) would be able to sue without being liable for freight or demurrage, paras 2.30–2.31 of the Report.

[10] *Borealis AB v. Stargas Ltd; The Berge Sisar* [1999] Q.B. 863.

[11] Within s. 3(1)(c).

[12] s. 3(2).

[13] s. 3(3).

[14] And therefore no title to sue in contract or tort, *The Aliakmon* [1986] A.C. 785.

[15] From *Brandt v. Liverpool, Brazil and River Plate Steam Navigation Co* [1924] 1 K.B. 575, as interpreted in *The Aramis* [1989] 1 Lloyd's Rep. 213. (Where an indorsee presented the bill of lading, paid the freight and took delivery of the goods, a contract could be implied between carrier and indorsee if the requirements of offer, acceptance and contractual intention were met.)

[16] *The Captain Gregos (No. 2)* [1990] 2 Lloyd's Rep. 395; see also *The Gudermes* [1993] 1 Lloyd's Rep. 331.

Recommendation (5)[17] of the Law Commission that the rule in *Grant v. Norway*[18] be abolished. Section 4[19] thus provides:

"A bill of lading which—

(a) represents goods to have been shipped on board a vessel or to have been received for shipment on board a vessel; and

(b) has been signed by the master of the vessel or by a person who was not the master but had the express, implied or apparent authority of the carrier to sign bills of lading,

shall, in favour of a person who has become the lawful holder of the bill, be conclusive evidence against the carrier of the shipment of the goods or, as the case may be, of their receipt for shipment."

This is reinforced by section 5(4)(a) which states that the provisions of the Act apply where the goods cease to exist.

The 1992 Act makes wide provision for the Secretary of State by statutory instrument to provide that the Act apply to EDI which will be of equivalent force and effect as as if the information had been in writing.[20]

Although the 1992 Act deals only with title to sue in contract, the right to sue in tort has not been excluded.[21]

If the carrier wrongly delivers the goods to a person not entitled thereto, the carrier is liable in *tort* for conversion.[22] This situation arises, in particular, if the consignee has resold the goods to a further purchaser and has transferred the bill of lading to the latter but prevails on the carrier to deliver the goods to him—the consignee—on arrival without return of the bill of lading.[23]

The Act does not make specific provision for multimodal transport documents but the Commissioners felt that by including "received for shipment" bills, multimodal documents were "capable of falling within its ambit."[24]

---

[17] p. 40.

[18] (1851) 10 C.B. 665.

[19] But note that this provision applies only to a bill of lading which is transferable, s. 2(2)(a) and para. 2.50 of the Report.

[20] s. 1(5). On EDI see Chap. 33.

[21] See *ante*, para. 5.24 of the Report. Actions in tort are dealt with in para. 2–030.

[22] *Chabbra Corporation Pte Ltd v. Jag Shakti (Owners); The Jag Shakti* [1986] A.C. 337; *The Winkfield* [1902] P. 42.

[23] In *The Jag Shakti* a pledgee was able to recover in full as was a bailee in *The Winkfield, ibid.*

[24] Para. 2.49 of the Report.

CHAPTER 16

CONTAINER TRANSPORT

16–001 The transportation of export goods is frequently carried out in containers. Scheduled ocean container operations now provide the key liner cargo services between the main markets of the industrialised world. Roll-on/roll-off operations also flourish on long-haul routes due to their "flexibility" while this same factor similarly contributes to the important growth of unitised services to developing areas of the world.[1] Other forms of unitised services, such as pallets, LASH barges[2] and trailers, are also used.

Containers are particularly suitable for multimodal transport.[3] If, for example, the goods have to pass through three stages of transportation, they are carried by land from an inland depot to the port of loading, then by sea, and finally again by land to an inland destination. They will travel in the same container from the place of loading to that of discharge and the physical labour as well as the cost of conveying them from one vehicle of transportation to the next is reduced. In addition, the danger of theft and pilferage is reduced as is the risk of damage through repeated handling of goods.[4] Container transport raises, as will be seen, difficult and largely unsolved legal problems. The failure so far to achieve a widely accepted international regulation[5] on multimodal transport does not make the task of finding solutions more easy.

The course of business in container transport

16–002 The course of business in container transport is that the exporter, having made arrangements with a forwarder or directly with the office of a container shipping

---

[1] Adapted from *Understanding the Freight Business* (3rd ed., Thomas Meadows & Co Ltd, 1984), p. 33. On containers generally, see Mark D. Booker, *Containers, Conditions, Law and Practice of Carriage and Use* (Twickenham, England, 1987). See also Malcolm Clarke, "Containers: Proof that Damage occurred during Carriage," in *International Carriage of Goods: Some Legal Problems and Possible Solutions* (ed. C. M. Schmitthoff and R. M. Goode, 1988), p. 64; Paul Budgen, *Freight Forwarding and Goods in Transit* (Sweet and Maxwell, 1998). Containers are also referred to as teus, "twenty foot equivalent units" and "boxes". Containers may be larger or smaller than 20 foot. The teu is generally used as the rule for measuring the carrying capacity of the specialised container vessels. These vessels are of unique design, many have no hatches. A vessel of 4,000teu capacity is not unusual.

[2] LASH stands for "Lighter-aboard-ship".

[3] A multimodal transport contract means a single contract for the carriage of goods by at least two different modes of transport—UNCTAD/ICC rules for multimodal transport documents: ICC publication no: 481—Also UN Convention on International Multimodal Transport of Goods, Geneva 1980, Art. 1.

[4] But not entirely avoided as the whole container may be stolen.

[5] See *post*, para. 16–005.

line, will send his goods to the nearest container loading depot of the forwarder or shipping line also called container freight stations (CFSs).[6]

If the exporter intends to stuff a full container load (FCL), the forwarder or shipping line will be prepared to send an empty container to the exporter for loading. If the exporter has arranged for the delivery of the goods to the overseas buyer's place of business, the container would be a door-to-door container. It is important that the door-to-door container is properly sealed with the carrier's seal. This is sometimes done by the shipper, and in other cases by the driver of the collecting vehicle. The exporter should make sure of this because, if there is a claim for shortage of or damage to the cargo carried in the container, the state of the carrier's seal provides an indication of what may have happened.

If the cargo is less than a full container load (LCL), the exporter will send it to the container freight station, where it will be consolidated with the goods of other exporters in a groupage container. On arrival at the place of destination it will be taken to a container freight station, where it will be "degrouped", *i.e.* the parcels within will be separated and delivered to the various consignees.

A case which illustrates certain of the aspects of the use of containers and the problems which may arise is *The Esmeralda I*,[7] decided by the Supreme Court of New South Wales. The plaintiff, an importer in Australia, bought a quantity of cutlery from a manufacturer in Brazil. The goods were to be carried in an FCL container on The Esmeralda I, a vessel chartered to the defendant carrier and loading in Rio Grande. The container was taken to the seller's premises and, after the goods were placed into it, the carrier's seal was affixed and the container was secured by a padlock. When the container arrived in Sydney, it was taken to the buyer's premises. There the seal, which was intact, was removed and the padlock forced. Of the 437 cardboard boxes of cutlery, allegedly loaded in the container, 118 boxes were missing. The plaintiff (the consignee) sued the defendant (the carrier) for damages. The bill of lading, which was a clean "shipped on board" bill, contained on its face the letters "FCL/FCL" and the following statement: "quantity contents if mentioned in the bill of lading were furnished by the shippers and were not and could not be ascertained or checked by the Master unless the contrary has been expressly acknowledged and agreed to".

There were further similar notices on the bill. The bill described the goods as "Container 20 with 437 cardboard boxes containing cutlery . . ." The words "said to contain—packed by shippers" were also printed on the bill. The action was dismissed. The clauses on the face of the bill of lading defeated the consignee's argument that the carrier was estopped from denying that he had received 437 cardboard boxes for shipment. The court accepted expert evidence

---

[6] Leggatt J. held in *Burke Motors Ltd v. Mersey Docks & Harbour Co* [1986] 1 Lloyd's Rep. 155 that a shipping line instructed to carry goods from England to Canada, which had stored them in a CFS prior to the arrival of the vessel, had acted as forwarder, and not yet as carrier; it is respectfully doubted that this decision is correct (CMS). There is a UN Convention on the Liability of Operators of Transport Terminals in International Trade, Vienna 1991; to date it has not been ratified by a sufficient number of States to bring it into force (five).

[7] *Ace Imports Pty Ltd v. Companhia de Navegação Lloyd Brasileiro; The Esmeralda I* [1988] 1 Lloyd's Rep. 206. See *post*, para. 16–004.

that in the letters FCL/FCL the first reference to FCL meant that the shipper wanted to ship whatever could go into a full container, and the second reference to this acronym meant that it was the importer who would unpack the whole container.[8]

Container leasing agreements

16–003 Containers, which are of various sizes, are not necessarily owned by the carrier. There are specialist companies which own containers and let them to carriers.[9] Container letting is a business of considerable size. The container leasing contract usually provides that, if the lessee retains the container beyond the stipulated time, he has to pay "demurrage", that is, liquidated damages.[10]

When the forwarder or shipping line has taken charge of the goods loaded in a full container or sent for groupage in a groupage container,[11] a receipt is issued. If the recipient is a shipping line, it may issue a container bill of lading. If the recipient is a forwarder, he may issue a FIATA combined transport bill of lading, or a combined transport document, or a house bill of lading, or any other form of receipt. No uniform practice exists in this respect.[12]

Legal problems of container transport

16–004 If the parties to a contract of international sale agree on container transport, the "critical point" for the delivery of the goods and the passing of the risk is different from that under a contract in which the traditional method of sea transport is envisaged. In the traditional forms of export contract, such as f.a.s., f.o.b., c.i.f. or c. and f., the critical point is in the port of shipment, and in an arrival contract it is in the port of destination.[13] If container transport is contemplated, the critical point is the place at which the carrier (or his agent) takes charge of the goods; this place may well be a container freight station inland.[14]

Standard terms take account of this situation. For example, if the parties to the contract of sale intend shipment in a container, the terms suggested are "Free Carrier" FCA , "Carriage Paid to" CPT, "Carriage and Insurance Paid to"

---

[8] The court found as a fact that the pilfering took place in Brazil before the FCL container was sealed and locked.

[9] In *The River Rima* [1988] 2 Lloyd's Rep. 193 the House of Lords held that containers supplied to a vessel were not "goods or materials supplied to a ship for her operation or maintenance" within the meaning of section 20(m) of the Supreme Court Act 1981 and that consequently the court could not exercise Admiralty jurisdiction *in rem* (arrest of the ship) in a claim arising from a leasing agreement between a container leasing company and a vessel.

[10] There exists a trade usage in England according to which a Customs clearance agent appointed by an importer is responsible to the forwarder for demurrage for retention of the forwarder's container if the return of the container is unreasonably delayed through the fault of the clearance agent: *Kuehne and Nagel Ltd v. W. B. Woolley (Scotland) Ltd* (unreported, Westminster County Court, August 15, 1973, Plaint. No. 73 50487).

[11] See *ante*, para. 16–002.

[12] See *Contracts for the Carriage of Goods*, Lloyds of London Press, Issue 13 1998 at 6.1.3.

[13] See Chap. 2, para. 2–046. The position is different if the contract is on terms ex works, FCA, or DAF.

[14] If the parties to the contract of sale, though agreeing on container transport, have provided for delivery at the buyer's place (door-to-door container), the critical point would be otherwise.

CIP. Other terms which may be used include "Carriage and Insurance Paid to Destination" CIP, "Delivered Duty Unpaid" DDU and "Delivered Duty Paid" DDP. What distinguishes these terms is that the means of the carriage of the goods is of no real consequence; it is sufficient that the goods are delivered whether by one or more means. A container or a pallet may be carried on most means of transport.[15]

The liability of the container operator

Containers, as has been observed, are largely used in multimodal transport. If **16–005** the goods conveyed in the container are lost or damaged in transit or delay occurs and it is sought to hold the container operator liable, a difficulty arises. The international Conventions applying to the various modes of international transport[16] differ considerably with respect to the conditions of liability of the carrier and the maximum limits of his liability. This difficulty is particularly marked in the European trade. Here, the liability for loss in sea transport is usually governed by the Hague or the Hague-Visby Rules, for air transport by the Warsaw Convention, and for land transport by the CMR or CIM. The Hague-Visby Rules hold the carrier liable only if he has acted negligently. On the other hand, the Warsaw Convention, and CMR as well as CIM provide, in principle, strict liability, but differ on the defences which the carrier may plead. In the case of air carriage, as well as carriage under CMR and CIM, the carrier may avoid liability if a few specified defences including inherent vice and force majeure can be relied upon. This difficulty is increased if it is impossible to ascertain during which phase of the multimodal transport the loss or damage occurred. At present an international regulation which provides a solution to this problem is not yet generally accepted.

The difficulties are compounded by the fact that in the eyes of the exporter, a multimodal transport operation constitutes one business transaction, irrespective of the various stages of the carriage of goods. The obvious suggestion is that a uniform system of liability should be adopted for the multimodal transport operator. Such an arrangement would make it unnecessary to inquire at which stage the loss of or damage to the goods occurred.[17] This system of liability is, in fact, accepted by the UN Convention on International Multimodal Transport of Goods, adopted at Geneva on May 24, 1980.[18] At the date of writing,[19] the Convention has only been adopted by a few States and does not form part of United Kingdom law. The principle of uniform liability is expressed in Article 16 of the Convention as follows:

---

[15] See *ante*, para. 15–002.
[16] See Chaps 15, 17 and 18 for reference to the Hague-Visby Rules, CMR, CIM and the various regimes applying to carriage by air.
[17] This solution was advocated in May 1972 by an international seminar on intermodal transport held in Genoa; see Lord Diplock, "A Combined Transport Document" [1972] J.B.L. 269.
[18] UN Doc. TD/MT/Conf/16. See *ante*, n. 3.
[19] The Convention will come into force one year after 30 countries have ratified it or have acceded to it.

"Basis of liability
1. The multimodal transport operator shall be liable for loss resulting from loss of or damage to the goods, as well as from delay in delivery, if the occurrence which caused the loss, damage or delay in delivery took place while the goods were in his charge as defined in Article 14, unless the multimodal transport operator proves that he, his servants or agents or any other person referred to in Article 15 took all measures that could reasonably be required to avoid the occurrence and its consequences.

2. Delay in delivery occurs when the goods have not been delivered within the time expressly agreed upon or, in the absence of such agreement, within the time which it would be reasonable to require of a diligent multimodal transport operator, having regard to the circumstances of the case.

3. If the goods have not been delivered within 90 consecutive days following the date of delivery determined according to paragraph 2 of this Article, the claimant may treat the goods as lost."

As regards the maximum liability of the multimodal transport operator, the Convention provides in Article 18(1) that his liability is limited to 920 units of account (SDRs) per package or other shipping unit or 2.75 units of account per kilogramme of gross weight of the goods lost or damaged, whichever is the higher. However, it adds in Article 19(3) that, notwithstanding this provision, if the international multimodal transport does not, according to the contract, include carriage by sea or inland waterways, his liability is limited to 8.33 units of account per kilogramme of gross weight of the goods lost or damaged. This latter limitation is similar to the rather low limitation provided by the CMR.

Until the Convention comes into operation and is given effect in the various national jurisdictions—and it may be some time before this is achieved—a regulation of the liability of the multimodal transport operator has to be provided on a contractual basis. As most international Conventions regulating the various modes of transportation are of mandatory character,[20] the contractual regulation has to proceed in two stages. It has to provide, first, that if it is known at which stage of the multimodal transport the loss occurred, the international Convention governing that mode of transport shall apply; and, secondly, if this cannot be ascertained, another regime specified in the contract shall apply, for example the regulation of the Hague or the Hague-Visby Rules or of the CMR.[21] This arrangement of the liability of the multimodal transport operator is known as the network liability system.[22]

The documents used in container transport—the combined transport document

16–006 It has already been observed that documents which differ in character and effect are used by multimodal transport operators. The ICC issued Uniform Rules for

---

[20] The Warsaw Convention, for example, contains in Art. 31 an express provision dealing with combined carriage, which includes an air leg. It states that in the case of combined carriage the parties may insert in the document of air carriage conditions relating to other modes of transport, provided that the provisions of the Convention are observed as regards the air carriage.
[21] The CMR so provide in Art. 2(1); see *post*, para. 18–006.
[22] See *post*, para. 16–007.

a Combined Transport Document[23] which could be incorporated into the contract of combined transport by agreement of the parties. The combined transport document, known as the CT document, is intended to be a "start-to-finish" document and to make it unnecessary to issue separate documents for every stage of the multimodal transport. The CT document may be issued in a negotiable or non-negotiable form, as the parties desire. By issuing a CT document, the combined transport operator accepts full responsibility for the performance of the combined transport, as well as liability, on the terms stated in the Uniform Rules, for loss or damage, and delay, throughout the entire combined transport.

After observing the operation and use of the Uniform Rules, a set of rules known as the UNCTAD/ICC Rules for Multimodal Transport Documents were developed. The introduction, on January 1, 1992, of these Rules was intended to set out provisions for multimodal transport documents based on existing provisions such as the ICC Uniform Rules for a Combined Transport Documents, ICC No. 298. They also provide a closer relationship with the Hague, Hague-Visby Rules and the Hamburg Rules. The Foreword to the Rules, ICC Publication No. 481, acknowledges that the Rules only cover "part of the customary contents of a multimodal transport document".

The Rules do not apply automatically and have to be incorporated into the contract between the exporter and the combined transport operator. The Negotiable FIATA Multimodal Transport Bill of Lading in its amended version[24] and the BIMCO/INSA COMBIDOC satisfy these requirements.

As the Rules are applied by contract, they cannot avoid adopting the system of network liability, but they provide their own maximum limits of compensation when the stage of transport where the loss or damage occurred is not known and consequently none of the international Conventions can be resorted to. The importance of the Rules is enhanced by the fact that according to the UCP (1993 Revision) such documents may be accepted by banks under a letter of credit unless the instructions state that a marine bill of lading shall be tendered.[25]

Container bills of lading

If a shipping line engages in combined transport, it may issue container bills of **16–007** lading. Such documents are genuine bills of lading. They are subject to the Hague or the Hague-Visby Rules by force of law, as far as the carriage by sea is concerned[26]; indeed, these Rules contain express provisions applying to the carriage of goods in a container, pallet or similar article of transport.[27]

---

[23] ICC Brochure 298, 1975 (Reprinted March 1985 and now superseded by the UNCTAD/ICC Rules for Multimodal Transport Documents, ICC Brochure No. 481, see below); see F.J.J. Cadwallader, "Uniform Rules for Combined Transport" [1974] J.B.L. 193.
[24] The current FIATA MTBL is dated 1992.
[25] Art. 26, see *ante*, para. 11–012.
[26] By contract they are normally extended to situations in which it cannot be ascertained at which stage of the transport the loss or damage occurred; see below this para.
[27] Hague-Visby Rules, Art. IV, r. 5(c); see *ante*, para. 15–045. An empty container was held to be a "consignment of goods" within the Conditions of Carriage of the Road Haulage Association (RHA), *Acme Transport Ltd v. Betts* [1981] 1 Lloyd's Rep. 131. A roll-on/roll-off lorry or trailer or a LASH barge is not likely to be considered a "package" within Art. IV, r. (5)(c). Scrutton, *Charterparties* (20th ed.), p. 451.

All container bills of lading are normally "received for shipment" bills and not "shipped on board" bills; it could not be otherwise in circumstances where the goods are received at a container freight station inland. All container bills of lading tend to adopt the network liability system. They usually provide that, when the stage where the loss of or damage to the goods cannot be ascertained, the liability of the carrier shall be determined with reference to the Hague or to the Hague-Visby Rules.

A typical clause will provide as follows[28]:

> **"3. Responsibility.** As regards carriage by sea this bill of lading, whether negotiable or not, shall have effect subject to the Hague Rules contained in the International Convention for the Unification of Certain Rules relating to bills of lading dated Brussels 25th August 1924, if and as enacted in the country of shipment.
>
> If in relation to sea carriage any term or condition contained in this bill is proved to be repugnant to or inconsistent with any compulsorily applicable statute or rule of law giving effect to the Hague Rules such term or condition shall be void to the extent of such repugnancy or inconsistency but no further and the Hague Rules enacted as mentioned in this article shall apply.
>
> Where by the nature of this bill of lading the contract of carriage is in respect of through transit commencing at and terminating at interior places which are expressly stated in the bill of lading, the carrier shall, subject to the terms hereof be responsible for the goods in the manner herein provided from the time they are received for shipment by his agents or servants, being sub-carriers or not, at the specified first place of despatch until delivery by his agents or servants, being sub-carriers or not, at a specified place of final destination.
>
> During the period before loading of the goods at the port of loading or after discharge of the goods at the port of discharge the carrier hereby accepts the same liability in respect of the goods as would have existed if every sub-contracting party had made a separate direct contract with the merchant on the standard terms and conditions of business of the sub-contracting party in respect of that part of the through transit cargo handling or warehousing undertaken by the sub-contracting party as modified by the effect of any legislation having compulsory application to such contract. Where the goods are in the hands of the carrier and not of a sub-contractor for any purpose whatsoever at any time before loading or after discharge they shall be subject to the Standard Conditions of Carriage of Goods of the carrier which include terms excluding carrier's liability for damage or loss and in other respects. If it cannot be established in whose custody the goods were when damage or loss occurred, the damage or loss shall be deemed to have occurred during the sea voyage and the appropriate Hague Rules Legislation shall apply. In any event where no financial limit of liability is laid down by any legislation which may affect the carrier's liability hereunder the financial liability of the carrier shall in no circumstances exceed its financial liability as laid down in the Hague Rules wherever the loss or damage in issue may have occurred."

It can be seen from the first sentence of the paragraph above that the carrier expressly acknowledges that compulsory rules of national law and/or one of the international carriage regimes will apply to the land part of the transport. The CMR, CIM or the Warsaw Convention may therefore apply to regulate liability in relation to that particular phase of the transit. It must also be noted that where there is doubt about the phase of transport during which the loss or damage occurred, the liability will be determined in accordance with the relevant rules governing the marine phase of the transport.

---

[28] The extract is from a Bill of Lading used by EUCON of Dublin, Rotterdam and other centres and is reproduced in part with their kind permission. "Merchant" is defined as meaning and including the shipper, consignee, holder of the bill of lading, the receiver and the owner of the goods. See the Bill of Lading used in *Finagra (U.K.) Ltd v. O.T. Africa Line Ltd* [1998] 2 Lloyd's Rep. 622.

"The carrier, as carrier or in any other capacity whatsoever, shall not be liable for loss or damage arising or resulting from delay, no matter what the cause thereof may be."[29]

Deck stowage

A container bill usually states, in the Terms and Conditions printed on the **16–008** reverse, that the shipowner shall be entitled to carry the goods on deck in containers. For example, in such terms:

"... may be carried on or under deck without notice to the shippers and if they are so carried the Hague Rules as incorporated herein shall be applicable notwithstanding carriage on or under deck and the goods and/or containers shall contribute in general average whether carried on or under deck."[30]

This, however, is only a liberty, it is not a statement that the shipowner has made use of it and that the goods are, in fact, carried on deck. If this is the case, the bill has to be marked accordingly on its face, so that a purchaser of the bill is aware that the goods are deck cargo. In an American case[31] which concerned the shipment of books from New York to Yokohama the container in which the books were carried was stowed on deck but the bill of lading did not contain an indication on its face to that effect. The ship encountered heavy weather when crossing the Pacific and the books were damaged by sea water. The court held that the shipowner had forfeited the defence of pleading the limitation of liability under the Hague Rules by stowing the cargo on deck; one of the reasons which the court gave was that "no consignee or assignee could tell from the bill whether it was below deck or on deck cargo".[32] In an English case[33] a forwarder promised an importer verbally to ship a container containing his goods below deck. Contrary to his promise he shipped them on deck and when the ship met a slight swell the container fell off and went to the bottom of the sea. The Court of Appeal held the forwarder liable for the loss.

Definition of "package or unit" in container transport

The container itself, as distinguished from the individual cargoes contained **16–009** therein, is normally shipped under an ordinary "shipped" bill of lading. As far as the transport by sea is concerned, it is important to ascertain whether the whole container or each of the individual cargoes contained within constitutes a "package or unit" within the meaning of the Hague-Visby Rules, Article IV, rule 5, which provides a maximum limit of liability in favour of the carrier in case of loss or damage to such a package or unit.[34] The Rules attempt to solve this problem by providing in Article IV, Rule (5)(c) a container clause which

---

[29] *ibid.*
[30] *ibid.* clause 7(ii).
[31] *Encyclopaedia Britannica Inc v. The Hong Kong Producer and Universal Marine Corp* [1969] 2 Lloyd's Rep. 536 at 542.
[32] *ibid.* at 542.
[33] *J. Evans & Sons (Portsmouth) Ltd v. Andrea Merzario Ltd* [1976] 1 W.L.R. 1078.
[34] See *ante*, paras 15–028, 15–029, 15–045.

was cited earlier.[35] According to the Hague-Visby Rules, the wording of the bill of lading issued by the carrier by sea is prima facie conclusive. If the bill only refers to "one container said to contain (specified merchandise)", then the container itself shall be considered as the package or unit, but if it enumerates the cargoes included in the container separately, each of those cargoes shall constitute a separate package or unit. If the bill mentions specifically one or two cargoes but not the other contents of the container, the separately mentioned items are regarded as separate packages for the purposes of maximum limitation of liability, and the rest of the container falls under the general limitation.

Therefore, briefly, if the bill describes the goods as "a container said to contain (specified merchandise)" the container is the package. If it refers to the goods, adding that they are packed in a container, "the goods" are the individual packages for the purposes of the Hague-Visby Rules. This would be in accordance with the Hague-Visby Rules, Article IV, rule 5(c) and Article 6(2)(a) of the Hamburg Rules and the synthesis of the decisions in relation to limitations of package liability.

Where the carrier has inserted terms on the bill of lading such as "said to contain" "particulars furnished by merchant", "quantity unknown" the bill provides no evidence against the carrier as to the truth of the assertion that a particular weight, quantity, etc. has been shipped, on the assumption that the carrier was not a party to the "stuffing" of the container.[36] In the foregoing circumstances the burden is on the cargo claimant to show that the number of items stated to have been placed in the container were in fact so placed. The bill of lading, subject to the disclaimers, is not conclusive. The decision in *The River Gurara*[37] is an illustration of the above in that, by inserting a number of packages on the face of the bill, the cargo claimant has at least ensured that the limitation may apply to each package or unit so enumerated. *The Esmeralda I*[38] turned on the fact that the FCL/FCL formula was used, together with the "said to contain" formulation which enabled the carrier to deny the cargo owners' entries on the bill, thereby placing the burden on the cargo claimant to prove the contents of the bill were true. In that case the judge was involved in consideration of a clause which referred to "receipt in apparent good order and condition . . .". Such a clause could only be interpreted as referring to the condition of the containers; it is axiomatic that the carrier could not possibly comment on the apparent order and condition of a package (and, of course, the quantity) *already* stuffed and sealed in a container.

The American courts held in *The Mormaclynx*[39] that bales of leather packed in a container were separate packages; the bill of lading referred to "1 container

---

[35] See *ante*, para. 15–045.

[36] *New Chinese Antimony Company Ltd v. Ocean Steamship Company Ltd* [1917] 2 K.B. 664; *The Atlas* [1996] 1 Lloyd's Rep. 642.

[37] *Owners of the Cargo lately aboard the River Gurara v. Nigerian National Shipping Line Ltd* [1998] 1 Lloyd's Rep. 225.

[38] *Ace Imports Pty Ltd v. Companhia de Navegaca Lloyd Brasileiro; The Esmeralda I* [1988] 1 Lloyd's Rep. 206.

[39] *Leather's Best Inc v. The Mormaclynx* [1970] 1 Lloyd's Rep. 527. This decision was followed in the Canadian case *The Tindefjel* [1973] 2 Lloyd's Rep. 253. See *Contracts for the Carriage of Goods by Land, Sea and Air*, Looseleaf, Lloyd's of London Press, notes at paras 6.2.4, 3.6.1 *et seq*.

s.t.c. 99 bales of leather".[40] In *The Kulmerland*,[41] on the other hand, the American courts treated the container as the package or unit; in that case the bill of lading stated "1 container said to contain machinery", without "indication to the carrier of the number of cartons or the intention of the shipper to contract on that basis".[42]

---

[40] As already stated the abbreviation "s.t.c" stands for "said to contain".

[41] *Royal Typewriter Co v. Division Litton Business Systems Inc v. M.V. Kulmerland and Hamburg-Amerika Linie* [1973] 2 Lloyd's Rep. 428. In *The Kulmerland* the American court did not consider the declaration of the goods in the bill of lading as the decisive criterion but attributed weight to the fact that the goods in the container were not packed for export ("the functional test") but Collier J. in *The Tindeffjell* referred to the vague declaration of the cargo in the bill issued in *The Kulmerland*. In another American case, *Insurance Company of North America v. S/S Brooklyn Maru, Japan Line Ltd; The Brooklyn Maru* [1975] 2 Lloyd's Rep. 512, the court likewise applied the "functional economics" (*sic*) test, but in later decisions, *e.g. Mitsui & Co Ltd v. American Lines* 1981 A.M.C. 331, 2nd Circuit (1981) the American courts abandoned the functional test because it penalised shippers who took advantage of the container by using lighter packaging for the goods carried within; see Timothy J. Armstrong, "Packaging Trends and Implications in the Container Revolution" 1981 Journal of Maritime Law and Commerce, Vol. 12, p. 427.

[42] *Per* Collier J. *The Tindeffjell* [1973] 2 Lloyd's Rep. 253 at 259.

CHAPTER 17

CARRIAGE OF GOODS BY AIR

History of the statutory scheme

17–001 The carriage of goods by air was regulated by the Carriage by Air Act 1932 which, like the Carriage of Goods by Sea Acts 1924 and 1971, gave effect to an international Convention. In respect of air carriage this was the Convention for the unification of certain rules relating to international air carriage, which was signed in Warsaw in 1929. Over the years it became clear that the Warsaw Convention required amendment. For example, the limitation of liability in the event of death or injury of a passenger was found to be too low.[1] An amendment was agreed at The Hague, on September 28, 1955; and is known as the Hague Protocol. The "Warsaw Convention, as amended at the Hague 1955" is scheduled to the Carriage by Air Act 1961 and came into force on June 1, 1967, in the United Kingdom, the Channel Isles, the Isle of Man and certain British territories overseas. The 1961 Act replaced the Carriage by Air Act 1932. Section 10 of that Act authorises legislation by order in council, to apply the amended Convention to carriage by air which is not otherwise subject to the Convention, where carriage involves a place of departure, destination or stopping place in a foreign State and a place of departure, destination or stopping in the United Kingdom.[2]

The basic Convention regulates the legal liabilities and relationships between carriers by air, on the one hand, and passengers, as well as cargo consignors and consignees, on the other. Neither the original nor the amended Warsaw Convention make it clear whether the "carrier" referred to is the carrier in contractual relationship with the passenger or consignor, or whether it is the carrier who actually performs the carriage. It was therefore necessary to supplement the Warsaw Convention by a further Convention which was signed in 1961 at Guadalajara in Mexico. This supplementary Convention aims at the unification of certain rules relating to international carriage performed by a person other than the contracting carrier. The Guadalajara Convention is embodied in the Carriage by Air (Supplementary Provisions) Act 1962, which applies to carriage governed by the original and the amended Warsaw Convention.[3]

---

[1] See generally Shawcross and Beaumont, *Air Law* (4th ed.) and H. Caplan, "Ratification of Hague Protocol by United Kingdom" [1961] J.B.L. 170. See also Chitty, *Contracts* (28th ed., 1999) Chap. 35.

[2] For an extensive examination of the application of section 10 see *Holmes v. Bangladesh Biman Corporation* [1989] 1 Lloyd's Rep. 444, particularly the judgment of Lord Bridge at 447. See also *Gurtner and Others v. Beaton and Others* [1993] 2 Lloyd's Rep. 369 at 388. Note that section 10 cannot be read to enable the amended Convention to be applied to carriage taking place wholly within the territory of a foreign State or between two foreign States).

[3] The text of the unamended Warsaw Convention is contained in Schedule 2 to the Carriage by Air Acts (Application of Provisions) Order 1967 (S.I. 1967 No. 480) the Amended Convention (*i.e.* the

Protocols 1 and 2 signed at Montreal in 1975 were intended to substitute the SDRs (Special Drawing Rights) of the IMF for the gold franc used originally in the Convention in the determination of the limit of the carrier's liability. Two additional Protocols, Nos. 3 and 4, were signed at Montreal in 1975. These again concerned limits of the carrier's liabilities. No. 3 relates to another Protocol concerning liability for passengers known as the Guatemala Protocol. No. 4 concerns cargo and postal items and the raising of the limits of liability in their respect. Protocols 1 and 2 are now in force in the United Kingdom as is Protocol No. 4 which came into force on May 21, 1999.[4] As far as non-Convention carriage is concerned, SDRs were substituted for gold francs with effect from October 4, 1985, but by virtue of the Carriage by Air Act 1961, and not by virtue of the 1979 Act.

Based on these international agreements, English statute law now provides a comprehensive but complex code of reasonable uniformity for the carriage of goods by air, not only for so-called international carriage, which is the subject of the Conventions, but also for what will be referred to below as non-Convention carriage.[5] This includes carriage which in the ordinary sense of the word is international but is not governed by the Conventions. By means of a series of Orders in Council, the system of law for carriage by air described above for the United Kingdom has been extended to various overseas territories.

Damage during "carriage by air"

So far as the destruction, loss of or damage to cargo is concerned, "carriage by **17–002** air" comprises the whole period during which the cargo is in the charge of the carrier, whether in an airport or on board an aircraft, or in the case of landing outside an airport in any place whatsoever. If surface carriage takes place outside an airport for the purpose of loading, delivery or transhipment of air cargo, any damage is presumed to have taken place during the carriage by air, subject to contrary proof.

Basic system of liability—an overview

The basic scheme of the carrier's liability is uniform in all the three regimes **17–003** recognised by English law. They apply equally to carriage for reward as to gratuitous carriage by an air transport undertaking. It is therefore convenient first to describe the basic system of liability and then to note the differences which exist in each of the three regimes, which are: carriage governed by

---

Warsaw Convention as amended by the Hague Protocol) and the Guadalajara Convention, with the exceptions, adaptations and modifications made in this Order set out in Schedule 1 to the Order.

[4] By the Carriage by Air and Road Act 1979 (Commencement No. 2 Order) S.I. 1997 No. 2565, Carriage by Air (Application of Provisions) Order 1967 (Fourth Amendment Order) S.I. 1998 No. 1058 and Carriage by Air Acts (Implementation of Protocol No. 4 Order) S.I. 1999 No. 1312 supplemented by S.I. 1999 No. 1737 respectively.

[5] Sometimes referred to as the United Kingdom rules, see *Holmes v. Bangladesh Biman Corporation* [1989] 1 Lloyd's Rep. 444 at 447.

the original Warsaw Convention, carriage governed by the amended Convention and non-Convention carriage, sometimes referred to as the United Kingdom rules.

The carrier of goods by air is liable without proof of fault for destruction or loss of, or damage to or delay of cargo if it occurs during the carriage by air. The Convention, to which effect is given in the United Kingdom by the Carriage by Air Acts, creates a statutory right of action.[6] The carrier has the right to use specified defences if he can, but he cannot contract out of liability or for a lower limit of liability. In return for this, the carrier can rely on the benefit of maximum limits for his liability, and even that liability arises only if the claimant can prove damage to that extent. The maximum limits of the air carrier's liability are:

(a) 17 SDRs per kilogramme[7]; or

(b) the value declared by the shipper for which any supplementary charge has been paid.

The conversion of SDRs into sterling on a particular day is effected by obtaining a certificate relating to the converted sterling value.[8]

Carrier's defences

17–004   The carrier is not liable for damage to cargo caused by delay if he proves that he and his servants or agents[9] have taken all necessary[10] measures to avoid the damage, or that it was impossible for him or them to take such measures, (see Article 20). The carrier will not be liable for damage or loss of cargo if the loss or damage resulted from one or more of the factors set out in Article 18(2), which are: inherent vice of cargo, defective packing by other than the carrier, act of war or act of public authority.

If the carrier proves that the damage was caused or contributed to by the negligence of the party claiming, the court may exonerate the carrier wholly or partly. (Article 21(2)).

---

[6] *Per* Lloyd J. in *American Express Co v. British Airways Board* [1983] 1 W.L.R. 701 at 707–708. See also *Malca-Amit Ltd and Ors v. British Airways Plc and Ors* (1999) Unrep. (LTL 4/5/99)—the standard of proof required in a claim (here for theft of diamonds) is on the balance of probabilities.
[7] See the Carriage by Air (Sterling Equivalents) Order 1999 (S.I. 1999 No. 2881) which revokes S.I. 1996 No. 244; it will be necessary to watch for further Sterling Equivalent Orders.
[8] The certificate is obtained from the Treasury; Carriage by Air and Road Act 1979, s.5. As to cargo claims whether in contract or tort, Art. 24(2) provides that any claims are subject to the provisions of the Convention including the maximum limits of liability. For a discussion on the provisions of Art. 24(1), claims in respect of passengers and baggage, see *Sidhu v. British Airways Plc* [1997] A.C. 430. See also [1998] L.M.C.L.Q. 476 for a New Zealand perspective.
[9] s.29 of the Air Navigation Act 1936 substituted "servants and agents" for "agents" in the English text of the Warsaw Convention scheduled to the Carriage by Air Act 1932, thereby correcting an error in the translation of *préposés* which appeared in the authentic French text of the Convention. The correction has been continued in force by the Carriage by Air Act 1961 and Orders made thereunder.
[10] Interpreted as reasonably necessary by Greer L.J. in *Grein v. Imperial Airways Ltd* [1937] 1 K.B. 50 at 69–71. On interpretation generally see C. Debattista [1997] J.B.L. 130.

Those who may claim

The persons who have rights of action are the consignor, in certain circum- **17–005** stances, and the consignee. The owner of the damaged or lost goods is entitled to sue the carrier, as his right of action is not expressly excluded by the Warsaw Convention.[11] It is thought, however, that the provisions in Article 26 of the Amended Convention, limiting the rights of the consignor and consignee to sue, would apply to the right of action of the owner. In the absence of fraud by the carrier, these rights of action are only exercisable provided that written complaints are made to the carrier within specified time limits in cases of damage or delay. Article 29 of the Amended Convention determines that the right to damages is extinguished if an action is not brought within two years reckoned from the date of actual or expected arrival at destination, or the date on which carriage stopped. Receipt of cargo without complaint by the person entitled to delivery is prima facie evidence of delivery in good condition.

The consignor has a right of action against the first carrier and the carrier who performed the carriage during which destruction, loss, damage or delay took place (the performing carrier), unless the first carrier has expressly assumed liability for the whole carriage. The consignor will have a right of action if, for example, he exercised a right of stoppage in transit under Article 12. The consignee has a right of action against the last carrier and the performing carrier. The owner of the damaged or lost goods has a right of action against the performing carrier. (Articles 13, 14, 30(3)).

Carriers who may be sued

   (a) a successive carrier: who is deemed to be a party to the original contract **17–006** of carriage so far as is relevant to the carriage performed under his supervision.

   (b) the contracting carrier: who, as a principal, makes an agreement for carriage with the consignor or the consignor's agent. In many cases the contracting carrier will be the first or sometimes the only carrier by air, but the contracting carrier may also be one who merely issues a waybill, or an aircraft charterer, or a cargo consolidator or forwarder.

   (c) the actual carrier: who by virtue of authority from the contracting carrier, performs the whole or part of the carriage and is neither a successive carrier nor a contracting carrier.

The first carrier, the performing carrier and the last carrier are jointly and severally liable respectively to the consignor and the consignee. The contracting carrier is liable for the whole of the carriage. The actual carrier is only liable for the part performed by him. At the claimant's option, written complaints may be made and actions may be brought against either the actual carrier or the contracting carrier, or against both together or separately.

---

[11] Art. 13(3), Art. 26. See *Gatewhite Ltd v. Iberia Lineas Aereas de Espana Sociedad* [1989] 1 Lloyd's Rep. 160.

Servants and agents of the carrier acting within the scope of their employment can claim the benefit of the limits of liability applicable to the carrier.[12] Acts and omissions of the actual carrier, including his servants and agents, are deemed to be those of the contracting carrier and vice versa, but the actual carrier's liability cannot exceed 17 SDRs per kilogramme by reason of:

(a) any act or omission of the contracting carrier;

(b) any special agreement entered into by the contracting carrier; or

(c) special declarations of value made to the contracting carrier,

unless in cases (b) and (c) the actual carrier has agreed to be bound.

When do the various regimes apply?

17–007 It is not a straightforward matter to determine when the various regimes apply, but the following may assist. Carriage of cargo for reward by aircraft or gratuitous air carriage by an air transport undertaking is governed by:

1. The original Warsaw Convention[13]

17–008 When, according to the contract between the parties, the places of departure and destination (regardless of breaks, miscarriage,[14] transhipment or numbers of consecutive contracts or successive carriers) are located:

(a) either in the territories of two State parties to the original Convention; or

(b) in the territory of a single such State with an agreed stopping place anywhere outside that State.

However, the original Convention does not apply to carriage "with a view to the establishment of a regular line of air navigation" or carriage "in extraordinary circumstances outside the normal scope of an air carrier's business".[15]

---

[12] Internationally, this is a feature of the amended Convention, but it was applied to actions arising in the English courts by section 4 of the Carriage by Air (Supplementary Provisions) Act 1962, now continued for this purpose in Article 25A of Part B of Schedule 2 to the Carriage of Air Acts (Application of Provisions) Order 1967 (S.I. 1967 No. 480). See now Contracts (Rights of Third Parties) Act 1999, s.6(5)(b) and s.6(8)(c), where it is provided that a third party may rely on the exclusions and limitations in a contract governed by a Convention. The Act applies to contracts entered into after May 11, 2000.
[13] Sched. 2 to the Carriage by Air Acts (Application of Provisions) Order 1967.
[14] See *Rotterdamsche Bank NV v. BOAC* [1953] 1 W.L.R. 493.
[15] There is no similar reservation of such a wide scope in the amended Convention.

2. The amended Convention[16]

When, according to the agreement between the parties, the places of departure **17–009** and destination (regardless of breaks, transhipment or numbers of consecutive contracts or successive carriers) are located:

(a) either in the territories of two States both of which are parties to the amended Convention; or

(b) in the territory of a single State party to the amended Convention with an agreed stopping place anywhere outside that State.

Difficulties can arise when the place of departure is in the territory of a State party to the original Convention, for instance, the United States of America, whilst the place of destination is in the territory of a State which is not only a party to the original Convention but has also become a party to the amended Convention, for instance the United Kingdom; in these circumstances, the only obligations which bind both of the States concerned are those contained in the original Convention.

For the purposes of actions in the English courts, the Carriage by Air (Parties to Conventions) Orders[17] certify those States and their associated territories which are parties to either or both the original and the amended Conventions.[18]

3. The non-Convention rules

When the carriage of cargo is governed neither by the original nor by the **17–010** amended Convention, for example if the place of destination is in a State which is a party to neither Convention, and there is no agreed stopping place in another State, then, whatever the place of departure, no part of the carriage would, as a matter of law, be governed by either of the two Conventions. In an action before the English courts the carriage would be governed by the non-Convention rules, even though the carriage is international in the ordinary meaning of that word but not within the technical meaning which governs the applicability of the two Conventions. The non-Convention rules do not apply to purely internal flights, which are flights where the contract of carriage is made and are performed wholly within the territory of one State.[19] In these cases the law of the country in question applies or, where that law allows, the law chosen by the parties as the applicable law of the contract. The non-Convention rules also govern[20]

---

[16] Carriage by Air Act 1961, s. 1 and Sched. 1.

[17] The Carriage by Air (Parties to Convention) Order 1977 (S.I. 1977, No. 240); the Carriage by Air (Parties to Convention) (Supplementary) Order 1977 (S.I. 1977 No. 1631); and the Carriage by Air (Parties to Convention) (Supplementary) Order 1978 (S.I. 1978 No. 1058). The latest is the Carriage by Air (Parties to Convention) Order 1999, S.I. 1999 No. 1313.

[18] *Phillipson v. Imperial Airways Ltd* [1939] A.C. 332 has very little practical application today.

[19] *Holmes v. Bangladesh Biman Corporation* [1989] 1 Lloyd's Rep. 444 (passenger killed in air crash on purely internal Bangladesh flight; the House of Lords held that the contract of carriage was governed by Bangladesh law and that the Order of 1967 did not apply).

[20] Carriage by Air Acts (Application of Provisions) Order 1967, Sched. 1.

carriage of mail or postal packages,[21] presumably of both a domestic and an international character.

Carriage governed by the original Warsaw Convention

Document of carriage

17–011　The document of carriage is called the air waybill (AWB). The carrier has the right to require the consignor to make out an air waybill and to demand a separate one for each package, and the carrier is required to accept it. Nevertheless, the absence, irregularity or loss of the document does not affect the validity of the contract or the operation of the Convention rules. The AWB is not a document of title. Each air waybill must be in three original parts and handed over with the goods. The First Part is marked "for the carrier" and signed by the consignor; the Second Part, marked "for the consignee", is signed by the consignor and the carrier and accompanies the goods; the Third Part is signed by the carrier and handed to the consignor after the goods have been accepted for carriage. The consignor must furnish the additional information and documents necessary for Customs and police purposes before the goods can be delivered to the consignee, and the consignor is liable to the carrier for any damage arising out of the absence or irregularity of such information or documents. This obligation of the consignor extends also to particulars and statements inserted by him in the air waybill, and if the carrier makes out the air waybill at the request of the consignor, he is deemed to have done so as the consignor's agent.

If the carrier accepts goods without an air waybill or if the air waybill does not contain any of the following particulars, then he cannot take advantage of the provisions of the Convention which would otherwise exclude or limit his liability as carrier:

(a) place and date of execution of the air waybill;

(b) places of departure and destination;

(c) agreed stopping places (which the carrier may alter in case of necessity);

(d) name and address of consignor;

(e) name and address of first carrier;

(f) name and address of consignee "if the case so requires";

(g) nature of the goods;

(h) number of packages, method of packing and the particular marks or numbers on them;

---

[21] Carriage by Air Acts (Application of Provisions) Order 1967, Art. 4.

(i) either the weight, quantity, volume or dimensions of the goods,[22]

(j) a statement that the carriage is subject to the rules relating to liability established by the Convention.[23]

The air waybill and the statements therein are prima facie evidence of the conclusion of the contract, receipt of the goods, the conditions of carriage, the weight, dimensions, packing and number of goods. Statements relating to quantity, volume or condition are not evidence against the carrier unless expressly stated on the air consignment note to have been checked in the presence of the consignor or they relate to apparent condition.

Basic liability

In addition to the basic defences, the carrier is not liable if he can prove that **17–012** "the damage was occasioned by negligent pilotage or negligence in the handling of the aircraft or in navigation and that in all other respects he and his agents have taken all necessary measures to avoid the damage". This defence is not available in case of injury or death of passengers. The wilful misconduct of the carrier will give rise to unlimited liability for passengers under Article 25. This Article, as worded in the unamended Warsaw Convention, denies the carrier reliance on the maximum limits of liability if his servants or agents were also guilty of "wilful misconduct".[24] The exception is also important for the air carriage of goods. In one case[25] two boxes of platinum were sent by air from South Africa to Philadelphia. The contract of air carriage was governed by the unamended Warsaw Convention. The platinum was transferred at Heathrow, London, from a South African plane to a plane bound for the United States. On this occasion, as the trial judge found, one of the boxes of platinum was stolen by one or several of the loaders. The Court of Appeal held that the plaintiffs, who were the owners, consignors and consignees, were entitled by way of damages to the full value of the platinum and that the carriers could not rely on the maximum limits of the Convention because the theft of the platinum by the loaders was "wilful misconduct" on the part of the loaders, for which the carriers were liable.

When calculating the carrier's limits of liability at 17 SDRs, under the

---

[22] The Court of Appeal decided to follow the original French text and the American translation and concluded that only one of these particulars need be given: *Corocraft Ltd v. Pan American World Airways Inc* [1969] 1 Q.B. 616.

[23] The formula used in IATA tickets and waybills is "Carriage hereunder is subject to the rules relating to liability established by the Warsaw Convention unless such carriage is not 'international carriage' as defined by the Convention." This formula has been approved in an American case, *Seth v. BOAC* [1964] 1 Lloyd's Rep. 268, and an English case, *Samuel Montagu & Co Ltd v. Swissair* [1965] 2 Lloyd's Rep. 363.

[24] The wording of Article 25 in the amended Warsaw Convention is different and the term "wilful misconduct" in not used therein.

[25] *Rustenburg Platinum Mines Ltd, etc. v. South African Airways, etc.* [1979] 1 Lloyd's Rep. 19. For the definition of "recklessness" (which term is used in Art. 25 of the amended Convention but which does not appear in the unamended Convention) see *Goldman v. Thai Airways International Ltd* [1983] 1 W.L.R. 1186, CA.

unamended Warsaw Convention, the weight of the damaged package ("Package weight") alone is decisive.[26]

Special rights of consignor and consignee

17–013 Unless varied by express provision in the air consignment note, the consignor and the consignee have the following rights:

The consignor—

(a) has the right of disposal prior to delivery to the consignee, subject to the production of the consignor's copy of the air consignment note to the carrier and payment of all expenses involved. (Article 12); and

(b) may enforce rights in his own name even if acting in the interests of another, subject to the fulfillment of all obligations of the consignor under the contract of carriage. (Article 14).

The consignee—

(a) has the right to require the carrier to hand over goods and the air consignment note on arrival at the destination on payment of proper charges and compliance with any other conditions set out in the air consignment note. (Article 13); and

(b) may enforce rights in his own name even if acting in the interests of another, subject to the fulfillment of all obligations of the consignor under the contract of carriage. (Article 14).

Procedure in the event of a claim

17–014 Unless otherwise stated in the air consignment note, the consignee can exercise his rights if the carrier admits loss of the goods, or if they have not arrived seven days after they should have arrived. Complaints by the person entitled to delivery must be made in writing either upon the air consignment note or separately, in cases of damage, forthwith after discovery, or at the latest within seven days of receipt,[27] and in cases of delay, within 14 days from the date on which the goods were placed at his disposal.[28] As to the jurisdiction for bringing a claim, Article 28 provides that an action for damages must be brought in the territory of one of the contracting states, either in the jurisdiction of the carrier's ordinary residence, or where the carrier has his principal place of business, or

---

[26] See *Datacard Corpn v. Air Express International Corp* [1983] 2 Lloyd's Rep. 81.

[27] Article 26(2). "Damage" includes partial loss: *Fothergill v. Monarch Airlines Ltd* [1981] A.C. 251. *Cf.* also *Rothmans of Pall Mall (Overseas) Ltd v. Saudi Arabian Airlines Corp* [1981] Q.B. 368.

[28] On the calculation of damages for delay see *Panalpina International Transport Ltd v. Densil Underwear Ltd* [1981] 2 Lloyd's Rep. 187.

has an establishment by which the contract was made, or the place of destination.[29]

Carriage governed by the amended Warsaw Convention

Document of carriage

The document of carriage is called the air waybill (AWB). All the provisions of **17–015** the original Convention relating to the air waybill apply to the air waybill under the amended Convention, with the most important exception of the particulars to appear therein and the penalties for omission. Articles 5 to 8 inclusive prescribe the requirements in relation to the air waybill, but those relating to the contents of the air waybill are considerably less onerous. The document shall contain, in accordance with Article 8:

(a) an indication of the places of departure and destination;

(b) if the places of departure and destination are within the territory of a single High Contracting Party, one or more agreed stopping places being within the territory of another state, an indication of at least one such stopping place; and

(c) an indication of the weight of the consignment.

If the requirements are not complied with, the contract of carriage will nevertheless subsist and be subject to the rules of the Convention, including the rules relating to limitation of liability (Article 9). The requirements contained in Articles 5 to 8 do not apply where the carriage is "performed in extraordinary circumstances outside the normal scope of an air carrier's business" (Article 34).

Basic liability

There are no defences in addition to the basic ones. The defence of negligent **17–016** pilotage has been dropped.

Servants and agents of the carrier enjoy the benefit of the same limits of liability as the carrier, if they have acted in the course of their employment. The aggregate liability of a carrier, his servants and agents cannot exceed the limit (if a limit applies). When calculating the limits of liability, the weight to be used is the weight of the package or packages concerned, and not necessarily the weight of all packages recorded on the same air waybill, unless the loss, damage or delay of one package affects the value of others on the same air waybill. The liability of the carrier is limited to 17 SDRs per kilogramme unless the consignor has declared a higher sum. Further, according to Article 25, the limits will not

---

[29] For an examination of Arts 28 and 29 see *Milor SRL v. British Airways plc* [1996] Q.B. 702 at 706.

apply if the carrier has caused the loss or damage intentionally or recklessly.[30] Article 18 allows the carrier to escape liability if he can prove that the loss or damage was a result of one or more of the following:

(a) inherent defect or vice of the goods;

(b) defective packing performed by other than the carrier or his servants;

(c) an act of war or an armed conflict;

(d) an act of public authority carried out in connection with the entry, exit or transit of the cargo.

Arbitration clauses are allowed if arbitration is to take place within one of the jurisdictions allowed by the Convention (Article 32).

Special rights of consignor and consignee

17–017 These have not been varied in the amended Convention.

Procedure in the event of a claim

17–018 The time limits for written complaints by the person entitled to delivery have been varied as follows:

(a) in cases of damage—the maximum is increased from 7 to 14 days[31];

(b) in cases of delay—the maximum is increased from 14 to 21 days. (Article 26).

Non-Convention carriage

17–019 The basic system of liability, including limits and times within which written complaint must be made for non-Convention carriage,[32] is exactly the same as those in the amended Convention, but there are no provisions whatsoever relating to documents of carriage or what has been described above as special rights of consignor and consignee.

The non-Convention rules were also applied to the carriage of mail or postal packages, because it became clear that at common law the sender of an airmail package had a right of direct action, without any limitation of liability against the air carrier.[33] The particular case involved carriage between London and

---

[30] See *Antwerp United Diamonds BVBA and The Excess Insurance Co Ltd v. Air Europe* [1995] 2 Lloyd's Rep. 224, where the relationship of Art. 25 to Art. 22 was examined; as to misconduct see *The Thomas Cook Group Ltd and others v. Air Malta Co Ltd (Trading as Air Malts)* [1997] 2 Lloyd's Rep. 399.

[31] On partial loss, see *Fothergill v. Monarch Airlines Ltd* [1981] A.C. 25.

[32] The rules applicable here are contained in Sched. 1 to the Carriage by Air Acts (Application of Provisions) Order 1967.

[33] *Moukataff v. BOAC* [1967] 1 Lloyd's Rep. 396, in which the senders of £20,000 in bank notes to Kuwait recovered the missing balance of over £17,000 from BOAC by reason of the theft of the money from a sealed mailbag by a BOAC employee who was convicted of the offence.

Kuwait, which would not have been governed by the original Warsaw Convention even if the package had been ordinary cargo instead of airmail, because Kuwait was not then a party to the Convention. In any event, the unamended Convention "does not apply to carriage performed under the terms of any international postal Convention" and the amended Convention "shall not apply to carriage of mail and postal packages". The point has now been dealt with by section 29(3) of the Post Office Act 1969 which protects the Post Office, its officers and persons "engaged in or about the carriage of mail" from civil liability for loss of or damage to a postal packet.[34] It has been held that an airline which carried mail could claim the protection of this section; in this case[35] American Express sent a postal packet containing travellers' cheques from Brighton, England, to a bank in Swaziland. The Post Office sent a sealed mailbag containing this consignment to British Airways at Heathrow airport in London for carriage to Johannesburg and on-carriage to Swaziland. The packet containing the traveller's cheques was stolen at the airport by a loader who was later convicted of theft. In proceedings by American Express the defendant airline pleaded successfully the protection of section 29(3). As the immunity from suit provided by this section is total, it cannot be said that this regulation is satisfactory, but it should not be overlooked that it is laid down in an Act of Parliament. For non-Convention carriage, Special Drawing Rights (SDRs) are already substituted for gold francs.[36]

IATA carriage

A further measure of uniformity in the rules relating to cargo is introduced by **17–020** the practices of members of the International Air Transport Association (IATA) who have for over 50 years been using a common form of air waybill and associated conditions of contract which appear on the reverse of the three Original copies, all of which have been revised from time to time. The IATA style of waybill and conditions of contract are used by IATA members for interline and online carriage, and also by non-members who either participate in interline carriage involving IATA members or merely wish to adopt the international standards set by IATA members. The format of the IATA air waybill is designed, amongst other things, to facilitate production of a copy air waybill which can easily be transmitted by electronic means, but is not a document of significance for legal purposes.

IATA conditions of contract cannot in any way derogate from the provisions of either the original or the amended Convention. Sample copies of the latest forms are made freely available to exporters on application to the leading IATA airlines.

Condition No. 4 of the IATA Conditions provides that in non-Convention situations, except as otherwise provided in the carrier's tariffs or the conditions

---

[34] The Post Office Act 1969, s. 33 imposes a limited liability in respect of registered inland packets.
[35] *American Express Co v. British Airways Board* [1983] 1 W.L.R. 701.
[36] The Carriage by Air Acts (Application of Provisions) (Second Amendment) Order 1979 (S.I. 1979 No. 931).

of carriage, the carrier's liability shall not exceed U.S. $20.00 or the equivalent per kilogramme of goods lost, damaged or delayed, in the absence of any declared value. The maximum limit is intended to be an approximation to the Convention limit of 17 SDRs, which is the limit set out in the IATA alternative air waybill per kilogramme. Thus, for all practical purposes, the Convention limits prevail in all but the most rare of situations internationally and are applied by law and by contract to all actions in the English courts, except if the flight is a purely internal flight.[37] Thus, a contract for the carriage of passengers or cargo from London to Manchester would be governed neither by the Convention (in its amended or unamended form), nor by the non-Convention Rules, but by its contractual terms, which would be subject to the provisions of the Unfair Contract Terms Act 1977 and the Unfair Terms in Consumer Contracts Regulations 1994.[38]

---

[37] See *Holmes v. Bangladesh Biman Corporation* [1989] 1 Lloyd's Rep. 444.
[38] See D. Grant, "Carriage—A United Kingdom Consumer's Perspective" [1998] J.B.L.123 for an informative article on the possible impact by the Unfair Terms in Consumer Contracts Regulations 1999 on the IATA General Conditions of Carriage. S.I. 1999 No. 2083 which implements E.C. Council Directive 93/13 and revokes S.I. 1994 No. 3159. S.I. 1999 No. 2083 came into force on October 1, 1999.

CHAPTER 18

CARRIAGE OF GOODS BY LAND

CARRIAGE BY RAIL AND ROAD

The international transport of goods overland is carried out by rail or road. Both **18–001** modes of transport are regulated by international Conventions.

International transport of goods by rail is governed by the International Convention concerning the Carriage of Goods by Rail (CIM)[1] of February 25, 1961. This Convention was given statutory force in the United Kingdom by the Carriage by Railway Act 1972 but this Act was repealed by the International Transport Conventions Act 1983, which continued to give effect to the CIM as part of the Convention Concerning International Carriage by Rail (COTIF) signed at Berne on May 9, 1980. CIM is appended to this Convention in Part 3 as Uniform Rules concerning the Contract for International Carriage of Goods by Rail (CIM).[2] The 1983 Act and, as far as the United Kingdom is concerned, COTIF, came into operation on May 1, 1985.[3]

International transport of goods by road is governed by the Convention on the Contract for the International Carriage of Goods by Road (CMR)[4] signed at Geneva on May 19, 1956. Effect was given to it in the United Kingdom by the Carriage of Goods by Road Act 1965 which embodies the CMR in its Schedule.[5] The 1965 Act came into operation on June 5, 1967.[6]

---

[1] CIM stands for *(Convention Internationale de Marchandises)* / *convention internationale concernant le transport des marchandises par chemin de fer.* For further reading on the carriage of goods on land: A. Messent and D. Glass, *CMR: Contracts for the International Carriage of Goods by Road* (2nd ed., 1995); M. A. Clarke, *International Carriage of Goods by Road: CMR* (3rd ed., 1997); M. A. Clarke, "Containers; Proof that Damage occurred during Carriage", in *International Carriage of Goods: Some Legal Problems and Possible Solutions* (ed. C. M. Schmitthoff and R. M. Goode, 1988), p. 64; D. A. Glass and C. Cashmore, *Introduction to the Carriage of Goods.* See also Dr. M. Clarke: The transport of goods in Europe: patterns and problems of uniform law. See [1999] L.M.C.L.Q. 36 for an excellent survey of the various transport regimes.

[2] The 1983 Act incorporates Cmnd. 8535 (1982), which contains COTIF; CIM is Appendix B of the COTIF, reproduced in Cmnd. 8535 at pp. 107 *et seq.* This version was subjected to amendments in 1990, in force June 1, 1991. There is also a protocol which made modifications to certain Articles. This Protocol became part of U.K. law by virtue of S.I. 1994 No. 1907 in force November 1, 1996. A revised CIM and COTIF was expected to come into force in 1999. The CIM revision results from among other matters, the recognition that rail carriage may only be one element in the carriage of goods and also that the party responsible for the railway system may not be the operator of the carrying service. For further information see *Contracts for the Carriage of Goods by Land, Sea and Air,* Lloyds of London Press.

[3] The International Transport Conventions Act 1983 (Certification of Commencement of Convention) Order 1985 (S.I. 1985 No. 612). COTIF was modified by means of a Protocol which came into force on November 1, 1996 by S.I. 1994 No. 1907.

[4] *Convention relative au contrat de transport des marchandises par route.*

[5] The 1965 Act is amended by the Carriage by Air and Road Act 1979 which replaces the references to gold francs in the CMR by references to SDRs.

[6] Carriage of Goods by Road Act 1965 (Commencement) Order 1967 (S.I. 1967 No. 819). The application of the 1965 Act has been extended by virtue of section 9 of the Act to Gibraltar, the Isle of Man and Guernsey.

The Parties to COTIF include practically all European countries and also some Asian and African countries.[7]

Carriage by rail

18–002 Increasing importance is attached to the international carriage of goods by rail. The factors contributing to this state of affairs include the interest in environmental protection and the consequent impetus to carry goods by rail and the opening of the Channel Tunnel, which meant that for the first time an "international" rail transit could commence in the United Kingdom without the necessity of conveying the rolling stock on a specially equipped train ferry.

Scope of application

18–003 As set out in Article 1, the Rules apply to all consignments of goods for carriage under a through consignment note made out for a route over the territories of at least two States. If a consignment commences in one State and terminates in that State but passes over the territory of another State in transit, the Rules will not apply if the lines of transit are operated by the railways of the State of departure or the States concerned have agreed that such consignments are not to be regarded as international. The revised Rules will no longer place an obligation on a railway to carry goods if certain conditions are met.[8] If goods are carried, they may be subject to other Regulations concerning the international carriage of goods by rail.[9]

Making the contract

18–004 Article 11 deals with the making of the contract between the consignor and the railway company. The consignor will make out the consignment note, one for each wagon load, which will correspond with the conditions prescribed by the Rules.[10] The contract comes into existence when the railway has accepted the goods for carriage together with the consignment note, which will be stamped with the stamp of the forwarding station. This stamped consignment will be evidence of the making and the content of the contract.[11] The consignor is responsible for the particulars in the consignment note, which may be verified by the railway,[12] and for the proper packing of the goods.[13] As for loading, the

---

[7] The International Transport Conventions Act 1983 provides that certification can be made by order in council as to Member States of COTIF, s.2(1).

[8] Art. 2 which imposed this requirement is to be abolished by the 1999 revision.

[9] Art. 4. Such as the Agreement on the International Carriage of Perishable Foodstuffs and its eponymous Act of 1976 and EC Council Directive 96/49 on the Carriage of Dangerous Goods by Rail.

[10] Arts 12 and 13. The consignment note may provide for "grand vitesse"—the goods must be dispatched within 12 hours and travel 300 kms every 24 hours, or "petite vitesse"—dispatch within 24 hours, 200 kms every 24 hours: Art. 27.

[11] Art. 11(3).

[12] Arts 18 and 21 respectively.

[13] Art. 19.

relative responsibilities are governed by the provisions in force at the loading station.

Liability

The railway accepting the goods is responsible for the entire journey, but each **18–005** railway, if more than one is used, becomes a party to the contract in the consignment note.[14] In the event of a claim against the railway arising out of the loss of or damage to goods, Article 55 provides that the claim may be made against the forwarding railway, the railway of destination or the railway on which the event giving rise to the proceedings took place. In the event that a claimant may choose between several railways, his choice is extinguished when action is brought against one.[15]

The action against the railway may be brought, according to Article 54, by the consignor until such a time as the consignee took possession of the consignment note, accepted the goods or asserted his right to delivery. The railway has a number of exclusions from liability which are set out in Article 36, which include loss or damage arising from, *inter alia*, defective packing, loading— where the consignor has carried out the loading—and inherent vice. The burden of proving the loss resulting from one of the matters set out in Article 36 falls on the railway.[16]

The railway's liability to compensate is limited to 17 units of account per kilogram of gross mass short and the refund of carriage charges and other amounts incurred in connection with the goods.[17] The compensation limits may not be relied upon by the railway if the loss or damage has been caused by its own wilful misconduct or gross negligence (Article 44). Any claim must be made in writing to the appropriate railway, and action must be brought within one year, or two years if the loss or damage was caused by wilful misconduct or in the event of fraud.[18]

Carriage by Road—CMR

Scope of application

The CMR[19] applies to every contract for the carriage of goods by road in **18–006** vehicles[20] for reward, when the place of taking over the goods and the place designated for delivery, as specified in the contract, are situated in two different

---

[14] Arts 35(1) and (2).
[15] Art. 55(4).
[16] Art. 37(1)—a third party may rely on excluding or limiting provisions. See Contracts (Rights of Third Parties) Act 1999, s.6(5)(b) and 6(8)(a).
[17] Art. 40 as amended.
[18] Arts 53 and 58 respectively.
[19] n. 4, *ante*. See Chitty, *Contracts* (28th ed., 1999), Chap. 36.
[20] "Vehicles" includes articulated vehicles, trailers and semi-trailers: Art. 1(2).

countries[21] of which at least one is a Contracting Party,[22] that is, a State which has accepted the Convention. All the Contracting Parties are European states.[23]

It should be noted that the Convention does not require that both the countries of dispatch and of destination should be Contracting Parties. A contract for the consignment by road of goods from the United Kingdom (a Contracting Party) to Saudi Arabia (not a Contracting Party) is governed by the CMR.

The Convention also applies where the carriage is carried out by States or by governmental institutions or organisations.[24] For the purposes of any proceedings brought in a court in the United Kingdom under the Convention, the provisions relating to those proceedings apply equally to an arbitration tribunal.[25] A contract for carriage may confer competence on an arbitration tribunal if the clause conferring competence provides that the tribunal applies the Convention.[26] The Crown is bound by the Act. The CMR does not apply to traffic between the United Kingdom and the Irish Republic.[27] Further, the CMR does not apply[28]:

(a) to carriage performed under an international postal Convention;

(b) to funeral consignments;

(c) to furniture removal.

The CMR further provides that, where the vehicle containing the goods is carried over part of the journey by sea, rail, inland waterways or air and, except in cases of emergency, the goods are not unloaded from the vehicle, the CMR shall apply to the whole of the carriage. The CMR thus applies in the frequent cases in which a container, particularly a groupage container, is taken by road on a trailer or similar vehicle from the territory of a Contracting Party to another country. If, however, the loss, damage or delay has occurred during the carriage by the other means of transport and was not caused by an act or omission of the carrier by road, the liability of the carrier by road is determined not by the CMR but by the applicable international Convention[29]; if there is no such Convention, the CMR applies. These provisions were applied in *Thermo Engineers Ltd v. Ferrymasters Ltd*,[30] a case which was discussed earlier.[31]

---

[21] For the purposes of the Convention, Jersey is not a "different country" from the United Kingdom: *Chloride Industrial Batteries Ltd v. F & W Freight Ltd* [1989] 1 W.L.R. 45.

[22] Art. 1(1). Even if a consignment note had not been issued, but there was in existence an all-embracing agreement for multiple deliveries, the CMR will apply, *Gefco. Gefco (U.K.) Ltd v. Mason* [1998] 2 Lloyd's Rep. 585.

[23] s.2 of the Act and Carriage of Goods by Road (Parties to the Convention) (Amendment) Order 1980 (S.I. 1980 No. 697).

[24] Art. 1(3) and s.6 of the Act.

[25] s.7—as to venue of jurisdiction, see Arts 31 and 39 and see also *Frans Maas Logistics (U.K.) Ltd v. CDR Tracking BV* [1999] 2 Lloyd's Rep. 179 at 183.

[26] Art. 33.

[27] Protocol of Signature, attached to the Act.

[28] Art. 1(4).

[29] Art. 2(1).

[30] [1981] 1 Lloyd's Rep. 200.

[31] See *ante*, para. 2–007.

Successive carriers

The CMR provides in Article 34 that, if the carriage by road is governed by a **18–007** single contract but performed by successive road carriers, each shall be responsible for the performance of the whole operation, the second and each successive carrier becoming a party to the contract of carriage under the terms of the consignment note by reason of his acceptance of the goods and consignment note. It must, however, be noted that a "single contract performed by successive carriers" is a contract under which a single consignment note is issued. If a consignment is split into several parcels and a separate consignment note is issued in respect of each, the carriers carrying these parcels are not successive carriers within Article 34.[32] In *ITT Schaub-Lorenz Vertriebsgesellschaft mbH v. Birkart Johann Internationale Spedition GmbH & Co KG* Bingham L.J. stated[33] "Where there are successive CMR carriers, a CMR carrier successfully sued by the sender or consignee can recover against a CMR carrier responsible for the loss or damage, but that carrier cannot escape liability by showing that he has delegated or subcontracted performance to a non-CMR carrier who was actually responsible." Except in the case of a counterclaim or set-off, legal proceedings in respect of liability for loss, damage or delay may be brought only against the first carrier, the last carrier or the carrier who was in control of the goods when the event which caused the loss, damage or delay occurred, but several carriers may be sued at the same time.[34] In the case of successive carriers the one responsible for the loss or damage is, as between the carriers, solely liable for compensation, but if it cannot be ascertained to which carrier liability is attributable, the compensation has to be borne by them proportionally.[35] If one of the carriers is insolvent, the share of compensation due from him has to be paid by the other carriers in proportion to the share of the payment for the carriage due to them.[36]

It is not always easy to decide whether the person with whom the owner of the goods contracts undertakes only to procure carriage, that is to act as a forwarder, or whether he contracts to carry, that is to act as carrier, even if he

---

[32] Art. 34. A "single contract performed by successive carriers" within Art. 34 is a contract under which a single consignment note is issued. If a consignment is split into several parcels and separate consignment notes are issued, one for each parcel, the carriers carrying these separate parcels are not "successive carriers" within Art. 34: *Arctic Electronics Co (U.K.) Ltd v. McGregor Sea & Air Services Ltd* [1985] 2 Lloyd's Rep. 510. This issue is of particular importance if the question of jurisdiction of the English courts under Art. 39(2) arises.

[33] [1988] 1 Lloyd's Rep. 487 at 493. The task of acceptance of the consignment note may be delegated. *Coggins T/A P.C. Transport v. LKW Walter I.T. AG* [1999] 1 Lloyd's Rep. 255 at 259.

[34] Art. 36. Despite the wording of Art. 36, the general rule, known as the rule in *Aries Tanker Corporation v. Total Transport Ltd* [1977] 1 W.L.R. 185 (see *ante*, para. 15-007), that a claim in respect of loss of or damage to the cargo cannot be asserted by way of deduction from freight, likewise applies to freight due under a contract of carriage to which the CMR applies: *R H & D International Ltd v. IAS Animal Air Services Ltd* [1984] 1 W.L.R. 573; *United Carriers Ltd v. Heritage Food Group (U.K.) Ltd* [1995] 2 Lloyd's Rep. 269.

[35] Art. 37.

[36] Art. 38. Art. 39(2) deals with the forum in which the carrier who has paid the goods owner can bring proceedings for recovery against the carriers concerned, who were responsible for the loss, damage or delay, see *Cummins Engine Co Ltd v. Davis Freight Forwarding (Hull) Ltd* [1981] 1 W.L.R. 1363, CA.

sub-contracts the actual carriage to another. In the former case the CMR does not apply to him but in the latter case it does. If a person has contracted to carry the goods to their destination by a single contract but does not take the goods into charge himself and arranges for them to be delivered direct to the actual carrier to whom he has sub-contracted the job, he is nevertheless the first carrier and the actual carrier is the successive carrier within Article 34 of the CMR. Apart from the contract of carriage with the first carrier, in the words of Megaw L.J.[37]: "the CMR Convention then sets out to create an artificial statutory contract between the actual carrier and the owner of the goods." The learned judge continued:

> "Looking at article 1(1), I think that the CMR Convention must have contemplated that for this purpose the company, or individual, with whom the owner of the goods contracts is the first carrier, whether or not he himself takes possession of the goods, and that all subsequent carriers are the successive carriers within the meaning of these provisions."

On the other hand, if the owner of the goods himself contracts with several contractors, each for a part of the journey, there is no single contract of carriage with the first contractor and the rules of the CMR on successive contractors do not apply, although the Convention may apply to the individual carriers.

The consignment note

18–008 The CMR provides that the contract of carriage by road shall be confirmed by a consignment note but that the absence of, or any irregularity in, the note shall not affect the validity of the contract, which will remain subject to the Convention.[38] The consignment note has to be made out in three original copies signed by the sender and the carrier. The first copy is handed to the sender, the second accompanies the goods, and the third is retained by the carrier. When goods are carried in different vehicles or are of a different kind or are divided into different lots, the seller or the carrier is entitled to require a separate consignment note for each vehicle or each kind or lot of goods.[39] The consignment note is neither a negotiable instrument, nor a document of title.

The consignment note is prima facie evidence of the making of the contract of carriage, the conditions of the contract and the receipt of the goods by the carrier.[40] If the consignment note does not contain a clausing relating to the condition of the goods, when received by the carrier, it is presumed that the goods and their packaging appeared to be in good order and condition and that,

---

[37] In *Ulster Swift Ltd v. Taunton Meat Haulage Ltd* [1977] 1 Lloyd's Rep. 346 at 360–361. See *Coggins, ante,* n. 33.
[38] Art. 4. For an unusual practice in the making out of the consignment note, see *Aqualon (U.K.) Ltd v. Vallana Shipping Corporation* [1994] 1 Lloyd's Rep. 669.
[39] Art. 5(1) and (2). The particulars to be set out in the consignment note are stated in Art. 6 and include the date, the place of making out the note, the name and address of the sender, carrier and consignee, a description of the goods including weight marks and numbers and if the goods are dangerous, their generally recognised description. See also Art. 22(1) and EU Council Directive 1994/55 regarding dangerous goods carried by road.
[40] Art. 9(1). As to the lack of a consignment note, see *Gefco, ante,* n. 22.

when the carrier took them over, their marks and numbers corresponded with the statements in the consignment note.[41]

For the purposes of the Customs or other formalities which have to be completed before delivery of the goods, the sender shall attach the necessary documents to the consignment note or place them at the disposal of the carrier and shall furnish him with all the information which he requires.[42]

The sender is entitled to deal with the goods, in particular by asking the carrier to stop the goods in transit, to change the place at which delivery is to take place, or to deliver the goods to a person other than the consignee designated in the consignment note.[43] However, that right ceases when the second copy of the consignment note has been handed over to the designated consignee or that consignee has required the carrier, against his receipt, to deliver up to him the second copy of the consignment note and the goods.[44] Furthermore, the consignee is entitled to dispose of the goods from the time when the consignment note is drawn up if the sender has made an entry to that effect on the consignment note.[45] If the sender, in exercising his right of disposal, has ordered the delivery of the goods to another person, that person is not entitled to name another consignee.[46] The sender who wishes to exercise the right of disposal has to produce the first copy of the consignment note to the carrier and the new instructions must be entered thereon; he must further give the carrier an indemnity and a division of the cargo on such a disposal is not permissible.[47] The right of the sender to stop the goods in transit given by these provisions should not be confused with the right of stoppage in transit of the seller under the contract of sale.[48] The right under the CMR exists against the carrier and is not dependent on the insolvency of the buyer, but the right under the Sale of Goods Act 1979 exists against the buyer and can be exercised only if the buyer has become insolvent.

When circumstances prevent delivery of the goods after their arrival at their destination, the carrier shall ask the sender for his instructions. If the consignee refuses to accept the goods, the sender is entitled to dispose of them without being obliged to produce the first copy of the consignment note, but despite his refusal the consignee may still require delivery as long as the carrier has not received instructions to the contrary from the seller.[49]

Liability of the carrier

The carrier is liable for the total or partial loss[50] of the goods and for damage **18–009** thereto occurring between the time when he takes over the goods and the time

---

[41] Art. 9(2).
[42] Art. 11.
[43] Art. 12(1).
[44] Arts 12(2) and 13.
[45] Art. 12(3).
[46] Art. 12(4).
[47] Art. 12(5).
[48] See *ante*, para. 5–016.
[49] Art. 15.
[50] On the meaning of "total loss" in the CMR see *post*, n. 75.

of delivery, as well as for delay in the delivery.[51] However, the carrier will be relieved of liability if the loss, damage or delay was caused:

(a) by the wrongful act or neglect of the claimant; or

(b) by the instructions of the claimant given otherwise than as the result of a wrongful act or neglect on the part of the carrier; or

(c) by inherent vice of the goods; or

(d) through circumstances which the carrier could not avoid and the consequences of which he was unable to prevent.[52]

If the carrier wishes to rely on the fourth of these grounds, it is not sufficient for him to show that he did not act negligently; he has to show that the loss could not be avoided.[53] In one case[54] the carrier, who was driving a consignment of shoes from Milan to England, parked the lorry in an unguarded lorry park in Milan in order for him and his assistant to have a meal. The only guarded lorry park was two hours away and to drive there would have involved breaking the driving period regulations. The alarm on the lorry was left on but thieves managed to by-pass it and to steal the lorry and its load. The carrier was held to be liable to the owner of the shoes because the loss was avoidable, as he and his assistant could have taken turns to guard the lorry. In another case involving the carriage of pickled pelts from Ayr to Salerno[55] the consignment was stolen by armed robbers between Rome and Naples. The owners of the goods alleged that as there was no security device on the vehicle and no extra driver the carrier could not rely on Article 17(2). The Judge held that in the circumstances of the robbery nothing could have saved the consignment and that the carriers were entitled to rely on the fact that the loss was caused by circumstances which were unavoidable. Longmore J. has indicated that for willful misconduct to be established there must be proved either an intention to do something which the actor knew to be wrong or a reckless act, in the sense that the actor was aware that loss might result from his act but did not care whether loss would result or not.[56]

The carrier cannot rely on any of the exemptions if the loss, damage or delay is caused by the defective condition of the vehicle,[57] *e.g.* if the tilt cover of the vehicle is porous and, as a result, the load is damaged by rain.[58] Further, the carrier is not relieved of liability by reason of the wrongful act or neglect of the

---

[51] Art. 17(1).

[52] Art. 17(2).

[53] The burden of proving that the loss could not be avoided rests on the carrier: Art. 18(1).

[54] *Michael Galley Footwear Ltd (in liq.) v. Laboni* [1982] 2 All E.R. 200. See also *J. J. Silber Ltd v. Islander Trucking Ltd* [1985] 2 Lloyd's Rep. 243 (armed robbery in Italy; carriers liable because they failed to discharge burden of proof imposed by Art. 18).

[55] *G.L. Cicatiello SrL v. Anglo European Shipping Services Ltd* [1994] 1 Lloyd's Rep. 678.

[56] In *National Semiconductors (U.K.) Ltd v. UPS Ltd and Inter City Trucks Ltd* [1996] 2 Lloyd's Rep. 212 at 214.

[57] Art. 17(3).

[58] *Walek & Co v. Chapman and Ball (International) Ltd* [1980] 2 Lloyd's Rep. 279.

person from whom he may have hired the vehicle or of the agents or servants of the latter.[59]

In addition, the CMR contains a catalogue of special risks which relieve the carrier from liability; among them are the use of open unsheeted vehicles when their use has been expressly agreed and specified in the consignment note.[60] The burden of proving that loss, damage or delay was due to one of the exemptions specified in Article 17(2) rests on the carrier.[61] If the carriage is performed in vehicles specially equipped to protect the goods from the effects of heat, cold, variation in temperature or the humidity of the air, the carrier cannot claim the benefit of the special risks exemptions otherwise applicable, unless he proves that all steps incumbent on him in the circumstances with respect to the choice, maintenance and use of such equipment were taken and he complied with any special instructions issued to him.[62]

The fact that the goods have not been delivered within 30 days following the expiry of the agreed time limit or, if no time limit has been agreed, within 60 days from the time when the carrier took over the goods, shall be conclusive evidence of the loss of the goods. The person entitled to make a claim may thereupon treat them as lost.[63]

If the goods are sent on "cash on delivery" (c.o.d.) terms and the carrier hands them over without insisting on payment in cash, he is liable for compensation not exceeding the amount of the charge defined in the term, without prejudice to his right of action against the consignee.[64] The compensation which the carrier is liable to pay in respect of total or partial loss of the goods is subject to a maximum limitation of liability. It is 8.33 SDRs per kilogram of gross weight short[65]; in addition, the carrier has to refund in full the carriage charges. Customs duties and other charges incurred in respect of the carriage of the goods.[66] In *James Buchanan & Co Ltd v. Babco Forwarding and Shipping U.K. Ltd*[67] a consignment of whisky for export from Glasgow to Iran was stolen from

---

[59] See Art. 17(3).
[60] Art. 17(4).
[61] Art. 18(1).
[62] Art. 18(4) and *Ulster Swift Ltd v. Taunton Meat Haulage Ltd* [1977] 1 Lloyd's Rep. 346.
[63] Art. 20.
[64] Art. 21. The carrier is, in principle, not authorised to accept a cheque instead of cash but it is thought he has implied authority to release the goods to the consignee if he has an unqualified binding undertaking of the consignee's bank that the cheque will be honoured. Sometimes the carrier is instructed to release the goods "contre attestation de blocage des fonds" (CABF arrangement); such a certificate would have to be given by the consignee's bank.
[65] Art. 23(3). The SDRs were introduced as "units of account" by the Carriage by Air and Road Act 1979, s.4(2), with effect from December 28, 1980 (Carriage by Air and Road Act 1979 (Commencement No. 1) Order 1980 (S.I. 1980 No. 1966 C.84)). The conversion of the SDRs into sterling for a particular day is ascertained from the Treasury and a certificate on the conversion value given by or on behalf of the Treasury is conclusive evidence of this value (1979 Act, s.5).
    Before the introduction of the SDRs the maximum limitation of liability was expressed as 25 gold francs; the reference to the gold franc was here to the Latin Union gold franc; the ascertainment of the value of this gold franc was uncertain. See L. Bristow, "Gold franc—Replacement of unit of account" [1978] 1 M.C.L.Q. 31.
[66] Art. 23(4). The fee for the survey of the damaged goods is recoverable as "other charges": *ICI plc v. MAT Transport Ltd* [1987] 1 Lloyd's Rep. 354 at 362.
[67] [1978] A.C. 141.

a lorry park in Woolwich. The export value of the whisky was some £7,000 but the Customs authorities demanded from Buchanan, the owners and consignors, excise duty of about £30,000. According to Customs law, Buchanan had to pay that duty. Buchanan then tried to recover that amount from the carriers. The House of Lords considered that claim as justified. The court decided that the excise duty constituted "other charges incurred in respect of the carriage of goods" within Article 23(4) and held that the carriers were liable for the full £37,000 because there was no limit placed on the items mentioned in paragraph 4 but, on the contrary, it was provided that the carrier had to pay them "in full".

In the case of delay, the measure of damages is limited to the carriage charges if the claimant can prove that he has suffered damage to that amount.[68]

The defences which exclude or limit the liability of the carrier are also available if the action is founded on tort and not on contract.[69] The agents and servants and any other persons of whose services the carrier makes use for the performance of the carriage may avail themselves of the same defences if they have acted within the scope of their employment.[70] Article 29 provides that the carrier may not avail himself of the provisions of the CMR relating to the limitation or exclusion of liability or the shifting of the burden of proof where he has been guilty of wilful misconduct, or such default which the tribunal seised of the matter considers wilful misconduct. The issue arose in *Laceys Footwear (Wholesale) Ltd v. Bowler International Freight Ltd*[71] where the carriers not only failed to effect insurance on the goods as required by the contract of carriage but also misdelivered the goods contrary to specific delivery instructions. The Court of Appeal determined that Articles 23 and 27 contain provisions which "fix" liability rather than exclude or limit it, so are therefore unaffected by the application of Article 29.

Time limits

18–010 If the consignee takes delivery of the goods and does not, in the case of apparent loss or damage at the time of delivery, or in the case of loss or damage which is not apparent, within seven days of delivery, send the carrier a notice of reservations, giving a general indication of the loss or damage, then the fact of taking delivery is prima facie evidence that he received the goods in the condition described in the consignment note.[72] No compensation is payable for delay in delivery unless a notice of reservations has been sent in writing to the carrier within 21 days from the time that the goods were placed at the disposal of the consignee.[73]

The period of limitation for bringing an action arising out of the contract of carriage under the CMR is one year. Nevertheless, in the case of willful miscon-

---

[68] Art. 23(5).
[69] Art. 28.
[70] Art. 28(2). See Contracts (Rights of Third Parties) Act 1999, ss.6(5)(b) and 6(8)(b) concerning a third party's ability to rely on excluding or limiting provisions in a contract governed by the CMR.
[71] [1997] 2 Lloyd's Rep. 369. See also *ante*, n. 56.
[72] Art. 30(1).
[73] Art. 30(3).

duct or such default as in accordance with the law of the court or tribunal dealing with the case is considered equivalent to willful misconduct, the period of limitation is three years.[74] According to Article 32(1), time begins to run:

(a) in the case of partial loss, damage or delay in delivery from the date of delivery;

(b) in the case of total loss,[75] from the 30th day after the expiry of the agreed time limit or, where no time limit is agreed, from the 60th day from the date when the goods were taken over by the carrier; or

(c) in all other cases on the expiry of three months after the making of the contract of carriage.[76]

Paragraph (a) of this provision applies only if two conditions are satisfied: there must be a partial loss, damage or delay, and the goods must have been delivered. Where the goods are not delivered within the time limits stated in Article 20(1),[77] they are conclusively presumed to be lost and consequently the starting point for the one year limitation period is determined by paragraph (b). If the case cannot be brought under either paragraph (a) or (b) of Article 32(1), the starting point for the one year period of limitation is determined by paragraph (c).[78]

The CMR allows the normal limitation period of one year, which is rather short, to be suspended if a written claim is made by the goods owner or somebody on his behalf against the carrier. This suspension, however, operates only until the date on which the carrier rejects the claim by notification in writing.[79] The object of this suspension is to enable the carrier to decide whether the claim is justified. Where there are successive carriers, the claimant must notify the carrier against whom he wants to make the claim. It is not sufficient for the claimant only to notify the first carrier and to leave it to him to notify the successive carriers because each of the carriers concerned must know that a claim is intended against him and be given the opportunity of stopping the suspension of the limitation period by rejecting the claim.[80]

---

[74] Art. 32(1). On "wilful misconduct" see also *Sidney G. Jones Ltd v. Martin Bencher Ltd* [1986] 1 Lloyd's Rep. 54 (driver falling asleep at the wheel) and the cases at nn. 54, 55, 56 and 71 *ante*.

[75] "Total loss" in Art. 32(1) of the CMR means, in the terminology of the Marine Insurance Act 1906, "actual total loss"; it does not include "constructive total loss": *ICI plc v. MAT Transport Ltd* [1987] 1 Lloyd's Rep. 354.

[76] See *Shell Chemicals U.K. Ltd and Shell U.K. Ltd v. P & O Roadtanks Ltd* [1993] 1 Lloyd's Rep. 114.

[77] These times limits are 30 days following the expiry of the agreed time limit or, if there is no agreed time limit, 60 days from the time the carrier took over the goods.

[78] *Worldwide Carriers Ltd v. Ardtran International Ltd* [1983] 1 Lloyd's Rep. 61 at 65. *Cf. William Tatton & Co Ltd v. Ferrymaster Ltd* [1974] 1 Lloyd's Rep. 203.

[79] Art. 32(2).

[80] *Worldwide Carriers Ltd v. Ardtran International Ltd, ante*; *Sidney G. Jones Ltd v. Martin Bencher Ltd* [1986] 1 Lloyd's Rep. 54; *Poclain SA v. SCAC SA* [1986] 1 Lloyd's Rep. 404 (authority of liability insurer of carrier to receive written claim); *ICI plc v. MAT Transport Ltd* [1987] 1 Lloyd's Rep. 354.

Nullity of stipulations contrary to the Convention

18–011 Apart from the internal arrangements between successive carriers,[81] any stipulation which would directly or indirectly derogate from the provisions of the CMR is null and void.[82] In particular, a benefit of insurance in favour of the carrier or any other similar clause or any clause shifting the burden of proof is null and void.[83]

---

[81] But in their internal arrangements carriers cannot abrogate Arts 37 and 38.
[82] Art. 41(1).
[83] Art. 41(2).

PART FOUR

INSURANCE OF GOODS IN TRANSIT

CHAPTER 19

MARINE AND AVIATION INSURANCE

It is customary to insure goods sold for export against the perils of the journey. **19–001** According to the method of transportation, marine, aviation or overland insurance is effected.

The term "marine insurance" is somewhat misleading because the contract of marine insurance can, by agreement of the parties or custom of the trade, be extended so as to protect the assured against losses on inland waters or land which are incidental to the sea voyage.[1] In the export trade extended marine insurance arrangements are made frequently in order to cover not only the sea voyage but also the transportation of goods from the warehouse of the seller to that of the overseas buyer.[2]

Marine insurance is an institution of great antiquity. It was known in Lombardy in the fourteenth century and the first English statute dealing with it was passed in 1601. Lloyd's Coffee House, the birthplace of Lloyd's of London, is first mentioned in the records in 1688. The law relating to marine insurance is codified in the Marine Insurance Act 1906,[3] the Schedule to which contains the standard form policy known as the *Lloyd's S.G. policy*. Since January 1, 1982 this has been replaced by the *Lloyd's Marine Policy*, and the Institute Cargo Clauses.[4] The three most important sets of clauses are known as Clauses A, B and C.

MARINE INSURANCE

Stipulations in the contract of sale

In an export transaction, the terms of the contract of sale normally provide **19–002** whether the costs of marine insurance shall be borne by the seller or by the buyer. If the goods are sold on f.o.b. terms, these costs have to be paid by the buyer and that is true even if the f.o.b. seller, by request of the buyer, has taken

---

[1] Marine Insurance Act 1906, s.2(1).

[2] On the transit clause (incorporating the warehouse to warehouse clause) see para. 19–022.

[3] References to sections on the following pages relate to this Act. The regulation of insurance business in the U.K. is governed by the Insurance Act 1982, as amended by the Financial Services Act, 1986, and that of Lloyd's by Lloyd's Act 1982; neither of these enactments call for discussion in this work.

[4] See *post*, para. 19–018. The full text of the Institute Cargo Clauses is reproduced in the Reference Book of Marine Insurance Clauses, (69th ed., Witherby, 1997). A commentary on these, and the Lloyd's Marine Policy form by Dr. Samir Mankabady is contained in 13 Journ. Marl. L. & Com. 527 (1982) and in the article by N. Leloir, "The Lloyd's Marine Policy and the Institute Cargo Clauses" [1985] J.B.L. 228 (Miss Leloir's article contains a useful comparative table).

out the policy.[5] If the goods are sold on c.i.f. terms, it is the duty of the seller to take out the policy and pay the costs of insurance.[6] In a c. and f. contract the seller need not insure, nor need the buyer (at whose risk the goods are carried), but if the c. and f. contract contains a clause "insurance to be effected by the buyer," or a clause in similar terms, that will normally place the buyer under a contractual obligation to insure and has not merely declaratory effect. The obligation to insure is thereby put into the reverse, and the buyer must take out the same policy which the seller would have been obliged to obtain had it been a c.i.f. contract.[7]

The marine insurance policy or the marine insurance certificate[8] forms part of the shipping documents.[9] Where goods are sold c.i.f. the seller is obliged to take out a marine insurance policy or certificate, which provides cover against the risks customarily covered in the particular trade in respect of the cargo and voyage in question, but he is not required to do more.[10] He need not take out an all risks[11] policy unless the parties have so agreed or it is demanded by the custom of the trade.

The assured, the insurer and the broker

19–003 The parties to a contract of marine insurance are known as the assured and the insurer. Insurers are either underwriting members of Lloyd's or marine insurance companies. The "Society of Lloyd's" has underwriting and non-underwriting members. The former, known as the "names," form groups called "syndicates," which conduct the actual underwriting through an underwriting agent. Every member of a syndicate is liable for a proportionate fraction of the risk, and thus the aim of all insurance is achieved, namely to spread the risk to many persons while, at the same time, providing indemnity for one person, the assured, if a loss occurs. The underwriting agent is usually, but not necessarily, a member of the syndicate or syndicates for which he acts. The duty of an underwriting agent is to conduct the affairs of the syndicate in good faith and for the benefit of the syndicate as a whole.[12] Insurance at Lloyd's is effected in "The Room," which is situated in London, and underwriting members accept only risks offered through Lloyd's brokers (who have access to The Room). A person who wishes to effect an insurance at Lloyd's has thus to employ the services of such a broker. The marine insurance companies have been early competitors of Lloyd's in the field of marine insurance, and can be approached directly or through an agent of the company (sometimes called an "underwriting agent," though his functions are

---

[5] See *ante*, para. 2–007.
[6] See *ante*, para. 2–020.
[7] *Reinhart Co. v. Joshua Hoyle & Sons Ltd* [1961] 1 Lloyd's Rep. 346; see para. 2–038.
[8] See *post*, para. 19–011.
[9] See *ante*, para. 2–021.
[10] In the cotton trade the ordinary insurance policy to be taken out under a c.i.f. contract includes "country damage," *i.e.* pre-shipment damage to the goods: *Reinhart Co. v. Joshua Hoyle & Sons Ltd* [1961] 1 Lloyd's Rep. 346, 353.
[11] On the meaning of "all risks" insurance, see *post*, para. 19–019.
[12] *Daly v. Lime Street Underwriting Agencies* [1987] 2 F.T.L.R. 277.

different from those of an underwriting agent at Lloyd's), or through an insurance broker.

In the normal course of business the exporter who wishes to have his goods insured does not approach the insurer directly but instructs an insurance broker to effect insurance on his behalf. Where the exporter is the regular client of an insurance broker, he forwards his instructions on a form supplied by the broker and gives the required particulars. The broker, who is usually authorised to place the insurance within certain limits as to the rates of premium, writes the essentials of the proposed insurance in customary abbreviations on a document called "the slip"[13] which he takes to Lloyd's or a marine insurance company. An insurer, who is prepared to accept part of the risk, writes on the slip the amount for which he is willing to insure and adds his initials; this is known as "writing a line." The presentation of the slip by a broker to an underwriter constitutes an offer and "writing a line" constitutes an acceptance by the underwriter.[14] Hence each line written on a slip gives rise to an immediately binding contract between the underwriter and the assured or reinsured for whom the broker is acting when he presents the slip. The broker then takes the slip to other insurers who successively write lines until the whole risk is covered.[15]

The broker then sends the assured a memorandum of the insurance effected which is conveniently executed on a duplicate form of the instructions. According to the nature of insurance which the broker was instructed to obtain, the memorandum assumes the form of a closed or open cover note.[16] A closed cover note is sent if the assured, in his instructions, has given full particulars as to cargo and shipment and the insurance has thus been made definite. An open cover note is sent if the instructions of the assured are so general and indefinite that further instructions are required from him defining the cargo, voyage or interest shipped under the insurance. This happens where the assured requires an "open cover"[17] or a "floating policy,"[18] or where he reserves the right to give "closing instructions."

The insurance broker should, as a matter of prudent business practice, notify the assured promptly of the terms of the insurance which he arranged for him and forward the cover note as soon as possible, but he is not under a legal duty to do so. In *United Mills Agencies Ltd v. R. E. Harvey, Bray & Co*,[19] the plaintiffs instructed the defendants, insurance brokers, to effect an open marine insurance on their goods, obtaining immediate cover. On April 2 the brokers reported that the cover was placed, and on April 4 they sent the assured the cover note which did not contain a clause covering the goods while at packers. In the night

---

[13] On the legal character of the slip, see *post*, para. 19–010. See especially Howard N. Bennett, "The Role of the Slip in Marine Insurance Law" [1994] I.M.C.L.Q. 94.
[14] *General Re-insurance Corporation v. Forsakringsaktiebolaget Fennia Patria* [1983] Q.B. 856; on this case, see *post*, para. 19–010. See also *The Zephyr* [1984] 1 Lloyd's Rep. 58 and *Touche Ross & Co v. Colin Baker* [1991] 2 Lloyd's Rep. 230, CA.
[15] *ibid.*
[16] The open cover note should not be confused with the type of insurance known as the "open cover"; see *post*, para. 19007.
[17] See *post*, para. 19–007.
[18] See *post*, para. 19–006.
[19] [1952] 1 T.L.R. 149.

of April 4–5 goods to the value of £8,000 were destroyed by fire at a warehouse of the packers. The action of the assured against the brokers for damages was dismissed. McNair J. held that the brokers had no knowledge that the goods in the hands of the packers were uninsured and that the brokers were not negligent by not insuring them in the hands of the packers or not informing the assured that they had not so insured them.[20] The judge rejected the contention of the assured that the brokers were under a duty to notify the assured at once of the terms of the insurance:

> "It was, no doubt, prudent to do so, both to allay the client's anxiety and possibly to enable the client to check the terms of insurance, but that was very different from saying it was part of the broker's duty."

The Standard Trading Conditions of the British International Freight Association (2000 Edition) provide that forwarders, who in practice often act as packers or procure packing, are not obliged to arrange insurance unless expressly instructed by the customer and, when arranging insurance, act as agents of the customer. Article 11(a) and (b) of the Standard Trading Conditions states:

> "(A) No insurance will be effected except upon express instructions given in writing by the Customer and all insurances effected by the Company are subject to the usual exceptions and conditions of the policies of the insurance company or underwriters taking the risk. Unless otherwise agreed in writing the Company shall not be under any obligation to effect a separate insurance on each consignment but may declare it on any open or general policy held by the Company.
> (B) Insofar as the Company agrees to arrange insurance, the Company acts solely as Agent for the Customer. The limits of liability under Clause 27(a)(ii) of these conditions shall not apply to the Company obligations under clauses 11(a) and (b) hereof."

The broker's position is anomalous; he is usually the agent[21] of the assured but is paid by the insurer. He is personally and solely responsible to the insurer for the payment of the premium while as between insurer and assured, by a legal fiction, the premium is regarded as paid. Bayley J.[22] put it thus:

> "As between the assured and the underwriter the premiums are considered as paid. The underwriter, to whom, in most instances, the assured are unknown, looks to the broker for payment, and he to the assured. The latter pays the premium to the broker only, who is a middleman between the assured and the underwriter. But he is not merely an agent, he is a principal to receive the money from the assured, and to pay it to the underwriter."

The historical origin of the rule is that underwriting members of Lloyd's refused,

---

[20] If they had acted negligently, the result would have been different; see *Osman v. J. Ralph Moss Ltd* [1970] 1 Lloyd's Rep. 313 where, in the case of motor insurance, it was held that the brokers were under a duty to advise and protect their clients: similarly *McNealy v. Pennine Insurance Co Ltd* [1978] R.T.R. 285, CA (a case of motor insurance also).

[21] On his duties as agent see *Anglo-African Merchants v. Bayley* [1970] 1 Q.B. 311; *North and South Trust Co v. Berkeley* [1971] 1 W.L.R. 470.

[22] In *Power v. Butcher* (1829) 10 B. & Cr. 329 at 340; see also *Amin Rasheed Corp v. Kuwait Insurance* [1982] 1 W.L.R. 961 at 967 where Bingham J. stated "There is the most compelling authority for the proposition that in placing insurance the broker acts as agent of the assured and not of the underwriter." The broker is entitled to sue and holds the proceeds as fiduciary for the assured, unless the agreement construed as a whole shows a contrary intention; *Transcontinental Underwriting Agency v. Grand Union Insurance Co Ltd* [1987] 2 Lloyd's Rep. 409.

at an early date, to deal with assured persons directly, and accepted insurance only from brokers whom they regarded as financially trustworthy. The rule in respect of marine insurance is laid down in the Marine Insurance Act 1906 in sections 53 and 54.[23] The general rule set out in section 53 is that the broker is responsible to the insurer for the premium and that the broker can recover premiums from the assured even if he had not paid them. This rule can only be displaced by clear words indicating that the parties intended to make such a change to their relationship.[24] Section 53(2) gives the broker a lien on the policy in respect of unpaid premiums and charges. The lien, however, may not be exercised where the broker had placed insurance for the benefit of a number of co-assured in respect of the liability of one of them.[25]

Kinds of marine insurance

Valued and unvalued policies

The Marine Insurance Act 1906 distinguishes between valued and unvalued **19–004** policies. A valued policy is a policy which specifies the agreed value of the subject-matter insured (s.27(2)); an unvalued policy[26] states merely the maximum limit of the sum insured and leaves the insurable value to be ascertained subsequently (s.28).

The main difference between these two types of policy is that in the case of a valued policy the value fixed by the policy is, in the absence of fraud, conclusive of the insurable value of the subject insured (s.27(3)), while in the case of an unvalued policy the value of the insured goods has to be proved by production of invoices, vouchers, estimates and other evidence. In the case of an unvalued policy, the insurable value of goods or merchandise is the prime cost of the goods, plus the expenses of and incidental to shipping and the charges of insurance upon the whole (s.16(3)).

The difference between valued and unvalued policies is of great practical importance. In a valued policy, the buyer's anticipated profits are normally included in the value declared by adding a percentage of, say, 10 or 15 per cent to the invoice value and the incidental shipping and insurance charges of the goods. In an unvalued policy, the buyer's anticipated profits cannot be included in the insurable value.

In export practice, valued policies are the rule and unvalued policies are rarely used. This tendency goes so far that, in the case of floating policies and open covers, where the assured cannot always declare the insurable value before

---

[23] Exceptionally, the broker may be regarded as the agent of the insurer: *Stockton v. Mason* [1978] 2 Lloyd's Rep. 430.

[24] *JA & Co Ltd (In Liquidation) v. Kadirga Denizcilik Ve Ticaret SA Chapman, The Times*, March 19, 1998. See also *Velos Group Ltd v. Harbour Insurance Services Ltd* [1997] 2 Lloyd's Rep. 461.

[25] *Eide U.K. Ltd v. Lowndes Lambert Group, The Times*, December 29, 1997, CA. In claiming against an assured for the non payment of premiums a broker is not entitled to arrest a vessel: *Bain Clarkson v. Owners of Sea Friends* [1991] 2 Lloyd's Rep. 283.

[26] Unvalued policies are sometimes called open policies. This term should not be confused with the open cover; see *post*, para. 19–007.

arrival of the goods or notice of their loss, special provision is made for the valuation of such shipments.[27]

The "insured value" is the agreed value (if any) specified in the policy; the "shipping value" is defined in identical terms with the definition of insurable value for unvalued policies, as set out in section 16(3). If there is the possibility of rising market prices during the transit of the goods, the assured who has covered the goods under an ordinary policy can obtain a so-called "*increased value*" policy. In all three versions of the Institute Cargo Clauses A, B and C, clause 14 includes wording which takes this practice into account. Clause 14 is reproduced at para. 19–032.

Voyage, time and mixed policies

19–005 Policies are also classified as voyage, time and mixed policies (s.25). Under a voyage policy the subject-matter is insured in transit from one point to another; under a time policy the subject-matter is insured for a fixed time. Under a mixed policy the subject-matter is insured both for a particular journey and a certain period of time.

In voyage policies, there is a warranty implied by s.39 that the carrying vessel will be seaworthy at the commencement of the voyage.[28] The duration of the insurance cover is governed by the transit clause in Institute Cargo Clauses A, B and C. Cover is provided from warehouse to warehouse and hence the transit clause extends the marine insurance to land risks incidental to the sea voyage. If the transit clause is deleted, the risk will commence and terminate at the sea ports. The transit clause is considered in more detail later in this chapter.[29]

Time policies[30] were rarely used in export transactions but are now found more frequently. These policies may cover a period exceeding 12 months[31]; they often contain the "*continuation clause*" under which the parties agree that:

> "should the vessel at the expiration of this policy be at sea, or in distress, or at a port of refuge or of call, she shall, provided previous notice be given to the underwriters, be held covered at a *pro rata* monthly premium to her port of destination."[32]

Mixed[33] policies are issued in the frequent instances where goods are insured under a contract for both voyage and time. Here the insurer is only liable under

---

[27] See *post*, para. 19–006.

[28] As to warranty, see para. 5–002.

[29] See *post*, para. 19–022.

[30] For a discussion of the nature of a time policy, see *Compania Maritima San Basilio SA v. Oceanus Mutual Underwriting Association (Bermuda) Ltd* [1977] Q.B. 49.

[31] s.25(2) of the Marine Insurance Act 1906, which, in principle, prohibited time policies exceeding 12 months, was repealed by the Finance Act 1959, s.30(5). S.23(2) to (5) of the Marine Insurance Act 1906 was also repealed by s.30(5) of the Finance Act 1959.

[32] The continuation clause in the Institute Time Clauses makes the prolongation of the risk dependent on notice being given to the insurer.

[33] For an example of a mixed policy see *The Al Jubail IV* [1982] 2 Lloyd's Rep. 637 where a vessel was insured for 12 months from the end of a voyage to the Gulf.

the insurance when a loss occurs during the period of insurance and while the ship is on the specified voyage.[34]

Floating policies

The floating policy lays down the general conditions of insurance, but not the **19–006** particulars of the individual consignments intended to be covered. These particulars are usually unknown to the assured when effecting the insurance. Notwithstanding this element of uncertainty, the floating policy covers automatically all shipments made thereunder and the assured is obliged to "declare" the individual shipments to the insurer promptly. The floating policy might cover, say, shipments to stated destinations within 12 months to the aggregate amount of £500,000. When the assured ships and declares a shipment of £30,000, the available cover is reduced to £470,000, and when the policy is fully declared, it is written off.[35]

The use of the floating policy has diminished. Open covers have taken their place in many cases. Brokers have also effected time policies instead, and the informal "slip" policy has taken the place of the floating policy in Lloyd's market.[36] A consideration of the floating policy is, however, still required because that type of policy forms the model on which the frequently used informal open cover is framed.

Under the floating policy it is usual to supply the assured with a book of declaration forms or certificates of insurance on which he declares the shipments as they go forward.

The Marine Insurance Act 1906 contains, in section 29, the following provisions on floating policies:

> "(1) A floating policy is a policy which describes the insurance in general terms, and leaves the name of the ship or ships and other particulars to be defined by subsequent declaration.
> (2) The subsequent declaration or declarations may be made by indorsement on the policy, or in other customary manner.
> (3) Unless the policy otherwise provides, the declarations must be made in the order of dispatch or shipment. They must, in the case of goods, comprise all consignments within the terms of the policy, and the value of the goods or other property must be honestly stated, but an omission or erroneous declaration may be rectified even after loss or arrival, provided the omission or declaration was made in good faith.
> (4) Unless the policy otherwise provides, where a declaration of value is not made until after notice of loss or arrival, the policy must be treated as an unvalued policy as regards the subject-matter of that declaration."

Section 29(4) discourages shippers from waiting until they have knowledge as to the safe arrival or otherwise of a particular shipment, before deciding whether or not to declare it. Were it not for this subsection, shippers could declare only losses. The effect of the subsection, however, is that such a practice

---

[34] A warranty of seaworthiness is also implied in respect of a mixed policy see *The Al Jubail IV, ante*, and *Lombard Insurance Co v. Kin Yuen Co; The Pab, Lloyd's List*, July 25, 1995.
[35] Arnould, *op. cit.*, para. 165.
[36] V. Dover, *A Handbook of Marine Insurance* (8th ed., London, H. F. and G. Witherby Ltd, 1975), p. 133.

would result in the subject-matter being treated as though the policy were an unvalued one. The value of the goods would accordingly be assessed by reference to the provisions of section 16(3).[37] However, the assured need not, and in fact sometimes cannot, declare the shipment before the ship sails. As seen above, section 29(3) of the Act provides that an omission or erroneous declaration may be rectified even after loss or arrival, provided the omission or declaration was made in good faith. Further, the insurer cannot refuse an individual risk which falls within the terms of the policy, although he is entitled to refuse a risk which the policy was not intended to cover, or a declaration which is made dishonestly.

The floating policy often contains a clause obliging the assured to make declarations of shipment as early as possible. It has been held[38] that an assured who, in breach of this undertaking, omitted to make a declaration at the earliest possible moment was not entitled to recover under the policy for loss suffered by him. The assured could not rely on section 29(3) because it was a case in which no declaration at all had been made within the express terms of the contract and, consequently, the insurer had lost the opportunity of reinsuring the risk.

The floating policy is not a time policy but an aggregation of voyage policies. The assured, who desires to avoid leaving some of his shipments unprotected, has to take out a further floating policy before the expiration of the current policy. This is a disadvantage of the floating policy, because if an assured forgets to take out a new policy the goods may be carried uninsured. This disadvantage is avoided if an "*always open*" open cover is taken out. In the case of a floating policy, the new policy which follows the old one, contains the clause:

"to follow and succeed policy No. . . . dated . . ."

The meaning of this clause is, in the words of Lord Blackburn,[39] "there being consecutive policies any loss declared is to be borne first by the earlier policies, and that it is not till after the earlier policy is exhausted, either by losses or declared adventures which have come in safe, that the underwriters on the policy which follows are to bear the loss, if any."

The floating policy often contains a clause limiting the risk per vessel, *e.g.* a policy granting cover for a total of £500,000 may provide:

"limit per bottom, £50,000."

The assured who wishes to ship in excess of the limit per vessel, should make arrangements for a separate additional cover prior to shipment.

The per bottom clause is regularly supplemented by a location clause, by which the insurer restricts to a fixed maximum sum his liability for accumulation of covered risks in one locality. The location clause is invariably inserted by underwriters where insuring land risks incidental to sea transit. The following is an example of the location clause:

---

[37] See *ante*, para. 19–004.
[38] In *Union Insurance Society of Canton Ltd v. George Wills & Co* [1916] 1 A.C. 281.
[39] In *Inglis v. Stock* (1885) 10 App.Cas. 263 at 269.

"In the case of loss and/or damage before shipment to the insured interest in any one locality the underwriter, notwithstanding anything to the contrary contained in this contract, shall not be liable in respect of any one accident or series of accidents arising out of the same event for more than his proportion of an amount up to, but not exceeding, the sum of £ . . . . . . in all taken in conjunction with preceding and/or succeeding insurances. The conveyance of the insured interest upon interior waterways or by land transit shall not be deemed to be shipment within the meaning of this clause."

The individual location risk is often limited to the same amount as the per bottom risk. As a result of the location clause, if goods accumulated in one warehouse prior to shipment are destroyed by fire, the insurers are only liable for the sum stated in the location clause, although the aggregate insurable value of the goods may far exceed that limit. Dover maintains[40] that the location clause limits only pre-shipment accumulations in one locality but not accumulations at the port of discharge or later. This view is supported by the present wording of the clause but the clause can, of course, be extended by agreement of the parties to limit the liability of the insurer for accumulations subsequent to the discharge from the overseas vessel.

The premium is often arranged at fixed rates for specified kinds of goods, *e.g.* textiles, hardware, motor-cars, etc. Sometimes a "held covered" clause[41] is added providing:

"other interests held covered at rates to be arranged."

The effect of such a clause is to bring within the ambit of the insurance cover voyages or goods not specifically mentioned in the policy. The assured is bound to give notice to the underwriters immediately he becomes aware of facts which fall within the held covered clause, otherwise the voyage and goods will not be held covered.[42] An underwriter receiving notice is bound to give insurance cover at a reasonable premium, being the market rate for a particular risk. A floating policy describes the type of goods, gives the rates of premium, and the voyages to be undertaken, but it does not specify the names of the ships to be used. For his own protection, an insurer will insist that the vessels used be of a particular class in the shipping register. He will insist on the attachment of the Institute Maintenance of Class Clause, under which the assured warrants that all the ships used will be of the specified class. This clause is in the form of a warranty pursuant to section 33, and failure to comply with it discharges the underwriter as from the time of the breach.

Open covers

The open cover, combined with the issue of insurance certificates, has become **19–007** a common and popular form of insurance in the export trade. The open cover is another method of effecting general insurance for recurring shipments, the details of which are unknown when the insurance is taken out. This method

---

[40] V. Dover, *loc. cit.*, *supra*, n. 36.
[41] The "held covered" clause is discussed at para. 19–013.
[42] *Thames and Mersey Insurance Co Ltd v. H. T. Van Laun & Co* [1917] 2 K.B. 48 (n. (1905)).

resembles, in many respects, the floating policy; in particular, the assured is also bound to declare all individual shipments effected thereunder, unless the contract of insurance otherwise provides.

The open cover, like the slip,[43] is not an insurance policy but is a document by which the underwriter undertakes subsequently to issue duly executed floating or specific policies within the terms of the cover. Open covers sometimes incorporate the *Institute Standard Conditions for Open Covers*[44] which are similar in wording to the Institute Standard Conditions for Floating Policies, except that they use the words "open cover" instead of "floating policies."

The open cover may be limited in time or may be permanent, while the floating policy is normally limited to twelve months. Where the open cover is perpetual in character ("always open"), a clause is inserted enabling both parties to give notice of cancellation of the cover within a stated time, *e.g.* thirty days or three months.

The open cover normally contains a maximum limit of the insurer's liability per bottom and a location clause like the floating policy.[45]

Special conditions are frequently laid down in the open cover for the determination of the insurable value. It is sometimes provided that if the value of a consignment is declared before the loss occurs, the declaration of value shall be binding. Where the loss occurs before the declaration, the basis of valuation shall be the prime cost of the goods plus expenses, freight, insurance and a fixed percentage of profit, usually 15 per cent. Sometimes it is stated that this amount is to be increased by the value of any duty payable or paid on the goods.

From the practical point of view, the difference between the floating policy and the open cover may be stated as follows. In the case of a floating policy the assured receives a formal policy document. In case of an open cover no formal policy is issued and the arrangement is more informal, but the assured is entitled to demand a policy if he requires it, for example if litigation ensues. In both cases the cover is written off, as declarations are made.

A recital of the main terms of the open cover is normally found on certificates of insurance issued under the cover in respect of individual shipments declared thereunder.[46]

If the open cover contains unusual conditions which an assignee of a certificate of insurance issued under it might not expect to be included in the contract of insurance, they should be printed specifically on the certificate. A mere reference to the open cover does not embody them, particularly if other conditions contained in the open cover are reproduced in the certificate. In one case[47] an open cover issued by a Swiss insurance company to a French firm of forwarders contained a provision that the insurers could only be sued in the commercial tribunals of the place where the contract was entered into, *i.e.* in the Swiss courts. Customers of the French forwarders sold a quantity of canned ham to an

---

[43] See *post*, para. 19–010.
[44] On Institute Clauses, see *post*, para. 19–018.
[45] See *ante*, para. 19–006.
[46] See below in the text.
[47] *MacLeod Ross & Co Ltd v. Compagnie d'Assurances Générales L'Helvetia of St. Gall* [1952] W.N. 56.

English company, and asked the French forwarders to insure it. The forwarders sent declarations of the consignment to the insurers, who issued certificates of insurance which, though referring to the open cover and reprinting some of its terms, did not state, or refer to, the provision giving exclusive jurisdiction to the Swiss courts. The documents, including the insurance certificates, were accepted by the buyers who claimed under the insurance for damage which, they alleged, was covered by the contract of insurance. In an action commenced by the buyers against the insurers in the English courts, the latter sought a stay of proceedings on the ground that the Swiss courts had exclusive jurisdiction. The English Court of Appeal refused the stay because, on the construction of the documents, the open cover and the certificates were separate contracts and the buyers were not bound by the clause relating to the jurisdiction of the Swiss courts in the open cover. In support of this view the judges in the Court of Appeal referred to the rule in *Phoenix Insurance Co of Hartford v. De Monchy.*[48]

Blanket policies

In the case of floating policies and open covers the assured has normally to **19–008** make declarations of the individual shipments falling under these insurances to the insurer. This is inconvenient to the exporter and requires a considerable amount of labour and cost where the various consignments are of small value or the voyage is of short duration. In these cases the assured will take out a "blanket policy" which usually provides that he need not advise the insurer of the individual shipments and that a lump sum premium—instead of a premium at several rates—shall cover all shipments.

The contract of insurance

It is now necessary to consider the rights and duties of the parties to the contract **19–009** of insurance.

The slip and the policy

It will be recalled from the opening paragraphs of the chapter that the intended **19–010** assured and the broker will decide on the particulars of the proposed cover. The broker will prepare a memorandum or slip. This will set out details of the proposed insurable property, the voyage or period of time for which the insurance is to be provided, a valuation of the subject matter, an indication of which policy form (A, B, or C) is required, an indication of any standard clauses to be incorporated such as the Institute War Clauses, and any other special terms or warranties. The broker will present this slip to underwriting syndicates, the first, known as "the leader," generally being a well established person of good reputation. The initialling of the slip by the underwriter amounts to an acceptance of risk by the underwriter and will create a binding contract between the parties in relation to the portion of the total risk accepted. In *General Reinsurance Cor-*

---

[48] (1929) 45 T.L.R. 543; see para. 19–011.

poration v. Forsakringsaktiebolaget Fennia Patria,[49] a Finnish insurance company sought to amend its reinsurance of a particular risk at Lloyds, London. An amendment slip was accepted by General Reinsurance for part of the amount stated on it. Before the total amount was underwritten, a loss occurred. Fennia Patria wanted to cancel the amendment because in the circumstances the unamended cover was more favourable to it. It was held, however, that a valid contract had been concluded between Fennia Patria and General Reinsurance and hence Fennia Patria could not cancel the amendment on the ground that the insured risk on the amended slip was not completely covered.

Once the slip has been initialled fully, the total risk is covered. The broker will take the slip to the signing office at Lloyd's where it will be signed, thereby executing the policy. A contract of marine insurance must be incorporated in a policy before it is admissible in evidence.[50] If there is any discrepancy between the policy and the slip, reference may be made to the slip.[51] In such a case, it is the terms of the slip that prevail.[52] If insurers wish to make their obligations as expressed in the policy differ from the obligations undertaken in the slip, they must reserve the power to make such alteration in the slip.[53]

Certificates of insurance; brokers' cover notes; letters of insurance

19–011 In export practice, much use is made of documents which, though lacking the legal characteristics of an insurance policy nevertheless acknowledge that insurance cover has been obtained. The most important of these documents are certificates of insurance, but brokers' cover notes and letters of insurance issued by the seller of the insured goods are occasionally used. The reasons for the popularity of these documents are explained by Bailhache J.[54] as follows:

> "The preparation of a policy of insurance takes some little time, particularly if there are a number of underwriters or several insurance companies, and when documents require to be tendered with promptness on the arrival of a steamer in order that expense may not be incurred through delay in unloading, or through the buyer not being ready to take delivery, it is not always practicable to obtain actual polices of insurance. In order to facilitate business in circumstances such as these, buyers are accordingly in the habit of accepting brokers' cover notes and certificates of insurance instead of insisting on policies."

---

[49] [1983] Q.B. 856, CA.

[50] Marine Insurance Act 1906, s.2.

[51] *ibid.* s.89. Stamp Duty is no longer payable upon policies of marine insurance: Finance Act 1970, Sched. 7, para. 1(2)(b).

[52] *Symington & Co. v. Union Insurance Society of Canton Ltd (No. 2)* (1928) 34 Com.Cas. 233 at 235, *per* Scrutton L.J.

[53] In principle the contract of insurance is subject to identical terms for all underwriters who have signed the slip: *Jaglom v. Excess Insurance Co Ltd* [1972] 2 Q.B. 250 at 257. The underwriters may also agree on "t.b.a. L/U" which means that they will be bound by "terms to be agreed with leading underwriters" without requiring further consultation: *American Airlines Inc v. Hope* [1973] 1 Lloyd's Rep. 233 at 245. On the liability of the broker to the underwriter if the broker indicates to reduce ("sign down") the underwriter's liability on the slip if the risk is oversubscribed, but the slip cannot be signed down, see *General Accident Fire and Life Assurance Co v. Tanter; The Zephyr* [1985] 2 Lloyd's Rep. 529, CA.

[54] In *Wilson, Holgate & Co v. Belgian Grain and Produce Co* [1920] 2 K.B. 1, 8.

The certificate of insurance is frequently used when an open cover has been obtained. It consists of two parts: the first part recites the main terms of the open cover under which the goods are insured[55]; the second part contains the declaration of the goods stating the value insured, the voyage and the marks, numbers and other particulars of the goods. The certificate is signed by the insurance broker who procured the open cover, or by the assured himself.

Certificates of insurance which are issued by an insurance broker or assured entitle the holder to demand the issue of a policy in the terms of the certificate and to claim for losses. According to older authorities[56] the buyer under a c.i.f. contract is not obliged, in English law, to accept a certificate of insurance in the place of an insurance policy unless he has agreed to do so or there is an established custom of the trade to that effect.

Brokers' cover notes are merely advice notes sent by brokers to their clients informing them that insurance cover has been obtained. Their practical value is less than that of certificates of insurance and, in the absence of stipulations to the contrary, the c.i.f. buyer need not accept a cover note in the place of a policy.

Rarely used letters of insurance, addressed by the seller (the assured) to the buyer, confirm that an insurance has been effected. Such an advice may or may not be correct; its value depends on the trust which the buyer reposes in the seller. Letters of insurance have no established status in law but are admissible in evidence against the seller (the assured) if litigation ensues.

The duty to disclose

A contract of marine insurance, like every contract of insurance, is a contract **19–012** based upon the utmost good faith (contract *uberrimae fidei*), and if the utmost good faith is not observed by either party[57] the contract may be avoided by the other party (s.17).[58] It follows from the confidential nature of the contract that the assured is bound to disclose to the insurer, before the contract is concluded, every material circumstance[59] which is, or in the ordinary course of business ought to be, known to him (s.18(1)). Section 18(2) provides that every circumstance is material which would influence the judgment of a prudent insurer in fixing the premium or determining whether he will take the risk. Thus, in one case[60] the goods were leather jerkins ex government surplus and were manufac-

---

[55] See *ante*, para. 19–007.

[56] *Diamond Alkali Export Corporation v. Fl. Bourgeois* [1921] 3 K.B. 443; *Phoenix Insurance Co of Hartford v. De Monchy* (1929) 45 T.L.R. 543.

[57] As to the insurer's duty see *Banque Keyser Ullman SA v. Skandia (U.K.) Insurance Ltd* [1989] 3 W.L.R. 25, CA. The duty to observe utmost good faith does not exist between the assignee of the benefit of the insurance and the insurer: *Bank of Nova Scotia v. Hellenic Mutual War Risks Association (Bermuda) Ltd; The Good Luck* [1989] 2 Lloyd's Rep. 238, CA.

[58] The duty of utmost good faith is a mutual duty, owed by the parties to each other. The duty of good faith extends to the making of a claim; however, the obligation not to make fraudulent claims would not be extended to embrace claims culpably made: *Manifest Shipping & Co Ltd v. Uni-Polaris Insurance Co Ltd; The Star Sea* [1997] 1 Lloyd's Rep. 360, CA.

[59] Circumstances are facts: they must be known, or should reasonably be known to the insured.

[60] *Anglo-African Merchants v. Bayley* [1970] 1 Q.B. 311 at 319–320. In *Woolcott v. Sun Alliance and London Insurance Ltd* [1978] 1 W.L.R. 493 it was held that the insurance company could avoid

tured at least 20 years earlier, but they were declared to the insurers simply as "new men's clothing in bales for export". The court held that there was a failure to disclose material facts and the assured could not recover under the policy when the goods were stolen.

Section 20 deals with the effect of various representations. A material repres-. entation must be true, otherwise the insurer can avoid the contract.[61] A material representation is one which would influence the judgment of a prudent insurer in fixing the premium or accepting the risk.[62] The section distinguishes between representations as to fact, and representations as to expectation or belief.[63] In the case of the former, the insurer cannot avoid the contract if the representation of fact is substantially correct.[64] In the case of the latter, the insurer cannot avoid the contract if the representation as to a matter of expectation or belief is made in good faith.[65]

Where the contract is concluded through an insurance broker or other agent, the agent must disclose to the insurer every material circumstance which is known to himself or has been communicated to him, or ought to be known by him, in addition to material circumstances that should be disclosed by the assured.[66] However, s.19(b) provides that a policy effected by the agent in ignorance of a material fact known to the assured cannot be avoided if it has come too late to the knowledge of the assured to be communicated to the agent. In *Pan Atlantic Insurance Co Ltd v. Pine Top Insurance Co Ltd*[67] the authorities relating to the duty of disclosure were reviewed in full. It was determined that in the event of non-disclosure the insurer was entitled to avoid the contract if the non-disclosure induced the making of the contract. For a material misrepresentation the insurer was only entitled to avoid if that misrepresentation had induced the making of the contract.[68] Materiality, in sections 18 and 20, was to be given an interpretation which accords with the natural and ordinary meaning of the words used.[69]

---

a fire insurance policy on the ground of material non-disclosure because the assured had failed to disclose that he had been convicted of robbery. See also *Lambert v. Co-operative Insurance Society Ltd* [1975] 2 Lloyd's Rep. 485.

[61] s.20(1).

[62] s.20(2).

[63] s.20(3).

[64] s.20(4).

[65] s.20(5).

[66] s.19. If the assured gives the broker full disclosure but the latter fails to pass it on to the insurer, the contract is voidable but the insurer may have waived his right to have further disclosure: *Roberts v. Plaisted* [1989] 2 Lloyd's Rep. 341. On the liability of the broker in such a case see *Forsikringsaktieselskapei Vesta v. J.N.E. Butcher Bain Dawes Ltd* [1989] 1 Lloyd's Rep. 331.

[67] [1994] 2 Lloyd's Rep. 427.

[68] For an application of *Pan Atlantic* see *St. Paul Fire and Marine Insurance Co (U.K.) Ltd v. McConnell Dowell Constructors Ltd* [1996] 1 All E.R. 96, CA where the insurers were entitled to avoid the policy subject to proof that they were induced to enter the contract on the terms in which they did. See also *Marc Rich & Co AG v. Portman* [1996] 1 Lloyd's Rep. 430 where it was argued that a non-disclosure was irrelevant as the insurers would have written the policy in any event. Potter J. dismissed the argument as the insurers had demonstrated that, despite their imprudence in not actively seeking information, they had been induced into making the contract on the basis of the non-disclosure.

[69] Per Lord Goff in *Pan Atlantic, ante.*

In the absence of inquiry, the following circumstances need not be disclosed (s.18(3)):

> "(a) Any circumstance which diminishes the risk.
> (b) Any circumstance which is known or presumed to be known to the insurer. The insurer is presumed to know matters of common notoriety or knowledge, and matters which an insurer in the ordinary course of his business, as such, ought to know.
> (c) Any circumstance as to which information is waived by the insurer.
> (d) Any circumstance which it is superfluous to disclose by reason of any express or implied warranty."

The exporter who wishes to insure goods sold for export will ask himself whether he has to give the insurer detailed information of the nature of the cargo, and especially of an unusual consignment or one of a particularly dangerous nature. The following rules emerge from the decisions of the courts[70]:

(1) Where the goods are an ordinary species of lawful merchandise which may fairly be described as a parcel of ordinary cargo, the exporter need not, in strict law, disclose details of the insured risk to the insurer, but where there is the slightest doubt which could be entertained by a reasonable person the exporter would be wise to disclose details.

(2) Where the goods are of an unusual and particularly dangerous kind, the duty of disclosure arises.[71]

(3) Where the cargo is tendered in such a manner—*e.g.* under a novel or unusual description—as to put an ordinary careful insurer on inquiry, and he fails to inquire, a waiver of information under section 18(3)(*c*) can be assumed.[72]

Once there is non-disclosure, be it fraudulent, negligent or innocent, the aggrieved party is entitled to elect whether he will avoid or affirm the contract. The right to avoid:[73]

> "exists from the time when the contract is made and continues until the underwriter, with full knowledge of the non-disclosure or misrepresentation, affirms or is deemed to have affirmed the contract . . . Full knowledge of the facts is essential before there can be any question of affirmation—being put on inquiry is insufficient . . . and even when the underwriter has full knowledge of the facts, he is entitled to a reasonable time in which to decide whether to affirm the contract. In a situation in which the underwriter has taken no action to affirm or repudiate the contract and a reasonable time for making up his mind has elapsed, he will be deemed to have affirmed the contract if either so much time has elapsed that the necessary inference is

---

[70] *Greenhill v. Federal Insurance Co Ltd* [1927] 1 K.B. 65; see further *Mann, Macneal Boyd v. Dubois* (1811) 3 Camp. 133 and *Carter v. Boehm* (1766) 3 Burr. 1905.

[71] Arnould, *op. cit.*, para. 654.

[72] Sargant L.J. in *Greenhill v. Federal Insurance Co Ltd* [1927] 1 K.B. 65 at 89.

[73] Whether the aggrieved party is also entitled to claim damages is very doubtful. It was held in *Banque Keyser Ullman SA v. Skandia (U.K.) Insurance Ltd* [1989] 3 W.L.R. 25, CA that such a claim could not be founded on contract or a statutory duty, but could only be brought in tort. See also *Banque Financière de la Cité v. Westgate Insurance Co* [1988] 2 Lloyd's Rep. 513. The claim cannot be founded on the Misrepresentation Act 1967, s.2, because the breach of duty consists merely of *silence* and not a positive act.

one of affirmation, or the assured has been prejudiced by the delay in making an election or the rights of third parties have intervened."[74]

Avoiding the contract necessitates returning the premium unless there is fraud (s.84).

The Rules for Construction of Policy, which are appended to the Act, provide that the term "goods" means goods in the nature of merchandise but, in the absence of any usage to the contrary, deck cargo and living animals must be insured specifically, and not under the general denomination of goods (r. 17). This definition still applies, although the Lloyd's S. G. Policy appended to the Marine Insurance Act 1906 is no longer used.

The "held covered" clause

19–013 In practice goods are normally specified in detail, and the assured has to take great care to describe the goods correctly. A material misdescription of the goods in the policy enables the insurer to avoid the contract on the ground of misrepresentation. This is even true where the erroneous description was due to the fact that the assured failed to realise the materiality of the description, or where he acted under an innocent mistake or where the misdescription was due to an accident. In view of these serious consequences the parties sometimes insert a "held covered" clause into the contract which covers, at any rate, innocent misdescription of the goods but obliges the assured to pay an additional premium if necessary. The clause "held covered at premium to be arranged" places the insurer on risk.[75] The following illustration of such a clause is taken from the Institute Cargo Clauses A, B and C[76]:

> "Where, after attachment of this insurance, the destination is changed by the Assured, *held covered at a premium and on conditions to be arranged subject to prompt notice being given to the Underwriters.*"

Even without express provision, a "held covered" clause is always subject to an implied term that the assured will give prompt notice to the insurer of any event which affects the clause.[77]

In one case,[78] the assured described a case of second-hand machinery simply as machinery, innocently believing that that description was sufficient, and the insurance policy contained a "held covered" clause. The machinery suffered breakage during the voyage and it was held that while the description of the subject-matter was a material misrepresentation which normally would entitle the insurer to rescind the contract, this defect was cured by the "held covered"

---

[74] *per* Donaldson J., *Liberian Insurance Agency v. Mosse* [1977] 2 Lloyd's Rep. 560 at 565.
[75] *American Airlines Inc v. Hope* [1973] 1 Lloyd's Rep. 233 at 241.
[76] Clause 10 of Institute of Cargo Clauses A, B and C.
[77] *Thames and Mersey Marine Insurance Company Ltd v. H.T. Van Laun & Co* [1917] 2 K.B. 48 (note), (1905); *Greenock S.S. Co v. Maritime Insurance Co* [1903] 1 K.B. 367.
[78] In *Hewitt Brothers v. Wilson* [1915] 2 K.B. 739. See further, *Kirby v. Consindit Società per Azioni* [1969] 1 Lloyd's Rep. 75.

clause and the insurers had to pay for the loss suffered by the assured but were entitled to an additional premium.

The exporter can obtain the protection of the "held covered" clause only if he has acted with the utmost good faith towards the insurer, this being an obligation which rests on him throughout the currency of the policy. In one case[79] the assured imported canned pork butts from France to the United Kingdom and effected an "all risks" policy[80] covering inherent vice and hidden defects and the condemnation of the goods by the authorities. The policy provided that the assured warranted that all tins were marked by the manufacturers with an indication of the date of manufacture and contained a "held covered" clause. Some of the tins were not properly marked, and when part of the consignment was rejected by the sub-purchasers of the assured, the assured claimed that, despite the inaccurate markings, they were protected by the "held covered" clause. McNair J. rejected the contention and decided in favour of the insurers on the ground that the assured had not been frank with their insurers and that the "held covered" clause could not have been invoked if, "at the time when the assured seeks to invoke the clause, they have been and are unable to correct the misdescription."[81]

In another instance, an assured failed to disclose that a cargo of enamelware he was exporting was an end of stock purchase bought at a very low price which had been touched up by overpainting. Further, it was not disclosed that the enamelware was packed in cartons, not wooden cases as stated. Here, the "held covered" clause contained in the policy was not applied in favour of the assured because the misdescription was of such a serious nature that no underwriter would have quoted a reasonable commercial rate for cover. The "held covered" clause was held to apply only where such a premium was applicable, but here, a very high extra premium would have been quoted.[82]

The insurable interest

It is a fundamental principle of insurance law[83] that the assured must have an **19–014** insurable interest in the subject-matter insured at the time of the loss.[84] If he has such an interest, an assured can recover for an insured loss occurring during the period of insurance cover, notwithstanding that the loss occurred prior to the insurance contract being concluded, unless the assured was aware of the loss and the underwriters were not.[85] In *Lucena v. Craufurd*[86] Lawrence J. defined an insurable interest in the following terms:

---

[79] *Overseas Commodities Ltd v. Style* [1958] 1 Lloyd's Rep. 553.
[80] The policy was actually an "all loss or damage" policy.
[81] *Overseas Commodities Ltd v. Style* [1958] 1 Lloyd's Rep. 553 at 559.
[82] *Liberian Insurance Agency Inc v. Mosse* [1977] 2 Lloyd's Rep. 560.
[83] Marine Insurance Act 1906, s.6.
[84] The provisions of s.6 are reiterated by Clause 11.1 Institute Cargo Clauses A, B and C.
[85] Institute Cargo Clauses A, B and C, Clause 11.2.
[86] (1806) 2 Bos. & P. (N.S.) 269, 302. A speculative interest does not amount to an interest unless agreed: *Cepheus Shipping Corporation v. Guardian Royal Exchange Assurance plc; The Capricorn* [1995] 1 Lloyd's Rep. 622.

"To be interested in the preservation of a thing, is to be so circumstanced with respect to it as to have benefit from its existence, prejudice from its destruction. The property of a thing and the interest divisible from it may be very different: of the first the price is generally the measure, but by interest in a thing every benefit and advantage arising out of or depending on such thing, may be considered as being comprehended."

Essentially, therefore, in order to have an insurable interest in property, a person must in some way suffer loss as a result of its damage, loss or destruction. The Marine Insurance Act 1906 states in section 5(1): "Subject to the provision of this Act, every person has an insurable interest who is interested in a marine adventure," and by section 5(2) it is provided that:

"In particular a person is interested in a marine adventure where he stands in any legal or equitable relation to the adventure or to any insurable property at risk therein, in consequence of which he may benefit by the safety or due arrival of insurable property or may be prejudiced by its loss or by damage thereto, or by detention thereof, or may incur liability in respect thereof."

If a person attempted to insure property in which he has no insurable interest, the contract is not one of insurance and is void. Such a contract is void both as being against public policy and also as being contrary to the statutory prohibition against contracts of marine insurance by way of gaming or wagering.[87] Such a contract is also void under section 18 of the Gaming Act 1845. An underwriter may agree to insure goods without seeking proof that the proposer has an insurable interest in them and such a policy is known as a ppi (policy proof of interest) policy. Although a ppi policy carries no legal obligation under the Marine Insurance Act and other statutes, an underwriter will ordinarily carry out his obligations in the usual way. Such a policy, being dependent on the underwriter's honour, is often referred to as an honour policy. Although it is unlikely that an underwriter would risk his reputation by refusing to pay out on such a policy, any action against a trustee in bankruptcy or receiver of such underwriter would fail.

If goods which are the subject matter of a contract of sale are insured, the question may arise whether the seller or the buyer has an insurable interest in them or whether both have such an interest. The answer depends on the terms of the contract of sale and the state of its performance. Clearly the party in whom the property in the goods is vested has an insurable interest. Possession of the goods, or the right to immediate possession, likewise constitutes an insurable interest.

It is thought that the party who bears the risk also has an insurable interest. The decision of the House of Lords in *Leigh and Sillivan Ltd v. Aliakmon Shipping Co Ltd*[88] does not affect this position; the House of Lords decided in this case that a buyer on c.i.f. or c. and f. terms, to whom only the risk, but no proprietary or possessory interest had passed, could not bring an action in the

---

[87] A policy effected "interest or no interest" or "without proof of interest other than the policy itself" or "without benefit of salvage to the insurer" or subject to any other like term, is deemed to be a gaming or wagering contract: Marine Insurance Act 1906, s.4(2). Provided there is no possibility of salvage, a policy may however be effected "without benefit of salvage," s.4(2).
[88] [1986] A.C. 785. See *ante*, para. 2–030.

tort of negligence against the carrier, but it did not deal with the question of the insurable interest. The buyer has always an insurable interest in the profits which he would have made on resale if the goods had arrived safely.

The unpaid seller has a contingent interest in the goods because he may have to exercise his right of stoppage in transit. He has also a defeasible interest in them until the buyer is deemed to have accepted the goods and thus lost his right to reject them. Similarly an f.o.b. seller or a c. and f. seller, who has not yet received the price, has a contingent interest in the goods during transit. Contingent and defeasible interests constitute insurable interests within the law (s.7(1)). They can—and should—be covered by a *seller's contingency insurance*.

Problems have occasionally arisen where unascertained goods are sold on f.o.b. terms and the buyer wishes to take out insurance. Normally, however, the goods are carried at his risk and this has been held sufficient to given him an insurable interest.[89]

A carrier has an insurable interest in the goods entrusted to him since he is, in principle, liable to the cargo owner for loss of or damage to the goods; he may insure the owner's goods and sue on the policy as trustee of the owner.[90]

An agent who is instructed by an overseas principal to buy goods may order these goods in the home market in his own name. This procedure is sometimes adopted by confirming houses.[91] If in these cases the agent has already shipped the goods and the insurance covering the transit risks has been arranged by the principal, the agent may find himself under a liability to the seller in the home market which would be onerous if the principal became insolvent. The agent would in this case have the right of stoppage in transit as if he were a seller,[92] but it is not always certain that the exercise of this right will lead to practical satisfaction.[93]

Under section 26(2) of the Marine Insurance Act 1906, the nature and extent of the interest of the assured in the subject-matter insured need not be specified in the policy. The Act refers to a number of insurable interests. For example, the insurer under a contract of marine insurance who has an insurable interest, may reinsure in respect of it,[94] but the original assured has no rights or interest in respect of such reinsurance and so can only proceed against his original insurer.[95] Where advance freight is payable, the person advancing the freight

---

[89] *Karlshamns Oljefabriker v. Eastport Navigation Co; The Elafi* [1981] 2 Lloyd's Rep. 679; *Leigh and Sillivan Ltd v. Aliakmon Shipping Co Ltd* [1986] A.C. 785; also *Inglis v. Stock* (1855) App. Cas. 263. By s.8 of the Marine Insurance Act 1906 a partial interest of any nature is insurable. Section 20A of the Sale of Goods Act 1979 meets many of the potential problems likely to arise.
[90] If under the terms of the contract of carriage he has incurred no risk (which will be a rare case), he cannot recover under the policy because mere possession of another person's goods (without incurring liability for them) does not constitute an insurable interest: *Scott v. Globe Marine Insurance Co Ltd* (1896) 1 Com.Cas. 370.
[91] See *ante*, para. 27–018.
[92] Sale of Goods Act 1979, s.38(2). See *ante*, para. 27–019.
[93] Insurance cover may be available to protect an agent against these eventualities on prior request to the underwriters.
[94] Marine Insurance Act 1906, s.9(1).
[95] *ibid.* s.9(2).

has an insurable interest in so far as the freight is not repayable in case of loss.[96] An assured has an insurable interest in respect of his insurance costs.[97] The owner of insurable property has an insurable interest in respect of the full value of such property, notwithstanding that some third party may have agreed, or be liable to indemnify him in the case of loss.[98]

The premium

19–015 Under section 52 the premium is payable to the insurer when he issues the policy, unless another arrangement is agreed upon by the parties or required by trade custom. It has been explained that in normal cases the broker is responsible solely and directly to the insurer for payment of the premium.

A proportionate part of the premium can be reclaimed where the assured has over-insured under an unvalued policy,[99] but not where he has done so under a valued policy because here the agreed valuation is, as a rule, binding on both parties. Where an over-insurance has been effected by double insurance, the assured who is covered only to the value of the insured interest can reclaim a proportionate amount of the several premiums paid by him. In case of loss the assured can claim the whole payment due to him from any one of the several underwriters and leave it to them to adjust the loss according to section 32(2) amongst themselves. In a few exceptional cases the assured is barred from recovering the overpaid portions of the premium.

1. If the double insurance was effected by the assured knowingly, or
2. If a claim has been paid for the full sum insured, or
3. If the policies were effected at different times and an earlier policy bore, at any time, the entire risk (s.84(3)(f), proviso).

Double insurance occurs only if the same insurable interest and the risk is insured twice or more frequently in excess of its value. It does not occur if two persons, *e.g.* the seller and the carrier, are interested in the same consignment and insure their (different) interests therein.[1]

The rates of premium require careful attention by the exporter, who has to rely here on the expert advice of his broker. The rates quoted normally include the cover under the Institute Cargo Clauses.

Assignment

19–016 When insured goods are sold or transferred, the insurance effected in respect of them does not automatically pass to the buyer. The assured, when conveying the property in the insured goods to the buyer, does not automatically assign the

---

[96] s.12; see *ante*, para. 15–010.
[97] s.13.
[98] s.14.
[99] s.84(2)(e).
[1] See *A. Tomlinson (Hauliers) Ltd v. Hepburn* [1966] A.C. 451.

"policy" (ss.15, 51). Insurance is not, as Arnould puts it, an "incident of the property insured."[2]

Normally, however, a contract to sell insured goods contains an express or implied condition that the seller shall assign the insurance to the buyer. In modern practice, the assignment is carried out by indorsing the policy in blank and delivering it to the buyer. Section 50 allows the assignee of the policy to sue in his own name. The consent of the insurer is not necessary for an assignment. As already observed,[3] the relationship between the insurer and the assignee is not one of utmost good faith. The policy can be assigned after a loss. An insurance policy is not a negotiable instrument.[4]

When insured goods are sold and the policy is assigned to the buyer, the buyer is entitled, in case of loss, to claim the full value of the insurance even if the cargo was sold at a price lower than the value insured. The seller cannot claim the difference between the insurance money and the purchase price.[5] The buyer, on the other hand, cannot claim the benefit of an insurance on "increased value" which the seller concludes as his own speculation and which he would not be bound to transfer to the buyer under the contract of sale.[6]

Risks covered and risks not covered ("exclusions")

The word "warranty" is used, in marine insurance, in a contradictory and con- **19–017** fusing manner. "First, it is used to denote a condition to be fulfilled by the assured. Secondly, it is used to denote a mere limitation on, or exception from, the general words of the policy."[7]

The first type of warranty is known as *promissory warranty*. These warranties are promises by the assured that certain facts exist; they take the following form:

> warranted professionally packed,
> or
> warranted no iron ore.
> or
> that the adventure insured is a lawful one.[8]

They are, in general legal terminology, conditions[9] which, if not exactly complied with, whether material to the risk or not, entitle the insurer to disclaim

---

[2] Arnould, *loc. cit.* para. 252.
[3] See *ante*, para. 19–012.
[4] See *Colonia Versicherung AG v. Amoco Oil Co* [1997] 1 Lloyd's Rep. 261, CA for an examination of assignment and subrogation.
[5] *Ralli v. Universal Marine Insurance Co* (1862) 31 L.J.Ch. 207; *Landauer v. Asser* [1905] 2 K.B. 184.
[6] *Strass v. Spiller and Bakers* (1911) 16 Com.Cas. 166. In this case the insurers had paid the insurance sum to the sellers and had not raised the question of an insurable interest remaining in the sellers after the sale; the buyers then claimed the insurance money from the sellers, but their claim was dismissed.
[7] Chalmers, *Marine Insurance* (10th ed., 1993), p. 51.
[8] Marine Insurance Act 1906, s.41. However, a contract for the sale and return of diamonds in West Germany was not affected by a deliberate misstatement of the value of goods in an invoice in order to avoid the German equivalent to VAT: *Euro-Diam Ltd v. Bathurst* [1990] 1 Q.B. 35.
[9] Diplock J. in *Vaughan Motors & Sheldon Motor Services Ltd v. Scottish General Insurance Co Ltd* [1960] 1 Lloyd's Rep. 479 at 481. On conditions generally, see p. 5–002, *ante*. It should be

liability from the date of their breach.[10] For example, in a situation where the carrying vessel was "warranted German FOM" (flag, ownership, management) the insurer was discharged from liability as the vessel was not in fact in German ownership, the criterion of nationality being held, on the facts, to be decisive.[11] Where a promissory warranty is broken, in English law the insurer may refuse to pay the insurance sum even if the breach of "condition" does not cause the loss suffered by the insurer.[12]

The second type of warranty is entirely different. It is known as an *exceptive warranty*, by which the insurer obtains exemption from liability in the indicated circumstances. These warranties are expressed by the words "warranted free . . ."; that means that the risk is not covered; *e.g.* the clause:

> "warranted free of loss or damage caused by strikers, locked-out workmen or persons taking part in labour disturbances, riots or civil commotions"

means that the insurer is not liable for any loss due to these causes.

The difference between "warranted" and "warranted free" is of fundamental importance for an exporter who wishes to obtain a clear idea of the protection which the policy provides for his shipments. In practice this confusing anti-quated terminology is usually avoided and it is stated that specified risks are covered and others are not covered. This terminology is used in the Institute Cargo Clauses A, B and C, where the section dealing with risks not covered is headed "Exclusions."

The Lloyd's Marine Policy and the Institute Cargo Clauses A, B and C

19–018 The form of policy is the *Lloyd's S.G. Policy*,[13] appended as a model form to the Marine Insurance Act 1906. This policy was adopted in 1779 and was a revision of earlier forms. It defied attempts to render it into a more modern and comprehensible form. The meaning of individual clauses had to be sought in numerous decisions of the courts over the two centuries during which it was in use. The existence of the guidelines to interpretation provided by these decisions was in itself a hindrance to redrafting the policy. Eventually change resulted from the strong criticism of the policy by the United Nations Commission on Trade and Development.[14] The Technical Clauses Committee of the Institute of

---

noted that the term "warranty," as used in insurance law, has a different meaning from that term as used in the law of contract generally.

[10] s.33(3). Where a promissory warranty is broken, in English law the insurer may refuse to pay the insurance sum even if the breach of the condition is not the cause of the loss suffered by the insurer.

[11] *The Tiburon* [1990] 2 Lloyd's Rep. 418.

[12] Other legal systems adopt a more lenient attitude, as evinced by Norwegian law, see *Forsikring-saktieselskapet Vesta v. J. N. E. Butcher, Bain Dawes Ltd* [1989] 1 Lloyd's Rep. 331.

Breach of a promissory warranty entitles the insurer to treat the insurance contract as voidable but (in spite of the wording of s.33) does not render the contract void: *Bank of Nova Scotia v. Hellenic Mutual War Risks Association (Bermuda) Ltd; The Good Luck* [1989] 2 Lloyd's Rep. 238, CA.

[13] "S.G." stands for ships and goods. There was formerly an S. Policy covering only ships and a G. Policy covering only goods, but they have fallen into disuse.

[14] UNCTAD Official Records TD/B/590.

London Underwriters succeeded in formulating a new policy, which was to replace the S.G. Policy, and five sets of clauses. The New Policy and Clauses were introduced on January 1, 1982 with a transitional period until March 31, 1983, the date set for the withdrawal of the old clauses. The new form is known as *Lloyd's Marine Policy* and the new cargo clauses are described as *Institute Cargo Clauses A, B and C* respectively. They are devised for use with the new policy form.

The Lloyd's Marine Policy form no longer contains the terms of insurance. It is simply a schedule into which the following information is to be inserted: the policy number, the names of the assured and the vessel, the voyage or period of insurance, the subject-matter insured and its agreed value (if any), the amount insured, the premium, clauses and endorsements to be attached, and a "catch-all" of special conditions and warranties.

The three sets of cargo clauses reflect a new approach when compared to the old forms. In addition, there are various other new clauses such as the Institute War Clauses (Cargo) and the Institute Strikes Clauses (Cargo).

Institute Cargo Clauses A, B and C list the cover which they provide, together with losses which are excluded under the policy. Institute Cargo Clauses A are considered as replacing the "all risks" cover which was available under the old S.G. Policy. Institute Cargo Clauses B and C cover specific perils, with Clauses C being by far the narrowest, providing cover against major casualties only. All three clauses cover general average and salvage charges.

Institute Cargo Clauses A

Clause 1 of the Institute Cargo Clauses A defines the cover provided by this **19–019** insurance. It states:

> "This insurance covers all risks of loss of or damage to the subject-matter insured except as provided in Clauses 4, 5, 6 and 7 below."

The "all risks" cover provided by Institute Cargo Clauses A does not, however, cover loss or damage caused by an inherent defect of the goods or insufficient packing, or by delay.[15]

Clauses 4, 5, 6 and 7 are exclusion clauses which will be considered later in detail.[16]

Institute Cargo Clauses B

The risks covered by this insurance are the following, except as provided in **19–020** clauses 4, 5, 6 and 7:

---

[15] See *post*, para. 19–024.
[16] See *post*, para. 19–024.

"1.1 loss of or damage to the subject-matter insured reasonably attributable to
1.1.1 fire or explosion,
1.1.2 vessel or craft being stranded ground sunk or capsized,
1.1.3 overturning or derailment of land conveyance,
1.1.4 collision or contact of vessel craft or conveyance with any external object other than water,
1.1.5 discharge of cargo at a port of distress,
1.1.6 earthquake volcanic eruption or lightning,
1.2 loss of or damage to the subject-matter insured caused by
1.2.1 general average sacrifice,
1.2.2 jettison or washing overboard,
1.2.3 entry of sea lake or river water into vessel craft hold conveyance container liftvan or place of storage,
1.3 total loss of any package lost over board or dropped whilst loading on to, or unloading from, vessel or craft."

Exclusion Clauses 4, 5, 6 and 7 are the same as those in Cargo Clauses A but Clause 4.7 excludes deliberate damage or destruction of the subject-matter insured.

Institute Cargo Clauses C

19–021 This insurance covers, except as provided by Clauses 4, 5, 6 and 7:

"1.1 loss of or damage to the subject-matter insured reasonably attributable to
1.1.1 fire or explosion,
1.1.2 vessel or craft being stranded grounded sunk or capsized,
1.1.3 overturning or derailment of land conveyance,
1.1.4 collision or contact of vessel craft or conveyance with any external object other than water,
1.1.5 discharge of cargo at a port of distress,
1.2 loss of or damage to the subject-matter insured caused by
1.2.1 general average sacrifice,
1.2.2 jettison."

Exclusion Clauses 4, 5, 6 and 7 are again applicable and are identical to those in Institute Cargo Clauses B.

The Transit Clause

19–022 It is appropriate at this point to consider the Transit Clause which is present in Institute Cargo Clauses A, B and C, and which is therefore applicable unless it is deleted. By this Clause, the liability of the insurer is extended to cover pre-shipment and post-shipment risks. The assured can, under this clause, for example, insure a consignment of goods from Birmingham to Paris, provided these places are named in the policy as the commencement and destination of the transit.[17] In Institute Cargo Clauses A, B and C the Transit Clause is supplemented by the Termination of Contract of Carriage Clause and these two Clauses are worded as follows:

---

[17] The clause does not cover damage to the goods before they reach the warehouse at the commencement of the transit: *Reinhart Co v. Joshua Hoyle & Sons Ltd* [1961] 1 Lloyd's Rep. 346, 354 and 358.

"8.1 This insurance attaches from the time the goods leave the warehouse or place of storage at the place named herein for the commencement of the transit, continues during the ordinary course of transit and terminates either

8.1.1 on delivery to the Consignees' or other final warehouse or place of storage at the destination named herein,

8.1.2 on delivery to any other warehouse or place of storage, whether prior to or at the destination named herein, which the Assured elect to use either

8.1.2.1 for storage other than in the ordinary course of transit or

8.1.2.2 for allocation or distribution,

or

8.1.3 on the expiry of 60 days after completion of discharge overside of the goods hereby insured from the oversea vessel at the final port of discharge, whichever shall first occur.

8.2 If, after discharge overside from the oversea vessel at the final port of discharge, but prior to termination of this insurance, the goods are to be forwarded to a destination other than that to which they are insured hereunder, this insurance, whilst remaining subject to termination as provided for above, shall not extend beyond the commencement of transit to such other destination.

8.3 This insurance shall remain in force (subject to termination as provided for above and to the provisions of Clause 9 below) during delay beyond the control of the Assured, any deviation, forced discharge, reshipment or transhipment and during any variation of the adventure arising from the exercise of a liberty granted to shipowners or charterers under the contract of affreightment.

If owing to circumstances beyond the control of the Assured either the contract of carriage is terminated at a port or place other than the destination named therein or the transit is otherwise terminated before delivery of the goods as provided for in Clause 8 above, then this insurance shall also terminate *unless prompt notice is given to the Underwriters and continuation of cover is requested when the insurance shall remain in force, subject to an additional premium if required by the Underwriters*, either

9.1 until the goods are sold and delivered at such port or place, or, unless otherwise specially agreed, until the expiry of 60 days after arrival of the goods hereby insured at such port or place, whichever shall first occur,

or

9.2 if the goods are forwarded within the said period of 60 days (or any agreed extension thereof) to the destination named herein or to any other destination, until terminated in accordance with the provisions of Clause 8 above."

Under the Transit Clause, with its additional Termination of Contract of Carriage Clause, the goods are covered from the time when they leave the warehouse at the place named in the policy for the commencement of the transit and continue to be covered until they are delivered to the final warehouse at the destination named in the policy or another warehouse, whether prior to or at the destination named in the policy. The policy provides an overriding time limit of 60 days[18] after the completion of discharge overside the overseas vessel at the final port of discharge. On the expiration of that time limit cover ceases even though the goods may not have reached a warehouse. If before the expiration of the 60 days but after discharge the goods are forwarded to a destination other than that named in the insurance, the cover terminates when the transit begins. The 60 days' cover is very valuable for the assured if, for some reason, the goods cannot proceed to the warehouse, for instance, if they are detained in the Customs shed because the buyer has not paid the import duties, and the assured cannot dispose of them quickly. The principle underlying these provisions is

---

[18] There exists also a so-called South American 60 day clause which appears to be similar to the Institute Clause except that it provides a 90 day extension for shipments via the Magdalena River.

that the assured shall be covered until he or his buyer can reasonably be expected to have made further insurance arrangements for the goods. If under the contract of carriage the goods are unloaded at a place other than the contemplated place of destination, due to circumstances beyond the control of the assured, they continue to be insured[19] (subject to the overriding time limit of 60 days) until they are forwarded to the agreed or another destination and have arrived at the final warehouse, or until they are sold and delivered. The word "warehouse" has been given its ordinary and natural meaning.[20]

The risks covered

19–023	Except as excluded by Clauses 4, 5, 6 and 7, discussed below, Institute Cargo Clauses A cover all risks of loss or damage to the subject-matter insured, whereas Clauses B and C only cover risks which are specifically referred to. A detailed consideration of these specific risks would go beyond the ambit of this work.

The exporter who, in order to save on the premium, does not wish to insure under Clauses A but prefers to insure under Clauses B or C, should make sure that the specific risks to which his cargo may be exposed are expressly covered, and also are not excluded by the provisions of Clauses B and C.

Risks not covered (the Exclusion Clauses)

19–024	*General Exclusion Clause.* Clause 4 is the General Exclusion Clause and, except for one particular exclusion which will be considered later, it is present in Institute Cargo Clauses A, B and C.

Clause 4.1 excludes "loss damage or expense attributable to wilful misconduct of the Assured." This clause mirrors section 55(2)(a) which states:

> "The insurer is not liable for any loss attributable to the wilful misconduct of the assured, but, unless the policy otherwise provides, he is liable for any loss proximately[21] caused by a peril insured against, even though the loss would not have happened but for the misconduct or negligence of the master or crew."[22]

"Wilful misconduct" is essentially a question of fact, but drawing a proper inference from the facts involves a consideration of the law.[23]

Clause 4.2 excludes "ordinary leakage, ordinary loss in weight or volume, or ordinary wear and tear of the subject-matter insured." The word "ordinary" refers to the normal transit losses which may arise from various causes such as

---

[19] See, *e.g. G. H. Renton & Co v. Palmyra Trading Corporation of Panama; The Caspiana* [1957] A.C. 149.
[20] *Leo Rapp Ltd v. McClure* [1955] 1 Lloyd's Rep. 292; *Reinhart Co v. Joshua Hoyle & Sons Ltd* [1961] 1 Lloyd's Rep. 346 at 358.
[21] On "proximately", see *post*, para. 19–030.
[22] Including wilful misconduct, though an assured cannot take advantage of his own wrong; see *Schiffshypotheken Bank zu Luebeck AG v. Compton; The Alexion Hope* [1987] 1 Lloyd's Rep. 60.
[23] For the interpretation of "wilful misconduct" see *Horabin v. British Overseas Airways Corp.* [1952] 2 All E.R. 1016; *Coutlas v. KLM (S.D.N.Y. 1961) Transport Laws of the World* iv/c/1 p. 303.

the nature of the goods themselves or their treatment in transit. When the ordinary leakage of one cargo damages a second cargo, the assured in respect of the second cargo can only recover if he is insured under Cargo Clauses A, but not if his insurance is based upon only Clauses B or C.

Clause 4.3 excludes "loss damage or expense caused by insufficiency or unsuitability of packing or preparation of the subject-matter insured (for the purpose of this Clause 4.3 'packing' shall be deemed to include stowage in a container or liftvan, but only when such stowage is carried out prior to attachment of this insurance or by the Assured or their servants)." The question of whether packing is suitable or sufficient is often determined according to what is customary in a particular trade. Where the packing is such that the cargo cannot withstand the usual conditions relating to a particular voyage, the assured cannot recover for any loss or damage caused or for any expenses incurred in replacing inadequate packing.[24] Loss of, or damage to, the contents of a container or liftvan will not be covered where they are loaded by the assured or his servants prior to or after the attachment of the insurance. This exclusion will not apply, however, when the stowing is done after the attachment of the insurance and without the assured or his servants being involved.

Clause 4.4 includes "loss damage or expense caused by inherent vice or nature of the subject-matter insured."[25] This exclusion clause covers situations where the goods insured are damaged or destroyed by an internal development. As an example, spontaneous combustion may occur within one cargo, damaging a second cargo. The owner of the first cargo cannot recover where the spontaneous combustion is the result of inherent vice, such as may be the case in a cargo of grain, but the owner of the second cargo can recover for his own loss under Clauses A, B or C since the risk of loss or damage due to fire and explosion is covered.

A difficulty arises where the loss or damage is caused not by the goods themselves but by insufficient packing. Sellers J. held in *F. W. Berk & Co Ltd v. Style*[26] that insufficiency of packing was an inherent vice of the goods—kieselguhr packed in bags—but the learned judge had found as a fact that the goods in no circumstances would have withstood the necessary handling and transport, and for that reason refused the assured's claim for the costs of re-bagging. Where, on the other hand, the packing would have been sufficient to withstand ordinary handling and transit but failed to protect the goods as the result of an extraneous event, that event—and not the insufficiency of packing—would be the proximate cause of the damage or loss and the assured could, it is thought, recover under the All Risks policy, now Clauses A. Another more recent example concerned a cargo of industrial leather gloves which sustained wetting damage in transit from Calcutta to Rotterdam. It was determined that moisture had been absorbed by the gloves prior to packing and containerisation. After containerisation the moisture within the gloves circulated within the container

---

[24] *F. W. Berk v. Style* [1956] 1 Q.B. 180.
[25] *Soya GmbH Mainz Kommandit-Gesellschaft v. White* [1983] 1 Lloyd's Rep. 122.
[26] [1956] 1 Q.B. 180. See also *Gee & Garnham v. Whittall* [1955] 2 Lloyd's Rep. 562, where aluminium kettles insured under an "all risks" policy arrived damaged; Sellers J. dismissed the claim of the assured, again treating insufficient packing as inherent vice of the goods.

and further damage was caused. It was held that the insurers could rely on the inherent vice exclusion; the gloves had deteriorated as a result of their natural behaviour and not their packing.[27]

Clause 4.5 excludes "loss damage or expense proximately caused by delay even though the delay is caused by a risk insured against (except expenses payable under [the general average] clause)." Therefore, although under the Transit Clause[28] the insurance will remain valid where a delay is beyond the control of the assured, he will not be protected in respect of any damage which is proximately caused by that delay. However, in the case of a general average act which causes a delay, the assured is entitled to recover his proportion of any expenses incurred during the period of the delay, such as, for example, his contribution to the wages of the crew.

Clause 4.6 excludes "loss damage or expense arising from insolvency or financial default of the owners managers charterers or operators of the vessel." If, due to financial difficulties, the carrier has to stop short of destination, the insurer will not have to pay the forwarding expenses incurred by the assured. Further, these expenses cannot be recovered under Clause 12, which is applicable only to expenses incurred where a voyage is terminated as a result of a peril insured against.

Clause 4.7 in Clauses B and C excludes "deliberate damage to or deliberate destruction of the subject-matter insured or any part thereof by the wrongful act of any person or persons." This clause is not to be found in Institute Cargo Clauses A. Where this clause is present, the insurer will not be liable for loss or damage caused by arson, scuttling or any form of sabotage or any other malicious acts, by which the subject-matter insured is deliberately damaged or destroyed. Where an assured wishes to remove this exception, a Malicious Damage Clause should be added.

Clause 4.7 in Cargo Clauses A, which is identical to Clause 4.8 in Clauses B and C, excludes "loss damage or expense arising from the use of any weapon of war employing atomic or nuclear fission and/or fusion or other like reaction or radioactive force or matter."

By section 55(2)(c) of the Marine Insurance Act 1906 "unless the policy otherwise provides, the insurer is not liable for . . . any loss proximately caused by rats or vermin. Under Clauses A such loss is covered since it is not expressly excluded, but where Clauses B and C are used, such loss is not covered even though not specifically excluded under the general exclusions clause, since the risk is not expressly provided for in the risks clauses.

Unseaworthiness and Unfitness Exclusion Clause. When the insured cargo is shipped, it is unlikely that the assured will have control over the vessel used, but by virtue of section 39, the assured's cover may be invalid if the vessel is unseaworthy. By Clause 5.2 of the Cargo Clauses, however, the "Underwriters waive any breach of the implied warranties of seaworthiness of the ship and fitness of the ship to carry the subject-matter insured to destination, unless the Assured or their servants are privy to such unseaworthiness or unfitness." Where

---

[27] *T.M. Noten BV v. Paul Charles Harding* [1990] 2 Lloyd's Rep. 283, CA.
[28] See para. 19–022, *ante*.

a vessel is sent to sea in a state of unseaworthiness in more than one respect and the assured is privy to only one, the insurer may only avoid liability if the loss or damage was attributable to the particular aspect of unseaworthiness to which the assured was privy according to s.39(5). The sub-section requires positive knowledge and consent or ignoring the true state of affairs on the part of the assured.[29]

Therefore, by Clause 5.2, the insurer is liable for any loss or damage which is insured against and which is not excluded where the assured or his servants have no knowledge of unseaworthiness or unfitness. Although not expressly stated, Clause 5.2 refers to the condition of the ship when it actually commences its voyage. This is made clear by the wording of Clause 5.1 which refers to the time of loading the cargo. It states:

"In no case shall this insurance cover loss damage or expense arising from unseaworthiness of vessel or craft, unfitness of vessel craft conveyance container or liftvan for the safe carriage of the subject-matter insured, where the Assured or their servants are privy to such unseaworthiness or unfitness, at the time the subject-matter insured is loaded therein."

Clause 5.1 is more comprehensive than Clause 5.2 in that it exempts the insurer as regards the unseaworthiness of a craft, for example a lighter, and also with respect to the unfitness of any conveyance or container used for carrying the goods, where the assured or his servants have knowledge of such unseaworthiness or unfitness. "Servants" in this context should not be confused with agents, and the knowledge of the assured's agents, such as stevedores, will not affect the insurer's liability.

War Exclusion Clause. Clause 6 is the War Exclusion Clause and is present in Cargo Clauses A, B and C. Deletion of Clause 6 will mean that war risks are covered in Clauses A, but not in Clauses B or C, since such perils are not present in the risks clause. Where an assured requires war risk cover, he should ask for the addition of the Institute War Clauses.

Strikes Exclusion Clause. This Clause 7 is present in all three Institute Cargo Clauses but its deletion would only enable an assured to recover for such risks where he is insured under Clauses A, since in Clauses B and C the peril is not within the specific risks covered.

Where an assured specifically wants cover for strikes and other labour disturbances, he should require the addition of the Institute Strikes Clauses.

Clause 7.3 excludes loss damage or expense "caused by any terrorist or any person acting from a political motive."

Minimising losses. The old S.G. Policy used to contain a "sue and labour" clause, which provided that it was lawful for an assured "to sue, labour and travel for, in and about the defence, safeguards, and recovery of the goods, ship, etc., without prejudice to this insurance." This clause has now been replaced by Clause 16 in Clauses A, B and C which states:

---

[29] See *Compañía Maritima San Basilio SA v. Oceanus Mutual Underwriting Association (Bermuda) Ltd; The Eurysthenes* [1976] 2 Lloyd's Rep. 171, CA; *Manifest Shipping & Co Ltd v. Uni-Polaris Insurance Co Ltd; The Star Sea* [1997] 1 Lloyd's Rep. 360, CA (and also at first instance [1995] 1 Lloyd's Rep. 651) for a discussion on privity.

"It is the duty of the Assured and their servants and agents in respect of loss recoverable
hereunder: to take such measures as may be reasonable for the purpose of averting or minimising such loss and to ensure that all rights against carriers, bailees or other third parties are
properly preserved and exercised and the Underwriters will, in addition to any loss recoverable
hereunder, reimburse the Assured for any charges properly and reasonably incurred in pursuance of these duties."

This clause is now called the Duty of Assured Clause. In conjunction with
section 78 of the Act it enables an assured to recover from the insurer any
expenses reasonably incurred pursuant to the clause, notwithstanding that the
insurer has already paid for a total loss. Recovery depends upon the reasonableness of the assured's assessment of the situation and if he has in all the
circumstances acted reasonably to avert a loss where there was a risk that the
insurers might have to bear it, then the assured can recover on proof of loss.[30]

General average[31]

19–025   The law of general average relates to general maritime law and affects two
relationships in which the exporter is involved, namely the contract of carriage
by sea which he concludes with the carrier, and the contract of insurance which
he concludes with the insurer.[32] The same general average act might affect both
contracts, and the rights and duties of the exporter under the contract of carriage
are different from those arising under the contract of insurance.

The general average act

19–026   A general average act occurs in the following circumstances. During the sea
voyage, three interests are at risk: the ship, the cargo and the freight. They form
a common adventure and they are exposed to the same risks. When these interests encounter a common peril, it may become necessary voluntarily to make
an extraordinary sacrifice or to incur an extraordinary expenditure in order to
preserve the property imperilled in the common adventure (s.66(2)). The ship
may encounter heavy weather and it may be necessary to jettison part of the
cargo or of the ship's equipment in order to lighten it. The sacrifice that is made
here is made for the benefit of all concerned in the common adventure and it is
only just and fair that the owners of all interests saved by a deliberate sacrifice
of a co-adventurer's property should contribute proportionately to his loss. The
situation which arises here is totally different from that arising, for example
where the cargo deteriorates owing to sea water entering a container carried on

---

[30] *Integrated Container Service Inc v. British Traders Insurance Co* [1984] 1 Lloyd's Rep. 154;
Netherlands Insurance Co Est. 1845 Ltd v. Karl Ljungberg & Co AB [1986] 2 Lloyd's Rep. 19 (PC
on appeal from Singapore; reimbursement for litigation costs expended by assured to preserve time
bar against carrier recoverable under "sue and labour" clause). See also *Royal Boskalis Westminster
BV v. Mountain* [1998] 2 W.L.R. 538.
[31] See Lowndes and Rudolf's *The Law of General Average and the York-Antwerp Rules*, D.J. Wilson
and J.H.S. Cooke (12th ed., Sweet & Maxwell, 1997).
[32] The law of general average might even affect a third relationship, namely the right of a cargo
owner to recover from another ship that negligently collided with the carrying ship, the general
average contribution which the cargo owner paid to the carrying ship in consequence of the collision;
Morrison Steamship Co v. Greystoke Castle [1947] A.C. 265.

a ship; this is a misfortune that befalls an individual interest and has to be borne by the owner of that interest alone, but he can cover this risk by taking out insurance under Institute Cargo Clauses A or B (though Cargo Clauses C would not cover him against this risk).

A general average act has thus to satisfy the following requirements (s.66(2)). It must be:

> "(1) an extraordinary sacrifice or expenditure,
> (2) purposely resorted to,
> (3) reasonably made or incurred,
> (4) in time of peril,
> (5) for the purpose of preserving the property imperilled in the common danger."

It must also appear:

> "(6) that the sacrifice or the expenditure was judiciously incurred.
> (7) that it is not included in those ordinary duties or expenses which are incidental to the navigation of the ship, and are paid out of the freight.
> (8) that it was not due to any wrongful act, for which the claimant is responsible."

The general average loss

A general average loss is expenditure caused[33] or a sacrifice incurred as the **19–027** result of a general average act (s.66(1)).

A general average loss may arise from a general average sacrifice, *e.g.* when cargo is jettisoned or, if the ship is in danger of foundering, where part of the cargo is loaded on boats and lost. Jettison of cargo does not constitute a general average act unless such cargo is carried in accordance with recognised customs of the trade.[34] A general average loss may also arise from general average expenditure, which is extraordinary expenditure incurred for the common benefit to secure the physical safety of ship and cargo, *e.g.* the expense of making and entering a port of refuge.[35] Reasonable costs incurred at the port of refuge for repair of the ship, warehousing the cargo, etc., are likely to be regarded as general average expenditure. It is at least general practice to allow costs of warehousing of the cargo at the port of refuge as general average expenditure, provided the ship put into the port of refuge in consequence of damage which was itself the subject of general average.[36]

The laws of maritime nations differ materially in their definition of general

---

[33] An indemnity paid to tugowners whose tugs were called in to tow a ship to safety is a "direct consequence" of a general average act and recoverable as general average expenditure; *Australian Coastal Shipping Commission v. Green* [1971] 1 Q.B. 456; see York-Antwerp Rules 1994, Rule C.
[34] See York-Antwerp Rules 1994, Rule I.
[35] Where a vessel suffering a breakdown in her diesel generator made a deviation to a port of refuge for repairs and the deviation was a reasonable deviation within the meaning of Art. IV r. 4 of the Hague Rules relating to Bills of Lading, the shipowners were entitled to claim general average from the cargo owners and their insurers; *Danae Shipping Corporation v. TPAO and Guven Turkish Insurance Co Ltd; The Daffodil B* [1983] 1 Lloyd's Rep. 499.
[36] Rules of Practice of the Association of Average Adjusters.

average.[37] It is to the credit of the International Law Association to have secured some measure of uniformity in this situation. The Association drafted standard rules dealing with the adjustment of general average which in their present form are known as the York-Antwerp Rules 1994.[38] These rules, though not having the force of law, are in practice frequently adopted by the parties. Sometimes the parties make other arrangements, *e.g.* they may provide that "average, if any, shall be adjusted according to the British Rule." Where the York-Antwerp Rules are not adopted and the parties have not made special arrangements, general average is adjusted in accordance with the law in force at the port of destination, and if the ship does not reach that port, at the port at which the journey is broken up.

General average and the contract of carriage by sea

19–028   It is now necessary to deal separately with the contracts of carriage by sea and insurance, so far as they are affected by the law of general average. In the law of maritime transport, where there is a general average loss, the party on whom it falls is entitled to a rateable[39] contribution from the other parties interested in the venture (s.66(3)). According to the circumstances this contribution may be a right or a duty of the cargo owner. If he suffers a general average loss, he is entitled to claim contribution from the shipowner and the other cargo owners. If their interest is lost and his is saved by their sacrifice or expenditure, he is liable to make a contribution to them.[40] These rights and duties arise from the contract of carriage by sea. They have no immediate connection with insurance and exist whether the cargo owner is insured or not. The cargo owner is not liable to contribute to general average expenditure if the York-Antwerp Rules were incorporated in the bill of lading and ship and cargo were completely lost after the expenditure was incurred.[41] The shipowner has, at common law, a lien on the cargo for general average contributions as long as he continues to be in possession of the goods. Sometimes the shipowner refuses to give up possession of the goods, unless the persons entitled thereto have signed an *average bond*,[42]

---

[37] There exists an International Convention on Salvage of 1989, reproduced in 20 *Journal of Maritime Law and Commerce* (1989), 589. This convention has nothing to do with general average loss or contribution but deals with the salvage award for the salvor.

[38] The first York-Antwerp Rules were those of 1924; they were in turn superseded by the 1950 version, which was in turn superseded by the 1974 version. The major amendment to the Rules contained in the 1994 version is the introduction of the Rule Paramount which provides: "In no case shall there be any allowance for sacrifice or expenditure unless reasonably made or incurred".

[39] The general average contributions of the shipowner and the cargo owner are calculated proportionally, according to the value of the interests involved: see Rule XVII for Contributory Values under the York-Antwerp Rules 1994 and see s.66(3) of the MIA 1906.

[40] Except where the claimant was at fault, *e.g.* the shipowner negligently failed to make the ship seaworthy; in that case the cargo owners do not lose their defences and counterclaims if they do not sue the shipowner within one year, as provided by the Hague Rules, Art. III, r. 6 (see *ante*, para. 15–048): *Goulandris Brothers Ltd v. B. Goldman & Sons Ltd* [1958] 1 Q.B. 74 (interpreting the York-Antwerp Rules 1950, Rule D). Further, *The Aga* [1968] 1 Lloyd's Rep. 431.

[41] *Chellew v. Royal Commission on the Sugar Supply* [1922] 1 K.B. 12.

[42] In principle the limitation period for a claim for general average contribution counts from the date of the sacrifice. But where the consignee of the cargo executes a Lloyd's standard form average bond in return for release of the cargo, he undertakes a new contractual obligation to contribute to general average and time begins to run from the date when the adjusters have completed their

that is a formal undertaking that they will pay their respective general average contributions after they have been ascertained, and have paid a deposit into a bank in the joint names of trustees nominated by the shipowner and the cargo owners. The cargo owner who has paid the deposit receives a general average deposit receipt, which states the name of the adjuster and which he has to produce when the refund found to be due to him is paid out. The average bond is normally concluded between the shipowner on the one hand and all cargo owners on the other. If, in an individual case, a cargo owner wishes to act on his own and to obtain possession of his cargo independently, he offers the shipowner an indemnity or guarantee issued by a bank. The adjustment of general average loss, *i.e.* the calculation of the individual contributions, is a complicated and often lengthy operation which is carried out by average adjusters.[43] The shipowner is entitled to appoint the average adjuster.

General average and the contract of insurance

The risks which may fall upon the cargo owner under the law of general average **19–029** are normally fully covered by his marine insurance. They are twofold: either physical loss of, or damage to, his goods, or liability to pay a general average contribution. The Marine Insurance Act provides in section 66(4) and (5):

> "(4) Subject to any express provision in the policy, where the assured has incurred a general average expenditure, he may recover from the insurer in respect of the proportion of the loss which falls upon him; and in the case of a general average sacrifice, he may recover from the insurer in respect of the whole loss without having enforced his right of contribution from the other parties liable to contribute.
>
> (5) Subject to any express provision in the policy, where the assured has paid, or is liable to pay, a general average contribution in respect of the subject insured, he may recover therefor from the insurer."

These provisions are implemented by the Institute Cargo Clauses. The General Average Clause in Cargo Clauses A, B and C is in identical terms.[44] It is worded as follows:

> "This insurance covers general average and salvage charges, adjusted or determined according to the contract of affreightment and/or the governing law and practice, incurred to avoid or in connection with the avoidance of loss from any cause except those excluded in Clauses 4, 5, 6 and 7 or elsewhere in this insurance."

It should be noted that a general average loss due to an event listed in one of the applicable Exclusion Clauses is not covered by this clause.[45]

---

statement: *Castle Insurance Co Ltd v. Hong Kong Islands Shipping Co Ltd; The Potoi Chau* [1984] A.C. 226, PC from Hong Kong. The expression "average bond" was described in the case as being "a common . . . though legally inaccurate description": *per* Diplock J.

[43] For the Rules of Practice of the Association of Average Adjusters, see Lowndes and Rudolf, *The Law of General Average and the York-Antwerp Rules*, D.J. Wilson and J.H.S. Cooke (12th ed., Sweet & Maxwell, 1997).

[44] In Cargo Clauses A, general average sacrifice is covered by the all risks cover. In Cargo Clauses B and C this risk is covered by an express provision.

[45] Although claims for a general average contribution have their origin in the common law, if they relate to events during the operation of a charterparty, they are claims arising out of the charterparty

By virtue of section 66(4) the cargo owner is enabled to claim, in respect of the loss suffered, payment of the insurance money from the insurer without becoming involved in the complications of the average adjustment. The underwriter, on payment of the insurance money, is subrogated to the rights of the assured under the contract of carriage by sea and is thus in a position to pursue the cargo owner for a claim for contribution.[46] This is, of course, an eminently practical solution; provided that there was no underinsurance the exporter can recover his loss from the insurer forthwith and leave the technicalities of the general average adjustment to him. The exporter, when advised of such loss, should lose no time in notifying the insurer, who is generally prepared to pay the deposit money and to sign the average bond or a similar undertaking. Where the exporter has already paid the deposit, the underwriter normally refunds it upon delivery of the general average deposit receipt, although in strict law he might not be bound to do so.[47]

Claims

Liability and causation

19–030 In order to recover for loss or damage under Institute Cargo Clauses A, B or C, it is not sufficient to show that the particular risk is covered by the Institute Cargo Clauses used. It must also be clear that liability has not been specifically excluded under Clauses 4, 5, 6 or 7.[48]

Initially, when it is intended to make a claim under the insurance, it must be considered whether the insurer is prima facie liable to reimburse the assured. It is stated in section 55(1) of the Marine Insurance Act 1906:

> "Subject to the provisions of this Act and unless the policy otherwise provides, the insurer is liable for any loss proximately caused by a peril insured against, but, subject as aforesaid, he is not liable for any loss which is not proximately caused by a peril insured against."

With the use of Institute Cargo Clauses A, the proximate cause test is applied to all the risks. Where Clauses B or C are used, it is expressly stated that with regard to certain of the risks covered, it is only necessary to show that loss or damage is reasonably attributable to the risk insured against. These risks are set out in Clause 1.1 of the Institute Cargo Clauses B and C. Where a claim is made under Clause 1.2 of the Institute Cargo Clauses B and C, the "proximately caused by" test is still applicable.

The cause which is proximate is that which is proximate in terms of efficiency

---

and are subject to an arbitration clause in the charterparty: *Union of India v. E. G. Aaby's Rederi A/S* [1975] A.C. 797.

[46] See *post*, para. 19–035.

[47] *Brandeis, Goldschmidt & Co v. Economic Insurance Co Ltd* (1922) 38 T.L.R. 609.

[48] Normally the cargo owner is a party to the insurance contract (either an original party or a party by assignment) and raises his claim directly under that contract. In exceptional circumstances, however, he has to rely on the statutory transfer of the right against the insurer under the Third Parties (Rights against Insurers) Act 1930; in *The Fanti. The Padre Island (No. 2)* [1989] 1 Lloyd's Rep. 239.

and is not necessarily the first in time.[49] The choice of which cause is proximate is made by applying commonsense standards. A good example is the case of *Reischer v. Borwick*.[50] Here a ship was insured against damage due to collision but not against perils of the sea. The ship ran against a snag[51] in a river and was holed. The leak was temporarily plugged and a tug was sent to tow the ship to the nearest dock for repairs. Unfortunately, whilst being towed, the motion of the ship through the water was such that the plug was dislodged and the ship began to sink. It was held that the proximate cause of the loss here was the collision with the snag and therefore the risk was covered by the insurance.

Where there are two dominant causes of damage, one covered by the Institute Cargo Clauses used and the other excluded under the clauses, the insurers can rely on the exclusion and hence avoid liability,[52] but if there is no exclusion, the insurers must indemnify the assured.[53]

Burden of proof

Where an assured wishes to recover under his insurance, the burden of proof is **19–031** initially on him to show that his loss or damage falls within a risk covered under the insurance, but if he relies, for example, on "the perils of the sea," he must prove the cause of the loss or damage with some degree of particularity.[54] He must also prove that they were undamaged when the insurance commenced.[55] In one case[56] the assured, an English company, bought essential oils from an Indonesian firm in Jakarta. These oils were to be used in the manufacture of soap and perfumes. The goods were insured under an Institute of London Underwriters Companics Combined policy, covering all risks and containing the usual warehouse to warehouse clause.[57] When the steel or iron drums containing the goods arrived they were found to contain water, with slight traces of essential oil. Mocatta J. dismissed the claim of the assured against the insurers. The learned judge held that the assured had not discharged the burden of proof upon them of establishing on the balance of probabilities that the oil in drums that they had agreed to buy ever started on the journey.

Once the assured has proved that the loss was due to an insured risk, the burden of proof shifts to the insurer and it is for him to show that the risk is not

---

[49] *Leyland Shipping Company Ltd v. Norwich Union Fire Insurance Society Ltd* [1918] A.C. 350.
[50] [1894] 2 Q.B. 548.
[51] This is a piece of timber embedded in a river or in the sea.
[52] *Wayne Tank and Pump Co Ltd v. Employers Liability Assurance Corporation Ltd* [1974] Q.B. 57 *per* Lord Denning M.R. (at 67C), Cairns L.J. (at 69B) and Roskill L.J. (at 75D).
[53] *J. J. Lloyd Instruments Ltd v. Northern Star Insurance Co Ltd; The Miss Jay Jay* [1987] 1 Lloyd's Rep. 264.
[54] *Rhesa Shipping Co SA v. Edmunds; The Popi M* [1985] 1 W.L.R. 948, HL; see also *Lamb Head Shipping Co v. Jennings; The Marel* [1994] 1 Lloyd's Rep. 624, CA.
[55] See para. 19–023 *ante*, where reference was made to *Reinhart Co v. Joshua Hoyle & Sons* [1961] 1 Lloyd's Rep. 346, 354 and 358. Also *Fuerst Day Lawson Ltd v. Orion Insurance Co Ltd* [1980] 1 Lloyd's Rep. 656, and *Electro Motion Ltd v. Maritime Insurance Co Ltd and Bonner* [1956] 1 Lloyd's Rep. 420; *National Justice Compañía Naviera SA v. Prudential Assurance Co Ltd; The Irakian Reefer* [1995] 1 Lloyd's Rep. 455, CA.
[56] *Fuerst Day Lawson Ltd v. Orion Insurance Co Ltd, supra.*
[57] The case arose before Lloyd's Marine Policy and the Institute Cargo Clauses A, B and C came into use.

in fact covered or is actually excluded.[58] The insurer may be able to rely on an exclusion clause, even when there is prima facie liability under a risk covered clause.

Preparation of claims

19–032 If the assured learns, even unofficially, that the goods might possibly be lost or damaged in transit he should forthwith inform his insurance broker and act on his advice. It is customary to employ brokers not only for the conclusion of a contract of insurance but also for the settlement of claims. If the consignee is informed that the goods have arrived damaged, he should immediately notify the Lloyd's local agent at the port of discharge, who will survey the goods and issue a *survey report*, unless the claim is for less than £3; in this case no survey report is required. The assured should further try to ascertain whether the loss is due to particular average or general average. A particular average loss is a loss to be borne by the particular interest incurring it alone and if such a loss is recoverable under the policy, the assured requires the following documents to support his claim: the policy, invoice, bill of lading and survey report. Other documents have to be added if necessary in the circumstances, for example the weight notes on loading and discharge if the loss is due to short weight, an extract from the ship's log or the master's protest if the loss is due to the perils of the sea.[59] The *master's protest* is a formal statement made by the master, often supported by members of the crew, before a consul or notary public and explaining the cause of damage. In the case of general average loss, the procedure indicated earlier[60] should be followed. The broker acting for the assured should not be employed by the insurer for the purpose of obtaining the report of a claims assessor.[61] Cargo policies payable abroad frequently embody a special red clause, known as the *"Important" Clause* (because it is headed by that word), specifying the requirements of the insurer as regards claims procedure. If the policy contains such a clause, the procedure set out therein must be followed punctiliously.

The Institute Cargo Clauses A, B and C all contain a set of clauses under the heading "Claims" and these are reproduced here:

> "11.1 In order to recover under this insurance the Assured must have an insurable interest in the subject-matter insured at the time of the loss.
> 11.2 Subject to 11.1 above, the Assured shall be entitled to recover for insured loss occurring during the period covered by this insurance, notwithstanding that the loss occurred before the contract of insurance was concluded, unless the Assured were aware of the loss and the Underwriters were not.
> 12. Where, as a result of the operation of a risk covered by this insurance, the insured transit is terminated at a port or place other than that to which the subject-matter is covered under this insurance, the Underwriters will reimburse the Assured for any extra charges properly and reasonably incurred in unloading storing and forwarding the subject-matter to the destination to which it is insured hereunder. This

---

[58] *M. Golodetz and Co Inc v. Czarnikow-Rionda Co Inc* [1980] 1 W.L.R. 495 at 513.
[59] Dover, *A Handbook of Marine Insurance* (8th ed., 1975), p. 618.
[60] See *ante*, para. 19–028.
[61] *North and South Trust Co v. Berkeley* [1971] 1 W.L.R. 471.

> Clause 12, which does not apply to general average or salvage charges, shall be subject to the exclusions contained in Clauses 4, 5, 6 and 7 above, and shall not include charges arising from the fault negligence insolvency or financial default of the assured or their servants.
>
> 13. No claim for Constructive Total Loss shall be recoverable hereunder unless the subject-matter insured is reasonably abandoned either on account of its actual total loss appearing to be unavoidable or because the cost of recovering, reconditioning and forwarding the subject-matter to the destination to which it is insured would exceed its value on arrival.
>
> 14.1 If any "Increased Value" insurance is effected by the Assured on the cargo insured herein the agreed value of the cargo shall be deemed to be increased to the total amount insured iunder this insurance and all Increased Value insurances covering the loss, and liability under this insurance shall be in such proportion as the sum insured herein bears to such total amount insured.
>
> In the event of claim the Assured shall provide the Underwriters with evidence of the amounts insured under all other insurances.
>
> 14.2 **Where this insurance is on Increased Value the following clause shall apply:**
> The agreed value of the cargo shall be deemed to be equal to the total amount insured under the primary insurance and all Increased Value insurances covering the loss and effected on the cargo by the Assured, and liability under this insurance shall be in such proportion as the sum insured herein bears to such total amount insured.
>
> In the event of claim the Assured shall provide the Underwriters with evidence of the amounts insured under all other insurances."

It can be seen that under Clause 12 the insurer undertakes to reimburse the assured for any charges, above the normal charges, which are properly and reasonably incurred in unloading, storing and forwarding the cargo to its destination and which result from the operation of a risk covered by the insurance.

The Corporation of Lloyd's has published *Lloyd's Survey Handbook* which, though primarily for the use of surveyors, contains valuable information for exporters and importers who wish to make a claim under cargo insurance policies.[62]

Total and partial loss

The law attaches a special technical meaning to the term "total loss," and treats **19–033** every loss that is not total as a partial loss. A partial loss occurs, for example, if 25 crated bicycles of a consignment of 100 are corroded by seawater, or if, owing to heating, a cargo of hay has to be sold at an intermediate port.

Total loss is either actual or constructive total loss. Section 57 provides that actual total loss (sometimes called "absolute total loss" occurs:

(1) where the subject-matter insured is destroyed, or
(2) where the assured has been irretrievably deprived thereof, or
(3) where the subject-matter has been so damaged that it has lost its commercial identity.

Constructive total loss, as far as goods are concerned, occurs according to section 60(2)(iii):

---

[62] Compiled and edited by the Controller of Agencies, Lloyd's, obtainable form Lloyd's.

"where the costs of repairing the damage and forwarding the goods to their destination would exceed their value on arrival."

The difference between actual and constructive total loss is that, in the former case, the subject-matter is so completely and irretrievably lost that the only course open to the assured is to recover the loss from the insurer, whereas in the latter case, the damage is repairable, though at considerable cost, and the assured is put to his election either to treat the loss as partial loss or to abandon the subject-matter to the insurer and treat the loss as total loss (s.61). Consequently, where the total loss is actual, the assured need not give the insurer notice of abandonment as this would be an empty form; but, where total loss is constructive, the assured has to give notice of abandonment in order to indicate which course he elects to take, and, if he fails to give notice with reasonable diligence, the loss is treated as a partial loss only (s.62). If the insurer declines to accept the notice of abandonment the assured must sue; the cause of action arises on the date of the casualty and not on the date of the service of the notice of abandonment.[63] If a constructive total loss of goods is followed by a justifiable sale by the master, this is treated as an actual total loss and no notice of abandonment is required, because the goods are in this case irretrievably lost and no benefit would accrue to the insurer if notice were given to him (s.62(7)).[64]

It is not always easy to say whether a loss is an actual or constructive total loss. Numerous cases have been decided on this issue but have not yielded, so far, well-defined principles. The best illustration is provided by an old case[65] where a vessel on which dates had been shipped was sunk during the course of the voyage and subsequently raised. On arrival at the port of discharge, the dates still retained the appearance of dates and were of value for distillation into spirits, but they were so impregnated with seawater and in such a condition of fermentation as to be no longer merchantable as dates. This was held to be an actual total loss of the dates.

Measure of indemnity

19–034 In case of a total loss, the assured is entitled, if the policy is a valued policy, to recover the sum fixed in the policy and if the policy is an unvalued policy, to recover the insurable value of the goods, subject to the limit of the sum insured (s.68).[66] The assured who has insured the goods at their arrival value plus estimated sales profits of the buyer[67] receives full indemnity.

---

[63] *The Kyriathi* [1993] 1 Lloyd's Rep. 137. *Asfar & Co v. Blundell* [1896] 1 Q.B. 123. See also *Terkol Rederierne v. Petroleo Brasileiro; The Badagry* [1985] 1 Lloyd's Rep. 395 (Effect of constructive total loss on substitution clause in charterparty).
[64] *Roux v. Salvador* [1836] 3 Bing, N.C. 85; see *Fraser Shipping Ltd v. Colton* [1997] 1 Lloyd's Rep. 586 for a recent example of a discussion on actual total loss and constructive total loss and the continuing difficulties in determination.
[65] *Asfar v. Blundell* [1896] 1 Q.B. 127, CA.
[66] ss. 67 and 68 are conclusive as to the insurer's liability; no additional special or general damages may be recovered: *The Italia Express (No. 2)* [1992] 2 Lloyd's Rep. 281.
[67] See *ante*, para. 19–004.

In case of partial loss of the goods, section 71 provides that the measure of damages is:

> (1) where part of the goods insured by a valued policy is lost, such proportion of the fixed value as the lost part bears to the whole insurable value of the insured goods;
> (2) where part of the goods insured by an unvalued policy is lost, the insurable value of the part lost;
> (3) where the whole or part of the goods insured arrives damaged, such proportion of the fixed value in case of a valued policy, or insurable value in the case of an unvalued policy, as the difference between the gross sound and damaged values at the place of arrival bears to the gross sound value."

In case of partial loss, where the goods are not lost but damaged, section 71 does not always give the assured full indemnity. As the percentage of the insurance sum which the insurer has to pay is calculated by comparison of the gross arrival value of the goods, if they had arrived sound, with the gross value of the damaged goods, the percentage remains constant and is independent of market fluctuations. The result would be different if the calculation were based on net values (*i.e.* values after deduction of freight charges).[68] The result of maintaining a constant measure of indemnity is that the assured, in making a claim, has a greater advantage in a falling market than in times of boom conditions. The effect of the calculation prescribed by section 71 will be seen from the following:

Illustration

Data
(1) Goods insured by valued policy at £600
(2) *Case I*: if arriving sound in gaining market, saleable at gross value of £800
(3) *Case II*: if arriving in sound losing market, saleable at gross value of £400
(4) In both cases, goods arrive damaged and are sold at gross price of 75 per cent of their sound value

	Case I	Case II
(a) Sound gross value	£800	£400
(b) Damaged gross value	600	300
Difference	£200=	£100=
	25 per cent	25 per cent

In each case, the insurers have to pay 25 per cent of £600=£150.

The measure of indemnity is not always ascertained as easily as in the preceding example. Where different species of property are insured under a single valuation and one species only is damaged, the value of the damaged goods must first be apportioned in the proportion which the damaged item bears to the different species before the ordinary rules of calculation can be applied.

The insurer's right of subrogation

On payment of the insurance money the insurer is entitled to be subrogated to **19–035** all rights and remedies of the assured in respect of the interest insured in so far as he has indemnified the assured. The purpose of subrogation is to prevent the assured from recovering more than once for the same loss, *e.g.* where goods are

---

[68] Dover, *loc. cit.*.

lost owing to a collision, the assured cannot claim the insurance money from the insurer and then sue the owners of the ship that negligently caused the collision. Under the doctrine of subrogation the right to sue the owners of the negligent ship passes from the insured to the insurer on payment of the insurance money. The insurer is subrogated to all rights of the assured arising from tort or contract, for example the assured's rights against the carrier under the contract of carriage. If the assured has already recovered damages from the third party, the insurer can claim from the assured the money received.[69]

The right of subrogation is subject to two qualifications:

(1) the insurer can only claim to stand in the shoes of the assured, he cannot acquire a better right than the latter possessed,[70] and

(2) unless the parties have otherwise agreed by way of a contractual subrogation clause, the insurer can claim to be subrogated to the rights of the assured only in so far as he has indemnified him.

The insurer can claim to be subrogated to the rights and remedies of the assured in case both of total and partial loss, but in the case of total loss he has an additional right, that is he becomes the owner of whatever remains of the interest he paid for (even if the value of that interest on salvage is greater than the insurance money paid by him).[71] If the insurer pays for partial loss only, the title in the subject-matter insured remains vested in the assured and any benefits derived from salvage may be retained by him (s.79).

In practice, the insurer invariably asks the assured, on payment of the insurance money, to sign a letter of subrogation and retains the documents, including the bill of lading, in order to prosecute the rights subrogated to him.

The right of subrogation should not be confused with the right of the insurer, on abandonment, to take over the subject-matter insured. Abandonment has significance only where there is a constructive total loss,[72] whereas subrogation applies to all cases where loss is paid, whether total or partial. In cases of abandonment, the property in the subject-matter passes but the claims for recovery of damages against third persons do not pass—as they do in the case of subrogation. In the case of subrogation, payment of the insurance money is a condition precedent to the passing of the assured's rights, but not so in the case

---

[69] See *Re R. Miller, Gibb & Co Ltd* [1957] 1 W.L.R. 703 (subrogation to ECGD of right to the price, after having paid the seller); *H. Cousins Ltd v. D & C Carriers Ltd* [1971] 2 Q.B. 230 (subrogation of interest after insurer had paid assured); *Pierce v. Bemis; The Lusitania* [1986] Q.B. 384 (insurers subrogated to hull and equipment of wrecked ship after having paid owners in respect of total loss). The insurer cannot, however, bring a second action in pursuance of a right of subrogation, where the insured has recovered in respect of the uninsured loss: *Hayler v. Chapman* [1989] 1 Lloyd's Rep. 490.

[70] Consequently, if the assured no longer exists, the insurer cannot sue the third party directly: *M. H. Smith (Plant Hire) v. D. L. Mainwaring* [1986] 2 Lloyd's Rep. 244. It would seem, however, that a timely assignment by the insured would avoid this problem, see below.

[71] But if, owing to depreciation of currency, the assured recovers more from the person liable for the loss than the insurer paid, the assured is entitled to retain the excess.

[72] See *ante*, para. 19–033.

of abandonment. This means that even in case of a constructive total loss, the insurer cannot pursue the assured's claims against third persons, for example negligent carriers, before he has paid the insurance money to the assured. If, however, the insurer has taken an assignment of the insured's rights, he can sue even before he has paid the insurance money.

Air Cargo Insurance

There are two principal methods for the insurance of cargo sent by air: **19–036**

(a) in the marine market via brokers, or

(b) mainly in the aviation market via the air waybill.

Of these two methods the first is the more usual, because those who are in the air cargo business can arrange annual policies to suit their own specific requirements.

Marine Clauses

Air cargo insurance taken out in the marine market is obtained under special **19–037** Institute Air Cargo Clauses. They are:

(a) Institute Cargo Clauses (Air) (Cl. 259),

(b) Institute War Clauses (Air Cargo) (Cl. 258), and

(c) Institute Strikes Clauses (Air Cargo) (Cl. 260).

The Institute Air Cargo Clauses are for use with Lloyd's Marine Policy form. They are modelled on the marine Institute Cargo Clauses, subject to suitable alterations.

The Institute Cargo Clauses (Air) are the standard form. The risks covered by this form are:

> "1. This insurance covers all risks of loss of or damage to the subject-matter insured except as provided in Clauses 2, 3 and 4 below."

This standard policy is thus an all risks policy but Clauses 2, 3 and 4 contain 14 exceptions, including exceptions for war and strikes.

The Institute War Clauses (Air Cargo) cover the following risks, subject to nine stated exceptions:

> "This insurance covers, except as provided in Clause 2 below, loss of or damage to the subject-matter insured caused by
>
> 1.1 war civil war revolution rebellion insurrection, or civil strife arising therefrom, or any hostile act by or against a belligerent power
> 1.2 capture seizure arrest restraint or detainment, arising from risks covered under 1.1 above, and the consequences thereof or any attempt thereat
> 1.3 derelict mines torpedoes bombs or other derelict weapons of war."

This policy thus covers the war risks excluded from the standard form. It neither includes nor excludes the risk of strikes or similar events. It is thought that these risks are not covered by this policy as they are not listed in the risks covered; Clause 2 contains the exceptions.

The Institute Strikes Clauses (Air Cargo) cover the following risks, subject to 11 stated exceptions:

> "This insurance covers, except as provided in Clause 2 below, loss of or damage to the subject-matter insured caused by
>
> > 1.1 strikers, locked-out workmen, or persons taking part in labour disturbances, riots or civil commotions
> > 1.2 any terrorist or any person acting from a political motive."

These Clauses thus also give cover against terrorist or political attacks. Again the exceptions are contained in Clause 2.

A comprehensive cover is provided only by a combination of all three Air Cargo Clauses and this cover is rated accordingly. Professional cargo shippers will have annual policies on which individual and bulk shipments may be made on a basis of regular declarations.

The Cargo Clauses (Air) and the War Clauses (Air Cargo) exclude dispatch by post but the Institute Strikes Clauses (Air Cargo) are silent on this point. As these Clauses are normally used in combination with the standard form, the exclusion of postal dispatch on this form would also make the Strikes Clauses inapplicable for posting.

Air waybill cover

19–038 In practice there is no uniformity of cover offered via the air carrier's air waybill; indeed, not all airlines offer this. Those that do will include a rubric on the face of the air waybill, whereby the shipper can choose to declare a value for the purpose of being insured via the air carrier's own policies which accept declarations from individual shippers. The terms of such policies are available on application to the carrier's principal offices and usually they will be based on the Institute Clauses noted above. Applying for insurance via the air waybill is obviously convenient for the non-professional or occasional shipper of cargo by air but it is seldom the choice of the professional cargo handler, who will have his own annual policy in the marine market.

For this reason, insurance via the air waybill is not a large-volume business and does not seem to be a prominent part of air cargo marketing, even though it has minor fringe benefits for the air carrier, such as generating a small commission and eliminating subrogation claims against the airline.

The air waybill in fact offers a cargo shipper three opportunities to declare a value:

(a) for carriage,

(b) for Customs,

(c) for insurance.

Declaring a value for carriage is unnecessary for cargo with a low value per kilogramme. If the value exceeds $20 kg or £13.80 kg then the shipment is eligible for a value declaration, for which a supplementary charge will be made. However, in certain jurisdictions the value of the limitation will fluctuate according to the free market price of gold. Professional cargo shippers do not consider declarations of value as cost-effective because this is not a normal form of insurance. Declaring an excess value for carriage merely has the effect of raising the carrier's limit of liability to the declared value. It is still necessary to prove the amount of loss *and* that the airline is legally liable. Where no value is declared, it is common to leave the rubric for declaring the value blank or to insert "NVD" (no value declared). The best practice for occasional or professional cargo shippers is to rely on individual insurance arrangements, as outlined above.

CHAPTER 20

EXPORT CREDIT GUARANTEES

20–001 A supplier of goods or services abroad may require insurance facilities covering risks which are peculiar to export transactions but which are not normally covered by commercial insurers. Apart from the risk of non-payment through various types of political risk, there may also be situations of commercial risk, such as a buyer's insolvency or protracted default. In order to safeguard himself against loss from such events, the exporter may look to the security afforded by an export credit guarantee.[1]

This type of cover has until recently been available primarily from the Export Credits Guarantee Department (the "ECGD"), which is a separate Government Department reporting to the Secretary of State for Trade and Industry. The Department was established in 1919 with a view to promoting British exports by insuring them against certain kinds of risk. Following the privatisation of its Insurance Services Group in 1991, the ECGD has concentrated its attention principally upon providing credit insurance and financing for capital goods and project exports which involve medium and long term credit arrangements. Insurance for export contracts for the sale of consumer goods or commodities on short payment terms[2] is now obtainable from private insurers, such as the Dutch group Nederlandsche Credietverzekering Maatschaappij (NCM).

The legislative basis for the export credit guarantees[3] offered by the ECGD is currently the Export and Investment Guarantees Act 1991,[4] Part 1 of which defines the ECGD's powers. Section 1 confers upon the Secretary of State[5] the power to make "arrangements for providing financial facilities or assistance for, or for the benefit of, persons carrying on business; and the facilities or assistance may be provided in any form, including guarantees, insurance, grants or loans".[6] Such arrangements may be made "with a view to facilitating, directly or indirectly, supplies by persons carrying on business in the United Kingdom of goods or services to persons carrying on business outside the United Kingdom".[7] The

---

[1] For a detailed discussion of export credit guarantees see Benjamin (1997), Chap. 24. See also *How ECGD can help Exporters: A Short Guide to ECGD Facilities*, available from the Export Credits Guarantee Department. Individual booklets on ECGD facilities are available from their offices at 2 Exchange Tower, Harbour Exchange Square, London E14 96S, Tel: 020 7512 7000; Fax: 020 7512 7649 and see *http://www.ecgd.gov.uk*.

[2] Up to two years: see *post*, para. 20–012.

[3] "Guarantee" includes an indemnity—see s.4(3) of the Export and Investment Guarantees Act 1991.

[4] Which took effect on October 23, 1991, repealing the Export Guarantees and Overseas Investment Act 1978.

[5] Whose functions are to be exercised and performed through the Export Credits Guarantee Department.

[6] s.1(4).

[7] s.1(1).

Secretary of State may also make arrangements for the purpose of rendering economic assistance to countries outside the United Kingdom.[8]

Section 2 of the Act sets out the Secretary of State's powers in relation to the granting of insurance for overseas investment. Such insurance may be granted to "any person carrying on business in the United Kingdom" to provide protection against risks of certain specified losses,[9] which may arise "in connection with any investment of resources by the insured in enterprises carried on outside the United Kingdom",[10] or "in connection with guarantees given by the insured in respect of any investment of resources by others in such enterprises, being enterprises in which the insured has any interest".[11]

By section 3 the Secretary of State is authorised to make arrangements which, in his opinion, are in the interests of the proper financial management of the ECGD portfolio, including a power to lend and to provide and take out insurance and guarantees.[12]

The ECGD's commitment limits are set out in section 6. Arrangements made under sections 1 and 2 of the Act may not exceed, in the case of commitments in sterling, £35,000 million,[13] and in respect of foreign currency transactions, 20,000 million[14] in special drawing rights.[15] Commitments under section 3 may not exceed £15,000 million where those commitments are expressed in sterling, nor 10,000 million in special drawing rights.[16] The Secretary of State has the power[17] to increase these limits by specified amounts (with the consent of the Treasury).

In circumstances in which the ECGD agreed to provide advice in relation to the extent of its cover and to the necessity of obtaining further insurance when a transaction had already been insured in another country, it has been held that a duty of care was owed to the enquirer. In one case[18] German main contractors contracted with the Saudi Arabian Government to build two stadiums in Jeddah and Daman. The German main contractors then contracted with a U.K. company that the latter should supply certain metal work for the stadiums. The U.K. sub-contractors who wanted to cover the credit risk were advised by an officer of the ECGD that, if the credit cover which the German main contractors obtained from Hermes Versicherung AG, the German counterpart to the ECGD, included the U.K. sub-contractors, there was no need to take out additional cover with the ECGD. The main contractors confirmed that their insurance included the sub-contractors, but the Hermes cover did not extend to a claim by the sub-contractors against the main contractors, and the latter failed to pay the

---

[8] s.1(2).
[9] Which are losses resulting directly or indirectly from war, expropriation, restrictions on remittances and other similar events—s.2(1).
[10] s.2(1)(a).
[11] s.2(1)(b).
[12] s.3(1) and s.3(2)(a) and (b).
[13] Under section 6(1)(a).
[14] Increased from 15,000 million by the Export and Investment Guarantees (Limit on Foreign Currency Commitments) Order 1995 (S.I. 1995 No. 1988).
[15] The unit of account of the International Monetary Fund.
[16] s.6(3).
[17] Under s.6(4).
[18] *Culford Metal Industries Ltd v. Export Credit Department, The Times*, March 25, 1981.

sub-contractors for the metal work supplied by him. The U.K. sub-contractors sued the ECGD for negligent advice. Neill J. held that there were two risks involved, *viz.* the Saudi risk, which was covered by Hermes, and the German risk, for which the sub-contractors were not covered and which should have been covered by an appropriate ECGD guarantee. The learned judge held that the ECGD had failed in their duty of care on the basis of the principles laid down in *Hedley Byrne v. Heller and Partners*[19] and was therefore liable in negligence.

THE EXPORT CREDITS GUARANTEE DEPARTMENT

20–002 The administration of the scheme of export credits guarantees is in the hands of the Exports Credits Guarantee Department. The insurance facilities offered by the ECGD are extensive and enable the exporter to eliminate export risks which are not covered by the usual marine and war risks policies. The premium rates charged by the ECGD vary in accordance with the risks involved and the country to which the export is intended. As the ECGD does not aim at making a commercial profit, actual premium rates are moderate. An exporter will find it easier to obtain advances from his bank for exports insured with the ECGD than if the transactions are not so covered, and the bank may provide finance at a lower interest rate than otherwise. An exporter may approach the ECGD either directly or through insurance brokers. By completing the appropriate proposal form, the exporter can obtain a quotation for the premium rates applicable to his class of business, free of charge and without an obligation to conclude an insurance.

FACILITIES OFFERED BY THE EXPORT CREDITS GUARANTEE DEPARTMENT

20–003 Most of the facilities currently offered by the ECGD are designed for the provision of medium and longer term credit insurance for major projects and for the export of high value capital goods and services.

The types of facility available include:

(a) guarantees of payment to banks which provide export finance;

(b) support for export finance at fixed, often favourable, interest rates;

(c) export insurance: insurance for non-payment on sale contracts for medium and longer term credit arrangements.

The ECGD also makes available insurance against the risk of unfair calling of bonds which the supplier may be required to provide.[20]

Some specific services provided by the ECGD are set out below.

---

[19] [1964] A.C. 465.
[20] See para. 20–009.

Supplier's credit finance facility

In this type of policy the insurer indemnifies the seller against loss from the **20–004**
buyer's inability to pay the price, either through insolvency or through political
risk. Under this facility, the supplier sells the buyer's bills of exchange or promissory notes to the bank once they gave been accepted, and the ECGD provides
a full guarantee to the bank in respect of any payment default which may subsequently arise. This type of cover is provided by means of a Master Guarantee
Agreement, which the ECGD issues to banks taking part in the scheme.

The ECGD ordinarily requires the bills and promissory notes provided by the
buyer to be freely negotiable and to be guaranteed by an acceptable third party.
In most instances the facilities are provided on a "without recourse" basis. The
exporter is thus able to receive the value of the buyer's negotiable instruments
upon endorsing them to his bank and the risk passes to the bank when it pays
the bills or notes. The minimum contract value under the scheme is presently
£25,000 and credit is offered for up to 85 per cent of the contract price, with
credit periods of a minimum of two years.

The Export Insurance Policy[21] is available to exporters in conjunction with
the Supplier Credit Facility and can provide cover for the period in between the
signature of the contract and the financing bank's purchase of bills or promissory
notes.

Where contractual and financial arrangements are complex, Buyer Credit
arrangements are more appropriate.

Buyer credits

Buyer Credits, which the ECGD makes available to banks making loans in **20–005**
respect of contracts of £1 million or more, may be used to finance major projects
or for exports of high value capital goods and services. Under this facility, the
exporter is able to offer credit of two or more years to an overseas buyer, whilst
the exporter himself is paid cash. Application must be made before the contract
is signed.

The overseas purchaser is normally required to pay direct to the supplier not
less than 15 per cent of the contract price out of his own resources prior to the
start of the credit period. The remainder is paid to the supplier direct from the
loan made to the buyer or a bank in his country by a U.K. bank[22] and guaranteed
by the ECGD as to 100 per cent of capital and interest against non-payment for
any reason. The repayment period must be at least two years and the ECGD's
premium is normally payable by the exporter.

The contractual relationships involved in a Buyer Credit are:

(a) a Supply Contract between the British supplier and the overseas buyer;

(b) a Loan Agreement between the British lender and the overseas buyer;

---

[21] Recently introduced, this replaces the previous Supplier Insurance Policy and Specific Guarantee
facilities.
[22] Which must be authorised under the terms of the Banking Act 1987 and approved by the ECGD.

(c) a Support Agreement containing the guarantee of repayment and given by the ECGD to the British lender;

(d) a Premium Agreement between the British supplier and the ECGD.[23]

This type of facility is designed to operate usually on a "disbursement" basis, which means that payment is triggered by the presentation of a Qualifying Certificate, evidencing the occurrence of certain events under the contract, such as shipment or delivery of goods or services. An alternative to this is the reimbursement basis in which, after making the initial down payment, the buyer pays all other sums direct to the exporter and draws down on the loan himself.

The new Supplemental Export Insurance Policy (EXIP), which affords protection prior to shipment or completion of a service, or in respect of direct payment risks, is available for use in conjunction with Buyer Credits.

Cover for lines of credit

20–006 Many governments or government agencies contemplating, for example, an electrification scheme, farm mechanisation or development of one or more industries prefer to arrange the credit facilities without at the same time committing themselves to any one supplier. To meet this need, and to promote openings for British goods generally, the ECGD will in many cases guarantee a *line of credit* offered by a British bank to the government or agency, and in some cases private sector institutions. If the borrower fails to repay any part of the finance, the ECGD guarantees that the U.K. bank will be paid in full.

General Purpose Lines of Credit, in which a bank may enable any importer to utilise the facility, take the form of a loan between a U.K. lender[24] and an overseas bank. The loan is used to finance a number of unrelated contracts between U.K. exporters and their buyers in the overseas market, and the U.K. lender then receives support from the ECGD by way of either a Supplier Credit Finance Facility or a Buyer Credit Guarantee.

In order that such agreements should not lead to any lengthening of credit terms, they are usually limited to sales of capital and project goods or services where the lengths of credit for individual contracts are between two and five years and are determined by the value of individual contracts (which may be as low as £25,000) and the type of goods being covered. The amount to be paid on or before shipment and the extent to which local costs in the buyer's country may be financed are also specified.

In addition, the ECGD provides Project Lines of Credit (PLOCs), which are available when purchases from a number of U.K. exporters are required for specified projects or programmes. In this instance, an agreed amount of finance

---

[23] Which will contain a right of recourse exercisable against the seller by the ECGD; see *Supplier Credit Finance Facility: A Brief Guide*, available from ECGD; see also *Export Credits Guarantee Department v. Universal Oil Products Co* [1983] 2 Lloyd's Rep. 152, where it was held that the provision in the recourse agreement obliging the exporter to pay back to the Department the amounts which it has paid to the financing bank under the bank guarantee is not in the nature of a penalty clause: consequently, such provision is enforceable as against the exporter.

[24] Who should hold a Master Guarantee Agreement with the ECGD.

is made available with reference to the specific project involved and the buyer/ borrower nominates individual contracts to be financed under the facility.

Project financing scheme

The ECGD provides a Project Financing Scheme in support of lenders prepared **20–007** to finance major new projects or large project expansions abroad. Project finance is the term used to describe lending in respect of major projects, when the lenders place primary reliance on the revenues of the new project for repayment, as well as using the assets and contracts of the project as security.

The scheme is made available for capital projects with a minimum ECGD supported loan of £20 million, although, exceptionally, lower value loans may be considered. The arrangement is based on the Buyer Credit system and offers lenders two options:

1) All Risks cover; and

2) Political Risk cover.

Applicants for project financing cover or project sponsors are expected to bear any internal expenses incurred by the ECGD, including the cost of any independent/specialist advice commissioned by the ECGD and external legal advice.

Export insurance policy

The Export Insurance Policy (EXIP) is offered directly to an exporter on the **20–008** basis of a completed proposal form and provides insurance against loss arising from non-payment by the buyer and certain specified political risks.

EXIP cover may be given either in conjunction with a Buyer Credit or Supplier Credit finance package (providing cover both for elements that are not being financed with ECGD support, and for the financed elements in the shipment or manufacturing period before the finance can be accessed). It may also be given on a "free-standing" basis, for a cash or credit contact where there is no ECGD support for finance.

The policy can be tailored to a particular contract, but it contains standard defined commercial and political risks. The usual insured percentage is 95 per cent, but lower percentages are available on request. The ECGD can also agree to reduced exposure cover, where the exporter's exposure to loss is significantly lower than the total value of his contract.

Versions of the EXIP are available to cater for sub-contracts and joint venture arrangements, whilst an optional plant confiscation clause can insure equipment used to perform a contract overseas.

Bond risk insurance

It is increasingly common for buyers to require the provision of bonds or guaran- **20–009** tees ensuring that sellers perform their contractual obligations. Since these instruments are usually unconditional and on demand, they represent a risk for exporters, who may be vulnerable to unfair calls or to calls made as a result of political events such as government actions.[25] In order to provide some protection in these circumstances, the ECGD makes a bond insurance policy (BIP) available as a supplement to their basic cover for an underlying contract.

Insurance for overseas investments

20–010 All companies carrying on business in the United Kingdom and their overseas subsidiaries are, in principle, eligible for cover under the ECGD's Overseas Investment Insurance scheme,[26] but U.K.-based subsidiaries or branches of foreign companies are excluded if they are merely acting as a conduit for an investment by their overseas parent. Cover is provided for contributions of resources to an enterprise; this includes equity capital in the form of cash, plant, machinery or know-how, as well as loans and loan guarantees advanced to overseas enterprises, which must be under a formal agreement and not tied to an export from the United Kingdom.

To qualify for cover, the investment must be new, *i.e.* investment which finances a new enterprise or is an injection of additional capital into an existing overseas enterprise. The investor must apply for cover before becoming irrevocably committed. Existing investment does not normally qualify, though it may be considered in circumstances where a direct investor is simultaneously injecting new resources (though not retained earnings) into the enterprise in the form of equity. The investor must intend to keep the capital in the overseas enterprise for at least three years.

The U.K. investor is offered insurance against losses arising from:

(a) expropriation, which includes nationalisation, confiscation of the investment or of the property of the overseas enterprise, and also against losses from indirect forms of expropriation ("creeping expropriation") caused by the host government with the intent of discriminating against the investor or the overseas enterprise;

(b) war—in which the host government is a participant, or losses arising from revolution or insurrection in the host country, as well as inability to operate due to war;

(c) restrictions on remittances: the standard commitment of the ECGD is normally for 15 years for 90 per cent of any loss arising in respect of the risks covered. An overall Maximum Insured Amount will be determined at the outset, within which the investor proposes a Current Insured Amount at the beginning of each 12 months of the contract of insurance. Cover is based on the initial investment earnings retained in the enterprise, and profits in the course of transfer to the United King-

---

[25] *e.g.* cancellation or non-renewal of export licences, war, hostilities, and civil disturbances where these actions prevent performance of the contract.

[26] See *Overseas Investment Insurance*, available from the ECGD.

dom. For loan investments cover is normally based on the total principal outstanding, plus accrued interest.

One Stop Shopping with the ECGD

The ECGD has a range of One Stop Shop arrangements with other export credit **20–011** agencies. These arrangements provide flexibility to source contracts from a number of countries and allow exporters and banks to deal with just one agency when sourcing from two or more countries.

There are two types of arrangement:

(a) Co-operation arrangements
These provide for either agency to consider supporting a contract with a percentage of goods/services from the other agency's country.

(b) Reinsurance arrangements
These arrangements cover export credit support and (where possible) interest rate support. The lead agency (normally the agency whose exporter is the main contractor) will provide support for the whole of the bid on its usual terms and will receive reinsurance from the export credit agency whose exporter is the sub-contractor.

Where the ECGD is the lead agency they are able to draw upon a full range of One Stop Shop arrangements to accommodate multi-country sourcing.

Comprehensive short term guarantees

Short term credits are normally covered by a standard type of policy known as **20–012** a comprehensive short term guarantee. In 1991, the Insurance Services Group of the ECGD, then the primary provider of this type of short term cover, was sold to the Dutch private credit insurer Nederlandsche Credietverzekering Maatschaappij NCM. NCM established a subsidiary, NCM Credit Insurance Ltd,[27] who are now the United Kingdom's major provider of cover for short term transactions. This category of cover is also available from other private insurers.[28]

NCM's "International" policy provides an example of this type of credit insurance. The policy provides cover for sales by U.K.-domiciled companies to buyers on credit terms of up to 180 days[29] and operates on a whole turnover basis, *i.e.* it covers all of the policy holder's eligible business with buyers in the countries for which NCM offers cover.[30] This effectively prevents the policy holder from electing to insure only potentially problematic contracts. A Credit

---

[27] 3 Harbour Drive, Capital Waterside, Cardiff CF1 6TZ, Tel: 0800 212131; Website: *http://www.ncmgroup.com.*
[28] *e.g.* Euler Trade Indemnity, Coface LBF.
[29] Which can be extended to up to two years by payment of a further premium.
[30] Currently over 250 countries.

Limit is established in respect of each overseas buyer and the exporter agrees[31] to declare all amounts due in respect of contracts to which the policy applies.

The premium is charged in relation to each such contract and is calculcated for each £100 required to be declared. An annual administrative charge is also payable. It is required that the contracts covered by the policy should set out in detail the nature and quantity of goods to be sold or services to be performed, with payment terms which are not to exceed the previously agreed maximum credit terms.[32]

Cover is continuous, remaining in force until either the insurer or the exporter decides to terminate it, which either may do annually. This type of policy protects the exporter from the time the goods are shipped[33] to the time of receipt of payment, though it can optionally include the "pre-credit" risk. Such policies are suitable for exporters who can readily dispose of the goods sold in the home or other overseas markets, in the event of the original overseas buyer becoming insolvent or the performance of the export contract becoming impossible.

This type of cover typically affords protection against the following categories of loss:

(a) the insolvency of the buyer;

(b) the buyer's failure to pay the amount due under the contract within six months of the date originally due;

(c) a moratorium decreed by the government of the buyer's country or by that of a third country through which payment must be effected;

(d) other measures or decisions of the government of a foreign country which in whole or in part prevents performance of the contract;

(e) political events, economic difficulties, or legislative or administrative measures which prevent or delay the transfer of payments or deposits made in respect of the contract;

(f) the operation of law in the buyer's country which has the effect of giving him a valid discharge of the debt under that law (though not under the proper law of the contract) notwithstanding that, owing to exchange rate fluctuations, such payments when converted into the currency of the contract, are less than the amount of the debt at the date of transfer;

(g) the occurrence outside the United Kingdom of war (including civil war, hostilities, rebellion and insurrection) revolution or riot, cyclone, flood earthquake, volcanic eruption or tidal wave which in whole or in part prevents performance of the contract;

(h) failure or refusal by a public buyer to fulfil the terms of the contract.

---

[31] See NCM International Policy, Art. 2A.
[32] See NCM International Policy, Art. 2A.
[33] See, *e.g.* NCM International Policy, Art. 2B.

The policy can cover up to 90 per cent of the value of goods and services for commercial loss and 95 per cent in the event of political causes of loss (with the customer bearing the risk of the uninsured percentage).

It should be noted that this type of cover does not protect the insured against:

(a) loss sustained in the event of failure by the insured, or by any person acting on his behalf, to fulfill the terms and conditions of the contract or to comply with the provisions of any law so as to affect the performance of the contract;

(b) loss caused by the ionising, radioactive, toxic, explosive or other hazardous or contaminating properties or effects of any explosive nuclear assembly or component thereto, nuclear fuel, combustion or waste;

(c) loss caused by failure to obtain import or export licences or other authorisations essential to the performance of the contract, or where performance of the contract would be in contravention of exchange control regulations;

(d) loss arising in connection with the third country where goods are to be despatched or payment is to be made from a country other than the buyer's country;

(e) loss caused by war between China, France, the United Kingdom, the Russian Federation and the United States.

NCM's Global Policy provides cover to U.K.—and non-U.K.—domiciled multi- **20–013** nationals. The cover afforded and the operation of the policy is broadly as for the International Policy, but policyholders can elect to specify both the currency and the language of the policy.

NCM's Compact Policy provides cover to businesses which are U.K.-domiciled with an insured turnover of up to £5 million. Cover is broadly comparable to that provided by the International Policy. The premium is assessed on the policy holder's anticipated annual shipments and is expressed as a monetary figure. This becomes the fixed price for one year's cover with no retrospective reconciliation at the end of the year. Policyholders are not required to make monthly declarations of their shipments and may elect to pay annually in advance, or by quarterly or monthly instalments.

PART FIVE

INTERNATIONAL COMMERCIAL DISPUTE RESOLUTION

CHAPTER 21

ENGLISH LAW AND FOREIGN LAW[1]

The exportation of goods involves parties in different jurisdictions. The resolu- **21–001** tion of any dispute between them falls within the province of English law known as private international law or the conflict of laws. This branch of law applies to international transactions and determines in an individual case the law applicable to the dispute and the jurisdiction of the courts which have to adjudicate upon the issue. These two questions do not coincide.[2] It is possible that, according to the rules of the conflict of laws, the dispute has to be heard by the English courts but that they would have to apply a foreign system of law. In the eyes of the English lawyer and the English courts, every system of law applied in another country is considered to be foreign law, and no distinction is drawn in this respect between the laws prevailing in countries which have founded their law on the common law, the Member States of the E.C., and other countries.

It is of great importance for the parties to know whether their contract is governed by English law or by a foreign system of law. In fact, from the legal point of view, this is one of the central problems[3] arising in an export transaction. It has been pointed out before that the rules of English and foreign law are often at variance; for example, the expression f.o.b. has a different meaning in English and American law.[4] The Sale of Goods Act 1979, as amended by the Sale and Supply of Goods Act 1994 and the Sale of Goods (Amendment) Act 1995, applies when an international contract is governed by English law but does not apply when it is governed by foreign law[5]; a contract may be regarded as frustrated by English law but as valid by foreign law; the provisions of the Law Reform (Frustrated Contracts) Act 1943 apply only to contracts governed by English law,[6] and so on. It is therefore desirable to have a choice of law clause in any contract with a foreign element as, in the event of dispute, uncertainty as to which law governs a contract can lead to expensive interlocutory proceedings.

In addition to addressing the law applicable to the contract, this Chapter deals with the extraterritorial effect of the legislative or administrative measures of foreign states. Also dealt with are the provisions under English law which protect our international trading interests. There are sections on foreign limitation periods, currency of account and payment, letters of request and foreign state

---

[1] Dicey and Morris, *Conflict of Laws* (13th ed., 2000) and *Halsbury's Laws*, Vol. 8(1).
[2] But they are not unrelated, *e.g.* a choice of English law may confer jurisdiction on the English court (RSC Ord. 11, r. 1(1)(d)(iii) (see now CPR, Pt. 6.20(5)(c))) and a choice of forum may infer a choice of law (Art. 3(1) of the Rome Convention).
[3] Another is the courts of the country which have jurisdiction.
[4] See *ante*, para. 2–006.
[5] See Chaps 4 and 5.
[6] See *ante*, para. 6–016.

immunity. This Chapter further deals with instances where an English court will refuse to enforce a contract which is contrary to the law of a foreign friendly state, or where its performance is illegal by the law of the place where it is to be performed. The different matter of the criminal consequences where an English exporter commits an offence under the law of a foreign country is also dealt with. Finally, there is a section on exchange control.

Proof of foreign law

21–002 Where it is clear that the contract is governed by a foreign system of law, this does not mean that the judge or arbitrator has to ascertain the rules of that legal system *ex officio*. In English law, it has long been established that foreign law is a question of fact, although it is "a question of fact of a peculiar kind."[7] A party seeking to establish that a contract is governed by a foreign law must plead and prove the foreign law in the same way as any other fact. The Rome Convention[8] does not apply to evidence and procedure[9] and thus the Convention does not alter the rule of English law that foreign law must be pleaded and proved. If foreign law is not pleaded then the dispute will be decided according to English law, and if foreign law is not proved to the satisfaction of the judge or arbitrator, English law will apply.[10]

In *Macmillan Inc v. Bishopsgate Investment Trust Plc (No. 4)*, it was held that where the concepts of the foreign law were not dissimilar to English law, the judge should apply his knowledge of common and statute law and was entitled to take a different view from an expert witness. The Court of Appeal was entitled, as was the judge, to take its own independent view on the question of construction, taking into account the relevant circumstances found by the judge.

Foreign law is proved by expert witnesses. An expert witness is "a person who is suitably qualified . . . on account of his knowledge or experience is competent"[11] to give evidence. However, where any question of foreign law has been determined by a specified higher court in England or by the Privy Council, any finding or decision on that question is admissible in evidence in subsequent proceedings. The foreign law shall be taken to be in accordance with that finding unless the contrary is proved, provided that the finding or decision is reported or recorded in citable form, that is, in a form in which it can be cited as an authority in an English court.[12] An English court takes judicial notice of European Community Law[13] and the House of Lords, in an English or Northern Irish appeal, takes judicial notice of Scots law and vice versa. As proving foreign law

---

[7] *Parkasho v. Singh* [1968] P. 233 at 250; *Dalmia Dairy Industries Ltd v. National Bank of Pakistan* [1978] 2 Lloyd's Rep. 223 at 286; *Bumper Development Corp v. Commissioner of Police of the Metropolis* [1991] 1 W.L.R. 1362 at 1370; *Macmillan Inc v. Bishopsgate Investment Trust Plc (No. 4)* [1999] C.L.C. 417.

[8] See *post*, paras 21–004 to 21–016.

[9] Art. 1(2)(h).

[10] *Bumper Development Corp v. Commissioner of Police of the Metropolis* [1991] 1 W.L.R. 1362. *Macmillan Inc v. Bishopsgate Investment Trust Plc (No. 4)* [1999] C.L.C. 417.

[11] Civil Evidence Act 1972, s.4(2).

[12] Civil Evidence Act 1972, s.4(2).

[13] European Communities Act 1972, s.3.

is likely to be costly and time-consuming, a party in English proceedings will plead foreign law only if this is to his advantage. Otherwise it is cheaper for him to have the issue determined in accordance with English law. For example in the *Romalpa* case,[14] it was probable that the contract was governed by Dutch law, but as neither party pleaded Dutch law, the case was decided according to English law. In many continental countries, judges and arbitrators have to ascertain the foreign law which in their view applies *ex officio*.

MEASURES OF CONFLICT AVOIDANCE

The need to avoid, or at least to reduce, the dangers of a conflict of laws in **21–003** international commercial transactions is obvious. Various international conventions have been adopted with this end in mind. The most important of these which affect international sales law are the two Hague Uniform Laws on International Sales appended to the Uniform Laws on International Sales Act 1967, the Vienna Convention on Contracts of International Sale and the Hague Convention on the Law applicable to International Sales of Goods.[15] The latter two Conventions have not yet been ratified by the United Kingdom.

The E.C. Convention on Jurisdiction and the Enforcement of Judgments in Civil and Commercial Matters, known as the Brussels Convention, is given legislative force in the United Kingdom by the Civil Jurisdiction and Judgments Act 1982. The Convention deals with procedural matters. It defines the international jurisdiction of the courts of the Member States by excluding—not wholly successfully—concurrent jurisdictions which invite "forum shopping", *i.e.* the choice by the litigant of the most favourable of several competent courts. The Convention also introduces an expeditious procedure for the recognition and enforcement of judgments of certain courts of the Member States throughout the E.C. Jurisdictional aspects of the Convention will be dealt with in Chapter 22 and the recognition and enforcement of judgments aspects in Chapter 24.

THE LAW GOVERNING THE CONTRACT—THE ROME CONVENTION

Since the last edition of this book the Contracts (Applicable Law) Act 1990 has **21–004** come into force[16] (except for sections 3(1), (2) and (3)(b)).[17] The Act implements the Convention on the Law Applicable to Contractual Obligations, known as the Rome Convention, which is appended to the Act as Schedule 1. Also appended to the Act are the Luxembourg[18] and Funchal[19] Conventions made on the accession of Greece, and Spain and Portugal respectively to the Rome Convention. The Brussels Protocol is appended as Schedule 3 but is not yet in force. The Rome Convention now applies to all contracts made after April 1, 1991 save for those specifically excluded by the Convention.[20]

---

[14] *Aluminium Industrie Vaassen BV v. Romalpa Aluminium Ltd* [1976] 1 W.L.R. 676.
[15] The Hague Uniform Laws and the Vienna Convention are considered in Chap. 32.
[16] April 1, 1991 (S.I. 1991 No. 707).
[17] These sub-sections concern the Brussels Protocol.
[18] Sched. 2.
[19] Sched. 3A.
[20] Art. 1(2), (3).

The common law rules for determining choice of law will not be dealt with, so for situations where they still apply, *i.e.* contracts made on or before April 1, 1991 and those excluded by the Convention, reference should be made to the earlier edition of this book.[21]

Broadly speaking, the Convention provides[22] for freedom of choice of law expressly or impliedly by the parties, but where there is no such choice the governing law will be that of the country most closely connected with the contract.[23] There are different provisions for certain consumer contracts[24] and individual employment contracts.[25]

Interpretation

21–005 To provide for uniform interpretation and application of the Convention by the courts of Member States, they shall have regard to its "international character".[26] As with all Community legislation the Rome Convention is to be interpreted purposively.[27] Reference may be made to the Giuliano and Lagarde Report on the Convention[28] as an aid to its interpretation. The Report[29] observes that Article 18 might enable parties to rely on decisions of courts of other Contracting States regarding interpretation. The Act provides that the Convention shall be interpreted in accordance with any relevant decision or principle laid down by the European Court.[30] It requires that judicial notice be taken of any decision or opinion of the European Court,[31] but those provisions which concern the Brussels Protocol are not yet in force. The Protocol itself is not yet in force, although it has been ratified by the United Kingdom. This Protocol provides for reference to the European Court by the House of Lords and courts from which no further appeal is possible and the courts of the Contracting States when acting as appeal courts[32] although, unlike the Brussels Convention,[33] it provides only that these courts *may* so refer.

Scope of the Convention

21–006 Article 1(1) provides:

"The rules of this Convention shall apply to contractual obligations in any situation involving a choice between the laws of different countries."

---

[21] See also Dicey and Morris, *Conflict of Laws* (11th ed., 1987); *Halsbury's Laws*, Vol. 8(1).
[22] Art. 3(1).
[23] Art. 4(1).
[24] Art. 5.
[25] Art. 6.
[26] Art. 18.
[27] See, *e.g.* Case No. 29/76 *LTU GmbH & Co v. Eurocontrol* [1976] E.C.R. 1541.
[28] Contracts (Applicable Law) Act 1990, s. 3(3)(a).
[29] At p. 38.
[30] s. 3(1).
[31] s. 3(2).
[32] Sched. 3, Art. 2(a), (b). The reference would be made under Art. 177 of the Treaty of Rome.
[33] See para. 22–013.

Undoubtedly, "contractual obligations" should be given an autonomous community meaning and should not be interpreted according to national law,[34] so that "contractual obligations" would probably encompass a wider range of obligations than those normally considered as contractual under English law.

The Giuliano and Lagarde Report[35] clarifies that the law of a country, in fact, means the legal system of a country. This is further explained by Article 19(1) which provides that where a State comprises several territorial units, each having its own rules of law, each territorial unit is a separate country for the purposes of determining the applicable law. Although Article 19(2) goes on to provide that the provisions of Article 19(1) need not be applied where there is a conflict solely between two such territorial units, the United Kingdom decided that the Convention rules "shall apply in the case of conflicts between the laws of different parts of the United Kingdom"[36] so that they apply to a conflict between English and Scots law.

Article 1(2) lists matters to which the rules of the Convention do not apply. They are:

(a) the status or legal personality of natural persons;

(b) wills and succession or family matters;

(c) obligations arising under bills of exchange, cheques and promissory notes and other negotiable instruments[37] to the extent that the obligations under such other negotiable instruments arise out of their negotiable character;

(d) arbitration agreements[38] and agreements on choice of court[39];

(e) questions governed by the law of companies;

(f) the ability of an agent to bind a principal to a third party[40];

---

[34] As with "matters relating to a contract" in Art. 5(1) of the Brussels Convention: Case 9/87 *SPRL Arcado v. SA Haviland* [1988] E.C.R. 1593; Case C-26/91 *Jakob Handle GmbH v. Traitements Mecano-chimiques des Surfaces* [1992] E.C.R. I-3967.

[35] At p. 10.

[36] Contracts (Applicable Law) Act 1990, s. 2(3).

[37] It is the *document* itself which must be the negotiable instrument, whereas if it is the *obligation* which is transferable, this is not excluded. Therefore "such documents as bills of lading, similar documents issued in connection with transport contracts, and bonds, debentures, guarantees, letters of indemnity, certificates of deposit, warrants and warehouse receipts are only excluded . . . if they can be regarded as negotiable instruments; and even then the exclusion only applies with regard to obligations arising out of their negotiable character. Furthermore, neither the contracts pursuant to which such instruments are issued nor contracts for the purchase and sale of such instruments are excluded." Whether a document is negotiable is a matter for the law of the forum: Giuliano and Lagarde Report, p. 11.

[38] This exclusion relates *only* to the agreement to arbitrate itself and not to the substantive contract. For the law applicable to arbitration agreements, see para. 23–007.

[39] These were excluded, *inter alia*, since each court decides the question of validity of agreement in accordance with its own law and where relationships within the E.C. were concerned aspects such as validity and form of the clause and consent would come within Art. 17 of the Brussels Convention, Giuliano and Lagarde Report, p. 11.

[40] The exclusion applies *only* to agent binding a principal to a third party and not to other numerous agency agreements, nor to the relationship between agent and principal and agent and third party, Giuliano and Lagarde Report, p. 13.

(g) constitution of trusts;

(h) evidence and procedure except for burden of proof.[41]

Insurance contracts covering risks in Member States are excluded by Article 1(3) but the Convention does apply to re-insurance contacts.[42]

Apart from the above, the Convention rules apply to all contracts made after April 1, 1991 and, it is important to note, the application of the rules is not confined to circumstances where there is a connection with a Contracting State, for Article 2 makes it clear that the law of a non-Contracting State may be applied.

Article 20 provides that present and future Community Law shall take precedence over national law and Article 21 provides that the Convention rules "shall not prejudice the application of international conventions to which a contracting state is, or becomes, a party". Thus, for example, the Hague-Visby Rules[43] will still apply to the carriage of goods by sea. Renvoi is excluded by Article 15.

The United Kingdom has exercised the reservation allowed by Article 22 not to apply the provisions of Articles 7(1) and 10(1)(e).[44] Article 7(1) permits effect to be given to the mandatory laws of another country whatever the law applicable to the contract and Article 10(1)(e) concerns the consequences of nullity of contract. However, it should be noted that it is the *consequences* of nullity that the United Kingdom has derogated from, not the material or formal validity of the contract, which is dealt with by Articles 8 and 9.

The applicable law

21–007 Two basic principles are adopted by the Convention. The first is that the parties may expressly or impliedly choose the law governing the contract[45] and that choice will be effective, subject to certain limitations which will be dealt with later. The second is that where there is no such express choice then the contract will be governed by the law of the country with which it is most closely connected.[46] Under English law, prior to the coming into force of the Convention, where there was no express or implied choice, the proper law of the contract was the system of law with which it had its closest and most real connection.[47] Although at first blush it may seem that English "proper law" authorities may aid interpretation of seemingly similar rules, reliance on them should be avoided, although they may have some persuasive value.

Freedom of choice

21–008 "A contract shall be governed by the law chosen by the parties. The choice must be express or demonstrated with reasonable certainty by the terms of the contract or the circumstances

---

[41] Art. 14.

[42] Art. 1(4).

[43] Implemented by the Carriage of Goods by Sea Act 1971.

[44] Contracts (Applicable Law) Act 1990, s. 2(2).

[45] Art. 3(1).

[46] Art. 4(1).

[47] *Amin Rasheed Shipping Corp v. Kuwait Insurance Co* [1984] A.C. 50.

of the case. By their choice the parties can select the law applicable to the whole or a part only of the contract."[48]

Where the parties have not expressly chosen the governing law, they may nevertheless have impliedly made a choice.[49] The Giuliano and Lagarde Report list some examples of matters which may imply a choice.[50] These are where:

(a) the contract is in a standard form known to be governed by a particular system of law, for example a Lloyd's policy of marine insurance[51];

(b) there is a previous course of dealing between the parties;

(c) there is a particular choice of forum;

(d) there is a reference to a specific provision, say to an Article or Articles of the French Civil Code;

(e) there is a choice of place of arbitration[52];

(f) there has been an express choice in related transactions between the same parties.

However the Report emphasises that a choice may only be implied where other circumstances of the case do not indicate a counter-intention and states that a choice may not be inferred where the parties had "no clear intention of making a choice."[53]

Article 3(1) permits *dépeçage* whereby different parts of the contract may be governed by different laws, although the Giuliano and Lagarde Report says this applies only when the contract is severable and the choice must be logically consistent. It would be unlikely for there to be one choice for the vendor and another for the purchaser for repudiation for non-performance.[54] The parties may not take advantage of the *dépeçage* provision in order to avoid manadatory rules.[55]

Article 3(2) permits the parties maximum flexibility to change at any time the law governing the contract, so long as this does not affect its formal validity under Article 9 or adversely affect the rights of third parties.

Where the parties have chosen a foreign law and all the relevant circumstances at the time of choice are connected with a single country, then the

---

[48] Art. 3(1).
[49] See *Egon Oldendorff v. Libera Corp (No. 2)* [1996] 1 Lloyd's Rep. 380 on whether choice is express or demonstrated with reasonable certainty.
[50] At p. 17.
[51] See *Gan Insurance Co Ltd v. Tai Ping Insurance Co Ltd* [1999] 2 All E.R. 54, QBD (Comm Ct). (where the Court of Appeal held that the judge was justified in relying on this example in the Giuliano and Lagarde Report to find that there was an inferred intention that the contract was governed by English law.)
[52] *Egon Oldendorff v. Libera Corp (No. 2)* [1996] 1 Lloyd's Rep. 380; in addition the standard clauses in the charterparty were well known in English law.
[53] *ibid.*
[54] At p. 17.
[55] Art. 7: Giuliano and Lagarde Report, p. 17. Mandatory rules will be dealt with later.

contractually non-derogatory mandatory rules of that country cannot be avoided.[56]

Article 3(4) which concerns existence and validity of consent to the choice of law, will be dealt with later.

Absence of express or implied choice

21–009
"To the extent that the law applicable to the contract has not been chosen in accordance with Article 3, the contract shall be governed by the law of the country with which it is most closely connected. Nevertheless, a severable[57] part of the contract which has a closer connection with another country may by way of exception be governed by the law of that other country."[58]

Contrary to the position at common law, in determining the law of the country with which the contract is most closely connected, the court may take account of matters which occurred after the conclusion of the contract.[59]

Article 4(2) provides:

"Subject to the provisions of paragraph 5[60] of this Article, it shall be presumed that the contract is most closely connected with the country where the party who is to effect the performance which is characteristic of the contract has, at the time of conclusion of the contract, his habitual residence, or, in the case of a body corporate or unincorporate, its central administration. However, if the contract is entered into in the course of that party's trade or profession, that country shall be the country in which the principal place of business is situated or, where under the terms of the contract the performance is to be effected through a place of business other than the principal place of business, the country in which that other place of business is situated."[61]

Characteristic performance is not the payment of money, it is "the performance for which payment is due, *i.e.* the delivery of goods, the granting of the right to make use of an item of property, the provision of a service, transport, insurance, banking operations, security, etc"[62] and in a contract of guarantee "the characteristic performance is always that of the guarantor, whether in relation to the principal debtor or the creditor."[63] The characteristic performance in a confirmed letter of credit transaction is that of the confirming bank.[64] Where performance was through a bank's London branch, this was "effected through a place of business other than the principal place of business" thus English law was the governing law of the contract.[65]

There are exceptions to the Article 4(2) presumption. First, it does not apply to either a right in, or a right to use, immovable property where the presumption

---

[56] Art. 3(3).
[57] The Giuliano and Lagarde Report, p. 23 emphasises that severance under this paragraph should be rare.
[58] Art. 4(1).
[59] Giuliano and Lagarde Report, p. 20.
[60] Which concerns certain consumer contracts, on which see *post*, para. 21–015.
[61] See *Hogg Insurance Brokers Ltd v. Guardian Insurance Co Inc* [1997] 1 Lloyd's Rep. 412 (where it made no difference that the claim was essentially one for negative declaratory relief).
[62] Giuliano and Lagarde Report, p. 20.
[63] *ibid.*
[64] *Bank of Baroda v. Vysya Bank Ltd* [1994] 2 Lloyd's Rep. 87.
[65] *ibid.*

is that a contract is most closely connected with the country in which the immovable property is situated.[66] However, as the Giuliano and Lagarde Report[67] points out, Article 4(3) would not extend to contracts for repair or construction of immovable property, since the subject-matter of such would not be the immovable property, but contracts for its repair or construction. The Report[68] also points out that the presumption is rebuttable and gives as an example two Belgian residents making a contract for rental of a holiday home in Italy, where it would be likely that the contract would be more closely connected with Belgium than Italy.

Secondly, it does not apply to a contract for the carriage of goods.[69] Where the country in which the carrier has his principal place of business is also the country where the goods were loaded or discharged, or the principal place of business of the consignor at the time the contract is concluded, it is presumed that the contract is most closely connected with that country.[70] The Giuliano and Lagarde Report states that " 'consignor' refers in general to any person who consigns goods to the carrier"[71] and " 'the carrier' means the party to the contract who undertakes to carry the goods, whether or not he performs the carriage himself."[72] Article 4(4) goes on to provide that single voyage charter-parties and other contracts whose primary purpose is the carriage of goods "shall be treated as contracts for the carriage of goods". The Giuliano and Lagarde Report states: "The wording of paragraph 4 is intended to make it clear that charterparties may be considered to be contracts for the carriage of goods in so far as that is their substance."[73] Where an arbitration clause provides for arbitration in a specified place, the circumstances may indicate that the law of that country should be the applicable law.[74] It may be that where there are related contracts between the same parties in a bill of lading and a charterparty, and a choice of law has been made in one of them, a court would be impelled to conclude that a choice of law had been made for the other.[75]

Thirdly, the presumption in Article 4(2) shall not apply where the characteristic performance cannot be determined and the Article 4(2)-(4) presumptions are to be "disregarded if it appears from the circumstances as a whole that the contract is more closely connected with another country" and are thus rebuttable.[76] This provision would seem to allow for a measure of judicial discretion where it is felt that particular circumstances do not sit comfortably with the foregoing presumptions.

---

[66] Art. 4(3).
[67] At p. 21.
[68] *ibid.*
[69] Art. 4(4).
[70] *ibid.*
[71] At p. 21.
[72] At p. 22.
[73] *ibid.*
[74] Giuliano and Lagarde Report, p. 17; *Egon Oldendorff v. Libera Corp (No. 2)* [1996] 2 Lloyd's Rep. 380.
[75] Giuliano and Lagarde Report, p. 17.
[76] Art. 4(5).

Limitations on applicable law and mandatory rules

21–010 The Convention contains several limitations on the application of the applicable law, whether expressly or impliedly chosen by the parties, or whether it is the law of the country most closely connected with the contract. However, it is important to note that these limitations do not nullify the applicable law, but rather limit its application, except in the case of certain consumer contracts and individual contracts of employment where there is no choice in accordance with Article 3,[77] or on grounds of public policy.[78]

Mandatory rules, which are referred to in Articles 3(3), 5, 6, 7(2)[79] and 9(6), are those rules from which there can be no contractual derogation. Examples are the Carriage of Goods by Sea Act 1971, enacting the Hague-Visby Rules, and certain provisions of the Financial Services Act 1986.

Article 3(3) provides that where the parties have chosen a foreign governing law and all the other relevant elements of the contract are connected with one country only, their choice will not prejudice the application of the mandatory rules of that country.

Article 7(2) provides that the Convention rules shall not restrict the application of the mandatory rules of the law of the forum, whatever the applicable law of the contract.

Article 9(6)[80] concerns the formal validity of a right in immovable property or a right to use immovable property. Where the law of the country in which the property is situated is subject to mandatory requirements, then the mandatory requirements regarding formal validity will be applied.

Finally, Article 16 allows that the application of a rule of law may be refused where its application is "manifestly incompatible" with the public policy of the law of the forum.

Scope of the applicable law

21–011 Article 10 provides:

> "1. The law applicable to a contract by virtue of Articles 3 to 6 and 12[81] shall govern in particular:
>
> (a) interpretation;
> (b) performance;
> (c) within the limits of the powers conferred on the court by its procedural law, the consequences of breach, including the assessment of damages in so far as it is governed by rules of law;
> (d) the various ways of extinguishing obligations, and prescriptions and limitation of actions;
> (e) the consequences of nullity of the contract.[82]

---

[77] Arts 5(3) and 6(2) respectively. Consumer and Employment contracts will be dealt with later.
[78] Art. 16.
[79] Art. 7(1) is not in force in the U.K.: s. 2(2) of the Act. See further para. 21–027.
[80] Set out at *post*, para. 21–012.
[81] Art. 12 concerns voluntary assignment.
[82] Para. 10(1)(e) is not in force in the U.K.: s. 2(2) of the Act.

2. In relation to the manner of performance and the steps to be taken in the event of defective performance regard shall be had to the law of the country in which performance takes place."

The Giuliano and Lagarde Report[83] points out that the words "in particular" mean that the list is not exhaustive. On the matter of "performance", the Report[84] considers that this covers everything necessary for performance and goes on to list matters which come within Article 10(1):

> "the diligence with which the obligation must be performed; conditions relating to the place and time of performance; the extent to which the obligation can be performed by a person other than the party liable; the conditions as to performance of the obligation both in general and in relation to certain categories of obligation (joint and several obligations, alternative obligations, divisible and indivisible obligations, pecuniary obligations); where performance consists of the payment of a sum of money, the conditions relating to the discharge of the debtor who has made the payment, the receipt, etc."[85]

However, regarding the manner of performance, referred to in Article 10(2), the Report[86] acknowledges that this cannot be given any precise meaning and feels that what is meant by "manner of performance" is a matter for the law of the forum. It goes on to suggest that included would be rules on Government holidays, how goods should be examined and steps to be taken if they are refused. Since Article 10(2) permits the court to consider the law of the place of performance, the court may consider whether such law is relevant and may apply that law in whole or in part in order to achieve justice between the parties.[87]

Although assessment of damages is a matter for the applicable law, the Report[88] emphasises that Article 10(c) provides that this is only in so far as the assessment of damages is governed by rules of law and that matters of fact will always be a matter for the forum.

Burden of proof, formal and material validity

The legal systems of different countries may not take a uniform view on the **21–012** issue of whether a particular aspect is classified as substantive or procedural and the Convention attempts to provide for any such differences.

Evidential and procedural matters are excluded from the Convention rules but without prejudice to Article 14,[89] which deals with the burden of proof. Article 14 provides that the burden of proof is governed by the applicable law of the contract, together with any presumptions or rules concerning burden of proof, so long as these presumptions or rules are contained in the *contract* law of the applicable law. This means that where such presumptions or rules are part of the general but not the contractual law of the applicable law, their application

---

[83] At p. 32.
[84] *ibid.*
[85] *ibid.*
[86] At p. 33.
[87] Giuliano and Lagarde Report, p. 33.
[88] At p. 33.
[89] Art. 1(2)(h).

is restricted. The Giuliano and Lagarde Report[90] gives as examples of general law the failure of one party to appear, which substantiates the claim of the other, or the silence of one party in response to a claim of the other being regarded as an admission.

Article 14(2) provides that a contract or act may be proved by any mode of proof recognised by the law of the forum, as long as it can be administered by the forum or, where the formal validity of a contract or act is in question, by any of the Article 9 rules.

Article 9, paragraphs 1 to 4 and 6 provide:

> "1. A contract concluded between persons who are in the same country is formally valid if it satisfies the formal requirements of the law which governs it under this convention or of the law of the country where it is concluded.
>   2. A contract concluded between persons who are in different countries is formally valid if it satisfies the formal requirements of the law which governs it under this Convention or of the law of one of those countries.
>   3. Where a contract is concluded by an agent, the country in which the agent acts is the relevant country for the purposes of paragraphs 1 and 2.
>   4. An act intended to have legal effect relating to an existing or contemplated contract is formally valid if it satisfies the formal requirements of the law which under this Convention governs or would govern the contract or of the law of the country where the act was done.
>
> . . .
>
>   6. Notwithstanding paragraphs 1 to 4 of this Article, a contract the subject matter of which is a right in immovable property or a right to use immovable property shall be subject to the mandatory requirements of the form of the law of the country where the property is situated if by that law those requirements are imposed irrespective of the country where the contract is concluded and irrespective of the law governing the contract."

Although it is not spelt out in Article 9 the Giuliano and Lagarde Report[91] states that the intention is that the law which would be applicable were the contract formally valid is to be applied to determine its validity. The Report[92] recognises that difficulties may arise where the contract is severable: "which of the laws governing the substance of the contract is to determine its formal validity?" The Report concludes that "it would seem reasonable to apply the law applicable to the part of the contract most closely connected with the disputed condition on which its formal validity depends."

The Report[93] further recognises the difficulty in determining where the contract was concluded. By way of clarification it states that where the contract is concluded by an agent and another party or between agents, the law of the country where they meet governs the formal validity of the contract regardless of the location of the principal(s). If the agent and another party or agents are in different countries when concluding the contract, the formal validity is between persons in different countries, even if the principal(s) were in the same country at the time. The Report[94] makes it clear that where the parties to the contract

---

[90] At p. 36.
[91] *ibid.*
[92] At p. 30.
[93] *ibid.*
[94] At p. 31.

are in different countries, the law of the country where the offer was made or that where it was accepted plays no part in determining its formal validity.

Regarding material validity, Article 8(1) provides that whether a contract or a contract term exists, or is valid, is to be determined by the law which would be applicable under the Convention rules if the contract or term were valid. This avoids "the circular argument that where there is a choice ... no law can said to be applicable until the contract is found to be valid."[95] Article 9(1) also applies to the question of the parties' consent as to choice of law.[96] However, on the matter of the existence but not the validity of consent,[97] Article 8(2) provides:

> "Nevertheless, a party may rely upon the law of the country in which he has his habitual residence to establish that he did not consent if it appears from the circumstances that it would not be reasonable to determine the effect of his conduct in accordance with the law specified in [paragraph 8(1)]."

The Giuliano and Lagarde Report[98] states that this paragraph was included to provide, *inter alia*, for a party's silence in the formation of the contract. It emphasises that "conduct" applies to both action and failure to act. All the circumstances of the case must be taken into account, particularly "the practices followed by the parties *inter se* as well as their previous business relationships." The Report points out that, under Article 8(2), a party who would have been bound under Article 8(1) could be released but not the converse. It is for the party seeking to rely on Article 8(1) to establish that it applies.[99]

Capacity

Article 11 provides that where a contract is made between parties in the same country and a natural person has capacity under the law of that country, he may only use the law of another country to establish his incapacity if the other party was aware of it at the time of the contract, or failed to be aware of it as a result of negligence. **21–013**

Voluntary assignment and subrogation

The law applicable to each of these in a contractual situation is dealt with by Articles 12 and 13 respectively. **21–014**

Specific contracts

Certain consumer contracts

Article 5 concerns the supply of goods or services or credit for their supply to a consumer, a consumer being a person to whom they are supplied outside his **21–015**

---

[95] At p. 30.
[96] Giuliano and Lagarde Report, p. 28.
[97] *ibid.*
[98] *ibid.*
[99] *Egon Oldendorff v. Libera Corp (No. 1)* [1995] 2 Lloyd's Rep. 64.

trade or profession. Where the parties have chosen the law to govern the contract between them, this choice shall not deprive the consumer of his protection under any mandatory rules afforded him by the law of the country of his habitual residence[1]:

> "—if in that country the conclusion of the contract was preceded by a specific invitation addressed to him or by advertising, and he had taken in that country all the steps necessary on his part for the conclusion of the contract, or
> —if the other party or his agent received the consumer's order in that country, or
> —if the contract is for the sale of goods and the consumer travelled from that country to another country and there gave his order, provided that the consumer's journey was arranged by the seller for the purpose of inducing the consumer to buy."[2]

If any of the foregoing circumstances apply, then in the absence of choice, the applicable law shall not be selected in accordance with Article 4 but shall be the law of the country in which the consumer has his habitual residence.[3] Article 5 does not apply to a contract of carriage or to a contract for the supply of services where these are to be supplied solely outside the country of consumer's habitual residence.[4] Despite the provisions of Article 4, Article 5 shall apply to a contract for a combination of travel and accommodation at an inclusive price.[5]

On the matter of formal validity, Articles 9(1) to (4) do not apply to a consumer contract and its formal validity is governed by the law of the country in which the consumer has his habitual residence.[6]

The Giuliano and Lagarde Report has, *inter alia*, the following to say about Article 5.[7] Its provisions are for the protection of the consumer, considered to be the weaker party, and should be so interpreted. However the consumer will not be protected if the other party did not know, or in all the circumstances could not reasonably be expected to have known, that he was acting as a consumer. Where a person is acting partly as a consumer and partly in the course of his trade or profession, then he is only afforded protection if he is acting primarily outside his trade or profession. Credit and cash sales and the sale of insurance are included but sales of securities are excluded.

Individual employment contracts

21–016 These are dealt with in Article 6. Where there is no contractual choice of law, the provisions of Article 4 do not apply. Instead, the contract will be governed in accordance with Article 6(2):

> "(a) by the law of the country in which the employee habitually carries out his work in performance of the contract, even if he is temporarily employed in another country; or

---

[1] The Convention contains no definition of what amounts to "habitual residence" nor does the Giuliano and Lagarde Report offer any enlightenment.
[2] Art. 5(2).
[3] Art. 5(3).
[4] Art. 5(4).
[5] Art. 5(5).
[6] Art. 9(5).
[7] At pp. 23 and 24.

(b) if the employee does not habitually carry out his work in one country, by the law of the country in which the place of business through which he was engaged is situated;

> unless it appears from the circumstances as a whole that the contract is more closely connected with another country, in which case the contract shall be governed by the law of that other country."

Where there is an Article 3 choice of law, then the chosen law will apply.[8] Nevertheless the employee will not be deprived of the protection of the mandatory rules of the law of the country which would apply in the absence of choice, as set out in Article 6(2).[9]

As in the case of consumer contracts, this Article is for the benefit of the weaker party. It does not apply to collective agreements.[10]

The Foreign Limitation Periods Act 1984

Every legal system provides a time bar for commencing proceedings in litigation **21–017** or arbitration. In English law the periods of limitation are laid down in the Limitation Act 1980. Generally speaking they are, in actions founded on a simple contract, six years after the cause of action accrued and in actions upon a deed, 12 years from that date. Special provisions apply for actions founded on tort or in actions based on fraud. Foreign legal systems provide other—and sometimes longer—periods of limitation.[11] The attempt to unify limitation periods in the international sale of goods has not significantly advanced.[12]

In English private international law the limitation of actions is classified as pertaining to the procedural rules,[13] but in many foreign legal systems it forms part of the substantive law. Consequently, if proceedings were brought in England upon a contract governed by foreign law, the judge or arbitrator had to apply the English periods of limitation, as laid down in the Limitation Act 1980, as part of the *lex fori*. A plaintiff could thus lose the benefit of a longer period of limitation which he may have enjoyed under the foreign law applying to the substantive contract, or a defendant the benefit of a shorter period of limitation. To remedy this injustice, Parliament passed the Foreign Limitation Periods Act 1984. The Act provides that, in principle, where a foreign law has to be applied by the English courts or an arbitrator in England, the foreign rules of limitation shall likewise apply (s.1(1)). The same is true if both the law of England and Wales and that of a foreign country have to be taken into account (s.1(2)). However there are exceptions to this principle. The foreign limitation rules shall not apply to the extent to which they conflict with English public policy (s.2(1)). It is expressly provided that such a conflict exists if the application of the foreign

---

[8] Giuliano and Lagarde Report, p. 25.

[9] Art. 6(1).

[10] *ibid.*

[11] See *e.g. Gotha City v. Sotheby's and Another; Federal Republic of Germany v. Same, The Times,* October 8, 1998 (German limitation period of 30 years applied but excluded on public policy grounds and English law; section 4 of the Limitation Act 1980 applied in order that time did not run in favour of a thief).

[12] UN Convention on the Limitation Period in the International Sale of Goods—see *post*, para. 32–032.

[13] The Rome Convention does not apply to procedure, Art. 1(2)(h).

limitation rules "would cause undue hardship[14] to a person who is, or might be made, a party to the action or proceedings" (s.2(2)). Where the foreign law allows an extension due to the absence of a party from the jurisdiction, that shall be disregarded (s.2(3)). The reference to the foreign law is to the internal foreign law and does not include a reference to the foreign private international law (s.1(5)).[15]

The decision of a foreign court on a limitation point shall be regarded as a decision "on the merits", *i.e.* on a substantive point of law, and this includes even a decision of the foreign court on the English rules on limitation (s.3).

As already indicated, the provisions of the Act apply to arbitration proceedings (s.5).

Article 10(1)(d) of the Rome Convention provides that limitation of actions is governed by the law applicable to the contract.

MONEY OF ACCOUNT AND OF PAYMENT—RECOVERY IN FOREIGN CURRENCY

21–018 The parties may agree that a monetary obligation, *e.g.* the purchase price, shall be expressed in one currency but that the debtor shall be at liberty to discharge this obligation in another. The currency in which the debtor's liability is measured is the *currency of account*, and the currency in which he may pay is the *currency of payment*. The effect of this distinction is that, if at the date of discharge the rate of exchange of the currency of payment has fallen against the currency of account, the buyer must acquire more currency of payment in order to satisfy his obligation. Thus, in one case[16] the Nigerian Produce Marketing Board sold Woodhouse a quantity of cocoa under contracts providing for delivery c.i.f. Liverpool. The purchase price was expressed in Nigerian currency, then the Nigerian pound,[17] which was equivalent to the pound sterling. In response to the request of the buyers, the sellers agreed that the buyers may pay the price in pounds sterling. Before payment was made, the pound sterling was devalued but the Nigerian pound retained its value. The House of Lords held that the money of account was still the Nigerian currency, notwithstanding the sellers' agreement to accept pounds sterling in discharge of the buyers' liability.

The distinction between the money of account and the money of payment has lost some of its importance, because it is now possible to obtain judgments in foreign currency in the English courts if the contractual obligation is expressed in that currency.[18] It is also possible to recover damages in contract or tort in

---

[14] On the interpretation of "undue hardship" see *Jones v. Trollope & Colls Cementation Overseas Ltd, The Times,* January 26, 1990; *The Komninos S* [1990] 1 Lloyd's Rep. 541 at first instance, reversed on appeal on other grounds; *Arab Monetary Fund v. Hashim* [1996] 1 Lloyd's Rep. 589.

[15] This provision is intended to exclude renvoi from the foreign law to English law.

[16] *Woodhouse AC Israel Cocoa SA v. Nigerian Produce Marketing Co* [1972] A.C. 741; see also *W. J. Alan & Co Ltd v. El Nasr Export & Import Co* [1972] 2 Q.B. 189; *President of India v. Lips Maritime Corporation; The Lips* [1988] A.C. 395 (freight and demurrage under a charterparty fixed in U.S. dollars but payable in "British external sterling"; delay in payment of demurrage is not a cause of action in damages).

[17] It is now called Naira.

[18] *Miliangos v. George Frank Textiles Ltd* [1976] A.C. 443; *Schorsch Meier GmbH v. Hennin* [1975] Q.B. 416.

foreign currency if the loss was sustained in that currency, and damages in a foreign currency were reasonably in the contemplation of the parties at the time the contract was concluded.[19] Arbitration awards can likewise be obtained in foreign currency in appropriate cases.[20] Further, judgments on a bill of exchange expressed in a foreign currency but payable in England may be obtained in the foreign currency.[21]

However the creditor is not obliged to claim payment in the foreign currency. If he prefers, he may make his claim in sterling.[22] In the words of Donaldson J.[23]:

"... it is for the plaintiff to select the currency in which to make his claim and it is for him to prove that an award or judgment in that currency will most truly express his loss and accordingly most fully and exactly compensate him for that loss ... while the currency of account is a factor of considerable importance, it is not decisive of the currency in which the plaintiff should make his claim and in which judgment should be given."

Payment of damages is to be made in the foreign currency or the sterling equivalent at the time of payment, although where the contract specifies an exchange rate between the moneys of account and payment, that rate must be applied.[24]

In the winding-up of an insolvent company or a voluntary liquidation, a foreign currency debt, and interest thereon, are converted into sterling on the date of the winding up order.[25] In the words of Mervyn Davies J.,[26] the original "'money of account' has, as against the bank [the creditor], by virtue of the liquidation, become sterling." The reason is that all creditors of the company should be treated equally in the winding-up. But in the winding-up of a wholly solvent company the position may be different; if the creditor is paid less than his full contractual foreign currency claim, the liquidator may well be obliged to make good the shortfall before distributing the surplus assets to the shareholders.[27]

The interest rate on foreign currency judgments was until recently the same

---

[19] *Jean Kraut AC v. Albany Fabrics* [1977] Q.B. 182; *Services Europe Atlantique Sud v. Stockholm Rederiaktiebolag Svea; The Folias and The Despina R* [1979] A.C. 685; *George Veflings Rederi A/ S v. President of India; The Bellami* [1978] 1 W.L.R. 982; *BP Exploration Co (Libya) Ltd v. Hunt (No. 2)* [1979] 1 W.L.R. 783; *Société Francaise Bunge SA v. Belcan NV; The Federal Huron* [1985] 2 Lloyd's Rep. 189; *Metaalhandel J.A. Magnus BV v. Ardfields Transport Ltd* [1988] 1 Lloyd's Rep. 197 (damages in foreign currency refused because they could not have been in the contemplation of the parties); *A G for Rep of Ghana v. Texaco Overseas Tankships Ltd; The Texaco Melbourne* [1994] 1 Lloyd's Rep. 473 (The House of Lords awarded damages in Ghanaian cedis since this was the currency in which the plaintiff's loss was felt despite the fact that they would have to expend U.S.$ for a replacement cargo and the dramatic fall in the cedi's exchange rate between the date of breach and the date of judgment.)

[20] *Jugoslavenska Oceanska Plovidba v. Castle Investment Co Inc* [1974] Q.B. 292; now Arbitration Act 1996, s. 48(4).

[21] *Barclays Bank International Ltd v. Levin Brothers (Bradford) Ltd* [1977] Q.B. 270.

[22] *Ozalid Group (Export) Ltd v. African Continental Bank Ltd* [1979] 2 Lloyd's Rep. 231.

[23] *ibid.* at 234.

[24] *The President of India v. Taygetos Shipping Co SA* [1985] 1 Lloyd's Rep. 155. See also *The Lash Atlantico* [1985] 2 Lloyd's Rep. 464.

[25] *Re Dynamics Corporation of America* [1976] 1 W.L.R. 757; and *Re Lines Bros Ltd* [1983] Ch. 1; *Re Lines Bros Ltd (No. 2)* [1984] 2 W.L.R. 905.

[26] *Re Lines Bros Ltd (No. 2)*, *ibid.* at 914.

[27] Brightman L.J. in *Re Lines Bros Ltd*, *ante*.

as for sterling judgments.[28] However, in line with the recommendations of the Law Commission,[29] Parliament has enacted the Private International Law (Miscellaneous Provisions) Act 1995 which provides by sections 1, 2 and 4 that the interest rate on foreign currency judgments shall be at the discretion of the court. There is a corresponding provision in the Arbitration Act 1996.[30]

FOREIGN STATE IMMUNITY

21–019 When an enterprise contracts with a foreign State[31] or a foreign State corporation and disputes occur, the question arises whether, if proceedings are commenced, the foreign State or State corporation can plead sovereign immunity and thereby evade its commercial obligations. Here, two theories are advanced. Under the doctrine of *absolute immunity*, the foreign State or State corporation can always plead immunity. Under the doctrine of *restrictive immunity*, a distinction is drawn between acts in the exercise of sovereign authority (*acta jure imperii*) and ordinary commercial transactions (*acta jure gestionis*).[32] Immunity is accorded to the former but refused to the latter.[33]

The State Immunity Act 1978 gives effect to the doctrine of restrictive immunity.[34] Section 3 of the Act provides:

"(1) A State is not immune as respects proceedings relating to—

    (a) a commercial transaction entered into by the State; or
    (b) an obligation of the State which by virtue of a contract (whether a commercial transaction or not) falls to be performed wholly or partly in the United Kingdom.

(2) This section does not apply if the parties to the dispute are States or have otherwise agreed in writing; and subsection (1)(b) above does not apply if the contract (not being a commercial

---

[28] Practice Direction [1976] 1 W.L.R. 83 as amended by Practice Direction [1977] 1 W.L.R. 184.
[29] Law Com. No. 124 (1983).
[30] s. 49.
[31] The E.C. is not a "State" within the meaning of the State Immunity Act 1978 and cannot claim immunity under it: *International Tin Council* cases [1988] 3 All E.R. 257, 316–320.
[32] See *Kuwait Airways Corp v. Iraqi Airways Co* [1995] 1 W.L.R. 1147 at 1160.
[33] English common law has adopted the principle of restrictive immunity: *I Congreso del Partido* [1983] 1 A.C. 244. Before this decision the restrictive doctrine was already applied by the Privy Council in *The Philippine Admiral* [1977] A.C. 373 and the Court of Appeal, *obiter*, in *Trendtex Trading Corporation v. Central Bank of Nigeria* [1977] Q.B. 529. On the concept of sovereignty ("*par in parem*") see *per* Lord Wilberforce in *I Congreso del Partido*, at 262. An entirely different matter is the rule of public international law sometimes referred to as the "Act of State" doctrine, according to which the courts will not adjudicate on transactions between foreign sovereign States: *Buttes Gas and Oil Co v. Hammer (No. 3)* [1982] A.C. 888. In *MacLaine Watson & Co Ltd v. International Tin Council* [1989] Ch. 253 (affirmed by HL in [1989] 3 W.L.R. 969), Kerr L.J. expressed doubt that the act of State nonjusticiability rule could be extended to claims based on commercial agreements. See also *per* Evans J. in *Amalgamated Metal Trading Ltd v. Department of Trade and Industry, The Times,* March 21, 1989. In the USA the Supreme court admitted the commercial activity exception to the act of State doctrine in the leading case of *Alfred Dunhill v. Republic of Cuba*, 425 U.S. 682 (1976); see Stephen J. Leacock, "The Commercial Activity Exception to the Act of State Doctrine revisited: Evolution of a Concept", in (1988) 13 North Carolina Journal of International Law & Commercial Relations, 1.
[34] The Act starts, as Lord Diplock observed in *Alcom Ltd v. Republic of Colombia* [1984] A.C. 580 at 600, by restating the absolute principle in s. 1(1) but it makes the principle subject to wide-ranging exceptions (ss. 2-17). In view of the wide scope of these exceptions, it is thought that the statement is the text is justified.

transaction) was made in the territory of the State concerned and the obligation in question is governed by its administrative law.

(3) In this section "commercial transaction" means—

    (a) any contract for the supply of goods or services;

    (b) any loan or other transaction for the provision of finance and any guarantee or indemnity in respect of any such transaction or any other financial obligation; and

    (c) any other transaction or activity (whether of a commercial, industrial, financial, professional or other similar character) into which a State enters or in which it engages otherwise than in the exercise of sovereign authority;

but neither paragraph of subsection (1) above applies to a contract of employment between a State and an individual."

It should be noted that in the cases mentioned in section 3(3)(a) and (b), the purpose of the transaction is irrelevant. Thus, a foreign State cannot claim immunity if it has purchased equipment for its army. However in the case of section 3(3)(c), transactions *jure imperii* are excluded and the State can rely on its immunity in such transactions.

The Act further deals with State corporations which enjoy separate legal personality.[35] Such a separate entity does not enjoy immunity, except if:

(a) the proceedings relate to anything done by it in the exercise of sovereign authority; and

(b) the circumstances are such that a State (or in the case of proceedings to which section 10 above applies, a State which is not a party to the Brussels Convention) would have been immune.

The central bank or other monetary authority of a foreign State is not regarded as a separate entity within the meaning of these provisions, even if under its own law it has that character, and its property is immune.[36] Where a State has agreed in writing to arbitration, it is not immune as respects proceedings in the courts of the United Kingdom which relate to arbitration; such an agreement may be entered into even before a dispute has arisen.[37]

It is possible to execute a judgment or arbitration award in respect of State property which is for the time being in use or intended for use for commercial purposes.[38] Such property is likewise subject to execution if it is intended to enforce a foreign judgment or arbitration award in the United Kingdom, provided that the conditions for such enforcement are satisfied. It is not, however, possible to obtain an injunction against a foreign State even in commercial matters[39]—a decided shortcoming of the Act—but an order for security in default of which leave would be given to enforce an arbitration award is not an injunc-

---

[35] In s. 14(2).

[36] s. 14(4); *Hispano Americana Mercantil SA v. Central Bank of Nigeria* [1979] 2 Lloyd's Rep. 277 (the immunity of a central bank under the U.K. Act of 1978 goes further than that under the U.S. Foreign Sovereign Immunities Act 1976 which protects only property of the bank "held for its own account").

[37] s. 9.

[38] s. 13(4). *cf. Alcom Ltd v. Republic of Colombia* [1984] A.C. 580.

[39] s. 13(2)(a).

tion.[40] It is, however, thought that one can obtain an injunction against a third party, *e.g.* a bank, which holds commercial property of the State, because that possibility is not expressly barred by the Act. The account of a foreign diplomatic mission with a U.K. bank cannot be attached by way of execution of a judgment against the mission, even if the money in the account is intended to be used for the day-to-day expenditure of the mission, because this is not a "commercial purpose" within section 13(4) of the Act. However the position is different if the judgment creditor can prove that the account was designated solely (subject to the *de minimis* rule[41]) to meet liabilities incurred in commercial transactions.[42]

The State Immunity (Merchant Shipping) Order 1997[43] made under the State Immunity Act 1978 preserves the immunity from execution of ships and cargoes owned by certain states which would otherwise be lost under section 13(4) of the State Immunity Act. Notice is required to be given to a consul of those States before a warrant of arrest is issued in an *in rem* action in respect of a ship or cargo on it which is owned by that State.

A foreign State can claim immunity for acts of torture of an individual within its own territory,[44] but the conduct of a foreign state is relevant in deciding whether, as a matter of public policy, an English court should refuse to give effect to a foreign law.[45]

In the United States the restrictive theory is also adopted[46] and forms the basis of the Foreign Sovereign Immunities Act 1976.[47]

EXTRATERRITORIAL EFFECT OF FOREIGN STATE MEASURES

21–020 Extraterritorial effect may be claimed by a State for its legislative or administrative measures or by a court for its judgments or orders. Extraterritorial claims of this character are attempts at exercising an "exorbitant" jurisdiction and should, in principle, be avoided. In practice, however, they are sometimes brought in order to give effectiveness to domestic law or for other—possibly economic or political—reasons. Foreign claims of extraterritoriality have, on occasion, come into conflict with the sovereignty of the United Kingdom and her trading interests.

Protective measures have been taken on two levels: Parliament has enacted

---

[40] *Soleh Boneh International Ltd v. Government of the Rep of Uganda* [1993] 2 Lloyd's Rep. 208.
[41] *De minimis non curat lex* (the law takes no account of trifles).
[42] *Alcom Ltd v. Republic of Colombia* [1984] A.C. 580. See also *Maclaine Watson & Co Ltd v. International Tin Council (No. 3)* [1989] 3 W.L.R. 969, HL.
[43] S.I. 1997 No. 2591, in force November 1, 1997.
[44] *Al-Adsani v. Government of Kuwait, The Times,* March 29, 1996.
[45] *Kuwait Airways Corporation v. Iraqi Airways Company (No. 5), The Times,* May 12, 1998. The facts of this case are set out at *post,* para. 21–026.
[46] In the U.S. the changeover from the absolute to the restrictive doctrine was accelerated by the so-called Tate letter of May 19, 1952, addressed by Mr. J.B. Tate, acting legal adviser to the State Department, to the then acting Attorney-General. The restrictive theory was applied by the Supreme Court in *Alfred Dunhill of London Inc v. Republic of Cuba* (1976) 96 S.C. 1854.
[47] See Kazimierz Grzybowski, "The United States Foreign Sovereign Immunities Act 1976" [1978] J.B.L. 111.

the Protection of Trading Interests Act 1980 and the courts have rejected extra-territorial claims of foreign courts conflicting with British sovereignty.

The Protection of Trading Interests Act 1980

The main provisions of this Act, as amended,[48] are:　　　　　　　　　**21–021**

(a) Where an overseas country takes, or proposes to take, measures regulating or controlling international trade and these measures damage or threaten to damage the trading interests of the United Kingdom,[49] the Secretary of State may order that persons carrying on business in the United Kingdom should notify him of such measures and he may issue directions prohibiting compliance with them.[50]

(b) If a request is made on a person inside the United Kingdom to produce to any court or authority of an overseas country a commercial document which is not within the territorial jurisdiction of that country or to furnish any commercial information to such overseas court or authority, or if such a requirement is imposed on a person inside the United Kingdom, the Secretary of State may prohibit compliance with such requirement if it is inadmissible by the Act.[51]

Section 2(2) provides that such requirement is inadmissible:

(i) if it infringes the jurisdiction of the United Kingdom or is otherwise prejudicial to the sovereignty of the United Kingdom; or

(ii) if compliance with the requirement would be prejudicial to the security of the United Kingdom or the relations of the government of the United Kingdom with the government of any other country.

Subsection (3) of this section provides, with respect to a request made by a person in an overseas country, that the requirement shall be inadmissible:

(i) if it is made otherwise than for the purposes of civil or criminal proceedings which have been instituted in the overseas country; or

(ii) if it requires a person to state what documents relevant to any such proceedings are or have been in his possession, custody or power

---

[48] By the Magistrates Courts Act 1980, Scheds 7 and 9, and the Civil Jurisdiction and Judgments Act 1982, s. 38. For a consideration of the Protection of Trading Interests Act 1980 see Lawrence Collins, "Blocking and Clawback Statutes: The United Kingdom Approach" [1986] J.B.L. 372 at 452.

[49] s. 1(1). Section 1(1), (3) are disapplied in so far as Council Regulation No. 2271/96 (protecting against the effects of the extraterritorial legislation adopted by a third country) applies and it is an offence to breach Arts 2 or 5 of the Regulation: Extraterritorial U.S. legislation (Sanctions against Cuba, Iran and Libya) (Protection of Trading Interests) Order 1996 (S.I. 1996 No. 3171).

[50] s. 1. Orders under this section were made in connection with the Trans-Siberian Pipeline (S.I. 1982 No. 885; see [1982] J.B.L. 360) and the *Laker* litigation (S.I. 1983 No. 90; this S.I. was considered in *British Airways Board v. Laker Airways Ltd* [1985] A.C. 58). Non-compliance with a requirement of the Secretary of State under s. 1 without reasonable excuse is punishable (s. 3).

[51] s. 2. Section 2 is disapplied in so far as the Council Regulation detailed in n. 49 above applies. Again, non-compliance without reasonable excuse is punishable (s. 3).

or to produce for the purposes of any such proceedings any documents other than particular documents specified in the requirement.[52]

(c) The Act further provides that a court in the United Kingdom shall not assist an overseas court[53] to obtain evidence in the United Kingdom if it is shown that the overseas request infringes the jurisdiction of the United Kingdom or is otherwise prejudicial to the sovereignty of the United Kingdom; and a certificate signed by or on behalf of the Secretary of State to that effect shall be conclusive evidence.[54]

(d) The Act further contains provisions directed against the recovery of multiple damages in the United Kingdom in excess of damages attributable to compensation. Such damages may be awarded in particular by the United States courts in anti-trust proceedings. They contain a punitive element, whereas damages in the United Kingdom are, in principle, of compensatory nature.[55]

Rejection of foreign extraterritorial claims by the courts—letters of request

21–022 The English courts reject claims by foreign courts or authorities if these claims, in the judgment of the English courts, infringe the sovereignty of the United Kingdom.[56] In particular, they will reject claims by U.S. courts or authorities to assist in the enforcement of U.S. anti-trust laws of extraterritorial character in the United Kingdom.[57]

Here, however, a difficulty arises. The English courts are bound by the Hague Convention on the Taking of Evidence Abroad in Civil or Commercial Matters of March 18, 1970, to which effect is given in the United Kingdom by the Evidence (Proceedings in Other Jurisdictions) Act 1975, to assist foreign courts

---

[52] This provision is directed against so-called "fishing expeditions", particularly in pre-trial proceedings, which are widely admitted in the United States; the purpose of such proceedings is to ascertain whether the enquirer has enough evidence to commence proceedings; on the other hand, the English courts will not restrain a litigant before them from making use of his right to obtain information by way of pre-trial proceedings in the American courts: *South Carolina Insurance Co v. Assurantie Maatschappij "De Zeven Provincien" NV* [1987] A.C. 24. But the problem may also arise in other contexts, see *Lonrho Ltd v. Shell Petroleum Co Ltd* [1982] A.C. 173; *Re State of Norway's Application (No. 2)* [1988] 3 W.L.R. 603; reversed by HL [1990] 1 A.C. 723 (see *post*, para. 21–022).
[53] Under the Evidence (Proceedings in Other Jurisdictions) Act 1975; see *post*, para. 21–022.
[54] s. 4.
[55] See further *ante*, para. 4–015.
[56] On the rejection of foreign revenue laws, penal laws, certain public laws, expropriatory laws claiming extraterritorial effect and certain discriminatory laws, see *post*, paras 21–024 to 21–026.
[57] *British Nylon Spinners Ltd v. Chemical Industries Ltd* [1953] Ch. 19; *Re Westinghouse Electric Corporation Uranium Contract Litigation MDL Docket No. 235 (No. 1 and No. 2)* [1978] A.C. 547. See also *Radio Corporation of America v. Rauland Corporation* [1956] 1 Q.B. 618 (request for pre-trial discovery in a U.S. patent action); *X AG v. Bank A* [1983] 2 All E.R. 464 (injunctions ordering non-compliance with subpoena of US court). But the English courts will not restrain a litigant before them from making use of the American pre-trial discovery procedure, see *"De Zeven Provincien"* case [1987] A.C. 24 at 43.

when requesting assistance in obtaining evidence situate in England and Wales. The request of the foreign courts is called *letters of request* or *letters rogatory*. The requirements of the 1975 Act for letters rogatory are strict; the procedure under this Act can only be used to obtain *evidence* but not to make *discovery*.[58] One of the requirements of the Act is that, if the production of documents is required, they must be sufficiently particularised.[59] However the letter of request procedure must not be used for an improper purpose. In one case,[60] where it was used on the intervention of the United States Department of Justice as a request for evidence for a grand jury investigation into an alleged anti-trust arrangement, letters rogatory were refused because, as Lord Wilberforce observed,[61] "the attempt to extend the grand jury investigation extraterritorially . . . was an infringment of United Kingdom sovereignty". Another illustration is provided by the *State of Norway's Application* cases.[62] A wealthy Norwegian shipowner had died domiciled in Norway. The Norwegian revenue alleged that he was the beneficial owner of a trust created in England and that he was liable to tax on his interest in the trust, which he had failed to declare. The representatives of the deceased denied these allegations and proceedings were pending on these matters in a court in Norway. That court requested the English courts to examine a director and an employee of an English merchant banking house which had acted as bankers to the trust. In the first case[63] the Court of Appeal, by a majority judgment, refused to comply with the letter of request on the ground that the request was too general and compliance with it would unjustifiably cause the bank to break its duty of confidentiality to a customer. The Norwegian court then particularised its request meticulously and repeated it and, in the second of these cases, was successful in the House of Lords.[64] The highest court held that the proceedings in the court of Norway fell within the definition of a civil or commercial matter both in English and Norwegian law. The House of Lords further held that the rule that the English courts would not assist in the direct or indirect enforcement of a foreign revenue law did not extend to the seeking of assistance in obtaining evidence to be used for the enforcement of a foreign revenue law in the foreign State.

Conversely, the English courts will refuse an application for (English) letters of request to be sent to a foreign court if the request is likely to cause embarass-

---

[58] *Re International Power Industries Inc NV* [1985] B.C.L.C. 128. See the seminal article by Lawrence Collins on "Problems of Enforcement in the Multinational Securities Market. A United Kingdom Perspective" in (1987) 9 University of Pennsylvania Journal of International Business Law, 487.

[59] *Re Asbestos Insurance Coverage Cases* [1985] 1 W.L.R. 331; *Minnesota v. Philip Morris Inc* [1998] I.L.Pr. 170. Evidence under the 1975 Act for a foreign court may be taken by videotape although such evidence might be inadmissible in the English courts: *J. Barber & Sons v. Lloyd's Underwriters* [1987] Q.B. 103.

[60] The *Westinghouse* case, *ante*. The *Westinghouse* case was decided before s. 4 of the Protection of Trading Interests Act 1980 (above in the text) came into force.

[61] *ibid.* at 616.

[62] [1990] 1 A.C. 723.

[63] *Re State of Norway's Application* [1987] Q.B. 433. See also *Minnesota v. Philip Morris Inc* [1998] I.L.Pr. 170.

[64] *Re State of Norway's Application (No. 2)* [1990] 1 A.C. 723.

ment to the foreign court[65]; the grant of such an application would contravene the comity of nations and would not be in accordance with the mutual respect which the courts of friendly nations show—or ought to show—to each other. The English courts will also refuse, save in exceptional circumstances, to make an order infringing a foreign State's sovereignty.[66]

The 1975 Act by section 9(4) precludes an English court from making an order "binding on the Crown or any other person in his capacity as an officer or servant of the Crown." In connection with the Lockerbie disaster the United States sought by a formal letter of request to examine a scientist employed by the Crown but who had since retired. It was held that the court had no jurisdiction to order him to submit to examination by a foreign court about knowledge obtained in his capacity as a Crown servant.[67]

The Criminal Justice (International Co-operation) Act 1990 provides by section 3 for evidence to be obtained overseas for use here, and by section 4 for U.K. evidence to be provided for use overseas by way of letters of request.[68]

THE EXCLUSION OF FOREIGN LAW

21–023 As a matter of international comity, the English courts recognise, in principle, the validity of the laws of a foreign country and will enforce a foreign judgment even where the remedy is one which is not recognised in English law.[69]

Exceptionally, however, the English courts will refuse to recognise or enforce foreign laws. The ultimate reason for such a refusal is that, in the judgment of the English courts, the foreign law in question is incompatible with the public policy of English law.[70] This common law rule is incorporated in several statutes.[71] Two points should be noted. The first is that although in general an English court will *recognise* a foreign law, it may refuse to *enforce* it if the result of its application is contrary to English public policy. There are rare instances where the foreign law is so repugnant that an English court may "refuse to recognise it as a law at all."[72]

The situations in which the English courts refuse the application of foreign law can be grouped under the following three headings.

---

[65] *Settobello Ltd v. Banco Totta and Acores* [1985] 1 W.L.R. 1050; see para. 6–010. See also *Buttes Gas and Oil Co v. Hammer (No. 3)* [1982] A.C. 888; *Maclaine, Watson & Co Ltd v. International Tin Council* [1989] 3 W.L.R. 969, see *ante*, para. 21–019, n. 33.
[66] *Mackinnon v. Donaldson, Lufkin and Jenrette Securities Corporation* [1986] Ch. 482 (order refused to produce under the Bankers' Books Evidence Act 1879 documents kept by a foreign bank abroad).
[67] *Lockerbie Air Disaster, Re, The Times*, May 20, 1992.
[68] See *post*, para. 21–028.
[69] *e.g. SA Consortium General Textiles v. Sun and Sand Agencies Ltd* [1978] Q.B. 279 (exemplary damages).
[70] *Vervaeke v. Smith* [1983] 1 A.C. 145.
[71] *e.g.* Foreign Judgments (Reciprocal Enforcement) Act 1984 s. 2; Civil Jurisdiction and Judgments Act 1982, Sched. 1, Art. 27(1) and Sched. 3C, Art. 27(1); The Rome convention, Sched. 1, Art. 16.
[72] *Oppenheimer v. Cattermole* [1976] A.C. 249 (Nazi decrees concerning German Jews).

Foreign confiscatory or nationalisation laws

While the English courts admit the validity of nationalisation or other expropria- **21–024** tory laws of a foreign State recognised[73] by the Government of this country[74] as far as property situate at the time of the expropriation in the territory of the foreign State is concerned,[75] they refuse to recognise the application of such laws to property situate at that time outside the territory of the foreign State, even if the expropriatory law claims to have extraterritorial effect.[76] Such a claim would be an excess of national sovereignty and an interference with the sovereignty of other States and this is contrary to the generally accepted principles of international law. If the foreign law does not claim to have extraterritorial effect then there is no question for the English court to consider.[77]

Foreign revenue laws, penal laws and other public laws of political or administrative character

The English courts will not enforce, directly or indirectly, revenue laws of **21–025** another country,[78] even if that country is a member of the Commonwealth or the E.C.[79] This rule applies to taxes, rates, Customs duties or other impositions levied in the overseas country. However, a request from a foreign state that evidence be taken in England in connection with tax proceedings is not a direct or indirect enforcement of its tax laws.[80]

Penal laws of a foreign country are likewise not enforceable directly or indirectly in the English jurisdiction.[81] "Penal laws" in the strict sense are "criminal laws"[82] but the term is given a wider meaning and includes discriminatory laws directed against a particular person,[83] family or business enterprise,[84] especially if these discriminatory measures are directed against a person or corporation resident in the United Kingdom[85] or if they contravene fundamental human rights. But, apart from the latter two cases, the English courts recognise, on the

---

[73] The Foreign Corporations Act 1991, s. 1 deals with matters concerning a body corporate in a territory which is not a recognised state.

[74] *Carl Zeiss Stiftung v. Rayner & Keeler (No. 2)* [1967] 1 A.C. 853; *Gur Corporation v. Trust Bank of Africa Ltd* [1987] Q.B. 599.

[75] *Luther v. Sagor* [1921] 3 K.B. 532; *Princess Paley Olga v. Weisz* [1929] 1 K.B. 718; *Williams & Humbert Ltd v. W&M Trade Marks (Jersey) Ltd* [1986] A.C. 368.

[76] *Lecouturier v. Rey* [1910] A.C. 262; *Frankfurther v. W.L. Exner Ltd* [1947] Ch. 629; *Redler Grain Silos Ltd v. BICC Ltd* [1982] 1 Lloyd's Rep. 435 at 438.

[77] *Lecouturier v. Rey* [1910] A.C. 262.

[78] *Re Visser* [1928] Ch. 877; *Indian Government v. Taylor* [1955] A.C. 491. See also the *In the State of Norway's Application* cases *ante. Buchanan and Macharg v. McVey* [1958] A.C. 516 (note).

[79] *QRS 1 Aps v. Frandsen* [1999] 3 All E.R. 289 (the Court of Appeal held the revenue claims exclusion in Article 1 of the Brussels Convention included indirect revenue claims and therefore the Convention did not apply).

[80] *State of Norway's Application* cases, *ante.*

[81] *Huntington v. Attrill* [1893] A.C. 150.

[82] *United States of America v. Inkley* [1988] 3 W.L.R. 304 (Florida judgment in civil proceedings for enforcement of a bail bond refused because the bail bond was given in penal proceedings).

[83] *Banco de Vizcaya v. Don Alfonso de Borbon y Austria* [1935] 1 K.B. 140.

[84] *The Rose Mary* [1953] 1 W.L.R. 246 (see on this case *Re Helbert Wagg & Co Ltd's Claim* [1956] Ch. 323 at 346).

[85] *Folliott v. Ogden* (1789) 1 H.Bl. 123.

principle in *Luther v. Sagor*,[86] a penal law in the wider sense if the foreign State has perfected its title to the expropriated assets in its own territory, *e.g.* if it has expropriated the shares of a local company even though the company has valuable assets outside the territory of the expropriating State.[87]

Direct enforcement is where a foreign state seeks enforcement of its revenue or penal laws. An example of indirect enforcement is where a third party seeks enforcement of a right but where the end result would amount to enforcement by a foreign state of its revenue or penal laws.[88]

Whether the English courts should refuse recognition to other public laws of a foreign country is controversial and the question remains to be decided despite discussion in a number of cases.[89] It is thought that there are two kinds of public laws; those which are of political or administrative character and those which are not. The latter class includes statutes designed to protect the natural environment[90] or to prevent the exportation of national art treasures without licence.[91] Public laws of the former type should be refused recognition but there is no justification in extending this refusal to public laws of the latter type, particularly as this country has enacted legislation having the same aims.

Other cases of public policy

21–026 It should, however, be emphasised that, to vary the words of a famous judge,[92] the categories of public policy are never closed. The English courts have a residual discretion to refuse the application of foreign laws in cases other than those mentioned in the preceding paragraphs, if they conclude that recognition would contravene heads of public policy which are not purely domestic.[93] In a recent case[94] arising out of Iraq's invasion of Kuwait, Iraq seized certain aircraft pursuant to an Iraqi resolution. The English court refused to recognise the Iraqi

---

[86] [1921] 3 K.B. 352.
[87] *Williams and Humbert Ltd v. W & H Trade Marks (Jersey) Ltd; Rumasa SA v. Multinvest (U.K.) Ltd (The Dry Sack litigation)* [1986] A.C. 368, HL.
[88] *Banco de Vizcaya v. Don Alfonso de Borbon y Austria* [1935] 1 K.B. 140.
[89] See, *e.g. Attorney-General of New Zealand v. Ortiz* [1982] Q.B. 349, and [1984] A.C. 1: *Att.-Gen (U.K.) v. Heinemann Publishers Australia Ltd* [1988] 165 C.L.R. 30 and *Att.-Gen (U.K.) v. Wellington Newspapers Ltd* [1988] 1 N.Z.L.R. 129 (the "Spycatcher" cases): *United States v. Ivey* [1995] 130 D.L.R. (4th) 674.
[90] *United States v. Ivey* [1995] 130 D.L.R. (4th) 674.
[91] The E.C. has implemented interlinked Regulations and Directives concerning the Export of Cultural Goods (Council Reg. No. 3911/92 as amended) and the Return of Cultural Objects Unlawfully Received from the Territory of a Member State (Directives 93/7 and 96/100). See further para. 26–005. The U.K. is not party to the Unidroit Convention on Stolen or Illegally Exported Cultural Objects, 1995.
[92] *Per* Lord Macmillan in *Donoghue v. Stevenson* [1932] A.C. 562 at 619.
[93] *Lemenda Trading Co Ltd v. African Middle East Petroleum Co Ltd* [1988] Q.B. 448 (alleged influence on foreign official for pecuniary gain held to contravene English and foreign public policy; Phillips J. (at 745): "Some heads of public policy are based on universal principles of morality . . . Where a contract infringes such a rule of public policy the English court will not enforce it, whatever the proper law of contract and wherever the place of performance"). See also *Mitsubishi Corporation v. Alafonzos* [1988] 1 Lloyd's Rep. 191; *E.I. Du Pont de Nemours v. I.C. Agnew* [1987] 2 Lloyd's Rep. 585 (English court better placed to decide a point on English public policy than foreign court); *Camdex International v. Bank of Zambia (No. 3)* [1997] 6 Bank L.R. 44.
[94] *Kuwait Airways Corporation v. Iraqi Airways Company, The Times*, May 12, 1998.

resolution on the ground that it was a clear contravention of international law and of the Charter of the United Nations. Moreover Iraq's invasion of Kuwait was not remote or irrelevant to the United Kingdom or its public policy.

A contract for a waiver of claims made under duress would be ineffective as a defence in an English court, on the ground of public policy.[95]

FOREIGN ILLEGALITY

Civil consequences

Under common law rules, the English courts will not enforce a contract to break **21–027** the laws of a foreign friendly state or where its performance is illegal by the law of the place where it is to be performed.[96] Thus, if the parties to a contract of export sale knowingly and deliberately agree to break the laws of a friendly country, *i.e.* a country with which the United Kingdom is not at war and the Government of which is recognised by the Government of this country, the English courts will not enforce such contract at the suit of one of the parties, because to do so would disregard the rules of international comity. This applies even if the laws which the parties intended to infringe were the revenue laws of another country, *i.e.* laws relating to Customs duties and quotas, import or export prohibitions, exchange control regulations[97] or taxation.

In *Regazzoni v. K.C. Sethia (1944) Ltd*[98] the Government of India prohibited the direct or indirect exportation of specified goods, including jute bags, to, among others, South Africa, because differences had arisen between the Governments of the two countries with respect to the treatment of Indian nationals in South Africa. Regazzoni, a Swiss merchant, bought from the defendants, a company incorporated in England and having Indian connections, a large quantity of jute bags c.i.f. Genoa; thence the goods were, as both parties knew, to be transhipped to South Africa. Both parties intended, as the court found, to infringe the prohibition of Indian law. The contract, which was governed by English law, was not carried out because the Indian Government did not sanction the exportation of the goods to Genoa, and the action by the buyer against the sellers for damages for non-delivery of the goods was dismissed by the English courts on

---

[95] *Royal Boskalis Westminster NV v. Mountain* [1988] 2 W.L.R. 538 (dredgers in Kuwait seized by Iraqi authorities and the waiver of claims was agreed in order to secure their release and that of employees).

[96] *Ralli Brothers v. Compañía Naviera Sota y Aznar* [1920] 2 K.B. 287; *Foster v. Driscoll* [1929] 1 K.B. 470; *Regazzoni v. K.C. Sethia (1944) Ltd* [1958] A.C. 301; *Ispahani v. Bank Melli Iran* [1998] Lloyd's Rep. Bank 133. But the mere fact that the contract is, or becomes, illegal by the law of the country in which the person who has to perform resides, is not sufficient unless that country is also the country in which the actual performance has to take place: *Toprak Mahsulleriofisi v. Finagrain Compagnie Commerciale, Agricole et Financiere* [1979] 2 Lloyd's Rep. 98 at 107. See also *Kleinwort Sons & Co v. Ungamische Baumwolle Industrie AG* [1939] 2 K.B. 678; *Libyan Arab Foreign Bank v. Bankers Trust Co* [1989] Q.B. 728 (these cases were decided before the introduction of the concept of "characteristic performance" into English law, see *ante*, para. 21–009).

[97] In *United City Merchants (Investments) Ltd v. Royal Bank of Canada* [1983] 1 A.C. 168 a different point arose. The agreement of the parties to infringe Peruvian exchange control regulations was invalid because it infringed *English* law, *viz.* the Bretton Woods Agreements Order 1946, and *not* because it aimed at the infringement of the laws of a *foreign* country, *viz.* Peru.

[98] [1958] A.C. 301; see also *Foster v. Driscoll* [1929] 1 K.B. 470.

the ground that it was against English public policy to enforce a contract intended by the parties to involve the breach of the laws of India.

The rule of which the *Regazzoni* case is an illustration is subject to certain
qualifications and exceptions.[99] First, the validity of the contract is not affected
where only one party, but not the other, is aware of the illegality.[1] Nor will it
be invalid where there was no intention to infringe a foreign law, unless it
violates the law applicable to the contract.[2] Secondly, where the transaction in
issue is completed and the illegality arises thereafter, or the illegality precedes
the transaction and is exhausted before the parties contract, their bargain is
unaffected by the illegality.[3] An ordinary sale in England of goods which, as
the seller knows or suspects, will be smuggled by the buyer into another country
is likely to be valid. Thirdly, foreign illegality affects only the contract in which
it arises but not supporting contracts. Thus, the fact that export invoices were
falsified in order to deceive the Customs authorities of the importer's country
did not prevent the exporter from recovering damages in this country from carriers when the exporter's goods were stolen from their lorry in transit to the
docks of London.[4] Further, where diamonds were exported to West Germany
on a sale or return basis and their price was understated in the invoice to save
German turnover tax, and part of the consignment was stolen in West Germany,
the English insurance contract, under which the diamonds were insured at their
correct value, was not tainted by the German illegality and the insurers were
liable under the policy.[5]

Since the coming into force of the Rome Convention, it is uncertain whether
the principle that an English court will not enforce a contract to break the laws
of a foreign friendly state, where its performance is illegal by the law of the
country where it is to be performed, will be upheld. It may well be restricted to
cases where English law is the governing law of the contract. Where the contract
is governed by a foreign law for the performance of an act which is illegal in a
country whose law is not the governing law of the contract, enforcement could
have been refused pursuant to Article 7(1)[6] of the Convention; however this is
not in force in the United Kingdom. In order to avoid enforcing such a contract,
an English court could only resort to Article 7(2)[7] if the principle could be

---

[99] Apart from the cases in which the English courts refuse to recognise or enforce foreign law, see
ante, paras 21–023 to 21–026.
[1] *Archbolds (Freightage) Ltd v. S. Spanglett Ltd* [1961] 1 Q.B. 374; *Fielding & Platt Ltd v. Najjar*
[1969] 1 W.L.R. 357; *Phoenix General Insurance Company of Greece SA v. Halvanon Insurance
Co Ltd* [1987] 2 W.L.R. 512 at 561; *SCF Finance Co Ltd v. Masri (No. 2)* [1987] 2 W.L.R. 58 at 78.
[2] *Regazzoni v. K.C. Sethia (1944) Ltd* [1958] A.C. 301; *Fielding & Platt Ltd v. Najjar* [1969] 1
W.L.R. 357.
[3] *Regazzoni v. K.C. Sethia (1944) Ltd* [1958] A.C. 301; see also *Mackender v. Feldia AG* [1967] 2
Q.B. 590. But in *Geismar v. Sun Alliance and London Insurance Ltd* [1978] 1 Q.B. 383 it was held
that a contract of insurance of goods illegally imported into this country was unenforceable on
grounds of public policy.
[4] *Pye Ltd v. BG Transport Service Ltd* [1966] 2 Lloyd's Rep. 300.
[5] *Euro-Diam Ltd v. Bathurst* [1990] 1 Q.B. 35.
[6] Which permits effect to be given to the "mandatory rules of the law of another country with
which the situation has a close connection".
[7] Which provides that the Convention rules shall not restrict the application of the mandatory rules
of the law of the forum, whatever the applicable law of the contract.

construed as a mandatory principle of English law, or to Article 16 on the grounds of public policy.[8]

An English court will not enforce a valid arbitration award where the contract was illegal under English law and the law of the place of performance on the ground of public policy, even though the foreign arbitrator considered the illegality to be of no consequence.[9]

Criminal consequences[10]

Questions governing the civil consequences of foreign illegality are different **21–028** from that of whether a British exporter who has committed a criminal offence under the laws of another country, or has conspired to commit such offence, can be convicted of it and punished in England.[11] Here, the position is that:

(a) The courts of this country do not enforce the criminal law of another country at the suit of that country, either directly or indirectly.[12]

(b) As a rule, an act committed abroad is not punishable in England.

(c) Exceptionally, however, certain acts committed abroad are made offences by the common law of England or United Kingdom statutes and are punishable in the English courts.

(d) Where an offence falls within the list of extraditable offences, and the United Kingdom has reciprocal arrangements for extradition with a foreign country, a person accused or convicted of such crime may be extradited to the country in question. Extradition to most foreign countries is regulated by the Extradition Act 1989[13] which consolidates four of the earlier Extradition Acts,[14] the Fugitive Offenders Act 1967 and the Criminal Justice Act 1988, Part I. Still in force is the Suppression of Terrorism Act 1978 which was passed to enable the United Kingdom to ratify the E.C. convention on the Suppression of Terrorism.

(e) The Proceeds of Crime Act 1995 makes further provision for the recovery of proceeds of criminal conduct and for facilitating the enforcement of overseas forfeiture and restraint orders.

---

[8] For a full discussion see Dicey and Morris, *loc cit*, Rule 175.

[9] *Soleimany v. Soleimany* [1999] Q.B. 785; see also *Eco Swiss China Time Ltd v. Benetton International NV* [1999] 2 All E.R. 44 (Comm).

[10] On Customs offences, see Chap. 26.

[11] See C.M. Schmitthoff, "Criminal Offences in Export Trade Law" [1957] J.B.L. 146.

[12] Denning L.J. in *Regazzoni v. KC Sethia (1944) Ltd* [1956] 2 Q.B. 490 at 515; affd [1958] A.C. 301 at 318. See *ante*, para. 21–027.

[13] The rule against the enforcement of foreign revenue laws does not apply to an extradition under the Extradition Acts if the offence committed in the foreign State is an extraditable offence, though directed against the foreign revenue authority: *R. v. Chief Metropolitan Stipendiary Magistrate, ex p. Secretary of State for the Home Department* [1988] 1 W.L.R. 1204. Conspiracy to import dangerous drugs into a foreign country (the U.S.) is an extraditable offence under the Extradition Acts and the bilateral treaty with the foreign country: *Government of the United States v. Bowe* [1990] 1 A.C. 500 (PC on appeal from the Bahamas).

[14] Of 1870, 1895, 1906 and 1932 but not the Extradition Act 1873.

(f) The Criminal Justice (International Co-operation) Act 1990 was enacted to enable the United Kingdom to cooperate more fully with foreign investigation and prosecution of criminal offences and in order that the European Convention on Mutual Assistance in Criminal Matters may be ratified. The Act provides for mutual service of process and provision of evidence,[15] including transfer of prisoners to give evidence, search for relevant material, and measures concerning offences at sea. Matters related to the proceeds of drug trafficking are consolidated, as is the Drug Trafficking Offences Act 1986, in the Drug Trafficking Act 1994.

The third of these rules, namely that an act committed abroad may be punishable in England by virtue of English law, was at least indirectly involved in *R. v. Reiss and John M. Potter Ltd*, decided by Barry J. at Leeds Assizes on December 10, 1956.[16] The accused had exported wool tops from Uruguay directly to Italy and Greece under certificates of origin obtained from the Bradford Chamber of Commerce, certifying falsely that the wool tops were of United Kingdom manufacture. The certificates of origin were obtained in this manner: the accused submitted the usual application forms to the Chamber of Commerce which, in perfect good faith and not suspecting that they contained false details, verified them. The legislation then in force[17] stated that it was an offence for any person who, being within the United Kingdom, aided and abetted, "*without the United Kingdom*", any act which, if committed in the United Kingdom, would be a misdemeanour. The accused were prosecuted and fined £5,000. The Trade Descriptions Act 1968, which has taken the place of that legislation, does not have extra-territorial effect and even provides that there shall be no prosecution in the United Kingdom if a false description is attached to goods intended for dispatch to a destination outside the United Kingdom.[18]

If goods are purchased in the United Kingdom under the false representation that they will be resold in an export market, but they are intended to be sold in the domestic market and the seller, relying on the misrepresentation, charges the (lower) export price, the fraudulent purchaser has committed the offence of obtaining property by deception, contrary to section 15 of the Theft Act 1968.[19] He further commits the tort of deceit and is liable to the seller in damages, which are assessed at the full market value of the goods.[20]

A person dispatching from England a forged end-user certificate purporting

---

[15] In *R. v. Secretary of State for the Home Department ex p. Fininvest SpA* [1997] 1 W.L.R. 743 concerning a letter of request from Italian prosecuting authorities, it was held that the term "evidence" in the Act had a different and wider meaning than earlier legislation and that the involvement of political parties and politicians in the alleged offences did not make the offences political.

[16] Unreported. The case is discussed in [1957] J.B.L. 147.

[17] s. 11 of the Merchandise Marks Act 1887 and 1953. These enactments were repealed by the Trade Descriptions Act 1968.

[18] Trade Descriptions Act 1968, s. 32, as amended (other particulars may be dispensed with by the Board of Trade).

[19] *R. v. Dearlove and Drucker* (the Oxo cubes case) [1988] Crim. L.R. 323; [1988] J.B.L. 167, CA. The offence is committed if the dual price structure contravenes Art. 81(1) of the E.C. Treaty.

[20] *Smith Kline & French Laboratories v. Long* [1989] 1 W.L.R. 1, CA.

to be issued by a foreign authority can be convicted for conspiracy to defraud the foreign authority if the conspiracy would be indictable here, which it would be if the acts to be done and the object to be achieved were in this country.[21] A conspiracy to commit an export offence abroad is only punishable as such if it constitutes, at the same time, a conspiracy to commit a crime in England, *e.g.* the crime of obtaining a pecuniary advantage by deception in England.[22] This rule applies even if the effect of the conspiracy to commit a crime abroad might cause economic loss to somebody in the United Kingdom. Thus, in one case[23] two persons conspired in the United Kingdom to affix on goods situated abroad faked labels of highly reputed merchandise produced in the United Kingdom and to sell these inferior goods under the false labels to a foreign buyer. The damage of such conspiracy to the British export trade was obvious. Nevertheless, the Court of Appeal held that the two wrongdoers could not be prosecuted in England, since the true object of the conspiracy was to defraud purchasers, abroad and an incidental consequence of the conspiracy was not an indictable offence.

Conversely, a conspiracy entered into abroad to commit a crime in England, continues in existence so long as there are two or more parties to it intending to carry out its design; if the conspirators, having still that intention, come to England, the English courts have jurisdiction to try them for conspiracy.[24] In exceptional cases, a dishonest or improper deal abroad by a person resident in England may be punishable in England as conspiracy to commit a public mischief to the prejudice of honest British traders, but the courts approach this crime with caution and circumstances must be very strong to persuade them that it has been committed.[25]

EXCHANGE CONTROL

Exchange contracts under the Bretton Woods Agreement[26]

Although exchange control was abolished in the United Kingdom in 1979, some **21–029** foreign countries still maintain exchange control regulations for the protection of their currency. If such a country is a member of the Bretton Woods Agreement—the United Kingdom is also a member—a contract qualifying as an "exchange contract", which involves the currency of the foreign country in question and is contrary to its exchange control regulations, is unenforceable in the English courts. This is provided by the Bretton Woods Agreements Order in Council 1946[27] which gives force in England to article VIII, section 2(b) of

---

[21] *Board of Trade v. Owen* [1957] A.C. 602.
[22] *R. v. Peter Stanley Cox* [1968] 1 W.L.R. 88; *R. v. Governor of Brixton Prison, ex p. Rush* [1969] 1 W.L.R. 165; *Attorney-General's Reference (No. 1 of 1982)* [1983] Q.B. 751.
[23] *Attorney-General's Reference (No. 1 of 1982)* [1983] 3 W.L.R. 72.
[24] *R. v. Doot* [1973] A.C. 807.
[25] See *R. v. Newland* [1954] 1 Q.B. 158; *Board of Trade v. Owen* [1957] A.C. 602. This principle was not applied in *Attorney-General's Reference (No. 1 of 1982)* [1983] Q.B. 751.
[26] Formerly the International Monetary Fund Agreement.
[27] S.R. & O. 1946 No. 36. This Order in Council was made under the Bretton Woods Agreements Act 1945, later largely repealed, but the Bretton Woods Agreement Order remains in force.

the Bretton Woods Agreement of 1944.[28] This provision is in the following terms:

> "Exchange contracts which involve the currency of any member and which are contrary to the exchange control regulations of that member maintained or imposed consistently with this agreement shall be unenforceable in the territories of any other member."

There is no definition of "exchange contracts". The English court[29] initially took the broad view that they mean "any contracts which in any way affect the country's exchange resources"[30] and they "should be liberally construed having regard to the objects of the Bretton Woods Agreement to protect the currencies of the states who are parties thereto".[31] Later the narrow view was adopted that an exchange contract is in principle only a monetary deal in currencies. The narrow view was subsequently aproved by the House of Lords.[32] However, a genuine commercial contract for the sale and purchase of merchandise or commodities is not an exchange contract, although the price is expressed in a foreign currency. Thus, a contract whereby Italian buyers purchased metal from English dealers but which had not been authorised by the Italian authorities did not qualify as an "exchange contract" and was enforceable against the buyers.[33] However, the Bretton Woods Agreement applied only to exchange contracts and did not affect the legality of banking arrangements entered into in contravention of a country's exchange controls.[34]

Disguised exchange contracts

21–030   An exchange contract may be made in the disguise of an innocent merchandise contract and would then be unenforceable. If a Member State of the Bretton Woods Agreement operates exchange control, a buyer in that State may induce the seller to invoice the goods at a higher price than the true price and ask him to transfer the excess to the buyer's account outside his, the buyer's, country. As far as the excess over the true price is concerned, the transaction is an exchange contract because it involves the transfer of currency from the buyer's country in breach of that country's exchange control regulations. This part of the contract is unenforceable in the English courts, but the part which represents the genuine merchandise transaction is enforceable. This was decided in *United City Merchants (Investments) Ltd v. Royal Bank of Canada; The American Accord.*[35] In this case Glass Fibres and Equipment Ltd, an English company,

---

[28] This is unaffected by the Rome Convention since Art. 21 provides that the Convention shall not prejudice the application of international conventions.

[29] *Sharif v. Azad* [1967] 1 Q.B. 605.

[30] *ibid. per* Lord Denning at 613.

[31] *ibid. per* Diplock L.J. at 618.

[32] *Wilson, Smithett & Cope Ltd v. Terruzzi* [1976] Q.B. 683. See Sir Joseph Gold, "Exchange Contracts, Exchange Control, and the IMF Articles of Agreement; Some Animadversions on Wilson, Smithett & Cope Ltd v. Teruzzi" 33 I.C.L.Q. (1984), 777.

[33] *Wilson, Smithett & Cope Ltd v. Terruzzi* [1976] Q.B. 683.

[34] *Ispahani v. Bank Melli Iran* [1998] Lloyd's Rep. Bank 133.

[35] [1983] 1 A.C. 168. See also *Overseas Union Insurance Ltd v. AA Mutual International Insurance Co Ltd* [1988] 2 Lloyd's Rep. 63 at 70 (reinsurance agreements did not contravene South African exchange control and were not disguised exchange contracts).

sold a glass fibre manufacturing plant to Vitrorefuerzos SA, a Peruvian company. At the request of the buyers, the sellers stated double the genuine purchase price in the invoice, which showed a price of $662,086 f.o.b. U.K. port. The arrangement between the parties was that the excess over the genuine purchase price should be transferred by the sellers to the United States into a "draw down" account, which was at the disposal of the buyers. The House of Lords held that the transaction, as far as the excess over the genuine purchase price was concerned, was an exchange contract in disguise and unenforceable as contravening the Bretton Woods Agreement. Lord Diplock observed that the court must take this point itself, even if not pleaded, and added:

> "But this does not have the effect of making an exchange contract that is contrary to the exchange control regulations of a Member State other than the United Kingdom into a contract that is illegal under English law or render acts undertaken in this country in performance of such a contract unlawful. Like a contract of guarantee of which there is no note or memorandum in writing it is unenforceable by the courts and nothing more."

Similarly, an agreement whereby airline tickets were bought in Iran (a member of the Bretton Woods Agreement) with Iranian currency for the purpose of obtaining a refund on them in pounds sterling in England was a disguised exchange contract. An action on a cheque given by the defendant who allegedly had obtained the refund would have amounted to enforcing an unenforceable contract and would have to be dismissed, provided, of course, that the transaction contravened Iranian exchange control regulations and these regulations were consistent with the Bretton Woods Agreement.[36]

Recognition of foreign exchange control regulations

The exchange control regulations of a foreign state are not classified as revenue **21–031** laws.[37] However where a foreign state seeks to have funds returned which were exported in violation of its exchange control regulations, whether directly or indirectly, it is unlikely that an English court would have jurisdiction to hear the action.[38] This is considered earlier.[39] However, the exchange control regulations of a foreign country, even if it is not a member of the Bretton Woods Agreement, are *recognised* by the English courts in so far as they will not enforce a contract deliberately aimed at the infringement of these regulations.[40]

---

[36] *Mansouri v. Singh* [1986] 1 W.L.R. 1393, CA.
[37] *Kahler v. Midland Bank* [1950] A.C. 24; *Re Lord Cable* [1977] 1 W.L.R. 7.
[38] *Re Lord Cable* [1977] 1 W.L.R. 7.
[39] See *ante*, paras 21–023 to 21–026.
[40] *ibid.*

CHAPTER 22

JURISDICTION[1]

22–001 Exporters must contemplate the possibility of a dispute arising out an international commercial transaction. When entering into an international contract, the exporter should ensure that it contains an unambiguous jurisdiction clause[2] which provides for the court of the country having jurisdiction to adjudicate in the event of any disputes between the parties.[3] Should an English exporter wish disputes to be settled by the English court, he should during negotiations endeavour to press for a jurisdiction clause which so provides. A choice of law clause is equally desirable.[4] If the contract fails to provide for jurisdiction and choice of law, the court which assumes jurisdiction over the dispute will determine the law to be applied to the contract in accordance with its own choice of law rules. Litigation concerning jurisdiction and/or choice of law can be extremely expensive.

If the exporter obtains a judgment he can then seek to enforce it against the defendants' assets within the jurisdiction or abroad.[5]

This Chapter is concerned primarily with jurisdiction *in personam*.[6] For *in personam* jurisdiction there are three relevant sets of rules, which are based on the domicile[7] of the defendant. They apply to:

(a) Those defendants not domiciled in E.C.[8] or EFTA[9] Contracting States. These are governed by the traditional law, which includes common law and statutory rules.

(b) Those defendants domiciled in E.C. or EFTA Contracting States, for whom the rules are set out in the Brussels and Lugano Conventions respectively.[10]

---

[1] See generally Dicey and Morris, *Conflict of Laws* (13th ed. 2000); *Halsbury's Laws*, Vol. 8(1).
[2] Or arbitration clause, see Chap. 23.
[3] But in certain circumstances an express jurisdiction agreement may be disregarded, see *post*, paras 22–008 and 22–010.
[4] See Chap. 21.
[5] See Chap. 24.
[6] An *in personam* action is against a person, including a company. An *in rem* action is against a *res*, usually a ship, on which see *post*, para. 22–033.
[7] See *post*, para. 22–002.
[8] European Community.
[9] European Free Trade Association.
[10] The European Community Convention on Jurisdiction and the Enforcement of Judgments in Civil and Commercial Matters 1968, the Brussels Convention, was enacted into U.K. law by the Civil Jurisdiction and Judgments Act 1982, which came into force on January 1, 1987. The Brussels Convention and the 1982 Act were amended to accommodate the accession of Greece (S.I. 1989 No. 1364), then on the accession of Spain and Portugal—also known as the San Sebastian Conven-

(c) Those defendants domiciled in the United Kingdom. These rules are set out in the Modified Convention.[11]

The domicile provisions for all three sets of rules are set out in sections 41–46[12] of the Civil Jurisdiction and Judgments Act as amended, hereafter referred to as "the 1982 Act".

In order for a legal action to commence, the defendant must be served with a claim form.[13] For a defendant domiciled in neither an E.C. nor an EFTA State it is necessary to obtain the permission of the court in order to serve a claim form out of the jurisdiction. The rules concerning service out on non-E.C. or EFTA domiciliaries are set out in the Rules of the Supreme Court, Order 11, rule 1(1)[13a]. For E.C. and EFTA domiciliaries, in accordance with Order 11, rule 1(2) no permission is required where the Brussels or Lugano Conventions[14] apply. Both rules will be quoted in full insofar as they are relevant to exporters.[15]

Also considered in this Chapter under the traditional rules are the circumstances in which the English court may stay an English action or restrain by injunction a foreign action.

This Chapter is concerned only with the jurisdictional aspects of the Conventions. The provisions for enforcement of judgments will be dealt with in Chapter 24.

There will also be a brief summary of freezing injunctions (previously Mareva Injunctions) and search orders (previously Anton Piller Orders), both of which are forms of interim relief. A freezing injunction freezes the defendants' assets to prevent their pre-trial dissipation and a search order may be granted in order to seize documents and other material to prevent their destruction.

Finally, there will be a brief summary of *in rem* jurisdiction.

DOMICILE

It is important to note that, for jurisdictional purposes, domicile is determined **22–002** in accordance with the extensive provisions of sections 41–46 of the 1982 Act, irrespective of whether or not a party is domiciled in an E.C. or EFTA Con-

---

tion (S.I. 1990 No. 2591) where the Convention itself was also amended, and again by the Civil Jurisdiction and Judgments Act 1991 (in force May 1, 1992 (S.I. 1992 No. 745), enacting the Lugano Convention into U.K. law. The Lugano Convention aims to strengthen legal and economic co-operation between the E.C. and EFTA States. It is a parallel Convention to the Brussels Convention and is thus also known as the parallel Convention. The provisions of the two Conventions are very largely the same. The Brussels Convention is appended as Sched. 1 and the Lugano Convention as Sched. 3C to the 1982 Act.

[11] This provides for allocation of jurisdiction between different parts of the U.K. and is appended as Sched. 4 to the 1982 Act. It will not be considered further.

[12] See *post*, para. 22–002.

[13] For how this is done see *post*, para. 22–029.

[13a] RSC Order 11 has been replaced by Part 6 of the Civil Procedure Rules (CPR).

[14] Hereafter referred to as "the Conventions".

[15] RSC Ord. 11, r. 1(1) when the traditional rules are considered and RSC Ord. 11, r. 1(2) when the Conventions are dealt with. Order 11 has been reenacted with amendments in Schedule 1 of the CPR, but see 13a, *infra*.

tracting State.[16] There are additional provisions in the Act for allocation of jurisdiction within the United Kingdom[17] and Scotland.[18]

Section 41 sets out the rules, subject to Article 52,[19] for determining whether an individual is domiciled in the United Kingdom, and if so, which part. Section 41(2) provides:

> "An individual is domiciled in the United Kingdom if:
>
> (a) he is resident in the United Kingdom; and
> (b) the nature and circumstances of his residence indicate that he has a substantial connection with the United Kingdom."

However, in essence, it is presumed that an individual is domiciled where he has been resident "for the last three months or more".[20]

Article 52 provides:

> "In order to determine whether a party is domiciled in a Contracting State whose courts are seised of a matter, the Court shall apply its internal law.
>
> If a party is not domiciled in the State whose courts are seised of the matter, then, in order to determine whether the party is domiciled in another Contracting State, the court shall apply the law of that State."

This means that a U.K. court will apply its law to decide if a party is domiciled in the United Kingdom. If it decides that the party is not domiciled in the United Kingdom, it must apply the national law of another state to determine if the person is domiciled in that state.

For an individual not domiciled in an E.C. or EFTA Contracting State, section 41(7) provides:

> "An individual is domiciled in a state other than a Contracting State if and only if—
>
> (a) he is resident in that state; and
> (b) the nature and circumstances of his residence indicate that he has a substantial connection with that state."

However, there is no "last three months or more" presumption.

If the defendant is a company, corporation or association, the 1982 Act provides[21] that its "seat" shall be treated as its domicile and for the purposes of Article 53, goes on to define "seat" for a U.K. corporation[22]:

---

[16] RSC Ord. 11, r. 1(4) (see now CPR, Pt 6.18(g)). The common law rules for determining domicile are of no relevance for determining jurisdiction.
[17] Art. 5, Sched. 4 of the 1982 Act.
[18] Sched. 8 of the 1982 Act.
[19] See below.
[20] s. 41(6)(b).
[21] s. 42(1).
[22] s. 42(3). A company may satisfy the test for the location of its seat, within the meaning of the Act, in relation to more than one State: *The Deichland* [1989] 3 W.L.R. 478 at 488. See also *The Rewia* [1991] 2 Lloyd's Rep. 325.

"A corporation or association has its seat in the United Kingdom if and only if

  (a) it was incorporated or formed under the law of a part of the United Kingdom and has its registered office or some other official address in the United Kingdom; or
  (b) its central management and control is exercised in the United Kingdom."

Article 53 of the Convention provides:

"For the purposes of this Convention, the seat of a company or other legal person or association of natural or legal persons shall be treated as its domicile. However, in order to determine that seat, the court shall apply its rules of private international law."

TRADITIONAL RULES

Where a defendant is not domiciled in an E.C. or EFTA Contracting State, the **22–003** English courts have jurisdiction over claims arising from contractual relations if:

1. the defendant is in England and Wales and is served with a writ there;
2. if, though he is not in England or Wales,

(a) he has submitted to the jurisdiction of the English courts; or

(b) the courts assume jurisdiction over him in accordance with the Rules of the Supreme Court, Order 11.[23]

Under 1 above, the English court has jurisdiction over a foreign defendant if he is validly served with a claim form, even if he is only within its jurisdiction on a fleeting visit.[24] This is known as "exorbitant" jurisdiction. However, the defendant may apply for a stay on the ground of *forum non conveniens*.[25]

Under 2(a) above, where a foreign defendant voluntarily submits to the jurisdiction of an English court, the court is normally prepared to exercise jurisdiction over him. It is not regarded as a voluntary submission if the defendant appears before the court solely to contest its jurisdiction. In proceedings in the English courts the defendant may dispute the jurisdiction of the court by virtue of CPR, Part 11.

If the defendant does more than merely contest the jurisdiction, that is if he takes any steps to defend on the merits, he is treated as having submitted to the jurisdiction of the court. An application to the English court for a stay of proceedings pending the outcome of proceedings in a foreign court does not amount to submission to the English jurisdiction,[26] nor does an application to discharge a freezing injunction issued against the defendant constitute a submission to the

---

[23] As reenacted in Schedule 1 of the CPR, see now CPR, Pt. 6.
[24] *Maharanee of Baroda v. Wildenstein* [1972] 2 Q.B.; *Colt Industries v. Sarlie* [1966] 1 All E.R. 673.
[25] See *post*, para. 22–007.
[26] *Williams & Glyn's Bank plc v. Astro Dinamico Compañía Naviera SA* [1984] 1 W.L.R. 438.

jurisdiction over the main action.[27] It seems that as long as the defendant expressly reserves the position that he contests the jurisdiction of the court, he will not be found to have submitted by making an application in the action,[28] by complying with an order for disclosure,[29] or by making an application for security for costs for his challenge to jurisdiction.[30]

Under 2(b) above, the circumstances under which the English court may assume jurisdiction are set out in RSC Order 11, rule 1(1)[30a].

RSC Order 11, rule 1(1)[31]

22–004
"Provided that the claim form is not a claim form to which paragraph (2) of this rule applies, a claim form may be served out of the jurisdiction with the permission of the Court if—

(a) relief is sought against a person domiciled within the jurisdiction;

(b) an injunction is sought ordering the defendant to do or refrain from doing anything within the jurisdiction (whether or not damages are also claimed in respect of a failure to do or the doing of that thing);

(c) the claim is brought against a person duly served within or out of the jurisdiction and a person out of the jurisdiction is a necessary or proper party thereto;

(d) the claim is brought to enforce, rescind, dissolve, annul or otherwise affect a contract, or to recover damages or obtain other remedy in respect of the breach of a contract, being (in either case) a contract which—

    (i) was made within the jurisdiction, or

    (ii) was made by or through an agent trading or residing within the jurisdiction on behalf of a principal trading or residing out of the jurisdiction, or

    (iii) is by its terms, or by implication, governed by English law, or

    (iv) contains a term to the effect that the High Court shall have jurisdiction to hear and determine any action in respect of the contract;

(e) the claim is brought in respect of a breach committed within the jurisdiction of a contract made within or out of the jurisdiction, and irrespective of the fact, if such be the case, that the breach was preceded or accompanied by a breach committed out of the jurisdiction that rendered impossible the performance of so much of the contract as ought to have been performed within the jurisdiction;

(f) the claim is founded on a tort and the damage was sustained, or resulted from an act committed, within the jurisdiction;

(g) . . .–(l). . .

(m) the claim is brought to enforce any judgment or arbitral award;

(n) . . .–(u). . ."

The application for permission to serve out

22–005 As the application is made without notice, the written evidence accompanying it must contain frank disclosure of the material facts on which it is based. Failure

---

[27] *Obikoya v. Silvernorth Ltd, The Times,* July 6, 1983. The adoption of English law as the proper law of the contract does not necessarily mean submission to the jurisdiction of the courts of this country: *Dundee Ltd v. Gilman & Co (Australia) Pty Ltd* [1968] 2 Lloyd's Rep. 394 (Sup. Ct. of N.S.W.). Where a foreign plaintiff has commenced proceedings in the English courts, he is regarded as having submitted to a counterclaim by the defendant: *Metal Scrap Trade Corp Ltd v. Kate Shipping Co Ltd* [1990] 1 W.L.R. 115; *Derby & Co Ltd v. Larsson* [1976] 1 W.L.R. 202; see also *Balkanbank v. Taher (No. 2)* [1995] 1 W.L.R. 1067.

[28] *Williams & Glyn's Bank, ante.*

[29] *The Xing Su Hai* [1995] 2 Lloyd's Rep. 15.

[30] Dicey & Morris, *loc cit.,* para. 11–111.

[30a] See now CPR, Pt. 6.20.

[31] RSC Ord. 11 includes a useful commentary on these rules, see 30a, *infra.*

to do this may lead to permission subsequently being set aside.[32] In addition, the claimant must show clearly that the case falls within the rule on which the application is based. The written evidence must be sufficiently full to establish the claimant's right to permission to the standards of proof governing the different elements of his application, and must set out sufficient facts to show that England is the forum conveniens.[33] It is for the applicant to satisfy the court that it is proper for it to exercise its discretion to grant permission. "No such permission shall be granted unless it shall be made sufficiently to appear to the Court that the case is a proper one for service out of the jurisdiction under this Order."[34]

Guidelines for the court in the exercise of its discretion under the *forum conveniens* and *forum non conveniens* doctrines are laid down in the judgment of Lord Goff in the *Spiliada*[35] case. The principles governing *forum conveniens*, where the court is exercising its discretion as to whether to grant the plaintiff leave to serve out, and *forum non conveniens*, where the defendant applies for a stay of an English action in order for the action to be heard in a foreign court, are the same except for the burden of proof. In Order 11[35a] cases the burden of proof is on the party applying for leave, whereas in stay cases the burden is on the party applying for a stay.

Stay of English proceedings and restraint of foreign proceedings

In cases with an international element, it may well be that proceedings have **22–006** been commenced in more than one jurisdiction between the same parties on the same cause of action, in circumstances where both the English and foreign court have jurisdiction to decide the matter. This is known as *lis alibi pendens*. In order to avoid the duplication of proceedings, with the accompanying risk of inconsistent judgments, and so that a case may be heard in the most appropriate forum to prevent injustice, the English court has a discretion[36] to stay an English action or restrain an action in a foreign court. The principles on which an action may be stayed or restrained are not the same.[37] Both applications have become increasingly important, one reason being to avoid "forum shopping", *i.e.* the claimant seeking the jurisdiction where it may be easier to prove his claim or where his award of damages may be greater.

Stay on the ground of forum non conveniens

Although the doctrine of *forum non conveniens* has been part of Scottish law **22–007** for many years, it was not until recently that the English courts finally followed

---

[32] *The Hagen* [1908] P. 189.

[33] These principles are derived from a number of cases but are conveniently set out in the House of Lords case *Seaconsar Far East Ltd v. Bank Markazi Jomhouri Islami Iran* [1993] 3 W.L.R. 756.

[34] RSC Ord. 11, r. 4(2), see now CPR, Pt 6.21(2A).

[35] *Spiliada Maritime Corp v. Cansulex Ltd* [1986] A.C. 460. This case will be considered in detail below.

[35a] Now CPR, Pt 6.

[36] Supreme Court Act 1981, s. 49(3) and also an inherent discretion.

[37] *Société Nationale Industriale Aerospatiale v. Lee Kui Jak* [1987] A.C. 871.

the Scottish lead in applying the doctrine to stay cases.[38] It had, however, been applied to applications for service out of the jurisdiction.

In *The Spiliada*,[39] after reviewing the development of the law, Lord Goff set out the principles to be considered by the court in a stay application[40] as follows:

> "(a) The basic principle is that a stay will only be granted on the ground of forum non conveniens where the court is satisfied that there is some other available forum, having competent jurisdiction, which is the appropriate forum for the trial of the action, *i.e.* in which the case may be tried more suitably for the interests of all the parties and the ends of justice.

> (b) . . . In general the burden of proof rests on the defendant to persuade the court to exercise its discretion to grant a stay . . . [but] if the court is satisfied that there is another available forum . . ., the burden will then shift to the plaintiff to show that there are special circumstances . . . which justice requires that the trial should nevertheless take place in this country . . .

> (c) It is significant that in all the leading English cases where a stay has been granted there has been another clearly more appropriate forum . . . the burden resting on the defendant is not just to show that England is not the natural or appropriate forum, but to establish that there is another available forum which is clearly or distinctly more appropriate . . . [If] the connection of the defendant with the English forum is a fragile one (for example, if he is served with proceedings during a short visit to this country), it should be all the easier for him to prove that there is another clearly more appropriate forum for the trial overseas.

> (d) . . . [t]he court will look first to see what factors there are which point in the direction of another forum. . . . So it is for connecting factors . . . that the court must first look; and these will include not only factors affecting convenience or expense (such as the availability of witnesses), but also other factors such as the law governing the relevant transaction . . . and the places where the parties respectively reside or carry on business.

> (e) If the court concludes at that stage that there is no other available forum which is clearly more appropriate for the trial of the action, it will ordinarily refuse a stay . . .

> (f) If, however, the court concludes at that stage that there is some other available forum which prima facie is clearly more appropriate for the trial of the action, it will ordinarily grant a stay unless there are circumstances by reason of which justice requires that a stay should nevertheless not be granted. In this inquiry, the court will consider all the circumstances of the case, including circumstances which go beyond those taken into account when considering connecting factors with the other jurisdiction. One such factor can be the fact, if established objectively by cogent evidence, that the plaintiff will not obtain justice in the foreign jurisdiction . . . [but here] the burden shifts to the plaintiff."

Of "a legitimate personal or juridical advantage"[41] Lord Goff said[42]: "Clearly, the mere fact that the plaintiff has such an advantage in proceedings in England cannot be decisive."[43] He went on to say: "The key to the solution of this problem lies . . . in the underlying principle. We have to consider where the case may be tried 'suitably for the interests of all the parties and for the ends of justice'." An important consideration was the "*Cambridgeshire* factor".[44]

---

[38] For development see Dicey and Morris, *loc cit.*, paras 12–007 to 12–010.
[39] *Spiliada Maritime Corp v. Cansulex Ltd; The Spiliada* [1987] A.C. 460.
[40] *ibid.*, at 476–478.
[41] *Per* Lord Diplock in *MacShannon v. Rockware Glass Ltd* [1978] A.C. 795.
[42] *The Spiliada* [1987] A.C. 460 at 482–484.
[43] Examples of "a legitimate personal or juridical advantage" to which he referred are: damages awarded on a higher scale, a more complete procedure of discovery, a power to award interest, a more generous limitation period, obtaining security for a claim (although the granting of a stay may be conditional on the retention of security), action time barred in the more appropriate forum.
[44] Experienced teams of lawyers and experts on both sides had been involved in a case concerning The Cambridgeshire in which the facts were very similar to those in *Spiliada*.

Since *Spiliada* a number of *forum non conveniens* cases have been considered by the English courts.[45]

Stays and exclusive foreign jurisdiction agreements

Where the parties have contractually agreed that a specified foreign court is to **22–008** have exclusive jurisdiction in the event of any disputes between them, the English court will, in general, hold them to their agreement by staying an action brought in an English court in breach of that agreement. The principles to be considered in granting a stay in such a situation were set out in *The Eleftheria*[46]:

"(1) ... the English court ... is not bound to grant a stay but has a discretion whether to do so or not.
(2) The discretion should be exercised by granting a stay unless strong cause for not doing so is shown.

---

[45] Including *EI du Pont de Nemours v. Agnew* [1987] 2 Lloyd's Rep. 399 (where there are public policy considerations in relation to a contract governed by English law, a stay will not be granted where the foreign court would apply its own law and public policy); *Banco SA v. The British Bank of the Middle East* [1990] 1 Lloyd's Rep. 504 (it will be unusual for a stay to be granted where the defendant had a very solid connection with England and, in addition, the foreign court would apply its own law (whereby the plaintiffs would not win) instead of the governing law of the contract); *Minories Finance Ltd v. Afribank Nigeria Ltd* [1995] 1 Lloyd's Rep. 134 (a stay would not be granted where expert witnesses are in England, there would probably be a considerable delay in getting Nigerian Exchange Control approval and remitting U.S. dollars, and probably a considerable delay in enforcing a judgment in Nigeria, whereas an English judgment could be enforced against assets in Ireland); *Milor Srl v. British Airways plc* [1996] 1 W.L.R. 1483; (the application of *forum non conveniens* was inconsistent with Art. 28 of the Warsaw Convention); *Mohammed v. Bank of Kuwait and the Middle East KSC* [1996] 1 W.L.R. 1483 (the circumstances at the time of an order and those at the time of the hearing should be taken into account when considering whether an alternative forum was available in order to consider whether substantial justice could be achieved there); *HIB Ltd v. Guardian Insurance Co Inc* [1997] 1 Lloyd's Rep. 412 (in a case governed by English law, it is inappropriate for a plaintiff to seek damages in a forum other than the most natural forum, particularly where it was inferred that the plaintiff wished to claim punitive damages for bad faith, which was available under the local foreign law but not English law); *Connolly v. RTZ Corporation* [1997] 3 W.L.R. 373 (as a general rule a stay will be refused even if no financial assistance is available to the claimant in the appropriate forum. Exceptionally, however, the fact that legal aid or a conditional fee arrangement was available in England would be a relevant factor if substantial justice could not be done without financial assistance, even if the foreign forum was clearly the most appropriate one; see also *Carlson v. Rio Tinto Plc* [1999] C.L.C. 551); *Owners of the ship Herceg Novi v. Owners of the ship Ming Galaxy: The Herceg Novi* [1998] 2 Lloyd's Rep. 454: a stay would be granted despite the availability of a higher limit of liability under the Convention on Limitation of Liability or Maritime Claims 1976, which applied in England, as opposed to the Convention Relating to the Limitation of the Liability of Owners of Seagoing Ships of 1957. It could not be said that the party bringing the English action would be deprived of a legitimate juridical advantage); *Askin v. ABSA Bank Ltd, The Times*, February 23, 1999 (it is for the defendant to establish the availability of an alternative appropriate forum, then for the plaintiff to establish that justice demanded an English trial. At that stage, the availability of the alternative forum in the broader sense becomes relevant); *Lubbe v. Cape Plc* and related appeals [2000] 1 W.L.R. 1545 (the House of Lords decided that although South Africa was the appropriate forum, a stay would lead to a denial of justice to the claimants since no legal aid was available there for personal injury claims and it was unlikely that they would be able to obtain legal representation on a contingency fee basis. In addition, there were no developed procedures in South Africa to deal with group actions, although this would not, on its own, be sufficient reason for a stay).

[46] [1970] P. 94 at 110. These principles were approved by the Court of Appeal in *The El Amria* [1982] 2 Lloyd's Rep. 119 and further approved by the House of Lords in *The Sennar (No. 2)* [1985] 1 W.L.R. 490.

(3) The burden of showing such strong cause is on the plaintiffs.

(4) In exercising its discretion the court should take into account all the circumstances of the case.

(5) In particular, but without prejudice to (4), the following matters, where they arise, may be properly regarded:

> (a) In what country the evidence on the issues of fact is situated, or more readily available, and the effect of that on the relative convenience and expense of trial as between the English and foreign courts.
>
> (b) Whether the law of the foreign court applies and, if so, whether it differs from English law in any material respects.
>
> (c) With what country either party is connected, and how closely.
>
> (d) Whether the defendants genuinely desire trial in the foreign country, or are only seeking procedural advantages.
>
> (e) Whether the plaintiffs would be prejudiced by having to sue in the foreign court because they would:
>
>> (i) be deprived of security for their claim;
>>
>> (ii) be unable to enforce any judgment obtained;
>>
>> (iii) be faced with a time bar not applicable in England;
>>
>> (iv) for political, racial, religious or other reasons be unlikely to get a fair trial."

In deciding whether to grant a stay on the basis that the action is time barred in the foreign court, the English court will take into account whether the party applying for the stay has acted reasonably in allowing his action to become time barred.[47] Thus, where a party had deliberately allowed the action to become time barred in the foreign juridisction without instituting proceedings there and the foreign court was clearly the most appropriate forum, a stay was refused.[48]

A stay was refused even though the action may have been time barred in the foreign forum; the fact that there was an amount of evidence in England but probably also in the foreign forum would not be sufficient to displace the contractual jurisdiction agreement,[49] nor was it appropriate to compare the way in which different well-established systems of law would approach the same set of facts.[50]

If the parties have contractually agreed the foreign forum and it was the natural and most appropriate forum, the fact that costs were not available to the winning party was not a sufficient disadvantage and the English action would be stayed.[51]

When an foreign exclusive jurisdiction clause is in contravention of an English statute it will be void.[52]

When a party seeks leave to serve out under RSC Order 11, rule 1[52a] and the contract contains an exclusive English jurisdiction clause, leave will normally be refused.[53]

---

[47] *Spiliada Maritime Corp v. Cansulex Ltd* [1987] A.C. 4650 at 483–484.

[48] *The Pioneer Container* [1994] 2 A.C. 324; *cf. Citi-March Ltd v. Neptune Orient Lines* [1996] 2 All E.R. 454 (although the plaintiffs had deliberately allowed their action in the foreign jurisdiction to become time barred, they had not acted unreasonably. England was clearly the appropriate forum and there was a risk of concurrent proceedings in England and Singapore and thus inconsistent decisions).

[49] *The Bergen (No. 2)* [1997] 2 Lloyd's Rep. 710.

[50] *ibid. Spiliada.*

[51] *The Nile Rhapsody* [1994] 1 Lloyd's Rep. 382.

[52] *The Hollandia* [1983] 1 A.C. 565.

[52a] See now CPR, Pt 6.20.

[53] *British Aerospace plc v. Dee Howard & Co* [1993] 3 Lloyd's Rep. 368.

Restraint of foreign proceedings

It is well established that the English courts have the discretion to restrain by **22–009** injunction[54] a party from instituting or continuing proceedings in a foreign court. Nevertheless, this is an indirect interference with the foreign court and therefore the English court must exercise caution,[55] especially where the foreign plaintiff has brought an action in his own court.[56] The principles to be applied by the court are not the same as for *forum non conveniens.*[57]

The leading case is now *Société Nationale Industrielle Aerospatiale v. Lee Kui Jak*[58] (hereafter referred to as *Aerospatiale*), where Lord Goff set out the basic principles relating to anti-suit injunctions:

(a) The jurisdiction is exercised when the "ends of justice" require it.

(b) The jurisdiction is exercised against a person not the foreign court.[59]

(c) The injunction must be an effective remedy against the person.

(d) The jurisdiction must be exercised with caution.

He recognised that these basic principles did not provide much guidance to judges in deciding whether to exercise their discretion to restrain foreign proceedings. He went on to say that the English court would only grant an injunction restraining a party from proceeding in a foreign court if maintaining such proceedings would be vexatious or oppressive to the defendant. As a general rule, the court must conclude that the English court is the natural forum. The court will not grant an injunction if it would be unjust to deprive the plaintiff of the advantages available to him in the foreign court.

Very shortly before *Aerospatiale*, the House of Lords[60] set out categories of cases where an injunction may be granted and stated that there were no others. They are:

(a) Where there is more than one available forum and England is one of them.

(b) Where by bringing proceedings abroad one party has invaded a legal or equitable right of the other party not to be sued abroad.

(c) Where the bringing of proceedings abroad would be unconscionable.

In *Aerospatiale*, Lord Goff said that these categories provided useful guidance but that the law was in a continuous state of development.

---

[54] Also known as an anti-suit injunction.
[55] *British Airways Board v. Laker Airways* [1985] A.C. 58; *Société Nationale Aerospatiale v. Lee Kui Jak* [1987] A.C. 871.
[56] *Metall und Rohstoff AG v. ACLI Metals Ltd* [1984] 1 Lloyd's Rep. 598.
[57] *Société Nationale Aerospatiale v. Lee Kui Jak* [1987] A.C. 871.
[58] [1987] A.C. 871.
[59] *i.e.* it is based on the English court's *in personam* jurisdiction over the party and not because it purports to have any extraterritorial jurisdiction over the foreign court.
[60] In *South Carolina Insurance Co v. Assurantie NV* [1987] A.C. 24.

Where there was an overwhelming case that England was the natural forum and the U.S. proceedings were oppressive, particularly in view of contingency fee arrangements and pre-trial discovery, the U.S. proceedings were restrained.[61]

If the plaintiff has no remedy in England,[62] a restraining injunction could be granted where the foreign action was unconscionable, such that it amounted to an infringement of an equitable right.[63] The case concerned anti-trust proceedings in the United States, in connection with an alleged conspiracy by airlines operating in the United States to put Laker Airways out of business. An injunction was refused since by operating in the United States, British Airways accepted that they were subject to U.S. law. However, in another Laker Airways case[64] Midland Bank was granted a restraining injunction. Unlike British Airways, their business activities had been carried on largely in England, and it would be unjust and unconscionable to allow Laker Airways to bring an anti-trust suit against them in the United States.

An unusual situation occurred in which a plaintiff sought to have his own English action stayed in favour of continuing his New York action against the same defendant. The defendant applied to have the New York action restrained. The court had thus to consider both applications. Since the defendant was resident and carrying on his activities in the jurisdiction, the English action would not be stayed. However, having decided that the English action would not be stayed, it would cause substantial injustice to the defendant if he had to fight on two fronts and an injunction restraining the New York action was granted.[65]

The House of Lords has held[66] that, as a general rule, comity required that in order to grant an anti-suit injunction the English court had to have a sufficient interest in, or connection with, the matter in question. The English court having no such interest,[67] an anti-suit injunction would not be granted even where the proceedings in Texas might be oppressive due, *inter alia*, to the absence at that time of the doctrine of *forum conveniens* in Texas, and where India was the appropriate forum.

Restraint and exclusive English jurisdiction agreement

22–010 Where the contract contains an express exclusive English jurisdiction clause, it is prima facie the policy of the court to hold the parties to their agreement. This is not an inflexible rule and the court has a discretion which would be exercised in favour of holding the parties to their bargain where there was no strong reason to the contrary.[68] The English court will not be cautious in granting an injunction restraining the foreign proceedings[69] where delay had caused no real prejudice

---

[61] *Simon Engineering plc v. Butte Mining plc (No. 2)* [1996] 1 Lloyd's Rep. 91.
[62] Called single forum cases.
[63] *British Airways Board v. Laker Airways Ltd* [1985] A.C. 58.
[64] *Midland Bank plc v. Laker Airways Ltd* [1986] Q.B. 689.
[65] *Advanced Portfolio Technologies Inc v. Ainsworth* [1996] F.S.R. 217.
[66] *Airbus Industrie GIE v. Patel* [1998] 2 W.L.R. 686.
[67] No proceedings had been instituted in England.
[68] *The Chaparral* [1968] 2 Lloyd's Rep. 158; *Shell International Petroleum Co Ltd v. Coral Oil Ltd* [1999] 1 Lloyd's Rep. 72.
[69] *The Angelic Grace* [1995] 1 Lloyd's Rep. 87 (foreign action commenced in breach of an arbitration agreement).

and the Texas action was for a negative declaration which ought not to be encouraged.[70] Moreover, the enforcement of a contractual promise was not an interference with the foreign court and an injunction was granted on condition that the applicant gave a satisfactory undertaking as to security.[71]

However, to grant an injunction restraining a party from enforcing a foreign judgment obtained in breach of a London arbitration clause, is a far greater interference in the foreign judicial process than restraining a foreign action brought in violation of such an agreement.[72] Where the defendant had boasted of his ability to manipulate the Sierra Leone legal system, this amounted to sufficient evidence of vexation and oppression for the injunction to be maintained, even though the plaintiff had submitted to the jurisdiction.[73]

THE BRUSSELS AND LUGANO CONVENTIONS

As mentioned in the introduction to this Chapter, no leave is required to serve **22–011** a writ on an E.C. or EFTA domiciled defendant where the provisions of RSC Order 11, rule 1(2)[73a] apply.

RSC Order 11, rule 1(2)

"A claim form may be served out of the jurisdiction on a defendant without the permission **22–012** of the Court provided that each claim against that defendant is either—

(a) a claim which by virtue of the Civil Jurisdiction and Judgments Act 1982 the Court has power to hear and determine made in proceedings to which the following conditions apply—

(i) no proceedings between the parties concerning the same cause of action are pending in the courts of any other part of the United Kingdom or of any other Convention territory, and

(ii) either—
the defendant is domiciled in any part of the United Kingdom or in any other Convention territory, or the proceedings begun by the claim form are proceedings to which Article 16 of Schedule 1, 3C or 4 refers, or the defendant is a party to an agreement conferring jurisdiction to which Article 17 of Schedule 1, 3C or 4 to that Act applies, or

(b) a claim which by virtue of any other enactment the High Court has power to hear and determine notwithstanding that the person against whom the claim is made is not within the jurisdiction of the Court or that the wrongful act, neglect or default giving rise to the claim did not take place within its jurisdiction."

RSC Order 11, rule 1A goes on to prescribe the period to be inserted in the claim form, within which service must be acknowledged or an admission served by the defendant, and rule 1B[73b] the period within which he must file a defence.

---

[70] *Sohio Supply Co v. Gatoil (U.S.A.) Inc* [1989] 1 Lloyd's Rep. 588.
[71] *Ultisol Transport Contractors Ltd v. Bouygues Offshore SA* [1996] 2 Lloyd's Rep. 140.
[72] *Industrial Maritime Carriers (Bahamas) Inc v. Sinoca International Inc (The Eastern Trader)* [1996] 2 Lloyd's Rep. 285.
[73] *A/S D/S Svendborg v. Wansa* [1996] 2 Lloyd's Rep. 559.
[73a] See now CPR, Pt. 6.19.
[73b] For Rules 1A and 1B see now CPR, Pt. 6.22 and 6.23 respectively.

Interpretation of the Conventions

22–013 A number of Official Reports may be consulted as an aid to interpretation of the Brussels Convention, amongst them those of Mr P. Jenard and Professor Peter Schlosser,[74] and on the Lugano Convention the report of Mr P. Jenard and Mr G. Möller.[75] Appellate courts may request the European Court of Justice (the E.C.J.) to give a preliminary ruling on questions of interpretation of the Brussels Convention[76] or, when they feel a decision is necessary in order to make a judgment, an appellate court may request a ruling and the House of Lords must so request.[77] An English court is bound by the principles laid down by, and any relevant decisions of, the E.C.J.

The Lugano Convention contains no provisions for reference to the E.C.J. Instead, it is provided that the courts of each Contracting State shall pay due account to the decisions of the courts of other Contracting States on the interpretation of the Convention.[78] It is further provided that a system is to be set up for an exchange of information and consultation between the contracting states, such information to be collated, and also for an exchange of views on the functioning of the Convention.[79] The E.C.J. should, when interpreting the Brussels Convention, take due account of rulings on the Lugano Convention by EFTA courts and vice versa.[80] The Lugano Convention provides[81] that it shall not prejudice the operation of the Brussels Convention. Consequently, if the dispute concerns persons in two E.C. Contracting States, the Brussels Convention applies; if it involves persons in two EFTA countries the Lugano Convention is applicable. Where one of the parties is domiciled in a Brussels Convention State and the other in a Lugano Convention country, no difficulty should arise since the rules of application are the same in both Conventions. The Conventions are drafted in a number of different languages and each language version is equally authentic.[82]

Area of application of the Conventions

22–014 The Conventions apply to civil and commercial matters,[83] whatever the nature of the court or tribunal, but do not extend to revenue,[84] customs or administrative measures.[85] They also do not apply to:

---

[74] [1979] O.J. C59/71. See s. 3(3) of the Act.
[75] [1990] O.J. C189/57. See s. 3B(2) of the Act.
[76] Sched. 2, Art. 2.
[77] Sched. 2, Art. 3.
[78] Protocol No. 2, Art. 1 of the Lugano Convention.
[79] *ibid.*, Arts 2–4.
[80] s. 3B(1) of the 1982 Act.
[81] Art. 54B.
[82] Art. 68.
[83] "Civil and commercial matters" are to be given a Community and not a national interpretation: Case 29/76 *LTU Lufttransportuntemehmen GmbH & Co KG v. Eurocontrol* [1976] E.C.R. 1541.
[84] *QRS 1 Aps. v. Frandsen* [1999] 3 All E.R. 289.
[85] Brussels Convention, Art. 1.

"1. The status or legal capacity of natural persons, rights in property arising out of matrimonial relationship, wills and succession;
2. Bankruptcy, proceedings relating to the winding up of insolvent companies or other legal persons, judicial arrangements, compositions and analogous proceedings;
3. Social security;
4. Arbitration."[86]

Jurisdiction provisions

The general rule,[87] subject to exceptions, is that E.C. and EFTA domiciliaries **22–015** shall be sued in the courts of the State of their domicile. However, the Conventions recognise the parties' freedom to agree which courts shall have jurisdiction in the event of any dispute between them.[88] They also recognise, subject to exceptions, the submission of a defendant to a court other than that which has jurisdiction except where he appears solely to contest jurisdiction.[89]

Special jurisdiction is provided for, in Articles 5 to 6A, for insurance contracts,[90] consumer contracts,[91] and exclusive jurisdiction for disputes relating to immovable property.[92] There are also provisions for a court's examination of the jurisdiction and admissability thereof,[93] for concurrent or related actions,[94] and applications for provisional, including protective, measures.[95]

Prorogation of jurisdiction

Article 17 of the Convention provides: **22–016**

"If the parties, one of more of whom is domiciled in a Contracting State, have agreed that a court or courts of a Contracting State are to have jurisdiction to settle any disputes which have arisen or which may arise in connection with a particular legal relationship, that court or those courts shall have exclusive jurisdiction. Such an agreement conferring jurisdiction shall be either—

    (a) in writing or evidenced in writing, or
    (b) in a form which accords with practices which the parties have established between themselves, or
    (c) in international trade or commerce, in a form which accords with a usage of which the parties are or ought to have been aware and which in such trade or commerce is widely known to, and regularly observed by, parties to contracts of the type involved in the particular trade or commerce concerned.

---

[86] Case C-190/89 *Marc Rich & Co v. Societa Italiana Impianti PA; The Atlantic Emperor* [1991] E.C.R. I-3855; but see *The Heidberg* [1994] 2 Lloyd's Rep. 287 where the question was whether the validity of an arbitration agreement was within the scope of the Conventions; *Lexmar Corp v. Nordisk Skibsrederforing* [1997] 1 Lloyd's Rep. 289 (exclusive jurisdiction clause in letters of undertaking pursuant to an order for security for costs made in an arbitration did not fall within the Art. 4(1) exclusion); Case C-391/95 *Van Uden Maritime BV v. Kommanditgesellschaft in Firma Deco-Line* [1999] All E.R. (E.C.) 258 (a court has the power under Art. 24 to make an order for an interim payment although the parties had agreed to arbitration and arbitration proceedings had been initiated).
[87] Art. 2.
[88] Art. 17: in the Conventions this is called prorogation of jurisdiction.
[89] Art. 18.
[90] Arts 7–12A.
[91] Arts 13–15.
[92] Art. 16.
[93] Arts 19 and 20.
[94] Arts 21–23.
[95] Art. 24.

. . .

. . .

. . .

> If an agreement conferring agreement was concluded for the benefit of only one of the parties,
> that party shall retain the right to bring proceedings in any other court which has jurisdiction
> by virtue of [these Conventions]"
> [Relates to employment contracts which will be considered later]

Concerning the "in writing" requirement, both parties must have clearly demonstrated their agreement for an exclusive jurisdiction clause to be upheld.[96] They must expressly agree the jurisdiction agreement itself, but it is not necessary for both parties to sign the agreement as long as the other party agrees in writing, which may itself be in a separate document.[97] An oral jurisdiction agreement can be confirmed if it is "evidenced in writing", and an oral agreement can be subsequently confirmed by one party if the other makes no objection.[98]

Where there was a valid exclusive jurisdiction clause, the designated court has exclusive jurisdiction in an action seeking a declaration that the contract containing the clause is void.[99] An express incorporation of the terms of a master agreement by the signing of a contract was binding and it did not matter that the person signing it had not seen the master agreement. He had agreed to its terms by signing the contract.[1]

The following questions have been referred to the E.C.J.[2]: (1) whether there was a valid jurisdiction agreement in an oral contract, and (2) whether for the purposes of Article 5(1)[3] an oral agreement designed solely to establish that the courts for a particular place had jurisdiction would be recognised.[4] In answer to (1) the E.C.J. held that an oral contract was binding if it was not challenged by the other party and the provisions of Article 17(c) were met. It was for the national court to determine whether a relevant practice existed and whether the parties ought to have been aware of it. In answer to (2), if an oral agreement specifying the place of performance was concerned with which courts were to have jurisdiction and not where the obligations under the contract were to be carried out, it did not fall within Article 5(1) but Article 17, provided it complied with the Article 17 rules.[5]

The parties may agree that more than one court is to have jurisdiction, known as a non-exclusive jurisdiction agreement.[6]

---

[96] Case 313/85 *Iveco Fiat SpA v. Van Hool SA* [1986] E.C.R. 3337.
[97] Case 25/76 *Partereenderei MS Tilly Russ v. Haven and Vervaebedriff Nova NV; The Tilly Russ* [1984] E.C.R. 2471.
[98] *ibid.* (a bill of lading).
[99] Case C-269/95 *Benincasa v. Dentalkit Sarl* [1998] All E.R. (E.C.) 135.
[1] *Crédit Suisse Financial Products v. Société Generale d'Enterprises* [1996] 5 Bank L.R. 220.
[2] Case C-106/95 *Mainschiffahrts Genossenschaft eg (MSG) v. Les Gravieres Rhenanes* [1997] All E.R. (E.C.) 385.
[3] See *post*, para. 22–018.
[4] See also Case 25/79 *Zegler v. Saltrini (No. 1)* [1980] E.C.R. 89.
[5] *ibid.*
[6] Case 23/78 *Meeth v. Glacetal Sarl* [1978] E.C.R. 2133 (if the German buyer were to sue the French seller, the French courts would have jurisdiction and if the French seller were to sue the German buyer, the German courts would have jurisdiction; see also *Kurz v. Stella Musical GmbH*

In relation to paragraph 3 of Article 17, the fact alone that the prorogated forum is that of the domicile of one of the parties to the contract does not support the conclusion that the jurisdiction clause was inserted for the benefit of that party only.[7]

The Conventions also allow in Article 18 an implied jurisdiction by a defendant's appearance before a court of a Contracting State which would not normally have jurisdiction. An appearance solely[8] to contest the jurisdiction shall not be regarded as conferring jurisdiction on that court.[9] This is spelt out in precise terms by section 33(1) of the 1982 Act.

Where there is a conflict between Articles 17 and 18, Article 18 prevails,[10] but not over the exclusive jurisdiction provisions of Article 16.[11]

General jurisdiction

The general rule is set out in Article 2: **22–017**

> "Subject to the provisions of this Convention, persons domiciled in a Contracting State shall, whatever their nationality, be sued in the courts of that State."

Article 3 states that domiciliaries of Contracting States may only be sued in the courts of another Contracting State in accordance with Articles 5 to 18. The exorbitant jurisdiction applicable under the English traditional rules, whereby a defendant can be served with a claim form[12] while on a temporary visit, is specifically excluded.

Although it was an important question, and necessary for the purpose of giving judgment, whether the plaintiff, who was domiciled in a non-Contracting State, had a right to bring proceedings in England under Article 2, the Court of Appeal exercised its discretion and refused to refer the matter to the E.C.J. in view of the delay and expense already involved and decided the matter on other grounds.[13]

Special jurisdiction

Article 5 sets out a number of exceptions to the Articles 2 and 3 general rule.[14] **22–018**
As far as is relevant in the context of international trade they are:

[1992] Ch. 196); *Mercury Communications v. Communications Systems International* LTL, June 1, 1999.
[7] Case 22/85 *Rudolf Anterist v. Crédit Lyonnais* [1986] 1 C.M.L.R. 333.
[8] The word "solely" has no meaning: Case 150/80 *Elefanten Schuh GmbH v. Jacqmain* [1981] E.C.R. 1671.
[9] For an E.C.J. interpretation of Art. 18 see Case 48/84 *Spitzley v. Sommer Exploitation SA* [1985] E.C.R. 787.
[10] *Elefanten Schuh, ante.*
[11] See *post*, para. 22–025.
[12] See *ante*, para. 22–003.
[13] *The Nile Rhapsody* [1994] 1 Lloyd's Rep. 382.
[14] Since these are exceptions they are to be strictly interpreted: see, *e.g.* Case 189/87 *Kalfelis v. Schroder* [1988] E.C.R. 5565.

"1. In matters relating to a contract, the courts for the place of performance of the obligation in question; in matters relating to individual contracts of employment, this place is that where the employee habitually carries out his work, or if the employee does not habitually carry out his work in any one country,[15] the employer may also be sued in the courts for the place where the business which engaged the employee was or is now situated;

2. . . . .

3. In matters relating to tort, delict or quasi-delict, the courts for the place where the harmful event occurred;

4. . . . .

5. As regards a dispute arising out of the operation of a branch, agency or other establishment, the courts for the place in which the branch, agency or other establishment is situated;

6. . . . .

7. [Relates to Admiralty claims which will be set out later in *in rem* jurisdiction]"

The phrase "matters relating to a contract" has to be interpreted by reference to the objectives of the Convention.[16] The claims of an independent agent for commission and compensation in case of wrongful repudiation of the agency agreement came within this concept,[17] as did a dispute as to the existence of a contract,[18] but not a claim for restitution where the contract is void,[19] nor a claim by a sub-purchaser against a manufacturer, as there was no direct contract between them.[20] An agent can claim commission from the buyer, pursuant to the contract between the buyers and sellers, on the basis that the buyers were trustees of the commission and this was a matter relating to a contract.[21] The duty to make fair representation was an obligation within Article 5(1) as it drew no express distinction between obligations arising in the context of negotiations, and those arising under or after the contract and was also a matter relating to a contract.[22]

The place of performance of the obligation in question is the place at which the contractual obligation on which the action is founded has to be performed and not just any contractual obligation.[23] If there is more than one claim then

---

[15] At this point the Brussels and Lugano Conventions differ and the Lugano Convention continues "this place shall be the place of business through which he was engaged".
[16] Case 9/87 *Arcado Sprl v. Haviland SA* [1988] E.C.R. 1593; Case C-26/91 *Jakob Handle GmbH v. Traitments Mechanochimiques des Surfaces* [1993] I.L.Pr. 5.
[17] *Arcado Sprl, ante.*
[18] Case 38/81 *Effer v. Kantner* [1982] E.C.R. 825; *Tesam Distribution Ltd v. Schuh Mode Team GmbH* [1990] I.L.Pr. 149; *Boss Group Ltd v. Boss France SA* [1997] 1 W.L.R. 351 (a defendant could not assert the existence of a contract in relation to proceedings in France and deny its existence in English proceedings. His assertion as to its existence in France was sufficient to ground jurisdiction in the English court); Case C-269/95 *Benincasa v. Dentalkit Srl* [1998] All E.R. (E.C.) 135.
[19] *Kleinwort Benson Ltd v. Glasgow City Council* [1999] 1 A.C. 153 in the House of Lords following a referral to the E.C.J. which ruled it had no jurisdiction.
[20] Case C-26/91 *Jakob Handle GmbH v. Traitments Mechnochimiques des Surfaces* [1993] I.L.Pr. 5.
[21] *Atlas Shipping Agency (U.K.) Ltd v. Suisse Atlantique Societe d'Armament Maritime SA* [1995] 6 I.L.Pr. 600.
[22] *Agnew v. Lansforsakringsbolagens AB* [1996] 4 All E.R. 978, disagreeing with *Trade Indemnity plc v. Forsakringsaktiebolaget Njord* [1995] 1 All E.R. 796.
[23] Case 14/76 *De Bloos Sprl v. Bouyer SA* [1976] E.C.R. 1497; *Viskase Ltd v. Paul Kiefal GmbH, The Times*, March 30, 1999 (the contractual obligation that goods had to be reasonably fit for their known purpose had to be performed at the time the goods were supplied and the place of performance was the place of delivery of the goods); *Chailease Finance Corp v. Credit Agricole Indosuez*

the principal claim must be identified.[24] The E.C.J. has confirmed[25] that the place of performance is to be determined by the national court under its own private international law rules. This still applies where the private international law rules of the national court would apply a Uniform Law, for example Article 59(1) of the Uniform Law on the International Sale of Goods,[26] which conflicts with Article 5(1).

In a case where there were two obligations of equal rank, the ECJ ruled that on a proper construction of Article 5(1), the same court did not have jurisdiction to hear the whole of an action founded on two obligations of equal rank arising from the same contract when, according to the conflict rules of the state where that court was situated, one of those obligations was to be performed in that state and the other in another contracting state. The ECJ observed that while there were disadvantages in having different courts ruling on different aspects of the same dispute, the plaintiff had the option, under Article 2, of bringing the entire claim before the courts of the place where the defendant was domiciled.[27] The court also held that Article 22[28] was intended to establish how related actions brought before the courts of different contracting states were to be dealt with. It did not confer jurisdiction, particularly where a court was seised pursuant to the rules of the Convention.

Employment contracts

The second part of Article 5(1) of the Brussels Convention has been amended **22–019** and now incorporates the E.C.J.'s decision in *Ivenel v. Schwab*,[29] which decided that where there was more than one obligation in an employment contract, the obligation under Article 5(1) was that which characterised the contract. This obligation is usually to carry out the work. To protect the employee the last part of Article 5(1) cannot be invoked by the employer, whereas it is possible, although unlikely, that under the Lugano Convention it could.

Where an employee works in more than one Contracting State, the place where he principally discharges his obligations towards his employer is the place where he has established the effective centre of his working activities and where

---

L.T.L. April 20 1999 (defendant could be sued in court of the jurisdiction where performance was due even where the place of performance of the obligation in question was not immediately ascertainable upon the making of the contract); *PRS Prodotti Siderurgici Srl v. Owners of the Sea Maas: The Sea Maas, The Independent*, July 7, 1999 (the fundamental obligation under a bill of lading incorporating the Hague Visby Rules was to exercise due diligence).

[24] Case 255/85 *Shenavai v. Kreischer* [1987] 3 C.M.L.R. 782; *Medway Packaging Ltd v. Meurer Maschinen GmbH* [1990] 2 Lloyd's Rep. 112; *Source Ltd v. TUV Rheinland Holding AG* [1997] 3 W.L.R. 365; *Raiffeisen Zentralbank Osterreich Aktiengesellschaft v. National Bank of Greece SA*, [1999] 1 Lloyd's Rep. 408 (the principal obligation could arise from an implied term).

[25] Case C-288/92 *Custom Made Commercial Ltd v. Stawa Metallabu GmbH* [1994] E.C.R. I-2913; Case 12/76 *Industrie Italiano Como v. Dunlop AG* [1976] E.C.R. 1473.

[26] About which see Chap. 32.

[27] Case C-420/97 *Leathertex Divisione Sintetica SpA v. Bodetex BVBA, The Times*, October 26, 1999.

[28] See *post*, para. 22–027.

[29] Case 133/81 [1982] E.C.R. 1891.

or from which he performs the essential part of his duties.[30] In relation to jurisdiction agreements, Article 17(5) provides:

> "In matters relating to individual contracts of employment an agreement conferring jurisdiction shall have legal force only if it is entered into after the dispute has arisen [here the Lugano Convention finishes but the Brussels Convention continues] or if the employee invokes it to seize courts other than those for the defendant's domicile or those specified in Article 5(1)."

Therefore, under both Conventions the agreement must be entered into *after* the dispute has arisen, but under the Brussels Convention the employee has an alternative and may invoke a pre-dispute agreement in accordance with the provision.

Tort

22–020 The E.C.J. has held[31] that "matters relating to tort, delict or quasi-delict" should not be interpreted in accordance with national law. The concept was an autonomous one which should be interpreted by reference to the system and objectives of the Convention. The phrase "included any action which sought to call into question the liability of a defendant and which did not involve matters relating to a contract under article 5(1) . . .". The E.C.J. acknowledged that inconvenience may be caused by different parts of a case having to be heard by different courts since a claim under Article 5(3) could not include elements of the same case based on non-tortious liabiity, but it was always possible that the actions could be related under Article 22.[32]

In *Bier v. Mines de Potasse D'Alsace*[33] the E.C.J. held that "the place where the harmful event occurred" meant "that the plaintiff has an option to commence proceedings either at the place where the damage occurred, or the place of the event giving rise to it". However, in a case where it was difficult to identify the place where the damage occurred, this was where the carrier delivered the goods.[34] In a case concerning an allegedly negligently issued inspection certificate by a defendant domiciled abroad, but where the certificate was relied upon by a plaintiff in England,[35] it was held, applying *Bier v. Mines de Potasse D'Alsace*, that the "harmful event" occurred in England. However, in subsequent cases of negligent misstatement, the *Minster* case has been distinguished[36] or not followed.[37]

In a libel claim, the plaintiff may bring an action for damages against the publisher either in the courts of the Contracting State where the publisher is established, which have jurisdiction to award damages for all the harm caused,

---

[30] Case C-383/95 *Rutten v. Cross Medical Ltd* [1997] I.C.R. 715.
[31] Case 189/87 *Kalfelis v. Schroder* [1988] E.C.R. 5565.
[32] On Art. 22 see *post*, para. 22–027.
[33] Case 21/76 [1976] E.C.R. 1735.
[34] Case 51/97 *Reunion Europeeane SA v. Spliethoffs Bevrachtingskantoor BV* [1999] I.L.Pr. 205.
[35] *Minster Investments Ltd v. Hyundai Precision and Industry Co Ltd* [1988] 2 Lloyd's Rep. 621.
[36] *Source Ltd v. TUV Rheinland Holding AG* [1997] 3 W.L.R. 365 (alleged negligent inspection of goods was "a matter relating to a contract" and did not come within Art. 5(3)).
[37] *Domicrest Ltd v. Swiss Bank Corp* [1999] 1 W.L.R. 364 (it was the negligent words rather than the receipt of them which most clearly identified the harmful event).

or before the courts of each Contracting State in which the publication was distributed.[38]

In a claim for financial loss, the harm flowing from the harmful event must be a direct and not an indirect consequence of the harmful event[39] and Article 5(3) cannot be construed so widely as to cover any place where the consequences of an event which had already caused damage elsewhere could be felt, and so did not include the place where a plaintiff suffered financial damage which arose from the original damage suffered by him in England.[40]

In a passing off action, the harm felt by the plaintiffs was to their goodwill in England and was a direct effect on their property in England so the place where the harmful event occurred was England.[41]

A claim for unjust enrichment is not within Article 5(3).[42]

Branch, agency or other establishment

The E.C.J. has strictly interpreted "branch, agency or other establishment" and **22–021** to come within the definition the defendant must have a fixed permanent address and be able to act on behalf of and bind the parent body[43] or give the impression to third parties that it was acting on behalf of the parent body.[44] In addition, the branch agency or other establishment must be subject to the direction and control of the parent body.[45]

The phrase "must arise out of the operation" has been interpreted by the E.C.J. to include the management of the branch, agency or other establishment, liability for its torts and undertakings entered into in its parent body's name.[46]

However, Article 5(5) did not presuppose that an undertaking, entered into by a branch in the name of its parent body, was to be performed in the Contracting State in which the branch is established.[47]

Co-defendants, third parties and counterclaims

Article 6 provides for alternative jurisdiction in the following cases: co- **22–022**

---

[38] Case C-68/93 *Shevill v. Presse Alliance SA* [1995] E.C.R. I-415.
[39] Case C-220/88 *Dumez France and Traboba v. Hessische Landesbank* [1990] E.C.R. 49 (cancelled bank loans causing financial loss to German subsidiary companies (direct loss) and to their parent companies in France (indirect loss)).
[40] Case C-364/93 *Marinari v. Lloyds Bank plc* [1995] E.C.R. I-2791.
[41] *Mecklermedia Corporation v. DC Congress GmbH* [1997] 3 W.L.R. 479; *cf. Modus Vivendi Ltd v. British Products Sanmex Ltd* [1996] F.S.R. 790.
[42] *Kleinwort Benson Ltd v. Glasgow City Council* [1997] 3 W.L.R. 923.
[43] Case 33/78 *Somafer SA v. Saar-Ferngas AG* [1978] E.C.R. 2183 (sales representative did not satisfy these requirements).
[44] Case 218/86 *SAR Schotte GmbH v. Parfums Rothschild SARL* [1978] E.C.R. 4905 (impression could be given by letterhead).
[45] Case 14/76 *De Bloos Sprl v. Bouyer SA* [1976] E.C.R. 1497 (exclusive distributor not within Art. 5(5)); Case 139/80 *Blanckaert and Willems v. Trost* [1981] E.C.R. 819 (independent commercial agent who negotiated orders and transmitted them to parent body not within Art. 5(5)).
[46] *SAR Schotte, ante.*
[47] Case C-439/93 *Lloyd's Register of Shipping v. Société Campenon Bernard* [1995] E.C.R. I-961.

defendants,[48] third parties,[49] counterclaims[50] and a combination of *in rem* rights in immovable property and a contractual claim against the same defendant.[51]

In the case of co-defendants, the courts of the place where any one of them is domiciled has jurisdiction. However, to ensure that it is not used to oust the jurisdiction of the court of the defendant, this provision must be strictly interpreted and the claims against them must be related, such that it is convenient for the court to hear them together and thus avoid irreconcilable judgments.[52] Article 6(1) does not permit a court which had accepted jurisdiction over a defendant not domiciled in a Contracting State to accept jurisdiction over a defendant domiciled in a Contracting State, on the ground that the cases were indivisible.[53]

The relevant time for assessing the domicile of one of the parties was at the time the writ is issued, not when it is served, and writs against co-defendants may be issued and served prior to service on the defendant.[54]

A third party may be sued in the court seised in the original proceedings but not if the proceedings were brought solely to remove him from the jurisdiction of the otherwise competent court. Article 6(2) applies as long as the court has jurisdiction over the plaintiff's claim and the domicile of the defendant is irrelevant.[55] It is sufficient if there is some nexus between the plaintiff's claim and that of the defendant against the third party.[56] Where the main action is inactive the defendant's claim did not come within Article 6(2), nor was it relevant that he was legally aided and would be unable to bring a claim in the courts of the third party's domicile.[57] Where there is an exclusive jurisdiction clause Article 17 prevails over Article 6(2).[58]

The E.C.J. has held that Article 6(3) applies only to claims by defendants which seek the pronouncement of a separate judgment or decree. It does not apply where a defendant raises as a defence a claim which he allegedly has against the plaintiff.[59]

Article 6a provides that where a court of a Contracting State has jurisdiction in actions relating to liability arising from the use or operation of a ship, it also has jurisdiction to claims for limiting liability.

---

[48] Art. 6(1).

[49] Art. 6(2).

[50] Art. 6(3).

[51] Art. 6(4).

[52] Case 189/87 *Kafelis v. Schroder* [1988] E.C.R. 5565; see also *Aiglon Ltd v. Gau Shan Co Ltd* [1993] 1 Lloyd's Rep. 164; *Holding Oil Finance Inc v. Marc Rich & Co AG* [1996] (it is an abuse of the process to improperly join English defendants in order to take advantage of Art. 6(1)).

[53] Case 51/97 *Reunion Europeeane SA v. Spliethoffs Bevrachtingskantoor BV* [1999] I.L.Pr. 205.

[54] *Canada Trust v. Stolzenberg (No. 2)* [1998] 1 W.L.R. 547; *Petrograde v. Smith* [1998] 2 All E.R. 346 (defendant was not domiciled in nor did he have any substantial connection with England when his remaining here was a condition of his bail).

[55] Case C-365/88 *Kongress Agentur Hagen GmbH v. Zeehaghe BV* [1990] E.C.R. I-1845.

[56] *Kinnear v. Flaconfilms NV* [1996] 1 W.L.R. 920.

[57] *Waterford Wedgwood plc v. David Nagli Ltd* [1998] FSR 92.

[58] *Hough v. P&O Containers* [1998] 2 Lloyd's Rep. 318.

[59] Case C-341/93 *Danvaern Production A/S v. Schuhfabriken Otterbech GmbH* [1995] E.C.R. I-2053.

Insurance contracts

Articles 7–12a provide for jurisdiction in matters relating to insurance. In general, in a claim arising from, or in connection with, an insurance contract, proceedings against the insurer may be taken in the courts of the Contracting State in which the insurer is domiciled[60] or in those of another Contracting State where the policyholder is domiciled.[61] However, an insurer may bring proceedings against the defendant irrespective of whether he is the policy-holder, the insured or a beneficiary only in the courts in which he is domiciled, but may bring a counterclaim in the court in which an original claim is pending.[62] The House of Lords has held that Article 11 applies to any insurer wherever domiciled and "counterclaim" applies to a counterclaim against an original plaintiff, which excludes the joinder of new parties as defendants to the counterclaim.[63]

    In respect of immovable property, the insurer may be sued in the courts of the Contracting State where the harmful event occurred.[64] In order to protect the weaker party (the insured), an exclusive jurisdiction clause is valid only if it is entered into after the dispute has arisen, or allows the insured to bring proceedings in courts other than those prescribed by Articles 7–11, or where both insurer and insured are domiciled in the same Contracting State and the jurisdiction clause stipulates that the courts of the state of domicile are to have jurisdiction, or where the insured is not domiciled in a Contracting State.[65] However an exclusive jurisdiction agreement is permitted for insurance contracts covering the risks set out in Article 12a,[66] the most important of which for the exporter is that an exclusive jurisdiction clause in an insurance contract relating to goods in transit by sea or air is binding. Article 12a also includes risks such as damage to seagoing ships, offshore installations and aircraft, including any financial loss such as freight or charter-hire or arising out of their use, where they are used for commercial purposes.

22–023

Consumer contracts

There are special jurisdiction provisions relating to consumer contracts in Articles 13-15. Although the exporter will not normally be dealing directly with consumers, these provisions are included because this work contains a chapter on Product Liability. In relation to consumer transactions involving the sale of goods or supply of services, or a credit element in relation to the sale of goods, the Conventions provide that the consumer can sue the seller, supplier or lender in the courts of the Contracting State where he (the consumer) is domiciled or

22–024

---

[60] Which includes a branch, agency or other establishment in a Contracting State where the insurer is not domiciled in a Contracting State.
[61] Art. 8.
[62] Art. 11.
[63] *Jordan Grand Prix Ltd v. Baltic Insurance Group* [1999] 2 W.L.R. 134.
[64] Art. 9.
[65] Art. 12.
[66] Art. 12(5).

where the seller, supplier or lender is domiciled. The seller, supplier or lender may only bring proceedings against the consumer in the courts of the Contracting State where the consumer is domiciled. The provisions regarding jurisdiction clauses in consumer contracts are similar to those set out above for contracts of insurance. Article 13 applies only where the defendant is domiciled or has a branch, agency or other establishment in a Contracting State. Where the defendant is not so domiciled, jurisdiction was to be determined by the law of the Contracting State in which proceedings were brought.[67] The E.C.J. has ruled that "consumer" had to be strictly construed to mean a private final consumer and did not extend to a person concluding a contract with the intention of pursuing a trade or profession.[68]

Exclusive jurisdiction

22–025 The cases in which the national courts of the Contracting States have exclusive jurisdiction, regardless of domicile, are listed in Article 16 of the Convention. These are: proceedings concerning *in rem* rights in immovable property situated in the Contracting State, except where the contract is for a tenancy for up to six months, the tenant is a natural person[69] and neither party is domiciled in the Contracting State in which the property is situated; the constitution, nullity or dissolution of companies or other legal persons or associations where the company or association has its seat; the registration of patents, trade marks, designs or similar rights of intellectual property where the deposit or registration has been applied for, has taken place or is deemed to have taken place under the terms of an international convention; and proceedings concerning the enforcement of foreign judgments where the judgment is to be enforced. Where a claim is within Article 16 the courts of any other Contacting State shall decline jurisiction.[70]

Jurisdiction and admissibility

22–026 Article 20 provides some safeguards for a defendant who is sued in the courts of a Contracting State other than the one in which he is domiciled. Where he does not enter an appearance the court shall decline jurisdiction, unless it has jurisdiction by virtue of the provisions of the Conventions. Further, the court shall stay proceedings where the plaintiff has not shown that the defendant has received the originating process in time to arrange his defence or has taken all steps necessary to ensure that the defendant has received it, except where service was in accordance with the provisions of the Hague Convention on the service abroad of judicial and extrajudicial documents in civil or commercial matters.

---

[67] Caes C-318/93 *Brenner v. Dean Witter Reynolds Inc* [1994] E.C.R. I-4275.
[68] Case C-269/95 *Benincasa v. Dentalkit Srl* [1998] All E.R. (E.C.) 135.
[69] Under the Lugano Convention the landlord must also be a natural person.
[70] Art. 19.

Lis pendens and related actions

If proceedings involving the same cause of action between the same parties are **22–027**
pending in the courts of one Contracting State (*lis pendens*), any court in another
Contracting State shall stay its proceedings *of its own motion* until the jurisdiction of the court first seised is established and where the jurisdiction of the court
first seised is established any other court shall decline jurisdiction.[71] If "related
actions" are brought in the courts of different Contracting States, the second
court has a discretion to order a stay and may do so on the application of one
of the parties. Actions are "related" if they are so closely connected that there is
a risk of irreconcilable judgments of the two courts concerned with the matter.[72]

Under Article 21 the parties in the two actions must be identical,[73] and where
they were not identical the second court seised was required to decline jurisdiction only to the extent to which the parties were the same as the parties to the
action in the court first seised, but the second court could decline jurisdiction
on the ground that the actions were related under Article 22.[74] However, the
E.C.J. has held subsequently that if it is established that the interests of the
parties in two actions are identical and indissociable, then the actions would
come within Article 21.[75] An *in personam* action by the ship-owner and an *in
rem* action against the ship have the same cause of action, the same object and
are between the same parties.[76]

Where the two cases both involved the same subject matter but the claims
were not identical, the enforceability of the contract was the subject matter
which equated to the "same cause of action" and the matter was therefore within
the provisions of Article 21.[77]

The Article 21 provision applies equally to defendants who are domiciled in
Contracting States and to those who are not.[78] The question as to which of
several competing national courts was first seised with the case depends on when
the case became pending in the courts according to the rules of their procedure.[79]

---

[71] Art. 21; *Davy International v. Voest Alpine Industrieanlagenblau GmbH* [1999] 1 All E.R. 103
(where concurrent Austrian and English proceedings were initiated prior to the coming into force
of the Lugano Convention, the English court is not required to stay its proceedings).
[72] Art. 22; *Virgin Aviatio v. CAD Aviation, The Times*, February 2, 1990 (in the exercise of judicial
discretion, a juridical advantage, such as the opportunity of obtaining summary judgment under RSC
Ord. 14 (now CPR, Pt 24) is only of subordinate importance).
[73] Case C-406/92 *The Maciej Rataj (sub. nom. The Tatry)* [1995] E.C.R. I-5439.
[74] *ibid.*, applied by the House of Lords in *Sarrio SA v. Kuwait Investment Authority* [1999] A.C. 32
(there should be a broad brush common sense approach to the question of whether actions were
related under Art. 22); *cf. Mecklermedia Corporation v. DC Congress GmbH* [1996] 3 W.L.R. 479.
[75] Case C-351/96 *Drouot Assurances SA v. Consolidated Metallurgical Industries* [1999] 2 W.L.R.
163.
[76] *The Maciej Rataj, ante.*
[77] Case 144/86 *Gubisch Maschinenfabrik KG v. Giulio Palumbo* [1987] E.C.R. 4861.
[78] Case C-351/89 *Overseas Union Insurance Ltd v. New Hampshire Insurance Ltd* [1991] E.C.R.
I-3317.
[79] Case 129/83 *Zelger v. Saltrini (No. 2)* [1984] E.C.R. 2397. See also *Dresser U.K. Ltd v. Fal-
congage Freight Management Ltd* [1992] Q.B. 502 (the English court is first seised on the date of
service of the writ) and *Neste Chemicals SA v. DK Line SA; The Sargasso* [1994] 3 All E.R. 180
(there are no exceptions, notwithstanding that the English court may have interlocutory jurisdiction
in respect of provisional relief, which is not jurisdiction over the substantive matter).

Where proceedings had been launched in another Convention's jurisdiction simply to harass and oppress a party who was already a litigant here, the court, under its inherent jurisdiction, may prohibit by injunction the plaintiff in the other jurisdiction from continuing the foreign process, in order to prevent abuse of process. This power was not limited to instances where jurisdiction was established under Article 21 or the court plainly possessed exclusive jurisdiction, for example, under Article 17.[80]

The Conventions and forum non conveniens

22–028 Where there are concurrent or related proceedings in Contracting States the doctrine of *forum non conveniens* does not apply. However, section 49 of the 1982 Act provides that the doctrine may be applied where it is not inconsistent with the Conventions. Where proceedings were commenced in England and a non-Convention country (Argentina), the Court of Appeal stayed the English proceedings on the ground of *forum non conveniens*, even though the defendant was domiciled here.[81] The House of Lords referred the case to the E.C.J. but the parties settled.

SERVICE ABROAD

22–029 Service abroad is effected in accordance with RSC Order 11, rules 5 to 10.[81a] Under rule 6, where the defendant is in a country which is party to a Civil Procedure Convention (other than the Hague Convention), he may be served through that country's judicial authorities or through a British Consular authority. Where the defendant is in a country which is party to the Hague Convention on the Service Abroad of Judicial and Extra-judicial Documents in Civil and Commercial Matters, signed at the Hague on November 15, 1965, he may be served through the authority designated under the Convention by that country. He may also be served through the judicial authorities or through a British consular authority, if the law of that country permits.

In addition to the multilateral Hague Convention, the United Kingdom has concluded a number of bilateral conventions on the facilitation of service of court documents abroad with some overseas countries and these conventions are still in force.

For service on a defendant in a country where there is no Civil Procedure Convention, this is effected through the government of that country if it is willing to effect service.

In general[82] the claim form must be accompanied by a translation in the official language of the country concerned or, where there is more than one official

---

[80] *Turner v. Grovit* [1999] 3 All E.R. 616.
[81] *Re Harrods (Buenos Aires) Ltd* [1992] Ch. 72; *Mercury Communications v. Communication Telecommunications Systems International* L.T.L. June 1, 1999 (where it was held that notwithstanding that Article 17 applied to a non-exclusive jurisdiction clause, the court nonetheless retained a discretion to decline jurisdiction on the ground of *forum non conveniens* if the interests of justice so required.).
[81a] See now CPR Pts 6.24 to 6.30.
[82] The Practice Direction, Service out of the Jurisdiction, supplements Order 11 and is very detailed.

language, in the language appropriate to the region where service is to be effected. The translation must be certified to be a correct translation by the person making it.

A request for service is then filed with the Central Office of the Supreme Court, together with a copy of the claim form. Documents are then sent by the Senior Master to the Parliamentary Under-Secretary of State to the Foreign Office, with the request that he arrange for the claim form to be served.

INTERIM REMEDIES

The freezing injunction

Its nature

The English court may grant an interim remedy against a party in the form of a **22–030** freezing injunction[83] restraining him from removing from the jurisdiction assets located there, or restraining him from dealing with any assets, whether located within the jurisdiction or not.[84] It is now granted by virtue of section 37 of the Supreme Court Act 1981; procedure and practice are governed by Part 25 of the Civil Procedure Rules, supplemented by extensive practice directions and the forms annexed thereto, and Part 1 of the CPR. The purpose of the freezing injunction is "simply to prevent the injustice of a defendant removing or dissipating his assets so as to cheat the plaintiff of the fruits of his claim";[85] it is not to improve the position of the plaintiff as against the other creditors.[86]

Part 25.2(1) provides that a freezing order may be made at any time, which includes before proceedings have started and after judgment has been given. However, Parts 25.2(2) and (3) go on to provide that it may only be granted before a claim is made if the matter is urgent or it is otherwise necessary to do so in the interests of justice, and if granted, the court may direct that a claim be made.

Previously, a freezing injunction could only be granted where the English court had jurisdiction over the substantive claim.[87] However this has been modified by Article 24 of the Brussels and Lugano Conventions, which provides that:

"Application may be made to the courts of a Contracting State for such provisional, including protective, measures as may be available under the law of that State, even if, under this

---

[83] Previously known as a *Mareva* injunction after *Mareva Compania Naviera SA v. International Bulkcarriers SA; The Mareva* [1975] 2 Lloyd's Rep. 509, CA, and renamed a "freezing injunction" in the Civil Procedure Rules, Part 25(1)(f). The Civil Procedure Rules (CPR) came into force on April 26, 1999. For further reading: Steven Gee, *Mareva Injunctions* (4th ed., 1997); Mark Hoyle, *The Mareva Injunction and Related Orders* (3rd ed., 1997), but note that these were published before the CPR came into force.

[84] CPR, Part 25(1)(f)(i) and (ii) which includes a worldwide freezing injunction.

[85] Per Lloyd J. in *P.C.W. (Underwriting Agencies) Ltd v. P.S. Dixon* [1983] 2 Lloyd's Rep. 197 at 202.

[86] *Town and Country Building Society v. Daisystar Ltd* (1989) 139 N.L.J. 1563, CA (abuse of Mareva procedure not to prosecute action but to use the injunction for the purpose of improving one's position against the other creditors).

[87] *The Siskina* [1979] A.C. 210.

Convention, the courts of another Contracting State have jurisdiction as to the substance of the matter."

Applications for worldwide freezing injunctions in support of proceedings in Contracting States have been granted by the English courts on the basis of Article 24 of the Conventions and section 25(1) of the Civil Jurisdiction and Judgments Act 1982.[88] Under section 25(3) of the Act, the English court has the power to grant interim relief in respect of proceedings commenced or to be commenced otherwise than in a Brussels or Lugano Contracting State and proceedings whose subject-matter is not within the scope of the 1968 Convention as determined by Article 1.[89] This is provided for in CPR, Part 25.4. However, in relation to section 25 and Article 24 proceedings, the court may refuse to grant the application if it considers that the fact that it has no jurisdiction over the substantive claim makes it inexpedient to grant it.[90]

A freezing injunction is a discretionary remedy. Neither Part 25 nor the Practice Direction state the grounds on which a freezing injunction may be granted, but it would seem that the court exercises its discretion in accordance with Parts 1.1 and 1.2 and no longer considers as relevant authorities decided prior to the coming into force of the Rules. This view would seem to be endorsed by Lord Woolf in *Ricardo Biguzzi v. Rank Leisure Plc*,[91] an appeal in a striking out application in which he stated at the end of his judgment: "The whole purpose of making the CPR a self-contained code was to send the message which now generally applies. Earlier authorities are no longer generally of any relevance once the CPR applies."

Parts 1.1 and 1.2 are central to the Rules and are set out in full below:

"The overriding objective

    1.1(1) These Rules are a new procedural code with the overriding objective of enabling the court to deal with cases justly.

    (2) Dealing with a case justly includes, so far as is practicable—

        (a) ensuring that the parties are on an equal footing;
        (b) saving expense;
        (c) dealing with the case in ways which are proportionate—

            (i) to the amount of money involved;
            (ii) to the importance of the case;
            (iii) to the complexity of the issues; and
            (iv) to the financial position of each party.

        (d) ensuring that it is dealt with expeditiously and fairly; and
        (e) allotting to it an appropriate share of the court's resources, while taking into account the need to allot resources to other cases.

    Application of the court of the overriding objective

---

[88] *Republic of Haiti v. Duvalier* [1989] 2 W.L.R. 261; *X v. Y* [1989] 3 W.L.R. 910 (both in support of French proceedings); *Credit Suisse Fides Trust SA v. Cuoghi* [1998] Q.B. 818 (in support of Swiss proceedings).
[89] S.I. 1997 No. 302 which came into force on April 1, 1997.
[90] s. 25(1)(2).
[91] [1999] 1 W.L.R. 1926.

1.2   The court must seek to give effect to the overriding objective when it—

  (a) exercises any power given to it by the Rules; or
  (b) interprets any rule.''

The applicant will normally apply for a freezing injunction without notice to the defendant, but in the affidavit in support of his application he must set out the facts on which he relies, including all material facts of which the court should be made aware.[92]

The freezing injunction is granted against an undertaking by the applicant to indemnify the other party and any others served with, or notified of, the order unless the court orders otherwise,[93] if the applicant loses the action and, in retrospect, the injunction was unjustified. The court may further order that the claimant shall provide a bank guarantee in respect of any order the court may make in the future as to damages.

Orders supporting the freezing injunction

In order to make the freezing injunction as effective as possible, the courts **22–031** may grant ancillary orders in its support. Two of these ancillary orders may be mentioned.

First, the court may order that a party provide information about the location of relevant property or assets which are or may be the subject of an application for a freezing order.[94]

Secondly, the court may order that the defendant shall surrender his passport and shall not leave the jurisdiction until the case is decided.[95]

If an injunction is granted and the claim is stayed other than by agreement of the parties, it will be set aside unless the court orders otherwise.[96] If a claim is struck out under Part 3.7 (non payment of certain fees), the injunction will cease after 14 days, unless the claimant applies to reinstate the claim before the expiry of the 14 days, and will continue until the hearing of the application unless the court orders otherwise.[97]

The search order

This is an order requiring a party to admit another party to premises for the **22–032** purposes of preserving evidence and property. It was previously known as an *Anton Piller* order, a name taken from a case decided in 1975[98] in which the order was granted by virtue of the court's inherent jurisdiction. This type of

---

[92] CPR, Part 25 Practice Direction—Interim Injunctions, para. 25 PD–003.
[93] CPR, Part 25 Practice Direction—Interim Injunctions, para. 25 PD–004.
[94] *ibid.* 25(1)(g). Relevant property means property (including land) which is the subject of a claim or as to which any question may arise on a claim: 25(1)(2).
[95] See *Bayer AG v. Winter* [1986] 1 W.L.R. 497.
[96] Part 25.10.
[97] Part 25.11: The Civil Procedure (Amendment) Rules 1999, S.I. 1999 No. 1008 (L.8).
[98] *Anton Piller KG v. Manufacturing Processes Ltd* [1976] Ch. 55.

order has been issued for a variety of reasons.[99] It has been granted to preserve evidence which might otherwise be removed, destroyed or concealed.[1] It has also been granted where it was alleged that confidential drawings might be secretly passed on to the competition[2]; where allegedly confidential information, including lists and evaluations of customers, might be used improperly[3]; and even after judgment in aid of execution, in order to prevent the destruction or concealment of documents.[4]

A statutory basis for the jurisdiction is now provided for in section 7 of the Civil Procedure Act 1997. Practice and procedure for search orders are governed by CPR, Part 25, supplemented by the extensive provisions contained in paragraph 7.1 of the accompanying Practice Direction.[5]

The search order is invariably granted to the applicant without notice. As with freezing injunctions, its grant is discretionary, such discretion being, it is thought, exercised in accordance with the overriding objectives set out in CPR, Parts 1.1 and 1.2.[6]

Applications are to be supported by affidavit evidence setting out the facts on which the applicant relies, and must include all material facts of which the court should be made aware.[7] Documents and articles which are the subject of the order are to be listed in an attached Schedule. The order is to be served by a "Supervising Solicitor"[8] and carried out under his supervision. The applicant indemnifies the respondent for any loss caused by the order or its carrying out.

Applications for interim injunctions are normally dealt with at a court hearing, but in cases of extreme urgency may be made by telephone.[9]

IN REM JURISDICTION

22–033 As mentioned in the introduction to this Chapter, an *in rem* action is an action against a *res*, which is usually a ship but might be cargo, freight, an aircraft or hovercraft. The *res* is arrested in order to provide security for the plaintiff's claim and the judgment or arbitral award is then enforced against the proceeds of sale of the *res*. Jurisdiction in Admiralty matters in the High Court, either *in rem* or *in personam*, is provided for by sections 20 and 21 of the Supreme Court Act 1981 and procedure is in accordance with Civil Procedure Rules, Part 49 and Practice Direction 49F which replaces, with modifications, RSC Order 75.

---

[99] Particularly to seize allegedly pirated video tapes (*Rank Film Distributors Ltd v. Video Information Centre (A Firm)* [1982] A.C. 380) or allegedly counterfeit goods (*Sony Corporation v. Time Electronics* [1981] 1 W.L.R. 1293).

[1] *Crest Homes plc v. Marks* [1987] A.C. 829; *Columbia Picture Industries Inc v. Robinson* [1987] Ch. 38.

[2] See n. 98, *supra*.

[3] *Vapormatic Co Ltd v. Sparex Ltd* [1976] 1 W.L.R. 939.

[4] *Distributori Automatici SpA v. Holford General Trading Co Ltd* [1985] 1 W.L.R. 1066.

[5] To which an example of a Search Order is annexed.

[6] See previous page.

[7] CPR, Part 25 Practice Direction—Interim Injunctions; and see *e.g. Memory Corp v. Sidhu, The Times*, May 31, 1999.

[8] Who must not be an employee or a member of the applicant's firm of solicitors; Practice Direction—Interim Injunctions 25 PD–004.

[9] See Practice Direction—Interim Injunctions 25 PD–003.

An *in rem* action requires that the *res* is arrested, or that security is provided in order to prevent arrest. This is done by filing an application to arrest, accompanied by an undertaking and a declaration on the relevant forms. The Admiralty Court then issues an arrest warrant.[10] The arrest of property may only be effected by the Marshal or his substitute.[11] This is done by serving the *in rem* claim form on the property by attaching it, or a copy, on the outside of the property in a position which may reasonably be expected to be seen. If the property is freight, service may either be on the cargo in respect of which freight was earned or on the ship which carried the cargo. Where the property is in the custody of a person who will not permit access to it, service is effected by leaving a copy of the *in rem* claim form with that person.[12] In order to be arrested a ship must be within the jurisdiction of the court and there is no provision for service out as for *in personam* jurisdiction.

There are many actions listed in the Supreme Court Act 1981 for which the court has Admiralty jurisdiction, the most relevant for the exporter being "any claim for loss of or damage to goods carried in a ship"[13] and "any claim arising out of any agreement relating to the carriage of goods in a ship or to the use or hire of a ship".[14] In these claims, amongst others, the carrying ship or a sister ship[15] may be arrested if "the relevant person"[16] was the beneficial owner of the ship as respects all the shares at the time when the action is brought, or in addition in the case of the carrying ship, where the demise charterer, or the person who is in possession or in control of it is "the relevant person".[17] "Charterer" is not limited to a "demise charterer" but includes time and voyage charterers,[18] a slot charterer, and a voyage charterer of part of a ship.[19] *In rem* claim forms may be issued against any or all of them and served on the first to come within the jurisdiction.

In accordance with the Arrest Convention,[20] the courts of the country in which the arrest is made have jurisdiction to determine the case on its merits.[21] Where there is an exclusive foreign jurisdiction clause, the English court has a discretion to stay its proceedings and will do so unless strong cause is shown why it should not.[22] Where there is a valid arbitration clause, a stay is mandatory.[23] However, in both cases the court may order that the arrested property, or bail or other security given to prevent or obtain release from arrest be retained, or

---

[10] CPR PD 49F, rule 6.
[11] *ibid*, rule 6.4(1).
[12] *ibid*, rule 2.2(a) and (b).
[13] s. 20(2)(g).
[14] s. 20(2)(h).
[15] This does not include a sister company, *The Evpo Agnic* [1988] 2 Lloyd's Rep. 411.
[16] This is the person who would be liable on the claim in an action *in personam*, s. 21(4)(b).
[17] s. 21(4).
[18] *The Span Terza* [1984] 1 W.L.R. 27.
[19] *MSC Mediterranean Shipping Co SA v. Owners of the Ship "Tychy"* [1999] 2 Lloyd's Rep. 11.
[20] International Convention for Unification of Certain Rules relating to the Arrest of Seagoing Ships 1952.
[21] Art. 7.
[22] *The El Amria* [1981] 2 Loyd's Rep. 119.
[23] Arbitration Act 1996, s. 9.

may make a stay conditional on the provision of equivalent security to satisfy any judgment or arbitral award.[24]

In practice, the shipowner will usually put up security for the claim and submit to the jurisdiction in order to obtain the release of the ship, since the value of the claim will normally be far less than the cost of the ship being idle and any subsequent claims that may result from her idleness. If he considers there is little or no defence to the claim, or it is not worth defending, he may well simply settle it without argument to obtain her release speedily. It is thus often not necessary to wait until the target ship enters British waters, as there are several countries where arrest is commonplace and the legal practitioners and legal systems are geared to completing the necessary documentation and effecting an arrest very quickly.

Until recently, *in rem* and *in personam* actions were thought to be separate and distinct actions, since one was against the ship and the other against the owner. However the House of Lords has now decided[25] that where a judgment *in personam* had been obtained in a foreign court on the same cause of action as that before the English court, the English *in rem* action was in reality an action against the owner and was barred by section 34 of the Civil Jurisdiction and Judgments Act 1982.[26]

The Brussels and Lugano Conventions have had some effect on the Admiralty jurisdiction of the High Court. Article 57 of the Conventions provides that their provisions do not affect any international conventions to which a Contracting State is a party and shall not prevent the assumption of jurisdiction in accordance with international conventions. The Arrest Convention is such a convention, so where an English court assumes jurisdiction under Article 7 of this Convention, the jurisdiction provisions of the Brussels and Lugano Conventions are ousted. However, in *The Maciej Rataj*[27] the E.C.J. held that although the jurisdictional rules of an international convention (here the Arrest Convention) precluded the jurisdictional provisions of the Conventions, the Conventions nevertheless applied in matters where the international convention was silent. The international convention contained no *lis alibi pendens* or related actions provisions, whereas the Conventions did.[28] In this case, the carrying ship (The Tatry) offloaded damaged cargo at European ports. The shipowners, aware that they were facing claims, commenced a limitation action (*in personam*) in Rotterdam against some of the cargo-owners, after which a sister ship of The Tatry, The Matiej Rataj, was arrested by cargo-owners in England. The ship-owners sought a stay of the English actions on the grounds that the Rotterdam court was the court first seised, or that the actions were related, or that the Rotterdam court

---

[24] Civil Jurisdiction and Judgments Act 1982, s. 26: Arbitration Act 1996, s. 11.

[25] *Republic of India v. India Steamship Co Ltd; The Indian Endurance No. 2* [1997] 3 W.L.R. 818, applying the dicta of Lord Brandon in *The August 8* [1983] 2 A.C. 450 at 456 and *The Deichland* [1990] 1 Q.B. 361.

[26] s. 34 provides: "No proceedings may be brought by a person in England and Wales . . . on a cause of action in respect of which judgment has been given in his favour in proceedings between the same parties, or their privies . . . in a court of an overseas country . . .".

[27] Case C-406/92 (*sub. nom. The Tatry*) [1994] E.C.R. I-5439.

[28] Arts 21 and 22 respectively of the Conventions, see *ante*, para. 22–027 on these Articles.

was the most appropriate forum. The E.C.J. held that for the purposes of Articles 21 and 22 there was no difference between *in personam* and *in rem* actions.

An English court has held[29] that there was a conflict between Article 7 of the Arrest Convention and Article 17 of the Conventions[30] and that the Arrest Convention prevailed.

The Conventions provide[31] for jurisdiction where a ship has been or could have been arrested:

> "A person domiciled in a Contracting State may, in another Contracting State, be sued:
>
> as regards a dispute concerning the payment of remuneration claimed in respect of the salvage of a cargo or freight the court under the authority of which the cargo or freight in question:
>
> > (a) has been arrested to secure such payment, or
> > (b) could have been so arrested, but bail or other security has been given;
>
> provided that this provision shall apply only if it is claimed that the defendant has an interest in the cargo or freight or had such an interest at the time of the salvage."

Article 5(7) was included in the Conventions to make provision for jurisdiction where property other than a ship is arrested. This is provided for in section 20 of the Supreme Court Act 1981 but not in the Arrest Convention which is restricted to the arrest of a ship. In addition, jurisdiction is granted under the Arrest Convention only when a ship has been arrested, not when it could have been arrested.[32]

---

[29] *The Bergen* [1997] 1 Lloyd's Rep. 380.
[30] See *ante*, para. 22–027.
[31] Art. 5(7).
[32] See Dicey and Morris, *loc cit*, paras 13–028 to 13–031.

CHAPTER 23

INTERNATIONAL COMMERCIAL LITIGATION—ARBITRATION

Extrajudicial dispute settlement and court proceedings

23–001 The possibility of a legal dispute arising is never absent in international trade transactions. The reasonable exporter, in spite of the care he has taken in the preparation of the contract of sale, has to contemplate acting against a buyer who is in breach of contract. In such circumstances, he may weigh the cost effectiveness of litigation and decide that it is better to cut his losses rather than engage in costly and protracted proceedings. There are, however, situations in which such a solution is neither possible nor desirable. It may be that the subject matter of the contract is too valuable for a loss to be absorbed, that third party interests are involved or that the breach is too flagrant to allow it to pass unchallenged. The question therefore arises as to the most convenient, expeditious and cost-effective way to settle the dispute.

Ideally, the exporter should consider this issue before entering into the contract of sale. When he has made his choice from the procedures available for dispute resolution, he should insist that a term giving full expression to the chosen procedure is inserted into the contract. It is common experience that agreement on this point is easier during the course of negotiation than when a dispute has arisen, as in the latter situation the aggrieved party has no means of compelling the other to agree to an extrajudicial procedure of dispute resolution. In these circumstances resort to the court is often the only way open to him.

If the exporter decides in favour of dispute resolution out of court he may insert into the contract of sale an alternative dispute resolution (ADR) clause which embraces mediation and conciliation or an arbitration clause. The difference between ADR and arbitration is to be found in the different aims of these procedures. The aim of ADR is to achieve the amicable settlement of a dispute by using the services of a third party, a mediator or conciliator, to facilitate such settlement. The aim of arbitration, on the other hand, is to achieve the resolution of a dispute through the appointment by parties adopting an adversarial stance of a private "judge" who will decide on the matters in dispute. Arbitration is thus closer to court proceedings than ADR.

For many reasons, not least in terms of cost, ADR is preferable to arbitration. ADR, however, will only succeed if the parties are well disposed towards it. Parties will only insert an ADR clause into their contract if the nature of their relationship is such that an amicable settlement can be hoped for. At the conclusion of an ADR process the parties may ask the mediator to draft the agreement reached as a consent award. The award is then enforceable as an arbitration award.

It is clear from developments in the Commercial Court, that disputing parties should be informed of the possibility of employing an ADR mechanism. In a Practice Statement[1] Waller J., stated that it was already the practice of the Commercial Court to ensure that the attention of parties in dispute was drawn to the possibility of exploring the use of ADR. He indicated that it would be the practice of the Commercial Court to take a further step, by inviting parties to take positive steps to set in motion ADR procedures, should the action before the court or any of the issues arising in it be particularly appropriate for settlement by ADR. The judge would, by way of assistance, be able to adjourn proceedings before him and extend time for compliance with the court's procedural rules. The judge could also offer an early neutral evaluation of the matters in dispute as a means of assisting in the resolution of those matters. The Statement recognises the virtues of ADR; saving costs, saving delays, settling disputes without damaging commercial relationships, offering a wider range of settlement options and ensuring better use of judicial resources.

The most commonly chosen alternative to court action as a means of dispute resolution is arbitration.

GENERAL ASPECTS OF ARBITRATION

Arbitration and litigation compared

It is a commonly held view that arbitration offers distinct advantages over litigation. First, parties to an international contract can remit the resolution of their dispute to judges of their own choice. This is a particular advantage to parties who reside in different countries, with different legal and cultural backgrounds, as they may be reluctant to submit the resolution of their dispute to the national court of their own countries. This may be so however well the commercial court of a particular country functions and administers justice.   **23–002**

Secondly, finality rather than meticulous legal accuracy is the preference of many involved in trade. An arbitration award is final,[2] whereas a judgment of a court may be appealed and further appealed so that considerable time lapses before the matter has been finally determined.

Thirdly, arbitration is confidential to the parties, its hearings (if there are any) are not open and the pleadings are not available for public perusal. In sensitive matters this is an advantage. Indeed, in the course of parliamentary debate prior to the passing of the Arbitration Act 1996 it was suggested that the Act should formally ensure the confidentiality of the documents used and the award made in an arbitration be confidential. This proposal was not enacted, but it is clear

---

[1] *Practice Statement (Alternative Dispute Resolution), The Times*, June 11, 1996 following *Practice Statement (Commercial Cases: Alternative Dispute Resolution)* [1994] 1 W.L.R. 14 and *Practice Direction (Commercial Court: Practice Guide)* [1994] 1 W.L.R. 1270.

[2] See the Arbitration Act 1996 s. 58 as to the effect of an award. Which is final as far as the arbitration tribunal is concerned, s.58(2). On arbitration see Bernstein, Tackaberry, Marriot and Wood, *Handbook Arbitration Practice* (Sweet and Maxwell, 1998); R. Merkin, *Arbitration Act 1996, An Annotated Guide* (LLP, 1996); A. Redfern and M. Hunter, *Law and Practice of International Commercial Arbitration* (Sweet and Maxwell, 1999).

from recent cases[3] that confidentiality is a term to be implied into an arbitration agreement. Finally, an arbitration award may be enforced as a judgment of the court (section 66 of the Arbitration Act 1996) if made in England and Wales. If made outside that territory, international conventions facilitate the recognition and enforcement of foreign arbitral awards and thereby make international execution relatively easy.

It is claimed that arbitration is speedier and cheaper than court proceedings. This is probably true in many cases but experience dictates that such claims be treated with a certain degree of scepticism. It remains to be seen whether this scepticism will be tempered by the operation of the new Arbitration Act in the light of the principles outlined in section 1:

> "The provisions of this Part are founded on the following principles, and shall be construed accordingly—
>
>> (a) the object of arbitration is to obtain the fair resolution of disputes by an impartial tribunal without unnecessary delay or expense; . . ."

Questions of fact and questions of law

23–003   In principle, questions of fact are decided by the arbitrator. The arbitrator also decides questions of law arising in the course of the arbitration. In the limited number of cases where review by the court is allowed in English law under the Arbitration Act, the court will accept the facts as found by the arbitrator and restrict its review to questions of law. Where the dispute concerns only facts, for example whether goods supplied are of the stipulated quality or description, or in accordance with sample, arbitration offers overwhelming advantages over litigation. Many of these so-called quality arbitrations are quickly and cost effectively disposed of, particularly if the arbitration is arranged under the rules of a trade association. It is rare that a dispute arising from them is later taken to court.

Where the facts of a particular matter are not disputed, and the dispute concerns the construction of a document or an issue of general importance in a particular trade, it has been suggested[4] that it may be cheaper and more expeditious to submit the dispute to the court. Such an option however has to be regarded in the light of s.1(c) of the Arbitration Act 1996 ". . . the court should not intervene . . ." and s.23(4) where the parties may agree to terminate the agreement. The thrust of the Act however is to strongly discourage submission to the court.

Where the dispute is one of fact and law—a mixed arbitration—the arbitrator's decisions on the legal issues may be subject to review by the court,[5]

---

[3] *Insurance Company v. Lloyd's Syndicate* [1995] 1 Lloyd's Rep. 272 and *Ali Shipping Corp v. Shipyard Trogir* [1998] 1 Lloyd's Rep. 643, CA. The term of confidentiality is implied by law into the pleadings, submissions, proofs of evidence and award. See also *Minmetals Germany GmbH v. Ferco Steel Ltd* [1999] C.L.C. 647.

[4] By, among others, Singleton L.J. in *K.C. Sethia (1944) Ltd v. Partabmull Rameshwar* [1950] 1 All E.R. 51 and Lord Donaldson in *Seaworld Ocean Line Co SA v. Catseye Maritime Co; The Kelaniya* [1989] 1 Lloyd's Rep. 30.

[5] See *post*, para. 23–019 for the circumstances where such review is possible or appropriate.

whereas the decision on the facts is not, unless it is obviously absurd. A typical example of an issue involving questions of fact and law is that of frustration. The circumstances alleged to have led to frustration raise questions of fact but the issue of what the facts are, and whether they satisfy the legal requirements of frustration and therefore lead to the termination of a contract, is solely a question of law. As Lord Diplock[6] observed:

"... the question of frustration ... is never a pure question of fact but does in the ultimate analysis involve a conclusion of law as to whether the frustrating event or series of events has made the performance of the contract a thing radically different from that undertaken by the contract."

In such situations the parties may find it expedient to appoint a judge of the Commercial Court as sole arbitrator or umpire. This is possible under Section 93 of the Arbitration Act 1996. The section makes it clear[7] that a judge may only act if he can be made available having regard to the state of business in the High Court. An appeal from the judge-arbitrator lies to the Court of Appeal[8] on the question of costs.

The characteristics of an arbitration

The contractual element

There can be no arbitration without the agreement of the parties to submit to **23–004** this method of dispute resolution.[9] The agreement itself may take the form of an arbitration clause in the original contract. For example, in the contract of export sale, such a clause will refer to future disputes. Alternatively, there may be an arbitration agreement subsequent to the conclusion of the original contract, particularly after the dispute has arisen.[10] Section 7 of the Arbitration Act provides that an arbitration agreement, unless otherwise agreed by the parties, be treated as a distinct agreement. The arbitration therefore "floats" clear of the agreement embodying the main obligations between the parties. The section enacts the so-called concept of separability which was fully acknowledged in *Harbour Assurance Co (U.K.) Ltd v. Kansa General Insurance Co Ltd.*[11] This section, taken together with section 30 of the Act, confirms that the arbitrator may decide on his own jurisdiction.[12] These sections resolve the long running questions as to whether the arbitration agreement is severable or not or whether the arbitration agreement was susceptible to a challenge to the main agreement. The Act therefore affirms the arrival of the continental jurisprudential notion

---

[6] In *Pioneer Shipping Ltd v. BTP Tioxide Ltd; The Nema* [1982] A.C. 724 at 738.
[7] Arbitration Act 1996, s. 93(2).
[8] Arbitration Act 1996, Sched. 2, para. 7(5).
[9] See ss. 1(b) and 6 generally as to the consensual nature of arbitration. See also *Kenya Railways v. Antares Pte Ltd; The Antares No. 1 and 2)* [1987] 1 Lloyd's Rep. 424.
[10] Arbitration Act 1996, s. 6 which generally defines an arbitration agreement.
[11] [1992] 1 Lloyd's Rep. 81.
[12] s. 30 states that the arbitral tribunal may rule on whether there is a valid arbitration agreement, s. 30(1)(a); whether the tribunal is properly constituted, s. 30(1)(b); and what matters have been submitted in accordance with the agreement, s. 30(1)(c).

of *compétence compétence (kompetenz kompetenz)*. A party may object to the substantive jurisdiction of the tribunal under the conditions, and in accordance with the procedure laid down in sections 31 and 32 of the Act.

The contractual nature of arbitration also had to be borne in mind when it was contended that the prolonged inactivity of the parties in the prosecution of the arbitration resulted in "frustration" of the arbitration by delay on the ground that after a lapse of time it is no longer possible to do justice between the parties.[13] This was not frustration in the legal sense, it was simply that inactivity by both parties may prompt the conclusion that the parties have agreed to abandon the arbitration or that one has repudiated the agreement and that the other has accepted that repudiation.[14] Both conclusions were possible owing to the contractual nature of the arbitration agreement. Prior to the Courts and Legal Services Act 1990, s. 102 inserting section 13A in the Arbitration Act 1950, the arbitrator had no power to strike out a claim for want of prosecution. This is now dealt with under section 41(3) of the Arbitration Act 1996 where the arbitrator, in the absence of contrary agreement by the parties may, in the event of inordinate and inexcusable delay, make an award dismissing the claim.

The judicial element of arbitration

23–005 The arbitrator, although chosen by the parties or otherwise appointed under the arbitration agreement, must approach the issues before him in the same spirit as a judge appointed by the state. He must act impartially; indeed the requirement of impartiality is one of the principles underlying the Arbitration Act 1996.[15] This requirement is further underlined in the general duty of the arbitral tribunal to act fairly and impartially between the parties[16] and by the fact that one of the limited grounds upon which the court may remove an arbitrator is that there are circumstances which give rise to justifiable doubts as to the impartiality of the arbitrator.[17] This provision covers not only actual bias but also imputed bias, that is, conduct which would lead a reasonable man to conclude that the arbitrator is biased.[18]

The arbitration must be conducted not only in accordance with the applicable procedural rules but also the arbitrator must observe the requirements of natural justice.[19] The arbitrator, like a judge, can order inspection of property,[20] in appropriate circumstances he may make an award in a foreign currency[21]; he may

---

[13] See *Bremer Vulkan Schiffbau und Maschinenfabrik v. South India Shipping Corporation* [1981] 1 A.C. 909 and *Food Corporation of India v. Antclizo Shipping Corporation* [1988] 1 W.L.R. 603. In the latter case it was suggested that where arbitrations have not been pursued for many years, the court should be empowered by legislation to dismiss the arbitration for want of prosecution.

[14] See *Bremer Vulkan, ante*, n. 14.

[15] Arbitration Act 1996, s. 1(a).

[16] *ibid.*, s. 33(1)(a).

[17] *ibid.*, s. 24(1)(a).

[18] The test of imputed bias is an objective one: *cf. Tracomin SA v. Gibbs Nathaniel (Canada) Ltd* [1985] 1 Lloyd's Rep. 586; see also *Cook International Inc v. BV Handelsmaattschappij Jean Delvaux* [1985] 2 Lloyd's Rep. 225.

[19] See the word "fair" in the Arbitration Act 1996, s. 1(a) and the notes above.

[20] Arbitration Act 1996, s. 38(4)(a).

[21] Arbitration Act 1996, s. 48(4).

order interest on that award[22] and he may, if the claimant is an individual ordinarily resident outside the United Kingdom or a company formed or controlled from outside the United Kingdom, order that security for costs be provided.[23] The arbitrator has the same powers as the court to order specific performance of a contract and rectification of a deed or document.[24] These powers are subject to the provisions of the arbitration agreement.

Ad hoc and institutional arbitration

In their arbitration agreement the parties may opt for *ad hoc* arbitration or for institutional arbitration. If they decide in favour of the former, they may agree on the identity of the arbitrator or leave his appointment to a third person, for example the President of the Law Society in London.[25] In *ad hoc* arbitrations it may be advisable for the parties to provide for the application of one of the standard sets[26] of Arbitration Rules in order to minimise procedural disputes and to enable a deadlock to be broken should one occur by the failure, for example, of the respondent to appoint his arbitrator or where the arbitration tribunal cannot agree a chairman.[27]

23–006

Often the parties will agree on arbitration under the rules of one of the institutions which provide facilities for the arbitral settlement of disputes arising in international trade transactions. The major international arbitration institutions are considered later.[28] Institutional arbitration offers some advantages over *ad hoc* arbitration. The institution usually offers administrative assistance with respect to the conduct of the arbitration and its rules contain a code of procedure to be followed. Whether the arbitration agreement provides for *ad hoc* or institutional arbitration, it should always specify the seat and the language of the arbitration.

The law governing the arbitration procedure

The law applicable to the arbitration procedure, sometimes referred to as the curial law, may be different from the law governing the contract. Thus, in a

23–007

---

[22] Arbitration Act 1996, s. 49. After amendment to the Arbitration Act 1950, s. 20 by the Private International Law (Miscellaneous Provisions) Act 1995, s. 3 the arbitrator was empowered to order the payment of interest after the date of the award, at his discretion, at a rate other than that applicable to a judgment debt. Before that the arbitrator only had the discretion to fix interest on the sum of the award up to the date of the award and after that date to order interest only at the rate applicable to a judgment debt.

[23] Arbitration Act 1996, s. 38(3), a new power which must be read in conjunction with the notes to RSC Ord. 23 and considered in the light of the fact that to order security against residents of E.C. countries may be constituting a breach of Art. 6 of the Treaty of Rome. See *Fitzgerald v. Williams* [1996] 2 All E.R. 171. See para. 23–017.

[24] See generally Arbitration Act 1996, s. 48(5).

[25] In the event of failure of appointment, see s. 18. See especially s. 18(3): application to the court to give directions for making appointments or making the appointment itself.

[26] Such as UNCITRAL Arbitration Rules, the Rules of Arbitration of the ICC, 1998.

[27] See also Arbitration Act 1996, s. 20.

[28] See para. 23–020.

case[29] in which the law governing the contract was English law, the parties held their arbitration in Scotland in accordance with the Scots law applicable to arbitration. The House of Lords decided that Scots law regulated the arbitration procedure whilst the arbitrator had to apply English law as the law governing the contract.

If the parties have adopted an international code of arbitration procedure, such as the UNCITRAL Arbitration Rules or the Rules of Arbitration of the ICC, there will usually be no need to go beyond this and to resort to a national law in order to ascertain the procedural rules. In this—restricted—sense one can talk of arbitration which is "transnational", or "anational". If, however, the international regulation contains a gap, reference will have to be made to the national legal system applicable to the arbitration procedure. This will normally be the law of the place where the arbitration is held but, exceptionally, another legal system may apply or may at least govern certain aspects of the curial law. Under the 1996 Act, the seat of the arbitration is defined in section 3 as the juridical seat of the arbitration which has been designated by the parties or by any arbitral or other institution with powers in that regard or by the tribunal, if so authorised by the parties. Section 2 provides that where the seat of the arbitration is in England, Wales or Northern Ireland, Part I of the Arbitration Act 1996 will apply whatever the curial law chosen by the parties may be.[30] Section 46 deals with the rules applicable to the substance of the dispute. The section provides that the tribunal shall decide the dispute in accordance with the law chosen by the parties or in accordance with other agreed considerations. If there is no choice on agreement the tribunal will apply the law determined by the conflict of law rules considered by the tribunal to be applicable.[31]

Application of the *lex mercatoria* in arbitration proceedings

23–008 The "transnational" or "anational" character of the legal regulation may extend to the substantive law of the contract. The parties may authorise the arbitrator to decide the substantive issues before him according to the "internationally accepted principles of law governing contractual relations" which, briefly, are referred to as the *lex mercatoria* (the law merchant)[32] or, if they leave the choice of the proper law to him, he may opt for the *lex mercatoria*. In one case,[33] which arose from an oil exploration agreement

---

[29] *Whitworth Street Estates (Manchester) Ltd v. James Miller & Partners Ltd* [1970] A.C. 583. See also *International Tank and Pipe SAK v. Kuwait Aviation Fuelling Co KSC* [1975] Q.B. 224; *Dalmia Dairy Industries Ltd v. National Bank of Pakistan* [1978] 2 Lloyd's Rep. 223 at 228.
[30] Arbitration Act 1996, s. 2.
[31] Note that the Brussels Convention, Art. 1(4) excludes arbitration. The Rome Convention does not apply to arbitration agreements—Art. 1, para. 2(d), see *Egon Oldendorff v. Liberia Corp [No. 2]* [1995] 2 Lloyd's Rep. 64.
[32] The Right Hon. Lord Justice Mustill, "The New Lex Mercatoria: The First Twenty-Five Years", in *Liber Amicorum for Lord Wilberforce* (ed. Bos and Brownlie, 1987), p. 149; O. Lando, "The Lex Mercatoria in International Commercial Arbitration" (1985) 34 I.C.L.Q. 747; C.M. Schmitthoff, "International Trade Usages", Inst. Internl. Bus. Law and Practice, 1987, I.C.C. Publication No. 440/4. *Cf.* also Felix Dasser, *International Schiedsgerichte und lex mercatoria* (Zürich, 1989).
[33] *Deutsche Schachtbau-und Tiefbohrgesellschaft mbH v. R' As al-Khaima National Oil Co* [1987] 3 W.L.R. 1023.

between an enterprise in a Middle Eastern State and a German company, DST, the arbitration clause provided for ICC arbitration to be held in Geneva. The ICC Rules of Arbitration[34] authorise the arbitrators, in the absence of any indication as to the proper law, to apply the law which they deem to be appropriate. Accordingly, the arbitral tribunal held that it would be inappropriate in the case before it to apply a national system of law, but that the substantive law governing the obligations of the parties was the "internationally accepted principles of law governing contractual relations". In English proceedings for the enforcement of the award, the Court of Appeal rejected the argument that the choice of an anational system of law contravened public policy. Sir John Donaldson M.R. said[35]:

> "I can see no basis for concluding that the arbitrators' choice of proper law—a common denominator of principles underlying the laws of various nations governing contractual relations—is outwith the scope of the choice which the parties left to the arbitrators."

As noted above, section 46 of the Arbitration Act 1996 provides that "the arbitral tribunal shall decide the dispute in accordance with the law chosen by the parties as applicable to the substance of the dispute or, if the parties agree, in accordance with such other considerations as are agreed by them or determined by the tribunal". It may be that "such other considerations" include the *lex mercatoria* and arbitrations *ex aequo et bono*.

Arbitration *ex aequo et bono*

The parties sometimes authorise the arbitrator to decide *ex aequo et bono*. Such **23–009** "equity" clauses are worded in different ways. Sometimes they provide that the arbitrator shall apply equitable considerations and in other cases they state that the agreement shall be interpreted "as an honourable engagement".[36]

An equity clause does not mean that the arbitrator may disregard the law and a clause purporting to give him this power would be void.[37] It means that, in interpreting the law and the contract between the parties, the arbitrator should take a common sense view and should not be bound by legal technicalities. In one case[38] in which the Court of Appeal interpreted an equity clause as authorising the arbitrator to take "the lenient view",[39] Lord Denning M.R. said of such a clause[40]:

---

[34] Then in operation. The matter is now covered by Art. 17(1) given effect January 1, 1998.
[35] *Deutsche Schachtbau, ante* at 1035.
[36] "Honourable engagement" provisions are often found in arbitration clauses of reinsurance agreements.
[37] What arbitrators may properly do will depend greatly on the width of such a clause. See *Eagle Star Insurance Co Ltd v. Yuval Insurance Co Ltd* [1978] 1 Lloyd's Rep. 357 and *Home Insurance Co v. Administratia Asigurarilor De Stat* [1983] 2 Lloyd's Rep. 674.
[38] *Home and Overseas Insurance Eagle Star, ante,* n. 34. See also *Overseas Union Insurance Ltd v. AA Mutual Insurance Co Ltd* [1988] 2 Lloyd's Rep. 63 and *Home and Overseas Co Ltd v. Mentor Insurance Co (U.K.) Ltd* [1989] 1 Lloyd's Rep. 473.
[39] *Per* Goff J. in the *Eagle Star* case.
[40] *Eagle Star, ante* at 362. See s.46(1)(a) and (1)(b).

"It only ousts technicalities and strict constructions. That is what equity did in the old days. And it is what arbitrators may properly do today under such a clause as this."

ENGLISH ARBITRATION

23–010 The statute law relating to arbitration is contained in the Arbitration Act 1996.[41] It applies to England, Wales and Northern Ireland. It consolidates the existing legislation (the Arbitration Acts of 1950, 1975 and 1979 and the Consumer Arbitration Agreements Act 1988), and introduces various reforms and some codification. The principle of non intervention by the courts, given a significant boost by the 1979 Act, is maintained and indeed is affirmed by section 1(c).[42] In this and other matters the new Act owes much to the UNCITRAL Model Law on International Commercial Arbitration[43] which provides in Article 5 "In matters governed by this Law, no court shall intervene except where so provided in this Law".

The arbitration agreement and the arbitrators

23–011 The Arbitration Act 1996 defines an arbitration agreement as an "agreement to submit to arbitration present or future differences whether they are contractual or not". Written agreements within the meaning of the Act need not be signed by the parties.[44] It is sufficient that the clause is expressed in writing and the contract wherein the clause appears has been accepted or acted upon by the parties. The agreement need not be contained in one and the same document. Lloyd L.J. said in one case concerning a GAFTA arbitration[45]:

> "For an agreement to be a written agreement to arbitrate it is unnecessary for the whole of the contract, including the arbitration agreement to be contained in the same document. It is sufficient that the arbitration agreement is itself in writing; indeed it is sufficient if there is a document which recognises the existence of an agreement between the parties . . . would hold that an arbitration agreement need not be signed and that the definition of s.32[46] of the Act is satisfied provided there is a document or documents in writing . . ."

---

[41] In force January 31, 1997: Arbitration Act 1996 (Commencement No. 1 Order) 1996 (S.I. 1996 No. 3146). *Practice Note (Arbitration: New Procedure)* [1997] 1 W.L.R. 391 referred to the new RSC Ord. 73 introduced by Rules of the Supreme Court (Amendment) 1996 (S.I. 1996 No. 3215). Commencing procedure is now governed by practice directions under CPR, Pt 49(2)(b). Allocation of proceedings is governed by the High Court and County Courts (Allocation of Arbitration Proceedings) (Amendment Order), S.I. 1999 No. 1010. Ss. 85–87 are not yet in force, see *post*, para. 23–016.

[42] s. 1(c), in matters governed by this Part the court should not intervene except as provided by this Part (Part 1 of the 1996 Act).

[43] As adopted by the United Nations Commission on International Trade Law on June 21, 1985.

[44] Arbitration Act 1996, s. 5(2)(a).

[45] *Excomm Ltd v. Ahmed Abdul-Qawi Bamaodah; The St. Raphael* [1985] 1 Lloyd's Rep. 403 at 408 and 409. See also *Zambia Steel & Building Supplies Ltd v. James Clark & Eaton Ltd* [1986] 2 Lloyd's Rep. 225. Now codified in s.5. See also s.6(2) and *Trygg Hansa Insurance Co v. Equitas Ltd* [1998] 2 Lloyd's Rep. 439.

[46] See now Arbitration Act 1996, s. 6(1).

An exchange by telex communication satisfies this test and constitutes an arbitration agreement in writing.[47] Oral arbitration agreements, which are rare in practice, are valid at common law, but not governed by the Arbitration Act 1996 and section 81 confirms this position. In such an agreement there is an element of uncertainty with respect to the implications and enforcement of the arbitration agreement. It is, therefore, preferable that the arbitration agreement should always be in written form although it need not be signed. It should be noted that if there is an arbitration agreement in a contract of sale or of partnership, it does not extend to the submission of claims under bills of exchange given by merchants in performance of those contracts unless there is a clear intention of both parties to that effect.

Examples of arbitration clauses

The following are examples of arbitration clauses[48]:   **23–012**

Example 1

> "Any dispute[49] arising out of or in connection with this contract including, any question regarding its existence, validity or termination, shall be referred to and finally resolved by arbitration under the Rules of the London Court of International Arbitration which Rules are deemed to be incorporated by reference into this clause."

Example 2

> "If any dispute should arise in connection with the interpretation and fulfilment of this contract, same shall be decided by arbitration in the city of . . . and shall be referred to a single arbitrator to be appointed by the parties hereto. If the parties cannot agree upon the appointment of the single arbitrator, the dispute shall be settled by three arbitrators, each party appointing one arbitrator, the third being appointed by . . ."

Section 15(3) provides that where there is no agreement on the number of arbitrators the tribunal shall consist of a sole arbitrator. Example 2 above resolves the difficulty of parties failing to agree an arbitrator.[50] If a third person has to make the appointment and refuses or fails to do so within the specified time or a reasonable time, any party to the arbitration agreement may give him notice

---

[47] *Arab African Energy Corp Ltd v. Olieprodukten Nederland BV* [1983] 2 Lloyd's Rep. 419. See also *Abdullah M. Fahem & Co v. Mareb Yemen Insurance and Tomen (U.K.) Ltd* [1997] 2 Lloyd's Rep. 738.

[48] Example 1 is the suggested clause of the London Court of International Arbitration. Example 2 is that of the London Maritime Arbitrators Association. A clause worded "suitable arbitration clause" in an English contract is not void on the ground of uncertainty. See *Hobbs Padgett & Co (Reinsurance) Ltd v. J.C. Kirkland Ltd* [1969] 2 Lloyd's Rep. 547. A clause providing for arbitration to be settled "in the customary manner" in a charter party was not invalid but meant that, as was usual in maritime disputes, two arbitrators should be appointed, one by each party: *Laertis Shipping Corporation v. Exportadora Española de Cementos Portland SA, The Laertis* [1982] 1 Lloyd's Rep. 613.

[49] On the meaning of "arising out of contract" and "under the contract" see para. 23–015.

[50] If the tribunal is to consist of three arbitrators, the arbitrators appointed by the parties will appoint the third as chairman, s.16(5)(b). As to "substitute" arbitrators see *Federal Insurance Co v. Transamerica Occidental Life Insurance Co* [1999] 2 Lloyd's Rep. 286.

to make the appointment. If he fails to do so within seven days, the provisions in sections 17 and 18, relating to failure to appoint, may be applied subject to the provisions of the arbitration agreement. Similarly, when the parties have to concur in the appointment of the arbitrator and fail to reach an agreement recourse may again be had to sections 17 and 18. The usual arrangement is that each party is entitled to appoint one arbitrator. Section 15 (2), a new provision , states that:

> "unless otherwise agreed by the parties, an agreement that the number of arbitrators shall be two or any other even number shall be understood as requiring the appointment of an additional arbitrator as chairman of the tribunal."

The procedure for appointing arbitrators, including any chairman, may be agreed by the parties. Again, in the event of failure to agree, the provisions in sections 17 and 18 may be invoked.

It may happen that one party desires to go to arbitration and appoints his arbitrator where more than one is required while the other party is unwilling to do so. Here, the former may serve the defaulting party with notice to appoint an arbitrator, and, if the defaulting party has not done so within seven clear days after the notice was served, the party who appointed an arbitrator may appoint his arbitrator as sole arbitrator and his award is binding on the parties.[51] The arbitrator must consent to act in this capacity before the appointment is effective.[52]

The former position under the Arbitration Act 1950, where there was a presumption in favour of the appointment of an umpire, has been changed by section 15(2). Under section 15(1) parties are free to agree on whether there is to be an umpire or a chairman:

> "The parties are free to agree on the number of arbitrators to form the tribunal and whether there is to be a chairman or umpire."

If an umpire is agreed upon the parties are, by virtue of section 21(1), free to agree on his functions.

Section 21(4) indicates the time when the umpire assumes his role:

> "Decisions, orders and awards shall be made by the other arbitrators unless and until they cannot agree on a matter relating to the arbitration.
>
> In that event they shall forthwith give notice in writing to the parties and to the umpire, whereupon the umpire shall replace them as the tribunal with power to make decisions, orders and awards as if he were sole arbitrator."

The arbitrators thus become in effect "functus officio."[53]

---

[51] Many arbitration clauses contain a time-limit for the appointment of arbitrators by the parties.

[52] *Tradax Export SA v. Volkswagenwerk AG* [1970] 1 Q.B. 537.

[53] Diplock J. in *Wessanen's Koninklijke Fabrikien v. Isaac Modiano & Sons Ltd* [1960] 1 W.L.R. 1243, suggested that arbitrators are "functus officio" and may only attend the hearing as representatives of the parties.

Qualifications

Section 24(1)(b) of the Arbitration Act 1996 states that the court may, upon **23–013** application, remove an arbitrator (and umpire) on the grounds, *inter alia*, that he does not possess the qualifications required by the arbitration agreement. Thus, it can be seen that the qualifications required will be those stated in the arbitration agreement. If the arbitration agreement provides that the arbitrators be "commercial men", they should be so. The pre-1996 Act cases in this area are few but it can, however, be discerned[54] that a practising member of the Bar is not to be considered as such, whereas a professional maritime arbitrator is.[55]

Jurisdiction of the tribunal

Once constituted the tribunal may, unless otherwise agreed by the parties, rule **23–014** on its own substantive jurisdiction. It may determine whether there is a valid arbitration agreement, whether the tribunal is properly constituted and therefore, presumably, whether the arbitrators are suitably qualified. It may also determine what matters have been submitted to arbitration.[56] The foregoing is a consequence, in turn, of section 7 which itself merely affirms the position at common law.[57] The tribunal, therefore, can rule on the validity of the arbitration agreement and whether the matters referred to them are within the agreement.

Disputes covered by the arbitration agreement

The arbitration agreement determines which disputes are submitted to the juris- **23–015** diction of the tribunal. The ambit of arbitration clauses varies and much depends upon the wording of such clauses, which should not be defective.[58] A formulation which is frequently adopted is that "all disputes arising out of the contract or in connection with it" shall be submitted to arbitration. The intention of the parties, when agreeing on such a wording, is that claims concerning an alleged relevant mistake or misrepresentation as well as extracontractual claims, such as *quantum meruit* or unjust enrichment,[59] or even in tort, if these claims are connected with the contract, are subject to the jurisdiction of the arbitrator. Asquith L.J. said in a case where the claim was founded on tort[60]:

---

[54] *ibid.*
[55] *Pando Compañía Naviera SA v. Filmo SAS* [1975] 1 Lloyd's Rep. 560.
[56] See Arbitration Act 1996, s. 30.
[57] In the case of *Harbour Assurance Co (U.K.) Ltd v. Kansa General Insurance Co Ltd* [1992] 1 Lloyd's Rep. 81.
[58] C.M. Schmitthoff, "Defective Arbitration Clauses" [1975] J.B.L. 9: also in *Essays*, p. 608.
[59] *Ashville Investments Ltd v. Elmer Contractors Ltd* [1988] 2 Lloyd's Rep. 73 (arbitration in a building contract; claim for rectification of contract arbitrable under "in connection" clause).
[60] In *Woolf v. Collis Removal Service* [1947] 2 All E.R. 260 at 263. See also *per* Sellers J. in *Government of Gibraltar v. Kenney* [1956] 2 Q.B. 410 at 422–423. *Fillite (Runcorn) Ltd v. Aqualift, The Times*, February 28, 1989 ("arising under" could not be read as including "and in connection with the contract"); *Ethiopian Oilseeds and Pulses Export Corporation v. Rio del Mar Foods Inc* [1990] 1 Lloyd's Rep. 86 ("arising out of" to be interpreted widely, it gives the arbitrator jurisdiction to decide on rectification of contract).

"We are of the opinion that, even if the claim in negligence is not a claim arising 'under the contract', yet there is sufficiently close connection between that claim and the transaction to bring the claim within the arbitration clause even though technically framed in tort."

A counterclaim is allowable in arbitration if it is within the ambit of the arbitration clause.[61]

In the case of frustration of contract the arbitrator may make an adjustment under the Law Reform (Frustrated Contracts) Act 1943.[62] An arbitrator has discretion under the Misrepresentation Act 1967, s.3, as amended by the Unfair Contract Terms Act 1977, s.8, to allow an exemption clause excluding liability for misrepresentation only if it satisfies the reasonableness test, as stated in the Unfair Contract Terms Act, and the onus of showing that it does is on the party claiming the exemption.

Stays

23–016 If the parties agree to abandon the arbitration and to take the dispute to court, no problem arises.[63] The original arbitration agreement is abrogated by a further agreement of the parties and the court will hear the case if it has jurisdiction.

Usually, however, the position is different. One of the parties may commence proceedings in court, contrary to the arbitration agreement, and the other, who wishes to abide by the agreement, applies to the court for a stay of court proceedings so that the arbitration may take its course.

That such an application can be made is provided by section 9(1). On hearing the application the court "shall grant a stay unless satisfied that the arbitration agreement is null and void, inoperative or incapable of being performed".[64] The parties will thus be held to their agreement, which position is consistent with the principles underpinning the Act.[65] The burden of proving why the court should not give effect to the arbitration agreement is on the party who commenced the proceedings.[66]

A recent case in relation to section 9 illustrates how courts approach the section and further underlines the difference between the new act and the old provisions which listed another ground upon which a court could refuse a stay, which was that there is no dispute between the parties. In *Halki Shipping Corporation v. Sopex Oils Ltd*[67] a demurrage claim arose. The charterparty contained an arbitration clause in respect to "any dispute arising from or in connection with the charterparty". The plaintiffs brought a claim in court and the defendants applied for a stay under section 9. In fact, the plaintiffs applied for summary

---

[61] A. Redfern and M. Hunter, *Law and Practice of International Commercial Arbitration* (Sweet and Maxwell, 1999), 242.

[62] *Government of Gibraltar v. Kenney* [1956] 2 Q.B. 410.

[63] On the question of terminating the arbitration agreement, see *ante*, para. 23–003.

[64] Arbitration Act 1996, s. 9(4). An agreement will be incapable of being performed as a result of some factor external to the parties and not merely the impecuniosity or insolvency of one of them, *The Rena K* [1978] 1 Lloyd's Rep. 545.

[65] Part I, s. 1(b): ". . . the parties should be free to agree how their disputes are resolved . . ." and s. 1(c): ". . . the court should not intervene . . ."

[66] *Per* Brandon J. in *The Eleftheria* [1969] 1 Lloyd's Rep. 237 at 242.

[67] [1998] 1 W.L.R. 726. See also *Jitendra Bhailbhai Patel v. Dilesh R. Patel* [1999] 3 W.L.R. 322.

judgment under CPR, Pt 24 on the basis that there was no dispute between the parties and therefore none to be referred to arbitration. The defendants did not admit liability. The judge at first instance granted a stay and dismissed the application. The plaintiffs appealed. The Court of Appeal held that the word "dispute" was to be given its ordinary meaning and embraced any claim which the other party did not admit or did not meet, whether or not there was an answer to the claim in law or in fact. By a majority, the Court held that once there was a dispute the Court was obliged by section 9 to grant a stay unless any of the circumstances in section 9(4) were present. The application to stay court proceedings must be made in time. This means that the party who wishes to apply for a stay must be mindful of the provisions of section 9(3):

> "An application may not be made by a person before taking the appropriate procedural step (if any) to acknowledge the legal proceedings against him or after he has taken any step in those proceedings to answer the substantive claim."

Section 11 deals with the position in Admiralty proceedings where a party commences an action *in rem* and proceedings are stayed under section 9. Here the court may order that the property arrested be retained as security for any arbitral award given in that dispute or order that the stay be granted on condition that an equivalent security be provided.[68]

The distinction made in the previous Acts between domestic and non-domestic arbitrations is preserved, for certain purposes, in the 1996 Act. "Domestic arbitration agreement" is defined in section 85.[69] An additional ground for not granting a stay of court proceedings is provided in section 86(2)(b) " that there are sufficient other reasons for not requiring the parties to abide by the arbitration agreement". Such sufficient other reasons in practice have been difficult to find.[70]

Any application to stay must be made in a proper manner and at the appropriate time, as the party seeking the stay may not make an application before acknowledgment of service and may not after taking any step in the court proceedings.[71] It is not exactly clear what "any step" means, but probably by analogy with considerations concerning submission to a jurisdiction, it embraces an attempt to defend the claim in court on its merits.

---

[68] s. 11(1)(a) and (b), see also *The Bazias 3* [1993] Lloyd's Rep. 101.
[69] An agreement to which none of the parties is an individual who is a national of or habitually resident in a State other than the U.K. or a body corporate incorporated in or whose central control is exercised in a State other than the U.K. and under which the seat of the arbitration is in the U.K., s. 85(2)(a) and (b); see *Hume v. AA Mutual International Insurance* [1996] L.R.L.R. 19. Ss. 85–87 relating to domestic arbitration agreements are not yet in force and may never be as such distinction may be contrary to the Treaty of Rome, see *Philip Alexander Securities and Futures v. Bamberger, The Times*, July 22, 1996, CA. These sections are unlikely to be brought into force and are included here only for information.
[70] *Bulk Oil (Zug) v. Trans-Asiatic Oil SA* [1973] 1 Lloyd's Rep. 129.
[71] Arbitration Act 1996, s. 9(3).

The powers of the tribunal

23–017 The powers of the tribunal in relation to procedural and evidential matters are
set out is section 34 of the Act. The scheme of the section ensures that the
agreement of the parties is of importance in relation to whatever powers may
be exercised, thereby ensuring that the whole arbitral procedure advances in
accordance with the parties' wishes and preferences. Section 34(1) provides that
it shall be for the tribunal to decide all procedural and evidential matters "subject
to the rights of the parties to agree any matter." Section 34 lists those procedural
and evidential matters. These include determining the location of proceedings,
the forms the submission of claim or defence are to take, matters relating to
discovery and evidence and, very significantly, under section 34(2)(g) "whether
and to what extent the tribunal itself should take the initiative in ascertaining
the facts and the law."

This gives the tribunal the option of determining whether to conduct the proceedings in the traditional adversarial manner or to employ an inquisitorial procedure. Prior to the Act it was generally assumed that only the parties could
authorise the latter being used.[72]

The tribunal may appoint experts to assist it,[73] order security for costs,[74] give
directions in relation to property which is the subject of the proceedings,[75] direct
that witnesses be examined on oath,[76] and order the preservation of evidence.[77]
Section 39 gives the tribunal the power, if the agreement of the parties so allows,
to make provisional awards such as an order for the payment of money or
disposition of property. The section should be read together with section 47
which allows the tribunal, unless otherwise agreed by the parties, to make
awards on different issues at different times. These sections ensure that the
tribunal can act expeditiously by making awards on separate discrete issues. The
powers are in addition to the tribunal's power to rule on its own jurisdiction[78]
and to make such a ruling in an award as to jurisdiction.[79]

Should either of the parties fail to do something necessary for the proper and
expeditious conduct of the arbitration, the tribunal may, unless the parties have
agreed otherwise, exercise certain powers. These powers are set out in section
41 and are extensive. They include the power to dismiss a claim if there has
been inordinate and inexcusable delay,[80] to proceed in the absence of a party
should a party, having received due notice, fail to attend or fail to make written

---

[72] *Town and City Properties (Development) Ltd v. Wilshier Southern Ltd and Gilbert Powell* (1988)
B.L.R. 114.
[73] s. 37. Unless otherwise agreed by the parties such an order or award may be challenged in the
courts. When considering such challenge the court ought to be guided by the principles set down in
Azov Shipping Co v. Baltic Shipping Co [1999] 2 Lloyd's Rep. 39. See para. 23–019 for challenges
to arbitral awards.
[74] s. 38(3).
[75] s. 38(4).
[76] s. 38(5). A party to arbitral proceedings may secure the attendance of a witness under the conditions laid down in s. 43.
[77] s. 38(6).
[78] s. 30.
[79] s. 31(4).
[80] s. 41(3).

submissions,[81] to dismiss a claim should a party fail to provide security for costs when ordered to do so[82] or exercise any of the options in section 41(7) if a party fails to comply with a peremptory order of the tribunal.[83]

The parties may agree on the remedies which the tribunal may provide; in the absence of such agreement the tribunal may make a declaration as to any matter to be determined or order payment of money in any currency, and has the same powers as the court to order a party to do or not do a thing, to specifically perform a contract (other than one relating to land), to order rectification or the setting aside of a deed[84] and to award interest on the award.[85]

The award

Section 52 provides that the parties are free to agree on the form of the award. **23–018** If there is no such agreement the award shall be in writing and signed by all the arbitrators or those assenting.[86] Formerly, the Arbitration Acts did not require the tribunal to state reasons for the award unless the parties so required. The position now is that, in accordance with section 52(4), the award must be reasoned unless otherwise agreed. The reasons should not be unduly long and need not set out the law extensively. Donaldson L.J. said:

> "All that is necessary . . . is that the arbitrators . . . should set out what, in their own view of the evidence, did or did not happen, and should explain succinctly why in the light of what happened they had reached their decision and what that decision was. They are not expected to analyse the law and the authorities."[87]

If no reasons are given or those that are given are not in sufficient detail, an application may be made to the court within 28 days for an order that the tribunal state its reasons in sufficient detail.[88] However, it must be noted that if the parties agree to dispense with reasons for the award, the agreement will be taken to be an agreement to exclude the court's jurisdiction.[89] The award must be notified to the parties without delay,[90] unless the tribunal exercises its right under section 56 to withhold the award for the non payment of the fees and expenses of the arbitrators. The award will be deemed to be made in England, Wales or Northern Ireland if the seat of the arbitration is there and it is immaterial where it was signed or dispatched. This provision under section 53 removes the difficulties created by the circumstance of an arbitrator signing in Paris an award in respect

---

[81] s. 41(4).
[82] s. 41(6). See s.41(5) and s.82 for the distinction between "order" and peremptory order.
[83] Such options include directing that a defaulting party may not rely on any allegation which is the subject matter of the order, draw such adverse inferences as are justified, or make such order for costs as the tribunal thinks fit.
[84] s. 48.
[85] s. 49.
[86] s. 52(3).
[87] *Westzucker GmbH v. Bunge GmbH* [1981] Com. L.R. 179 (also [1981] 2 Lloyd's Rep. 132–133 where the wording differs in inessential details) a case dealing with the 1979 Act. See also *Trave Schiffahrtsgesellschaft mbH & Co KG v. Ninemia Maritime Corporation (No.2)* [1986] Q.B. 802.
[88] s. 70(4).
[89] s. 69(7).
[90] s. 55(2).

of an arbitration whose seat was in England.[91] The tribunal shall award the costs of the arbitration to the successful party unless the tribunal consider it inappropriate to do so.[92] An award may, by section 66, be enforced as a judgment with the leave of the court.

The role of the court

23–019 In keeping with the principles of the Act,[93] the court[94] now enjoys only a limited role. It was seen above that the court can appoint an arbitrator under section 18 and remove an arbitrator on grounds of lack of qualifications under section 24. The court can assist, in respect of a party's failure to comply with a peremptory order of the tribunal, under the conditions set out in section 42. The court also enjoys powers, unless otherwise agreed, under section 43, securing the attendance of a witness and section 44 to assist the tribunal by making certain orders. These[95] include orders for the inspection, preservation or detention of property, the sale of goods which are the subject of proceedings and, importantly, the granting of an interim injunction or the appointment of a receiver.

This latter power will, of course, include the granting of a freezing order. These powers under sections 43 and 44 may be used even if the seat is outside England, Wales or Northern Ireland by virtue of section 2(3)(a) and (b)[96] but only if it is appropriate to do so.

The court may entertain an application under section 32 regarding a preliminary point of jurisdiction of the arbitral tribunal. It was seen above that the Act enables the tribunal to rule on its own substantive jurisdiction. Any objection must be made at the outset under section 31. The objecting party must not have taken the first step in the proceedings to contest the merits of any matter in relation to which he challenges the tribunal's jurisdiction.[97] The application under section 32 must be made with the agreement of all the other parties to the proceedings or with the permission of the tribunal. If the application is made with the permission of the tribunal the court must also be satisfied that the determination will produce substantial savings in costs, that the application was made without delay and that there is good reason for the court to decide the matter.[98] The strict conditions under which the application can be made are in keeping with the ethos of the Act and the preservation of the integrity of the tribunal in determining its own jurisdiction. A preliminary point of law may be

---

[91] *Hiscox v. Outhwaite (No. 1)* 3 All E.R. 641.
[92] s. 61(1) and (2). See *Smeaton, Hanscomb & Co Ltd v. Sassoon I. Setty, Son & Co (No. 2)* [1953] 1 W.L.R. 1481; see also *The Rozel* [1994] 2 Lloyd's Rep. 161.
[93] s. 1(c).
[94] The court is defined in s.105 and means the High Court or the county court. The High Court and County Courts (Allocation of Arbitration Proceedings Amendment Order) 1999 (S.I. 1999 No. 1010) allocates proceedings between the High Court and county court and provides for matters to be commenced in the Central London County Court Business List. See CPR, Pt 49 and the practice direction relating to arbitrations.
[95] s. 44(2)(a)–(e).
[96] See *Channel Tunnel Group Ltd v. Balfour Beatty Construction Ltd* [1993] 11 Lloyd's Rep. 291, HL and *Alfred C. Toepfer International GmbH v. Société Cargill France* [1998] 1 Lloyd's Rep. 379.
[97] s. 31(1).
[98] s. 32(2). See *Azov Shipping Co v. Baltic Shipping Co* [1999] 1 Lloyd's Rep. 68.

taken under section 45, the conditions to be fulfilled are similar to those set out in section 32(2).

As far as review of the award itself is concerned the 1979 Act inclined heavily in favour of finality as indicated by Lord Diplock in the important case of *The Nema*[99]:

> "... in weighing the rival merits of finality and meticulous legal accuracy there are, in my view, several indications in the Act itself of a Parliamentary intention to give effect to the turn of the tide in favour of finality in arbitral awards ... at any rate where this does not involve exposing arbitrators to a temptation to depart from 'settled principles of law'."

The drive for finality was confirmed by the fact that the 1996 Act adopts substantially the guidelines set out in that case for the judicial review of awards. The *"Nema* guidelines" indicated that the court's discretion in allowing judicial review should be exercised sparingly. The House of Lords distinguished between one-off contracts—those of singular occurrence—and contracts involving a question of general importance. A stricter test was to be applied to the former than to the latter. In the former class of cases the judge should only allow review if he concludes that the arbitrator was obviously wrong (now s.69(3)(c)(i)). The latter category of cases includes the interpretation of clauses in standard contracts and events that affect a significant number of transactions. Lord Diplock cited in this regard the closing of the Suez canal. In such a category, judicial review should only be allowed if there is "a strong prima facie case has been made out that the arbitrator was wrong in his construction"[1] (now s.69(3)(c)(ii)).

Section 69 sets out the conditions under which the court will review the award on a point of law. It should be noted that the parties can agree to oust the court's jurisdiction under the section. If a party wishes to appeal, that party requires the agreement of all the other parties or the leave of the court. To grant leave the court must be satisfied of the matters set out in s.69 above and that the rights of one or more of the parties will be substantially affected by the determination of the question and the question was one the tribunal was asked to determine and that it is just and proper for the court to determine the question.[2] Section 69(7) allows the court to confirm, vary, remit, or set aside in whole or in part the award.

The award may be challenged under sections 67 and 68. Section 67 allows appeals on the grounds that an award was made without jurisdiction. The matters which comprise "substantive jurisdiction" are those set out in sections 30 and 82.

Section 68 allows appeals on the basis of serious irregularity, the section lists in subsection 68(2): irregularities which would entitle a party to invoke the section. These include the failure by the tribunal to comply with its general duties under section 33, the tribunal exceeding its powers, failure to deal with all the issues, obtaining of an award by fraud or the award is contrary to public

---

[99] *Pioneer Shipping Ltd v. BTP Tioxide Ltd; The Nema* [1982] A.C. 724 at 739–740.
[1] *Antaios Compañía Naviera SA v. Salen Rederierna BA* [1985] A.C. 191 at 203 *per* Diplock L.
[2] s. 69(3)(a)(b)(d).

policy.[3] On successful application the court can make orders similar to those in section 69(7) above. The three sections are subject to the provisions of section 70 which include the requirement that the applicant exhaust any available arbitral appeal or review or procedure under the Act, such as section 57, and that the application be brought, within 28 days of the award or the applicant being notified. The court has power under section 12 to extend time for beginning arbitral proceedings. This section provides that a claim is barred or a claimant's right is extinguished unless some step has been taken within a fixed time. Such step may be the commencement of the arbitration proceeding or the triggering of other dispute mechanisms before the arbitration can commence. The court may extend time, if the claimant has exhausted any arbitral process for obtaining an extension. The court may grant the extension on such terms as it see fit. When considering the application, the court will examine all the "circumstances."[4]

INTERNATIONAL ARBITRATION

23–020 The various national laws on arbitration differ in material respects, although many countries adopt a liberal attitude to international commercial arbitration.[5] Various attempts have been made to devise an international procedure of commercial arbitration which commands wide acceptance. The most important of which will be considered below under the following headings:

    (a) UNCITRAL;

    (b) The ICC Court of Arbitration;

    (c) The London Court of International Arbitration;

    (d) The International Centre for the Settlement of Investment Disputes.

UNCITRAL

23–021 UNCITRAL itself does not provide arbitration facilities but has sponsored several measures which have made a notable contribution to the unification of the law of international arbitration.

The UNCITRAL Arbitration Rules

23–022 These Rules were adopted by UNCITRAL in 1976 and their use was recommended by the General Assembly of the United Nations on December 15, 1976. They are almost indispensible in *ad hoc* arbitrations and many arbitral institutions, which have adopted their own rules, allow the parties to use the UNCI-

---

[3] See *Egmatra AG v. Marco Trading Co* [1999] 1 Lloyd's Rep. 862.
[4] See *Vosnoc Ltd v. Transglobal Projects Ltd* [1998] 1 Lloyd's Rep. 711; *Grimaldi Compagnia v. Sekihyo Line* [1998] 2 Lloyd's Rep. 638 and *Harbour and General Works v. Environment Agency* [2000] 1 Lloyd's Rep. 65.
[5] See generally specialist publications of which the *International Arbitration Law Review* is one of several excellent examples in this area.

TRAL Rules in preference or refer to them in order to fill any gaps in their own rules.

The UNCITRAL Arbitration Rules do not have the force of law in any country. They may be adopted by the contracting parties. The following model clause is recommended for their adoption:

> "Any dispute, controversy or claim arising out of or relating to this contract, or the breach, termination or invalidity thereof, shall be settled by arbitration in accordance with the UNCITRAL Arbitration Rules as at present in force.
> *Note—Parties may wish to consider adding:*
>> (a) The appointing authority shall be . . . (name of institution or person);
>> (b) The number of arbitrators shall be . . . (one or three);
>> (c) The place of arbitration shall be . . . (town or country);
>> (d) The language(s) to be used in the arbitral proceedings shall be . . ."

The main characteristic of the UNCITRAL Arbitration Rules is that no arbitration shall fail on the ground that the parties cannot agree on an arbitrator or for any other reason no arbitrator can act. If no appointing authority has been agreed by the parties or if the appointing authority refuses to act or fails to appoint an arbitrator within 60 days of the receipt of a party's request, either party may request the Secretary-General of the Permanent Court of Arbitration at the Hague to designate an appointing authority.[6] Unless the parties have agreed upon the place where the arbitration is to be held, such place is determined by the arbitration tribunal.[7] It is further provided by Article 21(1) and (2) that the arbitration tribunal shall have the power to rule on objections that it has no jurisdiction and to determine the existence or the validity of a contract of which the arbitration clause forms part; for the purposes of this provision the arbitration clause is treated as independent of the other terms of the contract and a decision that the contract is null and void shall not entail *ipso facto* the invalidity of the arbitration clause.

Many national chambers of commerce and arbitration institutions have agreed to act as "appointing authority" under the UNCITRAL Arbitration Rules.

The UNCITRAL Conciliation Rules

In view of the practical difference between conciliation and arbitration UNCITRAL has prepared and in 1980 adopted the UNCITRAL Conciliation Rules which were recommended by the United Nations General Assembly on December 4, 1980. **23–023**

The UNCITRAL Conciliation Rules, like the Arbitration Rules, apply only if the parties have adopted them.

The Rules suggest the following Model Conciliation Clause:

> "Where in the event of a dispute arising out of or relating to this contract, the parties wish to seek an amicable settlement of that dispute by conciliation, the conciliation shall take place in accordance with the UNCITRAL Conciliation Rules as at present in force.

---

[6] UNCITRAL Arbitration Rules, Art. 6(2).
[7] *ibid.*, Art. 16(1).

(The parties may agree on other conciliation clauses)."

The conciliation commences when the invitation to conciliate under the Rules is accepted by the other party.[8] There may be one conciliator, or two or three.[9] If the parties do not agree on the person or persons of the conciliator they may enlist the assistance of an appropriate institution[10] but, unlike the UNCITRAL Arbitration procedure, there is no compulsory procedure for the appointment of a conciliator. The conciliator may make a proposal for a settlement agreement which the parties may either accept or reject.[11]

The parties undertake not to initiate, during the conciliation proceedings, any arbitral or judicial proceedings in respect of a dispute that is the subject of the conciliation proceedings, except in so far as is necessary to preserve the rights of a party.[12] The Rules do not provide what should happen if the conciliation attempt fails. The parties may have provided in their contract that in this case the dispute should go to arbitration; otherwise an aggrieved party is at liberty to take the matter to the court.

A person who has acted as conciliator shall not act as arbitrator if after the failure of the conciliation attempt the matter goes to arbitration,[13] but it is thought that this rule can be dispensed with if all parties agree.

The UNCITRAL model law on international commercial arbitration

23–024 In view of the great divergency of national arbitration laws, UNCITRAL has prepared and adopted in 1985 this Model Law. The General Assembly of the United Nations recommended on December 11, 1985 that all States should give consideration to the Model Law, in view of the needs of international commerce. It is to be hoped that the countries of the world will frame their national laws on this model and that thus uniformity of national legislations relating to arbitral procedure will be achieved. Even if followed by a country as a pattern for its own legislation, the Model Law as such does not have direct legal effect in a national jurisdiction. It has been stated[14]:

> "The idea is that the countries of the world should frame their own national arbitration laws on the UNCITRAL model, that they should know from it what the consensus of international lawyers is on controversial questions which arise when they draft or reform their own arbitration laws and that thus a degree of uniformity of the various arbitration regulations used in the world will be established."

As was seen above the Arbitration Act 1996 reflects the principles of the model law and indeed follows its format. The model law was adopted in Scotland by the Law Reform (Miscellaneous Provisions) Scotland Act 1990, s. 66.

---

[8] UNCITRAL Conciliation Rules, Art. 2.
[9] *ibid.*, Art. 3.
[10] *ibid.*, Art. 4(2).
[11] *ibid.*, Arts 7(4) and 13.
[12] *ibid.*, Art. 16.
[13] *ibid.*, Art. 19.
[14] C.M. Schmitthoff, "Extrajudicial Dispute Settlement", *Forum Internationale*, No. 6.

The ICC International Court of Arbitration

The ICC Court of Arbitration is the most important institution for the arbitral **23–025** settlement of international trade disputes.[15] It is widely used and enjoys the confidence and respect of businessmen all over the world and is also frequently resorted to in East-West trade.

The ICC International Court of Arbitration is not a governmental institution but is created by the International Chamber of Commerce. It has its seat at the headquarters of the ICC in Paris. The present Rules of Arbitration of the International Chamber of Commerce came into force on January 1, 1998.[16]

The following arbitration clause is recommended by the ICC when it is intended to submit differences to arbitration by its Court of Arbitration:

> "All disputes arising out of or in connection with the present contract shall be finally settled under the Rules of Arbitration of the International Chamber of Commerce by one or more arbitrators appointed in accordance with the said Rules.
>
> *Note:*
> Parties are reminded that it may be desirable for them to stipulate in the arbitration clause itself the law governing the contract, the number of arbitrators and the place and language of the arbitration. The parties' free choice of the law governing the contract and the place and language of the arbitration is not limited by the ICC Rules of Arbitration.
>
> Attention is called to the fact that the laws of certain countries require that parties to contracts expressly accept arbitration clauses, sometimes in a precise and particular manner."

Arbitration under the Rules of the ICC is open to members and non-members. A procedure for optional conciliation may be adopted under the ICC Rules of Conciliation which entered into force on January 1, 1998. An Administrative Commission for Conciliation is constituted at the ICC and for each dispute a Conciliation Committee of three members is set up by the President of the ICC. The party requesting conciliation may apply either through his National Committee or to the international headquarters of the ICC directly.

If no request for conciliation is made or the conciliation has failed, the dispute proceeds to arbitration. No person having sat on the Conciliation Committee for the settlement of the dispute in question may be appointed as arbitrator. The Court of Arbitration does not itself settle disputes but if the parties have not agreed on the arbitrator(s), the Court will appoint upon a proposal of a National Committee of the ICC if this fails the Court may request a proposal from another National Committee that it considers appropriate (Art. 9(3)); usually the National Committees have lists of competent and suitable persons to serve in that capacity. The sole arbitrator or the chairman of an arbitration tribunal shall be chosen from a country other than those of which the parties to the dispute are nationals. The arbitration is initiated (Art. 4(1)) by a request for arbitration to the Secretariat of the ICC Court of Arbitration, and the date when the request

---

[15] In *Bank Mellat v. GAA Development and Construction Co* [1988] 2 Lloyd's Rep. 44 at 48. Steyn J. referred to ICC arbitration as "the most truly international of all arbitral systems".
[16] Address: 38 Cours Albert 1c, 75008 Paris, France.

is received by the Secretariat is deemed to be the date of the commencement of the arbitral proceedings. Article 6(4) provides[17]:

> "Unless otherwise agreed, the Arbitral Tribunal shall not cease to have jurisdiction by reason of any claim that the contract is null and void or allegation that it is non-existent provided that the Arbitral Tribunal upholds the validity of the arbitration agreement. The Arbitral Tribunal shall continue to have jurisdiction to determine the respective rights of the parties and to adjudicate their claims and pleas even though the contract itself may be non-existent or null and void."

This provision constitutes an agreement of the parties to empower the arbitrator to decide on his own jurisdiction and to have jurisdiction even if the contract containing the arbitration clause is non existent, *i.e.* void *ab initio* or invalid or illegal when he gives his award.

The ICC Rules of Arbitration "provide a code that is intended to be self-sufficient in the sense that it is capable of covering all aspects of arbitrations conducted under the rules, without the need for any recourse to any municipal system of law or any application to the courts of the forum."[18] The three main characteristics of ICC arbitration are:

> "1. Before proceeding with the arbitration, the arbitrator shall draw up the *terms of reference* and obtain the signature of the parties thereto.[19]
> 2. Before the arbitrator signs the award, he shall submit it in draft form to the ICC Court of Arbitration in Paris for *scrutiny*[20]; and
> 3. The costs of arbitration shall be covered by a *deposit* which the parties normally have to pay to the Court in advance in equal parts."[21]

The object of the statement of the terms of reference is to determine with certainty the issues which are in dispute before the arbitrator. The scrutiny of the draft award by the ICC Court of Arbitration is intended to ensure that the award is enforceable in the country in which enforcement is sought. The requirement of a deposit will normally make it unnecessary for a national court to order in ICC arbitrations that a foreign claimant should provide security for costs.[22]

The award is deemed to be made at the place of the arbitration proceedings.[23] The Rules provide[24] that the award shall be "binding" on the parties who will be deemed to have waived their right to any form of recourse and in view of this provision the English courts have held[25] that the adoption of the ICC Rules of Arbitration may be treated as an advance exclusion agreement within the Arbitration Acts—excluding the judicial review on points of law. In normal

---

[17] Rules of Arbitration of the ICC 1998, Art. 4(2). A—prior—nomination of the arbitrator does not "commence" the arbitration: *Offshore International SA v. Banco Central SA* [1976] 2 Lloyd's Rep. 402 at 407.
[18] *Per* Kerr L.J. in *Bank Mellat v. Helliniki Techniki SA* [1984] Q.B. 291 at 304.
[19] Rules of Arbitration of the ICC, Art. 18(1) (2).
[20] *ibid.*, Art. 27.
[21] *ibid.*, Art. 30.
[22] *Bank Mellat v. Helliniki Techniki SA* [1984] Q.B. 291.
[23] Rules of Arbitration of the ICC, Art. 25(3).
[24] *ibid.*, Art. 28(6).
[25] *Marine Contractors Inc v. Shell Petroleum Development Co of Nigeria Ltd* [1984] 2 Lloyd's Rep. 77; *Arab African Energy Corporation Ltd v. Olieprokukten Nederland BV* [1983] 2 Lloyd's Rep. 419.

circumstances the finality of the ICC arbitration award is tus accepted by the English courts.

The London Court of International Arbitration

The London Court of International Arbitration is a tripartite organisation, spon- **23–026** sored by the London Chamber of Commerce, the City of London Corporation, and the Chartered Institute of Arbitrators, and is administered by the latter. Its seat is at the International Arbitration Centre in London. The Rules of the London Court of International Arbitation are known as the LCIA Rules.

The court recommends the adoption of the following arbitration clause:

> "Any dispute arising out of or in connection with this contract, including any question regarding its existence, validity or termination, shall be referred to and finally resolved by arbitration under the Rules of the London Court of International Arbitration, which Rules are deemed to be incorporated by reference into this clause.
>
> The following provisions may be suitable:
>
> The governing law of this contract shall be the substantive law of . . .
> The Tribunal shall consist of . . . (a sole or three) arbitrators). (In the case of a three member tribunal, the following words may be added . . . two of them shall be nominated by the respective parties).
> The place of the arbitration shall be . . . (city).
> The language of arbitration shall be . . ."

The Court has prepared several panels of arbitrators which contain the names of many prominent international personalities. A scale of arbitration fees is provided which are within moderate limits.

A number of trade associations provide their own machinery for international commercial arbitration. These standard contracts normally incorporate an arbitration clause providing for arbitration under the rules of the association in question.[26]

The International Centre for Settlement of Investment Disputes

An attempt has been made to approach the protection of foreign investors from **23–027** the procedural angle by providing machinery for the settlement of international investment disputes. This approach has been successful. In 1965 a *Convention on the Settlement of Investment Disputes between States and Nationals of Other States* was concluded in Washington.[27] This Convention has become effective. On June 30, 1988, it had been ratified by 89 countries, among them the United States, the United Kingdom, France and West Germany. The United Kingdom

---

[26] See *ante*, para. 23–011 where a GAFTA arbitration was in issue.
[27] The Convention entered into force on October 14, 1966. David M. Sassoon, "Convention on the Settlement of Investment Disputes" [1965] J.B.L. 334; J. Cherian, *Investment Contracts and Arbitration, The World Bank Convention on the Settlement of Investment Disputes* (Sijthoff, 1975).
On the *Multilateral Investment Guaranty Agency (MIGA)* see below. The MIGA Convention was approved by the Board of Governors of the World Bank in Seoul on October 10, 1985.

gave effect to it by the *Arbitration (International Investment Disputes) Act 1966*,[28] as amended.[29]

The Convention, which was sponsored by the International Bank for Reconstruction and Development, provides for the formation of an *International Centre for Settlement of Investment Disputes (ICSID)* at the principal office of the Bank in Washington.[30] The ICSID makes available facilities to which contracting States and foreign investors who are nationals of other contracting States have access on a voluntary basis for the settlement of investment disputes between them in accordance with rules laid down in the Convention. The method of settlement might be conciliation or arbitration, or conciliation followed by arbitration in case the conciliation effort fails. The initiative for such proceedings might come from a State as well as from an investor. The ICSID itself does not act as conciliator or arbitrator but maintains panels of specially qualified persons from which conciliators or arbitrators can be selected by the parties, and provides the necessary facilities for the conduct of the proceedings. Once a State and a foreign investor have agreed to use the facilities of the ICSID, they are required to carry out their agreement, to give due consideration to the recommendations of a conciliator and to comply with an arbitral award. In addition, all contracting States, whether parties to the dispute or not, are required to recognise arbitral awards rendered in accordance with the Convention as binding and to enforce the pecuniary obligations imposed thereby.

The United Kingdom Arbitration (International Investment Disputes) Act 1966, as amended, sets out the Convention in a schedule.[31] The Act itself provides that a person seeking recognition or enforcement of an award made under the Convention is entitled to have it registered in the High Court. The Act came into force on January 18, 1967.[32]

The *Convention establishing the Multilateral Investment Guarantee Agency* (MIGA) to which the United Kingdom has given effect by the Multilateral Investment Guarantee Agency Act 1988, provides an arbitration procedure for certain disputes; it further provides that, if the arbitration tribunal is not constituted within 60 days, the arbitrator or the president of the arbitration tribunal shall be appointed, at the joint request of the parties, by the Secretary General of ICSID.[33]

The ICSID has published four sets of Rules, *viz*. the Administrative and Financial Regulations, the Institution Rules, the Arbitration Rules and the Conciliation Rules. They, together with the Convention, are published in a document entitled "ICSID Basic documents".[34]

---

[28] The Convention entered into force for the U.K. on January 18, 1967 (Treaty Series No. 25/1967); Cmnd 3255. The Convention has been extended to various colonies and other territories; see S.I.s 1967 Nos. 159, 249, 585. 1968/1199 and 1979/572.

[29] By the Evidence (Proceedings in Other Jurisdictions) Act 1975, s. 8(2) and Sched. 2 and the Supreme Court Act 1981, Sched. 5.

[30] The address of the ICSID is: 1818 H Street, N.W. Washington D.C., 20433, USA.

[31] Act of 1966, s. 1(2).

[32] *ibid.*, s. 9(2); see *ante*, n. 24.

[33] Convention, Annex II, Art. 4(b). The Convention is reproduced as schedule to the Multilateral Investment Guarantee Agency Act 1988.

[34] Published in January 1985 (the pamphlet contains the documents as revised on September 26, 1984). The pamphlet also contains a flyleaf setting out the Schedule of Costs, as in January 1985.

CHAPTER 24

ENFORCEMENT OF FOREIGN JUDGMENTS AND ARBITRAL
AWARDS (ENFORCEMENT OF THE WTO AGREEMENT
THROUGH THE DISPUTE SETTLEMENT PROCEDURE)

Before embarking on litigation or arbitration outside the jurisdiction, exporters **24–001**
ought to be mindful of whether it is possible to enforce any judgment or arbitral
award obtained. It may be that the respondent to the claim has no assets, in
which case pursuit is probably a waste of time and expense, or it may be that
enforcement of a judgment or award is difficult or impossible. Similarly, the
exporter who has been successfully pursued outside the jurisdiction will need to
know if enforcement against him is possible within the jurisdiction. The first
part of this Chapter will deal with the issue of whether a judgment or award
obtained in another jurisdiction may be enforced against the assets of the judgment or award debtor in England and Wales. In general, judgments and awards
obtained overseas may be enforced. If the judgment has been obtained in a
Contracting State of the Brussels Convention reference must be made to that
Convention, otherwise reference must be made to the statutory or common law
methods of enforcement. If an arbitral award has been obtained in another jurisdiction, the New York Convention on the Recognition of Foreign Arbitral
Awards must be considered.

RECOGNITION AND ENFORCEMENT OF FOREIGN JUDGMENTS[1]

Brussels Convention

If the subject matter of the dispute is a civil or commercial matter and the **24–002**
judgment has been given in the court of a Contracting State of the Brussels
Convention[2] the question of recognition and enforcement will be considered
under that Convention. The following matters need to be addressed:

*Whether the Convention was in force in both countries, adjudicating and
enforcing, at the time of the institution of proceedings and at the time the
judgment was given*

In respect of this issue, Article 54 specifies that the "provisions of the Convention shall apply only to legal proceedings instituted . . . after its entry into force
in the State of origin and, where recognition or enforcement of a judgment . . .

---

[1] See generally, Dicey and Morris; *Conflicts of Law* (2000), Rules 34–52.
[2] As to the Brussels Convention and the Lugano Convention, see Chap. 22. The remarks here apply
to the Lugano Convention.

is sought , in the State addressed." The recognition provisions of the Convention will apply if these requirements are satisfied; if not regard must be had to the transitional provisions which apply to "new" Member States or signatories.[3] If neither provisions apply, the judgment may only be recognised and enforced in England and Wales by one of the means available under statute or common law.

Whether the judgment falls within the meaning of "judgment" under Article 25

"Judgment", the word used in the Article, admits of a very broad interpretation. It embraces most judicial orders and includes orders for costs,[4] orders for specific performance, injunctions and orders for delivery up It does not, however, include interlocutory orders which may be obtained *ex parte* such as freezing orders or search orders[5] nor will it include orders made to assist the course of the proceedings, such as orders to disclose evidence.

Whether there is some way in which the jurisdiction of the adjudicating court can be impeached

It is clear from Article 28 that the court of enforcement is bound by the findings on jurisdiction made by the adjudicating court. However, Article 28[6] also provides that a judgment will not be recognised if it conflicts with certain provisions of the Convention. These provisions concern the jurisdictional rules set out in sections 3, 4 and 5 and Article 59. Section 3 concerns jurisdiction in relation to insurance contracts, section 4 concerns jurisdiction in relation to consumer contracts, section 5 importantly deals with those circumstances where the court of a Contracting State has exclusive jurisdiction.[7] Article 59 deals with the circumstance where a State has assumed an obligation towards a third, non-Brussels Convention state, not to recognise judgments given in a Contracting State. Such agreements are rare and usually apply only to judgments given where the Contracting State has assumed jurisdiction under Article 3, that is, in the case of the United Kingdom, where the court assumed jurisdiction solely on the basis of the judgment debtor's temporary presence in the United Kingdom.[8]

Grounds for non-recognition

24–003   In addition to the matters set out in Article 28, Article 27 provides that a judgment shall not be recognised:

---

[3] See Chap. 22 for dates of the accession of Spain, Portugal, Austria, Sweden and Finland.
[4] Art. 25. The judgment must be given by a court of a contracting state: Case C-129/92 *Owens Bank Ltd v. Bracco* [1994] Q.B. 509.
[5] See *Denilauer v. Couchet Freres* [1980] E.C.R. 1553. A settlement reached in court is not a judgment: Case C-414/92 *Solo Kleinmotoren v. Emilio Boch* [1994] E.C.R. I–2237. But a judgment by consent is: *Landhurst Leasing plc v. Marcq* [1998] I.L.P.R. 822.
[6] In Art. 28(1).
[7] See Chap. 22.
[8] Such as the agreement between the U.K. and Canada (S.I. 1987 No. 468).

(a) If such recognition is contrary to public policy in the State in which recognition is sought. In one instance Donaldson M.R.[9] has said:

> "Considerations of public policy can never be exhaustively defined . . . It has to be shown that there is some element of illegality or that the enforcement of the award would be clearly injurious to the public good . . ."

It is a matter for determination by the recognising court precisely what constitutes public policy, but a difficulty may lie in the fact that under Article 29 no judgment may be reviewed as to its substance. The traditional bar to recognition under common law that the foreign judgment was tainted with fraud provides a case in point. The Schlosser Report[10] makes clear that this and any other illegality is a matter for the adjudicating court and therefore cannot provide a ground for non-recognition.[11] It is now clear that public policy considerations include observance of European Community competition rules.[12]

(b) Where it was given in default of appearance, if the defendant was not duly served with the documents which instituted the proceedings or with an equivalent document in sufficient time to enable him to arrange his defence.

This provision is to prevent recognition of a judgment in default. What constitutes due service is to be determined by the adjudicating court. It is established that there must not only be service but also time to prepare a defence.[13] If the judgment debtor has had a judgment in default entered against him it is no defence to recognition that he sought to have it set aside and that he was unsuccessful.[14]

(c) If the judgment is irreconcilable with a judgment given in a dispute between the same parties in the courts of the state in which recognition is sought.

Under the Convention such a situation should not arise. Obviously a judgment that a party found to be in default of a contract in an adjudicating court will not be recognised where the courts of the recognising State have reached the opposite conclusion.[15]

(d) If the court of the State of Origin, in order to arrive at its judgment, has decided a preliminary question concerning the status or legal capa-

---

[9] In *Deutsche Schachtbau-und Tiefbohrgesellschaft mbh v. Ras al Khaimah National Oil Co*; *Shell International Petroleum Co Ltd v. Rakoil* [1987] 2 Lloyd's Rep. 246.
[10] See generally, Schlosser Report, para. 192. [1979] O.J. C59/128.
[11] *Interdesco v. Nullifire* [1992] 1 Lloyd's Rep. 180.
[12] Case C-126/97 *Eco Swiss China Time Ltd v. Benetton International NV* [1999] C.L.R. 183.
[13] Case 305/88 *Isabelle Lancray v. Peters & Sickert* [1990] E.C.R. I-2725. And Case C-123/91 *Minalmet GmbH v. Brandeis* [1992] E.C.R. I-5661; *Noirhomme v. Walklate* [1992] 1 Lloyd's Rep. 427; C-78/95 *Hendrikman & Anor v. Magenta Druck & Verlag GmbH* [1997] 2 W.L.R. 349. "Duly served" may be deleted in proposed amendments to the Convention.
[14] Provided that he was within the adjudicating court's procedural time limits. See *Minalmet*, n. 13, *supra.*
[15] Art. 27(3). Case 144/86 *Gubisch Maschinenfabrik KG v. Giulio Palumbo* [1987] E.C.R. 4861. See also *Hoffman v. Krieg* [1998] E.C.R. 645.

city of natural persons, rights in property[16] in a way which conflicts with a rule of the private international law of the State in which recognition is sought, unless the same result would have been reached by the application of the rules of private international law of that State.

This is to prevent an adjudicating court from bringing within the scope of Article 1 matters which are outside it.

(e) If the judgment is irreconcilable with an earlier judgment given in a non-Contracting State involving the same cause of action and between the same parties, provided that this latter judgment fulfills the conditions necessary for its recognition in the State addressed.

The matter to be noted in this ground for non-recognition is that the non-Contracting State judgment must precede the judgment whose recognition is sought.[17]

Enforcement

24–004 Article 31 states that a judgment, given in a Contracting State and enforceable in that State, shall be enforced in another Contracting State, when on the application of any interested party, it has been declared enforceable there. Article 33 provides that it may be enforced in accordance with the procedure determined by the recognising State. The party seeking recognition must produce a copy of the judgment and documents which establish its enforceability in accordance with the law of the adjudicating State.[18]

The judgment creditor will make the application for registration *ex parte*[19] and may also seek protective measures against the property of the debtor under Article 39. These measures will afford the creditor some degree of security if the debtor is minded to appeal against the registration. Such appeal must be made within one month of the service of the order for registration. The appeal will be based on one of the grounds for non recognition cited above. If the appeal is unsuccessful the judgment may be enforced as if a judgment of the High Court.[20]

Enforcement under the common law or statute

24–005 The traditional means of enforcement of a foreign judgment is by action on the judgment. The established view of the English courts is that the foreign judgment will not be reopened and reviewed as to its merits. The doctrine of issue

---

[16] Art. 27(4) *i.e.* the matters set out in Art. 1 of the Brussels Convention.

[17] Art. 27(5). On issue estoppel see below n. 22.

[18] Arts 46 and 47.

[19] As to enforcement see generally, RSC Ord. 71. CPR, Part 50.1.3. The procedural law in this area was deemed too complex to be immediately reformed by the CPR.

[20] The High Court is the court set out in Art. 32. Interest is payable: Civil Jurisdiction and Judgments Act 1982, s. 7.

estoppel may be applied.[21] Issue estoppel may be raised when an issue brought before a competent court, including a foreign court which had, in accordance with the principles of private international law, jurisdiction to pronounce it and which has been determined by that court, is raised again in subsequent proceedings. The judge in the later proceedings may refuse to hear the issue anew[22] if the judgment is final, there is identity of the parties and the subject matter is the same in the earlier and later litigation.[23] It must however be noted that a judgment obtained by fraud will not be enforced in England and Wales.[24] Generally, to enforce a judgment, a judgment creditor may apply for summary judgment under CPR 24.2 on the basis that the judgment debtor has no real prospect of defending the claim successfully.

Enforcement under statute

There are two relevant acts; the Administration of Justice Act 1920, Part II, and **24–006** the Foreign Judgments (Reciprocal Enforcement) Act 1933.[25] Under the 1920 Act money judgments given in a part of the Commonwealth can be enforced in the United Kingdom upon registration, provided the territory in question has extended reciprocity to England and Wales. Under the 1933 Act the direct enforcement of money judgments is allowed in the United Kingdom by means of a number of bilateral treaties which are based on the principle of reciprocal treatment. Under the 1920 Act a judgment obtained in a relevant country[26] will be enforceable if registered within 12 months—longer with the discretion of the High Court—from the date of the judgment. Under the 1933 Act similar provisions obtain.

Conditions for enforcement

The conditions for enforcement under the common law, the 1920 Act and the **24–007** 1933 Act are similar. The judgment may only be enforced if the adjudicating court had jurisdiction over the judgment debtor, the judgment was for a fixed sum of money, was final and conclusive and was not to enforce a penal or revenue sanction. The following defences to recognition of the foreign judgment are available: the judgment was obtained by fraud, recognition would be contrary to public policy, the judgment is contrary to natural justice.

---

[21] *Charm Maritime Inc v. Minas Xenophon Kyriaku* [1987] 1 Lloyd's Rep. 433 at 440–441; *Carl Zeiss Stiftung v. Rayner & Keeler Ltd (No. 2)* [1967] 1 A.C. 853; *The Sennar (No. 2)* [1985] 1 W.L.R. 490; *The Speedlink Vanguard v. European Gateway* [1986] 2 Lloyd's Rep. 265 at 269; *Republic of India v. India Steamship Co Ltd* [1993] A.C. 410; *The Irini A (No. 2)* [1999] Lloyd's Rep. 189 at 193, *per* Tuckey J.
[22] *Adams v. Cape Industries plc* [1990] Ch. 433. See also *House of Spring Gardens v. Waite* [1999] 1 Q.B. 241.
[23] *Desert Sun Loan Corporation v. Hill* [1996] 2 All E.R. 847.
[24] *Jet Holdings Inc v. Patel* [1990] 1 Q.B. 335 see *post*, para. 24–013.
[25] As amended by the Civil Jurisdiction and Judgments Act 1982, s. 35(1) and Sched. 10.
[26] The countries which are parties to the 1920 Act include the Australian States, Malawi, Bermuda, Sri Lanka, New Zealand, Malta, Newfoundland, Jamaica, Trinidad, Ghana, Nigeria, Kenya, Tanzania, Uganda, Zimbabwe, Botswana, Malaysia, Singapore, Hong Kong, Cyprus, Gibraltar, the Falkland Islands.

Jurisdiction

24–008 The English court must be satisfied that the judgment debtor was within the jurisdiction of the adjudicating court. This requirement is satisfied in the following ways:

The defendant must have been present within the jurisdiction of the foreign court. It seems that mere presence as opposed to residence is sufficient.[27] A body corporate is present if it maintains a fixed place of business or a representative within the jurisdiction of the adjudicating court. The adjudicating court will have jurisdiction if the defendant has submitted to the jurisdiction by, for example, taking a step in the action. Taking a step in the action may involve entering a counterclaim or otherwise contesting the merits of the claimant's case. Contesting jurisdiction, on the other hand, is not submission at all.[28] Submission may also be through agreement, for example a jurisdiction clause in a contract conferring jurisdiction on the adjudicating court.

Fixed sum of money

24–009 Enforcement will only be allowed for a liquidated sum. This means that other orders such those for delivery up will not be enforceable.

Final and conclusive

24–010 A judgment will be final and conclusive as to the merits of the matter between the parties. The judgment must not be capable of being reopened, therefore a judgment in default or some sort of summary judgment will be insufficient to satisfy this requirement as neither judgment will be on the merits.[29] A judgment subject to appeal is, for these purposes,[30] final. A judgment is treated by the English courts as conclusive in circumstances where it is satisfied that a foreign court of competent jurisdiction has finally decided the matter between the parties.[31]

Penal or revenue sanctions

24–011 Foreign revenue, penal or other sanctions imposed by public law are not enforceable in England and Wales. Generally, this heading gives rise to little difficulty, however, save where damages are expressed to be a penalty or have the appear-

---

[27] See *Adams v. Cape Industries, ante,* n. 22.
[28] *Williams & Glynn's Bank v. Astro Dinamico* [1984] 1 W.L.R. 438. Also *The Eastern Trader* [1996] 2 Lloyd's Rep. 585 at 600, 602; *Akai Pty Ltd v. People's Insurance Co Ltd* [1998] 1 Lloyd's Rep. 90 at 97, 98.
[29] *Nouvion v. Freeman* (1889) 15 A.C. 1.
[30] See 1920 Act, s. 9(2) and 1933 Act, s. 5(1) regarding the effect of an appeal.
[31] In other words, if the judgment would satisfy the requirements for raising issue estoppel in the English Courts. See *ante,* para. 24–005. In *Black-Clawson International Ltd v. Papierwerke Waldhof-Aschaffenburg AG* [1975] A.C. 591 at 616 it was held that a German judgment dismissing a claim by an English company against a German defendant on the ground that it was statute-barred was not "conclusive". But see the Foreign Limitation Periods Act 1984 *ante,* Chap. 21.

ance of such. The enforcing court would in that circumstance direct its attention to the destination of the money awarded. If the ultimate destination was the coffers of a public authority, enforcement would not be possible.[32]

Defences

As summarised above, the following are available as defences to recognition of **24–012** a foreign judgment:

Fraud[33]

Based on the proposition that a party must not benefit from his own wrong, the **24–013** fraud defence allows the exception where an English court will reopen a case determined in a foreign court. The English court will do so reluctantly and review the merits to determine if a fraud has been carried out. Generally, it must be shown that the fraud was directed against the foreign court by presentation of false documents or of the presentation of perjured witnesses and that the fraud procured the judgment. In such circumstances, the English court has no difficulties reopening the matter. Difficulties arise if the judgment debtor could have raised the fraud in the adjudicating court but did not or if he had and the adjudicating court had considered it fully. The position is that the English court may still reopen the matter and effectively hear the case afresh even though such a course of action may be regrettable.[34]

Recognition contrary to public policy[35]

As stated above, public policy is a matter to be determined by the enforcing **24–014** court. It is determined in accordance with local principles of justice and fairness. A judgment will be refused recognition where to do so would offend basic norms of morality and justice.

Recognition contrary to natural justice

This defence, again, is a matter to be determined by the enforcing court. It **24–015** usually covers the situation where the judgment debtor was not served or properly served in the foreign proceedings. The defence can also cover breaches of substantial justice. In one instance[36] damages were awarded against a party by a foreign court which did not consider the evidence. In the Court of Appeal it was held that giving a judgment without weighing the evidence, or even hearing it, could be a breach of the common law view of substantial justice. The Court of Appeal's conclusion may well have been different had the judgment

---

[32] *SA Consortium General Textiles v. Sun & Sand Agencies Ltd* [1978] Q.B. 279.
[33] 1920 Act, s. 9(2)(a); 1933 Act, s.4(1)(a)(iv). *Tuvyahu v. Yoel Singh*, unreported.
[34] *Owens Bank v. Etoile Commerciale* [1995] 1 W.L.R. 44; *Owens Bank v. Bracco* [1992] 2 A.C. 443; [1992] C.L.J. 441.
[35] 1920 Act, s. 9(2)(f); 1933 Act, s. 4(1)(a)(v). *ED & F Man (Sugar) Ltd v. Haryanto Yani (No.2)* [1991] 1 Lloyd's Rep. 161.
[36] *Adams v. Cape Industries plc, ante.*

debtor been aware of the procedural issues and failed to raise them in the foreign court.[37]

Registration[38]

24–016 The judgment creditor will apply *ex parte* to register the foreign judgment within six years of its handing down or of the result of an appeal against it. Notice is then served on the judgment debtor who may apply to set the registration aside. A judgment in a foreign currency will be converted on the date of payment.

Judgments of the European Court of Justice

24–017 The judgments and orders of the E.C.J. are directly enforceable in the United Kingdom by virtue of the European Communities (Enforcement of Community Judgments) Order 1972 (S.I. 1972 No. 1590). Such enforcement is effected by registration in the High Court but it is first necessary that the Secretary of State appends an order of enforcement.

Enforcement of foreign arbitral awards

24–018 Generally, an arbitral award made in England and Wales may be enforced with the leave of the court by the same means as a judgment or order of the court. The party in whose favour an award has been made may apply for summary judgment.[39] The award may be challenged on the grounds that the arbitral tribunal lacked substantive jurisdiction, or the award was tainted by a serious irregularity.[40] With respect to foreign awards these may be enforced by means of section 99 of the Arbitration Act 1996 which applies to Foreign Awards which are not New York Convention awards. Such awards are those to which the Geneva Convention on the Execution of Foreign Arbitral Awards 1927 apply. The number of awards likely to be made under this Convention is so minute that it requires no further mention here.[41] Awards to which the New York Convention on the Recognition and Enforcement of Foreign Arbitral Awards 1958 applies can be enforced by virtue of section 101 of the Arbitration Act 1996 which provides that such an award will be "... binding on the persons as between whom it was made ..." Further, it may be enforced in the same manner as a judgment or order of the court to the same effect.[42] To be recognised the

---

[37] As to service of process see J. G. Collier "Fraud Still Unravels Foreign Judgments", Chap. 22. 1920 Act, s. 9(2)(c); 1933 Act, s. 4(1)(a)(iii).

[38] See RSC Ord. 71.

[39] Under CPR, Part 24.

[40] Arbitration Act 1996, ss. 67 and 68. See *Egmatra AG v. Marco Trading Corp* [1999] 1 Lloyd's Rep. 862 at 865 for an examination of s.68.

[41] Perhaps no more than two States are concerned, Arbitration Act 1950 Part II, s. 36(1) is retained.

[42] Arbitration Act 1996, s. 101(1) and (2); for meaning of "Court" see 2,105—High Court or county court. Awards obtained in a Brussels Convention State and registered there as a judgment may only be enforced in another Contracting State under the New York Convention, or other relevant Convention: *The Atlantic Emperor* [1992] 1 Lloyd's Rep. 342; *Arab Business Consortium International Finance and Investment Co v. Banque Franco-Tunisienne* [1996] 1 Lloyd's Rep. 485.

arbitration award must have been in writing which has the same meaning as the like requirement under section 5 of the Act.

Grounds for refusal of recognition

These are set out in section 103(2) of the Act and which are taken almost directly **24–019** from the Convention. They are:

(a) A party to the agreement was (according to the law applicable to him) under some incapacity; this would, presumably, apply to the situation where the party in question was a minor or suffered from other incapacitating factor.

(b) The arbitration agreement was not valid under the law to which the parties subjected it or, failing any indication thereon, under the law of the country where the award was made.

(c) The party against whom the award was made was not given proper notice of the appointment of the arbitrator or of the arbitration proceedings or was otherwise unable to present his case.

(d) The award deals with a difference not contemplated by or not falling within the terms of the submission to arbitration or contains decisions beyond the scope of the submission to arbitration; if the award contains decisions on matter not submitted to arbitration they may be excised from the award and the balance may be recognised.[43]

(e) The composition of the tribunal was not in accordance with the agreement of the parties or the law of the country where the arbitration took place.

(f) The award has not yet become binding on the parties, or it has been set aside or suspended by a competent authority of the country in which, or under the law of which, it was made.

Recognition or enforcement may also be refused if made in relation to a matter not capable of settlement by arbitration or contrary to public policy. This latter ground, set out under section 103(3), is of some significance. In *Westacre Investments Inc v. Jugoimport-SDPR Holding Co Ltd*[44] the judge reviewed the grounds for refusal to enforce an arbitral award; these included circumstances where an arbitrator had ignored illegality in the underlying transaction or has decided incorrectly that there was no illegality. These matters are in addition to those cited above where it was stated that a judgment would not be enforced where to do so would offend basic norms of morality and justice.[45]

---

[43] Arbitration Act 1996, s. 103(4).
[44] [1998] 2 Lloyd's Rep. 111, *per* Colman J. See also this case on appeal [1999] 2 Lloyd's Rep. 65; *Soleimany v. Soleimany* [1998] 3 W.L.R. 811; *J. Harris & F. Meisel* [1998] L.M.C.L.Q. 568.
[45] See *ante*, para. 24–003 regarding public policy; see also *Eco Swiss China Time Ltd v. Benetton International NV.*

Other

24-020 If an arbitral award is capable, under the law in force where it was made, of being registered as a judgment of the court or enforceable as a judgment of the court and that court is situated in a country to which the Administration of Justice Act 1920 or the Foreign Judgments (Reciprocal Enforcement) Act 1933 applies it may be enforced under the relevant provisions of those Acts.[46]

THE DISPUTE SETTLEMENT PROCEDURE OF WTO

24-021 The nature of the General Agreement on Tariffs and Trade (GATT) was succinctly indicated by the former Director-General of this organisation, Mr. Arthur Dunkel[47]:

> "The General Agreement on Tariffs and Trade is a multilateral treaty that lays down general rules, accepted by over 120 States, for the conduct of international trade relations. Since 1948, GATT has been the main forum for the liberalisation of trade barriers and for the settlement of international trade disputes."

As a result of the Uruguay Round of negotiations, which took seven years to complete and which concluded in December 1993, the World Trade Organisation came into being under the Marrakesh Agreement (the WTO Agreement). The WTO Agreement includes the GATT 1994 Agreement which amended the 1947 GATT Agreement. As under the original GATT, an elaborate system for the resolution of trade disputes is provided which builds upon the system set out in that agreement.

Exporter's standing

24-022 The first hurdle which the exporter wishing to make use of the WTO Agreement dispute procedure encounters is that the WTO Agreement, as has been seen, is an international treaty pertaining to public international law. It is normal in this branch of law—although there are exceptions—that only States which have acceded to the treaty may raise complaints about its breach but that such complaints cannot be lodged by private persons—individuals or companies resident in one of the contracting States—although they may be affected by a breach of the international treaty. In principle, only States are "Contracting Parties"—that is—WTO members. It follows that the ordinary exporter has no *locus standi* under the dispute resolution procedure and cannot set into motion its machinery, but he may approach the competent Ministry of his country—in the United Kingdom the Department of Trade and Industry—with a request to take up his case and to raise a complaint in accordance with the rules of the WTO Agreement. Whether the Minister will accede to this request is a matter for his discre-

---

[46] 1920 Act, s. 9(3)(a) and (5); 1933 Act, s. 10A.
[47] In his foreword to E. McGovern, *International Trade Regulation—GATT, The United States and the European Community* (Exeter, 1986). Mr. Dunkel was Director-General until 1993.

tion. This is a policy decision. As such, it is normally not subject to review by the courts.

The E.C. has *locus standi* under the WTO although it is not a "State". The Community has been accepted as a signatory to the protocols incorporating the results of the various Rounds and other WTO agreements.[48] It has been involved as a party in various trade disputes.[49] This is of importance to the exporter. If a discriminatory measure of a contracting State affects traders in several E.C. Member States, the E.C. Commission may be inclined to lodge a complaint under the WTO Agreement.

The WTO Agreement is described as a multilateral system for dispute settlement. It is designed to dispense with the need for unilateral action on the part of its members. The responsibility for settling disputes lies with the Dispute Settlement Body (DSB) who have the authority to establish panels of experts who will work to encourage the resolution of disputes, rather than render "judgments". The procedure runs to strict time limits. This is essential to the effective working of the dispute resolution mechanisms and also to the operation of the WTO. The 1995 complaint by Venezuela against the United States concerning gasoline imports provides an example of the operation of the time limits.

The law relating to WTO disputes

The procedure for the settlement of WTO Agreement disputes is now set out in **24–023**
Annex 2 of the Marrakesh Agreement, Understanding on Rules and Procedures Governing the Settlement of Disputes. This Annex specifically preserves the management of disputes as set out in Articles XXII and XXIII of GATT 1947. The major departure from the traditional procedure is the establishment of an Appellate Review, under Article 17 of the Understanding, Annex II.

The Annex provides for the settlement of disputes arising out of agreements listed in Appendix I of the Understanding and includes the WTO Agreement, Multilateral Agreement on Trade in Goods, Agreement on Trade-Related Aspects of Intellectual Property Rights, etc.

Under the procedure a Dispute Settlement Body ("DSB") is established to administer the rules and procedures . They will also have authority to establish panels, adopt panel reports and reports of the Appellate Body, and maintain surveillance of implementation of rulings, among other matters.[50]

Consultation between disputant Member States is encouraged by Article 4. This process has the advantage of being informal, confidential and undertaken without prejudice to other means of dispute settlement. Sixty days is the minimum time allowed to settle a dispute by this means after which a party is

---

[48] See J. Croome, *Reshaping the World Trading System, A History of The Uruguay Round* (WTO, 1995) for an account of the participation of The European Community. The WTO e-mail address for publications is: *publications@wto.org*. Website is *http://www.wto.org*. (Click on "About the WTO.")

[49] E.C. refunds on exports of sugar—Complaint by Brazil (1981); E.C. tariff treatment on imports of citrus (1985).

[50] Art. 2(1).

free to ask for a Panel to be established. The DSB is to be notified of any consultations.

Parties may volunteer to utilise the process set out in Article 5: "Good Offices, Conciliation and Mediation". The Director General may offer these facilities. Again, this process is subject to a minimum period of 60 days and is confidential.

Article 6 provides for the establishment of Panels by the DSB, whose terms of reference are set out in Article 7. These include the examination of the matter in dispute which has been referred to the DSB. The composition of these panels is set out in Article 8 and the rules therein are designed to ensure that the Panel is composed of experienced, independent Panelists. The Panels are empowered to examine other complaints made concerning the same matter (Article 9) and observe the interests of third parties. The panels must make an objective assessment of the matter before it and make such findings as will assist the DSB in the discharge of its functions (Article 11). The Panel has the right to seek any information from any individual or body, but if they are seeking information from within a particular jurisdiction, Article 13 requires the Panel to inform the authorities of that Member State.

The deliberations must be confidential (Article 14). The Panel will, in accordance with Article 15, following submissions and arguments, submit an interim report which may be commented upon by the parties. The Panel will then issue a final Panel report which will be circulated to the Members who have 10 days prior to the DSB meeting to consider the report to submit observations. The disputant parties have a right to participate in that meeting (Article 16). If, however, a party has indicated its intention to refer the matter to Appellate Review under Article 17, the DSB will postpone adoption of the Panel report. The Panel report will, in any event, be adopted at a DSB meeting if no party has indicated its intention to appeal within 60 days. The DSB, of course, may choose not to adopt the report. Article 22 provides for compensation and Suspension of Concessions as temporary measures in the event that rulings and recommendations are not observed within a reasonable time. There is a special provision for sympathetic allowances in respect of breaches by Least-Developed Country Members (Article 24). Article 25 preserves the right of disputant parties to refer matters to arbitration; the same means of "enforcement" will apply to arbitration awards (Article 25(4)).

PART SIX

CONSTRUCTION AND LONG TERM CONTRACTS

THE CONSTRUCTION OF WORKS AND INSTALLATIONS ABROAD

The contract for the construction of works and installations abroad has certain **25–001** typical characteristics. The parties to this international contract are often a foreign government department or Government corporation as employer and a company—or several companies jointly—incorporated in another country as contractor. Often, but not necessarily, the employer is an organisation in a country in the course of development and the contractor is incorporated in an industrialised country. Legally, this type of international contract is a contract for work, for the supply of goods, for services or a combination of these forms of contract; economically, it is a contract for the transfer of technology from one country to another. Illustrations of this type of contract are the undertaking of a contractor to build and equip in the country of the employer a hospital, a factory, an airport or a pipeline, but in some cases contractors are known to have undertaken to build whole ports or cities for the employer. The contract may be a turnkey contract, under which the contractor undertakes to hand over the installation ready for use, or it may proceed by stages, when each stage has to be tested and accepted by the employer.

Another feature of an international procurement contract is that it usually involves considerable amounts of money. Often the employer, particularly if it is an organisation in a developing country, cannot or will not finance the undertaking out of its own resources. Consequently, it has to be financed by public international bodies, such as the International Bank for Reconstruction and Development (IBRD, the World Bank), the International Development Association (IDA), both in Washington, D.C., or the European Investment Bank (EIB) or European Bank for Reconstruction and Development (EBRD), both of the European Community. While these financial institutions are usually loath to decree the precise terms on which their borrower, the employer, has to contract, some of them have established guidelines which they expect the parties to the international procurement contract to respect. Moreover, in recent years a more prescriptive approach to contract terms has been adopted as evidenced, for example, by the World Bank's publication in 1995 of their Standard Bidding Documents for the Procurement of Works.[1] Another aspect of the financial magnitude of these transactions is that they have given rise to various kinds of contract guarantees, such as tender guarantees, performance guarantees and

---

[1] *Standard Bidding Documents for the Procurement of Works* (published by The World Bank, January 1995).

repayment guarantees, some of which are dealt with in the ICC brochure on *Uniform Rules for Contract Guarantees.*[2]

A third feature of international procurement contracts is that their performance often extends over a considerable period of time. During that time the economic situation may change. For this reason it is usual to insert into this type of contract, in addition to the ordinary currency and *force majeure* clauses, special clauses, aimed at reducing the economic risk inherent in long term contracts, such as price adjustment clauses.

In recent years there has been a shift away from relatively straightforward arrangements between Government employer and foreign contractor, towards more complex structures involving a partnership between the public and private sectors. Often, this involves financing on a non-recourse basis from the international banking community. Frequently, such arrangements involve a BOO (Build Own Operate) BOT (Build Operate Transfer) or BOOT (Build Own Operate and Transfer) Scheme whereby, for example, the Government grants a 25 year concession to a consortium of private sector entities to build and operate a new infrastructure project, *e.g.* a motorway, airport, etc. The consortium arranges finance for the project and obtains its return out of the revenues of the project during the life of the concession. The construction contract is clearly a major element of any such scheme.

The UNCITRAL Legal Guide

25–002 The UNCITRAL Legal Guide on Drawing Up International Contracts for the Construction of Industrial Works[3] was adopted by that organisation in August 1987. It was published by the United Nations in 1988. The UNCITRAL Legal Guide is a comprehensive and detailed manual[4] intended to be of benefit to those charged with the task of drawing up international construction contracts. Its observations and the suggestions made in it aim at striking a just and fair balance between the interests of the employer and the contractor. The UNCITRAL Legal Guide deals with construction contracts on a global and not a regional level.

TYPES OF PROCUREMENT

Procurement by inviting tenders and by negotiation

25–003 From the legal point of view, there exist two methods of international procurement, *viz.* by inviting tenders from companies prepared to contract with the

---

[2] ICC Brochure No. 325 (1978).
[3] The UNCITRAL Legal Guide may be obtained through mail order, quoting sales number E.87.V.10, document A/CN.9/SER.B/2, by readers in Europe, Africa and northern Asia from United Nations Publications, Palais des Nations, CH-1211 Geneva 10, Switzerland, and by readers in North, Central and South America, southern Asia and the Pacific from United Nations Publications, Room DC2-0853, United Nations Headquarters, New York, New York 10017, USA. The UNCITRAL Legal Guide may also be purchased from bookshops and distributors throughout the world that stock United Nations publications. UNCITRAL is also working on a *Model Law on Procurement.*
[4] The preparation of the UNCITRAL Legal Guide took approximately seven years. The chairman of the Working Group was Mr. Leif Sevon of Finland.

employer (*appels d'offres*) or by negotiating the contract of work or supply with the contractor directly or through agents, without previously requiring competitive bids from intending contractors (*marchés de gré à gré*).

Of these two methods, procurement by tender is generally the preferred method. The World Bank requires competitive tendering as the normal method of procurement; it is stated in the Bank's *Guidelines*[5]:

> The Bank has found that, in most cases, these needs and interests can best be realised through international competitive bidding, properly administered, and with suitable allowance for preferences for domestically manufactured goods and, where appropriate, for domestic contractors for works under prescribed conditions. In such cases, therefore, the Bank requires its borrowers to obtain goods and works through international competitive bidding open to eligible suppliers and contractors.

Competitive tendering is usually taken to mean that the tenderer with the lowest price should be appointed. Quite often regulation requires the lowest tender to be accepted. However, there are risks in this approach: in his review of the construction industry in the United Kingdom "Constructing the Team", Sir Michael Latham[6] recommended that the best tender, not the lowest tender, should be accepted. He also recommended that the Department of the Environment should include the recommendation "that public authorities, including local authorities, should seek to evaluate all tenders on the basis of quality, likely cost-in-use and out-turn price and known past performance, as well as price. It should also state that auditors will be prepared to accept that price should not be the only criterion, provided that a clear audit trail is established by which quality is assessed".

To some extent the "best value" criterion is used in the European Commission's (E.C.) public procurement directive, which requires that the lowest price or "most economically advantageous" price is adopted. Those responsible for tendering processes need to have a procurement procedure, which takes account of these quality issues, as well as price. Especially with construction contracts, abnormally low bids all too often result in excessive claims, resulting in an out-turn of costs greater than might have been the case if a tender other than the lowest tender were accepted.

Open and selective tenders

There are two types of tender: the open and the selective. Under the open (or public) procedure "tenders are invited through advertisements or other forms of public notice from any eligible party. In the case of selective tenders a limited number of firms are invited by the [employer's] contracting agency to submit offers. The agency can select the tenderers either through its previous knowledge of the market or after a prequalification procedure, in which eligible firms are

---

[5] *Guidelines for Procurement under IBRD Loans and IDA Credits*, 5th printing, January 1999. Known as *The World Bank Guidelines* and obtainable from the Headquarters of the World Bank, 1818 H Street, NW, Washington DC 20433, USA.

[6] "Constructing the Team", Sir Michael Latham (HMSO, July 1994). Final Report of the Joint Government/Industry Review of Procurement and Contractual Arrangements in the United Kingdom Construction Industry.

invited to provide evidence of their ability to perform the services or produce the goods desired by the agency".[7] The prevalent method is selective competitive bidding, preceded by a prequalification procedure.

If the procurement is done without competitive bidding, the observations discussed in the previous Chapters apply to the contract between the employer and the contractor, but sometimes some of the special clauses noted in this Chapter are added.

The following observations deal only with the procurement by competitive tender.

The E.C. Directives on public procurement

25–004 The E.C. has issued several Directives dealing with the procurement procedures of Government and other public bodies and utilities of the Member States. It began with the 1971 Directive on public works and construction contracts[8] and the 1977 Directive on government procurement of supplies of goods and equipment.[9]

The main purpose of these E.C. measures was to provide equal opportunities in bidding for public sector contracts for suppliers and contractors from all E.C. countries and so to discourage discrimination against non-indigenous firms; further, tendering and award procedures should be open and above board.

However, these first Directives were largely unsuccessful in achieving their stated aims, as there was no effective means of ensuring compliance by the Member States. Governments tended especially to split contracts so that they would fall below the relevant thresholds. Also, key areas such as public water and energy utilities and public transport and telecommunications services were largely excluded from the application of these Directives.

The Commission issued a White Paper in 1985 highlighting the problems and attempted to address the situation by issuing several new Directives. The field is now governed by directives in five main areas.

Public works

25–005 Directive 93/37/EEC[10] consolidates the original Directive 71/305/EEC on this subject and the amendments to it contained in Directive 89/440/EEC and 97/52/EC.[11]

Supplies

25–006 Here, Directive 93/36/EEC[12] was issued, consolidating the original Directive 77/62/EEC and the amendments made to it, especially by Directives 80/767/EEC[13]

---

[7] Gösta Westring, *International Procurement* (2nd revised ed., International Trade Centre UNCTAD/GATT, 1985). See also the *GATT Agreement on Government Procurement*, Geneva, 1979.
[8] Directive 71/305/EEC [1971] O.J. L185/1.
[9] Directive 77/62/EEC [1977] O.J. L113/1.
[10] [1994] O.J. L111/4.
[11] [1989] O.J. L210/1. [1997] O.J. L328/1.
[12] [1993] O.J. L199/1.
[13] [1980] O.J. L215/1.

and 88/295/EEC and 97/52/EC.[14] The provisions on supplies are now in line with those on works and services.

Services

In addition to the above, Directive 92/50/EEC, as amended by 97/52/EC,[15] now **25–007** deals with the supply of services to entities covered by the supply and works Directives.

Utilities (formerly known as Excluded Sectors)

This area is covered by Directive 93/38/EEC,[16] which incorporates into the ori- **25–008** ginal Directive 90/531/EEC[17] (covering works and supplies) provisions extending the regulatory regime to services contracts awarded by certain utilities enjoying exclusive rights or special rights (for example, a water company). The Directive was recently amended by Directive 98/4/EC.[18]

Compliance

In order to ensure the efficacy of the above, two Directives relating to compli- **25–009** ance were also adopted :

(a) Directive 89/665/EEC[19] concerning the enforcement of the Works, Supplies and Services Directives (the Remedies Directive); and

(b) Directive 92/13/EEC[20] relating to the enforcement of procurement rules in the Utilities Sector (the Utilities Remedies Directive).

The procurement rules apply to contracts in excess of certain threshold values. The rules for calculating these values are detailed. The E.C. amended its public procurement measures following the WTO Government Procurement (GPA), which came into effect in January 1996. The changes were made in order to ensure that E.C.-based providers were not adversely affected by the changes in the thresholds which GPA introduced. The amendments were introduced to the Public Works, Supplies and Services Directives by Directive 97/52/EC[21] and to the Utilities Directive by Directive 98/4/EC.[22] The thresholds for the application of the E.C. public procurement rules are somewhat complicated by the fact that while some of the bodies covered by the E.C. rules are also covered by the GPA, others are not. All the figures quoted are net of VAT.

---

[14] [1988] O.J. L127/1.
[15] [1992] O.J. L209/1. [1997] O.J. L328/1.
[16] [1993] O.J. L199/84.
[17] [1990] O.J. L297/1.
[18] [1998] O.J. L101/1.
[19] [1989] O.J. L395/33.
[20] [1992] O.J. L76/7.
[21] [1997] O.J. L328/1.
[22] [1998] O.J. L101/1.

The threshold for contracts for works contracts awarded by contracting authorities and utilities, which are also covered by the GPA, is 5 million "Special Drawing Rights" (SDRs) (in 2000, £3,611,395). For other works contracts it is Euro 5 million (in 2000, £3,370,000).

In the case of public supply and service contracts for contracting authorities covered by the GPA, the threshold is SDR 130,000 (in 2000, £93,896). For other public contracting authorities it is Euro 200,000 (in 2000, £144,456). For Utilities covered by the GPA (water; electricity; urban transport including: railway, tramway, trolley bus or bus; and airport, maritime and port facilities) the threshold for supplies and services is SDR 400,000 (in 2000, £288,912). For utilities not covered by the GPA (gas, oil, coal and other solid fuels and rail services which are not urban transport) the threshold is Euro 400,000 (in 2000, £269,600). In the case of telecommunications it is Euro 600,000 (in 2000, £404,400). However, many of the activities of the telecommunication utilities in the E.C. are now exempt from the procurement rules, following the introduction of legislation in recent years, which has opened this sector up to full competition.

Contract structure

25–010 The traditional structure for a contract in a construction project involves three main parties or teams—the employer, the employer's professional team (architect or engineer, quantity surveyor) and the contractor's team (including both main contractor and subcontractors). The employer engages the professional team to prepare a specification and to design the project. These documents will be included in the tender, which will also be prepared by the employer's professional team. Following the tendering process, a contractor is then selected to carry out the work in accordance with the specification and designs supplied to him. The contractor will sublet various parts of the work to subcontractors. Sometimes the employer specifies ("nominates") which firms are to be appointed as subcontractors for certain aspects of the work.

In this structure, the architect or engineer usually has a dual role—he designs the project and then, once the contractor has been appointed, he supervises the work of the contractor on behalf of the employer. In such an arrangement, the design risk is with the employer and his professional advisers.

Under a turnkey, or design and build contract, which is most common with international projects, the contractor has a much wider role and his risk is greater: he is responsible both for the design and the construction of the project. The employer will still employ engineering and other consultants to prepare the specification and the initial design, including the performance specifications for the facilities. These documents will be provided to prospective contractors at the tender stage. However, the contractor will be responsible for the detailed engineering design as well as procurement and construction of the facilities. Here, most of the design risk as well as the construction risk lies with the contractor. Partly because of this, the contractor will usually have a relatively free hand not only with the detailed design of the work, but also with the selection of suppliers and subcontractors, provided that they meet the requirements of the specification which, in the case of, say, a process plant, will also include performance criteria.

Forms of contract

Because there are so many variable issues in a major international project, the **25–011** conditions of contract need to be carefully structured to meet the special circumstances in each case.

However, there are some forms designed for use internationally which provide useful models. Some of the most important are:

FIDIC Conditions of Contract[23]

Based in Lausanne, the Federation Internationale des Ingenieurs-Conseils **25–012** (International Federation of Consulting Engineers) have developed three forms of contract which are widely used, in particular in the English speaking world (other than the United States):

(a) The FIDIC Conditions of Contract for Civil Engineering Works, 4th Edition; 1987 (the "Red Book").

(b) The FIDIC Conditions of Contract for Electrical and Mechanical Work, 4th Edition (the "Yellow Book").

(c) The FIDIC Conditions of Contract for Fixed Price Turnkey Contracts, 1st Edition, 1994 (the "Orange Book").

Of these, perhaps the most widely used is the FIDIC Red Book which has been adapted for use in a number of jurisdictions on an official/semi-official basis— for example, in Dubai, Hong Kong and Poland.

In 1999, FIDIC published four new standard contracts to replace the documents mentioned above. These are:

Conditions of Contract for Construction,[24] which are recommended for building or engineering works designed by the Employer or by his representative, the Engineer. Under the usual arrangements for this type of contract, the Contractor constructs the works in accordance with a design provided by the Employer. However, the works may include some elements of Contractor-designed civil, mechanical, electrical and/or construction works.

Conditions of Contract for Plant and Design-Build,[25] which are recommended for the provision of electrical and/or mechanical plant, and for the design and execution of building or engineering works. Under the usual arrangements for

---

[23] FIDIC contracts can be obtained from the Association of Consulting Engineers, Alliance House, 12 Caxton Street, London SW1H OQL (website: *www.acenet.co.uk*) or from the headquarters of FIDIC, PO Box 86, CH-1000 Lausanne, 12- Chailley, Switzerland.
[24] The FIDIC Conditions of Contract for Construction (for Building and Engineering Works designed by the Employer) (1999).
[25] The FIDIC Conditions of Contract for Plant and Design-Build (for Electrical and Mechanical Plant and for Building and Engineering Works designed by the Contractor) (1999).

this type of contract, the Contractor designs and provides, in accordance with the Employer's requirements, plant and/or other works, which may include any combination of civil, mechanical, electrical and/or construction works.

Conditions of Contract for EPC/Turnkey Projects,[26] which may be suitable for the provision on a turnkey basis of a process or power plant, of a factory or similar facility, or of an infrastructure project or other type of development, where (i) a higher degree of certainty of final price and time is required, and (ii) the Contractor takes total responsibility for the design and execution of the project, with little involvement of the Employer. Under the usual arrangements for turnkey projects, the Contractor carries out all the Engineering, Procurement and Construction (EPC), providing a fully-equipped facility, ready for operation (at the "turn of the key").

Short Form of Contract,[27] which is recommended for building or engineering works of relatively small capital value. Depending on the type of work and the circumstances, this form may also be suitable for contracts of greater value, particularly for relatively simple or repetitive work or work of short duration. Under the usual arrangements for this type of contract, the Contractor constructs the works in accordance with a design provided by the Employer or by his representative (if any), but this form may also be suitable for contracts which include, or wholly comprise, Contractor-designed civil, mechanical, electrical and/or construction works.

The new FIDIC forms use similar wording wherever possible across the various documents. All of them now contain provision for disputes to be adjudicated by a Dispute Adjudication Board (DAB). Also, all the new books contain a provision limiting the contractor's liability, whereas such a clause was previously only to be found in the Orange Book. The new documents have been generally well received, although some concerns have been expressed on the Conditions of Contract for EPC and Turnkey ("Silver Book") by contractor organisations.

The forms are recommended for general use where tenders are invited on an international basis. Modifications may be required in some jurisdictions, particularly if the Conditions are to be used on domestic contracts. FIDIC considers the official and authentic texts to be the versions in the English language.

ENAA

25–013   The Engineering Advancement Association of Japan (ENAA) have prepared a model form of international contract for process plant construction,[28] specifically for use on a turnkey lump sum basis and a separate form for power plant construction. The ENAA documentation runs to five volumes and contains, in addition to forms of contract, useful guidance notes.

---

[26] The FIDIC Conditions of Contract for EPC Turnkey Projects (1999).
[27] The FIDIC Short Form of Contract (1999).
[28] The ENAA Model Form of International Contract for Process Plant Construction. The ENAA form can be obtained from Engineering Advancement Association of Japan, 4–6 Nishi-shinbashi, 1-chome, Minato-ku, Tokyo, 105 Japan, Fax: 0081 3350 0255 00.

UNIDO

The United Nations Industrial Development Organisation has issued a model **25–014** form of turnkey lump sum contract for the construction of a fertiliser plant.[29]

The Standard Bidding Documents for the Procurement of Works

The World Bank Standard Bidding Documents were published by the World **25–015** Bank, Washington D.C. in January 1995 (revised in 1999). The conditions of contract are based on the 4th Edition of the FIDIC Red Book referred to above. The World Bank's Bidding Document contains some additional clauses dealing with tax, illegal payments and other matters, as well as giving an alternative clause 67 which provides for the establishment of a Disputes Review Board (see *post*, para. 25–039). (A revised version can be anticipated to take into account the new FIDIC Conditions mentioned above.)

The Asian Development Bank

In their sample bidding documents[30] the Bank have adopted the FIDIC Orange **25–016** Book with some amendments.

A number of contract forms published in the United Kingdom are designed for international as well as domestic use, or can easily be adapted for international use. The Engineering & Construction Contract, published under the auspices of the Institution of Civil Engineers,[31] is written in plain English, intended for international use, with a variety of forms so that it can be adapted for all different types of contract structure—lump sum turnkey, build only, etc. The Institution of Chemical Engineers also produce contracts for process plant, both lump sum and cost plus,[32] which are often adopted for use internationally.

The prequalification procedure

There exists no internationally recognised standard procedure for prequalifica- **25–017** tion requirements. Sometimes the requirements are kept in general terms, *e.g.*:

> "In order to obtain the necessary application form, interested companies which can prove their fitness, technical and financial capacity, experience and tradition in such field of the . . . industry, are requested to contact . . ."

Sometimes the employer, if so requested, sends applicants a prequalification questionnaire. Where tenders are invited for work already begun, it is usual to exempt applicants who have already prequalified for previous stages from further prequalification.

Transactions financed by World Bank loans or IDA credits will normally

---

[29] UNIDO Model Form of Turnkey Lump Sum Contract for the Construction of a Fertiliser Plant. Available from UNIDO New York, New York, NY 10017, USA, Tel: 212 963 6890; Fax: 212 964 4116, UNIDO Geneva, Bocage, Palais des Nations, CH-1211 Geneva 10, Switzerland, Tel: 411 917 3367 or 917 3364; Fax: 411 917 0059.
[30] The Asian Development Bank Sample Bidding Documents (December 1996).
[31] The ICE Engineering and Construction Contract.
[32] The I.Chem. E. Model Form of Conditions of Contract for Process Plant.

require a prequalification procedure for bidders. The World Bank Guidelines provide[33]:

> "Prequalification is usually necessary for large or complex works, or in any other circumstances in which the high costs of preparing detailed bids could discourage competition, such as custom-designed equipment, industrial plant, specialized services, and contracts to be let under turnkey, design and build, or management contracting. This also ensures that invitations to bid are extended only to those who have adequate capabilities and resources. Prequalification may also be useful to determine eligibility for preference for domestic contractors where this is allowed. Prequalification should be based entirely upon the capability of prospective bidders to perform the particular contract satisfactorily, taking into account, *inter alia*, their (i) experience and past performance on similar contracts, (ii) capabilities with respect to personnel, equipment, and construction or manufacturing facilities and (iii) financial position. The invitation to prequalify for bidding on specific contracts should be advertised and notified . . . The scope of the contract and a clear statement of the requirements for qualification should be sent to those who reponded to the invitation."

The World Bank and IDA will normally wish to review prequalification procedures and to be notified of the list of prequalified firms and any reasons for exclusion of any applicant for prequalification. This has to be done before applicants are invited.[34] These international financial institutions wish to safeguard industry against arbitrary exclusion from prequalification and to ensure that fair play is observed.

The invitation to tender

25–018 The contracting agency of the employer will send those applicants who have qualified the tender documents. From the legal point of view they constitute an invitation to bid, *i.e.* to make an offer. Although in the legal context this is still a preliminary step, the tender documents are of the utmost importance, because they constitute the basis of any contract which may result. They are usually incorporated into the tender and again into the contract, when it is made, by reference.

The tender documents are usually divided into three parts: one which contains the conditions of contract; another which contains the technical details, such as the drawings, specifications and bill of quantities; and a third which contains detailed instructions to the intending bidder on how to submit his tender.

Four clauses which are often found in invitations to bid may be mentioned here.

First, the invitation will state that the employer is not bound to accept the lowest bid or any bid at all. Even without the addition of this clause the employer would not be bound to do so. Secondly, the employer may reserve the right to seek clarification of the bid from a bidder. Thirdly, if it is intended to give certain bids preference for non-commercial reasons, *e.g.* where domestic, political or regional preference is intended to be given, that should be stated clearly in the invitation to tender. In this connection, the World Bank Guidelines explain how to compare bids from domestic and other bidders.[35] Fourthly, the invitation

---

[33] World Bank Guidelines Art. 2.9.
[34] *ibid.* Appendix 1.
[35] *ibid.* Appendix 2.

should state that the employer shall be entitled to avoid the contract if it is proved that the contractor or any of his employees were engaged or involved in any form of bribery or corruption in connection with the contract.[36]

Furthermore, since bids are usually invited from tenderers in different countries, the tender documents should clearly state the currency or currencies in which bid prices may be expressed and the contract price will be paid.[37]

The tender

This is the offer made by the contractor to enter into a binding contract with the **25–019** employer on the terms of the tender documents. In English law and the laws of many other countries, the tender can be withdrawn by the contractor before it is accepted, but normally the right of withdrawal is restricted. The EDF Conditions[38] restrict it to the end of the tendering time.[39]

Any tender may be withdrawn, supplemented or amended prior to the date fixed for the receipt of tenders.

The FIDIC Conditions go further than that; their form of tender excludes the right of withdrawal for a specified time after the expiration of the tendering time.[40]

> "We agree to abide by this tender until . . . and it shall remain binding upon us and may be accepted at any time before that date."

In English law these restrictions of the right of withdrawal do not prevent the tenderer from withdrawing the tender after the expiration of the specified period (and also before its expiration,[41] provided that the withdrawal communication reaches the employer's contracting agency before acceptance). Here, however, the mechanism of the tender guarantee may operate: if the tenderer withdraws the tender contrary to his undertaking to be bound by it, it is arguable that the guarantee may be forfeit.

The tender incorporates the tender documents by reference and consequently both the conditions of contract and the technical details become part of the tender. The form of tender suggested by the FIDIC Conditions of Contract for Construction also contain the following significant provision which excludes the "subject to (formal) contract" interpretation[42]:

> "Unless and until a formal agreement is prepared and executed this letter of tender, together with your written acceptance thereof, shall constitute a binding contract between us."

---

[36] ICC Brochure No. 315 (1977) on *Extortion and Bribery in Business Transactions*, para. 3, pp. 10–11.
[37] World Bank Guidelines, Art. 2.29–2.33.
[38] The General Conditions for Public Works and Supply Contracts financed by the European Development Fund of the EEC (Brussels, February 14, 1972). These have now been updated by Decision No. 3/90 of the ACP/EEC Council of Ministers, and are known as The General Regulations and General Conditions of Works, Supplies and Service Contracts financed by the European Development Fund (generally known as The General Regulations and Conditions of Contract).
[39] EDF Conditions, Art. 40(1).
[40] FIDIC Contract, Part I. Tender form, cl. 4.
[41] On firm offers, see para. 3–006.
[42] FIDIC contract, Part I, Tender form, cl. 5.

The tender guarantee

25–020 Sometimes, the tenderer is asked to support his tender by a tender guarantee (tender bond) given by a bank, insurance company or other third party. The object of the tender guarantee is twofold: to indicate to the employer that the tenderer is in earnest and to protect the employer against the breach of any obligations which the tenderer undertakes by submitting his tender.

As far as the banks, insurance companies and other third parties are concerned, the *Uniform Rules for Contract Guarantees*, published by the ICC,[43] provide a useful regulation which applies, however, only if adopted by the parties. The Uniform Rules define a tender guarantee thus[44]:

> "('tender guarantee') means an undertaking given by a bank, insurance company or other party ('the guarantor') at the request of a tenderer ('the principal') or given on the instructions of a bank, insurance company, or other party so requested by the principal ('the instructing party') to a party inviting tenders ('the beneficiary') whereby the guarantor undertakes—in the event of default by the principal in the obligations resulting from the submission of the tender—to make payment to the beneficiary within the limits of a stated sum of money."

Under the Uniform Rules the tender guarantee expires:

(a) six months from the date of the guarantee[45];

(b) on acceptance of the tender by the employer by the award of a contract to the tenderer[46];

(c) by the award of the contract to another tenderer[47]; or

(d) if the employer expressly declares that he does not intend to place a contract.[48]

According to the Uniform Rules, a tender guarantee is valid only in respect of the original tender and does not cover any amendments not approved by the guarantor.[49] The Rules further provide that the employer who wishes to make a claim under the tender guarantee has to submit documentation supporting his claim within a specified time.[50] If the guarantee does not specify the documentation, a declaration from the employer is required that the contractor's tender has been accepted but he has failed either to sign the contract or to submit a performance guarantee. In addition, a declaration is required, addressed to the contractor, to have any dispute settled by arbitration, if not otherwise specified, in accordance with the Rules of the ICC Court of Arbitration or the UNCITRAL Arbitration Rules, at the option of the contractor. The Uniform Rules for Contract Guarantees fail to deal with a claim under the guarantee by the employer if the contractor withdraws the tender contrary to his undertaking to be bound by it.

---

[43] ICC Brochure No. 325 (1978) see *ante*, para. 25–001.
[44] *ibid.* Art. 2(a).
[45] *ibid.* Art. 4(a).
[46] *ibid.* Art. 5(2)(a).
[47] *ibid.* Art. 5(2)(b).
[48] *ibid.* Art. 5(2)(c).
[49] *ibid.* Art. 7(1).
[50] *ibid.* Arts 8 and 9.

The Uniform Rules provide[51] that, if a guarantee does not indicate the law applicable, it shall be governed by the law of the guarantor's place of business, and if he has several places of business by the law of the place of the branch which issued the guarantee.

The World Bank Guidelines provide[52] that bid security shall be released to unsuccessful bidders as soon as possible after it is determined that they will not be awarded the contract.

Opening of tenders

Both the World Bank Guidelines[53] and the EDF Conditions[54] require the bids **25–021** which are formally in order to be opened in public session, but the EDF Conditions do so only with respect to contracts for the supply of goods and not with respect to contracts for work.

The World Bank Guidelines state[55]:

> "Bids should be opened in public; *i.e.* bidders or their representatives should be allowed to be present. The name of the bidder and the total amount of each bid, and of any alternative bids, if they have been requested or permitted, should be read aloud and recorded, when opened and a copy of this record shall be promptly sent to the Bank."

Acceptance of tender

It has already been observed that the employer normally reserves in the tender **25–022** documents the right not to accept the lowest or any bid and to negotiate with tenderers about the clarification of their bids, or even to invite alternative bids. This is necessary in order to have a basis for comparison. The FIDIC letter of tender provides expressly:

> "We understand that you are not bound to accept the lowest or any tender you may receive."

The World Bank Guidelines provide similarly[56]:

> "The Borrower shall award the contract within the period of validity of bids, to the bidder who meets the appropriate standards of capability and resources and whose bid has been determined (i) to be substantially responsive to the bidding documents and (ii) to offer the lowest evaluated cost.[57]"

The contract—some key provisions

Construction contracts, particularly on large, complex infrastructure develop- **25–023** ments, present risks for the parties and the terms and conditions of the contract will address the sharing of those risks between employer and contractor. Money, time and quality are the three key elements of any construction project. In other

---

[51] *ibid.* Art. 10.
[52] World Bank Guidelines, Art. 2.14.
[53] World Bank Guidelines, Art 2.44.
[54] EDF Conditions, Art. 4.2.
[55] World Bank Guidelines, Art. 2.44.
[56] World Bank Guidelines, Art. 2.58.
[57] On the proceedings of an unsuccessful bidder in the E.C. Court of Justice concerning the Amarti River project, to be financed by the EDF, see Case 118/83 *CMC Cooperativa Muratori e Cementisti v. Commission* [1985] E.C.R. 2325.

words, project owners (as well as lenders) will want to see a contract structure which is designed to ensure that the contract is completed within the agreed price, within a specified time and to an adequate standard which, in the case of a production facility, means not only quality of work but also that the level of performance or output needs to meet the criteria specified by the employer.

Pricing

25–024   So far as cost is concerned, there is a balance to be struck between two elements—value for money and price certainty. That balance will change depending upon the pricing structure to be used. Although a lump sum or fixed price is most common, especially where lending institutions are concerned, there is a variety of pricing mechanisms which can be adopted on a construction contract:

Cost Plus Fee. Here, the employer pays the contractor the actual costs incurred by the contractor in carrying out the works, plus a fee to represent the contractor's management, overheads and profit. This fee can either be a fixed sum or a percentage of the total contract value.

From the employer's point of view, this arrangement allows him to know what profit the contractor is making on the project—the profit is not concealed in a lump sum figure. On the other hand, the contract price is more an estimate than a firm price for the work and, arguably, this method of pricing does not impose on the contractor the same incentive to keep costs under control as would be the case with a fixed price. From the contractor's point of view the risk is less than with a fixed price since his costs are being reimbursed, but the opportunity for a healthy profit, if things go right, is reduced.

Unit Price Method. Under this system the parties agree on a rate for each unit of the construction costs and the total price payable depends on the number of units used in the construction. Each unit rate will usually include an amount to represent the contractor's share of profit. Each element making up a construction unit may be materials—*e.g.* the quantity of cement—or calculated by reference to labour—*e.g.* cost per day of labour for specified works.

As with the Cost Plus type of contract such a pricing method does not make for certainty: if the work involves more units than originally anticipated, the employer has to bear the extra cost. Alternatively, if the contractor has underestimated the number of units required, then his profit is likely to be reduced.

With this method of pricing, it is important to have some system for ensuring that the unit rates do indeed reflect the likely cost of the contractor, otherwise there is scope for the contractor loading some units at the expense of others.

Lump Sum or Fixed Price. Here, the contractor undertakes to carry out the contract for a predetermined amount. The contractor is taking a greater risk than with the Cost Plus Fee arrangement: the price includes his estimate as to the overall cost, an allowance to cover the risks for which he is liable under the conditions of contract and contingency, plus a profit element. If the contractor has miscalculated, in particular with regard to the construction risk, his profit will be adversely affected and he could find that he makes a loss on the project. On the other hand, if costs are kept under control the profit can be maximised.

From the employer's point of view, the Fixed Price has much greater certainty and for this reason such an approach is preferred by financing institutions. However, especially where the contract is long term in nature, Fixed Price can produce difficulties and mechanisms designed to allow for fluctuation in price of, *e.g.* raw materials, may be appropriate even though such an arrangement to some extent moves away from the "Fixed Price" principle. Also, these contracts usually contain provisions allowing for changes in the price in specific circumstances, *e.g.* unforeseeable soil conditions.

Target Cost. This is something of a mixture between Fixed Price and Cost Plus Fee and is frequently coupled with the concept of a guaranteed maximum price (GMP). Here, the employer and contractor will agree the "target" cost for the overall contract—probably arrived at by reference to the Cost Plus Fee or Unit Price method. In order to encourage the contractor not to exceed the Target Cost, the contract often contains an incentive whereby any savings on the Target Cost are shared between employer and contractor. On the other hand, if the Target Cost is exceeded, the contractor will bear all or an agreed percentage of the cost overrun—hence the phrase "Guaranteed Maximum Price".

Pricing the risk and changing the contract price

One of the principal functions of a construction contract is to allocate risks as **25–025** between employer and contractor. The more the risk is imposed on the contractor, the less opportunity the contractor will have to claim extra costs on a Fixed Price or Target Cost Contract. However, when tendering for the contract, the contractor will evaluate the risks which are imposed on him and the greater the risk, the more his price is likely to be. This does not necessarily make for an economical solution for the employer.

For example, if the contract stipulates that the contract price is deemed to take account of all physical conditions at the site, whether or not these are foreseeable, the contractor will allow an amount in his tender to cover this risk. If there are no adverse conditions, the employer will, in effect, be paying a premium for a non-existent risk.

Most contract forms deal with such a situation by apportioning the risk. For example, the new FIDIC Conditions of Contract for Construction deal with ground conditions by providing in clause 4.12 for the contractor to give notice to the engineer if he encounters adverse physical conditions which he considers to have been "unforeseeable"—*i.e.* not reasonably foreseeable by an experienced contractor by the date for submission of the tender. If the engineer agrees with the contractor and the contractor suffers delay and/or incurs extra costs as a result of these conditions, then the engineer may grant an extension of time and/or contract price adjustment.

Thus, under the FIDIC Conditions, the risk is shared by employer and contractor, allowing the possibility of an extra cost but only if conditions which were not reasonably foreseeable by an experienced contractor do in fact arise.

There is an increasing trend towards Contractors becoming involved in sharing risk with clients on a longer term basis. Public–private partnerships are increasingly common internationally with the PFI (Private Finance Initiative) scheme, where the public sector enters into a long term contract with a private sector consortium for the design, construction, operation and maintenance of a facility—hospital, prison, etc. A detailed risk matrix is usually an element of these projects at tender stage, with the allocation of risk being clearly established between the parties. Moreover, with BOT schemes, the Contractor will be paid out of the income stream from the project and will thereby assume a substantial element of the long term risks.

Contract variations

25–026 Construction contracts usually contain a provision which allows the employer to request changes in the work as well as allowing the contractor to propose changes. Any changes, of course, are likely to affect the contract price.

Contracts increasingly nowadays contain provisions requiring the contractor to provide details of the cost and time impact which any change may have, before an instruction by the employer or engineer is issued to the contractor. Agreeing these details at the time that the change occurs avoids uncertainty and the potential for dispute at a later stage is substantially reduced.

The contract will usually specify the way in which changes to the contract are to be priced. It is usual for the terms and conditions to state that changes, whether alterations, additions or omissions, will be valued at the rates and prices set out in the contract, assuming that these are, in the opinion of the contract administrator or engineer, applicable. If the contract does not contain applicable rates or prices, then an alternative should be agreed or the applicable rates may be used as a basis for calculating the basis of the change. In the absence of agreement, the contract administrator or engineer will fix the appropriate rate and if there is a dispute, they will ultimately have to be determined by the courts or by arbitration.

Extensions of time

25–027 The contract will usually specify a date by which the works must be completed. During the course of the project, circumstances may arise which justify an extension to the completion date. Such circumstances may include, for example, delay by the employer in giving the contractor possession of the site; additional time needed by the contractor to comply with a change order which has been issued by the engineer; or an event of force majeure which causes delay.

An extension of time clause is an essential element of a construction contract and it does need to be carefully drafted. For example, the contractor should be required to notify the employer promptly when he becomes aware of an event which is likely to result in delay and which would justify an extension of the date for completion. The contractor should also be required to justify any requests for an extension, so that this can be assessed by the employer or his representative.

In addition, the contract should provide that an extension of time will not be granted for reasons which are due to some default on the part of the contractor.

The absence of a clause permitting an extension of time may have an adverse impact on the validity of the completion date and on the employer's right to claim liquidated damages for delay. If the contractor is unable to meet the completion due to some act or omission of the employer—for example, where the employer gives the contractor late possession of the site—then, under English law, if the contractor can show that he could not have completed the contract by the due date, he will not be liable for payment of liquidated damages for late completion. Instead, time will be "at large"—that is to say, the contractor is obliged to complete the work within a reasonable time but not by the date fixed in the contract since, by the employer's action or inaction, that date has become unachievable. By having a clause which permits an extension of time, the employer's right to claim liquidated damages will be retained: the contractor will seek and be given an extension of time and the liquidated damages provision will apply to the new completion date as it did to the original one.

Standard of design and work

The specification for the works will usually set out the standards of work- **25–028** manship and materials required.

The conditions of contract will impose quality standards and include warranties from the contractor concerning his performance, design, materials and workmanship.

In addition, where the contract is for the construction of an industrial or process facility, the contract will contain procedures for performance tests and the evaluation of the completed plant against the performance criteria contained in the specification.

Inspection and acceptance

The acceptance of the progressive stages of the work or the completed work is **25–029** an important incident in the performance of the contract because often payment, or part payment, is made dependent on it. This topic is usually regulated in the contract in some detail. Generally, the contract will provide for acceptance of the completed work in two stages—practical completion and final acceptance. Under this arrangement, the engineer will issue a certificate on practical completion, at which point the employer will take over responsibility for the works. The final certificate will be issued at the end of the "maintenance period" or "defects liability period", during which the contractor has both the right and the obligation to remedy any defect in the work for which he is responsible. At the end of this period, the duration of which is most frequently 12 months, the final certificate will be issued. Where there is a retention (see *post*, para. 25–035) it is common for half the retention to be released on practical completion and the remainder on the issue of the final certificate.

Assignment and sub-contracting

25–030 It is normal for the contractor to be prohibited from assigning his interest in the contract without the prior consent of the employer. However, it is usual to permit the contractor to sub-contract parts (but not the whole) of the contract. Where, for example, a hospital has to be built by a construction firm, it is probable that they will sub-contract x-ray and other clinical equipment to specialists. Indeed, the contractor is likely to sub-contract mechanical and electrical works, piling and other major elements of the project: the role of a main contractor is increasingly that of a manager of various specialists engaged to undertake the project. As with the FIDIC Conditions, it is usual to provide that the main contractor will be responsible for the acts, defaults or neglect of any sub-contractor as though they were his own.

The FIDIC Conditions contain provision for the appointment of "nominated sub-contractors". These are sub-contractors who have been selected by the employer, rather than the main contractor. Under the FIDIC Conditions of Contract for Construction, clause 5.4 provides that before the engineer issues a payment certificate or at any stage, he may ask the contractor to furnish reasonable evidence that the sub-contractors in question have been paid and, failing this, the employer may pay the sub-contractor directly. While under some jurisdictions, problems can arise with direct payments in the event of main contractor insolvency, such a provision has its uses: failure by a contractor to pay his sub-contractors is often a signal that the contractor is in financial difficulties. In order to ensure the smooth operation of a major contract, timely payment of sub-contractors is important. Even if the employer does not have the right to make direct payments, it is worth containing provisions in a contract which enable the employer to check whether sub-contractors have been paid and, if not, to withhold payment from the main contractor.

The engineer or contract administrator

25–031 Under the FIDIC Red Book and the new FIDIC Construction Contract and many other contracts, the employer appoints an engineer whose role is to issue instructions and decisions and to resolve disputes between employer and contractor as the project progresses. Although appointed by the employer, and thus in a contractual relationship only with the employer and not the contractor, the contract usually requires the engineer to act impartially in dealings between the employer and the contractor.

Although the engineer under this form of contract is not the employer's representative, it is often difficult for him to maintain a role of complete independence, not least since the employer will frequently in practice see the engineer as his representative in dealing with the contractor. Indeed, it is not unknown for the engineer to be an employee of the employer organisation.

Because of the difficulties in having a truly impartial engineer, there has been a shift in thinking in recent years. The new FIDIC Red Book provides that where, under the contract, the engineer is to agree or determine any matter, he shall "consult with each party in an endeavour to reach agreement. If agreement is not achieved, the Engineer shall make a fair determination in accordance with the Contract, taking due regard of all relevant circumstances."

The FIDIC Orange Book and the new FIDIC EPC Contract dispense with the engineer. Instead, they provide for the contract to be administered by the "Employer's Representative" whose role is to represent the employer and act with his authority. The employer's representative is not required to act impartially but where the contract requires him to agree or determine any matter, he is required to consult with the contractor in an endeavour to reach agreement, failing which he will issue his determination to the contractor with supporting particulars.

Payment

The contract will set out the basis upon which payment shall be made to the **25–032** contractor as the contract progresses. Under the FIDIC and many other contracts, the payment procedure will involve a process whereby at regular intervals, most frequently monthly, the engineer or contract administrator will certify the amount due to the contractor. At the end of each month the contractor will submit an application for payment to the engineer, the engineer will value this and then certify the amount payable. The employer will then make payment within a specified period.

In a lump sum turnkey contract it is not uncommon to have a payment schedule, so that certain amounts become due on certain dates or on the completion of certain activities, without the more traditional valuation method being adopted. Where there is a payment schedule, it is, nonetheless, important to ensure that the contract contains provisions which link payment to the progress of the work. Thus, if the work is not progressing in accordance with the programme, the employer or the engineer would have the right to adjust the payment schedule. Otherwise, there is clearly a risk that payment under the contract proceeds ahead of the work, with consequent risks for the employer.

Sometimes, a payment schedule is linked to milestones, that is to say key stages of the works, *e.g.* completion of the foundations. Payment due in respect of each milestone will only be made when the milestone is reached and occasionally a milestone payment is linked with a bonus for early completion, with a penalty if it is late.

Performance and repayment guarantees

It is usual for the contractor to provide a performance guarantee which is issued **25–033** by a bank, insurance company or other third party. The guarantee is intended to safeguard the employer against the failure of the contractor to perform his obligations under the contract. In most international contracts, the employer will require the performance guarantee (or performance bond) to be "on demand"— *i.e.* the party issuing the guarantee is required to pay the amount demanded up to the value of the guarantee, whenever this is requested by the employer and regardless of whether or not the call is properly made. The English courts have taken the view that it is necessary to show fraud before they will intervene to prevent the bank from making payment under an on-demand guarantee.

Performance guarantees issued by surety companies, however, are usually only payable after the employer is satisfied of the amount of loss which has been suffered, and quite frequently, only after the issue of an arbitration award or final judgment in the courts, which has not been honoured by the contractor.

If the employer makes an advance payment to a contractor at the commencement of the project, he will usually require an advance payment guarantee issued by a bank in his favour. This will protect the employer, in the event of a default or insolvency of the contractor, before the advance is repaid. Since the advance is usually recovered by way of deduction instalment payments as the contract progresses, so the advance payment guarantee is usually written so as to reduce in value to match the repayments.

Sometimes, the employer will be asked to provide a payment guarantee in favour of the contractor, in order to safeguard the contractor against the risk of the employer defaulting under his contractual obligations. The latest FIDIC Conditions now include a form of payment guarantee.

Liquidated damages and bonus clauses

25–034   International construction contracts often contain clauses providing for the payment of liquidated damages by the contractor if the work is not carried out within the stipulated times. The amount of the liquidated damages should be a reasonable estimate of the loss likely to be suffered; it should not be of punitive character, because in this case it would be a penalty and under English law may be set aside. Further, the clause should provide that no liquidated damages are payable if the contractor is prevented by an event beyond his control from completing the work. A bonus for early completion is incorporated occasionally to balance the liquidated damages clause.

Some contracts for process plant and similar facilities also contain provisions for performance-related liquidated damages if, *e.g.* the plant's production is less than the design capacity (but still at acceptable levels). In considering liquidated damages, it should be noted that these are usually limited, often to 10 per cent of the contract price, so they operate as a cap on the contractor's liability.

Retention money

25–035   It is usual in international construction contracts to provide for "retention". Under the terms of such a contract, the employer will usually retain a small percentage, say 5 per cent, of the amount certified as payable from each instalment payment until practical completion. The normal procedure is for 50 per cent of the retention to be released on practical completion, with the balance payable at the end of the defects liability period. Retention offers the employer some security, in addition to the security provided by performance guarantees, in the event of the default of the contractor. In those cases where there is a fixed schedule of payments under the contract, the "retention" element can be built into the payment schedule, so there is no need to apply a separate retention for making payments in accordance with the schedule.

Currency clauses

Particular attention has to be paid to the currency clauses, especially if the **25–036** employer has to make payment to joint contractors in different countries or to sub-contractors carrying on business in countries other than that of the main contractor. FIDIC Conditions contain provisions specifying the currency (or currencies) for the Contract Price and provision for fixed exchange rates and payment in the relevant currencies.

Insurance and indemnity clauses

The contractor will normally be required to insure the works during construction **25–037** and to insure against third party liability. If he fails to do so, the employer may insure himself for the account of the contractor. Depending on the location and nature of the project, it may be cheaper for the employer to arrange the insurance, in which case this will be reflected in the contract.

The contractor will under the contract indemnify the employer against any claims or liabilities in relation to works and third party risks for which the contractor is liable and in respect of which insurance cover is arranged.

Other contract clauses

An international construction contract normally incorporates many of the clauses **25–038** discussed earlier in this work, in particular:

(a) the force majeure clause;[58]

(b) the choice of law clause;[59]

(c) the arbitration clause;

(d) the waiver of immunity clause.[60]

Some of these clauses, such as the arbitration clause, have to be adapted to the special requirements of a long term construction contract.

Arbitration and the resolution of disputes

Dispute resolution clauses in international construction contracts have evolved **25–039** more, perhaps, than any other provisions over the past few years and FIDIC and the World Bank's Standard Bidding Documents reflect this evolution.

The FIDIC Red Book, in its 4th Edition, provides for any dispute to be settled

---

[58] See para. 32–015.
[59] See *ante*, para. 22–001.
[60] State Immunity Act 1978, ss. 2(2) and 9; see *ante*, para. 21–019.

initially by the engineer, within 84 days of a request from either party. If the engineer's decision is unacceptable to either party, then the matter is to be referred to arbitration and there is a 70-day period from the date of the decision with which this reference must be made. FIDIC Clause 67 also contains provision for amicable settlement before the arbitration commences: in effect, there is a 56-day moratorium.

The World Bank's Standard Bidding Document issued in 1995 substantially modified clause 67 of the FIDIC Red Book dealing with the resolution of disputes. Instead of having an engineer's decision followed by arbitration if this is not accepted, any disagreement over any action, certificate or instruction of the engineer is in the first place to be referred to a disputes review board or to a single disputes review expert: the World Bank has two versions, the first of which is mandatory for contracts with a value in excess of U.S.$50m. A disputes review board comprises three members, one each appointed by the employer and the contractor and the third member selected by the other two, unless they fail to agree, in which case the appointing authority named in the appendix will select the third member, who will act as chairman of the board. Each member of the board is to be experienced with the type of construction involved in the works and with the interpretation of contractual documents.

As well as amending clause 67 of the Red Book, the World Bank have produced a five page document setting out the dispute review board's rules and procedures. In addition to dealing with the actual method of resolving disputes, this document specifies the fees and expenses payable to the board and provides for site visits by the board at regular intervals. Clearly, the intention is to have an independent board whose members are familiar with the project and in a position to deal with disputes quickly.

Any party objecting to some action of the engineer or the other party will file a notice of dispute and the other party must respond within 14 days of receipt. If the dispute cannot be resolved, then either party may refer the dispute to the board by a written request for recommendation. The board must then reach its recommendations for a resolution of the dispute as soon as possible and in any event within 56 days of receipt of the request. The board's recommendation becomes final and binding on the parties if their recommendation is issued within the 56-day period and no notice of intention to commence arbitration is given by either party to the other within 14 days from receipt of the recommendation. Whether or not it has become final, the recommendation is admissible as evidence in any subsequent arbitration or litigation. Clearly, with experienced individuals making up the disputes review board, this provision is a powerful incentive to the parties not to take the dispute further.

If, however, the dispute is not resolved by the recommendation, then clause 67.3 of the World Bank document provides for arbitration under the UNCITRAL Arbitration Rules. The World Bank states, "Arbitration under the UNCITRAL Arbitration Rules is a form of unadministered or non-institutional arbitration". The Rules go on to refer to the fact that several arbitration centres do offer to provide administered arbitration under rules based on the UNCITRAL Rules and these include the regional centres for commercial arbitration in Cairo and Kuala Lumpur. The alternative World Bank procedure for reference to a disputes review expert is essentially the same, but here there is only one individual rather than a panel of three. The FIDIC Orange Book for lump sum turnkey contracts also contains provision for the establishment of a disputes review panel.

The new FIDIC Conditions largely adopt the World Bank's approach. Clause 20 of the new Red Book, for example, contains detailed provisions for the appointment of a Dispute Adjudication Board (DAB) of either one or three individuals. Every dispute must first be referred to the DAB for a decision, which must be given within 84 days from the reference and the parties are obliged to give effect to that decision. A dissatisfied party has 28 days in which to serve a notice of dissatisfaction, in which case the dispute will be finally determined by arbitration, before three arbitrators under the Rules of Arbitration of the ICC. As with the FIDIC Red Book, 4th Edition, there is provision for amicable settlement before the arbitration gets under way. If no notice of dissatisfaction is served, the DAB's decision becomes final and binding on the parties.

The new dispute resolution clauses are to be found in all the new FIDIC Conditions and they are far more elaborate than in previous editions. Clearly, the objective in having a Dispute Adjudication Board, with members who are familiar with the Project, is to have all disputes resolved quickly and to avoid the immense cost of lengthy arbitration proceedings, which have so often been a late feature of major construction contracts.

These new developments are to be welcomed: as well as avoiding the difficulties of having the engineer decide on disputes, the approach is a practical one, designed to produce a rapid decision issued by suitably qualified individuals who, from their own observations, know how the project is progressing. The chances of disputes going to arbitration will be greatly reduced.

In England, too, this trend has become enshrined in legislation: the Housing Grants, Construction and Regeneration Act 1996 has introduced a statutory right to adjudication in all contracts of "construction operations": under this legislation, which adopts a recommendation of the Latham Report, any party to a construction contract may refer a dispute to adjudication and the adjudicator is required to issue a decision within 28 days of the reference.

The growth of mediation and other alternative dispute resolution techniques is another aspect of this move away from formal litigation and arbitration, which have become so time consuming and expensive over the years.

PART SEVEN

CUSTOMS LAW

CHAPTER 26

GOVERNMENT REGULATION OF EXPORTS

The control and regulation of exports from the United Kingdom is governed by **26–001** various pieces of international, European and national legislation. The majority of legislation having a direct effect on exporters and suppliers of goods from the United Kingdom is administered by HM Customs and Excise. The scope of such legislation, however, is extremely wide; it may relate to prohibited or restricted exports, VAT, duty or excise or statistical requirements. The purpose of this Chapter is not to cover every aspect of Government regulation, but simply the main aspects. Areas not covered include animal health controls and the common agricultural policy (CAP). Moreover, whilst export licensing is considered, it should be emphasised that despite its importance, only 15 per cent of exports from the United Kingdom are subject to export licensing controls.[1]

EXPORT LICENSING REGULATIONS

The legislation relating to export licensing deals with "goods" only. This term **26–002** does not include banknotes, treasury bills, bills of exchange, promissory notes, stocks and shares, debentures and similar things in action and gold bullion; these were exclusively governed by exchange control regulations before these regulations were abolished in the United Kingdom.[2]

The present system of export licensing controls the exportation, from the United Kingdom, of specified goods which cannot be exported without the provision of an export licence issued by the Department of Trade and Industry (DTI). As regards strategic goods, the DTI was formerly empowered to exercise extraterritorial control but these powers appear to have lapsed. Further supernational vetting procedures are carried out under the Wassenaar Agreement, the agreed military list which is implemented in the United Kingdom by an amendment to the Export of Goods (Control) Order 1994.[3]

The general control of exports

The general powers of the DTI to regulate the exportation of goods are based **26–003** on the Import, Export and Customs Powers (Defence) Act 1939[4] which authorises the DTI to make "such provisions as the Department thinks expedi-

---

[1] Source: HM Customs and Excise.
[2] Exchange Control Act 1947, s. 22.
[3] See *post*, para. 26–004.
[4] In *R. v. Blackledge; R. v. Grecian; R. v. Mason; R. v. Phillips* (1995) 139 Sol. Jo. L.B. 139 it was held by the Court of Appeal that the subsequent Export of Goods (Control) Orders were valid under powers contained in the 1939 Act, an unrepealed statute.

ent" for the regulation of the importation into, or exportation from, the United Kingdom of all goods of a specified description. In exercise of these powers, the Secretary of State has issued the Export of Goods (Control) Order 1994[5] and the Export of Goods (Control) Order 1992[6] (in so far as it remains for antiques).[7]

The provisions of the Export of Goods (Control) Order apply to goods intended to be exported from the United Kingdom, but have no extraterritorial effect on goods situated outside the United Kingdom.

The exporter who wishes to ascertain whether an export licence is required in respect of the particular goods which he intends to export, should obtain a copy of the Order and all amendments to date, or inquire of the Export Control Organisation of the DTI.[8] The main types of goods which require a licence can be summarised as follows:

(a) nuclear-related goods, encompassing any material or equipment related to the production or processing of nuclear products;

(b) chemical weapons precursors and the associated equipment and technology required to produce such goods;

(c) biological products and associated processing equipment;

(d) military equipment, including, *inter alia*, any arms or ammunition, vehicles, military aircraft and ships;

(e) technology and equipment used in the development and production of weapons of mass destruction;

(f) dual-use goods, which may have a duplicitous function, *i.e.* both an innocent commercial use or a military use, including, *inter alia*, navigation equipment, cryptographic items, high powered computers, radar, certain aircraft parts and machine tool equipment[9];

(g) goods destined for countries subject to UN sanctions.[10]

A full list of prohibited goods; the *Prohibited List*, which is too lengthy and technical to reproduce here and is subject to frequent amendment, is provided in Schedule 1 to the Export of Goods (Control) Order 1994. The Export Control Organisation of the DTI will advise whether an export licence is required and provide the appropriate application form (which can now be completed electronically on computer disc). There are four principal forms of licence. The usual

---

[5] S.I. 1994 No. 1191. This replaced the Export of Goods (Control) Order 1987 (S.I. 1987 No. 2070). The 1994 Control Order is regularly amended (currently Amendment No. 3 of 2000 (S.I. 2000 No. 1396) applies).

[6] S.I. 1992 No. 3092.

[7] See *post*, para. 26–005.

[8] DTI Export Control Organisation on 020 7215 8070. The Export Control Organisation also has an Internet site: *http://www.dti.gov.uk/export.control*.

[9] Under Council Regulation 3381/94 and Council Decision 94/942 (as amended).

[10] Under the United Nations Act 1946. Currently, there are embargoes against Iraq (all goods), Libya, Angola and Sierra Leone (certain goods only) and arms embargoes against Liberia, Rwanda and Somalia.

type is an *Individual Licence*, applied for by a particular exporter and relating to particular goods; these are usually valid for two years. The second type is the *Open General Export Licence* which came into force in 1989 (OGEL). The OGEL removes the need to apply for individual licences for exports to scheduled destinations in Western Europe, North America, Japan and Australia. OGELs are usually open ended and do not have an expiry date. The third type is the *Open Individual Export Licence* (OIEL), which is specific to an individual exporter but covers regular shipments of certain goods to specified destinations. These are generally valid for two to three years, depending on the goods and the countries exported to. Finally, the fourth is the *Transhipment Licence*.

Even in the case of goods which, as a rule, require an export licence, exceptions are admitted. They are stated in article 3 of the Export of Goods (Control) Order 1994.

Any licence or other permission for the exportation of goods may be modified or revoked at any time by the Secretary of State (Article 7(1)).

Even when goods are only taken out of the country temporarily, if they are licensable they must be exported under the provisions of the relevant Order. Thus, a traveller in possession of licensable goods which they take abroad, "exports" them and has to declare them on leaving the country in compliance with what is now Article 6(1), even though they intend to return with them into the country and have insured them for the return journey.[11]

The exporter is not entitled to assign the authority to export goods which he is granted by licence, unless he is expressly authorised by the licence to do so. Normally, the licence is not transferable, but in the case of bulk shipments or similar exceptional cases the licence may be granted to "X, Y or any person or firm authorised in writing by them".

The export licence does not authorise the exporter to do an act prohibited by other enactments or regulations, such as regulations relating to Customs or postal movements and the granting of an export licence does not leave the holder immune from committing an offence under the Export of Goods (Control) Order.[12] Further, an export licence issued in the United Kingdom does not relieve the exporter from his duty to obtain an import licence in the country of importation if such a licence is required there and he has undertaken, under the terms of the contract of sale, to procure the import licence.

Strategic goods

The control of the export of strategic goods is covered by the provisions of the **26–004** 1994 Order, which only applies within the jurisdiction of the United Kingdom. Therefore, export controls of strategic goods do not have any extraterritorial effect.

Whereas previously the *CoCom* agreement existed on a supranational level, this agreement was disbanded in 1994. The export control lists were however

---

[11] *R. v. Berner* (1953) 37 Cr. App. R. 113.
[12] *R. v. Redfern and Dunlop Ltd (Aircraft Tyre Division)* (1992) 13 Cr. App. Rep. (S) 709. See *post*, para. 26–031.

maintained and the CoCom arrangements were replaced by the *Wassenaar Agreement*. This was signed in July 1996 and all participant nations[13] have agreed to implement controls to prevent the proliferation of military and dual-use goods, whilst not affecting legitimate civil transactions.[14] The military list is enforced in the United Kingdom in the Export of Goods (Control) Order 1994 (as amended) and came into force on November 1, 1996. The dual-use provisions are implemented through Council Regulation (E.C.) 3381/94 (Annex I), which was amended to take account of Wassenaar. Additionally, provisions have been incorporated into the Dual-Use and Related Goods (Export Control) Order 1995.

Antiques

26–005 The control of the export of antiques is administered by the Department for Culture, Media and Sport. The provisions in respect of these goods are contained in the Export of Goods (Control) Order 1992.[15] Section 4 refers to:

> "4. Any goods manufactured or produced more than 50 years before the date of exportation except:
> (1) postage stamps and other articles of philatelic interest;
> (2) birth, marriage or death certificates or other documents relating to the personal affairs of the exporter or the spouse of the exporter;
> (3) letters or other writings written by or to the exporter or the spouse of the exporter; and
> (4) any goods exported by, and being the personal property of, the manufacturer or producer thereof, or the spouse, widow or widower of that person."

In addition to national legislation, there is also E.C. law.[16] One of the consequences of this is to include water colour paintings within the scope of export controls. Further, two E.C. Directives exist, which relate to the "Return of Cultural Goods"[17]; these provide that where goods exported are significant in terms of national heritage of the exporting member state, and have been exported without a licence, they must be returned.

CUSTOMS REGULATIONS

Introduction

26–006 The principal function of Customs in international trade is the collection of duties and taxes. In addition, Customs often fulfil secondary functions in the

---

[13] Members of the Wassenaar Agreement include Argentina, Australia, Austria, Belgium, Bulgaria, Canada, Czech Republic, Denmark, Finland, France, Germany, Greece, Hungary, Ireland, Italy, Japan, Luxembourg, Netherlands, New Zealand, Norway, Poland, Portugal, Republic of Korea, Romania, Russian Federation, Slovak Republic, Spain, Sweden, Switzerland, Turkey, Ukraine, United Kingdom and United States of America.
[14] As protected by the United Nations Charter, Art. 51.
[15] S.I. 1992 No. 3092.
[16] Council Regulation 3911/92 as amended by Council Regulation 2469/96.
[17] Directive 93/7 and Directive 96/100. These Directives are enacted in U.K. law through S.I. 1994 No. 501 and S.I. 1997 No. 1719.

application of controls, on behalf of other government departments. These include, *inter alia*, the control of prohibited and restricted goods, the collection of statistical information and application of the Common Agricultural Policy (CAP).

Customs controls generally take place at the port or airport of exportation, although for authorised traders they may be carried out at the trader's premises under local export control (LEC).[18] An exception applies in respect of consignments moving between the Member States of the European Union, which since January 1, 1993, have no longer been regarded as *exports* but *supplies* of goods. Since the 1993 changes, exporters as well as other practitioners should treat trade within the European Union as separate from trade with other countries. Indeed, the Single Market has created a hybrid situation, in that it is not domestic trade, but is equally different from trade with countries outside of the European Union.

Whether trading within the European Union or with countries outside of the European Union, exporters are not generally expected to have an in depth knowledge of the legislative base for Customs requirements. In any case many of these requirements are interpreted for public consumption, in either the HM Customs and Excise Tariff[19] or in public notices.[20] However, it should be noted that public information is just that and cannot be relied upon in a court of law. Indeed, the Community Customs Code[21] requires exporters to have read and understood the relevant legislation,[22] much of which is held in Community law.[23]

The effect of the Single Market on Customs legisation

On January 1, 1993 momentous changes occurred in respect of customs legisla- **26–007** tion within the European Community. As a consequence of implementation of the Single European Act,[24] which laid down the timetable for the completion of the Single Market, all frontiers between the then 12 Member States of the E.C.[25] were removed, allowing for the free movement of goods.[26] This meant the

---

[18] Customs Public Notice 482 refers.

[19] The Tariff comprises three Volumes: Volume I contains General information; Volume II contains the list of commodity codes to describe goods and establish duty and tax rates; and Volume III provides more detailed information on completion of Customs declarations. The Tariff is available in good reference libraries, at local Customs offices or can be purchased from HMSO.

[20] Customs Public Notices are available free of charge from local HM Customs and Excise offices or from the Internet at Website *www.hmce.gov.uk*. A list of current Notices can be found in the Tariff, Vol. I, P. 15.

[21] See *post*, para. 26–012, n. 26.

[22] See *Gunzler Aluminium* [1995] T.75/95 E.C.J. (first instance) and *The Commissioners of Customs and Excise v. Invicta* [1997] Q.B.D. V and D R.56.

[23] Community law, in the form of Regulations, Directives and Decisions, is published in the *Official Journal of the European Communities*.

[24] Signed in 1986, implemented into U.K. legislation by the European Communities Act 1972, s.2(1).

[25] Belgium, Denmark, France, Germany, Greece, Ireland, Italy, Luxembourg, Netherlands, Portugal, Spain, United Kingdom.

[26] Art. 8 of the Single European Act 1986. The provisions now appear in the Treaty Establishing the European Community, Part Three, Articles 23–27 (as amended by the Treaty of Amsterdam 1997).

removal of all duties and quantitative restrictions, as well as procedural barriers such as systematic checks by the customs administrations at internal frontiers.[27] The Single Market changed customs procedures significantly, with the concepts of *export* and *import* being replaced by *supply* and *acquisition*[28] within the E.C.

In addition, from January 1, 1995, further changes were introduced under the Treaty of European Union,[29] including the expansion of the territory of the E.C. to include Austria, Finland and Sweden; the new grouping of 15 Member States forming the European Union.

Supply of goods to other Member States of the European Union

26–008 Whilst the Single European Act removed the frontiers between the Member States, some forms of control remain to take account of the payment of VAT and excise duty and the collection of statistical information. Although control of VAT and statistics now takes place in parallel with domestic VAT controls, the monitoring of excise still relies largely on accompanying documentation, with controls taking place at traders' or warehouse keepers' premises. Before goods can benefit from free movement between the Member States they must be in free circulation. This is defined as:

(a) goods which wholly originate in the European Union; and

(b) goods which satisfy the conditions of Articles 23 and 24 of the E.C. Treaty, being the goods coming from a non-European Union country which have been put into free circulation in the European Union.[30]

VAT

26–009 Previously, VAT had been collected at the frontiers as part of the declaration procedures to Customs. Since January 1993, this has no longer been the case. Instead, VAT is accountable in the member states of destination, through the national VAT system.[31]

When supplying goods to a customer in another Member State, the supplier must obtain and quote the customer's VAT registration number on the commercial invoice and zero-rate the supply (not charge VAT). The customer then accounts for the VAT on their national VAT return. For supplies to non-registered customers, as a VAT registration number cannot be quoted, the invoice must include VAT at the appropriate rate in the supplier's Member State

---

[27] Although some restrictions remained in respect of certain illicit drugs and other prohibited material; see *R. v. Henn* [1981] A.C. 850, which involved the supply of pornography. Article 30 of the E.C. Treaty applies.
[28] Referred to for statistical purposes as *"dispatches"* and *"arrivals"*.
[29] Signed in Maastricht on February 7, 1992.
[30] Previous Articles 9 and 10 (prior to the Treaty of Amsterdam). To meet this status all the taxes and duties must be paid on the goods at importation. Note that under the transit provisions (see *infra*), European Union goods which leave the Customs territory are deemed to lose their free circulation status, unless declared to the contrary.
[31] The changes were introduced by amendment to the Sixth VAT Council Directive 77/388.

and is accounted for on the supplier's VAT return. If, as a supplier, a trader is not registered, then no VAT can be charged.[32]

For all supplies of goods to other Member States, it is important for VAT purposes that evidence is retained in the trader's records that the goods left the United Kingdom. Such evidence may comprise, *inter alia*, a certificate of shipment[33] or a commercial transport document issued by the haulier. Other supporting information will include record of payment from abroad.[34] For VAT registered companies, additional boxes must be completed on the VAT return and the return must be accompanied by a VAT sales listing.[35] The latter identifies the VAT numbers and total value of sales to the individual companies traded with in other Member States, during the accounting period.[36]

The current VAT system introduced in January 1993 is transitional and is likely to be replaced at some stage by what is referred to as the definitive VAT system. Proposals for the definitive system have been produced by the Commission[37] and these are based on the VAT liability being moved to the Member States of supply. These proposals, however, are unlikely to be introduced until Member State governments can align their respective national VAT rates.

Statistics

Obtaining accurate statistical information is extremely important for business **26–010** and for government. For exports to countries outside of the E.U., information is collected via the Customs declaration.[38] However, within the E.U., with the removal of frontier formalities, other measures have been put in place. The system introduced is called Intrastat[39] and it requires suppliers of goods to other Member States who trade above a certain threshold[40] to report their supplies[41] on a monthly declaration.[42]

The legal basis for the Intrastat system lies in European law,[43] supplemented by the Statistics of Trade Act 1947; the Customs and Excise Management Act 1979, ss 145–148 and ss 150–154 and various statutory instruments.[44] The supply of accurate Intrastat information is important and should not be disregarded by suppliers. Although initially HM Customs and Excise took a pragmatic approach to the timeliness and quality of supply of Intrastat data, a number of

---

[32] In such instances, it is useful, although not a requirement, to include the following statement on the invoice; "*supply from non VAT registered company*".

[33] This is a prescribed document issued by the carrier. Note that the carrier may charge for issuing this document.

[34] Customs Notice 703 provides details of the requirements.

[35] VAT 101 Form. Required under the VAT Act 1994, Sched. 11, para. 2(3).

[36] For more information see Customs Notice 725—VAT in the Single Market.

[37] Commission Document DGXXI, COM 328(96) Final, dated July 10, 1996.

[38] The Single Administrative Document, Copy 2, see *post*, para. 26–013.

[39] For detailed information on Intrastat see Customs Notice 60.

[40] The current threshold is £233,000 of trade with other Member States. This figure is adjusted annually by an inflationary rise.

[41] Referred to as "*dispatches*" for statistical purposes.

[42] The Supplementary Statistical Declaration (SSD), Customs Form C 1500.

[43] The basic regulation is in Council Regulation 3330/91, the implementing provisions are held in Commission Regulation 3046/92.

[44] S.I. 1996 No. 2968, S.I. 1997 No. 2968, S.I. 1998 No. 2973 and S.I. 1999 No. 3269.

cases have shown that failure to comply with the requirements can result in heavy penalties.[45]

Excise

26–011 Excise is a duty levied on goods containing alcohol, tobacco or hydrocarbon oil and their derivatives. It is applied to all such goods irrespective of whether they are supplied domestically, to another Member State or to a non-E.U. country. Excise is a national tax and is accountable in the country of consumption.

Within the E.U. the rates of excise charged may vary considerably between the Member States and as a consequence strict controls are applied to the movement of such products. Trade in excise goods moves under one of three procedures: either in suspension[46] between authorised excise warehouse keepers; to an authorised receiver of excise goods in another Member State, where the excise must be accounted for on arrival in that Member State,[47] or as a distance sale, where the supply must be made duty paid.[48]

If a supplier of excise unpaid goods supplies such goods to an authorised receiver then the excise must be accounted for immediately upon arrival in the E.U. Member State of destination. Although suppliers do not have to be authorised to make such supplies,[49] they do have to fulfil certain obligations and may be liable as the supplier of the goods if they are not properly accounted for.[50]

Supplies can also be made of excise suspended goods between Customs authorised warehouse keepers within the E.U. This is a common method of deferring the payment of taxes until the goods are ready for consumption or sale. Warehouse keepers can either be the owners of the goods or can act on behalf of a third party.[51] Whatever the case, they are obliged to take effective measures to ensure the proper control and accounting of the goods.[52] All movements of excise suspended goods within the E.U. must be secured by a guarantee. This can be provided by the owner, the warehouse keeper or the transporter of the goods.

All such movements must be accompanied by an accompanying administrative document (AAD).[53] This is a four-part form which is used to confirm the delivery of the goods. The four copies are used as follows:

(a) Copy 1—for the consignor;

(b) Copy 2—for the consignee;

---

[45] Offences result in criminal penalties of up to £2,500 per offence (Level 4 on the Standard Scale). See *Commissioners Customs and Excise v. Dams International Ltd* (1994), unreported, in which the defendant received a penalty of £11,250 for failure to render Intrastat returns.
[46] Excise unpaid.
[47] This is known as the Registered Excise Dealer and Shipper (REDS) system in the U.K. Other Member States operate similar systems.
[48] For the supply of excise goods to private individuals.
[49] An authorisation system may be introduced by Customs and Excise in 2000.
[50] See Customs Notice 197.
[51] Where an owner stores his goods in an excise warehouse belonging to another party.
[52] Customs Notice 197.
[53] See Customs Notice 197, Appendix L.

(c) Copy 3—for return to the consignor;

(d) Copy 4—for the country of destination.

The basic legislation in respect of the movement and storage of excise goods in the E.U. is held in E.C. law,[54] supported by various national statutes.[55] Offences of handling goods subject to unpaid excise duty, or taking preparatory steps for the evasion of excise duty,[56] are treated as serious offences.[57] Where excise goods are stolen or lost, the owner is still liable for the duty. In *James Buchanan & Co Ltd v. Babco Forwarding and Shipping (U.K.) Ltd*,[58] a consignment of whiskey worth £7,000 (excluding excise duty) in transit to a destination abroad was stolen from the transporting vehicle in the United Kingdom; the owner had to pay the (unpaid) excise duty of some £30,000.[59]

Supply of goods to countries outside of the European Union

The basic policy for the export of goods from the United Kingdom has **26–012** remained unchanged and depends on the fiscal and restrictive character[60] of the goods intended to be exported. Where exportation does not involve the payment or refund of Customs duties and the goods are not of a restricted nature, these formalities are relatively simple, but where the payment or refund of Customs duties or licensing controls is involved, the procedure is more complicated.

Customs legislation and procedures for exports to non-E.U. destinations has also been affected by the completion of the Single Market. With the creation of a single customs territory, the European Commission,[61] with the support of Member States, has combined the various pieces of European Customs law into a single Code. This is the Community Customs Code[62] and its implementing Regulations.[63] This legislation has direct application upon Customs in the Member States and requires no further re-enactment into national law. It therefore forms the basis of Customs law in the United Kingdom and contains the

---

[54] Council Directive 92/12.
[55] The Customs and Excise Management Act 1979 (ss. 92 to 100); The Excise Goods (Holding, Movement, Warehousing and REDS) Regulations 1992 (S.I. 1992 No. 3135); The Excise Warehousing (etc.) Regulations 1988 (S.I. 1988 No. 809); Revenue Traders (Accounts and Records) Regulations 1992; as well as various Finance Acts.
[56] Contrary to the Customs and Excise Management Act 1979, s. 170.
[57] See *R. v. Dosanijh, The Independent*, May 5, 1998, where the Court of Appeal provided new guidance on sentencing of up to seven years (under Finance Act 1998, s. 12) for such offences.
[58] [1978] A.C. 141.
[59] See also the decision of the European Court in Cases 186 and 187/82 *Ministero delle Finanze v. Esercizio Maggazini Generali SpA* [1984] 3 C.M.L.R. 217.
[60] Fiscal character in terms of dutiable and taxable character and restrictive in terms of their prohibitive or restrictive nature.
[61] The European Commission is the body responsible for administering Community law and the functioning of the common market. Its constitutional establishment is held in Arts 211–219 of the Treaty of Rome (as amended).
[62] Council Regulation 2913/92.
[63] Commission Regulation 2454/93.

provisions governing the exportation and importation of goods with countries outside the E.U.[64]

Where European law does not apply, national legislation takes effect. The main statute in this regard is the Customs and Excise Management Act 1979, although this is surrounded and supported by numerous other Parliamentary Acts and Regulations.[65] Customs publish guidance on the provisions in these Acts in Customs notices,[66] which are available from local Customs offices.

The definition of an "exporter" held in the Customs and Excise Management Act 1979 has not been repealed, despite a definition now appearing in the Community Customs Code, which defines an exporter as ". . . the person on whose behalf the export declaration is made and who is the owner of the goods or has similar right of disposal over them at the time the declaration is accepted."[67]

Customs requirements

26–013　The basic requirement of Customs legislation, in respect of the exportation of goods, is that all such goods shall be entered under the export procedure.[68] In order for this to be carried out the goods must be declared to Customs.[69] The document required for this purpose is the Single Administrative Document (SAD).[70] This is a multi-function form; as well as serving as the export declaration, it also serves as the transit declaration.[71] Copies of the form are available free from local Customs offices.

Declarations can be made to Customs either directly or on behalf of third parties, acting as an agent or representative of the exporter,[72] which is common practice, bearing in mind the relative complexities of completing Customs formalities, particularly for the novice or irregular exporter. Customs declarations must be accurate; by signing a declaration the declarant is attesting to its accuracy, the authenticity of accompanying documents and compliance with any obligations in relation to the entry of the goods for export.[73]

---

[64] Note that the Community Customs Code does not govern the supply of goods between the Member States, provided they are in free circulation, that is to say, free from incumbent duties and not under Customs control. See the Code, Art. 1.

[65] See The Customs and Excise (General Reliefs) Act 1979; The Alcoholic Liquor Duties Act 1979; The Hydrocarbon Oils Duties Act 1979 and The Tobacco Products Duty Act 1979, known as "the Customs and Excise Acts 1979" (Customs and Excise Management Act 1979, s. 1(1)).

[66] Customs Notice 275 concerns the procedures for the exportation of goods. See also VAT Notice 703 on Exports and Removals of Goods from the U.K.

[67] Implementing regulations, Art. 788(1). Note the Customs and Excise Management Act 1979, s. 1(1) defines the exporter as, "in relation to goods for exportation or for use as stores, including the shipper of the goods and any person performing in relation to an aircraft functions corresponding with those of a shipper".

[68] Regulation 2913/92, Art. 161(2), with the exception of goods placed under the outward processing or transit procedure.

[69] *ibid.* Art. 161(4). See also Customs and Excise Management Act 1979, s. 53.

[70] Customs Form C88. This requirement for the SAD to be used is held in the implementing regulations to the Code, Art. 205 and Annex 37. Information is provided on the completion of the SAD in the Customs and Excise Tariff, Vol. III, P. I.

[71] For goods being imported into the E.U., it is also the import declaration.

[72] Such representatives may be *direct* (in the name of and on behalf of, another) or *indirect* (acting in one's own name but on behalf of another); Regulation 2913/92, Art. 5.

[73] Regulation 2454/93, Art. 199.

Customs also operate the computer system CHIEF[74] which processes export declarations electronically, removing the need in some instances to present a SAD.

The basic export declaration procedures can be grouped into two categories; normal and simplified procedures.

Normal declaration procedure

Sometimes referred to as "pre-entry", this requires the exporter to present the **26–014** SAD, Copies 1, 2 and 3 to Customs in the country where the exporter is established, accompanied by the appropriate supporting documents.[75] Copies 1 and 2 are retained by Customs, the latter forms the statistical declaration, and Copy 3 is returned to the declarant. If the goods are transiting other Member States before leaving the E.U., then this copy will need to be presented at the Customs office of exit[76] from the E.U., to verify the goods being exported and to certify their physical departure.[77] Once the consignment has been exported Copy 3 of the SAD must be retained in the exporter's records. As a relaxation of the above control procedure, consignments not subject to prohibition or restriction with a value of below Euro3,000 (£2,100) only have to be declared at the office of exit, negating the need to present them to Customs in the United Kingdom.[78]

For consignments declared using the Customs CHIEF system, the SAD may be replaced by a plain-paper declaration.[79] However, where a consignment will transit another Member State, as described above, then the exporter or declarant must ensure that the Member State of exit has agreed the use of the plain paper form.

Simplified declaration procedures

Simplified procedures permit relaxations to be applied, enabling exports to bene- **26–015** fit from swifter clearance or the provision of reduced information at the time of shipment. Such procedures are not generally available for dutiable or restricted goods. The Customs and Excise Management Act 1979[80] defines such goods as:

> "(a) goods from warehouse, other than goods which have been kept, without being warehoused, in a warehouse by virtue of section 92(4) below;
>
> (b) transit goods;
>
> (c) any other goods chargeable with any duty which has not been paid;
>
> (d) drawback goods;

---

[74] Customs Handling of Import and Export Freight.
[75] As required by Regulation 2913/92, Art. 62(2). The supporting documents include: the commercial invoice and any export licences or preferential duty documents.
[76] Regulation 2454/93, Art. 793.
[77] *ibid.*
[78] *ibid.*, Art. 794.
[79] Provided this conforms to the plain paper example in the Code. See Customs and Excise Tariff, Vol. III, P. 2, 2.1.1.
[80] Customs and Excise Management Act 1979, s. 52(1).

(e) goods with respect to the exportation of which any restriction is for the time being in force under or by virtue of any enactment;

(f) any goods required by or under any provision of this Act other than a provision of this Part or by or under a provision of any other Act to be entered before exportation or before shipment for exportation or as stores;

(g) goods incorporating or resulting from the use of inward processing goods or any goods which, following a determination by the Commissioners, are to be treated for customs purposes as inward processing goods in substitution for such goods."

The reference to dutiable goods also covers goods liable to levies under the Common Agricultural Policy (CAP). Further, the 1979 Act excludes explosives within the meaning of the Explosives Act 1875.[81]

The Community Customs Code provides for three simplified procedures:[82] incomplete declaration procedure,[83] simplified declaration procedure[84] and local clearance.[85] In the United Kingdom these procedures are available as part of a range of options for exporters.

Currently, the most popular is the *simplified clearance procedure* (SCP), although this is due to be phased out by Customs in 2001/2002. Approximately 65 per cent of U.K. exports are declared to Customs using SCP.[86] Originally introduced in the 1980's, SCP enables authorised exporters or their representatives to export goods by supplying only a minimum amount of information to Customs at the time of exportation, supplemented later by a full statistical declaration.[87] The procedure is intended to apply only where the declarant does not have all the information required for a full declaration at the time of exportation.[88] Application to use SCP must be made to Customs using form C274 (SCP), which is available from local Customs offices. Once authorised, the exporter or his representative will be issued a Customs registered number (CRN), which ensures access to the procedure.[89]

The initial export declaration under SCP can be made using the SAD Copy 2 (and Copy 3 if the consignment is exiting via another Member State) or a copy of a commercial document. For the majority of SCP entries lodged at ports, the Standard Shipping Note (SSN) is used as the initial declaration.[90] This is a four-part document designed by SITPRO[91] and fulfils a number of functions. It is used by the exporter as a delivery note, by the port authority as a cargo receiving document and by the haulier as a receipt of delivery to the port, as well as functioning as the Customs declaration. Exporters can use other commercial documents, provided

---

[81] Customs and Excise Management Act 1979, ss. 75 and 76.
[82] Regulation 2913/92, Art. 76.
[83] *ibid.* Art. 76(1)(a) and Regulation 2454/93, Arts 280 to 281.
[84] *ibid.* Art. 76(1)(b) and Regulation 2454/93, Art. 282.
[85] *ibid.* Art. 76(1)(c) and Regulation 2454/93, Arts 283 to 287.
[86] Source: HM Customs and Excise.
[87] See Customs Notice 275, para. 15.
[88] SCP therefore falls under the incomplete declaration procedure.
[89] The requirement for declarants to be pre-authorised to use SCP suggests that the procedure may be based on the *simplified declaration procedure* in Reg. 2454/93, Art. 282 and not under the *incomplete declaration procedure* in Arts 280–281, otherwise the legality of the authorisation procedure is questionable.
[90] Dangerous Goods Note (DGN) for hazardous consignments.
[91] The Simpler Trade Procedures Board, see Chap. 32.

they have been approved by Customs. Whatever document is used, it must show the declarant's CRN, plus a unique reference. These two numbers form the Export Consignment Identifier (ECI). For movements by air the ECI will be the CRN plus the Air Waybill number (with the airline prefix deleted).

In support of the initial declaration the declarant must submit a supplementary statistical declaration to the Customs Statistical Office within 14 days from the date of export. The supplementary declaration can also be submitted electronically through CHIEF.

For *low value consignments* there is a separate simplified procedure which, similar to SCP, permits the exporter to declare export consignments to Customs using a commercial document, a partially completed SAD Copy 2 or via CHIEF.[92] To qualify, the consignment cannot contain dutiable or restricted goods and must be below a value of £600 and weight less than 1,000kg. Irrespective of whether a commercial document or SAD Copy 2 is used as the pre-shipment declaration to Customs, if the consignment is to travel through other Member States, then the SAD Copy 3 must also accompany it and be marked "simplified exportation". No supplementary declaration is required under this procedure. If the goods require an export licence then the normal procedure, mentioned above, applies. In this case the exporter must present the licence with the full pre-shipment declaration.

Certain simplified procedures are available to assist regular exporters. These are generally based on the local clearance provisions in the Customs Code.[93] *Local Export Control* (LEC) is one such procedure. Exporters or their agents authorised to operate under LEC declare and Customs clear their goods at their inland premises, without the normal formalities having to be carried out at the port of export, consignments passing through the port accompanied by either SAD Copy 3 or an approved commercial document.[94] The supplementary declaration, providing full details of the export, must be submitted to Customs within 14 days of shipment. This can be lodged either using the SAD Copy 2, by submitting a paper schedule, electronically through the CHIEF system or using the Period Entry (Export) arrangements.

Period Entry (Exports) is a computer based simplified procedure, which enables exporters to declare goods at the time of exportation using a commercial document or SAD Copy 2. The subsequent supplementary declaration must be lodged with Customs electronically[95] during one of two accounting periods; either the beginning to the 15th of the month or the 16th to the end of the month.[96]

In addition to the range of simplified procedures currently available to exporters, Customs are also developing further facilities under the *Customs Freight Simplified Procedures* (CFSP) strategy.[97] The CFSP export system

---

[92] See Customs Notice 275, para. 16.
[93] Reg. 2913/92, Art. 76(1)(c) and Reg. 2454/93, Arts 283–287.
[94] See Customs Notice 482.
[95] Either on disc, tape or via a direct Customs link. For options concerning transmission of data see Customs Notice 278A.
[96] See Customs Notice 278.
[97] See Customs Notice 759.

currently being developed will enable exporters to declare their goods electronically, with the minimum of Customs intervention. Similar to Period Entry
(Exports), Customs controls are focused on traders' records and accounts and it
is envisaged that CFSP will eventually replace the current Period Entry
(Exports) system and SCP in 2001.

Information required to be declared to Customs

26–016 Whilst simplified procedures generally defer the requirement to supply information to Customs, the overall information requirement remains essentially
unchanged from that required under the normal declaration procedure. There are
in fact one or two key items of data which Customs rely upon and which are worthy
of individual note. The commodity code[98] is one example. This code identifies the
goods and allows Customs to apply the appropriate controls on exportation and
correct rates of duties and taxes at importation. The Tariff incorporates both the
Harmonised System[99] and the European statistical nomenclature[1] and common
Customs tariff. Updates to the codes and rates of duty are published in the Official
Journal of the European Communities. A list of commodity codes is contained in
the HM Customs and Excise Tariff, Volume II.[1a] The Tariff is updated on a
monthly basis in line with the Official Journal.[2] The commodity code for export
consignments[3] is an eight digit numerical code. Where the SAD is used for the
declaration, the code is declared in box 33.

Classifying goods can be a complex task. Not only does it require knowledge
of the goods, but also of the Tariff and structure of the nomenclature. For more
complex classifications it may be necessary to refer to the General Rules for the
interpretation of the Combined Nomenclature.[4] Reference may also be necessary
to the World Customs Organisation's Explanatory Notes in the International
Convention on the Harmonised Commodity Description and Coding System,[5]
although these only assist with interpretation and are not legally binding.[6] HM
Customs & Excise also provide a classification helpline, which can assist with
classification queries.[7]

---

[98] Sometimes referred to as the tariff number.
[99] Developed by the World Customs Organisation and applied under the Harmonised System Convention. Currently, there are 89 signatory countries to the Convention and a further 78 countries
apply the provisions without being signatories.
[1] The Harmonised System (HS) and European Statistical Nomenclature from the Combined
Nomenclature (CN). This is updated annually and is published in Reg. 2658/87 Annex I (as
amended).
[1a] Available for viewing as a looseleaf binder or in CD-ROM format at most reference libraries and
Customs offices, or purchasable from HMSO.
[2] Note that in the case of any discrepancies the *Official Journal* is law, whereas the tariff is merely
guidance and cannot be relied upon.
[3] With the exception of goods under the Common Agricultural Policy, which requires a further four
digits.
[4] See Reg. 2658/87, Annex I (as amended).
[5] Which are recognised by the courts: see European Court in Case 185/73 *Hauptzollamt Bielefeld
v. Offene Handelsgesellschaft in Firma HM König* [1974] E.C.R. 607.
[6] See Case C35/93 *Develop Dr Eisbein GmbH and Co v. Hauptzollamt Stuttgart-West* [1994] E.C.R.
I-2655.
[7] Telephone 01702 366077.

In addition to the commodity code, Customs require an accurate value of the goods for statistical purposes. The statistical value is the price charged to the buyer,[8] plus an adjustment to include all the costs up to the point of loading on the ship or aircraft.[9] The description which the *Tariff*[10] provides is:

> "The value to be declared is the cost, to the nearest pound sterling, of the goods to the purchaser abroad (or, if there is no sale, the price which the goods would fetch if sold to a purchaser abroad). It should include packing, inland and coastal transport in the U.K., dock dues, loading charges and all other costs, profits, charges and expenses (*e.g.* insurance and commission) accruing up to the point where the goods are deposited on board the exporting vessel or aircraft or at the Irish Land Boundary.
>
> For goods re-exported after process or repair in the U.K., the value to be declared must include the charge for the process and the value of the goods when imported."

The statistical value is declared in box 46 of the SAD.

Postal exports

Goods other than drawback goods[11] may be exported by parcel post without being pre-entered or post-entered for Customs. A Customs declaration has to be completed, which can be obtained from the Post Office or Parcel Force. The postal despatch documentation has to be affixed to the package, accompanied by the appropriate supporting documents.[12] Parcel Force provides a range of dispatch documents, depending on the standard of service required, for this purpose. Further information on postal documents and the services available can be obtained from Parcel Force offices.[13] On documentary requirements generally, the Simpler Trade Procedures Board is a useful source of information.[14] **26–017**

Customs trader records and accounts

Increasingly, Customs controls are moving away from the traditional frontier based approach, to controlling goods at traders' premises, using commercial records and accounts to verify the information in the export declaration.[15] The Community Customs Code requires that any person directly or indirectly involved in the trade of goods with Customs must retain and provide the relevant documentation.[16] Under the Customs and Excise Management Act 1979 traders **26–018**

---

[8] Or, if the consignment does not form part of a commercial sale, the price that *would* be charged to a buyer.

[9] This is essentially the f.o.b. value, although it is no longer referred to as such, as the value includes an "uplift": *Rolex Watch Co Ltd v. Commissioners of Customs and Excise* [1956] 1 W.L.R. 612.

[10] Vol. 3, P. 2.

[11] For a definition of drawback goods, see *post*, para. 26–023.

[12] Copies of the invoices, certificates of origin, etc., where required. These should be placed in a sleeve behind the postal document. It is inadvisable that supporting documents are placed inside the parcel, as Customs will be unable to view them without opening the packaging.

[13] Telephone 0800 224466.

[14] See Chap. 32.

[15] See Customs Notices 761 and 989 for an indication of what traders might expect during a Customs audit visit.

[16] Regulation 2913/92, Art. 14. Art. 16 requires that the period of retention is at least three calendar years.

must preserve records (including documentation) for a period not exceeding six years as specified by the regulations.[17] The Customs Traders (Accounts and Records) Regulations 1995[18] limit this period to four years.[19] The Regulations specify the form which records may take and this includes photocopies, computer disc, soundtrack or tape, as well as microfilm or other visual image.[20] A list of the documents and records which must be preserved is listed in Schedule 1 to the Regulations.

Generally, Customs audit based control is intended to facilitate trade, as it should result in a reduction in controls undertaken during the movement of the goods and consequently reductions in delays in transit times. Such a control approach is adopted for traders authorised to use the simplified procedures, such as CFSP and Period Entry.

Transit procedures

26–019 Customs transit procedures facilitate the movement of goods between countries by reducing the border formalities and removing the requirement to pay duties and taxes at each and every international frontier. There are currently three international transit systems in effect: the Common and Community transit systems and TIR.[21]

Common and Community transit

26–020 The Common and Community transit systems allow non-E.U. goods and certain E.U. goods not in free circulation[22] to transit Member States, EFTA[26] and Visegrad[27] countries unhindered. The legal provisions for the system are contained in the Community Customs Code[23] and its implementing regulations,[24] supported by national legislation.[25] The system is also extended to EFTA and Visegrad countries under the Convention on Common Transit.[28]

In relation to exports from the United Kingdom, the transit procedure only applies where goods either travel through EFTA or Visegrad countries to non-E.U. destinations, travel overland to EFTA or Visegrad countries, or are subject to special Community measures, such as the Common Agricultural

---

[17] Customs and Excise Management Act 1979, Art. 118A.
[18] S.I. 1995 No. 1203.
[19] *ibid.* Reg. 9.
[20] *ibid.* Sched. 2.
[21] The ATA Carnet system for the temporary importation of goods can also be used to transit countries en route, but is not a transit system.
[22] See *ante*, para. 26–008, n. 30.
[26] The European Free Trade Association (EFTA) countries include: Iceland, Liechtenstein, Norway, Switzerland.
[27] Visegrad comprises the Czech Republic, Hungary, Poland, Slovakia.
[23] Regulation 2913/92, Arts 91 to 97.
[24] Regulation 2454/93, Pt. II, Customs Approved Treatment or Use, Title II, Transit.
[25] The Customs and Excise Management Act 1979 and the Customs and Excise (Transit) Regulations 1993 (S.I. 1993 No. 1353) as amended by The Community Customs Code (Consequential Amendment of References) Regulations 1993 (S.I. 1993 No. 3014).
[28] [1987] O.J. L226.

Policy. Certain goods are exempt, including consignments covered by the TIR or ATA Conventions,[29] postal consignments and movements by rail, or under the Inter-container simplified procedure. A full list of examples where the transit procedure should or should not be used is provided in Customs Notice 750.

A definition of *Community Transit Goods* exists in the Customs and Excise Management Act 1979.[30] The term means:

"(a) in relation to imported goods, . . .—

(i) goods which have been imported under the internal or external Community transit procedure for transit through the United Kingdom with a view to exportation where the importation was and the transit and exportation are to be part of one Community transit operation; or

(ii) goods which have, at the port or airport at which they were imported, been placed under the internal or external Community transit procedure for transit through the United Kingdom with a view to exportation where the transit and exportation are to be part of one Community transit operation;

(b) in relation to goods for exportation, means—

(i) goods which have been imported as mentioned in paragraph (a)(i) of this definition and are to be exported as part of the Community transit operation in the course of which they were imported; or

(ii) goods which have, under the internal or external Community transit procedure, transited the United Kingdom from the port or airport at which they were imported and are to be exported as part of the Community transit operation which commenced at that port or airport.

[and for the purposes of paragraph (a)(i) above the Isle of Man shall be treated as if it were part of the United Kingdom]."

The objective of the transit system is to ensure that goods are not diverted onto a country's domestic market without proper accounting for taxes and duties. This is achieved by appointing a principal,[31] who is responsible for ensuring that transit formalities are carried out correctly and that the goods are presented to Customs in the country of destination. The principal must take out a guarantee to cover any potential loss of revenue in the event of the goods not arriving[32] and the SAD (Copies 1, 3, 4, 5 and 7) must accompany the consignment. The SAD copies are used as follows:

(a) Copy 1—Customs office of departure;

(b) Copy 3—CT principal, consignor or exporter;

(c) Copy 4—Customs office of destination, or T2L status;

---

[29] See *post*, para. 26–021.
[30] Customs and Excise Management Act 1979, s. 1(1).
[31] The principal can be the exporter, or a third party such as a warehouse keeper, freight forwarder or carrier.
[32] See Regulation 2454/93, Arts 359–374 and Customs Notice 750. There are three types of guarantee: *individual*—which covers only single movements; *comprehensive*—which covers unlimited numbers of movements (note that certain "high risk" goods may be excluded from this system); and *flat-rate*—a system relying on set-value vouchers. For certain goods the requirement for a guarantee may be waived (see Notice 750, Appendix E). Even if the principle acted in "good faith" and Customs were aware of fraudulent diversion of the goods (without any involvement of the principal) the principal is liable for the duty. *De Haan Beheer B.V. v. Inspecteor der Invoerrechten en Accijnzen et Rotterdam* [1999] All E.R. (E.C.) 803; Case C-61/98.

(d) Copy 5—Transit return copy to verify arrival;

(e) Copy 7—Statistical copy for the Member State of destination.

In addition, Copy 2 is required for export purposes as the statistical copy for the Member State of despatch. To enter goods to the system the completed SAD (copies as above),[33] together with evidence of the guarantee, must be presented to the Customs office of departure. Copy 1 is retained at that office, and the goods remain under the procedure until the guarantee is discharged by the Customs office of destination, which is also responsible for returning SAD Copy 5 to the office of departure to confirm that the consignment arrived. Consideration is being given to computerising the system by the year 2004[34] to help cope with the 18 million transit movements within Europe each year.[35] Moreover, it has been assessed by UCLAF[36] that between 1990 and 1994, Euro975 million[37] was lost in E.U. revenue, due to fraud in the transit systems. Despite this, the SAD-based procedure is likely to remain, or to operate in parallel with any electronic system, for the foreseeable future.

As well as functioning as a transit document, the SAD also provides an indication of the status of the goods. This is declared in box 1 and can be either T1, T2, T2L, T2F or T2LF.

A T1 declaration must be given for goods which originate, or which include goods originating in a non-E.U. country, and which:

(a) on arrival into the UK or another Member State were not subject to full import formalities, *i.e.* entry into free circulation by payment of customs duty, CAP and equivalent charges; or

(b) on importation into the U.K. or another Member State were not subject to full import formalities including payment of Customs duty, CAP or equivalent charges but the duties and/or charges have been, or are to be repaid in whole or part; or

(c) come under the Treaty establishing the European Coal and Steel Community and are therefore not in free circulation in the Community; or

(d) are Community goods listed in Regulation 2454/93, Article 310 *e.g.* CAP goods when export refund is being claimed.[38]

The T2 declaration applies where free circulation goods travel to another E.U. Member State via an EFTA or Visegrad country, travel overland to an EFTA or Visegrad destination or travel to or from certain special status territories. The declarations T2F and T2LF also relate to these territories.[39]

---

[33] For guidance on completion of the transit SAD see Customs Notice 751.
[34] Under the European Commission's "New Computerised Transit System" (NCTS).
[35] Source: European Commission.
[36] The European Commission Anti-Fraud Unit.
[37] Approximately £630 million.
[38] Customs Notice 750.
[39] See *ibid.*, p. 20.

Finally, it should be remembered that under the export procedure, consignments exported from the E.U. may either exit directly from the Member State from which they are dispatched, or they may travel through another Member State before finally exiting. For the latter, *such consignments do not move under the transit procedure.* Despite the fact that they must be declared to the Customs office of export, located in the Member State of dispatch and to the Customs office of exit, located at the final point of exit from the E.U., the procedure does not require the appointment of a principal or use of a guarantee.

The TIR and ATA Systems

The TIR[40] system is based on similar objectives to the Common and Community **26–021** transit systems, but applies between the contracting countries to the TIR Convention.[41] Unlike the Common and Community transit systems, TIR is based on the use of approved vehicles and containers. The general criteria for such vehicles is that they are secure, suitable for sealing by Customs and have permanent identification marks. Approval is carried out by one of two certifying organisations in the United Kingdom[42] and once approved, vehicles and containers must display a TIR plate.

For goods entered under the TIR system a TIR Carnet must be obtained from a guaranteeing authority.[43] This Carnet, essentially, has the same function as the SAD in Common and Community transit, and must be presented at the Customs offices of departure, transit and destination. Once the journey has been completed the carnet must be returned to the guaranteeing authority.

Since 1993, the European Union has been defined as a single territory for the purposes of the TIR Convention, therefore TIR carnets should not be used for movements between E.U. Member States. It may be used for movements involving Member States only if:

(a) it begins or ends in a non-Community country;

(b) it is routed to a Community Member State via a non-E.U. country; or

(c) the consignment is for split delivery to destinations in the Community and in other non-E.U. countries.

The ATA system enables the temporary exportation, transit and importation of goods in countries which are contracting parties to the agreement. The provisions of the ATA Convention (Admission Temporaire) are now contained in the Istanbul Convention on Temporary Admissions, agreed in Istanbul on June 26,

---

[40] Transports Internationaux Routiers.

[41] The Customs Convention on the International Transport of Goods Under the Cover of TIR Carnets (TIR Convention) 1975. The Convention was agreed under the auspices of the United Nations Economic Commission for Europe (UN/ECE). A full list of contracting countries is given in Customs Notice 464, Appendix B.

[42] The Vehicle Inspectorate is responsible for vehicle approval; for containers see Customs Notice 464, Appendix C.

[43] Currently the Road Haulage Association (RHA); telephone 01932 841515, and Freight Transport Association (FTA); telephone 01892 526171, are the only two issuing authorities in the U.K.

1990. The ATA system is applied to exports from the European Union through Regulation 2454/93, Article 797(1). The system is specifically intended for the temporary supply of samples and goods for show at exhibitions, although certain restrictions, specified in Article 797(1), are applied within the European Union.

The system operates on the basis of carnets and bank guarantees which secure the tax and duties, subject to the goods being re-imported: on application to a Chambers of Commerce, a carnet is issued. This must accompany the goods and is presented to Customs at the point of entry and exit to/from the territories visited. The carnet is finally endorsed by Customs on re-importation and, on presentation of the counterfoil to the Chamber of Commerce, the guarantee is discharged.

For countries not party to Istanbul or ATA Conventions, the "Duplicate List System" must be used. This requires the presentation to Customs at export of form C&E 1246 and an accompanying list of the goods temporarily exported. The list must also be presented at all points of entry and exit to/from the relevant Customs territories and any duties and taxes secured by deposit at each office of entry and reclaimed at each point of exit.

Details of the ATA and Duplicate List systems can be found in Customs Notices 104 and 236.

Duty suspense and relief schemes

26–022 There are a range of facilities provided for in Customs regulations, which enable duties and taxes to be relieved or suspended for certain goods. This applies where goods are being imported for repair or processing and re-exported, or merely to allow traders to store goods for periods of time in a suspended state until such time as they are to be used, consumed or sold. These schemes include *Outward Processing Relief* (OPR), *Outward Processing Textiles* (OPT), *Inward Processing Relief* (IPR), *Drawback* and a range of Customs warehousing facilities.

The provisions for such procedures are based on European legislation, although the authorisation for the procedures is currently still given at a national level.[44] There is also a range of documents which apply to the procedures, which have not been referred to in detail.[45] Examples of these documents can be found in the relevant legislation[46] and in the relevant notices provided by Customs.

Outward Processing, Inward Processing Relief and Drawback

26–023 Under the Outward Processing Relief (OPR) scheme, goods can be sent to non-E.U. countries for processing and returned with total or partial relief from

---

[44] By local Customs and Excise offices. Consideration is also being given to providing single European authorisations (SEA), which will allow multi-national companies to benefit from a single European wide authorisation.

[45] Examples include: the INF range of documents (see, for example, Information Sheet (INF) 1— Inward Processing).

[46] Regulation 2454/93, Annexes 82, 106, 110, 81, 98, 84, 70 *et al.*

taxes and duties in the processing country and on re-importation into the E.U.[47] The legal base for OPR is held in the Community Customs Code[48] and its implementing regulations.[49] Exporters wishing to use the scheme are required to be authorised by Customs and they must be able to demonstrate that the goods exported were part of a process to produce, or be incorporated into, another product. *Customs Notice 235* states that:

> "The OPR regime allows you to re-import Community goods which have been exported for process or repair, without paying duty on the exported goods, as long as you can show that the goods you exported were used to produce, or are incorporated into, the goods you are importing."

Textile products are excluded from OPR and must be entered under a separate scheme called Outward Processing Textiles (OPT). The benefits are the same as for OPR, but application for the OPT is lodged with the Department of Trade and Industry.[50]

The Inward Processing Relief (IPR) scheme is similar to OPR, but allows importers to receive goods from non-E.U. countries for incorporation into a process, again with total or partial relief from duty and taxes, provided they are re-exported and it can be demonstrated that the goods imported are part of the final exported product.[51] The legal base for IPR is also held in Community legislation.[52]

Both schemes have restrictions on goods which are eligible. Under OPR goods must be in free circulation[53] unless they are held under the IPR procedure and no refunds or remissions can be claimed at export.[54] The IPR scheme is even more restrictive in that one of the primary conditions for entering goods to the scheme is that authorisation must not harm Community suppliers, who produce the same goods, but are unable to match the non-E.U. products on the basis of price.[55] For certain sensitive commodities produced in the E.U. an economic test may be required. This is carried out by the Department of Trade and Industry (DTI) or the Ministry of Agriculture, Fisheries and Foods (MAFF) in the United Kingdom. Application for this type of authorisation must be submitted to the appropriate department, with supporting evidence that the equivalent goods are either not produced in the E.U. or that there is some other valid reason why the goods cannot be used.[56] For less sensitive products an economic test is

---

[47] See Customs Notice 235.
[48] Regulation 2913/92, Arts 145–160.
[49] Regulation 2454/93, Arts 748–787.
[50] DTI Import Licensing Branch, Queensway House, West Precinct, Billingham, Cleveland TS23 2NF. Telephone 01642 364343. See also Customs Notice 235.
[51] See Customs Notice 221.
[52] Regulation 2913/92, Arts 114–129 and Regulation 2454/93, Arts 549–649.
[53] See *ante*, para. 26–008, n. 30, Reg. 2913/92, Art. 146.
[54] See Customs Notice 235, para. 8.
[55] Regulation 2913/92, Art. 117(c).
[56] For example, the supplier cannot supply sufficient quantities, they cannot be produced within the required time scales or the price of the E.U. goods is so high that it negates any profitable interest in the venture.

not required and application for the scheme is made as part of the import declaration procedure, using the SAD.[57]

In addition to IPR, a Drawback scheme is also available. Drawback applies to goods which have previously been imported with all the relevant taxes and duties paid and are subsequently exported, either in the same state, or following a process, whether or not it has changed their form or character.[58] The relevant law on Drawback is contained in European and national legislation.[59]

Return of unused imports

26–024 Subject to certain conditions, an importer is entitled to be granted relief from the payment of any import duty. The Community Customs Code[60] states that:

"Community goods which, having been exported from the customs territory of the Community, are returned to that territory and released for free circulation within a period of three years shall, at the request of the person concerned, be granted relief from import duties.

However:

— the three year period may be exceeded in order to take account of special circumstances;
— where, prior to their exportation from the customs territory of the Community, the returned goods had been released for free circulation at reduced or zero import duty because of their use for a particular purpose, exemption from duty under paragraph 1 shall be granted only if they are to be re-imported for the same purpose.

Where the purposes for which the goods in question are to be imported is no longer the same, the amount of import duties chargeable upon them shall be reduced by any amount levied on the goods when they were first released for free circulation. Should the latter amount exceed that levied on the entry for free circulation of returned goods, no refund shall be granted."

Provisions concerning returned goods also exist in the implementing regulations to the Code,[61] Customs and Excise Management Act 1979[62] and specific provisions exist for VAT,[63] excise[64] and CAP goods.[65] Also note that import duties cannot be reclaimed for goods imported on approval, on sale or return, or on similar terms. For detailed information on returned goods see Customs Notice 236.

---

[57] By completing the applicable Customs Procedure Code (SAD, Box 37) and entering the notation that the goods are an IPR importation (SAD, Box 44). Reg. 2454/93, Art. 568(2).
[58] See Customs Notice 221 (Section IV) and for excise goods Notices 207 and 172 (Hydrocarbon Oil).
[59] Regulation 2913/92, Arts 114(1)(b) and Arts 124–128. Regulation 2454/93, Arts 551(2) *et seq.* and the Customs and Excise Management Act 1979, s.119 *et seq.* For Excise goods: Council Directive 92/12, as well as Customs and Excise Management Act 1979, s.133; the Finance Act 1992, s.2; and The Excise Drawback Regulations 1995 (S.I. 1995 No. 1046).
[60] Regulation 2913/93, Art. 185(1).
[61] Regulation 2454/93, Arts 844–856.
[62] s.123.
[63] The VAT (General) Regulations 1985, regs 45–46 (as amended).
[64] Customs and Excise duties (General Reliefs) Act 1979, ss.10–11.
[65] Regulation 3719/88.

Warehouse goods

As a facilitation measure for importers, import goods can be permitted entry **26–025** into the European Union without payment of taxes and duties and kept in an approved warehouse until such time as they are needed, when the goods must be entered to another Customs procedure. Where that procedure requires, the payment of taxes and duties then become liable.[66]

There are six types of Customs warehouse facilities[67] and a further additional excise warehouse facility.[68] In the United Kingdom, HM Customs operate four of the six types:

(a) *Type A*; a public warehouse,[69] under the responsibility of the warehouse keeper. Such public warehouses are available for use by any person and it is the responsibility of the warehouse keeper to ensure goods can be accounted for;

(b) *Type C*; a private warehouse,[70] where the warehouse keeper is the same as the depositor, but is not necessarily the owner of the goods. This type of warehouse is appropriate for individual traders and applies where the warehouse keeper is bound by the declaration to the warehouse procedure. The warehouse keeper is responsible for some or all the Customs documentation;[71]

(c) *Type D*; a private warehouse,[72] where the warehouse keeper is the same as the depositor, but is not necessarily the owner of the goods. This type of warehouse is similar to *Type C*, with the important difference that the tax and duty point (for valuation and duty and tax assessment purposes) is taken at the time when the goods are entered to the warehouse procedure,[73] as opposed to the time when the goods are removed from the warehouse, as is the case with *Type C* warehouses. This procedure is appropriate for individual traders and the warehouse keeper is bound by the declaration to the warehouse procedure. The latter is also responsible for some or all the Customs documentation;

(d) *Type E*; a private warehouse, where the warehouse keeper is the same person as the depositor of the goods, but is not necessarily the owner and it is the trader's system of stock control which is used to account for the goods.

---

[66] For example, where goods are entered from warehouse to free circulation, duties and taxes become payable. However, if re-exported, or entered to IPR (or another such Customs procedure), then the duties and taxes do not become liable.
[67] The six types are specified in the implementing regulations to the Code, Regulation 2454/93, Art. 504.
[68] See *ante*, para. 26–011 under "excise warehousing".
[69] Regulation 2913/92, Art. 99.
[70] *ibid.*
[71] See Customs Notice 232.
[72] Regulation 2913/92, Art. 99.
[73] Regulation 2913/92, Art. 112(3) (as amended by Regulation 82/97).

With the exception of *Type E*, the other warehouse types require a physical warehouse - a building where the goods are to be stored. For *Type E* approved traders, goods can be stored at any site or may be moved between any site, which has previously been notified to Customs.

For excise warehouses, a guarantee is necessary to secure the taxes and duties whilst the goods are in storage,[74] whereas for Customs warehouses, a financial guarantee is rarely required. Many dutiable commodities are stored in warehouses where they can be inspected by potential customers of the importer; taxes and duties become payable on release from the warehouse. As a general rule, no manufacturing process is allowed on goods whilst in a warehouse. However, some minor processes can be performed to:

(a) ensure warehoused goods are preserved; or

(b) improve their presentation or marketable quality; or

(c) prepare them for distribution or resale.[75]

Removals from a warehouse for export must be declared either under the normal or simplified procedures, using the SAD. In relation to shipments from bonded excise warehouses, the exporter must enter the name of the warehouse amongst other details on the SAD. The duly completed SAD must then be presented to the warehouse keeper, who is responsible for ensuring that the removal is recorded in the stock records. A copy of the SAD, stamped by Customs, is returned to the warehouse keeper as evidence of the goods having been exported.[76]

E.C. preference arrangements

26–026   Some countries, which are not members of the E.U., grant imports from an E.U. Member State preferential tariff treatment.[77] These countries are:

(a) the countries of the European Free Trade Association (EFTA), that is, Iceland, Norway and Liechtenstein (covered by the EEA[78]—European Economic Area) and Switzerland[79];

(b) Bulgaria, Romania, Hungary, Poland, Czech Republic, Slovakia and Slovenia[80];

---

[74] Such a guarantee is often referred to as a "bond", hence "bonded warehouses" and "bonded goods".

[75] Customs Notice 232.

[76] Note that for supplies to other E.U. Member States the SAD is replaced by the AAD, see *ante*, para. 26–011.

[77] Lower or zero rates of duty.

[78] European Economic Agreement, Arts 8–27.

[79] The EEC/Switzerland Agreement 1972 [1973] O.J. L338/73 (as amended).

[80] Through bilateral European Agreements. See Bulgaria [1994] O.J. L358/83 and [1994] O.J. L123/147 (as amended); Romania [1994] O.J. L357/2 and [1994] O.J. L123/476 (as amended); Hungary [1993] O.J. L347/2 and [1992] O.J. L410/391 (as amended); Poland [1993] O.J. L348/2 and [1992] O.J. L410/461 (as amended); Czech Republic [1994] O.J. L360/2 and [1994] O.J. L123/198 (as

(c) Baltic States—Estonia, Lithuania, and Latvia[81];

(d) Faroe Islands[82];

(e) Cyprus, Israel and Malta[83];

(f) Ceuta and Mililla[84];

(g) "Mashraq Group"—Egypt, Jordan, Lebanon, and Syria[85]; "Maghreb Group"— Algeria, Morocco and Tunisia[86];

(h) Some of the African, Caribbean and Pacific States (ACP) and Overseas Countries and Territories (OCT), details of which may be obtained from the Department of Trade and Industry;

(i) West Bank and Gaza.[87]

The exporter has to comply with certain requirements to enable his customer in the preference-giving non-E.U. country to claim preferential treatment.[88] The basic condition is that the exported goods must comply with the origin rules governing the particular preference. Those origin rules vary in the preference-giving countries and the exporter must satisfy himself that the goods he is exporting comply with the rules for the particular country of destination. The rules of origin are set out in Customs Notice 828. The exporter has to supply his customer with a prescribed certificate, which will normally be certificate EUR1 (C1299), endorsed by the Customs authority of the exporting country. For low-value exportations a declaration on the commercial invoice will suffice, or in some instances the EUR2 (C1297) form, neither of which need be endorsed by Customs. In the case of private exportations of little value, no form is required at all. It should, however, be emphasised that the use of the forms is not obligatory. Their use is necessary only if the exported goods qualify as originating and preferential admission into the importing country is to be claimed. A movement certificate must normally be produced for the Customs authorities of the importing country within a specified period after endorsement in the exporting country. For EFTA, Bulgaria, Czech Republic, Faroe Islands, Hungary, Israel, Poland, Romania, Slovakia, Slovenia, Baltic States and the West Bank/Gaza strip, the period is four months; for ACP/OCT countries, ten months; and for other countries; five months.

---

amended); Slovakia [1994] O.J. L359/2, [1997] O.J. L123/556 and [1997] O.J. L127/312 (as amended); Slovenia [1997] O.J. L62/5 (interim agreement only).
[81] Estonia [1994] O.J. L373/2; Lithuania [1998] O.J. L79/1; Latvia [1998] O.J. L79/9.
[82] [1997] O.J. L53/2 and [1997] O.J. L53/1.
[83] EEC Cyprus Agreement 1972 [1993] O.J. L133/2; EEC Israel Agreement [1975] O.J. L136/1; EEC Malta Agreement [1971] O.J. L61/2.
[84] [1987] O.J. L133/5 (as part of accession of Spain and Portugal).
[85] The Mashraq Group Agreements—Egypt [1978] O.J. L266/2 and [1987] O.J. L297/11; Jordon [1978] O.J. L268/2 and [1987] O.J. L297/19; Lebanon [1978] O.J. L267/2 and [1987] O.J. L297/29; Syria [1978] O.J. L269/2 and [1988] O.J. L327/58.
[86] The Maghreb Group Agreements—Algeria [1978] O.J. L263/2 and [1987] O.J. L297/2; Morocco [1978] O.J. L264/2 and [1978] O.J. L224/18; Tunisia [1978] O.J. L265/2 and [1987] O.J. L297/36.
[87] Interim Agreement on Trade and Co-operation [1997] O.J. L187/1.
[88] These requirements are stated in Customs Notice 827.

The exporter may be called upon to provide supporting evidence, showing that the particulars of the preference certificate are correct. Untrue information given to Customs and Excise is a Customs offence. If no verifying evidence is forthcoming when required, the Customs authorities of the importing country will normally require the importer to pay full non-preferential duties. This may be backdated to previous consignments of the same goods and they may also impose a penalty.

The range of goods admissible for preference in the preference-giving countries, the preferential rates of duty, the application of quota requirements and the consignment rules, vary considerably. Information about the availability of a preference and the preferential rate should, if required by the exporter, be sought from the customer in the country concerned or from the relevant country desk at the DTI, British Trade International Division.[89]

As a general rule, there can be no entitlement to both export relief in the E.U. and preferential tariff treatment in EFTA, Bulgaria, Czech Republic, Hungary, Poland, Romania, Slovakia, Slovenia, Baltic States, Israel, West Bank/Gaza Strip and the Faroe Islands. For exports to other countries, both can apply, provided the final product is deemed as originating in the E.U. Such relief includes suspension or reimbursement of import duties on goods which are exported in the form of compensating products[90] from an inward processing relief arrangement, but it does not include relief from CAP levies and variable charges, payments of export refunds, or relief from, or repayment of, excise duties.

CUSTOMS APPEALS

26–027 In January 1995 an appeal system was introduced into Customs and Excise law. The requirement for an appeal system was driven by two considerations: first, it was in response to changes in European legislation[91]; and secondly, in recognition of the cost for the appellant of pursuing a claim through the courts against decisions by the Commissioners of Customs and Excise, on what are often detailed technical matters.

The scope of the *VAT and Duties Tribunal* is extremely wide and covers any decision made in writing by the Commissioners since January 1, 1995. The Finance Act 1994, which contains the relevant provisions for the appeals procedure,[92] prescribes its scope[93] which is also explained in Customs Notice 990:

"...

- **Ancillary matters**—these generally involve the exercise of discretion by the Department [Customs]. They include authorisations and approvals and the conditions which attach to them, security, and restoration of seized goods ...

- **Other matters**—these are primarily about amounts of duty and penalties including excise duty assessments and penalties, the charge, rate or amount of customs duty, and Binding Tariff Information decisions."

---

[89] Address: 1–19 Victoria Street, London, SW1H 0ET, Tel: 020 7215 5000.
[90] The final product after processing has taken place.
[91] Regulation 2913/92, Art. 243.
[92] ss. 14–16.
[93] See *ibid.* and Sched. 5 to the 1994 Act.

It should be noted that the procedure only applies to VAT in respect of import VAT[94]; it does not cover complaints about the conduct of HM Customs officers,[95] nor does it apply to hypothetical matters.[96] Decisions associated with criminal matters,[97] compounding and seizure of goods (as being liable to forfeiture)[98] are also excluded, although the terms of restoration of goods are included.[99]

Since its instigation, the Tribunal has heard numerous cases on various matters, from post-clearance demands for duty and VAT[1] and errors made by Customs,[2] to cases concerning the classification of goods[3] and binding tarrif information.[4]

The appeal procedure itself comprises two stages: an *internal review* by a Customs officer senior to the officer who made the original decision and who has not been previously involved in that decision; and, if the appellant is not satisfied with the review decision, *an appeal to the independent VAT and Duties Tribunal*. Appellants have 45 days in which to request a review by Customs and a further 30 days from the date Customs advise their review decision, in which to lodge an appeal with the Tribunal,[5] although with the new Civil Procedure Rules these time limits will be viewed with underlying principles of fairness and justice.[6]

CUSTOMS OFFENCES

The concept of Customs offences

The Commissioners of Customs and Excise administer, in addition to the regula-   **26–028**
tion of Customs, the executive provisions of the law relating to export and ort

---

[94] For other aspects related to VAT there is a separate independent VAT tribunal system.
[95] See Customs Notice 1000.
[96] Such as advice on the classification of goods not yet imported. See Customs Notice 990.
[97] Regulation 2913/92, Art. 246.
[98] Except in so far as refusal to restore and the terms for restoration for the said goods. The question of the exclusion of forfeiture from the Appeals procedure is still under debate. It has been excluded by Customs on the grounds that it constitutes a decision in relation to criminal proceedings and therefore its inclusion would be contrary to Regulation 2913/92, Art. 246. However, it can be argued that forfeiture (and therefore seizure) is not a criminal procedure and consequently cannot legally be excluded from the Appeals system. In support of the latter argument, the European Court of Human Rights held in the case of *Air Canada v. United Kingdom*, Judgment May 5, 1995, Series A, No. 316 (App. No. 18465/91), that forfeiture does not constitute a criminal matter in respect of Article 6 of the European Convention on Human Rights. (See *post*, para. 26–030).
[99] See Finance Act 1994, Sched. 5, para. 2(1)(r). It is normal practice to seek restoration as quickly as possible to recover the goods and then, if necessary, appeal the restoration fee.
[1] *Commissioners of Customs and Excise v. Sidney Barlow Ltd* [1997] C64; *Commissioners of Customs and Excise v. Man About Town (Men's Wear) Ltd* [1997] C65; both cases involved the issue of invalid EUR1 Certificates for goods imported from Lesotho.
[2] *Commissioners of Customs and Excise v. Invicta Poultry Ltd and Fareway Trading* [1996] V and D.R. 291 (overturned on appeal [1997] Q.B.D. V and D.R. 56).
[3] *Commissioners of Customs and Excise v. Eastern Pharmaceuticals* [1995] C3 (the first classification appeal); *Commissioners of Customs and Excise v. Potter and Moore* [1997] C61.
[4] *Niko Surgical Ltd v. Commissioners of Customs and Excise* [2000] C118.
[5] Addresses for the Tribunal Centres can be found in Customs Notice 990.
[6] *Commissioners of Customs and Excise v. Eastwood Care Homes (Ilkeston) Ltd and Others, The Times*, March 7, 2000.

licensing, the regulation of the free movement of goods in the E.U., and VAT taxation. The measures dealing with these topics contain in many instances criminal as well as civil provisions, requiring that offences against them should have similar consequences to Customs offences. The concept of the Customs offence is thus much wider than merely constituting an infringement of the Customs and Excise Management Acts and regulations made thereunder.[7] Because of the wide and varied nature of Customs offences, it is not intended to cover each and every Customs offence in this Chapter, but merely to provide a summary of the main offences and an indication of Customs powers in this regard.

Customs offences and E.C. law

26–029 Generally, under the principle of subsidiarity, European Community law does not extend to the provision of offences and penalties; it does, however, place certain obligations on Member States. For example, in terms of Customs law and the TIR and ATA Conventions, the Community Customs Code implementing regulations[8] provides that "The customs administration of the Member States shall take the necessary measures to deal with any offence or irregularity and to impose effective penalties". Whilst E.C. law only places obligations on Member States in relation to offences, it can have a direct effect, even in areas where the Member States are deemed to have competence. In *R. v. HM Treasury, ex parte Centro-Com SrL*,[9] during a period when United Nation sanctions were in place against the former Yugoslavia, the applicant company exported medical goods from Italy to Montenegro under approval from the United Nations and the Italian Government. Several payments were made for the consignments from the Bank of Yugoslavia to the company's bank. However, U.K. Government policy dictated that only payments for exports from the United Kingdom would be permissible and the Bank of England stopped the transfer of funds. The applicant company claimed the action was contrary to common commercial policy and the E.C. Treaty.[10] Finding in favour of Centro-Com SrL, the European Court of Justice held that although competence for foreign and security policy lay with Member States, such policy must be consistent with Community law.[11] Whether damages might be claimed for such a breach is questionable after *Factortame*[12] and the test adopted in *Francovitch*,[13] which requires the breach to be "sufficiently serious" and damage to be caused.[14]

The completion of the Single Market also introduced new legislation in the

---

[7] Thus, the theft of export quotas may amount to a Customs offence: *Att.-Gen. of Hong Kong v. Daniel Nai-Keung* [1987] 1 W.L.R. 1339, PC.

[8] Commission Regulation 2454/93, Art. 454(3).

[9] Case C-124/95 [1997] Q.B. 683; [1997] All E.R. (E.C.) 193.

[10] Art. 113 (now Article 133, following the renumbering of the E.C. Treaty as a result of the Treaty of Amsterdam).

[11] In so holding, the E.C.J. found that the policy breached both the E.C. Treaty, Art. 113 and was an illegal quantitative restriction, contrary to the Common Rules for Export set out in Council Regulation 2603/69, Art. 1.

[12] *R. v. Secretary of State for Transport, ex p. Factortame (No. 5)* [1997] 22 L.S. Gaz. R. 31, QBD.

[13] Joined cases C-6/90 and C-9/90 *Francovitch v. Republic of Italy* [1991] ECR. I-5357.

[14] After *Mulder v. E.C. Council and E.C. Commission*, the answer is probably in the negative. See *Mulder v. E.C. Council and E.C. Commission* [1992] E.C.R. I-3061, ECJ, at para. 56.

United Kingdom, intended to promote co-operation between the Member States. Such mutual co-operation has been recognised in Customs law for some time,[15] but it was only in 1993 that provisions were introduced under, the Criminal Justice Act 1993, which specifically cover acts carried out in the United Kingdom that would lead to the committing of an offence in another Member State. Section 71 of the 1993 Act provides that:

"A person who in the United Kingdom assists in or induces any conduct outside the United Kingdom which involves the commission of a serious offence against the law of another Member State is guilty of an offence if:

(a) the offence involved is one consisting of or including the contravention of provisions of law of that Member State which relate to any matters specified in subsection(2);

(b) the offence involved is one consisting in or including the contravention of other provisions of that law so far as they have effect in relation to any of those matters; or

(c) the conduct is such as to be calculated to have an effect in relation to any of those matters."

Fines, forfeiture of goods and restoration

The Customs Acts provide heavy fines and terms of imprisonment for persons **26–030** contravening the Customs regulations.[16] In addition, the goods in respect of which the offence is committed may be treated as "prohibited goods" and declared as forfeited.[17] In particular, section 68 of the Customs and Excise Management Act 1979 provides that a person who exports, or brings to any place in the United Kingdom for the purpose of export, goods, the exportation of which is prohibited or restricted, shall be liable to a penalty of three times the value of the goods[18] or level three on the standard scale[19] which ever is greater, and the goods shall be liable to forfeiture. If the offence is committed knowingly, the penalty may be imprisonment.[20] The Customs authorities may also seize and subject to forfeiture any ship, aircraft or vessel that has been used to carry ds liable to forfeiture, provided that the owner is aware of the carriage the prohibited goods or that he could have discovered the goods had he used

---

[15] See Directive 76/308 on recovery of duties; Commission Regulation 1468/81 (replaced by Regulation 515/97) on mutual assistance between Community customs administrations in the agricultural sector; and the Customs and Excise Management Act 1979, s.9.

[16] As an example, the Customs and Excise Management Act 1979, s.170(3) provides for unlimited fines and terms of imprisonment of up to seven years and s.170(4) imprisonment up to 10 years.

[17] On service abroad under Sched. 3 to the Customs and Excise Management Act 1979, see *Commissioners of Customs and Excise v. IFS Irish Fully Fashioned Stockings Ltd* [1957] 1 W.L.R. 397. Forfeiture proceedings are procedures *in rem*—that is to say the penalty is not inflicted upon any specific person, as opposed to *in personam*; in which the penalty is imposed upon a specific person. The only question is whether the goods are liable to forfeiture; it is irrelevant who has imported them or whether they were unsolicited goods; *Lord Advocate v. Crookshanks* (1888) 15 R. 995; *Denton v. Jones* [1971] 1 W.L.R. 1426.

[18] On the calculation of the value of the goods, see *Byrne v. Low* [1972] 1 W.L.R. 1282.

[19] The standard scale for summary offences in England and Wales is prescribed in the Criminal Justice Act 1982, s.37. Level 3 equates to £1,000 within these jurisdictions.

[20] *Garrett v. Arthur Churchill (Glass) Ltd* [1969] 2 All E.R. 1141; [1970] 1 Q.B. 92. The stated case concerned the Customs and Excise Act 1952, s. 56(2), now replaced by the Customs and Excise Management Act 1979, s. 68(2).

due diligence.[21] As regards forfeiture a number of points should be noted.

The forfeiture of smuggled goods is only possible if the Customs authorities have lawfully seized them. There is an established procedure which must be undertaken before goods can be condemned as forfeit.[22] This is initiated by a "notice of seizure" by Customs.[23] Following this, if disputed, a "notice of claim" may be submitted by "any person claiming that any thing seized as liable to forfeiture is not so liable", and this must be lodged at any "office of Customs and Excise" within one month of the date of seizure.[24] At this stage, the legality of the seizure is in issue. Title to the goods remains with the claimant until such time as the court confirms the legality of the seizure and the goods are condemned as forfeit. During this period, the Commissioners may, if the seized goods are a living creature or are perishable, sell or destroy them.[25] However, if it is later found by the court that the goods were not liable to forfeiture then title always remains with the claimant and the seizure constitutes an illegal act. The Commissioners must return the goods or, where they have been destroyed or sold, the sum of their market value or proceeds of the sale and additionally, the Commissioners will be liable for damages. With respect to damages, however, the court may, if it sees fit, certify that there were reasonable grounds for the seizure, negating the Commissioner's liability.[26]

In *Att.-Gen. of New Zealand v. Ortiz*[27] a valuable Maori carving consisting of five wooden panels was exported from New Zealand without permission of the New Zealand Government and eventually purchased by Mr Ortiz, who acquired it in good faith. The exportation contravened the New Zealand Historic Articles Act 1962 which declared that articles exported without permission 'shall be forfeited' to the Crown. The Attorney-General of New Zealand claimed in the English courts that the carving was forfeited automatically to the Crown and became Crown property. The House of Lords dismissed the claim. Lord Bingham[28] said that "there being no seizure in the instant case, the conclusion is inescapable that the ownership of the carving and the right of possession have not become vested in the Crown". In United Kingdom Customs law this is even clearer, because the Customs Act uses the expression "shall be liable to forfeiture", and not, as the New Zealand Act states, "shall be forfeited".[29] In order to be liable to condemnation, forefeited goods must also be within the jurisdiction at the time of seizure. However, any subsequent determination that the goods were liable to condemnation is valid, even if the goods have subsequently been removed from the jurisdiction.[30]

---

[21] Customs and Excise Act 1979, s. 141(1)(a) as interpreted in *Customs and Excise Commissioners v. Air Canada* [1991] 2 W.L.R. 344, CA.

[22] See the Customs and Excise Management Act 1979, s.139 and Sched. 3.

[23] *ibid.*, Sched. 3, paras 1 and 2.

[24] *ibid.*, para. 3. The details to be shown in the claim are specified in para. 4.

[25] *ibid.*, para. 16(b).

[26] Customs and Excise Management Act 1979, s. 144(1).

[27] *Att.-Gen. of New Zealand v. Ortiz* [1984] A.C. 1.

[28] *ibid.* at 87.

[29] Although *Ortiz* concerned an issue about a New Zealand enactment, the ruling of the House of Lords applies equally to U.K. Customs law.

[30] *Hashwani v. Letherby* (1998) 162 J.P. 153, QBD.

The legality of the seizure quite often concerns a question of interpretation of the Customs Act. In *Travell v. Customs and Excise Commissioners*[31] the interpretation concerned section 141 of the Customs and Excise Management Act 1979. Section 141(1) is presented in two parts and provides that where an item has become liable to forfeiture, then (a) any means of transport or of carrying the goods also becomes so liable[32] and (b) any other thing mixed, packed or found with the item is also liable to forfeiture. It was held that due to the limited scope of the Customs and Excise Management Act, s. 141(1)(a) and (b) should be read disjunctively. Consequently, irrespective of whether items were so liable under section 141(1)(a), other items falling within the scope of section 141(1)(b) would also be liable to forfeiture and any such action would be lawful.

The powers of the Customs authorities in relation to the forfeiture of goods are capable of review under the provisions relating to the free movement of goods under the E.C. Treaty.[33] However, where such forfeiture concerns a matter of public morality, policy or security then it will be lawful.[34] Further, a claim based on legality of seizure under Community law *vis-à-vis* national legislation can rarely be relied upon. In *Customs and Excise Commissioners v. ApS Samex*[35] goods were seized by Customs after it became apparent that their importation contravened the conditions of the import licence, namely the date of importation was after the licence had expired. Counsel for the plaintiffs raised a number of points, two of which are relevant: the first claim was that HM Customs had acted *ultra vires* in seizing the consignment, as the only sanction available to them was refusal of entry to the United Kingdom; the second claim was that the seizure breached the Community law of proportionality. It was held that, on the first point, the sanctions adopted by Member States in legitimate pursuance of ensuring proper implementation of Community law were largely a matter for the Member States and on the second point, that proportionality was unlikely to succeed in such cases.

Recourse may also be made to the European Court of Human Rights under Article 1 of the First Protocol to the European Convention of Human Rights, which protects the peaceful enjoyment of one's possessions. However, the State authorities are permitted to control the free circulation of goods and, if necessary, to forfeit those goods where this can be justified on the grounds of public interest or to secure payment of taxes and duties. In the case of *Air Canada v.*

---

[31] [1998] C.O.D. 92; *The Independent*, November 4, 1997.
[32] s. 141(1)(a) lists ship, aircraft, vehicle, container (including article of passengers' baggage) or other thing whatsoever which has been used for the carriage, handling, deposit or concealment of the thing so liable for forfeiture.
[33] E.C. Treaty, Arts 23, 25, 28 and 29.
[34] E.C. Treaty, Art. 30. See also Case 121/85 *Conegate Ltd v. Commissioners of Customs and Excise* [1986] E.C.R. 1007, *Wright v. Commissioners of Customs and Excise* [1999] 1 Cr. App. R. 69, *R. v. Bow Street Metropolitan Stipendiary Magistrates, ex p. Noncyp Ltd* [1988] 3 W.L.R. 927, DC, and Case 34/79 *R. v. Henn* [1981] A.C. 850 on the application of the E.C. Treaty to seizures by Customs of books alleged to contravene the Obscene Publications Act 1959, but in free circulation in other Member States. However, where the Community provisions were to be harmonised, Art. 30 cannot be relied upon as a defence: Case C5/94 *R. v. Ministry of Agriculture, Fisheries and Food ex p. Hedley Lomas (Ireland) Ltd* [1996] E.C.R. I-2553.
[35] [1983] 1 All E.R. 1042.

United Kingdom[36] a quantity of cannabis resin was discovered on a passenger aircraft. The airline was warned of the consequences of not improving its security measures. However, further finds of cannabis were made on later flights, culminating with an £800,000 consignment of cannabis being discovered on an Air Canada aircraft at Heathrow in April 1987. Customs seized the aircraft under section 141(1) of the Customs Act and restored it on payment of £50,000.[37] The case was ultimately taken to the Court of Human Rights. On application for a ruling under Article 1 of Protocol No. 1, it was found that there was no breach of the said article and that the requirement to "pay £50,000 for the return of the aircraft which had been seized on 1 May 1987 was proportionate to the aim of controlling the use of aircraft involved in the importation of prohibited drugs". On a second application, under Article 6, which provides that under criminal proceedings everyone is entitled to a fair and public hearing, it was found that forfeiture does not constitute a criminal charge within the meaning of Article 6(1).[38]

In respect of restoration of goods, Customs are also under certain obligations; an explanation must be given of the sum demanded for restoration and an indication of the guidelines used to calculate that sum. In addition, Customs must in certain circumstances give due consideration to any decrease in the value of the said goods.[39]

Other aspects

26–031 Section 68(2) extends criminal liability to any person knowingly "concerned in the exportation" of goods which require an export licence. Activities which amount to being "concerned with exportation" are not limited to the act of actually taking the goods out of the country, but a person can be "concerned in the exportation" by doing things in advance of the time when the ship or aircraft leaves, *e.g.* by handing over the goods to the buyer's agent the night before the ship or aircraft leaves, knowing that the agent will take the goods out of the country without licence.[40] However, the Privy Council held in an appeal from Hong Kong that the offence of "causing" goods to be taken outside of Hong Kong in violation of local Customs requirements could not be committed by a person who handed over the goods inside Hong Kong territory to another who would take the goods outside the territory, even if the former knew that the goods would be smuggled out.[41] The case of *Att.-Gen.'s Reference No. 1*[42] has also reopened the issue. This case concerned the offence of being knowingly concerned in the fraudulent evasion of the prohibition of a controlled drug, contrary to the Customs and Excise Management Act, s. 170(2)(b), but the scope

---

[36] Judgment of May 5, 1955. Series A, No. 316 (App. No. 18465/91).
[37] Under Customs and Excise Management Act 1979, Sched. 3, para. 16.
[38] See Case A/281-A *Raimondo v. Italy* (1994) 18 E.H.R.R. 237, which confirmed that confiscation orders do not determine criminal charges.
[39] *R. v. Customs and Excise Commissioners, ex p. Tsahl* [1990] C.O.D. 230. See also *Allgemeine Gold- und Silberscheideanstalt v. Customs and Excise Commissioners* [1980] C.L.Y. 622.
[40] *Garrett v. Arthur Churchill (Glass) Ltd* [1969] 2 All E.R. 1141.
[41] *Att.-Gen. of Hong Kong v. Tse Hung-lit* [1986] 3 W.L.R. 320, PC.
[42] *The Times*, October 2, 1998.

of the ruling extends to import and export, duties and taxes. The court stated that section 170(2) should be given "the widest interpretation possible" and being "knowingly concerned in the fraudulent evasion" could be brought about without the defendant doing anything other than merely agreeing to some potential active participation, should the circumstances so require.[43] It further stated that knowledge by the defendant that there might be a fraudulent evasion is sufficient.

In respect of goods requiring an export licence, the granting of a licence does not prevent a person from being liable under the relevant Export of Goods (Control) Order, where he has knowingly attempted to export prohibited goods. This was held in the case of *R. v. Redfern and Dunlop Ltd (Aircraft Tyre Division)*,[44] which involved the exportation of military aircraft tyres destined for Iran, contrary to the Customs and Excise Act 1979, s.68(2) and the Export of Goods (Control) Order 1987 (S.I. 1987 No. 2070).[45]

Customs are responsible for controls in respect of the prohibition of counterfeit and pirated goods. Council Regulation 3295/94[46] provides that such goods are liable to forfeiture. The relevant sections in the Customs and Excise Management Act 1979 are 139, 144–146, 152-155, Schedule 3 and various statutory instruments.[47] For patented goods, where such goods are imported into the United Kingdom without being licensed by the owner of the patent, Customs must disclose the names of the importers to the owner of the patent, because the illicit importation constitutes a tort against the owner of the patent. Every person who, though innocently, becomes involved in the tortious acts of others, comes under a duty to assist the injured person by giving him full information by way of discovery, although he personally may not be liable in damages to the third person.[48]

It is also worthy of note that some Customs offences are absolute offences and require no *mens rea* for the offence to be complete. An example is the

---

[43] On what constitutes "fraudulent evasion" in relation to s.170(2) see *R. v. Latif and R. v. Shahzad, The Times*, March 17, 1994, CA, in which it was held to constitute "any conduct intended to lead to the prohibited importation [or exportation] of goods." However, it should be noted that "to evade" is to get around and does not confer dishonesty unless it is fraudulent: *R. v. Hurford-Jones* (1977) 65 Cr. App. R. 23.

[44] *R. v. Redfern and Dunlop Ltd (Aircraft Tyre Division)* (1992) 13 Cr. App. Rep. (S) 709.

[45] The case also established that the company would only be liable for the employee's actions if real managerial power was conferred upon him. Mere delegation of administrative function is not sufficient.

[46] As amended by Council Regulation is supplemented by implementing provisions in Commission Regulation 1367/95.

[47] The Counterfeit and Pirated Goods (Customs) Regulations 1995 (S.I. 1999 No. 1601) and the Counterfeit and Pirated Goods (Consequential Provisions) Regulations 1995 (S.I. 1999 No. 1618).

[48] See *Norwich Pharmacal Co v. Customs and Excise Commissioners* [1974] A.C. 133. Where a party obtained an Anton Piller injunction (see *Anton Piller Kg v. Manufacturing Processes Ltd* [1976] 1 All E.R. 779, CA and the Civil Procedure Act 1997, s.7), and his solicitors have retained documents, which they have taken away in safe custody, they must refuse the Customs and Excise Commissioners inspection of the documents, if the Commissioners investigate an alleged non-payment of VAT, until the court grants the Commissioners leave to inspect the documents: *Customs and Excise Commissioners v. A.E. Hamlin & Co* [1984] 1 W.L.R. 509. (Note that following the new Civil Procedure Rules, which came into force (in part) in April 1999, such injunctions are now referred to as "Search Orders", CPR, Pt. 25.1(h)).

Customs and Excise Management Act 1979, s. 167. This section contains two offences concerning untrue declarations:

> "(1) If any person either knowingly or recklessly—
>
> > (a) makes or signs, or causes to be made or signed, or delivers or causes to be delivered to the Commissioners or an officer, any declaration, notice, certificate or other document whatsoever; or
> >
> > (b) makes any statement in answer to any question put to him by an officer which he is required by or under any enactment to answer, being a document or statement produced or made for any purpose of any assigned matter, which is untrue in any material particular, he shall be guilty of an offence under this subsection and may be arrested; and any goods in relation to which the document or statement was made shall be liable to forfeiture. . . .
>
> (3) If any person—
>
> > (a) makes or signs, or causes to be made or signed, or delivers or causes to be delivered to the Commissioners or an officer, any declaration, notice, certificate or other document whatsoever; or
> >
> > (b) makes any statement in answer to any question put to him by an officer which he is required by or under any enactment to answer, being a document or statement produced or made for any purpose of any assigned matter, which is untrue in any material particular, then without prejudice to subsection (4) below, he shall be liable on summary conviction to a penalty of level 4 on the standard scale."

Whilst subparagraph 1 requires a person to act knowingly or recklessly, no such requirement exists in subparagraph 3. The consequence of this is that the offence is committed, irrespective of whether the person was or was not aware of the untrue nature of the information within it.[49]

There are also instances where *the burden of proof* in relation to certain Customs offences may be transferred from the Customs Commissioners to the defendant. In *R. v. Cohen*[50] the appellant was found in possession of Swiss watches, for which he provided no evidence of the duty having been paid and was charged under the Customs Consolidation Act 1876, s. 186.[51] The court held that where a party is in possession of dutiable goods and provides no evidence of the duty having been paid, then he may be guilty of an offence. However, if an explanation is provided and the defendant did not know, or it is uncertain whether the defendant knew, that the duty had not been paid on the goods, then he would not be liable.[52] Recent examples occur in respect of the permissible amounts of excise goods which may be brought into the U.K. from other E.U. Member States for personal consumption. In the Excise Duties

---

[49] See *Pearkes, Gunston and Tee Ltd v. Ward* [1902] 2 K.B. 1 on the absolute offences (relevant to s. 167(3)). Examples of s. 167(1) offences include: *R. v. Hayward* (1997), unreported, which concerned the causing of an untrue declaration for excise goods; *R. v. Hescroft* (1990) 154 J.P. 1042, CA (Criminal Division) where goods were "knowingly" undervalued; and *R. v. Cross* [1987] Crim. L.R. 43, CA in which the appellant was convicted of "recklessly" completing a document false in a material particular.

[50] [1951] 1 All E.R. 203.

[51] The provisions of which are now held in the Customs and Excise Management Act 1979, s. 154.

[52] See *Mizel v. Warren* [1973] 2 All E.R. 1149, which involved condemnation proceedings in respect of a second-hand bracelet purchased in the U.K. The Queen's Bench Division held that the onus of proof was with the respondent. In *Beck v. Binks* [1949] 1 K.B. 250 it was held that the offence of dealing with uncustomed goods with intent to defraud the Crown can be committed anywhere in the realm, not merely at the place of entry.

(Personal Reliefs) Order 1992[53] an amount of dutiable goods is specified, above which the Commission of Customs and Excise can presume that the consignment has been imported for commercial purposes. This presumption is rebuttable where the person who brought the goods into the country can convince the Commissioners that the goods are for personal consumption.[54]

In instances where the burden of proof shifts from the prosecution to the defence, the standard of proof required is lowered.[55]

Finally, Customs and Excise powers are covered by the Police and Criminal Evidence Act (PACE) 1984 and this confers upon them certain rights and restrictions. For example, in *R. v. Sanusi*.[56] the question was whether Customs officers had to inform a person of his right to see a solicitor prior to being interviewed. In considering PACE 1984[57] and the Police and Criminal Evidence Act 1984 (Application to Customs and Excise) Order 1985,[58] the Court of Appeal held that, although the 1985 Order did not directly apply, section 66 of the 1984 Act to Customs, section 67(9) effectively imposed the condition that the provisions of the code of practice must be observed and allowed the appeal.

The relationship between Customs and Excise and the Police is also relevant; in *Montes v. HM Advocate*[59] it was confirmed that police officers can lawfully act under instruction from an officer of Customs and Excise.

Customs powers under the Police and Criminal Evidence Act have recently been brought into question in the report by Sir Richard Scott,[60] which followed the prosecution of the directors of the Matrix Churchill company (Messrs. Henderson, Abraham and Allen). The report questions whether the definition of "assigned matter" in the 1979 Act, section 1 is adequate and whether the enforcement of export and import controls is within the definition.[61] Assigned matter is described as "any matter in relation to which the Commissioners are for the time being required in pursuance of any enactment to perform any duties". If the definition is found to be wanting, then it may have major implications for the powers conferred on Customs under PACE.

---

[53] S.I. 1992 No. 3155.
[54] *Customs and Excise Commissioners v. Carrier*, *The Times*, December 7, 1994. The case established that the presumption as to whether the goods were brought into the country for commercial purposes was a matter for the Commissioners.
[55] *R. v. Dunbar* [1958] 1 Q.B. 1. The burden of proof is lowered to "*on the balance of probabilities*".
[56] [1992] Crim. L.R. 43, CA.
[57] ss. 66 and 67(9).
[58] S.I. 1985 No. 1800.
[59] (1990) S.C.C.R. 654.
[60] Report of the Inquiry into the Export of Defence Equipment and Dual-Use Goods to Iraq and Related Prosecutions H.C. 115 of 1995–96.
[61] See the Scott Report, re: K 4.2(i).

CHAPTER 27

AGENCY ARRANGEMENTS[1]

SELF-EMPLOYED AGENTS ABROAD

The characteristic feature of this form of marketing is that the exporter enters **27–001** into direct relations with the customer abroad by means of a contract procured or concluded on his behalf, by a representative who resides abroad and who is not his employee.[2] The remuneration of a self-employed agent is usually based upon a commission on the price of the goods sold by or through him, while the remuneration of an employee is normally a fixed salary, sometimes augmented by bonuses or commissions. The relations between the principal and the self-employed commercial agent are now regulated by The Council Directive on the Co-Ordination of the Laws of the Member States Relating to Self-Employed Commercial Agents.[3] This Directive was implemented by The Commercial Agents (Council Directive) Regulations 1993.[4] The Regulations came into force on January 1, 1994. They are retrospective in that they apply to contracts entered into before they came into effect except, in respect of rights and liabilities accrued before January 1, 1994. The Regulations will be dealt with under the heading "Rights and Obligations of Agent and Principal"[5] but will also be referred to elsewhere in this Chapter where relevant.

Great care should be taken by an exporter who wishes to market his goods in a foreign country through the offices of a self-employed agent. A contract of agency creates a confidential relationship, and the agent has, in certain circumstances, implied authority to dispose of the principal's goods, to allow a customer credit terms or to receive the purchase price from him. The exporter should make searching inquiries about the personal reputation and financial standing of the agent before reposing his trust in him. These inquiries are often made through the exporter's bank or through his forwarder. When they result in a satisfactory reply, two further points should be observed. First, a precautionary measure is usually included in the contract,[6] for instance a short probationary period precedes the long-term commitment, or a minimum turnover is stipulated for a certain period, or the termination of the contract is provided for on short

---

[1] See generally Bowstead and Reynolds, *Agency* (16th ed., 1995); *Halsbury's Laws*, Vol. 1(2).

[2] But the U.K. exporter does not enter into relations with the overseas customer if his representative abroad is a commissionaire. Most European continental laws admit the concept of the commissionaire. On this concept and that of the commission agent in English law, see *post*, para. 27–015.

[3] Directive 86/653 [1986] O.J. L382/17.

[4] S.I. 1993 No. 3053, as amended by Commercial Agents (Council Directive) (Amendment) Regulations (S.I. 1993 No. 3173).

[5] See *post*, para. 27–010 *et seq.*

[6] In drawing up a contract reference may be made to ICC Publication No. 496—ICC Model Commercial Agency Contract and ICC Publication No. 512—The ICC Agency Model Contract: a Commentary (including disk).

notice, although here the provisions of the E.C. Regulations[7] in respect of self-employed commercial agents and minimum periods of notice prescribed by some foreign laws will have to be followed. Secondly, personal contact should be established and maintained between the principal and agent. No agency agreement of consequence should be concluded before the principal has met the agent in person; and regular visits of the principal to the agent, or vice versa, should maintain the high standard of mutual confidence which is an essential element in every successful agency agreement.

Assistance is available in finding an overseas agent.[8]

THE CONTRACT OF AGENCY

The legal nature of the contract of agency

27–002 An agent in the legal sense is a person who has authority from another person, the principal, to represent him or act on his behalf and legally bind him in relation to third parties. In the export trade, the authority which the exporter gives the self-employed agent abroad normally takes one of two forms: the agent may be authorised to *introduce* third parties in his territory to the principal, leaving the decision as to whether he wants to contract to the latter,[9] or the agent has authority to *conclude* contracts with third parties on behalf of the principal. In law, the term "agent" has a different meaning from that sometimes attributed to it in commercial parlance. It is wider in that it covers employees who conclude contracts with third parties on behalf of their employers, and it is narrower in so far as it does not include representatives who buy and sell in their own name. In one case[10] Scrutton L.J. referred to the well-known fact that "in certain trades the word 'agent' is often used without any reference to the law of principal and agent" and added that many difficulties have arisen from the habit of describing a purchaser as an agent.

A sole distributor is not an agent in the legal sense, because he does not act on behalf of the supplier and is not accountable to him. He buys goods from the supplier and resells them to his customers for his own profit.[11]

It is more difficult to define the legal character of a person who describes himself as a procurement agent. His business is to obtain goods for another person who has instructed him. The term "procuring agent" is ambiguous. He may act as an agent in the legal sense for the instructing party, or he may sell the goods to him. Whether he acts in the one or the other capacity depends on the construction of the contract between him and the instructing party.[12]

---

[7] Regs 14 and 15 *post*, para. 27–012.
[8] See Chap. 31.
[9] For a case in which the agent only had authority to introduce customers to his principal but not, without his prior consent, to accept orders, and was held not to be an agent see *Vogel v. R. and A. Kohnstamm Ltd* [1973] Q.B. 133. See also *Alpha Trading Ltd v. Dunnshaw-Patten Ltd* [1980] 2 Lloyd's Rep. 284.
[10] *W. T. Lamb & Sons v. Goring Brick Co* [1932] 1 K.B. 710 at 717.
[11] See Chap. 29.
[12] Bowstead and Reynolds, *Agency* (16th ed.), p. 27. On confirming houses, see *post*, paras 27–018 to 27–023.

Every agency agreement creates three relationships:

(a) that existing between the principal and the agent;

(b) that existing between the principal and the third party; and

(c) that existing between the agent and the third party.

The first is the internal arrangement between the principal and the agent, the contract of agency proper; it settles the rights and duties of these two parties, the scope of authority granted to the agent and the remuneration due to him.[13] The second is a normal contract of sale, but added thereto are certain features which arise from the fact that the seller concluded the contract through an agent. The third relationship only occurs in exceptional circumstances.

THE AGENT'S AUTHORITY

An agent's authority to act may be actual, implied, ostensible (or apparent), **27–003** usual, customary or by operation of law. Actual authority arises by agreement between principal and agent. For the remainder, the agency relationship arises although there is no such agreement between principal and agent, or where there is such agreement but the agent has exceeded his actual authority. An implied authority may arise from the relationsip between principal and agent or from conduct. An agency relationship may also occur where there is no agreement between principal and agent but where the principal has consented to the agent acting on his behalf and the agent has consented so to act.[14]

Actual authority

Actual authority is the express authority given to the agent by agreement with **27–004** the principal. "An 'actual' authority is a legal relationship between principal and agent, created by a consensual agreement to which they alone are parties. Its scope is to be ascertained by applying ordinary principles of construction of contracts, including any proper inference from the express words used, the usages of the trade, or the course of business between the parties."[15] Such an agreement may be by deed, in writing or oral.[16]

Disclosure of principal

An agent who discloses his representative capacity to a customer to whom he **27–005** sells the goods, acts merely as the mouthpiece or conduit of the principal, pro-

---

[13] In drawing up the contractual rights of duties of commercial agent and principal and the agent's remuneration, regard must be had for the E.C. Directive on these issues.

[14] *Yasuda Fire and Marine Insurance Co of Europe Ltd v. Orion Marine Insurance Underwriting Agency Ltd* [1995] Q.B. 174.

[15] *Per* Diplock L.J. in *Freeman and Lockyer v. Buckhurst Park Properties (Mangal) Ltd* [1964] 2 Q.B. 480 at 502.

[16] Although now see Directive 86/653, Reg. 13(1) for commercial agents.

vided that he has acted within the scope of his actual or ostensible authority. The contract of sale is concluded between the principal and the customer, and the agent normally disappears completely from the picture.[17]

The agent is not obliged to disclose his representative capacity to the third party. From the perspective of the third party, *viz.* the customer abroad, the following possibilities exist:

(a) The agent does not disclose the existence of his principal and concludes the contract in his own name. Here, he acts for an undisclosed principal; or

(b) The agent discloses his principal's existence but not his name, *e.g.* by signing a contract "on behalf of our principals". In this case he acts for an unnamed principal; or

(c) The agent discloses both the existence and the name of his principal. Here he acts for a named principal.

The first of these three cases is of considerable importance, as it reveals the difference between the concept of agency in common law countries, including England, and that prevailing in civil law countries, including most European continental countries. In English law, if an agent duly authorised by the principal, concludes a contract with a third party in his own name, *i.e.* without revealing his representative capacity, two rights arise: the third party's right of election and the principal's right of intervention. An undisclosed principal can sue and be sued on a contract made on his behalf by an agent acting within his actual authority.[18]

The third party, when discovering the true facts, may elect to sue the principal or the agent. This election must be unequivocal.[19] If the third party commences proceedings against either of these persons, this is strong evidence that he has elected to hold him alone liable, although this evidence may be rebutted; for instance, if the third party was not in possession of all relevant facts he can then still bring an action against the other.[20] However, there is little authority concerning at what point in any proceedings an unequivocal election has been

---

[17] Except if the agent undertakes personal liability to the third party, see *e.g.* the liability of the confirming agent to the supplier in the U.K., *post*, para. 27–023. If the agent signs a deed in his own name he is personally liable, even if he signs as "agent": *Plant Engineers (Sales) Ltd v. Davies* (1969) 113 S.J. 484. In accordance with the principle stated in the text, if an allegation of negligent misrepresentation is made by the third party and a claim is raised under the Misrepresentation Act 1967, s. 2(1), the principal, and not the agent, would be liable: *Resolute Maritime Inc v. Nippon Kaiji Kyokai; The Skopas* [1983] 1 W.L.R. 857. On the liability of the principal if the agent has made a fraudulent misrepresentation causing loss to the third party, see *Armagas Ltd v. Mundogas SA* [1986] A.C. 717 at 737. A sole Customs agent who innocently submits documents falsely showing the E.C. origin of goods and is personally liable to his Customs authorities for the differential import duties, cannot claim a waiver of the differentials under E.C. law: E.C.J. in Cases 98/83 and 230/83 *Van Gend en Loos NV v. E.C. Commission* [1984] E.C.R. 3763.
[18] *Siu Yin Kwan v. Eastern Insurance Co* [1994] 1 All E.R. 213, PC.
[19] *Clarkson-Booker v. Andjel* [1964] 2 Q.B. 775 at 792.
[20] *Clarkson-Booker Ltd v. Andjel* [1964] 2 Q.B. 775.

made.[21] It seems that, in general, the courts are slow to find that the third party has made an unequivocal election[22] and this will depend on the facts in each individual case. If the third party proceeds to judgment against either party, that would terminate his right to elect and an action against the other would then be barred.[23] But principal and agent are jointly liable for a tort, so the third party may proceed to judgment against either and then issue proceedings against the other under the Civil Liability (Contribution) Act 1978.[24]

The undisclosed principal has the corresponding right to intervene and make a direct claim against the third party. This right of intervention is acknowledged to be an anomaly, as it does not sit comfortably with the doctrine of privity of contract. However, the courts have justified this anomaly on the grounds of commercial convenience.[25] There are exceptions to the principal's right of intervention, but these are few and are largely restricted to cases where intervention is excluded by the terms of the contract[26] or where the identity of the principal is of great importance to the third party, *i.e.* he unequivocally intended to contract with only the agent[27] or would not have contracted with the principal had he known his identity.[28] The same principle applies in respect of the principal being sued by the third party.[29]

The third party's right of election and the principal's right of intervention enable these parties, even in the case of undisclosed agency, to create, in effect, a direct contractual bond between them. Thus, section 14(5) of the Sale of Goods Act 1979 applies to a disclosed or undisclosed principal and an undisclosed principal may be held liable for breach of section 14(2) or (3).[30]

In the other two cases the third party can sue only the principal. He can sue the agent only if the law in force in the territory in question so provides or the agent has undertaken personal liability to the third party or is liable by custom of the trade. The agent who does not disclose the existence of his principal does not normally escape liability (if the third party elects to sue him) by merely adding to his firm style a descriptive term such as "export and import agencies".[31] If, however, he signs the contract with the customer "as agents", or addresses letters to him "on behalf of", or "on account of" or "for", no personal liability attaches to him, even if he does not disclose the name of the

---

[21] See Reynolds, "Election Distributed" (1970) 86 L.Q.R. 317.
[22] *Clarkson-Booker v. Adjel* [1964] 2 Q.B. 775; *Pyxis Special Shipping Co Ltd v. Dritsas and Kaglis Bros Ltd; The Scaplake* [1978] 2 Lloyd's Rep. 380.
[23] *Priestly v. Fernie* (1865) 3 H.&C. 977.
[24] And see *New Zealand Guardian Trust v. Brooks* [1995] 1 W.L.R. 96; *Morris v. Wentworth-Stanley* [1999] Q.B. 1004.
[25] *Per* Lord Lindley in *Keighley, Maxstead & Co v. Durant* [1901] A.C. 240 at 260; *per* Lord Lloyd of Berwick in *Siu Yin Kwan v. Eastern Insurance Co Ltd* [1994] 1 All E.R. 213 at 220.
[26] *Per* McNair J.: *Finzel, Berry and Co v. Eastcheap Dried Fruit Co* [1962] 1 Lloyd's Rep. 370 at 375.
[27] *Greer v. Downs Supply Co* [1927] 2 K.B. 28.
[28] *Said v. Butt* [1920] 3 K.B. 497.
[29] In *Siu Yin Kwan v. Eastern Insurance Co Ltd* [1994] 1 All E.R. 213, PC, the principal, an insurance company, sought, unsuccessfully, to escape liability by arguing, *inter alia*, that a contract of insurance was a personal contract akin to a contract to paint a portrait.
[30] *Boyter v. Thomson* [1995] 2 A.C. 628.
[31] *The Swan* [1968] 1 Lloyd's Rep. 5 at 13.

principal.[32] Where an agent signs expressly in his capacity as director of the brokers for a charterer named in the contract, he is not acting for an undisclosed principal.[33] Sometimes it is clear from the circumstances that the person who acted did so as agent although he did not so indicate, for instance if the customer knew that he was merely a broker. In that case only the principal, but not the agent, is liable.[34]

The principal is in all three cases entitled to sue the customer in his own name. It has already been observed that, according to English law, he has this right even where the agent concluded the contract without disclosing the existence of the principal, provided the agent was duly authorised to act on his behalf. For example, where an English export house or other person has acted as agent in the legal sense for a foreign undisclosed principal (the customer) and the goods do not conform with the contract, the latter has a direct claim against the supplier in this country.[35] Some foreign laws differ in this respect from English law and provide that, when the contract is concluded by the agent in his own name, only he and not the undisclosed principal can sue on it. In view of this divergency, the exporter who wishes to reserve the right to sue the customer abroad for the purchase price should expressly provide in his contract with the agent that the agent should disclose his representative capacity when dealing with customers, or should, at least, require an undertaking from the agent to assign to him any claims against customers.

Implied, usual and customary authority

27–006 The agent's implied authority may be inferred from the relationship between the parties or from conduct. The agent may perform acts which are subordinate and incidental to those expressly authorised and "when it is inferred from the conduct of the parties and the circumstances of the case, such as when the board of directors appoint one of their number to be managing director. They thereby impliedly authorise him to do all such things as fall within the usual scope of that office."[36]

It is well established that the agent's implied authority also permits him to act in conformity with custom or what is usual, as long as these acts are reasonable and do not conflict with the scope of his express authority. Naturally what

---

[32] *Gadd v. Houghton* [1876] 1 Ex. D. 357. An agent who sells goods in his own name which involve a breach of the law relating to weights and measures is criminally liable, even if he is not guilty of negligence. But he is not liable if he sells them as agent for a named principal: *Lester v. Balfour Williamson Merchant Shippers Ltd* [1953] 2 Q.B. 168. An agent acting for an unnamed or undisclosed principal cannot appoint himself as principal, except in the rare cases in which the identity of the principal is immaterial: *Gewa Chartering BV v. Remco Shipping Lines Ltd; The Remco* [1984] 2 Lloyd's Rep. 205.

[33] *Yukong Line Ltd of Korea v. Rendsburg Investments Corporation of Liberia (No. 2)* [1998] 1 W.L.R. 294 (the agent was the beneficial owner of the charterer and immediately prior to the charterer's repudiation of a charterparty he transferred the funds in the charterer's account to another company owned by him and then closed the account).

[34] *N. & J. Vlassopulos Ltd v. Ney Shipping Ltd; The Santa Carina* [1977] 1 Lloyd's Rep. 478.

[35] *Teheran-Europe Co Ltd v. S. T. Belton (Tractors) Ltd* [1968] 2 Q.B. 545, CA.

[36] *Per* Lord Denning M.R. in *Hely-Hutchinson v. Brayhead Ltd* [1968] 1 Q.B. 549 at 583.

is customary or usual in the trade will vary according to the particular circumstances of each trade or profession.

Ostensible (or apparent) authority

Implied authority is to be distinguished from ostensible or apparent authority,[37] **27–007** although it may sometimes be difficult to draw the distinction.

In an ostensible (or apparent) authority the agent either has no actual authority to act on the principal's behalf or has exceeded his actual authority. If a third party is successful in establishing the existence of ostensible authority, the principal is liable. "Ostensible or apparent authority is the authority of an agent as it *appears* to others".[38] It is clear from the authorities that ostensible authority "operates as an estoppel, preventing the principal from asserting that he is not bound by the contract"[39] although among academic writers this is somewhat controversial.[40] "Actual authority and apparent authority are quite independent of one another. Generally they coexist and coincide, but either may exist without the other and their respective scope may be different."[41] The elements necessary to establish ostensible authority were set out by Slade J[42]:

> "Ostensible or apparent authority which negatives the existence of actual authority is merely a form of estoppel, indeed, it has been termed agency by estoppel, and you cannot call in aid an estoppel unless you have three ingredients: (i) a representation, (ii) a reliance on the representation, and (iii) an alteration of your position resulting from such reliance."

The representation must be made by the principal or by a person duly authorised by the principal[43]; it cannot be made by the agent.[44] Ostensible authority may sometimes be inferred from the position into which the agent has been placed. It has been held that a company secretary had ostensible authority to enter into contracts of an administrative, but not of a managerial, nature on behalf of his company,[45] and that a documentary credit manager of a bank had ostensible authority to sign a bank guarantee alone, although internal bank regulations

---

[37] *Gurtner v. Beaton* [1993] 2 Lloyd's Rep. 369; *First Energy (U.K.) v. Hungarian International Bank* [1993] 2 Lloyd's Rep. 194. In neither of these two cases did the agent have implied actual authority but he did have ostensible authority.

[38] *Per* Lord Denning M.R. in *Hely-Hutchinson v. Brayhead Ltd* [1968] 1 Q.B. 549 at 583; *per* Browne-Wilkinson L.J. in *Egyptian International Foreign Trade Co v. Soplex Wholesale Supplies Ltd* [1985] 2 Lloyd's Rep. 36 at 41.

[39] *e.g. per* Diplock L.J. in *Freeman & Lockyer v. Buckhurst Park Properties (Mangal) Ltd* [1964] 2 Q.B. 480 at 503; *per* Browne-Wilkinson L.J. in *Egyptian International Foreign Trade Co v. Soplex Wholesale Supplies Ltd; The Raffaella* [1985] 2 Lloyd's Rep. 36 at 41.

[40] See Bowstead and Reynolds, *Agency* (16th ed.), para. 8-029.

[41] *Per* Diplock L.J. in *Freeman & Lockyer v. Buckhurst Park Properties (Mangal) Ltd* [1964] 2 Q.B. 480 at 502.

[42] *Rama Corporation Ltd v. Proved Tin and General Investments Ltd* [1952] 2 Q.B. 147 at 149–150; see also *per* Diplock L.J. in *Freeman & Lockyer v. Buckhurst Park Properties (Mangal) Ltd* [1964] 2 Q.B. 480 at 506.

[43] *Armagas Ltd v. Mundogas SA* [1986] 2 All E.R. 385.

[44] *First Energy (U.K.) v. Hungarian International Bank Ltd* [1993] 2 Lloyd's Rep. 194; *Suncorp Insurance and Finance v. Milano Assicurazioni SpA* [1993] 2 Lloyd's Rep. 225.

[45] *Panorama Developments (Guildford) Ltd v. Fidelis Furnishing Fabrics Ltd* [1971] 2 Q.B. 711.

required two signatures.[46] The onus of proving that the "agent" had ostensible authority is on the person alleging it.[47]

Ratification

27–008   Where an agent exceeds his authority or has no actual or implied authority to act on behalf of another, but purports to conclude an agreement with a third party on behalf of his principal, then that purported principal may ratify the purported agreement. Once the purported principal has ratified the unauthorised agreement the ". . . ratification relates back and is deemed equivalent to an antecedent authority"[48] and "Ratification, as we all know, has a retroactive effect".[49] The effect of ratification by the principal puts all three parties in the same position *vis-à-vis* each other as where the agent has an express authority, *i.e.* both principal and third party may enforce the agreement against each other; the agent is no longer liable for exceeding his authority, nor personally liable to the third party, and has earned his commission.

However, in order to ratify an agreement the principal must be in existence, ascertainable (although he need not be named) and capable himself of entering into the agreement both at the time the agent purported to act on his behalf[50] and at the time of ratification.[51] It follows that since the purported principal must be ascertainable an undisclosed principal cannot ratify.[52] Ratification must be within the time set out in the agreement or within a reasonable time.[53]

The requirement that the purported principal must be capable himself of entering into the agreement at the time it was made and in existence meant that until relatively recently a company could not ratify an agent's unauthorised *ultra vires* agreement, nor one made on its behalf before it was formed. Now legislation provides that where a company lacks capacity to act under its memorandum any such act is nevertheless valid.[54] An agreement purportedly made by an unformed company or by a person as its agent is enforceable as between the party who purports to act for the company and a third party.[55] Section 36C(1) provides:

> "A contract which purports to be made *by or on behalf of* a company at a time when the company has not been formed has effect, subject to any agreement to the contrary, as one

---

[46] *Egyptian International Foreign Trade Co v. Soplex Wholesale Supplies Ltd; The Raffaelia* [1985] 2 Lloyd's Rep. 36. See also *First Energy (U.K.) v. Hungarian International Bank Ltd* [1993] 2 Lloyd's Rep. 194 in which the Court of Appeal held that the senior manager of a major branch of the bank was clothed with the authority to communicate that head office approval had been obtained for certain hire-purchase purchase agreements and that the Plaintiff was not obliged to check his authority with the head office; *Gurtner v. Beaton* [1993] 2 Lloyd's Rep. 369.
[47] *United Bank of Kuwait Ltd v. Hammoud* [1988] 1 W.L.R. 1051 at 1065.
[48] *Per* Jenkins L.J. in *Danish Mercantile Co Ltd v. Beaumont* [1951] Ch. 680 at 686.
[49] *Per* Harman J. *Boston Deep Sea Fishing and Ice Co Ltd v. Farnham (Inspector of Taxes)* [1957] 2 Lloyd's Rep. 238 at 244.
[50] *Boston Deep Sea Fishing and Ice Co Ltd v. Farnham (Inspector of Taxes)* [1957] 2 Lloyd's Rep. 238.
[51] *Dibbins v. Dibbins* [1896] 2 Ch. 348; *Presentaciones Musicales SA v. Secunda* [1994] Ch. 271.
[52] *Keighley Maxstead & Co v. Durant* [1901] A.C. 240.
[53] *Metropolitan Asylums Board Managers v. Kingham & Sons* (1890) 6 T.L.R. 217.
[54] Companies Act 1985, s. 35A(1) added by Companies Act 1989, s. 108(1).
[55] Companies Act 1985, s. 36C(1) added by Companies Act 1989, s. 130(4).

made with the person purporting to act for the company or as agent for it, and he is personally liable on the contract accordingly."

It can be seen that this section does not provide that the company may ratify acts done on its behalf before it was formed, but acts of directors in breach of their powers under the memorandum can be ratified by special resolution.[56]

A void agreement may not be ratified but a voidable one can be.[57] Ratification may be express or implied from conduct[58] or acquiescence. The purported principal acquiesces if he has full knowledge of all the facts and knows that he is regarded as principal, but takes no steps to make known within a reasonable time that he does not ratify the agreement.[59]

Agency by operation of law

The agent of necessity

Agency of necessity is the most important category of cases where agency arises **27–009** by operation of law. This occurs where an agent exceeds his authority and legitimately binds his principal in an emergency, in order to preserve or protect the principal's property or interest. An agency of necessity may also occur in an emergency where one person acts on behalf of another where there is no agency relationship between them, but this is unusual.

Where an agent is in possession of his principal's goods and has a limited authority only, for instance, not to sell from his stock unless expressly authorised by the principal, or to return the consignment to the principal or, perhaps, to dispatch to him goods bought on his behalf, circumstances of such urgent necessity might occur as to justify the use of exceptional measures for the protection of the principal's property. Mercantile law has evolved the doctrine of agency of necessity under which an agent is allowed, but not obliged, to exceed his authority in an emergency and do what is required for safeguarding his principal's property, including the sale of it where there is danger of deterioration or loss. But the conditions upon which an agency of necessity can be exercised are difficult to establish, and the courts are not prepared to extend them unduly.[60] These conditions are, first, that the action in excess of authority is required by an actual, definite and urgent commercial necessity, and secondly that the agent cannot communicate with the principal and obtain his instructions before disposing of the goods.[61] The term "agency of necessity" should, for reasons of clarity, be confined to a situation in which these two conditions are satisfied. It should not be applied to a situation in which a bailee incurs expenses to save the bailor's goods from deterioration where less stringent conditions apply and, in particular, inability to communicate with the owner of the goods is not a condition preced-

---

[56] s. 35(3).
[57] *Brook v. Hook* (1871) L.R. Exch. 89.
[58] *Maclean v. Dunn* (1828) 1 Moo. & P. 761.
[59] *Suncorp Insurance and Finance v. Milano Assicurazioni SpA* [1993] 2 Lloyd's Rep. 225.
[60] *John Koch Ltd v. C & H Products Ltd* [1956] 2 Lloyd's Rep. 59 at 65, *per* Singleton L.J.
[61] *China Pacific SA v. Food Corporation of India; The Winson* [1982] A.C. 939 at 965.

ent of the bailee's own right to reimbursement of his expenses.[62] There must be genuine necessity and any action taken by the agent must be reasonable. In 1920[63] London export merchants sent a parcel of goods to Batum through British carriers, who had establishments in Batum and Constantinople (now Istanbul), with instructions to deliver the goods to a local merchant. When the goods arrived, Batum was on the verge of serious disturbances; British residents had to evacuate the town and a clash between Soviet and White Russian forces seemed imminent. The carriers thereupon removed the goods to Constantinople when evacuating Batum and did not deliver them to the local merchant. The court ruled that they acted as agents of necessity and were not liable for any loss suffered by the exporters owing to the removal of the goods to Constantinople. Bailhache J. expressed the decisive test as follows[64]:

> "I have come to the conclusion that under all circumstances there never was a point of time that I can put my finger on and say 'here the defendants ought to have communicated with this country and if they had done so at that particular date there was a reasonable chance of getting a reply'."

It is extremely difficult to establish agency of necessity where there is no pre-existing agency relationship.[65] However, it has been long established that if the two conditions for agency of necessity are satisfied, the master of a vessel has power to act for the cargo owner in order to preserve the cargo, or may incur expenses on behalf of the shipowner in order to preserve the vessel.

Further, in the modern state of telecommunications, cases in which the agent is unable to communicate with the principal and to obtain his instructions with respect to the goods will rarely arise. But it is not beyond imagination that such a situation may still develop suddenly.

RIGHTS AND OBLIGATIONS OF AGENT AND PRINCIPAL

27–010 Until very recently the rights and obligations of commercial agent and principal were governed by the terms of their contract and the common law but many of these, particularly the obligations of a principal towards the agent, are now statutory. The E.C. Council Directive on the Co-Ordination of the Laws of the Member States Relating to Self-Employed Commercial Agents was adopted on December 18, 1986.[66] The Directive aims at harmonising the laws of the E.C. Member States between principal and self-employed agent and strengthening the position of the agent. The United Kingdom was allowed an extended period to adapt its laws to give effect to this Directive and The Commercial Agents (Council Directive) Regulations 1993 came into force on January 1, 1994.[67] It is important to note that the Regulations are retrospective and therefore apply

---

[62] *ibid.* 958, 962 and 964.
[63] *Tetley & Co v. British Trade Corporation* (1922) 10 Ll.L.R. 678.
[64] *ibid.* at 681.
[65] *Re Banque de Moscou, Royal Exchange Assurance v. The Liquidator* [1952] 1 All E.R. 1269 at 1278.
[66] Council Directive 86/653 [1986] O.J. L382/17.
[67] S.I. 1993 No. 3053 as amended by S.I. 1993 No. 3173.

to agency contracts which pre-date the Regulations, except where rights and liabilities of either agent or principal have accrued before they came into force.[68]

The Regulations govern relations between commercial agents and their principals.[69] A problem arises in connection with Regulation 1(3)[70] which provides that:

> "Regulations 3 to 22 do not apply where the parties have agreed that the agency contract is to be governed by the law of another Member State."

In *Ingmar (GB) Ltd v. Eaton Leonard Technologies Inc*[71] an English company acted as agent for a Californian company, the agreement stating that it was to be governed by the law of California. The Court of Appeal has formulated a question to the E.C.J., to determine the applicability of the Directive where the principal to an agency agreement was a company incorporated in a non-Member State, and the applicability where the express law of the contract was that of a foreign jurisdiction.

A commercial agent is[72]:

> ". . . a self-employed intermediary who has continuing authority to negotiate the sale or purchase of goods on behalf of another person (the 'principal'), or to negotiate and conclude the sale or purchase of goods . . . on behalf of and in the name of that principal."

Although the term "commercial agent" is alien to English lawyers, it is clear that the Regulations will apply to the usual agency relationship. It appears, however, that they would not apply to agents who are authorised only to introduce potential clients, leaving the negotiations and conclusion of any contract to the principal, since the definition refers to those who "negotiate" or "negotiate and conclude" a sale. Those who purchase and sell another's goods for their own account and so take a financial risk, are not strictly speaking agents in the legal sense, so the Regulations would not seem to apply to them. It is unclear whether the Regulations apply only to natural persons or whether legal persons are also included.

The definition refers to "sale or purchase of goods" and the Regulations would therefore seem not to apply to agents who negotiate services on behalf of a principal.

It is clear that the definition would include an agent acting for a named, and possibly also an unnamed, principal, but this is less certain, since it is possible that "on behalf of *and* in the name of *that* principal" may be interpreted to mean that the principal must be named. Still less certain is whether the definition includes the position where the principal is undisclosed. However, it is necessary to bear in mind that the Regulations, as all Community legislation, should be interpreted purposively.

---

[68] Reg. 23.
[69] Reg. 1(2). It is not possible to be both principal and agent and fall within the ambit of the Regulations: *AMB Imballaggi Plastici SRL v. Paciflex Ltd* [1999] 2 All E.R. (Comm) 249.
[70] See Bowstead and Reynolds, *Agency, loc cit.*, para. 11-008.
[71] [1999] Eu.L.R. 88.
[72] Reg. 2(1).

Excluded are duly authorised company officers[73] or partners[74] and insolvency practitioners.[75] Further, the Regulations do not apply to unpaid commercial agents,[76] those who operate on commodity exchanges or in the commodity market,[77] Crown Agents,[78] or those whose activities as commercial agents is secondary.[79] Paragraph 4 of the Schedule to the Regulations provides that it is indicative that such activity is secondary if:

> "(a) promotional material is supplied direct to potential customers;
> (b) persons are granted agencies without reference to existing agents in a particular area or in relation to a particular group;
> (c) customers normally select the goods for themselves and merely place their orders through the agent."

Paragraph 5 of the Schedule further provides that there is a presumption that mail order catalogue agents for consumer goods and consumer credit agents do not fall within paragraph 2 of the Schedule. The latter paragraph sets out circumstances which would negate the possibility that the agent's activities are secondary. In short, these are such as would be expected in a commercial agency relationship.

Duties of the agent to his principal

27–011 The duties of the self-employed agent are set out in Regulation 3 and no derogation is permitted.[80] There is a general requirement that the "agent must look after the interests of his principal and act dutifully and in good faith."[81] Regulation 3(2) requires that:

> "In particular the commercial agent must—
>
> (a) make proper efforts to negotiate and, where appropriate, conclude the transactions he is instructed to take care of;
> (b) communicate to his principal all the necessary information available to him;
> (c) comply with reasonable instructions given by his principal."

In case of breach, the law applicable to the contract shall determine the consequences.[82]

The following are the main common law duties of the agent, as far as relevant here, and it will be apparent that they accord largely with Regulation 3:

To use reasonable diligence. The agent has to carry out the duties which he has undertaken with customary and reasonable care, skill and diligence, and is

---

[73] Reg. 2(1)(i).
[74] Reg. 2(1)(ii).
[75] Reg. 2(1)(iii).
[76] Reg. 2(2)(a).
[77] Reg. 2(2)(b).
[78] Reg. 2(2)(c).
[79] Reg. 2(3)(4).
[80] Reg. 5(1).
[81] Reg. 3(1).
[82] Reg. 5(2).

responsible to the principal for any loss caused by a failure to observe these standards.[83] A selling agent has no authority to give the buyer a warranty with respect to the goods sold, unless such authority is given him expressly or impliedly, or arises from a trade custom.[84]

To disclose all material facts. The agent is obliged to disclose all facts[85] to his principal, which are likely to influence the latter when deciding whether to accept the customer's order or not. If, *e.g.* the principal has instructed the agent not to sell to X, and Y, a subsidiary company of X, ordered the goods from the agent, the latter, when forwarding the order to the principal, would have to point out that Y is known as being controlled by X. In particular, the agent is obliged to disclose to the principal any personal interest which he might have in the transaction. He must not buy the principal's goods without having first obtained the consent of the principal, nor must he act as agent for the buyer and receive double commission on the transaction without prior disclosure to the principal,[86] nor must his personal interest conflict with that of his principal.[87] A contract in which the agent has an undisclosed personal interest is voidable at the option of the principal.[88]

Not to accept bribes or to make secret profits. The agent must not accept a bribe, nor in other respects make a secret profit out of his representative position.[89] Where a bribe has been promised, the principal can claim it from the third party or, if it has been paid over, from the agent[90] together with interest.[91] He may also claim any profit made by investing the bribe[92] and is entitled to dismiss the agent without notice,[93] or to avoid the contract with the third party,[94] or to refuse to pay commission on the tainted transaction, or to claim damages for any loss which he has sustained through entering into the contract, but will have to elect whether to sue for damages or for the proceeds of the bribe.[95] These consequences ensue even when the bribe or secret profit has been accepted by the agent with the intention of not being influenced by it in his judgment, or

---

[83] *Beale v. South Devon Rly Co* (1864) 3 H.&C. 337.
[84] *Benmag v. Barda* [1955] 2 Lloyd's Rep. 354 where McNair J. found on the facts that the seller had authorised his agent to warrant to the buyer that a consignment of goat hair was of the same quality as an earlier consignment.
[85] *Dunne v. English* (1874) L.R. Eq. 524.
[86] *Anglo-African Merchants Ltd v. Bayley* [1970] 1 Q.B. 311 (insurance broker).
[87] *Boardman v. Phipps* [1967] 2 A.C. 46.
[88] *McPherson v. Watt* (1877) 3 App. Cas. 254.
[89] *Boston Deep Sea Fishing & Ice Co v. Ansell* (1888) 39 Ch. D. 339.
[90] *Reading v. Att.-Gen.* [1951] A.C. 507; *Grinstead v. Hadrill* [1953] 1 W.L.R. 696; *T. Mahesan S/O Thambia v. Malaysia Government Officers' Co-operative Housing Society Ltd* [1978] 2 W.L.R. 444. On the converse case of the liability of a principal whose agent bribes the servant of the third party, see *Armagas Ltd v. Mundogas SA* [1985] 3 W.L.R. 640 at 663 affd. [1986] 2 W.L.R. 1063, HL. Also *Logicrose Ltd v. Southend United Football Club Ltd* [1988] 1 W.L.R. 1256.
[91] *Boston Deep Sea Fishing & Ice Co v. Ansell* [1888] 39 Ch. 339.
[92] *Att.-Gen. for Hong Kong v. Reid* [1994] 1 A.C. 324 in which the decision in *Lister v. Stubbs* [1890] 45 Ch. D. 1 was doubted by the Privy Council. From the Privy Council's decision it seems now clear that the relationship of agent and principal is a fiduciary one.
[93] *Boston Deep Sea Fishing & Ice Co v. Ansell* [1888] 39 Ch. 339; Reg. 16.
[94] *Logicrose v. Southend Football Club* [1988] 1 W.L.R. 1256.
[95] *Mahesan S/O Thambiah v. Malaysia Government Officers' Co-operative Housing Society Ltd* [1979] A.C. 374.

when it can be proved that the interests of the principal have not been injured.[96] It is a matter of business morality as well as of the law that the standards of honesty required of the agent should be exacting; they are relaxed only if the principal knows that the agent receives a remuneration from the third party and has given his consent.

Not to divulge confidential information. The agent must not divulge confidential information or material which he has obtained in the course of his employment, to third parties during the existence or after termination of the agency agreement, nor must he use such information himself unfairly in order to compete with the principal.[97] Where an agent normally acts for several principals who may have conflicting interests, he must preserve the confidentiality of each principal.[98] The agent may divulge confidential information concerning the principal to the police, a public authority or, it would appear, even the press if the facts in question constitute a crime or fraud committed by the principal, or a serious matter contravening the public interest.[99]

However, he cannot be restrained from using the skill and experience which he gained when acting for the principal after termination of the agency agreement, unless the parties agreed upon a reasonable restraint of trade.[1] Regulation 20 provides that a restraint of trade clause must be in writing, must relate to the same geographical area and goods as those in the agency contract and may not be for a period exceeding two years after the termination of the contract. But Regulation 20(3) provides that the foregoing ". . . shall not affect any enactment or rule of law which imposes other restrictions on the validity or enforceability of restraint of trade clauses or which enables a court to reduce the obligations on the parties resulting from such clauses".

In one case[2] an international trade directory was published by a British publisher, who employed agents in certain districts of the European continent allotted to them exclusively. They were remunerated by a commission on the

---

[96] In certain circumstances criminal proceedings may be instituted against the agent under the Prevention of Corruption Acts 1906 and 1916 and here again, "if a person does what is called a double-cross, and does not do what he was bribed to do, that is no reason why he should be acquitted of taking a bribe"; *R. v. Carr* [1957] 1 W.L.R. 165 at 166.

[97] On confidentiality generally, see *Seager v. Copydex Ltd* [1967] 1 W.L.R. 923; *Thomas Marshall (Exports) Ltd v. Guinle* [1979] Ch. 227; *Fraser v. Thames Television Ltd* [1984] Q.B. 44. On the duty of confidentiality of an employee to his employer (and former employer) see *Faccenda Chicken Ltd v. Fowler* (1986) 136 N.L.J. 71, CA; see also *Speed Seal Products Ltd v. Paddington* [1985] 1 W.L.R. 1327 (injunction granted although allegedly confidential information already published earlier—a very exceptional case); *Johnson & Bloy (Holdings) Ltd v. Wolstenholme Rink plc* [1987] 2 F.T.L.R. 502.

[98] *Kelly v. Cooper* [1993] A.C. 205.

[99] *Initial Services Ltd v. Putterill* [1968] 1 Q.B. 396.

[1] *Roger Bullivant Ltd v. Ellis* [1987] I.C.R. 464 (injunction restraining confidential information after termination of contract restricted to contractual prohibition period). On the measure of damages for breach of confidentiality see *Dowson & Mason Ltd v. Potter* [1986] 1 W.L.R. 1419. On confidentiality after termination of contract generally, see *Lock International plc v. Beswick* [1989] 1 W.L.R. 1268.

[2] *Lamb v. Evans* [1893] 1 Ch. 218. See also *Nordisk Insulinlaboratorium v. C. L. Bencard (1934) Ltd* [1953] Ch. 430; *British Syphon Co Ltd v. Homewood* [1956] 1 W.L.R. 1190; *L. S. Harris Trustees Ltd (Trading as L. S. Harris & Co) v. Power Packing Services (Hermit Road) Ltd* [1970] 2 Lloyd's Rep. 65; *Baker v. Gibbons* [1972] 1 W.L.R. 693.

amounts received for advertisements. Apparently it was their habit to take down, in their own notebooks, information relating to the advertisers in their district, which was later produced in the directory. On terminating the agency agreement, the publisher successfully applied for an injunction to restrain the agents from using the material collected in their notebooks in their own interest or that of a rival publisher. It was argued on behalf of the agents that the advertisements, after publication in the directory, could be reprinted by anybody unless they were protected by copyright, but Kay L.J. dealt with this argument as follows:

> "The jurisdiction against these defendants is because these materials which they want to use were obtained by them when they were in the position of agents for the plaintiff, and, although the plaintiff might not be able to prevent anybody else in the world from publishing or using such materials as he is trying to prevent these defendants from using, that would be ño answer, because these defendants, from the position in which they were in, are put under a duty towards the plaintiff not to make this use of the material."

In an extreme case, in order to preserve material, the principal may apply to the court for a search order (*Anton Piller* order).[3]

To account to the principal. An agent is obliged to keep proper accounts of all agency transactions and to produce them to the principal in accordance with the terms of the agency agreement, or upon request by the principal.[4] The agent has to keep the customary office records and should keep the money and property of the principal separate from his own. He has to pay over to the principal all moneys actually received on behalf of the latter but, in the absence of contrary provisions in the agency agreement, is, in appropriate cases, entitled to a set-off or a lien on the principal's goods or money.[5] These rights of the agent can be exercised where money is owing from the principal, but the agent cannot claim these rights to retain arbitrarily expenses which have not been agreed upon.

Duties of the principal

For commercial agents these are now set out in the Commercial Agents (Council **27–012** Directive) Regulations 1993. Regulation 4, from which no derogation is permitted[6] provides that, like the agent, the principal must act "dutifully and in good faith."[7] Regulation 4 goes on to state that in particular the principal must provide the agent with the necessary documentation concerning the goods[8] and information to enable the agent to carry out the contract.[9] He must also advise the agent in reasonable time if he anticipates that the volume of business will be lower

---

[3] See *post*, para. 22–032.
[4] *Yasuda Fire & Marine Insurance Co of Europe v. Orion Marine Insurance Underwriting Agency* [1995] 2 Q.B. 174.
[5] *Rolls Razor Ltd v. Cox* [1967] 1 Q.B. 552.
[6] Reg. 5.
[7] Reg. 4(1).
[8] Reg. 4(2)(a).
[9] Reg. 4(2)(b).

than expected[10] and inform the agent of his acceptance, rejection or non-performance of any contract involving the agent.[11]

Part III, Regulations 6 to 12, of the Regulations deals in some detail with the question of the agent's remuneration. It will be seen that where an agent is paid commission, the parties' freedom to contract is considerably curtailed. Where there is no agreement as to the agent's remuneration, this shall be the remuneration which is customary where the agent works and where there is none then his remuneration shall be reasonable in the circumstances.[12] But Regulation 6(2) provides that the foregoing provision ". . . is without prejudice to the application of any enactment or rule of law concerning the level of remuneration". The remainder of the Regulations in this Part do not apply if the agent's remuneration is not wholly or in part commission.[13] It would therefore seem that if the agent is paid a fixed sum then Regulations 7 to 12 would not apply.

Regulation 7 provides that the agent is entitled to commission on transactions during the contract as a result of his action, or on transactions with a previous customer.[14] He is also entitled to commission on transactions where he has "an exclusive right to a specific geographical area or a specific group of customers."[15]

After termination of the contract the agent is entitled to commission if the order was placed before termination[16] (but not if the commission is payable to a previous agent, although the commission may be shared[17]), or if the transaction is largely due to him and occurs within a reasonable time after termination.[18]

Commission is due when[19]:

"(a) the principal has executed the transaction; or
 (b) the principal . . . should have executed the transaction; or
 (c) the third party has executed the transaction."

Further, "Commision shall become due at the latest when the third party has executed his part of the transaction or should have done so if the principal had executed his part of the transaction, as he should have."[20] Regulation 10(3) states that commission is to be paid no later "than on the last day of the month following the quarter in which it became due" and the remainder of the Regulation sets out when these quarter days shall be in the absence of agreement between the parties. No derogation is permitted from the latest date when commission is due or when it is to be paid, unless any variation is to the agent's advantage.[21]

---

[10] Reg. 4(2)(b).
[11] Reg. 4(2)(c).
[12] Reg. 6(1).
[13] Reg. 6(3).
[14] Reg. 7(1)(a) and (b).
[15] Reg. 7(2).
[16] Reg. 8(b).
[17] Reg. 9(1).
[18] Reg. 8(a).
[19] Reg. 10(1).
[20] Reg. 10(2).
[21] Reg. 10(4).

The agent's right to commission is "extinguished" only if the contract will not be executed and the principal is not to blame for its non-execution[22] and no derogation is permitted.[23] Commission already received by the agent for such a contract is to be refunded.[24]

To enable the agent to ascertain commission due to him, the principal must provide him with a statement of commission due within a prescribed time[25] and further he is entitled to all information available to the principal and extracts from the principal's books.[26] No derogation is permitted[27] but there is a saving for any enactment or rule of law which provides that the agent may inspect the principal's books.[28] Regulation 21 provides that no information should be disclosed where this would be contrary to public policy.

Regulation 13(1) provides that each part shall be entitled on request to receive from the other a signed written contract, which should include any terms subsequently agreed. This provision cannot be waived.[29]

Part IV, Regulations 14 to 20, deal extensively with termination of the agency contract.

If the parties continue to perform a contract beyond its fixed term then it is converted into a contract for an indefinite period.[30] In contracts for an indefinite term either party may give notice of termination,[31] the notice periods being[32]:

> "(a) 1 month for the first year of the contract;
> (b) 2 months for the second year commenced;
> (c) 3 months for the third year commenced and for the subsequent years;
>
> and the parties may not agree on any shorter periods of notice."

If the contract stipulates longer periods of notice then that for the principal shall not be shorter than that for the agent.[33] Unless otherwise agreed, the notice period must coincide with the end of a calendar month.[34] The notice periods also apply to a fixed term contract where it is converted to an indefinite period contract under Regulation 14 and the fixed term period shall be included in calculating the notice period.[35] A principal who intends that an agency contract should not run for more than the fixed period should therefore be careful that the contract does not overrun the fixed period. Regulation 16 allows for immediate termination if one party fails wholly or partly to perform his obligations under the contract, or where "exceptional circumstances" arise.

---

[22] Reg. 11(1).
[23] Reg. 11(3).
[24] Reg. 11(2).
[25] Reg. 12(1).
[26] Reg. 12(2).
[27] Reg. 12(3).
[28] Reg. 12(4).
[29] Reg. 13(2).
[30] Reg. 14.
[31] Reg. 15(1).
[32] Reg. 15(2).
[33] Reg. 15(3).
[34] Reg. 15(4).
[35] Reg. 15(5).

Regulation 17 provides for the agent's entitlement to be indemnified or compensated where the agency contract is terminated but, unless the contract provides otherwise, shall be entitled to compensation rather than an indemnity.[36] Where the agent is entitled to an indemnity, he shall be so entitled "if and to the extent that"—

> "(a) he has brought the principal new customers or has significantly increased the volume of business with existing customers and the principal continues to derive substantial benefits from the business with such customers; and
> (b) the payment of this indemnity is equitable having regard to all the circumstances and, in particular, the commission lost by the commercial agent on the business transacted with such customers."[37]

The agent's entitlement is a year's remuneration, calculated by averaging his remuneration over the preceeding five years, or the number of years if less than five.[38] In *Moore v. Puetta Pta Ltd*[39] it was held that under Regulation 17(3) the indemnity was to cover the entire period of the agency, including the period prior to the coming into force of the Regulations. The value to the principal of the customers introduced by the agent since termination was £92,000 net, but this was capped in accordance with Regulation 17(4) and so reduced to £64,526.33. While it is clear that an agent on contract for an indefinite period is entitled to be indemnified, his position on a fixed term contract is unclear although, since even on the expiry of a fixed term contract the principal may continue to benefit from the agent's work, it would seem fair that his part in the principal's increased business should be acknowledged.[40] This view appears to be reinforced by Regulation 19 which provides that there shall be no derogation from the agent's entitlement to indemnity or compensation to his detriment *before* the contract *expires*. Even if he is indemnified, the agent is not preluded from seeking damages.[41]

The agent is entitled to be compensated for damage suffered by the principal's termination of the contract,[42] which he is deemed to suffer in circumstances that[43]:

> "(a) deprive the commercial agent of the commission which proper performance of the agency contract would have procured for him whilst providing his principal with substantial benefits linked to the activities of the commercial agent; and/or
> (b) have not enabled the commercial agent to amortize the costs and expenses that he had incurred in the performance of the agency contract on the advice of his principal."

---

[36] Reg. 17(2).
[37] Reg. 17(3).
[38] Reg. 17(4).
[39] [1999] 1 All E.R. 174.
[40] See Bowstead and Reynolds, *Agency* (16th ed.), p. 709.
[41] Reg. 17(5).
[42] Reg. 17(6); *Page v. Combined Shipping and Trading Co* [1997] 3 All E.R. 656 (damages to reflect level of commission agent would have earned if the principal had not terminated the contract prematurely); *Duffen v. FRA BO SpA* [1999] E.C.C. 58 (agent entitled to common law damages and also compensation by way of augmentation rather than duplication under Reg. 17(6) following termination).
[43] Reg. 17(7).

Regulation 17(8) provides for indemnity or compensation if the agent dies, thus terminating the contact. In *Hackett v. Advanced Medical Computer Systems Ltd*[44] AMC argued that a letter from H's solicitor was unclear and that the statement of claim was limited to outstanding commission and did not include compensation under the Regulations. It was held that the letter was sufficient and it was not necessary to name any particular Regulation. It was enough to indicate an intention to pursue a claim. In applying the requirements of the Regulations, the court should avoid unnecessary formality.

The agent must notify the principal within a year of termination of his intention to claim indemnity or compensation.[45]

No indemnity or compensation is payable to the agent where the agent is at fault such as to justify immediate termination on the grounds set out in Regulation 16; or where the agent has terminated the contract, unless his termination is justified by the principal's actions; or because the agent is unable to continue due to age, infirmity or illness; or where with the principal's agreement he has assigned the agency contract to another.[46]

The following are the main duties of the principal at common law, but in so far as commercial agents are concerned they should be read in conjunction with the foregoing Regulations:

To pay commission. The principal has to pay the agent the agreed remuneration, which customarily is a commission payable on the purchase price of the business actually acquired by the agent. This method of remuneration is intended to operate as an incentive for the agent, but it sometimes tempts an unscrupulous agent to pay greater attention to the volume of effected sales than the financial soundness of the customers whose orders he solicits. The principal who wishes to protect himself against this contingency has several possibilities. The most effective is to lay down in the contract of agency that the commission shall be earned when the purchase price is received by the principal in cash. A frequent provision of this type is that:

"commission shall be paid at a rate of ... per cent on all moneys received by the principal as purchase price for goods sold by the agent."

Another possibility is to arrange *del credere* terms[47] whereby the agent, usually on payment of an additional commission, undertakes to indemnify the principal for any loss sustained through an insolvency of customers introduced by him.

It is advisable to state expressly when the commission is earned. If the contract is silent on this point, the normal intention of the parties is that the agent can claim the commission when the contract of sale is concluded, for example when the principal accepts the customer's order. It is customary to distinguish the date when the commission is payable from that when it is earned, and to provide that the commission shall be payable some time later than it was earned,

---

[44] [1999] C.L.C. 160.
[45] Reg. 17(9).
[46] Reg. 18.
[47] See *post*, para. 27–016.

or at certain fixed dates. If the contract does not deal with this matter and no contrary trade usages exist, the agent can claim commission immediately it is earned. Advances on unearned commission, must normally be repaid on termination of the agency agreement.[48]

The agent is entitled to commission when he has earned it in accordance with the terms of the contract. The courts will not imply into the contract a term whereby the agent is entitled to commission, if this would be contrary to the express terms.[49]

When the agent only has authority to introduce customers, the principal has full discretion to accept or reject the customer's order, and the agent cannot claim commission on orders which the principal elects to refuse, unless the parties have agreed on special terms, for example that commission shall be paid on the introduction of or inquiries from potential customers, or established trade usages can be proved allowing commission on a reduced scale. However, the principal must not prevent the agent by a wrongful act or omission from earning his commission, and the agent can recover damages for the actual loss sustained if the principal contravenes this rule. These damages may in appropriate cases be commensurate to the lost commission. In one case[50] a principal was introduced by an agent to a Dutch buyer who wanted to buy a quantity of cement that was to be shipped c. & f. to a port in Iran. The principal accepted the introduction and contracted with the buyer accordingly. The buyer opened a letter of credit in favour of the seller (the principal) and the latter provided a performance guarantee in favour of the buyer. Later, the principal decided not to perform the contract of sale. He met a claim by the buyer by forfeiting the performance guarantee and making an additional payment. The agent claimed damages for the lost commission. The court held that he was entitled thereto. It was an implied term in the contract of agency that the principal would not deprive the agent of his commission by breaking the contract with the third party. Lawton L.J. expressed this principle in a graphic manner[51]:

> "The life of an agent in commerce is a precarious one. He is like the groom who takes a horse to the water-trough. He may get his principal to the negotiating table but when he gets him there he can do nothing to make him sign, any more than the groom can make a horse drink. . . . Once the signing has been done, the agent is in a different position altogether, because by that time the principal has accepted the benefit of the agent's work. In these circumstances, he ought not to be allowed to resile from his obligations to the agent . . . the whole relationship of principal and agent depends upon the principal accepting his obligations to the agent once the agent has done his work and the principal has accepted the benefit of it."

Where commission is to be paid on the purchase price received by the principal, and the customer repudiates the contract before paying the price, the principal is not bound to sue the customer in order to enable the agent to earn his commission, but if he receives some compensation from the customer the agent would

---

[48] *Bronester Ltd v. Priddle* [1961] 1 W.L.R. 1294.
[49] *Marcan Shipping (London) Ltd v. Polish Steamship Co; The Manifest Lipkowy* [1989] 2 Lloyd's Rep. 138.
[50] *Alpha Trading Ltd v. Dunnshaw-Patten Ltd* [1981] Q.B. 290.
[51] *ibid.* at 308.

appear to be entitled to a reasonable remuneration, which may be a good deal less than full commission.[52]

If the agent himself is in breach of his obligations under the contract of agency but nevertheless a contract of sale has been concluded between the principal and the third party, the agent forfeits his commission if he has acted in bad faith. However, he is still entitled to it if the breach was committed honestly and in good faith.[53]

Three points require particular attention when the agent's commission is discussed by the parties: the reimbursement of the agent for expenses, the payment of commission on orders emanating from the agent's territory but received directly by the principal, and commission due on repeat orders. These matters should be dealt with in the contract in precise terms.

It happens sometimes—though more often in the home trade than in the export trade—that the principal agrees to pay the agent a fixed sum at monthly or other intervals "on account of the commission which will accrue to him". Such an arrangement would make the agent a servant of the principal rather than constitute him an independent contractor. If, in such a case, on the termination of the agency the payments by the principal exceed the commission earned by the agent, the agent has to repay the principal the excess, unless the agency agreement contains an express or implied provision to the contrary.[54] As this point often gives rise to disputes, it is advisable to cover it in advance by an express term in the agency agreement.

Agent's expenses and indemnity. The self-employed sales agent abroad who solicits orders for an exporter cannot claim his trading expenses from the principal, unless this is expressly agreed upon in the contract of agency. If the agent, with the approval of the principal, incurs liabilities in the course of his duties, for instance if he sues a defaulting customer in the courts of the country where the customer resides, he is entitled to be indemnified for any losses sustained or liabilities incurred by him.

Orders emanating from agent's territory but not procured by him. In principle, the agent is entitled to commission if the transaction for which commission is claimed is the direct result of his efforts. The agent can therefore claim commission if the customer with whom he has negotiated eventually orders goods directly from the principal, or if the customer whom he introduces offers a lower price than the list price and the principal decides to accept the offer at the lower price. He cannot claim commission if the customer places an unsolicited order with the principal, or if the order has been obtained by the principal himself or other agents. These rules of law are frequently modified by the contract parties or a custom of the trade, which may provide that the agent shall be entitled to commission on all transactions emanating from his territory. These arrangements

---

[52] *Boots v. E. Christopher & Co* [1951] 2 All E.R. 1045.
[53] *Robinson Scammell & Co v. Ansell* [1985] 2 E.G.L.R. 41.
[54] *Rivoli Hats Ltd v. Gooch* [1953] 1 W.L.R. 1190; *Clayton Newbury Ltd v. Findlay* [1953] 1 W.L.R. 1194.

are particularly frequent when an agent is appointed as exclusive agent for a defined territory.

Repeat orders. It depends on the intention of the parties, as evinced in the agency agreement, whether the agent is entitled to commission on repeat orders. Two questions have to be distinguished here: is the agent entitled to commission on repeat orders during the currency of the agency agreement, and is he so entitled after its termination?

As regards the first of these questions, the parties frequently arrange in the agency agreement expressly that commission shall be payable on repeat orders, *e.g.* by providing that the agent shall be entitled to commission on "repeats on any accounts introduced by" him,[55] or sometimes by stating generally that commission shall be due on all orders from customers introduced by him.[56] If the parties have failed to make express provision on this point, the principles stated above under the previous heading apply. In other words, if the first order was the direct result of the agent's efforts, he is entitled to commission on the repeat order, because they have to be considered as the continued effect of his original efforts. It is irrelevant whether these repeat orders are placed with the agent or with the principal directly.

The second question raises more difficult legal problems. The difficulty arises if, after termination of the agency contract by notice, mutual agreement or death of the agent, the principal has accepted repeat orders which, if the agency had not been terminated, would have carried a commission for the agent. Here, it can be argued that the principal appropriates the fruits of his former agent's labours after termination of his relationship with him. Nevertheless, unless the parties have otherwise provided in the agency agreement,[57] the rule is that no remuneration is payable on transactions between the principal and third parties arising after termination of the authority, whether such transactions are due to the agent's introduction or not.[58] However, the rule allows exceptions and it is not easy to determine whether in a particular case the rule applies or an exception should be admitted. Generally speaking, where the agency agreement was concluded for a limited time, the rule applies,[59] but where it was concluded for an indefinite time, exceptions to the rule have occasionally been allowed.[60] However, the question is always one of construction of the relevant contractual terms. The modern tendency is not to allow commission on repeat orders after termination of the agency agreement but, as observed, each case has to be decided on its own merits.[61] Even in cases in which, according to these principles, the agent is entitled to commission after termination, his claim is only

---

[55] *Levy v. Goldhill* [1917] 2 Ch. 297.

[56] *Roberts v. Elwells Engineers Ltd* [1972] 2 Q.B. 586.

[57] *Marshall v. NM Financial Management Ltd* [1997] 1 W.L.R. 1527 (the contractual provision for renewal commission after termination was conditional upon a restraint of trade provision. This was struck out and the agent was entitled to renewal commission).

[58] *Halsbury's Laws of England* (4th ed.), Vol. 1(2) (reissue), para. 120.

[59] *Weare v. Brimsdown Lead Co* (1910) 103 L.T.R. 429.

[60] *Levy v. Goldhill* [1917] 2 Ch. 297; *Bilbee v. Hasse & Co* (1889) 5 T.L.R. 677; *Salomon v. Brownfield* (1896) 12 T.L.R. 239; *Wilson v. Harper, Son & Co* [1908] 2 Ch. 370; *British Bank Ltd v. Novimex Ltd* [1949] 1 K.B. 623; *Sellers v. London Counties Newspapers* [1951] 1 K.B. 784.

[61] *Crocker Horlock Ltd v. B. Lang & Co Ltd* [1949] 1 All E.R. 526.

for a lump sum representing monetary compensation for loss of commission on the repeat orders. He cannot claim a declaration and an account for the future, because that would amount to an annuity "to the crack of doom."[62]

Exclusive trading rights

The agency agreement may provide that the self-employed agent shall have sole, **27–013** or exclusive, or sole and exclusive trading rights in a particular territory.[63] The character of the agency is here territorial and not personal. The agent is normally paid commission on all sales emanating from his territory, whether procured by his own efforts or those of other persons,[64] and he usually undertakes to promote systematically in the territory reserved to him the distribution of the principal's goods by an organisation of sub-agents, advertisements or other means. Agency agreements are, as far as the exclusivity of trading rights is concerned, similar to distribution agreements, but the essential difference between an agent, who contracts on behalf of a principal, and a distributor, who contracts on his own account and for his own benefit, remains.[65] In particular, the contract of agency should state expressly that the agent has to sell in the principal's name. In one case,[66] the terms of an exclusive agency contract were summed up by Lord Simon L.C. as follows:

> "By a written contract dated February 19, 1938, the respondents, manufacturers of steel in Sheffield, as principals appointed the appellants, whose business address was in New York, to be sole selling agents of their tool steels in a wide area of territories including the western hemisphere (excluding USA and Argentine), Australia, New Zealand and India. The appellants were to sell in the name of the respondents, the respondents fixing f.o.b. prices and the appellants charging the purchaser with such excess price over f.o.b. prices as they could obtain. Any excess price over the f.o.b. price was for the credit of the appellants and the respondents were to account to the appellants in respect of such excess price after the respondents had received payment in full from the purchaser. The duration of the agreement was to be for three years from April 1, 1938, as a minimum. The agreement contained an arbitration clause."

An exclusive agency agreement, as such, is not prohibited by Article 81(1) of the E.C. Treaty but may contravene it if it contains clauses which have as their object or effect the distortion of competition in the common market. However, the E.C. Commission has granted important exemptions *en bloc* from the general prohibition of Article 81(1). The regulation of European Community Law, affecting exclusive distribution and agency agreements, will be considered later on.[67]

SPECIAL TYPES OF AGENTS

Commercial practice has evolved certain types of agency agreements which play **27–014** an important role in the export trade.

---

[62] *Per* Lord Denning M.R., *Roberts v. Elwells Engineers Ltd* [1972] 2 Q.B. 586 at 593.
[63] On the meaning of the terms "sole" and "exclusive", see Chap. 29.
[64] And see Reg. 7(2), *ante*, para. 27–012.
[65] *ibid.*
[66] *Heyman v. Darwins Ltd* [1942] A.C. 356 at 357 (in this case the remuneration of the agent did not consist of a commission).
[67] See paras 29–011 and 29–012.

The Commission agent

27–015 The agent whom the British exporter appoints in an overseas country may be classified by the agent's own law as a commissionaire. Most European continental countries and other legal systems founded on the civil law recognise commissionaires as a special class of self-employed commercial agents. The term "commissionaire" is sometimes rendered in English as "commission agent" or "commission merchant" but this translation is confusing, because the civil law and common law concepts of this type of agency are fundamentally different.

A commissionaire is a person who internally, *i.e.* in his relationship to his principal, is an agent but externally, *i.e.* in his relationship to the third party, is a seller or buyer in his own name. Where a commissionare has acted for the principal, no privity of contract can be constituted between the principal and the third party.[68] As an agent, the commissionaire is accountable to his principal for the profit from the transaction, must use reasonable diligence in the performance of his duties, and must not make an undisclosed profit or take a bribe. The principal, on the other hand, cannot claim the price from the third party directly, nor is he liable in contract for any defects of the goods.

In civil law countries a distinction is drawn between direct and indirect agency. A direct agent is an agent who discloses his agency quality to the third party. An indirect agent is a person who, though being an agent, treats with the third party in his own name. The commissionaire is an indirect agent.

This form of commercial activity is, of course, also known in English law. Indeed, it is widely used, *e.g.* by confirming houses.[69] In English law, the institution of an agent acting for an undisclosed principal[70] fulfils the function of the commissionaire in civil law. If duly authorised, he is a true agent of his principal but he appears to be a seller or buyer in his own name as far as the third party is concerned.

There is, however, a fundamental difference between the commissionaire of civil law and the English commission agent.[71] The commissionaire relationship is always a two-contract relationship and privity of contract can never be established between the principal and the third party.[72] But the third party and undisclosed principal can enter into direct contractual relationship with each other by the third party's election or the principal's intervention[73] and thus a one-contract relationship can be constituted between them.

A commission agent who has himself paid the price to the third party has the same rights against the goods as an unpaid seller, *viz.* the right of lien, stoppage in transit and resale. This is provided by the Sale of Goods Act 1979, s.38(2).[74]

---

[68] Except by assignment.
[69] See *post*, paras 27–018 to 27–023.
[70] See *ante*, para. 27–005.
[71] See C. M. Schmitthoff, "Agency in International Trade. A Study in Comparative Law", Academy of International Law, 129 Receuil des Cours (1970, Vol. 1), pp. 109, 135. *Essays*, p. 306.
[72] Except by assignment.
[73] See *ante*, para. 27–005.
[74] See *ante*, para. 5–016.

These rights are of great value to him if his principal does not repay him or cannot do so because he has become insolvent.

The del credere agent

A del credere agent is an agent who undertakes to indemnify the principal for any **27–016** loss which the latter may sustain, owing to the failure of a customer introduced by the agent to pay the purchase price. The advantages of the del credere arrangement are evident: the principal is not sufficiently in touch with the foreign market in which the agent operates to judge the financial soundness of the customer who orders goods; credit terms cannot always be avoided if it is desired to market the goods on a competitive basis, and even where no credit terms are granted, the exporter might find himself entangled in complicated and costly insolvency proceedings if the customer fails. These pitfalls are avoided by the agent agreeing to accept the del credere for the customers introduced by him and, incidentally, the principal can be assured that the agent will not place considerations of turnover higher than the solvency of the customers whose orders he solicits. It is usual to pay an additional commission, called the del credere commission, to the agent who accepts a del credere responsibility. The del credere agreement need not be evidenced in writing; it is a contract of indemnity against loss and not a contract of guarantee.[75] The del credere agent undertakes merely to indemnify the principal if the latter, owing to the insolvency of the buyer or some analogous cause, is unable to recover the purchase price, but the agent is not responsible if a perfectly solvent buyer refuses to pay the price on the ground that the principal has not duly performed the contract.[76] Lord Ellenborough expressed this rule in 1817 as follows[77]: "The (del credere) commission imports that if the vendee does not pay, the factor will; it is a guarantee from the factor to the principal against any mischief to arise from the vendee's insolvency. But it varies not an iota the rights subsisting between vendor and vendee."

By an announcement of December 24, 1962,[78] the E.C. Commission indicated that it did not consider exclusive dealing arrangements with commercial agents as falling within the prohibition of Article 81(1) of the E.C. Treaty, provided that the agent did not assume a financial risk other than that implied in the usual del credere obligation.[79]

The agent carrying stock (the mercantile agent)

Agents resident abroad have either authority to solicit or accept orders and **27–017** pass them on to the principal, who then dispatches the goods to the customer

---

[75] Consequently, s. 4 of the Statute of Frauds 1677, which provides, *inter alia*, that a contract of guarantee, to be enforceable, must be evidenced in writing, does not apply (this provision of s. 4 is not repealed by the Law Reform (Enforcement of Contracts) Act 1954).
[76] *Gabriel & Sons v. Churchill & Sim* [1914] 3 K.B. 1272.
[77] In *Hornby v. Lacy* (1817) 6 M. & S. 166 at 171.
[78] See *post*, para. 29–012.
[79] This announcement does not bind the Commission or the courts. In particular, the legal form of agency must not be used as a device to evade the competition rules of the E.C. The Commission

directly, or they are entrusted with a store or consignment of stock lines, spare parts, etc. and have authority to supply customers directly from their store. Agents of the latter type are mercantile agents within the meaning of the Factors Act 1889. According to the Act, a mercantile agent is an agent who in the customary course of his business has authority to sell goods, or to consign goods for sale, or to buy goods or to raise money on the security of goods.[80] The problem that arises with respect to these consignment agents is that they may dispose of their principal's goods contrary to his instructions and without due authority. Great uncertainty would be imported into business transactions if the deals of consignment agents in goods entrusted to them were invalid for lack of authority, particularly as these agents often do not disclose their representative capacity and the third party has no means of ascertaining the internal arrangement between the principal and agent. The Factors Act 1889 aims at the protection of third parties dealing in good faith with the consignment agent and provides in particular that, where such an agent, in his capacity of mercantile agent with the consent of the principal is in possession of goods or documents of title to the goods, any sale or other disposition transacted by him in the ordinary course of business in respect of these goods is as valid as if it were expressly authorised by the principal, provided the third party did not know of the lack of the mercantile agent's authority.[81] The Act cannot be invoked in export transactions if the contract between the agent residing abroad and the customer there is governed by the law of the foreign country where the contract is concluded or to be performed,[82] but the laws of many foreign countries embody rules corresponding to the provisions of the Factors Act 1889. On the other hand, the Act provides a valuable protection in import transactions, as shown in the following case[83]: importers obtained an advance from Lloyd's Bank on the security of bills of lading in respect of certain merchandise and the bank returned the bills of lading to the importers in order to enable them to sell the goods. On receipt of the bills of lading, the importers gave the bank a trust receipt,[84] wherein they acknowledged their holding of the documents under lien of the bank and agreed to clear the goods as trustees of the bank. The importers, who were in financial difficulties, pledged the bills of lading, in breach of trust, with the Bank of America, which was unaware of the true position. The court decided that the importers received the documents of title as mercantile agents of Lloyd's Bank and that the pledging of the documents with the Bank of America was valid as against Lloyd's Bank.

---

and the E.C.J. will always look at the realities of the situation: *Re Pittsburgh Corning Europe* [1973] C.M.L.R. D.2; *Re Sugar Cartel* [1975] E.C.R. 1663; [1976] 1 C.M.L.R. 295.

[80] s. 1(1). The expression "factor" in the title of the 1889 Act is an antiquated term which is not used in the Act itself. The Act refers to "mercantile agents".

[81] s. 2(1). The mercantile agent must be in possession of the goods or documents of title when he disposes of them: *Beverley Acceptances Ltd v. Oakley* [1982] R.T.R. 417.

[82] See Chap. 21.

[83] *Lloyd's Bank v. Bank of America National Trust and Savings Association* [1937] 2 K.B. 631; [1938] 2 K.B. 147.

[84] On release under a trust receipt see *ante*, para. 10–005.

The confirming house

In the export trade an overseas importer may buy in the United Kingdom through **27–018** a confirming house resident in the United Kingdom,[85] although in recent years the number of independent confirming houses has decreased, many having been absorbed by banks. In modern practice these confirming houses are called export houses.[86] Business enterprises carrying on these activities are, of course, also established in other countries, notably the United States.

Nature of the confirming house

The term "confirming house" has no definite meaning in law or in commercial **27–019** practice. A confirming house usually enters into two legal relationships, namely, with its overseas customer, who asks it to procure certain goods for him, and with the seller in the home market, with whom it places the order or indent. The relationship with the overseas customer is normally that between principal and agent, whereas the relationship with the seller in the home market depends on the nature of the contract which the confirming house concludes with him. Three possibilities exist in that respect: first, when placing the order with the seller, the confirming house may buy from the seller; in that case it enters into a direct contract of sale and is liable for the price and for the acceptance of the goods as a buyer. The fact that the seller knows that the goods are destined for export and even knows the name of the overseas buyer is not relevant. The second possibility is that the confirming house places the order with the seller "as agents on behalf of our principals", either naming them or not; in that case the contract of sale is made directly between the seller and the overseas buyer and the confirming house does not intend to make itself liable for the price. The first and the second possibility are diametrically opposed; in the first case the confirming house places its client's order as a principal and in the second it does so as an agent. A third arrangement is possible and, indeed, this is the typical confirming arrangement: the confirming house may place the client's order as agent of the overseas importer, but may indicate at the same time that it intends to hold itself personally responsible for the price. This type of confirmation is described by McNair J.[87] as follows:

> "The critical question is: What is the meaning of 'confirming order' or what is the meaning of 'confirming house'? . . . It seems to me, using the word in its ordinary sense, 'to confirm' means that the party confirming guarantees that the order will be carried out by the purchaser. In that sense he adds confirmation or assurance to the bargain which has been made by the primary contractor, just as a bank which confirms that a credit has been opened by the buyers in favour of the seller guarantees that payment will be made against the credit if the proper documents are tendered."

---

[85] The following observations are founded on C.M. Schmitthoff's *Legal Aspects of Export Sales* (3rd ed., 1978), pp. 8–10.
[86] Their trade association is the British Exporters' Association, Broadway House, Tothill Street, London SW1H 9NP. Tel: 020 7222 5419, Fax: 020 7799 2468.
[87] In *Sobell Industries Ltd v. Cory Bros & Co Ltd* [1955] 2 Lloyd's Rep. 82 at 89; *per* Donaldson J. in *Teheran-Europe Co Ltd v. S.T. Belton (Tractors) Ltd* [1968] 2 Q.B. 53 (this part of the judgment was affirmed by the Court of Appeal in [1968] 2 Q.B. 545).

This third arrangement produces, as far as the liability for the price is concerned, the same effect as the first one; it is the normal and typical confirmation transaction into which the confirming house enters.

In practice, confirming houses, when carrying out orders received from their customers abroad, use two types of forms: one in which they order the goods from the supplier in the home market under their own liability, and another in which they merely pass on the order of the overseas importer as his agent; they use whatever form is appropriate in the case in question.

It should be noted that in the first of these cases the confirming house acts as agent and buyer at the same time. It is clearly established that a person may combine these two qualities in the same transaction. Thus, Roche J. said[88]:

> "Between a commission agent . . . and the foreign principal there is no relation except that of agency; but as between the British seller and the commission agent . . . as buyer there is no party to the contract except the commission agent . . . on that side."

The Sale of Goods Act 1979 makes express provision for the protection of an agent, such as the confirming agent, who has himself paid, or is directly responsible for, the price: section 38(2) of that Act provides that he shall have the same rights against the goods as an unpaid seller: namely, the rights of lien, of stoppage in transit, and resale.[89]

The activities of export houses are of great benefit to international trade. By entering into an absolute obligation to the supplier, either by ordering the goods in its own name or by confirming the overseas order, the export house provides, in effect, non-recourse finance to the supplier. At the same time it often allows the overseas purchaser credit and thus enables him to place the order.

Obligations of the confirming house

27–020 The confirming house, which has made itself liable to the supplier, is under a personal obligation to the supplier to pay the price for the goods. If before the execution of the transaction the overseas customer cancels the order without valid reason, the confirming house is still bound to pay the price to the supplier; its position is similar in this respect to that of the confirming bank under a bankers' letter of credit.[90] If the confirming house has performed this obligation, it is entitled to be indemnified by the customer for what it has paid to the supplier and, in appropriate cases, can recover damages.[91]

As regards the client, the confirming house undertakes to give the supplier proper shipping instructions but—and this has to be emphasised—it does not undertake liability for the conformity of the goods with the contract, and in

---

[88] In *R. & J. Bow Ltd v. Hill* (1930) 37 Ll.L.R. 46 (the learned judge referred in this case to the famous case of *Ireland v. Livingstone* (1872) L.R. 5 HL 395); see further *Basma v. Weekes* [1950] A.C. 441 at 454; *Brown & Gracie Ltd v. F. W. Green & Co Pty Ltd* [1960] 1 Lloyd's Rep. 289 at 303.

[89] This interest can be covered by the confirming house by insurance, see Chap. 19. On the rights of the unpaid seller against the goods see Chap. 5.

[90] *Hamzeh Malas & Sons v. British Imex Industries Ltd* [1958] 2 Q.B. 127, see Chap. 11.

[91] *Anglo-African Shipping Co of New York Inc v. J. Mortner Ltd* [1962] 1 Lloyd's Rep. 610, CA.

particular for their quality and quantity.[92] If a dispute of this character arises, the customer must make a direct claim against the supplier; in this respect the confirming house, if it has merely confirmed the customer's order, has acted for an undisclosed principal.[93] In order to have certainty about the confirming house's position in this type of case, it is advisable for confirming houses, which intend to hold themselves personally responsible to the supplier, to use the third form of transaction—the actual confirmation—rather than the first form under which they are buyers from the supplier.

Confirming houses often insert express clauses in their contracts with the customer and the supplier, to make this position clear. A typical clause is this:

> "By confirming the order, we undertake full responsibility to pay the supplier for all goods delivered in accordance with our confirmation, but it is expressly agreed that we are to incur no other liability whatsoever in respect of the said contract and are not to be made parties to any litigation or arbitration relating thereto."

As already observed, the confirming house has a special lien on the goods and bills of lading *vis-à-vis* the customer and is, in this respect, in the same position as an unpaid seller.[94] But where the confirming house has allowed the customer credit, it does not have a general lien entitling it to retain goods or bills of lading for an indebtedness of the customer resulting from earlier transactions, unless such a general lien is contractually granted to the confirming house; the confirming house is not in the position of a factor, who by custom of trade, has a general lien.[95]

The contracts into which an English confirming house enters often provide that they shall be governed by English law and that the parties submit to the jurisdiction of the English courts.

Insolvency of the confirming house

If the confirming house becomes insolvent, the question arises whether the seller **27–021** can still claim the price from the overseas buyer. If the confirming house has re-ordered the goods from the seller, the answer is clear: the seller can claim the price from the buyer on the contract of purchase originally placed by the buyer. If the confirming house has confirmed the buyer's order, the position is more difficult. If the intention of the parties was that the obligation of the confirming house shall be the sole obligation to the seller, there would be no claim against the overseas buyer. That conclusion would, however, be exceptional. Normally, the confirmation by the confirming house, like the confirmation of the advising bank under a letter of credit, provides only conditional discharge and the seller has still his claim against the overseas buyer.[96]

---

[92] Provided that it has passed on the instructions of the customer correctly to the supplier.
[93] *Teheran-Europe Co Ltd v. S. T. Belton (Tractors) Ltd* [1968] 2 Q.B. 545, CA.
[94] Sale of Goods Act 1979, s. 38(2).
[95] *Tellrite Ltd v. London Confirmers Ltd* [1962] 1 Lloyd's Rep. 236.
[96] *Cf*. Chap. 11.

Illustrations

27–022 Two illustrations of transactions in which the confirming agent was held to be personally liable to the supplier may be added. In *Rusholme*'s case[97] the plaintiffs, manufacturers in England, received in May 1951, through their Australian agents, orders for shirting material from an Australian importer; the orders provided "terms—confirmation and payment by" the defendants, a confirming house in London. The confirming house then ordered the shirting material from the manufacturers. The order stated "Purchased by [the confirming house], holders of Purchase Tax No. Central 2/3793 of goods as stock intended for export". There was nothing on the order to show that it had reference to another transaction except the words: "In confirmation of your agents' Indent No. 14". The order was accepted by the manufacturers by a letter of June 7 in these words: "We thank you for the above order for [name of the Australian importer] and have pleasure in confirming same herewith": then the terms of the contract were set out. Owing to an Australian trade recession before the delivery date the Australian importer cancelled the orders and the confirming house refused to accept delivery. Pearce J. found that the manufacturers would not have accepted the orders without the interposition of an English confirming house and held that the orders by the confirming house to the manufacturers constituted the true contracts between the parties and that the confirming house was liable to pay damages for non-acceptance of the goods. The learned judge said with respect to that order form:

> "The document means what it says, namely, that the defendants are assuming liability as between themselves and the plaintiffs. It would have been easy for the defendants to put a different wording in the document had the intention been otherwise. The defendants at first claimed that their wording 'Purchased by S. G. Read & Co. (London) Ltd.' was inserted on the compulsion of the Board or Trade as a condition of the defendants holding a purchase tax certificate; but in cross-examination Mr. Read had to admit that this was not so. He could have set out in terms that they were purchasing only as agents."

In *Sobell Industries Ltd v. Cory Bros & Co Ltd*[98] Sobell obtained a considerable order for radio sets from a firm in Istanbul and insisted on confirmation by Cory who, in addition to other activities, carried on the business of export merchants and shippers. Cory thereupon placed an order for the same goods in their own name with Sobell. The Turkish buyers accepted only part of the goods and the confirming house—Cory—likewise refused to accept the balance of the goods. The sellers successfully sued the confirmers for damages for non-acceptance of the goods. McNair J. founded his judgment on a very short point; he held that the contract was contained in the order by the confirming house to the sellers and that it was clear from that order that the confirming house acted as principal.

Whether an English confirming house is personally liable to a supplier in this country depends entirely on the terms of the contract between him and the confirming house. If the contract discloses an intention to constitute privity of

---

[97] *Rusholme & Bolton & Roberts Hadfield Ltd v. S. G. Read & Co (London) Ltd* [1955] 1 W.L.R. 146.
[98] [1955] 2 Lloyd's Rep. 82.

contract between these two parties, the confirming house is liable, but if the contract shows that privity of contract shall only be constituted between the customer and the supplier, the confirming house acting merely as agent of the customer, there is no liability on the part of the confirming house.

Confirmation by confirming house and by bank

It should not be thought that the confirmation by a confirming house has the **27–023** same effect as that by a bank in all circumstances. Where the confirming house merely adds its own confirmation to that of the customer,[99] this is true to a certain extent, although the confirming house gives shipping instructions to the supplier and the bank does not do so. But where the confirming house itself places the order with the U.K. supplier,[1] the position is fundamentally different. In this case the confirming house, in the words of McNair J.,[2] confirms "the contract as a whole". The confirmed credit has, thus, the merit of safety, in view of the financial status of the confirmer, but the acceptance of personal liability of the confirming house by way of a purchasing order has the additional merit of giving the seller protection in contingencies which are not purely financial.

The freight forwarder

The services of freight forwarders are of great value to those engaged in the **27–024** export trade, and particularly to small firms which do not possess their own export organisations and shipping department. Forwarders have a specialised knowledge of the intricacies of carriage by sea, air and land[3] and are, in particular, acquainted with the constantly changing Customs formalities at home and abroad, the rates and rebates of freight, the practices of sea and air ports, the groupage of sea or air cargoes in container transport[4] and the package and handling of export goods. They also undertake on occasion the inspection of goods[5] and the collection of debts from customers abroad.

The forwarder acting as principal or as agent

A forwarder may act as a principal or as an agent. Historically, forwarders acted **27–025** as agents on behalf of their customers[6] but the practice has changed and in modern circumstances they often carry out other services, such as packing, warehousing, cartage, lighterage, insurance, or, in container transport, the groupage or consolidation of parcels of various customers into one container. Often they

---

[99] See *ante*, para. 27–019.
[1] *ibid.*
[2] In *Sobell Industries Ltd v. Cory Bros & Co* [1955] 2 Lloyd's Rep. 82 at 89.
[3] The activities of forwarders in connection with the reservation of freight space for cargoes are described in para. 15–003.
[4] On container transport see Chap. 16.
[5] *PSA Transport v. Newton, Lansdowne & Co* [1956] 1 Lloyd's Rep. 121 (port dues and wharfage charges payable before release of the goods for inspection not included in agents' agreed charges and agents entitled to be reimbursed).
[6] For this reason they were known as forwarding agents.

act as carriers. It follows that, in law, they may qualify more often as principals than as agents. Nevertheless, it has to be ascertained in every individual case in which legal capacity the forwarder acted.[7] The answer depends on the construction of the contract between the forwarder and his customer and the facts of the case.

If the forwarder acts as the customer's agent, his duty is to procure with due diligence others who perform the carriage, storage, packing or handling of the goods. The customer, through the intermediaryship of the forwarder, enters into direct contractual relations with the others. In this case the forwarder is under the usual duties of an agent, unless they are modified by his contract with the customer. In particular, he is accountable to him, but, as will be seen, this duty is usually qualified by the trading conditions of the forwarder.

If the forwarder acts as a principal, he enters into a contract of services with the customer. He is the only person with whom the customer is in contractual relations, even though the actual services which the forwarder has undertaken are carried out by others. The profit which the forwarder makes, when contracting with the actual operators, is his own affair and he is not accountable for it to the customer.

The forwarder, when acting as agent, will often charge a commission, and, when acting as principal, an "all-in" price. However, the method of remuneration is not the decisive factor and not even an indicative guide. It is just one of the details which, in the factual matrix of the case, have to be taken into consideration. In modern practice a forwarder acting as agent may charge a fixed price, known as an uplift price, and, vice versa, a forwarder acting as principal may describe his remuneration as commission. In one case[8] Donaldson J. said: "The reference to a commission is equivocal" and held that, although the remuneration was described as commission, the forwarder had acted as principal.

The Standard Trading Conditions (1989 edition) of the British Institute of Freight Forwarders recognise that today the activities of the forwarder as principal and as agent are of equal importance.[9]

The capacity of the forwarder is particularly difficult to determine when he is instructed to arrange for the *carriage* of goods, and this is obviously the most frequent practical problem. The question here is whether the forwarder has acted as carrier, *i.e.* as principal, or as forwarding agent whose duty was only to procure carriage on behalf of the customer.[10] The difficulty is enhanced by the

---

[7] In *Cory Brothers Shipping Ltd v. Baldan* [1997] 2 Lloyd's Rep. 58 the forwarding agents who gave no notice that they were acting as agents were held personally liable for unpaid freight.

[8] *Salsi v. Jetspeed Air Services Ltd* [1977] 2 Lloyd's Rep. 57 at 60.

[9] See para. 16–010 where The Standard Trading Conditions are considered. BIFA's revised Standard Trading Conditions took effect in May 2000.

[10] *Per* Rowlatt J. in *Jones v. European & General Express Co Ltd* (1920) 90 L.J.K.B. 159 at 160. See also *Chas. Davis (Metal Brokers) Ltd v. Gilyott & Scott Ltd* [1975] 2 Lloyd's Rep. 422; *Elektronska Industrija Oour TVA v. Trqansped Oour Kintinentalna Spedicna* [1986] 1 Lloyd's Rep. 49 (defendants describing themselves as "full load and groupage services specialists to Yugoslavia— full loads to all European countries" held to have contracted as carriers within the CMR). See also, *passim, Sidney G. Jones Ltd v. Martin Bencher Ltd* [1986] 1 Lloyd's Rep. 54 at 64.

distinction drawn in modern international transportation Conventions[11] between the contractual and the actual carrier. The contractual carrier is a person who has contracted to move the goods from one place to another, although he does not carry out the transportation himself but leaves this task to the actual carrier with whom he has contracted. The CMR Convention, which deals with the international carriage of goods by road,[12] provides[13] that, where a carriage governed by a single contract is performed by successive carriers, each of them shall be responsible for the performance of the whole operation, and it has been held[14] that a forwarder who merely contracted to move the goods from one country to another was a carrier within the meaning of the Convention. But in other cases the courts held[15] that the forwarder had acted as agent. It is also possible for the forwarder to act in a "hybrid" character,[16] *e.g.* as a carrier for the land segments of the journey and as forwarding agent for the sea leg.[17] As already observed, it is always a question of construction of the contract and the facts whether the forwarder has acted as a carrier or as forwarding agent in a particular case. Bean J. expressed this conclusion, when observing[18] that "at the end of the day it was very much a matter for the trial judge whether forwarding agents were in fact acting as principals or agents."

The forwarder as bailee

If a dispute involving the forwarder as carrier cannot be resolved by reference **27–026** to the provisions of the international convention applying to the particular mode of transport[19] or the Forwarders' Standard Trading Conditions or other terms of the contract, it may become necessary to resort to the common law concept of bailment because the carrier, who has possession of the owner's (bailor's) goods, is undoubtedly the bailee of those goods. A bailment arises if a person (the bailee) has possession of another person's (the bailor's) goods by consent of the latter and undertakes to deal with them as directed by the bailor. The carrier,

---

[11] Guadalajara Convention of 1961 (air transport, see Chap. 17); CMR (road transport, see Chap. 18).
[12] Effect is given to this Convention in the U.K. by the Carriage of Goods by Road Act 1965, see Chap. 18.
[13] In Art. 34.
[14] *Ulster-Swift Ltd v. Taunton Meat Haulage Ltd* [1977] 1 Lloyd's Rep. 346; *Tetroc Ltd v. Cross-Con (International) Ltd* [1981] 1 Lloyd's Rep. 192.
[15] *Marston Excelsior Ltd v. Arbuckle, Smith & Co Ltd* [1971] 2 Lloyd's Rep. 306; *Hair & Skin Trading Co Ltd v. Norman Airfreight Carriers Ltd* [1974] 1 Lloyd's Rep. 443; *Motor Vespa SA v. Mat (Brittania Express) Ltd* [1979] 1 Lloyd's Rep. 175 at 179. In *Harlow & Jones Ltd v. P. J. Walker Shipping & Transport Ltd* [1986] 2 Lloyd's Rep. 141 Bingham J. held that the forwarders acted as agents, and not as principals, but that, in their capacity as agents, they had warranted that the freight would not exceed a stated sum, so that the risk of excess freight had to be borne by them.
[16] *Per* Beattie J. in *The Maheno* [1977] 1 Lloyd's Rep. 81, 86, 88, N.Z. See also *Burke Motors Ltd v. Mersey Docks & Harbour Co* [1986] 1 Lloyd's Rep. 155, 161–162.
[17] *ibid.*
[18] In *Hair and Skin Trading Co Ltd v. Norman Airfreight Carriers Ltd* [1974] 1 Lloyd's Rep. 443 at 445.
[19] See *ante*, para. 15–001.

the warehouseman and the goods repairer are typical examples of bailees, as long as they have the bailor's goods in their charge. The main duty of a bailee for reward was defined by Lord Denning M.R.[20] as the "duty to take reasonable care to keep [the bailor's goods] safe."

Difficulties arise, in particular, if the bailee, with the consent of the bailor, allows a sub-bailee to take charge of the bailor's goods. In *Transcontainer Express Ltd v. Custodian Security Ltd*[21] Duty Free Distributors (U.K.) Ltd, an English company, bought 400 cases of brandy from a French supplier in Machecoul. Duty Free contracted with Transcontainer to carry the brandy from Machecoul to Feltham in Middlesex. Transcontainers sub-contracted the leg of carriage from Dover to Feltham to Crossland Haulage Ltd. The warehouse in Feltham was not able to take delivery of the goods and the driver of Crossland took them to the East India Dock, where the defendants Custodian Security Ltd provided a security service. There the brandy was stolen. Transcontainer paid Duty Free £5,620.16 (exclusive of duty) by way of damages and the duty of £49,458.46 to Customs and Excise. Transcontainer claimed to recover these sums from the defendants Custodian, founding their claim on the tort of negligence. The Court of Appeal dismissed the action because, according to the principle in *Aliakmon*,[22] they were not entitled to sue in negligence since they were neither the owners of the goods nor did they have possession of them, but it was doubtful whether they had "an immediate right of possession" which would have given them a "possessory title"; as this question was not argued in the court of first instance, the Court of Appeal left this important point undecided. The sub-bailee is under the same duty to take reasonable care as the main bailee.[23]

A further problem is whether a defence available to the sub-bailee against the main bailee can be pleaded by him against the bailor. This question has to be answered in the affirmative if the sub-bailee is employed by the main bailee with the consent of the bailor. In *Singer Co (U.K.) Ltd v. Tees and Hartlepool Port Authority*[24] Singer contracted with J. H. Bachman (U.K.) Ltd to crate and deliver machines to U.K. ports; the machines were to be shipped from there to Brazil. Bachman took the machines to one of the defendants' docks for loading on the vessel *Serra Dourada* but in the loading process the machines were badly damaged. Singer claimed damages from the defendant port authority, which denied that its employees had been negligent. Bachman had acted as principal, and not as agent of Singer. The Court of Appeal held that Bachman had implied authority from Singer to employ the port authority for the loading of the machines; the limitation of liability provisions in the port authority's

---

[20] In *Morris v. C. W. Martin & Sons Ltd* [1966] 1 Q.B. 716, 726.
[21] [1988] 1 Lloyd's Rep. 128.
[22] See *ante*, para. 2–030.
[23] In *Metaalhandel J. A. Magnus BV v. Ardfields Transport Ltd* [1998] 1 Lloyd's Rep. 197, Metaalhandel, a Dutch company, asked the forwarder (Ardfields) to store some tungsten near London. Ardfields contracted with Jones Transport to store the goods in Ashfield, Middlesex. The goods were handed over by Jones's employee to an unauthorised person and disappeared. Although Ardfields never had possession of the goods they were held liable as "quasi-bailees" because they had failed to check the system of safeguarding applied by the sub-bailee (Jones).
[24] [1988] 2 Lloyd's Rep. 164.

(sub-bailee's) general conditions could be pleaded against Singer (the bailor), and these limitation provisions were reasonable and not invalid under the Unfair Contract Terms Act 1977. In the result, Singer's claim was dismissed.

In *The Pioneer Container*[25] the Privy Council held that where the owner gave **27–027** his consent to the carrier to sub-contract the carriage of goods "on any terms", this was wide enough to embrace consent to an exclusive jurisdiction clause, the incorporation of which would have been in accordance with reasonable commercial expectations and the sub-bailee could rely on it against the owner.[26]

The Privy Council also confirmed[27] that where goods have been sub-bailed with the authority of the owner, the obligation of the sub-bailee towards the owner was that of bailee for reward and the owner could proceed directly against the sub-bailee under the law of bailment, without having to rely on the contract of sub-bailment between the bailee and the sub-bailee.

Further duties of the forwarder

Further, where shipping agents were employed by importers for the clearance **27–028** of imports through Customs but, in the course of dealing with their customers, did not make Customs entries without specific instructions from their customers, they were held not to be liable for failing to make such Customs entries before the date when the import duty for the goods went up.[28] Where a freight charge quoted by a forwarder to his customers is based on the weight and measurement of the goods, the customers are liable to make additional payment to the forwarder, if he has to pay higher freight on the ground that the measurements of the goods are greater than originally stated.[29]

According to the custom of the London freight market, forwarders, who by request of their customers book freight space on board a ship, are personally liable for dead freight to the carrier, if the customers fail to load the goods and the ship sails with the space unfilled; in this case the forwarders are entitled to be indemnified by their customers.[30]

---

[25] [1994] 2 A.C. 324.

[26] Applying the *dicta* of Lord Denning M.R. in *Morris v. C. W. Martin & Son Ltdz* [1966] 1 Q.B. 716 at 729 (also applied at first instance in the *Singer* case *ante*); contrast *The Forum Craftsman* [1985] 1 Lloyd's Rep. 291, where the owners could not rely on an exclusive jurisdiction clause in their contract with the bailees against sub-bailees, since the sub-bailees were not party to that contract.

[27] *The Pioneer Container, ante.*

[28] *World Transport Agency v. Royte* [1957] 1 Lloyd's Rep. 381.

[29] *Brushfield Sargent & Co Ltd v. Holmwright Engineering Co Ltd* [1968] 1 Lloyd's Rep. 439. But the forwarder cannot claim additional freight when he has given a firm quotation without finding out whether the goods which he has undertaken to transport have any peculiar characteristics: *S. Zimmermann & Son Ltd v. Baxter, Hoare & Co Ltd* [1965] 1 Lloyd's Rep. 88. If, after a firm charge has been agreed, the forwarder demands a surcharge and this demand amounts in law to economic duress (a concept which English law recognises and which is much more severe than commercial pressure), the customer need not pay the surcharge: *Atlas Express Ltd v. Kafco (Importers and Distributors) Ltd* [1989] 3 W.L.R. 389.

[30] *Anglo-Overseas Transport Co Ltd v. Titan Industrial Corporation (United Kingdom) Ltd* [1959] 2 Lloyd's Rep. 152. Similarly, air agents who undertake personal liability are entitled to be indemnified by the customer, if the latter ought to have known that the air agents rendered themselves

Travelling Representatives Abroad

27–029 Another form of marketing is for an exporter to send travelling representatives abroad. Their task is to solicit orders from new customers or to maintain contact with already existing customers. They usually produce on their visits samples of their principal's goods or exhibit them in local showrooms. The customer who wishes to place a repeat order normally sends it directly to the principal's head office. Travelling representatives often visit their customers at regular intervals in order to show them a new range of samples.

Since the establishment of the Single Market in the E.C. in 1992, visits by travelling representatives in this regional "home" market may become more widely used than formerly. Generally speaking however, this method of marketing is not as effective as maintaining a permanent presence in the target territory, by independent distributors or self-employed agents, or, better still, by local branches or subsidiaries.

Travelling representatives and their luggage are subject to the laws of the overseas countries which they visit, and these laws vary greatly. Three points have to be borne in mind here: does the traveller require a licence when soliciting or accepting orders, are taxes payable by the principal in respect of the traveller's activities, and is Customs duty payable on the samples which he carries?

In most countries a business traveller representing a principal resident abroad does not require a Government licence when pursuing his activities. That is certainly true with respect to Member States of the E.C. which are visited by the travelling representative of a principal resident in another Member State, but it also applies in the case of U.K. travelling representatives visiting countries outside the E.C., such as Australia, New Zealand, Canada, the United States, Brazil and Peru. Only in some African and South American countries does such a travelling representative have to obtain a licence before engaging in business.

In some countries transient traders' taxes are levied on principals represented by travelling representatives. Sometimes these taxes are State and sometimes municipal revenues. They provide a serious obstacle to the free movement of international trade. The Conventions on relief from double taxation, which the U.K. Government has concluded with various overseas governments, aim at the exemption of U.K. firms from this form of taxation.

The Customs regulations of most countries provide special facilities for the importation of bona fide trade samples by travelling representatives. In some countries, samples which are of no commercial value are admitted free of duty. Generally, however, trade samples are liable to Customs duties, but it is often sufficient for a deposit to be paid to the Customs authorities. In other cases where the duty has to be paid, a refund or drawback is allowed when the samples are exported within a stated time, *e.g.* six or 12 months.

---

personally liable: *Perishable Transport Co Ltd v. Spyropoulos (London) Ltd* [1964] 2 Lloyd's Rep. 379.

CHAPTER 28

BRANCH OFFICES AND SUBSIDIARIES ABROAD—FOREIGN ACQUISITIONS

Often the most effective method of overseas marketing is the establishment of **28–001** a local branch or subsidiary in the country to which the exports are directed. The progressive intensification of international trade and, on the regional level, the establishment of a Single Market by the E.C. in 1992 favour this form of marketing. In many countries national corporations expand into transnational groups of companies,[1] sometimes of global dimension. The medium-sized exporter should not ignore this form of overseas marketing. He will often find that trading through overseas branches or subsidiaries opens new markets for his products, is profitable and contains a considerable growth element.

In the E.C. a national of a Member State, and this includes a company having its seat in it,[2] is entitled to establish agencies, branches or subsidiaries in any other Member State[3] and Article 43 of the E.C. Treaty provides that, within the framework of the Treaty, any restrictions of this right shall be abolished.[4] This freedom of establishment has been characterised by the European Court of Justice as "one of the fundamental principles of the Community".[5] The E.C.J. has also pointed out that the provisions of the Treaty guaranteeing this freedom are of direct application.[6] Consequently, national restrictions of this right are, in principle, invalid. The E.C.J. has also held[7] that Article 43 precluded legislation of a Member State whose effect was to deny a particular form of tax relief, where the majority of subsidiaries controlled by a holding company were estab-

---

[1] See "Groups of Companies", C. M. Schmitthoff and R. M. Goode, ed., Vol. 2 of the International Commercial Law Series, 1990.

[2] Art. 48 of the E.C. Treaty.

[3] Arts 43–48 of the E.C. Treaty; Treaty on Economic Union (Maastricht Treaty) Title II, Art. G(1).

[4] For a discussion of the right of establishment of companies see Case 81/87 *R. v. HM Treasury and Commissioners of Inland Revenue, ex p. Daily Mail and General Trust plc* [1988] 3 C.M.L.R. 713; in this case the E.C.J. held that the freedom of establishment did not entitle a national company to transfer its residence (the central management and control) from one Member State to another while retaining its status as a company incorporated under the legislation of the original Member State, and a provision in the tax law of the Member State of origin of the company requiring consent of the Treasury to such a transfer did not contravene the prohibition of Arts 43 and 48.

[5] In the *Daily Mail* case, *ante*. See also Case 270/83 *Re Tax Credits, E.C. Commission v. France* [1987] 1 C.M.L.R. 401 (tax credit discrimination against foreign E.C. branches and subsidiaries infringes Art. 43 and the risk of tax evasion could not derogate from the effect of Art. 43); Case 79/85 *DHM Segers v. Bestuur van de Bedrijfsvereniging voor Bank-en Verzekeringswezen, Groothandel en Vrije Beroepen* [1987] 2 C.M.L.R. 247 (sickness benefit could not be refused in the Netherlands to a director (who was a Dutch national) of a company incorporated in England on the grounds that the company was not incorporated in the Netherlands).

[6] In the *Daily Mail* case, *ante*.

[7] *Imperial Chemical Industries plc v. Colmer (Inspector of Taxes)* [1999] 1 W.L.R. 108.

lished in other Member States. This preclusion did not apply however, where the majority of the subsidiaries were established in non-Member countries.

BRANCH OFFICES AND SUBSIDIARIES ABROAD

The choice between branches and subsidiaries

28–002 The exporter who wishes to establish a permanent presence in an overseas country will ask himself whether it is more advantageous to establish a branch office in that country or to work through a subsidiary incorporated there. There is no general answer to this question and it depends on the circumstances of the individual case. Two matters have to be considered: first, whether the local legislation, particularly relating to employment, companies, taxation and foreign investment, is more favourable to one of these alternatives; and secondly, whether the exporter wishes to co-operate with local interests. In the latter case, if he does not wish to adopt the form of joint venture or another form of joint export co-operation, the form of a local subsidiary is preferable, though the exporter should aim at obtaining the control over it, *e.g.* by retaining the majority of votes. But even if he does not intend such co-operation, the preference may well be for a wholly-owned subsidiary.

The legal distinction between branches and subsidiaries

28–003 The decisive difference between these two types of business organisation is that the subsidiary has a separate and independent legal personality in the overseas country in which it is incorporated, but a branch office is merely an emanation of the exporter in the overseas country and, through it, he is himself present in that country.

A subsidiary which requires bank credit might be unable to offer sufficient security and the bank may ask for a guarantee by the parent company to secure the debts of the subsidiary.[8] No such guarantee is required in the case of a branch office, because its debts are automatically those of the head office.

A particular problem arises in the E.C. In this region some Directives aiming at harmonisation of the national company laws of the Member States impose strict requirements of disclosure and accountability on companies incorporated in them.[9] The national laws giving effect to these Directives apply to subsidiaries incorporated in a Member State and branches[10] of a company incorporated in another Member State or in a non-E.C. country. The Eleventh Directive assimilates the disclosure requirements of branches to those of subsidiaries.[11] As far as

---

[8] Sometimes, the bank will accept a "letter of comfort" from the parent company but normally such a letter does not constitute an obligation of the latter to be liable for the debts of the subsidiary: see *ante*, para. 3–012.

[9] Particularly the First (68/151), Fourth (78/660) and Seventh (83/349) Directives, see *Palmer's Company Law* (27th ed. (Looseleaf)), Vol. 3, Part 16. For text of Directives see the E.C.'s website: *www.europa.eu.int*.

[10] The Eleventh Directive.

[11] ss. 690A and Sched. 21A inserted in the Companies Act 1985 by the Overseas Companies and Credit and Financial Institutions (Branch Disclosure) Regulations 1992 (S.I. 1992 No. 3179).

U.K. law is concerned, the adoption of this Directive does not make a material difference, because a company incorporated outside Great Britain and having an established place of business in Great Britain has to register as an "oversea company" and, as such, has to give far-reaching disclosure.[12] However, its implementation now means that that there is a distinction between an overseas company's "place of business" and its "branch", although there is no definition of "branch" in the Directive.[13]

BRANCH OFFICES ABROAD

Jurisdiction over the head office

The difference between branches and subsidiaries abroad is also important if a **28–004** claimant in the overseas country, in which the permanent representation is established, wishes to commence proceedings against the exporter's enterprise. The jurisdiction of the courts in the overseas country is governed by the procedural law of those courts.[14] The considerations which may be relevant are indicated when the reverse case is examined, *viz.* the case of an overseas enterprise establishing a permanent presence in the United Kingdom.

The "oversea company" in the United Kingdom

If a company incorporated in a country other than Great Britain establishes a **28–005** branch office, *i.e.* a place of business, in this country, the company must register as an "oversea company" under the Companies Act 1985.[15] One of the requirements of the Act is that it shall deliver to the Registrar of Companies the name and address of a person resident in Great Britain and authorised to accept service of proceedings and notices on behalf of the oversea company.[16] In brief, the oversea company, which has established a branch office in Great Britain, can be sued in the English courts like any other person ordinarily resident here.

The subsidiary registered in this country of a company incorporated elsewhere will have its registered office either in England and Wales or in Scotland and

---

[12] Companies Act 1985, s. 691 *et seq.*; see *post*, para. 28–005.

[13] For the purposes of Art. 5(5) of the Brussels Convention on Jurisdiction and Enforcement of Judgments in Civil and Commercial Matters of 1968, the E.C.J. held that a branch was an entity whose place of business had the appearance of permanency and which could negotiate business with third parties who would nevertheless be aware that there was a legal link with a parent body: Case 33/78 *Somafer SA v. Saar-Ferngas AG* [1978] E.C.R. 2183; see *ante*, para. 22–021.

[14] If the overseas country is an E.C. or EFTA Member State and has given effect to the Brussels Convention, Art. 5(5) may be relevant. It provides that, as regards a dispute arising out of the operation of a branch, agency or other establishment, the courts of the place in which the branch, agency or other establishment is situated shall have jurisdiction; see *ante*, para. 22–021.

[15] s. 691 *et seq.*

[16] s. 691(1)(b)(ii). If the company has made default of this obligation, the document may be sent by post to its place of business (s. 695) for details see *Palmer's Company Law* (27th ed., *loc. cit*, Vol. 1, para. 2.517). An oversea company, which has duly nominated a person authorised to accept service, can be served with process on him even after it has notified the Registrar of Companies that it has discontinued to have a place of business in Great Britain: *Rome v. Punjab National Bank (No. 2)* [1989] 1 W.L.R. 1211, CA.

can be sued in the courts of these countries like any other company registered here.

Dealings between branches

28–006 Exceptionally, *e.g.* in string contracts[17] in the commodity trade, dealings between two branches of the same legal entity are treated like dealings between two separate legal entities, provided that these dealings are regarded in the trade as genuine trading transactions.[18] Foreign branches of banks are treated as separate from the head office, but this principle has its limits in that a judgment obtained against a foreign branch is enforceable against its head office in England.[19]

SUBSIDIARY COMPANIES ABROAD

28–007 The favoured form of intensive export marketing is the establishment of a subsidiary company in the country into which exports are directed.

The overseas subsidiary

28–008 The overseas subsidiary is incorporated under the law of that country. It possesses an independent and separate legal personality and enjoys in the country of its incorporation the same status as an indigenous trading corporation. The control of the overseas subsidiary is vested in the parent firm which, *e.g.* is resident in the United Kingdom. It is exercised by various means, such as holding a majority of shares in, or a majority of the voting power of, the subsidiary company, or by reservation of the right to appoint its directors or managers, but these examples are illustrative only and not exhaustive.[20]

The overseas subsidiary is capable of entering into the same contractual relations with the parent firm as can be entered into by every other enterprise trading in the overseas country. The relations between these two enterprises may be ordinary contracts of sale concluded on f.o.b., c.i.f. or other trade terms; or the parent firm may arrange a sole distribution agreement with the subsidiary, or employ it as its commission agent or resident representative abroad. The observations made elsewhere in this book in regard to these different forms of trading apply here, *mutatis mutandis*. The form of a subsidiary company is particularly well suited when several U.K. exporters combine in export marketing, or when a U.K. exporter associates with an overseas concern in the production or distribution of certain goods. The overseas subsidiary is, thus, the ideal trading instrument for joint ventures. In view of the wide discretionary powers permitted by

---

[17] A string contract is a series of contracts under which a dealer (A) sells goods to another dealer (B), and so on, possibly through the whole alphabet, and only the last in the series takes delivery of the goods. In the oil trade, these contracts are colloquially called "daisy chain" contracts: *Voest Alpine Intertrading GmbH v. Chevron International Oil Co Ltd* [1987] 2 Lloyd's Rep. 547.

[18] *Bremer Handelsgesellschaft mbH v. Toepfer* [1980] 2 Lloyd's Rep. 43, 47, 51 (the case concerned a soya meal transaction under a GAFTA form).

[19] *Libyan Arab-Foreign Bank v. Barbers Trust Co* [1989] 3 W.L.R. 314 at 332.

[20] *British American Tabacco Co Ltd v. Inland Revenue Commissioners* [1943] A.C. 335.

the company laws of most countries, it is not difficult to arrange the distribution of control in the subsidiary and the participation in its profits and losses in harmony with the agreement between its constituent members.

A different question is whether the parent company can be regarded as being within the jurisdiction of the court, by virtue of the subsidiary having its place of business there. As the parent and the subsidiary are two different legal persons, the question has, in principle, to be answered in the negative. Exceptionally, the courts are prepared to "lift the veil of corporateness", *e.g.* if it can be proved that the subsidiary acted as agent of the parent or was merely a sham or facade.[21] In addition, legislation may effectively provide for "lifting the veil",[22] particularly the taxing Acts, and the E.C.J. will do so in certain circumstances.[23]

The multinational enterprise

By establishing one or several subsidiaries overseas, the British parent company **28–009** becomes a multinational or, as it is sometimes called, transnational enterprise. Such an enterprise has been defined as "a combination of companies of different nationality, connected by means of shareholdings, managerial control, or contract and constituting an economic unit."[24]

On the international level no effective regulation of multinationals has yet been established. The United Nations have constituted two bodies, a Commission and a Centre on Transnational Corporations. Both have been operative since 1975. The aim is to produce a UN code of conduct of multinational enterprises. Many other UN organisations and agencies and regional groupings have also made proposals or published codes in this area.[25] The OECD first published Guidelines for Multinational Enterprises in 1976. These are reviewed every seven years. The current Guidelines were adopted on June 27, 2000.[26]

On the national level two legal problems arise with respect to multinational enterprises. First, the interests of the host country in which the subsidiary is formed may conflict with those of the home country in which the controlling company has its seat. If the United Kingdom is the host country, the Protection of Trading Interests Act 1980 enables the Secretary of State to prohibit the U.K. subsidiary of an overseas parent from complying with the directions of its parent, if he considers that compliance would damage the trading interests of the United Kingdom.[27]

---

[21] *Adams v. Cape Industries plc* [1990] Ch. 433; *Customs and Excise Commissioners v. Hare* [1996] 2 All E.R. 391 (where the veil was lifted in the case of companies used for criminal activities, in particular for large scale fraud). For "lifting the veil", see further *Palmer's Company Law (loc. cit.)*, Vol. 1, paras 2.1519 *et seq.* and *Halsbury's Laws*, Vol. 7(1), para. 93.

[22] *e.g.* Companies Act 1985, s. 227(1) (group accounts).

[23] *e.g.* under Arts 81 and 82 of the E.C. Treaty which concern Competition, see Chap. 29; Cases 6-7/73 *Instituto Chemioterapic Italiano SpA and Commercial Solvents Corp v. E.C. Commission* [1974] E.C.R. 223 where the parent and subsidiary were held to be one undertaking; see also *post*, para. 29–004.

[24] C. M. Schmitthoff, "The Multinational Enterprise in the United Kingdom", in *Nationalism and Multinational Enterprise*, H. R. Hahlo, J. Graham South and Richard W. Wright (eds.) (Sijthoff, Leiden, 1973), 24 *Essays*, 717.

[25] See D. Sauermann, "The Regulation of Multinational Corporations and Third World Countries", in *South African Yearbook of International Law*, Vol. II, 1985–1986, p. 55.

[26] See OECD website: *www.oecd.org*.

[27] See *ante*, para. 21–021.

Secondly, in some circumstances the veil of separate legal status of the various constituent companies of the multinational enterprise is pierced and the multinational is treated as an economic unit. In particular, in the competition law[28] of the E.C. the European Court has assumed jurisdiction[29] over a parent company incorporated in a non-Member State and having a subsidiary in a Member State, if that subsidiary "does not determine its behaviour on the market in an autonomous manner but essentially carries out the instructions of the parent company."[30]

The proposed European company[31]

28–010 The E.C. authorities have proposed since 1970 to create a new form of company, namely the European Company (société Européenne, societas Europea, SE). Since then the SE has been the subject of several draft and amended proposals and consultative documents. The latest is the Draft Regulation of April 1996, on which the Department of Trade and Industry produced a Consultative Document in 1997. One of the stumbling blocks was the requirement of worker participation and the Commission set up the Davignon Group to consider this matter. The Group produced its Report in May 1977. The Transnational Information and Consultation Directive, requiring that employees be informed and consulted through European Works Councils, was implemented by the Transnational Information and Consultation of Employees Regulations 1999 which came into force on January 15, 2000.[32] However, the Directive is limited to organisations having at least 1000 employees in Member States and at least two establishments in different Member States, each of which employs at least 150 workers.

According to the proposal, an SE may be formed by at least two companies having a branch or subsidiary in different Member States other than where either have their central administration. Companies whose head offices are outside the Member States may form an SE if the SE has its registered office in a Member State, provided it was formed under the law of that State and its link with it is "genuine" and "permanent". Provision is made for mergers. An SE must be a public liability company with a share capital of 100,000 Euros or more, registered in the Member State in which it has its head office and governed by the law of that state. At the time of writing the Commission's amended proposals are before the Council.[33]

OVERSEAS SUBSIDIARIES IN ENGLISH AND FOREIGN LAW

Overseas subsidiaries in English law

28–011 According to the U.K. Companies Act 1985 an overseas subsidiary of a British company is, in principle, treated in the same manner as if the subsidiary was incorporated in the United Kingdom.[34]

---

[28] Arts 81–82 of the E.C. Treaty, see Chap. 29.
[29] *e.g.* the *ICI* and *Commercial Solvents* cases, *ante.*
[30] In the *ICI* case, at 629.
[31] See *Palmer's Company Law*, *loc. cit.*, Vol. 3, Part 16.
[32] S.I. 1999 No. 3323.
[33] See the E.C.'s website: *www.europa.eu.int.*
[34] Overseas subsidiaries are sometimes promoted as partnerships, and not as companies.

The E.C. has issued various Company Directives affecting the relationship of parent and subsidiary companies. The Seventh Company Directive[35] deals with consolidated accounts and the Eighth Company Directive[36] with the qualifications and the position of auditors of companies of the accounting documents required by the fourth and seventh Directives.[37] The Companies Act 1989 amends and augments the 1985 Act and seeks, *inter alia*, to implement in the United Kingdom the Seventh and Eighth E.C. Company Directives. This legislation introduces, for the purposes of group accounts, the new concepts of parent and subsidiary undertakings (which are wider than those of holding and subsidiary companies in the unamended 1985 Act) and recasts the provisions of the unamended 1985 Act dealing with accounts and audit contained in Part VII of the Act, in order to make them conform with the requirements of the two E.C. Directives.[38]

The Companies Act 1985 provides[39] that a company shall be deemed the subsidiary of another (the holding) company if—

"(1) A company is a 'subsidiary' of another company, its 'holding company', if that other company—

(a) holds a majority of the voting rights in it, or
(b) is a member of it and has the right to appoint or remove a majority of its board of directors, or
(c) is a member of it and controls alone, pursuant to an agreement with other shareholders or members, a majority of the voting rights in it,

or if it is a subsidiary of a company which is itself a subsidiary of that other company."

The 1985 Act further provides for an extension of publicity of the company's affairs and lays down in particular that, as a matter of principle, group accounts shall be prepared by the holding company.[40] Group accounts have to consist of[41]:

"(a) a consolidated balance sheet dealing with the state of affairs of the parent company and its subsidiary undertakings, and
(b) a consolidated profit and loss account dealing with the profit or loss of the parent company and its subsidiary undertakings."

A parent company is exempted from preparing group accounts if it is itself a subsidiary and its immediate parent company is established under the law of an

---

[35] Directive 83/349.
[36] Directive 84/253.
[37] The Ninth Company Directive will deal with the conduct of groups of companies. Its Draft has not yet been submitted to the Council by the Commission.
[38] The sections of the 1985 Act most affected by the implementation of the Seventh and Eighth E.C. Directives are ss. 221 to 262A which have been amended and augmented by the Companies Act 1989.
[39] s. 736(1). These provisions are explained in s. 736A and a detailed treatment is contained in *Palmer's Company Law, loc. cit.*, Parts 6–9 and A1.
[40] s. 227(1).
[41] s. 227(2).

E.C. Member State, subject to certain provisos.[42] There are several exceptions to the obligation to include subsidiaries into the group accounts.[43]

Reference has already been made earlier to the Eleventh Directive and the disclosure requirements concerning branches. The Twelfth Directive[44] provides for single-member private limited-liability companies.

Overseas subsidiaries in foreign law

28–012   When it is intended to establish a subsidiary in an overseas country, the legal position in that country is an important factor to be considered, in addition to extra-legal factors, such as the political and economic stability of the country, the cost of labour, raw material and transport, the size of the market and the membership of the country to a regional trade group.

Broadly speaking, there are four branches of foreign law to which the U.K. exporter must give attention when deciding to form an overseas subsidiary; *viz.* the law relating to companies, employment, taxation and foreign investment. A detailed treatment of these topics is beyond the scope of this work, inasmuch as the foreign regulations change constantly. Obviously, the exporter has to obtain competent advice on the legal position in the overseas country in which he intends to set up a subsidiary. In the following, it is intended to indicate in a general way the different attitudes which legal systems may adopt in the areas mentioned.

Foreign company law

28–013   The principle of free registration of a company under the general laws of the country, without the requirement of a special Government licence, is recognised in many overseas countries. In another group of countries, Government permission has to be obtained for the formation of the company but can be refused only for specified reasons. In a third group of countries, a Government licence is required, which may be refused on grounds of administrative expediency and discretion.

Generally speaking, the laws of the Member States of the E.C.,[45] and many Commonwealth countries, do not restrict the participation of non-residents or foreign shareholders or directors. In other countries, however, whether industrially developed or in the course of development, legal restrictions exist.

A number of national laws impose restrictions on aliens on matters such as equity participation in a company or joint venture, ownership of land and mineral rights, or requirements that promoters, directors or managers be resident and/or nationals. In view of the changing economic conditions, it is not possible to make general statements as to the restrictions and requirements of individual countries. They have to be ascertained with the relevant authority of each coun-

---

[42] s. 228.
[43] s. 229.
[44] Directive 89/667.
[45] See *Company Law in Europe*, Thomas, ed., Butterworths (Looseleaf) for a country by country summary for setting up a company in Europe.

try in every individual case and they may vary in the country in question from case to case.

Foreign employment law

The laws of foreign countries often contain employee protection legislation. **28–014** Such legislation applies to a subsidiary incorporated in the country in question and controlled by aliens, in the same manner as to individual alien employers. The general trend of this protectionist legislation will be considered later in this Chapter.

Foreign tax law

The provisions of foreign tax law applying to overseas subsidiaries of British con- **28–015** cerns vary considerably in the various countries. It is obvious that the incidence of taxation is one of the major considerations when a decision is taken whether to set up a subsidiary in the target country. It is perhaps less obvious that what matters is not merely the legal regulation, but the realities of the tax position, and, in particular, the administrative discretion vested in the revenue authorities which, in many foreign countries, are not supervised by the ordinary courts. In some countries the revenue authorities have little discretion in the assessment and collection of taxes; in others a foreign enterprise is treated apparently or actually preferentially, because it is the policy of the country to attract foreign capital and it may be that, occasionally, the rates of taxation can be settled by negotiation before the foreign subsidiary is formed. In other countries, on the other hand, while the rates of taxation for foreign and domestic enterprises are the same and the law does not admit open discrimination, the practical effect of taxation is such that its impact is greater on foreign than on domestic enterprises and, from the practical point of view, a considerable degree of discrimination may result.

   Sometimes the operations of an overseas subsidiary attract taxation both in this country and in the country in which it is constituted. In these cases the question arises whether the exporter qualifies for double taxation relief in this country.

   In the United States, some States apply to branches or subsidiaries carrying on activities in the State the concept of "unitary business", *i.e.* they treat the branch or subsidiary and the parent as a unit and claim to tax the income of the whole enterprise, irrespective of whether it is earned inside or outside the State. The Supreme Court upheld a unitary tax imposed by California in 1983,[46] and even after the passing of the Outer Continental Shelf Act,[47] which, in principle, prohibits the application of State tax laws to the Outer Continental Shelf, admitted a unitary tax law imposed by Iowa.[48] This claim of extraterritorial application of tax law is a serious obstacle to the free flow of international trade.

---

[46] *Container Corporation of America v. Franchise Tax Board* 463 U.S. 159 (1983).
[47] 67 Stat. 29, 43 U.S.C. para. 1331 *et seq.* (1982 ed. and Supp. III).
[48] *Shell Oil Company v. Iowa Department of Revenue* (Supreme Court Opinion of November 8, 1988) see 57 L.W. 4001 (1988); in this case, which concerned Outer Continental gas, the court held that the Act was not applicable.

Foreign investment law

28–016 *National investment legislation.* Many overseas countries, which wish to develop their own industry with the help of foreign private investors, have enacted legislation granting special privileges to foreign interests prepared to transfer technology by building up an industry in the country in question, either on their own or in collaboration with local industrialists.

The investment privileges which national legislations normally provide, subject to many conditions and often not as generous as they appear at the first glance, relate to:

(a) *Exchange control regulations.* The investor is allowed to transfer home profits and to repatriate his invested capital and any capital gain.

(b) *Customs regulations.* Free entry or entry at a reduced rate is allowed for machinery required to set up or expand the new industry and sometimes also for the goods produced.

(c) *Relief from taxation.* Hereunder fall relief from, or preferential rates of, national or municipal taxation, stamp duties and similar imposts; such relief is normally limited to a specified "running in" period; and

(d) *Public credit facilities* whereby the investor may be eligible for grants or loans.

The developing countries are important potential markets for industrial goods, but it is only possible to take advantage of this potential if private investors in the developed countries are prepared to risk their capital and—more important than finance—to apply their knowledge and experience to the development of industries in those parts of the world. Here, the danger exists that the exporter, possibly after having been invited into the capital-importing country by favourable investments legislation and having sunk considerable capital into his subsidiary in that country, is threatened by expropriation.

Various measures have been adopted to alleviate this fear. In some cases Governments have undertaken in concession agreements or other contracts with foreign private investors not to expropriate their assets except in the case of overriding public interest and in that event to pay just and fair compensation without delay. However, these arrangements do not provide effective protection to the foreign investor. If they are broken by the Government which made them or—more likely—by its successor, the private investor is often helpless.

The general rules of international law at present afford little protection to the private investor. In the absence of an undertaking to the contrary, international law considers a sovereign State to be at liberty to carry out non-discriminatory measures of any kind in its own territory, including measures amounting to the expropriation of property of aliens, but in the modern view the expropriating State must pay the alien full, fair and speedy compensation. The English courts consider as effective an expropriation or nationalisation decree of a foreign country, the Government of which is recognised by the Crown, unless:

(a) the decree or order attempts to attach property situate outside the territory of the expropriating State;

(b) the decree is unenforceable under other rules of English private international law[49]; or

(c) the decree constitutes a breach of international law, *e.g.* a breach of an undertaking or obligation of that State.

Attempts have been made to extend the protection which international law provides for the private investor, by creating an international investments code, a multilateral Convention, the signatories of which would undertake definite obligations protecting foreign private investment in their countries. OECD countries commenced negotiations for a Multilateral Agreement on Investments in 1995. At the OECD Ministerial meeting in May 1999, the Secretary-General reported that a period of consultation and assessment took place in 1998 but that negotiations were no longer taking place.[50] Without international protection, manufacturers are often reluctant to invest capital in the building of factories in a less developed country, unless the investment is grant aided[51] or the political risk is covered by insurance. In the United Kingdom such cover might be provided by the Export Credits Guarantee Department.[52]

The settlement of international investment disputes

An attempt has been made to approach the protection of foreign investors from **28–017** the procedural angle, by providing machinery for the settlement of international investment disputes by means of arbitration. In 1965 a Convention on the Settlement of Investment Disputes between States and Nationals of Other States was concluded in Washington. The United Kingdom gave effect to it by the Arbitration (International Investment Disputes) Act 1966,[53] as amended.[54] This Act was considered earlier in the context of arbitration generally.[55]

The procedure under the Washington Convention is not the only method of settling international investment disputes by arbitration. The agreement under which the investment is carried out sometimes provides[56] that in the case of

---

[49] See *ante*, paras 21–023 to 21–026.
[50] OECD website: *www.oecd.org*.
[51] *e.g.* by a loan of the World Bank, a credit of IDA, or a grant from the European Development fund. See further *The Law of Financing and Payment in International Trade* (ed. Norbert Horn), Chap. 11, 1989 (Vol. 5 of *Studies in Transnational Economic Law*).
[52] See Chap. 20.
[53] The Convention entered into force for the U.K. on January 18, 1967 (Treaty Series No. 25/1967) Cmnd. 3255. The Convention has been extended to various overseas territories, etc. See S.I. 1967 Nos. 159, 249, 585.
[54] By the Evidence (Proceedings in other Jurisdictios) Act 1975, s. 8(2) and Sched. 2; the Administration of Justice Act 1977, s. 4 and Sched. 5; the Judicature (Northern Ireland) Act 1978, Sched. 5; and the Supreme Court Act 1981, Sched. 5.
[55] See *ante*, para. 23–027.
[56] Or the parties so agree when the dispute has arisen.

disputes an *ad hoc* arbitration tribunal[57] shall be constituted, or the dispute should be settled under the rules of the ICC Court of Arbitration.[58]

FOREIGN ACQUISITIONS

28–018   An enterprise which is cash rich or has a leverage facility[59] may consider expanding its export potential by acquiring a company established in an overseas country. It can then utilise the marketing outlets of that company for the distribution of its own products and need not build up a permanent representation from the beginning in that market.

The usual, and best, method of a foreign acquisition is that of an agreed take-over bid.[60] The bidding company will purchase the equity, or at least the majority of the voting shares, in the target company from its shareholders. The effect of this transaction is that the target company has become a subsidiary of the bidding company and the observations made earlier on subsidiary companies abroad[61] apply to the acquired company.[62]

If it is intended to establish a permanent representation abroad, in addition to the general considerations which have to be taken into account, two special areas of law have to be examined: the local law relating to take-overs and the competition law of the country in question.

The law relating to take-overs

28–019   Many countries have laws and regulations dealing with this subject. In the United Kingdom, if a foreign company makes a take-over bid on a company incorporated in this country, the provisions of the Companies Acts 1985 and 1989 have to be considered.[63] They apply to all types of companies, whether public or private companies. If the company to be acquired is a public company, the shares in which are traded at the International Stock Exchange, the provisions of the City Code on Take-overs and Mergers and the Rules governing Substantial Acquisitions of Shares, as well as the Regulations of the Stock Exchange, have to be taken into consideration.[64]

Since the mid-1970's there has been discussion concerning E.C. regulation of

---

[57] See *ante*, para. 23–006.

[58] See *ante*, para. 23–025.

[59] Leverage means financing an acquisition by means of capital borrowed from a bank. This is also called debt financing.

[60] If the target company is a public company, the shares of which are traded at a stock exchange, there may, of course, also be a hostile take-over.

[61] See *ante*, paras 28–007 to 28–008.

[62] There exist also other methods of foreign acquisitions, including mergers across borders. The Council proposal for the Tenth Directive on cross-border mergers of public limited companies aims to harmonise laws on cross-border mergers. The proposal has been sent to the European Parliament for its consideration: see E.C. website, *ante*. The E.C. Merger Regulation (Regulation 4064/89 as amended) came into force in September 1990.

[63] Particularly ss. 428 to 430F of the 1985 Act as substituted by the Financial Services Act 1986, s. 172, Sched. 12. These sections aim mainly at the protection of minority shareholders in the offeree company.

[64] See *Palmer's Company Law, loc. cit.,* paras 12.301 *et seq.*

take-over bids. The recent E.C. Commission Proposal for a Thirteenth Directive on Company Law Concerning Takeover Bids is appended to a DTI Consultative Document of April 1996. In June 1997, the European Parliament amended and supported the draft directive and an amended proposal was presented by the Commission in November 1997, which is being examined by the Council.[65] The U.K. Government remains opposed to it, although continuing to propose amendments.[66]

A U.K. company which wishes to acquire a foreign company needs to obtain expert advice on the acquisition law of the country in question. In addition, great care must be taken that a takeover bid does not infringe the relevant competition law.[67]

The Personnel Employed in Overseas Branches and Subsidiaries

A branch or subsidiary abroad is normally staffed by two types of employees **28–020** who work in co-operation, namely U.K. personnel which the exporter has sent abroad and local personnel. From the legal point of view, this distinction is important. The contracts of employment with the former type of employee will normally be expressly governed by English law and will thus have to satisfy the requirements of the English law of employment as well as of the law of the country in which the branch or subsidiary is situate, but the contracts with the latter type of employee have only to comply with the local foreign law, unless the parties have agreed that they shall be governed by English law, in which case only the mandatory provisions of foreign law apply.[68]

Arrangements between exporters and employees on overseas service vary widely, according to the nature of the goods intended to be exported and the circumstances existing in the country where the branch office is situated. Sometimes the U.K. executive has merely to supervise the staff of local sales agents and to assist them with his technical knowledge, but sometimes he is engaged in the marketing operations directly. In some companies it is usual to post rising young managers on foreign service for a limited period of time, to give them an opportunity of gaining experience and of proving that they are worthy of consideration for further promotion.

English employment law

The contract of service between a U.K. enterprise and an employee ordinarily **28–021** resident in the United Kingdom but posted on foreign service is normally governed by English (or Scots) law, because the contract will normally contain a choice of law clause to that effect. If there is no choice of law clause, the

---

[65] See E.C. website.
[66] *ibid.*, para. 16.435.
[67] See Chap. 29.
[68] See *ante*, para. 21–010; *Cf. Sayers v. International Drilling Co NV* [1971] 1 W.L.R. 1176 (Dutch company recruiting European personnel to work on oil rig; contract between Dutch employers and English employee governed by Dutch law).

governing law will be in accordance with the Rome Convention.[69] However two additional aspects have to be taken into account: first, the provisions of the British employee protection legislation, much of which cannot be contracted out, may apply; and secondly, in some overseas countries protective employee provisions, which are likewise of mandatory character, are also applied to employees who are not ordinarily resident in the country in question but have worked there for some time. Further, The Working Time Regulations 1998 as amended by the Working Time Regulations 1999,[70] which limit the working week to 48 hours, night shifts to eight hours and provide for three weeks' paid holiday per annum, may need to be considered.

As far as U.K. law is concerned, the Employment Rights Act 1996[71] as amended by the Employee Relations Act 1999[72] constitutes a comprehensive code containing provisions for the protection of employees working in Great Britain. It demands the delivery, to the employee, of written particulars of the terms of employment, prescribes minimum periods of notice for the termination of the contract of employment, contains provisions for unfair dismissal, redundancy payment, maternity pay and the right to return to work, and deals with other rights arising in the course of employment, such as, *e.g.* the right to have time off for trade union activities. It also secures to some extent the position of the employee in the insolvency of the employer.[73] The Race Relations Act 1976[74] and Sex Discrimination Act 1975 may likewise be relevant.

28–022   The Employment Rights Act 1996, s. 196, provides that certain maternity rights, unfair dismissal, time off for trade union activities, redundancy payment and protection against the insolvency of the employer do not extend to employees who ordinarily work outside Great Britain. However, by section 32(3) of the Employment Relations Act 1999, it is provided that section 196 "shall cease to have effect". Thus, there is now no legislative distinction between employees working in Great Britain and those employed to work abroad. However, for the U.K. legislation to apply "[t]here must be some proper connection with the U.K."[75]

The earlier Employment Acts also distinguished between those partly employed in Great Britain and partly abroad. This distinction has been abolished by the coming into force of section 32 of the 1999 Act.[76]

For jurisdictional purposes, the E.C.J. has held that where a contract of employment is performed in more than one E.C. State "the place where he habitually carries out his work" is the place where he has established the effect-

---

[69] See *ante*, para. 21–016.

[70] The Regulations extend only to Great Britain (s.1(2)). However, virtually identical legislation applies in other E.C. states.

[71] This is a Consolidation Act.

[72] As at June 6, 2000, the Act was largely in force.

[73] Employment Rights Act 1996, ss. 182–190.

[74] *Barclays Bank plc v. Kapur* [1991] 2 W.L.R. 401, CA. (Asian employees who had served with the bank in East Africa and opted for transfer to the U.K. alleged that the bank did not count their African service for pension purposes whereas they did so in the case of European employees. The House of Lords decided that the complaints related to "an act extending over a period" within s. 68(7)(b) of the Race Relations Act and accordingly the action was not time barred.)

[75] Minister of State McCartney, *Hansard* H.C., Vol. 336, ser. 131, col. 31.

[76] October 25, 1999.

ive centre of his working activities, or from which he in fact performs the essential part of his duties. That is where it is least expensive for the employee to sue his employer or defend proceedings against him by his employer.[77]

Restraint of trade clauses

A stipulation restraining the employee from trading after the termination of the **28–023** contract is invalid in English law if the stipulation is unreasonably wide in the area of application or in point of time, or covers more goods or kinds of transactions than is reasonable.

Foreign employment law

Free movement of employees in the E.C.

Where it is intended to employ U.K. personnel in an overseas branch or subsidi- **28–024** ary, the first question is whether that branch or subsidiary is established in another Member State of the E.C., or in a country which is not a member of the Community.

In the former case, the E.C. Treaty and the secondary legislation made thereunder apply. The Treaty provides valuable privileges for workers of the Member States of the Community.[78] It is laid down that progressively the free movement of persons shall be secured within the Community and discrimination based on nationality shall be abolished between workers of the Member States as regards employment, remuneration and other conditions of work and employment,[79] and men and women are entitled to equal pay.[80] Moreover, the Treaty provides that the restriction of the freedom of establishment of nationals of a Member State in the territory of another Member State shall be prohibited and states[81]:

> "... Such prohibition shall also apply to restrictions on the setting up of agencies, branches or subsidiaries by nationals of any Member State established in the territory of any Member State."

It follows that no discriminatory requirements can be imposed in any of the other

---

[77] Case C-383/95 *Rutten v. Cross Medical Ltd* [1997] E.C.R. I-57; *ante*, para. 22–019.
[78] The Treaty draws a distinction between persons in salaried or wage-earning employment who are described as workers and are given the freedom of movement, and self-employed person who have the freedom (or right) of establishment. Arts 39–42 apply to the former, and Arts 43–47 to the latter.
[79] E.C. Treaty, Art. 39.
[80] E.C. Treaty, Art. 141 and see *Pickstone v. Freemans Plc* [1987] 3 W.L.R. 811 where it was held that Art. 119 (now Art. 141) was directly applicable although the claim did not come within the Equal Pay Act 1970 as amended; see also Case C-218/98 *Abdoulaye v. Régie Nationale des Usines Renault SA, The Times*, October 20, 1999.
[81] *ibid.* Art. 43; see *Reyners v. Belgian State* [1974] 2 C.M.L.R. 305; *Van Duyn v. Home Office* [1975] 1 C.M.L.R. 1; *Van Binsbergen v. Bestuur van de Bedrijfsvereniging voor de Metaalnijverheid* [1975] 1 C.M.L.R. 298; *Thieffry v. Conseil de l'Ordre des Avocats a la Cour de Paris* [1977] 2 C.M.L.R. 373; *Patrick v. Ministre des Affaires Culturelles* [1977] 2 C.M.L.R. 523; *R. v. HM Treasury and Commissioners of Inland Revenue, ex p. Daily Mail and General Trust plc* [1989] 2 W.L.R. 908.

Member States of the Community against the employment of U.K. personnel in branches or subsidiaries of British enterprises, except if limitations are justified on grounds of public policy, public security or public health.[82]

The articles of the E.C. Treaty, guaranteeing employees the freedom of movement, like those guaranteeing enterprises the right of establishment, are "fundamental principles of the Community"[83] and any national prohibition or discriminatory measure infringing them is invalid.

Legislation pertaining to foreigners in non-E.C. countries

28–025   In the countries which are not Member States of the E.C., the business activities of U.K. citizens are governed by legislation pertaining to foreigners. The permission to enter the country does not, as a matter of course, imply the right to engage in business there. Such legislation varies greatly in different countries; the foreigner is usually required to obtain permission from a government department before allowed to commence business.

Foreign legislation protecting security of employment

28–026   It has already been noted that in many countries, including Great Britain, legislation exists which is aimed at the protection of the employee in the event of the termination of his service agreement, by providing that he shall be entitled to notice of a specified length or to compensation. However, the qualifying conditions, the periods of notice and the amounts of compensation frequently differ from those applicable in Britain.

The exporter is well advised, before entering into a service agreement with an employee in an overseas country, to ascertain whether such legislation is in operation in that country.

Of particular importance in this connection are the various national provisions dealing with unfair dismissal. The regulation of English law has already been indicated. The question whether the foreign legislation protecting security of employment can be contracted out by providing that the contract of employment shall be governed by English law is difficult to answer; it depends in every case on whether the foreign legislation in question is mandatory in character.

---

[82] Art. 39(3); see Case 41/74 *Van Duyn v. Home Office* [1974] E.C.R. 1337; *Roland Rutili v. French Minister of the Interior* [1976] 1 C.M.L.R. 140; Case 43/75 *Defrenne v. Sabena* [1976] E.C.R. 455. See also *Stanton v. INASTI* [1989] 3 C.M.L.R. 761 (person self-employed in one Member State and employed in another).

[83] The *Daily Mail* case, *ante*; and see Case 19/92 *Kraus v. Land Baden Wurtemburg* [1993] E.C.R. I-1663 on national restrictions relating to E.C. freedoms.

CHAPTER 29

THE COMPETITION LAW OF THE EUROPEAN COMMUNITY
AND OF THE UNITED KINGDOM

Among the tasks and activities of the European Community, the safeguarding **29–001**
of legitimate competition and the controlling of restrictive trade practices and
monopoly situations is of paramount importance. Such legal regulation exists
on two levels, that of the E.C. and that of the national laws of the Member
States. The former is of great practical importance to the exporter. The latter, as
far as the United Kingdom is concerned, is of lesser significance to those
engaged in international trade. However, when fully implemented, the competition law of the United Kingdom will mirror, significantly, the competition law
of the E.C. In this Chapter the competition law of the E.C. and then that of the
United Kingdom will be addressed.

THE BASIC PROVISIONS OF E.C. COMPETITION LAW

The basic provisions on competition are contained in Articles 81 and 82 of the **29–002**
E.C. Treaty, as amended by the Treaty of Amsterdam.[1] The former prohibits as
incompatible with the common market certain restrictive trade practices which
may affect trade between the Member States and have as their object or effect
the prevention, restriction or distortion of competition in the common market.
Agreements that fall within the prohibition and do not merit exemption under
Article 81 (3) are void (Art. 81(2)) and cannot be enforced in the courts of the
Member States.[2] Article 82 prohibits the abuse of a dominant position within
the common market, as far as it may affect trade between Member States. The
following is the wording of these two articles:

Article 81

"1. The following shall be prohibited as incompatible with the common market: all agreements **29–003**
between undertakings, decisions by associations of undertakings and concerted practices which
may affect trade between Member States and which have as their object or effect the prevention, restriction or distortion of competition within the common market, and in particular those
which:

---

[1] The whole chapter of the EEC Treaty on the Rules on Competition comprises Arts 81 to 86.
Treaty of Amsterdam 1997. For further reading: C. Bellamy and G. Child, *Common Market Law of
Competition* (4th ed., 1993 and 1997 supplement); Korah, *Competition Law; Cf.* 1999 E.C.L.R. 445.
For a well structured and comprehensive view see M. Furse, *Competition Law of the U.K. & E.C.*
(Blackstone Press, 1999). See *www.EUROPA.eu.int/EUR-LEX/en/dat.*
[2] See *Brasserie de Haecht v. Wilkin (No. 2)* [1973] C.M.L.R. 287; *BRT v. SABAM* [1977] 2 C.M.L.R
238; see Notice on Cooperation between National Courts and the Commission in applying Arts 81
and 82 [1993] O.J. C39/S. See also Case C-126/97 *Eco Swiss China Time Ltd v. Benetton International NV* [1999] C.L.R. 183: note the scheme of Art. 81 is likely to be altered from 2002.

(a) directly or indirectly fix purchase or selling prices or any other trading conditions;
(b) limit or control production, markets, technical development, or investment;
(c) share markets or sources of supply;
(d) apply dissimilar conditions to equivalent transactions with other trading parties, thereby placing them at a competitive disadvantage;
(e) make the conclusion of contracts subject to acceptance by the other parties of supplementary obligations which, by their nature or according to commercial usage, have no connection with the subject of such contracts.

2. Any agreements or decisions prohibited pursuant to this Article shall be automatically void.
3. The provisions of paragraph 1 may, however, be declared inapplicable in the case of:

— any decision or category of decisions by associations of undertakings;
— any concerted practice or category of concerted practices;
which contributes to improving the production or distribution of goods or to promoting technical or economic progress, while allowing consumers a fair share of the resulting benefit, and which does not;

(a) impose on the undertakings concerned restrictions which are not indispensable to the attainment of these objectives;
(b) afford such undertakings the possibility of eliminating competition in respect of a substantial part of the products in question."

Article 82

29–004   "Any abuse by one or more undertakings of a dominant position within the common market or in a substantial part of it shall be prohibited as incompatible with the common market in so far as it may affect trade between Member States. Such abuse may, in particular, consist in:

(a) directly or indirectly imposing unfair purchase or selling prices or other unfair trading conditions;
(b) limiting production, markets or technical development to the prejudice of consumers;
(c) applying dissimilar conditions to equivalent transactions with other trading parties, thereby placing them at a competitive disadvantage;
(d) making the conclusion of contracts subject to acceptance by the other parties of supplementary obligations which, by their nature or according to commercial usage, have no connection with the subject of such contracts."

These Articles are to be regarded in the light of the provisions of Part 1 of the Treaty, particularly Article 3(g) concerning the task of ensuring that competition in the Community will not be distorted. They are further amplified by secondary legislation[3] and other measures of the Community. They are interpreted by numerous decisions of the Commission and the European Court of Justice. It is clear from the foregoing that European competition law, while allowing broad exceptions, is strict and may expose an offender to heavy fines.[4]

The ambit of Community competition law is wide. The provisions place prohibitions on "undertakings", a word which is construed very widely to embrace all those entities which exercise an economic function, from the obvious, for example a corporation, to the obscure, a group of opera singers. Even inventors exploiting their inventions under a patent licence are "undertakings" within the

---

[3] Mainly founded on Art. 8 of the E.C. Treaty.
[4] Arts 15 and 16 of Reg. 17/62; see *ICI v. Commission* [1972] C.M.L.R. 557; *Re Polypropylene* [1986] O.J. L230/1. In Case 92/163 *Tetra Pak II* [1992] O.J. L72/1 the fine was ECU 75m. In Case 98/273 *Volkswagen* [1998] O.J. L124/61 a fine of ECU 102m. was imposed. These fines may of course be appealed against.

competition rules.[5] As to whether companies in the same group of companies could be treated as different undertakings for the purposes of Article 81, the case of *Viho Europe BV v. Commission of the European Communities (supported by Parker Pen Ltd, intervener)*[6] is of some assistance. The case concerned whether a company and its subsidiaries together form a single economic unit. The Sixth Chamber of the Court of Justice determined that the decisive factor was the degree of autonomy, in deciding their own course of action, which the subsidiary enjoyed. If the company and subsidiaries were to be treated as a single entity, they could not enter arrangements in breach of Article 81, although they could fall foul of Article 82.

Article 81 catches a concerted practice, which has been defined as a form of coordination between undertakings ". . . which, without having reached the stage where an agreement properly so called has been concluded, knowingly substitutes practical cooperation between them for the risks of competition."[7] Parallel behaviour, such as identical price increases, is not sufficient to prove concerted behaviour, conscious parallelism is. Activity wherein undertakings show sensitivity to the marketing practices of their competitors may not be regarded as concerted. To determine whether behaviour is to be regarded as concerted the Commission will analyse the prevailing market structure.

Article 81 applies to horizontal as well as vertical arrangements,[8] market-sharing agreements,[9] price-fixing agreements,[10] agreements with exclusive dealers,[11] forms of co-operation, joint ventures,[12] and patent,[13] trade mark,[14] franchising agreements,[15] copyright[16]; or licensing agreements.[17] Community competition law applies to the supply of services as well as goods.[18] Agreements with indirect effect on competition are also caught, such as agreements to exchange detailed information about prices, customers, turnover, capacity avail-

---

[5] An undertaking "encompasses every entity engaged in economic activity, regardless of legal status and the way in which it is financed": *Hofner and Elser v. Macrotron GmbH* [1993] 4 C.M.L.R. 306.

[6] C-73/95 [1996] E.C.R. 1–5457; [1997] All E.R. (E.C.) 163.

[7] *ICI v. Commission* [1972] C.M.L.R. 557.

[8] *De Geus v. Bosch* [1962] C.M.L.R. 1; *Consten and Grundig v. Commission* [1966] C.M.L.R. 418; *ICI, ante.* Although Reg. 2790/99 will exempt vertical agreements and concerted practices from the provisions of Art. 81(1): [1999] O.J. L336. Horizontal agreements are those which are concluded between undertakings at the same level of production whereas vertical agreements refer to those in which parties are at differing levels of supply or production and the affected competition is between them and third parties.

[9] *Re Polypropylene* [1988] O.J. L230/1; *Dunlop* [1994] E.C.R. II-441.

[10] *Distillers Co v. E.C. Commission* [1980] 3 C.M.L.R. 121.

[11] *Re Pioneer Hi-Fi* [1980] 1 C.M.L.R. 457; *Hasselblad (GB) v. E.C. Commission* [1984] 1 C.M.L.R. 559; Cases 25 and 26/84 *Ford Werke AG v. Commission* [1985] 3 C.M.L.R. 528.

[12] *Re Rockwell/Iveco* [1983] 3 C.M.L.R. 709.

[13] *Re Davidson Rubber Co* [1972] C.M.L.R. D52.

[14] *Sirena SRL v. Eda SRL* [1971] C.M.L.R. 260; *Van Zuylen Freres v. Hag AG* [1974] 2 C.M.L.R. 127.

[15] Case 161/84 *Pronuptia de Paris GmbH v. Schillgalis* [1986] 1 C.M.L.R. 414 but see later Regulation 4087/88. See 29–016.

[16] *Deutsche Grammophon GmbH v. Metro-SB-Grossmarkte GmbH & Co KG* [1971] C.M.L.R. 631.

[17] See *Nungesser v. Commission* [1982] E.C.R. 2015 to examine the E.C.J.'s treatment of this area of E.C. law. See 29–015.

[18] *Verband der Sachversicherer eV v. E.C. Commission* [1987] E.L.R. 265 on insurance.

able, etc.[19] Even the acquisition of shares in order to influence the commercial conduct of a competitor may be within the prohibition of Article 81(1).[20]

Articles 81(1) and (2) and 82 have direct effect and therefore are to be applied in the national jurisdiction. Indeed, the European Court of Justice (E.C.J.) has ruled that national judges are bound to apply E.C. competition law whether or not the matter has been raised by the parties themselves.[21] An agreement which is prohibited by Article 81(1) is void by virtue of Article 81(2) unless it has been duly notified and thus gained provisional validity until it is decided whether it is a prohibited agreement and, if so, whether it falls under an exemption within Article 81(3). A non-notifiable agreement is valid. If an agreement is void because it is prohibited by Article 81(2), the question arises whether the offending clauses can be severed from the other clauses of the agreement. It is thought that this should be possible unless the severance would change the whole character of the agreement. In English law an infringement of Article 81 or 82 may give rise to an action for compensation by a person who suffered loss as the result of such infringement.[22]

In principle, the prohibitions of Articles 81 and 82 apply only to arrangements which may affect trade between the Member States. The concept of trade needs comment here for two reasons. Trade includes within its definition all commercial activity within the community whether of manufacture or the provision of services, such as banking, insurance and the provision of satellite time for broadcasting. Trade also encompasses trade with countries in the European Economic Area such as Norway, Iceland and Liechtenstein and other states with which the Community has concluded association agreements. This appears to exclude from the application of Community law arrangements operative only outside the Community[23]; or only inhibiting exports to countries outside the Community.[24] On the other hand, an arrangement restricted to one Member State might affect trade between Member States and be caught by Article 81(1) because it might hinder the economic penetration of the national market by competitors from other Member States.[25] Consequently, an arrangement operative only within one Member State is subject to Community law if it obstructs the importation of the goods in question into that country from the other Member States or otherwise affects imports and exports between the Member States. Further, in certain circumstances the competition law of the Community claims to have extra-territorial effect.[26] Of paramount interest to the exporter is the

---

[19] *Re Cobelyn* [1977] 2 C.M.L.R. D28; *Re Fatty Acids* [1987] O.J. L311/7.

[20] *British-American Tobacco Co Ltd v. E.C. Commission* [1988] 4 C.M.L.R. 24.

[21] *BRT v. SABAM* [1974] 2 C.M.L.R. 238; *Garden Cottage v. Milk Marketing Board* [1984] A.C. 130, HL, where an alleged breach of Art. 86 (now 82) was held to be the alleged breach of a statutory duty in the United Kingdom. See also *Eco Swiss China Time Ltd. v. Benetton International NV, supra,* n.2.

[22] *Garden Cottage Foods Ltd v. Milk Marketing Board* [1984] A.C. 130, HL.

[23] *Rieckermann/AEG-Elotherm* [1968] C.M.L.R. D78.

[24] *Bulk Oil (Zug) AG v. Sun International (No. 2)* [1986] 2 C.M.L.R. 732.

[25] *Vereiniging van Cementhandelaren v. E.C. Commission* [1973] C.M.L.R. 7; Case 123/83 *Bureau National Interprofessionnel du Cognac v. Clair* [1985] 2 C.M.L.R. 430.

[26] See *ICI ante,* n.7 and *Re Woodpulp Cartel* [1988] 4 C.M.L.R. 901.

prohibition by European Community Law of restrictions on parallel imports or exports.

Agreements prohibiting parallel exports or imports

Article 81(1) prohibits in principle clauses under which a supplier imposes on **29–005** an exclusive dealer an obligation not to supply goods—the subject-matter of the exclusive dealing agreement—outside the assigned territory to another part of the E.C. An obligation not to import such goods is also similarly prohibited. Thus, in *Consten and Grundig v. Commission*[27] the German company Grundig appointed the French company Consten its sole dealer for France, the Saar and Corsica with respect to Grundig products. The agreement contained a clause according to which Consten undertook not to sell articles liable to compete with Grundig products and not to export the goods to which the contract related directly or indirectly to other countries. Grundig had imposed similar restrictions on the sole concessionaires in other countries, including Germany. Consten was permitted to register and use in France the trade mark GINT which was carried by all goods manufactured by Grundig. Another French company, UNEF, bought Grundig products from German dealers and sold them in France more cheaply than the goods marketed by Consten. Consten commenced proceedings against UNEF in the French courts and the matter was referred to the E.C.J. The E.C.J. held that the restrictions on exports and imports imposed on Consten and the other sole concessionaires of Grundig infringed Article 81(1). The same decision was given with respect to the exercise and use of the trade mark GINT in France because that industrial property right was, in effect, used to create an artificial national division of the Common Market.

The Commission thus relies on the possibility of parallel imports to reduce national price differences. It hopes that where price differences are great it will pay someone to buy in the low priced market and sell in the higher. Restraints on exports or imports are so inimical to the Common Market that few have been exempted under Article 81(3). In "The Distillers Co. Ltd Case"[28] Distillers' conditions of sale for U.K. trade customers prohibited these customers from selling outside the United Kingdom whisky and other liquor produced by Distillers. The effect of this prohibition was that Distillers could operate a double pricing policy, enabling them to charge less for the same brand of liquor in the United Kingdom than in the other E.C. countries. The Commission held that Distillers' conditions of sale for United Kingdom trade customers infringed Article 81(1) and refused to declare the provision inapplicable under subsection (3) of that Article. It would appear, however, that in reaching their conclusion in this case, the Commission had failed to make a thorough appraisal of the facts, as the Court in *Grundig/Consten* had emphasised they should. The promotional needs in the several markets were very different.[29]

---

[27] [1966] C.M.L.R. 418. See *Centrafarm BV v. Sterling Drug Inc* [1974] 2 C.M.L.R. 480; Case 266/87 *R. v. Pharmaceutical Society of Great Britain* [1989] 2 C.M.L.R. 751 (U.K. legislation prohibiting pharmacists to supply equivalent imported medicines, if doctor prescribes a proprietary brand, valid).
[28] [1978] 1 C.M.L.R. 400. *A. Bulloch and Co and others v. The Distillers Company Ltd.*
[29] See *ante*, n. 28.

In *BASF-Accinauto*[30] a dealer in BASF paints had an agreement with BASF that should he receive any orders from outside his territory, he would refer them to BASF. The purpose was that BASF could then have the order dealt with by the appointed dealer in the territory of the party making the order. It was determined that the overall effect of such an agreement, with which the dealer did not always comply, was to prevent parallel imports.[31]

In the case of standard conditions agreed upon by a manufacturer with exclusive dealers who have special technical qualifications, the Commission may insist that clauses prohibiting the import and export to another Member State must be removed but will then approve the conditions.[32]

Regulation 17/62

29–006 The procedure for the application of Articles 81 and 82 is set out in Council Regulation 17 of 1962, as amended.[33] In general, agreements, decisions and concerted practices of the kind described in Article 81(1) must be notified to the Commission[34] and failure to notify, intentionally or negligently, may expose the offender to heavy fines.[35] There are exceptions from the duty to notify but in the excepted cases the arrangement may be notified at the discretion of the parties.[36] Each party to an arrangement described in Article 81(1) is entitled to notify the Commission.

For the purposes of Articles 81 and 82, an undertaking which is resident in a non-Member State but has in a Member State a subsidiary which must act according to its instructions, is regarded as being resident in the Common Market because it forms an economic unit with the subsidiary.[37] Conversely, a wholly-owned subsidiary which enjoys no real autonomy in the market is regarded as being part of the same economic unit as its parent company and agreements between those two companies do not fall within the ambit of Article 81(1).[38] If, however, the subsidiary is to some extent autonomous, it will be treated as a separate undertaking.[39] Furthermore, an undertaking established in a non-Member State which is a party to an agreement that may have effect in the Common Market is subject to the jurisdiction of the

---

[30] Case 95/477 *BASF Lacke-Farbon AG and Accinauto SA* [1995] O.J. L272/17.
[31] See *Consten, ante.*
[32] *Re Kodak* [1970] C.M.L.R. D19; *Re Omega* [1970] C.M.L.R. D49.
[33] Regulation 17/62 was supplemented by Regs 27/62, 99/63, 118/63, 1133/68, 2822/71, 1699/75.
[34] Regulation 17/62, Arts 4 and 5.
[35] *ibid.* Art. 15(2) see n. 4 *ante.* See 98/C 9/03 *Guidelines on the method of setting fines imposed pursuant to Art.15(2) Regulation No. 17 and Article 65(5) of the Treaty.*
[36] Regulation 17/62, Art. 4(2). An agreement which could appreciably affect imports or exports cannot benefit from the exception: *IAZ International Belgium v. E.C. Commission* [1984] 3 C.M.L.R. 276.
[37] *ICI v. Commission* [1972] C.M.L.R. 557; *Commercial Solvents Corpn v. Commission* [1974] 1 C.M.L.R. 309 (the *Zoja* case).
[38] *Re Christiani and Nielsen* [1970] C.M.L.R. D19.
[39] *Eurim Pharm GmbH v. Johnson & Johnson* [1981] 2 C.M.L.R. 287; *Viho Europe v. Commission, ante.*

Community authorities.[40] In these respects the Community authorities claim extraterritorial jurisdiction.[41]

The control of restrictive arrangements in E.C. competition law

The prohibitions of Article 81(1) are worded very widely. Their unmitigated **29–007** application would lead to results which are unacceptable to the trade in the Community. For this reason Article 81(3) authorises the Commission to grant exemption from the prohibitions of Article 81(1), subject to certain conditions. These exemptions may be individual exemptions, which can be obtained by applying for a declaration of inapplicability of Article 81(1); or they may be block exemptions, which apply to a whole class of commercial activities.

Negative clearance and declaration of inapplicability

If an undertaking considers that the arrangement to which it is a party is outside **29–008** the prohibition of Article 81(1) and wishes to obtain official confirmation of that view, it can apply to the Commission for negative clearance which, however, is only granted "on the basis of the facts in its possession".[42] If the agreement falls within Article 81(1) but the conditions of Article 81(3) regarding exemptions are satisfied, the Commission, on the application of a party, can grant a declaration of inapplicability of Article 81(1).[43] This can only be done when the arrangement is duly notified.[44] Given the small numbers of formal decisions taken by the Commission, the more likely outcome is a "comfort letter" from the Commission telling the parties either that, in its view, the arrangement is not caught by Article 81(1) or that it is likely to satisfy the criteria for exemption under Article 81(3), and that it is closing its file. Before doing this, it may ask the parties to abrogate certain anti-competitive provisions in their agreement. It is proposed to discontinue the use of comfort letters from 2002.

A case in which the Commission formally refused to grant a declaration of inapplicability of Article 81(1) concerned the British Net Book Agreement entered into by British publishers and aimed at collective retail price maintenance for books.[45] The decision of the Commission applied to the extent that trade between Member States was affected by the Agreement. The decision was noteworthy because the Net Book Agreement was one of the few arrangements

---

[40] *Beguelin Import v. SAGL Import-Export SA* [1972] C.M.L.R. 81; *Re Pittsburgh Corning Europe-Formica-Belgium-Hertel* [1973] C.M.L.R. D2; *Re Wood Pulp Cartel: A. Ahlstrom OY* [1988] 4 C.M.L.R. 901.
[41] *Re Wood Pulp, ante* at 915 for basis of the E.C.J. judgment.
[42] Regulation 17/62, Art. 2.
[43] It may, however, require the parties to modify their agreement. This can have unfortunate consequences when one of the parties is no longer able to negotiate with the other from a position of strength. This consideration, it is believed, has sometimes led parties to run the risk of a fine rather than notify.
[44] *Distillers Company v. E.C. Commission* [1980] 3 C.M.L.R. 121; *Zinc Cartel* [1984] O.J. L220/17.
[45] Commission decision of December 13, 1988; see [1989] 4 C.M.L.R. 87.

upheld by the U.K. Restrictive Practices Court.[46] The notification of an arrangement and applications for negative clearance or inapplicability of Article 81(1) are made on combined form A/B.[47]

Measures providing block exemption and notices

29–009 In order to eliminate obviously innocuous arrangements, the Community made use of its powers under Article 81(3) to declare inapplicable the prohibition of Article 81(1) to certain categories of arrangements, in brief, to grant them block exemptions. It also published notices specifying agreements which in its view did not fall within Article 81(1). The most important of these exemptions, for exporters, relate to exclusive agency contracts, exclusive distribution agreements, exclusive purchasing agreements, patent licensing, specialisation agreements and research and development agreements. The Commission has also issued notices declaring its policy on co-operation agreements and agreements of minor importance. These measures require individual consideration.

Agreements of minor importance

29–010 The Commission stated as early as in 1964[48] that an agreement did not infringe the prohibition of Article 81 if it did not distort the Common Market to an "appreciable" extent. By subsequent notices,[49] the Commission has sought to attach a concrete meaning to the term "appreciable". In its Notice on Agreements of Minor Importance,[50] it reasserts its desire "to facilitate co-operation between undertakings where such cooperation is economically desirable without presenting difficulties from the point of view of competition policy".[51] The Notice then provides that an agreement is not regarded as infringing Article 81(1) if it satisfies the following test:

> "9. The Commission holds the view that agreements between undertakings engaged in the production or distribution of goods or in the provision of services do not fall under the prohibition in Article 81(1) if the aggregate market shares held by all of the participating undertakings do not exceed, on any of the relevant markets:
>
>> (a) the 5% threshold, where the agreement is made between undertakings operating at the same level of production or of marketing ('horizontal' agreement);
>> (b) the 10% threshold, where the agreement is made between undertakings operating at different economic levels ('vertical' agreement)."

---

[46] The RPC has been abolished by the Competition Act 1998; see *post*, para. 29–020 *et seq.*
[47] The most recent version of the form is founded on Commission Reg. 3385/94 [1994] O.J. L377/28.
[48] In *Grossfillex-Fillistorf* [1964] C.M.L.R. 237. In *Volk v. Etablissements Vervaecke SPRL* [1969] C.M.L.R. 273 the European Court held that an agreement may escape the prohibition of Article 85(1) if the position of the parties was too weak to influence trade between the Member States.
[49] See 97/C/ 372/04 *Notice on agreements of minor importance which do not fall within the meaning of Article 81(1) of the Treaty establishing the European Community.* A Notice of the Commission is a declaration of policy on the part of the Commission; it does not prevent the European Court from interpreting Art. 81 differently.
[50] See n. 49, *ante.*
[51] The previous notice is to be found in [1986] O.J. C231/2.

Where there is a mixed agreement or one difficult to classify as horizontal or vertical the 5 per cent threshold applies. By Article 10 an excess by no more than one tenth in the market shares stated in Article 9 above in the course of two successive financial years is deemed not to fall foul of Article 81(1).

Exclusive agency contracts

By an Announcement of December 24, 1962 on Exclusive Agency Contracts **29–011** made with Commercial Agents[52] the Commission indicated that in certain circumstances restrictive provisions in agreements between principals and agents do not fall within Article 81. This applies only to dependent agents who accept no financial risk, do not act as independent dealers for other suppliers, and who are prepared to take detailed instructions from their principals.[53] Such an agent may be treated as an auxiliary organ, forming an integral part of the principal's business.[54] The definition of an agent by the Commission is closer to that used in the common law than to that in the European continental countries. The Commission understands by an agent a person who has acted on behalf of a principal, and regards it as irrelevant whether he has acted in the name of the principal or in his own name, provided that he does not accept the financial risk of the transaction.[55] The Announcement states:

> "The Commission regards as the decisive criterion, which distinguishes the commercial agent from the independent trader, the agreement—express or implied—which deals with responsibility for the financial risks bound up with the sale or with the performance of the contract. Thus the Commission's assessment is not governed by the way the 'representative' is described. Except for the usual del credere guarantee, a commercial agent must not, by the nature of his functions, assume any risk resulting from the transaction. If he does assume such risks his function becomes economically akin to that of an independent trader and he must therefore be treated as such for the purposes of the rules of competition.
>
> An intermediary is regarded as an independent dealer, and not an agent within the meaning of the Announcement, if he—
>
> > is required to keep or does in fact keep, as his own property, a considerable stock of the products covered by the contract, or
> > is required to organise, maintain or ensure at his own expense a substantial service to customers free of charge, or does in fact organise, maintain or ensure such a service, or
> > can determine or does in fact determine prices or terms of business."

The leading case in this area is *Eirpage*[56] where non exclusive agents were appointed to market a paging system. The agency agreements were notified and after some amendments insisted on by the Commission exemption was granted. The agreements included, among other matters, the freedom for the agent to promote their own services before that of Eirpage, no absolute obligation to

---

[52] The Announcement is published in J.O. of December 24, 1962, 139/2921.
[53] *Pittsburgh Corning (Europe)* [1973] C.M.L.R. D2 and D7-8; *Suiker Unie* [1976] 1 C.M.L.R. 295.
[54] See Bellamy and Child, *Common Market Law of Competition, loc cit.*
[55] The only financial risk which he may assume is the *del credere* risk; on del credere agents, see *ante*, para. 27–016.
[56] [1991] O.J. L306/22.

Eirpage rather a freedom to promote their own interests and no obligations not to compete after the termination of the agreement.

Exclusive distribution agreements

29–012   A block exemption, Regulation 1983/83 of the Commission,[57] exempts certain exclusive distribution agreements from the prohibition of Article 81(1). This regulation is limited in time; the exemption was originally granted only until December 31, 1997 but was extended to December 31, 1999.

The Regulation exempts the agreements[58] to which only two undertakings are a party and whereby one party agrees with the other to supply certain goods for resale within the whole or a defined area of the Common Market[59] only to that other. Certain additional clauses may be included in the exempt agreement. The most important of them are[60]:

> "(a) the obligation not to manufacture or distribute goods which compete with the contract goods;
> (b) the obligation to obtain the contract goods for resale only from the other party;
> (c) the obligation to refrain, outside the contract territory and in relation to the contract goods, from seeking customers, from establishing any branch and from maintaining any distribution depot".

The exemption is available notwithstanding that the exclusive distributor undertakes all or any of the following obligations in accordance with Article 2(3):

> "(a) to purchase complete ranges of goods, or minimum quantities;
> (b) to sell the contract goods under trade marks, or packed and presented as specified by the other party;
> (c) to take measures for promotion of sales, in particular:
>
> — to advertise
> — to maintain a sales network or stock of goods
> — to provide customer and guarantee services
> — to employ staff having specialised or technical training."

On the other hand, an exclusive distribution agreement is not exempt in the following cases where[61]:

> "(a) manufacturers of identical goods or of goods which are considered by users as equivalent in view of their characteristics, price and intended use enter into reciprocal exclusive distribution agreements between themselves in respect of such goods;
> (b) manufacturers of identical goods or of goods which are considered by users as equivalent in view of their characteristics, price and intended use enter into a non-reciprocal exclusive distribution agreement between themselves in respect of such goods unless at least one of them has a total annual turnover of no more than 100 million ECU;

---

[57] [1983] O.J. L173/1 corrected by O.J. [1983] L281/24 and amended by [1995] O.J. L1/1. See Korah, "Exclusive Dealing Agreements in the EEC" (1984) ELC; also [1984] 21 C.M.L.R. 53.
[58] See para. 29–004.
[59] Reg. 1983/83. Art. 1.
[60] *ibid.* Art. 2(1).
[61] *ibid.* Art. 3.

(c) users can obtain the contract goods in the contract territory only from the exclusive distributor and have no alternative source of supply outside the contract territory;

(d) one or both of the parties makes it difficult for intermediaries or users to obtain the contract goods from other dealers inside the common market or, in so far as no alternative source of supply is available there, from outside the common market, in particular where one or both of them:

1. exercises industrial property rights so as to prevent dealers or users from obtaining outside, or from selling in, the contract territory contract goods properly marked or otherwise properly marketed contract goods;

2. exercises other rights or takes other measures so as to prevent dealers or users from obtaining outside, or from selling in , the contract territory contract goods."

Exclusive purchasing agreements

There is also a block exemption for certain kinds of exclusive purchasing agree- **29–013** ments. This is under Regulation 1984/83. The Regulation has four Titles; the first is of general application and the next two are devoted respectively to beer and petrol products. The fourth Title contains miscellaneous provisions. The first Title sets out the general principles of exemption. The agreement must be one between two undertakings under which:

"one party, the reseller, agrees with the other, the supplier, to purchase certain goods for sale only from the supplier or from a connected undertaking or from another undertaking the supplier has entrusted with the sale of his goods."

As in Regulation 1983/83, an agreement will not be exempt in certain cases where:

"(a) manufacturers of identical goods or of goods which are considered by users as equivalent in view of their characteristics, price and intended use enter into reciprocal exclusive purchasing agreements between themselves in respect of such goods;

(b) manufacturers of identical goods or of goods which are considered by users as equivalent in view of their characteristics, price and intended use enter into a non-reciprocal exclusive purchasing agreement between themselves in respect of such goods, unless at least one of them has a total annual turnover of no more than 100 million ECU;

(c) the exclusive purchasing obligation is agreed for more than one type of goods where these are neither by their nature nor according to commercial usage connected to each other;

(d) the agreement is concluded for an indefinite duration or for a period of more than five years."

The scheme of Titles II and III is similar to Title I but there are some differences to take account of the peculiarities of the markets in question.[62]

Joint research and development, joint ventures and specialisation agreements

The Commission wishes to encourage enterprises, in particular of small and **29–014** medium size, to co-operate with a view to enabling them to compete with

---

[62] Regulation 84/83, Recital 12.

stronger undertakings. In furtherance of this policy, which was mentioned earlier,[63] Regulations have been promulgated;[64] granting block exemptions to research and development agreements[65] and specialisation agreements.[66] Cooperative joint ventures create difficulties in respect of Article 81(1). An assessment will be required to ascertain whether the joint venture is between non competitors, which is likely to raise few difficulties, or between competitors, which would probably be prohibited. Exemptions have also been granted in individual cases.[67]

Patent and know-how licensing agreements

29–015 Regulation 2349/84 granted a block exemption to certain closely defined patent licensing agreements. The Regulation contained a list of "white" clauses which fall under the exemption from the general prohibition of Article 81(1), and a list of "black" clauses which are not exempted and consequently are prohibited. The block exemption covering know-how licensing agreements was issued as Regulation 556/89. Regulation 240/96 applies Article 81 (3) to Certain Categories of Technology Transfer Agreements and takes the place of the previous Block Exemptions. The format of the Regulation is similar to that of Regulation 2349/84 in that there is a comprehensive list of "white" clauses and "black" clauses. The white list contained in the Regulation deals with matters relating to, among others, obligations not to disclose know-how, non-assignment of the license, enforcement of the rights which are the subject matter of the agreement, obligations concerning the marking of the products, etc. Specifically prohibited by Article 4 are export bans generally, limits on the numbers to be sold, restrictions on customers, etc. The Regulation is too complex to be considered here. In drafting any licensing agreement, reference should be made to the text of the Regulation.

Franchising agreements and agreements relating to intellectual property rights

29–016 On November 30, 1988 the Commission issued block exemption Regulation 4087/88 concerning franchising agreements.[68] Other rules relating to intellectual property rights are to be found in Directive 89/104 relating to Trade Marks, Directive 91/250 (Protection of computer programs) and Regulation 40/94 on the Community Trademark.

---

[63] That is the facilitation of cooperation between small and medium sized companies.
[64] For details of these Regulations see Bellamy and Child (4th ed., 1993 and supplement 1997), Chap. 7.
[65] Regulation 418/85. This Regulation expires on December 31, 2000 (Reg. 2236/97).
[66] Regulation 417/85. This Regulation expires on the same date as Regulation 418/85.
[67] Exemptions were granted in: *ACEC/Berliet* [1968] C.M.L.R. D35; *Henkel/Colgate* [1981] C.M.L.R. D31; *Re Davidson Rubber* [1972] C.M.L.R. D52; *Re European Music Satellite Venture* [1984] 3 C.M.L.R. 162; *Transocean Marine Paint Association* [1989] 4 C.M.L.R. 84.
[68] See *Pronuptia, ante.*

Maritime transport and air transport

The application of Articles 81 and 82 to maritime transport is covered by Regu- **29–017**
lation 4056/86.[69] The Regulation sets out procedural rules governing investigations of the Commission into cases of suspected infringements and provides
block exemption for agreements between members of liner conferences[70] complying with the provisions of the Regulation. Regulations have also been promulgated on air transport.[71]

ABUSE OF DOMINANT POSITION

The European Court has given Article 82 of the E.C. Treaty a wide interpreta- **29–018**
tion. The "dominant position" referred to in that Article relates to a position of
economic strength which enables an enterprise to prevent effective competition
being maintained in the relevant market by giving it the power to behave to an
appreciable extent independently of its competitors, customers and ultimately
the consumers.[72] An abuse of a dominant position may already exist where an
undertaking of considerable strength in the market attempts further to increase
its share in a particular market by taking over a rival enterprise.[73]

It is also an abuse of a dominant position if an undertaking which is in control
of certain raw material cuts off the supply of that material to a customer who
needs it for the production of goods which are in competition with goods produced by the enterprise that has a monopoly with respect to the raw material.[74]
In this case a dominant position is abused although the measure objected to
applies to different stages of the production.

In circumstances like these it is not easy to determine what is a relevant
market in which an undertaking has a dominant position. The "relevant market"
is determined by two criteria: the particular features of the product in question
and the geographical area in which it is marketed. The product market is determined by the application of a relatively narrow test. The court held in *United
Brands Co v. Commission*[75] that bananas constituted a market which was sufficiently distinct from that of other fresh fruit to form a separate relevant market
for the purposes of Article 82. Even a relatively small company may enjoy a

---

[69] There are also Regulations concerning the freedom to provide shipping services between Member
States and Member States and Third Countries Regulation 4055/86 and a Regulation safeguarding
free access to cargoes in ocean trades: Reg. 4058/86.
[70] Regulation 870/95.
[71] Regulations 3975/87 and 3976/87 on the application of the competition rules to air transport.
[72] *United Brands Co v. Commission* [1978] 1 C.M.L.R. 429 at 486–487; *Hoffman La Roche v. E.C.
Commission* [1979] 3 C.M.L.R. 211; *Argyll Group plc v. Distillers Co plc* [1986] 1 C.M.L.R. 764.
(Abuse must be an act having a significant and abnormal effect distorting the market).
[73] *Europemballage Corpn and Continental Can Co Inc v. Commission* [1973] C.M.L.R. 199; *British-
American Tobacco Co Ltd v. E.C. Commission* [1988] 4 C.M.L.R. 24.
[74] *Commercial Solvents Corpn v. Commission* [1974] 1 C.M.L.R. 309 (the *Zoja* case). Abuse of a
dominant position can occur on the demand as well as the supply side: *Eurofima* [1973] C.M.L.R.
217. Predatory price undercutting by a large undertaking in order to keep a small competitor away
from a particular market may be abuse of a dominant position: *ECS/AKZO* [1986] 3 C.M.L.R. 273.
[75] [1978] 1 C.M.L.R. 429 at 483–484. See also 97/C372/03 *Commission Notice on the definition of
relevant market for the purposes of Community competition law* [1997] O.J. C372.

dominant position with respect to some of its products; thus, in one case[76] a Swedish enterprise supplied only 12 or 13 per cent of cash registers in the common market countries and was found not to have a dominant position with respect to cash registers, but the parts of the cash registers marketed by that company were not interchangeable with those of other registers, so that the users of its cash registers were utterly dependent on the Swedish company with respect to the supply of spare parts; the Commission ruled that the Swedish company had a dominant position with respect to the spare parts of its cash registers, but the E.C.J. quashed this decision on the ground that trade between Member States was not affected.[77]

In another case[78] a U.K. car manufacturer, British Leyland, had to issue "certificates of conformity" required by Government regulations in order to enable dealers to sell the manufacturer's cars. It was alleged that, in order to prevent the reimportation of cars from another Member State (to which they were imported to save tax), the manufacturer refused certificates of conformity on reimported cars or charged excessive fees for the certificates. The E.C.J. held that the manufacturer had an "administrative monopoly" and had abused its dominant position, contrary to Article 82.

Infringement of Article 82 of the E.C. Treaty can be a basis for the issue of a freezing order or other relief in the national courts,[79] or a defence to an action for infringement.[80] Proceedings may however be suspended on a satisfactory undertaking being given.[81]

Generally speaking, the grant to its customers by a dominant enterprise of a quantity discount (which is linked solely to the volume of purchases) is not an abuse of its dominant position, but a loyalty discount (which tends to prevent the customers from obtaining their supplies from competing manufacturers) is an abuse under Article 82.[82]

Powers of Commission to obtain information and to conduct investigations

29–019 The Commission has extensive powers to obtain information. It may request an undertaking to give it information essential to the performance of its functions in enforcing the competition rules,[83] and may send an inspector to the premises of an undertaking for an "on the spot" investigation, such as to examine docu-

---

[76] *Liptons Cash Registers & Business Equipment Ltd v. Hugin Kassaregister AB* [1978] 1 C.M.L.R. D19.

[77] *Hugin Kassaregister AB v. E.C. Commission* [1979] 3 C.M.L.R. 345.

[78] *British Leyland plc v. E.C. Commission* [1987] 1 C.M.L.R. 185.

[79] *Garden Cottage Foods Ltd v. Milk Marketing Board* [1983] A.C. 130.

[80] *British Leyland Motor Corporation Ltd v. TI Silencers* [1981] 2 C.M.L.R. 75; *ICI Ltd v. Berk Pharmaceuticals* [1981] 2 C.M.L.R. 91. But, if a Eurodefence is pleaded, a sufficient nexus between the alleged actions of the plaintiff and the alleged breaches of a dominant position must be particularised. See also *Leyland Daf v. Automotive Products plc* [1994] B.C.L.C. 245.

[81] *IBM* [1984] 3 C.M.L.R. 147.

[82] *Nederlandsche Banden-Industrie Michelin NV v. Commission* [1985] 1 C.M.L.R. 282.

[83] Giving the Commission the wrong information is a ground for the maximum penalty being imposed under Reg. 17/62, Art. 15(1): *Community v. Comptoir Commercial D'Importation* [1982] 1 C.M.L.R. 440.

ments, ask oral questions, and so on.[84] In pursuing its investigation, the Commission must, however, have regard to the legitimate interests of undertakings that their business secrets should not be disclosed.[85] Regulation 17 provides in Article 19 the right of the undertaking or association of undertakings, under investigation, to a hearing. This important right, one of the general principles on which Community law is founded, is amplified by Regulation 2842/98.

THE COMPETITION LAW OF THE UNITED KINGDOM[86]

The competition law of the United Kingdom has been radically reformed by the **29–020** Competition Act 1998. The date of enactment was November 9, 1998 and the new law came into force on March 1, 2000. There are transitional provisions set out in Schedule 13 dealing with agreements made before the date of enactment, agreements made in the transitional period and agreements made after the Act came into force. These are dealt with below. The overall scheme of the Act is to prohibit an agreement or behaviour which has an impact on trade within the United Kingdom and which has as its object or effect the prevention, restriction and distortion of competition, the so-called Chapter 1 prohibition. Also prohibited is the abuse of a dominant position by one or more undertakings if it may affect trade within the United Kingdom, the Chapter II prohibition.

The similarity in approach between domestic and Community legislation is striking and corresponds to the aim of ensuring a closer alignment between United Kingdom and Community law in this area. Section 60 (1) ensures that the approach to be taken in the interpretation of the Competition Rules is consistent with the "treatment of corresponding questions arising in Community law in relation to competition within the Community". There are certain transitional arrangements in force.

Competition Act 1998

The Act repeals prior legislation and excludes from its provisions mergers and **29–021** concentrations, competition scrutiny under other enactments, planning obligations and other general exclusions and professional rules. The Director General of Fair Trading (DGFT) has powers under section 4 to grant exemptions from the competition rules on notification by an individual. The exemption is however

---

[84] Reg. 17/62, Arts 11 and 14.
[85] For the power to request information see Art. 11 of Reg. 17; for the power to conduct investigations see Art. 14. It was held by the European Court in Cases 46/87 and 227/88 *Hoechst AG v. Commission* [1991] 4 C.M.L.R. 410 that the Commission, when conducting an on-the-spot investigation, does not require a search warrant even though such a warrant is prescribed for a national investigation under national competition law; they may not, however, use force. On confidentiality see E.C. Treaty, Art. 287; Regulation 17, Art. 20; and *AKZO Chemie BV and AKZO Chemie U.K. Ltd v. E.C. Commission* [1987] 1 C.M.L.R. 231.
[86] See, *inter alia*, J. Nazerali and D. Cowan, "Importing the E.U. Model into U.K. Competition Law: A Blueprint for Reform or a Step into 'Euroblivion'?" [1999] E.C.L.R. 55; J. Maitland-Walker, "The New U.K. Competition Law Regime" [1999] E.C.L.R. 51. Certain provisions of the competition law have been brought into force by The Competition Act 1998 (Commencement No. 1) Order, S.I. 1998 No. 2750, (No. 2 Order), S.I. 1998 No. 3136, (No. 3 Order), S.I. 1999 No. 505, (No. 4 Order), S.I. 1999 No. 2859.

subject to cancellation if there has been a material change of circumstance. As with Community law there are block exemptions available which will apply to particular categories of agreement. The creation of categories will be affected by Orders made by the Secretary of State on the recommendation of the DGFT. Agreements exempt from Community law, either by virtue of a Regulation or by exemption granted by the Commission, will also be exempt under the Act. There is provision for the immunity of "small agreements". This does not include price fixing agreements.

Notification

29–022 Parties to any agreement which may fall foul of the Chapter I prohibition may notify the agreement to the Office of Fair Trading. There are two notification procedures; one involves notification to the DGFT for guidance and the other for a decision. The former process involves the DGFT giving guidance as to whether the agreement may be in breach of the Chapter I prohibition. The DGFT may also indicate whether the agreement may be exempted by a block exemption, or any other available exemption. The latter process involves a request for a formal decision as to whether the agreement is in breach of the prohibition or whether an individual exemption may be granted. There is an immunity from penalty for the period between the notification and the time the application is determined in respect of both notifications.

Enforcement

29–023 The DGFT has been given powers of investigation under Chapter III. These powers are similar to the powers of the Commission under Regulation 17 and in some respects are stronger. The Chapter also gives the DGFT the power to, among other matters, enter premises without a warrant, subject to the service of a written notice of the intended entry. The notice must also specify the subject matter of the investigation and the nature of the offences which may be committed by, for example, supplying false information, destroying documents, etc. If the notice cannot be served, entry may be effected in any event on production of evidence of authorisation and a document containing the subject matter and the purpose of the investigation. Fines and imprisonment are available for the supply of false or misleading information or the destruction of documents. For infringements the DGFT has power to fine an undertaking up to 10 per cent of turnover.

Appeals

29–024 Section 45 provides for the creation of a body known as the Competition Commission. This body has been given the functions which were formerly exercised by the Monopolies and Mergers Commission. The Competition Commission will also entertain appeals against the decisions of the DGFT. The decisions which may be appealed are set out in section 46(3): decision of infringement of Chapter I prohibition, decision of infringement of Chapter II prohibition or the grant or not of an individual exemption. A third party with sufficient interest in the relevant decision may also have standing to appeal. The appeal itself is decided by a tribunal against whose determination appeal may be made to the court on a point of law or the amount of a penalty.

The Act has stimulated more than passing comment about certain issues, for example the fact that prohibited agreements are "void" and not "automatically void" as provided in Article 81 of the E.U. Treaty. It may be that an English Court may take a view that circumstances may change and that which may have been void is not any longer so.[87] Quite what the impact of this difference is remains to be seen but section 60(1) above is intended to ensure that questions in relation to competition within the United Kingdom are to be dealt with in a manner consistent with the treatment of corresponding questions arising in Community law.

This section is also invoked to cover the lack of provision relating to individual enforcement of the domestic competition rules. It may be suggested that sections 60(1) and (2)(b), which ensure that there is no inconsistency between a determination of a question by a domestic court and the principles laid down by the Treaty and any relevant decision of the E.C.J. may enable a domestic court to imply such rights. Articles 81 and 82 are directly effective, that is they give an individual rights which may be enforced in the national courts. Whether the 1998 Act confers rights of enforcement on individuals is yet to be decided. To enable an individual to enforce would be consistent with the norms of Community law, but the manner of treatment by domestic courts of these rights leaves room for uncertainty. It is suggested that an individual would have a remedy in the enforcement of Community law in any event.

---

[87] See Maitland-Walker and his remarks on *Passmore v. Morland* and others; *op. cit.* n. 86.

CHAPTER 30

SOLE DISTRIBUTION AGREEMENTS, LICENSING AND FRANCHISING

30–001 The main concern of the exporter who is intent on expanding his sales abroad is to devise a well-planned marketing strategy. Obviously he will first engage in intensive market research, utilising the sources of information described in the next chapter.[1] He will soon discover that the economic, social and political conditions in the various overseas countries are so different that his approach to marketing his goods abroad must be very flexible. An organisational scheme suitable for one country may be totally unsuitable for another.

The establishment of a single market in the E.C. in 1992[2], created a favourable climate for direct purchases by buyers in a Member State from sellers in others, but even in the countries of the Community differences founded on linguistic problems, customary sales techniques and traditional customer preferences will remain. It may therefore be necessary for the exporter even in this regional market to contemplate the establishment of local outlets for his products.

The various legal forms of overseas marketing can be grouped as follows:

1. The exporter may conclude a *sole distribution* or a *licensing* or *franchising agreement* with an importer abroad; or

2. he may entrust his representation to an *exclusive agent* abroad or ask his overseas customers to use the services of a *confirming house* in this country; or

3. he may provide his own unincorporated or corporate marketing organisation in the overseas country by establishing a *branch office* or *subsidiary* there, or by a *foreign acquisition*, *i.e.* by acquiring an enterprise already carrying on business in the target country and possibly having established market outlets there; or

4. he may combine with an enterprise in the overseas country in a *joint venture* or adopt another form of joint export organisation, *e.g.* the *European Economic Interest Grouping (EEIG)*.

Since the choice of the marketing organisation most appropriate to the circumstances is greatly influenced by the competition law of the E.C. and

---

[1] Chap. 31.
[2] Provided by the Single European Act 1986.

the United Kingdom, a chapter dealing with these topics is included in this work.

NATURE OF SOLE DISTRIBUTION AGREEMENTS

Sole and exclusive agreements

In distribution agreements, and in agency agreements, which are dealt with in **30–002** Chapter 27, the distributor or agent is often granted "sole" or "exclusive" rights of representation. The law does not attach a definite meaning to these terms. It has, therefore, to be ascertained in every case what the parties meant by them. The best course for the parties is to spell out in their agreement the precise rights which they intend the representative to have. If these rights are not defined in the contract, it should be borne in mind that in modern commercial usage the following meaning is often attributed to the terms "sole" and "exclusive":

1. Both terms imply that the principal shall not be entitled to appoint another distributor or agent for the territory of the representative.

2. If the representation is "sole", the principal himself may undertake sales in the territory of the representative on his own account without any liability to the representative.

3. If the representation is "exclusive", the principal is not allowed himself to compete with the representative in the allotted territory. This interpretation is supported by the definition of the word "exclusive" in the Copyright Designs and Patents Act 1988, s.92(1), where the term "exclusive licence" is defined.

Sometimes a distribution or agency agreement provides that the representative shall have "sole and exclusive" rights of representation.

Sole distribution agreements distinguished from contracts of sale and from agency agreements

Sole distribution agreements,[3] as customary in the export trade, are different **30–003** from contracts of sale and agency agreements. They provide, in essence, that the seller, a United Kingdom manufacturer or merchant, grants the buyer, an overseas merchant, sole trading rights within a particular territory with respect to goods of a specified kind while the buyer may undertake to rely on the seller

---

[3] See Rudolf Graupner, "Sole Distributorship Agreements—a Comparative View" (1969) 18 I.C.L.Q. 879; J. A. Wade, "The Sole Distributor in Comparative and Private International Law", in *Hague-Zagreb Essays 4 on the Law of International Trade*, p. 213, edited by C. C. A. Voskuil and J. A. Wade (1983, T.M.C. Asser Instituut, The Hague). On exclusive sales agreements in French law and on the law of the E.C., see R. Plaisant, *Les contrats d'exclusivité* in (1964) 17 *Rev. Trim. de Droit Commercial* 1; Thomas E. Carbonneau, "Exclusive Distributorship Agreements in French Law" (1979) 28 I.C.L.Q. 91. Van Houtte, *The Law of International Trade* (Sweet & Maxwell, 1995); A. Juasas, *International Encyclopedia of Agency and Distribution Agreements* (Kluwer, 1997).

as the sole source of supply whenever desirous of buying goods of the specified kind in the United Kingdom.[4] Where such a contract is concluded between a manufacturer of computers in the United Kingdom and, say, an Indian importer, the former is not entitled to appoint another distributor for his computers in India, nor, if that is the intention of the parties, is the latter at liberty to buy competitive makes of computers in this country. The sole distribution agreement is not a contract of sale of specific goods. It merely lays down the general terms on which later individual contracts of sale will be concluded. Sometimes the sole distribution agreement contains a stipulation on the part of the buyer to buy a quantity of specified goods which have to be delivered by instalments or on call. Even where such a stipulation is not agreed upon, the sole distribution agreement is not merely a contract to conclude a contract, but an agreement which is presently effective. Although its mandatory clauses are dependent on the conclusion of individual contracts of sale in the future, its restrictive clauses are immediately effective and remain in force for the duration of the agreement even when individual sales are never concluded. Where the exclusive buyer resides in a region or country which has strict laws safeguarding competition, such as the E.C. or the United States, great care has to be taken that the proposed agreement does not infringe these laws.[5]

Further, the sole distributor is not an agent of the British manufacturer or trader in the legal sense, although in commercial language he is sometimes loosely referred to as such.[6] Unlike an agent in the legal sense, the sole distributor does not act on behalf of the British principal and is not accountable to him for the profits derived from the resale of the goods in his own territory. The profit of the sole distributor is normally the difference between the buying and selling price whereas the profit of the agent is usually the commission which he earns when concluding a sales contract on behalf of his principal or when the principal concludes a sales contract with a customer introduced by the agent.

The sole distribution agreement has some affinity with a contract granting exclusive agency rights. In both contracts an area or territory is defined where the exclusive trading rights are to be operative. The sole distribution agreement differs from the exclusive agency agreement also in another aspect; the contracts which are concluded within its framework are proper contracts of sale by which the overseas merchant—the distributor—buys in his own name and when he resells the goods in his territory no contractual bond is established between the re-purchaser and the British exporter.[7] The sole distribution agreement has thus a distinct advantage over the exclusive agency agreement. The British exporter is not concerned with the credit of a multitude of buyers in the foreign territory, but he sells to one person only whose credit and commercial standing is well known to him or is at least relatively easily ascertainable.

---

[4] For details see *post*, para. 30–010.
[5] See Chap. 29.
[6] See *ante*, para. 27–014 for types of agent.
[7] A commission agent or *commissionaire* in the continental sense (see *ante*, para. 27–014) is not a sole distributor because, although he resells the goods in his own name, he acts on behalf of his principal and is accountable to him for the profits of the transaction. He is a true agent, as this term is understood in English law. He usually receives a commission.

Sole distribution agreements and licensing and franchising agreements

The sole distribution agreement is sometimes described by commercial men as **30–004** the grant of a sales licence. From the legal point of view, this is an inaccurate description because the distribution agreement provides for the conclusion of straightforward contracts of sale and not for the grant of licences.

Licensing and franchising agreements are very different from sole distribution agreements. By a licensing agreement the owner of an intellectual property right authorises another person, the licensee, to use that right, subject to certain conditions. The intellectual property right may be a patent, trade mark, (unregistered) business name or a particular business method. A franchise agreement is a contract whereby the franchisor grants the franchisee a licence to carry on a particular business under a name belonging to the franchisor and making use of his business methods, which the franchisor communicates to the franchisee. Normally the franchisor is entitled under this agreement to exercise a strict degree of control over the franchised business during the period of the licence.[8] Licensing and franchising agreements will be considered later on.[9]

Export distribution agreements

A sole distribution agreement might further be concluded between an exporter **30–005** in this country and a manufacturer or wholesaler here. In this case the exporter, who is sometimes referred to as "exporter distributor", is granted the exclusive right of distributing the manufacturer's goods abroad, either anywhere or in a specified market. Two types of export distribution agreements are in use and the contract should make it clear in unambiguous terms which type is intended: under some export distribution agreements the distributor undertakes to place annually orders of a fixed amount with the manufacturer, and under other agreements he merely undertakes to place such orders if and when he receives them from his customers abroad; although in the latter case—as in the former—the export distributor undertakes to place the order in his own name (and not as agent of the overseas customer) and to hold himself personally liable for the price, the nature of his obligation differs; in the latter case the distributor is only liable if he fails diligently[10] to pass on to the manufacturer such customers' orders as are received by him while in the former case he is liable to order goods of the stipulated value whether he receives such orders or not. The importance of this distinction became evident in the following case[11]: the defendants, a confirming house, undertook to act as exclusive export distributors of the plaintiffs, manufacturers of water taps and other sanitary fittings, for certain foreign coun-

---

[8] See generally M. M. Bynger, *Franchising* (FT Law and Tax, 1995); a useful nation-by-nation guide is found in M. Mendelsohn and M. Brennan, *International Encyclopedia of Franchising* (Kluwer Law International, 1999).

[9] See *post*, para. 30–015.

[10] He must use his best endeavours; see *Ault & Wiborg Paints Ltd v. Sure Service Ltd, The Times*, July 2, 1983; see *post*, para. 30–008.

[11] *James Shaffer Ltd v. Findlay Durham & Brodie* [1953] 1 W.L.R. 106. See also the Canadian case of *Wingold v. Wm. Looser & Co* [1951] 1 D.L.R. 429 and the Scottish case *R. J. Dempster Ltd v. Motherwell Bridge and Engineering Co Ltd* [1964] S.C. 308.

tries. The agreement was for 15 years but could be cancelled at the end of 10 years by giving six months' notice. Under clause 2(k) of the agreement the export distributors undertook to "pass on to the manufacturers customers' orders for the goods amounting to not less in volume than the volume of goods which at present price would amount to the value of £80,000." The agreement continued in operation for about 15 months when the amount of orders had fallen short of the stipulated value, mainly because in some foreign countries the issue of import licences for the goods in question was suspended. A dispute arose between the parties on the exact meaning of clause 2(k). The manufacturers maintained that the distributors were bound to place annually £80,000 worth of orders while the latter contended that they were only obliged to give them whatever orders they received from their customers. The manufacturers contended that the distributors had repudiated the agreement and claimed damages resulting, first, from the breach of clause 2(k) during the currency of the agreement and, secondly, from the repudiation of the entire contract. The Court of Appeal held that clause 2(k) obliged the export distributors to place annually £80,000 worth of orders with the manufacturers whether they received such orders from their customers or did not receive them, but that the construction which the distributors put on the clause, though being erroneous, was adopted in good faith and did not evince an intention to repudiate the entire contract.[12] The court awarded the plaintiffs damages for non-performance of the distributors' undertakings during the 15 months in which the contract was in operation, but dismissed the claim for damages resulting from the repudiation of the contract which, in view of the long currency of the contract, would have been heavy.

30–006   When interpreting the clauses of a sole distribution agreement, it must be borne in mind that the parties intend to build up an enduring relationship. Minor deviations from the terms of the contract cannot be used as an excuse to treat the whole contract as repudiated although they may give rise to a claim for damages. This is particularly true if, without obligation on his part, the sole distributor has incurred considerable expense in order to promote the sales of the producer's goods. Thus in *Decro-Wall SA v. Marketing Ltd*[13] Decro-Wall, a French company, gave the sole distributing rights of their goods—decorative tiles—in the United Kingdom to Marketing, a small but reputable company. The

---

[12] Repudiation occurs only if there is clear and unequivocal conduct of a party evincing his intention not to be bound by the contract, see *The Mercanaut* [1980] 2 Lloyd's Rep. 183 at 185; *Woodar Investment Development Ltd v. Wimpey Construction U.K. Ltd* [1980] 1 W.L.R. 277, HL. The repudiation must be accepted in order to terminate the contract; such acceptance does not, of course, mean abandonment of the claim for damages by the aggrieved party: *MSC Mediterranean Shipping Co SA v. BRE-Metro Ltd* [1985] 2 Lloyd's Rep. 239. There can be no acceptance without knowledge of the innocent party that a repudiation has occurred; the innocent party must have the option of electing whether to accept the repudiation or not: *Fercometal Sarl v. Mediterranean Shipping Co SA; The Simona* [1988] 3 W.L.R. 200 at 206, HL; *State Trading Corporation of India Ltd v. M. Golodetz Ltd* [1988] 2 Lloyd's Rep. 182, 1988. For the measure of damages in repudiation cases see *Lusograin Comercio Internacional de Cereas Ltda v. Bunge AG* [1986] 2 Lloyd's Rep. 654.
[13] [1971] 1 W.L.R. 361; see also *Evans Marshall & Co Ltd v. Bertola SA* [1975] 2 Lloyd's Rep. 373 (the contract of sole distributorship contains an implied term according to which the supplier must not charge the distributor prices which would prevent him from making a reasonable commercial profit).

sole distribution agreement was of indefinite duration and thus determinable by reasonable notice. Marketing was highly successful in building up a market in the United Kingdom. Two years after the conclusion of the agreement there were already 780 points of sale of Decro-Wall products in the United Kingdom. Marketing spent some £30,000 on advertising Decro-Wall products and had engaged at least six extra salesmen. There were, however, some minor differences between the parties due to slow payment by Marketing, although in the end it always paid fully; Marketing also alleged delayed deliveries by Decro-Wall. The managing director of Marketing thereupon submitted a new plan for smaller but more regular deliveries but that plan was rejected by Decro-Wall. Decro-Wall then appointed another company in the United Kingdom its sole concessionaire. Decro-Wall alleged that its contract with Marketing had been repudiated by the latter by its failure to pay the bills punctually and purported to accept that repudiation. Decro-Wall sued Marketing in the English courts for the outstanding bills and also for a declaration that Marketing had ceased to be its sole concessionaire in the United Kingdom. Marketing, by its counterclaim, asked for a declaration that it was still the sole concessionaire of Decro-Wall in the United Kingdom. The Court of Appeal held that Marketing had not repudiated the agreement by its failure to pay outstanding bills punctually, as time was not of the essence of the payments, that the agreement between the parties still subsisted and could only be terminated by reasonable notice and that, in the circumstances, the length of such notice was 12 months.

CLAUSES IN SOLE DISTRIBUTION AGREEMENTS

Sole distribution agreements require careful drafting. An infinite variety of **30–007** arrangements is possible here. The parties have complete liberty of contracting and should use that discretion for the purpose of creating by their contract a charter of trading which is fair and equitable to both of them, and closely adapted to the particular requirements of their trade and can be relied upon, whether the market is a seller's or a buyer's market. In view of the variety of forms admitted by the law, it is impossible to give an exhaustive catalogue of the clauses embodied in these agreements. It is believed that the main points to be considered are indicated under the following heads which are illustrated by contract clauses when necessary.

Definition of the territory

The following points have to be considered by the parties: **30–008**

(1) The geographical definition of the territory which may consist of several political units, *e.g.* the Scandinavian countries, or of one political unit, *e.g.* Sweden, or of part of a political unit, *e.g.* the city of Stockholm.

(2) The extension of the territory at a future date. Sometimes such extension is merely expressed as a moral claim, sometimes the buyer—the sole distributor—is given a legal right to claim the extension on the happening of certain events, *e.g.* when the sales in his own territory have reached a certain amount over a fixed period.

(3) The seller's obligation not to sell directly to customers in the territory. In earlier agreements it was usual to provide that the seller should insert a clause into his contracts with his home buyers and overseas buyers (other than the contracting party) prohibiting the direct or indirect sale of the goods in the territory of the exclusive dealer. In modern practice such an undertaking is normally omitted, as far as the Member States of the E.C. are concerned, because such restrictions are likely to infringe the competition law of the E.C.[14]

(4) The seller's obligation to refer direct enquiries from consumers in the territory to the buyer.

(5) The buyer's obligation to pass on enquiries from outside the territory to the seller.

(6) The buyer's obligation to keep customers'—retailers'—lists and to supply them to the seller on request.

(7) The territory in which the buyer is bound to buy exclusively from the seller. Here again, the former practice of providing that the buyer shall not buy any goods of the specified description from another source of supply than the buyer is now usually abandoned in the E.C. because of the danger that such restrictions may contravene the provisions of the E.C. Treaty or of national legislations.

Definition of the price

30–009 Sometimes the distribution agreement contains provisions relating to the ascertainment of the price which the distributor shall pay when ordering goods under that agreement. The difficulty is here that the distribution agreement is intended to be of considerable duration but that the prices of the goods, which shall be bought from time to time by way of individual sales contracts under the terms of the distribution agreement may be affected by inflation or other events or may fluctuate if quoted on world markets, as, *e.g.* is the case with crude oil, minerals or commodities.

The parties refer sometimes in the distribution agreement to a definite price ruling on a particular date, such as the date of conclusion of the sales contract or the delivery of the goods, *e.g.* the f.o.b. spot price for crude oil of the grade in question quoted at Rotterdam at the date of the bill of lading. In other cases the parties agree that the distributor shall pay the *most favoured customer (m.f.c.) price, i.e.* the best price which the supplier would obtain from another customer

---

[14] See *ante*, Chap. 29.

at the critical date, possibly subject to a rebate. When an m.f.c. price is agreed upon, it is usual to allow the supplier a list of exempted customers and to provide that sales to them shall not be taken into account when determining the m.f.c. price. This list includes, among others, the holding company, the subsidiaries, associated and connected companies of the supplier. An example of an m.f.c. price clause is this:

> "For the supplies in accordance with clause 1 of this agreement [the distributor] will pay [the supplier], unless otherwise agreed, the lowest f.o.b. price charged under comparable conditions to any customer of [the supplier], except if supplied to a company on the attached list, such price to be reduced by a rebate of 18 per cent."

Definition of the goods

(1) The contract may only refer to some lines produced or traded by the **30–010** seller and not to his whole range of production or trade.

(2) A good method of defining the goods in question is to append to the contract a schedule of identifying them by the seller's catalogue number.

(3) Sometimes goods are described generally as "all kinds and types of goods, machinery and equipment designed for use in the . . . industry."

(4) The contract should cease to apply with respect to goods which the seller discontinues to manufacture or trade.

(5) The contract should allow for an extension to new lines manufactured or traded by the seller where the new lines are used in the same trade as the goods covered by the agreement.

Sole buying and selling rights

(1) A contract need not provide for sole buying and selling rights as con- **30–011** current terms and is valid if only establishing sole selling rights or sole buying rights. In practice, reciprocal agreements provide mutual satisfaction and are preferable to agreements whereby only one party is granted sole trading rights; but all depends here on the requirements of the particular trade. Where these matters are not regulated expressly in the distribution agreement, a term may have to be implied that the distributor shall use his best endeavours to promote the supplier's goods. It was held in one case[15] that in the circumstances of the contract such implied term was not inconsistent with the distributor being at liberty to promote similar goods made by competitors of the supplier but required him to treat the supplier favourably, at least as favourably

---

[15] *Ault & Wiborg Paints Ltd v. Sure Service Ltd, The Times,* July 2, 1983, CA; (the case dealt with a domestic transaction). What constitutes a breach of the contractual obligation on the part of the distributor to use his best efforts on behalf of the supplier was discussed in the Australian case *US Surgical Corporation v. Hospital Products Ltd* [1983] 2 N.S.W.L.R. 157.

as he treated the competitors. The decision demonstrates the need for regulating these matters expressly in the contract, subject, of course, to the mandatory provisions of the competition rules of the E.C. and the national legislation.[16]

(2) The contract should put it beyond doubt that the overseas importer acts as buyer and not as agent of the seller. The following clause illustrates this point:

> "It is agreed and understood that the buyer is not the agent or representative of the seller for any purpose whatever, and that the buyer has no authority or power to bind the seller, or to contract in the name of, and to create a liability against, the seller in any way or for any purpose, but on the other hand it is understood that the buyer stands in the relation of an independent contractor with the exclusive rights to buy the seller's . . . machinery, and to resell, handle and deal in the same on his own account and responsibility in the said territory as hereinbefore set forth."

(3) The seller may ask for a clause obliging the buyer to offer the seller's goods in the market. The following clause is here sometimes found:

> "During the life of this contract the buyer agrees vigorously, diligently, and in good efficient salesmanlike manner, to solicit orders for and to bring to the attention of buyers or potential buyers within the territory, the seller's entire line of . . . machinery and equipment, all to the end that as large a volume of sales of the seller's said machinery and equipment can and will be made to the ultimate users thereof in the territory as the circumstances of competition and general business from time to time permit."

(4) The seller asks sometimes that orders representing a minimum value shall be ordered within a fixed time; sometimes the agreement gives the seller an option of giving notice of termination if the orders placed by the buyer do not represent a minimum value for a fixed period.

Advertising, market information, protection of patents and trade marks

30–012 (1) The seller is normally not interested in the proceeds of the sale of goods in the territory, as his overseas contractor stands in the position of a buyer and not of an agent. The seller is, however, interested in seeing a demand created in the overseas market for his goods and having his trade mark advertised if the goods are distributed under that mark. The buyer is, therefore, sometimes asked to undertake certain minimum obligations with respect to the advertising of the goods. The following clause illustrates this point:

> "All exhibiting, soliciting of orders, and advertising either by circulars or by paid advertisements in journals or magazines circulating in the territory, of the . . . machines and equipment of the seller shall be under the exclusive control and at the expense of the buyer, but the buyer agrees during the life of this contract to provide and pay for not less than 12 full-page advertisements per annum, appearing at regular monthly intervals in the national journals or magazines of the . . . industry circulating generally throughout the territory, and the buyer at his own expense will at the time

---

[16] See *ante*, Chap. 27.

of issue dispatch to the seller a copy of each such monthly journal or magazine in which such advertisements of the seller's machinery or equipment appears."

(2) It is sometimes provided that the distributor shall visit certain prospective customers at regular intervals.[17]

(3) The buyer is often asked to provide the seller with market information which is accessible to him, *e.g.*:

> "The buyer agrees to the best of his ability to provide the seller at intervals or at such reasonable times as the seller may request information concerning any developments in the territory relating to the demand, the reactions of the ultimate users, the activities of the competitors, or other matters or circumstances relating to this contract as far as such information is reasonably accessible to the buyer, and the latter agrees to do all such acts and things as may be necessary or helpful to extend and improve the sale of the seller's . . . machinery and equipment in the territory, and to extend and maintain the public goodwill towards the seller's said machinery and equipment."

(4) Due protection should be provided for the seller's patents and trade marks,[18] and the seller sometimes asks generally for an undertaking on the part of the buyer not to make, imitate or copy the goods.

Other clauses

(1) The contract should embody the appropriate provisions of the seller's **30–013** general conditions of sale which have been discussed earlier.[19]

(2) The contract is usually concluded for an indefinite time, and either party is given the right of terminating the agreement upon a fixed date, *e.g.* the end of every calendar year, on having given notice a fixed number of days or months prior to that date. Sometimes the seller's right to terminate the agreement depends on the purchases by the buyer falling below a certain minimum value over a fixed period.

Where the contract contains no provision for its termination, a party is entitled to give the other party notice of reasonable length.[20] In agreements in the commercial field, such as exclusive sales agreements, there is no presumption in favour of permanence.[21]

---

[17] In *L. Schuler AG v. Wickman Machine Tool Sales Ltd* [1974] A.C. 235 the sole distributor agreement concerned panel presses and the sole distributor undertook to visit the six largest United Kingdom motor manufacturers at least once every week. Failure to comply with this clause was held not to be a breach of a condition although the clause was described in the contract as a condition.

[18] In *Sport International Bussum BV v. Hi-Tec Sports Ltd (No. 1)* [1998] R.P.C. 329, the Dutch owner of a trade mark granted a distributor the exclusive right to use his trade mark in the U.K.; the Court of Appeal held that a term had to be implied into the distribution agreement that after its termination the distributor was not only prevented from using the owner's trade mark in the U.K. but also from using it in any other country without licence by the owner.

[19] See *ante*, para. 32–015.

[20] See *Decro-Wall SA v. Marketing Ltd* [1971] 1 W.L.R. 361.

[21] *Martin-Baker Aircraft Co Ltd v. Canadian Flight Equipment Ltd* [1955] 2 Q.B. 556 at 571; *Tower Hamlets London Borough Council v. British Gas Corporation* (1982) 79 L.S.Gaz. 1025; *The Times*, March 23, 1982.

Laws Relating to Restrictive Practices

30–014 The sole distribution agreement must further conform with the laws relating to restrictive trade practices and restraints of trade, as in force in the E.C., the United Kingdom and in the countries in which the agreement is intended to operate.

As far as E.C. law is concerned, an exclusive sales agreement may contravene the prohibitions of Articles 81 and 82 of the E.C. Treaty or the relevant provisions of the U.K. Competition Act 1998.

Licensing and Franchising Agreements

30–015 It was stated earlier[22] that the exporter who owns a patent, trade mark or other form of intellectual or industrial property in relation to goods may exploit such ownership abroad through licensing another to exploit that property overseas. The licensor therefore avoids the necessity of providing the capital needed in the designated territory to exploit the property and further avoids the commercial risk of the transactions carried out in relation to the goods. The licensor needs to be mindful of certain important matters when drawing up the licence. They are quality control, the question of taxation and the impact of European Community or other relevant laws. Quality control may generally be ensured by a provision that samples of the goods sold abroad will be tested on a regular basis. The question of taxation relates to the issue of whether tax is deductible at source or not and the consequences of such deduction for the licensor. The provisions of European Community law in relation to licensing are to be looked at in relation to the prohibitions contained in Article 81 of the Treaty.[23]

European Community law affects the conditions under which property rights may be licensed as the granting of licenses whose terms ensure that the parties eliminate competition from other parties will be regarded as being in breach of Article 81 and therefore void.[24] The commission have, however, developed block exemptions[25] so that parties drawing up such agreements may refer to those exemptions to discern what clauses are permitted and what clauses are specifically prohibited, the so-called "white-list" and "black-list". If the parties are unable to determine whether a clause falls within or without those lists they may still have recourse to the Commission to seek an individual exemption.[26] In relation to lesser industrialised nations the licensor must pay heed to any relevant laws relating to the transfer of technology. Such laws are generally designed to mitigate the inequality of bargaining power between a licensor from an industrialised nation and a potential licensee from one less industrialised.

---

[22] See Introduction.
[23] See Chap. 29—E.C. Competition Law.
[24] See Chap. 29 generally.
[25] For example, Regulation 240/96 on the application of Art. 81(3) to certain categories of Technology Transfer Agreements [1996] O.J. L31/2.
[26] Under Art. 81(3).

FRANCHISING

The course of business

Where it is desired that the licensee operates under the corporate image already **30–016** established by the licensor franchising, a particular form of licensing, may be adopted. Under this arrangement the licensee will carry on the licensed business under the franchisor's name, style, get up, etc., and indeed in accordance with a system already developed by the franchisor. The purpose is to ensure that the retail outlets, wherever they may be, are easily recognised by the customer, who is therefore not able to distinguish between the outlets owned and run by the franchisor and those run by the franchisee. The difference is behind the scenes. The franchisee will own the outlets maintained by him and risks his own capital.

Such arrangements are mainly associated in the mind of the public with catering outlets such as "fast-food" and coffee chains but of course franchising arrangements are not confined to this trade. The franchise industry is not only involved with provision to customers (members of the public) but also in provision of goods and services to other businesses. Such is the nature and size of the franchising industry that in certain areas there may be a franchise association whose members will subscribe to the Code of Ethics which was established by the International Franchise Association. The ICC have produced a Model Franchising Contract with a detailed commentary to which potential franchisors may make reference.[27]

FRANCHISING AGREEMENTS AND E.C. LAW

The case of *Pronuptia de Paris GmbH v. Schillgalis*[28] concerning distribution **30–017** franchises, resulted in the creation of a block exemption, Regulation 4087/88,[29] covering franchise agreements. In *Pronuptia* the claimants were a subsidiary of Pronuptia de Paris SA, who traded in wedding dresses and other products connected with weddings under the trademark "Pronuptia de Paris". The respondent, Schillgalis, was a franchisee who had been granted exclusive rights to use the Pronuptia de Paris trade mark for marketing Pronuptia goods and services in the district of Hamburg, Oldenberg and Hanover. The franchisors undertook not to open up any other Pronuptia retail outlets or to provide goods or services covered by the agreement to third parties in the districts mentioned. A dispute arose between franchisor and franchisee concerning licensing fees. The German referred the matter to the E.C.J. which held that, in principle, a franchising agreement whose purpose it was to protect the franchisor's know-how or the identity and reputation of the distribution network did not infringe Article 81(1). Clauses, however, which resulted in a division of markets between franchisor

---

[27] Doc. 460-13/15. The ICC are working on a refined model franchising contract. For up-to-date information contact their website. Website: *www.iccwbo.org*.

[28] Case 161/84 [1986] 1 C.M.L.R. 414, see also *Computerland* [1987] O.J. L222/12; Case 87/100 *Yves Rocher* [1987] O.J. L8/49; *Charles Jourdan* [1989] O.J. 35/31.

[29] Regulation 4087/88 on the application of Art. 81(3) of the Treaty to categories of franchise agreements. [1988] O.J. L359/46.

and franchisee or between franchisees could restrict competition contrary to that Article. In particular, the clause in the agreement prohibiting the sale of Pronuptia goods or offering Pronuptia services on premises other than those specified, might be restrictive because it would prevent the respondent from opening a second retail outlet in her district.

BLOCK EXEMPTION

30–018 Regulation 4087/88 applies only to retail distribution and services franchises. It does not apply to industrial franchises involving the manufacturing of goods.[30] It therefore covers agreements whereby a combination of goods and services are provided to end-users; it does not apply to wholesale franchise agreements. The Regulation contains a list of restrictions of competition which are exempted[31] and these involve obligation to conduct the business only from the contract premises, not to seek sales outside the territory, not to compete with the franchise goods, etc. The Regulation sets out in the usual form a set of "white-list" clauses and "black-list" clauses.[32] Agreements within the guidelines need not be notified. Those not within require notification but are subject to the so-called "opposition" procedure[33] which means that the agreement will be exempted if the Commission do not oppose it within six months, running from the date of notification. Those notifying must make express reference to Article 6. Any Member State may oppose exemption within three months.[34] The Regulation continued in force until December 31, 1999. Potential Franchisors may also note the Commission Notice on agreements of minor importance of 1997.[35]

---

[30] Art. 1(3), Recitals (4) and (5).
[31] Art. 2.
[32] Arts 3 and 4.
[33] Art. 6.
[34] Art. 7.
[35] 97/C/372/04 and Chap. 29, n. 49.

PART NINE

MARKET INFORMATION

CHAPTER 31

MARKET INFORMATION FOR EXPORTERS—MARKET RESEARCH

Direct market research

An enterprise which wants to engage in export transactions, whether on the **31–001** global or E.C. level, will first engage in an exploration of the markets to which it wishes to target its exports.

The exporter may engage in his own market research. He may have in-house experts or he may call in independent marketing experts or other consultants. He may visit the overseas markets himself or send out appointed representatives. He may have received approaches or inquiries from importing or commission houses abroad, or may have been contacted directly by overseas customers, who have read his advertisements in the home or overseas press, or may have obtained his address by other means.

In his direct market research the exporter can obtain valuable assistance from British Trade International, his local chamber of commerce, which is likely to have an export department, or from his trade association.

GOVERNMENT SERVICES FOR EXPORTERS—BRITISH TRADE INTERNATIONAL

British Trade International was established in May 1999. It has lead responsibil- **31–002** ity within Government for trade development and promotion on behalf of British business. It brings together the joint work of the Foreign & Commonwealth Office (FCO) and the Department of Trade and Industry (DTI) in support of British trade and investment overseas.

It combines in a single operation all trade development and promotion work currently undertaken locally in the English regions by the Business Link network, trade support services provided nationally, and the commercial work overseas of over 200 embassies and other diplomatic posts. British Trade International's website[1] has details of current export services, overseas markets and other trade information.

The Government's trade promotion policy is guided by advice from 200 businessmen and women who serve on the British Trade International Board[2] and its Area Advisory Groups and Small Firms Committee.

---

[1] *www.brittrade.com.*
[2] For further information: British Trade International Trade Board, Room 917, Kingsgate House, 66–74 Victoria Street, London SW1E 6SW; Tel: 020 7215 4943, Fax: 020 7215 4653.

Business Links

31–003 Through the Business Link network,[3] small and medium sized businesses can easily find the help and support they need to grow and compete successfully. Now open throughout England, Business Links bring together all the most important business support services including:

(a) A reliable and comprehensive business enquiry and information service; providing detailed and specific research, or fast and focused response, depending on the exporter's needs.

(b) Personal, reliable advice from independent Personal Business Advisers trained to help the exporter identify and pursue business opportunities.

(c) Innovation and Technology, Design, and Export Counsellors for specialist support.

(d) In-depth diagnostic reviews and consultancy support to help the business grow and develop.

(e) Events, promotions, conferences, seminars and networking opportunities where the exporter can meet and work with other local business people.

These resources and more, are focused on companies with the potential to grow. Those wanting to start new businesses also have access to Business Link information and resources.

Some advice and services are free and many Business Links will offer initial consultation free of charge. Other services may be offered on a subsidised basis, and some may be charged in full.

Export Market Information Centre (EMIC)

31–004 The EMIC library[4] has telephone directories, country reports, visitor guides and doing business guides, covering all the major export markets.[5] If the exporter is unable to visit the EMIC in person, a professional researcher can carry out research on his behalf, at a cost of £40 per half hour. This service is a joint venture partnership between the Institute of Export and Business & Trade Statistics Ltd.[6]

Alternatively, under the *Export Market Research Scheme*, export marketing research staff can help the exporter draw up an appropriate specification for the

---

[3] For further information: The national Business Link signpost number: 0345 567 765; Scottish Trade International: Tel: 0141 228 2808, Fax: 0141 221 3712; The National Assembly for Wales: Tel: 029 2082 5097, Fax: 029 2082 3964; Trade International Northern Ireland: Tel: 028 9023 3233.
[4] Kingsgate House, 67–74 Victoria Street, London SW1E 6SW.
[5] For further information: Tel: 020 7215 5444/5445, Fax: 020 7215 4231, e-mail: *emic@xpd3.dti.uk;* website: *www.brittrade.com/emic.*
[6] For further information: Tel: 020 7215 5707, Fax: 020 7233 6853, e-mail: *emirs@ash001.ots.dti-.gov.uk.*

research work, to be carried out by his in-house staff or by a professional marketing research consultant. "The Export Zone" will help and encourage new and existing British Exporters. The website[7] will point users to the best organisations to help them break into new, or build on existing, markets.[8] In addition, companies with fewer than 500 employees may be eligible for a grant of up to 50 per cent of the agreed costs of approved marketing research projects.

Tailored Market Information Reports for U.K. companies can be produced by Commercial Officers at Embassies and other missions overseas. Reports can include: basic market information, identification and assessment of potential agents/distributors, customised local contact lists, market assessments for the exporter's product or service, advice on market approach, information about potential local business contacts, and general information on local investment opportunities. Costs range from £50 to over £1,000, depending on the number of hours of research required for the enquiry. For reports costing £600 or more, the exporter may be eligible for a refund of up to 50 per cent of the value of the service, to offset the cost of a visit to the chosen market within six months of receiving the report.[9]

Export Promoters are senior executives with practical experience of exporting, seconded to British Trade International from industry. They can offer expert advice and information based on first hand experience, including specific opportunities within the markets they cover.[10]

Export Explorer[11] was launched by the British Trade International's Business in Europe Directorate as part of the Government's package for helping small businesses into new export markets. This is a new scheme for first time or inexperienced exporters focusing on Western Europe. *Export Explorer* is an integrated package of help and advice, which will enable small and medium sized businesses to experience Western European markets for £99, excluding travel and accommodation. It comes in two tailor made packages: *Market Explorer* and *Trade Fair Explorer*. The purpose of *Market Explorer* is to give potential exporters their first taste of a possible export market and focuses on those countries which offer the best opportunities for "first timers". *Trade Fair Explorer* concentrates on some of the world's great marketplaces. This gives firms the opportunity to see at first hand the marketplace for their products.

Programme Arranging Service.[12] Some Posts can arrange a programme of visits to potential business contacts in advance of the exporter's arrival. This service is chargeable, costing £80 for up to two hours work and £40 per hour thereafter. At selected Posts, Commercial Offices are able to accompany the exporter on his programme of visits to potential business contacts.

---

[7] *www.britishchambers.org.uk/exportzone.*
[8] For further information: British Chambers of Commerce (BCC), Tel: 01203 694554, Fax: 01203 694690.
[9] For further information: Local Business Link, Scottish Trade International, British Trade International or Trade International Northern Ireland.
[10] For further information: Tel: 020 7215 5000 and ask for the relevant Country Helpdesk.
[11] For further information: Business in Europe Desk: Tel: 020 7215 8885, Fax: 020 7215 8884, Internet: *www.brittrade.com/explorer.*
[12] For further information: Local Business Link, Scottish Trade International, The National Assembly for Wales or Trade International Northern Ireland.

Grant-Supported Missions.[13] An effective way of visiting a chosen market is with a trade mission. Grant support is available for visiting markets, as part of a sponsored mission. These grants are managed through sponsor bodies, such as Trade Associations, Chambers of Commerce or Business Links. Trade missions are also organised by Scottish Trade International, The National Assembly for Wales and Trade International Northern Ireland.

Grant-supported Trade Fairs.[14] Exhibiting at Trade Fairs and participating in seminars abroad are highly effective ways of showing a product to the market and keeping abreast of market trends. Practical and financial assistance is available when an exporter exhibits as part of a U.K. group at selected trade fairs. Grant support may be available amounting to nearly half the cost of space and a 15 sq.m. stand, inclusive of display aids and services. The exporter may also be eligible for travel grants for up to two U.K.-based personnel to staff the stand.

Overseas Seminars.[15] These are designed to increase overseas awareness of U.K.-produced hi-tech goods and services and their commercial prospects. Held as either stand-alone promotions or as part of a trade show, these seminars concentrate on specific sectors and target an invited audience of decision makers and end users. Groups organised by sponsors, *e.g.* trade associations, can receive travel grants and assistance of up to 45 per cent towards costs incurred in staging the event.

Inward Missions.[16] This programme enables groups of buyers, other influential business people and journalists from overseas markets to come to Britain to meet manufacturers, service providers and to attend trade fairs. Financial assistance may include contributions towards their travel, accommodation and briefing or debriefing costs.

The TradeU.K. Export Sales Lead Service[17]

31–005 This service takes the bringing together of buyers and potential suppliers a stage further, allowing potential overseas customers who are looking for British suppliers to be matched up. Already, 53,000 U.K. exporters are listed on TradeU.K.'s National Exporters Database (NED). Entry on the Database is free of charge.

Services provided by the Central Office of Information.[18] On behalf of British Trade International, the Central Office of Information offers a range of export publicity services for the British Trade International-supported groups of companies taking part in overseas trade fairs and outward missions:

---

[13] For further information: British Trade International Country Helpdesk: Tel: 020 7215 5000, Export Services Directorate: Tel: 020 7215 4740/4915, Fax: 020 7215 8126.
[14] For further information: British Trade International Country Helpdesk: Tel: 020 7215 5000, Export Services Directorate: Tel: 020 7215 2425, Fax: 020 7215 2424.
[15] For further information: Export Services Directorate: Tel: 020 7215 2400, Fax: 020 7215 2424.
[16] For further information: Export Services Directorate: Tel: 020 7215 2400, Fax: 020 7215 2424.
[17] For further information: TradeU.K. Customer Service Department, The Dialog Corporation PLC, The Communications Building, 48 Leicester Square, London WC2H 7DB. Tel: 020 7925 7810, Fax: 020 7925 7770, e-mail: *export@dialog.com.* website: *http//www.tradeuk.com.*
[18] For further information: Commercial Publicity, Room 303, Central Office of Information, Hercules House, Hercules Road, London SE1 7DU. Tel: 020 7261 8422, Fax: 020 7928 9034.

(a) *Preview*: A press release highlighting the products or services being offered by the exporter's group as a whole.

(b) *New Products From Britain*: A professionally written article of around 300 words about a product or service not previously publicised in a country. It is distributed to the trade press before the event.

(c) *Made in Britain leaflet*: A colour leaflet describing the exporter's products or services, illustrated by a photograph, written by COI's professional journalists in a style appropriate to the chosen market and translated into any language.

(d) *Catalogues*: Published in DL (1/3 A4), A4 or A5 format for use by both the group sponsor and participating companies before and at the event.

(e) *Newsletters*: A newsletter can act as an effective marketing tool, turning a straight forward catalogue into an interesting read. News about developments in the exporter's industry, trade with the country to be visited, and interviews can all be published.

(f) *Supplement*: A guaranteed number of pages promoting the group's products and services at a particular overseas exhibition. The supplement is aimed primarily at the pre-show issue of a leading trade journal in the host country.

The Export Credits Guarantee Department[19]

Regulated by the Export and Investment Guarantees Act 1991, and responsible **31–006** to the Secretary of State for Trade and Industry, ECGD offers insurance to exporters and guarantees to banks for capital goods sold on cash and medium- to long-terms. Overall, ECGD issues guarantees for around £4 billion per annum. ECGD offers four main services to the U.K. exporting community, which:

(a) enable exporters to offer finance packages providing credit to buyers, whilst receiving cash on delivery through the provision of guarantees to banks in the U.K.;

(b) enable exporters to offer finance at favourable fixed interest rates;

(c) give exporters confidence to sell overseas, by providing insurance against non-payment on export contracts;

(d) protect U.K. companies investing overseas against certain political risks.

---

[19] For further information: Export Credit Guarantee Department, PO Box 2200, 2 Exchange Tower, Harbour Exchange Square, London E14 9GS. Tel: 020 7512 7887, Fax: 020 7512 7649. See also Chap. 20.

Other help available

31–007 Other help is available from the National Languages for Export Campaign,[20] Infrastructure and Energy Projects Directorate (IEP),[21] Joint Environmental Markets Unit (JEMU),[22] Simpler Trade Procedures Board (SITPRO),[23] Export Control and Non-Proliferation Directorate,[24] Action Single Market,[25] and Technical Help to U.K. Exporters.[26]

Export Publications

31–008 Many excellent trade publications exist, which keep the exporter informed of the constantly changing market conditions in the overseas markets, and of the legal and consular requirements abroad. It is perhaps invidious to specify only some of these publications, but it is thought that the following are particularly useful for the exporter.

British Trade International publications

31–009 A wide range of exporting titles can be purchased,[27] written by the commercial staff of the Foreign and Commonwealth Office based overseas and British Trade International export staff, or consultants that are experts in their field. They include:

(a) *Exporting*: This free British Trade International brochure describes the range of British Trade International services for exporters. Much of the information in this brochure is contained in the previous section.

(b) *Hints to exporters*: This is a series of booklets, each about exporting to a different country abroad. They are regularly updated and contain valuable information on currency and exchange regulations, passport and entry formalities, methods of doing business, local holidays, economic factors, social customs and many other useful tips for visiting British businessmen and women.

(c) *Sector Reports and General Reports*: These are market research reports on sectors/areas where export opportunities have been identified.

(d) *Project Lists*: These identify opportunities for U.K. exporters in major projects and contracts overseas.

---

[20] Tel: 020 7215 8146/8155, Fax: 020 7215 4856.
[21] Tel: 020 7215 5000.
[22] Tel: 020 7215 1055, Fax: 020 7215 1089.
[23] Tel: 020 7215 0800, Fax: 020 7215 0824, and see para. 32–017.
[24] Tel: 020 7215 8070, Fax: 020 7215 8564.
[25] Tel: 020 7215 4212, Fax: 020 7215 4489.
[26] Tel: 020 8996 7111, Fax: 020 8996 7048.
[27] To receive a free British Trade International Export Publications Catalogue or purchase titles, contact the British Trade International Publications Orderline—Tel: 0870 1502 500: Export publications website: *www.brittrade.com/publications*.

(e) *Countertrade and Offset—A Guide for Exporters*: This is a new and completely revised and extended edition.

Websites for exporters:

This website covers internet sites giving company details, statistical data or **31–010** information on multilateral development agencies. In addition this contains websites for over 130 overseas markets. The full text is available on the internet.[28]

Croner's Reference Book for Exporters

This is a comprehensive loose-leaf publication[29] comprising three volumes **31–011** which contain valuable information for exporters, including country by country information. Also included are matters relating to export control and Customs procedures. The work is kept up-to-date by a regular amendment service. Included in the subscription are *Export Digest*, published monthly, *Exporter's Briefing*, a fortnightly newsletter, and *Exporter's Bulletin*, published bi-monthly.

Tate's Export Guide

Published bi-monthly, this spiral bound A-4 book[30] consists mainly of a sum- **31–012** mary of current documentation, regulations and exporting procedures, on a country by country basis. The General Section contains a succinct and informative summary of matters to be considered by, and of interest to, the exporter. Included in the subscription is *Tate's Export Briefing* published regularly. Tate's also publish *The Scottish Exporter*.

Export Today

This is the official journal of the *Institute of Export*.[31] It is published every two **31–013** months and contains valuable articles of topical interest to the exporter and other useful information. The Institute also commissions annually a *Survey of International Services Provided to Exporters*.

Business Matters and International Business Matters

These are published monthly and bi-monthly respectively by the London Cham- **31–014** ber of Commerce.[32] Business Matters includes a section on international matters

---

[28] *www.brittrade.com/emic.*
[29] Obtainable from Croner Publications Ltd, Croner House, London Road, Kingston upon Thames, Surrey KT2 6SR, Tel: 020 8547 3333, Fax: 020 8549 7275, e-mail: *info@croner.co.uk.*
[30] Obtainable from Tate Publishing Ltd, Waybill House, 1 Fitzhamon Court, Wolverton Mill, Milton Keynes MK12 6BA, Tel: 01908 221162, Fax: 01908 313800, e-mail: *tatefreight@btinternet.com.*
[31] Address: Export House, 64 Clifton Street, London EC2A 4HB, Tel: 020 7247 9812, Fax: 020 7377 5343. Website: *www.export.org.uk.*
[32] A list of London Chamber of Commerce and Industry services and publications can be obtained from the London Chamber of Commerce, 33 Queen Street, London EC4R 1AP, Tel: 020 7248 4444, Fax: 020 7489 0391, e-mail: *lc@londonchamber.co.uk*; website: *www.londonchamber.co.uk.*

and both publications contain valuable information for the exporter. The same is true of journals published by other chambers of commerce. Many trade journals also publish export information.

Euronews

31–015 This is the monthly newsletter of the Euro Info Centres (EICs)[33] of which there are a number in the U.K. and across Europe. EICs provide information to small and medium-sized businesses wishing to do business in Europe and assistance, via the British Cooperation Centre, in seeking new markets.

Eurostat

31–016 The E.C. operates a Statistical Office known as Eurostat.[34] It publishes updated information on all economic and social activities of the E.C. and the Member States, as well as their main trading partners.

---

[33] London addresses: (1) Euro Information Centre, London Chamber of Commerce, *ante* and (2) Euro Information Centre, 25 Maddox Street, London W1R 9LE, Tel: 020 7629 2151, Fax: 020 7629 2057; website: *www.euro.info.org.uk.*
[34] The London address of Eurostat is: 1 Drummond Gate, London SW1V 2QQ, Tel: 020 7533 5678, Fax: 020 7533 5689, website: *www.ons.gov.uk.* For information e-mail: *inso@ons.gov.uk.*

PART TEN

STANDARDISATION, UNIFICATION, ELECTRONIC COMMERCE
AND EDI

STANDARDISATION OF TERMS AND UNIFICATION OF INTERNATIONAL SALES LAW

When discussing in Chapter 2 the terms used in the export trade, it was stated **32–001** that these terms were not always interpreted in the same manner in all countries and that this may lead to misunderstandings amongst those engaged in international trade.[1] To avoid this, frequent attempts have been made to standardise the terms on which export and import business is transacted.

Such attempts can be classified into three groups.[2] First, uniform rules of general character have been issued, which are intended to apply to all types of international trade transactions. Sometimes, the uniform rules have, or are intended to have, the force of law; sometimes they are intended to apply only if adopted by the parties to the contract. Secondly, in some types of business, mainly in the trade in commodities or in capital goods, there are standard contract forms relating to specified international transactions, which normally apply only if used by the parties to the contract. Thirdly, exporters and importers frequently incorporate general terms of business into their contracts, which are intended to apply to all transactions between them, unless they are expressly excluded. In addition to the above, this Chapter also has a section on the simplification of export documentation.

UNIFORM RULES OF GENERAL CHARACTER

The most important sets of uniform rules applying to international trade transac- **32–002** tions are formulated by international organisations which have as their object, or as one of their objects, the harmonisation of international trade law. These organisations are intergovernmental,[3] regional,[4] or non-governmental.[5] They prepare international conventions, formulate rules for adoption by the parties in their contract, or engage in other harmonising activities. They are known as the formulating agencies.[6] The most important of these, and the measures which they promote, are noted below.

Many of the measures sponsored by the formulating agencies are accepted and applied by the international business community. In view of the progressive global integration of international trade, the activities of these organisations are

---

[1] See *ante*, para. 2–001.
[2] See Mario Matteuci, "The Unification of Commercial Law" [1960] J.B.L. 137.
[3] *e.g.* UNCITRAL and Unidroit.
[4] *e.g.* the E.C.
[5] *e.g.* The International Chamber of Commerce.
[6] See C. M. Schmitthoff, *Commercial Law in a Changing Economic Climate* (2nd ed., 1981), 24 *Essays*, 219.

of importance. The documents which the formulating agencies have produced are numerous, but access is now made easier with the advent of the website.

United Nations Commission on International Trade Law

32–003 In 1966 the United Nations decided to take an interest in the progressive harmonisation of the law of international trade. They constituted the United Nations Commission on International Trade Law (UNCITRAL) which became operative on January 1, 1968. The Commission consists of 36 Member States which are arranged in the following five groups:

(a) African States (nine States);

(b) Asian States (seven States);

(c) Eastern European States (five States);

(d) Latin American States (six States);

(e) Western European and other States (nine States).

The objective of UNCITRAL is to further the progressive harmonisation and unification of the law of international trade. The Secretariat of UNCITRAL is in Vienna.

UNCITRAL publishes a Yearbook containing the substantive documents related to the work of the Commission and its working groups. It has also published a book on UNCITRAL,[7] which is a document of considerable interest. It gives a brief summary of the constitution of UNCITRAL, its working methods and activities, and surveys the various topics on the programme of harmonisation by the Commission. It contains in the Annexes the text of all conventions and other measures prepared and finalised by the Commission.[8]

UNCITRAL is currently pursuing work in the fields of electronic commerce, privately-financed infrastructure projects and assignment in receivables financing.

The most important UNCITRAL texts are as follows:

International conventions

32–004 The *United Nations Convention on Contracts for the International Sale of Goods*[9] was adopted by the United Nations in April 1980 at Vienna. It is intended to supersede the two Hague Conventions on the Uniform Laws on International Sales of 1964. The Vienna Convention came into operation on January 1, 1988 after the required number of ratifications and successions was received. It has not yet been given effect in the United Kingdom.

---

[7] 1986 ed.: UN sales No. E.86.V.8 Published in 1986 (a new edition is in preparation).
[8] General information on UNCITRAL's work and texts of legal instruments resulting from its work is available at the UNCITRAL Website: *http://www.uncitral.org*. Additional information may be obtained from the UNCITRAL Secretariat, e-mail: *uncitral@unov.un.or.at*.
[9] See paras 32–026 to 32–031.

The *United Nations Convention on Independent Guarantees and Stand-by Letters of Credit*, 1996.[10]

The *Convention on the Limitation Period in International Sale of Goods* was recommended by the United Nations in 1974. This Convention was amended for the purposes of aligning it with the Vienna Convention on Contracts for the International Sale of Goods (1980) by a Protocol to the Convention.[11]

The *United Nations Convention on the Carriage of Goods by Sea*, 1978 was adopted by a United Nations conference at Hamburg in 1978. The so-called Hamburg rules adopted by that Convention were jointly prepared by UNCITRAL and UNCTAD (United Nations Conference on Trade and Developments). They are intended to replace the Hague Rules and the Hague-Visby Rules relating to Bills of Lading.[12] The Hamburg Rules have not yet been given effect in the United Kingdom.

The *United Nations Convention on the Liability of Operators of Transport Terminals in International Trade*, 1991.

The *United Nations Convention on International Bills of Exchange and International Promissory Notes*, 1988.

Model Laws

The *UNCITRAL Model Law on International Commercial Arbitration* was **32–005** adopted by the United Nations in 1985.[13] It has been used as a model for national legislation in a large number of jurisdictions.

The *UNCITRAL Model Law on Procurement of Goods, Construction and Services*, 1994, is designed to assist States in reforming and modernising their laws on procurement procedures.

The *UNCITRAL Model Law on Electronic Commerce*, adopted in 1996,[14] is intended to facilitate the use of modern means of communications and storage of information, such as electronic data interchange (EDI), electronic mail, telegram, telex and telecopy, with or without the use of such support as the Internet.

The *UNCITRAL Model Law on Cross-Border Insolvency*, adopted in 1997, has as its purpose the promotion of modern and fair legislation in cases where the insolvent debtor has assets in more than one State.

The *United Nations Model Law on International Credit Transfers*, 1992.

Other instruments

The *UNCITRAL Arbitration Rules*, adopted by the United Nations in 1976, pro- **32–006** vide a framework for international commercial arbitration.[15] They are widely used by individual parties and also as a model for the arbitration rules of arbitral institutions.

---

[10] See *ante*, para. 12–001.
[11] See *ante*, para. 32–032.
[12] See *ante*, para. 15–020.
[13] See *ante*, para. 23–024.
[14] See generally Chap. 33.
[15] See *ante*, para. 23–022.

The *UNCITRAL Conciliation Rules* were adopted by the United Nations in 1980.[16]

The *UNCITRAL Notes on Organizing Arbitral Proceedings* were adopted by the United Nations in 1996.

Legal guides

32–007 The *UNCITRAL Legal Guide on International Countertrade Transactions*, 1992.[17]

The *UNCITRAL Legal Guide on Drawing Up International Contracts for the Construction of Industrial Works*, 1987.

The *UNCITRAL Legal Guide on Electronic Funds Transfers*, 1987.

International Chamber of Commerce publications

32–008 The International Chamber of Commerce, which has consultative status under the Charter of the United Nations, has contributed valuable publications which ease the flow of international trade and are from time to time referred to in this work. Only a few are mentioned below.[18]

Incoterms, which have the sub-title *International Rules for the Interpretation of Trade Terms*, were published by the International Chamber of Commerce and have been amended from time to time; the edition in use at the time of writing is *Incoterms 2000*. The *ICC Guide to Incoterms 2000* became available as from November 1, 1999. Exporters and importers who wish to use them for an individual contract should specify that the contract is governed by the provisions of "Incoterms". Sometimes exporters, particularly in Europe, provide in their general terms of business that all their contracts shall be governed by Incoterms, unless otherwise agreed in a particular instance.[19]

The *Uniform Customs and Practice for Documentary Credits* (1993 Revision)[20] is widely adopted throughout the world[21] and banking associations and individual banks. The *Uniform Rules for Collections* (1995)[22] is also widely used.

The *ICC Rules of Conciliation and Arbitration* (1998).[23] The ICC Court of Arbitration is a popular arbitral tribunal for the settlement of disputes arising from international commercial contracts, but has jurisdiction only if the parties

---

[16] See *ante*, para. 23–023.

[17] See generally Chap. 14.

[18] A complete list of ICC publications can be obtained from ICC's headquarters in Paris (38 Cours Albert 1er, 75008 Paris, Tel: 33 1 49 53 29 33, Fax: 33 1 49 53 29 02, website: *www.iccbooks.com*.

[19] See, *e.g. The Albazero* [1975] 3 W.L.R. 491 at 498.

[20] ICC Brochure No. 500, see Chap. 11. There are a number of other ICC publications on Documentary Credits.

[21] A list of countries which have adopted UCP is obtainable from the National Committees of the ICC or its headquarters in Paris, website: *www.iccwbo.org*.

[22] Brochure No. 522, see *ante*, para. 10–002.

[23] ICC Publication No. 581, see *ante*, para. 23–025. There are a number of other ICC publications on international arbitration.

have agreed to ICC arbitration. Arbitration may be preceded by optional conciliation.

For commercial agency contracts the *ICC Model Commercial Agency Contract*[24] is helpful; also the *ICC Model Distributorship Contract (Sole Importer—Distributor)*.[25]

UNCTAD/ICC Rules for a Combined Multimodal Transport Documents.[26] This publication concerns the adoption of a single combined transport document for the transportation of goods in containers by means of two or more modes (multimodal) of transport. The issue of such a document avoids the need to issue a series of separate transport documents for each stage of the transport.[27]

Uniform Rules for Contract Guarantees[28] deals with the issue of performance and bank guarantees supporting obligations arising in international contracts.

Force Majeure and Hardship.[29] This brochure offers suggestions for the adoption of force majeure and hardship clauses, particularly in long term contracts or contracts involving complex projects, such as turn-key contracts or public works. The arrangements suggested in this document are intended to enable the parties to provide in their contract for any unforeseen eventuality.

American Uniform Commercial Code

The characteristic feature of the American unification of commercial law is that **32–009** it was not carried out by the federal legislation but by the adoption of a uniform law, the Uniform Commercial Code. Work on the Uniform Commercial Code commenced in 1942 as a joint project of the American Law Institute and the National Conference of Commissioners on Uniform State Laws. In 1951 the first official text of the Code was adopted by the two sponsoring organisations. The present Official Text is constantly under review, with amendments being made to individual articles necessitated by changes in commercial law and practice and technological developments. Although the UCC has been enacted by all the U.S. States, the wording of the enactment may vary from State to State.

The Code deals, *inter alia*, with sales,[30] including the terms of export sales,[31] negotiable instruments,[32] bank deposits and collections,[33] letters of credit,[34] funds transfers,[35] bills of lading and other documents of title,[36] funds transfers[37] and leases.[38]

---

[24] Brochure No. 496. Also available is the ICC Model Agency Contract: a Commentary—including diskette (No. 512).
[25] Brochure No. 518.
[26] Brochure No. 481.
[27] See Chap. 16.
[28] Brochure No. 325, see *ante*, para. 12–001.
[29] Brochure No. 421. See *ante*, paras 6–017 to 6–021.
[30] Art. 2 of the Uniform Commercial Code.
[31] See *ante*, para. 2–037.
[32] Art. 3.
[33] Art. 4.
[34] Art. 5.
[35] Art. 4A.
[36] Art. 7.
[37] Art. 6.
[38] Art. 2A.

STANDARD CONTRACT FORMS APPLYING TO SPECIFIED INTERNATIONAL
TRANSACTIONS

32–010 The international trade in many commodities and capital goods is conducted on the basis of standard contract forms. Some of these are issued by international trade associations, of which those of the United Kingdom have worldwide reputation. Others are drafted by the United Nations Economic Commission for Europe. Others again are used in construction contracts for works and installations abroad.

All types of standard contracts have in common that they apply only if the parties to a contract of sale adopt them and that they normally can be varied by agreement of the contracting parties.

Standard conditions issued by trade associations

32–011 The following trade associations are examples of those who provide standard commodity contracts[39]:

(a) the Confederation of British Wool Textiles;

(b) the Cocoa Association of London Ltd;

(c) the Federation of Oil, Seed and Fats Associations (FOSFA);

(d) the Grain and Feed Trade Association (GAFTA);

(e) the London Jute Association;

(f) the London Metal Exchange;

(g) the Sugar Association of London;

(h) the Timber Trade Federation of the United Kingdom.

Some of the above, together with some other trade associations, are members of the British Federation of Commodity Associations.

Model contracts sponsored by United Nations Economic Commission for Europe[40]

32–012 Various sets of general conditions of sale and standard forms of contract have been drafted by working parties convened by the United Nations Economic Commission for Europe.[41]

Notable amongst them are:

---

[39] A list of these markets and trade associations is provided in the Arbitration (Commodity Contracts) Order 1979 (S.I. 1979 No. 754).
[40] For activities of UN/ECE see their website: *www.unece.org*.
[41] The UN/ECE forms can be obtained from United Nations Distribution and Sales Section, Palais des Nations, CH-1211 Geneva. For the activities of UN/ECE see their website: *www.unece.org*.

Form

(a) 188—For the Supply of Plant and Machinery for Export;

(b) 574—For the Supply of Plant and Machinery for Export;

(c) 188A—For the Supply and Erection of Plant and Machinery for Import and Export;

(d) 574A—For the Supply and Erection of Machinery for Import and Export;

(e) 188B—Listing Additional Clauses for Supervision of Erection of Engineering Plant and Machinery abroad;

(f) 574B—Listing Additional Clauses for Supervision of Erection of Engineering Plant and Machinery abroad;

(g) 188D—Listing Additional Clauses for Supervision of Erection of Engineering Plant and Machinery abroad;

(h) 730—For the Export of Durable Consumer Goods and Engineering Articles.

Form 188 and its variations are used between enterprises of free market economy, and Form 574 and its variations are for use between enterprises of socialist economy and for the East–West trade, while Form 730 can be used for international trade between any enterprises.[42]

Further, the Economic Commission for Europe has published a series of interconnected Guides dealing with major international contracts for the construction of works and installations,[43] although it should be noted that these and the General Conditions referred to above have not been revised for upwards of 20 years. The ECE has more recently published additional General Conditions and Guides,[44] including Guides for the economies in transition.[45]

---

[42] On the difference between these forms, see [1965] J.B.L. 100 and [1966] J.B.L. 71. Of further importance is the "Preface to the General Conditions of Sale, Standard Forms of Contract and Commercial Arbitration Instruments prepared under the auspices of the United Nations Economic Commission of Europe".

[43] Guide for use in drawing up contracts relating to the international transfer of know-how in the engineering industry (Trade/222/Rev. 1); Guide on drawing up contracts for large industrial works (ECE/Trade/117); Guide on drawing up international contracts on industrial co-operation (ECE/Trade/124); Guide for drawing up international contracts between parties associated for the purpose of executing a specific project (ECE/Trade/131); Guide for drawing up international contracts on consulting engineering, including some related aspects of technical assistance (ECE/Trade/145); Guide on drawing up international contracts for services relating to maintenance, repair and operation of industrial and other works (ECE/Trade/154); East-West Joint Venture Contracts (ECE/Trade/165); International Counterpurchase Contracts (ECE/Trade/169); International Buy-Back Contracts (ECE/Trade 176); Guide on new forms of industrial co-operation (1988); Juridical Guide for the creation of East-West joint ventures on the territory of socialist countries (1988).

[44] Guide for drawing up international contracts on consulting engineering, including some related aspects of technical assistance (ECE/Trade/145); Guide on drawing up international contracts for services relating to maintenance, repair and operation of industrial and other works (ECE/Trade/154).

[45] Guide on Legal Aspects of Privatisation in Industry (ECE/Trade/180); Management Development in East-West Joint Ventures: A Guide for Managers in the Economies in Transition (ECE/Trade/185).

The Economic Commission for Europe has sponsored model contracts for the sale of fresh fruit and vegetables, dry and dried fruit and potatoes.

Model contract forms used in construction contracts

32–013 The main model contract forms used in construction contracts are listed and considered in an earlier chapter[46] and will therefore not be repeated here.

The International Bank for Reconstruction and Development (IBRD)[47] has published Guidelines for Procurement under IBRD Loans and IDA Credits (January 1995, most recently revised January 1999) and Guidelines for Selection and Employment of Consultants by World Bank Borrowers (January 1997).

Also set out in Chap. 25 are the various E.C. Directives concerning tendering for public works.

The model contract forms sponsored by the United Nations Economic Commission for Europe, which are listed in the preceding paragraph, are also used in international construction work. UNCITRAL has also published a Legal Guide on Drawing up International Contracts for Construction of Industrial Works (1988).

GENERAL TERMS OF BUSINESS ADOPTED BY INDIVIDUAL EXPORTERS

32–014 The importance, for international sales, of well-drafted general terms of business can hardly be exaggerated. They are particularly important where neither uniform conditions of export sales nor standard contract forms are used. Litigation can often be avoided when the seller is able to refer the buyer to a clause in his printed terms of business which was embodied in the quotation or acceptance, and the fact that these terms apply to all transactions concluded by the seller adds persuasive force to his argument.

Some important clauses

32–015 The most important clauses which the exporter should incorporate in his general terms of business are:

(a) *General clause* which subjects every contract of sale to the seller's conditions of sale;

(b) *Retention of title clause* which provides that until the seller receives the purchase price fully in cash,

(i) the seller retains the legal property in the goods and is given the irrevocable right to enter the premises of the buyer at any time and without notice in order to retake possession of the goods; and

(ii) the buyer may resell the goods only as an agent of the seller and only in the ordinary course of business to a bona fide repurchaser,

---

[46] See *ante*, Chap. 25.
[47] Known as the World Bank, website: *www.worldbank.org*.

and, if he does so, shall receive the proceeds of the resale as an agent of and trustee for the seller and shall place the proceeds of sale in a separate account in the name of the seller.[48]

(c) *Price escalation clause* which provides that unless firm prices and charges are agreed upon, the seller shall be entitled to increase the agreed prices and charges in the same proportion in which the prices or charges of the goods or their components, including costs of labour to be paid or borne by the seller, have been increased between the date of the quotation and the date of the delivery[49];

(d) *Interest* which provides where payment is made after the agreed date, interest shall be paid at a specified rate[50];

(e) *Force majeure clause* (an illustration of this clause was given earlier)[51];

(f) *Choice of law clause* which specifies that the contract be governed by English law;

(g) *Arbitration* which provides that any disputes between the parties are to be settled by arbitration, or

(h) *Jurisdiction*, providing for the jurisdiction of the English courts.[52]

It is emphasised that the above clauses are indicated here only in very general terms. The exporter is advised to ask his solicitor to frame appropriate general terms of business, which should be revised from time to time.

Standard terms in domestic transactions

The Unfair Contract Terms Act 1977 provides[53] that where one of the con-   **32–016** tracting parties deals on the other's written standard terms of business, the party who inserted the standard terms cannot rely on them in order to exclude or restrict his liability, except if the standard term in question satisfies the test of reasonableness. The same rules apply if the party who inserted the standard terms wishes to rely on them in order to avoid performance of the contract.

These provisions will not, however, normally concern the exporter because they do not apply to international supply contracts, as defined in section 26 of the Act.[54]

---

[48] For a discussion of the various types of reservation of title clauses and their effectiveness in English law see *ante*, paras 4–007 to 4–009.

[49] Several variants of the price escalation or "rise and fall" clause are in use. Sometimes, a "rise" clause is inserted into a c.i.f. contract; the clause provides for an increase of the purchase price if the freight and insurance charges are raised. It may also be necessary to insert provisions dealing with the exchange rate risk (or at least to cover this risk by an appropriate financial arrangement).

[50] *e.g.* 3 per cent above the base lending rate of the National Westminster Bank plc.

[51] See *ante*, paras 6–017 to 6–021.

[52] On the question of whether arbitration or litigation is preferable, see *ante*, para. 23–002.

[53] In s. 3.

[54] See *ante*, para. 3–019.

SIMPLIFYING INTERNATIONAL TRADE

32–017 The Simpler Trade Procedures Board (SITPRO),[55] is the United Kingdom's trade facilitation agency. SITPRO is a Department of Trade and Industry sponsored activity, which exists to facilitate and simplify international trade. It achieves this by working with commercial bodies, government departments and business to rationalise and standardise international trade law and procedures. This activity covers the whole business process, including logistics, banking and Customs. Its objectives in these areas can be summarised as:

(a) encouraging the alignment and simplification of legislation and reduction in burdens on business, through new trader, based control techniques and single transmission of data;

(b) promoting the use of simpler payment methods and standard contractual terms;

(c) providing a system of aligned standardised documents for international trade; and

(d) encouraging the use of electronic commerce.

SITPRO's current priorities are directed towards introducing practical solutions to promote the use of electronic commerce[56] such as the "Electra" project, which is aimed at enabling parties to use both paper documents and EDI in the same transaction. This takes account of the reality of international trade practice— that not all parties in an international business process are capable of handling EDI messages and that the current message structures are quite complex.

SITPRO is also renowned for its work with HM Customs & Excise and the European Commission (with the latter as a member of EUROPRO[57]). Activities include simplification of Customs export procedures, use of export data for import purposes, completion of the Single Market and alignment of Customs legislation. SITPRO is also involved with the World Customs Organisation (WCO) on the revision of the Kyoto Convention,[58] which was completed at the end of 1999 and is to be ratified in 2001.

Historically SITPRO is perhaps best known for the U.K. Aligned Series of Export Documents. This system, which is based on UN/ECE Recommendations,[59] simplifies the completion and reading of documentation by standardising the format and position of data fields, thus aiding completion by computer. Information is keyed in only once, allowing the computer to manage and print

---

[55] Website: *www.sitpro.org.uk*, e-mail: *info@e-sitpro.org.uk*.
[56] See *post*, para. 33–001.
[57] The trade facilitation organisation of the E.U. and EFTA countries.
[58] Simplification and Harmonisation of Customs Procedures.
[59] United Nations Economic Commission for Europe, Centre of Expertise for Administration, Commerce and Transport (UN/ECE CEFACT), Recommendation No. 1—United Nations Layout Key.

off the required forms. This reduces time, effort and error rates[60] and consequently cuts costs.

The range of documents in the U.K. Aligned system are held in the publication "*Top Form*".[61] The documents include invoices, bills of lading, sea and air way bills, certificates of origin, Customs documents (the Single Administrative Document, EUR1, Intrastat declaration, etc.), insurance documents and a range of banking forms. The savings for exporters using the Aligned System have been assessed as substantial, reducing administrative costs by up to 50 per cent.[62] Further, with the standardisation of the data fields to UNTDED standards,[63] the transition from supplying paper documents to transmitting data by electronic commerce is made much simpler.

As well as working to facilitate international trade, SITPRO provides free fact sheets on a range of subjects, including general exporting, getting paid and specific country information. A set of letter of credit checklists and management guidelines for exporters are also available. In addition, there is a direct help-line for exporters needing technical advice.[64]

The activities of the national trade facilitation organisations generally are co-ordinated at the highest level by the United Nations Economic Commission for Europe Centre of Expertise for Administration, Commerce and Transport (UN/ECE CEFACT[65]). UN/ECE CEFACT has its own trade facilitation work programme as well as being responsible for the administration of the world standard for EDI—UN/EDIFACT.

THE UNIFORM LAWS IN THE UNITED KINGDOM

The Uniform Laws on International Sales Act 1967

This enactment introduces the two Uniform Laws adopted by the Hague Conference of 1964 into the law of the United Kingdom. They are appended to the Act as Schedules 1 and 2. The Act of 1967 was activated and the two Uniform Laws came into force in the United Kingdom on August 18, 1972.[66]   **32–018**

Application of Uniform Laws only if adopted by parties

The Order in Council which gives effect to the two Uniform Laws provides that   **32–019** the Uniform Law on Sales shall only apply if it has been chosen by the parties

---

[60] Errors in export documents can prove extremely costly, either in terms of misdeclarations to Customs, or under letter of credit transactions, causing the documents to be rejected by the banks. On the latter, several surveys assessing letter of credit rejections show a rejection rate of between 55 and 70 per cent. A significant proportion of these rejections are due to documentary errors.

[61] The current edition is *Top Form* 2 (1997). *Top Form* is available from SITPRO, who can be contacted through the Department of Trade and Industry, Tel: 020 7215 5000.

[62] Quoted as saving four thousand U.K. exporters at least £40m a year; Institute of Directors, "Director's Guides to Exporting", 1992, p. 79.

[63] UN/ECE Trade Data Elements Directory.

[64] SITPRO helpline Tel: 020 7215 0800.

[65] Formerly UN/ECE Working Party 4.

[66] Vienna Convention, *post*, paras 32–026 to 32–031; Limitation Period Convention, *post*, para. 32–032.

to the contract[67]; the Uniform Law on Formation has only ancillary character and applies only to contracts to which the Uniform Law on Sales is applied.[68]

While such a restriction considerably reduces the usefulness of the Uniform Laws, it might lead to a difficulty if one party to the contract is resident in the United Kingdom and the other in a country in which the Uniform Laws apply automatically (unless excluded by the parties). This raises a problem of private international law, namely that it has to be determined whether the applicable law of the contract is English or foreign law.[69] In the latter case, the Uniform Laws apply to an English party who has not adopted them in the contract, but in the former, they apply only if adopted by the parties.

Mandatory provisions of applicable law cannot be contracted out of

32–020 When the parties adopt the Uniform Laws—and they may adopt them even if the conditions for the application of the Uniform Laws are not satisfied—the parties cannot, by so doing, contract out of the mandatory provisions of the law which would have been applicable if they had not chosen the Uniform Laws.[70] As far as the law of the United Kingdom is concerned, the only provisions which are mandatory by statute[71] are those aiming at the protection of the consumer in the domestic sale of goods, namely those contained in the Unfair Contract Terms Act 1977, ss. 2 to 7. As already stated, these provisions apply only to domestic sales. They do not apply to international supply contracts.[72] As regards the latter type of contract, exemption clauses, if freely negotiated, are perfectly valid.

Further, by adopting the Uniform Laws, the parties cannot contract out of provisions directly founded on public policy.

GENERAL LIMITATIONS OF UNIFORM LAWS

32–021 It is recognised that two of these general limitations are the restriction of these Laws to cases in which the parties have chosen them as the applicable law of the contract[73] and the rule that the parties cannot exclude the mandatory provisions of the applicable law by their adoption of the Uniform Laws.[74] There are, however, further limitations which may be introduced by States when ratifying the Conventions to which the Uniform Laws are appended.

---

[67] This regulation was admitted by the 1967 Act s. 1(3). The United Kingdom was entitled to restrict the scope of the Uniform Law on Sales in this manner by virtue of Art. V of the First Convention.
[68] 1967 Act., Sched. 2, Art. 1.
[69] See *ante*, Chap. 21.
[70] Uniform Laws on International Sales Act 1967, s. 1(4); this section was amended by the Unfair Contract Terms Act 1977, Sched. 4, and by the Sale of Goods Act 1979, Sched. 2, para. 15. Also Uniform Law of Sales, Art. 4.
[71] Unfair Contract Terms Act 1977, s. 27(2).
[72] Unfair Contract Terms Act 1977, s. 26.
[73] Uniform Law on Sales, Art. 4.
[74] Art. II of both Conventions.

Restriction to contracts between parties in Convention States

The Uniform Laws, as drafted, apply to all cases in which the parties to the **32–022** contract have their places of business in the territories of different States or, if they have no place of business, are habitually resident in different States.[75] The Laws do not require that the places of business or habitual residence should be in the territories of Contracting States; in brief, they do not require reciprocity in that respect. However, a State, when ratifying the Conventions embodying the Uniform Laws, may stipulate that it will apply them only if each of the parties to the contract has his place of business or habitual residence in the territory of a different State which likewise has ratified the Conventions.[76] The United Kingdom, when enacting the Uniform Laws of International Sales Act 1967, has made use of this qualification.[77]

A State which adopts this qualification introduces into its law an unfortunate complication. It has two legal regimes applying to international sales contracts, one in respect of residents in Convention States and the other in respect of residents in other foreign countries.

CONTRACTS OF INTERNATIONAL SALE

The Uniform Laws apply only to contracts for the international sale of goods. **32–023** They do not apply to domestic transactions.[78]

A contract of international sale, within the meaning of the Uniform Laws in the form adopted by the 1967 Act, is defined[79] as a contract of sale of goods entered into by parties whose places of business are in the territories of "different contracting States",[80] in each of the following cases:

(a) where the contract involves the sale of goods which are at the time of the conclusion of the contract in the course of carriage or will be carried from the territory of one State to the territory of another;

(b) where the acts constituting the offer and the acceptance have been effected in the territories of different States;

---

[75] Uniform Law on Sales, Art. 1(1) and (2).

[76] Both Conventions, Art. III.

[77] 1967 Act, s. 1(1). See also the reference to "Contracting Parties" in Art. 1(1) of the First Convention, contained in Sched. 1 of the 1967 Act. For a list of contracting states see *http://www.uncitral.org*.

[78] Unless a State introduces legislation applying them to domestic transactions or the parties to home transaction adopt them.

[79] Uniform Law on Sales, Art. 1. This definition should be compared with that of the international supply contract in section 26 of the Unfair Contract Terms Act 1977; see *ante*, para. 3–019.

[80] Two or more States may declare that they do not consider themselves as "different States" for the purposes of the Uniform Laws, because their law of sale and their law on the formation of the contract of sale are substantially the same; see the two Conventions, Art. II, and the two Uniform Laws, Art. 1(5). Such a declaration of conformity can, *e.g.* be made between the United Kingdom, on the one hand, and Australia, New Zealand and Canada (with the exception of Quebec) on the other hand, if the latter States decide to adopt the Uniform Laws.

(c) where delivery of the goods is to be made in the territory of a State
other than that within whose territory the acts constituting the offer and
the acceptance have been effected.

Where a party to the contract does not have a place of business, the habitual
residence of the party shall determine his *situs*. The nationality of the parties is
irrelevant for the determination of the international character of the contract.[81]
Further, the Uniform Laws apply to contracts of sale regardless of the commercial or private character of the parties.[82]

THE UNIFORM LAW ON INTERNATIONAL SALES

32–024 The Uniform Law on Sales does not define the trade terms customary in international trade[83] but provides[84]:

1. The parties shall be bound by any usage which they have expressly or
   impliedly made applicable to their contract and by any practices which
   have been established between themselves.

2. They shall also be bound by usages which reasonable persons in the
   same situation as the parties usually consider to be applicable to their
   contract. In the event of conflict with the present Law, the usages shall
   prevail unless agreed by the parties.

3. Where expressions, provisions or forms of contract commonly used in
   commercial practice are employed, they shall be interpreted according
   to the meaning usually given to them in the trade concerned.

Consequently, where the parties have agreed on a trade term, such as f.o.b. or
c.i.f., the regulation intended by that term takes precedence over the provisions
of the Law. Further, the Law does not prevent the parties from agreeing on a
uniform interpretation of these trade terms, *e.g.* by embodying into their contract
Incoterms or a similar text.

The Uniform Law does not use the distinction between conditions and warranties which, as we have seen,[85] the Sale of Goods Act, 1979 adopts. It distinguishes, however, between two types of breach of contract, namely a fundamental
and a non-fundamental breach. A fundamental breach occurs[86]:

> "wherever the party in breach knew, or ought to have known, at the time of the conclusion
> of the contract, that a reasonable person in the same situation as the other party would not
> have entered into the contract if he had foreseen the breach and its effects."

---

[81] Uniform Law on Sales, Art. 1(3).
[82] *ibid.* Art. 7.
[83] See *ante*, Chap. 2.
[84] In Art. 9 of the Uniform Law on Sales. (All references to articles in this section are to the Uniform
Law on Sales (1967 Act, Sched. 1), unless stated otherwise.)
[85] See *ante*, para. 5–003.
[86] Art. 10.

The principle of the Law is that where a breach is of fundamental nature, the person who suffers it may declare the contract as avoided. However, if the breach is not fundamental the contract continues to be in existence, subject to the right of the wronged party to claim damages. This is similar in effect to the English concept of the innominate term, discussed earlier.[87] These rules may be illustrated by reference to the case of a seller who has failed to deliver the goods on time, *i.e.* at the date agreed in the contract. It depends here on the importance which the parties have attached to timely delivery. If the failure to deliver on time constitutes a fundamental breach, the buyer has the choice between requiring performance of the contract or declaring the contract avoided; if he does not exercise this choice within a reasonable time, the contract is automatically avoided.[88] On the other hand, if the failure of timely delivery does not amount to a fundamental breach, the buyer may grant the seller an additional period of reasonable length, and failure to deliver within this period would turn the non-fundamental breach into a fundamental breach.[89]

Of further interest are the provisions of the Uniform Law on the rights of the buyer if the seller tenders or delivers "non-conforming goods", *i.e.* goods which fail to conform with their description in the contract or with the stipulated quantity or quality. Such a failure will normally constitute a fundamental breach of the seller's obligation to deliver the goods contracted for.[90] In these cases the buyer loses his right to rely on lack of conformity:

1. if he fails to notify the seller promptly[91] after he has discovered that lack or ought to have discovered it, but in no circumstances, not even in the case of hidden defects, can notice of lack of conformity be given after two years from the date when the goods were handed over, unless a longer guarantee was stipulated in the contract.[92] The notice of lack of conformity must specify the nature of the defects[93]; or

2. if he fails to take the matter to the court, by action or defence, within one year after having given notice of lack of conformity, except if he has been prevented from relying on lack of conformity by fraud on the part of the seller or if he claims reduction of the price in an action for payment of the price by the seller.[94]

If the buyer has given due notice of lack of conformity, he is entitled:

---

[87] See *ante*, para. 5–004.
[88] See Art. 26(1). This rule is subject to exceptions, see Art. 26(2) and (3). "Avoidance of the contract" does not mean that the contract is null and void from the beginning, it merely releases both parties from their obligations thereunder (Art. 78). In the case of avoidance of the contract the buyer may be entitled to damages (Art. 84).
[89] See Art. 27.
[90] Art. 33.
[91] *i.e.* "within as short a period as possible" (Art. 11).
[92] Art. 39(1).
[93] Art. 39(2).
[94] Art. 49.

1. to demand performance of the contract by the seller.[95] But where the court would not order specific performance in respect of similar contracts not governed by the Law—as is the case in England—it is not compelled by the Law to order specific performance of an international contract[96]; or

2. to declare the contract as avoided, but only if the lack of conformity constitutes a fundamental breach[97] or;

3. to reduce the price[98]; and

4. in addition, to claim damages.[99]

If the lack of conformity does not constitute a fundamental breach, the seller is entitled, even after the date fixed for the delivery of the goods, to make a second tender of conforming goods or to remedy the defect, "provided that the exercise of this right does not cause the buyer either unreasonable inconvenience or unreasonable expense".[1] Here again, however, the buyer can turn the non-fundamental breach into a fundamental one by fixing an additional period for further delivery or for remedying the defect.[2]

THE UNIFORM LAW ON FORMATION

32–025 This Law, as adopted by the U.K. Uniform Laws on International Sales Act 1967, is ancillary to the Uniform Law on Sales, *i.e.* it applies only to contracts of international sale "which, if they were concluded, would be governed by the Uniform Law on the International Sale of Goods".[3] This curious provision postulates a retrospective consideration. One has first to assume that the contract was validly concluded, then to satisfy oneself that it falls within the ambit of the Uniform Law on Sales, and if that condition is satisfied, one has to revert to the primary assumption and to examine whether the contract was or was not validly concluded.

Three provisions of the Law on Formation deserve special mention. First, the Law attempts to reconcile the different attitude of English and European continental law to the problem of the firm offer. In English law an offer can, in principle, always be revoked until it is accepted. In short, unless the offer is by deed, rendered irrevocable by statute,[4] or supported by consideration, the concept of a binding offer is not admitted in English law.[5] In most European contin-

---

[95] Art. 41(1)(a).
[96] First Convention, Art. VII.
[97] Art. 41(1)(b).
[98] Art. 41(1)(c).
[99] Art. 41(2).
[1] Art. 44(1).
[2] Art. 44(2).
[3] Uniform Law on Formation, Art. 1. (All references to articles in this section are to the Uniform Law on Formation (1967 Act, Sched. 2), unless stated otherwise.)
[4] See Companies Act 1985, s. 82(7).
[5] American law differs in this respect from English law; the Uniform Commercial Code (Official text), s. 2-205, allows in certain circumstances firm offers.

ental laws, on the other hand, an offeror is bound by his offer unless he has excluded its binding character. The compromise adopted by the Uniform Law on Formation is that in principle an offer can be revoked but such a revocation is excluded—

1. if the offer states a fixed time for acceptance or otherwise indicates that it is firm or irrevocable; or

2. if the revocation is not made in good faith or in conformity with fair dealing.[6]

Secondly, the Uniform Law on Formation attempts to solve the problem of an acceptance containing additional stipulations. In English law, if such stipulations are contained in the acceptance, the offer is normally regarded as rejected and the acceptance constitutes a counter-offer, which may or may not be accepted by the original offeror. Logical as this rule is, it is iniquitous if the additional terms are only immaterial or trifling.[7] The Uniform Law provides that in principle an acceptance containing additions, limitations or other modifications shall be a rejection of the offer and a counter-offer, but if these additional or different terms do not alter the terms of the offer materially, the reply including these additions or modifications shall constitute the acceptance, unless the offeror promptly objects to the discrepancy.[8]

Thirdly, the Uniform Law deals with the case of the late acceptance. Here it is provided that such an acceptance may be treated by the offeror as having arrived in due time if he promptly so informs the acceptor.[9] Further, if the delay in the receipt of the acceptance is due to unusual circumstances and the communication of the acceptance would have arrived in time if the transmission had been normal, the acceptance is deemed to have been communicated in due time, unless the offeror has promptly informed the acceptor that he considers his offer as lapsed.[10]

UN CONVENTION ON CONTRACTS FOR THE INTERNATIONAL SALE OF GOODS (1980)

The Vienna Convention and the Hague Uniform Laws

It has already been observed that the Vienna Convention came into operation **32–026** on January 1, 1988.[11]

---

[6] Art. 5(2) and (3).

[7] Here again, modern American law adopts a different solution in the Uniform Commercial Code (Official text), s.2-207.

[8] Art. 7. This provision is referred to in *Butler Machine Tool Co Ltd v. Ex-Cell-O Corporation (England) Ltd* [1979] 1 W.L.R. 401 at 406; see *ante*, para. 3–018.

[9] Art. 9(1).

[10] Art. 9(2).

[11] The main literature on the Vienna Convention (in English) is: J. O. Honnold, *Uniform Law for International Sales* (Kluwer Law International, 1999); C. M. Bianca and M. J. Bonnell (eds), *Commentary on the International Sales Law. The 1980 Vienna Sales Convention*, 1987; P. Schlechtriem, *Uniform Sales Law. The UN Convention on Contracts for the International Sale of Goods*; H.

Although founded on the Hague Uniform Laws, the Vienna Convention differs from them in form and, in some respects, in substance.

As regards form, the subject-matter of the two Uniform Laws is contained in the Vienna Convention in one document. The Vienna Convention consists of four Parts:

    I. Sphere of Application and General Provisions.

    II. Formation of the Contract.

    III. Sale of Goods.

    IV. Final Provisions.

Part II deals with offer and acceptance and the conclusion of the contract and is founded on the 1964 Uniform Law on Formation. Part III, which is based on the 1964 Uniform Law on International Sales, is subdivided into the following chapters:

    I. General Provisions.

    II. Obligations of the Seller.

    III. Obligations of the Buyer.

    IV. Passing of the Risk.

    V. Provisions common to the obligations of the Seller and the Buyer.

Chapter V of Part III contains provisions on anticipatory breach,[12] damages and exemptions,[13] and avoidance of contract.[14] It also contains provisions on the preservation of the goods.[15]

The Convention provides that a Contracting State, by declaration on accession, may adopt only Part II (on formation of contract) or Part III (on sale of goods).[16]

As regards substance, the Vienna Convention has greatly simplified the regulation contained in the Uniform Laws and has made it more flexible. A German scholar comments on these features of the Convention[17]:

> "The tendency to avoid inflexible and irrevocable legal remedies . . . influenced the formulation of the remedy provisions in the 1980 Convention. The need for greater judicial discretion in particular cases also became clear, such as in the requirement that a measure or waiting period should be 'reasonable'. The new provisions on time limitations for giving notice in a timely manner (Articles 39 and 44) show especially clearly the strongly felt need for flexible rules to accommodate the buyer's difficulties."

Haddad, *Remedies of the Unpaid Seller in International Sale of Goods under ULIS and 1980 UN Convention*, 1985. For the current list of signatories and general information see *http://www.uncitral.org*.

[12] Arts 71 and 72.

[13] Arts 74 to 77, 79 and 80.

[14] Arts 81 to 84.

[15] Arts 85 to 88.

[16] Art. 92.

[17] P. Schlechtriem, *loc. cit.*, n. 11.

Applicability of the Vienna Convention

The sphere of application of the Vienna Convention[18] is different from that of **32–027**
the Uniform Laws. While the latter are intended to apply in principle to all
international sales but enable an acceding State to restrict their application to
sales contracts between parties who have their place of business or habitual
residence in Contracting States,[19] the Vienna Convention—realistically—
restricts its application to contracts between parties who have their place of
business in different Contracting States, or to cases in which the proper law
of the contract is that of a Contracting State. Article 1(1) of the Convention
provides:

> "This Convention applies to contracts of sale of goods between parties whose places of business are in different States:
>
> (a) when the States are Contracting States; or
> (b) when the rules of private international law lead to the application of the law of a Contracting State."

A state may not become a party to the Vienna Convention if it wishes to provide
that the Convention shall only apply if parties to a contract have adopted it.[20]
However, it does allow parties to exclude its application, or to derogate from or
vary the effect of its provisions by their contract.[21] The effect of this regulation
in the United Kingdom is that: under the 1967 Act the Uniform Laws apply
only if the parties "contract in". When the Vienna Convention is introduced
into United Kingdom law, parties who do not wish to be subject to the Convention regulation will have to "contract out".

The Vienna Convention and the national law

While the Uniform Law on International Sales is intended to be a self-contained **32–028**
code as regards the topics regulated by it, and expressly excludes the rules of
private international law,[22] the draftsmen of the Vienna Convention were aware
that measures of conflict avoidance can reduce the dangers of a conflict of laws
but cannot completely exclude them. For this reason they have linked the Vienna
Convention with the national systems of private international law. This linkage
occurs in two respects.

First, the Vienna Convention (like the Uniform Sales Law) does not regulate
all incidents of the international sales transaction. It does not regulate:

---

[18] The Convention, by virtue of Article 2, does not apply to sales (a) of goods for personal, family
or household use (with a slight qualification); (b) by auction; (c) on execution or otherwise by
authority of law; (d) of stocks, shares, investment securities, negotiable instruments or money; (e)
of ships, vessels, hovercraft or aircraft; (f) electricity. The Convention likewise does not apply to
barter arrangements.
[19] The United Kingdom has made use of this qualification.
[20] This qualification is provided by Art. V of the First Convention of 1964 and the United Kingdom
availed itself of it by the Uniform Laws on International Sales Act 1967, s. 1(3); see *ante*, para. 32–
019.
[21] Art. 6.
[22] See *ante*, Chap. 21.

(a) the special trade terms for the delivery of goods and the fixing of the price[23]; and

(b) the passing of property in the goods.[24]

Secondly, the Convention contains an express reference to national systems of private international law for the filling of gaps in the Convention. Article 7(2) provides:

> "Questions concerning matters governed by this Convention not expressly settled in it are to be settled in conformity with the general principles on which it is based or, in the absence of such principles, in conformity with the law applicable by virtue of the rules of private international law."

A good illustration of the linkage between the Vienna Convention and national law is provided by American law. The Convention is part of the federal law of the USA[25] and, as such overrides the Uniform Commercial Code, which is state law in the States which have given effect to it,[26] except if the parties have excluded the application of the Convention in whole or part,[27] or in so far as a particular topic is not regulated by the Convention. These topics include important parts of Article 2 of the UCC—this is the Article dealing with Sales—such as the special trade terms[28] and the provisions on passing of title, reservation for security and good faith purchasers.[29] The same relationship exists between the Vienna Convention and other national systems of law. It will therefore be necessary in many cases to ascertain the national law governing the international sales contract.

The central position of the Vienna Convention

32–029 The Vienna International Sales Convention is intended to be the centrepiece of international harmonisation of trade law. A number of other associated Conventions are linked to it, each dealing with a specialised subject and being self-contained, but taking account of the provisions of the International Sales Con-

---

[23] See *ante*, para. 32–024.

[24] Art. 4(b). The reason for this exclusion is that the regulation of the passing of property in the various legal systems is so different that a uniform rule cold not be established; see *ante*, para. 4–002. In addition, the Convention does not regulate the law governing the alleged invalidity of a contract on general grounds, such as fraud, misrepresentation, incapacity and so on (Art. 4(a)). Product liability is likewise not regulated by the Convention (Art. 5).

[25] UCC.

[26] These are all USA States and jurisdictions, except Louisiana. The effect is that the Vienna Convention is law in Louisiana but Article 2 of the UCC is not.

[27] By virtue of Article 6 of the Convention. If the parties adopt in their contract the law of a Contracting State, their adoption would include the adoption of the State's private international law and they would then again adopt the Convention; if they wish to exclude the Convention, they have to adopt the *domestic* law of the Contracting State. Thus, a choice of law clause in favour of the law of New York makes the Convention applicable, but a choice of law clause in favour of New York *domestic* law does not have this effect.

[28] ss. 2-319 to 2-324 of the UCC.

[29] ss. 2-401 to 2-403. s. 2-402 deals with the rights of the seller's creditors against the sold goods. But the provisions of s. 2-201 of the UCC, which requires evidence in writing for sales contracts of $500 or more, is excluded by Art. 11 of the Vienna Convention and the USA has not declared Art. 11 to be inapplicable.

vention. Thus, the UN Limitation Period Convention of 1974 was amended by the Vienna Conference of 1980 on the same day as the Conference approved the International Sales Convention, in order to make it conform to the latter.[30] Other of these linked Conventions are the Hague Convention on the Law applicable to Contracts for the International Sale of Goods of 1986[31] and the Geneva Convention on Agency in the International Sale of Goods in 1983.[32] The two Ottawa Conventions on International Factoring and International Financial Leasing of 1988[33] are also linked to the Vienna Convention.

Some features of the Vienna Convention

Fundamental and non-fundamental breach

The Convention adopts many concepts of the Uniform Sales Law of 1964, but **32–030** has refined them and made them more useful. It retains the distinction between fundamental and non-fundamental breach of the sales contract but defines fundamental breach in a more objective manner.[34] The definition of fundamental breach in the Vienna Convention[35] should be compared with that of the Uniform Law on International Sales.[36] The Vienna Convention definition is as follows:

> "A breach of contract committed by one of the parties is fundamental if it results in such detriment to the other party as substantially to deprive him of what he is entitled to expect under the contract, unless the party in breach did not foresee and a reasonable person of the same kind in the same circumstances would not have foreseen such a result."

From the practical point of view, the objective test of fundamental breach considerably restricts the cases in which avoidance of the international sales contract can be claimed under the Vienna Convention.

Specific performance and repair of non-conforming goods

The Vienna Convention entitles the buyer to demand specific performance, **32–031** delivery of substitute goods for non-conforming goods and even repair of such goods. Article 46 of the Convention provides:

> (1) The buyer may require performance by the seller of his obligations unless the buyer has resorted to a remedy which is inconsistent with this requirement.
>
> (2) If the goods do not conform with the contract, the buyer may require delivery of substitute goods only if the lack of conformity constitutes a fundamental breach of contract and a

---

[30] See *post*, para. 32–032.
[31] See *ante*, para. 32–026.
[32] See *ante*, para. 27–030.
[33] Not ratified by the United Kingdom.
[34] The definition of fundamental breach in the Uniform Sales Law has been criticised as being too subjective.
[35] Art. 25 of the Vienna Convention.
[36] Art. 10 of the Uniform Law; see *ante*, para. 32–024.

> request for substitute goods is made either in conjunction with notice given under Article 39[37] or within a reasonable time thereafter.
>
> (3) If the goods do not conform with the contract, the buyer may require the seller to remedy the lack of conformity by repair, unless this is unreasonable having regard to all the circumstances. A request for repair must be made either in conjunction with notice given under Article 39[38] or within a reasonable time thereafter.

These remedies are different from those normally available in English law. In English law the normal remedy for the breach of a condition, such as the supply of non-conforming goods, is a claim for damages. A claim for the repair of such goods is unknown to the common law.

UN CONVENTION ON THE LIMITATION PERIOD IN THE INTERNATIONAL SALE OF GOODS (1974)

32–032 This Convention was signed June 14, 1974 in New York. It was the first project of UNCITRAL which reached fruition. This Convention was amended by a Protocol, adopted by the UN Conference at Vienna on April 11, 1980, the same day when the Convention on Contracts for the International Sale of Goods was approved. The purpose of the Protocol is to align the provisions of the Limitation Convention with those of the Contracts for the International Sale of Goods Convention. The United Kingdom has not ratified the Limitation Convention.[39]

The Convention is intended to replace a variety of conflicting national laws, which provide limitation periods ranging from six months to 30 years. The basic aim of the Convention is to establish a uniform time limit that prevents the pressing of claims at such a late date that evidence has become unreliable.

The Convention[40] limits to four years the period within which a buyer or seller may press claims based on a contract for the international sale of goods.[41] The sphere of application of the Limitation Convention is assimilated by the 1980 Protocol to that of the International Sales Convention of that year.[42]

The Convention contains provisions specifying exactly when the limitation period begins to run, which is usually the case when the claim becomes due. It also states when the limitation period ceases to run, under what circumstances it can be extended, how it can be modified by the parties and how it is calculated. In the case of a breach of contract, the limitation period begins on the date of

---

[37] Article 39 provides that the buyer loses the right to rely on non-conformity if he does not give the seller notice specifying the defects within a reasonable time, and in any event he loses that right if he does not give such notice within two years from the date when the goods were handed over, unless a longer guarantee was given.

[38] Michael Will, the commentator of Article 46 in *Bianca and Bonnell* (see n. 11, *ante*), states that the common law admits a claim for specific performance in equity only if damages would be an inadequate remedy. He then states: "interestingly enough, the two opposing approaches appear to be less different in practice". It is thought that this comment is correct because the aggrieved buyer will normally prefer to claim damages.

[39] Position.

[40] The Convention, as amended by the 1980 Protocol, does not apply to the sales to which the International Sales Convention does not apply; see n. 18, *ante*. The exclusions in the unamended Limitation Convention are worded slightly differently.

[41] Art. 8 of the Limitation Convention.

[42] See para. 32–027. In the unamended Limitation Convention the sphere of application was different.

the breach. When the buyer finds a defect in the goods supplied or discovers that they do not otherwise conform to the terms of the contract, the limitation period starts from the date when the goods were handed over to him or their delivery is refused by him. The limitation period for claims based on fraud begins on the date on which the fraud is discovered or reasonably could be discovered.

The limitation period ceases to run when one party begins judicial or arbitral proceedings against the other. In the case of other proceedings, including those in which a party presses a claim upon the death or insolvency of the other party, the period ceases to run once the claim is asserted. When a party making a claim is prevented by circumstances beyond his control from starting legal proceedings, he may have a one-year extension from the time when those circumstances cease to exist. The overall limit for extensions of the limitation period is 10 years from the date when the period began to run. A circumstance occurring in another Contracting State that affects the cessation or extension of the limitation period shall be taken into account, provided that the creditor has taken all reasonable steps to inform the debtor of it as soon as possible.

CHAPTER 33

ELECTRONIC COMMERCE AND ELECTRONIC DATA
INTERCHANGE

33–001 Over the past decade changes in trade practice have placed demands on business for reduced costs and quicker supply times in both international and domestic trade. These changes have necessitated better planning and speedier supply of information, resulting in the increasing use of alternative methods of communication such as electronic commerce and electronic data interchange (EDI).

Although often confused, electronic commerce and EDI are not the same thing. Electronic commerce is a generic term and embraces EDI as well as other electronic communication technologies, such as electronic mail and the Internet. It can thus be defined as any form of business or administrative transaction or business information exchange which is executed using information or communications technology.

The growth of electronic commerce and its influence on trade practice has been phenomenal. With the arrival of the Internet, communications have undergone a mini-revolution. It is currently assessed that there are 80 million Internet users world-wide and this figure is growing at a rate of 20 per cent every month.[1] This has provided new opportunities with E-mail[2] and the World Wide Web[3] offering a full range of communication options. Orders can be placed and paid for although, due to the Internet's structure, the level of security is highly questionable and sending payment details over the Internet presents a considerable risk unless information is encrypted.

It is also wise when trading with partners on the Internet to operate under a form of code of practice or "interchange agreement" to clarify the ground rules. A standard form electronic commerce interchange agreement has been produced by UN/ECE CEFACT.[4]

EDI is also becoming more popular but its use is not increasing at the same rate as the Internet. EDI is different from other forms of electronic commerce, in that it comprises structured, computer-recognisable, messages. A good definition of EDI is given as[5]:

> "The electronic transfer of computer processable data relating to a business or administrative transaction using an agreed standard to structure the data."

---

[1] Source: SITPRO.

[2] The transfer of messages electronically, with the possibility of attaching other computer files and graphics.

[3] A format which enables businesses to advertise goods and services electronically, with links directly between buyers and sellers.

[4] CEFACT Internet Interchange Agreements. Information on these agreements is available from the e-centre: see *post*, n.7.

[5] P. Jones and D. Marsh, *Essentials of EDI Law* (1993 ed.), p. 5.

In a pure EDI environment, there is little or no human intervention and computers communicate with each other directly, supplying and processing data. The functionality of EDI is extremely diverse and exchanges of information between computers can mean changes in production levels within a company, speedier processing of orders and preparation of consignments for shipment. Moreover, EDI in international trade is now not only being used in business to business communications, but in submitting declarations to Customs (although often such declarations have to be supported by paper documents).[6]

The use of electronic commerce and EDI is likely to increase over the next five years; exporters would be well advised to familiarise themselves with the terminology and keep abreast of developments. Relevant information can be obtained from the e-centre[7] or SITPRO.[8]

Standardisation of EDI methods of communication

The major hurdle which electronic commerce and EDI in particular have had to **33–002** overcome is the ability for two or more parties, each with different computers and using different software, to be able to talk to each other. To resolve this, agreed standards and practices have been introduced. Although initially driven by various industry sectors, organisations such as UN/ECE have developed what have now become global standards. At present these relate mainly to EDI, although some national codes of practice for electronic commerce do exist.[9]

UN/EDIFACT Standard

The UN/EDIFACT[10] rules were developed by UN/ECE CEFACT[11] and have **33–003** become the world standard for EDI message structures. EDIFACT operates on the principle that parties need established message formats if they are to be able to communicate, but within these formats there is a degree of flexibility that enables users to define their own requirements. Not only does EDIFACT specify the overall message structure, but also data content, with mandatory and optional data items. These are all presented within structured message segments and each data item must be qualified.

---

[6] Mainly to verify authenticity of the information submitted and for evidential purposes. Although unnecessary, Government departments still tend to insist on supporting paper documents. In the U.K. the requirement for paper can be traced back as far as the Statute of Frauds 1677, s. 4, which introduced a general requirement for a written and signed record of transactions and has never been repealed. See H. B. Thomsen and B. S. Wheble, *Trading with EDI—The Legal Issues* (IBC Books, 1989), Chaps 4.4–4.6.

[7] e-centre UK, 11 Kingsway, London WC2B 6AR. Tel: 020 7655 9000, website: *www.e-centre.org.uk,* e-mail: *info@e-centre.org.uk.*

[8] The Simpler Trade Procedures Board (SITPRO), 151 Buckingham Palace Road, London SW1W 9SS. Tel: 020 7215 5000, website: *www.sitpro.org.uk,* e-mail: *info@e-sitpro.org.uk.*

[9] The Netherlands introduced a code of practice for using the Internet in 1998; however, no such code exists in the U.K. yet.

[10] United Nations/Electronic Data Interchange for Administration, Commerce and Transport.

[11] There also exists EDIFACT Syntax Guidelines and EDIFACT Syntax Implementation Guidelines. Information on these documents can be obtained from the e-centre U.K. in London or from the International Standards Organisation (ISO) in Geneva.

The adoption of the EDIFACT standard is optional, although given its wide acceptance as the world EDI standard, its use is recommended.

UNTDED and UNTDID

33–004 The United Nations Trade Data Elements Directory (UNTDED) and Trade Data Interchange Directory (UNTDID) support the UN/EDIFACT standard. UNTDED provides the definition, size and format of data elements and other conditions of use. UNTDID, on the other hand, contains protocols for the application of EDI, such as the UNCID Rules,[12] message design guidelines and a directory of UN/ECE standard electronic messages (UNSM).

Interchange agreements

33–005 In addition to the international standards which exist for EDI protocols and message structures, businesses intending to trade, either using electronic commerce or EDI, should draw up interchange agreements with their partners. Such agreements are necessary to avoid legal uncertainties in respect of some key areas of practice. The standard clauses in such agreements normally cover validity and formation of contract, integrity and confirmation of messages, security measures, storage of data, liability and force majeure. UN/ECE CEFACT,[13] the European Commission in Europe[14] and the e-centre in the U.K.[15] all provide model standard interchange agreements, which can be used as a basic framework document.

Other legal issues

33–006 Although it is not intended to cover every legal issue related to electronic commerce in this Chapter, it is worth considering one or two important points.

Electronic commerce and contract law

33–007 Generally, the fundamental rules of contract law remain unaffected by electronic commerce. Indeed, it is important when drawing up interchange agreements that the terms of the agreement do not impeach upon the main terms in the contract of sale. The only exception is in relation to *offer* and *acceptance*, most importantly the communication of acceptance.[16] For electronic communication, bearing in mind the statement of Lord Wilberforce in *Brinkibon v. Stahag Stahl und*

---

[12] Published in January 1988 and sponsored by the ICC and UN/ECE, the *Uniform Rules of Conduct for Interchange of Trade Data by Teletransmission* (UNCID) have largely been replaced by individual interchange agreements.

[13] UN/ECE Recommendation No. 26—*Commercial Use of Interchange Agreements for Electronic Data Interchange*, ECE/Trade/208, Geneva, 1996.

[14] E.C. Commission Recommendation of October 19, 1994 relating to the legal aspects of electronic data interchange (94/820/E.C.) [1994] O.J. L338/98.

[15] e-centre Interchange Agreement, 3rd Edition, dated December 1993.

[16] On offer, acceptance and communication of acceptance see Chap. 3.

Stahwarenhandels GmbH[17] and in order to avoid any ambiguity, such points should be clarified in any interchange agreement avoiding potential for litigation.[18]

Selling on the Internet—Legal Issues

The modern export company may wish to consider advertising on the Internet. **33–008** However, there are a number of issues that need to be considered carefully before placing advertisements for the sale of goods on a company website. For example, two distinct contractual issues arise. The first concerns the terms of the contract between the Internet service provider[19] and the exporter, the second, the contractual issues of respect of customers visiting and ordering goods from the website.

On the former, usually the Internet service provider[20] will advise a set of standard terms. However, even if this is the case, it is important to ensure that these terms cover all the necessary requirements and eventualities and clearly define the areas of responsibility. Such issues as maintenance of the site, site updates, customer support and the procedure in the event of termination of contract are specifically covered. Also the contract should specify the delineation of responsibility for providing the text and links to other sites on the Internet. It is not possible to give full detailed advice here on this aspect, however, information can be obtained from the e-centre.[21]

In respect of the contract between the exporter and his customer, consideration needs to be given to the impact of local consumer laws and the status of the information on the exporter's website. For example, does the web page constitute an "invitation to treat" or an "offer of goods for sale".[22] If properly worded it should be an invitation to treat, which needs to be followed by offer and acceptance. To move to the offer stage, the customer must be given the opportunity to read the terms and conditions and, only after having verified that they have read (and accepted) these terms, should they be able to progress to the next stage of formal offer.[23] Other issues include identification of the parties—to ensure that the party being traded with exists and is legitimate, method of payment, as well as the impact of European Legislation. For example, in respect of consumers, the E.C. Distance Selling Directive,[24] requires a seven-day cooling-off period and, unless otherwise specified, the contract must be performed within 30 days of acceptance.[25]

---

[17] [1983] 2 A.C. 34, set out in para. 3–008.
[18] See P. Jones and D. Marsh, *Essentials of EDI Law* (1993 ed.), p. 53.
[19] The party providing the website technology upon which the exporter's advertising material and communication links will appear.
[20] Also referred to as the host or Website Provider.
[21] See *supra.*, n.7.
[22] See Chap. 3.
[23] The restriction on progressing before having acknowledged the terms of reference is usually achieved by linking the terms and conditions to the web page by what is known as hypertext. This prevents progress to the next web page before a certain action has been carried out.
[24] Directive 97/7 Art. 6, para. 1.
[25] *ibid.* Art. 7.

Authentication of messages

33–009 The authenticity of electronic messages is also a major concern to businesses wishing to use electronic commerce. Indeed, a recent DTI survey stated that 69 per cent of businesses in the United Kingdom cited security as a major inhibitor to trading over the Internet.

Generally, the issue of authentication has focused on the development of the electronic signature. In terms of English law what constitutes a signature is not defined and the law is sufficiently flexible to provide for all forms, including electronic codification and encryption. However, the laws of other countries, particularly in Europe, are not so flexible and what constitutes a signature tends to be more precisely defined. This is proving problematic and consequently, the European Commission has issued a communication on electronic signatures and encryption[26] and is currently drafting an E.C. Directive on the subject. Changes to English law are also being considered[27] and legislation is likely to be introduced enabling Government to licence trusted third parties, who can offer certification to support electronic signatures, which are reliable enough to be recognised as equivalent to written signatures. UNCITRAL[28] is also working on the development of Uniform Rules on Electronic Signatures.

Negotiability

33–010 Related closely to the issue of the electronic signature is the question of EDI and negotiable documents, primarily the bill of lading. With the paper document, transfer of title is fulfilled by transferring the original bill of lading to the buyer of the goods.[29] However, in an electronic environment this is difficult to replicate. A number of solutions have been investigated, including using an electronic bill of lading, by controlling changes in title to goods through irrevocable, but transferable instructions to the carrier, or by appointing an independent electronic data registry, or replacing the bill of lading with a sea waybill, which is non-negotiable.[30]

Concerning the latter, in the past the use of non-negotiable documents has been unattractive, as they enabled the carrier to evade liability.[31] However, with the introduction of the Carriage of Goods by Sea Act 1992, this has now been rectified.[32] Consequently, the use of non-negotiable documents, where possible,

---

[26] Commission Document Com. (1998) 297/2.
[27] Following the issuing of a public consultation paper "*Licensing of Trusted Third Parties for the provision of Encryption Services*", by the DTI, the Electronic Communications (EC) Act 2000 came into force in May 2000. See *post*, para. 33–012.
[28] United Nations Commission on International Trade Law.
[29] See paras 15–019 and 15–038. The Carriage of Goods by Sea Act 1992 provides by s. 1(5) that regulations may be made so as to apply the provisions of the Act to paperless transaction involving EDI.
[30] *ibid.*
[31] The Hague Visby Rules only apply where the contract for carriage is governed by a Bill of Lading (Art. 1(b)), thus the Rules do not apply to contracts involving sea waybills.
[32] See para. 15–052.

is recommended.[33] Generally, with the exception of the international commodity trade, bills of lading are no longer necessary even for documentary credit transactions, although having said this, and noting that sea waybills are acceptable under ICC UCP Rules,[34] banks are still less inclined to accept non-negotiable documents under documentary credit transactions, as they consider that they do not afford the same level of control and security over the goods. Some countries indirectly require such documents at importation for exchange control purposes. Sea waybills do, however, have a number of advantages, not least that they do not have to be presented at the destination for the goods to be released.

Where negotiability *is* required other options have been considered. The CMI Rules on Electronic Bills of Lading (1990) provide for the use of irrevocable instructions from the shipper (the original "Holder" being the person having the "Right of Control and Transfer") to the carrier. These instructions notify the carrier of a new Holder. The system relies on unique codes (referred to as "private keys"), which are cancelled and replaced upon each transfer to a new Holder. Although workable, the CMI Rules have yet to be widely adopted in practice. Another alternative is the use of trusted third parties to operate an *electronic data registry*, recording changes in title to goods. Bolero Operations Limited is currently trialing such a system with SWIFT (who is providing the data registry) and the TT Club.[35] Bolero provides a secure electronic delivery service as well as a data registry, and initially thirteen countries are involved.[36] It remains to be seen whether data registry services are adopted widely by industry. A disadvantage of such services is that they operate within a closed membership environment, so when non-members become involved, title documents must revert to paper.

Admissibility of electronic data under English law

It has long been accepted that electronic messages, whether they be EDI messages or another certified form, are admissible as evidence in Court. This has previously been affirmed in common law[37] and in the Civil Evidence Act 1968.[38] More recently the Civil Evidence Act 1995 introduced clear provisions for the submission of electronic data in civil proceedings, which are now widely accepted.[39] Under criminal law, the restrictions that previously existed in the **33–011**

---

[33] UN Recommendation No. 12 "Measures to Facilitate Maritime Transport Document Procedures" also recommends the use of non-negotiable documents.

[34] Art. 24 UCP 500 (1993) and see para. 11–012.

[35] This approach was initially adopted by Chase Manhattan Bank with the "SEADOCS" project and later by the "Bolero" project. Information on the latter can be obtained from Bolero Operations Ltd, Holland House, 1–4 Holland Street, London EC3A 5AE, website: *www.boleroproject.com*.

[36] Belgium, Brazil, China (Hong Kong), France, Germany, Italy, Japan, Norway, Singapore, Spain, Taiwan, the United Kingdom and the United States of America.

[37] See *R. v. Sang* (1978) 2 All E.R.

[38] CEA 1968, s. 5.

[39] CEA 1995, s. 1(1), states that in civil proceedings evidence shall not be excluded on the ground that it is hearsay. CEA 1995, s. 9 is relevant in respect of records of business. CEA 1995, s. 13, defines a "document" as anything in which information of any description is recorded. This is equally applied to a "copy" .

Police and Criminal Evidence Act 1984, s.69(1) in respect of computer reports[40] were repeated in April 2000 by the Youth Justice and Criminal Evidence Act 1999, s.60. However, such evidence may still be caught by the hearsay rule. The adduction of computer generated evidence will be assisted greatly by the Electronic Communications Act 2000, but its true effect on criminal evidential procedure is yet to be seen.

Electronic Communications Act

33–012 For some time it has been recognised that statutory provisions would facilitate the use of electronic commerce in the U.K. This would provide some stability in the law, whilst introducing measures which are consistent with the E.U. draft Directive on Electronic Signatures and other international guidelines and model laws.[41] The Government responded with the Electronic Communications Act, which was passed on May 25, 2000.[42]

The Act is drawn from developing policy[43] and focuses on four issues, reflecting the three parts of the legislation:

(a) cryptography service provides;

(b) facilitation of electronic communication through data storage provision and recognition of electronic signatures;

(c) amendments to the Telecommunications Act 1984 in respect of telecommunications licensing and other general aspects.

In respect of cryptography service providers,[44] the Act requires the Secretary of State to provide and maintain a register of approved providers.[45] To appear in the register, providers have to meet certain objective criteria.[46] Inclusion in the list is voluntary. The main purpose of such providers is to verify and authenticate data, and from this perspective the provisions will assist with admissibility and evidential issues in the courts.

The Act also introduces requirements in respect of the handling of electronic data by the service provider. Notably, improper disclosure of information is made a criminal offence,[47] attracting on indictment, up to two years imprisonment, a fine or both, or on summary conviction, a fine.

---

[40] Namely that such records were inadmissible unless it was demonstrated that, at the material time, the computer was operating satisfactorily and is reliable. See *R. v. Shepherd* [1993] A.C. 380, HL.
[41] The UNCITRAL Model Law on Electronic Commerce and the OECD Cryptography Guidelines (March 1997).
[42] "*Promoting Electronic Commerce*—See also Consultation on the draft Legislation and the Government's Response to the Trade and Industry Committee's Report", Cm. 4417.
[43] See the Competitiveness White Paper, Cm. 4176 (December 1998); The Modernising Government White Paper, Cm. 4310 (March 1999); *Information of Our Age: The Government Vision* (URN 98/677; 4-98).
[44] Electronic Communications Act, Part I, sections 1–6.
[45] Section 1.
[46] Section 2.
[47] Section 4.

Part II of the Act[48] specifically provides for the admissibility of electronic signatures and authenticating certificates in legal proceedings.[49] In this respect the Act supports the Civil Evidence Act 1995—the matter of authenticity and probity being left to the courts.[50] A particularly interesting aspect is the "power of modification" in section 8. This has wide ramifications, potentially impacting on legislation such as the Statute of Frauds 1677, the Companies Act 1985 and the Carriage of Dangerous Goods by Road Regulations 1996.[51] Section 8(1) provides power to the relevant Minister to vary primary legislation under his portfolio through Statutory Instrument. Certain safeguards are included, which limit this power, not least a duty to only apply the provision where it can be assured that records will be kept.[52] Also, parties who have not previously expressed an intention to use electronic communication may not be required to transfer to a paperless environment.[53] It should be noted, however, that section 8(7) excludes HM Customs & Excise (as well as the Inland Revenue) from the provisions in section 8(3).[54]

Part III introduces changes to the Telecommunications Act 1984, s. 12,[55] including new provisions for modifying telecommunications licences, allowing modifications to be made efficiently and in a non-discriminating manner, as required by European law.[56]

The progress of the Act through Parliament was somewhat slow due to concern expressed with the provisions on disclosure and access to information and encryption keys in respect of human rights.[57] As a consequence, these requirements were removed and are being considered under a separate Act.

UNCITRAL Model Law on Electronic Commerce

Consideration of legal issues in relation to international trade and electronic **33–013** commerce would not be complete without reference to the *UNCITRAL Model Law on Electronic Commerce*. The Model was drawn up by UNCITRAL in 1996 in recognition of inadequate national legislation which existed around the world. Comprising 17 articles, the Model covers the main legal issues, including, *inter alia*, requirements for writing (Article 6), original information (Article 8), signature (Article 7), admissibility and probative value (Article 9) and actions related to contracts of carriage of goods (Article 11).

---

[48] Section 7–10.
[49] Section 7(1).
[50] See *infra*, para. 33–011.
[51] S.I. 1996 No. 2095, although in respect of this legislation it is unlikely that the Secretary of State for the Department of Transport Environment Regions would agree to such a provision.
[52] Section 8(3).
[53] Section 8(6)(a).
[54] Primarily because the provisions are already in the Finance Act 1999, Part VIII, sections 132–133.
[55] Clause 20.
[56] See The EC Telecommunications Services Licensing Directive (Directive 97/13).
[57] Under the European Convention on Human Rights (E.C.H.R.), Article 8. In response (and meeting the requirements of the Human Rights Act 1998, s. 19), the Secretary of State for Trade and Industry stated in Parliament that "In my view the provisions of the Electronic Communications Bill are compatible with the Convention rights".

Introduction of the UNCITRAL Model into national law is variable, although this is not unexpected. To date it has been enacted in Singapore (July 1998) and the U.S. State of Illinois has incorporated certain provisions into its State law. Colombia and the U.S. State of Connecticut are likely to implement the Model shortly. Growing interest has also been shown in South East Asia, particularly Thailand and Korea.[58] The U.K. Electronic Communications Act is consistent with the provisions of the UNCITRAL Model Law.

---

[58] Source: UNCITRAL, Brussels 1998.

INDEX

ABUSE OF DOMINANT POSITION
  Commission's powers
    information, to obtain 29–017
    investigations, to conduct 29–017
  interpretation of, 29–018
  prohibition on
    E.C. 20–002—29–004
    U.K. 29–018
ACCEPTANCE 3–007—3–013
  communication of 3–008
  deemed 5–006
  e-mail, by 3–008
  electronic data exchange, by 3–008
  fax, by 3–008
  forms of 3–010, 3–011
    countersigned 3–011
  goods, of. *See* GOODS
  letter of credit transaction 3–008
  post, by 3–008
  seller's general conditions
    incorporation of current 3–014
    subject to 3–013, 3–014
  telegram, by 3–008
  telex, by 3–008
  unconditional 3–007
  unqualified 3–007
ADVERTISING
  buyer's obligations 30–012
AGENCY ARRANGEMENTS
  agent
    authority of 27–003—27–009
      actual 27–004, 27–005
      apparent 27–007
      customary 27–006
      generally 27–003
      implied 27–006
      necessary 27–009
      ostensible 27–007
      ratification 27–008
      usual 27–006
    carrying stock 27–017
    duties of 27–010, 27–011
    freight forwarder, as 27–025
    orders emanating from but not procured
      by 27–012
    protection of 15–047
    rights and obligations of 27–010—
      27–013
  bribes 27–011
  commission, payment of 27–012
  confidential information 27–011
  contract of agency 27–002
    exclusive 29–011
  Convention on Agency in the International
    Sale of Goods 27–030
  disclosure 27–005, 27–011

AGENCY ARRANGEMENTS—*cont.*
  E.C. Directive on self-employed commercial
    agents 27–010
  exclusive trading rights 27–013
  expenses 27–012
  forwarder as bailee 27–026, 27–027
  franchise agreements and 30–004
  indemnity 27–012
  operation of law, by 27–009
  principal
    accounting to 27–011
    duties of 27–012
    rights and obligations of 27–010—
      27–013
  reasonable diligence 27–011
  repeat orders 27–012
  secret profits 27–011
  self-employed agents abroad 27–001
  sole distribution agreements distinguished
    30–003
  special types 27–014—27–028
  travelling representatives abroad 27–029
AGENT CARRYING STOCK 27–017
AGENT OF NECESSITY 27–009
AIR CARGO INSURANCE
  air waybill cover 19–038
  generally 19–036
  marine clauses 19–037
AIR TRANSPORT
  airway bill 15–001
  Article 81, application of 29–016
  c.i.f. 2–035
  consignment note 15–001
  documents 11–012
AIRPORT
  f.o.b. contract 2–018
  free carrier (FCA) 2–018
AMERICAN UNIFORM COMMERCIAL CODE 2–004,
    32–009
  arrival/ex ship/delivered ex ship clauses
    defined 2–042
  c.i.f. variants 2–037
  common ownership rule 4–005
  f.o.b., meaning 2–006
  frustration and 6–001
  loading operation 2–013
  passing of the risk under 4–010
ANTICOMPETITIVE PRACTICE
  prohibition on
    E.C. 29–002—29–004
    U.K. 29–018
ANTIQUES
  control of export 26–005
ANTON PILLER ORDER, 22–001. *See* SEARCH
    ORDER
ARBITRATION
  ad hoc 23–006

701

ARBITRATION—*cont.*
agreement 23–011
  disputes covered by 23–015
characteristics 23–004, 23–005
clause, 22–001, 23–012, 25–038,
  32–015
contractual element 23–004
enforcement 24–018
English 23–010—23–019
  arbitration agreement 23–011
  arbitrators 23–011
    appointment of 23–012
    powers 23–005
    qualifications 23–013
    two 23–012
  award 23–018
  counterclaim 23–015
  court's role 23–019
  disputes covered by agreement 23–015
  examples of arbitration clauses 23–012
  judicial review 23–019
  jurisdiction of the Tribunal 23–014
  Nema guidelines 23–019
  statutory framework 23–010
  staying proceedings 23–016
  Tribunal
    jurisdiction 23–014
    powers 23–017
equity clause 23–009
ex aequo et bono 23–009
fact, questions of 23–003
foreign award
  enforcement 24–001, 24–018, 24–020
  recognition, grounds for refusal of 24–
    019
GATT, and 24–021—24–023
general aspects 23–002—23–009
Geneva Convention, 1927 24–018
ICC International Court of Arbitration
  23–025, 32–008
ICC Rules of Conciliation and Arbitration
  23–007, 23–008, 23–025, 32–008
institutional 23–006
international 23–020—23–023
International Centre for Settlement of
  Investment Disputes (ICSID) 23–027
judge-arbitrator, appeal from 23–003
judicial element 23–005
law
  governing 23–007
  merchant 23–008
  questions of 23–003
lex mercatoria, application of 23–008
litigation compared 23–002
London Court of International Arbitration
  23–026
mixed 23–003
New York Convention, 1958 24–001,
  24–018
UNCITRAL 23–021
  Arbitration Rules 23–007, 23–022,
    25–039, 32–006

ARBITRATION—*cont.*
UNCITRAL—*cont.*
  Conciliation Rules 23–023, 32–006
  Model Law on International Commercial
    Arbitration 23–010, 23–024, 32–005
ARREST CONVENTION 22–033
ARRIVAL CONTRACT 2–035, 2–042
ASIAN DEVELOPMENT BANK 25–016
ATA CARNET SYSTEM, 26–019 n.21, 26–020,
  26–029
AVERAGE BOND 19–028

BAILEE
  forwarder as 27–026, 27–027
BANK
  definitions 10–002
  indemnities
    letters of credit and 11–037
BANK GUARANTEE
  absolute undertaking 12–002
  buyer, procured by 12–002, 12–003
  common law, at 12–001
  conditional 12–001
  demand performance 12–001, 12–004
    fraudulent 12–005
    unfair 12–005
  indemnity contract distinguished 12–001
  international trade, in 12–001
  performance guarantee 12–002
  seller, procured by 12–002, 12–004, 12–005
BARTER
  contracts of 14–002
  meaning 14–007
BATTLE OF FORMS 3–018
BILLS OF EXCHANGE
  avalised 9–009
  characteristics 9–004
  claused 9–007
  definition 9–004
  deregulation 9–004
  dishonour of 10–003
  documentary 9–008
  foreign 9–005
  generally 9–001
  holder in due course 9–004
  irregular 9–004
  nature of 9–004
  negotiation by exporter 9–011
  parties to 9–004
  payable on demand 9–004
  payment by 9–003
    open account, on 9–002
    place of 9–004
    time of 9–004
  proceedings on 9–012
  set, drawn in 9–010
  sight 9–004, 9–009
  time 9–004, 9–009
  UN Convention 9–006
BILLS OF LADING 2–022, 15–002, 15–003,
  15–004
  accomplished 15–003

Bills of Lading—*cont.*
arbitration clause 15–023, 15–048
on board 15–025
Brussels Protocol, 1968 15–020
Carriage of Goods By Sea Act, 1971
documentary application 15–022
territorial application 15–021
charterparty 11–012, 11–102, 15–002,
15–023
indemnity 15–040
claused 15–026, 15–036
clean 15–026, 15–036
fraudulent issue
effect of, 15–039 n.61
clean transport document 15–036
container 15–028, 16–007, 16–008
dangerous goods, clause as to 15–050
date of 15–035
delivery order 15–003, 15–034
description of goods in 15–036
document of title, as 15–038
electronic 33–010
evidence, as
contract of carriage, of 15–037
receipt of goods, of 15–036
FIATA combined transport (FBL) 15–001,
15–028, 16–006
goods causing damage, clause as to
15–050
groupage 15–029
Hague Rules, 1921 15–020
Hague-Visby rules 15–020
Hamburg Rules 15–020
house 15–029
indemnities and 15–039
international rules as to 15–020
marine 11–012
nature of 15–019
negotiable 15–024
non-negotiable 15–024
non-production of 15–038
particulars 15–003
passing of property in goods 15–038
received 15–025
receipt, as 15–036
release of goods without production of
15–038
shipped 15–025
ship's manifest 15–003
stale 15–032
switch 15–031
through 15–027
on-carriage by air, covering 15–030
types of 15–023
various parts in hands of different persons
15–003
Branch Offices
abroad 28–004—28–006
dealings between 28–006
generally 28–001
jurisdiction over head office 28–004
oversea company 28–005

Branch Offices—*cont.*
personnel employed in 28–020—28–026
aliens legislation in non-E.C. countries
28–025
English employment law 28–021—
28–023
foreign employment law 28–024—
28–026
free movement in E.C. 28–024
partly in U.K. partly outside 28–022
restraint of trade clauses 28–023
security of, foreign legislation protecting
28–026
subsidiaries
choice between 28–002
legal distinction between 28–003
Bretton Woods Agreement 21–029
British Net Book Agreement 29–008
British Trade International 31–002
Brussels Convention 21–003
application of 22–014
foreign judgment
enforcement/recognition 24–002
interpretation 22–013
jurisdiction
admissibility 22–026
consumer contract 22–024
employment contract 22–019
exclusive 22–025
forum non conveniens 22–028
general 22–017
insurance contract 22–023
lis pendens and related actions 22–027
prorogation of 22–016
provisions 22–015, 22–033
special 22–018

C. and F. 2–038
Carriage and Insurance Paid (CIP)
2–040
Carriage by Air
air waybill (AWB) 17–015
IATA 17–020
basic system of liability 17–003, 17–012,
17–016
damage during 17–002
International Air Transport Association
(IATA) 17–020
liability
carrier's defences 17–004
carriers who may be sued 17–006
claimants 17–005
rights 17–013, 17–017
non-Convention rules 17–010, 17–019
procedure in event of claim 17–014, 17–018
regimes governing 17–007—17–010
statutory scheme 17–001
Warsaw Convention 17–001, 17–003,
17–008, 17–011–17–014
amended 17–005, 17–009, 17–015—
17–018
Carriage by Land 18–001—18–011

CARRIAGE BY RAIL
  Convention governing (CIM), 18–001—
      18–005. *See also* CIM
  generally 18–002
CARRIAGE BY ROAD
  Convention governing (CMR), 18–001. *See
      also* CMR
CARRIAGE BY SEA 2–029
  agents' duties 5–003
  Article 81, application of 29–016
  bill of lading, 15–003, 15–004, 15–019—
      15–040. *See also* BILLS OF LADING
  carrier's liability 15–041—15–048
    agents, protection of 15–047
    cargoworthiness, as to 15–041
    claim for loss of/damage to goods
        15–048
    discharge of goods 15–041
    due diligence 15–041
    excepted perils 15–042—15–044
      burden of proof 15–043
      insurance and 15–044
      generally 15–041
    Hague-Visby Rules 15–045
    independent contractors 15–047
    limitation of 15–046
    maximum limits 15–045
    seaworthiness 15–041
    servants
      negligence of 15–041
      protection of 15–047
    time limit 15–048
    tort, in 2–030
  charterparty 5–002, 5–004
  container, by 15–002
  contract of 15–004
    bill of lading, covered by 15–004
    charterparty 15–004
    conclusion of 15–005
      shutting out goods 15–006
    special oral term may override 15–005
  course of business in 15–003
  dangerous goods 15–050
  delivery order 15–003, 15–034
  example 15–003
  excepted perils 15–042
    burden of proof 15–043
    insurance, and 15–044
  freight, 15–007—15–018. *See also* FREIGHT
  general average and 19–028
    claims and contributions, 15–049. *See
        also* GENERAL AVERAGE
  generally 15–003
  Law Commission Report 2–030
  mate's receipt 15–003
  mode of delivery 15–003
  multimodal 15–001
  non-negotiable documents recommended
      33–010
  place of delivery 15–003
  proceedings by cargo owner 2–030, 15–051,
      15–052

CARRIAGE BY SEA—*cont.*
  rights to sue in respect of 2–030, 15–052
  shipowner's liability 15–041, 15–050
  traditional methods 15–002
  unimodal transport 15–001
CARRIAGE PAID TO (CPT) 2–041
CARRIER
  liability in tort
    c.i.f. contract, under, 2–030. *See also*
        FREIGHT FORWARDER
CEFACT INTERNET INTERCHANGE AGREEMENTS
    33–001
CERTIFICATE
  inspection, of 2–025, 4–013
    pre-shipment 4–014, 5–005
  origin, of 2–025
  provision of 4–011
  quality, of 2–025, 4–012
    in personam 4–012
    in rem 4–012
  shipping 11–029
CHARTERPARTY 15–002, 15–004
  bill of lading 11–012, 15–023, 15–040
CHOICE OF LAW CLAUSE 3–017, 21–008,
    22–001, 25–038, 32–015
C.I.F. 2–019—2–037
  American practice 2–037
  carrier
    contractual relations 2–028, 2–029
    liability in tort 2–030
  consular fees 2–027
  contracts expressed to be 2–035
  contractual relations
    buyer and carrier 2–029
    seller and carrier 2–028
  date of arrival of goods
    determinant for payment of price 2–037
  definitions 2–020
  delivered weight 2–037
  destination, port of 2–032
  duties of buyer 2–020
  export duties 2–027
  feeding stuff 2–027
  generally 2–019
  import duties 2–027
  inaccurate documents 2–026
  intention of parties 2–035
  loss of goods 2–034
  net landed weight 2–037
  not true contracts 2–035
  out-turn 2–037
  payment of price 2–031
  purpose of contract 2–020
  refusal to accept goods 2–036
  rescission of contract 2–031
  responsibilities of parties 2–027
  risk, passing of 2–027
  seller's obligations 2–019, 2–020
  shipment, port of 2–032
  shipping documents, 2–021. *See also*
      SHIPPING DOCUMENTS
  significance of 2–019

C.I.F.—*cont.*
  specified elements to be borne by buyer,
      where 2–037
  tender of goods afloat 2–033
  transhipment 2–032
  Uniform Commercial Code 2–037
  variants of contract 2–037
C.I.F. and C. 3–039
C.I.F. and C. and I. 3–039
C.I.F. and E. 3–039
CIM
  liability 18–005
  making the contract 18–004
  scope of application 18–003
CLEAN COLLECTION
  definition 10–002
CMR
  cash on delivery (c.o.d.) 18–009
  consignment note 18–008
  defences 18–009
  delay 18–009
  liability 18–009, 18–010
  limitation period 18–010
  measure of compensation 18–009
  nullity of stipulations contrary to 18–011
  scope of application 18–006
  special risks 18–009
  successive carriers 18–007
  time limits 18–009
COLLECTION
  meaning 10–002
COLLECTION ARRANGEMENTS 4–001
  definitions 10–002
  delivery of documents contrary to
      instructions 10–004
  dishonoured bill, where 10–003
  documentary bill lodgement for 10–001
  release under trust receipt 10–004
  representative in case of need 10–002
  Uniform Rules 10–002
COMFORT LETTERS 3–012
COMMERCIAL AGENT
  definition 27–010
  independent trader distinguished 29–011
COMMISSION AGENT 27–015
COMMON AGRICULTURAL POLICY (CAP)
  levies under 26–015
COMMUNICATION
  meaning 3–008
COMPETITION LAW OF E.C.
  abuse of dominant position 29–004
      Commission powers 29–017
      interpretaion, 29–018
  agreements
      Article 81, application of 29–004,
          29–007, 29–010
      exclusive distribution 29–012
      exclusive purchasing 29–013
      franchising 29–015
      intellectual property rights, as to 29–015
      joint ventures 29–014
      know-how licensing 29–015

COMPETITION LAW OF E.C.—*cont.*
  minor importance, of 29–010
  parallel imports/export, prohibiting
      29–005
  patent licensing 29–015
  research and development 29–014
  restrictive, control of 29–007
  specialisation 29–014
  air transport 29–016
  ambit 29–004
  Article 81
      application of 29–004
          procedure 29–006
      block exemptions 29–009, 29–012—
          29–016
      declaration of inapplicability under
          29–008
      direct effect of 29–004
      negative clearance under 29–008
      notices 29–009
      provisions 29–002, 29–003
  Article 82
      application of 29–004
          procedure 29–006
      Commission powers 29–017
      direct effect of 29–004
      interpretation, 29–018
      provisions 29–002, 29–004
  basic provisions 29–002
  block exemptions 29–009, 29–012—29–016
  declaration of inapplicability 29–008
  exclusive agency contracts 29–011
  generally 29–001
  maritime transport 29–016
  negative clearance 29–008
  notices 29–009
  powers of Commission
      information, to obtain 29–017
      investigations, to conduct 29–017
  Regulation 17/62 29–006
  restrictive arrangements, as to 29–007
COMPETITION LAW OF U.K.
  appeals 29–022
  block exemptions 29–019
  Chapter I prohibition 29–018
  Chapter II prohibition 29–018
  Competition Commission
      establishment 29–022
      functions 29–022
  Director General of Fair Trading (DGFT)
      enforcement by 29–021
      notification to 29–020
      powers 29–019, 29–021
  enforcement 29–021
  notification 29–020
  reform of 29–018
  relationship to E.C. law 29–022
  statutory provisions 29–019
COMPREHENSIVE SHORT TERM GUARANTEE
      20–012
CONDITION
  breach of, effect of 5–003

CONDITION—*cont.*
classification of 5–003
definition 5–003
FIDIC 25–012
warranty distinguished 5–003
CONFIRMATION SLIP 3–010
CONFIRMING HOUSE 27–018—27–023
confirmation by 27–023
bank, and by 27–023
examples of transactions 27–022
generally 27–018
insolvency of 27–021
liability of English agent acting as foreign
principal 27–022
nature of 27–019
obligations of 27–020
CONFLICT OF LAWS
avoidance measures 21–003
choice of law clause 21–008, 22–001
Contracts (Applicable Law) Act, 1990
21–004
currency of account/payment 21–018
exclusion of foreign law 21–023—21–026
confiscatory 21–024
generally 21–023
nationalisation laws 21–024
public laws of political/administrative
nature 21–025
public policy 21–026
revenue laws 21–025
extraterritorial effect of foreign state
measures 21–020—21–022
foreign illegality 21–027, 21–028
civil consequences 21–027
criminal consequences 21–028
foreign judgment
enforcement 24–002, 24–004
common law, under 24–005
conditions for 24–007
jurisdiction 24–008
liquidated sum only, for 24–009
statute, under 24–005, 24–006
final and conclusive 24–010
penal/revenue sanction 24–011
recognition 24–002
defences to 24–003, 24–012, 24–013
generally 1–004, 4–002, 21–001
law governing contract, 21–004—21–017
See also ROME CONVENTION
letters of request (rogatory) 21–002, 21–022
limitation periods 21–017
proof of foreign law 21–002
Protection of Trading Interests Act, 1980
21–021
recovery in foreign currency 21–018
rejection of foreign extraterritorial claims by
the courts 21–022
Rome Convention, 21–002, 21–004—
21–017. *See also* ROME CONVENTION
State immunity 21–019
CONSTRUCTION CONTRACT
generally 25–001

CONSTRUCTION CONTRACT—*cont.*
key provisions, 25–023. *See also*
INTERNATIONAL PROCUREMENT
CONTRACT
CONTAINER TRADE TERMS 2–046
CONTAINER TRANSPORT
bills of lading 15–028, 16–007, 16–008
combined transport document 16–006
contract of export sale, and 16–004
course of business 16–002
deck stowage 16–008
documents used in 16–006
FIATA combined transport bill of lading
15–029, 16–006
generally 16–001
leasing agreement 16–003
legal problems 16–004
liability, basis for 16–005
network liability system 16–005
operator's liability 16–005
package or unit, definition 16–009
CONTAINERS
packing in 7–009
CONTRACT
acceptance, 3–007—3–013. *See also*
ACCEPTANCE
agency, of 27–002
applicable law 21–004—21–017
battle of forms 3–018
certainty, effect of lack of 3–015
condition. *See* CONDITION
conduct, by 3–009
formation of. *See* FORMATION OF CONTRACT
frustration of. *See* FRUSTRATION
implied term 5–003
incomplete, effect of 3–015
indemnity, of 12–001
innominate terms. *See* INNOMINATE TERMS
international supply 3–019
law governing, 3–017, 21–004—21–017. *See
also* CONFLICT OF LAWS
offer 3–006, 3–005
passing of property. *See* PASSING OF
PROPERTY
performance of. *See* PERFORMANCE OF
CONTRACT
repudiation 5–003, 5–004
sale, of
standard terms 3–017, 32–010
time of the essence, where 5–012
unfair terms 3–019, 5–003
warranty. *See* WARRANTY
CONTRACT OF SALE
export transactions based on 1–002
overseas, 1–004. *See also* VIENNA
CONVENTION 1980
sole distribution agreement distinguished
30–003
CONTRIBUTORY NEGLIGENCE
product liability and 8–007
CONVENTION ON AGENCY IN THE INTERNATIONAL
SALE OF GOODS 27–030

CONVENTION ON LIMITATION OF LIABILITY FOR
    MARITIME CLAIMS 15–046
COUNTERTRADE
  additional risks 14–003
  barter
    contract of 14–002
    meaning 14–007
  buy-back agreement 14–008
  buyer
    definition 14–006
  disposal transaction 14–010
  ECGD cover 14–003
  economic background 14–003
  framework agreement 14–004, 14–012
  generally 14–001
  importance of 14–003
  off-set arrangements 14–009
  oil 14–011
  reciprocal sales agreement 14–005
  sale, contract of 14–002
  switch transaction 14–010
  types of transaction 14–004—14–012
COURT PROCEEDINGS 23–001
CUSTOMS
  Community Code 26–012, 26–015
  functions 26–006
  law
    antiques 26–005
    generally 26–003
    strategic goods, 26–004. *See also*
        CUSTOMS REGULATIONS, CUSTOMS
        OFFENCES
  registered number 26–015
CUSTOMS OFFENCES
  absolute 26–031
  burden of proof 26–031
  concept 26–028
  E.U. law 26–029
  export of goods without licence 26–031
  fines 26–030
  forfeiture of goods 26–030
  P.A.C.E. and 26–031
  patented goods 26–031
  restoration 26–030
  single market, effect of the 26–029
CUSTOMS REGULATIONS 26–006—26–018
  appeals 26–027
  CHIEF computer system 26–013, 26–014,
      26–015
  Community goods 26–008–26–011
    excise duty 26–011
    free movement of 26–008
    statistics 26–010
    value added tax (VAT) 26–009
  drawback scheme 26–023
  duty suspense and relief schemes 26–022
  E.C. preference arrangements 26–026
  generally 26–006
  goods outside the EU 26–012—26–017
    basic policy 26–012
    Community Customs code 26–012,
        26–015

CUSTOMS REGULATIONS—*cont.*
  goods outside the EU—*cont.*
    normal declaration procedure 26–014
    requirements 26–013
    simplified declaration procedure 26–015
  government regulation of exports 26–001
  information required 26–016
  Inward Processing Relief (IPR) scheme
      26–023
  licensing regulations 26–002
  offences. *See* CUSTOMS OFFENCES
  Outward Processing Relief (OPR) scheme
      26–023
  postal exports 26–017
  pre-entry of goods 26–014
  return of unused imports 26–024
  Single Administrative Document (SAD) 26–
      013, 26–014, 26–015, 26–020
  Single Market, effect of the 26–007
  statistics, collection of 26–010
  tariff requirements 26–016
  trader records/accounts 26–018
  transit procedures 26–019—26–021
    ATA Convention 26–020
    common and Community 26–020
    EFTA countries, through 26–020
    generally 26–019
    TIR system 26–020, 26–021
    Visregard countries, through 26–020
  warehouse goods 26–025

DAMAGE
  definition 8–006
DAMAGES
  breach, for
    condition, of 5–003
    contract, of 5–001
    innominate term, of 5–004
    warranty, of 5–003
  defective product, caused by 8–006
  failure to open/pay credit 11–021
  liquidated 4–015
  loss on resale, for 5–017
  mitigation 5–003
  product liability and 8–009
DANGEROUS GOODS
  packing 7–012
DE MINIMIS RULE 5–003
DEFECTIVE PRODUCT
  damages for 8–009
  definition 8–006
DEL CREDERE AGENT 27–016
DELAY
  frustrating contract 6–004
DELIVERED AT FRONTIER (DEF) 2–044
DELIVERED DUTY PAID/UNPAID (DDP/DDU)
    2–045, 4–010
DELIVERED EX QUAY (DEQ) 2–043
DELIVERED EX SHIP (DES) 2–042
DELIVERY
  definition 4–003
  docks, to 2–004

DELIVERY—*cont.*
goods, of 4–003
order 15–003, 15–034
DEMAND GUARANTEE
autonomy 12–004
definition 12–004
fraudulent 12–005
unfair 12–005
Uniform Rules 12–004
DISPUTE SETTLEMENT
alternative mechanism for, 23–001. *See also*
ARBITRATION
procedure of WTO/GATT 24–021, 24–022
DOCK DUES
f.a.s 2–004
f.o.b. 2–005
DOCUMENTARY CREDIT. *See* LETTERS OF CREDIT
DOCUMENTS
air transport 11–012
definitions 10–002
delivery of
contrary to instructions 10–004
role of 1–004
insurance 11–014
release of
trust receipt, under 10–005
transport 11–012, 15–002
combined 16–006
freight forwarders, issued by 11–012
multimodal 11–012
DOMICILE 22–002
DRAFT EUROPEAN CONVENTION ON THE SIMPLE
RESERVATION OF TITLE 4–008

E-MAIL 33–001
acceptance by 3–008
E.C.
competition law. *See* COMPETITION LAW OF
E.C.
E.C. CONVENTION ON JURISDICTION AND
ENFORCEMENT OF JUDGMENTS, 22–001.
See also BRUSSELS CONVENTION
ECONOMIC LOSS
recovery of 8–009
ELECTRONIC COMMERCE
authentication of messages 33–009, 33–012
contract law, and 33–007
electronic data interchange distinguished
33–001
legal issues 33–006—33–012
negotiability 33–010
statutory provisions proposed 33–012
ELECTRONIC DATA INTERCHANGE (EDI)
acceptance by 3–008
admissibility of 33–011, 33–012
definition 33–001
electronic commerce distinguished 33–001
negotiability 33–010
standardisation of methods of
communication 33–002—33–005
ENGINEERING ADVANCEMENT ASSOCIATION OF
JAPAN (ENAA) 25–013

EQUITABLE ESTOPPEL
doctrine of 5–012
ESTOPPEL
convention, by, 5–012 n.98
equitable 5–012
issue 24–005
rejection and 5–011
EUROPRO 32–017
EX QUAY CLAUSE 2–002, 2–043
EX SHIP CLAUSE 2–042
EX STORE CLAUSE 2–002
EX WAREHOUSE CLAUSE 2–002
EX WORKS CLAUSE 2–002
EXAMINATION OF GOODS. *See* GOODS
EXCEPTIVE WARRANTY 19–017
EXCHANGE CONTROL
arbitration awards in foreign currency
21–032
Bretton Woods Agreement 21–029
disguised exchange contracts 21–030
English judgments in foreign currency
21–032
foreign regulations 21–031
EXCLUSIVE DISTRIBUTION AGREEMENT
meaning 30–002
EXPORT CREDIT GUARANTEES
administration of scheme 20–002
generally 20–001
legislative basis 20–001
NCM'S international policy 20–012
compact 20–013
global 20–013
Secretary of State's powers 20–001
EXPORT CREDIT GUARANTEES DEPARTMENT
bond risk insurance 20–009
buyer credit arrangements 20–005—
20–011
commitment limits 20–001
duty of care 20–001
export insurance policy 20–008
facilities offered 20–003
function 20–002
Insurance Services Group, privatisation of
20–001
lines of credit
cover for 20–006
general 20–006
project (PLOC) 20–006
one-stop shopping with 20–011
overseas investments insurance 20–010
powers 20–001
project financing scheme 20–007
services offered 20–003—20–011
specific 20–004—20–011
types of 20–003
short term 20–008, 20–012
Supplemental Export Insurance Policy
(EXIP) 20–005
supplier's credit arrangements 20–004
unfair demand, covering 12–005
EXPORT DISTRIBUTION AGREEMENT
30–005

EXPORT LICENCE
  duty to procure
    c.i.f. contract 2–027
    f.a.s. contract 2–004
    f.o.b. contract 2–017
  frustration of contract 6–012
  goods requiring 26–003
EXPORT LICENSING
  antiques 26–005
  general control of exports 26–003
  individual licence 26–003
  prohibited goods 26–003
  regulations 26–002—26–005
  strategic goods 26–004
  transhipment licence 26–003
  Wassenaar Arrangement 26–004
EXPORT PROHIBITION 6–009
EXPORT PUBLICATIONS
  British Trade International publications
    31–009
  Business Matters 31–014
  Croner's *Reference Book for Exporters*
    4–014, 31–011
  Euronews 31–015
  Eurostat 31–016
  Export Today 31–013
  generally 31–008
  International Business Matters 31–014
  Tates Export Guide 31–012
EXPORT QUOTA
  frustration of contract 6–012
EXPORT TRANSACTION
  contract of sale, based on 1–002
  generally 1–001
  means of 1–005
  nature of 1–004
  parties to 1–005
  works and installations, for construction of
    1–003
EXPORTER
  definition 26–012
EXTRAJUDICIAL DISPUTE SETTLEMENT 23–001,
  25–039

FACTORING
  average maturity 13–005
  credit management 13–005
  direct 13–003
  disclosed 13–002, 13–004, 13–005
  essence of international 13–002
  generally 13–001
  indirect 13–003
  legal forms 13–004
  Ottawa Convention 13–001
  price collection service 13–005
  undisclosed 13–002, 13–004, 13–006
  Unidroit Convention on International
    Factoring 13–007
F.A.S. 2–003, 2–004
FIATA COMBINED TRANSPORT BILL OF LADING.
  See BILLS OF LADING
FIDIC Conditions of Contract 25–012, 25–039

FINANCIAL LEASING. *See* INTERNATIONAL
  FINANCIAL LEASING
F.O.B. 2–005—2–018
  additional services, contract with 2–007,
    2–008
  airport 2–018
  American practice 2–006
  buyer contracting with carrier 2–007
  classic 2–007, 2–008
  Commonwealth, in the 2–006
  examination of goods 2–015
  export licence, duty to procure 2–017
  freight and marine insurance 2–008
  loading operation 2–013
  meaning 2–006
  multi-port terms 2–016
  nomination of suitable ship, 2–004, 2–007,
    2–009—2–012. *See also* SUITABLE SHIP
  passing of property 2–014
  responsibilities of parties 2–005, 2–009—
    2–018
  significance 2–005
  simple 2–007
  strict 2–007
  types of contract 2–007
  U.K., in the 2–006
  Uniform Commercial Code 2–006
  values 2–008
FORCE MAJEURE CLAUSE 32–008, 32–015
  construction contract 25–038
  defeated by events 6–021
  standard contract in commodity trade 6–019
  too vague, where 6–020
  two-stage 6–018
  types of 6–017
FOREIGN ACQUISITIONS
  generally 28–018
  take-overs, law as to 28–019
FOREIGN ILLEGALITY
  civil consequences 21–027
  criminal consequences 21–028
FOREIGN LAW. *See* CONFLICT OF LAWS
FORFAITING
  essence of 13–009
  generally 13–008
  leasing agreement 13–013
  primary 13–011
  secondary 13–011
  security
    avalised bills of exchange 13–010
    bank guarantee as 13–012
  supply agreement 13–013
  Unidroit Convention on International
    Financial Leasing 13–013
FORMATION OF CONTRACT 3–001—3–019
  acceptance 3–001—3–014
  battle of forms 3–018
  certainty requirement 3–015
  comfort letter as to 3–012
  conduct, by 3–009
  generally 3–001
  inquiry 3–002

FORMATION OF CONTRACT—*cont.*
  instantaneous 3–008
  invitation OF 3–002
  letter of intent as to 3–012
  negotiations 3–002—3–004
  offer 3–005, 3–006
  parol evidence rule 3–016
  quotation 3–003
  standard terms
    agreement to 3–017
  tender 3–004
FORUM NON CONVENIENS
  Conventions and 22–028
  principles for 22–005
  stay on grounds of 22–007
FRANCHISE AGREEMENT
  agency and 30–004
  black list clauses 30–015, 30–016
  course of business 30–016
  E.C. block exemption 29–015, 30–015,
    30–016
  meaning 1–005, 30–004
  nature of 1–005
  opposition procedure 30–016
  sole distribution agreement and 30–004
  white list clauses 30–015, 30–016
FRANCO-DOMICILE 2–045, 4–010
FREE ARRIVAL STATION CLAUSE
  f.a.s. and 2–004
FREE CARRIER 2–003, 2–005
FREE CARRIER AIRPORT 2–018
  Vienna Convention 2–004
FREE DELIVERY 2–045
FREE TO DOCKS 2–004
FREEZING INJUNCTION
  application for 22–030
  discretionary remedy 22–030
  nature 22–030
  orders supporting 22–031
  worldwide 22–030
FREIGHT
  advance 15–010
  back 15–013
  calculation 15–008
  collect bill of lading and 15–011
  dead 15–014
  definition 15–007
  lump sum 15–009
  payment, liability for 15–017
  prepaid 15–010
  primage, and 15–015
  pro rata 15–012
  rates fixed by shipping conferences 15–016
  shipowner's lien 15–018
FREIGHT FORWARDER
  agent, as 27–025
  bailee, as 27–026, 27–027
  duties 27–028
  generally 27–024
  principal, as 27–025
  Standard Trading Conditions 19–003,
    27–025

FREIGHT FORWARDER—*cont.*
  transport documents issued by 11–012
FRUSTRATION
  apportionment of performance 6–014
  conditions for 6–006—6–014
  delay, by 6–004
  effect of 6–015, 6–016
    common law, at 6–015
    statutory 6–016
  force majeure, 6–017—6–021. *See also*
    FORCE MAJEURE
  fundamental change in circumstances, where
    6–011
  illegality, where 6–008—6–010
  inordinate delay 6–011
  licences/quotas, where export and import
    6–012
  matter of degree, may be 6–003
  meaning 6–002
  partial 6–013
  principles of 6–001
  prohibitions, where export and import 6–009
  self-induced 6–005
  Shatt-el-Arab cases 6–011
  subject-matter destroyed, where 6–007
  Suez Canal cases 6–011
FUNGIBLE
  definition, 4–005 n.20

GENERAL AGREEMENT ON TARIFFS AND TRADE
  (GATT)
  arbitration 24–023
  complaints procedure 24–022
  consultation 24–023
  dispute settlement procedure 24–021,
    24–023
  exporter's standing 24–022
  law relating to disputes 24–023
  locus standi 24–022
  nature 24–021
  nature of 24–021
  Panels 24–023
    report 24–023
GENERAL AVERAGE
  act 19–026
  carriage by sea contract, and 19–028
  insurance contract, and 19–029
  law of 19–025
  loss 19–027
GOODS
  acceptance of 5–001, 5–006
  ascertained 4–006
  carriage by sea 7–008
  dangerous 7–012
  definition, 8–006 n.29
  delivery of 1–004, 4–003
  examination of 2–015, 5–005
  part of bulk, forming 4–005
  rejection of 2–026, 5–001, 5–007
    estoppel and 5–011
    property in 5–010
    right in c.i.f. contracts 2–026, 5–008

GOODS—*cont.*
 rejection of—*cont.*
  two bills of lading, where 5–009
  unascertained 4–005
  unpaid seller's right against 5–013
GOVERNMENT PROHIBITION 6–010
GOVERNMENT REGULATION OF EXPORTS
 ˙generally 26–001
GUARANTEE
 meaning 12–001

HAGUE CONVENTION ON THE LAW APPLICABLE
 TO INTERNATIONAL SALES OF GOODS
 21–003
HAGUE RULES 15–020
HAGUE-VISBY RULES 7–008, 7–009, 15–001,
 15–004, 15–020, 15–033, 32–004
HAMBURG RULES 15–020
˙HARDSHIP CLAUSE 32–008

ICC COURT OF ARBITRATION. *See* ARBITRATION
 rules. *See* ARBITRATION
ILLEGALITY
 export and import prohibitions 6–009
 government prohibitions 6–010
 war, outbreak of 6–008
IMPORT LICENCE
 frustration of contract 6–012
IMPORT PROHIBITIONS 6–009
IMPORT QUOTA
 frustration of contract 6–012
INCOTERMS 2–001, 2–003, 32–008
 arrival/ex ship/delivered ex ship clauses
  defined 2–042
 documentation required by 2–004
 free carrier 2–005
 loading operation 2–013
INNOMINATE TERM 5–001
 application 5–004
 concept 5–004
INSOLVENCY
 definition, 5–014 n.10
INSOLVENT BUYER
 rights against 5–014, 5–016
INSPECTION
 certificate 2–025, 4–013
 pre-shipment (PSI) 4–014, 5–005
INSTITUTE CARGO CLAUSE
 A 2–023, 19–019
 B 19–020
 C 19–021
 claims 19–030
 exclusion clauses 19–024
 general average clause 19–029
 general exclusion clause 19–024
 Lloyd's Marine Policy and 19–018
 minimising losses 19–024
 risks covered 19–023
 strikes exclusion clause 19–024
 transit clause 19–022
 unfitness exclusion clause 19–024
 unseaworthiness exclusion clause 19–024

INSTITUTE CARGO CLAUSE—*cont.*
 war exclusion clause 19–024
INSURANCE
 air cargo. *See* AIR CARGO INSURANCE
 American practice 2–023
 document 2–023, 11–014
 Export Credits Guarantees Department,
  20–001. *See* EXPORT CREDITS
  GUARANTEES DEPARTMENT
 freight and marine
  f.o.b. contract, and 2–008
 letter of credit requirements 11–014
 marine. *See* MARINE INSURANCE
 open cover 2–023
 packing regulations 7–010
 product liability 8–011
 usual Lloyd's conditions, on 2–023
 value 2–023
INTELLECTUAL PROPERTY RIGHTS
 E.C. block exemption 29–015
INTERCHANGE AGREEMENTS
 form, proposals for standard 33–001
 standard clauses 33–005
INTEREST
 clause providing for 32–015
INTERNATIONAL CHAMBER OF COMMERCE 2–001,
 10–002, 11–002
 publications 11–003, 32–008
INTERNATIONAL CONVENTION FOR UNIFICATION
 OF RULES RELATING TO THE ARREST OF
 SEAGOING SHIPS 22–033
INTERNATIONAL FINANCIAL LEASING
 essence of 13–012
 leasing agreement 13–013
 supply agreement 13–013
 Unidroit Convention 13–013
INTERNATIONAL PROCUREMENT CONTRACT
 acceptance 25–029
 administration of 25–031
 arbitration 25–039
  clause 25–038
 assignment 25–030
 bonus clause 25–034
 characteristics 25–001
 choice of law clause 25–038
 competitive tendering 25–003
 compliance 25–009
 currency clause 25–036
 dispute resolution 25–039
 extension of time 25–027
 features 25–001
 force majeure clause 25–038
 forms of 25–011–25–016
 inspection 25–029
 insurance and indemnity clause 25–037
 inviting tenders, by 25–003, 25–018
 key provisions 25–023
 liquidated damages 25–034
 negotiation, by 25–003
 open tendering, 25–003
 payment for 25–032
 performance guarantee 25–033

INTERNATIONAL PROCUREMENT CONTRACT—
  cont.
  pricing 25–024
    changing the 25–025
    risk, the 25–025
  procedure 25–017—25–022
    invitation to tender 25–018
    prequalification 25–017
    tender 25–019—25–022
  public
    E.C. Directives on 25–004—25–009
    works 25–005
  repayment guarantee 25–033
  retention money 25–035
  selective tendering, 25–003
  services 25–007
  standard of design/work 25–028
  structure 25–010
  sub-contracting 25–030
  supplies 25–006
  tender 25–019
    acceptance of 25–022
    guarantee 25–020
    opening of 25–021
  types of, 25–003, 25–003
  UNCITRAL legal guide 25–002
  utilities 25–008
  variation 25–026
  waiver of immunity clause 25–038
INTERNATIONAL SUPPLY CONTRACT
  definition 3–019
INTERNET
  CEFACT Internet Interchange Agreements
    33–001
  growth of 33–001
INTRASTAT 26–010
INTRATERMS 2–001
  arrival/ex ship/delivered ex ship clauses
    defined 2–042
  documentation required by 2–004
  free carrier 2–005
  loading operation 2–013
INVOICE
  c.i.f. transaction 2–024
  commercial 7–003, 11–013
  correct 7–002
  discounting 13–006
  generally 7–001
  letter of credit transaction 7–004, 11–013
  official requirements 7–005
  pro forma 7–001
  true 7–002

JOINT VENTURE
  E.C. competition law as to 29–014
  nature of 1–005
JUDGMENT
  interpretation 24–002
JUDICIAL REVIEW 23–019
JURISDICTION
  admissibility, and 22–023
  arbitration outside 24–001

JURISDICTION—*cont.*
  Brussels Convention as to 22–015, 22–033
  clause 3–017, 22–001, 32–015
  consumer contract 22–024
  domicile 22–002
  employment contract 22–019
  exclusive agreements 22–008, 22–010,
    22–025
  foreign judgment
    enforcement of 24–002—24–017
  forum non conveniens 22–005, 22–007,
    22–028
  general rule 22–003, 22–017
  in personam 22–001, 22–033
  in rem 22–033
  insurance contract 22–023
  interim remedies 22–032—22–033
  lis pendens and related actions 22–027
  litigation outside 24–001, 24–004
  Lugano Convention as to 22–015, 22–033
  Order 11 rule 1(1) 22–004, 22–012
  prorogation of 22–016
  service out of 22–005
  special 22–018
  traditional rules, 22–003—22–010. *See also*
    LITIGATION

KNOW-HOW LICENSING AGREEMENT
  block exemption 29–015

LETTERS OF CREDIT 4–001
  acceptance 11–022
  anomalous situations 11–037—11–043
  anticipatory 11–032
  assignment of benefit 11–035
    transfer distinguished 11–036
  autonomy 11–006
  back-to-back 11–033
  bank indemnity, and 11–037
  characteristics 11–001
    conditional 11–040
  confirmed 11–001, 11–023
    conditionally 11–029
    irrevocable and 11–026
    localisation device, as 11–028
    recourse and reimbursement of bank
      11–027
    seller, by 11–029
    variants 11–029
  countervailing 11–033
  damages for failure to open/pay 11–021
  deferred payment 11–022
  definition 11–001
  documents tendered to bank 11–008
    discrepancy of 11–010
    linkage of 11–016
    rejection of 11–010
    several to be read together 11–015
    time for examination 11–009
    transport 11–012
    UCP provisions as to 11–011
  essence of 11–001

LETTERS OF CREDIT—*cont.*
expiry date 11–019
fraud affecting 11–042
evidence of 11–043
generally 11–001
insurance documents 11–014
invoice 7–004, 11–013
irrevocable 11–001, 11–023
confirmed, and 11–026
unconfirmed, and 11–025
kinds of 11–001, 11–022
law governing 11–020
negotiation 11–022
opened, 11–023, n.77
overriding 11–033
packing 11–032
payment
at sight 11–022
deferred 11–022
reserve, under 11–038
principles governing 11–005
recourse of confirming bank 11–027
red clause 11–032
reimbursement of confirming bank 11–027
revocable 11–001, 11–023
unconfirmed, and 11–024
revolving 11–031
shipment date 11–019
short-circuiting 11–039—11–041
stages of transaction 11–004
standby 11–030, 32–004
strict compliance, doctrine of 11–007
teletransmission 11–017
time of opening 11–018
transferable 11–034, 11–036
assignment of benefit distinguished
11–036
unconfirmed 11–001, 11–023
irrevocable and 11–025
revocable and 11–024
Uniform Customs and Practice (UCP) (1993
Revision) 11–002, 32–008
application 11–003
transfer under 11–036
LICENSING 1–005, 30–004, 30–015
LIEN
rights of 5–013, 5–014, 5–015
shipowner, of 15–018
unpaid seller, of 5–014, 5–015
LIMITATION OF ACTIONS
breach of contract, where 5–001
foreign 21–017
generally 21–017
LINER CONFERENCES
Code of Conduct for 5–016
LIQUIDATED DAMAGES 4–015
LIS PENDENS 22–006, 22–027
LITIGATION
concurrent proceedings 22–005
extrajudicial dispute settlement and 23–001
jurisdiction 22–001
assumed by English courts 22–004

LITIGATION—*cont.*
jurisdiction—*cont.*
Brussels Convention, 22–011—22–028.
See also BRUSSELS CONVENTION
English courts 22–003, 22–004
exclusive agreement as to 22–008,
22–010, 22–016
forum non-conveniens 22–005, 22–007,
22–028
lis pendens 22–006, 22–027
Lugano Convention, 22–011—22–028.
See also LUGANO CONVENTION
outside 22–004, 22–005, 24–001
limitation periods 5–001, 21–017
restraint of
English action 22–010
foreign action 22–006, 22–009
service out of jurisdiction 22–004, 22–011,
22–029
leave, application for 22–005, 22–012
stay of proceedings
English action 22–006
foreign action 22–008
forum non conveniens, on grounds of
22–007
submission to English jurisdiction, 22–003.
See also CONFLICT OF LAWS,
JURISDICTION
LLOYD'S MARINE POLICY 2–023, 7–010
LOADING
meaning 2–013
LONDON COURT OF INTERNATIONAL
ARBITRATION 23–026
LUGANO CONVENTION
application of 22–014
interpretation 22–013
jurisdiction
admissibility, and 22–026
consumer contract 22–024
employment contract 22–019
exclusive 22–025
forum non conveniens 22–028
general rule 22–017
insurance contract 22–023
lis pendens and related actions 22–027
prorogation of 22–016
provisions 22–015, 22–033
special rule 22–018

MAREVA INJUNCTION, 22–001. *See also*
FREEZING INJUNCTION
MARINE BILL OF LADING 11–012
MARINE INSURANCE
assignment 19–016
assured 19–003
blanket policy 19–008
broker 19–003
broker's cover note 19–011
certificate of insurance 19–011
claims 19–030—19–035
burden of proof 19–031
causation 19–030

MARINE INSURANCE—*cont.*
  claims—*cont.*
    liability 19–030
    measure of indemnity 19–034
    partial loss 19–033
    preparation of 19–032
    total loss 19–033
  continuation clause 19–005
  contract of 19–009–19–017
    sale, stipulations in 19–002
  duty to disclose 19–012
  exceptive warranty 19–017
  exclusions 19–024
  floating policy 19–003, 19–006
  general average, 19–025—19–029. *See also*
    GENERAL AVERAGE
  held covered clause 19–013
  increased value policy 19–004
  Institute Cargo Clauses A, B, C, 19–019—
    19–024. *See also* INSTITUTE CARGO
    CLAUSE
  insurable interest 19–014
  insured value 19–004
  insurer 19–003
  kinds of 19–004—19–008
  letter of insurance 19–011
  Lloyd's Marine Policy 19–018
  Lloyds policy 19–018
  measure of indemnity 19–035
  mixed policy 19–005
  open cover 19–003, 19–007
  premium 19–014
  promissory warranty 19–017
  red clause 19–032
  risks covered 19–017
  seller's contingency 19–014
  shipping value 19–004
  slip and the policy 19–010
  subrogation right 19–035
  termination of contract of carriage clause
    19–022
  time policy 19–005
  unvalued policy 19–004
  valued policy 19–004
  voyage policy 19–005
  warranties 19–017
MARITIME TRANSPORT. *See* CARRIAGE BY SEA
MARKET INFORMATION
  provided by buyer. *See also* EXPORT
    PUBLICATIONS, MARKET RESEARCH
MARKET RESEARCH
  Business Links 31–003
  direct 31–001
  Export Credits Guarantee Department
    31–006
  Export Market Information Centre (EMIC)
    31–004
  export publications 31–008—31–016
  government assisted 31–002—31–007
  Trade U.K. Export Sales Lead Service
    31–005
MATE'S RECEIPT 15–003

MERCANTILE AGENT 27–017
MERCHANT
  definition, 16–007 n.28
  finance 13–014
MULTIMODAL TRANSPORT
  containers 16–001
  documents 11–012

NON-RECOURSE FINANCE 13–014

OFFER 3–005
  counter 3–007
  firm 3–006
OIL COUNTERTRADE 14–011

PACKAGE OR UNIT
  definition 16–009
PACKING
  containers, in 7–009
  dangerous goods 7–012
  import regulations 7–011
  insurance law, in 7–010
  law of carriage of goods, in 7–008
  sale of goods, in 7–007
  suitable, obligation to provide 7–006
PAROL EVIDENCE RULE 3–016
PASSING OF PROPERTY 2–014, 4–004
  ascertained goods 4–006
  retention of title clause, 4–007—4–009. *See
    also* RETENTION OF TITLE CLAUSE
  specific goods 4–006
  unascertained goods 4–005
PASSING OF RISK. *See* RISK
PATENT LICENSING AGREEMENT
  block exemption 29–015
PAYMENT
  Bills of Exchange, by 9–003
  open account, on 9–002
  sight, on 9–002
PENALTIES AND LIQUIDATED DAMAGES 4–015
PERFORMANCE OF CONTRACT
  acceptance of goods 5–001
  apportionment of 6–014
  ascertained goods 4–006
  certificates, provision of 4–012
    inspection, of 4–013
    quality, of 4–012
  construction. *See* CONSTRUCTION CONTRACT
  delivery of goods 4–003
  English law 4–002
  foreign law 4–002
  generally 4–001
  liquidated damages 4–015
  passing of property, 4–004. *See also* PASSING
    OF PROPERTY
  passing of risk 4–009, 4–010
  penalties 4–015
  relaxation of strict 5–012
  unascertained goods 4–005
PORT RATES
  f.a.s. 2–004
  f.o.b. 2–005

PRICE ESCALATION CLAUSE 32–015
PRIVATE INTERNATIONAL LAW. *See* CONFLICT OF
  LAWS
PRODUCER
  definition 8–006
PRODUCT
  definition 8–006
PRODUCT LIABILITY
  American law 8–012—8–014
    generally 8–012
    reform of 8–014
    Restatement (Second) of Torts s. 402A
      8–013
    unavoidably unsafe product, 8–013 n.70
  basis of 8–002
  causation 8–007
  Consumer Protection Act, 1987 8–002,
    8–005
  contract of sale, arising from 8–003
  contributory negligence 8–007
  damages and 8–009
  defective products, for 8–006
  defences, 8–007, 8–013 n.70
  definitions 8–006
  E.C. Directive on 8–002, 8–004, 8–005
  English law 8–003—8–009
  examples 8–008
  fault liability 8–002
  insurance 8–011
  joint and several 8–006
  limitation periods 8–003, 8–007
  procedural aspects 8–010
  producer, definition 8–006
  qualified liability 8–002
  statutory cause of action 8–006
  strict liability 8–002
  unlimited 8–006
PROPERTY
  rejected goods, in 5–010
  use of term, 4–006 n.23

REGISTRABLE CHARGE 4–008, 4–009
RESALE
  right of unpaid seller 5–014, 5–017
RETENTION OF TITLE CLAUSE
  definition, 4–007 n.33
  extended 4–009
  generally 4–007, 32–015
  simple 4–008
RISK
  accidental loss 4–010
  deterioration of goods 4–010
  passing of 4–010
ROMALPA CLAUSE 4–009
ROME CONVENTION ON THE LAW APPLICABLE TO
  CONTRACTUAL OBLIGATIONS 11–020
  applicability 21–005
  assignment 21–014
  burden of proof 21–012
  capacity 21–013
  choice of law 21–007
    absence of 21–009

ROME CONVENTION ON THE LAW APPLICABLE TO
  CONTRACTUAL OBLIGATIONS—*cont.*
  Community law and 21–006
  consumer contracts 21–015
  employment contracts 21–016
  generally 21–004
  interpretation 21–005
  limitations 21–010
  principles 21–006
  scope of 21–006, 21–011
  subrogation 21–014
  validity 21–012

SALE OF GOODS ACT, 1979
  condition within the meaning of 5–004
  delivery of goods under 2–027, 4–002,
    4–003
  examination/acceptance/rejection of goods
    5–001, 5–005—5–007
  frustration under 6–007
  marine insurance under 2–008, 2–038
  packing under 7–007
  passing of property under 2–014, 2–027,
    4–002—4–009
  passing of the risk under 4–010
  product liability under 8–003
  rights of the unpaid seller under 5–014—
    5–017
SEA WAYBILL
  advantages 33–009
  electronic data interchange, replaced by
    15–033
  non-negotiable 11–012, 15–033, 33–010
  replacing bill of lading 33–010
SEARCH ORDER 22–032
SEAWORTHINESS 15–041
SHIP
  suitable. *See* SUITABLE SHIP
SHIPOWNER'S LIEN 15–018
SHIPPING CONFERENCES
  freight rates fixed by 15–016
SHIPPING DOCUMENTS 2–021—2–026
  bill of lading 2–022
  delay in presenting, effect of 2–031
  inspection, certificate of 2–025
  insurance document, 2–023. *See also*
    INSURANCE
  invoice 2–024
  origin, certificate of 2–025
  quality, certificate of 2–025
  rejection right, 2–026. *See also* C.I.F.
SIGNATURE
  electronic, as to 33–009, 33–012
SIMPLER TRADE PROCEDURES BOARD (SITPRO)
  26–015
  EDI guidance from 33–001
  objectives 32–017
SOLE DISTRIBUTION AGREEMENT
  advertising 30–012
  agency agreement distinguished 30–003
  clauses in 30–007—30–013
    drafting 30–007

SOLE DISTRIBUTION AGREEMENT—*cont.*
  clauses in—*cont.*
    general 30–013
    interpretation 30–006
  contract of sale distinguished 30–003
  export distribution agreement 30–005
  franchising agreement distinguished 30–004
  generally 30–001
  goods, defining 30–010
  licensing agreement distinguished 30–004
  market information 30–012
  meaning 30–002
  nature 1–005, 30–002—30–006
  patents, protection of 30–012
  price, defining 30–009
  restrictive practices and 30–014
  sales licence and 30–004
  sole buying and selling rights 30–011
  territory, defining 30–008
  trade marks, protection of 30–012
SPECIAL TRADE TERMS
  arrival 2–042
  c. and f. 2–038
  carriage and insurance paid (CIP) 2–040
  carriage paid (CPT) 2–041
  c.i.f. 2–001, 2–019—2–037
  c.i.f. and c. 2–039
  c.i.f. and c. and i. 2–039
  c.i.f. and e. 2–039
  container trade terms 2–046
  delivered at frontier (DAF) 2–044
  delivered duty paid/unpaid (DDP/DDU)
    2–045
  ex quay 2–001, 2–002, 2–043
  ex ship 2–042
  ex store 2–002
  ex warehouse 2–002
  ex works 2–001, 2–002
  f.a.s. 2–003, 2–004
  f.o.b. 2–001, 2–005—2–018
  free carrier 2–003
  generally 2–001
STANDARD SHIPPING NOTE (SSN) 26–015
STANDARDISATION OF TERMS
  American Uniform Commercial Code
    32–009
  construction industry, used by 32–013
  general terms of business 32–014—32–016
    important clauses 32–015
  generally 32–001
  home transactions 32–016
  Incoterms 32–008
  International Chamber of Commerce
    publications 32–008
  standard contract forms 32–010—32–013
  trade associations, issued by 32–011
  UN Commission on International Trade Law
    (UNCITRAL) 32–003—32–007
  UN Economic Commission for Europe
    (UNECE), issued by 32–012
STANDBY LETTER OF CREDIT. *See* LETTERS OF
  CREDIT

STOPPAGE IN TRANSIT 5–013, 5–014, 5–016
STRATEGIC GOODS
  control of export 26–005
SUBSIDIARY COMPANIES
  branch offices and
    choice between 28–002
    legal distinction between 28–003
  European company, proposals for 28–010
  favoured method of export marketing
    28–007
  generally 28–001
  multinational enterprise 28–009
  overseas 28–008
    English law, in 28–011
    foreign law, in 28–012
      company 28–013
      dispute settlement 28–017
      employment 28–014
      investment 28–016, 28–017
      tax 28–015
  personnel employed in 28–020—28–026
    aliens legislation in non-E.C.countries
      28–025
    English law as to 28–021—28–023
    foreign law as to 28–024—28–026
    foreign legislation protecting security
      28–026
    free movement in the E.C. 28–024
    generally 28–020
    partly in U.K. partly outside 28–022
    restraint of trade clauses 28–023
SUITABLE SHIP
  buyer's duty to nominate 2–004, 2–009
  failure to nominate 2–011
  f.o.b. contract and 2–004, 2–007, 2–009—
    2–012
  meaning 2–010
  nomination 2–004, 2–007, 2–009
    substitute vessel, of 2–012
    time for 2–009—2–012
SUPPLIER
  definition 8–006
SURETYSHIP. *See* BANK GUARANTEE

TELETRANSMISSION
  instructions communicated by, 11–017. *See*
    also ELECTRONIC DATA INTERCHANGE
    (EDI)
THIRD PARTY RIGHTS 5–016
TIR CARNET SYSTEM 26–019, 26–020, 26–021
TITLE
  use of term, 4–006 n.23
TORT
  liability of carrier in
    c.i.f. contract, under 2–030
TRADE ASSOCIATIONS
  standard conditions issued by 32–011
TRADE MARKS
  protection of 30–012
TRANSIT
  meaning 5–016
  stoppage in 5–013, 5–014, 5–016

TRANSPORT DOCUMENTS. *See* DOCUMENTS

UN COMMISSION ON INTERNATIONAL TRADE
    LAW (UNCITRAL) 2–002, 12–001,
    23–021, 32–003–32–007
  Arbitration Rules 23–007, 23–022, 25–039,
    32–006
  Conciliation Rules 23–023, 32–006
  electronic commerce, on 33–012
  electronic signatures, on 33–009, 33–013
  legal guides 25–002, 32–007
  Model Laws 23–010, 23–024, 32–005,
    33–009, 33–013
  most important texts 32–004
UN CONVENTION ON CONTRACTS FOR
    INTERNATIONAL SALE OF GOODS, 4–002,
    32–004. *See* VIENNA CONVENTION
UN CONVENTION ON INTERNATIONAL
    MULTIMODAL TRANSPORT OF GOODS
    15–001, 16–004
UN CONVENTION ON THE LIMITATION PERIOD IN
    THE INTERNATIONAL SALE OF GOODS
    4–002, 32–004, 32–032
UN ECONOMIC COMMISSION FOR EUROPE
    (UNECE)
  model contracts sponsored by 32–012
UN INDUSTRIAL DEVELOPMENT ORGANISATION
    (UNIDO) 25–014
UN TRADE DATA ELEMENTS DIRECTORY
    (UNTDED) 33–004
UN TRADE DATA INTERCHANGE DIRECTORY
    (UNTDID) 33–004
UN/ECE CEFACT
  standard electronic messages (UNSM)
    33–001, 33–004
UN/EDIFACT STANDARD 33–003, 33–004
UNCITRAL LEGAL GUIDE 25–002
UNCITRAL. *See* UN COMMISSION ON
    INTERNATIONAL TRADE LAW
    (UNCITRAL)
UNDERTAKINGS
  meaning 29–004
UNFAIR CONTRACT TERMS 5–003
UNIDROIT CONVENTION ON INTERNATIONAL
    FACTORING 13–007
UNIDROIT CONVENTION ON INTERNATIONAL
    FINANCIAL LEASING 13–013
UNIFORM CUSTOMS AND PRACTICE FOR
    DOCUMENTARY CREDITS (UCP) 11–002,
    15–023, 15–032, 32–008, 33–010
  application 11–003
  transfer, as to 11–036
UNIFORM LAW OF FORMATION
  application only if adopted by parties
    32–019
  breach of contract 32–024
  contract of international sale 32–023
  customary trade terms 32–024
  formation, on 32–025
  general limitations 32–021, 32–022
  international sales, on 32–024
  mandatory provisions of proper law cannot
    be contracted out 32–020

UNIFORM LAW OF FORMATION—*cont.*
  "non-conforming" goods 32–024
  restriction to
    contracts between parties in Convention
      States 32–023
  U.K. 32–018
  Uniform Laws on Internationals Sales Act
    1967 32–018
UNIFORM LAWS ON INTERNATIONAL SALES
    4–002
  examination/acceptance of goods under
    5–001
  passing of the risk 4–010
  U.K. 32–018
UNIFORM RULES FOR A COMBINED TRANSPORT
    DOCUMENT 16–006, 32–008
UNIFORM RULES FOR COLLECTIONS (1995
    REVISION) 10–002, 32–008
UNIFORM RULES FOR CONTRACT GUARANTEES
    (URGG) 12–001, 25–020, 32–008
UNIFORM RULES FOR DEMAND GUARANTEES
    12–004
UNPAID SELLER
  lien of 5–014, 5–015
  resale rights 5–014, 5–017
  rights of 5–013—5–017
    definition 5–014
    goods, against 5–013
  stoppage in transit. *See* STOPPAGE IN TRANSIT
  third party rights against 5–016
URUGUAY ROUND 4–014

VIENNA CONVENTION, 1980 2–004, 21–003
  applicability 32–027
  central position of 32–029
  contract performan 4–002
  ex works clause 2–002
  factoring and 13–007
  f.a.s. contracts 2–004
  f.c.a. contracts 2–004
  fundamental breach, as to 32–030
  goods
    acceptance 5–001
    examination 5–001
  Hague Convention and 21–003
  Hague Uniform Laws, based on 32–026
  national law, and 32–028
  non-fundamental breach, as to 32–030
  passing of risk 4–010
  repair of non-conforming goods, as to
    32–031
  specific performance, as to 32–031
  trade terms 2–001

WAIVER
  doctrine of 5–012
WAR
  outbreak of, effect of 6–008
WAREHOUSE
  interpretation, 2–002 n.12
WARRANTY
  breach of, effect of 5–003

WARRANTY—*cont.*
  condition distinguished 5–003
  exceptive 19–017
  promissory 19–017
WARSAW CONVENTION 15–001, 17–001
WASSENAAR ARRANGEMENT 26–004
WORKS AND INSTALLATIONS ABROAD
  export transactions, 1–003. *See*
      INTERNATIONAL PROCUREMENT
      CONTRACT
WORLD BANK
  Standard Bidding Documents for the
      Procurement of Works 25–015, 25–039

WORLD BANK—*cont.*
  tenders
    guidelines as to 25–020, 25–021
  transaction financed by
    prequalification procedure
      25–017
WORLD CUSTOMS ORGANISATION (WCO)
  32–017
WORLD TRADE ORGANISATION (WTO)
  24–021
  Government Procurement Agreement (GPA)
    25–009
WORLD WIDE WEB 33–001